POPULATION

FACTS AND METHODS OF DEMOGRAPHY

POPULATION
FACTS AND METHODS OF DEMOGRAPHY

Nathan KEYFITZ

UNIVERSITY OF CALIFORNIA
Berkeley

Wilhelm FLIEGER SVD

UNIVERSITY OF SAN CARLOS
Cebu City, Philippines

W. H. FREEMAN AND COMPANY
San Francisco

Printed in the United States of America

International Standard Book Number: 0-7167-0931-7

Library of Congress Catalog Card Number: 70-141154

1   2   3   4   5   6   7   8   9

TO THE STATISTICIANS
OF THE SEVENTY COUNTRIES
WHOSE DATA ARE THE STARTING POINT
OF THESE CALCULATIONS

Preface

To think of population today is to think of growth. Although the science of demography deals with much more than population increase, it is the phenomenon of growth that commands the attention of experts and the public alike. This volume is no exception: in it we examine the way in which changing birth and death rates affect the growth of populations throughout the world.

Before World War II the human race was increasing by about 20 million per year; now it is increasing annually by more than 70 million. The part that the United States contributes to annual global increase is less than 2 million, yet even here population growth may have a part in the deterioration of the environment. For poorer countries the increase has the terrifying aspect of a condemnation to deepening poverty; the control of both population and poverty through economic development is itself forestalled by population growth. The high valuation set on human life when there was less of it is being eroded. Perception of the operative relations is inhibited by obsolete ways of looking at population, inherited from long past epochs when natural death rates were several times greater than they are now; one of these obsolete perspectives is that which associates large and growing population with national greatness.

Formal demography helps to describe and analyze population growth. It applies mathematical models to the processes of birth and death, recognizing divisions of population by age and sex. This book includes accounts of the models most commonly used, the computer programs by which these models are implemented, and instances of the use of these models to draw conclusions about the population trends of the present day. The rates of birth and death are related to marriage, housing, schooling, income, occupation, and other cultural and social variables, whose treatment is also part of demography. We have not been able to incorporate data on these in this book. Our numbers deal with the process of population growth itself.

Most national official data bearing on rates of birth and death in the late 1960's are represented here. Every country that has usable vital statistics is shown for at least one year. We are grateful to the many national statistical agencies that responded with unpublished materials and clarifications to our pleas for information; we were dependent also on national publications and the United Nations for much of our data base.

All data that we were given are shown as Table 1 of the Main Tables of this volume—population and deaths by age and sex, and births by age of parent.

Everything else, that is to say the remaining seven tables for each country, city, or other area, was computed by us. Before computers were available no one made such calculations centrally, and life tables and population projections were customarily produced in national statistical offices, or else not calculated at all. The computer enables us to go from simple distributions by age and sex to the implied probabilites of living and dying. These and numerous other quantities are calculated by uniform methods, described in Part III.

This book summarizes but does not repeat in detail the material contained in our *World Population*, published by The University of Chicago Press in May of 1968. In that earlier work we tried to collect together whatever historical materials on population, births, and deaths were available for whole countries. We were able to go back to 1780 for Sweden; to 1851 for France; to 1861 for England and Wales; to the beginning of the twentieth century for Belgium, the Netherlands and Luxemburg; to World War I for Canada, Australia, and the United States. The Summary Table included as Part II of this book shows 42 main facts for all of the populations with which we have worked, an overlap made possible by the University of Chicago Press.

The quality and qualifications of his materials are a main preoccupation of the demographer and Part V contains an account of the general factors bearing on the accuracy of demographic data. The tight space restrictions under which we worked for the first volume prevented our publishing the extensive documentation. Our practice was to punch up with each set of data all descriptive footnotes available, as well as the reference to the source. In the present book these notes and references are shown in Part V, covering most of the populations printed out in the Main Tables.

While the accuracy of a single number—that the population of China in 1953 was 583 million—cannot by itself be assessed, sets of numbers can be checked for coherence. In some instances the published numbers at the several ages do not add to the official total; in others the sex ratio at birth is far from that usual in human populations. We tried to resolve the conflicting figures in such cases by seeking an alternative source of information.

More extensive computation revealed deeper errors in the data. The computer occasionally told us that numbers of deaths that looked satisfactory at first glance implied that people would live the impossibly high average of 80 years. Births as officially published were often grossly out of accord with the age-distribution of the population. Our usual course was to eliminate sets of data containing such errors, and to include only what was testified to officially *and* implied nothing impossible. We did not eliminate sets of data that were merely doubtful; the official figures for Romania show it to have lower mortality than any other country of Europe or America; despite our scepticism we allowed Romania to remain in the Summary Table. Spain, included in the Main Tables, also shows mortality so low as to arouse doubts on completeness. To present such computed results as expectation of life and the standardized death rate along with the raw data is in effect to warn the reader of possible errors in the sources.

The computer helped also by combining groups of countries. Sets of data on European countries are virtually complete for each of the years 1955, 1960, and 1965, and we accordingly aggregated Europe's 26 countries, as well as some sub-groups of these such as the Common Market Six. No other continent permits such consolidation, but we do show Central America (five countries) and the West Indies (seven countries), as well as partial totals for Africa and South America, in the Summary Table.

We have also gone down to some subpopulations within nations. Included are main cities where we could obtain them, and certain urban and rural totals. Life tables and other demographic calculations for such areas have not been plentiful. For three countries—the United States, Canada, and Australia—an exhaustive set of states or provinces is shown in the Summary Table.

A major feature of this book is the inclusion of computer programs, which are expressed in as universal a FORTRAN IV as we could manage. In exactly the form here shown they have worked on seven different installations in the United States. Computers are now available on all continents and demographic software is needed. We hope the international exchange of such software will be furthered by our effort.

The twelve separate programs listed in Part III produce life tables, projections, intrinsic rates, and other quantities needed in formal demography. Our aims in the development of these programs included readability, associated with brevity and directness in the program, economy of computer time and storage, as well as machine-independence. They are so documented that the reader who has other problems than those we were directly concerned with can adapt them to his purposes.

Demographic theory is also provided in Part III, beginning with the life table, and continuing through population projection, analysis of a population projection in its matrix form, the Lotka equation and its solution, standardization, and other matters. The level of exposition is that of a first course in calculus and we have tried to make it self-contained. A considerable part of the core of formal demography has been compressed into these pages, though we cannot pretend that the whole of the mathematics of population is included.

Our contribution is the linking of data and theory. Theory helps to interpret the data, to bring out their bearing on current population issues. It helps equally to check the data by seeing how well their elements of population, births, and deaths as fitted into models are consistent with one another. The interpretation as well as the checking are aided by the computer, and we not only give our own computed results, but also make available a collection of programs. The student may apply these as they stand to his own data; he can read and criticize them to develop his computing skill; he can take them as a base for making more elaborate computations and solving problems beyond those we deal with.

The collaboration of which this book is the result began with the collection of data by Flieger and development of methods of analysis by Keyfitz. The large program that produced the analysis of Part IV and the Summary Table of Part II was written by Flieger; the simplified programs presented in Part II were due to Keyfitz, except for the one called LOTKA. The text was written by Keyfitz. We are indebted to Roger Avery, Lee Jay Cho, James Cramer, Prithwis Das Gupta, James G. Dobbins, Elizabeth Eisenberg, Griffith Feeney, Judith Guthartz, David Klassen, Ruth Meade, Geoffrey McNicoll, Frank Oechsli, James A. Palmore, Beresford Parlett, James Pick, Robert Retherford, Robert Schoen, Robert K. Sembiring, Peter Smith, and Belinda Wong for help at many points; Arthur Van Horn drew the charts. The research was supported financially by NSF grant GZ995, by NIH research contract 69-2200, and by teaching grants to the Department of Demography, University of California at Berkeley, from the National Institute of General Medical Sciences (5 TO1 GMO1240) and the Ford Foundation. Among those who helped test our programs on their installations were Francisco Bayo, James Beshers, Paul Meier, James Sakoda, Joel Smith, Zenas Sykes, C. J. Thomas, Vincent Whitney, H. H. Winsborough, and Theodore Woolsey. The Statistical Office of the United Nations, the United States Bureau of the Census, and the National Center for Health Statistics helped with advice and data. The University of Chicago Press has encouraged the production of this book by allowing the reprinting of some of the numbers in the Summary Table shown in our *World Population*, published in 1968 and now in its second printing. We also thank the editors and publishers of *Rapid Population Growth: Consequences and Policy Implications*, prepared by a Study Committee of the Office of the Foreign Secretary, National Academy of Sciences (Baltimore: Johns Hopkins Press, 1971), and of *Environment: Resources, Pollution and Society*, edited by William W. Murdoch (Stamford, Conn.: Sinauer Associate, 1971), for permission to use parts of the text of those books. Our greatest debt is to the national statisticians who provided us with numbers, and many of whom engaged tirelessly in correspondence with us. It is to them that we dedicate our book.

Berkeley, California   NATHAN KEYFITZ
December, 1970   WILHELM FLIEGER SVD

Contents

PART I

WORLD POPULATION ENTERS THE SEVENTIES:
Some Conclusions from the Statistics

CHAPTER 1

Types of Human Populations

Individuals enter the human community by birth, and they leave it by death; at certain points in life they may generate sons and daughters. From this simple observation follows the entire process of the increase and decline of human populations. Whether death occurs on the average at 30 years or at 70; whether a woman bears two children or three on the average; such facts determine whether populations grow or remain stationary, and whether the planet as a whole becomes overloaded and deteriorates, or remains hospitable to human societies.

Numbers of people are by no means the whole subject of demography, but they are its starting point both historically and logically. The printout tables that follow present most of the material available on national populations and their birth and death rates; the introductory text initiates the analysis of that material by calculating summary constants and relating them to one another; it sketches the body of theory that makes intelligible the numerical aspects of population growth and decline. All that can be attempted here is to provide some examples of the analysis, mostly using the simple one-sex model for females.

Our discussion starts with a classification of national populations according to their rates of death and of birth.

A Threefold Classification

Parts of the present-day world, for instance the countries of tropical Africa reported in this book, show patterns of human mortality corresponding to those that prevailed in Europe during the eighteenth century and earlier. The mortality patterns of the underdeveloped countries of Asia and Latin America are similar to those of North America and Europe during the 1930's and 1940's. The most advanced countries present new features—for instance, a strikingly lower mortality for women than for men. The range of death rates in the contemporary data compiled in this book reveals in cross section the several phases of the demographic transition of the past two centuries.

The remarkable variation of mortality in the 1960's may be seen in the expectations of life (defined on page 4) of children just born. In Guinea, Cameroon, and Togo, for example, the expectation of life at age zero is about 40 years; the chance that a child will survive until he or she can have children in turn is only about one-half. Near the other extreme are girl children in the United States, with an expectation of about 75 years, and with a much better than 90 percent chance of living through the period of reproduction. The Summary Table that is included as Part II of this book shows that the range from 40 to 75 years in expectation of life is nearly as wide as that shown by Europe during the past 200 years; Sweden's expectation of life for females at age zero went from 36.56 in 1785 to 76.58 in 1967.

In respect of births also the present is a time of large contrasts. The range from the 50 births per thousand persons in some underdeveloped countries, through the 18 per thousand that has become the dominant pattern in the developed world, down to the 15 per thousand of Eastern Europe, is wider than the range found in any previous period. Just as digging-stick agriculture and even preagricultural hunting and food-gathering coexist in the 1970's with successful expeditions to the moon, so do primitive and advanced demographic regimes. The coexistence of these dissimilar regimes is uncomfortable and presumably transitory, like the coexistence of primitive and advanced technologies.

In many individual countries the arithmetical incongruities between modern death rates and traditional birth rates are a special feature of the present time. As low death rates spread through the world, it becomes clear that they must be accompanied by low birth rates if economic and ecological disaster is to be avoided.

The change from a preindustrial to a modern regime as seen in perspective has been called the demographic transition. All countries concerned in it started with high mortality and relatively high fertility, a condition that goes back to the dawn of the human race and extends well into the era of official statistics. Through official statistics—those for Sweden and some other European countries, given in detail in our *World Population* (The University of Chicago Press, 1968) and summarized here in Part II—we can follow the changes that occurred with modernization.

First came a fall in the death rate, so that the expectation of life of persons in advanced countries moved from about 40 years in 1850 to about 50 in 1900. Some 50 years were needed for an increase of 10 years in the expectation of life at age zero. Today's developing countries show an increase of 10 years each 20 or 25 years. Ceylon's expectation, for example, rose by more than two years in the four years 1963–67 (page 82), and Taiwan's by more than two years during the period 1962–66.

If human affairs were logically arranged, birth control would be adopted simultaneously with the diminution of disease that in effect constitutes death control. The rate of increase of populations would not change, but only the manner of increase; the waste of the preindustrial regime, with its high infant and child mortality, would be eliminated, but the virtually zero net increase of traditional regimes would be retained.

Given that it takes time for the fact of death control to influence reproductive practices, the populations of Europe had an advantage in that their death rates declined slowly. A fall in the death rate calls for a fall of the same amount in the birth rate if the previous balance is to be maintained. That the death rates of under-developed countries have fallen much faster than those of Europe makes the task of controlling births now facing them all the more urgent and difficult.

Preliminary Definitions. Let us define here in preliminary fashion some of the terms required for more detailed study of birth and death rates. Other quantities are defined in Part III, where their computation is also presented.

If a population contains P individuals on July 1 and B births occur during the calendar year, then the *crude birth rate* is B/P; it is crude in the sense that it takes no account of age and sex. If deaths during the calendar year number D, the *crude death rate* is D/P.

The information needed to compute such rates, and the rates themselves, are included in the Main Tables (Part IV) of this book for the population of each country. Ireland in 1968, for example, had $P = 2,909,688$, $B = 61,004$, and $D = 33,157$ (Table 1, Data Input to Computations, page 446). Hence, the crude birth rate multiplied by 1000 is $1000B/P = 20.97$, and the crude death rate multiplied by 1000 is $1000D/P = 11.40$, both of which are shown in Table 5, Observed and Projected Vital Rates (page 447). The crude rate of natural increase is the difference, $20.97 - 11.40 = 9.57$ per thousand population. (Multiplying rates by 1000 is a convention of demographic analysis.)

If the P individuals of a population include $_5P_x$ females aged x to $x + 4$ at last birthday, and if the D deaths include $_5D_x$ deaths of females in this same age range, then the *age-specific death rate* for females at ages x to $x + 4$ is $_5M_x = {_5D_x}/{_5P_x}$. Here, as elsewhere in this book, the beginning of the age interval is given at the lower right of symbols such as P, B, and D, the length of the interval at the lower left. (Where the context makes clear what the length of the interval is, the symbol on the lower left may be omitted.)

Looking again at Irish female data for 1968, and taking $x = 45$ as an example, we see that $_5D_{45}$ is 374, and $_5P_{45}$ is 81,524, so that $_5M_{45} = {_5D_{45}}/{_5P_{45}} = 0.00459$, as shown in the second to last column of Table 3, Life Table for Females (page 446). From such information the full life tables, included as Tables 2 and 3, of each of our printouts are calculated; detail of the calculation and the theory behind it appears in Chapter 7. The l_x column of Tables 2 and 3 is printed out at five-year intervals and for age 1. This is 100,000 times the probability of living from age 0 to each age x; 100,000 times the probability that a girl just born would live to age 45, computed from the data for Ireland in 1968, is $l_{45} = 94567$, according to the third column of Table 3 (page 446.)

Another important column is $_5L_x$, the stationary population between ages x and $x + 4$ inclusive; this is the sum of all the l_x (not shown in the table, but estimated by a smooth curve through $l_{x-5}, l_x, l_{x+5}, l_{x+10}$) between l_x and l_{x+5} or

$$_5L_x = \int_0^5 l_{x+t}\, dt.$$

If 100,000 females are born each year, subject to the mortality of Ireland, 1968, we would have the population $_5L_{45} = 467,789$, as shown in the fifth column of Table 3. Finally, the average future years of life for persons of age x is

$$\mathring{e}_x = \int_0^\infty l_{x+t}\, \frac{dt}{l_x}$$

or $\mathring{e}_{45} = 31.24$ years for Irish women 45 years old, according to the third-to-last column of Table 3. The quantity $\mathring{e}_0$, the *expectation of life* at age 0, is a summary description of the age-specific death rates of a population, usually referring to a given moment of time.

We use such ratios as $\mathring{e}_0$ to examine in detail the three patterns of birth and death by which contemporary populations can be classified.

High Birth and High Death Rates.   Most of the populations in this first category are in tropical Africa. An example for which recent official data are available is Madagascar (an island off the mainland of Africa), which had 6,163,000 inhabitants in 1966. Its crude birth rate was 45.75 per thousand population (page 313), and its crude death rate 25.31 per thousand, making its rate of increase about 2 percent per year. Our life tables for Madagascar, 1966, show $\mathring{e}_0$ to be 37.6 years for males and 38.5 years for females. The probability $l_{50}/100,000$ that a boy just born will live to age 50 is 0.386, and a girl 0.401. These expectations and probabilities may be compared with those of Europe at the beginning of the nineteenth century (see Summary Table, Part II). Sweden, for example, in the five years around 1800, had $\mathring{e}_0$ values of 36.0 and 38.9 years for males and females, respectively, and l_{50} of 0.417 and 0.456. Madagascar's mortality pattern resembles those of Europe about 1800.

Similar death rates prevail in Cameroon, in the Central African Republic, in

Togo, for which less recent official figures are available, and probably in a considerable part of the rest of tropical Africa, for which no official figures at all are to be had. These high death rates, which today are found in only a minority of the world's population, appear to be on their way out.

Tropical Africa's birth rates do not resemble those of Europe in 1800. The crude birth rate of Madagascar in 1966, reported as 45.74 per thousand, is half again as high as Sweden's in 1800, which was 31.21. The difference is important for the rate of increase; Sweden's increase was about 5 per thousand, while that of Madagascar is 20 per thousand.

No one knows how many of the world's populations are in the category of birth and death rates typified by Madagascar. Tropical Africa contains about 250 million people; parts of Asia and Latin America probably have similar birth and death rates but no official records; they contain at most an additional 250 millions; the total in this category is probably less than half a billion.

High Birth and Low Death Rates. This category includes most of the underdeveloped world. Up-to-date official information on some of the populations is lacking, though it is not as scarce as for the high death rate countries. Obviously, it is the countries with high birth and low death rates whose populations are increasing most rapidly. Honduras is typical of these, with a birth rate in 1966 of 44.2 per thousand population, and a death rate of 8.7. Its $\mathring{e}_0$ is 59.2 years for males and 60.7 for females; $l_{50}/100,000$ for a boy just born is 0.741, and for a girl 0.764. These mortality figures contrast sharply with those for Madagascar, though births of the two countries are at about the same level.

A population with a birth rate of about 44 per thousand and a death rate of about 9 will grow at $3\frac{1}{2}$ percent per year. Furthermore, the real birth rate of Honduras and similar countries may be even higher than that calculated from registered births. For this category as a whole we may speak conservatively of a birth rate of 40 per thousand and a death rate of 10 per thousand, producing a growth by natural increase of 3 percent per year. Again we cannot say with precision what part of the world is in this category, but it is certainly more than half; let us say that it includes a round two billion people.

One way to see the meaning of a rate of increase is to translate it into doubling time t, obtained as the solution of the equation

$$(1 + r)^t = 2,$$

where r is the fraction of increase per year. The solution for t, obtained by taking natural logarithms and expanding $\ln(1 + r) = r - r^2/2 + \ldots$, is

$$t \cong \frac{\ln 2}{r - \dfrac{r^2}{2}} \cong \frac{0.693}{r - \dfrac{r^2}{2}},$$

if terms in r^3 and higher may be disregarded, or very nearly $t = 0.70/r$ for values of r in the range 0–0.04. Hence the rule that doubling time is obtained by dividing the percentage annual increase into 70; according to this rule Honduras's annual increase of 3.5 percent implies a doubling time of $70/3.5 = 20$ years. For Madagascar, which has a 2 percent increase, the doubling time is 35 years. For Sweden in 1800, which had a 0.5 percent increase, the doubling time was 140 years.

Thus if these rates remained constant over the course of 140 years, the population of Honduras would double 7 times, or, in other words, be multiplied by $2^7 = 128$; the population of Madagascar would double 4 times, or be multiplied by 16; and that of Sweden, 1800, would have been multiplied only by two. While the rates of increase 3.5 percent, 2.0 percent, and 0.5 percent do not seem very different, the numbers 128, 16, and 2 as factors are different indeed. Sweden actually continued to increase at somewhat more than the 0.5 percent rate, and in fact doubled in about 90 years, due to a fall in its death rate and despite emigration. If the population of Honduras were to double 7 times, it would number a quarter of a billion persons. Such a consideration makes us certain that the 3.5 percent increase for Honduras cannot continue; either its birth rate will come down or its death rate will go up.

Low Birth and Low Death Rates.   For this group of countries we do not face the difficulty of deciding whether those that publish vital statistics are typical; they all have good official statistics, and we can even add and obtain aggregate figures, as though they were a single country. We have done this for the countries of Europe, whose 1965 population was 442 million. (Only for Northern Ireland were 1965 figures unavailable.) The European consolidated 1965 birth rate was 18.0 per thousand, the death rate 10.2, and hence the rate of natural increase was 7.8. The United States, for which the 1967 figures for these three items are 17.8, 9.4, and 8.4 per thousand, obviously falls in the same demographic category as Europe. Similar also are Canada, Australia, and New Zealand, and the USSR is not very different. Japan is an extreme member of the group, with 1966 figures of 13.8, 6.8, and 7.0 per thousand; its birth and death rates are lower, but its rate of natural increase is, at least for the moment, very similar to those of the countries whose populations are mostly of European descent.

The death rates appear to be continuing to drop in the countries of this category, probably at a declining rate. The consolidated life table for European males, for instance, goes from an $\mathring{e}_0$ of 64.9 years in 1955 to 66.6 in 1960, but only to 67.7 in 1965. The expectation of life for European males is rising by about one year every five years now, for European females a year and a half. In the United States the male expectation of life has been approximately constant over the last few years; the female expectation has increased by two years in a decade.

We can (with much more confidence than for the sizes of the preceding groups)

TABLE A

Projection from present birth and death rates for each of three groups of populations.

Aspects of number and growth	Rates and locations of populations		
	High birth, high death	High birth, low death	Low birth, low death
	Tropical Africa, parts of Asia	Asia, Latin America	Europe, North America, Oceania, USSR, Japan
Total number of persons ca. 1970, in billions	0.5	2.0	1.0
Percent increase per year	2	3	0.7
Time needed to double, in years	35	23	100
Doublings per century	3	4	1
Total number of persons ca. 2070, in billions	4	32	2

speak of this group of the world's populations as containing nearly one billion people, a little less than 30 percent of the current world total, and increasing at about 0.7 percent per year.

Table A presents in summary form conclusions on the three groups of populations. During the course of a century they would double 3 times, 4 times, and once, respectively, making totals of 4, 32, and 2 billions.

Prospects for Change in Present Rates

The very approximate scheme of Table A allows us to think about the consequences for the world's future population of the continuance of present rates. The first conclusion is that they cannot continue for a century; if they did the world would contain 38 billion people by the year 2070.

Serious problems will arise if even the low birth, low death rate group continues to increase at the present rate of 0.7 percent per year for a century; its population presses heavily on the environment now.

The same is true *a fortiori* for the other two groups. We can suppose that the death rate for tropical Africa will go down, and some further decline in the death rate for the underdeveloped world as a whole is in immediate prospect. These trends may be seen in the data on the few and small countries in these groups for which we have official statistics over a series of recent years. Mauritius had a crude death rate of 12.86 per thousand in 1955, which by 1966 had fallen to 8.83; the Mauritian $\mathring{e}_0$

increased by 6 years for males and by 7 years for females during the eleven-year period. In Jamaica $\overset{\circ}{e}_0$ increased by 7 years for males and by 9 years for females from 1951 to 1963; in Mexico it increased by 4 years for both males and females from 1960 to 1966. Advances in the expectation of life at age zero of 5 years per decade are typical for the underdeveloped world.

Declines in birth rates are conspicuous in some of the countries around the rim of Asia: the crude birth rate of Taiwan fell from 44.20 per thousand in 1956 to 31.88 in 1966; that of Hong Kong from 34.40 in 1961 to 25.84 in 1966; that of Ceylon from 39.35 in 1953 to 31.58 in 1967; that of Singapore from 43.22 in 1957 to 25.99 in 1967. These are the parts of Asia with the longest and most intense contact with the outside world, and the least prejudice against birth control. Equally encouraging is the fact that in an underdeveloped country of Latin America, Costa Rica, the crude birth rate underwent a similar fall, from 55.45 per thousand in 1960 to 41.75 in 1966.

Increases in crude birth rates during recent periods are not unheard of. Jamaica's went from 33.87 per thousand in 1951 to 39.79 in 1963; Honduras's from 42.38 in 1957 to 44.20 in 1966; French Guiana's from 31.95 in 1961 to 35.21 in 1964. This last increase undoubtedly reflects improved registration of births, and we do not know to what extent the other increases do as well. But a rise in birth rates with the onset of modernization is not *a priori* unlikely; the relaxation of former constraints on reproduction (that permitting remarriage of widows in India is the clearest example) in general precedes the adoption of modern means of limiting reproduction, and in the interval between the one event and the other the birth rate may rise.

Though the rates of today cannot continue, it is worth noting further in what direction they are pointing. That the world population in 2070 would contain 38 billion persons is half the story; the other half is that 36 of the 38 billion would be the children and grandchildren of those who are now poorest. Today's developed countries would then contain—rather than about one-third of the world's population as they do now—only about one-twentieth of it. And since development of the countries that are poor today could not occur in the face of such population growth, we have to imagine 36 billion wretchedly poor versus 2 billion rich, the latter being those of European or Japanese descent. Separated so sharply by race and income, as well as by the pace of reproduction, the two groups would hardly be congenial occupants of the planet. The avoidance of so dismal a predicament is the strongest argument for contraception and development.

The Sweden-Honduras Resemblance and Contrast

Looking at countries in different stages of development today reveals the most striking contrasts in our collection of data, particularly in birth rates. But more

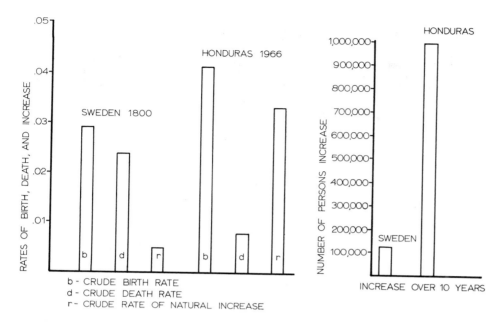

FIGURE 1

Crude rates and natural increase—Sweden, 1800, and Honduras, 1966.

surprising, some very large differences also appear between countries in the same stage of development. The evolutionary viewpoint implicit in many studies suggests that Europe in the early nineteenth century was in the same stage as the tropics are in today. By comparing population data, however, we shall see some dramatic differences according as the stage was reached in the nineteenth century or today.

We continue with the comparison of Honduras, 1966, and Sweden, 1800. The population of Honduras in 1966 was 2,363,000, that of Sweden in 1800 was 2,352,000; for all practical purposes the two numbers are identical. Sweden's income was probably much higher, but both were rugged countries with long stretches of coastline, whose labor forces were principally engaged in agriculture.

With a decidedly lower death rate and a higher birth rate, Honduras has a very much higher rate of natural increase; projecting the Swedish population forward from 1800 with the age-specific birth and death rates of 1798–1802, we find 10 years later a population of 2,478,000, a gain of about 126,000, while for Honduras we calculate that after 10 years the population would number 3,398,000, a gain of more than 1,000,000. Honduras is having to assimilate a natural increase about 8 times as large as that faced by Sweden (Figure 1).

Age differences are also large. In Honduras 51.48 percent of the population is less than 15 years old; in Sweden only 32.60 was less than 15. The burden of providing

10

TABLE B
The three phases of the demographic transition—comparisons for selected countries.

Populations of European descent—over two centuries	Birth rate 1000b	Death rate 1000d	Percent under 15	Other populations around the world—present day only	Birth rate 1000b	Death rate 1000d	Percent under 15
				HIGH BIRTH AND HIGH DEATH RATE PHASE			
Sweden, 1800	29.38	25.08	32.60	Subsaharan Africa			
				Cameroon (West), 1964	45.57	24.06	48.57
				Madagascar, 1966	46.70	24.17	46.51
				HIGH BIRTH AND LOW DEATH RATE PHASE			
England and Wales, 1861	31.73	21.53	35.65	North Africa			
Sweden, 1860	30.64	19.23	33.48	Algeria, 1965	45.19	9.52	47.23
				Tunisia, 1960	40.54	16.92	40.85
				Asia			
				Ceylon, 1967	35.14	9.04	41.86
				India, 1961	41.22	20.00	41.09
				Taiwan, 1966	34.48	6.00	43.69
				Latin America			
				Honduras, 1966	44.05	8.41	51.48
				Mexico, 1966	43.31	8.66	46.26
				Puerto Rico, 1965	28.93	6.53	38.67
				Venezuela, 1965	43.96	6.36	45.41
				LOW BIRTH AND LOW DEATH RATE PHASE			
North America							
Canada, 1966–68	17.52	10.12	32.07				
United States, 1967	17.75	10.36	30.32				
Europe, 1965	17.46	10.83	25.23				

Note: The birth rates *b* and death rates *d* used in this table are those called *intrinsic* in demography, and they are taken from column 15 and 17 of the Summary Table; percent under 15 is from colunm 5. Definitions are given in Chapter 5.

schools and other facilities for the young is thus much greater for Honduras.

It is true that Sweden had a greater proportion of people beyond the main working ages, with 5.49 percent older than 65 years. In Honduras only 1.76 percent of the population is older than 65. But this small disadvantage for Sweden was more than offset by her fewer children. One way of looking at the matter is through the dependency ratio, the number of persons younger than 15 and older than 65 per hundred persons between those two ages. We find that the dependency ratio of Honduras is 113.89, and that Sweden's was 61.53. (In this respect Honduras is extreme, but several other underdeveloped countries show dependency ratios higher than 100.00.)

Less difference appears between Honduras of 1966 and Sweden of 1800 in mortality at older than at younger ages. Men of 70 had an expectation of life in Sweden of 6.82 years; in Honduras the figure is 8.63 years. At the youngest ages, on the other hand, the contrast is dramatic: infant mortality (deaths of children less than 1 year old) is 37.24 per thousand live births in Honduras, and was 248.96 in Sweden. It is not likely that any difference in completeness of registration can be responsible for such a gap.

Without trying to force the analogy, we may use the general demographic similarities already noted as categorizing the three types of present-day populations (high birth and high death rates, high birth and low death rates, and low birth and low death rates) as if they were successive phases in the "evolution" or "demographic transition" of populations. Table B further illustrates the correspondence between these three phases as they have been expressed among the populations of Europe and as they are being expressed today by other populations. Tropical Africa shows high birth and high death rates, corresponding to those of Europe up to the early nineteenth century; Asia and Latin America show high birth rates but much lower death rates, corresponding to those of Europe of the late nineteenth century; Europe and America have low birth rates and low death rates. Our approach uses both cross-sectional (of a number of countries at the same point of time) and longitudinal (of one country at different times) comparisons. Table C and Figure 2 show the longitudinal picture for Sweden, as a kind of base to which the cross-sectional variation of the present day may be referred and contrasted. Though the

TABLE C
The demographic transition in Sweden—birth and death rates per 1000 population.

Five-year period, centered on	Crude rates		Rates standardized by age and sex on United States, 1960	
	Birth	Death	Birth	Death
1780	34.51	25.92	29.88	29.00
1800	31.21	25.88	27.48	31.11
1825	34.73	21.59	31.03	25.27
1850	31.46	20.54	28.49	25.71
1875	30.96	19.22	29.88	22.60
1900	26.79	16.19	26.20	17.38
1925	17.50	11.91	15.06	12.63
1950	16.64	9.85	15.05	9.12

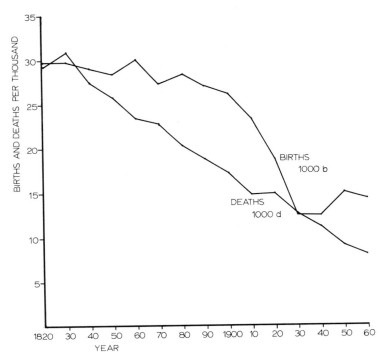

FIGURE 2
The demographic transition in Sweden shown with standardized rates.

European birth rate of 1800 had apparently not yet started its modern decline, it was decidedly lower than those of most present-day underdeveloped countries. (The rates of Table B are intrinsic, defined in Chapter 9, those of Table C are crude.)

Sweden 60 years later corresponds to present-day Asia and Latin America, at least in that some fall had taken place in its death rate but none in its birth rate. But the fall in Sweden's death rate was less dramatic than that of the countries in the second phase today—the drop was from about 25 to about 20 per thousand; in parts of Asia and Latin America today the death rate has dropped to about 7 per thousand. Even the death rate of India, which has only begun to fall, has probably improved as much in the last 20 years as Sweden's did in the 50 years, 1800–1850.

In births, the countries of Asia and Latin America are much above Europe of 1860. Most stand at 40–45 births per thousand; Europe's second-phase birth rates were 30–35 per thousand. We can distinguish countries in the second phase that are moving into the third phase, that of the developed countries—according to both their vital rates and their national incomes—including Taiwan, Puerto Rico, and Hong Kong.

As populations settle into the third phase, they assume something like a steady condition, a birth rate of about 17, and a death rate of 10. But even the durability of this is relative—a natural increase of 7 per thousand means a doubling in 100 years. Is accommodation of such an increase possible, even for rich populations? Does wealth increase the population-carrying capacity of a given territory?

On the one hand, the advance of technology enables man to use the environment more effectively—he can synthesize materials from available resources to replace those formerly produced only from scarce resources. Fabrics like nylon, made out of coal, enable more people to be clothed for the same cost to the environment in raw materials than do fabrics of cotton and wool. Modern fertilizers permit the available combination of land and the sun's energy to support more people than could traditional agriculture.

On the other hand, the increase of wealth allows and encourages human use of more and more-varied commodities. We have increased the bank account of the natural environment by technology, but we also draw larger checks on it. Higher agricultural yields can support a larger population if diet remains the same, but this effect is at least in part offset when they are accompanied by a shift from a cereal to a meat diet. Though with more wealth we can make nature do more for us, our extended activities result in pollution of air and water, overmining, overfishing, and overgrazing. The danger of bankrupting nature seems at least as immediate for the world's rich as for the world's poor. The American and European population increase of 7 per thousand per year, along with increasing per capita use of material goods, is in the long run impossible in a fixed environment. At some time in the future they will have to reduce their population growth; the only question is when. For a given population the precondition of increasing consumption is recognition that the technical processes which contribute to the modern standard of living damage the environment in different degrees; advanced countries will presumably learn to draw their satisfactions from activities less damaging to the landscape in which they have to live.

The data compiled in this book permit further comparisons and contrasts on a continental basis.

Continental Comparisons

Europe is the continent with whose statistics the exigent user can be most nearly satisfied. It inherits an ancient tradition of vital registration and census-taking. It and the United States and Canada have produced an extensive literature on the enumeration errors in total and by age for population, births, and deaths, some of which will be summarized in Part V.

Our technique of putting data—those contained in Table 1 of each set of the

Main Tables of this book—on punch cards and letting the computer do the rest lent itself well to aggregation. We simply added through the decks of data cards for the several countries, and came up with a European total set of data for each of three years—1955, 1960, and 1965. Our regular program was then applied to these data just as it was to data on individual countries, and we obtained the life tables, intrinsic rates, and other results shown (beginning on page 526). A start had been made on this in *World Population*, which gives European computations for 1961; in all we have, therefore, aggregated European data for four years.

What made us want to aggregate these data was the similarity among European countries, comparable with that among states of the United States, as can be ascertained from the Summary Table (pages 72–107). The expectation of life at birth, $\mathring{e}_0$, for males in 1965 was 67.62 for Belgium, 67.61 for West Germany, 67.68 for Italy. Such small variation makes us question the value of studying the countries separately in all their details. It is true that the Netherlands shows the somewhat higher male $\mathring{e}_0$ of 71.14, and Poland is lower with 66.39, but many of the differences are no greater than the margin of error in any one of the figures.

Changes over a period of time are also similar enough among the countries that the continental summary reports the trends in each. The aggregated data on Europe showed increases in the male expectation of life at age zero from 64.88 in 1955, to 66.57 in 1960, to 67.69 in 1965, a total increase of about three years for the decade, but with apparent deceleration. Table D gives a transatlantic comparison. The Common Market countries, as of 1965, have 11 million fewer people than the United States, though in 1955 the two were equal in population; Europe as a whole —up to the boundaries of the USSR—has more than double the population of the United States.

The expectation of life is nearly equal on the two sides of the ocean, with the United States behind for males, and ahead for females. On infant mortality— deaths of children less than one year old per thousand births—Europe goes from 52.68 in 1955, to 39.74 in 1960, to 30.93 in 1965, a striking decrease. The United States shows 29.73, 26.83, and 24.08 at the three dates, a lower rate and a smaller drop. Comparing infant mortality of the United States with that of the Common Market countries reveals a clear convergence, as the latter fell from 40.16 to 32.15 to 25.34 over the same ten years. During the decade 1955–1965, Europe's overall standardized death rate for all ages and both sexes so decreased that at the end of the decade it was almost the same as that of the United States.

Birth rates also are converging. In 1955 the United States was near the peak of its postwar baby boom, while Europe's smaller boom was well past. Since that time the birth rate in the United States has fallen drastically, while that in Europe as a whole has remained relatively constant, and that in the Common Market has gently risen. Convergence towards a uniform 16–18 births per thousand population is suggested by the figures of the Summary Table.

TABLE D

Demographic comparison of the United States and Europe, 1955, 1960, and 1965.

Parameter and year	United States	Europe	European Common Market
Population, in 1000's			
1955	164,301	405,480	164,304
1960	179,990	422,786	172,227
1965	193,818	441,791	182,706
1965 area, in sq km	9,363,000	4,953,000	1,164,000
1965 density per sq km	20.7	89.2	157.0
$\overset{\circ}{e}_0$, males			
1955	66.45	64.88	66.32
1960	66.84	66.57	67.07
1965	66.87	67.69	67.99
$\overset{\circ}{e}_0$, females			
1955	72.61	69.66	71.29
1960	73.40	71.70	72.60
1965	73.83	73.33	74.05
Infant mortality, per 1000 births			
1955	29.73	52.68	40.16
1960	26.83	39.74	32.15
1965	24.08	30.93	25.34
Death rate standardized on United States, 1960, per 1000			
1955	9.68	10.75	10.25
1960	9.39	10.12	9.93
1965	9.30	9.45	9.17
Birth rate, per 1000			
Crude			
1955	25.16	19.26	17.39
1960	23.92	18.60	17.96
1965	19.61	18.04	18.08
Standardized on U.S., 1960			
1955	23.37	16.69	15.45
1960	23.92	16.67	16.17
1965	19.20	16.69	16.97
Intrinsic			
1955	26.86	17.32	15.78
1960	27.65	17.40	16.75
1965	21.29	17.46	17.74
Rate of natural increase— intrinsic, per 1000			
1955	19.88	5.06	3.13
1960	21.13	5.97	5.23
1965	12.65	6.62	7.33

Other Groupings

The statistics shown for Europe and its subdivisions are relatively satisfactory. In the first place, all the countries that may reasonably be counted as being within the area are included, with exceptions totalling less than one percent of the population of the area. Second, each of the countries provides statistical data of high accuracy. Third, the countries resemble one another, demographically and otherwise, a homogeneity required if aggregates and averages are to be useful. None of these statements applies to other continents, and we have thus had to be satisfied with less comprehensive totals for other parts of the world.

For the five countries of Central America—Panama, Honduras, Guatemala, Costa Rica, and Nicaragua—the necessary population, birth, and death statistics are available for at least one year of the period 1964–66, and, when added, provide information on a total population given at 11,247,000. Of this population, 47.55 percent is under the age of 15 years. The crude birth rate is 43.19 per thousand and the death rate 10.80 per thousand. Projection at the rates of the present time gives a population of 18.5 million by 1980, and an ultimate rate of increase of 3.26 percent per year. Rough accuracy of the official birth statistics is suggested by our independent estimate of 45 births and 11 deaths per thousand, which we obtained by using the age distribution and deaths alone in methods described in Chapter 11.

Our West Indies data include seven areas (Barbados, Guadaloupe, Jamaica, Martinique, Puerto Rico, St. Lucia, and Trinidad) for 1963 or 1964, and we have aggregated these to obtain a total population of 6,172,000 persons. Considerably more demographic movement than in Central America is visible here. For example, the stable age distribution that would eventuate from the current age-specific rates of birth and death is much farther from the observed age distribution. The proportion of the population under 15 years of age, 41.69 percent, is lower than in Central America, and the reported birth rate of 34.15 per thousand is much lower. Expectation of life at age zero is 64 years for males, compared with 57 in Central America, and 68 for females compared with 59. One feature of modern mortality is an increasingly favorable expectation of life for women, and the West Indies shows a four-year advantage for women compared with a two-year advantage for women in Central America.

The aggregation of such South American countries as provide data is less justifiable. Aside from the fact that only 54 million persons, one-third of the total population, is included in the available statistics, we face great heterogeneity among countries, ranging in degree of modernization from Ecuador to Uruguay. Similar heterogeneity occurs among the countries of Southeast Asia around 1960, between the extremes of Taiwan and Laos. Hence South America and Southeast Asia appear only in the Summary Table, where 42 numbers are shown for each. We calculated life tables and other quantities for these regions, but decided they were not repre-

TABLE E

Mortality and fertility for five European countries and their principal cities.

Countries and cities	Rates per 1000, standardized on England and Wales, 1961		Expectation of life $\overset{\circ}{e}_0$		Intrinsic rates of		Dependency ratio
	Birth	Death	Males	Females	Birth	Death	
Denmark, 1966	16.60	10.52	70.42	75.10	18.03	9.87	54.59
Copenhagen, 1966	14.29	11.29	68.30	74.61	15.13	11.97	47.85
England and Wales, 1966–68	16.72	11.17	68.72	74.92	18.08	9.90	55.51
Greater London, 1967	15.71	10.07	69.39	76.98	16.34	10.42	48.82
Finland, 1966	14.78	13.71	65.98	73.17	15.71	11.98	52.96
Helsinki, 1966	12.06	13.57	65.63	73.45	12.02	15.18	41.34
West Germany, 1966	16.05	11.83	67.57	73.55	17.03	10.99	53.66
West Berlin, 1966	11.48	12.50	66.42	72.92	11.00	16.48	51.95
Dusseldorf, 1966	12.61	12.09	67.46	73.96	12.22	14.77	43.95
Hamburg, 1966	12.90	11.83	68.17	73.97	12.82	14.17	48.62
Sweden, 1958–62	14.13	9.99	71.55	75.22	14.29	12.43	51.86
Stockholm, 1960	12.15	10.99	69.02	74.91	11.63	15.05	44.94

sentative enough to deserve space among the Main Tables of this book.

In addition to the aggregation of countries into regions and continents, we show some subdivisions of countries. For Canada, the United States, and Australia, provinces or states are given for one period of time. We also obtained data on some cities.

Cities and Countryside. Fertility and mortality statistics for cities provide less reliable measurements than those for whole countries. We had particular difficulty in ensuring that city areas were identically defined for population, birth, and death statistics. A serious distortion derives from the custom of recording as the place of birth or death the locality at which the event occurs, rather than the normal residence of the person; many persons who reside in suburban or rural communities are born and die in hospitals in nearby cities. Intercensal populations of cities are affected by migration; we have annual data on intercountry moves, but not on intercity moves. These problems, and others, are severe enough that demographic literature contains relatively few life tables, intrinsic rates, and similar calculations for cities.

Our own collection of data on 15 cities is only a small beginning, but nonetheless it makes some statements about the relations of cities to the countries of which they are a part. Table E gives for five European countries and for some cities within them the main facts on birth and death rates that we have computed. These statistics bear on such questions as: (1) Do city-dwellers live longer than residents of the countryside? (2) Do city-dwellers have larger families? (3) How close does the population of a city come to maintaining its size from births to its own residents?

The most precise measure at our disposal for comparisons of mortality is *direct standardization*. This is the calculation of the overall death rate that would be sustained by the given population if, having the actual death rates age for age in each sex that it does, it had the age-sex distribution of the standard population (see Chapter 12 for details and a computer program). Because one standard population is not appropriate for all comparisons, we have applied three standard populations, England and Wales, the United States, and Mexico, in Table 6 of the Main Tables for each population. In Table E some of these numbers are extracted for European cities; the standard selected for this purpose is England and Wales, 1961.

Stockholm has higher death rates than Sweden; the directly standardized rate on England and Wales, 1961, shows 10.99 (that is, it would have 10.99 deaths per year per thousand persons with its actual age-specific death rates if it had the 1961 age-sex constitution of England and Wales) compared with only 9.99 for Sweden as a whole. In expectation of life Stockholm is about 1.4 years lower than Sweden, if we average the sexes. The intrinsic death rate (defined on page 51) is 15.05 per thousand for Stockholm, and 12.43 for Sweden. If we can trust the basic data, these various measures decisively show that Stockholm has higher mortality than the rest of Sweden.

At the other extreme, London seems to have a lower mortality than does England and Wales. In between are the cities of West Germany, whose mortalities are very close to that of the country as a whole. The conclusion from this very small collection of data is that if on the average European city death rates are higher than those of the countries to which they belong, the difference is small.

For births there is a clearcut difference—each of the cities in Table E has a lower rate than the country in which it is found. Our standardization has made due allowance for the sex ratio as well as for age distribution. The results come out nearly the same using either the United States, 1960, or England and Wales, 1961, as standards. Even more than with mortality, we would have to allow for income, schooling, and other differences to comment on the pure effect of cities on fertility.

Of the cities of Table E only Copenhagen and London are maintaining their size from their own births. All the others show intrinsic death rates greater than intrinsic birth rates. Such intrinsic rates tell us what would happen if the age-specific rates of birth and death continued, disregarding migration. We see that the population of Stockholm, for example, would decrease by about 0.3 percent per year. North American cities, on the other hand, were reproducing themselves, and would grow substantially if present rates continued, even in the absence of migration, to judge from our limited data on cities of the United States and Canada.

Cities tend to have a favorable—that is to say, low—dependency ratio. For instance, that of Helsinki is just slightly more than 41 (compared with Finland's 53). The dependency ratios of most other European and American cities are either less than 50 or not much more, a result of low birth rates and the tendency of persons of working age to migrate to urban centers.

Underdeveloped countries have dependency ratios far higher than 50 for all types of communities: Taiwan, for instance, has 78.73 for urban, 86.99 for semi-urban, and 91.71 for rural. Even here the city is somewhat better off than the country as a whole.

Ethnic Groups

We would like to have presented more data on ethnic divisions within countries, such as those for West Malaysia. Some cultures assign a competitive value to population size. The Sinhalese in Ceylon compare their population growth with that of the Tamils; the Malays in Malaysia compare theirs with that of the Chinese; those of African origin in Trinidad are interested in how they stand numerically against those of Indian origin. The concern for numbers is a natural one in a democracy, where political power is formally determined by votes. And rivalry to produce more voters in the next generation can act against the economic and ecological necessity of overall population limitation.

CHAPTER 2

What the Age Structure Can Tell Us

Changes in Age Distributions

The data and analysis of this book emphasize age. From changes of age distribution flow important consequences for the educational, economic, and political life of the community. Hauser (1969), using censuses up to 1950, finds that in the United States the fifties was the decade of the elementary school child; the sixties the decade of the college student and young worker. Let us see to what extent our more recent material can elaborate on this.

The Summary Table shows that the percentage of persons less than 15 years old was 31.76 in 1920, and that this percentage fell steadily to a low of 25.12 in 1940, and then rose to a high of 31.30 in 1962 (page 72). It also shows for 1960 different percentages for White and Nonwhite, with the former at 30.33 and the latter at 37.68. But these overall percentages are less dramatic than the absolute numbers in smaller age intervals, some of which appear in Table F, together with projected numbers up to 1980.

That during the 1950's the 5–9 age group increased by $5\frac{1}{2}$ million does indeed make that the decade of the primary school child. The 1960's show the same $5\frac{1}{2}$ million increase in the 15–19 age group. This is, of course, no coincidence: most of the same individuals were 15–19 years old in the 1960's who had been 5–9 in the 1950's. Also, in the 1960's, the 20–24 age group, which had decreased during the previous decade, suddenly increased by 6 million. During the 1970's this age group is expected to increase by a further $3\frac{1}{2}$ million.

Such an increase means different things for different sectors of the population.

Educational facilities are strained to provide enough places for the same proportion of very large cohorts as had been provided for the previous smaller ones. The military has a more plentiful supply of fighting manpower at its disposal. Employers have more workers in prospect, attractive in proportion as they are skilled. To the young people themselves such an increase means they must compete for jobs, but apparently the jobs are to be found in a rapidly increasing and evolving system of production.

Official projections of college enrollments rise considerably faster than the figures for the relevant age groups (U.S. Bureau of the Census, 1968). Total college enrollment increased by 50 percent during the 1950's, and is expected to double during the 1970's—from 3,570,000 in 1960 to more than 7 million. Record *proportions* of the age group 15–24, themselves of record *absolute* size, are expected to attend college during the coming years.

Consistent with changes in the age figures, the number of marriages held about constant during the 1950's, at slightly more than half a million a year, then began to increase in the 1960's, reaching 1,913,000 in 1967, with about three-quarters of these being first marriages (United States Bureau of the Census, 1968). First marriages may be seen in terms of the number of young persons reaching marrying age each year. Suppose, as a rough approximation, that the age group 20–24 is the pertinent one; that one-fifth of it comes to marrying age each year, and that it takes two people from the age group to make a marriage. Then the number of couples eligible for first marriage will be about one-tenth of the 20–24 age group; thus, from Table F, the number of eligible couples increases from about 1,100,000 in 1960 to 1,700,000 in 1970, and to 2,000,000 in 1980.

Not everyone gets married; not everyone who gets married does so at age 20–24; not everyone who gets married at age 20–24 founds a new household and equips a home. But in the United States a high proportion of the population does all of

TABLE F
Observed numbers of persons in the United States 5–24 years old from 1950 to 1965; projected numbers from 1970 to 1980, using age-specific birth and death rates of 1965, without allowance for migration; in thousands.

Year	5–9	10–14	15–19	20–24
1950	13,388	11,225	10,636	11,426
1955	17,151	13,343	11,029	10,310
1960	18,826	16,909	13,351	10,850
1965	20,518	18,956	16,954	13,333
1970	20,358	20,477	18,893	16,858
1975	19,761	20,317	20,408	18,785
1980	22,488	19,722	20,248	20,291

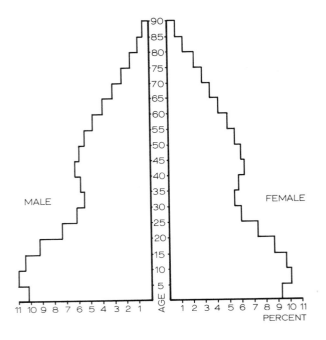

FIGURE 3,A
Population pyramid for United States, 1967.

these things. Hence the age distribution of the population is important to the housing market, among other matters. Such considerations motivate an interest in comparative study of age distributions.

Population Charts

The age and sex distribution of a population is sometimes called a population pyramid (not to be confused with the food pyramid of ecology). Figure 3 shows population pyramids for the United States, Venezuela, and Madagascar. That for the United States has a narrow waist, reflecting the low birth rate of the 1930's, and a bulge for the subsequent baby boom. Venezuela's shows a taper or narrowing towards the older ages. Madagascar's is also a taper, but it exhibits a curious lack of symmetry between males and females of ages 20–24 years, an asymmetry possibly due to errors in the statistics. The stable population theory developed below explains the taper of Venezuela, the fact that the United States has more women than men at the oldest ages, and other features of the distributions given in this volume.

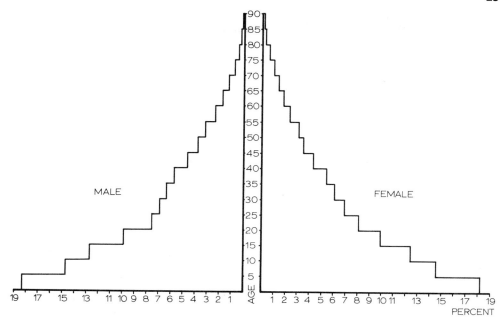

FIGURE 3,B
Population pyramid for Venezuela, 1965.

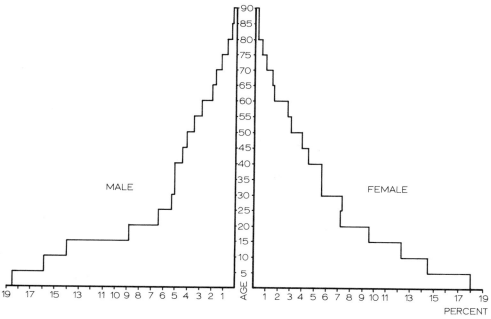

FIGURE 3,C
Population pyramid for Madagascar, 1966.

Graphical methods have in the past been extensively used for the presentation of demographic results. Once conclusions had been drawn from a set of numbers, charts were made to present these conclusions to the reader. Now, however, that data bases have become large, charts have a new function: they serve to examine the data. Instead of asking a draftsman to draw selected charts, we program the computer to provide charts for each of hundreds of populations. Glancing at the charts enables us to see analogies and contrasts that would be more difficult to see in the numbers.

The population pyramid is one example of such graphical assistance. The print-out of Figure 4,A and 4,B shows not only the observed age distribution for males and females, but also the life table distribution (whose theory is given on page 133) for the same population. We could exhibit other sorts of contrasts: for example, one observed population against another, males against females. The only limit on this use of the computer is the fineness of grain that it permits showing: if each page has 60 rows and 130 columns, we can put dots or other symbols in 60×130 possible positions. We can show more positions by running several pages together. Finer detail is available with a cathode ray tube, or with a computer-controlled pen that draws on draftsman's paper. Whatever the method, the demographer now has computerized visual representation to help him examine large masses of numerical data.

Stability in the One-Sex Model

Let us think about the age distribution of women in a population in which birth and death rates have been constant for a long time. Many purposes can be served by analysis of the female side alone, so we will avoid the complication of a two-sex model. The analysis cannot be better arranged than in the form devised by Leonhard Euler in a paper written in 1760. We go back to Euler for this part of the exposition, not only because he introduced the idea of a stable population, but because no one has written on it more clearly. (We require, however, neither his old-fashioned French nor his even more outdated notation.)

Two principles, said Euler, are sufficient to develop a theory of age distributions. The first is the principle of fixed mortality, by which out of a cohort of B births the number of survivors x years later can be written as Bl_x. Let l_x be defined as the probability of surviving to age x and $l_0 = 1$. (This is somewhat more logical than making $l_0 = 100,000$ as elsewhere in this volume and in demographic writing generally.) From l_x we can find the expectation of life of an individual, the value of an annuity to him, and many other matters.

But, like the modern demographer, Euler was not primarily interested in expected values for an individual. He was interested in whole populations, and for

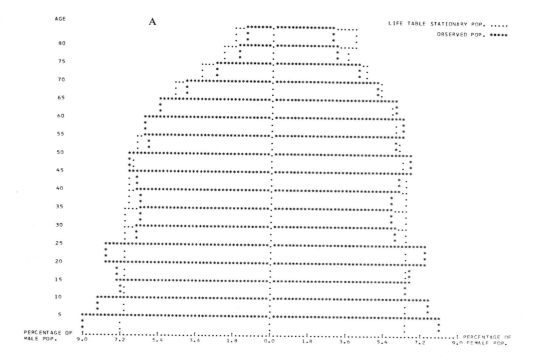

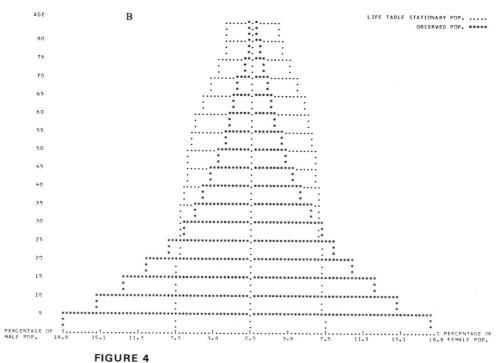

FIGURE 4

Population pyramids for two countries, as drawn by computer.
A: England and Wales, 1968.   B: Mexico, 1966.

this he needed a second principle, which he called the principle of multiplication. Euler's multiplication is the law of geometric increase that Malthus employed 40 years later—simply that if the number of births exceeds the number of deaths, then the population will increase, and if the ratio of increase to population is constant then both the total population and total births will increase geometrically.

These principles suffice to set up the stable model, including the determination of age distribution. For if the births one year (say, this year) are B, the births next year will be $e^r B$, where e^r is the supposed fixed ratio of increase; the births the year following will be $e^{2r} B$, etc. Now we think forward to 100 years in the future. (For simplicity, we can assume that everyone who would then be older than 100 years had died.) Suppose, as Euler did, that all the births of a given year occur on one day, say July 1. Then the population 100 years hence would consist in the births of this year times the chance of living to age 100, which is Bl_{100}; plus the births of next year, Be^r, multiplied by l_{99}, or $Be^r l_{99}$; the births of the year after that times l_{98}, or $Be^{2r} l_{98}$, etc.; ending with the births of the year 100 years from now, Be^{100r}. Adding over the 100 years, we obtain as the total population at the time

$$Bl_{100} + Be^r l_{99} + Be^{2r} l_{98} + \ldots + Be^{100r},$$

where the first term is people 100 years old, the second people 99 years old, etc. Factoring out Be^{100r} and reversing the order of the terms gives the total population at the time, say P_{100}:

$$P_{100} = Be^{100r}(1 + l_1 e^{-r} + l_2 e^{-2r} + \ldots + l_{100} e^{-100r}),$$

where the first term in the parentheses refers to age 0, the second to age 1 year, etc.

Dividing both sides by the population P_{100}, and remembering that the ratio of births to population in any year is to be a constant according to the principle of multiplication, say b, then we have the identity

$$1 = b + bl_1 e^{-r} + bl_2 e^{-2r} + \ldots + bl_{100} e^{-100r}.$$

The several terms on the right-hand side are for the several ages in the population starting with zero, and they add to one. The proportion of the population zero years old is b, one year old is $bl_1 e^{-r}$, $\ldots$. This is the stable age distribution.

We have followed Euler through his demonstration that the stable age distribution depends only on the life table column that is called l_x in modern notation and the overall rate r by which the population increases. With the fixed life table and the supposition of constant increase, the age distribution is completely determinate. A modern treatment would be more realistic only in dispensing with the assumption that the annual births occur on a single day at mid-year. The argument applies to men as well as to women, or to both sexes added together, but not to the two in interaction; hence it is called a one-sex model.

We can avoid complications arising from the fact that births are really spread over each year by translating Euler's result into continuous terms. If the sought-after proportion of the population between age a and $a + da$ is $c(a)da$, then we have

$$c(a)da = be^{-ra}l_a da,$$

obtained simply by reducing to da the time interval of one year that Euler used.

Euler pointed out that one use of this result is that if we know the age distribution, say from a census, and we know the birth rate and the rate of natural increase, then we can infer the probability of living to each separate age:

$$l_a = \frac{c(a)e^{ra}}{b},$$

as follows directly from the preceding expression for $c(a)da$.

Application to Inference from Incomplete Data

This result of Euler's has had considerable application in recent years (Arriaga, 1968, and others). We do have censuses for many countries that have not set up accurate death registration systems, and Euler's deduction from his expression for age distribution is a powerful tool, applicable wherever rates can be assumed to be approximately fixed.

The age distribution that Europe would have if it retained its life table of 1965 and had a rate of natural increase of $r = 0.035$ is shown as the bottom histogram of Figure 5. If its life table were the same and its r were 0.025, it would be as shown in the next higher curve, and so on up the table. Hence, when we look at an age distribution we ought to be able to identify it with one of such a sequence of curves.

The theory as given in this simple version requires that past rates of birth and death have been fixed. This assumption of stability is a serious restriction on application of the theory. To escape from it requires a complication of the mathematics that need not be entered into here.

Euler ended his researches on stable population theory at about this point, and the next development along the line of our present interest had to wait 200 years for Ansley Coale. Coale observed that if we know the life table l_x and the proportion α of persons less than 25 years old, say, then we can uniquely infer r, the rate of increase of the population. With the fixed (but unknown) rate of increase, the known life table l_x, and proportion α less than 25, we have the equation

$$\alpha = \frac{\displaystyle\int_0^{25} e^{-rx} l_x \, dx}{\displaystyle\int_0^{100} e^{-rx} l_x \, dx}.$$

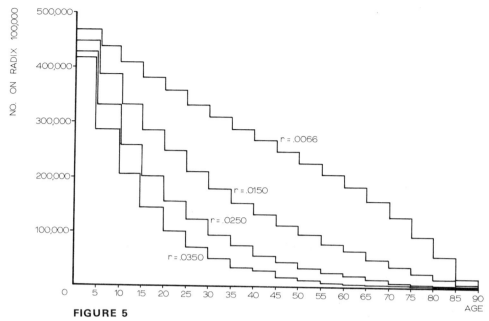

FIGURE 5

Europe, 1965—hypothetical age distribution with actual life table and several values of r, female.

To solve this equation for r is difficult if we insist on a closed form, which is to say if we want to express r as a general function of α and the l_x's. Since the equation is typical of many in mathematical demography, it is instructive to consider how it can be solved in practice.

One way is to construct tables of stable age distribution for various l_x and r. This was the method used by Coale and Demeny (1966). Their procedure is to leaf through the book of tables to find the case with the same α and l_x as the problem, and note what r it shows. The method may be made as precise as necessary by having finely graduated tables and then interpolating.

An alternative method is iteration on a computer. We take out of the integral in the numerator the factor e^{-10r}, to put it in the form $e^{-10r} \int_0^{25} e^{-r(x-10)} l_x dx$, which plainly has the identical value. In the same way we take out of the denominator the factor e^{-20r}, and again multiply within the integral so as not to change anything. Combining these two factors gives us e^{10r} outside the ratio of integrals. Dividing both sides by the ratio of integrals, taking logarithms, and dividing by 10 results finally in

$$r = \frac{1}{10} \ln \left(\frac{\alpha \int_0^{100} e^{-r(x-20)} l_x \, dx}{\int_0^{25} e^{-r(x-10)} l_x \, dx} \right).$$

This is exactly the same equation as that with α on the left given earlier, since each change made works in exactly the same way on both sides. And yet we are in sight of a solution for r. Take an arbitrary value of r on the right; with this and the known l_x evaluate both integrals; multiply by α and take the logarithm, and so obtain an improved value of r, say r^*. Entering this in its turn on the right-hand side permits further improvement in r. After about four cycles no further changes in r occur, and the iteration can be stopped. When the process converges, we know it must converge to the right answer; since the second form of the equation is really equivalent to the first, any r that satisfies one must satisfy the other. For this and many other equations, then, all we do is manipulate into a form whose right-hand side is relatively insensitive to the value of the unknown, then choose an arbitrary value of the unknown to start with and iterate until no further change occurs. An infinite number of forms is possible, and, as long as convergence occurs fairly quickly we need not be very discriminating about which we use. The continuous form above has to be altered to the five-year age intervals of l_x, a minor technical problem discussed in Chapter 10.

As an example of the use of this method, consider some data on Colombia, 1965. Solution of the equation for r just given, using the observed $\alpha = 0.643$ and l_x from a Colombian life table, provides the value of $r = 0.0333$. All this is from the female age distribution only. The identical calculation may be applied to the male side, using the proportion of males less than 25 years old and the male life table. The estimate of r so obtained is 0.0329. When we look up the vital statistics as officially registered we find a birth rate of 0.0384 and a death rate of 0.0099, giving a rate of natural increase of 0.0285.

Our calculation from the census gave the rates of increase of 0.0333 for females and 0.0329 for males; the births less deaths calculation gives the much lower 0.0285 for both sexes. Which shall we accept? Further evidence is available, including the probable under-registration of births that would make the births less deaths figure too low. From this we can safely assume that the actual rate of natural increase is much closer to our estimate, say 3.3 percent, than it is to the official vital statistics.

Many other equations are used in the burgeoning part of demography that makes inferences from incomplete data. The field has been developed by Bourgeois-Pichat, Brass, Coale, Demeny, Henry, Lopez, Thompson, and others. We shall use their methods in Chapter 11, where the program INFER is developed.

The Stable Model and Actuality

We have indirectly tested Euler's model by showing that it gives a reasonable estimate of the rate of natural increase but a more direct test is desirable. We may make such a test by noting the distribution of a population as observed in a census and comparing this with what the distribution would be on Euler's stable model.

This comparison has been made for some 700 populations, and the smallest difference appears in England and Wales, 1881, disregarding hypothetical and cohort data. At that time the percent distributions of females in the observed and stable populations included the numbers:

Age	Observed	Stable	Difference (Observed − Stable)
0–4	13·2	13·1	0·1
5–9	11·8	11·4	0·4
10–14	10·5	10·4	0·1
15–19	9·6	9·5	0·1
20–24	9·1	8·6	0·5
. . .	. . .	. . .	. . .

A measure of the difference between the observed and the stable is Δ, the index of dissimilarity, the sum of the positive differences in percentage. For England and Wales in 1881 the index was $\Delta = 1.4$, apparently the record low for all times and places (column 9 of the Summary Table, page 104). The United States in 1967 showed a much greater value: $\Delta = 6.2$ (Table 8, page 361, and Summary Table, page 72). The record high is the index of Japan, 1966, of $\Delta = 26.3$. Europe's instability as measured by Δ is similar to that of the United States.

For many purposes of analysis a model is indispensable, and the stable model is especially convenient. But we can trust what it tells us only up to a certain point. Comparing, for instance, Venezuela with the United States in proportions of the population less than 15 years old (page 76), we note that the observed percentages are 45.4 and 30.9 for 1965, or that Venezuela has an excess of 14.5 percentage points. If we make the same comparison by means of the stable model we obtain 46.5 versus 28.4, or 18.1 points more for Venezuela. The stable model gives a difference in the right direction but about 25 percent too high. We might have been warned against using the model in this instance by the fact that Δ for the United States was more than 6. It seems prudent to use the stable model principally for populations of low Δ, though even for others the model tells us something.

Explanation of Differences in Proportions

As the second application of Euler's stable population model we try to explain the fact that 45.4 percent of Venezuela's population is less than 15 years old. The high dependency determined by the size of the younger age groups is a hindrance to development; resources must be devoted to caring for and educating children

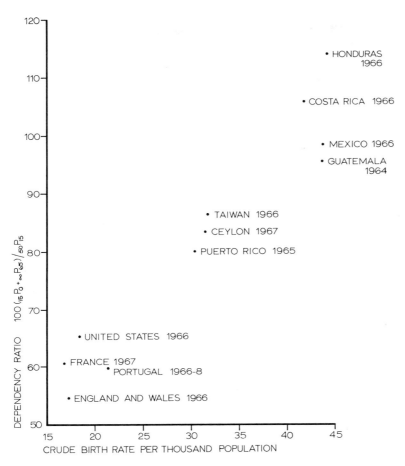

FIGURE 6

Relation of dependency ratio and crude birth rate.

that could otherwise go into building factories. Since resources are finite, the country can *either* have fewer children with good prospects for productive employment *or* many children whom there will not be the equipment to employ when they grow up.

Such considerations motivate us to compare data on other countries when they were in a corresponding stage of economic growth. We note, for instance, that Sweden, ca. 1805, had only 32.74 percent of its population younger than 15 years.

As already mentioned, demographers find it useful to add the young and old populations together and express the total as a ratio to the population of working age. If age 15 separates children from adults, and age 65 separates the labor force from those older, as is conventionally assumed for this purpose, then the children may be designated as $_{15}P_0$, those of labor force age as $_{50}P_{15}$, and the old as $_\infty P_{65}$. In this notation the beginning of the interval is shown by a subscript on the lower right and the length of the interval by a subscript on the lower left. Thus, we may write

$$\text{dependency ratio} = \frac{_{15}P_0 + {_\infty P_{65}}}{_{50}P_{15}} \times 100.$$

The dependency ratio was 61.75 for Sweden, 1805, and 93.81 for Venezuela, 1965. Each person of working age in Venezuela had, on the average, more than half again as many dependents as did the person of working age in Sweden. Sweden's lower proportion of children gave it a substantial advantage over Venezuela in the possibilities of industrial investment when the two were at similar stages of development.

We see by Figure 6 how close is the relation for various countries between the birth rate and the dependency ratio. Since the largest element in the latter is the number of children, this result is not surprising. We certainly expect that insofar as death rates are about the same the country with the higher birth rate will have more children less than 15 years old. But we are also interested in the fact that the percentage older than 65 was 2.99 in Venezuela and 5.43 in Sweden. We proceed to an analysis that will show most of this difference in the older than 65 to be due to *birth* rates.

A Technique for Decomposition

We may ask to what extent is the difference between Sweden and Venezuela in any function of age due to the difference between their birth rates and to what extent is it due to the difference between their death rates. To answer such a question we need a model in which we can first vary births, then deaths; without a model we can only note that Sweden had a much higher death rate than does Venezuela—24.9 per thousand compared with 7.1—and that, on the other hand, Venezuela has a higher birth rate than did Sweden—43.5 compared with 31.3—and this ends the matter. Luckily we find that Δ for the departure of the observed ages from those on the stable model is as low as 1.6 for Sweden, 1805, and 3.4 for Venezuela, 1965. These low values encourage us to proceed using Euler's formulation. We need look no further for a model that will allow us to perform an experiment: specifically to ascertain what proportion of the population would be less than 15 years old in a country that age by age had the death rates of Sweden, 1805, and the birth rates of Venezuela, 1965. By comparing this hypothetical population with that of Sweden, 1805, we obtain a pure indicator of the effect of fertility when mortality is held constant.

The percentage less than 15 years old in Sweden, 1805, was 31.3. The percentage less than 15 years old in the hypothetical population with Swedish death rates and Venezuelan birth rates is 43.6. Hence the effect of the higher Venezuelan fertility is to raise the proportion less than 15 years old by 12.3 percentage points. These numbers are found in the first section of Table G, which is arranged to show effects of all combinations of the mortality and fertility rates of five countries. The fertility for each entry is that of the population at the top of the column; the mortality is that of the population at the beginning of each row. The numbers for the five countries themselves are found along the diagonal in each section.

What was the effect of mortality? To ascertain this for the percentage of the population less than 15 years old, we compare the Swedish population with that of a hypothetical country having Swedish birth rates and Venezuelan death rates. Sweden's percentage was 31.3, and that of the hypothetical population 34.2, or only 2.9 percentage points higher than Sweden's.

This gives the answer we seek: of the difference between Sweden's 31.3 percent less than 15 and Venezuela's 47.7 percent, 12.3 was due to fertility differences and 2.9 percent to mortality differences. If we do the calculation in the other direction— starting with Venezuela rather than Sweden—we obtain 13.5 percent and 4.1 percent, the discrepancy being due to interaction. Interaction here means that the birth effect is not quite the same in the presence of Swedish mortality as in the presence of Venezuelan mortality, which introduces an uncertainty into the conclusion. We can say that, in this instance, the effect of fertility in determining what percentage of a population is less than 15 years old is three or four times as important as the effect of mortality.

Any other difference between the age distributions of the two populations can be similarly analyzed. The dependency ratio was 58.9 for Sweden and is 102.1 for Venezuela. Of the difference about 29 is due to fertility and 14 to mortality, where we average the two ways of making the calculation. The mean age of the population is 21.1 years for Venezuela and was 29.1 for Sweden. Of the difference about 7 years are due to fertility and 1 year to mortality.

Consider the second section of Table G, percentage of population 65 years old and older. The first figure derives from Venezuelan birth and death rates; the next figure down the diagonal from those of the United States. To what extent is the large difference—2.8 percent compared with 13.5—due to the difference in birth rates between the two countries, and to what extent to the difference in death rates? By comparing along the first line, which is to say holding both populations at Venezuela's death rate but allowing each to have its own birth rate, we explain almost the whole difference, as we do again by comparing along the second line, holding both at the United States' death rates. Comparing down the columns, on the other hand, which is to say holding birth rates fixed, but allowing each country to retain its own death rates, we find very little of the overall difference reflected. Evidently the proportion at any age in the two countries, including the proportion

TABLE G
Features of age distribution and rates of increase obtained by combinations of female birth and death rates from five countries: Venezuela, 1965; United States, 1967; Madagascar, 1966; England and Wales, 1968; and Sweden, 1803–1807.

Age-specific death rates of	Age-specific birth rates of				
	Venezuela	United States	Madagascar	England	Sweden
PERCENTAGE OF POPULATION LESS THAN 15 YEARS OLD					
Venezuela	47.7	23.9	47.8	23.6	34.2
United States	48.5	24.5	48.6	24.2	34.8
Madagascar	45.0	22.0	45.2	21.8	32.1
England	48.5	24.5	48.6	24.2	34.8
Sweden	43.6	21.0	43.8	20.8	31.3
PERCENTAGE OF POPULATION 65 YEARS OLD AND OLDER					
Venezuela	2.8	13.1	2.8	13.3	7.1
United States	2.8	13.5	2.8	13.7	7.3
Madagascar	2.7	12.0	2.7	12.2	6.5
England	2.8	13.1	2.7	13.3	7.1
Sweden	2.5	10.9	2.5	11.0	5.8
DEPENDENCY RATIO					
Venezuela	102.1	58.8	102.4	58.7	70.3
United States	105.4	61.1	105.6	60.9	72.5
Madagascar	91.3	51.5	91.8	51.3	62.8
England	105.2	60.3	105.5	60.1	72.1
Sweden	85.6	46.7	86.2	46.6	58.9
MEAN AGE					
Venezuela	21.1	35.5	21.0	35.7	28.3
United States	20.8	35.4	20.8	35.7	28.2
Madagascar	22.0	36.0	21.9	36.2	29.0
England	20.8	35.2	20.8	35.5	28.1
Sweden	22.5	36.1	22.4	36.2	29.1
INTRINSIC RATE OF NATURAL INCREASE, $1000r$					
Venezuela	38.5	4.9	38.6	4.5	19.5
United States	40.7	7.1	40.8	6.7	21.5
Madagascar	22.3	−11.3	22.5	−11.6	3.8
England	41.0	7.4	41.1	7.0	21.8
Sweden	24.3	−9.4	24.6	−9.6	6.4

of old people, differs in the long run mainly because they differ in birth rates.

All this is based on the stable model, and constitutes the most exact treatment possible at this level of simplicity. In fact the observed percentages 65 years old and older were 2.99 for Venezuela and 9.50 for the United States, a ratio of about three to one compared with the five to one of the stable model. To this degree of approximation Table G permits analysis of observed differences; the analysis will be most trustworthy where the populations most closely approximate the stable model.

Unstable Populations

Explaining differences for the several age groups between the proportions observed and those computed using the stable model can in itself be instructive. The United States census of 1960 may be taken as an example of an age distribution differing considerably from the stable. The value of Δ was 10.0, rather larger than those we find for Europe or the United States at most times of their history. The proportion less than 5 years old, computed using the stable model, was too high, 12.7 compared with 10.9 in the observed, due to the drop in the birth rate that had started about 1957–58. On the other hand, the computed proportion was low for the ages 35–39, 6.0 percent compared with the observed 7.0 percent, reflecting the high birth rates of the early 1920's. For Europe the effects of wars are superimposed on those of prosperity and depression.

The method that evolves for analyzing age distributions has three stages. The first is to compare the observed age distribution with that computed using the stable model; this tells us what is explainable entirely in terms of the current rates of birth and death, without appeal to historical factors. The second stage is to see to what extent the departures of the observed from the stable can be attributed to recent trends in births and deaths. The third stage is to explain residual discrepancies by extraordinary historical events, including wars, which reduce the numbers of males in their twenties, immigration, which tends to increase the numbers of males in their twenties, and famines, which especially reduce the number of young children.

Three kinds of populations appear in demographic discussion: observed, stationary, and stable, the last two being models only. The stable population has the fraction $be^{-ra}l_a da$ of its total between ages a and $a + da$, the stationary has $bl_a da$ between a and $a + da$. In the stationary population the birth rate b is $1/\mathring{e}_0$, the reciprocal of life expectancy; it is the special case of the stable where $r = 0$. See Part III for methods of calculating these quantities.

CHAPTER 3

Accounting for the Sex Ratio

Sex-Age Distribution

On the whole the population of the United States contains more females than males, but the difference is by no means uniform through the several age groups. Figure 7 shows that there are more males up to age 20, and from then on more females, with the largest differences after about age 65. Demographers usually discuss such matters in terms of the sex ratio, defined as the number of males per hundred females, either in the population as a whole, or in a particular age interval.

Essentially the same method of study that worked for age distribution will be found helpful in accounting for the varied sex ratios in observed populations. Our analysis, as before, will start with the current age-specific rates of birth and death, now on the two sexes separately, from which a stable model may be constructed; what is left unexplained by this stable model can be referred to trends affecting the rates in recent years; what is still unexplained can be pursued by study of migration, sudden changes in death rates due to wars, epidemics, and other historical events. The method is implied in the treatment by Hawley (1950).

To convert the one-sex model used for the analysis of ages into the (very primitive) two-sex model needed now, we must add one item of data: the sex ratio at birth, say s. If s boys are born for each girl, and B girls are born in the current year, then the number of boys born is sB. By exactly the same argument as was used by Euler, we can now write down the sex-age distribution if the regime of mortality and fertility is fixed, and population is increasing in a geometrical sequence with a ratio e^{5r} of increase over any five-year period. Births, as well as each age-sex group, are all

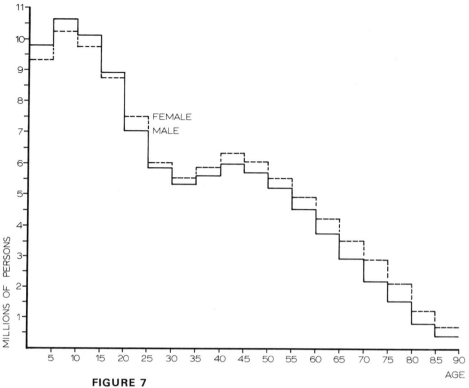

FIGURE 7
Male and female populations by age, United States, 1967.

supposed increasing at this ratio in our stable model. The survivors to the end of the first five-year period in a group of B female births per year will be $B \int_0^5 l_t dt$, which we will write $(B)(_5L_0)$, or simply BL_0 wherever the context shows that five-year age intervals are meant. The survivors in the female age group 5–9 will be BL_5, etc. Since male births are sB, male survivors at the end of the first five-year period are sBL_0^*, and at the end of the second five-year period sBL_5^*, etc., where an asterisk distinguishes the male from the female life table. Then the ratio of males to females in the successive age groups is $sL_0^*/L_0, sL_5^*/L_5, \ldots$

Note that the sex ratio at any age in this model, which is closed to migration, depends only on the two life tables and on the sex ratio at birth. It depends not at all on either the ratio of increase r or the birth rate. On entering the numbers for the United States, 1965, at ages 70–74 in the result of the preceding paragraph we have

$$sL_{70}^*/L_{70} = 1.0472 \, \frac{224{,}489}{326{,}260} = 0.7205.$$

This may be compared with the observed ratio of men to women in the United

States, 1965, of 0.7856. Similar comparisons for other ages are shown in Table H.

For the oldest age groups the model shows a steadily falling sex ratio with age, as does the observed population. In fact, the calculated sex ratio falls even lower than the observed. The difference between male and female mortality has increased in recent years, and this accounts for the observed ratio being higher than that calculated on the stable model; the discrepancy is in one sense a lag of the observed behind the stable. For example, the value of $sL_{40}*/L_{40}$ for 1939–41 was 1.0131, compared with 1.0084 shown for 1965 in Table H, a small difference, but in the right direction. The trend in $sL_{40}*/L_{40}$ is generally downward over 45 years, a measure of the greater improvement of female than of male survivorship:

1919–21	1.0310
1929–31	1.0155
1939–41	1.0131
1949–51	1.0150
1959–61	1.0118
1965	1.0084

Some of the discrepancies of Table H are due to heavy immigration of males into the United States during the early part of the century, which raises the observed sex ratios but is not taken into account in the stable model.

The model fits especially badly at ages 20 and 40. This is partly due to many members of the armed forces being abroad, and thus not in the observed population, but implicitly included in the stable population. Incompleteness of enumeration of young men in the 1960 census is also part of the cause, since it lowers the 1965 estimates that constitute our "observed."

TABLE H
Comparison of observed sex ratios and those calculated on the stable model for the United States, 1965.

Age	Observed			Calculated on stable assumption, with $s = 1.0472$		
	Males in 1000's	Females in 1000's	Ratio	L_x*	L_x	sL_x*/L_x
0–4	10,432	10,002	1.0430	486,168	489,235	1.0406
20–24	6,539	6,794	0.9624	476,823	484,298	1.0310
40–44	6,033	6,378	0.9459	453,348	470,778	1.0084
60–64	3,710	4,099	0.9051	345,754	410,024	0.8831
80–84	820	1,175	0.6979	94,580	180,614	0.5484

TABLE I

Observed sex ratios and those calculated on the stable model for Austria, 1965.

Age Group	Observed	Stable sL_x^*/L_x	Ratio of observed to stable
35–39	0.9459	1.0116	0.94
40–44	0.7293	1.0034	0.73
45–49	0.7317	0.9925	0.74
50–54	0.7617	0.9772	0.78
55–59	0.7841	0.9487	0.83
60–64	0.7984	0.8939	0.89
65–69	0.6956	0.8133	0.86
70–74	0.5947	0.7183	0.83
75–79	0.5524	0.6196	0.89
80–84	0.5340	0.5330	1.00
85+	0.4783	0.4234	1.13

Further illustrations of the way that age and sex distributions reflect the history of a country are to be found in the calculation for Austria, which suffered the impact of two wars in this century (Table I).

Mortality Differences Between the Sexes

For at least the past two generations in advanced countries female mortality has been lower than male mortality. In the United States life table for 1920 the expectation of life at age zero was 54.5 for males and 56.4 for females. The difference increased at an accelerating pace, and by 1967 the expectation for males was 67.0 and that for females 74.2, a difference of more than 7 years. The probability of male survivorship L_x^* increased much less than L_x for females. We noted in the examples of the preceding section that this caused the stable sex ratios sL_x^*/L_x to fall towards the end of life.

Expectation of life at age 1 is free of the factor of higher male infant mortality, but we find the expectation for males to be 67.7 and that for females 74.7, again a difference of 7 years.

Even if we eliminate all ages up to 50, we still find women 5.5 years ahead. After that the difference decreases more rapidly, being 2.65 by age 70. This difference in expectation in favor of females at the oldest ages is a newer phenomenon than the overall difference in their favor; in 1920 the female $\mathring{e}_{70}$ was only 0.3 of a year more than the male.

To what extent does the rise of the female expectation relative to that of the male hold in other advanced countries? It certainly holds for England and Wales, where the female had an advantage of 2.5 years in 1861; this had grown to 6.2 years by 1966–68. The difference for France is the record high: we calculate, for 1967, 68.0 for the male $\dot{e}_0$ and 75.5 for the female. For the aggregation of Europe as a whole we note a difference in favor of the female of 5.1 years as of 1960, and of 5.5 years for the Common Market countries. By 1965 the difference for Europe had risen to 5.6 years, with the expectation for males at 67.7 and for females at 73.3; the Common Market difference had increased to more than 6 years (page 118).

The mortality of underdeveloped countries has fallen almost to the same level as that of the developed ones. Aside from tropical Africa, where mortality is like that of eighteenth century Europe, the countries of the Third World resemble Europe and America in the 1920's, as we saw earlier. The underdeveloped countries tend today to have mortality differences between the sexes; values of female $\dot{e}_0$ about 5 years greater than those of male $\dot{e}_0$ are common.

TABLE J
Ratio of male to female mortality, United States and Europe.

Age interval from	United States, 1967	Europe,* 1965
0	1.30	1.25
1	1.25	1.15
5	1.38	1.05
10	1.72	1.15
15	2.51	2.18
20	2.80	2.33
25	2.26	1.92
30	1.81	1.73
35	1.68	1.64
40	1.72	1.57
45	1.79	1.62
50	1.95	1.78
55	2.07	1.95
60	2.10	1.95
65	1.91	1.80
70	1.82	1.57
75	1.56	1.39
80	1.33	1.27
85+	1.08	1.13

*West of the USSR, omitting only Northern Ireland. The population included numbered 442,000,000.

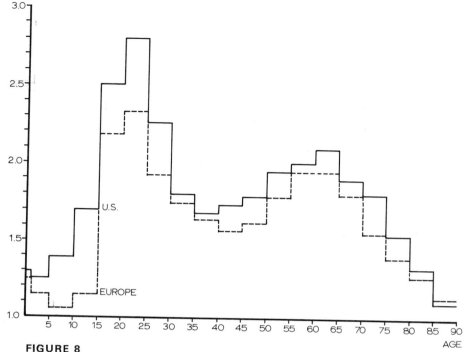

FIGURE 8

Ratio of male to female mortality by age for the United States, 1967, and Europe, 1965.

Expectation of life is only one measure of the difference in overall mortality between the sexes. It rests on an implicit weighting of the several age groups according to the stationary age distribution, and this is not the same for males and females; the stationary female population contains more old people by virtue of the same difference in mortality that we are trying to compare. Also the stationary age distribution for both males and females is much more weighted than the observed age distribution towards the older ages, at least for growing populations. Expectations of life are a good way of assessing prospects for individuals, but they tend to underestimate differences between populations.

A more complete analysis would start by considering individual categories of age and sex, calculating the age-specific rates for males and for females, and then the ratio of the male to the female rate. Table J shows the result for the United States, 1967, and for our aggregation of Europe as a whole.

The ratios of the death rates of the two sexes show a characteristic pattern. They start with male infant mortality 25 or 30 percent higher than female, then decline slightly, then rise to a point at which male mortality is 2.5 times as high as female (this is for the 20–24 age group), then decline again to a low about age 35–39, then rise again to age 60, where male mortality is about twice female; finally they descend to near equality by age 85 and older. The pattern of three peaks (a minor one at age 0

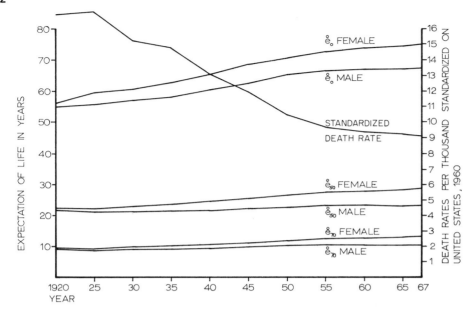

FIGURE 9
Male and female life expectancies, and death rates standardized by age and sex,
for the United States, 1920–1967.

and major ones about ages 20 and 60) and three troughs (a minor one about age 5 and major ones about ages 40 and 85), shown in Figure 8, is repeated from country to country.

These surprising differences between the sexes, with male mortality more than double female at the peak, are a modern phenomenon. They appear rather less conspicuously in eighteenth century Sweden, in tropical Africa today, and among Nonwhites in the United States. In places and times of heavy mortality males and females show no such uniform relation.

Figure 9 shows how male and female mortality have diverged in recent years. The divergence appears in the expectation of life at all three ages given. Note that the slope for $\dot{e}_0$ is somewhat more sharply upward than those for $\dot{e}_{50}$ and $\dot{e}_{70}$, but that the slope of the standardized rate is much greater than that of any of the $\dot{e}$'s.

Further study of mortality requires analysis by cause of death, of which an example is given in Table K. The peak in motor-vehicle accidents for males at ages 15–24 is striking, both in relation to males of other ages and to females. Notable also is the very much greater male mortality due to heart disease, excepting only the last age group.

Age patterns of mortality can be significantly different, even among countries having the same overall mortality. For example, males in England and Wales, 1966–68, have on the whole the same mortality as males in the United States, 1967,

TABLE K
Deaths by age and sex from two causes in the United States, 1967.

Age group	Motor-vehicle accidents		Arteriosclerosis and degenerative heart diseases	
	Male	Female	Male	Female
0–14	3,669	2,243	28	15
15–24	12,169	3,477	113	57
25–34	5,689	1,528	1,058	362
35–44	4,257	1,513	10,284	2,229
45–54	4,144	1,675	36,923	8,698
55–64	3,467	1,616	74,186	24,748
65–74	2,702	1,583	100,689	59,220
75+	2,017	1,152	121,786	132,604
Totals	38,114	14,787	345,067	227,933

Source: *Vital Statistics of the United States, 1967. Mortality*, Vol. 2.

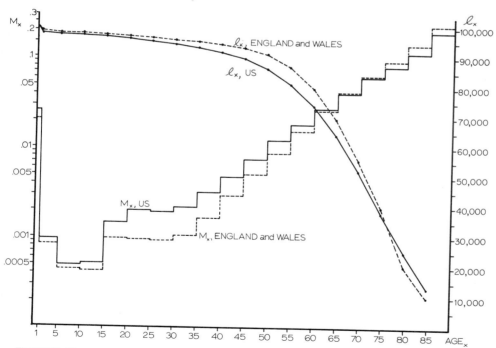

FIGURE 10

Comparison of male age-specific death rates M_x, United States, 1967, and England and Wales, 1966–1968, and l_x columns from the corresponding life tables.

yet large differences appear in individual ages. With surprising consistency (Figure 10) male mortality in the United States is higher at the ages younger than 65 years and lower at the ages above 65. Since the l_x curve in effect cumulates the age-specific rates, we are not surprised that the probability of living to any age less than 75 is greater in England and Wales, and of living from birth to ages above 75 is greater in the United States.

When we standardize on the United States, 1960, male mortality of England and Wales is lower by 0.04 per thousand (9.12 for the United States and 9.08 for England and Wales); when we standardize on England and Wales, 1961, the male mortality of the United States is lower by 0.07. A more precisely balanced equality of overall mortality could hardly be asked for.

CHAPTER 4

Policy Dilemmas and the Future

The study of fertility confronts us with painful dilemmas. We like people, and children especially, yet we have to admit that in a finite world there can be too many of them. The countries of western Europe and northern North America rose to wealth and power as their populations increased; must we say that developing countries of today have too many people before they even start the process of development? Are observers quicker to perceive the ill effects of overpopulation in countries other than their own, perhaps as an unconscious expression of their nationalism? Whether or not outsiders can be unbiased, population problems can best be dealt with by the nations concerned. In recent times this has meant by government policy. Some authority (political, economic, or spiritual) must find the means to discourage parents from having more children than the economy and ecology can accommodate.

The powerlessness of governments to change the birth rate by persuasion is suggested by the vain efforts—for example, in nineteenth century France—to keep the number of births up, and is also shown in many underdeveloped countries of today by their lack of success in lowering the number of births. If persuasion is ineffective, and the pressure of material necessity is decisive, then governments ought to see that parents of large families are disadvantaged economically, as they were in all social classes in nineteenth century Europe. But the operation of such sanctions against having many children involves hardships for children already born. Could a tax be imposed that parents would be unable to shift to the innocent offspring? One way would be to require parents to pay a tax in advance of conceiving, but this raises even more bitter conflicts of values.

Whether or not parents were required to pay a tax, could they be compelled to demonstrate assets equal to the cost of raising their children before being given permission to conceive? Childbearing would be greatly reduced by this requirement, and the financial support of the children would be guaranteed. The present system, under which children's expenses are covered by parents as they are incurred, amounts to buying children on the installment plan. Installment buying encourages improvidence and results in the purchase of more children (or other commodities) than would be bought if full payment were required at delivery of the article. But installment buying of children would be much harder to limit than, say, installment buying of automobiles, or stock-exchange dealings on margin.

Taxes on large families and other disincentives will not be acceptable until the crush of population is much more severe than it is at present. As the pressure of population becomes generally apparent, a sequence of changes will occur. First, abortion will become acceptable—this is already happening. Then the tax exemption for third and later children will be removed. Then contraception may become compulsory for families who have had three children. The visible harm of increasing population density is yet far short of what would make the last restraint seem proper to an electorate. Possibly births will be curbed voluntarily before density imposes extreme measures, but this no one can yet foretell. We would like to see disincentives that allow the maximum choice to individual couples, yet result in a near-zero average increase.

Overpopulation presents different problems depending on whether a country is rich or poor. The overpopulated poor country is faced with unemployment and hunger. If a rich country is overpopulated, the shortages are of space, air, and clean water. The residents of a rich country are more-or-less fully employed, and each uses many times the space, air, and water that are consumed by the citizen of a poor country.

What makes the problem difficult and provides fuel for endless controversy is that increasing population size in both rich and poor countries is only one of many factors that produce discomfort; those who wish to concentrate on other factors can argue that there is no population problem. We could, in principle, clean up the air and water even if populations were much larger than those of today. Western Europe approaches the United States' standard of living with seven times its population density, yet has no more trouble with air, water, and garbage; the United States could solve its pollution problems if it were prepared to sacrifice other aims. The poorest and most densely populated country could accumulate capital if its people would work hard and intelligently enough and postpone their rewards for doing so. But all undertakings become more difficult as there are more people. This interaction of population growth with other variables of the economy and the ecology is what makes the population problem so obscure and so persistent.

In the past some intergroup differences contributed to a stabilizing process.

When rural fertility was higher than urban, the needs of the cities for more people could be filled by migration from the rapidly growing countryside. Rural people of high fertility came to the cities; in response to the new kind of life, their children had few children; the city death rate was high; more migrants from the countryside were welcome. The same applied to income categories, with the fertile poor taking the place of rich families that died out.

Two circumstances interfere with population stability today. One is the fact that many populations are increasing today at faster rates than have prevailed in the past, and this means much greater differentials. Victorian England was growing faster than Victorian India, but still at an annual rate of less than two percent. Now many countries are increasing at between three and four percent per year, while others are stationary.

Moreover, in the past it has often been the populations of rich countries that grew faster and those of the poor countries that grew more slowly. In a rich country, rapid increase could dilute prosperity; in a poor one, high death rates could check poverty. This constituted a negative feedback of a kind that can be stable. But now the rich countries have the lowest rates of increase; the poor grow faster and hence become poorer. Insofar as poverty is, in turn, a cause of increase, we have a positive feedback system that is notoriously unstable; national differences do not tend to disappear but to grow larger.

Some, though by no means all, of these issues may be examined with the help of our data. We hope that the statistics that follow will contribute evidence for and against the hypotheses just mentioned and others.

CHAPTER 5

The Columns of the Summary Table Defined

In the Summary Table, included as Part II of this book, are 42 facts regarding each of 752 populations. The 42 facts are in columns spread over four pages and include the observed and projected populations; a description of age structure; the crude, standardized, and intrinsic rates of birth and death; age-specific death rates; life table probabilities; life expectancies; and some of the parameters of reproduction. The meaning of most of the numbers is readily accessible to common sense, but some are narrowly technical and specialized.

Observed and Projected Populations (columns 1–3)

1. Observed at Mid-Year. Ideally this number would be the total of a census count made on July 1 of the year given, or at the July 1 mid-point of the three- or five-year period given. For many of the populations the number shown is an extrapolation from a preceding census, made by the official statistical agency of the country. In many cases some further interpolation by ourselves was required, for instance when official sources gave the population at the beginning of each calendar year only. The number is in thousands; Algeria, the first country named, is estimated to have had 12,134,000 inhabitants on July 1, 1965.

2, 3. Populations Projected Over 5 and 10 Years. Each projection was made by our computer program, using the births and deaths shown by age in Table 1 of the Main Tables for the population (Part IV of this book). To make the projection we assumed that age-specific birth and death rates of the given period would persist unchanged and that the population is closed to migration. The survivors from each date to the next are supplied by the life tables (calculated earlier in our program) for the two sexes (see Chapter 7 for details). The calculation of each projected population is female dominant, which is to say, births are attributed exclusively to mothers, except for the projections in the last section (those numbered 733–752), which were calculated using a male-dominant model. The population of Algeria, under continuance of 1965 age-specific birth and death rates, would grow to 14,362,000 by mid-1970, and to 16,991,000 by 1975. The numbers of columns 1–3 are shown in thousands.

Age Structure (columns 4–9)

4. Total Reproductive Value. This value, also given in thousands, is the girl children that would be born in the future to the women in the population, again assuming that age-specific birth and death rates persist. Here, however, these rates are discounted like a debt, at the intrinsic rate of natural increase (column 17). The individual reproductive value of a girl child just born is 1, of a girl of 15 somewhat more than 1, of a woman of 50 zero; those of the various age groups are shown in Table 8 of the Main Tables (Part IV). This total over all ages given in column 4 of the Summary Table is the biological potential at the observed rates of the population. Further discussion and definition of reproductive value appears on page 187.

5, 6, 7. Percentages of the Population Younger Than 15 Years, 15–64 Years Old, and 65 and Older. These three age groups represent biological and economic immaturity, the working and reproductive ages, and superannuation. That fully 47.23 percent of the population of Algeria was less than 15 and that only 48.34 percent was 15–64 (that is to say, about one child for each person of working age) contrasts with the percentages in developed countries, in which for each child there are two persons of working age. Ages are in completed years, so that 15–64 means exact age 15 to exact age 65. The three numbers in columns 5, 6, and 7 summarize the population distribution of Table 1 of the Main Tables.

8. Dependency Ratio. The dependency ratio contains in its numerator the number of persons younger than 15 years plus those 65 and older, $_{15}P_0 + {}_\infty P_{65}$, and in its denominator those who are 15–64 years old, $_{50}P_{15}$:

$$\text{dependency ratio} = \frac{{}_{15}P_0 + {}_\infty P_{65}}{{}_{50}P_{15}} \times 100.$$

Following convention we have multiplied by 100.

9. Departure From Stability.   The observed age distribution described broadly in columns 5–7 is in some instances highly irregular when analyzed into finer groups, owing to the effects of wars and other historical events, and especially owing to abrupt or gradual changes in birth rates; Δ, the index of dissimilarity between observed and stable age distributions, is a measure of such irregularity. If the existing regime of mortality and fertility were to continue over a long enough period (and there was no migration), the distribution would gradually come to have a smooth and simple stable form related to the stationary age distribution of the life table (see page 162). The measure Δ tells us how far the existing age distribution departs from the one that would ultimately be reached if no further changes occurred in the age-specific birth and death rates. It is calculated by taking the observed female percentage distribution at each age (given in Table 1 of the Main Tables), and subtracting the corresponding percentage of the female stable age distribution. The sum of the positive differences is Δ. For Algeria Δ is 3.8, which is on the low side; for the Central African Republic Δ is 19.8, which is high, possibly because of age misstatement.

Vital Rates Per Thousand Population (columns 10–17)

10. Crude Birth Rate.   The crude birth rate is obtained by dividing total births by population. Referring to Table 1 for Algeria, 1965 (page 308), we find 528,928 births and 12,133,775 population; the first divided by the second gives 0.04359, which is 43.59 per thousand population. Here, and in the column headings that follow, "crude" means that no account is taken of age.

11. Crude Death Rate.   The crude death rate is similarly obtained: total deaths for Algeria, 1965, were 121,023, which divided by the population gives 0.00997, or 9.97 per thousand.

12. Crude Rate of Increase.   The difference between the last two ratios is 43.59 − 9.97 = 33.62 per thousand population. This, the crude rate of natural increase, tells us that during 1965 the Algerian population increased by 3.362 percent of its mid-year population, disregarding migration.

13. Standardized Birth Rate.   The directly standardized rate given in this column reports how many births per thousand there would have been in the given country and time period if age-specific rates were those given, but the weighting among ages and sexes were that of the United States, 1960. The standardized birth rate of Mauritius fell from 37.71 per thousand in 1955 to 35.40 per thousand in 1966, a decline not nearly as sharp as that shown by its crude birth rate (column 10), which fell from 41.69 per thousand in 1955 to 34.92 in 1966. This drop in the crude rate is a fact, but for its interpretation we have to know that the proportion of women of reproductive age in Mauritius decreased over this interval; a rough indication of this decrease is given by the percentage of the population in the age group 15–64 (column 6), which fell from 54.99 percent to 52.40. In making the calculation of column 13 births were attributed to mothers (that is, female dominance was assumed), except in the last section (page 121), which contains results based on the male-dominant model.

14. Standardized Death Rates. The need to standardize is especially great for mortality comparisons. The crude death rate in Mauritius fell from 12.86 per thousand to 8.83 between 1955 and 1966, according to column 11, a drop of 31 percent. But if the population was younger in the later period, then not all of this decrease is a genuine drop in mortality, and column 14 tells us how much was: it shows a drop from 19.47 per thousand to 15.22, or only 22 percent. The remainder of the decrease in the crude rate of column 11 is due to the lowering of the average age between 1955 and 1966, a lowering partly attributable to the faster rate of natural increase resulting from improved survivorship of young children.

Standardized rates permit comparisons between populations of different places as well as of different times. Mauritius, 1966, shows a crude death rate (column 11) of 8.83 per thousand, compared with the United States' 9.51. Can United States mortality be higher than that of Mauritius? Hardly; when both are standardized on the United States, 1960, as in column 14, the death rate of Mauritius is more than 60 percent higher: 15.22 per thousand compared with 9.33. The standardized rate adjusts for Mauritius' higher proportion of children.

15, 16, 17. Intrinsic Rates of Birth, Death, and Natural Increase. As a closed population is projected forward in time with fixed age-specific rates, its age distribution moves to a fixed or stable form. The intrinsic rates are those that would prevail after the age distribution has become stable. The intrinsic rates are not properties of future population, but a summary of the existing regime of mortality and fertility. They tell us the consequence of a continuance of the current age-specific rates, and are uninfluenced by the initial age distribution of the population.

In Mauritius, the continuance of 1966 age-specific birth and death rates would cause the overall or crude birth rate to rise from its observed 1966 value of 34.92 to 38.89 ultimately. The death rate would change little, and the rate of natural increase would rise from 26.10 to 30.54.

Infant Mortality (column 18)

18. Rate Per Thousand Births. Dividing the deaths of children less than one year old during a calendar period by the births in the same period and multiplying by 1000 gives infant mortality for both sexes together. For Algeria we divided the 46,602 deaths of children less than one year old by the 528,928 births (Table 1, page 308), to obtain 88.11 deaths per thousand births. Infant mortality is a widely used indicator, but it is not actually a true rate; the births of this year are not the appropriate denominator for this year's deaths.

Age-Specific Death Rates (columns 19–22)

19, 20. 1000_4M_1—Death Rates for Ages 1–4, Shown for Males and Females Separately. In 1966 in Mauritius the number of deaths of boys 1–4 years old (Table 1, page 314) was 362, and the mid-period male population of this age was 50,250. The 7.20 given in column 19 of the Summary Table is obtained by dividing 362 by 50,250 and then multiplying by 1000. Note the rapid drop in age-specific death rates shown by Mauritius males, and the even greater drop by females, presumably resulting from the eradication of malaria. The decrease in age-specific death rates in Mauritius between 1955 and 1966 may be compared with that of European countries during the first third of the twentieth century (see page 101 of the Summary Table for Sweden).

21, 22. 1000_5M_{50}—Death Rates for Ages 50–54, Shown for Males and Females Separately. For Algeria, the number for males in column 21 comes from the deaths of men in the age group 50–54, numbering 1584 (Table 1, page 308), divided by the male population in the same age group, 181,817, multiplied by 1000: $(1584/181,817) 1000 = 8.71$. This value is about the same as that for European countries; in general the disparities in mortality rates among countries diminish at the older ages.

Life Table Values (columns 23–34)

23, 24. q_0—Probability of Dying during the First Year of Life for Males and Females Just Born. The numbers given in these columns are obtained from the life tables of each country, being the first numbers of Tables 2 and 3 of the Main Tables (Part IV). Death registrations provide the numbers of deaths, which are given in Table 1, and the exposure to risk of death is determined from the estimated number alive at mid-year. The technique of calculation, and especially of deriving probabilities from rates, is discussed in Chapter 6, which includes the computer program for the life table.

Notice, as we did for infant mortality, the dramatic decrease in probability of dying in the first year for many countries. That of Canada, for instance, drops from $q_0 = 0.1016$ to $q_0 = 0.0237$ for males between 1930–32 and 1966–68.

25, 26. l_{50}—Survivors to Age 50 per 100,000 Births. The l_{50} shown is 100,000 times the probability of living to age 50 for a baby just born. Like most other life table values in this book it does not apply to any real group, but is synthesized from the death rates at the several ages for the period in question. The l_{50} describes decreases in mortality up to the end of the reproductive ages; that of males in Mauritius rose from 68,937 in 1955 to 78,841 in 1966; from 1930–32 to 1966–68 that of Canadian females rose from 75,808 to 93,060. In other words, the chance that a girl baby will survive to the end of the reproductive period is 0.93 on the Canadian age-specific rates of 1966–68, compared with 0.76 on those of 1930–32.

27, 28. $\mathring{e}_0$—Life Expectancy at Age Zero. The expectation of life is the sum of the probabilities of living to subsequent ages. If a child just born has a probability l_1/l_0 of living through his first year, l_2/l_0 of living through his second year, etc., then his expectation of life is the sum of these probabilities, $\sum_{x=1}^{\omega} l_x/l_0$, covering completed years, plus an adjustment for the fraction of a year that he lives beyond the last birthday that he celebrates. In continuous terms $\mathring{e}_0 = \int_0^{\omega} l_x dx$. The expectation of life at age zero may be shown to be the same as the average age at death in the stationary population.

The expectation $\mathring{e}_0$ for males in Mauritius rose from 53.30 years in 1955 to 59.48 in 1966, or by 6 years, and by 7 years for females during the same period. In Jamaica $\mathring{e}_0$ increased by 8 and 9 years for males and females respectively between 1951 and 1963. Improvement in $\mathring{e}_0$ of more than 5 years per decade is common in the under-developed countries. But Honduras hardly increased at all in the 9 years shown; can improving death registration be hiding a decrease in mortality?

29, 30. $\mathring{e}_1$—Expectation of Life at Age 1. In general the expected subsequent length of life implied by the age-specific death rates for a given period is $\mathring{e}_x = \int_0^{\omega-x} l_{x+t} dt/l_x$. We can call $\mathring{e}_1$ a conditional expectation, applicable if the child reaches age 1. Because of infant mortality, $\mathring{e}_1$ is higher than $\mathring{e}_0$; for Algerian females, $\mathring{e}_1$ is 71.91 years compared with 66.85 for $\mathring{e}_0$.

31, 32. $\mathring{e}_{50}$—Expectation of Life at Age 50. This expectation is conditional on the person's reaching age 50. Increases in $\mathring{e}_{50}$ appear over time, but of much smaller amount than those for $\mathring{e}_0$. In England and Wales, males gained only about 3 years in $\mathring{e}_{50}$ during the last century, while females gained 7 years.

33, 34. $\mathring{e}_{70}$—Expectation of Life at Age 70. This expectation is conditional on the person's reaching age 70. Variation over time is small. In Canada the gain since 1931 of nearly 3 years for women contrasts with virtually no increase for men; this is similar to the United States as shown in Figure 9.

Fertility Measures (Females) (columns 35–42)

35. General Fertility Rate.   The general fertility rate is 1000 times the number of births of both sexes in a year divided by the number of women in the 15–44 year age group. Looking at the Main Tables for Algeria (Table 1, page 308) we find 528,928 births during 1965 and 2,308,879 women in the 15–44 age group at mid-year; 1000 times the ratio of the first of these numbers to the second is 229.08, as shown in column 35 of the Summary Table. The corresponding figure for the United States, 1967, is 87.65.

The general fertility rate takes some account of the age-sex distribution and so is superior to the crude birth rate for comparing fertility among countries.

36. Total Fertility Rate.   This is the sum through all ages of the age-specific fertility rates. In Algeria, 1965, 67,477 children were born to mothers in the 15–19 age group, and the number of women in this age group was estimated to be 545,658. The age-specific birth rate (Table 1, page 308) was thus $67,477/545,658 = 0.1237$. Assuming that the average rate of the five-year age group is appropriate to each of the five years, we multiply the 0.1237 by 5 to obtain 0.618. Adding such numbers through the several ages of mother gives the 6.86 shown as the total fertility rate of Algeria, 1965. This is a synthetic estimate from cross-sectional data of the number of children born to a woman in the course of her reproductive life.

37. Gross Reproduction Rate, GRR.   If we had counted only female children in determining the age-specific birth rates that were added together to give the total fertility rate, we would have obtained the GRR. Following common practice imposed by lack of data on sex of child by age of mother, the total fertility rate was multiplied by the proportion of females in births to mothers of all ages. For Algeria, 1965, the 6.86 of column 36 was multiplied by 0.4912 to provide the 3.37 shown in column 37.

The gross reproduction rate is the number of female children that a female just born may expect to bear during her reproductive life, calculated from the data of the given period, if the possibility of death before the end of the reproductive period is ignored.

From another point of view, the GRR is a standardized birth rate: the number of female children expected to be born in a standard population consisting of one woman in each of the ages of reproduction.

38. Net Reproduction Rate, NRR. The basic demographic measure denoted by NRR or R_0 is the sum of the age-specific rates for the several ages, after each has been multiplied by the probability of living to that age. For each age the probability of surviving to each age, multiplied by the birth rate at that age, is called the net maternity function, and R_0 is the total of the net maternity function. In symbols: $R_0 = \sum {_5L_x F_x}/l_0$, where $_5L_x$ is the number of women in the stationary population of ages x to $x + 4$, and F_x is the corresponding age-specific birth rate for girl children. The proportion of all births that are females is taken as applying to each separate age.

The NRR is a replacement ratio, the number of girl children expected to be born to a female just born, on the regime of mortality and fertility in question. If the regime remains fixed, the NRR gives the ratio of numbers in successive female generations. To say that the NRR of Algeria, 1965, was 2.76 is to say that the mortality and fertility of that year were such as to multiply the population by 2.76 per generation. A NRR of less than unity tells us that the age-specific birth and death rates are not high enough to replace the population, a situation found in some western countries in the 1930's and currently in some countries of eastern Europe. Hungary, for example, had an NRR of 0.93 in 1967, following a low of 0.82 early in the 1960's.

39. The Mean Age at Childbearing μ for the Net Maternity Function. To proceed from the NRR, a measure of replacement per generation, to a clearly defined annual rate, we need to take further account of the ages at which women have their children. One way of summarizing these is by their mean μ, calculated by multiplying each value of the variable (in this case age) by the number of women in the distribution showing that value, and then dividing by the total number of women. With grouped data and a maternity function equal to $_5L_x\ F_x$ births in the age group x to $x + 4$, the mean μ is

$$\mu = \frac{\sum_x \left(x + 2\frac{1}{2}\right) {_5L_x F_x}}{\sum_x {_5L_x F_x}},$$

where the summations go through the values $x = 10, 15, 20, \ldots, 50$. As we will see in the discussion concerning column 41, μ is slightly greater than the length of generation for an increasing population.

The mean μ for women varies from a low of about 26 years (the United States, 1967, value of 26.28 is one of the lowest in our collection) to 33.13, the figure for Sweden, 1860. Western countries have shown a decreasing μ during the present century, Sweden, for example, in the amount of 6 years. Such decreases are due partly to younger ages at marriage, partly to less childbearing at ages beyond 30.

56 WORLD POPULATION ENTERS THE SEVENTIES

40. The Variance of the Distribution of Ages at Childbearing, σ^2. The third parameter of the net maternity function, its variance, tells how widely the ages scatter about the mean. It is defined as

$$\sigma^2 = \frac{\sum\limits_{x}\left(x + 2\frac{1}{2} - \mu\right)^2 {}_5L_xF_x}{\sum\limits_{x} {}_5L_xF_x},$$

The σ^2 for the United States has fallen from 45.30 in 1930 to 34.85 in 1967; women are now having their children closer together in time.

In general, the higher the fertility rates the greater the spread of ages at childbearing as measured by σ^2 or its square root σ. Conversely, the lower the fertility rates the smaller the spread of maternal ages: women stop having children at a younger age when the birth rate is low.

41. Mean Length of Generation, T. Lotka's T, the length of generation, is the time in which a population growing at the rate r (given in column 17) will increase in the ratio of the net reproduction rate (column 38). The rate r, taken as compounded momently, implies that the population is e^r times as large at the end of a year as at the beginning, and at the end of T years it is e^{rT} times as large. By the definition of T this is equal to the net reproduction rate; we have the equation

$$e^{rT} = R_0$$

to be solved for T. The solution by taking logarithms is

$$T = \frac{\ln R_0}{r}.$$

For the United States in 1967 R_0 was 1.212, and $1000r$ was 7.38, which gives $T = (\ln 1.212)/0.00738 = 26.1$.

For an increasing population the length of generation T defined in this way is slightly less than μ, the mean age at childbearing in the stationary population, but the difference is small. For the United States, 1967, μ was 26.3. Even for a population of very rapid growth like Algeria, μ exceeds T by only one year.

42. The Second Root of the Characteristic Equation, r_2. The intrinsic rate r of column 17 is the most useful single summary figure for a set of age-specific rates of birth and death—it is the fixed rate at which the population would ultimately increase if those age-specific rates were to continue. The population would ultimately approach Qe^{rt}, where Q is a suitable constant. But the immediate increase would, in general, be irregular, depending on the initial age distribution. A closer approximation to the population growth would be $Qe^{rt} + Q_2e^{r_2t} + Q_3e^{r_3t}$. The major irregularities take the form of waves whose length and rate of disappearance are expressed by r_2.

The root r_2 is a complex number, say $x + iy$, where i, conventionally designated as imaginary, is the square root of minus one, $(-1)^{1/2}$, and x and y are real. The root r_3 is then $x - iy$. For Algeria the real part is -0.0244; the wave will be $e^{-0.0244t}$ times as important t years later as at the outset. Thus after about a generation, say $t = 29$ years, $e^{-0.0244t} = e^{-0.0244 \times 29} = 0.49$, so that the amplitude of the wave will be only 0.49 times as great. This tells how rapid the approach to stability is under the action of a fixed regime of mortality and fertility.

The imaginary part iy of $r_2 = x + iy$ tells how long the waves will be: their length is $2\pi/y$, where $\pi = 3.14159$ is the ratio of the circumference of a circle to its diameter. For Algeria, 1965, $2\pi/y$ is $2(3.14159)/0.2141 = 29.3$ years.

The closeness of $2\pi/y$ to T, the length of generation, is not a coincidence. When a disturbance occurs in the age distribution of a population, for example that caused by a famine or an epidemic, insofar as it strikes baby girls, the consequent hollow in the age distribution means fewer births in the next generation. That these echoes should repeat at intervals of a generation, and that they should gradually fade away, is a property of any reproduction process in which births are spread over a range of maternal ages.

Populations Included and Their Sequence

In the Summary Table that follows, the first 651 rows are for countries, with some provinces and states, and the above definitions of the 42 quantities were written with them in mind. They are arranged first by continents; then within continents by countries in alphabetical order; within countries by date starting with the earliest; then for the given country and date such divisions as states or ethnic groups, in the few cases where these are shown. The sequence is that of the United Nations, adhered to through 20 editions of their *Demographic Yearbook;* we saw no need for originality in regard to the sequencing. This list, starting with Algeria, 1965, in Africa, and ending with New Zealand, 1967, in Oceania, and the USSR, 1959, is the main corpus of our results.

Following it we include cities, arranged alphabetically within continents and countries, beginning with Montreal, 1966, and ending with Sydney, 1966. This is followed by such supranational groupings as seemed worth making, given the incomplete statistics for many continents. That statistics for such groupings are incomplete is indicated in the Summary Table by the abbreviation *inc.*

Beyond these are cohort materials for the United States and Sweden, the results from performing the same computations on a different arrangement of the same data. Thus to constitute the United States, 1910, cohort we assembled the population and deaths data for children less than five years old in 1910, those for children 5–9 years old in 1915, and so on. In assembling cohorts we also included from each period births by mothers of the appropriate age: mothers 15–19 years old for 1925, 20–24 years old for 1930, and so on for the cohort born in 1905–10.

The last group of data in the Summary Table is based on the male-dominant model. Instead of attributing births to mothers, this model attributes them to fathers; projection at fixed rates produces a number of births in each period proportional to the number of males in the "childbearing" ages. Not all of the 42 columns are affected; total population, the crude rates of birth, death, and natural increase, and the life table quantities merely repeat what was given earlier for the same populations calculated on the female-dominant model. Projections, intrinsic rates, and the analysis of the net maternity (paternity) function do not give the same numbers on the male as on the female model. The net paternity function is obtained from births by age of father, and all the constants derived from it, including R_0, μ, and σ^2, refer to characteristics of fathers and boy children.

The footnotes showing sources for at least the most recent data are given in Part V. Where we had to make gross adjustments to official figures, or where such figures were lacking and we resorted to model tables from Coale and Demeny (1966), this fact is indicated by the word *hypothetical* (or the abbreviation *hyp*) in the stub of the Summary Table.

PART II

SUMMARY TABLE

SERIES NUMBER	AREA AND YEAR		POPULATION, IN 1000'S			AGE STRUCTURE					
			Observed at mid-year	Projected		Total re-productive value (in 1000's)	Percent at age			Dependency ratio (× 100)	Departure from stability (Δ percent)
				5 years	10 years		< 15	15–64	⩾ 65		
			1	2	3	4	5	6	7	8	9
	AFRICA										
1	Algeria	1965	12134	14362	16991	7178	47.23	48.34	4.43	106.87	3.8
2	Cameroon (West)	1964	1031	1167	1320	610	48.57	50.33	1.10	98.69	4.2
3	Cen. African Rep.	1960	1028	1115	1171	502	40.02	58.99	0.99	69.50	19.8
4	Guinea	1955	2582	2712	2809	1579	42.12	54.56	3.32	83.28	7.3
5	Madagascar	1966	6163	6824	7586	3779	46.51	49.54	3.95	101.89	4.0
6	Mauritius	1955	551	634	727	284	41.85	54.99	3.16	81.84	4.4
7	(Excl. dep.)	1956–58	588	680	785	309	42.97	54.20	2.83	84.50	4.8
8		1959–61	639	735	849	329	44.30	52.62	3.08	90.03	4.0
9		1962	682	791	917	358	45.31	51.47	3.22	94.29	5.7
10		1963	701	819	966	385	45.36	51.39	3.25	94.58	6.4
11		1964	722	838	985	387	45.28	51.42	3.30	94.51	5.7
12		1965	741	854	994	387	44.89	51.73	3.38	93.31	4.0
13		1966	759	874	1011	397	44.16	52.40	3.44	90.85	3.9
14	Reunion	1961	346	403	470	208	45.00	51.54	3.46	94.04	5.0
15		1963	372	437	518	221	45.00	51.48	3.52	94.26	5.4
16	Seychelles	1960	42	46	55	20	38.51	55.29	6.20	80.87	10.2
17	South Africa,	1957	1322	1542	1795	811	43.88	52.88	3.24	89.11	2.0
18	Colored	1958	1363	1580	1831	837	44.14	52.75	3.11	89.61	1.9
19		1960	1497	1744	2040	929	45.17	51.66	3.17	93.58	1.7
20		1961	1549	1810	2117	950	45.10	51.76	3.14	93.20	1.9
21	White	1950–52	2649	2864	3090	867	31.75	61.77	6.48	61.89	3.6
22		1953–55	2801	3034	3277	919	31.87	61.50	6.63	62.61	3.4
23		1956–58	2954	3197	3459	967	31.90	61.36	6.74	62.96	3.3
24		1960	3065	3324	3615	1023	32.35	60.89	6.76	64.21	3.6
25		1961	3129	3389	3681	1021	32.40	60.92	6.68	64.15	3.3
26	Togo	1961	1544	1729	1917	1015	47.94	48.27	3.79	107.15	10.5
27	Tunisia	1960	4182	4863	5610	2385	40.85	54.51	4.64	83.45	3.4
	NORTH AMERICA										
29	Barbados	1959–61	234	259	292	98	38.06	55.73	6.21	79.44	6.8
30		1962	233	255	290	97	38.82	54.76	6.42	82.63	5.6
31		1963	239	262	292	101	40.53	53.33	6.14	87.53	5.6
32		1965	244	271	303	99	38.92	54.30	6.78	84.13	5.7
33	Canada	1930–32	10372	11062	11814	3717	31.59	62.85	5.56	59.12	7.8
34		1940–42	11507	12243	13002	3606	27.81	65.50	6.69	52.67	7.4
35		1950–52	13657	14875	16049	4469	30.14	62.07	7.79	61.12	4.4
36		1960–62	17769	19413	21219	6019	33.74	58.58	7.68	70.71	5.1
37		1963	18402	20008	21835	6167	33.65	58.66	7.69	70.48	4.0
38		1964	18771	20343	22140	6182	33.41	58.91	7.68	69.76	3.7
39		1965	19100	20490	22099	5995	33.07	59.24	7.69	68.80	5.1
40		1966–68	19933	21089	22415	5685	32.07	60.18	7.75	66.16	9.6

VITAL RATES PER THOUSAND POPULATION								INFANT MOR-TALITY RATE per 1000 births	AGE-SPECIFIC DEATH RATES				
Crude (both sexes)			Standardized on U.S., 1960 (both sexes)		Intrinsic (females)				1000_4M_1		1000_5M_{50}		SERIES NUMBER
Birth 10	Death 11	Increase 12	Birth 13	Death 14	Birth 15	Death 16	Increase 17	18	Males 19	Females 20	Males 21	Females 22	
43.59	9.97	33.62	45.01	9.52	45.19	9.52	35.66	88.11	13.73	13.05	8.71	5.75	1
49.67	25.69	23.98	41.52	34.64	45.57	24.06	21.51	137.93	40.08	38.55	48.79	38.28	2
47.49	25.43	22.06	32.43	33.83	37.69	25.09	12.59	190.44	28.67	25.36	49.17	14.67	3
54.04	42.47	11.57	40.47	42.27	47.07	36.83	10.24	246.16	59.29	49.93	74.05	31.76	4
45.75	25.31	20.44	44.48	25.10	46.70	24.17	22.53	103.58	30.45	34.92	27.72	18.83	5
41.69	12.86	28.83	37.71	19.47	41.61	11.18	30.43	71.48	15.63	18.25	23.31	13.33	6
42.40	12.16	30.24	39.60	20.22	43.06	10.44	32.62	74.31	10.93	12.34	23.59	11.82	7
39.31	10.70	28.61	37.43	17.71	41.19	9.78	31.40	72.42	8.59	10.20	23.30	11.93	8
38.00	9.28	28.72	38.32	14.91	41.46	8.38	33.08	67.28	5.90	7.29	18.56	9.53	9
40.14	9.56	30.58	40.99	16.15	43.84	8.56	35.28	66.04	7.90	8.37	17.77	10.75	10
37.93	8.56	29.37	38.94	14.49	41.99	7.70	34.28	59.35	5.68	6.77	15.68	9.27	11
35.39	8.55	26.83	36.00	14.24	39.22	8.07	31.15	66.34	7.15	7.23	15.47	8.85	12
34.92	8.83	26.10	35.40	15.22	38.89	8.35	30.54	64.92	7.20	7.44	15.36	7.67	13
43.94	11.56	32.38	42.55	16.61	43.87	10.80	33.08	126.77	10.53	10.88	19.25	10.38	14
44.35	10.92	33.43	43.70	15.74	43.89	8.83	35.06	70.26	8.66	9.57	23.54	9.11	15
41.27	9.94	31.32	37.98	11.50	40.21	6.68	33.54	51.92	7.07	3.14	9.08	14.11	16
47.58	16.26	31.32	41.92	20.20	45.99	14.71	31.28	151.65	21.50	21.14	22.46	14.30	17
46.95	16.86	30.09	41.42	21.26	45.61	15.27	30.34	155.35	22.81	24.10	23.63	15.06	18
46.76	15.61	31.15	42.51	19.14	46.44	14.26	32.18	128.57	19.89	18.76	20.11	14.78	19
46.12	15.45	30.67	41.97	18.69	46.20	13.37	32.84	128.40	20.32	19.73	22.03	14.16	20
25.14	8.58	16.56	21.66	10.82	23.98	8.77	15.21	35.87	2.55	2.02	13.33	8.28	21
24.79	8.41	16.38	22.00	10.46	24.52	8.19	16.32	33.53	2.01	1.80	13.17	7.35	22
24.72	8.58	16.14	22.31	10.48	25.03	7.89	17.14	31.29	1.91	1.59	12.66	6.72	23
24.90	8.74	16.16	22.90	10.67	25.93	7.61	18.32	29.55	1.77	1.52	13.56	7.19	24
24.20	8.63	15.57	22.15	10.55	24.99	7.61	17.38	28.09	1.55	1.29	13.13	7.26	25
54.53	28.97	25.56	46.33	29.53	50.34	23.13	27.21	128.62	47.36	43.62	34.86	21.05	26
43.57	12.04	31.53	41.32	12.84	40.54	11.64	28.90	88.87	21.01	19.90	13.11	9.40	27
30.86	9.42	21.44	28.35	11.56	31.83	8.16	23.67	76.16	4.19	3.55	9.64	9.01	29
29.48	9.07	20.41	26.47	11.41	30.11	7.60	22.51	59.26	4.28	2.45	12.59	7.64	30
28.28	8.75	19.53	25.85	11.64	28.23	8.38	19.85	64.29	3.74	3.51	9.38	5.90	31
27.97	7.81	20.16	25.53	9.94	28.02	7.34	20.68	36.66	2.00	2.37	8.37	4.90	32
23.13	10.23	12.90	20.83	13.67	22.23	13.20	9.03	97.76	6.58	5.80	10.62	9.24	33
22.36	9.81	12.55	18.57	12.11	19.73	12.38	7.34	67.57	4.35	3.72	10.68	8.19	34
27.24	8.94	18.31	22.93	10.06	25.15	8.20	16.95	42.19	2.03	1.68	10.36	6.50	35
25.76	7.77	17.99	24.77	8.67	27.58	6.32	21.26	27.28	1.22	0.99	9.46	5.21	36
24.38	7.82	16.56	23.84	8.65	26.54	6.57	19.97	25.90	1.20	0.90	9.43	5.12	37
23.35	7.61	15.74	22.86	8.41	25.23	6.84	18.39	24.55	1.13	0.91	9.50	5.09	38
21.14	7.63	13.52	20.64	8.44	22.47	7.81	14.67	22.50	1.04	0.88	9.80	5.26	39
18.11	7.43	10.69	16.84	8.23	17.52	10.12	7.40	21.81	1.03	0.83	9.46	4.99	40

continued

LIFE TABLE VALUES

SERIES NUMBER	AREA AND YEAR		Probability of dying in first year, q_0		Survivors to age 50 per 100,000 births, l_{50}		Expectancy, $\overset{\circ}{e}_0$		Expectancy, $\overset{\circ}{e}_1$		Expectancy, $\overset{\circ}{e}_{50}$
			Males 23	Females 24	Males 25	Females 26	Males 27	Females 28	Males 29	Females 30	Males 31
	AFRICA										
1	Algeria	1965	0.0946	0.0836	74243	75509	63.02	66.85	68.57	71.91	29.70
2	Cameroon (West)	1964	0.1455	0.1212	38018	40841	34.27	38.09	39.04	42.28	12.99
3	Cen. African Rep.	1960	0.2125	0.1905	36315	39883	34.26	38.26	42.41	46.18	14.68
4	Guinea	1955	0.2459	0.2054	21607	24347	24.30	27.34	31.10	33.31	13.53
5	Madagascar	1966	0.1098	0.1261	38574	40128	37.58	38.49	41.16	42.99	16.92
6	Mauritius	1955	0.0764	0.0599	68937	71557	53.30	56.58	56.68	59.16	17.57
7	(Excl. dep.)	1956-58	0.0766	0.0644	70013	72103	53.82	57.48	57.26	60.40	17.06
8		1959-61	0.0757	0.0624	74166	75038	56.15	59.11	59.73	62.02	18.01
9		1962	0.0721	0.0563	77327	78649	58.83	62.35	62.37	65.04	19.60
10		1963	0.0692	0.0569	77583	77758	58.54	61.47	61.87	64.16	19.54
11		1964	0.0632	0.0502	78451	79565	60.13	63.72	63.17	66.07	20.36
12		1965	0.0699	0.0569	78477	80708	59.83	64.25	63.30	67.11	20.44
13		1966	0.0694	0.0585	78841	79833	59.48	63.71	62.89	66.64	20.14
14	Reunion	1961	0.1247	0.1082	66311	74136	52.21	60.01	58.61	66.25	18.95
15		1963	0.0733	0.0694	70966	76069	55.58	62.40	58.95	66.03	18.28
16	Seychelles	1961	0.0552	0.0575	75255	84889	61.92	69.21	64.51	72.42	23.97
17	South Africa,	1957	0.1463	0.1296	59400	65571	47.67	52.53	54.78	59.30	18.74
18	Colored	1958	0.1500	0.1323	58547	65059	46.87	51.73	54.08	58.56	18.16
19		1960	0.1502	0.1320	60754	66318	48.76	53.45	56.32	60.53	19.71
20		1961	0.1284	0.1142	61379	68069	49.85	54.56	56.14	60.54	19.75
21	White	1950-52	0.0390	0.0307	83025	87963	64.50	70.15	66.11	71.36	22.41
22		1953-55	0.0359	0.0293	83803	89356	64.94	71.30	66.34	72.44	22.32
23		1956-58	0.0343	0.0265	83602	89684	64.80	71.57	66.09	72.51	22.23
24		1960	0.0350	0.0274	83291	89692	64.51	71.49	65.84	72.50	21.97
25		1961	0.0257	0.0199	84539	90860	65.28	72.16	66.00	72.61	21.92
26	Togo	1961	0.1456	0.1169	33429	44242	33.57	40.27	38.22	44.55	16.41
27	Tunisia	1960	0.1182	0.1066	69198	71431	55.66	63.23	62.07	69.73	24.44
	NORTH AMERICA										
29	Barbados	1959-61	0.0761	0.0677	81129	83825	62.90	67.39	67.07	71.26	23.00
30		1962	0.0611	0.0525	82626	86661	63.11	69.32	66.20	72.14	22.14
31		1963	0.0662	0.0564	82299	86093	64.18	68.38	67.71	71.46	23.44
32		1965	0.0387	0.0391	86736	88427	66.95	71.23	68.63	73.11	23.46
33	Canada	1930-32	0.1016	0.0805	73959	75808	59.00	61.36	64.64	65.71	23.75
34		1940-42	0.0722	0.0563	79168	82282	62.28	65.79	66.11	68.69	23.51
35		1950-52	0.0456	0.0358	84921	88857	66.18	70.81	68.33	72.42	23.87
36		1960-62	0.0299	0.0232	87931	92452	68.41	74.29	69.51	75.06	24.27
37		1963	0.0284	0.0222	88063	92580	68.46	74.42	69.46	75.11	24.23
38		1964	0.0273	0.0207	88130	92899	68.61	74.95	69.53	75.53	24.30
39		1965	0.0247	0.0194	88463	92946	68.75	75.00	69.49	75.48	24.22
40		1966-68	0.0237	0.0192	88463	93060	68.89	75.47	69.56	75.93	24.32

[62]

Expectancy, $\overset{o}{e}_{70}$			General fertility rate	Total fertility rate	Gross reproduction rate	Net maternity function					SERIES NUMBER
Females 32	Males 33	Females 34	35	36	37	Total, NRR 38	Mean, μ 39	Variance, σ^2 40	Generation, T 41	Complex root, r_2 42	
33.58	16.01	18.32	229.08	6.86	3.37	2.76	29.51	57.00	28.500	$-0.0244+0.2141$	1
16.65	6.18	9.13	231.38	6.19	2.81	1.72	25.96	58.86	25.326	$-0.0903+0.2714$	2
22.43	7.31	10.85	174.72	4.96	2.47	1.39	26.47	40.66	26.205	$-0.0409+0.2383$	3
16.34	7.87	8.36	217.59	6.13	3.06	1.31	26.63	52.32	26.361	$-0.1079+0.3122$	4
20.15	8.02	8.82	225.27	6.77	3.29	1.88	28.56	57.15	27.908	$-0.0397+0.2177$	5
21.44	7.19	8.60	200.77	5.73	2.81	2.30	28.15	47.77	27.411	$-0.0236+0.2199$	6
21.82	7.00	8.78	209.97	6.01	2.95	2.45	28.24	47.42	27.448	$-0.0206+0.2195$	7
22.15	8.45	9.35	196.92	5.71	2.80	2.37	28.22	46.53	27.474	$-0.0240+0.2235$	8
23.67	8.62	10.21	197.08	5.86	2.87	2.50	28.46	45.25	27.697	$-0.0187+0.2250$	9
23.27	8.32	9.71	207.11	6.26	3.08	2.66	28.54	45.38	27.732	$-0.0170+0.2246$	10
24.43	8.36	10.40	195.05	5.96	2.94	2.60	28.63	43.86	27.867	$-0.0147+0.2251$	11
24.94	8.70	10.87	179.42	5.51	2.72	2.39	28.65	44.13	27.947	$-0.0180+0.2226$	12
24.89	8.29	10.44	174.12	5.42	2.69	2.35	28.66	44.27	27.968	$-0.0187+0.2229$	13
25.35	8.44	11.57	214.56	6.49	3.21	2.63	30.01	46.06	29.225	$-0.0106+0.2110$	14
25.43	8.34	11.95	217.99	6.67	3.27	2.81	30.25	45.37	29.439	$-0.0068+0.2106$	15
28.22	8.78	15.42	200.23	5.83	2.88	2.60	29.35	50.56	28.501	$-0.0260+0.2200$	16
22.20	8.82	10.48	222.22	6.41	3.18	2.39	28.71	52.92	27.887	$-0.0335+0.2244$	17
21.83	8.19	9.98	220.33	6.34	3.13	2.33	28.71	53.48	27.901	$-0.0364+0.2235$	18
22.77	9.30	10.32	225.50	6.49	3.23	2.46	28.77	51.95	27.936	$-0.0283+0.2230$	19
22.68	9.11	10.41	222.93	6.41	3.20	2.49	28.65	51.13	27.808	$-0.0278+0.2248$	20
26.38	10.17	11.72	112.44	3.35	1.63	1.53	28.25	38.13	27.954	$-0.0261+0.2252$	21
26.87	10.07	12.00	113.23	3.40	1.66	1.57	28.09	36.80	27.780	$-0.0241+0.2281$	22
26.90	10.02	12.00	115.17	3.45	1.69	1.60	27.85	35.43	27.530	$-0.0222+0.2305$	23
26.78	9.65	11.94	118.49	3.55	1.73	1.65	27.70	34.33	27.371	$-0.0199+0.2332$	24
26.67	9.50	11.76	115.19	3.44	1.67	1.60	27.51	33.75	27.204	$-0.0207+0.2350$	25
20.12	10.96	9.50	251.95	7.06	3.59	2.14	28.75	56.50	27.978	$-0.0414+0.2155$	26
33.25	12.15	19.88	208.18	6.34	3.02	2.35	30.34	51.32	29.596	$-0.0154+0.2137$	27
26.75	9.63	11.96	146.15	4.30	2.11	1.90	27.63	47.11	27.056	$-0.0330+0.2218$	29
26.89	9.03	12.25	135.92	4.01	2.00	1.84	27.73	46.24	27.197	$-0.0306+0.2185$	30
26.52	9.45	10.92	133.94	3.91	1.90	1.73	28.17	51.36	27.648	$-0.0337+0.2115$	31
27.63	9.55	12.76	131.09	3.86	1.88	1.77	28.05	50.02	27.518	$-0.0338+0.2119$	32
24.82	10.10	10.67	103.97	3.19	1.55	1.31	29.75	42.56	29.554	$-0.0285+0.2058$	33
25.49	9.97	10.96	97.06	2.85	1.39	1.24	29.12	40.89	28.959	$-0.0317+0.2112$	34
26.85	10.43	11.68	122.70	3.53	1.71	1.61	28.41	39.32	28.061	$-0.0250+0.2217$	35
28.41	10.72	12.67	125.96	3.83	1.86	1.79	27.79	37.47	27.379	$-0.0221+0.2319$	36
28.46	10.69	12.68	119.60	3.68	1.79	1.73	27.76	36.61	27.385	$-0.0221+0.2317$	37
28.81	10.82	13.02	114.22	3.53	1.72	1.66	27.80	36.60	27.453	$-0.0232+0.2307$	38
28.79	10.69	12.93	103.06	3.19	1.55	1.50	27.75	37.09	27.470	$-0.0277+0.2288$	39
29.22	10.83	13.34	86.41	2.60	1.27	1.22	27.46	36.61	27.316	$-0.0354+0.2288$	40

SERIES NUMBER	AREA AND YEAR		POPULATION, IN 1000'S			AGE STRUCTURE					
			Observed at mid-year	Projected		Total re-productive value (in 1000's)	Percent at age			Dependency ratio (× 100)	Departure from stability (Δ percent)
				5 years	10 years		<15	15–64	≥65		
			1	2	3	4	5	6	7	8	9
41	Prince Edward	1930–32	88	93	98	31	31.92	58.19	9.89	71.84	4.9
42	Island	1940–42	95	101	109	32	30.19	60.38	9.43	65.62	3.9
43		1950–52	98	106	117	37	33.41	56.72	9.87	76.31	7.2
44		1960–62	105	118	131	40	36.02	53.53	10.45	86.80	11.2
45		1963	107	119	135	43	35.68	53.96	10.36	85.31	11.6
46		1964	107	121	133	42	35.40	54.43	10.17	83.72	9.8
47	Nova Scotia	1930–32	513	543	576	182	32.54	59.53	7.93	67.96	5.7
48		1940–42	579	618	660	191	29.24	62.62	8.14	59.71	5.5
49		1950–52	643	704	763	220	32.62	58.83	8.55	69.98	3.9
50		1960–62	738	808	895	263	34.77	56.62	8.61	76.62	7.0
51		1963	756	825	917	266	34.52	56.91	8.57	75.74	5.8
52		1964	760	828	909	267	34.34	57.05	8.61	75.28	5.4
53	New Brunswick	1930–32	409	443	476	169	35.42	57.88	6.70	72.78	4.2
54		1940–42	458	495	540	176	31.91	60.99	7.10	63.95	4.2
55		1950–52	516	575	642	209	35.69	56.74	7.57	76.23	5.0
56		1960–62	599	666	746	235	37.98	54.17	7.85	84.58	7.2
57		1963	614	675	758	238	37.36	54.81	7.83	82.44	6.0
58		1964	617	680	760	237	36.95	55.29	7.76	80.86	6.2
59	Quebec	1930–32	2878	3133	3423	1314	35.55	59.64	4.81	67.68	7.0
60		1940–42	3338	3626	3937	1302	31.92	62.79	5.29	59.24	7.1
61		1950–52	4066	4505	4945	1568	33.70	60.58	5.72	65.09	4.2
62		1960–62	5270	5789	6364	1933	35.40	58.78	5.82	70.13	3.9
63		1963	5476	5979	6545	1955	34.84	59.24	5.92	68.82	4.2
64		1964	5570	6064	6624	1941	34.46	59.57	5.97	67.86	5.0
65	Óntario	1930–32	3435	3596	3760	1012	27.92	65.25	6.83	53.26	8.0
66		1940–42	3794	3959	4120	968	24.43	67.61	7.96	47.91	7.1
67		1950–52	4611	4948	5253	1304	27.02	64.28	8.70	55.56	6.1
68		1960–62	6245	6777	7344	1966	32.21	59.64	8.15	67.67	7.6
69		1963	6459	6981	7565	2034	32.39	59.44	8.17	68.24	6.5
70		1964	6597	7122	7715	2054	32.22	59.60	8.18	67.79	5.4
71	Manitoba	1930–32	700	745	799	238	31.22	64.25	4.53	55.63	13.4
72		1940–42	730	772	817	214	26.19	67.53	6.28	48.08	11.4
73		1950–52	778	841	898	238	28.72	62.84	8.44	59.12	4.8
74		1960–62	922	1002	1096	303	32.56	58.40	9.04	71.22	7.4
75		1963	951	1031	1123	312	32.54	58.41	9.05	71.20	7.0
76		1964	959	1034	1122	307	32.42	58.53	9.05	70.86	5.3
77	Saskatchewan	1930–32	922	1004	1101	358	35.38	61.24	3.38	63.29	11.8
78		1940–42	895	960	1034	293	29.93	64.89	5.18	54.11	12.8
79		1950–52	833	909	989	279	30.72	61.19	8.09	63.43	3.5
80		1960–62	926	1016	1119	320	34.05	56.70	9.25	76.38	7.5
81		1963	934	1024	1131	329	34.31	56.36	9.33	77.42	8.0
82		1964	944	1030	1136	329	34.21	56.46	9.33	77.13	7.0
83	Alberta	1930–32	732	792	866	264	32.63	63.85	3.52	56.63	9.8
84		1940–42	797	857	916	251	28.71	66.09	5.20	51.31	10.2
85		1950–52	943	1042	1136	316	30.58	62.30	7.12	60.53	5.0
86		1960–62	1335	1489	1659	478	35.25	57.77	6.98	73.12	6.0
87		1963	1407	1560	1727	495	35.54	57.54	6.92	73.79	4.6
88		1964	1434	1576	1736	492	35.58	57.50	6.92	73.92	4.4
89	British	1930–32	695	714	737	167	24.64	69.84	5.52	43.18	15.9
90	Columbia	1940–42	821	852	875	188	21.47	70.18	8.35	42.49	8.8
91		1950–52	1169	1242	1304	312	26.18	63.00	10.82	58.73	7.9
92		1960–62	1632	1756	1892	496	31.26	58.58	10.16	70.71	9.7
93		1963	1699	1816	1955	508	31.30	58.76	9.94	70.19	7.1
94		1964	1742	1850	1973	505	31.04	59.19	9.77	68.93	5.0

VITAL RATES PER THOUSAND POPULATION

Crude (both sexes)			Standardized on U.S., 1960 (both sexes)		Intrinsic (females)			INFANT MOR-TALITY RATE per 1000 births	1000$_4M_1$		1000$_5M_{50}$		SERIES NUMBER
Birth 10	Death 11	Increase 12	Birth 13	Death 14	Birth 15	Death 16	Increase 17	18	Males 19	Females 20	Males 21	Females 22	
21.40	11.06	10.34	23.13	10.76	23.23	11.56	11.67	73.61	5.00	5.30	5.66	6.37	41
22.04	11.08	10.96	21.57	10.97	23.06	10.88	12.19	73.97	3.27	2.93	8.28	8.01	42
27.88	9.22	18.66	28.15	8.41	30.43	6.19	24.25	35.88	1.11	1.34	6.75	6.10	43
26.65	9.53	17.13	31.05	8.22	33.40	5.01	28.39	31.81	1.33	0.77	8.73	4.00	44
27.56	9.15	18.41	32.22	7.89	34.87	4.21	30.66	22.49	1.11	1.92	13.70	4.58	45
25.49	9.17	16.32	30.06	8.14	31.87	4.88	26.99	25.58	0.92	1.17	11.11	3.75	46
22.46	11.90	10.56	22.05	12.91	23.39	12.59	10.80	86.23	5.69	5.46	11.82	9.36	47
24.24	11.25	12.98	20.41	12.23	22.20	11.71	10.49	73.35	3.91	4.49	10.39	8.83	48
27.12	9.14	17.97	24.46	9.48	26.89	7.40	19.49	39.54	1.74	1.41	10.32	6.66	49
26.18	8.39	17.78	26.87	8.47	30.14	5.80	24.33	30.67	1.13	1.13	9.90	5.42	50
25.09	8.42	16.67	25.82	8.45	28.77	5.90	22.87	27.64	1.26	0.75	9.37	4.96	51
24.09	8.40	15.69	24.99	8.38	27.86	6.11	21.75	24.10	1.11	1.08	9.73	5.65	52
26.22	11.57	14.65	25.89	13.67	27.74	11.83	15.91	98.41	7.61	6.46	9.64	9.75	53
26.67	11.16	15.51	24.02	13.03	25.89	11.36	14.54	90.99	5.84	5.71	10.29	8.51	54
31.73	9.31	22.43	29.15	10.27	32.01	7.02	24.99	57.04	2.37	2.00	8.98	6.62	55
27.50	7.88	19.62	29.22	8.61	32.11	5.45	26.66	29.64	1.36	1.12	8.70	5.06	56
25.68	7.84	17.84	27.43	8.53	29.99	5.72	24.27	27.46	0.94	0.75	9.14	5.90	57
24.85	7.67	17.18	26.58	8.36	29.29	5.78	23.51	24.45	1.25	1.10	10.96	4.81	58
28.89	11.99	16.90	26.05	16.03	27.43	13.87	13.55	136.51	9.87	8.71	12.23	10.46	59
26.77	10.08	16.69	22.15	13.74	23.63	12.05	11.58	87.07	6.09	5.11	12.12	9.32	60
30.04	8.47	21.58	24.75	11.24	26.80	8.47	18.33	54.11	2.46	2.00	11.61	7.53	61
25.94	6.91	19.02	23.84	9.42	25.95	7.19	18.76	31.64	1.44	1.14	10.17	5.59	62
24.41	6.98	17.43	22.53	9.40	24.68	7.60	17.08	30.13	1.28	1.08	9.84	5.36	63
23.49	6.74	16.75	21.68	9.01	23.45	7.75	15.71	25.88	1.29	1.01	9.93	5.48	64
20.12	10.63	9.49	17.22	13.30	18.26	14.24	4.03	81.25	4.82	4.12	10.94	9.33	65
19.24	10.26	8.97	15.76	11.55	16.41	13.46	2.95	52.34	2.76	2.20	11.45	7.97	66
25.11	9.57	15.55	21.08	9.96	23.20	8.50	14.70	34.65	1.64	1.27	10.73	6.06	67
25.24	8.25	16.99	24.22	8.87	27.32	6.27	21.06	23.58	1.07	0.85	9.94	5.36	68
24.01	8.30	15.71	23.70	8.85	26.63	6.42	20.21	22.78	1.20	0.84	9.94	5.32	69
23.15	7.91	15.24	22.96	8.40	25.59	6.52	19.07	20.28	0.99	0.67	9.91	5.13	70
20.42	7.78	12.64	18.27	11.81	19.27	13.02	6.25	77.05	4.65	3.92	9.14	8.56	71
20.66	8.78	11.88	16.63	11.21	17.30	13.29	4.02	60.42	3.70	3.33	8.60	7.85	72
25.71	8.53	17.18	21.48	9.26	23.26	8.52	14.74	36.18	1.85	1.73	8.61	5.60	73
25.11	8.06	17.05	25.32	8.01	28.20	5.97	22.23	28.03	1.22	1.13	7.83	4.93	74
23.93	8.34	15.59	24.54	8.14	27.63	6.21	21.42	25.18	1.45	1.03	7.58	4.95	75
22.69	8.05	14.64	23.40	7.80	25.86	6.54	19.32	23.95	1.06	1.15	8.49	4.81	76
23.22	6.66	16.56	22.80	11.11	24.28	10.64	13.64	76.17	4.48	3.73	7.53	7.78	77
20.84	7.12	13.72	18.50	10.06	19.21	11.54	7.68	53.07	3.38	3.05	7.46	7.36	78
26.38	7.73	18.65	23.51	8.73	25.66	7.58	18.08	36.09	2.26	1.91	6.76	5.61	79
25.72	7.55	18.17	27.18	7.30	30.25	5.28	24.97	26.81	1.07	1.04	6.86	4.06	80
25.21	7.97	17.24	27.49	7.46	30.65	5.21	25.43	27.77	1.12	0.81	7.44	3.80	81
24.03	7.81	16.22	26.39	7.22	29.33	5.44	23.89	24.68	1.12	0.77	6.92	3.69	82
23.62	7.43	16.19	22.02	12.05	23.84	11.23	12.61	72.89	4.67	4.35	9.10	7.99	83
22.15	7.81	14.34	18.74	11.00	20.12	11.44	8.69	52.52	3.92	3.31	8.21	7.65	84
28.90	7.55	21.35	24.29	9.20	27.05	7.18	19.87	34.79	1.87	1.69	8.84	6.15	85
29.14	6.75	22.40	27.62	7.87	31.23	5.20	26.03	26.88	1.11	0.86	8.11	4.29	86
27.33	6.71	20.62	26.42	7.84	29.80	5.37	24.43	23.64	1.23	0.63	8.61	4.85	87
25.22	6.61	18.61	24.66	7.61	27.73	5.76	21.97	21.79	1.30	1.03	7.69	4.54	88
15.09	8.95	6.15	14.19	11.85	14.12	16.29	-2.17	54.28	4.76	4.40	11.13	7.86	89
18.55	10.43	8.12	15.06	11.08	15.29	14.00	1.30	44.66	4.07	2.85	11.48	6.77	90
24.24	10.07	14.18	20.92	9.42	23.06	8.49	14.57	31.70	1.91	1.75	10.68	6.56	91
23.87	8.99	14.88	24.68	8.10	28.03	5.93	22.10	24.21	1.26	0.96	9.14	4.98	92
22.06	8.85	13.22	22.95	7.89	25.83	6.46	19.38	23.04	0.93	0.86	8.96	4.47	93
20.61	9.22	11.40	21.17	8.24	23.52	7.24	16.28	20.48	1.11	1.25	9.33	5.04	94

continued

LIFE TABLE VALUES

SERIES NUMBER	AREA AND YEAR		Probability of dying in first year, q_0		Survivors to age 50 per 100,000 births, l_{50}		Expectancy, $\mathring{e}_0$		Expectancy, $\mathring{e}_1$		Expectancy, $\mathring{e}_{50}$
			Males 23	Females 24	Males 25	Females 26	Males 27	Females 28	Males 29	Females 30	Males 31
41	Prince Edward	1930-32	0.0770	0.0624	78113	76824	63.73	64.72	68.03	68.01	26.47
42	Island	1940-42	0.0777	0.0621	80555	81310	64.13	66.17	68.51	69.54	25.41
43		1950-52	0.0399	0.0297	87811	89572	69.72	72.63	71.61	73.84	26.32
44		1960-62	0.0363	0.0253	87558	91791	68.93	74.70	70.52	75.64	25.48
45		1963	0.0298	0.0129	88104	94270	69.11	76.24	70.23	76.24	25.23
46		1964	0.0335	0.0158	86129	93630	68.28	76.03	69.64	76.25	25.38
47	Nova Scotia	1930-32	0.0894	0.0723	73528	74772	59.72	61.80	64.56	65.60	24.38
48		1940-42	0.0779	0.0610	76201	79752	61.12	64.86	65.26	68.06	23.85
49		1950-52	0.0434	0.0331	84881	89313	66.82	71.62	68.84	73.06	24.55
50		1960-62	0.0329	0.0268	86937	91828	68.44	74.24	69.76	75.28	24.89
51		1963	0.0313	0.0225	87560	92588	68.59	74.79	69.80	75.51	24.62
52		1964	0.0261	0.0209	88347	92695	68.77	74.87	69.61	75.46	24.31
53	New Brunswick	1930-32	0.1028	0.0809	72936	73817	58.75	60.52	64.45	64.82	24.32
54		1940-42	0.0943	0.0762	76496	77637	60.42	62.80	65.68	66.96	23.71
55		1950-52	0.0614	0.0475	83614	86774	65.54	69.60	68.81	72.06	24.56
56		1960-62	0.0317	0.0260	87190	91771	68.51	73.89	69.75	74.86	24.91
57		1963	0.0290	0.0245	86590	92328	68.21	74.55	69.24	75.42	24.65
58		1964	0.0261	0.0216	87889	92925	68.76	74.81	69.59	75.46	24.61
59	Quebec	1930-32	0.1385	0.1096	68130	69132	54.62	56.65	62.35	62.58	23.06
60		1940-42	0.0925	0.0708	75310	78045	59.40	62.55	64.43	66.29	22.84
61		1950-52	0.0581	0.0453	82738	86603	64.23	68.54	67.18	70.78	23.12
62		1960-62	0.0346	0.0270	86909	91658	67.35	72.87	68.76	73.88	23.73
63		1963	0.0319	0.0269	87312	91683	67.53	72.89	68.75	73.90	23.65
64		1964	0.0282	0.0221	87377	92218	67.86	73.84	68.83	74.51	23.82
65	Ontario	1930-32	0.0848	0.0681	76173	79002	60.40	63.22	64.98	66.82	23.36
66		1940-42	0.0565	0.0439	82131	85761	63.92	67.94	66.73	70.05	23.10
67		1950-52	0.0377	0.0294	86272	90360	66.69	71.77	68.29	72.94	23.41
68		1960-62	0.0258	0.0202	88631	92891	68.32	74.47	69.12	75.00	23.64
69		1963	0.0252	0.0194	88515	93000	68.21	74.67	68.97	75.14	23.57
70		1964	0.0226	0.0170	89087	93681	68.84	75.45	69.42	75.75	23.89
71	Manitoba	1930-32	0.0819	0.0638	78097	80297	62.18	64.92	66.71	68.33	24.50
72		1940-42	0.0621	0.0532	81460	83711	64.12	66.98	67.34	69.72	24.23
73		1950-52	0.0386	0.0315	86768	89942	67.85	71.93	69.57	73.26	24.72
74		1960-62	0.0309	0.0236	88717	93049	69.53	75.27	70.74	76.08	25.22
75		1963	0.0268	0.0225	89347	92299	69.74	74.74	70.65	75.46	25.18
76		1964	0.0251	0.0217	89010	93168	69.90	75.53	70.69	76.20	25.26
77	Saskatchewan	1930-32	0.0800	0.0637	80260	81239	63.86	65.67	68.39	69.12	25.46
78		1940-42	0.0563	0.0456	83529	85717	66.18	68.75	69.11	71.02	25.42
79		1950-52	0.0377	0.0326	87202	90032	68.81	72.48	70.49	73.91	25.71
80		1960-62	0.0300	0.0223	88793	93224	70.59	76.23	71.77	76.96	26.43
81		1963	0.0322	0.0219	88959	93153	70.32	76.05	71.65	76.75	26.14
82		1964	0.0266	0.0215	88611	93199	70.82	76.36	71.75	77.03	26.57
83	Alberta	1930-32	0.0782	0.0599	78184	79783	62.26	64.41	66.52	67.49	24.55
84		1940-42	0.0565	0.0445	81941	84484	64.57	67.66	67.42	69.80	24.40
85		1950-52	0.0386	0.0287	86186	90191	67.85	72.06	69.57	73.18	24.99
86		1960-62	0.0299	0.0224	88512	92969	69.58	75.51	70.72	76.24	25.38
87		1963	0.0268	0.0194	88525	93526	69.77	75.64	70.69	76.14	25.47
88		1964	0.0250	0.0176	88468	93477	69.75	76.40	70.53	76.76	25.40
89	British	1930-32	0.0584	0.0460	76525	79986	61.78	65.22	64.59	67.35	24.06
90	Columbia	1940-42	0.0497	0.0364	79381	85046	63.13	68.67	65.42	70.26	23.58
91		1950-52	0.0342	0.0274	84734	89692	66.64	72.25	67.99	73.28	24.07
92		1960-62	0.0267	0.0207	87930	92786	68.88	75.43	69.76	76.02	24.74
93		1963	0.0264	0.0187	88118	93038	69.27	75.75	70.14	76.19	25.00
94		1964	0.0239	0.0161	87964	93075	68.63	75.59	69.31	75.82	24.32

| Expectancy, $\mathring{e}_{70}$ | | | General fertility rate | Total fertility rate | Gross reproduction rate | Net maternity function | | | | | SERIES NUMBER |
Females 32	Males 33	Females 34	35	36	37	Total, NRR 38	Mean, μ 39	Variance, σ^2 40	Generation, T 41	Complex root, r_2 42	
27.95	11.60	12.85	109.88	3.53	1.66	1.42	30.19	41.56	29.938	−0.0226+0.2028	41
26.71	10.76	11.89	109.15	3.31	1.62	1.43	29.60	43.57	29.321	−0.0280+0.2080	42
28.12	11.54	12.65	142.79	4.32	2.11	2.00	29.14	41.71	28.626	−0.0179+0.2168	43
29.19	11.37	13.43	151.86	4.79	2.30	2.21	28.54	41.21	27.948	−0.0175+0.2282	44
29.48	11.50	12.92	155.06	4.96	2.43	2.35	28.53	38.82	27.918	−0.0113+0.2268	45
29.61	11.11	13.61	141.90	4.64	2.22	2.15	28.86	39.02	28.323	−0.0129+0.2240	46
25.68	10.77	11.56	108.97	3.37	1.63	1.37	29.36	46.00	29.099	−0.0320+0.2065	47
26.02	10.40	11.54	109.30	3.13	1.53	1.34	28.49	43.01	28.251	−0.0345+0.2151	48
27.37	10.91	12.28	128.08	3.75	1.81	1.71	28.10	42.38	27.670	−0.0294+0.2232	49
28.78	11.32	13.08	134.70	4.14	2.02	1.93	27.58	39.95	27.082	−0.0248+0.2354	50
28.82	11.10	13.05	129.34	3.98	1.93	1.86	27.61	38.31	27.162	−0.0231+0.2329	51
28.85	11.32	13.36	124.66	3.85	1.88	1.81	27.84	38.96	27.408	−0.0230+0.2306	52
24.96	10.47	11.01	126.23	3.95	1.93	1.60	29.96	46.27	29.579	−0.0249+0.2044	53
25.47	10.00	10.93	122.20	3.67	1.79	1.52	29.38	45.38	29.041	−0.0283+0.2082	54
26.96	10.45	11.79	151.98	4.47	2.19	2.02	28.72	43.88	28.162	−0.0227+0.2202	55
28.47	11.04	12.65	144.72	4.50	2.18	2.08	28.05	40.37	27.497	−0.0202+0.2317	56
28.81	10.87	12.97	133.87	4.23	2.04	1.96	28.20	39.89	27.704	−0.0207+0.2281	57
28.81	11.01	12.95	128.77	4.09	2.00	1.92	28.17	38.71	27.696	−0.0193+0.2272	58
23.94	9.81	10.20	126.33	3.97	1.93	1.51	30.91	41.86	30.609	−0.0192+0.1998	59
24.48	9.65	10.47	112.05	3.39	1.64	1.41	30.23	40.84	29.985	−0.0231+0.2048	60
25.75	10.06	11.08	130.96	3.81	1.85	1.70	29.48	39.32	29.101	−0.0189+0.2137	61
27.38	10.44	11.95	121.11	3.68	1.79	1.71	28.88	38.05	28.506	−0.0204+0.2207	62
27.41	10.38	11.98	113.43	3.48	1.70	1.62	28.73	37.26	28.395	−0.0217+0.2217	63
27.98	10.58	12.38	108.81	3.35	1.63	1.56	28.71	36.85	28.411	−0.0224+0.2216	64
24.59	9.84	10.45	88.18	2.64	1.29	1.12	28.90	41.81	28.815	−0.0359+0.2100	65
25.48	9.85	10.89	83.27	2.42	1.18	1.09	28.14	38.88	28.077	−0.0382+0.2178	66
26.87	10.21	11.64	113.21	3.24	1.57	1.49	27.64	37.80	27.354	−0.0288+0.2270	67
28.24	10.29	12.52	123.13	3.74	1.82	1.76	27.23	35.90	26.844	−0.0225+0.2372	68
28.40	10.23	12.60	118.01	3.67	1.78	1.72	27.27	34.95	26.909	−0.0217+0.2367	69
28.81	10.62	13.03	113.45	3.55	1.72	1.67	27.32	35.04	26.975	−0.0224+0.2358	70
25.88	10.55	11.44	89.44	2.80	1.37	1.20	29.70	41.85	29.566	−0.0305+0.2060	71
26.01	10.18	11.33	87.82	2.56	1.25	1.12	29.03	40.23	28.943	−0.0343+0.2109	72
27.52	10.67	11.97	115.12	3.31	1.60	1.51	28.26	38.41	27.963	−0.0266+0.2226	73
29.27	11.01	13.20	127.05	3.91	1.90	1.83	27.59	36.91	27.170	−0.0209+0.2343	74
28.93	10.88	12.90	121.85	3.79	1.86	1.79	27.63	36.22	27.229	−0.0205+0.2330	75
29.40	11.20	13.33	115.71	3.61	1.76	1.69	27.61	36.62	27.244	−0.0232+0.2325	76
26.28	10.89	11.43	110.51	3.50	1.70	1.49	29.76	43.11	29.459	−0.0260+0.2080	77
26.83	10.71	11.80	94.51	2.84	1.38	1.25	29.56	41.37	29.395	−0.0301+0.2081	78
28.13	11.06	12.31	123.52	3.62	1.76	1.66	28.55	39.06	28.183	−0.0230+0.2224	79
30.13	11.68	13.63	135.58	4.19	2.05	1.97	27.70	37.86	27.212	−0.0197+0.2347	80
29.95	11.57	13.65	135.29	4.25	2.07	2.00	27.67	37.01	27.183	−0.0173+0.2356	81
30.24	11.74	13.86	129.30	4.08	1.99	1.92	27.78	36.88	27.329	−0.0179+0.2329	82
25.58	10.33	10.92	110.66	3.38	1.65	1.44	29.20	42.29	28.924	−0.0288+0.2128	83
26.11	10.01	11.26	99.35	2.89	1.41	1.28	28.78	41.11	28.589	−0.0337+0.2159	84
27.41	10.90	11.90	131.29	3.74	1.83	1.73	27.96	38.53	27.569	−0.0241+0.2284	85
29.48	11.18	13.28	143.47	4.26	2.08	2.00	27.20	37.75	26.694	−0.0211+0.2411	86
29.20	11.18	13.04	135.71	4.08	1.98	1.92	27.15	37.42	26.682	−0.0228+0.2413	87
30.02	11.32	13.81	125.74	3.81	1.86	1.80	27.19	37.14	26.774	−0.0241+0.2404	88
26.05	10.46	11.66	71.08	2.18	1.07	0.94	28.76	39.10	28.808	−0.0401+0.2118	89
26.69	10.26	11.73	83.34	2.33	1.13	1.04	27.89	36.10	27.868	−0.0379+0.2221	90
27.80	10.77	12.33	111.38	3.23	1.57	1.48	27.41	36.69	27.136	−0.0285+0.2310	91
29.38	11.00	13.41	121.57	3.81	1.86	1.80	26.97	35.12	26.573	−0.0213+0.2412	92
29.56	11.26	13.43	112.74	3.55	1.74	1.68	27.06	34.98	26.710	−0.0233+0.2388	93
29.24	10.69	13.37	104.43	3.27	1.59	1.55	27.09	35.49	26.789	−0.0273+0.2367	94

	AREA AND YEAR		POPULATION, IN 1000'S			AGE STRUCTURE					
			Observed at mid-year	Projected		Total reproductive value (in 1000's)	Percent at age			Dependency ratio (× 100)	Departure from stability (Δ percent)
				5 years	10 years		<15	15–64	≥65		
SERIES NUMBER			1	2	3	4	5	6	7	8	9
95	Costa Rica	1960	1166	1455	1790	739	46.36	50.90	2.74	96.46	7.5
96		1963	1341	1640	2003	852	47.75	49.07	3.18	103.79	4.3
97		1964	1396	1687	2038	865	47.72	49.11	3.17	103.61	3.2
98		1966	1541	1836	2191	898	48.24	48.58	3.18	105.87	2.3
99	Dominican	1960	3039	3498	4055	1692	47.29	49.74	2.97	101.03	8.5
100	Republic	1966	3498	4043	4693	1969	44.57	51.86	3.57	92.83	7.0
101	El Salvador	1961	2527	3030	3614	1520	44.80	52.02	3.18	92.23	4.1
102	Greenland	1960	32	38	46	18	44.25	53.65	2.10	86.38	5.8
103	Grenada	1960	89	104	125	52	47.67	47.14	5.19	112.15	9.0
104		1961	92	107	131	54	47.68	47.13	5.19	112.18	8.8
105	Guatemala	1964	4440	5121	5922	2644	46.05	51.18	2.77	95.41	2.3
106	Honduras	1956–58	1768	2070	2422	970	45.27	51.63	3.10	93.67	1.4
107		1959–61	1940	2289	2702	1092	47.34	50.01	2.65	99.97	1.8
108		1962	2068	2470	2946	1211	48.72	48.92	2.36	104.40	1.9
109		1963	2137	2543	3033	1258	49.41	48.38	2.21	106.70	2.2
110		1964	2209	2651	3177	1339	50.10	47.84	2.06	109.04	2.2
111		1965	2284	2720	3248	1353	50.79	47.30	1.91	111.44	3.5
112		1966	2363	2831	3398	1447	51.48	46.76	1.76	113.89	3.1
113	Jamaica	1951	1430	1593	1762	597	36.15	60.06	3.79	66.51	3.5
114		1952	1457	1626	1804	601	36.18	60.05	3.77	66.53	3.5
115		1956	1564	1792	2043	688	38.01	58.08	3.91	72.18	5.8
116		1960	1632	1918	2244	815	42.02	53.68	4.30	86.29	7.0
117		1961	1646	1924	2254	825	43.37	52.28	4.35	91.29	6.3
118		1962	1663	1940	2272	846	44.50	51.09	4.41	95.74	6.1
119		1963	1696	1984	2334	885	45.12	50.44	4.44	98.24	6.4
120	Martinique	1961	288	330	380	151	42.38	52.75	4.87	89.57	5.4
121		1963	308	349	396	154	42.16	52.88	4.96	89.12	4.3
122	Mexico	1959–61	34997	41401	48866	20819	44.42	52.15	3.43	91.77	2.5
123		1962	38543	45581	53854	22343	45.85	50.87	3.28	96.59	1.5
124		1966	44145	52407	62252	25927	46.26	50.43	3.31	98.32	1.5
125	Nicaragua	1963	1546	1852	2218	882	48.25	48.83	2.92	104.80	3.3
126		1965	1655	1978	2368	937	48.34	48.76	2.90	105.08	3.4
127	Panama	1960	1000	1179	1389	517	43.45	52.98	3.57	88.73	1.8
128		1962	1075	1273	1508	547	43.35	53.04	3.61	88.55	2.3
129		1966	1221	1440	1696	615	43.45	52.98	3.57	88.75	1.6
130	Puerto Rico	1960	2362	2700	3123	1084	42.46	52.31	5.23	91.15	4.1
131		1963	2513	2840	3231	1047	39.82	54.68	5.50	82.88	3.6
132		1964	2572	2902	3281	1050	39.11	55.26	5.63	80.98	3.1
133		1965	2626	2962	3352	1044	38.67	55.56	5.77	80.00	2.8
134	St. Kitts - Nevills -	1960	57	64	75	32	45.72	49.29	4.99	102.89	11.3
135	Anguilla	1961	59	68	79	32	45.73	49.29	4.98	.	102.91	11.5
136	St. Lucia	1960	87	101	118	52	44.26	50.95	4.79	96.25	7.8
137	Trinidad and	1954	698	818	948	331	40.77	55.34	3.89	80.70	9.8
138	Tobago	1955	721	843	979	346	41.45	54.79	3.76	82.52	8.8
139		1956–58	765	880	1019	357	42.31	54.13	3.56	84.74	5.8
140		1959–61	831	966	1133	410	42.36	53.41	4.23	87.24	4.4
141		1962	900	1048	1231	436	42.57	53.84	3.59	85.73	3.0

VITAL RATES PER THOUSAND POPULATION

Crude (both sexes)			Standardized on U.S., 1960 (both sexes)		Intrinsic (females)			INFANT MORTALITY RATE per 1000 births	1000$_4M_1$		1000$_5M_{50}$		
Birth 10	Death 11	Increase 12	Birth 13	Death 14	Birth 15	Death 16	Increase 17	18	Males 19	Females 20	Males 21	Females 22	SERIES NUMBER
55.45	8.63	46.82	51.90	14.78	51.50	7.35	44.15	69.75	7.03	7.68	9.29	6.97	95
49.79	8.48	41.31	49.85	11.70	49.45	7.93	41.52	88.15	7.17	7.87	8.81	5.97	96
46.87	8.79	38.09	46.90	11.37	47.38	8.20	39.18	76.14	7.42	7.75	8.01	6.91	97
41.75	7.39	34.37	42.40	10.36	43.44	6.84	36.60	64.01	5.18	6.04	7.94	5.94	98
36.23	8.89	27.34	34.76	10.24	35.94	9.45	26.50	98.32	12.21	11.31	6.60	6.74	99
36.10	7.64	28.46	34.98	10.06	35.91	9.07	26.84	83.55	9.80	9.50	8.70	7.16	100
49.42	11.28	38.14	44.05	13.21	46.39	10.68	35.70	70.65	16.73	16.31	12.56	10.47	101
48.85	7.85	40.99	44.65	14.89	44.41	6.83	37.59	64.31	5.62	2.09	10.94	5.68	102
44.97	11.56	33.42	43.83	12.59	47.48	8.33	39.15	81.92	14.01	11.76	8.96	7.82	103
44.60	11.07	33.53	44.13	12.26	46.66	8.17	38.50	64.61	13.93	12.38	16.61	7.08	104
44.23	15.38	28.85	40.92	18.80	43.86	15.43	28.44	87.98	25.27	26.97	17.12	13.48	105
42.38	10.58	31.80	38.72	12.63	40.47	10.54	29.93	56.50	17.04	17.29	11.23	10.76	106
42.42	9.26	33.17	39.62	12.26	41.12	9.08	32.04	47.00	13.61	13.67	12.27	9.51	107
44.55	9.02	35.53	42.17	13.62	43.42	8.70	34.73	40.43	12.91	12.78	13.30	11.32	108
43.83	9.13	34.70	41.72	14.68	43.18	8.66	34.52	42.83	13.08	12.76	12.65	10.51	109
45.52	9.30	36.21	43.71	14.78	44.63	8.92	35.71	42.16	13.91	13.60	12.55	11.45	110
43.03	8.60	34.44	41.76	14.89	42.49	8.43	34.06	36.22	12.17	12.02	11.78	10.35	111
44.20	8.67	35.52	43.68	16.44	44.05	8.41	35.64	37.24	12.38	12.20	12.25	11.14	112
33.87	12.05	21.82	26.61	17.89	31.25	11.99	19.25	87.91	12.06	10.32	17.94	13.94	113
33.27	11.47	21.79	26.27	17.41	30.53	11.45	19.08	79.52	12.14	10.63	16.17	13.34	114
37.21	9.38	27.82	31.31	14.95	35.96	8.14	27.82	59.19	8.08	6.66	13.18	10.21	115
41.91	8.77	33.14	36.86	11.07	41.17	6.53	34.65	51.57	7.23	5.96	11.29	9.65	116
40.18	8.62	31.56	36.69	11.20	40.68	6.48	34.21	48.93	6.74	5.83	11.72	8.08	117
39.03	8.52	30.51	36.82	11.07	40.96	6.49	34.47	48.88	7.07	5.65	12.62	9.52	118
39.79	8.91	30.89	38.49	11.73	42.01	6.71	35.30	50.18	7.07	6.51	11.52	9.44	119
36.66	7.94	28.72	36.03	10.82	37.73	6.97	30.76	56.43	6.47	5.86	13.46	9.24	120
33.20	8.17	25.03	33.36	11.16	35.01	6.72	28.29	38.76	4.84	4.87	16.24	9.25	121
46.14	11.32	34.83	42.33	15.12	44.14	11.19	32.95	102.00	13.81	14.49	13.16	9.76	122
44.25	10.46	33.79	41.99	14.29	43.26	9.61	33.65	76.70	11.67	12.40	12.90	9.32	123
43.96	9.61	34.35	43.07	13.33	43.31	8.66	34.65	63.33	9.73	10.28	12.12	8.35	124
43.72	7.50	36.22	40.26	12.05	42.73	7.38	35.35	54.63	8.74	7.30	8.00	7.82	125
43.05	7.32	35.74	39.56	9.82	41.79	7.34	34.46	51.73	8.23	8.56	9.40	7.37	126
41.25	8.39	32.87	37.31	11.11	41.77	8.08	33.69	57.47	9.57	9.38	8.74	8.00	127
41.54	7.32	34.22	37.51	10.30	41.61	6.97	34.65	43.43	7.40	7.73	10.42	7.50	128
40.44	7.52	32.92	36.57	10.30	40.85	7.12	33.73	45.41	8.44	8.49	9.15	8.32	129
32.31	6.69	25.62	30.05	8.61	33.46	6.20	27.26	43.75	2.91	3.24	9.88	7.28	130
30.82	6.90	23.91	26.62	9.34	29.75	6.81	22.94	47.19	2.22	2.44	9.65	6.03	131
30.70	7.22	23.48	26.12	9.39	29.38	7.03	22.36	53.01	2.54	2.80	9.41	5.62	132
30.32	6.74	23.58	25.73	8.29	28.93	6.53	22.40	42.82	1.66	2.02	9.54	5.08	133
42.53	13.39	29.14	44.35	14.70	46.71	9.67	37.04	101.36	16.09	11.84	12.38	7.37	134
42.26	12.11	30.15	44.60	13.45	46.04	8.68	37.36	83.84	15.79	10.00	12.82	9.35	135
48.89	14.77	34.12	45.23	14.21	47.77	12.61	35.16	107.07	25.24	17.89	14.01	8.47	136
41.93	9.76	32.18	37.74	14.27	43.37	8.07	35.30	72.58	4.41	3.77	13.92	14.26	137
41.92	10.35	31.57	38.00	15.27	42.94	7.69	35.25	68.40	4.45	3.61	14.93	13.46	138
37.46	9.46	28.00	34.68	15.35	39.98	7.63	32.35	64.90	4.18	3.63	13.87	12.27	139
38.66	8.36	30.30	35.35	12.79	39.68	6.63	33.06	56.97	3.48	2.75	15.36	11.45	140
37.88	7.18	30.70	34.25	12.43	38.50	5.97	32.53	38.50	2.05	1.80	14.85	10.26	141

continued

LIFE TABLE VALUES

SERIES NUMBER	AREA AND YEAR		Probability of dying in first year, q_0		Survivors to age 50 per 100,000 births, l_{50}		Expectancy, $\mathring{e}_0$		Expectancy, $\mathring{e}_1$		Expectancy, $\mathring{e}_{50}$
			Males 23	Females 24	Males 25	Females 26	Males 27	Females 28	Males 29	Females 30	Males 31
95	Costa Rica	1960	0.0707	0.0606	80444	82791	63.16	65.18	66.93	68.36	24.20
96		1963	0.0920	0.0738	78560	81458	62.64	65.24	67.96	69.40	25.50
97		1964	0.0953	0.0792	77852	81009	62.37	65.26	67.91	69.84	25.63
98		1966	0.0694	0.0588	81821	84240	65.02	67.74	68.94	70.96	25.55
99	Dominican Republic	1960	0.1017	0.0828	75357	78085	62.68	65.46	68.73	70.34	28.64
100		1966	0.0975	0.0849	77576	79814	63.61	66.06	69.45	71.16	27.97
101	El Salvador	1961	0.0930	0.0768	67086	72923	56.35	60.65	61.09	64.66	25.17
102	Greenland	1960	0.0715	0.0601	77952	79373	60.23	64.90	63.85	68.03	22.32
103	Grenada	1960	0.0860	0.0698	74704	81001	58.65	65.05	63.13	68.91	22.61
104		1961	0.0677	0.0615	79820	79967	60.54	65.02	63.91	68.25	22.07
105	Guatemala	1964	0.1067	0.0900	58096	61253	49.25	50.87	54.09	54.86	22.20
106	Honduras	1956-58	0.0584	0.0497	67418	70455	58.35	60.08	60.94	62.20	26.66
107		1959-61	0.0489	0.0414	70140	74718	59.51	62.51	61.55	64.19	25.51
108		1962	0.0422	0.0358	70839	75410	59.30	61.67	60.89	62.95	24.27
109		1963	0.0442	0.0382	71440	75978	58.53	61.72	60.22	63.16	23.20
110		1964	0.0441	0.0372	71943	75425	58.39	60.62	60.07	61.94	22.81
111		1965	0.0389	0.0311	73334	76759	59.13	61.53	60.51	62.49	22.66
112		1966	0.0327	0.0296	74101	76430	59.24	60.70	60.23	61.53	22.04
113	Jamaica	1951	0.0884	0.0769	69843	71692	55.20	58.13	59.51	61.94	20.50
114		1952	0.0814	0.0690	71692	74004	58.16	59.59	61.97	62.98	23.27
115		1956	0.0615	0.0515	78369	81142	61.07	64.68	64.05	67.17	22.04
116		1960	0.0555	0.0450	80369	84330	63.41	67.91	66.11	70.09	23.67
117		1961	0.0513	0.0447	81313	84515	63.47	68.07	65.88	70.23	23.06
118		1962	0.0512	0.0459	82052	84653	63.88	67.92	66.31	70.17	23.33
119		1963	0.0557	0.0478	81065	83844	62.89	67.15	65.57	69.50	22.66
120	Martinique	1961	0.0611	0.0475	79076	81640	63.09	68.21	66.17	70.59	23.60
121		1963	0.0408	0.0326	80992	82690	63.63	68.75	65.32	70.05	22.52
122	Mexico	1959-61	0.1020	0.0891	67078	71880	55.64	58.61	60.92	63.31	23.75
123		1962	0.0781	0.0676	70966	75405	58.27	61.12	62.18	64.52	23.81
124		1966	0.0723	0.0605	72643	77810	59.49	62.82	63.09	65.85	23.90
125	Nicaragua	1963	0.0605	0.0498	76330	80227	62.78	65.90	65.80	68.33	25.83
126		1965	0.0558	0.0501	76259	81068	64.55	67.88	67.34	70.44	27.89
127	Panama	1960	0.0637	0.0553	78300	79182	62.74	65.23	65.98	68.03	25.06
128		1962	0.0511	0.0424	80899	82322	65.05	67.29	67.53	69.25	25.68
129		1966	0.0498	0.0411	81396	82602	64.99	67.21	67.38	69.07	25.50
130	Puerto Rico	1960	0.0471	0.0372	83426	87793	67.41	72.03	69.73	73.81	26.24
131		1963	0.0497	0.0407	83133	88902	66.54	72.02	69.01	74.06	25.29
132		1964	0.0579	0.0433	82620	88611	66.32	71.77	69.38	74.00	25.68
133		1965	0.0463	0.0360	84618	89794	68.03	73.74	70.32	75.48	26.17
134	St. Kitts - Neville - Anguilla	1960	0.1040	0.0859	72343	76694	56.57	61.26	62.10	65.99	22.19
135		1961	0.0908	0.0713	76546	77536	64.05	62.70	69.40	66.49	29.24
136	St. Lucia	1960	0.1145	0.1110	66353	69098	54.31	57.98	60.28	64.18	24.58
137	Trinidad and Tobago	1954	0.0736	0.0631	76530	77324	59.85	62.08	63.58	65.25	21.13
138		1955	0.0715	0.0558	76794	78809	59.11	62.37	62.64	65.04	19.98
139		1956-58	0.0674	0.0558	79057	81559	60.13	63.20	63.46	65.92	20.11
140		1959-61	0.0600	0.0486	80987	84099	61.88	66.43	64.81	68.81	21.02
141		1962	0.0434	0.0362	83570	86092	63.73	67.82	65.61	69.36	21.13

FERTILITY MEASURES (FEMALES)

| | Expectancy, $\mathring{e}_{70}$ | | General fer-tility rate | Total fer-tility rate | Gross repro-duction rate | Net maternity function | | | | | SERIES NUMBER |
| | | | | | | Total, NRR | Mean, μ | Variance, σ^2 | Generation, T | Complex root, r_2 | |
Females 32	Males 33	Females 34	35	36	37	38	39	40	41	42	
25.26	10.36	10.21	271.98	7.91	3.89	3.43	29.01	49.33	27.922	−0.0137+0.2237	95
26.40	11.19	11.34	253.80	7.61	3.70	3.23	29.23	48.80	28.208	−0.0122+0.2208	96
26.86	11.86	12.26	238.86	7.15	3.49	3.03	29.25	49.30	28.272	−0.0144+0.2188	97
27.11	11.57	12.00	215.20	6.45	3.15	2.82	29.30	50.51	28.362	−0.0178+0.2147	98
29.73	13.71	14.14	177.54	5.31	2.57	2.15	29.64	49.65	28.970	−0.0234+0.2084	99
29.16	13.26	13.43	169.94	5.36	2.65	2.24	31.05	74.68	30.061	−0.0457+0.1917	100
26.88	12.65	14.01	230.77	6.71	3.30	2.69	28.60	50.23	27.696	−0.0202+0.2239	101
24.93	7.89	10.85	233.99	6.83	3.20	2.90	29.28	51.73	28.312	−0.0178+0.2219	102
26.89	10.51	12.80	233.42	6.68	3.33	2.87	27.87	45.78	26.968	−0.0171+0.2314	103
26.98	10.87	12.35	232.15	6.70	3.29	2.85	28.19	49.01	27.251	−0.0200+0.2252	104
22.56	11.07	10.34	211.10	6.22	3.04	2.21	28.61	53.39	27.841	−0.0310+0.2169	105
26.78	13.69	13.64	202.71	5.90	2.82	2.30	28.60	50.29	27.835	−0.0253+0.2210	106
26.61	12.10	12.75	206.20	6.03	2.90	2.45	28.80	52.50	27.955	−0.0244+0.2178	107
24.69	10.86	11.28	218.91	6.40	3.10	2.64	28.88	53.69	27.943	−0.0247+0.2157	108
24.45	9.54	10.50	216.56	6.33	3.07	2.63	28.90	53.03	27.974	−0.0239+0.2148	109
23.50	9.29	9.72	226.16	6.63	3.20	2.72	29.00	52.99	28.043	−0.0221+0.2145	110
23.50	8.68	9.38	215.04	6.33	3.04	2.61	29.12	53.77	28.197	−0.0229+0.2112	111
22.44	8.63	9.10	222.09	6.63	3.20	2.76	29.53	59.00	28.472	−0.0263+0.2097	112
23.23	7.40	9.41	141.56	4.07	2.02	1.67	27.15	45.13	26.703	−0.0433+0.2333	113
23.66	9.47	9.57	139.64	4.02	1.99	1.67	27.23	45.68	26.784	−0.0432+0.2340	114
24.90	8.14	9.85	165.13	4.79	2.35	2.09	27.18	43.90	26.560	−0.0299+0.2390	115
26.61	10.81	12.85	196.17	5.61	2.78	2.53	27.62	47.52	26.794	−0.0279+0.2314	116
26.63	9.88	12.35	194.12	5.58	2.75	2.51	27.70	48.16	26.866	−0.0280+0.2281	117
26.42	10.30	12.18	193.97	5.60	2.77	2.53	27.76	47.12	26.942	−0.0251+0.2278	118
26.13	9.55	11.92	201.45	5.85	2.87	2.60	27.94	47.95	27.088	−0.0241+0.2251	119
28.07	11.37	14.05	178.16	5.50	2.75	2.48	30.29	44.50	29.581	−0.0091+0.2093	120
27.40	11.17	13.68	161.21	5.08	2.53	2.33	30.56	44.12	29.910	−0.0089+0.2058	121
24.84	10.99	10.96	219.11	6.45	3.14	2.54	29.06	46.26	28.280	−0.0172+0.2153	122
25.04	10.78	10.86	215.45	6.40	3.10	2.59	29.14	46.48	28.335	−0.0169+0.2148	123
25.30	11.12	11.03	216.34	6.57	3.17	2.71	29.72	52.34	28.799	−0.0200+0.2119	124
26.93	11.03	12.24	213.99	6.15	2.99	2.64	28.29	47.06	27.447	−0.0210+0.2277	125
29.13	15.19	15.62	209.10	6.02	2.92	2.57	28.28	49.82	27.415	−0.0267+0.2236	126
27.31	10.95	12.67	201.06	5.70	2.82	2.45	27.43	45.23	26.660	−0.0244+0.2371	127
27.37	11.94	12.87	202.58	5.72	2.81	2.51	27.34	45.13	26.557	−0.0246+0.2382	128
27.30	11.91	12.89	197.76	5.58	2.75	2.45	27.34	45.51	26.574	−0.0274+0.2392	129
29.11	12.31	13.69	156.88	4.61	2.26	2.10	27.86	47.20	27.213	−0.0372+0.2372	130
28.52	11.59	12.99	142.51	4.07	1.98	1.85	27.38	46.65	26.832	−0.0490+0.2879	131
28.56	11.81	12.97	140.89	4.00	1.95	1.81	27.14	46.33	26.614	−0.0636+0.2709	132
29.74	12.57	14.10	138.86	3.94	1.92	1.81	26.98	45.56	26.463	−0.0500+0.2536	133
24.90	10.02	9.88	225.59	6.74	3.23	2.72	27.91	48.31	27.007	−0.0263+0.2263	134
25.08	18.65	10.82	225.12	6.74	3.21	2.77	28.27	50.27	27.322	−0.0221+0.2166	135
27.09	13.24	12.89	234.50	6.89	3.37	2.63	28.34	49.93	27.455	−0.0239+0.2258	136
23.39	9.98	11.50	199.34	5.74	2.83	2.50	26.75	44.79	25.959	−0.0338+0.2426	137
22.69	9.14	11.04	201.17	5.78	2.82	2.52	27.00	45.43	26.199	−0.0312+0.2394	138
22.37	8.79	10.23	183.57	5.29	2.59	2.34	26.99	43.21	26.284	−0.0295+0.2397	139
24.49	9.10	11.33	186.68	5.40	2.64	2.43	27.59	43.34	26.864	−0.0215+0.2335	140
24.56	8.94	11.44	181.03	5.23	2.56	2.40	27.60	43.53	26.885	−0.0230+0.2325	141

			POPULATION, IN 1000'S			AGE STRUCTURE					
				Projected		Total re-productive value (in 1000's)	Percent at age			Dependency ratio (× 100)	Departure from stability (Δ percent)
	AREA AND YEAR		Observed at mid-year	5 years	10 years		<15	15–64	≥65		
SERIES NUMBER			1	2	3	4	5	6	7	8	9
142	Trinidad and	1964	951	1097	1267	443	42.57	53.90	3.53	85.54	2.3
143	Tobago	1966	995	1125	1278	437	42.41	54.00	3.59	85.20	4.4
144	cont	1967	1010	1131	1274	423	42.35	54.06	3.59	84.99	6.8
145	United States	1919–21	106630	114320	121973	38162	31.76	63.53	4.71	57.39	5.1
146		1924–26	115829	123468	131185	38771	31.02	63.98	5.00	56.29	5.6
147		1929–31	122988	128673	134271	36127	29.27	65.29	5.44	53.18	10.3
148		1934–36	127252	131841	136188	33436	27.02	66.85	6.13	49.59	12.3
149		1939–41	131684	137302	142370	33094	25.12	67.99	6.89	47.07	9.8
150		1944–46	131976	139827	146727	36661	26.63	65.71	7.66	52.18	5.8
151		1949–51	151345	161830	171206	41083	27.01	64.83	8.16	54.26	6.5
152		1954–56	164301	176915	189512	47890	29.70	61.74	8.56	61.98	9.8
153		1959–61	175990	193552	208810	54285	31.17	59.58	9.25	67.85	10.0
154	Nonwhite	1959–61	20599	22972	25734	7972	37.68	56.18	6.14	77.99	10.4
155	White	1959–61	155392	170319	182576	46037	30.33	60.01	9.66	66.62	9.3
156	United States	1962	185888	198993	214142	55621	31.30	59.39	9.31	68.40	8.3
157		1963	188656	201179	215740	55738	31.20	59.49	9.31	68.09	6.7
158		1964	191369	203704	218011	56001	31.08	59.59	9.33	67.81	5.3
159		1965	193818	204696	217455	54607	30.91	59.72	9.37	67.44	4.3
160		1966	195857	205644	217258	53196	30.67	59.91	9.42	66.91	5.2
161	Nonwhite	1966	23493	25677	28314	8523	38.32	55.57	6.11	79.95	4.8
162	White	1966	172364	180011	189061	44705	29.62	60.50	9.88	65.28	5.6
163	United States	1967	197863	207159	217995	52115	30.32	60.18	9.50	66.16	6.2
164	Alabama	1959–61	3279	3563	3886	1068	33.93	58.08	7.99	72.20	6.3
165	Alaska	1959–61	228	257	289	81	35.51	62.11	2.38	61.01	10.2
166	Arizona	1959–61	1309	1446	1598	451	34.77	58.30	6.93	71.53	8.1
167	Arkansas	1959–61	1792	1926	2093	547	31.89	57.23	10.88	74.74	10.8
168	California	1959–61	15776	16970	18261	4493	30.31	60.93	8.76	64.11	10.1
169	Colorado	1959–61	1761	1907	2070	543	32.44	58.54	9.02	70.83	7.2
170	Connecticut	1959–61	2543	2704	2880	721	29.48	60.95	9.57	64.06	11.4
171	Delaware	1959–61	448	484	527	140	32.17	59.82	8.01	67.16	11.1
172	Florida	1959–61	4968	5317	5693	1391	29.62	59.21	11.17	68.90	12.2
173	Georgia	1959–61	3959	4309	4702	1268	33.57	59.06	7.37	69.33	6.1
174	Hawaii	1959–61	636	707	781	213	34.41	60.98	4.61	64.00	6.2
175	Idaho	1959–61	670	733	811	226	34.69	56.58	8.73	76.75	9.1
176	Illinois	1959–61	10115	10801	11546	2934	29.77	60.56	9.67	65.13	12.1
177	Indiana	1959–61	4679	5033	5446	1415	31.78	58.66	9.56	70.45	9.1
178	Iowa	1959–61	2766	2958	3191	838	31.11	57.01	11.88	75.42	12.4
179	Kansas	1959–61	2186	2343	2529	642	30.86	58.11	11.03	72.08	10.9
180	Kentucky	1959–61	3049	3284	3563	944	32.25	58.13	9.62	72.03	8.1
181	Louisiana	1959–61	3272	3598	3977	1140	35.25	57.33	7.42	74.41	8.5
182	Maine	1959–61	972	1041	1128	298	31.05	57.96	10.99	72.55	12.5
183	Maryland	1959–61	3113	3367	3647	954	32.01	60.68	7.31	64.79	9.5
184	Massachusetts	1959–61	5163	5466	5800	1478	28.76	60.14	11.10	66.29	12.9
185	Michigan	1959–61	7855	8515	9252	2509	33.13	58.71	8.16	70.32	9.0
186	Minnesota	1959–61	3428	3723	4066	1146	32.85	56.77	10.38	76.14	11.9
187	Mississippi	1959–61	2187	2406	2673	797	35.82	55.46	8.72	80.33	10.4
188	Missouri	1959–61	4332	4598	4904	1219	29.28	59.07	11.65	69.31	12.6
189	Montana	1959–61	677	735	805	225	33.67	56.63	9.70	76.57	10.7
190	Nebraska	1959–61	1416	1525	1647	431	30.88	57.49	11.63	73.95	12.8
191	Nevada	1959–61	286	311	339	85	30.58	63.05	6.37	58.61	10.9
192	New Hampshire	1959–61	609	647	694	179	30.07	58.77	11.16	70.15	13.5
193	New Jersey	1959–61	6085	6442	6810	1667	28.83	61.93	9.24	61.45	11.8
194	New Mexico	1959–61	957	1081	1226	371	37.93	56.68	5.39	76.42	6.1
195	New York	1959–61	16827	17716	18620	4475	27.57	62.37	10.06	60.33	11.1
196	North Carolina	1959–61	4574	4966	5413	1443	33.39	59.76	6.85	67.33	4.0
197	North Dakota	1959–61	635	698	774	225	34.42	56.32	9.26	77.57	9.9

VITAL RATES PER THOUSAND POPULATION								INFANT MOR-TALITY RATE per 1000 births	AGE-SPECIFIC DEATH RATES				
Crude (both sexes)			Standardized on U.S., 1960 (both sexes)		Intrinsic (females)				$1000_4 M_1$		$1000_5 M_{50}$		SERIES NUMBER
Birth 10	Death 11	Increase 12	Birth 13	Death 14	Birth 15	Death 16	Increase 17	18	Males 19	Females 20	Males 21	Females 22	
34.65	7.02	27.63	31.35	12.98	35.38	6.36	29.02	35.32	2.31	2.15	14.47	9.97	142
30.22	7.09	23.12	27.02	15.24	31.59	7.03	24.57	41.79	2.21	1.77	13.91	10.20	143
28.18	6.71	21.47	25.26	20.00	28.97	7.57	21.39	35.77	2.25	2.00	12.65	9.86	144
27.34	12.49	14.85	22.11	16.90	24.67	14.43	10.23	88.79	9.22	8.39	14.83	13.82	145
25.11	11.84	13.27	20.42	17.03	22.81	13.77	9.04	73.90	7.14	6.37	16.29	13.81	146
20.83	11.43	9.40	16.66	15.39	17.99	15.48	2.51	68.06	6.13	5.38	16.19	12.72	147
18.67	11.18	7.49	14.71	14.77	15.32	16.48	-1.16	63.74	5.05	4.39	16.25	11.83	148
19.56	10.64	8.92	15.08	13.06	15.78	14.84	0.94	54.48	3.15	2.72	14.89	10.23	149
23.26	10.63	12.63	17.37	11.95	18.77	11.89	6.88	43.18	2.18	1.86	14.22	8.88	150
24.45	9.64	14.81	20.53	10.45	23.17	8.80	14.37	33.91	1.55	1.30	13.22	7.76	151
25.16	9.28	15.88	23.37	9.68	26.86	6.98	19.88	29.73	1.23	1.04	12.17	6.66	152
23.92	9.39	14.53	23.92	9.39	27.65	6.52	21.13	26.83	1.15	0.96	12.26	6.36	153
31.90	10.04	21.86	29.60	12.54	35.82	6.84	28.98	45.72	2.12	1.74	17.65	11.16	154
22.58	9.34	13.25	22.82	9.05	26.09	6.68	19.41	23.57	1.01	0.83	11.61	5.56	155
22.66	9.45	13.21	22.74	9.38	26.15	6.91	19.24	25.36	1.05	0.91	12.27	6.34	156
21.95	9.61	12.34	21.82	9.54	24.85	7.36	17.50	25.27	1.08	0.91	12.30	6.37	157
21.27	9.40	11.87	21.00	9.29	23.77	7.67	16.10	24.64	1.05	0.87	12.06	6.39	158
19.61	9.43	10.18	19.20	9.30	21.29	8.64	12.65	24.08	1.01	0.85	12.16	6.28	159
18.41	9.51	8.90	17.77	9.33	19.30	9.60	9.70	23.72	1.01	0.85	12.23	6.24	160
26.09	9.73	16.36	23.78	12.41	28.55	8.13	20.41	38.81	1.65	1.42	19.09	12.00	161
17.37	9.48	7.88	16.90	8.97	17.96	10.03	7.93	20.63	0.90	0.73	11.51	5.60	162
17.79	9.36	8.44	16.71	9.12	17.75	10.36	7.38	22.45	0.96	0.76	12.00	6.16	163
24.79	9.01	15.78	23.71	10.05	27.49	7.17	20.32	32.55	1.39	1.35	13.64	7.56	164
31.35	5.47	25.88	29.76	10.44	34.73	5.69	29.04	40.00	2.00	1.58	11.45	6.38	165
27.59	7.72	19.87	26.82	9.29	31.00	5.88	25.12	33.16	1.91	1.54	12.49	6.16	166
22.74	9.72	13.02	24.21	8.76	28.11	6.38	21.74	27.98	1.37	1.26	11.54	6.04	167
23.51	8.48	15.04	23.36	8.83	27.08	6.40	20.68	24.51	1.07	0.87	11.70	6.15	168
24.53	8.58	15.95	23.76	8.63	27.39	6.38	21.01	27.80	1.19	0.91	10.82	5.47	169
22.35	9.33	13.02	22.86	9.10	26.05	6.65	19.40	22.42	0.83	0.71	10.88	5.62	170
26.18	9.10	17.08	25.27	9.98	29.69	6.03	23.66	25.86	0.88	0.83	13.65	7.19	171
23.15	9.48	13.67	23.73	8.78	27.57	6.59	20.98	31.19	1.64	1.23	13.65	6.99	172
25.25	8.68	16.57	23.53	10.19	27.42	7.13	20.30	32.63	1.36	1.29	15.59	8.51	173
27.20	5.40	21.80	25.05	8.15	28.65	6.00	22.65	23.43	0.76	0.82	9.28	7.22	174
25.50	8.16	17.34	26.74	8.39	31.20	5.28	25.92	23.29	1.46	1.08	9.10	5.39	175
23.61	10.09	13.53	23.81	9.74	27.65	6.56	21.09	25.47	1.07	0.92	12.60	6.60	176
24.07	9.57	14.50	23.81	9.27	27.60	6.36	21.25	24.51	1.01	0.87	11.73	6.16	177
23.17	10.28	12.90	24.78	8.33	28.57	5.72	22.85	21.79	0.96	0.78	9.71	4.84	178
23.36	9.57	13.79	24.17	8.20	27.90	5.91	21.99	22.84	1.01	0.80	10.37	4.85	179
23.78	9.65	14.13	23.96	9.38	27.47	6.66	20.81	28.66	1.25	1.02	12.39	5.78	180
27.52	8.84	18.68	26.42	10.17	31.01	6.19	24.82	32.38	1.47	1.29	14.34	7.58	181
23.95	11.09	12.86	25.18	9.51	29.38	5.99	23.39	26.93	1.23	0.98	11.04	5.81	182
24.86	8.86	16.00	24.11	10.37	28.11	6.69	21.43	28.42	1.17	0.91	14.00	7.18	183
22.33	10.82	11.51	23.15	9.44	26.19	6.70	19.50	22.57	0.86	0.72	12.21	6.01	184
24.91	8.59	16.33	24.75	9.41	28.68	6.13	22.55	24.53	0.98	0.79	11.53	6.28	185
25.49	9.11	16.38	26.94	8.32	30.57	5.24	25.33	21.93	0.98	0.86	10.00	4.92	186
27.35	9.73	17.62	28.05	10.14	32.76	6.27	26.49	41.03	1.76	1.61	13.09	7.54	187
22.59	10.95	11.64	23.58	9.13	27.01	6.56	20.45	25.37	1.15	0.87	11.87	5.98	188
25.82	9.59	16.23	27.31	9.32	31.71	5.45	26.26	25.76	1.28	1.07	12.08	6.44	189
24.22	9.87	14.35	25.53	8.21	29.35	5.52	23.83	23.47	0.98	0.78	9.94	4.73	190
26.07	8.81	17.26	25.15	10.47	30.10	6.40	23.69	32.60	1.43	1.23	14.20	7.55	191
22.58	11.00	11.58	24.19	9.37	28.32	6.07	22.25	23.74	1.08	0.89	11.83	5.61	192
21.84	9.78	12.06	22.23	9.84	25.53	7.22	18.31	25.13	1.01	0.88	12.40	6.71	193
31.64	6.64	25.00	29.15	9.00	34.05	5.36	28.69	33.45	1.79	1.46	10.63	5.77	194
21.45	10.57	10.88	21.30	9.96	24.24	7.71	16.54	25.20	1.06	0.84	12.53	6.57	195
24.23	8.12	16.11	22.26	9.99	25.52	7.53	17.99	32.83	1.30	1.20	14.12	6.79	196
26.33	8.41	17.92	28.42	8.21	32.15	5.00	27.15	24.26	1.15	0.83	9.31	4.64	197

continued

LIFE TABLE VALUES

SERIES NUMBER	AREA AND YEAR		Probability of dying in first year, q_0		Survivors to age 50 per 100,000 births, l_{50}		Expectancy, $\overset{\circ}{e}_0$		Expectancy, $\overset{\circ}{e}_1$		Expectancy, $\overset{\circ}{e}_{50}$
			Males 23	Females 24	Males 25	Females 26	Males 27	Females 28	Males 29	Females 30	Males 31
142	Trinidad and	1964	0.0383	0.0320	84714	86589	64.04	67.68	65.58	68.91	21.06
143	Tobago	1966	0.0459	0.0348	83727	87872	63.55	68.00	65.60	69.45	20.94
144	*cont*	1967	0.0385	0.0322	84468	87409	64.11	68.37	65.66	69.63	21.20
145	United States	1919–21	0.0932	0.0740	66288	68376	54.49	56.41	59.06	59.89	21.76
146		1924–26	0.0782	0.0621	69933	73156	56.34	59.01	60.09	61.89	21.01
147		1929–31	0.0723	0.0575	71096	75218	57.27	60.67	60.71	63.35	21.18
148		1934–36	0.0680	0.0537	73251	78106	58.53	62.58	61.78	65.11	21.30
149		1939–41	0.0585	0.0460	77634	82423	61.14	65.58	63.92	67.72	21.71
150		1944–46	0.0467	0.0366	78734	85631	62.26	68.11	64.30	69.69	22.17
151		1949–51	0.0372	0.0287	83853	88854	65.28	70.86	66.80	71.95	22.67
152		1954–56	0.0327	0.0252	85560	90739	66.45	72.61	67.69	73.49	23.07
153		1959–61	0.0297	0.0228	86162	91317	66.84	73.40	67.87	74.10	23.10
154	Nonwhite	1959–61	0.0493	0.0388	76610	82829	61.23	66.69	63.39	68.38	21.44
155	White	1960	0.0263	0.0198	87392	92509	67.58	74.33	68.40	74.83	23.28
156	United States	1962	0.0281	0.0215	86404	91431	66.93	73.52	67.86	74.13	23.02
157		1963	0.0280	0.0215	86233	91366	66.68	73.42	67.59	74.02	22.79
158		1964	0.0271	0.0211	86204	91450	66.90	73.72	67.76	74.30	23.04
159		1965	0.0266	0.0206	86259	91493	66.87	73.83	67.69	74.37	22.96
160		1966	0.0258	0.0200	86081	91519	66.75	73.86	67.51	74.36	22.88
161	Nonwhite	1966	0.0413	0.0341	75507	83576	60.77	67.49	62.38	68.86	20.79
162	White	1966	0.0226	0.0171	87558	92712	67.61	74.80	68.17	75.10	23.10
163	United States	1967	0.0247	0.0191	86195	91726	66.98	74.22	67.67	74.66	23.05
164	Alabama	1959–61	0.0348	0.0286	82838	88772	65.06	71.73	66.40	72.83	22.77
165	Alaska	1959–61	0.0459	0.0314	82374	89546	64.88	71.36	67.00	72.67	23.39
166	Arizona	1959–61	0.0365	0.0279	83288	90075	65.38	73.72	66.85	74.83	23.15
167	Arkansas	1959–61	0.0305	0.0242	84927	90870	67.11	74.00	68.21	74.82	24.22
168	California	1959–61	0.0272	0.0207	87096	91808	67.62	74.48	68.50	75.05	23.47
169	Colorado	1959–61	0.0313	0.0228	86314	91680	67.71	74.49	68.89	75.23	24.22
170	Connecticut	1959–61	0.0255	0.0185	88748	92996	68.14	74.22	68.91	74.61	23.22
171	Delaware	1959–61	0.0296	0.0209	86458	91204	66.38	72.77	67.40	73.32	22.36
172	Florida	1959–61	0.0347	0.0260	84036	89935	66.47	74.00	67.85	74.97	23.89
173	Georgia	1959–61	0.0369	0.0266	82438	88993	64.45	71.82	65.91	72.78	22.16
174	Hawaii	1959–61	0.0261	0.0195	89542	92190	69.86	74.24	70.72	74.72	24.93
175	Idaho	1959–61	0.0264	0.0192	86733	92267	68.06	75.14	68.89	75.61	24.40
176	Illinois	1959–61	0.0283	0.0215	86433	91301	66.64	73.03	67.58	73.63	22.66
177	Indiana	1959–61	0.0276	0.0204	87094	92092	67.34	73.85	68.24	74.38	23.20
178	Iowa	1959–61	0.0241	0.0186	88274	93047	68.81	75.48	69.50	75.90	24.28
179	Kansas	1959–61	0.0261	0.0192	87994	92753	68.79	75.48	69.63	75.91	24.51
180	Kentucky	1959–61	0.0309	0.0250	84719	90913	66.58	73.24	67.70	74.11	23.52
181	Louisiana	1959–61	0.0352	0.0278	83487	89672	64.97	71.86	66.33	72.90	22.39
182	Maine	1959–61	0.0300	0.0226	86569	91799	66.83	73.61	67.89	74.31	22.97
183	Maryland	1959–61	0.0312	0.0243	85723	90658	65.68	72.10	66.79	72.89	21.88
184	Massachusetts	1959–61	0.0257	0.0185	88085	92581	67.46	73.87	68.23	74.26	22.70
185	Michigan	1959–61	0.0273	0.0207	87405	91875	67.36	73.49	68.24	74.04	23.05
186	Minnesota	1959–61	0.0248	0.0182	88232	93296	68.86	75.39	69.60	75.78	24.40
187	Mississippi	1959–61	0.0442	0.0351	82011	87856	64.75	71.04	66.74	72.62	23.28
188	Missouri	1959–61	0.0276	0.0219	86670	91584	67.24	73.94	68.14	74.59	23.31
189	Montana	1959–61	0.0293	0.0210	84531	91214	66.19	73.85	67.18	74.43	23.29
190	Nebraska	1959–61	0.0265	0.0193	88139	92965	68.82	75.59	69.69	76.07	24.48
191	Nevada	1959–61	0.0358	0.0276	82310	88675	64.06	72.06	65.43	73.11	21.79
192	New Hampshire	1959–61	0.0265	0.0199	87748	92597	67.13	74.18	67.95	74.68	22.73
193	New Jersey	1959–61	0.0276	0.0216	87584	91819	67.01	72.84	67.90	73.44	22.49
194	New Mexico	1959–61	0.0367	0.0281	83674	89943	66.44	73.43	67.96	74.54	24.40
195	New York	1959–61	0.0279	0.0213	86762	91434	66.68	72.71	67.59	73.29	22.53
196	North Carolina	1959–61	0.0361	0.0278	82648	89964	64.91	72.41	66.33	73.47	22.60
197	North Dakota	1959–61	0.0268	0.0206	87947	93083	68.98	75.27	69.87	75.85	24.86

FERTILITY MEASURES (FEMALES)

Females 32	Expectancy, $\hat{e}_{70}$		General fertility rate 35	Total fertility rate 36	Gross reproduction rate 37	Net maternity function					SERIES NUMBER
	Males 33	Females 34				Total, NRR 38	Mean, μ 39	Variance, σ^2 40	Generation, T 41	Complex root, r_2 42	
24.01	8.86	11.18	165.64	4.79	2.33	2.19	27.71	43.18	27.065	$-0.0248+0.2282$	142
23.98	8.36	10.39	145.17	4.13	2.06	1.94	27.55	44.50	26.998	$-0.0331+0.2282$	143
24.44	8.11	10.71	136.38	3.86	1.89	1.78	27.45	44.14	26.966	$-0.0352+0.2281$	144
22.42	9.35	9.68	116.55	3.38	1.64	1.33	28.42	46.45	28.172	$-0.0392+0.2131$	145
22.28	8.76	9.29	106.64	3.12	1.51	1.29	28.16	46.51	27.938	$-0.0425+0.2136$	146
22.97	9.19	9.98	87.34	2.55	1.24	1.07	27.90	45.30	27.844	$-0.0475+0.2138$	147
23.56	9.19	10.14	77.51	2.25	1.10	0.97	27.61	44.08	27.635	$-0.0518+0.2157$	148
24.42	9.45	10.59	80.27	2.31	1.13	1.03	27.18	40.54	27.156	$-0.0481+0.2240$	149
25.33	9.84	11.10	92.43	2.67	1.30	1.21	27.45	39.19	27.306	$-0.0387+0.2238$	150
26.50	10.21	11.82	108.11	3.15	1.54	1.46	26.56	37.34	26.281	$-0.0356+0.2388$	151
27.40	10.49	12.37	118.87	3.60	1.75	1.68	26.47	36.03	26.104	$-0.0288+0.2440$	152
27.89	10.46	12.61	119.13	3.69	1.80	1.73	26.37	34.62	25.994	$-0.0248+0.2475$	153
24.78	10.04	11.77	153.14	4.51	2.24	2.08	25.94	39.82	25.358	$-0.0327+0.2560$	154
28.24	10.40	12.58	113.02	3.53	1.72	1.66	26.45	33.61	26.110	$-0.0243+0.2462$	155
27.91	10.41	12.62	113.37	3.51	1.71	1.65	26.42	34.26	26.074	$-0.0256+0.2460$	156
27.82	10.23	12.56	109.62	3.37	1.64	1.58	26.48	34.23	26.168	$-0.0271+0.2441$	157
28.10	10.48	12.82	106.07	3.24	1.58	1.53	26.53	34.39	26.247	$-0.0285+0.2423$	158
28.17	10.40	12.86	97.66	2.96	1.45	1.39	26.52	35.12	26.291	$-0.0334+0.2402$	159
28.18	10.35	12.84	91.27	2.74	1.34	1.29	26.35	35.19	26.173	$-0.0376+0.2409$	160
25.03	11.01	13.54	125.86	3.61	1.78	1.68	25.83	40.92	25.398	$-0.0464+0.2497$	161
28.54	10.30	12.82	86.41	2.61	1.27	1.23	26.47	33.98	26.326	$-0.0366+0.2398$	162
28.43	10.42	13.07	87.65	2.57	1.25	1.21	26.28	34.85	26.145	$-0.0394+0.2406$	163
27.51	10.76	12.98	121.13	3.64	1.77	1.69	26.12	38.05	25.724	$-0.0352+0.2516$	164
27.04	10.10	11.74	158.06	4.57	2.25	2.13	26.63	40.38	26.036	$-0.0271+0.2537$	165
29.17	10.97	13.65	135.78	4.13	2.01	1.91	26.26	36.15	25.795	$-0.0231+0.2529$	166
28.92	11.38	13.51	121.05	3.71	1.82	1.74	25.94	37.77	25.516	$-0.0340+0.2589$	167
28.74	10.68	13.15	115.01	3.60	1.75	1.69	25.85	33.28	25.496	$-0.0255+0.2538$	168
28.99	10.99	13.18	121.01	3.67	1.79	1.72	26.11	34.40	25.742	$-0.0254+0.2525$	169
27.80	10.27	12.31	109.84	3.55	1.73	1.68	27.06	31.32	26.746	$-0.0180+0.2388$	170
27.06	10.04	11.96	125.57	3.89	1.90	1.84	26.18	34.06	25.767	$-0.0223+0.2497$	171
29.35	11.85	14.07	117.89	3.64	1.77	1.70	25.61	34.37	25.242	$-0.0290+0.2570$	172
27.39	10.88	13.30	121.07	3.60	1.76	1.68	25.85	37.01	25.459	$-0.0345+0.2541$	173
28.23	11.46	13.24	128.12	3.88	1.87	1.81	26.54	31.71	26.164	$-0.0166+0.2455$	174
29.34	10.85	13.45	133.00	4.13	2.02	1.94	26.12	34.22	25.662	$-0.0182+0.2567$	175
27.41	10.06	12.24	118.17	3.68	1.80	1.73	26.49	33.90	26.118	$-0.0232+0.2452$	176
27.94	10.26	12.44	120.11	3.67	1.79	1.73	26.10	34.61	25.723	$-0.0261+0.2525$	177
29.22	10.71	13.07	124.15	3.84	1.88	1.82	26.55	33.64	26.152	$-0.0195+0.2485$	178
29.36	10.96	13.25	122.24	3.73	1.82	1.76	26.08	33.85	25.695	$-0.0230+0.2535$	179
28.02	10.69	12.51	121.55	3.67	1.79	1.71	26.25	38.90	25.837	$-0.0361+0.2517$	180
27.19	10.51	12.73	135.84	4.06	1.99	1.89	26.19	36.31	25.725	$-0.0255+0.2525$	181
27.90	10.09	12.45	126.08	3.89	1.90	1.83	26.29	33.42	25.884	$-0.0204+0.2507$	182
26.76	9.82	12.00	117.94	3.71	1.81	1.74	26.13	34.70	25.747	$-0.0259+0.2496$	183
27.61	10.08	12.24	113.24	3.59	1.75	1.69	27.40	32.50	27.070	$-0.0180+0.2346$	184
27.62	10.09	12.33	122.99	3.83	1.87	1.81	26.60	33.87	26.203	$-0.0210+0.2459$	185
28.98	10.70	12.97	135.14	4.17	2.04	1.98	27.35	35.04	26.889	$-0.0162+0.2396$	186
27.50	10.65	12.66	143.27	4.30	2.11	1.99	26.48	39.78	25.943	$-0.0305+0.2492$	187
28.33	10.57	12.76	117.95	3.63	1.76	1.70	26.22	35.87	25.844	$-0.0294+0.2491$	188
28.43	10.38	12.76	136.64	4.22	2.05	1.97	26.36	35.00	25.890	$-0.0188+0.2540$	189
29.39	10.89	13.17	129.91	3.95	1.92	1.86	26.48	33.55	26.073	$-0.0187+0.2498$	190
27.89	9.61	12.68	124.10	3.87	1.90	1.81	25.44	32.77	25.044	$-0.0222+0.2617$	191
28.07	9.91	12.39	118.49	3.75	1.85	1.79	26.52	33.12	26.138	$-0.0199+0.2479$	192
26.96	9.96	11.94	106.25	3.45	1.68	1.63	26.81	31.64	26.506	$-0.0206+0.2408$	193
28.90	11.17	13.28	153.17	4.48	2.20	2.10	26.36	38.66	25.796	$-0.0240+0.2565$	194
26.98	9.90	11.76	105.04	3.30	1.61	1.55	26.89	32.22	26.608	$-0.0230+0.2389$	195
27.67	10.62	12.69	114.24	3.41	1.66	1.59	25.98	36.49	25.643	$-0.0345+0.2511$	196
29.07	11.03	12.88	143.15	4.40	2.14	2.07	27.27	35.95	26.774	$-0.0165+0.2430$	197

SERIES NUMBER	AREA AND YEAR		POPULATION, IN 1000'S			AGE STRUCTURE					
			Observed at mid-year	Projected 5 years	Projected 10 years	Total re-productive value (in 1000's)	Percent at age <15	15–64	≥65	Dependency ratio (× 100)	Departure from stability (Δ percent)
			1	2	3	4	5	6	7	8	9
198	Ohio	1959–61	9741	10451	11246	2931	31.72	59.04	9.24	69.37	9.0
199	Oklahoma	1959–61	2335	2491	2671	648	29.97	59.34	10.69	68.50	8.8
200	Oregon	1959–61	1774	1887	2025	504	30.83	58.79	10.38	70.11	9.4
201	Pennsylvania	1959–61	11349	11975	12669	3148	29.11	60.92	9.97	64.15	10.4
202	Rhode Island	1959–61	862	912	963	238	28.37	61.21	10.42	63.36	12.3
203	South Carolina	1959–61	2392	2613	2868	809	35.68	58.00	6.32	72.42	4.8
204	South Dakota	1959–61	683	746	822	233	33.57	55.92	10.51	78.84	12.1
205	Tennessee	1959–61	3579	3845	4148	1064	31.62	59.72	8.66	67.45	5.3
206	Texas	1959–61	9622	10518	11521	3065	33.11	59.11	7.78	69.19	7.6
207	Utah	1959–61	896	1003	1126	341	37.53	55.74	6.73	79.43	4.9
208	Vermont	1959–61	391	419	458	124	31.45	57.33	11.22	74.41	13.3
209	Virginia	1959–61	3982	4306	4668	1213	31.98	60.74	7.28	64.65	5.7
210	Washington	1959–61	2863	3071	3318	845	31.27	58.95	9.78	69.63	10.0
211	West Virginia	1959–61	1866	1990	2144	555	32.17	58.56	9.27	70.77	6.3
212	Wisconsin	1959–61	3967	4287	4657	1282	32.11	57.70	10.19	73.33	12.5
213	Wyoming	1959–61	331	361	395	105	33.74	58.41	7.85	71.21	7.4
	SOUTH AMERICA										
214	Argentina	1961	21097	22575	24015	6448	29.87	64.95	5.18	53.96	8.6
215		1964	22038	23600	25141	7735	29.86	64.09	6.05	56.03	8.4
216	Brazil *hypothetical*	1950	51944	59589	68167	30521	41.86	55.69	2.45	79.56	3.4
217	Chile	1953–55	6597	7281	8027	3103	37.36	58.65	3.99	70.50	4.8
218		1959–61	7736	8632	9647	3788	39.80	56.00	4.20	78.57	2.3
219		1962	8145	9107	10185	3955	39.79	55.95	4.26	78.71	2.3
220		1964	8391	9364	10468	3976	39.63	56.00	4.37	78.56	3.0
221		1965	8584	9681	10915	4112	39.74	55.89	4.37	78.90	1.5
222		1966	8922	9910	11029	4012	40.02	55.55	4.43	80.04	4.8
223		1967	9137	10110	11209	3949	39.84	55.69	4.47	79.55	6.3
224	Colombia	1964	17505	20196	23432	9980	46.64	50.36	3.00	98.58	4.5
225		1965	17993	20812	24200	10297	46.64	50.36	3.00	98.58	4.1
226	Ecuador	1965	5109	6006	7080	3135	46.98	49.86	3.16	100.58	2.1
227	French Guiana	1961	33	35	39	14	37.83	55.56	6.61	80.00	8.8
228		1964	34	38	43	16	38.57	55.08	6.35	81.55	11.7
229	Guyana	1954	454	526	609	228	42.37	54.10	3.53	84.85	7.2
230		1955	467	543	636	237	42.97	53.60	3.43	86.55	7.0
231		1956	480	561	657	248	43.59	53.05	3.36	88.48	7.0
232		1961	568	668	799	304	46.32	50.25	3.43	99.01	5.4
233	Peru	1961	9907	11239	12749	5156	43.33	52.66	4.01	89.88	4.5
234		1963	10980	12678	14645	6577	44.15	52.43	3.42	90.75	2.9
235	Uruguay	1963	2648	2786	2919	746	28.00	64.19	7.81	55.80	3.3
236	Venezuela	1963	8144	9732	11605	4459	45.17	51.95	2.88	92.51	3.1
237		1964	8427	10079	12033	4632	45.30	51.76	2.94	93.21	3.2
238		1965	8722	10450	12505	4817	45.41	51.60	2.99	93.81	3.4
	ASIA										
239	Ceylon	1953	8162	9355	10663	4098	39.70	56.80	3.50	76.08	4.7
240		1962	10444	11955	13656	4993	40.68	55.87	3.45	78.99	5.2

[76]

| VITAL RATES PER THOUSAND POPULATION | | | | | | | | INFANT MOR-TALITY RATE per 1000 births | AGE-SPECIFIC DEATH RATES | | | | |
| Crude (both sexes) | | | Standardized on U.S., 1960 (both sexes) | | Intrinsic (females) | | | | 1000_4M_1 | | 1000_5M_{50} | | |
Birth 10	Death 11	Increase 12	Birth 13	Death 14	Birth 15	Death 16	Increase 17	18	Males 19	Females 20	Males 21	Females 22	SERIES NUMBER
23.73	9.49	14.24	23.32	9.47	27.01	6.62	20.39	24.57	0.99	0.75	12.16	6.31	198
21.89	9.69	12.20	22.23	8.59	25.59	6.83	18.76	25.48	1.37	0.99	11.83	5.43	199
21.16	9.47	11.69	22.61	8.70	26.08	6.61	19.47	24.56	1.13	0.91	10.91	5.09	200
21.40	10.61	10.79	21.77	10.07	24.99	7.45	17.54	25.08	1.00	0.74	13.11	6.66	201
21.46	10.30	11.15	22.65	9.48	25.76	6.89	18.87	23.39	0.91	0.79	12.33	5.92	202
25.08	8.46	16.62	23.46	11.01	27.47	7.56	19.91	33.99	1.76	1.58	17.37	10.01	203
25.98	9.36	16.62	28.36	8.51	32.29	5.08	27.21	26.26	1.24	1.02	10.01	4.24	204
23.04	9.07	13.97	21.78	9.51	24.91	7.59	17.31	30.64	1.17	1.13	12.47	6.30	205
25.80	7.87	17.93	24.61	8.77	28.55	6.19	22.36	29.34	1.31	1.18	11.42	5.92	206
29.21	6.70	22.51	27.78	8.35	31.50	5.13	26.37	20.42	1.12	0.83	10.16	5.27	207
24.08	11.17	12.91	25.83	9.41	29.99	5.70	24.29	26.32	1.16	0.94	11.39	5.68	208
24.21	8.52	15.69	22.74	10.01	26.36	7.19	19.17	30.74	1.17	1.02	13.71	7.15	209
22.83	9.23	13.60	23.90	8.79	27.78	6.08	21.70	24.07	1.08	0.78	11.18	5.76	210
21.58	9.62	11.96	21.75	9.55	24.62	7.53	17.09	27.67	1.10	1.11	12.90	6.19	211
24.92	9.47	15.45	26.39	8.77	30.16	5.52	24.63	23.25	1.01	0.77	10.28	5.19	212
25.43	8.11	17.32	25.49	8.96	29.50	5.87	23.63	27.85	1.45	0.88	10.29	5.65	213
22.54	8.36	14.17	18.54	11.86	19.85	11.43	8.41	61.43	3.58	3.57	12.13	6.76	214
21.86	7.84	14.02	19.98	10.00	19.06	10.91	8.15	53.05	3.08	3.14	11.84	6.01	215
44.00	16.00	28.00	37.97	20.77	40.04	15.84	24.20	119.64	19.80	19.58	19.32	14.44	216
32.70	12.76	19.94	27.42	17.75	30.41	13.41	17.00	148.15	10.41	10.49	16.07	11.10	217
33.79	12.12	21.67	30.61	15.85	33.53	11.73	21.80	135.43	8.33	8.35	15.27	9.28	218
33.69	11.65	22.05	30.42	15.10	33.23	11.26	21.97	129.99	7.54	7.58	16.51	9.55	219
32.81	11.21	21.60	29.05	14.68	31.99	10.94	21.05	119.28	7.19	7.25	16.44	9.59	220
34.27	10.68	23.59	30.45	14.00	33.42	9.93	23.49	100.11	5.23	5.30	15.48	8.64	221
30.06	10.21	19.85	27.20	13.34	29.96	10.00	19.96	108.30	4.98	4.89	15.55	8.94	222
28.43	9.50	18.92	25.51	12.70	28.08	9.69	18.39	99.92	4.00	3.84	15.84	8.90	223
37.92	10.02	27.91	35.92	13.21	38.40	10.06	28.35	89.20	12.34	12.47	11.71	9.73	224
38.39	9.91	28.47	36.37	13.32	38.82	9.88	28.95	80.12	12.07	12.55	10.90	9.24	225
44.32	11.78	32.54	43.36	13.23	44.82	11.50	33.31	93.55	17.23	18.29	9.86	8.38	226
31.95	14.60	17.35	33.09	17.74	35.89	9.57	26.32	70.65	12.13	6.10	20.78	9.86	227
35.21	11.58	23.63	36.82	14.01	40.34	6.32	34.02	44.52	4.50	4.23	26.94	8.86	228
42.86	12.91	29.95	38.20	19.50	43.67	9.91	33.76	80.92	9.45	8.66	26.51	19.75	229
43.22	11.90	31.32	39.06	18.83	44.07	9.22	34.86	75.38	8.68	7.34	22.29	16.90	230
43.15	11.20	31.95	39.42	18.06	44.77	8.70	36.07	73.19	7.23	6.82	20.68	13.51	231
41.93	8.78	33.15	40.39	14.07	43.95	6.97	36.98	49.38	5.01	4.40	17.38	12.00	232
36.17	11.17	25.00	33.17	13.14	35.03	11.57	23.46	96.06	16.17	16.78	11.05	8.49	233
38.36	10.02	28.34	38.39	11.92	37.73	10.17	27.56	80.87	14.44	14.98	10.40	7.47	234
21.58	11.28	10.30	18.67	12.53	20.07	11.27	8.79	61.83	1.74	1.86	14.04	7.83	235
43.41	7.18	36.23	41.14	10.80	43.54	6.84	36.70	55.58	5.91	6.39	12.58	8.23	236
43.35	7.23	36.13	41.45	10.84	43.65	6.59	37.06	48.71	5.98	6.29	11.49	8.49	237
43.51	7.06	36.45	41.82	10.97	43.96	6.36	37.59	47.68	5.45	5.73	10.97	8.29	238
39.35	10.90	28.45	34.41	14.32	37.47	11.83	25.64	86.66	16.25	19.64	9.16	8.55	239
35.50	8.51	26.99	32.53	13.55	34.80	8.40	26.40	42.26	8.39	9.83	8.35	7.33	240

continued

LIFE TABLE VALUES

SERIES NUMBER	AREA AND YEAR		Probability of dying in first year, q_0		Survivors to age 50 per 100,000 births, l_{50}		Expectancy, $\overset{\circ}{e}_0$		Expectancy, $\overset{\circ}{e}_1$		Expectancy, $\overset{\circ}{e}_{50}$
			Males 23	Females 24	Males 25	Females 26	Males 27	Females 28	Males 29	Females 30	Males 31
198	Ohio	1959-61	0.0270	0.0211	87237	91995	67.29	73.42	68.15	74.00	23.01
199	Oklahoma	1959-61	0.0282	0.0216	85991	91623	67.47	74.87	68.42	75.52	23.94
200	Oregon	1959-61	0.0275	0.0201	86478	92244	67.51	74.88	68.44	75.41	23.79
201	Pennsylvania	1959-61	0.0275	0.0216	86980	91788	66.58	72.63	67.46	73.23	22.26
202	Rhode Island	1959-61	0.0255	0.0202	89109	92780	67.79	73.68	68.56	74.20	22.62
203	South Carolina	1959-61	0.0372	0.0290	80602	87588	63.13	70.36	64.56	71.46	21.39
204	South Dakota	1959-61	0.0303	0.0210	85859	92441	67.62	75.04	68.72	75.65	24.47
205	Tennessee	1959-61	0.0333	0.0264	84966	90429	66.41	72.83	67.69	73.80	23.30
206	Texas	1959-61	0.0322	0.0250	85752	91103	67.11	74.32	68.34	75.22	23.80
207	Utah	1959-61	0.0223	0.0178	87641	92844	68.70	75.08	69.26	75.44	24.41
208	Vermont	1959-61	0.0294	0.0219	86714	92675	66.96	74.11	67.98	74.76	23.03
209	Virginia	1959-61	0.0338	0.0261	84716	90567	65.62	72.42	66.91	73.35	22.40
210	Washington	1959-61	0.0273	0.0198	87448	92535	67.73	74.83	68.63	75.33	23.52
211	West Virginia	1959-61	0.0304	0.0237	84500	91131	66.25	73.19	67.32	73.97	23.18
212	Wisconsin	1959-61	0.0254	0.0201	88161	92888	68.38	74.52	69.16	75.04	23.94
213	Wyoming	1959-61	0.0319	0.0225	84455	91841	66.56	74.30	67.75	75.00	24.02
	SOUTH AMERICA										
214	Argentina	1961	0.0630	0.0541	81169	85736	62.53	68.16	65.72	71.04	22.07
215		1964	0.0567	0.0475	82928	87468	64.97	70.95	67.86	73.48	23.78
216	Brazil *hypothetical*	1950	0.1406	0.1188	56375	60077	47.16	50.18	53.82	55.89	20.13
217	Chile	1953-55	0.1427	0.1249	64791	70567	52.04	56.56	59.66	63.59	20.71
218		1959-61	0.1300	0.1162	67298	73664	54.17	59.19	61.23	65.94	21.53
219		1962	0.1258	0.1111	67541	74734	54.76	60.36	61.60	66.87	21.78
220		1964	0.1160	0.1031	69061	76306	55.70	61.29	61.97	67.30	21.74
221		1965	0.1060	0.0922	71812	78216	57.84	62.69	63.67	68.04	22.56
222		1966	0.1022	0.0884	72060	79159	58.26	64.34	63.86	69.56	22.75
223		1967	0.0906	0.0795	73612	80902	59.24	66.16	64.11	70.85	22.56
224	Colombia	1964	0.0911	0.0775	72435	75847	58.23	61.56	63.02	65.70	23.79
225		1965	0.0878	0.0738	72511	76162	58.23	61.71	62.81	65.59	23.55
226	Ecuador	1965	0.1096	0.0935	70108	72148	57.09	60.16	63.07	65.33	25.21
227	French Guiana	1961	0.0661	0.0691	69952	75856	54.31	61.52	57.13	65.06	17.49
228		1964	0.0570	0.0354	76359	83954	58.71	67.42	61.24	68.88	19.14
229	Guyana	1954	0.0847	0.0674	70868	72628	54.34	57.50	58.34	60.63	17.68
230		1955	0.0764	0.0662	73655	75143	56.00	58.76	59.61	61.91	18.21
231		1956	0.0746	0.0639	74714	76215	56.63	60.15	60.17	63.23	18.32
232		1961	0.0555	0.0487	78073	81084	59.87	64.46	62.37	66.75	19.88
233	Peru	1961	0.0972	0.0840	69358	71439	57.43	59.94	62.57	64.40	25.28
234		1963	0.0819	0.0727	72891	74327	60.53	62.78	64.89	66.67	26.52
235	Uruguay	1963	0.0747	0.0555	80020	86244	61.37	68.16	65.31	71.15	21.20
236	Venezuela	1963	0.0579	0.0490	79589	82747	63.34	67.10	66.22	69.54	24.19
237		1964	0.0543	0.0452	79877	83322	63.65	67.35	66.29	69.52	24.30
238		1965	0.0532	0.0444	80356	83984	63.90	67.70	66.47	69.83	24.17
	ASIA										
239	Ceylon	1953	0.0902	0.0742	73805	71173	58.99	58.18	63.80	61.81	24.63
240		1962	0.0439	0.0368	82263	80831	64.10	64.42	66.03	65.87	23.70

FERTILITY MEASURES (FEMALES)

Females 32	Expectancy, $\mathring{e}_{70}$ Males 33	Females 34	General fertility rate 35	Total fertility rate 36	Gross reproduction rate 37	Net maternity function Total, NRR 38	Mean, μ 39	Variance, σ^2 40	Generation, T 41	Complex root, r_2 42	SERIES NUMBER
27.53	10.24	12.24	116.67	3.60	1.76	1.70	26.38	33.71	26.025	−0.0237+0.2472	198
29.42	10.94	13.49	112.68	3.42	1.66	1.60	25.43	34.06	25.101	−0.0289+0.2632	199
29.02	10.62	13.15	109.89	3.50	1.70	1.64	25.87	31.90	25.547	−0.0225+0.2559	200
26.73	9.83	11.84	105.03	3.37	1.65	1.59	26.73	33.05	26.429	−0.0238+0.2411	201
27.38	10.00	12.05	108.98	3.51	1.71	1.66	27.04	32.77	26.716	−0.0210+0.2390	202
26.52	10.80	13.31	120.43	3.60	1.76	1.67	26.01	37.10	25.631	−0.0337+0.2522	203
29.22	10.83	13.11	142.54	4.39	2.13	2.05	26.94	35.93	26.446	−0.0176+0.2468	204
27.86	10.67	12.60	111.00	3.34	1.63	1.56	25.95	36.73	25.622	−0.0358+0.2520	205
29.16	10.98	13.63	126.59	3.78	1.84	1.77	25.91	35.70	25.501	−0.0286+0.2550	206
28.93	10.93	12.95	145.09	4.29	2.09	2.02	27.08	36.70	26.584	−0.0197+0.2418	207
28.03	9.96	12.41	127.50	4.00	1.96	1.89	26.72	33.55	26.301	−0.0169+0.2465	208
27.26	10.25	12.41	114.87	3.49	1.71	1.63	26.01	35.85	25.659	−0.0314+0.2513	209
28.76	10.55	12.92	117.37	3.70	1.80	1.74	26.01	31.98	25.651	−0.0201+0.2538	210
27.81	10.56	12.37	107.31	3.35	1.62	1.56	26.18	36.05	25.864	−0.0321+0.2525	211
28.29	10.48	12.47	131.63	4.09	2.00	1.93	27.08	34.14	26.763	−0.0165+0.2411	212
28.74	10.57	13.02	129.15	3.94	1.90	1.82	25.80	33.72	25.392	−0.0212+0.2599	213
26.40	9.12	11.18	97.68	2.84	1.39	1.26	28.16	45.36	27.967	−0.0390+0.2174	214
28.42	11.27	12.96	97.54	3.05	1.43	1.31	33.18	45.57	32.985	−0.0202+0.1897	215
22.16	8.77	9.54	192.12	5.78	2.80	2.01	29.53	49.96	28.909	−0.0232+0.2088	216
23.54	9.05	10.16	140.72	4.19	2.07	1.64	29.44	51.09	28.990	−0.0303+0.2099	217
24.70	9.50	10.80	155.69	4.67	2.30	1.87	29.30	47.25	28.775	−0.0218+0.2120	218
25.29	9.87	11.39	154.97	4.64	2.28	1.88	29.26	46.95	28.734	−0.0217+0.2117	219
25.27	9.93	11.38	149.28	4.43	2.18	1.82	29.08	48.62	28.553	−0.0268+0.2118	220
25.31	11.28	11.39	156.59	4.64	2.28	1.95	29.06	49.35	28.469	−0.0262+0.2118	221
26.62	11.23	13.00	139.69	4.15	2.04	1.76	28.89	48.95	28.388	−0.0262+0.2124	222
27.44	11.16	14.01	131.81	3.89	1.91	1.68	28.72	49.45	28.254	−0.0304+0.2122	223
										−0.0340+0.2128	
25.65	11.24	12.11	181.06	5.49	2.71	2.27	29.60	50.90	28.873	−0.0208+0.2146	224
25.49	11.05	12.17	183.35	5.56	2.75	2.31	29.61	50.93	28.863	−0.0203+0.2149	225
27.72	11.53	13.50	221.32	6.62	3.26	2.59	29.41	52.33	28.539	−0.0209+0.2171	226
24.24	6.72	10.59	168.70	5.05	2.42	2.08	28.52	49.47	27.859	−0.0326+0.2174	227
25.83	7.75	10.71	183.32	5.63	2.80	2.55	28.32	43.67	27.561	−0.0157+0.2269	228
20.69	7.93	9.06	206.75	5.82	2.86	2.43	27.08	44.24	26.323	−0.0262+0.2378	229
20.83	7.81	8.98	210.99	5.95	2.91	2.51	27.21	44.57	26.425	−0.0253+0.2361	230
21.98	7.86	9.49	213.46	6.01	2.98	2.59	27.20	43.64	26.399	−0.0218+0.2374	231
24.02	8.46	11.45	215.57	6.16	2.99	2.70	27.65	43.59	26.841	−0.0195+0.2334	232
27.23	11.65	12.32	171.53	5.07	2.45	1.96	29.36	52.61	28.737	−0.0285+0.2135	233
28.56	13.55	14.13	184.80	5.99	2.90	2.35	32.32	103.14	30.973	−0.0204+0.2331	234
25.85	9.23	11.06	96.45	2.86	1.39	1.27	27.76	42.60	27.562	−0.0390+0.2224	235
26.83	11.35	12.87	216.01	6.28	3.07	2.75	28.50	49.11	27.598	−0.0208+0.2270	236
26.63	11.09	12.62	216.27	6.32	3.09	2.79	28.61	49.44	27.693	−0.0191+0.2255	237
26.59	10.88	12.26	217.54	6.38	3.13	2.83	28.63	49.42	27.699	−0.0188+0.2255	238
25.13	10.71	10.62	188.54	5.28	2.58	2.06	28.69	38.68	28.173	−0.0136+0.2204	239
24.90	9.80	10.22	172.93	4.96	2.43	2.14	29.35	41.08	28.787	−0.0120+0.2127	240

	AREA AND YEAR		POPULATION, IN 1000'S			AGE STRUCTURE					
			Observed at mid-year	Projected		Total re-productive value (in 1000's)	Percent at age			Depen-dency ratio (× 100)	Departure from stability (Δ percent)
SERIES NUMBER				5 years	10 years		<15	15–64	≥65		
			1	2	3	4	5	6	7	8	9
241	Ceylon	1963	10585	12062	13796	5238	41.75	54.65	3.60	82.97	3.9
242	*cont*	1967	11701	13230	15043	5513	41.86	54.53	3.61	83.37	5.8
243	China Mainland *hyp*	1953	582800	640600	698400	295661	35.95	59.67	4.38	67.57	8.0
244	China (Taiwan)	1956	9368	11188	13220	5356	44.18	53.36	2.46	87.40	3.9
245		1959–61	10612	12439	14483	5648	45.13	52.40	2.47	90.85	3.8
246		1962	11330	13166	15261	5805	45.92	51.59	2.49	93.82	3.7
247		1963	11698	13546	15677	5910	45.90	51.58	2.52	93.88	4.2
248		1964	12070	13898	16032	5912	45.64	51.79	2.57	93.10	4.8
249		1965	12443	14239	16385	5888	45.17	52.21	2.62	91.52	5.3
250		1966	13021	14891	17175	6029	43.69	53.67	2.64	86.33	4.5
251	Urban	1966	3833	4343	4940	1608	41.85	55.95	2.20	78.73	7.5
252	Semi-urban	1966	3849	4395	5064	1785	43.79	53.48	2.73	86.99	4.8
253	Rural	1966	5339	6151	7180	2640	44.95	52.16	2.89	91.71	3.8
254	Cyprus	1950–52	502	555	611	199	34.64	59.24	6.12	68.79	3.6
255		1953–55	523	574	632	196	34.56	59.03	6.41	69.42	3.9
256		1956–58	546	598	659	192	34.45	58.76	6.79	70.16	3.3
257		1959	567	621	684	198	34.21	58.77	7.02	70.15	4.0
258		1960	573	633	698	213	36.71	57.38	5.91	74.25	6.5
259	Hong Kong	1961	3161	3580	3987	1326	40.76	56.43	2.81	77.21	9.6
260		1966	3732	4144	4635	1529	40.45	56.30	3.25	77.62	7.3
261	India *hypothetical*	1961	439235	490700	546700	232275	41.09	55.99	2.92	78.60	1.9
262	Indonesia *hyp*	1961	96371	108472	120735	51164	42.15	55.35	2.50	80.67	8.3
263	Iran *hypothetical*	1956	19441	21926	24735	12607	43.98	53.96	2.06	85.32	3.8
264	Israel, Jewish population	1949	919	1019	1110	302	28.93	67.41	3.66	48.33	12.1
265		1950–52	1304	1468	1616	454	30.40	65.61	3.99	52.43	9.3
266		1953–55	1505	1666	1827	504	32.53	63.01	4.46	58.70	7.6
267		1956–58	1715	1879	2049	569	34.53	60.90	4.57	64.19	6.7
268		1960	1885	2059	2241	624	34.87	60.22	4.91	66.06	6.7
269		1963	2115	2294	2502	688	33.77	60.70	5.53	64.74	5.9
270		1964	2209	2402	2626	727	33.45	61.04	5.51	63.82	6.7
271		1965	2269	2473	2714	755	32.70	61.25	6.05	63.28	6.3
272		1966	2323	2530	2774	768	31.99	61.61	6.40	62.30	6.0
273		1967	2363	2557	2784	761	31.33	62.09	6.58	61.04	5.7
274	Japan	1939–41	72265	77047	82402	32715	36.05	59.24	4.71	68.80	3.4
275		1950–52	84260	91250	98798	32647	35.18	59.90	4.92	66.93	7.3
276		1953–55	87982	93482	99277	28985	33.95	60.86	5.19	64.30	15.1
277		1956–58	90860	95506	100243	26405	31.94	62.65	5.41	59.61	19.1
278		1959–61	93224	97809	102554	24950	30.18	64.12	5.70	55.97	19.8
279		1962	94558	99501	104153	24237	28.83	65.27	5.90	53.21	19.8
280		1963	95912	100893	105927	24333	27.77	66.19	6.04	51.06	19.2
281		1964	96916	102295	107762	24503	26.52	67.32	6.16	48.55	17.9
282		1965	98003	103810	109798	25183	25.79	67.95	6.26	47.17	15.3
283		1966	98859	102417	105962	21470	24.97	68.60	6.43	45.77	26.3
284	Korea *hypothetical*	1960	24989	28844	33066	13649	43.10	53.63	3.27	86.45	3.9
285	Kuwait	1966	491	605	732	255	38.03	60.28	1.69	65.89	8.4
286	Malaysia (West)	1966	8541	9894	11520	4418	44.17	52.15	3.68	91.76	3.1
287	Malays	1966	4253	4995	5873	2317	45.61	51.24	3.15	95.14	3.6
288	Chinese	1966	3175	3633	4201	1574	42.30	52.86	4.84	89.16	5.1
289	Indians, Pakistanis	1966	978	1127	1323	500	45.00	52.75	2.25	89.57	6.1

VITAL RATES PER THOUSAND POPULATION | INFANT MORTALITY RATE | AGE-SPECIFIC DEATH RATES

Crude (both sexes)			Standardized on U.S., 1960 (both sexes)		Intrinsic (females)			INFANT MORTALITY RATE per 1000 births	$1000_4 M_1$		$1000_5 M_{50}$		SERIES NUMBER
Birth 10	Death 11	Increase 12	Birth 13	Death 14	Birth 15	Death 16	Increase 17	18	Males 19	Females 20	Males 21	Females 22	
34.56	8.66	25.90	32.65	12.65	35.14	9.04	26.09	55.78	8.39	10.37	8.99	7.03	241
31.58	7.51	24.07	29.95	11.16	32.47	7.92	24.55	47.78	5.86	6.72	8.79	6.44	242
41.59	20.99	20.59	35.17	24.71	42.09	20.09	22.00	176.52	23.71	26.68	21.98	17.83	243
44.20	7.91	36.29	42.16	14.72	41.96	7.08	34.88	33.10	9.34	10.09	14.90	9.67	244
39.62	6.96	32.65	37.66	13.45	38.94	6.84	32.10	33.56	7.61	8.39	13.06	7.97	245
37.37	6.44	30.94	35.58	12.94	37.59	6.53	31.06	31.27	6.28	6.48	12.38	7.34	246
36.27	6.13	30.14	34.66	12.51	36.85	6.37	30.49	28.43	5.84	6.01	10.93	7.34	247
34.54	5.74	28.80	32.90	11.87	35.47	6.18	29.29	25.53	4.73	5.16	11.22	6.79	248
32.68	5.46	27.22	31.06	11.33	34.13	6.15	27.98	23.66	4.75	4.65	10.75	6.67	249
31.88	5.36	26.52	30.95	11.37	34.48	6.00	28.48	20.19	4.16	4.37	10.70	6.81	250
29.74	4.48	25.26	26.66	10.74	30.32	6.36	23.96	15.60	3.03	3.17	9.96	6.70	251
31.53	5.45	26.08	30.56	11.54	34.09	6.02	28.07	19.93	4.03	4.41	11.17	6.81	252
33.67	5.92	27.74	34.75	11.66	37.85	5.85	32.00	23.27	4.99	5.11	10.99	6.88	253
28.07	7.91	20.16	24.79	10.39	26.01	8.86	17.14	62.98	5.57	5.36	6.22	4.29	254
26.19	6.54	19.65	22.99	9.56	24.38	7.98	16.40	45.55	3.39	2.50	5.54	3.33	255
25.82	6.21	19.61	22.52	9.26	24.45	7.62	16.83	31.53	2.03	2.94	6.14	3.57	256
25.42	6.01	19.41	22.28	9.81	23.26	7.85	15.41	33.70	1.92	2.44	7.65	4.60	257
25.31	5.58	19.72	22.80	7.46	23.98	7.15	16.83	29.86	1.73	1.60	4.07	2.82	258
34.40	5.93	28.47	32.26	11.22	34.13	6.55	27.58	37.72	4.27	4.37	14.15	7.03	259
25.84	5.01	20.83	28.85	10.74	31.20	5.80	25.41	23.83	2.28	2.16	11.03	5.87	260
41.30	19.48	21.82	36.49	24.07	41.22	20.00	21.22	165.64	20.09	26.30	20.57	18.21	261
44.98	18.37	26.60	35.88	24.94	40.46	17.26	23.20	109.40	28.28	23.96	20.87	15.46	262
51.00	26.39	24.61	47.73	30.27	52.28	26.22	26.06	195.55	32.08	35.93	27.27	22.16	263
29.35	6.70	22.65	21.50	11.72	23.64	9.91	13.72	54.99	4.72	4.87	8.93	8.85	264
31.89	6.44	25.46	25.56	10.15	28.28	7.78	20.50	46.09	3.45	3.28	8.12	5.80	265
28.30	6.18	22.12	24.10	9.85	27.07	7.48	19.59	35.13	2.29	2.16	8.12	6.07	266
25.48	6.01	19.47	22.94	9.57	25.70	7.65	18.04	32.76	1.62	1.67	7.18	5.77	267
23.86	5.52	18.34	22.66	8.32	25.30	7.28	18.02	27.90	1.56	1.41	6.83	5.38	268
21.93	6.02	15.91	21.52	8.71	23.84	7.77	16.08	22.91	0.88	1.05	6.76	5.90	269
22.24	6.20	16.04	22.04	8.80	24.41	7.51	16.90	24.03	1.02	0.92	6.73	5.37	270
22.61	6.38	16.24	22.32	8.52	24.83	7.21	17.63	22.78	0.96	0.95	7.03	5.43	271
22.38	6.33	16.05	21.85	8.23	24.30	7.27	17.03	21.60	1.07	0.95	6.88	4.66	272
21.45	6.63	14.82	20.62	8.49	22.62	7.92	14.69	20.76	1.00	0.78	7.15	5.40	273
29.04	16.49	12.54	26.97	21.56	28.61	16.75	11.86	98.14	20.61	20.17	19.66	13.84	274
25.64	9.93	15.71	21.32	14.33	23.34	11.99	11.35	55.95	7.66	7.60	12.73	9.53	275
20.34	8.29	12.05	16.15	12.58	17.06	13.60	3.46	44.56	5.03	4.90	11.50	8.21	276
17.92	7.93	9.99	13.59	11.99	13.83	15.37	-1.54	38.36	3.54	3.30	11.11	7.51	277
17.24	7.48	9.76	12.77	10.98	12.71	15.60	-2.89	31.01	2.66	2.25	10.10	6.69	278
17.05	7.48	9.57	12.40	10.88	12.23	15.77	-3.54	26.44	2.04	1.70	9.76	6.40	279
17.30	6.99	10.31	12.56	9.96	12.38	15.15	-2.77	23.79	1.81	1.41	9.21	5.85	280
17.71	6.94	10.77	12.84	9.73	12.74	14.61	-1.87	20.36	1.63	1.31	8.99	5.66	281
18.61	7.15	11.46	13.54	9.97	13.85	13.58	0.27	18.50	1.56	1.21	8.93	5.58	282
13.77	6.78	6.99	10.10	9.31	8.68	19.36	-10.67	19.26	1.43	1.13	8.52	5.33	283
42.13	12.20	29.93	38.73	17.31	40.64	12.22	28.41	83.35	10.62	12.49	15.34	12.35	284
51.46	5.73	45.74	54.56	11.62	53.55	5.91	47.64	37.87	4.05	3.76	9.66	10.38	285
36.21	7.42	28.79	36.07	11.05	38.06	7.20	30.86	48.06	5.20	5.14	12.75	8.95	286
40.40	8.41	31.99	38.75	12.66	41.39	8.26	33.13	57.72	7.01	6.81	12.97	10.98	287
31.80	6.16	25.65	33.58	8.74	34.15	5.43	28.72	30.94	2.77	2.49	12.24	5.97	288
34.32	7.68	26.63	35.66	14.88	43.37	8.09	35.28	51.26	4.64	5.77	13.66	13.44	289

continued

LIFE TABLE VALUES

SERIES NUMBER	AREA AND YEAR		Probability of dying in first year, q_0		Survivors to age 50 per 100,000 births, l_{50}		Expectancy, $\mathring{e}_0$		Expectancy, $\mathring{e}_1$		Expectancy, $\mathring{e}_{50}$
			Males 23	Females 24	Males 25	Females 26	Males 27	Females 28	Males 29	Females 30	Males 31
241	Ceylon	1963	0.0631	0.0526	79378	78948	63.04	63.44	66.26	65.95	24.54
242	*cont*	1967	0.0443	0.0395	82315	83877	65.14	66.81	67.15	68.54	24.50
243	China Mainland *hyp*	1953	0.1633	0.1534	51166	51429	43.55	44.01	50.99	50.92	19.07
244	China (Taiwan)	1956	0.0339	0.0307	78933	82015	60.15	64.78	61.25	65.82	19.77
245		1959-61	0.0344	0.0313	80746	84247	61.86	66.36	63.06	67.49	20.93
246		1962	0.0317	0.0296	81821	85596	62.76	67.37	63.81	68.41	21.27
247		1963	0.0290	0.0268	82354	86146	63.47	67.97	64.35	68.83	21.65
248		1964	0.0266	0.0236	83115	87399	64.13	68.96	64.88	69.61	21.83
249		1965	0.0245	0.0221	83927	88230	64.81	69.69	65.42	70.26	22.19
250		1966	0.0229	0.0206	84585	88423	65.19	69.83	65.71	70.29	22.15
251	Urban	1966	0.0180	0.0168	86861	90082	66.45	71.10	66.66	71.31	22.24
252	Semi-urban	1966	0.0229	0.0196	84451	88730	64.98	69.95	65.49	70.35	21.89
253	Rural	1966	0.0260	0.0236	82973	87049	64.47	68.93	65.17	69.58	22.28
254	Cyprus	1950-52	0.0603	0.0605	84808	86602	66.97	69.35	70.25	72.79	26.08
255		1953-55	0.0455	0.0427	88071	91001	69.94	72.77	72.26	75.00	26.94
256		1956-58	0.0291	0.0326	86316	91431	70.07	73.87	71.16	75.34	27.37
257		1959	0.0316	0.0343	88523	92686	70.58	74.38	71.87	76.02	26.87
258		1960	0.0276	0.0275	91416	93880	72.81	75.64	73.87	76.77	27.44
259	Hong Kong	1961	0.0499	0.0411	83311	87344	63.03	70.33	65.33	72.33	21.12
260		1966	0.0255	0.0206	86928	90966	65.90	72.69	66.62	73.21	21.64
261	India *hypothetical*	1961	0.1461	0.1521	54954	51561	46.02	44.03	52.84	50.86	19.38
262	Indonesia *hypothetical*	1961	0.1478	0.1263	52696	57950	44.13	47.53	50.73	53.35	18.81
263	Iran *hypothetical*	1956	0.2075	0.1954	41916	42143	37.35	37.55	46.04	45.58	17.46
264	Israel, Jewish population	1949	0.0588	0.0465	84888	86645	64.90	67.52	67.94	69.80	23.50
265		1950-52	0.0476	0.0413	85585	87974	66.56	69.56	68.87	71.54	24.51
266		1953-55	0.0360	0.0324	88285	90114	68.02	70.83	69.55	72.19	24.27
267		1956-58	0.0339	0.0299	88764	91094	68.49	71.52	69.89	72.71	24.46
268		1960	0.0295	0.0250	90599	92177	70.50	73.31	71.63	74.19	25.56
269		1963	0.0247	0.0201	91029	92907	70.69	72.84	71.47	73.34	25.27
270		1964	0.0272	0.0205	90525	92396	70.26	73.22	71.21	73.75	25.09
271		1965	0.0264	0.0194	90769	92926	71.00	73.73	71.92	74.18	25.76
272		1966	0.0241	0.0191	91304	93029	71.26	74.29	72.01	74.73	25.72
273		1967	0.0221	0.0187	90681	93489	70.59	74.14	71.17	74.55	25.21
274	Japan	1939-41	0.0991	0.0857	58167	59969	47.71	50.54	51.92	54.24	18.68
275		1950-52	0.0568	0.0500	75622	78049	59.42	62.75	61.97	65.03	21.43
276		1953-55	0.0468	0.0411	80719	83526	62.54	66.49	64.59	68.32	22.03
277		1956-58	0.0418	0.0356	82987	86184	63.83	68.21	65.60	69.72	22.06
278		1959-61	0.0340	0.0278	85161	88750	65.50	70.34	66.79	71.34	22.61
279		1962	0.0292	0.0238	86549	90237	66.26	71.21	67.24	71.94	22.53
280		1963	0.0257	0.0209	87321	91122	67.29	72.43	68.05	72.97	23.18
281		1964	0.0230	0.0185	87849	91634	67.72	72.94	68.31	73.31	23.30
282		1965	0.0215	0.0168	88306	92085	67.76	72.96	68.24	73.20	23.06
283		1966	0.0192	0.0151	88731	92552	68.49	73.72	68.83	73.85	23.61
284	Korea *hypothetical*	1960	0.0955	0.0906	68221	68331	54.80	55.69	59.55	60.21	21.19
285	Kuwait	1966	0.0519	0.0503	83326	84123	64.69	67.05	67.21	69.59	23.30
286	Malaysia (West)	1966	0.0542	0.0442	80524	82098	63.52	66.76	66.13	68.83	23.50
287	Malays	1966	0.0659	0.0527	78107	78066	61.61	62.76	64.94	65.23	23.19
288	Chinese	1966	0.0348	0.0281	84751	89338	66.53	74.04	67.92	75.17	23.89
289	Indians, Pakistanis	1966	0.0550	0.0504	79513	78178	62.55	60.34	65.17	62.52	22.59

FERTILITY MEASURES (FEMALES)

Females 32	Males 33	Females 34	General fertility rate 35	Total fertility rate 36	Gross reproduction rate 37	Total, NRR 38	Mean, μ 39	Variance, σ^2 40	Generation, T 41	Complex root, r_2 42	SERIES NUMBER
25.26	10.33	10.43	168.69	5.00	2.45	2.12	29.29	39.34	28.756	−0.0116+0.2156	241
25.84	10.34	10.69	154.49	4.59	2.26	2.03	29.35	40.58	28.836	−0.0138+0.2156	242
20.47	8.16	8.64	199.47	5.98	2.91	1.88	29.36	49.61	28.797	−0.0268+0.2111	243
24.16	7.45	9.93	211.21	6.45	3.14	2.80	30.36	45.53	29.556	−0.0067+0.2123	244
24.79	8.25	10.22	196.84	5.79	2.81	2.54	29.73	41.67	29.045	−0.0074+0.2183	245
24.98	8.33	10.21	190.32	5.49	2.66	2.44	29.30	39.53	28.676	−0.0070+0.2228	246
25.20	8.52	10.29	185.11	5.35	2.59	2.39	29.25	38.82	28.642	−0.0066+0.2235	247
25.50	8.72	10.60	175.81	5.10	2.47	2.30	28.96	36.73	28.413	−0.0059+0.2266	248
25.82	9.06	10.74	165.17	4.83	2.34	2.19	28.52	34.67	28.023	−0.0058+0.2304	249
25.78	8.96	10.85	161.74	4.82	2.34	2.20	28.23	33.83	27.733	−0.0048+0.2335	250
26.06	9.16	11.22	143.40	4.16	2.02	1.92	27.73	31.06	27.340	−0.0073+0.2354	251
25.78	8.75	10.69	160.12	4.76	2.32	2.18	28.27	33.08	27.796	−0.0042+0.2328	252
25.64	9.05	10.77	177.35	5.40	2.62	2.44	28.51	35.73	27.926	−0.0029+0.2327	253
27.90	10.37	10.99	126.55	3.80	1.84	1.66	30.02	43.19	29.642	−0.0210+0.2087	254
28.46	10.76	11.30	118.85	3.53	1.73	1.62	29.69	42.93	29.323	−0.0234+0.2117	255
29.22	11.86	11.84	118.95	3.48	1.70	1.60	28.34	40.08	27.993	−0.0264+0.2274	256
29.11	11.88	12.05	116.75	3.44	1.63	1.55	28.73	39.95	28.407	−0.0262+0.2218	257
29.48	11.37	12.26	119.07	3.52	1.69	1.62	29.06	40.55	28.710	−0.0241+0.2184	258
27.65	9.00	12.35	175.77	4.97	2.40	2.21	29.36	38.82	28.810	−0.0092+0.2199	259
27.39	8.77	11.52	131.89	4.46	2.16	2.07	29.09	34.43	28.633	−0.0076+0.2218	260
20.24	8.21	8.47	195.08	5.55	2.69	1.77	27.58	51.35	27.027	−0.0444+0.2266	261
20.04	7.85	8.12	195.58	5.47	2.65	1.88	27.77	50.14	27.182	−0.0454+0.2264	262
18.76	7.53	7.88	249.14	7.29	3.53	2.03	27.79	46.76	27.176	−0.0332+0.2292	263
25.07	9.60	9.71	115.08	3.32	1.60	1.47	28.17	35.34	27.919	−0.0237+0.2230	264
26.38	10.46	11.20	132.17	3.92	1.90	1.76	27.92	40.98	27.490	−0.0247+0.2258	265
26.21	10.16	10.90	125.49	3.71	1.80	1.70	27.53	38.93	27.139	−0.0254+0.2329	266
26.36	10.15	11.19	121.58	3.54	1.72	1.63	27.60	36.87	27.254	−0.0240+0.2318	267
27.62	11.18	12.37	119.57	3.50	1.71	1.64	27.79	35.74	27.456	−0.0210+0.2314	268
26.51	10.94	11.39	106.80	3.34	1.61	1.56	27.86	33.31	27.576	−0.0193+0.2309	269
27.16	10.61	12.19	107.34	3.43	1.65	1.59	27.80	32.31	27.513	−0.0175+0.2310	270
27.37	11.62	12.34	108.52	3.47	1.68	1.63	27.93	32.51	27.636	−0.0162+0.2300	271
27.93	11.54	12.58	106.50	3.39	1.66	1.60	27.94	32.33	27.652	−0.0164+0.2292	272
27.55	10.78	12.28	101.15	3.20	1.55	1.51	28.10	32.04	27.853	−0.0185+0.2267	273
21.99	7.44	8.93	132.36	4.13	2.02	1.43	30.66	38.09	30.427	−0.0189+0.2042	274
24.32	8.71	10.25	109.89	3.30	1.60	1.39	29.42	31.27	29.231	−0.0172+0.2147	275
25.26	8.84	10.67	86.57	2.51	1.22	1.10	28.98	27.44	28.932	−0.0223+0.2171	276
25.48	8.72	10.57	74.76	2.13	1.03	0.96	28.43	23.41	28.452	−0.0245+0.2217	277
26.21	9.01	10.97	70.93	2.01	0.98	0.92	27.88	19.69	27.914	−0.0229+0.2263	278
26.22	8.75	10.75	69.23	1.96	0.95	0.91	27.74	17.56	27.772	−0.0216+0.2270	279
26.98	9.33	11.39	69.26	1.98	0.96	0.93	27.78	16.96	27.802	−0.0202+0.2265	280
27.18	9.37	11.47	69.56	2.03	0.99	0.95	27.76	16.53	27.778	−0.0189+0.2268	281
26.91	9.07	11.18	72.56	2.14	1.04	1.01	27.68	16.47	27.679	−0.0170+0.2277	282
27.48	9.55	11.65	53.29	1.60	0.77	0.74	27.58	17.99	27.688	−0.0298+0.2270	283
22.84	8.86	9.52	201.20	5.94	2.88	2.27	29.52	43.88	28.883	−0.0142+0.2174	284
25.57	9.54	10.28	308.66	8.30	4.03	3.67	28.42	46.74	27.305	−0.0082+0.2285	285
26.39	11.40	12.94	182.80	5.53	2.68	2.41	29.24	46.49	28.513	−0.0146+0.2202	286
24.22	11.26	11.53	198.13	5.92	2.89	2.52	28.74	48.20	27.937	−0.0176+0.2245	287
30.05	11.69	15.18	163.72	5.16	2.49	2.35	30.35	42.59	29.723	−0.0078+0.2131	288
20.51	10.26	8.46	200.84	6.08	2.97	2.63	28.16	44.20	27.380	−0.0145+0.2331	289

SERIES NUMBER	AREA AND YEAR			POPULATION, IN 1000'S			AGE STRUCTURE					
				Observed at mid-year	Projected		Total re-productive value (in 1000's)	Percent at age			Dependency ratio (× 100)	Departure from stability (Δ percent)
					5 years	10 years		<15	15–64	⩾65		
				1	2	3	4	5	6	7	8	9
290	Pakistan	*hypothetical*	1961	93832	107358	122882	56178	44.79	52.81	2.40	89.36	0.1
291	Philippines	*hyp*	1960	27420	32616	38742	17101	45.69	51.58	2.73	93.87	3.1
292	Ryukyu Islands		1965	930	1004	1100	356	38.86	55.27	5.87	80.93	8.2
293	Sarawak		1961	745	859	983	371	44.47	52.51	3.02	90.45	6.2
294	Singapore		1957	1450	1723	2031	772	42.88	54.97	2.15	81.91	4.8
295			1962	1714	1972	2276	843	45.96	51.81	2.23	93.05	4.6
296			1966–68	1956	2180	2453	855	42.78	54.39	2.83	83.85	9.4
297	Thailand		1960	26273	30107	34407	13859	43.19	54.01	2.80	85.14	7.2
298	Turkey	*hypothetical*	1960	27506	31383	35591	15112	41.25	55.22	3.53	81.09	7.4
	EUROPE											
299	Albania		1955	1381	1594	1832	826	39.05	55.13	5.82	81.38	5.1
300	Austria		1950–52	6933	7002	7030	1450	22.91	66.49	10.60	50.39	6.8
301			1953–55	6940	7022	7072	1443	22.88	65.86	11.26	51.83	6.8
302			1956–58	6966	7113	7238	1540	21.77	66.51	11.72	50.37	7.5
303			1959–61	7048	7238	7414	1594	22.04	65.74	12.22	52.13	10.4
304			1962	7130	7333	7523	1641	22.62	64.77	12.61	54.37	10.4
305			1963	7172	7382	7575	1664	22.77	64.45	12.78	55.14	11.1
306			1964	7215	7430	7618	1665	22.99	64.03	12.98	56.19	10.8
307			1965	7255	7424	7578	1647	23.27	63.53	13.20	57.40	10.0
308			1966–68	7323	7478	7626	1629	23.85	62.50	13.65	60.01	8.1
309	Belgium		1900	6637	6992	7386	2754	31.87	61.92	6.21	61.51	2.5
310			1903–07	7202	7582	7964	2712	30.37	63.63	6.00	57.15	11.2
311			1908–12	7416	7718	8035	2624	30.52	63.13	6.35	58.42	8.0
312			1919–21	7408	7635	7852	2166	25.55	67.97	6.48	47.13	10.3
313			1923–25	7752	7988	8176	2026	23.28	69.75	6.97	43.37	8.2
314			1928–32	8062	8230	8335	1981	22.99	69.47	7.54	43.93	9.5
315			1933–37	8279	8360	8377	1811	23.74	67.96	8.30	47.15	11.6
316			1938–42	8295	8252	8182	1757	22.34	68.56	9.10	45.84	10.8
317			1943–47	8370	8441	8482	1870	21.02	69.04	9.94	44.85	6.7
318			1948–52	8647	8817	8949	1909	20.94	67.97	11.09	47.13	5.4
319			1953–57	8827	9007	9139	1922	21.63	66.93	11.44	49.43	4.5
320			1958–62	9153	9359	9529	2025	23.53	64.50	11.97	55.04	6.3
321			1963	9290	9495	9696	2117	23.81	63.80	12.39	56.74	6.8
322			1964	9378	9623	9860	2146	23.83	63.67	12.50	57.04	7.1
323			1965	9464	9672	9874	2123	23.87	63.49	12.64	57.50	6.0
324			1966	9525	9709	9895	2106	23.89	63.29	12.82	58.00	4.5
325	Bulgaria		1950–52	7284	7699	8066	2027	26.73	66.57	6.70	50.21	11.4
326			1953–55	7468	7859	8193	1878	26.47	66.59	6.94	50.17	13.7
327			1956–58	7651	8007	8316	1787	26.49	66.23	7.28	50.98	11.9
328			1959–61	7867	8207	8522	1729	26.07	66.42	7.51	50.55	10.7
329			1962	8013	8327	8624	1705	25.43	66.70	7.87	49.92	9.8
330			1963	8078	8405	8708	1687	25.08	66.92	8.00	49.44	10.8
331			1964	8144	8482	8786	1665	24.66	67.19	8.15	48.84	11.6
332			1965	8200	8503	8770	1618	23.88	67.56	8.56	48.03	12.5
333			1966–68	8310	8597	8851	1617	23.45	67.69	8.86	47.72	10.3
334	Czechoslovakia		1930	13964	14482	14894	4177	25.67	67.68	6.65	47.76	13.2
335			1935	14339	14540	14650	3558	26.86	65.94	7.20	51.66	17.3
336			1950–52	12532	13211	13808	3404	26.00	66.00	8.00	51.51	6.5

[84]

VITAL RATES PER THOUSAND POPULATION								INFANT MOR-TALITY RATE per 1000 births	AGE-SPECIFIC DEATH RATES				
Crude (both sexes)			Standardized on U.S., 1960 (both sexes)		Intrinsic (females)				$1000\,_4M_1$		$1000\,_5M_{50}$		
Birth 10	Death 11	Increase 12	Birth 13	Death 14	Birth 15	Death 16	Increase 17	18	Males 19	Females 20	Males 21	Females 22	SERIES NUMBER
47.23	20.29	26.94	43.81	25.60	48.70	21.44	27.26	156.94	22.26	28.43	21.72	19.00	290
47.08	10.87	36.22	43.80	14.76	44.37	11.00	33.37	64.35	14.84	13.76	13.29	10.96	291
23.71	8.00	15.71	21.23	11.47	22.69	8.96	13.73	14.01	2.39	2.73	13.77	6.32	292
36.97	8.02	28.95	33.97	12.21	36.93	8.27	28.66	49.95	6.25	5.53	15.62	10.63	293
43.22	7.38	35.84	42.73	14.13	43.61	6.22	37.39	44.49	4.56	4.67	17.68	10.03	294
34.42	5.94	28.48	35.35	15.67	37.27	5.56	31.71	27.25	2.50	2.69	15.11	9.39	295
25.99	5.45	20.54	26.31	13.39	28.97	6.78	22.19	24.77	1.83	1.78	12.58	7.16	296
36.46	8.44	28.01	33.82	12.27	33.47	9.80	23.67	49.06	11.40	10.42	13.61	8.89	297
45.71	16.55	29.16	42.05	21.50	44.59	16.56	28.04	90.20	17.15	20.37	19.17	15.53	298
44.39	15.02	29.36	45.79	14.40	44.74	15.35	29.39	104.05	31.42	38.85	11.30	6.57	299
15.08	12.37	2.71	13.47	12.10	13.17	16.02	-2.84	63.37	2.57	2.29	12.12	6.99	300
15.15	12.15	3.00	14.05	11.21	14.01	14.53	-0.52	50.71	2.00	1.70	10.94	6.31	301
16.95	12.54	4.41	16.42	10.92	17.28	11.80	5.48	44.58	1.82	1.54	10.55	5.95	302
18.06	12.45	5.61	17.63	10.35	18.73	10.52	8.21	38.44	1.70	1.30	10.28	5.44	303
18.69	12.74	5.95	18.15	10.29	19.56	9.90	9.67	34.00	1.23	1.14	9.81	5.32	304
18.80	12.77	6.03	18.23	10.22	19.83	9.70	10.13	32.32	1.50	1.13	9.56	5.21	305
18.55	12.35	6.20	17.97	9.77	19.37	9.75	9.62	29.45	1.35	1.19	9.63	5.33	306
17.91	12.99	4.91	17.44	10.18	18.71	10.17	8.55	28.54	1.38	1.06	9.15	5.31	307
17.39	12.88	4.52	17.12	9.95	18.16	10.34	7.82	26.69	1.14	0.95	9.74	5.27	308
29.43	19.44	9.99	24.89	22.89	27.97	18.37	9.61	194.86	19.19	17.94	19.87	13.49	309
26.38	16.40	9.98	19.59	20.37	21.17	18.56	2.61	168.52	17.84	16.84	16.77	11.90	310
23.92	15.85	8.07	19.44	19.75	21.26	17.90	3.36	155.31	16.69	15.66	16.16	11.77	311
20.38	14.36	6.02	16.09	17.74	16.84	18.58	-1.74	106.34	14.35	12.99	13.49	11.35	312
19.69	13.25	6.45	15.41	15.99	15.94	17.49	-1.55	95.95	11.43	10.30	13.00	10.32	313
18.44	13.66	4.79	14.27	15.99	14.66	18.26	-3.60	93.95	8.50	7.38	13.66	10.26	314
15.83	12.82	3.01	12.72	14.60	12.46	19.11	-6.64	82.18	6.23	5.42	13.06	9.26	315
14.02	14.52	0.50	12.24	16.05	11.92	19.83	-7.91	84.19	5.51	4.71	14.91	10.50	316
16.21	14.06	2.15	14.72	14.87	14.77	16.56	-1.79	80.55	4.61	4.61	14.54	8.41	317
16.78	12.36	4.42	15.36	11.17	15.80	13.27	2.53	45.35	2.18	1.84	12.09	6.90	318
16.78	12.09	4.69	15.44	10.45	15.92	12.46	3.46	38.24	1.63	1.29	10.78	5.77	319
17.00	11.80	5.20	16.51	9.62	17.34	10.84	6.50	25.60	1.21	1.00	10.12	5.13	320
17.14	12.56	4.57	17.22	10.01	18.42	10.33	8.08	28.02	1.26	0.96	11.14	5.37	321
17.15	11.74	5.41	17.34	9.33	18.48	10.02	8.47	25.35	0.95	0.82	9.74	5.18	322
16.43	12.16	4.27	16.71	9.56	17.67	10.52	7.15	23.69	1.08	0.83	10.31	5.24	323
15.86	12.14	3.73	16.09	9.49	16.90	11.00	5.90	24.73	1.05	0.81	9.74	5.25	324
22.39	10.79	11.61	16.93	12.84	17.44	15.04	2.40	103.94	8.73	8.66	9.90	6.83	325
20.27	9.12	11.15	15.40	11.01	15.38	14.77	0.60	88.58	5.61	5.72	8.59	5.82	326
18.61	8.61	10.00	14.75	10.38	14.76	14.40	0.36	66.09	4.78	4.67	7.87	5.48	327
17.58	8.48	9.10	14.73	9.84	14.91	13.62	1.29	47.80	3.02	2.89	7.95	5.39	328
16.74	8.69	8.05	14.36	9.71	14.50	13.57	0.93	37.89	2.17	1.85	7.52	5.05	329
16.36	8.18	8.18	14.15	9.03	14.06	13.68	0.37	36.44	1.97	2.04	7.33	4.76	330
16.08	7.92	8.16	14.02	8.61	13.70	13.61	0.09	33.61	1.77	1.66	7.14	4.53	331
15.34	8.17	7.17	13.40	8.61	12.77	14.31	-1.55	31.73	1.55	1.41	7.15	4.90	332
15.61	8.63	6.97	13.64	8.98	13.28	14.09	-0.81	31.09	1.50	1.37	7.58	4.69	333
21.78	13.92	7.86	15.50	17.28	16.43	18.74	-2.30	153.21	8.75	8.45	14.65	10.25	334
17.03	13.30	3.73	12.59	16.73	12.21	21.15	-8.95	126.60	7.22	6.42	13.72	10.18	335
22.75	11.19	11.56	19.54	12.51	21.42	11.23	10.19	74.30	2.95	2.73	11.63	6.91	336

continued

LIFE TABLE VALUES

SERIES NUMBER	AREA AND YEAR		Probability of dying in first year, q_0		Survivors to age 50 per 100,000 births, l_{50}		Expectancy, $\mathring{e}_0$		Expectancy, $\mathring{e}_1$		Expectancy, $\mathring{e}_{50}$
			Males 23	Females 24	Males 25	Females 26	Males 27	Females 28	Males 29	Females 30	Males 31
290	Pakistan *hypothetical*	1961	0.1563	0.1619	52533	49262	44.38	42.45	51.53	49.58	18.98
291	Philippines *hyp*	1960	0.1084	0.0864	67392	71700	55.40	58.68	61.09	63.19	23.83
292	Ryukyu Islands	1965	0.0157	0.0135	82206	88178	63.88	70.78	63.90	70.75	21.07
293	Sarawak	1961	0.0721	0.0515	75944	77345	60.63	64.38	64.32	66.86	22.68
294	Singapore	1957	0.0469	0.0388	80470	83609	60.20	66.46	62.14	68.12	18.68
295		1962	0.0309	0.0220	85191	88789	63.14	68.42	64.15	68.95	19.33
296		1967	0.0265	0.0213	86961	90713	64.45	70.38	65.19	70.90	19.94
297	Thailand	1960	0.0833	0.0629	71131	74783	58.68	64.43	62.99	67.73	24.67
298	Turkey *hypothetical*	1960	0.1325	0.1255	58360	58328	48.27	48.72	54.60	54.66	19.83
	EUROPE										
299	Albania	1955	0.1078	0.1104	67261	65952	54.55	55.40	60.09	61.22	25.23
300	Austria	1950-52	0.0681	0.0523	81590	86371	62.82	68.05	66.39	70.79	22.35
301		1953-55	0.0553	0.0419	84143	88628	64.52	69.96	67.29	72.01	22.65
302		1956-58	0.0477	0.0375	84254	89596	64.77	70.84	67.01	72.59	22.62
303		1959-61	0.0414	0.0327	85524	90729	65.65	72.06	67.47	73.49	22.74
304		1962	0.0365	0.0292	86734	91310	66.27	72.49	67.78	73.66	22.61
305		1963	0.0349	0.0278	86734	91558	66.35	72.65	67.74	73.72	22.69
306		1964	0.0324	0.0248	87010	92009	66.80	73.27	68.03	74.13	22.97
307		1965	0.0306	0.0251	87009	92186	66.58	73.00	67.67	73.87	22.58
308		1966-68	0.0304	0.0227	86766	92434	66.63	73.41	67.71	74.11	22.76
309	Belgium	1900	0.1866	0.1566	55119	59303	45.11	48.55	54.39	56.51	19.42
310		1903-07	0.1640	0.1380	59770	63758	48.17	51.67	56.56	58.89	20.34
311		1908-12	0.1527	0.1280	61817	65251	49.34	52.77	57.17	59.47	20.28
312		1919-21	0.1086	0.0852	64917	68557	52.54	55.82	57.89	59.99	21.44
313		1923-25	0.0988	0.0784	69524	73259	55.47	59.28	60.51	63.30	21.79
314		1928-32	0.0986	0.0768	70326	74549	55.93	59.76	61.02	63.70	21.53
315		1933-37	0.0870	0.0679	73507	77947	58.20	62.26	62.72	65.77	22.00
316		1938-42	0.0893	0.0689	70345	78222	56.14	62.01	60.62	65.57	20.95
317		1943-47	0.0847	0.0663	71786	79332	57.42	63.35	61.71	66.83	21.64
318		1948-52	0.0495	0.0379	83079	87996	64.50	69.54	66.84	71.28	22.74
319		1953-57	0.0417	0.0323	86496	90740	66.30	71.50	68.18	72.88	22.93
320		1958-62	0.0283	0.0217	88314	92450	67.70	73.40	68.66	74.02	23.19
321		1963	0.0305	0.0241	87556	92157	66.87	72.97	67.97	73.77	22.62
322		1964	0.0284	0.0221	88086	92551	67.73	73.88	68.71	74.54	23.27
323		1965	0.0256	0.0207	88470	92674	67.62	73.75	68.39	74.31	22.87
324		1966	0.0267	0.0216	88682	92698	67.74	73.79	68.59	74.42	22.98
325	Bulgaria	1950-52	0.1059	0.0875	74220	77572	58.78	62.72	64.71	67.70	23.80
326		1953-55	0.0904	0.0756	79819	82923	62.68	66.56	67.89	70.99	24.61
327		1956-58	0.0689	0.0571	83289	86342	65.11	68.68	68.91	71.82	24.78
328		1959-61	0.0497	0.0425	85919	88823	66.90	70.44	69.39	72.55	24.61
329		1962	0.0397	0.0338	87295	90681	67.79	71.47	69.58	72.96	24.47
330		1963	0.0388	0.0320	87701	90827	68.67	72.18	70.43	73.56	25.23
331		1964	0.0356	0.0298	88330	91561	69.34	73.27	70.89	74.52	25.48
332		1965	0.0343	0.0274	88665	92105	69.39	73.66	70.85	74.73	25.37
333		1966-68	0.0357	0.0293	88184	91937	68.86	72.93	70.40	74.12	24.99
334	Czechoslovakia	1930	0.1498	0.1249	65371	69736	52.40	55.97	60.58	62.91	21.67
335		1935	0.1273	0.1035	68734	73325	54.59	58.25	61.51	63.95	21.61
336		1950-52	0.0771	0.0629	80197	84824	62.03	66.63	66.20	70.09	22.52

FERTILITY MEASURES (FEMALES)

Females 32	Expectancy, $\mathring{e}_{70}$ Males 33	Females 34	General fertility rate 35	Total fertility rate 36	Gross reproduction rate 37	Net maternity function Total, NRR 38	Mean, μ 39	Variance, σ^2 40	Generation, T 41	Complex root, r_2 42	SERIES NUMBER
19.87	8.00	8.27	235.83	6.67	3.25	2.08	27.55	51.20	26.846	−0.0401+0.2316	290
24.69	11.21	11.23	221.25	6.71	3.25	2.63	29.82	45.96	29.041	−0.0116+0.2170	291
26.59	8.77	11.52	108.99	3.29	1.58	1.49	29.48	28.06	29.282	−0.0107+0.2154	292
26.20	11.30	13.22	176.51	5.20	2.54	2.23	28.75	48.14	28.046	−0.0247+0.2229	293
24.74	7.91	11.19	215.83	6.55	3.17	2.90	29.34	43.33	28.517	−0.0065+0.2209	294
23.73	7.30	9.08	187.41	5.43	2.63	2.49	29.45	42.36	28.762	−0.0103+0.2187	295
24.93	7.06	10.10	130.86	4.06	1.98	1.89	29.17	38.88	28.721	−0.0153+0.2208	296
29.51	12.57	15.72	170.66	5.17	2.44	2.03	30.60	49.73	29.994	−0.0192+0.2046	297
21.36	8.38	8.94	226.78	6.41	3.11	2.20	28.89	51.29	28.165	−0.0279+0.2169	298
28.77	11.45	13.38	222.55	7.02	3.43	2.43	31.16	59.44	30.286	−0.0203+0.2079	299
25.64	9.25	10.46	68.79	2.07	1.00	0.92	27.97	38.68	28.028	−0.0435+0.2166	300
26.25	9.41	10.77	72.26	2.17	1.05	0.99	27.87	37.37	27.878	−0.0417+0.2200	301
26.57	9.39	10.96	81.83	2.54	1.24	1.16	27.79	35.99	27.682	−0.0351+0.2238	302
27.18	9.51	11.38	89.40	2.72	1.32	1.25	27.53	36.87	27.370	−0.0344+0.2271	303
27.20	9.29	11.28	92.19	2.80	1.36	1.30	27.45	37.00	27.262	−0.0335+0.2282	304
27.20	9.32	11.37	91.94	2.81	1.38	1.32	27.39	36.51	27.199	−0.0322+0.2284	305
27.59	9.61	11.73	90.60	2.77	1.35	1.30	27.39	36.89	27.208	−0.0332+0.2282	306
27.20	9.22	11.37	88.18	2.68	1.31	1.26	27.28	37.13	27.116	−0.0352+0.2284	307
27.43	9.36	11.52	87.94	2.63	1.28	1.23	26.89	37.73	26.738	−0.0402+0.2309	308
21.49	7.84	8.52	125.67	3.84	1.87	1.32	28.79	27.64	28.651	−0.0167+0.2157	309
22.41	8.33	9.25	104.99	2.99	1.46	1.08	29.06	32.10	29.017	−0.0257+0.2078	310
22.57	8.28	9.19	102.55	3.00	1.47	1.10	28.80	28.34	28.744	−0.0233+0.2136	311
22.96	8.71	9.39	83.13	2.48	1.20	0.95	28.88	27.76	28.908	−0.0273+0.2121	312
24.13	8.76	9.72	81.47	2.38	1.16	0.96	28.66	28.00	28.681	−0.0280+0.2137	313
23.57	8.67	9.61	77.09	2.20	1.08	0.90	28.44	28.17	28.497	−0.0309+0.2148	314
24.22	8.92	10.04	69.20	1.97	0.96	0.83	28.08	28.90	28.182	−0.0359+0.2168	315
23.69	8.21	9.58	61.49	1.89	0.92	0.80	28.71	35.37	28.856	−0.0423+0.2117	316
24.75	8.76	10.12	72.04	2.27	1.09	0.95	29.01	35.39	29.049	−0.0350+0.2119	317
25.97	9.65	10.91	78.74	2.37	1.15	1.07	28.72	35.88	28.676	−0.0327+0.2149	318
26.54	9.62	11.01	82.05	2.39	1.16	1.10	28.49	34.32	28.426	−0.0314+0.2184	319
27.39	9.75	11.52	88.49	2.56	1.24	1.20	28.01	33.57	27.891	−0.0297+0.2253	320
27.08	9.60	11.40	86.08	2.68	1.30	1.25	27.78	32.21	27.638	−0.0276+0.2283	321
27.83	9.99	11.93	85.54	2.69	1.31	1.26	27.74	32.02	27.594	−0.0270+0.2286	322
27.59	9.69	11.73	82.04	2.60	1.26	1.22	27.58	32.06	27.463	−0.0289+0.2297	323
27.65	9.74	11.80	79.48	2.50	1.22	1.17	27.47	32.13	27.371	−0.0305+0.2303	324
26.47	10.51	12.33	93.27	2.62	1.27	1.07	26.67	35.98	26.628	−0.0430+0.2395	325
27.21	10.88	12.63	86.44	2.38	1.15	1.02	26.19	35.05	26.173	−0.0460+0.2459	326
26.98	10.76	11.61	81.97	2.28	1.11	1.01	25.65	32.28	25.641	−0.0429+0.2524	327
26.94	10.52	11.41	78.65	2.28	1.11	1.03	25.09	29.95	25.067	−0.0394+0.2578	328
26.72	10.13	11.03	73.89	2.22	1.08	1.02	25.13	29.49	25.119	−0.0394+0.2567	329
27.42	10.86	11.72	71.33	2.19	1.06	1.01	25.03	28.44	25.028	−0.0391+0.2568	330
28.12	11.04	12.30	69.64	2.17	1.05	1.00	24.87	28.14	24.870	−0.0396+0.2590	331
28.14	10.84	12.36	66.44	2.07	1.00	0.96	24.91	28.06	24.929	−0.0411+0.2576	332
27.49	10.57	11.53	68.47	2.11	1.02	0.98	24.68	26.22	24.691	−0.0380+0.2602	333
23.43	9.15	9.71	85.86	2.45	1.19	0.94	28.59	39.17	28.633	−0.0421+0.2135	334
23.31	8.75	9.36	70.82	1.95	0.95	0.77	28.37	37.81	28.548	−0.0485+0.2139	335
25.28	9.42	10.23	102.92	3.02	1.46	1.32	27.38	37.30	27.182	−0.0353+0.2317	336

SERIES NUMBER	AREA AND YEAR		POPULATION, IN 1000'S			AGE STRUCTURE				Dependency ratio (× 100)	Departure from stability (Δ percent)
			Observed at mid-year	Projected		Total reproductive value (in 1000's)	Percent at age				
				5 years	10 years		< 15	15–64	⩾ 65		
			1	2	3	4	5	6	7	8	9
337	Czechoslovakia	1953–55	12952	13585	14162	3351	27.23	64.59	8.18	54.83	6.5
338	cont	1956–58	13358	13939	14512	3310	27.74	63.89	8.37	56.52	5.4
339		1959–61	13654	14109	14593	3096	27.23	63.95	8.82	56.38	7.0
340		1962	13860	14281	14767	3102	26.54	64.38	9.08	55.34	6.1
341		1963	13952	14497	15093	3223	26.06	64.64	9.30	54.71	6.1
342		1964	14058	14622	15239	3253	25.70	64.76	9.54	54.43	6.4
343		1965	14156	14639	15167	3187	25.33	64.85	9.82	54.19	6.1
344		1966	14240	14677	15133	3077	24.86	65.03	10.11	53.77	6.7
345	Bohemia, Moravia	1966	9826	10017	10202	1887	22.69	66.37	10.94	50.68	7.7
346	Slovakia	1966	4414	4658	4935	1188	29.70	62.05	8.25	61.14	5.9
347	Czechoslovakia	1967	14305	14687	15070	2963	24.36	65.24	10.40	53.30	8.1
348	Denmark	1950–52	4304	4483	4643	1039	26.39	64.41	9.20	55.25	5.4
349		1953–55	4407	4583	4759	1051	26.55	63.84	9.61	56.64	4.8
350		1956–58	4488	4660	4838	1052	26.42	63.48	10.10	57.54	4.8
351		1959–61	4581	4751	4937	1059	25.23	64.19	10.58	55.77	4.8
352		1962	4647	4822	5012	1073	24.27	64.80	10.93	54.33	4.5
353		1963	4684	4883	5093	1096	23.97	64.93	11.10	54.01	5.0
354		1964	4720	4916	5121	1091	23.84	64.91	11.25	54.06	4.6
355		1965	4758	4961	5164	1103	23.78	64.84	11.38	54.24	4.8
356		1966	4797	5000	5207	1108	23.81	64.68	11.51	54.61	4.8
357		1967	4839	5013	5172	1056	23.84	64.49	11.67	55.06	4.1
358	Finland	1930	3654	3792	3917	1164	28.01	65.51	6.48	52.65	10.0
359		1950–52	4047	4312	4567	1272	30.13	63.21	6.66	58.19	4.5
360		1953–55	4187	4437	4677	1264	30.55	62.59	6.86	59.76	4.6
361		1956–58	4324	4551	4791	1257	30.71	62.24	7.05	60.68	4.3
362		1959–61	4430	4649	4890	1248	30.40	62.30	7.30	60.53	4.9
363		1962	4505	4711	4953	1239	29.05	63.44	7.51	57.63	4.6
364		1963	4543	4761	5014	1246	28.34	64.03	7.63	56.16	4.8
365		1964	4580	4792	5029	1227	27.67	64.55	7.78	54.93	5.2
366		1965	4612	4796	5013	1200	27.06	65.01	7.93	53.82	5.8
367		1966	4639	4828	5032	1179	26.54	65.37	8.09	52.96	6.2
368	Urban	1966	2102	2207	2300	507	24.61	68.16	7.23	46.71	7.6
369	Rural	1966	2537	2621	2732	674	28.14	63.06	8.80	58.56	7.5
370	France	1851	35791	36406	36902	13941	27.31	66.21	6.48	51.04	4.4
371		1854–58	36016	36090	36074	13455	27.51	66.10	6.39	51.30	4.8
372		1861	37397	37964	38397	14264	27.11	66.19	6.70	51.08	3.9
373		1864–68	38027	38477	38817	13934	26.97	65.79	7.24	51.99	2.5
374		1871	36731	35128	33665	12847	27.76	64.77	7.47	54.40	7.0
375		1872	36106	36777	37333	13271	27.06	65.52	7.42	52.63	2.4
376		1874–78	36824	37415	37970	13192	27.12	65.24	7.64	53.28	1.9
377		1879–83	37541	37937	38297	13677	27.13	64.85	8.02	54.20	3.0
378		1884–88	37934	38209	38502	13443	26.96	65.00	8.04	53.84	4.2
379		1889–93	38135	38146	38226	12941	26.23	65.48	8.29	52.71	4.6
380		1894–98	38278	38495	38744	12698	25.99	65.67	8.34	52.27	4.6
381		1899–1903	38473	38707	38948	12139	26.12	65.68	8.20	52.25	3.3
382		1904–08	38868	39102	39326	11829	26.00	65.67	8.33	52.30	3.3
383		1909–13	39215	39382	39522	10888	25.74	65.89	8.37	51.76	5.2
384		1920–22	40228	40761	41118	10450	22.48	68.38	9.14	46.25	5.3
385		1924–28	40295	40604	40775	9962	22.51	68.33	9.16	46.35	5.8
386		1929–33	41225	41363	41249	9572	23.07	67.55	9.38	48.04	6.0
387		1934–38	40957	40784	40465	8958	24.57	65.47	9.96	52.74	6.8
388		1945–47	40282	41269	42185	10248	21.49	67.39	11.12	48.38	6.5
389		1949–53	42056	43473	44782	10594	23.12	65.44	11.44	52.82	8.2
390		1954–58	43843	45179	46315	10697	24.95	63.51	11.54	57.46	6.4
391		1959–63	46163	47647	49194	11445	26.43	61.85	11.72	61.68	6.8
392		1965	48919	50679	52687	12023	24.58	62.87	12.55	59.06	7.4
393		1966	49164	50994	53036	12048	25.44	62.28	12.28	60.57	6.3
394		1967	49548	51189	53036	11890	25.28	62.24	12.48	60.67	4.9

VITAL RATES PER THOUSAND POPULATION / INFANT MORTALITY RATE / AGE-SPECIFIC DEATH RATES

| Crude (both sexes) | | | Standardized on U.S., 1960 (both sexes) | | Intrinsic (females) | | | INFANT MORTALITY RATE per 1000 births | $1000\,_4M_1$ | | $1000\,_5M_{50}$ | | SERIES NUMBER |
Birth 10	Death 11	Increase 12	Birth 13	Death 14	Birth 15	Death 16	Increase 17	18	Males 19	Females 20	Males 21	Females 22	
20.68	10.17	10.51	18.43	11.25	20.21	10.40	9.81	40.13	2.11	1.89	10.80	6.27	337
18.71	9.65	9.06	17.55	10.40	19.16	10.36	8.80	31.40	1.60	1.41	10.09	5.77	338
15.93	9.35	6.58	15.39	9.73	16.18	11.74	4.44	24.51	1.40	1.15	9.32	5.30	339
15.69	10.01	5.68	15.03	10.44	15.83	12.03	3.80	23.17	1.25	1.01	9.36	5.13	340
16.92	9.54	7.37	16.06	9.78	17.22	10.90	6.32	23.42	1.26	0.97	9.21	5.06	341
17.16	9.59	7.57	16.12	9.63	17.25	10.80	6.45	22.08	1.25	0.96	8.70	5.13	342
16.37	9.96	6.42	15.21	9.88	15.96	11.82	4.13	25.44	1.40	1.00	9.30	5.20	343
15.63	9.98	5.65	14.26	9.75	14.53	12.76	1.78	23.79	1.30	0.90	9.35	5.19	344
14.37	10.77	3.60	12.97	9.85	12.57	14.45	−1.88	21.92	1.10	0.69	9.69	5.28	345
18.45	8.24	10.22	17.08	9.41	18.57	10.12	8.45	27.02	1.63	1.28	8.43	4.93	346
15.10	10.10	5.00	13.40	9.70	13.16	13.91	−0.75	22.86	1.17	0.89	9.70	4.96	347
18.05	9.02	9.03	16.44	9.33	17.33	11.31	6.01	30.09	1.53	1.14	7.54	6.01	348
17.51	8.93	8.58	16.59	8.86	17.49	10.89	6.60	26.97	1.32	0.94	7.54	5.45	349
16.84	9.13	7.71	16.54	8.58	17.47	10.62	6.84	23.60	1.05	0.84	7.65	5.32	350
16.48	9.40	7.08	16.25	8.47	17.22	10.68	6.54	22.25	1.04	0.80	7.34	5.05	351
16.74	9.76	6.99	16.33	8.53	17.35	10.48	6.87	20.26	0.85	0.83	7.76	4.68	352
17.60	9.77	7.82	16.94	8.43	18.16	9.96	8.20	19.84	0.98	0.85	7.45	4.80	353
17.66	9.92	7.74	16.75	8.44	17.73	10.12	7.61	18.98	0.94	0.67	7.56	4.78	354
18.03	10.06	7.97	16.85	8.47	17.94	10.04	7.90	18.72	0.93	0.82	7.72	4.98	355
18.41	10.29	8.13	16.91	8.56	18.10	9.90	8.20	16.95	0.83	0.75	7.70	5.00	356
16.82	9.89	6.94	15.21	8.14	15.67	11.30	4.38	15.81	0.77	0.64	8.01	4.89	357
20.59	13.20	7.39	16.97	15.58	17.28	17.13	0.15	75.14	9.11	8.57	16.43	10.30	358
23.51	9.89	13.62	19.99	12.78	21.64	10.11	11.53	37.76	2.32	1.81	15.20	7.11	359
21.53	9.35	12.18	19.07	12.22	20.72	9.96	10.76	32.29	2.04	1.45	13.60	6.37	360
19.81	9.12	10.70	18.23	11.54	19.74	10.16	9.58	25.97	1.86	1.60	13.50	5.94	361
18.62	8.97	9.64	17.60	11.01	19.02	10.18	8.85	22.54	1.33	1.05	13.28	5.59	362
18.08	9.52	8.56	17.01	11.56	18.34	10.53	7.81	20.82	1.22	0.81	13.30	5.59	363
18.11	9.25	8.86	17.02	11.09	18.29	10.42	7.87	18.61	1.19	0.88	14.26	5.83	364
17.56	9.28	8.28	16.36	10.89	17.40	10.93	6.47	17.44	1.15	0.85	13.80	5.46	365
16.89	9.64	7.25	15.52	11.42	16.25	11.70	4.55	17.61	1.08	0.74	14.27	5.17	366
16.75	9.39	7.36	15.04	11.00	15.71	11.98	3.72	14.98	0.87	0.82	13.31	4.95	367
18.78	8.63	10.14	13.95	11.15	14.29	13.07	1.22	14.26	0.73	0.71	13.93	5.27	368
15.07	10.01	5.06	16.34	10.93	17.33	10.87	6.46	15.72	1.00	0.92	12.84	4.66	369
27.14	22.33	4.81	22.76	27.14	24.47	25.39	−0.92	237.84	37.22	37.36	17.26	15.09	370
26.03	24.99	1.04	21.54	25.45	23.25	26.92	−3.67	223.07	39.62	39.26	19.55	18.11	371
26.88	23.17	3.70	22.82	26.75	24.43	25.45	−0.99	234.52	40.28	39.76	16.88	15.57	372
26.35	23.44	2.91	22.50	26.90	24.44	24.43	0.01	216.59	34.61	34.78	18.89	15.78	373
22.49	31.95	−9.46	19.52	34.91	20.94	31.63	−10.69	244.77	46.48	43.85	26.88	21.98	374
26.75	21.96	4.79	22.93	24.97	24.94	23.23	1.71	209.78	30.79	31.16	18.21	14.90	375
25.82	22.28	3.54	22.33	24.74	24.50	22.39	2.11	200.65	28.24	27.71	18.75	15.20	376
24.86	22.41	2.45	21.89	24.91	24.12	23.12	0.99	222.54	29.21	28.70	19.22	15.36	377
24.03	22.34	1.69	20.83	24.96	22.64	23.36	−0.72	218.52	29.45	28.46	19.28	15.54	378
22.63	22.51	0.12	19.47	25.25	21.05	23.26	−2.21	217.43	26.96	26.09	19.21	15.22	379
22.25	20.90	1.35	18.95	23.47	20.43	21.87	−1.44	208.69	21.01	20.09	18.75	13.97	380
21.86	20.63	1.22	18.48	23.13	20.11	20.83	−0.72	172.58	17.29	16.48	19.39	13.99	381
20.57	19.80	0.77	17.56	22.29	18.88	19.64	−0.77	136.52	15.32	14.62	19.44	13.55	382
19.29	18.51	0.78	16.22	20.77	17.32	19.69	−2.37	126.90	12.66	12.26	18.96	12.85	383
19.93	17.00	2.93	16.09	17.97	16.92	18.13	−1.21	109.09	6.85	6.41	15.60	10.98	384
18.78	17.13	1.65	15.13	18.09	15.84	18.36	−2.52	90.83	8.62	8.02	17.18	11.62	385
17.54	16.43	1.11	14.38	17.20	14.93	18.12	−3.18	79.84	7.22	6.59	16.87	10.74	386
15.53	15.73	−0.21	13.42	15.96	13.65	18.07	−4.42	68.33	5.79	5.11	17.32	10.41	387
19.28	13.98	5.30	17.88	13.88	18.84	13.81	5.03	106.44	4.86	4.21	12.37	7.39	388
19.83	13.01	6.81	18.46	11.62	19.94	10.75	9.20	47.94	2.45	2.13	12.53	6.90	389
18.40	11.88	6.52	17.38	10.30	18.52	10.50	8.02	32.47	1.78	1.53	11.69	5.95	390
18.07	11.32	6.76	18.03	9.39	19.39	9.42	9.97	23.23	1.30	1.09	10.75	5.18	391
17.63	11.05	6.58	18.10	8.66	19.42	9.03	10.39	18.25	1.02	0.81	10.58	4.91	392
17.50	10.69	6.81	17.84	8.68	19.21	9.14	10.07	18.01	0.97	0.79	10.67	5.09	393
16.90	10.90	6.00	17.00	8.77	18.04	9.78	8.25	17.13	0.94	0.77	10.74	5.14	394

continued

LIFE TABLE VALUES

SERIES NUMBER	AREA AND YEAR		Probability of dying in first year, q_0		Survivors to age 50 per 100,000 births, l_{50}		Expectancy, $\overset{\circ}{e}_0$		Expectancy, $\overset{\circ}{e}_1$		Expectancy, $\overset{\circ}{e}_{50}$
			Males 23	Females 24	Males 25	Females 26	Males 27	Females 28	Males 29	Females 30	Males 31
337	Czechoslovakia	1953-55	0.0429	0.0348	85211	89404	65.29	69.97	67.20	71.49	22.55
338	cont	1956-58	0.0343	0.0269	87031	91186	66.67	71.61	68.03	72.58	22.96
339		1959-61	0.0269	0.0210	87961	92483	67.58	72.97	68.44	73.53	23.26
340		1962	0.0256	0.0198	88346	92824	67.13	72.81	67.89	73.28	22.50
341		1963	0.0259	0.0199	88034	92883	67.46	73.40	68.25	73.89	23.02
342		1964	0.0243	0.0187	88412	93151	67.73	73.65	68.41	74.05	23.09
343		1965	0.0275	0.0217	88033	92726	67.32	73.22	68.25	73.83	22.94
344		1966	0.0266	0.0200	87896	93210	67.32	73.67	68.15	74.17	22.94
	Bohemia,										
345	Moravia	1966	0.0247	0.0181	88323	93497	67.25	73.87	67.95	74.22	22.56
346	Slovakia	1966	0.0299	0.0234	87083	92710	67.78	73.35	68.87	74.11	24.08
347	Czechoslovakia	1967	0.0253	0.0197	87931	93200	67.38	73.77	68.12	74.25	22.88
348	Denmark	1950-52	0.0334	0.0252	88694	91206	69.42	71.99	70.81	72.85	25.26
349		1953-55	0.0300	0.0226	89644	92106	70.05	72.92	71.21	73.60	25.38
350		1956-58	0.0269	0.0192	90414	92867	70.37	73.78	71.31	74.22	25.23
351		1959-61	0.0247	0.0189	90633	93057	70.56	74.09	71.34	74.51	25.26
352		1962	0.0227	0.0170	90763	93463	70.32	74.46	70.95	74.74	24.81
353		1963	0.0227	0.0161	90816	93298	70.43	74.53	71.06	74.74	24.92
354		1964	0.0212	0.0158	90884	93684	70.31	74.83	70.83	75.03	24.70
355		1965	0.0220	0.0155	90855	93516	70.20	74.69	70.78	74.86	24.62
356		1966	0.0198	0.0142	91017	93744	70.23	74.81	70.64	74.88	24.49
357		1967	0.0177	0.0117	91498	93822	70.66	75.41	70.93	75.30	24.67
358	Finland	1930	0.0785	0.0647	64466	69789	53.87	58.20	57.42	61.20	21.80
359		1950-52	0.0403	0.0330	80682	87911	62.28	68.78	63.88	70.12	20.76
360		1953-55	0.0359	0.0271	83284	90078	63.72	70.29	65.08	71.24	21.07
361		1956-58	0.0280	0.0228	84346	90870	64.70	71.15	65.56	71.80	21.38
362		1959-61	0.0250	0.0192	85285	92154	65.38	72.19	66.05	72.60	21.56
363		1962	0.0231	0.0178	85294	92611	65.11	72.26	65.65	72.56	21.09
364		1963	0.0201	0.0166	85690	92901	65.53	72.68	65.87	72.90	21.27
365		1964	0.0199	0.0145	85805	93032	65.64	72.81	65.97	72.88	21.34
366		1965	0.0200	0.0147	85572	93323	65.32	72.83	65.64	72.91	21.04
367		1966	0.0165	0.0135	86394	93431	65.98	73.17	66.08	73.16	21.27
368	Urban	1966	0.0156	0.0135	86652	93475	65.60	73.31	65.64	73.31	20.61
369	Rural	1966	0.0173	0.0135	86116	93388	66.17	73.09	66.33	73.08	21.71
370	France	1851	0.2203	0.1918	44993	46425	38.34	39.65	48.07	47.97	20.39
371		1854-58	0.2103	0.1802	40744	43964	35.91	38.17	44.37	45.48	19.39
372		1861	0.2186	0.1891	45218	46210	38.29	39.60	47.90	47.75	20.49
373		1864-68	0.2039	0.1762	46020	47833	39.30	40.93	48.27	48.60	19.71
374		1871	0.2267	0.1974	26702	35600	28.61	33.71	35.89	40.91	17.79
375		1872	0.1996	0.1693	46063	48978	40.04	42.40	48.93	49.97	20.39
376		1874-78	0.1917	0.1627	48350	51220	41.33	43.72	50.06	51.15	19.97
377		1879-83	0.2093	0.1782	46617	49924	40.22	42.85	49.77	51.07	20.22
378		1884-88	0.2062	0.1755	46794	50459	40.40	43.12	49.81	51.22	20.07
379		1889-93	0.2070	0.1724	48128	52615	40.90	44.09	50.49	52.20	19.52
380		1894-98	0.1984	0.1662	50996	55944	43.03	46.59	52.61	54.81	19.84
381		1899-1903	0.1680	0.1404	53496	58242	45.02	48.53	53.05	55.40	19.49
382		1904-08	0.1264	0.1045	57488	62249	48.07	51.61	53.97	56.59	19.41
383		1909-13	0.1275	0.1057	59389	64656	49.18	53.14	55.32	58.38	19.61
384		1920-22	0.1113	0.0904	64688	68847	52.88	56.61	58.48	61.20	20.72
385		1924-28	0.0950	0.0757	65642	70829	53.37	57.67	57.94	61.36	20.19
386		1929-33	0.0845	0.0666	67790	73693	54.85	59.64	58.88	62.87	20.26
387		1934-38	0.0736	0.0566	69636	77116	56.27	62.14	59.72	64.85	20.35
388		1945-47	0.1090	0.0873	73260	79427	57.90	63.69	63.96	68.76	22.45
389		1949-53	0.0519	0.0404	82604	87556	63.88	69.63	66.37	71.55	22.29
390		1954-58	0.0356	0.0276	85602	90674	66.03	72.43	67.46	73.48	22.70
391		1959-63	0.0258	0.0197	87428	92386	67.46	74.23	68.24	74.72	23.12
392		1965	0.0202	0.0157	88095	93093	68.27	75.48	68.67	75.67	23.48
393		1966	0.0205	0.0153	87771	93091	68.10	75.45	68.52	75.62	23.44
394		1967	0.0191	0.0146	87820	93166	68.04	75.47	68.36	75.58	23.28

FERTILITY MEASURES (FEMALES)

	Expectancy, $\mathring{e}_{70}$		General fertility rate	Total fertility rate	Gross reproduction rate	Net maternity function					SERIES NUMBER
Females 32	Males 33	Females 34	35	36	37	Total, NRR 38	Mean, μ 39	Variance, σ^2 40	Generation, T 41	Complex root, r_2 42	
25.63	9.41	10.32	98.94	2.85	1.38	1.30	27.20	35.85	27.013	$-0.0350+0.2358$	337
26.28	9.71	10.76	93.05	2.72	1.32	1.26	26.69	33.24	26.541	$-0.0345+0.2418$	338
26.89	9.89	11.16	79.96	2.40	1.16	1.12	26.00	29.56	25.934	$-0.0342+0.2499$	339
26.51	8.95	10.66	76.30	2.34	1.14	1.10	25.87	28.17	25.808	$-0.0329+0.2507$	340
27.12	9.49	11.24	80.52	2.50	1.22	1.18	25.94	27.87	25.850	$-0.0299+0.2490$	341
27.20	9.53	11.37	80.69	2.51	1.22	1.18	26.03	28.09	25.933	$-0.0300+0.2478$	342
27.09	9.42	11.24	76.61	2.37	1.15	1.11	25.99	28.31	25.931	$-0.0328+0.2476$	343
27.26	9.42	11.37	72.95	2.22	1.08	1.05	25.82	27.82	25.793	$-0.0352+0.2488$	344
27.24	9.21	11.37	67.07	2.02	0.98	0.95	25.32	25.36	25.346	$-0.0370+0.2521$	345
27.33	10.03	11.38	86.04	2.66	1.30	1.25	26.64	31.11	26.497	$-0.0305+0.2435$	346
27.35	9.47	11.45	70.36	2.09	1.01	0.98	25.65	27.41	25.657	$-0.0379+0.2501$	347
26.53	10.54	10.98	84.38	2.54	1.23	1.18	27.65	36.28	27.536	$-0.0356+0.2261$	348
26.99	10.72	11.26	84.31	2.57	1.24	1.20	27.38	34.67	27.257	$-0.0342+0.2302$	349
27.44	10.71	11.57	83.20	2.56	1.24	1.20	27.09	33.14	26.975	$-0.0329+0.2340$	350
27.68	10.69	11.62	81.15	2.52	1.23	1.19	26.95	31.69	26.844	$-0.0313+0.2353$	351
27.83	10.46	11.72	81.48	2.54	1.24	1.20	26.88	31.21	26.771	$-0.0305+0.2360$	352
27.93	10.57	11.91	85.40	2.63	1.28	1.24	26.85	31.23	26.712	$-0.0293+0.2362$	353
28.06	10.48	11.93	85.73	2.60	1.26	1.22	26.73	31.02	26.606	$-0.0300+0.2369$	354
28.01	10.46	11.99	87.81	2.61	1.27	1.23	26.72	30.97	26.586	$-0.0296+0.2370$	355
27.95	10.20	11.86	90.21	2.62	1.27	1.24	26.58	30.48	26.450	$-0.0293+0.2379$	356
28.43	10.62	12.39	82.82	2.36	1.15	1.12	26.45	30.26	26.383	$-0.0333+0.2379$	357
24.56	10.43	10.69	85.83	2.60	1.26	1.00	30.59	45.04	30.585	$-0.0354+0.1966$	358
25.02	8.77	10.03	103.19	3.08	1.50	1.40	29.32	41.26	29.069	$-0.0287+0.2125$	359
25.35	8.69	10.03	98.12	2.94	1.43	1.36	28.94	40.57	28.715	$-0.0312+0.2157$	360
25.76	8.95	10.27	93.46	2.82	1.37	1.31	28.59	39.74	28.390	$-0.0335+0.2194$	361
26.10	9.12	10.46	89.75	2.72	1.33	1.28	28.33	38.33	28.158	$-0.0336+0.2231$	362
25.86	8.68	10.18	85.32	2.64	1.29	1.24	28.16	37.15	28.009	$-0.0337+0.2253$	363
26.15	8.99	10.47	84.43	2.64	1.29	1.25	28.11	37.27	27.958	$-0.0335+0.2253$	364
26.19	9.10	10.53	80.83	2.53	1.23	1.20	28.05	37.74	27.925	$-0.0360+0.2248$	365
26.07	8.65	10.18	76.97	2.40	1.17	1.14	28.03	38.15	27.942	$-0.0375+0.2228$	366
26.36	8.76	10.47	76.04	2.32	1.14	1.11	27.82	37.35	27.751	$-0.0381+0.2240$	367
26.42	8.48	10.71	76.32	2.15	1.06	1.03	27.06	34.72	27.038	$-0.0401+0.2291$	368
26.35	8.92	10.32	75.75	2.53	1.24	1.20	28.39	38.45	28.261	$-0.0346+0.2206$	369
20.77	8.16	8.25	116.74	3.48	1.70	0.97	29.68	37.34	29.697	$-0.0325+0.2040$	370
19.60	7.68	7.68	111.57	3.30	1.61	0.90	29.29	38.45	29.369	$-0.0371+0.2048$	371
20.99	8.38	8.49	117.12	3.49	1.70	0.97	29.27	38.84	29.290	$-0.0353+0.2057$	372
20.61	7.95	8.14	116.00	3.44	1.68	1.00	29.14	39.06	29.148	$-0.0354+0.2069$	373
19.14	7.25	7.83	101.34	3.00	1.46	0.73	28.68	38.63	28.895	$-0.0476+0.2070$	374
21.67	8.48	9.05	118.38	3.52	1.72	1.05	28.99	38.16	28.956	$-0.0344+0.2097$	375
21.23	8.13	8.69	115.00	3.43	1.67	1.06	28.94	38.13	28.896	$-0.0343+0.2102$	376
21.43	8.75	9.09	111.82	3.36	1.66	1.03	28.99	38.12	28.968	$-0.0348+0.2094$	377
21.25	8.63	8.87	107.13	3.19	1.56	0.98	29.10	38.06	29.110	$-0.0355+0.2080$	378
20.84	7.95	8.39	99.96	2.99	1.46	0.94	29.28	39.14	29.325	$-0.0371+0.2070$	379
21.49	8.15	8.71	97.43	2.91	1.43	0.96	29.42	40.74	29.448	$-0.0375+0.2070$	380
21.45	7.72	8.53	95.88	2.84	1.39	0.98	29.09	40.67	29.100	$-0.0393+0.2099$	381
21.68	7.68	8.52	90.44	2.69	1.32	0.98	29.90	44.60	29.917	$-0.0385+0.2041$	382
22.14	7.71	8.72	84.82	2.50	1.22	0.93	28.55	39.05	28.602	$-0.0422+0.2132$	383
23.29	8.24	9.36	83.78	2.48	1.21	0.97	28.72	37.85	28.748	$-0.0386+0.2131$	384
23.09	8.02	9.24	79.13	2.33	1.14	0.93	28.33	37.77	28.377	$-0.0418+0.2158$	385
23.39	8.04	9.40	76.27	2.22	1.09	0.91	27.99	37.98	28.055	$-0.0448+0.2182$	386
24.01	8.20	9.87	71.13	2.07	1.02	0.88	27.86	36.87	27.951	$-0.0452+0.2199$	387
25.86	9.10	10.73	87.53	2.77	1.35	1.16	28.89	35.19	28.795	$-0.0296+0.2167$	388
26.37	9.08	11.00	95.78	2.86	1.39	1.30	28.55	34.44	28.382	$-0.0258+0.2207$	389
27.40	9.43	11.66	94.57	2.69	1.32	1.25	28.40	33.72	28.257	$-0.0275+0.2218$	390
28.24	9.75	12.17	95.24	2.80	1.37	1.32	28.10	33.30	27.923	$-0.0259+0.2273$	391
29.06	10.17	12.89	86.95	2.81	1.37	1.33	27.81	32.53	27.633	$-0.0250+0.2298$	392
29.01	10.23	12.88	86.60	2.77	1.35	1.31	27.30	32.50	27.125	$-0.0278+0.2337$	393
28.98	10.07	12.83	83.63	2.64	1.29	1.25	27.30	32.36	27.164	$-0.0294+0.2326$	394

		POPULATION, IN 1000'S				AGE STRUCTURE				
		Observed at mid-year	Projected		Total re-productive value (in 1000's)	Percent at age			Depen-dency ratio (× 100)	Departure from stability (Δ percent)
SERIES NUMBER	AREA AND YEAR		5 years	10 years		<15	15–64	⩾65		
		1	2	3	4	5	6	7	8	9
395	East Germany	1952	18328	18731	19085	4008	22.17	66.50	11.33	50.37	8.3
396	(Incl. East	1953–55	18059	18458	18814	3850	21.47	66.58	11.95	50.20	8.7
397	Berlin)	1956–58	17517	17784	17940	3527	20.56	66.45	12.99	50.48	7.5
398		1959–61	17241	17523	17679	3491	21.08	65.24	13.68	53.28	8.9
399		1962	17102	17350	17505	3463	22.47	63.37	14.16	57.81	9.4
400		1963	17155	17468	17676	3513	23.00	62.71	14.29	59.45	9.6
401		1964	16992	17245	17420	3499	23.61	61.94	14.45	61.44	9.8
402		1965	17032	17223	17359	3465	23.86	61.57	14.57	62.42	9.0
403		1966	17064	17232	17362	3440	23.83	61.36	14.81	62.97	8.0
404		1967	17082	17192	17303	3309	23.81	61.14	15.05	63.56	6.8
405	West Germany	1960	55585	57144	58389	12587	21.33	67.82	10.85	47.45	7.1
406	(Incl. West	1961	56175	57947	59286	12720	21.70	67.22	11.08	48.77	7.4
407	Berlin)	1962	56938	58630	59875	12727	21.94	66.79	11.27	49.72	6.4
408		1963	57587	59299	60576	13002	22.19	66.36	11.45	50.71	7.1
409		1964	58266	60145	61501	13160	22.40	65.91	11.69	51.71	7.7
410		1965	59012	60623	61771	13124	22.56	65.52	11.92	52.62	7.3
411		1966	59638	61236	62397	13250	22.76	65.08	12.16	53.66	7.1
412		1967	59873	61327	62382	13147	23.01	64.51	12.48	55.02	6.0
413	Greece	1956–58	8096	8576	9031	2179	26.22	66.03	7.75	51.44	12.7
414		1959–61	8327	8779	9172	2100	26.11	65.77	8.12	52.04	12.8
415		1962	8451	8860	9216	2089	25.70	65.69	8.61	52.24	12.5
416		1963	8480	8874	9222	2066	25.64	65.67	8.69	52.27	13.2
417		1964	8510	8913	9272	2081	25.61	65.51	8.88	52.64	10.6
418		1965	8550	8951	9309	2057	25.56	65.41	9.03	52.89	10.4
419		1966–68	8716	9141	9530	2098	25.25	65.34	9.41	53.05	7.8
420	Hungary	1950–52	9423	9810	10147	2382	25.00	67.06	7.94	49.12	5.6
421		1953–55	9706	10218	10684	2545	25.49	66.32	8.19	50.78	5.9
422		1956–58	9839	10169	10450	2265	25.94	65.54	8.52	52.57	5.3
423		1959–61	9984	10192	10368	2047	25.32	65.65	9.03	52.33	10.3
424		1962	10061	10158	10240	1919	24.79	65.71	9.50	52.19	12.7
425		1963	10088	10231	10345	1921	24.32	65.92	9.76	51.70	13.0
426		1964	10120	10258	10374	1889	23.80	66.15	10.05	51.18	13.2
427		1965	10148	10265	10365	1872	23.28	66.37	10.35	50.65	12.0
428		1966	10179	10354	10506	1887	22.76	66.61	10.63	50.13	10.6
429		1967	10215	10410	10595	1943	22.29	66.79	10.92	49.72	7.5
430	Iceland	1920	94	100	107	39	33.16	59.89	6.95	66.98	2.5
431		1950	143	158	176	49	30.56	61.89	7.55	61.58	4.4
432		1955	158	177	193	55	33.24	59.20	7.56	68.94	6.1
433		1960	176	196	219	63	34.80	57.14	8.06	75.02	6.7
434		1962	182	203	222	64	34.97	56.76	8.27	76.18	4.9
435		1965	192	213	233	67	34.53	57.04	8.43	75.31	3.9
436	Ireland	1926	2976	3081	3197	1038	29.20	61.66	9.14	62.19	3.5
437		1936	2972	3053	3149	975	27.64	62.70	9.66	59.48	3.3
438		1946	2961	3102	3251	992	27.85	61.51	10.64	62.57	3.6
439		1951	2958	3065	3190	949	28.93	60.37	10.70	65.63	4.3
440		1955–57	2895	3029	3178	946	30.09	58.97	10.94	69.57	6.1
441		1960–62	2815	2953	3132	955	31.18	57.63	11.19	73.54	10.1
442		1966	2884	3038	3246	997	31.22	57.58	11.20	73.67	10.2
443		1967	2899	3066	3275	992	31.28	57.51	11.21	73.88	9.1
444		1968	2910	3067	3276	987	31.34	57.45	11.21	74.09	8.8
445	Italy	1931	41225	43392	45620	15293	29.79	62.90	7.31	58.98	6.3
446		1936	42493	44362	46213	14665	30.98	61.48	7.54	62.64	8.1
447		1950–52	47043	49053	51006	13157	26.38	65.40	8.22	52.89	9.1
448		1955	48782	50861	52778	12726	25.55	65.60	8.85	52.43	7.5
449		1960–62	50521	52627	54520	12745	24.78	65.79	9.43	52.00	5.5
450		1964	52130	54668	56974	13783	24.24	66.04	9.72	51.42	4.2
451		1965	52686	54965	57039	13087	24.30	65.77	9.93	52.05	4.5
452		1966	53128	55473	57573	13076	24.35	65.58	10.07	52.49	4.7

VITAL RATES PER THOUSAND POPULATION

Crude (both sexes)			Standardized on U.S., 1960 (both sexes)		Intrinsic (females)			INFANT MORTALITY RATE per 1000 births	$1000\,{}_4M_1$		$1000\,{}_5M_{50}$		SERIES NUMBER
Birth 10	Death 11	Increase 12	Birth 13	Death 14	Birth 15	Death 16	Increase 17	18	Males 19	Females 20	Males 21	Females 22	
16.70	12.09	4.60	15.42	11.34	15.91	13.68	2.23	61.76	2.74	2.29	10.31	6.48	395
16.35	11.93	4.42	15.23	10.68	15.58	13.34	2.23	52.73	2.31	1.95	9.30	5.94	396
15.72	12.54	3.18	14.55	10.35	14.65	13.70	0.95	46.70	2.17	1.70	8.83	5.61	397
17.13	13.27	3.86	15.53	10.27	16.14	12.31	3.83	39.21	1.88	1.48	8.73	5.47	398
17.42	13.68	3.74	16.05	10.21	16.93	11.55	5.38	32.21	1.68	1.33	8.70	5.51	399
17.57	12.94	4.63	16.29	9.62	17.19	11.21	5.98	32.09	1.63	1.25	8.27	5.30	400
17.18	13.31	3.87	16.21	9.76	17.17	11.16	6.01	28.89	1.35	1.11	8.34	5.23	401
16.50	13.52	2.98	15.76	9.84	16.44	11.57	4.87	24.76	1.43	1.05	8.27	5.19	402
15.70	13.22	2.48	15.34	9.55	16.02	11.74	4.28	22.89	1.24	1.05	8.45	5.36	403
14.80	13.29	1.51	14.87	9.51	15.28	12.20	3.08	21.36	1.21	0.92	8.66	5.25	404
17.43	11.57	5.86	15.55	10.51	16.05	12.24	3.81	35.08	1.45	1.18	9.59	5.27	405
18.03	11.17	6.86	16.11	9.93	16.74	11.57	5.18	33.48	1.51	1.19	9.36	5.33	406
17.89	11.32	6.56	15.94	9.92	16.52	11.59	4.93	30.14	1.30	1.09	9.34	5.24	407
18.30	11.69	6.62	16.34	10.12	17.11	11.20	5.91	28.13	1.34	1.08	9.40	5.26	408
18.29	11.05	7.23	16.43	9.45	17.08	10.96	6.12	26.00	1.21	0.91	9.17	5.12	409
17.70	11.48	6.21	16.13	9.69	16.74	11.21	5.54	24.17	1.18	0.96	9.38	5.32	410
17.61	11.51	6.10	16.33	9.63	17.03	10.99	6.04	23.61	1.17	0.93	9.26	5.27	411
17.03	11.48	5.55	16.01	9.49	16.60	11.18	5.43	22.86	1.12	0.88	9.29	5.18	412
19.33	7.38	11.95	14.70	8.51	14.24	13.41	0.83	41.04	2.56	2.47	7.18	4.37	413
18.74	7.42	11.32	14.24	8.35	13.69	13.59	0.10	39.67	2.05	1.84	6.63	4.06	414
18.01	7.88	10.13	14.12	7.96	13.60	13.53	0.07	40.64	1.90	1.85	6.84	4.28	415
17.48	7.88	9.60	13.86	8.12	13.20	13.89	-0.69	38.55	1.57	1.49	6.38	3.90	416
17.99	8.16	9.83	14.52	8.33	14.24	12.99	1.25	36.32	1.56	1.38	6.98	3.85	417
17.71	7.87	9.85	14.50	7.99	14.15	12.87	1.28	34.04	1.35	1.19	6.58	3.86	418
18.27	8.15	10.12	15.29	8.00	15.22	11.98	3.24	34.26	1.21	1.10	6.54	3.78	419
20.24	11.47	8.76	16.52	13.23	17.43	13.96	3.47	80.03	3.54	3.26	11.89	7.72	420
22.00	10.87	11.13	18.43	12.34	20.06	11.50	8.56	63.76	2.65	2.42	10.17	6.84	421
17.56	10.36	7.21	15.32	11.39	15.75	13.60	2.15	60.30	2.13	1.93	9.72	6.26	422
14.62	10.08	4.55	13.02	10.76	12.42	15.89	-3.47	49.17	1.66	1.46	8.92	5.80	423
12.93	10.76	2.16	11.60	11.25	10.44	18.21	-7.77	47.95	1.83	1.57	8.94	5.82	424
13.12	9.90	3.22	11.72	10.15	10.52	17.63	-7.11	42.91	1.46	1.40	8.48	5.46	425
13.06	9.96	3.09	11.62	9.98	10.36	17.64	-7.28	41.30	1.25	1.24	8.32	5.27	426
13.11	10.65	2.45	11.63	10.47	10.51	17.59	-7.08	40.37	1.45	1.21	8.66	5.22	427
13.61	10.02	3.59	12.10	9.69	11.01	16.71	-5.70	38.38	1.23	1.01	8.59	5.30	428
14.58	10.72	3.85	12.97	10.14	12.38	15.32	-2.94	36.99	1.29	1.07	8.62	5.21	429
27.90	14.44	13.46	25.87	16.29	25.84	14.35	11.49	88.56	13.00	13.74	15.35	9.93	430
28.69	7.86	20.82	25.30	8.43	26.72	6.77	19.95	22.40	1.51	1.17	6.71	6.05	431
28.48	6.95	21.53	26.29	7.41	29.02	5.48	23.54	23.19	1.20	0.77	6.96	4.68	432
27.93	6.63	21.30	27.60	7.14	30.04	5.05	24.99	13.50	1.50	1.01	8.42	4.83	433
25.82	6.77	19.04	25.99	7.25	28.61	5.39	23.22	17.24	1.35	0.88	8.57	4.65	434
24.55	6.71	17.83	24.29	7.17	27.63	5.67	21.96	15.04	1.58	1.21	5.84	6.46	435
20.55	14.02	6.53	20.66	14.82	21.49	15.08	6.41	82.06	9.62	9.54	12.58	13.42	436
19.55	14.33	5.23	19.68	14.64	20.64	14.61	6.02	80.29	7.28	6.92	13.77	12.61	437
22.94	14.00	8.94	22.15	13.35	22.96	11.75	11.21	66.30	3.94	3.56	12.16	11.34	438
21.26	14.33	6.93	21.48	13.22	22.59	10.62	11.97	45.37	2.76	2.41	11.78	9.59	439
21.14	12.09	9.05	22.69	10.71	23.61	8.76	14.85	35.88	1.69	1.35	10.17	7.91	440
21.59	11.99	9.60	25.40	10.02	26.34	7.23	19.11	28.64	1.33	1.14	9.38	7.17	441
21.57	12.18	9.40	25.84	10.24	26.84	6.85	20.00	24.95	0.98	0.91	9.89	7.12	442
21.15	10.83	10.32	25.12	9.17	26.09	6.83	19.26	24.43	0.94	0.65	9.17	6.34	443
20.97	11.40	9.57	24.66	9.63	25.83	6.94	18.89	20.98	0.91	0.65	8.62	6.13	444
24.83	14.78	10.04	21.02	17.13	22.08	15.93	6.15	115.25	16.54	16.59	12.36	9.49	445
22.65	13.88	8.78	18.71	16.06	19.57	15.84	3.73	102.19	14.15	13.73	11.98	8.96	446
18.59	9.98	8.61	15.63	11.43	15.78	14.13	1.65	68.22	4.46	4.39	10.03	6.16	447
17.82	9.16	8.66	15.17	9.82	15.17	13.32	1.85	50.91	2.54	2.40	9.10	5.11	448
18.32	9.62	8.70	15.71	9.75	15.91	12.31	3.60	43.54	1.96	1.81	9.22	4.99	449
19.49	9.40	10.09	16.99	9.12	17.37	10.98	6.39	36.09	1.55	1.42	8.68	4.79	450
18.80	9.83	8.97	16.60	9.33	17.03	11.16	5.87	36.02	1.47	1.25	8.87	4.86	451
18.44	9.30	9.14	16.42	8.71	16.65	11.08	5.58	34.91	1.28	1.18	8.45	4.72	452

continued

LIFE TABLE VALUES

SERIES NUMBER	AREA AND YEAR		Probability of dying in first year, q_0		Survivors to age 50 per 100,000 births, l_{50}		Expectancy, $\mathring{e}_0$		Expectancy, $\mathring{e}_1$		Expectancy, $\mathring{e}_{50}$
			Males 23	Females 24	Males 25	Females 26	Males 27	Females 28	Males 29	Females 30	Males 31
395	East Germany	1952	0.0644	0.0520	82760	86237	64.28	68.32	67.69	71.05	23.50
396	(Incl. East	1953-55	0.0566	0.0443	84903	88215	65.68	69.83	68.60	72.05	23.77
397	Berlin)	1956-58	0.0504	0.0395	85824	89333	66.19	70.79	68.69	72.69	23.69
398		1959-61	0.0423	0.0333	86709	90363	66.69	71.51	68.63	72.96	23.49
399		1962	0.0355	0.0268	87608	91137	67.25	72.07	68.72	73.04	23.45
400		1963	0.0351	0.0272	87805	91397	67.73	72.65	69.19	73.67	23.86
401		1964	0.0320	0.0244	88189	91753	67.79	72.77	69.03	73.58	23.59
402		1965	0.0272	0.0213	88642	92080	67.99	72.95	68.88	73.53	23.43
403		1966	0.0248	0.0199	88960	92471	68.38	73.32	69.11	73.80	23.62
404		1967	0.0231	0.0176	89278	92767	68.45	73.55	69.06	73.86	23.51
405	West Germany	1960	0.0378	0.0299	86908	91084	66.47	71.84	68.07	73.05	22.89
406	(Incl. West	1961	0.0363	0.0284	87098	91371	66.91	72.43	68.42	73.54	23.28
407	Berlin)	1962	0.0328	0.0256	87553	91769	67.10	72.77	68.37	73.68	23.09
408		1963	0.0305	0.0241	87752	91902	67.04	72.74	68.14	73.54	22.85
409		1964	0.0283	0.0223	87932	92274	67.59	73.58	68.55	74.25	23.31
410		1965	0.0264	0.0208	88402	92520	67.61	73.44	68.44	74.00	23.03
411		1966	0.0267	0.0206	88229	92520	67.57	73.55	68.42	74.09	23.08
412		1967	0.0255	0.0196	88267	92717	67.71	73.84	68.48	74.31	23.17
413	Greece	1956-58	0.0401	0.0392	87998	90017	69.54	72.56	71.43	74.51	26.23
414		1959-61	0.0395	0.0371	88690	91083	70.09	73.33	71.97	75.15	26.39
415		1962	0.0419	0.0367	88910	91191	70.11	73.72	72.16	75.52	26.38
416		1963	0.0385	0.0363	89020	91460	70.20	73.72	72.01	75.48	26.25
417		1964	0.0374	0.0331	88943	91877	69.87	73.75	71.57	75.26	25.84
418		1965	0.0348	0.0312	89604	92308	70.57	74.32	72.11	75.71	26.23
419		1966-68	0.0349	0.0310	89907	92649	70.65	74.50	72.19	75.87	26.13
420	Hungary	1950-52	0.0865	0.0700	77618	82614	60.58	65.09	65.30	68.98	22.49
421		1953-55	0.0694	0.0554	82564	86427	63.52	67.43	67.24	70.37	22.83
422		1956-58	0.0643	0.0504	82965	87712	64.26	68.79	67.67	71.43	23.33
423		1959-61	0.0526	0.0417	85607	89519	65.87	70.30	68.52	72.36	23.40
424		1962	0.0507	0.0414	85732	89649	65.66	70.16	68.15	72.18	23.00
425		1963	0.0473	0.0394	86147	90009	66.60	71.28	68.90	73.20	23.73
426		1964	0.0443	0.0354	86796	90987	67.03	71.86	69.12	73.49	23.77
427		1965	0.0435	0.0345	86950	91022	66.71	71.56	68.73	73.11	23.30
428		1966	0.0431	0.0351	87344	91252	67.47	72.22	69.50	73.84	23.96
429		1967	0.0425	0.0349	86737	91223	66.86	71.95	68.83	73.54	23.50
430	Iceland	1920	0.0837	0.0834	62680	67997	53.31	56.72	57.15	60.84	22.65
431		1950	0.0203	0.0236	85017	90022	68.71	73.84	69.13	74.61	25.87
432		1955	0.0250	0.0201	87884	93465	70.81	76.32	71.62	76.88	26.84
433		1960	0.0165	0.0100	89935	94214	72.53	75.93	72.74	75.70	27.47
434		1962	0.0207	0.0131	88809	93695	71.45	76.53	71.95	76.54	26.92
435		1965	0.0150	0.0149	88758	94124	71.41	76.55	71.49	76.70	26.69
436	Ireland	1926	0.0851	0.0703	70573	69939	57.47	57.86	61.79	61.21	23.20
437		1936	0.0837	0.0683	73320	73524	58.42	59.55	62.72	62.89	22.50
438		1946	0.0692	0.0558	78353	78901	61.43	63.63	64.98	66.38	22.60
439		1951	0.0497	0.0377	82535	84854	63.58	66.18	65.89	67.77	22.04
440		1955-57	0.0394	0.0303	87324	89469	67.11	70.22	68.86	71.41	23.43
441		1960-62	0.0312	0.0244	88857	91266	68.12	71.88	69.31	72.67	23.52
442		1966	0.0269	0.0208	89721	92452	68.07	72.39	68.95	72.92	22.86
443		1967	0.0259	0.0206	90216	92667	69.12	73.47	69.95	74.01	23.82
444		1968	0.0215	0.0190	89650	92421	68.69	73.21	69.20	73.62	23.37
445	Italy	1931	0.1131	0.1009	67046	69412	53.80	55.92	59.62	61.16	22.28
446		1936	0.1027	0.0884	69219	72783	55.39	58.28	60.70	62.89	22.41
447		1950-52	0.0694	0.0604	81636	85157	63.83	67.42	67.57	70.74	23.92
448		1955	0.0533	0.0455	84703	88580	66.39	70.77	69.11	73.13	24.57
449		1960-62	0.0459	0.0380	86377	90416	66.83	72.05	69.04	73.88	23.90
450		1964	0.0404	0.0337	87269	91395	67.71	73.17	69.56	74.71	24.22
451		1965	0.0384	0.0306	87588	91750	67.68	73.18	69.37	74.48	23.90
452		1966	0.0373	0.0306	88247	92941	68.44	74.24	70.09	75.58	24.43

[94]

FERTILITY MEASURES (FEMALES)

Females 32	Expectancy, $\mathring{e}_{70}$ Males 33	Females 34	General fertility rate 35	Total fertility rate 36	Gross reproduction rate 37	Total, NRR 38	Mean, μ 39	Variance, σ^2 40	Generation, T 41	Complex root, r_2 42	SERIES NUMBER
26.02	9.75	10.60	75.6C	2.39	1.15	1.06	27.17	34.02	27.131	$-0.0388+0.2318$	395
26.43	9.83	10.77	75.5C	2.36	1.14	1.06	26.95	33.95	26.909	$-0.0407+0.2337$	396
26.74	9.79	10.96	75.31	2.25	1.09	1.03	26.67	32.64	26.649	$-0.0413+0.2355$	397
26.78	9.66	10.89	85.45	2.40	1.16	1.11	26.30	33.23	26.237	$-0.0404+0.2413$	398
26.74	9.50	10.83	88.14	2.48	1.20	1.15	26.02	33.25	25.927	$-0.0408+0.2452$	399
27.27	9.92	11.32	88.45	2.51	1.22	1.17	26.00	33.08	25.898	$-0.0402+0.2450$	400
27.11	9.68	11.16	87.48	2.5C	1.22	1.17	26.13	32.70	26.031	$-0.0386+0.2432$	401
27.05	9.45	11.08	84.42	2.44	1.18	1.14	26.20	32.15	26.118	$-0.0384+0.2425$	402
27.21	9.70	11.25	8C.53	2.38	1.16	1.12	26.10	30.66	26.031	$-0.0373+0.2432$	403
27.22	9.61	11.28	75.95	2.30	1.11	1.08	25.40	29.59	25.350	$-0.0407+0.2507$	404
26.63	9.37	10.78	82.C4	2.41	1.17	1.12	28.83	33.44	28.759	$-0.0287+0.2179$	405
27.10	9.78	11.24	85.87	2.50	1.21	1.16	28.65	33.36	28.558	$-0.0279+0.2200$	406
27.18	9.59	11.26	85.1C	2.47	1.20	1.15	28.54	32.87	28.453	$-0.0277+0.2206$	407
27.0C	9.37	11.11	86.95	2.54	1.23	1.18	28.51	32.33	28.410	$-0.0259+0.2207$	408
27.65	9.84	11.76	87.07	2.55	1.24	1.19	28.54	32.42	28.437	$-0.0253+0.2200$	409
27.34	9.56	11.49	85.2C	2.5C	1.21	1.17	28.47	32.89	28.369	$-0.0264+0.2200$	410
27.47	9.57	11.56	85.94	2.53	1.23	1.19	28.28	33.06	28.175	$-0.0271+0.2215$	411
27.63	9.63	11.70	84.C1	2.48	1.21	1.16	28.14	33.35	28.041	$-0.0291+0.2223$	412
28.58	11.50	12.24	8C.33	2.27	1.09	1.02	29.20	33.37	29.183	$-0.0286+0.2133$	413
28.74	11.49	12.20	79.70	2.20	1.06	1.00	28.73	31.47	28.729	$-0.0287+0.2163$	414
29.07	11.70	12.78	77.98	2.19	1.06	1.00	28.59	31.49	28.594	$-0.0299+0.2174$	415
28.87	11.39	12.44	75.09	2.15	1.04	0.98	28.47	31.63	28.480	$-0.0311+0.2179$	416
28.56	11.07	12.17	77.34	2.25	1.09	1.04	28.21	31.55	28.187	$-0.0300+0.2204$	417
28.91	11.39	12.45	76.42	2.25	1.09	1.04	28.09	32.16	28.069	$-0.0307+0.2210$	418
28.89	11.27	12.35	79.17	2.37	1.14	1.09	27.82	31.63	27.764	$-0.0293+0.2237$	419
24.94	9.24	10.21	86.79	2.55	1.23	1.10	27.11	37.97	27.039	$-0.0450+0.2314$	420
25.02	9.16	9.94	97.88	2.85	1.37	1.26	27.20	36.88	27.032	$-0.0377+0.2324$	421
25.72	9.64	10.39	81.25	2.37	1.14	1.06	26.28	34.50	26.245	$-0.0465+0.2421$	422
26.15	9.55	10.61	68.84	2.01	0.97	0.91	25.78	32.30	25.843	$-0.0498+0.2484$	423
25.93	9.07	10.31	59.79	1.8C	0.87	0.82	25.69	31.16	25.825	$-0.0523+0.2475$	424
26.89	9.76	11.21	59.72	1.82	0.88	0.83	25.80	30.00	25.915	$-0.0488+0.2452$	425
26.89	9.82	11.08	58.91	1.8C	0.87	0.83	25.73	28.78	25.845	$-0.0466+0.2458$	426
26.52	9.24	10.74	59.C6	1.81	0.88	0.83	25.65	28.13	25.756	$-0.0456+0.2467$	427
27.13	9.95	11.28	61.41	1.88	0.91	0.86	25.57	28.11	25.659	$-0.0443+0.2478$	428
26.84	9.56	10.97	65.88	2.01	0.97	0.93	25.55	27.59	25.598	$-0.0413+0.2478$	429
25.23	9.7C	10.76	127.37	3.94	1.88	1.43	31.16	40.57	30.922	$-0.0193+0.1976$	430
28.98	11.39	13.10	132.58	3.87	1.83	1.76	28.69	44.23	28.236	$-0.0264+0.2155$	431
29.99	11.73	13.75	139.65	4.02	1.97	1.91	27.98	43.66	27.449	$-0.0291+0.2233$	432
28.82	12.51	12.62	142.36	4.22	2.04	1.99	28.03	44.72	27.458	$-0.0302+0.2249$	433
29.81	12.22	13.16	132.51	3.98	1.94	1.89	28.02	44.21	27.497	$-0.0306+0.2252$	434
29.74	12.41	13.39	124.8C	3.71	1.87	1.82	27.75	45.48	27.241	$-0.0362+0.2246$	435
23.68	10.24	11.17	97.46	3.14	1.53	1.23	31.86	33.16	31.747	$-0.0164+0.1937$	436
23.37	9.85	10.59	94.CC	2.98	1.46	1.21	31.87	34.67	31.764	$-0.0174+0.1927$	437
24.58	9.35	11.03	1C9.77	3.37	1.63	1.42	31.37	35.49	31.164	$-0.0147+0.1970$	438
23.68	8.64	9.46	106.65	3.27	1.59	1.45	31.48	34.15	31.260	$-0.0130+0.1973$	439
25.59	9.64	10.54	110.29	3.45	1.68	1.59	31.46	34.68	31.185	$-0.0101+0.1981$	440
26.33	9.74	11.07	119.10	3.87	1.89	1.80	31.23	34.42	30.882	$-0.0070+0.2012$	441
26.19	9.20	10.95	118.74	3.95	1.91	1.84	30.80	35.26	30.429	$-0.0080+0.2045$	442
27.17	10.17	11.77	116.45	3.84	1.86	1.79	30.73	35.98	30.363	$-0.0094+0.2045$	443
26.91	9.70	11.47	115.48	3.78	1.83	1.77	30.53	35.67	30.181	$-0.0104+0.2060$	444
23.67	8.84	9.41	1C5.C6	3.2C	1.56	1.20	30.35	44.45	30.212	$-0.0280+0.1990$	445
23.98	8.99	9.63	99.25	2.86	1.39	1.12	30.45	40.49	30.373	$-0.0284+0.2002$	446
26.21	9.91	10.74	79.79	2.4C	1.17	1.05	29.77	38.07	29.740	$-0.0311+0.2059$	447
27.48	10.39	11.67	79.CC	2.34	1.14	1.06	29.44	35.59	29.403	$-0.0292+0.2107$	448
27.62	10.12	11.62	83.77	2.42	1.18	1.11	29.14	35.05	29.071	$-0.0286+0.2128$	449
28.15	10.53	12.07	87.31	2.62	1.27	1.21	29.85	34.64	29.734	$-0.0231+0.2094$	450
27.86	10.19	11.78	84.43	2.55	1.24	1.18	28.56	37.09	28.450	$-0.0290+0.2154$	451
28.51	10.65	12.42	83.68	2.52	1.23	1.17	28.58	37.38	28.467	$-0.0296+0.2151$	452

SERIES NUMBER	AREA AND YEAR		POPULATION, IN 1000'S			AGE STRUCTURE					
			Observed at mid-year	Projected 5 years	Projected 10 years	Total reproductive value (in 1000's)	Percent at age <15	15–64	≥65	Dependency ratio (× 100)	Departure from stability (Δ percent)
			1	2	3	4	5	6	7	8	9
453	Luxembourg	1903–07	245	259	274	110	32.48	61.58	5.94	62.38	2.0
454		1908–12	259	270	287	107	32.66	61.35	5.99	62.99	2.4
455		1913–17	260	270	276	94	30.41	63.47	6.12	57.54	5.9
456		1918–22	261	267	271	83	27.94	65.81	6.25	51.95	9.4
457		1920–24	259	267	279	84	26.95	66.74	6.31	49.85	7.0
458		1923–27	274	284	290	83	25.56	68.12	6.32	46.81	7.2
459		1925–29	283	289	300	83	24.72	68.95	6.33	45.02	7.3
460		1928–32	298	308	318	82	24.60	69.04	6.36	44.85	9.0
461		1933–37	297	300	302	69	24.56	68.35	7.09	46.33	15.3
462		1938–42	295	298	294	64	22.78	69.18	8.04	44.55	13.4
463		1943–47	292	292	292	62	20.80	70.19	9.01	42.46	11.0
464		1945–49	290	291	289	60	19.95	70.65	9.40	41.53	9.7
465		1948–52	297	300	301	60	19.34	70.91	9.75	41.03	8.3
466		1953–57	309	314	316	60	19.26	70.54	10.20	41.77	6.8
467		1958–62	318	321	323	62	20.74	68.58	10.68	45.83	5.7
468		1963	330	337	340	64	21.31	67.80	10.89	47.50	4.7
469		1966	334	338	346	70	22.54	65.73	11.73	52.12	4.6
470	Malta	1959–61	329	357	391	124	36.66	56.12	7.22	78.18	3.8
471		1962	329	355	388	118	35.26	57.38	7.36	74.29	5.4
472		1963	328	347	375	111	34.40	58.07	7.53	72.21	8.1
473		1964	324	344	367	108	33.60	58.65	7.75	70.51	8.2
474		1965	319	330	350	100	32.91	58.20	8.89	71.82	10.4
475		1966	317	328	348	94	32.09	59.79	8.12	67.27	12.8
476	Netherlands	1901	5166	5572	6024	2595	34.74	59.26	6.00	68.74	1.5
477		1902	5234	5663	6137	2572	34.68	59.31	6.01	68.61	1.6
478		1903–07	5461	5910	6399	2615	34.67	59.21	6.12	68.86	1.4
479		1908–12	5860	6319	6818	2646	34.51	59.37	6.12	68.44	2.4
480		1913–17	6337	6818	7339	2708	33.82	60.22	5.96	66.06	3.1
481		1918–22	6790	7260	7755	2790	32.72	61.37	5.91	62.93	3.5
482		1923–27	7307	7865	8472	2830	32.00	62.12	5.88	60.96	4.5
483		1928–32	7856	8390	8954	2844	30.79	63.07	6.14	58.55	6.4
484		1933–37	8387	8884	9392	2747	29.70	63.84	6.46	56.65	9.4
485		1938–42	8856	9361	9871	2745	27.99	65.05	6.96	53.71	7.3
486		1943–47	9218	9904	10576	3195	27.80	64.92	7.28	54.04	3.8
487		1948–52	10114	10903	11670	3304	29.30	62.96	7.74	58.82	4.0
488		1953–57	10751	11487	12205	3337	29.90	61.72	8.38	62.03	3.7
489		1958–62	11487	12260	13075	3529	29.99	61.01	9.00	63.92	3.8
490		1963	11966	12775	13671	3649	28.75	61.89	9.36	61.57	3.7
491		1964	12127	12960	13873	3665	28.48	62.06	9.46	61.14	3.7
492		1965	12295	13082	13953	3620	28.26	62.17	9.57	60.84	3.3
493		1966	12456	13206	14032	3565	28.05	62.28	9.67	60.56	3.0
494		1967	12598	13345	14146	3521	27.85	62.34	9.81	60.40	3.6
495	Norway	1950–52	3296	3447	3568	807	24.60	65.73	9.67	52.13	7.3
496		1953–55	3394	3548	3683	829	25.46	64.49	10.05	55.05	6.4
497		1956–58	3492	3648	3789	862	26.15	63.37	10.48	57.81	6.4
498		1959–61	3581	3731	3892	883	25.92	63.05	11.03	58.62	7.1
499		1962	3639	3789	3957	890	25.25	63.32	11.43	57.93	7.1
500		1963	3667	3812	3979	903	25.00	63.39	11.61	57.73	7.7
501		1964	3694	3858	4046	914	24.84	63.38	11.78	57.78	7.9
502		1965	3723	3891	4078	917	24.75	63.28	11.97	58.04	7.7
503		1966	3753	3922	4103	916	24.71	63.12	12.17	58.43	7.2
504		1967	3784	3948	4124	911	24.68	62.96	12.36	58.82	6.5
505	Poland	1960	29577	31663	33734	9036	33.60	60.50	5.90	65.29	7.5
506		1962	30324	32075	33891	8759	33.13	60.75	6.12	64.62	8.7
507		1965	31182	32801	34601	8497	31.41	61.93	6.66	61.47	9.3
508	Portugal	1950–52	8459	8991	9545	3071	29.46	63.51	7.03	57.45	5.1
509		1953–55	8570	9108	9674	3004	29.36	63.31	7.33	57.95	4.6
510		1956–58	8680	9234	9801	2988	29.27	63.11	7.62	58.45	2.9

Crude (both sexes)			Standardized on U.S., 1960 (both sexes)		Intrinsic (females)			INFANT MORTALITY RATE per 1000 births	AGE-SPECIFIC DEATH RATES $1000_4 M_1$		$1000_5 M_{50}$		
Birth 10	Death 11	Increase 12	Birth 13	Death 14	Birth 15	Death 16	Increase 17	18	Males 19	Females 20	Males 21	Females 22	SERIES NUMBER
30.57	18.95	11.61	28.82	22.24	30.73	17.39	13.33	179.52	15.56	16.20	19.76	13.12	453
27.94	17.75	10.19	26.32	21.62	28.16	17.04	11.12	173.54	14.62	15.01	19.73	11.96	454
22.26	17.28	4.98	20.37	21.43	21.93	18.66	3.28	147.31	14.87	15.66	18.27	12.96	455
19.38	15.87	3.51	17.05	20.05	17.70	19.62	-1.92	118.96	13.75	13.84	16.61	13.08	456
20.91	14.46	6.44	18.05	18.60	19.07	17.58	1.49	124.95	10.75	10.86	15.40	11.91	457
20.44	13.75	6.69	17.12	17.52	18.33	17.02	1.30	120.35	8.58	8.17	15.17	10.86	458
20.78	14.05	6.73	17.09	17.74	18.14	17.21	0.93	119.94	8.82	8.14	15.94	10.71	459
20.15	13.34	6.80	16.07	16.76	16.78	17.09	-0.31	97.34	7.34	6.88	15.30	10.50	460
15.55	12.57	2.97	12.23	15.51	11.88	20.23	-8.34	88.57	5.54	5.20	14.34	10.40	461
14.72	12.94	1.78	12.01	15.04	11.51	20.18	-8.67	80.91	5.11	4.22	13.55	9.19	462
14.54	13.26	1.29	12.41	14.51	11.91	19.40	-7.49	78.06	5.28	4.44	13.29	8.63	463
14.55	12.65	1.90	12.67	13.54	12.22	18.26	-6.04	65.93	3.82	3.68	12.26	8.38	464
14.99	12.00	2.99	12.97	12.22	12.69	16.80	-4.11	58.75	2.87	2.66	11.69	7.91	465
15.90	11.91	3.99	13.64	11.06	13.70	14.80	-1.09	43.42	2.32	1.82	11.07	7.42	466
15.80	11.63	4.17	14.38	10.30	14.71	13.23	1.48	33.12	1.52	1.50	11.63	5.41	467
15.50	11.91	3.59	14.85	10.33	14.98	12.98	1.99	28.76	1.29	1.64	10.71	7.29	468
15.54	12.12	3.42	15.07	10.29	16.11	11.92	4.19	26.76	1.04	1.58	12.22	6.72	469
25.10	8.72	16.38	22.61	11.00	24.74	8.00	16.74	34.43	1.19	0.92	9.36	6.47	470
22.84	8.63	14.20	20.95	10.87	22.56	8.92	13.64	35.77	1.43	0.65	8.85	5.62	471
20.33	9.09	11.25	18.78	10.43	20.02	10.06	9.96	33.60	0.71	1.08	9.38	4.65	472
19.76	8.52	11.24	18.04	10.47	19.35	10.37	8.98	34.62	0.94	0.58	9.01	5.71	473
17.63	9.40	8.23	15.99	10.83	16.75	11.97	4.79	33.80	1.01	0.94	8.62	5.69	474
16.82	9.02	7.80	15.05	10.86	15.15	13.11	2.04	30.15	1.08	0.92	8.42	6.40	475
32.60	17.42	15.18	30.61	20.14	31.41	16.63	14.78	115.82	38.10	33.12	13.68	11.87	476
32.24	16.47	15.77	30.14	19.46	30.75	15.67	15.08	94.90	33.77	30.99	14.58	11.40	477
31.31	15.48	15.83	28.98	18.30	29.85	14.92	14.93	96.16	29.57	26.41	13.02	10.86	478
28.95	13.95	15.01	26.63	16.98	27.66	13.94	13.72	102.34	18.11	16.67	12.60	10.82	479
27.25	12.77	14.49	24.87	15.88	25.94	13.29	12.64	93.84	12.14	11.40	11.84	10.31	480
26.41	13.19	13.22	23.82	16.44	24.79	14.24	10.55	86.94	13.76	12.71	11.74	10.70	481
24.61	9.95	14.67	22.05	12.96	22.89	11.75	11.14	48.24	10.67	8.11	9.36	9.23	482
22.77	9.64	13.13	19.90	12.69	20.63	12.26	8.37	53.37	5.87	4.92	8.90	9.16	483
20.41	8.71	11.70	17.29	11.48	17.73	12.85	4.89	41.94	3.74	3.18	8.21	8.24	484
20.69	9.33	11.35	17.37	11.71	18.02	12.46	5.56	39.89	3.71	3.12	8.78	7.87	485
25.83	10.82	15.01	22.14	12.85	23.01	10.91	12.10	53.66	5.74	4.90	10.33	7.58	486
23.23	7.56	15.67	20.77	8.83	21.41	8.95	12.46	26.61	1.82	1.52	7.21	5.40	487
21.43	7.60	13.84	19.89	8.33	20.64	8.81	11.83	20.42	1.46	1.23	7.01	4.73	488
21.07	7.64	13.43	20.43	7.85	21.53	7.99	13.54	16.72	1.34	0.97	7.12	4.19	489
20.88	8.00	12.88	20.56	7.93	21.78	7.77	14.01	16.13	1.16	0.78	7.48	4.11	490
20.69	7.70	12.99	20.35	7.56	21.52	7.77	13.75	15.07	1.13	0.86	7.12	4.16	491
19.94	7.97	11.97	19.56	7.73	20.68	8.16	12.52	14.48	1.08	0.76	7.85	4.02	492
19.24	8.07	11.17	18.65	7.75	19.73	8.64	11.09	14.70	1.08	0.82	7.69	4.21	493
18.95	7.92	11.02	17.98	7.53	18.87	8.96	9.91	13.37	1.10	0.74	7.67	4.06	494
18.76	8.68	10.08	16.40	8.07	16.43	11.28	5.15	26.57	1.59	1.33	6.91	4.57	495
18.59	8.51	10.08	17.48	7.66	18.08	9.87	8.20	21.82	1.43	1.06	6.65	4.41	496
18.16	8.80	9.36	18.48	7.66	19.49	8.98	10.51	20.93	1.27	0.99	6.88	4.02	497
17.45	9.09	8.36	18.71	7.61	19.83	8.68	11.15	18.86	1.14	0.87	6.67	3.71	498
17.11	9.43	7.68	18.63	7.73	19.95	8.57	11.38	17.96	1.19	0.74	7.29	3.98	499
17.26	10.05	7.21	18.76	8.13	20.27	8.53	11.74	17.27	1.27	0.68	6.98	3.90	500
17.75	9.52	8.23	19.12	7.66	20.35	8.36	11.99	16.97	1.17	1.01	7.02	3.67	501
17.80	9.49	8.32	18.94	7.55	20.08	8.38	11.71	16.79	0.97	0.70	7.64	3.38	502
17.87	9.60	8.27	18.68	7.52	19.82	8.46	11.36	14.55	1.09	0.75	6.88	3.69	503
17.65	9.57	8.08	18.08	7.44	19.15	8.74	10.41	14.75	1.04	0.72	7.16	3.81	504
22.35	7.58	14.77	19.30	10.22	20.77	10.10	10.67	60.87	1.75	1.61	9.49	5.45	505
19.77	7.89	11.88	17.46	10.78	18.50	11.18	7.32	54.85	1.62	1.44	9.86	5.64	506
17.52	7.45	10.07	16.16	9.90	16.85	11.57	5.28	41.75	1.37	1.16	8.73	4.97	507
24.60	12.17	12.43	20.91	14.94	21.54	13.87	7.67	109.97	13.50	12.87	12.13	6.78	508
23.71	11.36	12.35	20.18	13.69	20.90	13.03	7.87	103.05	11.18	10.54	10.98	6.36	509
24.06	11.54	12.52	20.45	13.64	21.51	12.51	9.00	99.44	9.93	9.64	11.18	6.04	510

[97]

continued

LIFE TABLE VALUES

SERIES NUMBER	AREA AND YEAR		Probability of dying in first year, q_0		Survivors to age 50 per 100,000 births, l_{50}		Expectancy, $\mathring{e}_0$		Expectancy, $\mathring{e}_1$		Expectancy, $\mathring{e}_{50}$
			Males 23	Females 24	Males 25	Females 26	Males 27	Females 28	Males 29	Females 30	Males 31
453	Luxembourg	1903-07	0.1736	0.1447	54915	60554	45.75	49.15	54.30	56.41	19.58
454		1908-12	0.1694	0.1394	56664	62470	46.64	50.52	55.09	57.65	19.71
455		1913-17	0.1450	0.1223	57669	62382	47.52	50.85	54.53	56.89	19.77
456		1918-22	0.1200	0.0996	61554	64914	50.08	52.86	55.87	57.66	20.17
457		1920-24	0.1245	0.1039	64796	69086	52.02	55.21	58.38	60.57	20.75
458		1923-27	0.1209	0.0998	66703	71940	53.51	57.12	59.83	62.42	21.14
459		1925-29	0.1203	0.1003	65969	71613	53.13	56.96	59.36	62.28	20.96
460		1928-32	0.0986	0.0827	68738	74258	55.20	58.93	60.20	63.22	21.07
461		1933-37	0.0941	0.0717	71580	77652	56.99	61.25	61.89	64.96	21.49
462		1938-42	0.0865	0.0656	72881	79081	57.83	62.31	62.28	65.67	21.68
463		1943-47	0.0822	0.0649	73348	79602	58.31	62.97	62.51	66.32	21.96
464		1945-49	0.0690	0.0557	77305	82483	60.82	64.91	64.31	67.73	22.20
465		1948-52	0.0634	0.0488	80857	85735	62.88	67.28	66.12	69.72	22.55
466		1953-57	0.0488	0.0347	83727	89166	64.79	69.99	67.10	71.50	22.79
467		1958-62	0.0366	0.0278	86506	91247	66.44	71.91	67.95	72.96	22.93
468		1963	0.0329	0.0229	86744	91398	66.87	71.99	68.14	72.68	23.28
469		1966	0.0295	0.0242	86972	91535	66.29	72.63	67.30	73.42	22.12
470	Malta	1959-61	0.0367	0.0297	88124	92047	66.74	71.03	68.28	72.19	22.43
471		1962	0.0363	0.0332	88495	91793	67.07	70.92	68.59	72.35	22.68
472		1963	0.0366	0.0283	88066	92030	66.78	70.89	68.31	71.95	22.39
473		1964	0.0351	0.0321	89952	91982	67.97	71.21	69.44	72.57	22.88
474		1965	0.0380	0.0276	88884	92587	67.71	71.07	69.38	72.08	23.13
475		1966	0.0300	0.0294	90045	92832	67.97	71.24	69.07	72.38	22.70
476	Netherlands	1901	0.1206	0.0961	58146	61553	47.40	50.66	52.84	55.00	21.64
477		1902	0.1004	0.0792	61272	63957	49.54	52.23	54.02	55.68	21.51
478		1903-07	0.1001	0.0817	63396	65977	51.18	53.81	55.83	57.55	21.99
479		1908-12	0.1057	0.0862	68042	69750	54.09	56.30	59.44	60.57	22.13
480		1913-17	0.0975	0.0786	71036	72328	56.29	58.29	61.34	62.24	22.39
481		1918-22	0.0911	0.0725	68822	69876	55.31	57.00	59.82	60.43	22.39
482		1923-27	0.0511	0.0424	79092	79930	62.22	63.66	64.56	65.46	23.71
483		1928-32	0.0581	0.0445	80937	81859	63.28	64.71	66.16	66.71	23.66
484		1933-37	0.0458	0.0354	84122	85416	65.76	67.19	67.90	68.65	24.19
485		1938-42	0.0438	0.0334	82673	86297	64.90	67.72	66.86	69.04	23.85
486		1943-47	0.0573	0.0452	74800	82795	60.48	65.64	63.14	67.73	23.58
487		1948-52	0.0292	0.0229	89197	91691	70.07	72.54	71.17	73.24	25.76
488		1953-57	0.0228	0.0173	90860	93154	71.03	74.02	71.68	74.32	25.69
489		1958-62	0.0186	0.0143	91502	94187	71.39	75.43	71.73	75.52	25.61
490		1963	0.0180	0.0137	91486	94472	71.01	75.80	71.31	75.85	25.13
491		1964	0.0168	0.0129	91376	94570	71.31	76.28	71.52	76.27	25.47
492		1965	0.0160	0.0126	91595	94580	71.14	76.17	71.29	76.14	25.13
493		1966	0.0166	0.0124	91534	94528	71.05	76.14	71.25	76.10	25.12
494		1967	0.0148	0.0119	91543	94625	71.20	76.59	71.27	76.51	25.21
495	Norway	1950-52	0.0292	0.0227	88685	92139	70.59	73.98	71.70	74.69	26.57
496		1953-55	0.0242	0.0186	89993	93428	71.38	75.13	72.14	75.54	26.59
497		1956-58	0.0231	0.0180	90360	93880	71.33	75.48	72.01	75.86	26.29
498		1959-61	0.0211	0.0159	90526	94333	71.29	75.89	71.83	76.11	26.08
499		1962	0.0204	0.0148	90502	94588	70.98	76.02	71.46	76.16	25.71
500		1963	0.0189	0.0151	90827	94583	70.83	75.47	71.19	75.63	25.31
501		1964	0.0185	0.0149	90828	94727	71.27	76.08	71.60	76.23	25.76
502		1965	0.0186	0.0150	90607	94746	71.10	76.51	71.44	76.67	25.64
503		1966	0.0165	0.0127	91287	94915	71.41	76.62	71.60	76.60	25.59
504		1967	0.0163	0.0130	90973	95163	71.36	76.85	71.54	76.86	25.64
505	Poland	1960	0.0642	0.0514	83332	88416	64.85	70.69	68.29	73.51	23.73
506		1962	0.0584	0.0462	83639	89063	64.56	70.68	67.55	73.09	22.95
507		1965	0.0447	0.0344	85689	90936	66.39	72.32	68.49	73.89	23.50
508	Portugal	1950-52	0.1091	0.0955	70110	75790	55.86	60.95	61.66	66.35	22.58
509		1953-55	0.1030	0.0893	74416	79610	58.34	63.47	64.00	68.66	22.91
510		1956-58	0.0993	0.0866	75366	80678	58.87	64.05	64.32	69.10	22.70

Expectancy, $\stackrel{\circ}{e}_{70}$			General fertility rate	Total fertility rate	Gross reproduction rate	Net maternity function					SERIES NUMBER
Females 32	Males 33	Females 34	35	36	37	Total, NRR 38	Mean, μ 39	Variance, σ^2 40	Generation, T 41	Complex root, r_2 42	
21.07	8.14	8.60	144.36	4.39	2.14	1.51	30.99	39.45	30.719	−0.0168+0.1998	453
21.47	8.12	8.55	133.85	4.02	1.94	1.40	30.49	40.61	30.254	−0.0217+0.2021	454
21.46	7.88	8.40	102.26	3.11	1.52	1.10	30.57	40.76	30.496	−0.0277+0.1982	455
21.75	8.07	8.62	85.10	2.61	1.25	0.94	30.47	39.55	30.513	−0.0322+0.1987	456
22.19	8.49	8.87	89.84	2.76	1.34	1.05	30.31	38.73	30.281	−0.0292+0.2020	457
22.53	8.64	9.02	88.16	2.63	1.29	1.04	29.93	38.96	29.907	−0.0313+0.2042	458
22.52	8.50	8.95	89.80	2.62	1.28	1.03	29.61	38.67	29.575	−0.0327+0.2061	459
22.72	8.54	9.06	86.45	2.47	1.19	0.99	29.27	38.67	29.272	−0.0354+0.2083	460
23.19	8.77	9.38	66.55	1.88	0.91	0.78	29.22	37.04	29.389	−0.0412+0.2067	461
23.50	8.99	9.50	63.32	1.85	0.89	0.77	29.22	34.95	29.383	−0.0384+0.2071	462
24.05	9.23	9.73	62.89	1.91	0.92	0.80	29.44	33.99	29.579	−0.0361+0.2058	463
24.39	9.23	9.86	62.82	1.96	0.94	0.84	29.07	32.15	29.183	−0.0351+0.2110	464
25.04	9.51	10.33	66.32	2.01	0.97	0.89	28.70	31.87	28.773	−0.0342+0.2145	465
25.76	9.68	10.82	73.74	2.12	1.03	0.97	28.16	31.37	28.186	−0.0334+0.2206	466
26.58	9.61	10.93	77.07	2.24	1.09	1.04	27.62	30.31	27.604	−0.0320+0.2275	467
26.39	10.22	10.88	76.81	2.31	1.10	1.06	27.42	29.60	27.409	−0.0312+0.2301	468
26.92	9.36	11.45	76.10	2.35	1.16	1.12	27.26	29.94	27.198	−0.0302+0.2316	469
25.24	9.01	10.43	117.77	3.49	1.70	1.63	29.35	40.05	28.998	−0.0238+0.2152	470
25.34	9.06	10.62	103.30	3.24	1.55	1.48	29.15	39.30	28.869	−0.0268+0.2167	471
25.00	9.11	9.64	90.72	2.90	1.39	1.33	28.98	38.92	28.784	−0.0310+0.2168	472
25.49	9.54	10.81	86.96	2.79	1.36	1.30	29.09	38.70	28.906	−0.0308+0.2156	473
25.02	10.55	−9.94	77.11	2.47	1.20	1.15	29.39	38.65	29.289	−0.0334+0.2103	474
25.08	9.56	10.06	73.03	2.33	1.11	1.06	29.20	42.15	29.160	−0.0369+0.2167	475
22.97	8.81	9.37	147.17	4.65	2.27	1.59	31.88	37.40	31.594	−0.0120+0.1945	476
22.84	8.71	9.14	145.08	4.58	2.22	1.61	31.91	37.41	31.615	−0.0117+0.1944	477
23.22	8.94	9.48	140.22	4.40	2.15	1.60	31.88	37.33	31.591	−0.0118+0.1944	478
23.25	8.99	9.49	129.27	4.05	1.97	1.54	31.84	37.58	31.573	−0.0133+0.1944	479
23.48	9.17	9.62	120.67	3.79	1.84	1.49	31.73	38.08	31.474	−0.0150+0.1948	480
23.23	9.08	9.50	115.41	3.63	1.76	1.39	31.61	38.18	31.403	−0.0172+0.1948	481
24.25	9.66	10.07	107.06	3.36	1.63	1.42	31.77	37.86	31.549	−0.0160+0.1940	482
24.14	9.55	9.91	97.75	3.03	1.47	1.30	31.81	37.65	31.648	−0.0180+0.1929	483
24.67	9.84	10.16	87.15	2.63	1.28	1.17	31.72	39.27	31.615	−0.0223+0.1918	484
24.79	9.53	10.10	87.92	2.66	1.29	1.19	30.81	36.58	30.707	−0.0225+0.2002	485
25.01	9.60	10.18	111.31	3.38	1.63	1.45	31.02	35.32	30.798	−0.0146+0.2007	486
26.95	10.83	11.25	105.71	3.17	1.54	1.47	30.94	36.31	30.703	−0.0152+0.2011	487
27.62	10.85	11.56	102.37	3.05	1.48	1.43	30.41	35.46	30.189	−0.0170+0.2056	488
28.50	11.02	12.09	103.69	3.15	1.53	1.49	29.75	34.07	29.503	−0.0162+0.2120	489
28.71	10.78	12.24	100.72	3.18	1.54	1.50	29.36	33.36	29.110	−0.0163+0.2155	490
29.16	11.27	12.68	99.41	3.15	1.53	1.49	29.21	32.96	28.973	−0.0166+0.2166	491
29.02	10.94	12.53	95.88	3.03	1.47	1.43	28.98	32.82	28.761	−0.0184+0.2183	492
29.01	10.93	12.53	92.72	2.89	1.41	1.37	28.75	32.52	28.556	−0.0201+0.2200	493
29.41	11.08	12.89	91.37	2.79	1.36	1.32	28.55	32.09	28.385	−0.0215+0.2215	494
28.32	11.45	12.12	86.73	2.52	1.22	1.16	29.65	39.36	29.540	−0.0299+0.2073	495
28.72	11.62	12.38	90.13	2.70	1.31	1.27	29.03	38.41	28.864	−0.0295+0.2144	496
28.84	11.43	12.31	92.02	2.86	1.39	1.35	28.59	37.20	28.383	−0.0283+0.2202	497
28.98	11.30	12.49	90.20	2.90	1.41	1.37	28.27	35.88	28.065	−0.0272+0.2240	498
28.93	11.10	12.41	88.27	2.89	1.41	1.37	27.83	34.92	27.623	−0.0277+0.2283	499
28.35	10.77	11.72	89.15	2.90	1.42	1.38	27.81	34.58	27.595	−0.0269+0.2280	500
28.97	11.21	12.38	91.85	2.96	1.43	1.39	27.73	34.35	27.515	−0.0264+0.2290	501
29.38	11.17	12.67	92.65	2.93	1.41	1.38	27.68	34.78	27.469	−0.0276+0.2290	502
29.34	11.02	12.68	93.78	2.89	1.40	1.36	27.55	34.47	27.340	−0.0281+0.2304	503
29.49	11.17	12.87	93.16	2.80	1.36	1.33	27.43	34.21	27.247	−0.0294+0.2312	504
27.52	10.18	11.96	106.05	2.99	1.44	1.34	27.47	37.38	27.258	−0.0351+0.2338	505
26.96	9.38	11.34	92.90	2.71	1.30	1.22	27.33	35.59	27.193	−0.0365+0.2357	506
27.40	9.74	11.61	80.02	2.51	1.21	1.15	27.21	34.36	27.111	−0.0369+0.2365	507
25.94	9.19	10.60	104.89	3.21	1.55	1.26	30.38	43.13	30.205	−0.0286+0.2020	508
26.35	9.30	10.80	102.42	3.10	1.50	1.27	30.19	42.79	30.011	−0.0292+0.2042	509
26.22	9.16	10.63	105.36	3.14	1.53	1.30	29.72	42.58	29.522	−0.0299+0.2076	510

SERIES NUMBER	AREA AND YEAR		POPULATION, IN 1000'S			AGE STRUCTURE					
			Observed at mid-year	Projected 5 years	Projected 10 years	Total re-productive value (in 1000's)	Percent at age <15	15–64	≥65	Dependency ratio (× 100)	Departure from stability (Δ percent)
			1	2	3	4	5	6	7	8	9
511	Portugal	1959–61	8865	9454	10057	3008	29.18	62.90	7.92	58.98	2.7
512	*cont*	1962	9008	9624	10254	3031	29.11	62.77	8.12	59.31	2.4
513		1963	9074	9648	10242	2979	29.08	62.70	8.22	59.49	2.6
514		1964	9143	9744	10360	3003	29.05	62.63	8.32	59.66	2.6
515		1965	9234	9810	10400	2942	29.02	62.56	8.42	59.84	2.9
516		1966–68	9415	9958	10489	2859	28.87	62.52	8.61	59.94	3.6
517	Romania	1956–58	17824	18962	19976	5117	27.76	65.69	6.55	52.23	7.3
518		1959–61	18407	19237	19949	4617	28.08	65.01	6.91	53.84	11.6
519		1962	18691	19290	19822	4257	27.88	64.87	7.25	54.15	14.4
520		1963	18813	19459	20034	4171	27.61	65.06	7.33	53.72	15.1
521		1964	18927	19559	20123	4088	27.07	65.37	7.56	52.97	16.0
522		1965	19027	19575	20080	4064	26.33	65.75	7.92	52.10	14.9
523		1966	19136	20042	20602	3976	25.62	66.16	8.22	51.15	19.1
524	Spain	1950	27849	29119	30378	8617	26.23	66.54	7.23	50.28	10.6
525		1960	30401	32307	34122	8907	27.35	64.47	8.18	55.10	4.2
526		1962	30895	32749	34526	8983	27.57	63.96	8.47	56.34	3.3
527		1963	31160	33061	34904	9179	27.67	63.72	8.61	56.93	2.9
528		1966	32102	34046	35934	9369	27.88	63.12	9.00	58.43	3.3
529		1967	32431	34392	36326	9572	27.98	62.90	9.12	58.99	3.0
530	Sweden	1778–82	2104	2197	2292	1114	31.92	63.16	4.92	58.32	3.1
531		1783–87	2147	2193	2238	1078	31.35	63.43	5.22	57.65	3.9
532		1788–92	2161	2219	2272	1100	31.94	62.61	5.45	59.73	2.1
533		1793–97	2274	2374	2470	1163	32.50	62.05	5.45	61.16	2.3
534		1798–1802	2352	2414	2478	1171	32.60	61.91	5.49	61.53	2.2
535		1803–07	2418	2497	2579	1184	32.74	61.83	5.43	61.75	1.6
536		1808–12	2380	2371	2379	1231	31.93	62.90	5.17	58.99	1.8
537		1813–17	2450	2553	2657	1235	31.61	63.22	5.17	58.19	1.9
538		1818–22	2573	2692	2806	1312	32.07	62.51	5.42	59.97	2.8
539		1823–27	2749	2931	3113	1382	34.13	60.35	5.52	65.69	4.3
540		1828–32	2876	2980	3090	1468	35.10	59.56	5.34	67.91	3.0
541		1833–37	3004	3166	3341	1542	35.21	59.65	5.14	67.66	2.8
542		1838–42	3123	3267	3437	1585	33.86	61.43	4.71	62.80	2.2
543		1843–47	3296	3471	3668	1677	33.31	61.86	4.83	61.66	2.2
544		1848–52	3462	3662	3880	1740	32.91	62.30	4.79	60.52	2.0
545		1853–57	3625	3795	3971	1851	33.21	61.91	4.88	61.52	2.1
546		1858–62	3824	4094	4354	1960	33.48	61.34	5.18	63.02	2.3
547		1863–67	4092	4356	4617	2053	34.02	60.60	5.38	65.02	2.2
548		1868–72	4164	4363	4568	1991	34.02	60.58	5.40	65.08	2.9
549		1873–77	4362	4621	4895	2153	33.66	60.93	5.41	64.14	2.9
550		1878–82	4572	4856	5164	2164	32.66	61.54	5.80	62.50	2.5
551		1883–87	4664	4962	5277	2148	32.82	60.66	6.52	64.85	2.2
552		1888–92	4780	5053	5334	2101	33.29	59.16	7.55	69.02	2.2
553		1893–97	4896	5175	5476	2092	32.96	58.97	8.07	69.57	2.4
554		1898–1902	5117	5401	5707	2140	32.49	59.19	8.32	68.94	2.4
555		1903–07	5278	5575	5902	2105	32.07	59.53	8.40	67.98	2.1
556		1908–12	5499	5813	6151	2095	31.80	59.77	8.43	67.31	1.6
557		1913–17	5696	5942	6218	1997	31.04	60.63	8.33	64.93	4.2
558		1918–22	5876	6088	6314	1923	29.39	62.22	8.39	60.70	5.5
559		1923–27	6045	6225	6414	1735	27.49	63.78	8.73	56.80	10.8
560		1928–32	6131	6232	6331	1524	25.04	65.81	9.15	51.94	14.8
561		1933–37	6242	6313	6367	1358	22.53	68.26	9.21	46.50	16.9
562		1938–42	6356	6490	6593	1361	20.52	70.11	9.37	42.63	11.5
563		1943–47	6636	6909	7128	1547	21.51	68.66	9.83	45.65	6.5
564		1948–52	7017	7225	7379	1506	23.30	66.52	10.18	50.35	6.7
565		1953–57	7262	7427	7568	1488	23.75	65.33	10.92	53.07	6.1
566		1958–62	7480	7636	7791	1499	22.39	65.85	11.76	51.86	5.5
567		1965	7734	7962	8177	1587	20.94	66.38	12.68	50.65	5.8
568		1966	7808	8033	8237	1575	20.94	66.19	12.87	51.08	5.5
569		1967	7868	8074	8248	1557	20.96	65.96	13.08	51.61	5.0

VITAL RATES PER THOUSAND POPULATION

Crude (both sexes)			Standardized on U.S., 1960 (both sexes)		Intrinsic (females)			INFANT MORTALITY RATE per 1000 births	1000₄M₁		1000₅M₅₀		SERIES NUMBER
Birth 10	Death 11	Increase 12	Birth 13	Death 14	Birth 15	Death 16	Increase 17	18	Males 19	Females 20	Males 21	Females 22	
24.23	10.99	13.24	20.69	12.64	21.64	11.88	9.76	97.67	8.88	8.41	9.80	5.44	511
24.44	10.75	13.69	20.98	12.14	21.89	11.31	10.58	90.81	7.56	7.23	9.73	5.07	512
23.38	10.80	12.58	20.18	12.20	21.02	11.33	9.69	80.68	6.84	6.33	9.62	5.28	513
23.75	10.60	13.15	20.58	11.78	21.40	11.05	10.35	77.17	6.69	6.25	9.65	5.22	514
22.77	10.31	12.47	19.84	11.37	20.64	10.86	9.77	69.50	5.32	5.00	9.32	4.51	515
21.38	10.29	11.10	18.82	10.89	19.46	11.10	8.35	61.72	4.32	4.03	8.84	4.45	516
22.89	9.60	13.29	17.79	12.29	19.04	12.82	6.23	81.10	5.15	5.04	9.77	6.96	517
18.93	9.23	9.70	15.02	11.58	15.12	14.75	0.38	76.36	3.81	3.71	9.58	6.39	518
16.16	9.23	6.93	13.24	11.65	12.81	16.29	-3.48	60.80	2.61	2.59	9.22	6.27	519
15.67	8.28	7.39	13.05	10.25	12.30	16.20	-3.90	55.98	2.57	2.36	8.45	5.52	520
15.18	8.06	7.13	12.73	9.79	11.82	16.34	-4.52	49.42	2.50	2.37	8.23	5.50	521
14.63	8.59	6.04	12.36	10.26	11.96	16.24	-4.28	44.62	2.12	2.07	8.38	5.80	522
14.30	8.23	6.07	12.18	9.50	10.56	16.56	-6.01	46.60	2.20	2.10	8.19	5.55	523
20.07	10.93	9.14	16.07	13.41	16.12	15.52	0.60	87.88	7.52	7.34	11.86	6.99	524
21.53	8.63	12.90	18.02	9.52	18.60	10.51	8.09	36.99	2.14	1.87	8.58	5.10	525
21.03	8.78	12.25	18.02	9.48	18.64	10.33	8.31	32.86	1.87	1.58	8.56	5.19	526
21.26	8.84	12.42	18.44	9.44	19.14	9.97	9.17	32.45	1.75	1.53	8.80	5.04	527
20.61	8.40	12.21	18.50	8.58	19.13	9.55	9.58	28.08	1.16	1.04	8.04	4.57	528
20.72	8.45	12.27	18.77	8.57	19.40	9.34	10.06	26.13	1.07	0.90	7.87	4.52	529
34.51	25.92	8.59	25.88	29.00	31.16	25.26	5.90	211.62	45.87	44.30	20.79	16.09	530
31.60	27.26	4.34	26.92	31.24	28.57	27.17	1.40	231.45	46.69	44.46	24.50	18.64	531
33.64	27.71	5.93	28.71	31.52	30.61	26.25	4.36	255.30	37.81	36.63	26.90	20.67	532
33.97	24.88	9.09	29.57	28.94	31.40	23.82	7.58	194.30	35.48	33.25	22.37	17.54	533
31.21	25.88	5.33	27.48	31.11	29.38	25.08	4.31	248.96	37.14	35.75	25.53	19.46	534
31.27	24.89	6.39	28.03	29.31	29.97	23.53	6.44	223.07	31.16	29.14	25.95	20.61	535
32.20	33.09	-0.90	28.32	39.19	31.19	30.45	0.74	260.08	48.21	45.19	36.86	28.76	536
33.03	24.67	8.36	28.74	25.19	30.58	23.35	7.23	216.98	35.52	32.80	25.21	19.09	537
34.29	24.90	9.39	29.82	29.31	31.44	23.10	8.34	206.69	34.51	31.89	26.82	20.03	538
34.73	21.59	13.14	31.03	25.27	32.37	18.85	13.51	178.35	22.24	20.59	25.08	17.25	539
32.52	25.82	6.70	29.83	30.91	31.85	22.61	9.25	203.99	31.85	29.42	31.91	22.00	540
32.63	22.13	10.51	30.84	26.84	32.28	20.02	12.25	185.99	24.56	22.45	27.55	19.08	541
30.54	21.73	8.81	29.09	27.34	30.60	20.61	10.00	184.61	25.32	23.67	26.48	19.43	542
30.73	21.20	9.53	28.89	26.54	30.10	20.04	10.05	174.16	27.01	24.75	25.75	17.52	543
31.46	20.54	10.93	28.49	25.71	29.53	19.39	10.14	165.60	25.55	23.19	24.96	16.95	544
32.06	22.83	9.23	28.31	27.57	29.47	22.05	7.42	164.80	34.54	32.11	24.90	18.81	545
34.10	19.87	14.23	30.17	23.40	30.64	19.23	11.42	150.76	30.68	28.75	20.57	15.00	546
32.76	19.70	13.06	29.86	23.52	30.38	18.83	11.55	148.04	30.36	28.10	18.99	14.23	547
29.15	19.40	9.75	27.27	23.97	28.04	19.41	8.62	157.70	28.14	26.49	20.20	14.61	548
30.96	19.22	11.74	29.88	22.60	30.25	18.92	11.33	155.36	27.52	26.34	17.74	13.13	549
29.52	17.56	11.96	28.47	20.34	28.82	17.76	11.06	131.33	26.38	25.34	15.16	11.70	550
29.55	17.05	12.50	28.33	19.37	28.64	16.79	11.85	121.69	23.90	22.71	14.72	11.11	551
27.92	16.75	11.17	27.00	18.70	27.57	16.15	11.42	115.87	19.54	18.78	14.36	11.27	552
27.17	15.88	11.29	26.61	17.31	27.00	15.41	11.59	106.93	16.80	16.42	13.38	10.43	553
26.79	16.19	10.59	26.20	17.38	26.81	15.33	11.48	106.84	16.15	15.38	13.74	11.04	554
25.68	15.00	10.68	24.92	15.82	25.58	14.27	11.31	90.16	12.18	11.47	12.91	10.03	555
24.72	14.11	10.61	23.47	14.84	24.23	13.56	10.66	69.78	12.16	11.10	12.17	9.81	556
21.95	13.83	8.13	20.23	14.71	20.84	14.57	6.27	51.40	14.14	12.69	11.70	9.44	557
20.99	14.19	6.80	18.68	14.97	19.15	15.80	3.35	46.42	14.39	12.52	11.35	9.95	558
17.50	11.91	5.59	15.06	12.63	15.01	16.19	-1.18	42.01	9.54	7.99	9.83	8.98	559
15.20	12.01	3.18	12.52	12.62	11.97	18.83	-6.87	42.55	8.49	7.21	9.85	8.93	560
13.95	11.62	2.33	11.12	11.90	10.15	20.17	-10.01	37.26	6.83	5.25	9.43	8.30	561
15.76	11.14	4.62	12.48	11.05	11.96	17.11	-5.15	31.31	5.17	4.01	8.97	7.39	562
19.81	10.69	9.12	16.43	10.10	17.00	12.19	4.81	23.71	3.65	2.88	7.95	6.51	563
16.64	9.85	6.79	15.05	9.12	15.23	12.51	2.71	18.92	2.05	1.64	7.25	5.68	564
14.81	9.65	5.15	14.58	8.52	14.58	12.54	2.04	16.27	1.65	1.26	6.53	4.83	565
14.02	9.82	4.19	14.39	8.01	14.29	12.43	1.85	15.57	1.14	0.90	6.25	4.36	566
15.88	10.11	5.77	15.63	7.63	16.01	10.83	5.17	13.51	0.75	0.54	6.76	4.18	567
15.80	10.05	5.75	15.33	7.46	15.40	11.15	4.26	12.56	0.80	0.52	6.59	3.98	568
15.42	10.14	5.28	14.75	7.45	14.61	11.73	2.88	12.85	0.60	0.46	6.70	3.85	569

continued

LIFE TABLE VALUES

SERIES NUMBER	AREA AND YEAR		Probability of dying in first year, q_0		Survivors to age 50 per 100,000 births, l_{50}		Expectancy, $\mathring{e}_0$		Expectancy, $\mathring{e}_1$		Expectancy, $\mathring{e}_{50}$
			Males 23	Females 24	Males 25	Females 26	Males 27	Females 28	Males 29	Females 30	Males 31
511	Portugal	1959–61	0.0974	0.0853	77108	82334	60.16	65.57	65.62	70.65	23.34
512	*cont*	1962	0.0918	0.0784	78064	83693	60.95	66.69	66.08	71.34	23.43
513		1963	0.0812	0.0710	79616	84939	61.71	67.41	66.14	71.53	23.10
514		1964	0.0779	0.0679	79725	85111	62.10	67.71	66.32	71.62	23.37
515		1965	0.0712	0.0604	81270	86598	63.12	68.95	66.94	72.36	23.37
516		1966–68	0.0638	0.0545	82232	87632	63.97	69.73	67.30	72.73	23.49
517	Romania	1956–58	0.0821	0.0705	80334	83496	62.12	65.73	66.65	69.69	23.16
518		1959–61	0.0776	0.0665	81921	85150	63.26	67.06	67.56	70.83	23.35
519		1962	0.0618	0.0541	83983	87236	64.44	68.21	67.68	71.11	22.97
520		1963	0.0576	0.0496	84474	88117	65.91	69.73	68.92	72.35	24.32
521		1964	0.0514	0.0437	85304	89090	66.69	70.66	69.30	72.87	24.59
522		1965	0.0471	0.0390	85996	89559	66.57	70.60	68.85	72.45	23.94
523		1966	0.0508	0.0415	85832	89486	71.26	73.54	74.06	75.71	29.61
524	Spain	1950	0.0873	0.0780	73985	78766	58.68	63.44	63.27	67.79	22.68
525		1960	0.0399	0.0317	86945	90418	67.91	72.38	69.72	73.74	24.67
526		1962	0.0355	0.0283	87521	91050	68.18	72.77	69.68	73.88	24.50
527		1963	0.0361	0.0269	87537	91389	68.14	73.01	69.68	74.02	24.47
528		1966	0.0294	0.0241	88631	92523	69.25	74.37	70.34	75.20	24.85
529		1967	0.0279	0.0221	88795	92853	69.24	74.55	70.23	75.23	24.69
530	Sweden	1778–82	0.1974	0.1768	41184	44587	36.00	38.52	43.76	45.71	19.04
531		1783–87	0.2134	0.1913	37393	41684	33.58	36.56	41.59	44.12	17.99
532		1788–92	0.2318	0.2059	35455	42299	33.34	37.32	42.29	45.90	17.83
533		1793–97	0.2185	0.1943	43594	47257	37.45	40.18	46.82	48.79	18.55
534		1798–1802	0.2268	0.2016	41683	45649	35.99	38.89	45.45	47.61	17.56
535		1803–07	0.2072	0.1818	43836	47560	37.81	40.59	46.60	48.53	17.63
536		1808–12	0.2384	0.2081	29265	35682	28.99	32.76	36.95	40.27	15.12
537		1813–17	0.2041	0.1765	42788	47788	37.33	40.76	45.81	48.42	17.83
538		1818–22	0.1953	0.1696	42519	47816	37.42	40.90	45.41	48.18	17.44
539		1823–27	0.1715	0.1473	48318	55346	41.96	46.40	49.58	53.36	18.10
540		1828–32	0.1941	0.1662	40344	48284	36.77	41.27	44.54	48.43	16.36
541		1833–37	0.1780	0.1531	45314	52617	40.25	44.67	47.89	51.68	17.76
542		1838–42	0.1770	0.1520	45156	52219	39.97	44.21	47.49	51.07	17.61
543		1843–47	0.1690	0.1441	47238	54172	40.78	45.20	48.00	51.74	17.77
544		1848–52	0.1622	0.1364	47818	55665	41.54	46.28	48.51	52.53	18.04
545		1853–57	0.1611	0.1377	44015	50167	38.75	42.60	45.12	48.34	18.11
546		1858–62	0.1481	0.1266	50997	55718	43.07	46.54	49.49	52.23	19.68
547		1863–67	0.1464	0.1246	51583	56946	43.35	47.18	49.71	52.84	19.62
548		1868–72	0.1548	0.1319	51313	56332	43.11	46.87	49.94	52.93	19.16
549		1873–77	0.1524	0.1303	51200	56084	43.64	47.22	50.42	53.24	20.36
550		1878–82	0.1317	0.1110	55697	59092	46.58	49.53	52.59	54.66	21.56
551		1883–87	0.1234	0.1023	57500	61006	48.08	51.13	53.80	55.91	21.94
552		1888–92	0.1182	0.0974	59870	62710	49.78	52.44	55.40	57.06	22.03
553		1893–97	0.1088	0.0910	61825	64433	51.51	54.09	56.76	58.47	22.71
554		1898–1902	0.1095	0.0902	61690	64642	51.53	54.26	56.82	58.60	22.62
555		1903–07	0.0935	0.0765	65302	67602	54.28	56.77	58.84	60.44	23.13
556		1908–12	0.0736	0.0598	68080	70716	56.35	58.95	59.80	61.68	23.43
557		1913–17	0.0556	0.0440	69027	71449	56.98	59.58	59.31	61.30	23.41
558		1918–22	0.0506	0.0394	66203	69548	55.96	58.71	57.91	60.10	23.75
559		1923–27	0.0461	0.0355	75805	77984	61.46	63.77	63.41	65.10	24.28
560		1928–32	0.0470	0.0356	76853	78916	62.02	64.11	64.06	65.47	24.18
561		1933–37	0.0411	0.0314	79844	82308	63.75	66.15	65.46	67.28	24.26
562		1938–42	0.0345	0.0264	82797	85896	65.62	68.42	66.95	69.27	24.44
563		1943–47	0.0260	0.0200	85500	88109	67.63	70.16	68.42	70.59	25.02
564		1948–52	0.0212	0.0160	89388	92040	70.04	72.76	70.55	72.94	25.35
565		1953–57	0.0182	0.0139	90681	93557	70.94	74.18	71.24	74.22	25.57
566		1958–62	0.0177	0.0130	91546	94261	71.55	75.22	71.83	75.20	25.73
567		1965	0.0146	0.0119	91746	94547	71.75	76.14	71.81	76.05	25.69
568		1966	0.0145	0.0105	91717	94860	71.89	76.52	71.94	76.33	25.81
569		1967	0.0142	0.0113	91620	94772	71.87	76.58	71.90	76.45	25.77

| Expectancy, e_{70} | | | General fertility rate | Total fertility rate | Gross reproduction rate | Net maternity function | | | | | SERIES NUMBER |
Females 32	Males 33	Females 34	35	36	37	Total, NRR 38	Mean, μ 39	Variance, σ^2 40	Generation, T 41	Complex root, r_2 42	
26.99	9.49	11.05	107.65	3.18	1.54	1.33	29.57	41.58	29.354	$-0.0292+0.2090$	511
27.20	9.64	11.25	109.51	3.22	1.56	1.36	29.55	42.18	29.319	$-0.0293+0.2088$	512
27.00	9.24	10.98	105.33	3.10	1.50	1.33	29.66	42.36	29.443	$-0.0294+0.2073$	513
27.15	9.57	11.23	107.63	3.16	1.52	1.36	29.65	42.74	29.421	$-0.0295+0.2074$	514
27.32	9.59	11.24	103.99	3.05	1.47	1.33	29.61	43.05	29.392	$-0.0308+0.2076$	515
27.32	9.85	11.35	98.95	2.89	1.40	1.28	29.45	45.17	29.256	$-0.0354+0.2064$	516
25.51	9.64	10.53	98.29	2.74	1.33	1.18	27.21	38.94	27.087	$-0.0431+0.2307$	517
25.87	9.83	10.71	83.85	2.31	1.12	1.01	26.43	38.54	26.427	$-0.0558+0.2397$	518
25.54	9.20	10.29	71.34	2.04	0.99	0.91	26.06	36.91	26.131	$-0.0591+0.2448$	519
26.63	10.34	11.07	68.47	2.01	0.97	0.90	25.92	36.78	25.998	$-0.0602+0.2455$	520
26.99	10.54	11.32	65.74	1.96	0.95	0.89	25.90	35.26	25.990	$-0.0560+0.2459$	521
26.48	9.83	10.87	62.98	1.91	0.95	0.89	25.99	34.80	26.067	$-0.0539+0.2441$	522
29.92	17.76	14.99	61.35	1.88	0.91	0.85	26.05	34.78	26.159	$-0.0551+0.2420$	523
26.08	9.39	10.90	81.14	2.47	1.20	1.02	30.63	36.58	30.623	$-0.0277+0.2020$	524
27.76	9.93	11.54	95.20	2.78	1.35	1.27	29.97	33.27	29.825	$-0.0201+0.2097$	525
27.74	9.78	11.49	93.58	2.78	1.35	1.28	29.88	33.04	29.735	$-0.0193+0.2101$	526
27.76	9.78	11.48	94.92	2.84	1.38	1.31	30.01	32.09	29.853	$-0.0175+0.2097$	527
28.52	10.58	12.29	93.14	2.85	1.39	1.33	29.92	33.54	29.747	$-0.0188+0.2098$	528
28.47	10.35	12.23	94.46	2.89	1.41	1.35	30.16	35.50	29.973	$-0.0189+0.2081$	529
20.30	8.03	8.16	145.21	4.53	2.21	1.21	32.24	43.29	32.108	$-0.0216+0.1892$	530
19.63	7.57	8.08	132.36	4.08	2.00	1.05	32.05	42.50	32.024	$-0.0256+0.1893$	531
19.17	7.49	7.82	142.10	4.35	2.12	1.15	32.15	42.48	32.055	$-0.0226+0.1895$	532
19.81	7.38	7.78	145.27	4.48	2.19	1.27	32.19	41.75	32.022	$-0.0195+0.1905$	533
19.14	6.82	7.32	134.23	4.16	2.03	1.15	32.18	41.84	32.082	$-0.0224+0.1895$	534
19.02	7.25	7.67	136.02	4.25	2.08	1.23	32.19	42.10	32.051	$-0.0210+0.1903$	535
16.58	6.35	6.69	136.67	4.30	2.10	1.02	31.92	40.76	31.906	$-0.0259+0.1907$	536
19.41	7.31	7.81	139.11	4.35	2.13	1.26	32.23	40.64	32.074	$-0.0191+0.1903$	537
19.29	7.26	7.86	144.96	4.52	2.20	1.31	32.35	41.08	32.168	$-0.0182+0.1899$	538
20.43	7.63	8.45	153.08	4.71	2.30	1.54	32.28	41.21	31.993	$-0.0140+0.1917$	539
18.44	6.81	7.40	144.89	4.52	2.21	1.35	32.32	40.08	32.123	$-0.0171+0.1906$	540
19.80	7.47	8.09	145.21	4.67	2.28	1.48	32.44	39.70	32.180	$-0.0139+0.1910$	541
19.64	7.27	7.92	132.55	4.40	2.16	1.38	32.62	38.15	32.419	$-0.0144+0.1897$	542
20.00	7.35	7.95	132.55	4.37	2.13	1.39	32.83	37.82	32.631	$-0.0135+0.1884$	543
20.27	7.44	8.16	134.26	4.30	2.10	1.39	32.97	37.88	32.772	$-0.0131+0.1876$	544
19.67	7.49	8.08	135.69	4.28	2.09	1.28	33.04	38.20	32.894	$-0.0156+0.1864$	545
21.47	8.32	8.95	145.69	4.56	2.23	1.46	33.13	39.25	32.899	$-0.0124+0.1864$	546
21.44	8.01	8.83	143.23	4.51	2.20	1.46	33.02	39.85	32.774	$-0.0130+0.1869$	547
21.29	7.79	8.70	130.16	4.12	2.01	1.33	32.96	39.15	32.780	$-0.0152+0.1866$	548
22.38	8.43	9.35	139.76	4.53	2.20	1.44	32.70	41.34	32.452	$-0.0150+0.1880$	549
23.36	8.84	9.77	132.72	4.32	2.10	1.43	32.47	41.50	32.232	$-0.0159+0.1897$	550
23.65	9.08	9.91	135.06	4.30	2.09	1.46	32.36	41.89	32.102	$-0.0156+0.1904$	551
23.54	9.09	9.77	130.78	4.10	2.00	1.44	32.22	42.29	31.970	$-0.0167+0.1909$	552
24.38	9.58	10.35	127.33	4.04	1.96	1.44	32.02	42.31	31.764	$-0.0173+0.1919$	553
24.27	9.50	10.23	124.95	3.98	1.94	1.43	31.68	42.79	31.419	$-0.0188+0.1936$	554
24.75	9.86	10.54	119.66	3.79	1.84	1.42	31.43	42.96	31.175	$-0.0200+0.1948$	555
24.94	9.93	10.60	115.27	3.57	1.73	1.39	31.15	43.73	30.905	$-0.0220+0.1960$	556
24.97	9.79	10.49	100.04	3.08	1.50	1.21	31.00	44.27	30.859	$-0.0267+0.1951$	557
24.89	9.98	10.55	92.97	2.85	1.38	1.11	30.64	44.00	30.560	$-0.0308+0.1969$	558
25.42	10.19	10.81	75.59	2.30	1.12	0.96	30.53	44.37	30.557	$-0.0350+0.1958$	559
25.16	10.07	10.54	64.03	1.91	0.93	0.81	29.99	44.35	30.154	$-0.0418+0.1971$	560
25.32	10.06	10.59	58.04	1.70	0.83	0.74	29.61	42.75	29.832	$-0.0450+0.1995$	561
25.70	10.04	10.57	65.12	1.92	0.93	0.86	29.18	40.38	29.293	$-0.0412+0.2056$	562
26.22	10.37	10.83	86.02	2.52	1.22	1.15	28.87	39.28	28.772	$-0.0326+0.2118$	563
26.78	10.53	11.08	77.45	2.31	1.12	1.08	28.16	39.77	28.104	$-0.0391+0.2164$	564
27.48	10.58	11.41	72.95	2.25	1.09	1.06	27.66	36.86	27.619	$-0.0395+0.2233$	565
28.18	10.68	11.80	70.15	2.23	1.08	1.05	27.45	33.87	27.417	$-0.0360+0.2267$	566
28.93	10.74	12.46	79.23	2.41	1.18	1.15	27.08	33.03	26.994	$-0.0325+0.2297$	567
29.15	10.90	12.55	79.51	2.37	1.15	1.12	26.98	32.98	26.901	$-0.0338+0.2301$	568
29.26	10.90	12.61	78.14	2.28	1.10	1.08	26.92	32.52	26.874	$-0.0348+0.2306$	569

			POPULATION, IN 1000'S			AGE STRUCTURE					
			Observed at mid-year	Projected		Total re-productive value (in 1000's)	Percent at age			Depen-dency ratio (× 100)	Departure from stability (Δ percent)
SERIES NUMBER	AREA AND YEAR			5 years	10 years		<15	15–64	≥65		
			1	2	3	4	5	6	7	8	9
570	Switzerland	1950–52	4749	4904	5028	1122	23.55	66.93	9.52	49.40	5.3
571		1953–55	4927	5081	5205	1155	24.11	66.11	9.78	51.24	5.2
572		1956–58	5117	5298	5444	1204	24.19	65.89	9.92	51.78	4.5
573		1959–61	5429	5643	5837	1294	23.49	66.30	10.21	50.82	3.4
574		1962	5584	5825	6044	1350	23.05	66.48	10.47	50.41	3.3
575		1963	5663	5924	6176	1398	22.88	66.59	10.53	50.17	3.8
576		1964	5773	6069	6343	1431	22.71	66.85	10.44	49.60	4.4
577		1965	5852	6137	6411	1434	22.96	66.35	10.69	50.70	3.8
578		1966	5917	6188	6445	1441	23.31	65.82	10.87	51.92	3.4
579		1967	5990	6252	6495	1431	23.33	65.59	11.08	52.46	4.0
	United Kingdom										
580	England, Wales	1861	20132	21461	22853	10369	35.65	59.70	4.65	67.48	3.1
581		1871	22794	24237	25781	11946	36.12	59.15	4.73	69.06	1.7
582		1881	26050	28084	30287	13234	36.41	59.01	4.58	69.47	1.4
583		1891	29091	30812	32770	14283	35.00	60.27	4.73	65.92	3.8
584		1901	32616	34554	36574	14415	32.37	62.95	4.68	58.86	7.8
585		1911	36116	37861	39559	13569	30.56	64.21	5.23	55.74	10.3
586		1921	37895	39800	41596	12128	27.70	66.25	6.05	50.95	8.2
587		1931	39993	40615	41033	9516	23.76	68.80	7.44	45.35	13.6
588		1941	38743	38876	38713	8268	22.05	67.98	9.97	47.10	13.2
589		1945–47	40595	41880	42742	9545	21.66	67.39	10.95	48.38	5.7
590		1950–52	43800	44454	44805	9008	22.23	66.78	10.99	49.75	4.8
591		1955–57	44667	45432	46004	9235	22.76	65.66	11.58	52.30	4.6
592		1960–62	46166	47478	48795	10305	22.93	65.11	11.96	53.58	9.3
593		1963	47028	48486	50007	10766	22.64	65.41	11.95	52.88	9.8
594		1964	47401	49137	50829	10946	22.70	65.24	12.06	53.28	9.8
595		1965	47763	49366	50930	10900	22.83	64.97	12.20	53.93	9.0
596		1966	47985	49464	50918	10830	23.04	64.65	12.31	54.68	8.1
597	Urban	1966	37844	39018	40216	8543	22.77	64.85	12.38	54.19	8.4
598	Rural	1966	10141	10478	10824	2289	24.08	63.89	12.03	56.52	5.9
599	England, Wales	1966–68	48301	49684	50997	10712	23.20	64.30	12.50	55.51	6.6
600	Urban	1967	38094	39253	40367	8438	22.92	64.51	12.57	55.03	6.8
601	Rural	1967	10207	10543	10868	2265	24.23	63.55	12.22	57.34	4.7
602	N. Ireland	1966	1425	1513	1613	480	28.92	60.98	10.10	63.98	9.2
603	Scotland	1950–52	5100	5230	5344	1240	24.64	65.37	9.99	52.96	2.9
604		1955–57	5145	5310	5465	1261	25.05	64.71	10.24	54.53	3.9
605		1960–62	5184	5379	5593	1322	25.72	63.75	10.53	56.85	8.0
606		1963	5205	5403	5619	1345	25.58	63.71	10.71	56.95	9.3
607		1964	5206	5431	5673	1357	25.61	63.50	10.89	57.48	9.6
608		1965	5203	5405	5623	1334	25.75	63.19	11.06	58.25	8.7
609		1966	5190	5367	5570	1309	25.86	62.86	11.28	59.08	7.8
610	Yugoslavia	1950–52	16477	17902	19405	6419	30.83	63.50	5.67	57.48	7.0
611		1953–55	17267	18765	20316	6524	31.97	62.12	5.91	60.97	6.3
612		1956–58	18005	19265	20447	5847	30.21	63.66	6.13	57.08	10.0
613		1961	18582	19818	21016	5626	31.22	62.60	6.18	59.75	9.5
614		1965	19507	20700	21911	5548	29.68	63.62	6.70	57.19	9.0
615		1966	19735	20976	22236	5445	29.27	63.66	7.07	57.10	9.8
	OCEANIA										
616	Australia	1911	4473	4862	5272	1744	31.66	64.03	4.31	56.17	7.3
617		1921	5456	5862	6261	1912	31.73	63.85	4.42	56.63	8.4

VITAL RATES PER THOUSAND POPULATION								INFANT MOR-TALITY RATE per 1000 births	AGE-SPECIFIC DEATH RATES				
Crude (both sexes)			Standardized on U.S., 1960 (both sexes)		Intrinsic (females)				$1000\,_4M_1$		$1000\,_5M_{50}$		
Birth 10	Death 11	Increase 12	Birth 13	Death 14	Birth 15	Death 16	Increase 17	18	Males 19	Females 20	Males 21	Females 22	SERIES NUMBER
17.56	10.18	7.39	15.45	10.39	15.87	12.59	3.28	30.98	2.05	1.64	9.73	6.33	570
17.06	10.09	6.96	14.88	9.99	15.17	12.79	2.38	28.75	1.73	1.42	9.51	5.78	571
17.60	9.90	7.70	15.10	9.52	15.37	12.27	3.11	24.33	1.67	1.16	8.81	5.24	572
17.60	9.40	8.19	15.83	8.80	16.34	11.20	5.14	23.91	1.39	1.06	8.54	4.83	573
18.68	9.87	8.81	16.56	9.26	17.35	10.67	6.68	24.76	1.30	1.08	8.27	4.76	574
19.42	10.06	9.36	17.24	9.42	18.33	10.04	8.29	25.18	1.41	0.91	8.42	4.67	575
19.55	9.29	10.27	16.99	8.74	17.81	10.10	7.71	23.64	1.22	0.96	8.53	4.12	576
19.11	9.49	9.62	16.53	8.53	17.09	10.45	6.65	17.85	1.19	0.87	7.57	4.38	577
18.55	9.43	9.12	15.92	8.44	16.31	10.89	5.42	17.09	1.22	1.03	8.42	4.62	578
17.93	9.21	8.73	15.27	8.15	15.46	11.32	4.14	17.48	1.02	0.84	7.92	3.95	579
34.59	21.61	12.98	29.74	25.35	31.73	21.53	10.20	178.12	35.67	35.05	19.51	16.17	580
34.98	22.59	12.40	30.69	26.38	33.03	21.78	11.25	182.43	34.15	33.34	21.68	17.32	581
33.92	18.88	15.04	29.90	23.33	32.20	18.18	14.03	145.84	25.90	24.75	21.30	16.56	582
31.42	20.21	11.21	26.77	26.33	29.71	19.70	10.01	176.72	27.29	26.12	25.38	19.41	583
28.51	16.91	11.60	22.56	22.09	24.76	18.61	6.15	176.56	21.33	20.47	20.75	15.89	584
24.40	14.61	9.78	18.92	19.34	20.37	17.98	2.39	146.54	18.24	17.37	17.34	13.19	585
22.40	12.10	10.30	17.46	15.56	18.46	15.60	2.86	88.40	10.90	9.99	13.62	10.34	586
15.80	12.29	3.51	12.21	14.96	11.86	19.74	-7.88	70.11	8.06	7.05	13.42	9.71	587
14.95	13.54	1.41	11.23	13.82	10.32	20.51	-10.19	63.05	5.58	5.00	13.29	8.51	588
19.56	12.20	7.36	15.77	11.28	16.22	13.21	3.01	48.67	2.47	2.08	11.23	6.99	589
15.59	11.85	3.74	13.99	10.84	14.10	13.88	0.22	29.47	1.37	1.16	10.71	6.32	590
15.61	11.60	4.00	15.11	9.87	15.54	12.10	3.45	24.56	1.02	0.90	9.84	5.57	591
17.58	11.81	5.77	17.88	9.59	19.28	9.51	9.77	22.38	0.98	0.79	9.25	5.33	592
18.16	12.18	5.98	18.33	9.84	20.00	9.16	10.85	21.68	0.98	0.83	9.49	5.31	593
18.48	11.28	7.20	18.63	9.05	20.18	8.86	11.32	19.91	0.87	0.73	9.22	5.21	594
18.06	11.50	6.56	18.14	9.13	19.62	9.10	10.52	19.00	0.87	0.76	9.38	5.19	595
17.71	11.75	5.96	17.70	9.29	19.03	9.44	9.59	19.00	0.92	0.75	9.39	5.37	596
17.78	11.94	5.84	17.72	9.24	18.99	9.37	9.62	19.62	0.94	0.75	9.63	5.39	597
17.45	11.01	6.44	17.62	8.51	18.80	9.28	9.52	16.64	0.84	0.75	8.35	5.07	598
17.26	11.61	5.65	17.03	9.08	18.08	9.90	8.18	18.55	0.87	0.73	9.10	5.23	599
17.28	11.42	5.86	17.01	8.75	17.91	9.83	8.08	18.97	0.82	0.72	9.49	5.33	600
17.02	10.53	6.49	16.95	8.07	17.85	9.64	8.22	15.98	0.87	0.63	8.02	5.06	601
23.44	11.54	11.90	24.15	10.63	25.04	7.56	17.49	25.42	1.39	0.99	9.85	5.96	602
17.88	12.50	5.38	15.63	12.30	16.44	13.12	3.31	38.75	1.80	1.53	13.06	7.61	603
18.52	11.96	6.56	16.96	11.21	18.27	11.01	7.25	30.32	1.28	0.94	12.16	6.73	604
19.73	12.15	7.58	18.96	10.93	20.92	9.31	11.61	27.71	1.16	0.93	11.81	6.52	605
19.73	12.59	7.14	19.40	11.20	21.63	8.97	12.67	26.32	1.21	0.92	11.85	6.59	606
20.04	11.72	8.32	19.80	10.33	21.90	8.62	13.28	24.03	0.91	0.89	11.50	6.57	607
19.35	12.08	7.26	19.23	10.55	21.11	8.99	12.12	23.12	1.02	0.78	11.18	6.24	608
18.60	12.27	6.33	18.58	10.62	20.34	9.39	10.95	23.19	1.03	0.78	11.47	6.81	609
29.08	13.00	16.08	23.21	15.81	25.17	13.81	11.36	117.68	12.12	12.57	13.15	9.06	610
27.95	11.52	16.43	22.05	14.00	24.00	12.82	11.18	109.62	8.86	9.69	11.98	8.40	611
24.43	10.29	14.14	18.56	12.88	19.69	13.66	6.03	103.25	7.21	8.13	10.12	7.11	612
22.72	9.01	13.71	18.03	11.29	19.22	12.35	6.87	83.71	4.29	4.57	8.77	6.11	613
20.92	8.74	12.18	17.36	10.94	18.37	12.33	6.05	71.88	3.36	3.62	8.56	5.76	614
20.26	8.09	12.17	17.05	9.98	17.76	11.88	5.88	62.14	2.56	2.63	8.67	5.46	615
27.32	10.70	16.61	22.74	15.40	24.53	12.24	12.29	71.96	6.60	6.15	15.34	10.72	616
24.96	9.91	15.05	20.27	13.77	21.63	12.61	9.01	66.94	7.11	6.10	12.87	9.41	617

continued

LIFE TABLE VALUES

SERIES NUMBER	AREA AND YEAR		Probability of dying in first year, q_0		Survivors to age 50 per 100,000 births, l_{50}		Expectancy, $\overset{\circ}{e}_0$		Expectancy, $\overset{\circ}{e}_1$		Expectancy, $\overset{\circ}{e}_{50}$
			Males 23	Females 24	Males 25	Females 26	Males 27	Females 28	Males 29	Females 30	Males 31
570	Switzerland	1950-52	0.0342	0.0262	86473	90411	66.78	71.20	68.13	72.11	23.40
571		1953-55	0.0313	0.0249	87371	91438	67.40	72.15	68.57	72.98	23.56
572		1956-58	0.0267	0.0208	88015	92556	68.03	73.17	68.89	73.72	23.85
573		1959-61	0.0270	0.0198	88943	93070	68.83	74.32	69.74	74.82	24.24
574		1962	0.0271	0.0214	88658	92977	68.44	73.91	69.34	74.53	23.92
575		1963	0.0281	0.0211	88546	93143	68.18	74.03	69.15	74.62	23.70
576		1964	0.0267	0.0197	89158	93490	68.92	74.85	69.80	75.35	24.21
577		1965	0.0219	0.0176	89976	93867	69.57	75.13	70.12	75.47	24.35
578		1966	0.0205	0.0157	89994	94062	69.58	75.32	70.03	75.52	24.33
579		1967	0.0211	0.0151	89953	94231	69.73	75.88	70.23	76.05	24.56
	United Kingdom										
580	England, Wales	1861	0.1771	0.1435	46852	49675	40.51	43.03	48.14	49.18	19.72
581		1871	0.1785	0.1488	44038	48666	39.22	42.43	46.66	48.78	19.13
582		1881	0.1467	0.1199	51672	55977	44.18	47.38	50.72	52.79	19.16
583		1891	0.1760	0.1412	49592	54934	41.94	45.64	49.82	52.08	17.52
584		1901	0.1735	0.1422	55105	60396	45.40	49.39	53.86	56.52	19.30
585		1911	0.1459	0.1209	61469	66223	49.36	53.33	56.73	59.61	20.26
586		1921	0.0927	0.0721	70423	74609	55.98	59.94	60.66	63.57	21.62
587		1931	0.0762	0.0574	74039	78409	58.15	62.34	61.92	65.11	21.43
588		1941	0.0678	0.0527	73948	80904	58.54	64.63	61.78	67.20	21.60
589		1945-47	0.0522	0.0408	82756	86482	63.97	68.94	66.48	70.87	22.66
590		1950-52	0.0324	0.0250	87679	90671	66.44	71.50	67.66	72.33	22.21
591		1955-57	0.0270	0.0209	89579	92420	67.71	73.29	68.58	73.86	22.55
592		1960-62	0.0246	0.0190	90038	93071	68.10	73.97	68.81	74.39	22.70
593		1963	0.0238	0.0185	90052	93059	67.87	73.87	68.52	74.26	22.39
594		1964	0.0230	0.0181	90196	93228	68.53	74.68	69.14	75.06	23.03
595		1965	0.0214	0.0163	90379	93394	68.53	74.75	69.02	74.99	22.89
596		1966	0.0214	0.0164	90392	93487	68.40	74.68	68.88	74.92	22.75
597	Urban	1966	0.0223	0.0170	90195	93317	68.12	75.08	68.67	75.37	22.54
598	Rural	1966	0.0179	0.0142	91039	94002	69.67	75.69	69.94	75.77	23.83
599	England, Wales	1966-68	0.0206	0.0161	90697	93602	68.72	74.92	69.16	75.14	22.94
600	Urban	1967	0.0209	0.0169	90800	93549	68.83	75.63	69.29	75.92	23.01
601	Rural	1967	0.0172	0.0134	91678	94260	70.31	76.32	70.54	76.35	24.26
602	N. Ireland	1966	0.0285	0.0252	89045	92081	66.96	72.17	67.92	73.03	22.07
603	Scotland	1950-52	0.0421	0.0329	84877	87696	64.39	68.65	66.21	69.97	21.43
604		1955-57	0.0332	0.0256	87319	90862	65.91	71.10	67.17	71.96	21.66
605		1960-62	0.0313	0.0227	87928	91732	66.14	71.91	67.27	72.57	21.58
606		1963	0.0288	0.0225	87712	91620	65.82	71.89	66.76	72.54	21.15
607		1964	0.0279	0.0220	88258	92069	66.65	72.76	67.55	73.39	21.79
608		1965	0.0256	0.0204	88270	91973	66.55	72.66	67.29	73.17	21.62
609		1966	0.0262	0.0207	88202	92117	66.57	72.54	67.36	73.07	21.73
610	Yugoslavia	1950-52	0.1134	0.1006	69499	72430	55.28	58.19	61.31	63.66	22.24
611		1953-55	0.1055	0.0973	75617	77218	58.76	61.13	64.66	66.69	22.67
612		1956-58	0.1003	0.0920	78156	79741	60.53	63.14	66.24	68.50	23.23
613		1961	0.0824	0.0745	81798	84263	63.55	66.82	68.24	71.17	23.98
614		1965	0.0754	0.0696	82945	85885	64.43	67.99	68.67	72.05	24.05
615		1966	0.0639	0.0595	84775	87625	66.05	70.17	69.54	73.59	24.55
	OCEANIA										
616	Australia	1911	0.0753	0.0607	71738	75546	57.35	61.11	60.99	64.04	21.13
617		1921	0.0709	0.0560	73760	77694	59.05	63.06	62.53	65.78	22.30

FERTILITY MEASURES (FEMALES)

Females 32	Expectancy, $\mathring{e}_{70}$ Males 33	Females 34	General fertility rate 35	Total fertility rate 36	Gross reproduction rate 37	Total, NRR 38	Mean, μ 39	Variance, σ^2 40	Generation, T 41	Complex root, r_2 42	SERIES NUMBER
26.19	9.60	10.86	80.24	2.39	1.16	1.10	29.30	33.15	29.238	−0.0268+0.2124	570
26.67	9.74	11.07	78.95	2.30	1.12	1.07	29.15	33.11	29.113	−0.0282+0.2131	571
27.07	9.83	11.28	82.04	2.34	1.14	1.09	28.95	33.33	28.893	−0.0286+0.2149	572
28.04	10.23	11.96	83.18	2.46	1.20	1.16	28.68	31.54	28.597	−0.0256+0.2192	573
27.73	9.97	11.67	87.32	2.57	1.25	1.21	28.45	31.83	28.338	−0.0254+0.2219	574
27.74	9.74	11.56	90.34	2.68	1.31	1.26	28.35	31.03	28.211	−0.0230+0.2231	575
28.39	10.23	12.09	89.42	2.64	1.29	1.24	28.38	31.18	28.257	−0.0234+0.2220	576
28.43	10.27	12.25	87.42	2.57	1.24	1.21	28.34	31.14	28.227	−0.0244+0.2222	577
28.52	10.27	12.23	84.73	2.47	1.20	1.16	28.35	31.11	28.258	−0.0254+0.2214	578
28.99	10.48	12.58	82.09	2.37	1.16	1.12	28.28	31.39	28.210	−0.0270+0.2217	579
21.05	8.37	9.07	147.10	4.52	2.21	1.37	30.78	42.03	30.554	−0.0224+0.1971	580
20.58	8.33	8.86	151.65	4.67	2.29	1.41	30.80	41.75	30.556	−0.0213+0.1975	581
20.89	8.27	9.08	146.97	4.55	2.23	1.54	30.89	40.62	30.590	−0.0179+0.1985	582
19.27	7.47	8.18	132.06	4.08	2.00	1.36	30.90	39.14	30.696	−0.0203+0.1982	583
21.30	8.41	9.29	114.19	3.45	1.69	1.21	30.85	36.48	30.727	−0.0226+0.1992	584
22.46	8.47	9.52	97.90	2.90	1.42	1.07	30.37	35.96	30.324	−0.0266+0.2015	585
23.96	8.89	10.10	89.63	2.68	1.31	1.09	29.67	34.90	29.622	−0.0279+0.2072	586
23.92	8.50	9.82	64.29	1.88	0.92	0.79	29.02	34.74	29.162	−0.0399+0.2089	587
25.05	8.88	10.53	58.42	1.74	0.84	0.74	28.63	36.37	28.830	−0.0464+0.2118	588
26.28	9.51	11.22	81.59	2.44	1.18	1.09	28.81	34.51	28.757	−0.0309+0.2151	589
26.28	8.97	10.91	72.06	2.17	1.05	1.01	28.09	33.28	28.091	−0.0351+0.2213	590
27.20	9.21	11.56	76.66	2.35	1.14	1.10	27.67	32.17	27.614	−0.0325+0.2271	591
27.54	9.27	11.74	89.51	2.78	1.35	1.30	27.42	31.91	27.253	−0.0262+0.2315	592
27.41	8.99	11.63	90.93	2.85	1.38	1.34	27.36	31.64	27.182	−0.0250+0.2320	593
28.19	9.60	12.36	92.60	2.89	1.40	1.36	27.35	31.85	27.159	−0.0249+0.2319	594
28.13	9.46	12.30	91.24	2.81	1.37	1.33	27.24	32.35	27.062	−0.0268+0.2326	595
28.01	9.29	12.18	90.12	2.74	1.33	1.29	27.08	32.40	26.914	−0.0284+0.2338	596
28.52	9.07	12.84	90.27	2.74	1.33	1.30	27.10	32.73	26.930	−0.0288+0.2332	597
28.79	9.74	12.96	89.53	2.74	1.33	1.29	27.02	30.94	26.863	−0.0267+0.2359	598
28.20	9.40	12.35	88.59	2.64	1.28	1.25	27.03	32.56	26.889	−0.0300+0.2333	599
29.01	9.53	13.31	88.50	2.63	1.28	1.24	27.05	33.15	26.908	−0.0310+0.2326	600
29.31	10.08	13.53	88.12	2.63	1.28	1.25	26.97	31.01	26.834	−0.0282+0.2355	601
26.29	9.19	10.73	116.86	3.70	1.79	1.72	31.23	33.14	30.924	−0.0058+0.2037	602
24.83	8.78	10.13	80.58	2.42	1.17	1.10	28.60	34.12	28.543	−0.0309+0.2167	603
25.66	9.02	10.66	87.45	2.63	1.28	1.22	28.08	32.72	27.952	−0.0280+0.2238	604
26.02	8.94	10.87	97.64	2.94	1.43	1.38	27.72	32.39	27.526	−0.0243+0.2291	605
26.01	8.62	10.96	97.36	3.01	1.47	1.41	27.63	31.42	27.422	−0.0220+0.2301	606
26.76	9.18	11.64	99.00	3.07	1.49	1.44	27.63	31.96	27.407	−0.0222+0.2299	607
26.63	8.94	11.40	96.60	2.98	1.44	1.39	27.53	32.28	27.322	−0.0241+0.2303	608
26.46	8.89	11.25	93.80	2.88	1.39	1.35	27.40	32.75	27.210	−0.0263+0.2309	609
24.41	9.36	10.13	120.70	3.58	1.73	1.38	28.92	44.79	28.656	−0.0339+0.2200	610
24.86	9.58	10.65	119.67	3.40	1.64	1.37	28.63	43.56	28.375	−0.0351+0.2219	611
25.58	10.00	11.05	104.88	2.87	1.39	1.18	27.99	42.07	27.857	−0.0426+0.2267	612
26.48	10.28	11.32	100.96	2.79	1.35	1.21	27.43	42.39	27.282	−0.0439+0.2376	613
26.69	10.15	11.29	89.10	2.69	1.30	1.18	27.02	37.90	26.901	−0.0371+0.2408	614
27.80	10.52	12.33	86.24	2.64	1.27	1.17	26.82	37.75	26.703	−0.0385+0.2412	615
23.73	8.78	9.89	114.85	3.47	1.70	1.45	30.31	42.51	30.038	−0.0228+0.2028	616
24.92	9.55	10.66	106.63	3.10	1.51	1.31	29.79	41.82	29.593	−0.0277+0.2055	617

SERIES NUMBER	AREA AND YEAR		POPULATION, IN 1000'S			AGE STRUCTURE					
			Observed at mid-year	Projected		Total reproductive value (in 1000's)	Percent at age			Dependency ratio (× 100)	Departure from stability (Δ percent)
				5 years	10 years		<15	15–64	⩾65		
			1	2	3	4	5	6	7	8	9
618	Australia	1933	6630	6886	7137	1758	27.48	66.04	6.48	51.42	14.5
619	cont	1947	7579	8107	8582	2127	25.22	66.75	8.03	49.81	6.0
620		1950–52	8422	8960	9430	2313	27.05	64.93	8.02	54.02	6.0
621		1953–55	8987	9565	10102	2513	28.52	63.18	8.30	58.29	6.0
622		1956–58	9640	10288	10948	2769	29.55	62.00	8.45	61.29	6.9
623		1959–61	10275	10996	11788	3042	30.11	61.43	8.46	62.78	7.3
624		1962	10705	11456	12293	3184	29.98	61.51	8.51	62.58	6.2
625		1963	10916	11659	12497	3222	29.85	61.67	8.48	62.16	5.4
626		1964	11136	11822	12604	3207	29.73	61.85	8.42	61.68	3.6
627		1965	11360	12019	12767	3186	29.53	62.05	8.42	61.18	3.5
628		1966	11550	12196	12929	3197	29.37	62.09	8.54	61.06	3.8
629	New South Wales	1966	4234	4438	4672	1117	28.30	62.98	8.72	58.76	4.0
630	Queensland	1966	1664	1771	1892	486	30.43	60.60	8.97	65.02	4.2
631	South Australia	1966	1092	1153	1229	307	30.13	61.39	8.48	62.89	5.2
632	Tasmania	1966	371	398	426	111	32.40	59.79	7.81	67.25	4.8
633	Victoria	1966	3219	3413	3629	916	29.26	62.16	8.58	60.88	3.0
634	Western Austr.	1966	837	895	962	246	31.10	61.24	7.66	63.28	4.7
635	Capital Terr.	1966	96	105	116	32	33.16	63.92	2.92	56.43	12.1
636	Northern Terr.	1966	37	41	45	13	30.75	66.79	2.46	49.72	10.0
637	Australia	1967	11810	12490	13251	3265	29.29	62.24	8.47	60.69	3.8
638	Fiji Islands	1956	343	404	481	187	46.09	50.75	3.16	97.05	2.1
639		1963	435	511	602	217	44.79	51.99	3.22	92.35	3.7
640		1964	449	527	618	229	44.50	52.26	3.24	91.34	3.5
641		1966	477	552	646	230	43.83	52.86	3.31	89.17	5.9
642	New Zealand	1951	1833	1960	2076	534	28.48	61.95	9.57	61.44	7.2
643		1952	1876	2010	2143	560	29.02	61.42	9.56	62.81	8.2
644		1953–55	1966	2115	2254	594	29.90	60.58	9.52	65.07	8.5
645		1956–58	2089	2254	2432	656	30.69	59.89	9.42	66.96	10.2
646		1959	2181	2359	2561	703	31.43	59.36	9.21	68.46	10.9
647		1961	2260	2456	2684	747	31.82	59.09	9.09	69.23	11.6
648		1963	2543	2773	3039	850	32.94	58.67	8.39	70.44	8.7
649		1965	2635	2843	3085	842	32.65	59.03	8.32	69.41	4.5
650		1966–68	2729	2939	3181	854	32.59	59.13	8.28	69.11	4.2
	UNION OF SOVIET SOCIALIST REPUBLICS										
651	USSR hypothetical	1959	208827	223690	237044	60574	29.88	63.89	6.23	56.51	10.0
	NORTH AMERICA--CITIES										
	Canada										
652	Montreal	1966	1224	1284	1340	283	25.37	67.03	7.60	49.20	8.8
653	Toronto	1966	665	702	729	154	24.02	64.98	11.00	53.90	5.1
654	Vancouver	1966	410	420	424	83	22.16	64.38	13.46	55.34	6.3
	United States										
655	Chicago	1960	3562	3794	4017	996	27.17	63.07	9.76	58.56	15.6
656	Nonwhite	1960	843	953	1072	322	36.49	58.77	4.74	70.17	14.2
657	White	1960	2719	2836	2955	675	24.29	64.40	11.31	55.29	15.8
658	Washington	1960	767	819	867	205	25.35	65.60	9.05	52.44	13.9

VITAL RATES PER THOUSAND POPULATION

Crude (both sexes)			Standardized on U.S., 1960 (both sexes)		Intrinsic (females)			INFANT MORTALITY RATE per 1000 births	AGE-SPECIFIC DEATH RATES				
									$1000_4 M_1$		$1000_5 M_{50}$		
Birth 10	Death 11	Increase 12	Birth 13	Death 14	Birth 15	Death 16	Increase 17	18	Males 19	Females 20	Males 21	Females 22	SERIES NUMBER
16.78	8.92	7.87	14.10	11.81	14.10	15.47	-1.37	41.74	3.92	3.51	11.61	8.40	618
24.06	9.69	14.37	15.95	10.43	21.75	9.31	12.44	28.26	2.03	1.63	11.84	7.51	619
23.18	9.56	13.61	19.97	10.57	21.99	8.94	13.05	25.07	1.79	1.46	10.89	6.75	620
22.71	9.05	13.66	20.78	9.90	23.13	8.15	14.98	23.68	1.70	1.37	10.19	6.28	621
22.65	8.81	13.84	21.84	9.68	24.40	7.46	16.94	21.92	1.43	1.17	10.02	5.73	622
22.62	8.65	13.97	22.44	9.52	25.28	7.01	18.27	21.10	1.23	1.04	9.88	5.43	623
22.15	8.70	13.44	22.04	9.32	24.74	7.10	17.64	20.66	1.09	0.93	10.08	5.69	624
21.59	8.69	12.90	21.48	9.30	24.03	7.36	16.67	19.96	1.00	0.91	10.12	5.57	625
20.58	9.03	11.54	20.30	9.69	22.38	8.09	14.29	19.07	1.08	0.92	10.28	5.67	626
19.62	8.78	10.84	19.13	9.46	20.94	8.64	12.29	18.62	1.07	0.88	10.69	5.55	627
19.27	9.00	10.28	18.60	9.54	20.23	8.99	11.24	18.17	1.09	0.73	10.39	6.00	628
18.48	9.38	9.10	17.64	9.78	18.96	9.76	9.21	18.89	1.01	0.83	11.07	6.35	629
20.25	8.76	11.50	20.26	8.98	22.34	8.02	14.32	18.37	1.27	0.98	10.79	6.38	630
18.80	8.30	10.51	18.59	8.76	20.15	8.70	11.45	17.63	0.97	0.70	9.58	4.97	631
20.17	8.46	11.71	15.86	9.47	22.29	8.07	14.22	16.15	0.94	0.93	9.50	4.79	632
19.99	8.81	11.18	19.24	9.38	21.12	8.44	12.68	17.22	0.92	0.69	10.05	5.36	633
20.40	7.90	12.51	19.99	8.91	22.06	7.92	14.14	19.39	1.18	0.74	9.17	5.23	634
23.86	4.06	19.80	19.30	8.88	21.56	8.04	13.52	17.89	0.63	0.44	8.87	5.56	635
33.93	7.51	26.42	28.79	13.63	32.62	8.05	24.57	42.55	4.12	5.46	14.94	9.26	636
19.42	8.70	10.72	18.37	9.24	19.96	9.02	10.94	18.26	0.97	0.85	10.08	5.90	637
41.06	7.57	33.49	38.58	12.31	41.18	7.02	34.16	46.01	4.81	4.69	12.22	9.18	638
38.01	5.78	32.24	33.84	9.93	36.77	6.06	30.71	28.85	3.26	2.88	12.97	9.86	639
37.85	6.06	31.79	34.18	10.31	36.76	5.93	30.84	31.82	4.33	3.58	13.90	8.48	640
34.94	5.21	29.73	30.98	8.55	33.49	5.82	27.68	25.28	2.53	2.64	10.78	9.40	641
24.36	9.55	14.81	21.96	9.73	24.19	7.81	16.38	23.72	1.41	1.19	8.84	6.63	642
24.77	9.28	15.49	22.77	9.40	25.37	7.34	18.04	22.68	1.34	1.20	9.22	6.90	643
24.53	8.92	15.61	23.27	8.97	25.82	6.90	18.91	20.77	1.40	1.24	8.70	5.99	644
24.90	9.07	15.83	24.90	9.11	27.94	6.15	21.80	20.28	1.23	1.02	8.31	5.43	645
25.10	9.09	16.02	25.75	8.98	29.09	5.83	23.26	20.41	1.17	1.23	8.04	4.92	646
25.53	9.03	16.51	26.49	8.90	29.99	5.50	24.49	19.13	1.03	1.04	8.78	5.09	647
25.43	8.81	16.62	25.91	9.18	29.18	5.78	23.39	19.88	1.25	0.99	8.74	5.57	648
22.83	8.72	14.12	22.71	9.14	25.42	6.87	18.55	19.51	1.17	1.00	9.62	5.83	649
22.43	8.70	13.73	21.69	9.19	24.62	7.08	17.55	18.13	1.15	0.99	9.60	5.81	650
21.98	7.30	14.68	15.94	10.19	16.47	11.58	4.88	33.07	0.98	0.81	9.23	5.00	651
18.56	8.57	9.98	14.91	9.96	14.83	12.64	2.19	24.44	0.89	0.90	12.47	5.84	652
20.88	10.13	10.75	17.84	8.88	19.41	9.08	10.34	20.95	0.62	0.85	11.37	5.52	653
15.62	12.08	3.53	14.38	8.52	13.87	12.73	1.13	21.53	0.98	0.51	11.24	5.31	654
25.06	11.76	13.29	24.29	11.36	28.55	6.98	21.57	28.33	1.36	1.17	15.91	8.28	655
36.78	9.72	27.06	31.25	13.18	38.61	6.44	32.17	38.04	1.96	1.80	19.65	14.82	656
21.42	12.40	9.02	21.93	10.83	25.08	7.50	17.58	23.15	1.04	0.84	15.12	6.96	657
26.23	11.49	14.74	22.97	11.39	26.89	7.90	18.99	36.24	1.36	1.02	17.90	8.94	658

continued

LIFE TABLE VALUES

SERIES NUMBER	AREA AND YEAR		Probability of dying in first year, q_0		Survivors to age 50 per 100,000 births, l_{50}		Expectancy, $\overset{\circ}{e}_0$		Expectancy, $\overset{\circ}{e}_1$		Expectancy, $\overset{\circ}{e}_{50}$
			Males 23	Females 24	Males 25	Females 26	Males 27	Females 28	Males 29	Females 30	Males 31
618	Australia	1933	0.0450	0.0359	81209	83909	63.55	67.33	65.53	68.83	22.73
619	cont	1947	0.0303	0.0240	86186	89258	66.35	70.98	67.42	71.71	22.84
620		1950-52	0.0274	0.0217	86523	90455	66.28	71.68	67.14	72.27	22.49
621		1953-55	0.0260	0.0205	87469	91521	67.06	72.70	67.84	73.21	22.90
622		1956-58	0.0237	0.0192	88053	92180	67.50	73.35	68.13	73.78	22.98
623		1959-61	0.0231	0.0182	88368	92488	67.67	73.87	68.26	74.24	22.96
624		1962	0.0228	0.0176	88360	92800	67.80	74.20	68.37	74.52	23.03
625		1963	0.0219	0.0173	88523	92651	67.86	74.17	68.37	74.48	22.97
626		1964	0.0210	0.0165	88339	92505	67.46	73.82	67.90	74.06	22.58
627		1965	0.0205	0.0162	88571	92612	67.75	74.13	68.16	74.34	22.79
628		1966	0.0208	0.0161	88548	92782	67.60	74.06	68.03	74.27	22.66
629	New South Wales	1966	0.0217	0.0160	88136	92452	67.14	73.74	67.62	73.94	22.29
630	Queensland	1966	0.0203	0.0168	87484	91866	67.83	74.33	68.23	74.60	23.39
631	South Australia	1966	0.0198	0.0149	89565	93674	68.61	75.24	68.99	75.37	23.30
632	Tasmania	1966	0.0180	0.0145	88305	92653	67.79	73.95	68.03	74.03	22.94
633	Victoria	1966	0.0191	0.0158	89132	93322	67.98	74.51	68.30	74.70	22.73
634	Western Austr.	1966	0.0229	0.0179	88908	93190	68.12	75.10	68.71	75.47	23.25
635	Capital Terr.	1966	0.0220	0.0131	90255	93141	68.74	75.22	69.28	75.22	23.22
636	Northern Terr.	1966	0.0594	0.0445	78219	81397	60.07	66.61	62.84	68.69	20.36
637	Australia	1967	0.0206	0.0159	88480	92916	67.79	74.48	68.21	74.68	22.85
638	Fiji Islands	1956	0.0490	0.0393	81163	80936	63.49	64.91	65.75	66.55	22.60
639		1963	0.0274	0.0291	83301	85609	66.14	69.65	66.99	70.73	23.57
640		1964	0.0331	0.0291	82845	86893	64.97	70.10	66.18	71.19	23.05
641		1966	0.0265	0.0243	84673	87348	68.09	73.57	68.93	74.39	25.46
642	New Zealand	1951	0.0274	0.0190	87643	91586	67.85	72.32	68.76	72.71	23.73
643		1952	0.0236	0.0208	88515	91796	68.51	72.61	69.16	73.14	23.99
644		1953-55	0.0233	0.0173	89164	92466	68.88	73.61	69.52	73.90	24.09
645		1956-58	0.0223	0.0174	89482	92880	68.88	73.97	69.44	74.27	23.88
646		1959	0.0218	0.0181	89653	92923	69.04	74.09	69.57	74.45	23.90
647		1961	0.0232	0.0166	89873	93327	69.08	74.35	69.71	74.60	23.84
648		1963	0.0221	0.0169	89032	92729	68.49	74.13	69.03	74.39	23.54
649		1965	0.0231	0.0169	88790	92748	68.20	74.18	68.80	74.45	23.36
650		1966-68	0.0200	0.0151	88863	92874	68.21	74.33	68.59	74.47	23.23
	UNION OF SOVIET SOCIALIST REPUBLICS										
651	USSR hypothetical	1959	0.0336	0.0261	88808	92649	67.73	72.87	69.08	73.82	23.21
	NORTH AMERICA--CITIES										
	Canada										
652	Montreal	1966	0.0253	0.0227	87707	91969	66.67	73.34	67.40	74.03	21.98
653	Toronto	1966	0.0219	0.0194	88636	92818	67.71	75.46	68.22	75.94	22.54
654	Vancouver	1966	0.0224	0.0205	87164	91720	67.92	75.43	68.47	76.00	23.47
	United States										
655	Chicago	1960	0.0333	0.0260	83264	88948	64.09	70.67	65.29	71.55	21.08
656	Nonwhite	1960	0.0440	0.0374	76685	82684	60.88	66.11	62.67	67.66	20.50
657	White	1960	0.0279	0.0199	85549	91163	65.27	72.23	66.14	72.69	21.22
658	Washington	1960	0.0448	0.0370	79874	86085	62.70	69.98	64.63	71.66	21.11

Females 32	Expectancy, $\hat{e}_{70}$ Males 33	Females 34	General fertility rate 35	Total fertility rate 36	Gross reproduction rate 37	Net maternity function Total, NRR 38	Mean, μ 39	Variance, σ^2 40	Generation, T 41	Complex root, r_2 42	SERIES NUMBER
25.64	9.54	10.99	71.86	2.16	1.05	0.96	29.14	41.02	29.174	−0.0385+0.2071	618
26.37	9.80	11.37	106.69	3.08	1.50	1.42	28.46	35.69	28.230	−0.0245+0.2210	619
26.47	9.34	11.26	107.00	3.09	1.50	1.44	28.02	35.32	27.780	−0.0255+0.2257	620
27.03	9.60	11.64	108.55	3.22	1.57	1.51	27.77	34.42	27.498	−0.0238+0.2302	621
27.36	9.58	11.72	111.25	3.39	1.65	1.59	27.59	33.52	27.293	−0.0211+0.2330	622
27.72	9.58	11.99	112.74	3.48	1.70	1.64	27.49	32.79	27.177	−0.0189+0.2346	623
27.89	9.69	12.16	109.69	3.42	1.67	1.62	27.51	32.54	27.206	−0.0190+0.2337	624
27.91	9.73	12.26	106.49	3.33	1.63	1.57	27.49	32.94	27.206	−0.0205+0.2334	625
27.57	9.38	11.90	101.03	3.14	1.52	1.48	27.51	33.40	27.264	−0.0233+0.2311	626
27.83	9.56	12.12	95.77	2.96	1.44	1.40	27.39	33.31	27.172	−0.0255+0.2315	627
27.67	9.40	12.10	94.08	2.88	1.40	1.36	27.29	33.37	27.098	−0.0268+0.2318	628
27.46	9.30	12.08	89.35	2.73	1.32	1.28	27.25	33.07	27.091	−0.0283+0.2305	629
28.40	10.15	12.80	102.53	3.13	1.52	1.47	27.33	34.88	27.065	−0.0263+0.2332	630
28.47	9.87	12.59	92.17	2.89	1.40	1.36	27.23	32.27	27.040	−0.0255+0.2345	631
27.59	9.59	11.87	101.37	3.07	1.50	1.46	26.70	33.97	26.451	−0.0281+0.2414	632
27.90	9.35	12.16	96.74	2.98	1.46	1.41	27.59	32.05	27.377	−0.0223+0.2302	633
28.69	9.69	12.83	101.32	3.10	1.50	1.46	26.92	31.57	26.682	−0.0229+0.2382	634
28.61	9.30	12.78	101.10	2.99	1.49	1.45	27.78	32.08	27.541	−0.0204+0.2281	635
26.31	7.05	13.63	158.43	4.34	2.12	1.92	27.22	51.27	26.577	−0.0397+0.2214	636
28.05	9.63	12.45	94.66	2.85	1.39	1.34	27.26	32.80	27.068	−0.0261+0.2323	637
24.56	9.27	10.73	201.68	5.91	2.88	2.59	28.66	49.69	27.815	−0.0238+0.2298	638
27.19	11.02	13.02	182.29	5.20	2.51	2.32	28.16	47.42	27.436	−0.0249+0.2397	639
27.11	10.36	12.77	180.73	5.27	2.55	2.38	28.76	46.18	28.046	−0.0202+0.2337	640
30.58	13.91	17.22	165.10	4.78	2.32	2.17	28.57	45.85	27.927	−0.0241+0.2340	641
26.51	10.06	11.31	116.58	3.40	1.65	1.58	28.30	33.08	28.019	−0.0180+0.2255	642
26.79	10.19	11.54	119.98	3.53	1.72	1.65	28.26	33.24	27.942	−0.0170+0.2267	643
27.46	10.34	11.98	121.15	3.61	1.75	1.69	28.16	32.56	27.838	−0.0155+0.2285	644
27.62	9.90	11.94	125.71	3.87	1.88	1.82	27.85	31.77	27.487	−0.0127+0.2326	645
27.77	9.97	12.01	129.13	4.00	1.95	1.89	27.68	31.43	27.299	−0.0113+0.2344	646
27.79	10.12	11.99	132.63	4.12	2.01	1.95	27.65	31.93	27.248	−0.0105+0.2350	647
27.81	9.63	12.10	130.85	3.99	1.93	1.87	27.28	36.43	26.842	−0.0188+0.2338	648
27.86	9.81	12.36	116.14	3.52	1.70	1.65	27.23	34.48	26.895	−0.0222+0.2372	649
27.89	9.71	12.36	113.80	3.36	1.64	1.59	26.85	33.50	26.541	−0.0224+0.2404	650
26.84	9.31	10.83	89.58	2.46	1.20	1.15	28.49	39.04	28.387	−0.0365+0.2201	651
27.50	9.46	12.11	79.31	2.27	1.10	1.06	25.98	37.39	25.941	−0.0441+0.2350	652
29.18	9.87	13.62	94.16	2.71	1.34	1.30	25.66	38.44	25.453	−0.0418+0.2414	653
29.78	10.33	13.87	75.31	2.20	1.07	1.03	26.16	36.30	26.136	−0.0420+0.2315	654
26.00	9.35	11.59	122.70	3.74	1.83	1.75	26.33	34.78	25.937	−0.0255+0.2451	655
23.83	10.38	12.77	161.17	4.74	2.35	2.21	25.26	38.60	24.635	−0.0340+0.2688	656
26.50	9.25	11.52	108.84	3.39	1.65	1.59	26.78	32.63	26.484	−0.0234+0.2397	657
26.88	10.04	12.48	117.71	3.50	1.71	1.61	25.61	37.68	25.236	−0.0395+0.2494	658

	AREA AND YEAR		POPULATION, IN 1000'S			AGE STRUCTURE					
			Observed at mid-year	Projected		Total re-productive value (in 1000's)	Percent at age			Depen-dency ratio (× 100)	Departure from stability (Δ percent)
SERIES NUMBER				5 years	10 years		<15	15–64	⩾65		
			1	2	3	4	5	6	7	8	9
	ASIA--CITIES										
	China (Taiwan)										
659	Kaohsiung	1964	559	647	744	265	45.55	52.91	1.54	89.02	8.1
660		1966	620	707	814	274	44.10	54.25	1.65	84.33	8.0
661	Taipei	1964	1066	1212	1368	438	40.69	57.24	2.07	74.71	8.4
662		1966	1164	1314	1473	450	39.33	58.56	2.11	70.78	9.1
	Indonesia										
663	Djakarta	1961	2885	3287	3684	1490	40.28	58.48	1.24	71.00	11.6
	EUROPE--CITIES										
	Denmark										
664	Copenhagen	1966	667	673	673	114	16.94	67.63	15.43	47.85	12.7
	Finland										
665	Helsinki	1966	513	533	543	108	20.37	70.76	8.87	41.34	9.3
	East Germany										
666	East Berlin	1961	1056	1047	1021	170	16.91	65.74	17.35	52.13	14.2
	West Germany										
667	West Berlin	1961	2204	2135	2044	278	13.04	68.91	18.05	45.11	10.6
668		1966	2191	2119	2026	304	13.97	65.81	20.22	51.95	12.7
669		1967	2174	2093	1995	297	14.31	64.97	20.72	53.93	11.3
670	Duesseldorf	1964	705	720	723	126	17.90	70.61	11.49	41.62	10.1
671		1966	696	701	704	121	18.23	69.47	12.30	43.95	7.4
672	Hamburg	1964	1860	1870	1857	312	16.61	68.50	14.89	45.99	9.4
673		1966	1851	1850	1830	318	17.22	67.29	15.49	48.62	7.4
	Sweden										
674	Stockholm	1959	806	817	822	140	20.05	68.59	11.36	45.79	7.5
675		1960	808	816	819	142	19.38	68.99	11.63	44.94	7.3
	United Kingdom										
676	Greater London	1967	7804	8064	8275	1642	20.52	67.20	12.28	48.82	7.6
	OCEANIA--CITIES										
	Australia										
677	Sydney	1966	2446	2559	2675	621	25.87	65.00	9.13	53.83	3.4
	POOLED POPULATIONS										
	Africa										
678	Subsaharan inc	1961-63	5677	6395	7159	3300	45.07	52.19	2.74	91.62	6.7
	United States										
679	Low Mortality	1959-61	58507	63161	68423	17700	31.52	58.99	9.49	69.53	9.8
680	Medium Mortality	1959-61	86634	92585	99171	25383	30.44	60.11	9.45	66.35	10.0
681	High Mortality	1959-61	34815	37514	40576	10761	32.08	59.65	8.27	67.66	8.3
682	Central America	1964-66	11247	13232	15611	6532	47.55	49.73	2.72	101.09	1.9
683	West Indies	1963-64	6172	7058	8099	2838	41.69	53.43	4.88	87.16	2.5
684	South America inc	1963-65	54070	62397	72167	29608	43.96	52.49	3.55	90.51	1.9
685	Southeast Asia inc	1960-61	161421	184362	208750	87959	43.12	54.29	2.59	84.21	6.4

VITAL RATES PER THOUSAND POPULATION								INFANT MOR-TALITY RATE per 1000 births	AGE-SPECIFIC DEATH RATES				
Crude (both sexes)			Standardized on U.S., 1960 (both sexes)		Intrinsic (females)				$1000_4 M_1$		$1000_5 M_{50}$		
Birth 10	Death 11	Increase 12	Birth 13	Death 14	Birth 15	Death 16	Increase 17	18	Males 19	Females 20	Males 21	Females 22	SERIES NUMBER
34.69	4.38	30.31	30.88	12.12	34.21	5.90	28.31	21.45	3.33	3.48	9.59	7.38	659
31.76	4.24	27.52	27.92	11.70	32.34	6.00	26.34	17.16	2.82	3.34	11.18	5.45	660
30.66	4.05	26.61	27.20	9.86	30.17	6.16	24.02	11.05	2.88	3.49	9.21	6.15	661
27.98	3.94	24.04	24.38	9.44	27.71	6.65	21.06	9.64	3.05	2.86	8.74	6.41	662
45.97	16.73	29.25	31.84	25.16	37.67	18.17	19.50	109.08	29.39	27.58	22.46	23.15	663
15.88	13.66	2.22	14.60	9.18	15.13	11.97	3.16	17.28	0.71	0.43	10.05	5.37	664
17.86	9.78	8.08	12.31	10.98	12.02	15.18	-3.16	14.42	0.43	0.84	14.56	5.12	665
15.61	16.75	-1.14	14.47	10.67	14.38	13.73	0.65	33.06	1.26	1.49	10.53	6.24	666
10.53	16.21	-5.68	10.72	10.27	9.32	18.98	-9.66	32.67	1.45	0.97	10.20	5.46	667
11.90	17.98	-6.08	11.71	10.23	11.00	16.48	-5.48	26.45	0.97	0.68	11.41	6.20	668
11.60	18.31	-6.71	11.50	10.15	10.53	17.10	-6.57	25.58	1.01	0.73	10.77	5.75	669
15.81	10.86	4.95	12.73	9.62	11.97	15.12	-3.15	25.30	1.16	0.74	9.87	5.16	670
15.30	12.01	3.29	12.86	9.90	12.22	14.77	-2.56	19.33	1.12	0.96	10.70	5.55	671
14.91	12.83	2.09	12.85	9.00	12.13	14.62	-2.48	19.00	1.00	0.78	8.53	5.08	672
14.81	14.10	0.71	13.14	9.58	12.82	14.17	-1.35	18.41	0.64	0.81	9.08	5.49	673
13.01	9.63	3.39	12.61	8.59	11.65	14.85	-3.20	16.58	0.71	0.40	7.93	4.10	674
12.67	10.24	2.43	12.38	8.96	11.63	15.05	-3.42	17.68	0.58	0.52	8.77	5.22	675
17.21	10.93	6.28	16.03	8.30	16.34	10.42	5.92	18.39	0.77	0.70	8.73	4.83	676
18.60	10.27	8.34	17.09	10.39	18.23	10.38	7.85	18.41	1.13	0.75	11.46	7.19	677
48.05	22.37	25.68	35.78	24.55	44.67	19.89	24.78	139.46	33.58	31.07	34.06	19.47	678
24.12	8.83	15.30	24.34	8.67	28.15	6.11	22.04	24.71	1.17	0.95	11.23	5.74	679
23.19	9.76	13.42	23.16	9.61	26.66	6.81	19.84	25.12	1.08	0.90	12.29	6.35	680
24.20	9.45	14.75	23.55	10.24	27.38	7.03	20.35	29.82	1.29	1.11	14.04	7.45	681
43.19	10.80	32.40	40.84	14.30	43.10	10.54	32.56	64.24	15.25	16.06	12.72	10.44	682
34.15	7.84	26.32	31.00	13.47	34.61	6.85	27.75	48.12	4.44	4.38	11.19	7.52	683
38.29	9.84	28.45	36.20	12.70	38.24	9.48	28.76	78.68	10.82	11.27	11.73	8.42	684
43.55	14.68	28.87	36.46	20.20	39.61	14.43	25.18	87.98	21.84	19.05	17.99	13.21	685

continued

LIFE TABLE VALUES

SERIES NUMBER	AREA AND YEAR		Probability of dying in first year, q_0		Survivors to age 50 per 100,000 births, l_{50}		Expectancy, $\mathring{e}_0$		Expectancy, $\mathring{e}_1$		Expectancy $\mathring{e}_{50}$
			Males 23	Females 24	Males 25	Females 26	Males 27	Females 28	Males 29	Females 30	Males 31
	ASIA--CITIES										
	China (Taiwan)										
659	Kaohsiung	1964	0.0244	0.0210	85288	89447	65.02	69.68	65.63	70.16	21.56
660		1966	0.0186	0.0177	85552	90056	65.50	70.88	65.74	71.14	21.59
661	Taipei	1964	0.0130	0.0132	88666	90666	68.11	71.95	68.00	71.91	23.10
662		1966	0.0117	0.0114	89056	91054	68.66	72.35	68.47	72.17	23.57
	Indonesia										
663	Djakarta	1961	0.1319	0.1228	53032	55450	44.54	46.13	50.24	51.53	18.21
	EUROPE--CITIES										
	Denmark										
664	Copenhagen	1966	0.0219	0.0141	89204	92687	68.30	74.61	68.82	74.67	22.92
	Finland										
665	Helsinki	1966	0.0136	0.0158	85988	93050	65.63	73.45	65.54	73.62	20.67
	East Germany										
666	East Berlin	1961	0.0368	0.0282	87070	89878	66.01	71.29	67.52	72.35	22.13
	West Germany										
667	West Berlin	1961	0.0350	0.0317	87074	90118	66.40	72.01	67.80	73.36	22.43
668		1966	0.0311	0.0218	87139	91369	66.42	72.92	67.55	73.54	22.21
669		1967	0.0276	0.0229	87562	91291	66.80	72.77	67.69	73.48	22.28
670	Duesseldorf	1964	0.0278	0.0235	88929	91623	68.06	73.65	69.00	74.42	23.24
671		1966	0.0240	0.0152	89202	92956	67.46	73.96	68.11	74.09	22.32
672	Hamburg	1964	0.0209	0.0170	89251	93055	68.53	74.63	68.99	74.91	23.36
673		1966	0.0207	0.0170	89516	93151	68.17	73.97	68.60	74.24	22.79
	Sweden										
674	Stockholm	1959	0.0200	0.0136	90488	93899	69.53	75.45	69.95	75.49	23.86
675		1960	0.0205	0.0155	90409	93172	69.02	74.91	69.46	75.09	23.32
	United Kingdom										
676	Greater London	1967	0.0195	0.0161	91186	93695	69.39	76.98	69.77	77.24	23.41
	OCEANIA--CITIES										
	Australia										
677	Sydney	1966	0.0229	0.0169	87900	92111	66.52	73.07	67.07	73.32	21.67
	POOLED POPULATIONS										
	Africa										
678	Subsaharan *inc*	1961-63	0.1524	0.1290	43658	49937	39.28	44.56	45.28	50.10	17.46
	United States										
679	Low Mortality	1959-61	0.0285	0.0216	86741	91847	67.73	74.60	68.71	75.24	23.90
680	Medium Mortality	1959-61	0.0287	0.0220	86531	91526	66.82	73.19	67.79	73.83	22.86
681	High Mortality	1959-61	0.0337	0.0263	84372	90012	65.34	71.89	66.61	72.83	22.26
682	Central America	1964-66	0.0694	0.0596	69517	72432	57.09	59.12	60.32	61.84	23.60
683	West Indies	1963-64	0.0530	0.0431	82200	86223	64.06	68.41	66.63	70.48	23.13
684	South America *inc*	1963-65	0.0856	0.0731	73616	77231	59.15	63.01	63.66	66.95	23.77
685	Southeast Asia *inc*	1960-61	0.1241	0.1059	59311	63902	48.87	52.24	54.74	57.38	20.39

FERTILITY MEASURES (FEMALES)

Females 32	Expectancy, $\mathring{e}_{70}$ Males 33	Females 34	General fertility rate 35	Total fertility rate 36	Gross reproduction rate 37	Net maternity function Total, NRR 38	Mean, μ 39	Variance, σ^2 40	Generation, T 41	Complex root, r_2 42	SERIES NUMBER
24.92	8.25	10.16	170.17	4.79	2.34	2.22	28.74	38.90	28.180	-0.0075+0.2313	659
25.98	9.62	11.11	152.67	4.35	2.14	2.04	27.47	30.98	27.045	-0.0056+0.2381	660
26.64	9.61	11.63	150.01	4.22	2.04	1.95	28.32	35.45	27.878	-0.0117+0.2297	661
26.70	9.84	12.00	132.16	3.80	1.84	1.78	27.64	32.13	27.293	-0.0115+0.2355	662
18.90	7.94	8.10	185.25	4.83	2.34	1.66	26.59	47.81	26.117	-0.0683+0.3042	663
28.04	9.55	12.31	83.10	2.25	1.11	1.08	25.67	30.10	25.622	-0.0390+0.2430	664
26.85	8.76	11.21	70.13	1.90	0.94	0.92	27.02	32.94	27.068	-0.0406+0.2268	665
26.51	9.21	11.28	81.99	2.22	1.07	1.02	25.56	33.92	25.582	-0.0492+0.2438	666
27.25	9.40	11.61	55.68	1.66	0.81	0.77	26.46	31.65	26.627	-0.0483+0.2312	667
27.23	9.12	11.68	64.82	1.81	0.89	0.86	27.64	32.18	27.729	-0.0380+0.2206	668
27.18	9.28	11.70	63.87	1.77	0.87	0.83	27.50	32.33	27.613	-0.0399+0.2208	669
28.11	10.10	12.40	69.63	1.97	0.95	0.92	27.60	30.75	27.637	-0.0356+0.2233	670
27.59	9.23	11.92	69.74	1.99	0.96	0.93	27.29	32.19	27.330	-0.0380+0.2255	671
28.15	9.85	12.19	69.52	1.99	0.96	0.93	27.62	29.62	27.666	-0.0334+0.2228	672
27.49	9.37	11.60	71.90	2.04	0.99	0.96	27.98	30.48	28.005	-0.0319+0.2211	673
28.53	10.07	12.27	61.14	1.95	0.94	0.92	27.38	31.87	27.436	-0.0377+0.2249	674
28.32	9.63	12.14	59.40	1.92	0.93	0.91	27.58	31.97	27.641	-0.0374+0.2236	675
30.35	9.40	14.80	84.97	2.47	1.21	1.17	27.42	33.47	27.314	-0.0308+0.2263	676
26.90	8.88	11.69	86.18	2.64	1.28	1.24	27.46	32.43	27.324	-0.0272+0.2269	677
22.11	10.50	11.76	215.13	6.04	2.97	1.95	27.59	53.60	26.923	-0.0452+0.2291	678
28.94	10.87	13.22	122.15	3.75	1.83	1.76	26.15	34.40	25.757	-0.0243+0.2520	679
27.51	10.18	12.23	114.80	3.58	1.74	1.68	26.53	34.14	26.180	-0.0245+0.2447	680
26.97	10.20	12.34	117.68	3.62	1.77	1.69	26.25	35.80	25.871	-0.0287+0.2481	681
24.52	11.12	11.37	211.64	6.21	3.03	2.48	28.71	53.14	27.842	-0.0279+0.2182	682
26.00	9.56	11.02	163.05	4.73	2.31	2.13	27.88	47.40	27.209	-0.0326+0.2259	683
26.46	11.12	12.41	183.35	5.56	2.72	2.30	29.82	63.38	28.929	-0.0241+0.2212	684
21.95	8.93	9.32	195.83	5.58	2.69	2.03	28.71	49.69	28.081	-0.0317+0.2201	685

SERIES NUMBER	AREA AND YEAR		POPULATION, IN 1000'S			AGE STRUCTURE					
			Observed at mid-year	Projected		Total reproductive value (in 1000's)	Percent at age			Dependency ratio (× 100)	Departure from stability (Δ percent)
				5 years	10 years		<15	15–64	≥65		
			1	2	3	4	5	6	7	8	9
686	Europe	1955	4C548C	422900	438300	104834	25.22	65.55	9.23	52.54	4.2
687		1960	422786	439700	455700	105730	25.84	64.48	9.68	55.08	3.6
688		1965	441791	459000	475700	107866	25.23	64.27	10.50	55.59	3.1
689	European Common	1955	164304	169662	174395	39792	23.95	65.96	10.09	51.61	4.2
690	Market	1960	172227	178136	183408	41750	24.35	65.20	10.45	53.37	4.1
691		1965	182706	189283	195423	43904	24.05	64.56	11.39	54.91	4.6
692	European Free	1955	85574	87645	89369	19221	23.79	65.55	10.66	52.56	3.9
693	Trade Area	1960	88885	91732	94573	21002	24.37	64.52	11.11	54.99	5.3
694		1965	91523	94928	98315	21814	23.63	64.64	11.73	54.70	6.5
695	European Members	1955	93269	99845	105425	26674	27.04	65.29	7.67	53.18	6.6
696	of COMECON	1960	96730	100938	104881	24047	27.95	63.70	8.35	56.98	6.0
697		1965	99740	102943	106256	22686	26.84	63.93	9.23	56.43	6.9
	COHORTS										
698	United States	1910	155303	154510	153505	33481	20.66	64.27	15.07	55.61	1.7
699		1915	167208	166751	166101	35607	20.54	64.16	15.30	55.86	0.8
700		1920	172077	172449	172596	38084	20.79	63.66	15.55	57.09	3.0
701		1925	181415	183555	185320	40782	20.57	63.79	15.64	56.77	7.7
702		1930	173702	177943	181722	39693	20.08	64.47	15.45	55.11	12.8
703	Sweden	1780	2426	2468	2510	1162	28.76	64.11	7.13	56.00	4.3
704		1785	2435	2489	2540	1185	28.58	64.21	7.21	55.73	4.7
705		1790	2545	2609	2666	1234	28.35	64.04	7.61	56.13	5.7
706		1795	2815	2893	2960	1328	27.84	63.97	8.19	56.34	6.6
707		1800	2851	2926	2993	1346	27.45	64.13	8.42	55.94	6.6
708		1805	2858	2949	3034	1326	27.25	64.09	8.66	56.03	7.5
709		1810	2793	2865	2924	1341	26.74	64.21	9.05	55.76	5.9
710		1815	3165	3274	3366	1424	25.99	64.17	9.84	55.81	8.0
711		1820	3564	3689	3806	1579	25.60	64.13	10.27	55.94	8.6
712		1825	4136	4309	4467	1760	25.52	63.82	10.66	56.68	9.3
713		1830	4086	4224	4354	1770	25.62	63.55	10.83	57.36	7.2
714		1835	4173	4336	4499	1781	25.77	63.11	11.12	58.45	7.9
715		1840	4091	4247	4399	1746	26.07	62.70	11.23	59.47	7.0
716		1845	4319	4467	4610	1797	26.45	62.26	11.29	60.63	5.2
717		1850	4346	4489	4646	1827	27.28	61.39	11.33	62.89	5.4
718		1855	4589	4732	4884	1919	27.50	61.10	11.40	63.68	4.3
719		1860	5029	5187	5363	2048	27.78	60.79	11.43	64.49	4.2
720		1865	5291	5435	5605	2108	28.28	60.24	11.48	66.00	3.5
721		1870	4940	5043	5169	1903	28.34	59.90	11.76	66.94	2.9
722		1875	5335	5421	5518	1943	27.82	59.84	12.34	67.11	2.3
723		1880	5862	5942	6035	1956	26.51	60.55	12.94	65.16	1.8
724		1885	6119	6165	6227	1883	25.97	60.58	13.45	65.08	1.6
725		1890	6567	6566	6582	1822	25.15	60.87	13.98	64.30	3.1
726		1895	6853	6796	6744	1688	24.09	61.37	14.54	62.95	6.1
727		1900	7355	7232	7112	1627	23.02	61.95	15.03	61.44	9.9
728		1905	7909	7749	7589	1624	22.20	62.33	15.47	60.45	11.6
729		1910	8464	8300	8136	1689	21.38	62.82	15.80	59.19	10.2
730		1915	8457	8325	8193	1665	20.68	63.31	16.01	57.95	7.5
731		1920	8114	8030	7941	1571	20.19	63.64	16.17	57.12	4.6
732		1925	8249	8178	8102	1520	19.65	64.02	16.33	56.22	3.1

VITAL RATES PER THOUSAND POPULATION

Crude (both sexes)			Standardized on U.S., 1960 (both sexes)		Intrinsic (females)			INFANT MOR-TALITY RATE per 1000 births	1000₄M_1		1000₅M_{50}		SERIES NUMBER
Birth 10	Death 11	Increase 12	Birth 13	Death 14	Birth 15	Death 16	Increase 17	18	Males 19	Females 20	Males 21	Females 22	
19.26	10.43	8.83	16.69	10.75	17.32	12.26	5.06	52.68	3.05	2.93	9.96	5.88	686
18.60	10.20	8.40	16.67	10.12	17.40	11.44	5.97	39.74	2.08	1.90	9.34	5.32	687
18.04	10.20	7.84	16.69	9.45	17.46	10.83	6.62	30.93	1.44	1.25	9.01	5.05	688
17.39	10.55	6.83	15.45	10.25	15.78	12.66	3.13	40.16	2.02	1.78	10.12	5.64	689
17.96	10.71	7.24	16.17	9.93	16.75	11.52	5.23	32.15	1.59	1.37	9.79	5.16	690
18.08	10.69	7.39	16.97	9.17	17.74	10.41	7.33	25.34	1.21	0.99	9.49	5.03	691
16.50	11.12	5.37	15.32	10.28	15.66	12.66	3.00	35.76	2.51	2.34	9.76	5.79	692
17.56	10.98	6.58	17.31	9.72	18.35	10.42	7.92	30.42	1.87	1.61	9.03	5.22	693
18.47	11.13	7.34	17.94	9.32	19.16	9.64	9.53	25.09	1.45	1.27	8.95	4.99	694
23.09	10.03	13.06	19.27	11.30	20.44	10.71	9.73	68.04	3.42	3.29	9.93	6.32	695
18.71	9.40	9.31	16.24	10.69	16.97	12.26	4.72	51.96	2.20	2.01	9.04	5.61	696
16.00	9.45	6.56	14.45	10.22	14.71	13.19	1.52	35.70	1.54	1.30	8.53	5.22	697
16.41	17.31	-0.90	15.59	13.67	14.72	17.23	-2.50	119.11	13.30	12.26	12.48	6.39	698
16.16	16.57	-0.41	15.54	12.50	14.89	15.85	-0.96	95.68	9.47	8.58	12.16	6.27	699
17.16	16.43	0.73	16.35	12.22	16.11	14.63	1.48	93.30	9.95	9.17	12.16	6.28	700
18.73	15.92	2.81	17.74	11.33	18.30	12.38	5.92	73.58	6.72	6.04	12.16	6.28	701
21.06	15.47	5.58	19.88	10.99	21.71	10.46	11.25	69.38	6.02	5.22	12.16	6.28	702
32.91	28.53	4.38	28.88	30.70	30.43	25.81	4.62	211.62	45.87	44.30	31.91	22.00	703
33.85	27.81	6.04	29.46	30.60	30.96	25.87	5.09	231.45	46.69	44.46	27.55	19.08	704
34.24	27.21	7.04	29.93	29.57	31.30	25.25	6.04	255.30	37.81	36.63	26.48	19.43	705
33.93	26.46	7.47	30.07	28.20	31.24	24.13	7.12	238.48	35.48	33.25	25.75	17.52	706
33.97	26.35	7.62	30.44	28.22	31.64	24.55	7.09	248.96	37.14	35.75	24.96	16.95	707
33.95	25.69	8.25	30.50	26.69	31.51	23.06	8.45	223.07	31.16	29.14	24.90	18.81	708
33.85	26.86	6.99	30.68	27.87	31.73	25.01	6.71	260.08	48.21	45.19	20.57	15.00	709
32.70	24.15	8.56	29.93	24.41	30.60	21.78	8.82	216.98	35.52	32.80	18.99	14.23	710
32.23	23.16	9.07	29.94	23.17	30.25	20.81	9.43	206.69	34.51	31.89	20.20	14.61	711
31.37	21.44	9.92	29.32	20.90	29.24	18.70	10.55	178.35	22.24	20.59	17.74	13.13	712
30.81	22.52	8.29	28.74	21.96	28.75	20.17	8.58	203.99	31.85	29.42	15.16	11.70	713
30.62	21.52	9.10	28.78	20.51	28.68	18.68	9.99	185.99	24.56	22.45	14.72	11.11	714
30.15	21.54	8.61	28.34	20.53	28.27	18.88	9.39	184.61	25.32	23.67	14.36	11.27	715
28.55	21.13	7.42	26.99	20.01	26.89	18.90	7.99	174.16	27.01	24.75	13.38	10.43	716
28.61	21.46	7.15	27.52	20.01	27.49	18.77	8.72	165.60	25.55	23.19	13.74	11.04	717
28.02	21.56	6.45	27.08	20.11	27.20	19.31	7.89	164.80	34.54	32.11	12.91	10.03	718
26.87	20.81	6.06	26.19	19.20	26.44	18.43	8.01	150.76	30.68	28.75	12.17	9.81	719
25.62	20.50	5.11	25.44	18.84	25.69	18.33	7.36	148.04	30.36	28.10	11.70	9.44	720
24.33	20.52	3.82	24.45	18.79	24.72	18.75	5.97	157.70	28.14	26.49	11.35	9.95	721
23.11	20.52	2.59	23.44	18.20	23.64	18.82	4.83	155.36	27.52	26.34	9.83	8.98	722
21.75	19.48	2.28	21.80	16.95	22.01	18.07	3.94	131.33	26.38	25.34	9.85	8.93	723
20.00	18.94	1.06	19.92	16.10	19.95	17.90	2.05	121.69	23.90	22.71	9.43	8.30	724
17.77	18.21	-0.45	17.51	15.19	17.06	18.37	-1.32	120.73	19.54	18.78	8.97	7.39	725
15.44	17.71	-2.27	15.18	14.28	14.13	19.36	-5.22	106.93	16.80	16.42	7.95	6.51	726
13.30	17.34	-4.04	13.18	13.65	11.51	20.93	-9.42	106.84	16.15	15.38	7.25	5.68	727
11.78	16.46	-4.68	11.86	12.36	9.95	21.44	-11.49	90.16	12.18	11.47	6.53	4.83	728
11.63	15.91	-4.28	11.90	11.50	10.05	20.43	-10.38	69.78	12.16	11.10	6.25	4.36	729
12.26	15.55	-3.30	12.52	10.96	10.91	18.84	-7.93	51.40	14.14	12.69	6.25	4.36	730
13.09	15.30	-2.21	13.13	10.48	11.94	17.14	-5.19	46.42	14.39	12.52	6.25	4.36	731
13.21	14.81	-1.60	13.15	9.74	12.16	16.12	-3.96	42.01	9.54	7.99	6.25	4.36	732

[117]

continued

LIFE TABLE VALUES

SERIES NUMBER	AREA AND YEAR		Probability of dying in first year, q_0		Survivors to age 50 per 100,000 births, l_{50}		Expectancy, $\overset{\circ}{e}_0$		Expectancy, $\overset{\circ}{e}_1$		Expectancy, $\overset{\circ}{e}_{50}$
			Males 23	Females 24	Males 25	Females 26	Males 27	Females 28	Males 29	Females 30	Males 31
686	Europe	1955	0.0585	0.0485	83986	87744	64.88	69.66	67.90	72.20	23.40
687		1960	0.0439	0.0359	86525	90292	66.57	71.70	68.61	73.36	23.47
688		1965	0.0336	0.0271	87874	91850	67.69	73.33	69.04	74.37	23.64
689	European Common	1955	0.0439	0.0357	85683	89841	66.32	71.29	68.36	72.91	23.53
690	Market	1960	0.0357	0.0285	87310	91406	67.07	72.60	68.55	73.73	23.28
691		1965	0.0277	0.0219	88279	92491	67.99	74.05	68.92	74.71	23.50
692	European Free	1955	0.0399	0.0324	87032	90315	66.53	71.52	68.28	72.91	23.08
693	Trade Area	1960	0.0344	0.0275	88377	91782	67.52	72.94	68.92	74.00	23.33
694		1965	0.0280	0.0223	89060	92578	68.08	73.95	69.03	74.63	23.33
695	European Members	1955	0.0771	0.0627	81500	85591	63.21	70.11	67.48	73.78	23.44
696	of COMECON	1960	0.0573	0.0465	84690	88778	65.40	70.19	68.36	72.61	23.55
697		1965	0.0388	0.0306	86965	91235	67.00	72.04	68.69	73.31	23.49
	COHORTS										
698	United States	1910	0.1206	0.0996	69203	74203	55.04	61.56	61.54	67.33	22.95
699		1915	0.0992	0.0800	73400	78773	57.81	64.67	63.14	69.27	22.98
700		1920	0.0977	0.0775	74373	80568	58.33	65.71	63.61	70.20	22.98
701		1925	0.0780	0.0617	77670	83989	60.67	68.21	64.77	71.67	22.98
702		1930	0.0735	0.0586	79500	85311	61.82	69.12	65.70	72.40	22.98
703	Sweden	1780	0.1974	0.1768	38311	43616	34.36	37.89	41.71	44.95	17.33
704		1785	0.2134	0.1913	37541	43279	34.23	37.79	42.41	45.64	17.75
705		1790	0.2318	0.2059	38253	44284	34.78	38.52	44.17	47.41	18.25
706		1795	0.2185	0.1943	39557	45877	35.86	39.92	44.78	48.46	18.54
707		1800	0.2268	0.2016	39125	45488	35.52	39.43	44.83	48.29	18.89
708		1805	0.2072	0.1818	40623	47888	36.84	41.32	45.38	49.42	19.38
709		1810	0.2384	0.2081	38515	44980	34.78	39.02	44.56	48.18	19.84
710		1815	0.2041	0.1765	44172	50236	39.08	43.32	48.01	51.53	20.74
711		1820	0.1953	0.1696	46739	52174	40.76	44.75	49.56	52.81	21.20
712		1825	0.1715	0.1473	50753	55910	44.24	48.03	52.32	55.27	22.03
713		1830	0.1941	0.1662	48297	53781	42.11	46.10	51.17	54.21	22.38
714		1835	0.1780	0.1531	51501	56701	44.43	48.38	52.97	56.06	22.63
715		1840	0.1770	0.1520	51331	56419	44.20	48.20	52.63	55.78	22.76
716		1845	0.1690	0.1441	52295	56901	44.85	48.59	52.90	55.71	23.23
717		1850	0.1622	0.1364	52629	57014	44.90	48.61	52.52	55.23	23.25
718		1855	0.1611	0.1377	52478	56305	44.72	47.93	52.24	54.52	23.56
719		1860	0.1481	0.1266	54843	58370	46.52	49.54	53.54	55.67	23.74
720		1865	0.1464	0.1246	55676	58992	47.09	49.98	54.10	56.04	23.90
721		1870	0.1548	0.1319	55723	58600	47.03	49.67	54.58	56.16	24.12
722		1875	0.1524	0.1303	56536	58796	47.76	50.05	55.28	56.49	24.62
723		1880	0.1317	0.1110	59122	61536	49.78	52.25	56.27	57.73	24.90
724		1885	0.1234	0.1023	61022	63485	51.27	53.99	57.43	59.10	25.06
725		1890	0.1182	0.0974	63045	65717	52.80	55.80	58.82	60.78	25.28
726		1895	0.1088	0.0910	65451	68282	54.49	57.70	60.10	62.44	25.49
727		1900	0.1095	0.0902	67647	70676	55.67	59.25	61.47	64.09	25.63
728		1905	0.0935	0.0765	72714	75164	58.96	62.35	64.01	66.49	25.76
729		1910	0.0736	0.0598	76352	78801	61.24	64.66	65.08	67.75	25.80
730		1915	0.0556	0.0440	78709	81357	62.67	66.23	65.33	68.25	25.80
731		1920	0.0506	0.0394	80590	83957	63.85	67.87	66.22	69.63	25.80
732		1925	0.0461	0.0355	83679	87225	65.95	70.12	68.12	71.69	25.80

FERTILITY MEASURES (FEMALES)

Expectancy, $\mathring{e}_{70}$			General fertility rate	Total fertility rate	Gross reproduction rate	Net maternity function					SERIES NUMBER
Females 32	Males 33	Females 34	35	36	37	Total, NRR 38	Mean, μ 39	Variance, σ^2 40	Generation, T 41	Complex root, r_2 42	
26.80	9.74	11.29	87.84	2.58	1.25	1.15	28.50	36.90	28.405	$-0.0327+0.2185$	686
27.20	9.73	11.35	89.00	2.58	1.25	1.18	28.10	35.91	27.993	$-0.0324+0.2233$	687
27.83	9.92	11.87	84.79	2.58	1.26	1.20	27.85	35.07	27.723	$-0.0313+0.2255$	688
26.93	9.77	11.20	80.59	2.39	1.16	1.09	28.95	34.79	28.893	$-0.0301+0.2146$	689
27.31	9.68	11.37	86.98	2.50	1.22	1.16	28.81	34.59	28.716	$-0.0286+0.2176$	690
28.08	9.99	12.09	85.96	2.63	1.28	1.23	28.31	34.17	28.180	$-0.0270+0.2213$	691
26.92	9.49	11.29	78.80	2.37	1.15	1.09	28.21	35.42	28.159	$-0.0347+0.2209$	692
27.48	9.64	11.59	87.65	2.68	1.30	1.24	27.84	33.93	27.700	$-0.0293+0.2266$	693
27.96	9.69	12.02	91.30	2.78	1.35	1.30	27.58	34.33	27.410	$-0.0289+0.2286$	694
29.02	9.95	14.85	103.41	2.98	1.44	1.30	27.55	37.63	27.358	$-0.0355+0.2304$	695
26.66	9.76	10.97	88.54	2.51	1.21	1.13	26.58	35.43	26.494	$-0.0422+0.2417$	696
26.85	9.52	10.97	73.40	2.24	1.09	1.04	26.34	32.49	26.319	$-0.0412+0.2431$	697
28.25	10.42	12.97	80.13	2.38	1.16	0.93	27.14	42.90	27.198	$-0.0535+0.2157$	698
28.27	10.42	12.97	78.88	2.37	1.16	0.97	27.54	41.12	27.560	$-0.0449+0.2157$	699
28.27	10.42	12.97	83.24	2.50	1.22	1.04	27.75	39.69	27.723	$-0.0407+0.2162$	700
28.27	10.42	12.97	90.36	2.72	1.33	1.18	27.68	36.02	27.570	$-0.0317+0.2207$	701
28.27	10.42	12.97	102.33	3.08	1.50	1.35	27.04	31.83	26.850	$-0.0259+0.2342$	702
19.66	7.52	8.30	142.49	4.37	2.14	1.16	32.29	42.31	32.186	$-0.0221+0.1886$	703
19.93	7.68	8.29	145.08	4.46	2.18	1.18	32.31	41.96	32.198	$-0.0214+0.1885$	704
20.23	8.15	8.79	147.71	4.53	2.21	1.21	32.38	41.12	32.245	$-0.0198+0.1886$	705
20.84	8.10	9.13	149.41	4.55	2.22	1.26	32.40	40.73	32.244	$-0.0187+0.1890$	706
21.03	8.15	9.17	151.15	4.61	2.25	1.26	32.25	40.07	32.106	$-0.0189+0.1901$	707
21.48	8.73	9.64	151.13	4.62	2.26	1.31	32.25	40.98	32.070	$-0.0183+0.1903$	708
21.93	8.83	9.71	150.64	4.65	2.27	1.24	32.34	40.68	32.202	$-0.0195+0.1894$	709
22.76	9.29	10.06	147.18	4.53	2.21	1.33	32.55	40.98	32.362	$-0.0173+0.1887$	710
23.08	9.37	10.04	146.70	4.53	2.21	1.36	32.92	40.51	32.722	$-0.0154+0.1867$	711
23.77	9.71	10.47	143.46	4.43	2.16	1.41	33.12	39.05	32.900	$-0.0130+0.1860$	712
24.00	9.68	10.31	140.59	4.34	2.11	1.33	33.02	37.86	32.853	$-0.0141+0.1869$	713
24.35	9.82	10.54	140.77	4.35	2.12	1.39	33.08	38.85	32.876	$-0.0137+0.1871$	714
24.52	9.82	10.55	137.90	4.29	2.09	1.36	32.86	38.73	32.666	$-0.0146+0.1878$	715
24.84	10.04	10.69	131.52	4.08	1.99	1.30	32.74	39.20	32.572	$-0.0163+0.1877$	716
24.71	10.03	10.52	133.79	4.17	2.03	1.33	32.53	37.51	32.354	$-0.0154+0.1901$	717
24.94	10.13	10.60	132.40	4.11	2.00	1.29	32.22	38.52	32.063	$-0.0178+0.1911$	718
25.04	10.12	10.58	127.07	3.98	1.93	1.29	32.00	39.05	31.837	$-0.0186+0.1922$	719
25.15	10.11	10.69	122.95	3.87	1.88	1.26	31.80	39.14	31.644	$-0.0196+0.1930$	720
25.26	10.25	10.81	118.73	3.72	1.81	1.21	31.49	38.49	31.367	$-0.0213+0.1949$	721
25.71	10.60	11.16	115.54	3.57	1.74	1.16	31.18	37.98	31.087	$-0.0231+0.1969$	722
26.16	10.77	11.48	108.86	3.34	1.62	1.13	30.65	37.98	30.572	$-0.0259+0.2004$	723
26.63	10.76	11.66	100.14	3.05	1.48	1.06	30.15	37.86	30.106	$-0.0293+0.2031$	724
27.18	10.75	11.83	88.92	2.69	1.31	0.96	29.57	37.04	29.599	$-0.0336+0.2062$	725
27.63	10.75	11.84	77.72	2.34	1.13	0.86	29.07	36.47	29.173	$-0.0388+0.2097$	726
27.96	10.75	11.84	67.73	2.03	0.99	0.76	28.83	38.34	29.020	$-0.0465+0.2091$	727
28.17	10.75	11.84	60.47	1.82	0.88	0.71	29.32	41.93	29.574	$-0.0480+0.2009$	728
28.23	10.75	11.84	60.25	1.81	0.88	0.73	29.75	40.32	29.972	$-0.0412+0.1977$	729
28.23	10.75	11.84	63.70	1.91	0.93	0.79	29.48	34.35	29.621	$-0.0349+0.2041$	730
28.23	10.75	11.84	67.67	2.03	0.99	0.86	28.70	30.87	28.781	$-0.0337+0.2145$	731
28.23	10.75	11.84	68.00	2.04	0.99	0.89	27.96	32.45	28.024	$-0.0385+0.2214$	732

SERIES NUMBER	AREA AND YEAR / MALE-DOMINANT CALCULATIONS	POPULATION, IN 1000'S			AGE STRUCTURE					
		Observed at mid-year	Projected		Total re-productive value (in 1000's)	Percent at age			Depen-dency ratio (× 100)	Departure from stability (Δ percent)
			5 years	10 years		< 15	15–64	⩾ 65		
		1	2	3	4	5	6	7	8	9
	NORTH AMERICA									
733	Canada 1966	19521	20719	22080	6589	32.75	59.51	7.74	68.02	5.5
734	Trinidad and Tobago 1956-58	765	876	1005	435	42.31	54.13	3.56	84.74	5.1
735	United States 1959-61	179990	192935	207070	61599	31.17	59.58	9.25	67.85	10.3
736	1962	185888	198456	212769	63189	31.30	59.39	9.31	68.40	9.0
737	1963	188656	200735	214695	63635	31.20	59.49	9.31	68.09	8.0
738	1964	191369	203317	217197	63896	31.08	59.59	9.33	67.81	6.7
739	1966	195857	205610	217453	61835	30.67	59.91	9.42	66.91	5.4
740	Nonwhite 1966	23493	25693	28420	10401	38.32	55.57	6.11	79.95	7.0
741	White 1966	172364	179958	189153	51528	29.62	60.50	9.88	65.28	5.1
	SOUTH AMERICA									
742	Chile 1964	8391	9366	10486	4805	39.63	56.00	4.37	78.56	2.0
743	Peru 1963	10980	12688	14678	6841	44.15	52.43	3.42	90.75	2.1
	ASIA									
744	Cyprus 1956-58	546	600	665	199	34.45	58.76	6.79	70.16	3.1
	EUROPE									
745	Belgium 1966	9556	9732	9911	2326	23.91	63.19	12.90	58.25	3.2
746	Hungary 1964	10120	10259	10380	2306	23.80	66.15	10.05	51.18	9.5
747	1967	10197	10387	10585	2383	22.53	66.70	10.77	49.93	6.0
748	Norway 1963	3667	3803	3953	1009	25.00	63.39	11.61	57.73	6.1
749	Romania 1966	19136	20011	20518	4701	25.62	66.16	8.22	51.15	20.4
750	UK: England, 1960-62	46166	47431	48643	11630	22.93	65.11	11.96	53.58	7.2
751	Wales 1964	47401	49093	50740	12374	22.70	65.24	12.06	53.28	7.6
	OCEANIA									
752	New Zealand 1966	2683	2877	3116	945	32.61	59.10	8.29	69.23	4.1

| VITAL RATES PER THOUSAND POPULATION | | | | | | | | INFANT MOR- TALITY RATE | AGE-SPECIFIC DEATH RATES | | | | |
| Crude (both sexes) | | | Standardized on U.S., 1960 (both sexes) | | Intrinsic (females) | | | per 1000 births | 1000_4M_1 | | 1000_5M_{50} | | SERIES NUMBER |
Birth 10	Death 11	Increase 12	Birth 13	Death 14	Birth 15	Death 16	Increase 17	18	Males 19	Females 20	Males 21	Females 22	
19.14	7.52	11.62	18.26	8.33	20.23	8.74	11.50	22.93	1.06	0.87	9.77	4.96	733
37.46	9.46	28.00	37.30	15.35	38.38	7.84	30.55	61.04	4.18	3.63	13.87	12.27	734
23.65	9.39	14.26	23.65	9.39	27.48	6.57	20.92	26.83	1.15	0.96	12.26	6.36	735
22.42	9.45	12.97	22.85	9.38	26.59	6.77	19.81	25.36	1.05	0.91	12.27	6.34	736
21.72	9.61	12.11	22.12	9.54	25.74	7.06	18.68	25.24	1.08	0.91	12.30	6.37	737
21.05	9.40	11.65	21.44	9.29	24.78	7.31	17.48	24.64	1.05	0.87	12.06	6.39	738
18.41	9.51	8.90	18.66	9.33	21.40	8.58	12.82	23.72	1.01	0.85	12.23	6.24	739
26.09	9.73	16.36	27.60	12.41	31.67	7.34	24.33	38.81	1.65	1.42	19.09	12.00	740
17.37	9.48	7.88	17.52	8.97	19.94	8.96	10.98	20.63	0.90	0.73	11.51	5.60	741
32.81	11.21	21.60	33.54	14.68	34.18	10.63	23.55	114.30	7.19	7.25	16.44	9.59	742
38.36	10.03	28.34	38.61	11.92	39.53	10.06	29.47	80.87	14.44	14.98	10.40	7.47	743
25.82	6.21	19.61	23.63	9.26	27.54	6.72	20.82	31.53	2.03	2.94	6.14	3.57	744
15.81	12.10	3.71	14.97	9.44	16.53	11.23	5.31	24.73	1.05	0.81	10.01	5.41	745
13.06	9.96	3.09	11.76	9.98	12.39	15.34	-2.95	40.00	1.25	1.24	8.32	5.27	746
14.60	10.74	3.86	13.08	10.28	14.26	13.64	0.62	36.99	1.28	1.06	8.13	4.94	747
17.26	10.05	7.21	17.67	8.13	19.40	8.98	10.42	16.87	1.27	0.68	6.98	3.90	748
14.30	8.23	6.07	11.59	9.50	11.46	15.58	-4.12	46.60	2.20	2.10	8.19	5.55	749
17.58	11.81	5.77	16.91	9.59	19.14	9.59	9.55	21.64	0.98	0.79	9.25	5.33	750
18.48	11.28	7.20	17.63	9.05	20.01	8.94	11.07	19.91	0.87	0.73	9.22	5.21	751
22.43	8.86	13.57	21.60	9.33	24.76	7.06	17.70	17.68	1.18	1.07	9.47	5.59	752

continued

LIFE TABLE VALUES

SERIES NUMBER	AREA AND YEAR / MALE-DOMINANT CALCULATIONS		Probability of dying in first year, q_0		Survivors to age 50 per 100,000 births, l_{50}		Expectancy, $\overset{\circ}{e}_0$		Expectancy, $\overset{\circ}{e}_1$		Expectancy, $\overset{\circ}{e}_{50}$
			Males 23	Females 24	Males 25	Females 26	Males 27	Females 28	Males 29	Females 30	Males 31
	NORTH AMERICA										
733	Canada	1966	0.0244	0.0195	88356	92902	68.74	75.24	69.45	75.73	24.25
734	Trinidad and Tobago	1956–58	0.0674	0.0558	79057	81559	60.13	63.20	63.46	65.92	20.11
735	United States	1959–61	0.0297	0.0228	86162	91317	66.84	73.40	67.87	74.10	23.10
736		1962	0.0281	0.0215	86404	91431	66.93	73.52	67.86	74.13	23.02
737		1963	0.0280	0.0215	86233	91366	66.68	73.42	67.59	74.02	22.79
738		1964	0.0271	0.0211	86204	91450	66.90	73.72	67.76	74.30	23.04
739		1966	0.0258	0.0200	86081	91519	66.75	73.86	67.51	74.36	22.88
740	Nonwhite	1966	0.0413	0.0341	75507	83576	60.77	67.49	62.38	68.86	20.79
741	White	1966	0.0226	0.0171	87558	92712	67.61	74.80	68.17	75.10	23.10
	SOUTH AMERICA										
742	Chile	1964	0.1160	0.1031	69061	76306	55.70	61.29	61.97	67.30	21.74
743	Peru	1963	0.0819	0.0727	72891	74327	60.53	62.78	64.89	66.67	26.52
	ASIA										
744	Cyprus	1956–58	0.0291	0.0326	86316	91431	70.07	73.87	71.16	75.34	27.37
	EUROPE										
745	Belgium	1966	0.0271	0.0219	88763	92737	67.75	73.84	68.63	74.49	22.99
746	Hungary	1964	0.0443	0.0354	86796	90987	67.03	71.86	69.12	73.49	23.77
747		1967	0.0438	0.0353	86474	91087	66.69	71.82	68.74	73.44	23.45
748	Norway	1963	0.0189	0.0151	90827	94583	70.83	75.47	71.19	75.63	25.31
749	Romania	1966	0.0508	0.0415	85832	89486	71.26	73.54	74.06	75.71	29.61
750	UK: England,	1960–62	0.0246	0.0190	90038	93071	68.10	73.97	68.81	74.39	22.70
751	Wales	1964	0.0230	0.0181	90196	93228	68.53	74.68	69.14	75.06	23.03
	OCEANIA										
752	New Zealand	1966	0.0202	0.0145	88936	92833	68.04	74.22	68.43	74.31	23.02

Expectancy, $\mathring{e}_{70}$			General fertility rate	Total fertility rate	Gross reproduction rate	Net paternity function					
Females 32	Males 33	Females 34	35	36	37	Total, NRR 38	Mean, μ 39	Variance, σ^2 40	Generation, T 41	Complex root, r_2 42	SERIES NUMBER
29.07	10.79	13.20	91.52	2.95	1.51	1.42	30.84	49.94	30.624	−0.0253+0.2117	733
22.37	8.79	10.23	184.04	6.01	3.06	2.66	33.05	63.75	32.090	−0.0173+0.2025	734
27.89	10.46	12.61	121.97	3.83	1.96	1.84	29.55	46.23	29.067	−0.0170+0.2272	735
27.91	10.41	12.62	115.95	3.70	1.90	1.78	29.53	45.62	29.074	−0.0171+0.2267	736
27.82	10.23	12.56	111.94	3.58	1.84	1.72	29.58	45.22	29.153	−0.0177+0.2254	737
28.10	10.48	12.82	108.10	3.47	1.78	1.67	29.62	45.02	29.222	−0.0191+0.2241	738
28.18	10.35	12.84	94.23	3.02	1.55	1.45	29.33	47.34	29.026	−0.0259+0.2247	739
25.03	11.01	13.54	138.92	4.47	2.26	2.02	29.70	60.58	28.988	−0.0200+0.2338	740
28.54	10.30	12.82	88.40	2.84	1.46	1.38	29.29	44.87	29.038	−0.0266+0.2233	741
25.27	9.93	11.38	158.27	5.42	2.75	2.17	33.66	70.58	32.839	−0.0328+0.2004	742
28.56	13.55	14.13	184.21	6.14	3.16	2.55	32.48	46.43	31.771	−0.0037+0.1948	743
29.22	11.86	11.84	127.48	3.75	1.92	1.78	28.20	57.62	27.602	−0.0383+0.2353	744
27.71	9.78	11.88	77.15	2.42	1.24	1.17	30.10	40.25	30.069	−0.0262+0.2136	745
26.89	9.82	11.08	61.23	1.91	0.99	0.92	29.73	38.72	29.794	−0.0327+0.2178	746
26.76	9.47	10.85	67.72	2.13	1.10	1.02	29.39	37.87	30.789	−0.0289+0.2197	747
28.35	10.77	11.72	86.12	2.84	1.45	1.38	31.45	45.48	31.204	−0.0228+0.2050	748
29.92	17.76	14.99	61.43	1.88	0.97	0.88	30.12	42.01	30.216	−0.0352+0.2147	749
27.54	9.27	11.74	89.01	2.73	1.41	1.34	30.52	42.22	30.314	−0.0227+0.2119	750
28.19	9.60	12.36	90.18	2.85	1.47	1.40	30.37	42.48	30.128	−0.0203+0.2133	751
27.80	9.48	12.28	109.01	3.49	1.79	1.70	30.22	45.77	29.851	−0.0153+0.2179	752

DEMOGRAPHIC THEORY
AND COMPUTATION

CHAPTER 6

Mortality and the Making of Life Tables

In Part III certain models making up formal demography are introduced in sequence, with special attention to the life table, population projection, and stable population.

The life table is our first subject, because it is the oldest and simplest demographic model, and more elaborate models depend on it. We will first examine how the life table is interpreted and used, and then see how it is constructed. This reversal of the natural order is a convenience in exposition: once the interpretation of the table, its notation, and its applications are clear, the method of construction follows readily.

Probabilities of Living and Dying

The life table was orginally developed to express probabilities pertaining to individual persons. For this purpose, a fundamental column is the $_nq_x$, the probability of dying in the next n years for a person of age x. We see for the United States, 1967 (Table 2, page 360), that the probability of a man exactly 40 years old dying within 5 years (that is, before he reaches age 45) was $_5q_{40} = 0.02334$. (The method by which this is calculated from data is set forth in a later section of this chapter, and revolves around equation (1).) A man of 45 years in this same population stood a chance $_5q_{45} = 0.03681$ of dying before reaching age 50.

Chances of living through the n years are the complements of these, or $1 - {_nq_x}$.

If we designate the chance of living to age 45 for a person of age 40 by the ratio l_{45}/l_{40}, then this ratio must be equal to $1 - {}_5q_{40}$, that is,

$$l_{45} = l_{40}(1 - {}_5q_{40}) = l_{40} - l_{40}\,{}_5q_{40}.$$

The absolute value of the l_x column has no meaning; we use as probabilities only the ratios of the l_x among themselves. Following custom l_0 is set equal to 100,000 in all our tables, but any other number would have served, and for theoretical argument $l_0 = 1$ is more convenient.

What about the chance ${}_{10}q_x$ of a person's dying in the 10 years following a given age x? This is $(l_x - l_{x+10})/l_x$. Introduce a quantity ${}_nd_x$ defined as the difference between l_x and l_{x+n}, ${}_nd_x = l_x - l_{x+n}$. The quantity ${}_nd_x$, also being dependent in its absolute value on the arbitrary magnitude l_0, provides an alternative expression for the probability of dying:

$$ {}_nq_x = \frac{l_x - l_{x+n}}{l_x} = \frac{{}_nd_x}{l_x}.$$

For $n = 10$ we have

$$ {}_{10}q_x = \frac{l_x - l_{x+10}}{l_x} = \frac{{}_{10}d_x}{l_x},$$

or for United States males of age 40 on 1967 mortality $(2139 + 3294)/91628 = 0.05929$. More generally, the chance that a man of age x will live to age y and then die between ages y and $y + n$ is

$$\frac{l_y - l_{y+n}}{l_x} = \frac{{}_nd_y}{l_x}.$$

To save space in this book we have shown only 19 values of the life table functions. To find an intermediate value the reader would interpolate, perhaps assuming a uniform spread of deaths through the five-year interval of age, so that

$$ {}_td_x = \frac{t}{5}({}_5d_x), \qquad t < 5,$$

and

$$l_{x+t} = l_x - \frac{t}{5}({}_5d_x).$$

If this linear interpolation between the l_x is not precise enough, the reader can resort to a second- or third-degree curve. More extensive and elaborate interpolation is provided for by the program POLATE described in Chapter 13.

Still thinking of an individual person, we may draw from the life table the number of years of life he may expect out of the next five years. This is a sum or integral; he has a probability $l(x + t)/l_x$ of living through the short age interval $x + t - dt$ to $x + t$, and so the time he is expected to live during this interval is $[l(x + t)/l_x]dt$.

Adding this quantity through the elements dt covering the range from 0 to 5 and proceeding to the limit $dt = 0$ gives the integral, designated $_5L_x/l_x$,

$$\frac{_5L_x}{l_x} = \frac{1}{l_x} \int_0^5 l(x + t)\, dt,$$

as years of life expected between ages x and $x + 5$. As long as there is some chance of dying between ages x and $x + 5$ the expected value $_5L_x/l_x$ will be less than 5. (Parentheses, as in $l(x + t)$, are used for continuous functions, and subscripts, as in l_x, are used for discrete values.)

By an extension of the preceding argument we can obtain the expected number of years of life the person of age x may expect during the next n years:

$$\frac{_nL_x}{l_x} = \frac{1}{l_x} \int_0^n l(x + t)\, dt,$$

this being a way of defining $_nL_x$. For the special case in which n is very large, so that $x + n$ is greater than the oldest possible age, this becomes the complete expectation of life, $\mathring{e}_x$, and $_\infty L_x$ is usually written T_x, giving

$$\mathring{e}_x = \frac{_\infty L_x}{l_x} = \frac{T_x}{l_x} = \frac{1}{l_x} \int_0^\infty l(x + t)\, dt.$$

The columns T_x and $\mathring{e}_x$ are both tabulated in all of the life tables in this book. The T_x furnishes the number of years of life expected in any age interval, say y to $y + n$, for a person now aged x:

$$\frac{T_y - T_{y+n}}{l_x}.$$

For example, a forty-year-old man might want to know the expected number of years of retirement he could look forward to on the United States, 1967, mortality. If the retirement age is 65, then the expected number of years of retirement is

$$\frac{T_{65}}{l_{40}} = \frac{833199}{91628} = 9.09 \text{ years.}$$

This quantity increases as he moves towards age 65, at which time his expected years of retirement is 13.00.

The expectation of life at birth, $\mathring{e}_0$, is often used as an indication of the level of mortality. The $\mathring{e}_0$ of United States males has risen from 62.26 to 66.98, or by nearly 5 years during the two decades since World War II. At the same time, the $\mathring{e}_0$ of United States females has risen from 68.11 to 74.22, or by about 6 years. The greater decrease in female mortality is indicated, but as we shall see in the discussion of standardization (Chapter 12) the amount of the decrease is grossly understated by $\mathring{e}_0$. Standardization provides a better method for comparing mortality; it is more effective than the life table in holding age constant, and it avoids the excessive weighting of older ages implicit in the life table.

The Attrition of Cohorts

The discussion thus far in this chapter provides necessary definitions of life table symbols, but, as they are given in terms of probabilities for individuals, it does not embrace the main *demographic* uses of the life table. These uses concern aggregates of individuals, the simplest of which is a group born at the same moment of time; this is an example of what demographers call a *cohort*. If members number l_0 and do not leave the group except by death, then we can say that one year later there will be l_1 of them, five years later $l_5, \ldots, x$ years later l_x. These numbers of survivors are expected values, obtained by supposing that the probabilities applying to individuals will be exactly applicable to the group as a whole, a supposition that underlies the *deterministic model*.

The various quantities of the life table as interpreted in the deterministic model all derive from l_x. The $_nq_x$ is the proportion of the l_x (that is, those still alive at age x) who are expected to die before reaching age $x + n$:

$$_nq_x = \frac{l_x - l_{n+x}}{l_x} = 1 - \frac{l_{x+n}}{l_x}.$$

The $_nL_x = \int_0^n l(x + t)\, dt$ is the expected number of person-years lived between ages x and $x + n$. The $T_x = {_\infty}L_x$ is the total number of person-years lived by the cohort beyond age x. $T_x/l_x = \mathring{e}_x$ is the number of person-years lived per person—that is, the average number of person-years lived, beyond age x.

Moreover, we can think of the $_nL_x$ years lived in the interval between x and $x + n$ as being divided into two parts: the years lived by the part $_nd_x$ of the cohort that died during the interval, and the years lived in the interval by those who were still alive at the end of it. Suppose that the average number of years lived in the interval by the $_nd_x$ who died during it is $_na_x$; we would like to express $_na_x$ in terms of previously defined life table columns. The total years lived in the interval by those dying during it would be $_nd_x \, _na_x$. The l_{x+n} (that is, those who were still alive at the end of the interval) each lived n years in the interval. Hence the total years $_nL_x$ is the sum of two components:

$$_nL_x = {_nd_x} \, {_na_x} + nl_{x+n},$$

which we will regard as an equation for $_na_x$ giving

$$_na_x = \frac{_nL_x - nl_{x+n}}{_nd_x}.$$

Wherever the deaths $_nd_x$ in the cohort are rising from age to age, more individuals will die in the second half of the interval than in the first, and the quantity $_na_x$ will be greater than $n/2$. This is true for most of the range of the life table, but it is not true at the youngest and the oldest ages, when the number of deaths in the cohort declines. That infant mortality tends to be concentrated in the first hours and days after birth is reflected in an $_1a_0$ much smaller than 0.5. The quantity $_na_x$ is shown in all the life tables of our *World Population* but not in this book.

We have so far discussed a cohort of individuals born at a certain moment. But in practice births are spread over time. To follow actual populations we consider births taking place at annual rate l_0 throughout a five-year or other finite period. This is still called a cohort, and time is measured from the end of the five-year period of births. It includes $l_0 dt$ individuals born between time t and $t + dt$ (where $-5 \leq t \leq 0$), and the expected number of these surviving to time zero when they would be age t is $l(t)dt$. Adding the births of the five years prior to age zero we obtain the same $\int_0^5 l(t)dt = {_5L_0}$ we met before. The capacity of one set of life table columns to represent seemingly different things reflects the ingenuity of its design: continuous births at rate l_0 per year produce at the end of five years a cohort numbering $_5L_0$, the same quantity that before was taken to be the expected number of years to be lived before age 5 for a child just born. Five years later, as further application of this argument shows, the cohort numbers $_5L_5$, and similarly for later times and ages; x years later it numbers $_5L_x$.

By following such a cohort beyond age x, when it has fallen to $_5L_x$, to age $x + 5$, when it numbers $_5L_{x+5}$, we can see that the proportion surviving over the five years is $_5L_{x+5}/_5L_x$.

Under the heading of population *projection*, demographers make much use of the ratio $_5L_{x+5}/_5L_x$. If the number of males in the United States in the 40–44 age group in 1967 is 5,992,000, or in general $_5P_{40}$, then these can be seen as survivors of a cohort born 40–45 years before. By identifying the observed $_5P_{40}$ with the $_5L_{40}$ survivors of the theoretical cohort, we can say that if $_5L_{40}$ individuals have $_5L_{45}$ survivors, then $_5P_{40}$ individuals will have $(_5P_{40}/_5L_{40})_5L_{45} = {_5P_{40}}(_5L_{45}/_5L_{40})$ survivors. We can then say that the cohort of 5,992,000 will diminish to 5,992,000 × 439,814/453,179 = 5,815,000. This is the number projected as surviving until 1972, when they will be 45–49 years old, on the 1967 life table. In general, the number expected to survive for five years is $_5P_x(_5L_{x+5}/_5L_x)$.

In applying this in practice we have to bear in mind that:

1. We are talking about expected values; even if the probabilities properly apply to individuals any actual cohort will vary by chance from the expected value; the relative variation will be smaller the larger the population.

2. The life table from which the survivorship ratio was obtained may not be appropriate to the future.

3. The cohort is assumed to be *closed*, entry being possible only by birth and

departure only by death. For application to a population in which substantial migration occurs, the argument would require modification.

4. Births usually do not take place evenly through a one-year or five-year interval in a real population.

To elaborate the last qualification, suppose the births at time $-t$ were $B(-t)l_0$; then the integral we need for the initial value of the cohort is not $_5L_0$ as before, but $_5L_0'$:

$$_5L_0' = \int_0^5 B(-t)l(t)\, dt,$$

and a similar weighting under the integral sign would apply to later ages, with every L being replaced by L'. If in particular the births were increasing steadily in the ratio e^{rt}, then we would define $_nL_x'$ as

$$_nL_x' = \int_0^n e^{-rt}l(x+t)\, dt.$$

In principle, projection ought to be carried out with the ratio $_5L_{x+5}'/_5L_x'$ rather than $_5L_{x+5}/_5L_x$, but in practice this refinement is usually disregarded, even though we may know that the r contained in $_nL_x'$ is large enough, say 0.03, to make some noticeable difference. (See the program STABLE in Chapter 10, where $_nL_x'$ appears as VLLP(I), and an estimate of the difference between $_5L_x'$ and $_5L_x$ appears in the output.)

We have thus discussed three kinds of cohort: (1) l_0 births at a moment of time; (2) $5l_0$ births spread evenly over five years; (3) $B(-t)l_0 = e^{-rt}l_0$ births occurring at time $-t$, $0 \le t \le 5$ added through the five-year interval.

One further variable, not printed out in our life tables, but essential for the theory used in their construction, is the mortality for a small interval of age dx. The number surviving in the cohort up to age x is $l(x)$, and the number up to age $x + dx$ is $l(x + dx)$, so the deaths over the interval dx are $l(x) - l(x + dx)$. This corresponds to an annual number of deaths equal to the same difference divided by dx:

$$\text{Deaths over interval } x \text{ to } x + dx \text{ on a per-year basis} = \frac{l(x) - l(x + dx)}{dx}.$$

The limit of this as dx tends to zero is minus the derivative of $l(x)$ with respect to x, for any form of $l(x)$ that admits a derivative.

Finally, to produce an age-specific rate $\mu(x)$, we must divide deaths by the number living, which if dx is small may be supposed to be $l(x)$ throughout the period x to $x + dx$:

$$\mu(x) = \frac{l(x) - l(x + dx)}{l(x)dx} = -\frac{1}{l(x)} \cdot \frac{dl(x)}{dx}.$$

What will be important for later work is that $l(x)\mu(x)dx$ is the number of deaths in the cohort during the short period dx.

The Stationary Population

A third aspect of the life table, quite different from either probability or cohort but discussible in the same notation, is its portrayal of a stationary population. In the second kind of cohort the births occur at a uniform annual rate l_0 for five years; suppose now that the l_0 births per year continue not for five years only, but indefinitely. Then, if there is no migration, after a hundred or so years a certain population, with a certain age-constitution, will have come into existence. Consider it in cross section at a moment in which a census might be taken. The count in that census of persons of ages x to $x + 4$ years would be $_5L_x$; the total population would number T_0; the proportion of the population between x and $x + 4$ years old would be $_5L_x/T_0$; the proportion older than x years would be T_x/T_0. The number of births in any year being l_0, and the number of the population being T_0, the crude birth rate would be l_0/T_0, which is the reciprocal of the expectation of life $\mathring{e}_0$. The number of deaths between ages x and $x + 4$ would be $_5d_x$, and the central death rate $_5m_x = {_5d_x}/{_5L_x}$. The total number of deaths occurring in a year would be the sum of the $_5d_x$ over all x, and this is bound to equal l_0, so the death rate, like the birth rate, would be l_0/T_0 or $1/\mathring{e}_0$.

Such an account suggests that the life table is a simplified model of the actual population from which it is derived. In the degree that the actual population has a birth rate close to its death rate, and that these have persisted over a long period of time, the fit will be close. For observed populations that are consistently increasing the birth rate will be higher, and the age distribution will be younger, than the corresponding parameters of the life table derived from them.

The main tables of this book permit comparisons of observed age distributions with the stationary model. For a population that is increasing slowly, like Austria, 1966–68, the observed proportion of a particular age, say less than 15 years old, will be similar to the proportion less than 15 in the stationary model, based on the death rates only: 22.0 percent compared with 19.9 percent for females. To be able to explain the age distribution in terms of the mortality schedule helps to make sense of census data on age. For a population growing rapidly, say Guatemala, 1964, the observed proportion of females younger than 15 years, 45.2 percent, is much greater than the proportion calculated from the stationary model, 24.5 percent. The stationary model here requires modification to what is known as the stable model to allow for the rate of increase. Such modification is computed by PROJECT (Chapter 7) and STABLE (Chapter 10) and discussed in the introduction to these programs, as well as in Part I.

The Fundamental Equation

Our construction of a life table revolves around a relation between the observed age-specific death rate $_5M_x$, five-year age intervals being used for this presentation, and the corresponding ratio obtained from the life table. We use these intervals because reliable data are rarely available on intervals shorter than five years. We first set down an equation incorporating the observations and the desired parameter of the model; the latter will be l_x, the survivors to age x out of l_0 births. From the equation incorporating the given $_5M_x$ and the unknown l_x column of the life table, we will seek a numerical solution for the l_x. To suppose the life table made, at least in symbolic terms, may seem to avoid the problem, but in fact this is a common technique in mathematics.

Assume that a continuous function $p(x + t)$ underlies the observed age distribution within the interval x to $x + 5$. This means that the number of individuals in the population between ages $x + t$ and $x + t + dt$ exposed to the risk of death is designated $p(x + t)dt$. Though $p(x + t)$, analogous to the $l(x + t)$ of the life table, is unknown, no interpretation of the observed death rates $_5M_x$ is possible without some supposition in regard to $p(x + t)$. The death rate $\mu(x + t)$ in the interval $x + t$ to $x + t + dt$ may be applied to the $p(x + t)\, dt$ to obtain the number of deaths $p(x + t)\mu(x + t)\, dt$ and this quantity may be added through the five years from x to $x + 5$. The corresponding population is the sum of $p(x + t)\, dt$ through the five years. Then the observed death rate $_5M_x$ can be equated to the ratio of integrals given by these definitions:

$$_5M_x = \frac{\int_0^5 p(x + t)\mu(x + t)\, dt}{\int_0^5 p(x + t)\, dt} = \frac{-\int_0^5 \frac{p(x + t)}{l(x + t)}\, dl(x + t)}{\int_0^5 p(x + t)\, dt}, \tag{1}$$

using the definition of $\mu(x + t)$ of page 132. The numerator is a theoretical representation of $_5D_x$, the number of deaths, and the denominator of $_5P_x$, the exposed population. This equation (whether or not the calculator is aware of it) is the inescapable starting point for any attempt to calculate a life table. The various possible ways of solving it will provide different approximations to the life table; the l_x column obtained from a given set of observed $_5M_x$ is not unique.

The Assumption that $p(x + t)$ is $l(x + t)$

Suppose first that the distribution $p(x + t)$ within the age group is the same as that of the life table $l(x + t)$. Then by integration in the numerator of (1), we transform it to

$$_5M_x = \frac{l_x - l_{x+5}}{\int_0^5 l(x+t)\,dt}. \tag{2}$$

To make (2) determinate we need a further assumption on the form of $l(x+t)$. If $l(x+t)$ is a straight line from l_x to l_{x+5}, which is to say if the deaths in the stationary population are uniformly distributed through the five years, then we have

$$_5M_x = \frac{l_x - l_{x+5}}{\frac{5}{2}(l_x + l_{x+5})}, \tag{3}$$

an equation that is readily solvable for the desired ratio l_{x+5}/l_x:

$$\frac{l_{x+5}}{l_x} = \frac{1 - \dfrac{5M_x}{2}}{1 + \dfrac{5M_x}{2}}, \tag{4}$$

where $_5M_x$ is abridged to M_x. The complement of l_{x+5}/l_x is $_5q_x = 1 - l_{x+5}/l_x$, which to the same approximation is

$$_5q_x = \frac{5M_x}{1 + \dfrac{5M_x}{2}}.$$

We have assumed too much in this first attack on (1), and solved for l_{x+5}/l_x in the form (4) at the cost of weakening the relation between the life table and the data. A solution should be possible that provides a tighter agreement of the l_{x+5}/l_x with the observed M_x. We cannot avoid a supposition on the form of $p(x+t)$ as well as on the integration of $l(x+t)$ or some other function, but these can be more realistic.

What about retaining the replacement of $p(x+t)$ in (1) by $l(x+t)$, and so still reducing (1) to (2), but allowing a more satisfactory shape than a straight line for $l(x+t)$ in (2)? If $l(x+t)$ is assumed to be a cubic curve, then the integral $_5L_x = \int_0^5 l(x+t)\,dt$ may be expressed in terms of four successive ordinates:

$$_5L_x = \int_0^5 l(x+t)\,dt = \frac{65}{24}(l_x + l_{x+5}) - \frac{5}{24}(l_{x-5} + l_{x+10}). \tag{5}$$

In order to derive (5) we use as the third-degree curve through l_{x-5}, l_x, l_{x+5}, and l_{x+10} the form

$$l_{x+t} = l_x + \frac{t}{5} \Delta l_x + \frac{(t)(t-5)}{(25)(2!)} \Delta^2 l_x + \frac{(t)(t-5)(t-10)}{(125)(3!)} \Delta^3 l_{x-5},$$

where

$$\Delta l_x = l_{x+5} - l_x,$$
$$\Delta^2 l_x = \Delta l_{x+5} - \Delta l_x,$$
$$\Delta^3 l_x = \Delta^2 l_{x+5} - \Delta^2 l_x.$$

This is Newton's advancing-difference formula with third differences constant, and may be verified to pass through the four required values. Integrating it from $t = 0$ to $t = 5$ produces (5).

Substituting $_5 L_x$ from (5) in (2) gives a result that, unlike (3) does not permit solution for each age interval separately, and we must think of all the l_x together as the unknowns in a set of simultaneous linear equations; the l_x would be collectively determinate once the arbitrary l_0 was chosen.

Rather than solve a large set of linear equations directly, we attain the same result by iteration. The improved l_{x+5}^* is

$$l_{x+5}^* = l_x^* \frac{1 - \frac{65}{24} M_x + \frac{5}{24} M_x \left(\frac{l_{x+10} + l_{x-5}^*}{l_x^*} \right)}{1 + \frac{65}{24} M_x}, \tag{6}$$

obtained by solving (2) with (5) entered in the denominator of its righthand side for the unknown l_{x+5}/l_x. From an arbitrary initial set of l_x, (6) permits calculation of improved values, working from the youngest to the oldest ages. These improved values can be further improved in a second series of applications of (6). After four or so applications no further change in any of the l_x will appear when these are shown as whole numbers on a radix or base $l_0 = 100,000$.

Iterative procedures are used at many points in this book. In every case they are derived by an algebraic transformation of an equation so as to put the desired quantity on the left and everything else on the right. An especially simple instance appears in (19), solving a quadratic equation for r, the intrinsic rate. The general principle is to manipulate an equation of the form $f(r) = 0$ into the equivalent $r = g(r)$, then treat the r on the left as an improved value, writing it r^* (page 186).

Of course, $f(r) = 0$ can yield $r^* = g(r)$ in many ways, and it is by no means indifferent which is used. It may be shown that the condition for convergence is that the derivative $g'(r)$ must be less than unity, and for rapid convergence it must be much less than unity. A part of the argument is given in the solution of (22).

The derivation of (6) is complicated by requiring not one variable r, but four distinct variables l_{x-5}, l_x, l_{x+5}, and l_{x+10}, or at least the three ratios between them. The principle of iteration is unaffected by this complication.

A More General Form for $p(x + t)$

If in fact the births from year to year have been increasing, then within each five-year interval the observed population will be slightly younger than the stationary population of the life table discussed on page 133. Under mild restrictions, in an increasing population at ages for which mortality is rising, the death rate $_5m_x$ in the life table, defined as

$$_5m_x = \frac{_5d_x}{_5L_x} = \frac{l_x - l_{x+5}}{_5L_x},$$

will be slightly higher than the observed $_5M_x$.

We want to allow for the increasing population within the five-year interval. To do so we revert to (1), but this time replace $p(x + t)$ with $e^{-rt}l(x + t)$. If the successive cohorts within a five-year interval are increasing in a constant ratio, r will be greater than zero; if they are decreasing, r will be less than zero. If the age distribution is highly irregular, so that the constant ratio does not apply, then r is a kind of average of the change within the five-year period.

Now entering $p(x + t) = e^{-rt}l(x + t)$ in (1) gives

$$_5M_x = \frac{\int_0^5 e^{-rt}l(x + t)\mu(x + t)\,dt}{\int_0^5 e^{-rt}l(x + t)\,dt},$$

and on integration by parts in the numerator and rearranging we have, again dropping the prescript and writing M_x for $_5M_x$,

$$l_{x+5}^* = e^{5r}\left[l_x^* - (M_x + r)\int_0^5 e^{-rt}l(x + t)\,dt\right]. \tag{7}$$

This result is exact, given the form $p(x + t) = e^{-rt}l(x + t)$. If $r = 0$, it reduces to

$$l_{x+5}^* = l_x^* - M_x\,_5L_x, \tag{8}$$

as it ought to. To emphasize that (7) is a generalization of the commonsense (8), we will write the integral $\int_0^5 e^{-rt}l(x + t)\,dt$ as $_5L_x'$, so that (7) becomes

$$l_{x+5}^* = e^{5r}[l_x^* - (M_x + r)_5L_x']. \tag{9}$$

In order to implement (9) we still need to evaluate the integral $_5L_x'$. This is readily achieved by the same (5) but now with $e^{-rt}l_{x+t}$, $t = -5, 0, 5, 10$, replacing l_{x+t}. We go down the successive ages and apply (7) as we go, always using the latest values for the l_x from which the integral $_5L_x$ is assembled. The current values l_{x-5}^* and l_x^* would be entered naturally if only one cell is provided for each of the l_x, and as successive iterates of the l_x are calculated they replace the previous occupants of those cells. We cannot use the value from the new iterate l_{x+10}^* since it has not yet been created at the time l_{x+5}^* is being calculated. The only value that we can do something about is l_{x+5}, where we would like in effect to enter l_{x+5}^*. This is attained by replacing $_5L_x'$ in (9) by $_5L_x' + 5/2\,(l_{x+5}^* - l_{x+5})\,e^{-5r}$ and then solving to reach

$$l_{x+5}^* = \frac{e^{5r}\left[l_x^* - (M_x + r)\left(_5L_x' - \frac{5}{2}\,e^{-5r}l_{x+5}\right)\right]}{1 + \frac{5}{2}(M_x + r)}. \tag{10}$$

Alternatively, the constant 5/2 in (10) may be replaced by 65/24.

The value of r is readily estimated from two or three successive age groups. With an arbitrary r we calculate $_5L_{x-5}'$ and $_5L_{x+5}'$, and then identify the observed population in the corresponding age groups, $_5P_{x-5}$ and $_5P_{x+5}$, with the stable population over the same range. This gives as the improved r^*

$$r^* = \frac{1}{10}\ln\left(\frac{\dfrac{_5P_{x-5}}{_5L'_{x-5}}}{\dfrac{_5P_{x+5}}{_5L'_{x+5}}}\right). \tag{11}$$

The iteration on (10) alternates with that on (11), so that in each cycle we use the most recent set of l_x and the most recent r.

The difficulties of curve fitting, along with problems of defective enumeration, make it necessary to devise special methods for the youngest and oldest ages; these methods are more primitive than those for the main body of the table.

Youngest Ages

For each of the three intervals 0, 1–4, 5–9, counting age at last birthday, we assume a value for $_na_x$, the average years lived in the interval by those dying in the interval. For 0 this is the empirical regression,

$$a_0 = 0.07 + 1.7M_0, \tag{12}$$

obtained from a number of countries in which day, month, and year of birth are available. For 1–4, $_4a_1$ may be assumed to be 1.5 years without great loss of accuracy; for 5–9, $_5a_5$ is put at 2.5 years. If the rate r of increase of successive cohorts is taken as zero, then $p_{x+t} = l_{x+t}$, and $_nd_x/_nL_x$ or $(l_x - l_{x+n})/_nL_x$ can be equated to the observed M_x. This and the definition of $_na_x$ just given provide two equations in each of the first three age intervals

$$l_x - l_{x+n} = {_nL_x}\,M_x,$$
$$_nL_x = (l_x - l_{x+n})_na_x + nl_{x+n},$$

which may be solved without iteration for the unknown $_nL_x$ and l_{x+n}.

Terminating the Table

For the oldest age interval the simplest procedure is again to accept that $p(x + t) = l(x + t)$ in (1), which is to say to suppose that $_\infty m_x$, the final age-specific rate in the life table, is the same as $_\infty M_x$, the final observed rate. This avoids our having to judge what is the oldest age to which an individual can live. Refinement is discouraged, moreover, by inaccuracy in age statement by older people, and especially in that very different errors appear in the death registration, which provides the numerator, from those in the census count, which provides the denominator of $_\infty M_x$.

If $_\infty m_x = {_\infty M_x}$, then from the definition $m_x = (l_x - l_\infty)/L_x$ and the fact that $l_\infty = 0$, it follows that $_\infty M_x = l_x/_\infty L_x$, and hence

$$_\infty L_x = \frac{l_x}{_\infty M_x}, \tag{13}$$

where x is the start of the terminal age interval. Having $l_\infty = 0$ gives $_\infty q_x = 1$, and no further assumptions are needed. For example, to find the expectation of life at this age x we have

$$\mathring{e}_x = \frac{\int_0^\infty l(x + t)\, dt}{l_x} = \frac{1}{_\infty M_x};$$

the expectation of life is taken to be the reciprocal of the terminal death rate.

This completes our statement of such parts of mortality theory as are needed for calculating a life table from observed population and deaths. We now go on to the program by which this theory is implemented.

Life Table and Other Programs

Each chapter of this part of the book includes a program that translates the demographic theory into FORTRAN. Twelve programs are shown in all, along with their input and output, covering operations on birth and death data given by age and sex. The series starts with LIFE, which checks the data, makes a life table, and punches out cards that will be useful in some of the subsequent programs. It includes PROJECT, which projects forward the population by age and sex on the age-specific rates of the initial period. The calculation of the elements of the matrix operator that also performs this projection is accomplished in MATRIX: the matrix permits birth and death rates to be analyzed separately from the initial age distribution. The parameters for the Lotka and Leslie theory are calculated in LOTKA, ROOT, and ZEROS. Inferences from incomplete data in INFER, along with standardization and graduation are the objectives of subsequent programs.

The programs as they stand have been tested on a CDC6400 and an IBM360 at the University of California at Berkeley; a UNIVAC1108 at Oakland, California; a GE635 at the University of Kansas. Each time that we ran them on a new installation we had to make changes, and in such a fashion as not to lose compatibility with the machines used before. The result was to reduce the FORTRAN IV with which we started to a more basic form; we had to get rid of mixed mode, of complex arithmetic, and other features that seem to be treated differently on different machines. We are especially grateful to James B. Pick for helping us on this effort to achieve portability. After the four-way compatibility was attained we had help in testing from other installations, including those at the University of Chicago, Brown University, University of Wisconsin, and University of Pennsylvania. In most instances the programs required no change at all; in one or two they required alteration of the input statements.

Whether a given procedure is the best numerical approximation to the parameters it professes to calculate is in some instances controversial. We have met the difficulty by incorporating three methods for the intrinsic rate of natural increase, and two for the stable age distribution, so that the user can see the numerical effect on his own problem. Those with an extreme concern for accuracy at the computing level may be consoled by the thought that the discrepancies due to methods are trifling compared with errors in demographic data.

The several tasks that have been accomplished in the book and are reported in the printouts of Part IV are here represented by separate programs. We did not think it necessary to tie them together in a sequence of subroutines, as was done in the preparation of the book. The separate programs can be employed one at a time for specific limited purposes; the user can easily combine such of them as he wishes to use together.

The programs rest on procedures that are somewhat simpler than those used for the book. The life table given as the subroutine LIF in particular requires only about 180 executable statements, compared with twice that number in the original out of which the book was made. We here abandon several of the devices used to make the main printouts of the book, on the ground that they do not increase accuracy sufficiently to trouble the reader with them. One instance is the fitting of a hyperbola to the first ages of life in order to infer the L_x from the l_x; instead we use a separation factor (SEP in the program) ascertained by regression on the M_0. Hence many of the numbers that result differ in the last decimal place from those of the main printouts.

In respect of output the programs here are more extensive than those that produced the book. Thus DIRECT not only produces direct standardization, but also decomposes the difference between the crude rates of two populations into a rates component, a composition component, and interaction. The real root is calculated by three different methods in ROOT, the results necessarily differing from one another, as do different finite approximations to an integral. The program for complex roots (ZEROS) not only shows the first pair, which alone are published in this book, but goes on to all the other roots, sweeping out each pair as it is found, and finally arranging the set in order of absolute value. Thus the programs of this section are not only simpler and more intelligible than those that produced the book, but they provide results that we did not calculate before because we did not have the space to print them out.

Two kinds of readers are envisaged for the present Part III—the reader interested in following the methods and logic of our programs, and the reader who is indifferent to details and merely wants to calculate a life table, an intrinsic rate, or some other quantity. All that the latter needs to know is how to prepare his data.

Input. Since calculating a life table is usually the first step of a larger population analysis, we have devised a standard data deck, like the one used to make the main printouts of this book, in which population and deaths are punched by age and sex, along with births by age of mother (or age of father for the male-dominant analysis).

The program LIFE can be used without change if data on births are not available by substituting two blank cards for the birth distribution. The computing and printing of the life table are performed by the subroutine LIF, the input to which is just the distributions of population and deaths for one sex, all arranged on four punch cards. A short main program could be written to call LIF if one wishes to calculate a life table for one set of data. To suppress the punchout the researcher need only remove four cards, those for statements 79, 80, 82 in LIFE and 181 in the subroutine LIF.

The standard data deck consists of 14 or more cards including ones for footnotes. These are displayed in Exhibit 1.

Card 1 contains the name of the country or other population, the calendar year or years, and such additional identification as is needed; it is read in *A* (for alphabetical) format, and once read can only be printed out unchanged.

Card 2 contains the year again (or middle year if three or five years are used) punched in columns 1–4, total population (columns 10–18), total deaths (columns 19–27), total births (columns 28–36), male births (columns 37–45), female

EXHIBIT 1
Specimen data and source deck.

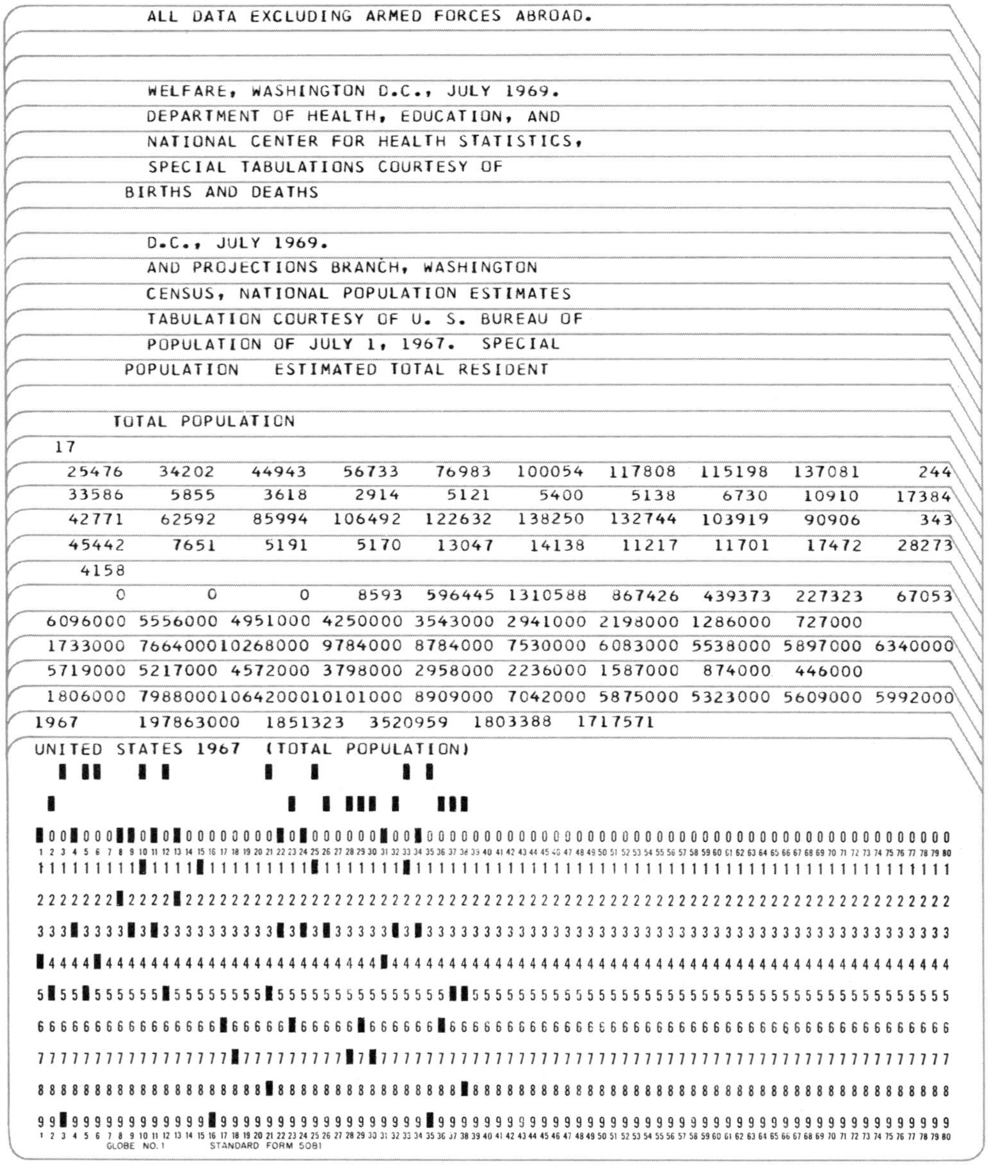

```
ALL DATA EXCLUDING ARMED FORCES ABROAD.


        WELFARE, WASHINGTON D.C., JULY 1969.
        DEPARTMENT OF HEALTH, EDUCATION, AND
        NATIONAL CENTER FOR HEALTH STATISTICS,
        SPECIAL TABULATIONS COURTESY OF
        BIRTHS AND DEATHS

        D.C., JULY 1969.
        AND PROJECTIONS BRANCH, WASHINGTON
        CENSUS, NATIONAL POPULATION ESTIMATES
        TABULATION COURTESY OF U. S. BUREAU OF
        POPULATION OF JULY 1, 1967.  SPECIAL
        POPULATION   ESTIMATED TOTAL RESIDENT

        TOTAL POPULATION
   17
        25476     34202     44943     56733     76983    100054    117808    115198    137081       244
        33586      5855      3618      2914      5121      5400      5138      6730     10910     17384
        42771     62592     85994    106492    122632    138250    132744    103919     90906       343
        45442      7651      5191      5170     13047     14138     11217     11701     17472     28273
         4158
            0         0         0      8593    596445   1310588    867426    439373    227323     67053
      6096000   5556000   4951000   4250000   3543000   2941000   2198000   1286000    727000
      1733000  7664000 10268000   9784000   8784000   7530000   6083000   5538000   5897000   6340000
      5719000   5217000   4572000   3798000   2958000   2236000   1587000    874000    446000
      1806000   7988000 10642000 10101000   8909000   7042000   5875000   5323000   5609000   5992000
   1967       197863000   1851323   3520959   1803388   1717571
  UNITED STATES 1967  (TOTAL POPULATION)
```

```
GLOBE NO.1    STANDARD FORM 5081
```

Note: The maximum number of cards is 53 (12 data cards, 1 counter card, 1–20 source cards, and 1–20 adjustment cards.)

births (columns 46–54). This is in F (for floating-point) format, which means it consists of numbers, not necessarily integers, on which computation will be carried out.

Cards 3 and 4 contain data on the male population, showing age groups 0, 1–4, 5–9, . . ., 85+, punched in columns 1–8, 9–16, 17–24, . . ., 73–80. This is signified in the program as 10F8.0 format, which is used for the cards 3 to 12.

Cards 5 and 6 contain data on the female population in the same age intervals.

Cards 7 and 8 contain data on births by age of mother in the same age intervals, with blanks or zeros for less than 10 or more than 55.

Cards 9 and 10 contain data on male deaths in the same age intervals.

Cards 11 and 12 contain data on female deaths in the same age intervals.

Card 13 contains a two-digit number in columns 3 and 4 indicating how many footnote cards follow. It may also contain a number in Column 8 to indicate source cards.

Cards 14 . . . up to possible 53 are footnote cards, of which up to 20 are for sources and up to 20 for description of adjustments.

The cards of Exhibit 1 are the input to the first program, LIFE, with its subroutine LIF. LIFE reads the cards, adds the several ages, and checks to see that the added total agrees with the punched total. After it has made the life table, it punches out the original population and birth cards and $_nL_x$ for age x equal to 0, 1, 5, 10, . . . , 85, again in format 10F8.0. and prints the source cards. The punched-out deck of 12 cards—cards 1 to 8 of the input-deck plus two cards for the male $_nL_x$ and two for the female $_nL_x$—is then the input for several of the remaining programs.

The glossary that is included as Exhibit 2 should make it easier to follow this and later programs.

The programs that follow were developed independently of those that made the Main Tables of Part IV. Here we wanted simpler and more flexible versions, suitable for modification by the user. The results agree closely; the expectation of life at age 0 for Mexico, 1966, males, for example, is 59.508 on page 156 and 59.49 on page 344; for females the corresponding numbers are 62.835 and 62.82.

144

EXHIBIT 2
Glossary of mathematical symbols and FORTRAN names of demographic variables.

Description	Symbol	FORTRAN name
OBSERVATIONS		
Total population	P	TPP
Total births	B	TBB
Total deaths	D	TDD
Crude birth rate	$b = B/P$	CBR
Crude death rate	$d = D/P$	CDR
Crude rate of natural increase	$r = b - d = \dfrac{B-D}{P}$	CRI
Indexing of age	x	I
Population in five-year age groups	${}_5P_x$	PP(I)
Population at age 0	P_0	PP(1)
Population at age 1–4	${}_4P_1$	PP(2)
Population at age 5–9	${}_5P_5$	PP(3)
Population at age 10–14	${}_5P_{10}$	PP(4)
. . .	. . .	. . .
Population at age 80–84	${}_5P_{80}$	PP(18)
Population at age 85+	${}_\infty P_{85}$	PP(19)
Births by mother's age in five-year age groups	${}_5B_x$	BB(I)
Deaths in five-year age groups	${}_5D_x$	DD(I)
Male population in five-year age groups	${}_5P_x{}^*$	PPM(I)
Female population in five-year age groups	${}_5P_x$	PPF(I)
Male deaths in five-year age groups	${}_5D_x{}^*$	DDM(I)
Female deaths in five-year age groups	${}_5D_x$	DDF(I)
Age-specific death rates for five-year age groups	${}_5M_x$	VMM(I)
Age-specific death rates for single years of age	${}_1M_x$	SMM(I)
Age-specific fertility rates for five-year age groups	F_x	FF(I)
LIFE TABLE—STATIONARY MODEL		
Number attaining age x	l_x	VL(I)
Probability of dying within five years	${}_5q_x = 1 - l_{x+5}/l_x$	QX(I)
Number dying within five-year interval	${}_5d_x = l_x - l_{x+5}$	DX(I)
Stationary population age x to $x+4$	${}_5L_x = \int_0^5 l(x+t)dt$	VLL(I)

Locally stable population	$_5L_x' = \int_0^5 e^{-rt}l(x+t)dt$	VLLP(I)
Mean years lived in interval by those dying during it	$_5a_x = \dfrac{_5L_x - 5l_{x+5}}{_5d_x}$	VA(I)
Central death rate	$_5m_x = {_5d_x}/{_5L_x}$	VM(I)
Stationary population age x to the end of life	T_x	TT(I)
Expectation of life	$\mathring{e}_x = T_x/l_x$	E(I)
Local rate of increase	r_x	VR(I)
Ratio of increase over five years	$s = e^{5r}$	S
Separation factor	f	SEP

STABLE MODEL

Net reproduction rate	$\mathbf{R}_0 = \sum\limits_x {_5L_x}F_x/l_0$	RR
Intrinsic rate of natural increase	r	R
Intrinsic birth rate	b	B
Intrinsic death rate	d	D
Improved r in iteration	$r*$	RSTAR
Stable age distribution in five-year age groups with radix l_0	$_5K_x = e^{-r(x+2.5)}{_5L_x}$	VKK(I)
Continuous stable age distribution	$k(x) = e^{-rx}l(x)$	VK(I)

STANDARDIZATION

Title of standard population		NAMEST
Age distribution of standard population	SP_x	STPP(I)
Deaths in standard population	SD_x	STDD(I)
Age-specific death rates in standard population	SM_x	STMM(I)
Total of standard population	$SP = \sum SP_x$	SP
Total of standard deaths	$SD = \sum SD_x$	SPSM

(Given population: same, but with S or ST replaced by V)

Total deaths of given population	$VD = \sum VP_x VM_x$	VPVM
Expected deaths with standard age distribution and given age-specific rates	$\sum SP_x VM_x$	SPVM
Expected deaths with given age distribution and standard rates	$\sum VP_x SM_x$	VPSM
Directly standardized death rate	$\sum SP_x VM_x/SP$	SRD
Indirectly standardized death rate	$\left(\dfrac{VD}{\sum VP_x SM_x}\right)\left(\dfrac{SD}{SP}\right)$	SRI

Program LIFE

```
C
C                          LIFE
C
C
C     READS INPUT, CHECKS ITS CONSISTENCY, AND PUNCHES A
C     STANDARD DECK FOR USE AS INPUT TO OTHER PROGRAMS.
C     ALSO CALLS LIF, WHICH COMPUTES AND PRINTS A LIFE TABLE
C     AND PUNCHES 'LL(X).'
C
C
C     INPUT STARTS WITH 12 CARDS AS FOLLOWS
C        TITLE CARD (19A4)
C        TOTALS CARD IN FORMAT (I4,5X,I9,5F9.0) CONTAINING
C           THE YEAR (IDATE) IN COLUMNS 1-4
C           TOTAL POPULATION (ITPP) IN COLUMNS 10-18
C           TOTAL DEATHS (TDD) IN COLUMNS 19-27
C           TOTAL BIRTHS (TBB) IN COLUMNS 28-36
C           MALE BIRTHS (TBBM) IN COLUMNS 37-45
C           FEMALE BIRTHS (TBBF) IN COLUMNS 46-54
C           THE NUMBER OF YEARS TO WHICH THE BIRTH AND DEATH DATA
C              APPLY (YEARS) IN COLUMNS 55-63.  IF THE NUMBER OF YEARS
C              IS NOT PUNCHED, THE DEFAULT VALUE IS ONE YEAR.
C        MALE POPULATION BY AGE (PPM (I)), 2 CARDS IN FORMAT (10F8.0)
C        FEMALE POPULATION BY AGE (IPPF (I)), 2 CARDS IN FORMAT (10I8)
C        BIRTHS BY AGE OF MOTHER (BB (I)), 2 CARDS IN FORMAT (10F8.0)
C        MALE DEATHS BY AGE (DDM (I)), 2 CARDS IN FORMAT (10F8.0)
C        FEMALE DEATHS BY AGE (DDF (I)), 2 CARDS IN FORMAT (10F8.0)
C
C     AGE GROUPS ARE 0,1-4,5-9,10-14,... 85+, UNKNOWN
C     (20 CATEGORIES).
C
C     NEXT ARE THE NUMBERS NN AND MM IN FORMAT (2I4), FOLLOWED BY
C     NN CARDS CONTAINING THE SOURCE NOTES AND MM CARDS DESCRIBING
C     ADJUSTMENTS.  IF THERE ARE NO NOTES, THE DATA DECK ENDS
C     WITH A CARD PUNCHED 1 IN COLUMN 4 AND A BLANK CARD.
C
C     SETS OF THE ABOVE INPUT MAY BE REPEATED INDEFINITELY.  THE
C     PROGRAM TERMINATES EXECUTION WHEN A BLANK TITLE CARD IS READ.
C
      DIMENSION NAME(19),NOTE(19),PPM(20),PPF(20),BB(20),DDM(20),DDF(20)     1
     A,IAGE(19),IPPM(20),IPPF(20),IBB(20),IDDM(20),IDDF(20)                  2
C
C        COLUMNS 1-76 OF THE TITLE CARD ARE STORED IN 'NAME.'
C        COLUMNS 77-80 OF THE TITLE CARD MUST ALWAYS BE BLANK.
C
      READ 50,NAME,IRK                                                      3
   50 FORMAT (19A4,A4)                                                      4
   52 PRINT 54,NAME                                                         5
```

```
   54 FORMAT (1H1 19A4//)                                               6
      READ 56,IDATE,ITPP,TDD,TBB,TBBM,TBBF,YEARS                        7
   56 FORMAT (I4,5X,I5,5F9.0)                                           8
      READ 58,IPPM,IPPF                                                 9
   58 FORMAT (10I8/10I8/10I8/10I8)                                     10
      READ 59,BB,DDM,DDF                                              11
   59 FORMAT (10F8.0)                                                 12
C        THE DATA HAVE BEEN READ.
C
C        READ AND PRINT SOURCE NOTES (A MINIMUM OF ONE NOTE CARD IS
C        REQUIRED--IF THERE ARE NO NOTES IT WILL BE BLANK).
      READ 60,NN,MM                                                   13
      N = NN + MM                                                     14
   60 FORMAT (2I4)                                                    15
      DO 62 I=1,N                                                     16
      READ 50,NOTE                                                    17
   62 PRINT 64,NOTE                                                   18
   64 FORMAT (1X 19A4)                                                19
      IF (N .GT. 23) PRINT 54,NAME                                    20
C        NOTES HAVE BEEN PRINTED.
C
C        ADJUST THE BIRTHS AND DEATHS TO A ONE-YEAR INTERVAL
C        IF THE INPUT APPLIES TO MORE THAN ONE YEAR.
      IF (YEARS .LE. 0.0 .OR. IFIX(YEARS) .EQ. 1) GO TO 68            21
      RECIP=1.0/YEARS                                                 22
      TDD=TDD*RECIP                                                   23
      TBB=TBB*RECIP                                                   24
      TBBM=TBBM*RECIP                                                 25
      TBBF=TBBF*RECIP                                                 26
      DO 66 I=1,20                                                    27
      BB(I)=BB(I)*RECIP                                               28
      DDM(I)=DDM(I)*RECIP                                             29
   66 DDF(I)=DDF(I)*RECIP                                             30
C
C        CHECK TO ASCERTAIN IF EACH TOTAL EQUALS THE SUM OF THE AGES.
   68 ITPPM = 0                                                       31
      ITPPF = 0                                                       32
      TTBB = 0.                                                       33
      TDDM = 0.                                                       34
      TDDF = 0.                                                       35
      DO 70 I=1,20                                                    36
      ITPPM=ITPPM+IPPM(I)                                             37
      ITPPF=ITPPF+IPPF(I)                                             38
      TTBB = TTBB + BB(I)                                             39
      TDDM = TDDM + DDM(I)                                            40
   70 TDDF=TDDF + DDF(I)                                              41
      ID1=ITPPM+ITPPF-ITPP                                            42
      ID2=TTBB-TBB                                                    43
      ID3=TDDM+TDDF-TDD                                               44
      IF(IABS(ID1)+IABS(ID2)+IABS(ID3).LT.1) GO TO 74                 45
      PRINT 72,ID1,ID2,ID3                                            46
   72 FORMAT (/// 29H DISCREPANCY IN POPULATION IS I10 /               47
     B 25H DISCREPANCY IN BIRTHS IS I10 / 25H DISCREPANCY IN DEATHS IS 48
     C I10)                                                           49
      GO TO 96                                                        50
C
C        NEXT, PRINT THE DATA.
C
C        FIRST, SET UP THE STUB OF THE TABLE.
```

```
      74 IAGE(2)=C                                                            51
         DO 76 I=3,19                                                         52
      76 IAGE(I)=IAGE(I-1)+5                                                   53
         IAGE(1)=C                                                            54
         IAGE(2)=1                                                            55
C
C
C        CONVERT THE DATA TO INTEGERS FOR PRINTING AND PUNCHING.
         ITTBB = TTBB                                                         56
         ITCDM = TDDM                                                         57
         ITCDF = TDDF                                                         58
         DC 78 I=1,2C                                                         59
         IBB(I)=BB(I)                                                         60
C
C        ELIMINATE POSSIBLE MINUS ZEROS.
         IF (IBB(I) .LE. C) IBB(I)=0                                          61
         IDDM(I)=DDM(I)                                                       62
      78 IDDF(I)=DDF(I)                                                       63
C
C        PRINT THE TABLE.
         PRINT 8C                                                            64
      80 FORMAT (/// 3X 3HAGE 9X 1CHPOPULATION 11X 6HBIRTHS 12X6HDEATHS 12X   65
        D 3HAGE /12X 4HMALE 7X 6HFEMALE 20X 4HMALE 7X 6HFEMALE /)             66
         PRINT 82,(IAGE(I),IPPM(I),IPPF(I),IBB(I),IDDM(I),IDDF(I),IAGE(I),    67
        E I=1,19)                                                            68
      82 FORMAT (I5,5I12,I9)                                                  69
         PRINT 84,IPPM(2C),IPPF(20),IBB(20),IDDM(20),IDDF(20)                70
      84 FORMAT (/1X 7HUNKNCWN I9,4I12,5X 7HUNKNOWN )                         71
         PRINT 85,ITPPM,ITPPF,ITTBB,ITDDM,ITDDF                             72
      85 FORMAT (5X,5(5X,7H------- ) / 7H0 TOTAL,I10,4I12,6X,5HTOTAL )        73
C
C        CONVERT THE DATA TO REALS FOR DISTRIBUTION OF POPULATION.
         TPPM = ITPPM                                                         74
         TPPF = ITPPF                                                         75
         DO 86 I = 1,20                                                       76
         PPM(I)=IPPM(I)                                                       77
      86 PPF(I)=IPPF(I)                                                       78
C
C        DISTRIBUTE THE UNKNOWN CATEGORY OF POPULATION.
         DO 87 I=1,19                                                         79
         PPM(I)=PPM(I)*IPPM/(TPPM-PPM(20))                                    80
         PPF(I)=PPF(I)*TPFF/(TPPF-PPF(20))                                    81
         DDM(I)=DDM(I)*TDDM/(TDDM-DDM(20))                                    82
         DDF(I)=DDF(I)*TDDF/(TDDF-CDF(20))                                    83
         IPPM(I)=PPM(I)+.5                                                    84
      87 IPPF(I)=PPF(I)+.5                                                    85
C
C        PUNCH A NEW DATA DECK.
         ITDD=TDD                                                             86
         ITBB=TBB                                                             87
         ITBBM=TBBM                                                           88
         ITBBF=TBBF                                                           89
         IBB(18)=TBBM                                                         90
         IBB(19)=TBBF                                                         91
         IBB(20)=TBB                                                          92
         PUNCH 5C,NAME                                                        93
         PUNCH 88,IDATE,ITPP,ITDD,ITBB,ITBBM,ITBBF,YEARS                     94
      88 FORMAT (I4,5X 5I9,F9.3)                                              95
         PUNCH 90,IPPM,IPPF,IBB                                               96
```

```
   90 FORMAT (10I8)                                                       97
C
C        COMPUTE AND PRINT THE MALE LIFE TABLE.
         PRINT 92
   92 FORMAT (21H1LIFE TABLE FCR MALES )                                  98
         CALL LIF (PPM,DDM)                                               99
C                                                                        100
C        COMPUTE AND PRINT THE FEMALE LIFE TABLE.
         PRINT 94
   94 FORMAT (23H1LIFE TABLE FCR FEMALES )                               101
         CALL LIF (PPF,DDF)                                              102
C                                                                        103
C        CHECK FOR ANOTHER SET CF DATA.
   96 READ 50,NAME
         DO 98 I=1,1C                                                    104
         IF (NAME(I) .NE. IBK) GC TO 52                                  105
C        BLANK CARD AFTER LAST STACKED DATA SET TERMINATES PROGRAM.      106
   98 CONTINUE
         STOP                                                            107
         END                                                             108
                                                                         109



      SUBROUTINE LIF (PP,DD)                                             110
C
C     PRODUCES A LIFE TABLE THAT ITERATES TO THE DATA.
C
C     INPUT IN FORMAT (10F8.0) IS --
C        1) POPULATICN PP(I) FCR AGES 0,1-4,5-9,... 85+, AT LAST
C           BIRTHDAY (2 CARDS)
C        2) DEATHS DD(I) FOR THE SAME AGE GROUPS, OVER ONE YEAR OR THE
C           AVERAGE PER YEAR CF SOME OTHER PERIOD (2 CARDS)
C
      DIMENSICN PP(20),DD(2C),VMM(20),VR(20),VL(20),VLLP(20),            111
     A IAGE(20),QX(20),IPP(2C),IDD(20),L(20),LL(20),NDX(2C),VM(20),     112
     B VA(20),ITT(20),E(20),TT(2C)                                      113
C
C
C     LIFE TABLE VARIABLES
C        VMM(I) = AGE-SPECIFIC DEATH RATES
C        VR(I) = RATE CF INCREASE FOR ITH AGE GROUP--LOCAL R
C        SEP = SEPARATICN FACTCR FOR AGE ZERO
C        VL(I) = NUMBER SURVIVING COLUMN OF LIFE TABLE
C        VLLP(I) = NUMBER LIVING IN LOCALLY OR SECTIONALLY STABLE
C                  PCPULATICN--ALSO STORES STATIONARY POPULATION
C        LL(I) = NUMBER LIVING IN STATIONARY POPULATICN
C
C     SET INITIAL VALUES IN ARRAYS.
      DO 11 I=1,19
      IPP(I)=PP(I)+.5                                                    114
      IF (IPP(I) .EQ. C) PP(I)=1.                                       115
      VMM(I) = DD(I)/PP(I)                                              116
   11 VR(I)=.CC00C1                                                     117
      SEP = .C7 + 1.7*VMM(1)                                            118
      VL(1) = 1CCC00.                                                   119
      VL(2) = VL(1)*(1. - SEP*VMM(1))/(1. + (1. - SEP)*VMM(1))          120
                                                                        121
```

```
      VL(3) = VL(2)*(1. - 1.5*VMM(2))/(1. + 2.5*VMM(2))          122
      DO 13 I=3,19                                                123
      VL(I+1) = VL(I)*(1. - 2.5*VMM(I))/(1. + 2.5*VMM(I))         124
   13 VLLP(I) = 2.5*(VL(I) + VL(I+1))                             125
      VL17=VL(17)                                                 126
C
C        THE FOLLOWING QUOTIENTS ARE COMPUTED ONCE AND STORED TO
C        AVOID RE-COMPUTING THEM MANY TIMES IN THE DO-LOOPS AHEAD.
      CNSTA=10./3.                                                127
      CNSTB=5./12.                                                128
      CNSTC=65./24.                                               129
      CNSTD=5./24.                                                130
C
C        THE MAIN ITERATIVE LOOP IS FROM HERE TO STATEMENT 21.
      DO 21 J=1,1C                                                131
C
C        REVISE LL(X) FOR AGES 5-9 AND 85+.
      VLLP(3)=2.5*(VL(3)+VL(4)/EXP(5.*VR(3)))                     132
      VLLP(19)=CNSTA*VL(19)-CNSTB*VL(18)                          133
C        VLLP(I) IS USED FIRST TC STORE THE SECTIONALLY STABLE
C        POPULATION AND LATER THE STATIONARY POPULATION.
C
C        PERFORM THE ITERATION FOR EACH AGE GROUP (10-14,... 80-84).
      DO 15 I=4,18                                                134
C
C        DEFINE S AS EXP (5*R) TC AVOID RECALCULATING EXPONENTIALS.
      S = EXP(5.*VR(I))                                           135
C
C        COMPUTE THE NEW ITERATE FOR VLLP(I).
      VLLP(I)=CNSTC*(VL(I)+VL(I+1)/S)-CNSTD*(VL(I-1)*S+VL(I+2)/S**2)  136
C
C        COMPUTE NEW ITERATE FCR L(X).
      VL(I+1)=S*(VL(I)-(VMM(I)+VR(I))*(VLLP(I)-CNSTC*VL(I+1)/S)) /  137
     C (1.+CNSTC*(VMM(I)+VR(I)))                                  138
C
C        COMPUTE NEW ITERATE FCR AGE-SPECIFIC INCREASE RATE VR(I).
      WW=(PP(I-1)/VLLP(I-1))/(PP(I+1)/VLLP(I+1))                  139
      VR(I)=.00001                                                140
      IF (WW .GT. 1.0) VR(I)= .1 * ALOG (WW)                      141
      IF (VR(I) .GT. .04)  VR(I) = .04                            142
   15 CONTINUE                                                    143
C
C        TEST FCR CONVERGENCE.
      IF (ABS (VL17 - VL(17)) .LT. 1.) GO TO 25                   144
      VL17=VL(17)                                                 145
   21 CONTINUE                                                    146
      PRINT 23                                                    147
   23 FORMAT (50H0  CONVERGENCE WAS NOT ATTAINED WITH 10 ITERATIONS  )  148
      RETURN                                                      149
C        THE ITERATION FOR L(X) IS COMPLETE.
C
C        THE REMAINING COLUMNS OF THE LIFE TABLE WILL NOW BE COMPUTED
C        STARTING WITH THOSE CALCULATED FROM TOP TO BOTTOM.
   25 DO 27 I=1,19                                                150
      IAGE(I)=5*I-10                                              151
      QX(I)=1.0-VL(I+1)/VL(I)                                     152
      NDX(I)=VL(I)-VL(I+1) + 0.5                                  153
      IF (I .LT. 4 .OR. I .EC. 19) GO TO 27                       154
      VLLP(I)=CNSTC*(VL(I)+VL(I+1)) - CNSTD*(VL(I-1)+VL(I+2))     155
   27 CONTINUE                                                    156
```

```
C
C           SOME OF THE ABOVE COMPUTATIONS MUST BE MODIFIED
C           FOR THE LOWEST AND HIGHEST AGE GROUPS.
            NDX(19)=VL(19)+0.5                                          157
            QX(19)=1.0                                                  158
            IAGE(1)=0                                                   159
            IAGE(2)=1
            VLLP(1)=SEP*VL(1) + (1.0-SEP)*VL(2)                         160
            VLLP(2)=1.5*VL(2) + 2.5*VL(3)                               161
            VLLP(3)=2.5*(VL(3)+VL(4))                                   162
            VLLP(19)=VL(19)/VMM(19)                                     163
            TT(19)=VLLP(19)                                             164
C                                                                       165
C
C           THE NEXT LOOP COMPUTES FROM THE BOTTOM TO THE TOP.
C           TO DO THIS, INDEX I TAKES ON VALUES 19,18,... 1 AS J=1,19.
            DO 29 J=1,19
            I=20-J                                                      166
            VM(I)=(VL(I)-VL(I+1))/VLLP(I)                               167
            VA(I)=(VLLP(I)-5.0*VL(I+1))/(VL(I)-VL(I+1))                 168
            IF (I .NE. 19) TT(I)=TT(I+1)+VLLP(I)                        169
C                                                                       170
   29 E(I)=TT(I)/VL(I)
C                                                                       171
C
C           AGAIN, SOME VALUES REQUIRE ADJUSTMENT.
            VA(1)=SEP
            VA(2)=1.5                                                   172
            VA(3)=2.5                                                   173
            VA(19)=E(19)                                                174
C                                                                       175
C
C           IN ORDER TO SUPPRESS DECIMAL POINTS CONVERT TO INTEGERS
C           BEFORE PRINTING.
            DO 31 I=1,19
            IDD(I)=DD(I)                                                176
            L(I)=VL(I)+0.5                                              177
            LL(I)=VLLP(I)+0.5                                           178
   31 ITT(I)=TT(I)+0.5                                                  179
C                                                                       180
      PRINT 33
   33 FORMAT (//4H0AGE 7X2HPP 8X2HDD 8X4HQ(X) 6X4HL(X) 7X4HD(X) 5X      181
     E 5HLL(X) 5X3HAGE /)                                               182
C                                                                       183
C
      PRINT THE FIRST SIX COLUMNS OF THE LIFE TABLE.
      PRINT 35, (IAGE(I),IPP(I),IDD(I),QX(I),L(I),NDX(I),LL(I),IAGE(I),
     D I=1,19)                                                          184
   35 FORMAT (1X I3,I11,I9,F12.6,3I10,I7)                               185
      PRINT 37                                                          186
   37 FORMAT (///4H0AGE 6X4HM(X) 7X4HA(X) 6X5HTT(X) 6X4HR(X) 5X4HE(X) 6X  187
     F 5HMM(X) 5X3HAGE /)                                              188
C                                                                       189
C
      PRINT THE SECOND SIX COLUMNS OF THE LIFE TABLE.
      PRINT 39,(IAGE(I),VM(I),VA(I),ITT(I),VR(I),E(I),VMM(I),
     G IAGE(I),I=1,19)                                                  190
                                                                        191
   39 FORMAT (1XI3,F11.6,F10.3,I12,F9.4,F10.3,F11.6,I6)                 192
C
C           PUNCH LL(X) FOR FUTURE PROGRAMS--FORMAT (10I8).
      LL(20)=0
      PUNCH 41,LL                                                       193
   41 FORMAT (10I8)                                                     194
      RETURN                                                            195
      END                                                              196
                                                                        197
```

```
ENGLAND AND WALES 1968
1968          48593000    576880    819272    421130    398142
   414700  1716200  1980500  1716000  1734800  1857200  1538700  1504100  1508800  1540800
  1626400  1411600  1458300  1292800   991000   631100   399200   206600   101100        0
   393600  1631200  1882500  1633100  1681800  1838900  1500800  1426100  1443300  1522100
  1644900  1488800  1585300  1483800  1280500  1033400   753600   464300   275100        0
        0        0        C      222    81853   295946   240807   125316    58083    15904
     1140        1        C        0        C        0        0        0        0        0
     8707     1490      869      677     1545     1712     1347     1554     2447     4653
     8275    13023    23368    34785    43710    43426    42011    32675    27037        0
     6275     1194      573      431      624      740      794     1077     1739     3153
     5569     7848    12601    19196    27233    37936    47724    49949    58913        0
        1

MEXICO 1966
1966          44145000    424141   1940565   1004002   936563
   896000  3266000  3445999  2837000  2290000  1839000  1497000  1238000  1044000   881000
   713000   575000   484000   399000   292000   195000   122000    62439    39562        0
   868000  3126000  3271000  2712000  2235000  1838000  1538000  1311000  1110000   938000
   777000   630000   514000   409000   304000   209000   130000    66502    42498        0
        0        0        C     3390   213986   537112   491128   328540   241290   107736
    17383        0        C        0        C        0        0        0        0        0
    68108    31788     7574     3644     4371     5477     5820     5813     7200     6809
     6796     6970     8510     9823    11098     9233     8634     6807    10773        0
    54788    32138     6811     2988     3404     4192     4557     4393     5428     4662
     4936     5260     6413     8357     9418     8863     8484     8288    15513        0
        1
```

```
ENGLAND AND WALES 1968
  AGE          POPULATION           BIRTHS           DEATHS              AGE
             MALE      FEMALE                    MALE      FEMALE

    0        414700    393600          C         8707      6275          0
    1       1716200   1631200          C         1490      1194          1
    5       1980500   1882500          C          869       573          5
   10       1716000   1633100        222          677       431         10
   15       1734800   1681800      81853         1545       624         15
   20       1857200   1838900     295946         1712       740         20
   25       1538700   1500800     240807         1347       794         25
   30       1504100   1426100     125316         1554      1077         30
   35       1508800   1443300      58083         2447      1739         35
   40       1540800   1522100      15904         4653      3153         40
   45       1626400   1644900       1140         8275      5569         45
   50       1411600   1488800          1        13023      7848         50
   55       1458300   1585300          0        23368     12601         55
   60       1292800   1483800          C        34785     19196         60
   65        991000   1280500          C        43710     27233         65
   70        631100   1033400          C        43426     37936         70
   75        399200    753600          0        42011     47724         75
   80        206600    464300          0        32675     49949         80
   85        101100    275100          C        27037     58913         85

UNKNOWN           0         0          C            0         0     UNKNOWN
              -------   -------    -------      -------   -------

TOTAL     23629900  24963100     819272       293311    283569       TOTAL
```

LIFE TABLE FOR MALES

AGE	PP	DD	Q(X)	L(X)	D(X)	LL(X)	AGE
0	414700	8706	0.C206C9	10CCC0	2061	98157	0
1	1716199	1489	0.C03465	97939	339	390908	1
5	1980499	868	0.C02191	976CC	214	487464	5
10	1715999	676	0.CC1977	97386	193	486493	10
15	1734799	1544	0.CC4445	971S3	432	484939	15
20	1857199	1711	0.CC4598	96761	445	482692	20
25	1538699	1346	0.CC4370	96316	421	480540	25
30	1504099	1553	0.CC5159	95896	495	478314	30
35	1508799	2446	0.CC8C8C	954C1	771	475270	35
40	1540799	4652	0.014597	94630	1419	469931	40
45	1626399	8274	0.C25168	93211	2346	460750	45
50	1411599	13022	0.C45200	90865	4107	444965	50
55	1458299	23367	0.C77259	86758	6703	418289	55
60	1292799	34784	0.126664	80055	10140	376445	60
65	991000	43709	0.200187	69915	13996	315912	65
70	631100	43425	0.295219	55919	16508	238820	70
75	399200	42010	0.415613	39411	16380	155344	75
80	206600	32674	0.5583C5	23031	12858	81302	80
85	101100	27036	1.C00CC0	10173	10173	38039	85

AGE	M(X)	A(X)	TT(X)	R(X)	E(X)	MM(X)	AGE
0	0.020996	0.106	6864567	0.00C0	68.646	0.020996	0
1	0.000868	1.500	6766411	C.00C0	69.088	0.000868	1
5	0.000439	2.500	6375503	C.00CC	65.323	0.000439	5
10	0.000396	2.735	5888039	0.0127	60.461	0.000395	10
15	0.000891	2.621	5401546	C.00C0	55.575	0.000891	15
20	0.000922	2.495	4916607	C.0061	50.812	0.000922	20
25	0.000876	2.524	4433915	C.02C3	46.035	0.000875	25
30	0.001034	2.647	3953375	C.0059	41.226	0.001033	30
35	0.001622	2.75C	3475062	C.00C0	36.426	0.001622	35
40	0.003020	2.731	2999793	C.00C0	31.700	0.003020	40
45	0.005092	2.739	2529863	C.0028	27.141	0.005088	45
50	0.009230	2.721	2069114	C.0019	22.771	0.009226	50
55	0.016024	2.688	162415C	C.00CC	18.720	0.016024	55
60	0.026936	2.65C	1205861	C.0053	15.063	0.026907	60
65	0.044304	2.595	829416	C.0222	11.863	0.044107	65
70	0.069125	2.530	513505	C.0232	9.183	0.068810	70
75	0.105441	2.454	274684	C.0093	6.970	0.105238	75
80	0.158156	2.367	119341	C.00C0	5.182	0.158156	80
85	0.215123	3.739	38039	C.00C0	3.739	0.267428	85

LIFE TABLE FOR FEMALES

AGE	PP	DD	Q(X)	L(X)	D(X)	LL(X)	AGE
0	393600	6274	0.C15716	1C0CC0	1572	98581	0
1	1631199	1193	0.CC2923	98428	288	392994	1
5	1882499	572	0.0C1520	98141	149	490330	5
10	1633099	430	0.C01319	97992	129	489641	10
15	1681799	624	0.CC1854	97862	181	488872	15
20	1838899	739	0.C02011	97681	196	487929	20
25	1500799	793	0.CC2651	97484	258	486811	25
30	1426099	1076	0.CC3776	97226	367	485279	30
35	1443299	1738	0.C06CC9	96859	582	482969	35
40	1522099	3152	0.C10309	96277	993	479115	40
45	1644899	5568	0.C16797	95284	1601	472722	45
50	1488799	7847	0.026037	93684	2439	462729	50
55	1585299	12600	0.C39C25	91245	3561	447961	55
60	1483799	19195	0.C62862	87684	5512	425635	60
65	1280499	27232	0.101552	82172	8345	391454	65
70	1033400	37935	0.169360	73827	12503	339658	70
75	753600	47723	0.275469	61324	16893	265709	75
80	464300	49948	0.424249	44431	18850	175218	80
85	275100	58912	1.CC0C00	25581	25581	119454	85

AGE	M(X)	A(X)	TT(X)	R(X)	E(X)	MM(X)	AGE
0	0.015942	0.097	7483C52	C.0000	74.831	0.015943	0
1	0.000732	1.500	7384472	C.0000	75.024	0.000732	1
5	0.000304	2.500	6991478	C.0000	71.239	0.000304	5
10	0.000264	2.551	6501148	0.0110	66.344	0.000264	10
15	0.000371	2.576	6C11508	C.0CC0	61.428	0.000371	15
20	0.000403	2.581	5522637	C.0051	56.538	0.000402	20
25	0.000531	2.637	5C347C9	C.0235	51.646	0.000529	25
30	0.000757	2.683	4547898	0.0C89	46.777	0.000755	30
35	0.001205	2.724	4C62619	C.0000	41.944	0.001205	35
40	0.002072	2.714	3579650	C.0000	37.181	0.002071	40
45	0.003386	2.688	31C0536	C.00C0	32.540	0.003386	45
50	0.005271	2.667	2627815	C.0000	28.050	0.005271	50
55	0.007949	2.68C	2165C86	C.0000	23.728	0.007949	55
60	0.012950	2.681	1717126	C.0C53	19.583	0.012937	60
65	0.021317	2.675	1291491	C.0116	15.717	0.021267	65
70	0.036812	2.642	90C038	0.0129	12.191	0.036710	70
75	0.063576	2.578	56C381	C.0168	9.138	0.063328	75
80	0.107579	2.51C	294672	C.0000	6.632	0.107579	80
85	0.148957	4.670	119454	C.0000	4.670	0.214151	85

MEXICO 1966

AGE	POPULATION		BIRTHS	DEATHS		AGE
	MALE	FEMALE		MALE	FEMALE	
0	896000	868000	0	68108	54788	0
1	3266000	3126000	0	31788	32138	1
5	3445999	3271000	0	7574	6811	5
10	2837000	2712000	3390	3644	2988	10
15	2290000	2235000	213986	4371	3404	15
20	1839000	1838000	537112	5477	4192	20
25	1497000	1538000	491128	5820	4557	25
30	1238000	1311000	328540	5813	4393	30
35	1044000	1110000	241290	7200	5428	35
40	881000	938000	107736	6809	4662	40
45	713000	777000	17383	6796	4936	45
50	575000	630000	0	6970	5260	50
55	484000	514000	0	8510	6413	55
60	399000	409000	0	9823	8357	60
65	292000	304000	0	11098	9418	65
70	195000	209000	0	9233	8863	70
75	122000	130000	0	8634	8484	75
80	62439	66502	0	6807	8288	80
85	39562	42498	0	10773	15513	85
UNKNOWN	0	0	0	0	0	UNKNOWN
	-------	-------	-------	-------	-------	
TOTAL	22116000	22029000	1940565	225248	198893	TOTAL

LIFE TABLE FOR MALES

AGE	PP	DD	Q(X)	L(X)	D(X)	LL(X)	AGE
0	895999	68107	0.071652	100000	7165	94262	0
1	3265999	31787	0.038008	92835	3528	362518	1
5	3445998	7573	0.010929	89306	976	444092	5
10	2836999	3643	0.006379	88330	564	440214	10
15	2289999	4370	0.009563	87767	839	436888	15
20	1838999	5476	0.014869	86928	1293	431576	20
25	1496999	5819	0.019323	85635	1655	424177	25
30	1237999	5812	0.023305	83980	1957	415245	30
35	1043999	7200	0.034015	82023	2790	403360	35
40	881000	6808	0.037992	79233	3010	388801	40
45	713000	6795	0.046716	76223	3561	372480	45
50	575000	6969	0.059105	72662	4295	353037	50
55	484000	8509	0.084606	68367	5784	328002	55
60	399000	9822	0.116621	62583	7299	295475	60
65	292000	11097	0.174624	55285	9654	252789	65
70	195000	9232	0.212635	45631	9703	204152	70
75	122000	8633	0.302905	35928	10883	152649	75
80	62439	6806	0.428833	25045	10740	98517	80
85	39562	10772	1.000000	14305	14305	52533	85

AGE	M(X)	A(X)	TT(X)	R(X)	E(X)	MM(X)	AGE
0	0.076013	0.199	5950763	0.0000	59.508	0.076013	0
1	0.009733	1.500	5856501	0.0000	63.085	0.009733	1
5	0.002198	2.500	5493983	0.0000	61.518	0.002198	5
10	0.001280	2.449	5049892	0.0257	57.171	0.001284	10
15	0.001921	2.681	4609678	0.0389	52.522	0.001909	15
20	0.002995	2.631	4172791	0.0400	48.003	0.002978	20
25	0.003901	2.584	3741215	0.0377	43.688	0.003888	25
30	0.004713	2.621	3317039	0.0335	39.498	0.004695	30
35	0.006917	2.579	2901794	0.0286	35.378	0.006897	35
40	0.007742	2.553	2498434	0.0291	31.533	0.007729	40
45	0.009560	2.575	2109634	0.0329	27.677	0.009532	45
50	0.012165	2.608	1737154	0.0292	23.907	0.012122	50
55	0.017635	2.608	1384117	0.0209	20.245	0.017583	55
60	0.024701	2.610	1056115	0.0222	16.875	0.024619	60
65	0.038190	2.552	760640	0.0314	13.759	0.038007	65
70	0.047527	2.526	507851	0.0349	11.130	0.047349	70
75	0.071293	2.520	303699	0.0400	8.453	0.070770	75
80	0.109018	2.513	151050	0.0000	6.031	0.109018	80
85	0.220132	3.672	52533	0.0000	3.672	0.272307	85

LIFE TABLE FOR FEMALES

AGE	PP	DD	Q(X)	L(X)	D(X)	LL(X)	AGE
0	868000	54787	0.060004	100000	6000	95063	0
1	3125999	32137	0.040093	94000	3769	366577	1
5	3270999	6810	0.010357	90231	935	448818	5
10	2711999	2987	0.005468	89296	488	445207	10
15	2234999	3403	0.007627	88808	677	442454	15
20	1837999	4191	0.011394	88131	1004	438270	20
25	1537999	4556	0.014746	87127	1285	432510	25
30	1310999	4392	0.016671	85842	1431	425790	30
35	1109999	5427	0.024221	84411	2045	417066	35
40	938000	4661	0.024583	82366	2025	406869	40
45	777000	4935	0.031389	80342	2522	395648	45
50	630000	5259	0.041116	77820	3200	381521	50
55	514000	6412	0.060944	74620	4548	362495	55
60	409000	8356	0.097986	70072	6866	334156	60
65	304000	9417	0.144822	63206	9154	293892	65
70	209000	8862	0.193173	54053	10441	244830	70
75	130000	8483	0.283724	43611	12374	188052	75
80	66502	8287	0.477139	31238	14905	119594	80
85	42498	15512	1.000000	16333	16333	44744	85

AGE	M(X)	A(X)	TT(X)	R(X)	E(X)	MM(X)	AGE
0	0.063120	0.177	6283550	0.0000	62.835	0.063120	0
1	0.010281	1.500	6188487	0.0000	65.835	0.010281	1
5	0.002082	2.500	5821911	0.0000	64.522	0.002082	5
10	0.001097	2.390	5373094	0.0282	60.172	0.001102	10
15	0.001531	2.658	4927887	0.0356	55.489	0.001523	15
20	0.002291	2.626	4485433	0.0360	50.895	0.002281	20
25	0.002970	2.569	4047164	0.0326	46.452	0.002963	25
30	0.003361	2.611	3614654	0.0300	42.108	0.003351	30
35	0.004902	2.560	3188865	0.0292	37.778	0.004890	35
40	0.004977	2.549	2771799	0.0297	33.652	0.004970	40
45	0.006374	2.597	2364931	0.0326	29.436	0.006353	45
50	0.008386	2.632	1969284	0.0332	25.306	0.008349	50
55	0.012545	2.668	1587763	0.0306	21.278	0.012477	55
60	0.020548	2.640	1225268	0.0306	17.486	0.020433	60
65	0.031146	2.581	891112	0.0335	14.098	0.030980	65
70	0.042648	2.564	597220	0.0391	11.049	0.042407	70
75	0.065799	2.575	352389	0.0400	8.080	0.065261	75
80	0.124628	2.545	164338	0.0000	5.261	0.124628	80
85	0.348118	2.740	44744	0.0000	2.740	0.365029	85

CHAPTER 7

Population Projection

Demographic analysis of statistical information on present or past populations typically takes the form of asking what would happen if the observed rates were to continue. The future population that is so projected is a logical construct, an artifact designed to help understand the observed population.

Nearly all demographic measures implicitly use this device of projecting a future population; even crude birth and death rates tell us (though not entirely satisfactorily) by their difference, the rate of natural increase, how fast a population is growing. We know little when we observe only that so many births occurred last year in a country, but if we also know the number of deaths and the number of persons in the population, and that the rate of natural increase is 2 percent, then we can note that a doubling of the population in 35 years is implied by those births.

In this chapter the reference to the future is explicit; we shall see how to calculate the effect of the given age-specific rates of mortality and fertility on the subsequent population, always supposing that the rates continue. Prediction is not the object here, since in fact rates will change. The future is affected by the variables of many disciplines: psychology, ecology, economics, and politics among others. We cannot pretend to estimate in what direction and by how much rates will change for each of the 90 or so countries represented in this book.

If the reader requires predictions, he will have to modify our projections according to his views on the likely changes in mortality and fertility for the country in question, as well as its migration prospects. Forecasts of change involve different uncertainties for more and for less developed countries. For the more developed, fertility seems to move in waves of unequal amplitude and length, and even the once steady downtrend of mortality has shown some hesitation in recent years. For the less developed the great unknown is when the birth rate will start to fall.

Survival of Those Alive at the Beginning of the Interval

Survival of persons from one point of time to another has in effect been covered in the discussion of the life table, where the survivors of a cohort were designated $_5L_x$. We may think of the persons of a given age in a given country, caught at a moment of time in a census or equivalent estimation procedure, as a cross section of a cohort. We know that they were not all born in that country, and we are not following them from birth, but only from the starting point of the projection; nonetheless their attrition will be in the ratio of the successive $_5L_x$.

Thus the $_5P_x$ initially aged x to $x + 4$ will in the course of five years diminish to $_5P_x(_5L_{x+5}/_5L_x)$ aged $x + 5$ to $x + 9$. A minor point, mentioned in Chapter 6, is that this ratio supposes that they may be regarded as the result of a uniform number of births. If the distribution by age within the interval x to $x + 4$ is the outcome of births increasing at rate r, then the cohort diminishes according to $_5L'_x = \int_0^5 e^{-rt}l(x + t)\, dt$ for successive x. However, the program PROJECT uses the conventional $_5L_x$ rather than $_5L'_x$.

The computer program can be seen as a worksheet in which the cells are the numbers of persons in successive age groups at five-year intervals subsequent to the date of observing the initial population. The continuation of cohorts by the ratios $_5L_{x+5}/_5L_x$ is equivalent to filling in diagonal lines on the worksheet. United States girl children younger than five years old in 1967 numbered 9,397,000, and these multiplied by the survival factor $_5L_5/_5L_0$ for females, $9,397,000 \times 488,523/490,021$, come to 9,368,000, which is the projected number of females 5–9 years old in 1972 shown in the Main Tables (page 361). Similar calculations give projected numbers for other ages. In the resulting collection of numbers in the various age groups, the number younger than five years in 1972 is necessarily left blank. The 0–4 age group of 1972 arises from the births of 1967–72, and calculation of these is the second task in a population projection.

Survivors Among the Group of Children Born During the Interval

Our model is female dominant: all births are attributed to women. After the projection to the end of the interval of the women initially present we calculate the woman-years of exposure to the risk of childbearing as the arithmetic mean of the initial and final numbers multiplied by 5. The initial number of females aged x to $x + 4$ years old is $_5P_x^{(0)}$, and the final number in this age group five years later as obtained by following the cohort five years younger is $_5P_x^{(1)}$. The exposure is taken as the average of initial and final numbers times 5: $5[(_5P_x^{(0)} + _5P_x^{(1)})/2]$, thought of as a number of women-years. Insofar as the population is increasing geometrically this is slightly too high; with geometric increase the mean exposure will be somewhat less than the arithmetic mean of the initial and final values. (A better approximation would be one-third of the arithmetic mean plus two-thirds of the geometric mean of $_5P_x^{(0)}$ and $_5P_x^{(1)}$ all multiplied by five, but for simplicity we have stayed with the arithmetic mean.) Note that all women, married and not married, are regarded as "exposed" for this purpose.

The number of women-years over the five-year time period is then multiplied by the age-specific birth rate to generate the total number of children born during the five years. For example, the number of U.S. women 20–24 years in 1967 was 7,530,000, and the projection of those 15–19 along the cohort line gave 8,755,000 for 1972. The arithmetic mean of these two numbers is $\frac{1}{2}(7,530,000 + 8,755,000) =$ 8,142,500. The age-specific birth rate F_{20} for 1967 was 1,310,588/7,530,000 = 0.1740, counting both sexes of children. Since we want the rate for girl children only we must multiply by the ratio of girls to total among all babies, 1,717,571/ 3,520,959 = 0.4878, to obtain as the age-specific birth rate for girls 0.1740 × 0.4878 = 0.0849. Multiplying the average exposure of 8,142,500 by 5 and then by 0.0849 gives 3,456,000. Adding together similar numbers for other ages of mother gives the expected number of female births during 1967–72.

But births are not strictly what we want. We need the number of children born that survive to 1972, the end of the five-year period. These are obtained by multiplying the births by $_5L_0/5l_0$, thus giving in this example, 9,017,000 females 0–4 in 1972.

On this female-dominant model the boy births are obtained from the ratio of boy babies to girl babies, which provides in effect the birth rate to women of boy babies· Once we have the number of boy births the survivors to the end of the five years are obtained by using the $_5L_0$ of the male life table.

The Projection as a Whole

The following of persons down cohort lines and the generating of new cohorts embrace the whole of population projection. The two steps repeated provide numbers for each sex, at each age, and at each point of time required.

Despite the artificiality of the model it provides us with some useful results. Populations that have had violent ups and downs in birth rates reflect this in the projections. The United States is an illustration. In projections from 1967, the starting point of the calculation shown on pages 360 and 361, the number of persons

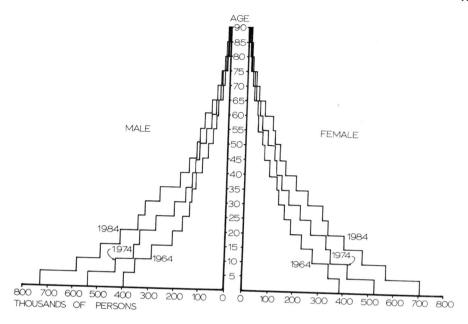

FIGURE 11

Population of Guatemala, 1964, by age and sex, and projection to 1974 and 1984.

in the 5–9 age group falls between 1967 and 1972, while those of working ages rise sharply. The 20–24 age group, for instance, rises from 14,572,000 in 1967 to 17,585,000 in 1972; the rate of increase of this group then slows as we project further into the future. Other examples of short-term projections have appeared in Part I. Figure 11 shows what happens to the age pyramid of a rapidly growing population in the projection with fixed rates.

Though treating these projections as predictions is necessarily the responsibility of the reader, especially in view of our application of fixed rates and the lack of any allowance for migration, yet in their gross outlines, and in particular for the part of the population already born, the numbers given in Table 4 of each set of Main Tables are realistic for most of the countries shown. That table projects only 15 years beyond the date to which the data refer, but the reader can extend the projection as far as he wishes with the program **PROJECT**. The program continues to project to the point at which the population becomes stable (up to 500 years) in the version here contained; it prints out only the first 25 years unless instructed otherwise.

The Stable or Ultimate Population

No projection of up to 500 years with fixed rates of birth and death can have any meaning in detail. The purpose of this part of the calculation is to find out what would happen with the indefinite continuance of the age-specific rates. We want to know the ultimate distribution by age for each sex; the ultimate sex ratio; the ultimate crude rates of birth, death, and natural increase. All of these ratios converge to their limiting values before the projection has extended through 500 years, at least to the number of digits required for our analysis.

If we think of the observed age-sex distribution of a population as being influenced by the "accidents" of earlier fluctuations in births and deaths, then we are curious about what the age distribution would be after the effects of these accidents work themselves out. That is called the stable age distribution, as we have seen. In particular, we would like to know what set of ages, distributed as the stable, would produce the same ultimate curve of population as do the observed ages.

To find this stable equivalent, the program PROJECT carries the population forward to stability, and then calculates the ratio of one point of time to that five years earlier. This ratio is the λ of our earlier discussion, here worked out from the grand total of the population projected, say, 375 years into the future to that 370 years into the future. The program then in a sense carries the projection back to the beginning, by dividing the projection to 375 years or 75 cycles by λ^{75}. This is a fitting of a stable age-sex distribution, but a special kind of fitting. The stable equivalent is such that it may be carried forward either by multiplying by the scalar λ or by projecting, and either way it will join the same ultimate projected values. Comparison of the stable equivalent with the observed age-sex distribution tells whether the latter is (temporarily) favorable or unfavorable to overall mortality and fertility.

Finally the program provides the ultimate fixed rates of birth, death, and natural increase, each calculated on an annual basis with instantaneous compounding.

Note that the projection as carried out above remains essentially a one-sex model. We do indeed calculate males as well as females, but the number of male births is a simple multiple of the number of female births. This way of handling the males in a model in which the number of women determines births is the *female dominance* to which reference has been made earlier. The alternative of male dominance is applied for those countries, seven in number, for which we were able to obtain births by age of father (pages 556–564).

Program PROJECT

```
C
C                          PROJECT
C
C
C       PROVIDES A POPULATION PROJECTION WITH FIXED AGE-SPECIFIC
C       RATES OF BIRTH AND DEATH, AS WELL AS ULTIMATE OR INTRINSIC
C       RATES OF BIRTH, DEATH, AND NATURAL INCREASE, AND AGE
C       DISTRIBUTION.  THE MODEL IS FEMALE-DOMINANT, I.E. THE NUMBER
C       OF BIRTHS AT EACH STAGE OF PROJECTION IS DETERMINED BY THE
C       NUMBER OF WOMEN.
C
C       THE INPUT IS THE STANDARD DECK PRODUCED BY PROGRAM
C       'LIFE', MODIFIED ONLY BY PUNCHING THE DESIRED TERMINAL YEAR OF
C       THE PROJECTION IN COLUMNS 65-68 OF THE TOTALS CARD WHICH IS
C       SECOND IN THE DECK OF 12 CARDS.  IF NO PUNCH FOR TERMINAL YEAR,
C       PROGRAM PRINTS OUT 25 YEARS PROJECTION.
C
C       IF OUTPUT OF 'LIFE' IS NOT AVAILABLE, THE INPUT
C       WOULD BE MADE UP AS FOLLOWS--
C         TITLE CARD (1 CARD IN FORMAT 19A4)
C         ONE CARD IN FORMAT (I4, 32X, 2F9.0, 9X, I5) THAT CONTAINS
C           THE YEAR OF INITIAL POPULATION, TOTAL MALE BIRTHS, TOTAL
C           FEMALE BIRTHS, AND THE DESIRED TERMINAL YEAR FOR
C           THE PROJECTION
C         THE FOLLOWING FIVE DISTRIBUTIONS EACH CONTAINING 20 NUMBERS
C           PUNCHED ON TWO CARDS IN FORMAT (10F8.0) ACCORDING TO
C           AGE GROUPS (0,1-4,5-9,...,85+, UNKNOWN)--
C             OBSERVED MALE POPULATION
C             OBSERVED FEMALE POPULATION
C             BIRTHS BY AGE OF MOTHER
C             MALE STATIONARY POPULATION LL(X) FROM THE LIFE TABLE
C             FEMALE STATIONARY POPULATION LL(X) FROM THE LIFE TABLE
C
C       SETS OF THE ABOVE INPUT MAY BE REPEATED INDEFINITELY.  THE
C       PROGRAM TERMINATES EXECUTION WHEN A BLANK TITLE CARD IS READ.
C
C       ARRAYS
C       PP=POPULATION NUMBER IN 5-YEAR AGE GROUPS
C       BB=BIRTHS TO MOTHERS IN 5-YEAR AGE GROUPS
C       VLL=LIFE TABLE STATIONARY AGE DISTRIBUTION
C       FF=AGE-SPECIFIC BIRTH RATES
C       'NAME' IS USED TO STORE THE CONTENTS OF THE TITLE CARD
C
      DIMENSION NAME(19),VLL(40),PP(41,6),PP1(40),BB(20),FF(20),JJ(41),    1
     A V(41),IYEAR(7),PPA(20),PPB(20),VLLA(20),VLLB(20)                    2
C
C       COLUMNS 1-76 OF THE TITLE CARD ARE STORED IN 'NAME'
C
      EQUIVALENCE (PP1,PPA),(PP1(21),PPB),(VLL,VLLA),(VLL(21),VLLB)         3
```

```
C
      Q=0.                                                          4
      READ 1,NAME,IBK                                               5
    1 FORMAT (20A4)                                                 6
    3 PRINT 5,NAME                                                  7
    5 FORMAT (1H1 19A4)                                             8
      READ 7,IYEAR(1),TBBM,TBBF,LYEAR                               9
    7 FORMAT (I4,32X 2F9.0,9X I5)                                  10
C
C         CLEAR ARRAYS IN WHICH PROJECTION IS TO BE STORED.
      DO 8 I=1,41                                                  11
      DO 8 J=1,6                                                   12
      PP (I,J)=0                                                   13
    8 CONTINUE                                                     14
C
C         N IS THE NUMBER OF TWENTY-FIVE YEAR PROJECTION CYCLES TO
C         BE PRINTED.
      N=1+(LYEAR-IYEAR(1)-1)/25                                    15
      IF (LYEAR.EQ.0) N=1                                          16
C
C         READ INPUT
      READ 9,PPA,PPB,BB,VLLA,VLLB                                  17
    9 FORMAT (10F8.0)                                              18
      PRINT 11                                                     19
   11 FORMAT (1H0/16X 5HMALES 20X 7HFEMALES 12X 6HBIRTHS)          20
C         S IS THE SEX RATIO AT BIRTH.
      S=TBBM/TBBF                                                  21
C
C         SET AGES IN ARRAY JJ.
      JJ(2)=0                                                      22
      DO 19 I=3,19                                                 23
      JJ(I)=JJ(I-1)+5                                              24
   19 JJ(I+20)=JJ(I)                                               25
      JJ(1)=0                                                      26
      JJ(2)=1                                                      27
C
C         PRINT INPUT DATA.
      PRINT 21                                                     28
   21 FORMAT (3X1HX 6X5HPP(X) 7X5HLL(X) 9X5HPP(X) 7X5HLL(X) 8X5HBB(X) 29
     D 4X 1HX /)                                                   30
      PRINT 23,(JJ(I),PP1(I),VLL(I),PP1(I+20),VLL(I+20),BB(I),JJ(I), 31
     E I=1,19)                                                     32
   23 FORMAT (1X I3,2F12.0,F14.0,2F12.0,I5)                        33
      PRINT 25,S                                                   34
   25 FORMAT (1H0/21H SEX RATIO AT BIRTH = F10.6)                  35
      JJ(2)=0                                                      36
      JJ(22)=0                                                     37
C         THE ARRAY JJ CONTAINS THE INITIAL YEAR OF EACH 5-YEAR AGE GROUP
C         STARTING WITH JJ(2) = 0 FOR MALES AND JJ(22) = 0 FOR FEMALES.
C         CHANGE IS BECAUSE AGES FOR PROJECTION OUTPUT (0, 5, 10,...)
C         ARE SLIGHTLY DIFFERENT FROM THOSE FOR DATA INPUT (0, 1, 5,...).
C
C         THE INITIAL AGE DISTRIBUTION IS ENTERED IN THE FIRST COLUMN
C         OF THE MATRIX PP.
      DO 27 I=1,40                                                 38
   27 PP(I,1)=PP1(I)                                               39
C
C         THE AGE GROUPS 0 AND 1 - 4 ARE COMBINED AND PLACED IN THE
C         POSITION OF THE 1 - 4.
```

```
          VLL(2) = VLL(2) + VLL(1)                                             40
          VLL(22) = VLL(22) + VLL(21)                                          41
          PP(2,1) = PP(2,1) + PP(1,1)                                          42
          PP(22,1) = PP(22,1) + PP(21,1)                                       43
          DO 29 I=4,12                                                         44
       29 FF(I)=BB(I)/PP1(I+20)                                                45
C
C         THIS CCNCLUDES THE PREPARATORY WORK.   NOW FOR THE
C         PROJECTION PROPER, STARTING WITH SURVIVORSHIP.
C         SUCCESSIVE COLUMNS CF PP ARE FILLED WITH THE POPULATION
C         PROJECTED FORWARD FIVE YEARS, USING THE LIFE TABLE SURVIVAL
C         RATIOS.
C
C         I INDEXES ACES
C         J INDEXES YEARS WITHIN 25-YEAR PROJECTION CYCLE
C         L INDEXES 25-YEAR CYCLES.
C
          DO 67 L=1,2C                                                         46
          DO 35 J=2,6                                                          47
          DO 31 I=3,19                                                         48
          PP(I,J) = PP(I-1,J-1)*VLL(I)/VLL(I-1)                                49
       31 PP(I+20,J) = PP(I+19,J-1)*VLL(I+20)/VLL(I+19)                        50
C
C         THE NUMBER OF MALE AND FEMALE BIRTHS DURING THE JTH 5-YEAR
C         PERIOD THAT SURVIVE TC THE END OF THE PERIOD ARE STORED
C         RESPECTIVELY IN PP(2,J) AND PP(22,J).
C         BIRTHS MUST BE  CCNVERTED INTO SURVIVORS TO THE END OF EACH
C         FIVE-YEAR PERIOD.
          PP(22,J) = C.                                                        51
          DO 33 K=4,12                                                         52
       33 PP(22,J) = PP(22,J) + .5*VLL(22)*(PP(K+20,J-1) + PP(K+20,J))         53
         1 *FF(K)/((1. + S)*10000C.)                                          54
          PP(2,J) = S*PP(22,J)*VLL(2)/VLL(22)                                  55
          PP(20,J) = C.                                                        56
       35 PP(40,J) = C.                                                        57
C
C         THE TOTAL MALES, TOTAL FEMALES, AND GRAND TOTAL ARE STORED
C         RESPECTIVELY IN PP(20,J), PP(40,J), AND PP(41,J).
          PP(20,1) = C.                                                        58
          PP(40,1) = C.                                                        59
          DO 39 J=1,6                                                          60
          IYEAR(J+1) = IYEAR(J) + 5                                            61
          DO 37 I=2,19                                                         62
          PP(20,J) = PP(2C,J) + PP(I,J)                                        63
       37 PP(40,J) = PP(4C,J) + PP(I+20,J)                                     64
       39 PP(41,J) = PP(2C,J) + PP(40,J)                                       65
C
C         IF THE PROJECTICN IS PAST LYEAR, DON'T PRINT IT.
          IF (L .GT. N) GC TC 59                                              66
          PRINT 41,(IYEAR(J),J=1,6)                                           67
       41 FORMAT(1H1 6I12/)                                                   68
C
C         PRINT FIRST HALF CF SIX PROJECTIONS.
          PRINT 43,(JJ(I),(PP(I,J),J=1,6),JJ(I),I=2,19)                       69
       43 FORMAT (1X I2,6F12.0,I4)                                            70
          K=20                                                                71
C
C         PRINT TCTALS FOR MALES.
          PRINT 47,(PP(K,J),J=1,6)                                            72
       47 FORMAT (3HOTM 6F12.C,4H  TM /1H0 )                                  73
```

```
C
C             PRINT SECOND HALF OF SIX PROJECTIONS.
        PRINT 43,(JJ(I),(PP(I,J),J=1,6),JJ(I),I=22,39)                     74
        K=40                                                              75
C
C             PRINT TOTALS FOR FEMALES.
        PRINT 53,(PP(K,J),J=1,6)                                          76
     53 FORMAT (3H0TF 6F12.0,4H  TF /1H0 )                                77
C
C             PRINT GRAND TOTALS.
     55 PRINT 57,(PP(41,J),J=1,6)                                         78
     57 FORMAT (3H  T 6F12.0,3H  T )                                      79
C             A TWENTY-FIVE YEAR PROJECTION CYCLE HAS BEEN PRINTED.
C
C             ALAM IS CALCULATED AS THE RATIO OF THE TOTAL PROJECTED
C             POPULATION AT ONE TIME TO THAT FIVE YEARS BEFORE. (IT IS THE
C             SAME AS THE DOMINANT ROOT OF THE PROJECTION MATRIX).
C             FROM THE LATEST PROJECTION, THE TOTAL POPULATION IS CARRIED
C             BACKWARD TO THE INITIAL YEAR BY MEANS OF ALAM, WHICH
C             APPROXIMATES THE STABLE POPULATION EQUIVALENT.
     59 ALAM=PP(41,6)/PP(41,5)                                            80
        A=ALAM**(-5*L)                                                    81
        QSTAR=PP(41,6)*A                                                  82
        Q=QSTAR                                                           83
C
C             THE LAST PROJECTION IS PLACED IN THE FIRST POSITION FOR THE
C             NEXT SERIES OF PROJECTIONS.
        DO 65 I=1,41                                                      84
     65 PP(I,1) = PP(I,6)                                                 85
     67 IYEAR(1) = IYEAR(6)                                               86
C
C             THE PROJECTION IS NOW COMPLETED.
C             WE PROCEED TO ANALYSIS OF THE STABLE CONDITION.
C
C             COMPUTE THE AGE-SEX-SPECIFIC POPULATION EQUIVALENT.
     69 DO 70 I=1,41                                                      87
     70 V(I)=PP(I,6)*A                                                    88
C
C             THE STABILIZED POPULATION IS USED TO COMPUTE THE FEMALE STABLE
C             OR INTRINSIC RATES OF BIRTH B, DEATH D, AND NATURAL INCREASE R.
        BBS=0.0                                                           89
        DO 71 I=4,12                                                      90
     71 BBS = BBS + PP(I+20,6)*FF(I)/(1.+S)                               91
        B = BBS/PP(40,6)                                                  92
        R = ALOG(ALAM)/5.                                                 93
        D = B - R                                                         94
C
C             PRINT STABLE OR INTRINSIC RATES.
        PRINT 73                                                          95
     73 FORMAT (1H1,7X,40HSTABLE EQUIVALENT TO ORIGINAL POPULATION,//     96
       1 22X, 5HMALES, 8X,7HFEMALES//)                                    97
        PRINT 75,(JJ(I),V(I),V(I+20),I=2,19)                             98
     75 FORMAT (10X,I3,2F15.0)                                            99
        PRINT 79,V(20),V(40),V(41)                                       100
     79 FORMAT (/15X,2HTM,F11.0,2X,2HTF,F11.0// 11X,5HTOTAL,F17.0)       101
        PRINT 81                                                         102
     81 FORMAT (1H0/1H0 10X 15HINTRINSIC RATES )                         103
        PRINT 85,B,D,R                                                   104
     85 FORMAT (1H0 10X 10HBIRTH RATE F12.5/11X 10HDEATH RATE F12.5 /    105
```

```
      A 8X 16HNATURAL INCREASE F9.5)                                        106
        NN = (L - 1)*25                                                     107
        PRINT 87,NN                                                         108
     87 FORMAT (1H0/11X 33HBASED CN POPULATION PROJECTED TO  I4,6H YEARS )  109
     89 READ 1,NAME                                                         110
        DO 91 I=1,1C                                                        111
        IF (NAME(I).NE.NAME(19)) GO TO 3                                    112
     91 CONTINUE                                                            113
        PRINT 93                                                            114
     93 FORMAT (11H1END CF JOB )                                            115
        STOP                                                                116
        END                                                                 117
```

ENGLAND AND WALES 1968
```
1968        48593000   576880    819272    42113C    398142     -0.
 414700 1716200 1980500 1716C00 1734800 185720C 1538700 1504100 1508800 1540800
1626400 1411600 145830C 1292800  99100C  63110C  399200  206600  101100       0
 393600 1631200 1882500 1633100 1681800 18389CC 1500800 1426100 1443300 1522100
1644900 1488800 158530C 1483800 1280500 1C33400  753600  464300  275100       0
      0       0       0     222   81853  295946  240807  125316   58083   15904
   1140       1       C       C       C       0       0       0  421130  398142  819272
  98157  390908  487464  486493  484940  482693  480541  478315  475271  469932
 460751  444967  418291  376447  315914  238822  155344   81302   38039       0
  98581  392994  49C33C  489641  488871  487929  486812  485280  482970  479116
 472723  462731  447963  425638  391456  33966C  265710  175219  119454       0
```

MEXICO 1966
```
1966        44145000   424141  1940565  1C040C2   936563     -0.
 896000 3266000 3445999 2837C00 2290000 18390C0 1497000 1238000 1044000  881000
 713000  575000  484000  399000  292000  195000  122000   62439   39562       0
 868000 3126000 3271000 2712C00 2235C00 1838000 1538000 1311000 1110000  938000
 777000  630000  51400C  40900C  304C0C  209000  130000   66502   42498       0
      0       0       0    3390  213986  537112  491128  328540  241290  107736
  17383       C       C       0       0       0       0 1004002  936563 1940565
  94262  362518  444C92  440214  436888  431577  424178  415246  403362  388803
 372482  353039  328004  295478  25279C  2C4153  152650   98518   52533       0
  95064  366577  448818  445208  442455  438270  432511  425791  417068  406870
 395649  381523  362496  334158  293893  244831  188052  119594   44744       0
```

ENGLAND AND WALES 1968

X	MALES PP(X)	LL(X)	FEMALES PP(X)	LL(X)	BIRTHS BB(X)	X
0	414700.	98157.	393600.	98581.	0.	0
1	1716200.	390908.	1631200.	392994.	0.	1
5	1980500.	487464.	1882500.	490330.	0.	5
10	1716000.	486493.	1633100.	489641.	222.	10
15	1734800.	484940.	1681800.	488871.	81853.	15
20	1857200.	482693.	1838900.	487929.	295946.	20
25	1538700.	480541.	1500800.	486812.	240807.	25
30	1504100.	478315.	1426100.	485280.	125316.	30
35	1508800.	475271.	1443300.	482970.	58083.	35
40	1540800.	469932.	1522100.	479116.	15904.	40
45	1626400.	460751.	1644900.	472723.	1140.	45
50	1411600.	444967.	1488800.	462731.	1.	50
55	1458300.	418291.	1585300.	447963.	0.	55
60	1292800.	376447.	1483800.	425638.	0.	60
65	991000.	315914.	1280500.	391456.	0.	65
70	631100.	238822.	1033400.	339660.	0.	70
75	399200.	155344.	753600.	265710.	0.	75
80	206600.	81302.	464300.	175219.	421130.	80
85	101100.	38039.	275100.	119454.	398142.	85

SEX RATIO AT BIRTH = 1.057737

	1968	1973	1978	1983	1988	1993	
0	2130900.	2096609.	2146001.	2206212.	2319898.	2432227.	0
5	1980500.	2123924.	2089745.	2138975.	2198989.	2312302.	5
10	1716000.	1976554.	2119693.	2085582.	2134714.	2194608.	10
15	1734800.	1710522.	1970244.	2112926.	2078924.	2127899.	15
20	1857200.	1726761.	1702596.	1961114.	2103135.	2069291.	20
25	1538700.	1848919.	1719062.	1695005.	1952370.	2093758.	25
30	1504100.	1531572.	1840354.	1711098.	1687153.	1943326.	30
35	1508800.	1494527.	1521824.	1828641.	1700208.	1676415.	35
40	1540800.	1491850.	1477738.	1504728.	1808098.	1681108.	40
45	1626400.	1510697.	1462703.	1448867.	1475330.	1772773.	45
50	1411600.	1570684.	1458944.	1412594.	1399232.	1424789.	50
55	1458300.	1326973.	1476520.	1371479.	1327908.	1315347.	55
60	1292800.	1312418.	1194228.	1328815.	1234282.	1195069.	60
65	991000.	1084916.	1101380.	1002195.	1115140.	1035808.	65
70	631100.	749168.	820165.	832612.	757631.	843014.	70
75	399200.	410505.	487303.	533484.	541580.	492808.	75
80	206600.	208928.	214845.	255039.	279208.	283445.	80
85	101100.	96663.	97752.	100520.	119326.	130634.	85
TM	23629840.	24272112.	24901040.	25529808.	26233056.	27024560.	TM
0	2024800.	1992338.	2039273.	2096490.	2204522.	2311264.	0
5	1882500.	2019671.	1987292.	2034108.	2091180.	2198938.	5
10	1633100.	1879854.	2016832.	1984499.	2031249.	2088241.	10
15	1681800.	1630531.	1876897.	2013660.	1981378.	2028054.	15
20	1838900.	1678559.	1627389.	1873280.	2009779.	1977560.	20
25	1500800.	1834690.	1674716.	1623663.	1868991.	2005178.	25
30	1426100.	1496076.	1828916.	1669445.	1618553.	1863109.	30
35	1443300.	1419311.	1488954.	1820210.	1661498.	1610848.	35
40	1522100.	1431782.	1407985.	1477072.	1805684.	1648239.	40
45	1644900.	1501790.	1412677.	1389197.	1457362.	1781590.	45
50	1488800.	1610131.	1470046.	1382817.	1359833.	1426557.	50
55	1585300.	1441285.	1558743.	1423129.	1338684.	1316434.	55
60	1483800.	1506293.	1369456.	1481060.	1352204.	1271968.	60
65	1280500.	1364639.	1385325.	1259478.	1362119.	1243611.	65
70	1033400.	1111068.	1184074.	1202023.	1092828.	1181888.	70
75	753600.	808410.	869169.	926280.	940321.	854900.	75
80	464300.	496952.	533096.	573162.	610823.	620082.	80
85	275100.	316532.	338792.	363433.	390748.	416423.	85
TF	24963040.	25539840.	26069568.	26592944.	27177680.	27844832.	TF
T	48592880.	49811952.	50970608.	52122752.	53410736.	54869392.	T

STABLE EQUIVALENT TO ORIGINAL POPULATION

	MALES	FEMALES
0	2023621.	1922980.
5	1948062.	1852555.
10	1877738.	1786730.
15	1807773.	1722951.
20	1737903.	1660861.
25	1671025.	1600429.
30	1606440.	1540867.
35	1541662.	1481122.
40	1472247.	1419089.
45	1394151.	1352301.
50	1300379.	1278477.
55	1180643.	1195378.
60	1026224.	1096984.
65	831773.	974410.
70	607307.	816585.
75	381529.	616968.
80	192856.	392948.
85	87148.	258734.

TM 22688416.   TF 22970304.

TOTAL   45658736.

INTRINSIC RATES

BIRTH RATE   0.01733
DEATH RATE   0.01037
NATURAL INCREASE   0.00695

BASED ON POPULATION PROJECTED TO 475 YEARS

MEXICO 1966

X	MALES		FEMALES		BIRTHS	
	PP(X)	LL(X)	PP(X)	LL(X)	BB(X)	X
0	896000.	94262.	868000.	95064.	0.	0
1	3266000.	362518.	3126000.	366577.	0.	1
5	3445999.	444092.	3271000.	448818.	0.	5
10	2837000.	440214.	2712000.	445208.	3390.	10
15	2290000.	436888.	2235000.	442455.	213986.	15
20	1839000.	431577.	1838000.	438270.	537112.	20
25	1497000.	424178.	1538000.	432511.	491128.	25
30	1238000.	415246.	1311000.	425791.	328540.	30
35	1044000.	403362.	1110000.	417068.	241290.	35
40	881000.	388803.	938000.	406870.	107736.	40
45	713000.	372482.	777000.	395649.	17383.	45
50	575000.	353039.	630000.	381523.	0.	50
55	484000.	328004.	514000.	362496.	0.	55
60	399000.	295478.	409000.	334158.	0.	60
65	292000.	252790.	304000.	293893.	0.	65
70	195000.	204153.	209000.	244831.	0.	70
75	122000.	152650.	130000.	188052.	0.	75
80	62439.	98518.	66502.	119594.	1004002.	80
85	39562.	52533.	42498.	44744.	936563.	85

SEX RATIO AT BIRTH = 1.072006

	1966	1971	1976	1981	1986	1991	
0	4162000.	5000904.	5932196.	7075935.	8447482.	10063604.	0
5	3445999.	4046390.	4861992.	5767415.	6879384.	8212835.	5
10	2837000.	3415907.	4011053.	4819534.	5717049.	6819309.	10
15	2290000.	2815563.	3390096.	3980746.	4783119.	5673851.	15
20	1839000.	2262161.	2781334.	3348882.	3932352.	4724971.	20
25	1497000.	1807471.	2223378.	2733649.	3291467.	3864934.	25
30	1238000.	1465477.	1769410.	2176559.	2676083.	3222157.	30
35	1044000.	1202569.	1423536.	1718770.	2114267.	2599495.	35
40	881000.	1006318.	1159163.	1372154.	1656732.	2037954.	40
45	713000.	844018.	964075.	1110504.	1314554.	1587186.	45
50	575000.	675782.	799961.	913751.	1052537.	1245936.	50
55	484000.	534225.	627861.	743233.	848955.	977898.	55
60	399000.	436005.	481249.	565600.	669532.	764769.	60
65	292000.	341356.	373015.	411723.	483887.	572804.	65
70	195000.	235819.	275679.	301246.	332507.	390787.	70
75	122000.	145806.	176327.	206131.	225249.	248623.	75
80	62439.	78737.	94101.	113799.	133034.	145372.	80
85	39562.	33295.	41985.	50178.	60681.	70938.	85
TM	22115936.	26347680.	31386320.	37409696.	44618720.	53223296.	TM
0	3994000.	4714641.	5592623.	6670892.	7963929.	9487540.	0
5	3271000.	3883057.	4583680.	5437276.	6485593.	7742714.	5
10	2712000.	3244689.	3851822.	4546810.	5393541.	6433426.	10
15	2235000.	2695229.	3224624.	3828001.	4518692.	5360187.	15
20	1838000.	2213860.	2669735.	3194121.	3791792.	4475950.	20
25	1538000.	1813847.	2184769.	2634651.	3152147.	3741966.	25
30	1311000.	1514103.	1785664.	2150823.	2593715.	3103170.	30
35	1110000.	1284141.	1483084.	1749081.	2106759.	2540578.	35
40	938000.	1082858.	1252741.	1446820.	1706312.	2055245.	40
45	777000.	912131.	1052993.	1218191.	1406918.	1659253.	45
50	630000.	749258.	879565.	1015397.	1174697.	1356686.	50
55	514000.	598581.	711892.	835700.	964758.	1116113.	55
60	409000.	473818.	551787.	656240.	770369.	889339.	60
65	304000.	359717.	416724.	485298.	577165.	677542.	65
70	209000.	253251.	299666.	347157.	404283.	480814.	70
75	130000.	160531.	194519.	230170.	266648.	310525.	75
80	66502.	82675.	102091.	123707.	146380.	169578.	80
85	42498.	24881.	30931.	38196.	46283.	54765.	85
TF	22028960.	26061184.	30868816.	36608416.	43469872.	51655232.	TF
T	44144896.	52408864.	62255136.	74018112.	88088592.	104878528.	T

```
         STABLE EQUIVALENT TO ORIGINAL POPULATION

                 MALES           FEMALES

         0      4209486.         3968526.
         5      3439206.         3242339.
        10      2864919.         2702802.
        15      2389361.         2257271.
        20      1983502.         1878967.
        25      1638270.         1558250.
        30      1347738.         1289138.
        35      1100167.         1061142.
        40       891163.          869934.
        45       717456.          710891.
        50       571447.          576073.
        55       446164.          459962.
        60       337758.          356316.
        65       242831.          263352.
        70       164802.          184364.
        75       103554.          119001.
        80        56163.           63598.
        85        25167.           19996.

      TM  21581872.   TF  22529088.

   TOTAL        44110976.



   INTRINSIC RATES

      BIRTH RATE       0.04329
      DEATH RATE       0.00850
   NATURAL INCREASE    0.03479


      BASED ON POPULATION PROJECTED TO  475 YEARS
```

CHAPTER 8

The Leslie Model

For understanding the effect of a regime of age-specific rates of birth and death the projection discussed and programmed in the preceding pages suffers from the handicap of confounding the rates with the initial age distribution. We want a description of the process that separates out the birth and death rates from the age distribution of the population on which these are assumed to operate. Leslie (1945, 1948) showed that the projection can be arranged as the multiplication of a vector containing the number of individuals at the various ages by a matrix operator that embodies the effects of birth and death. This matrix operator constitutes an especially instructive arrangement of birth and death rates. It enables us not only to find the action of birth and death in the long run, as in the program PROJECT, but also to trace their short-term effects and to analyze these effects into understandable components.

The matrix expression has the incidental advantage of enabling us to write formulas more compactly. Moreover, the matrix turns out to be a simple one, containing mostly zeros. (The advantage for analysis of a largely empty matrix is a disadvantage for computing; it requires more storage and time for manipulation than the arithmetic executed as in the program PROJECT.)

Given a set of age-specific birth and death rates contained in a vertical vector $\{P_0\}$, we want to assemble a matrix operator M capable by premultiplication of moving the population five years on a growth trajectory identical with that of the population projection. We then find $\{P_1\}$, the population five years later, as $\{P_1\} = M\{P_0\}$. We will exemplify here the part of the process referring to females less than 50 years old, supposing this range to include all the ages of childbearing.

The 10×10 matrix that results contains positive elements only in its first row and subdiagonals. It has the appearance

$$
\begin{bmatrix}
0 & \frac{1}{2}\left(\frac{_5L_{10}}{_5L_5}F_{10}\right){_5L_0} & \frac{1}{2}\left(F_{10}+\frac{_5L_{15}}{_5L_{10}}F_{15}\right){_5L_0} & \cdots & . & \frac{1}{2}\left(F_{45}\right){_5L_0} \\[2ex]
\frac{_5L_5}{_5L_0} & 0 & 0 & \cdots & 0 & 0 \\[2ex]
0 & \frac{_5L_{10}}{_5L_5} & 0 & \cdots & 0 & 0 \\[2ex]
0 & 0 & \frac{_5L_{15}}{_5L_{10}} & \cdots & 0 & 0 \\[2ex]
\vdots & \vdots & \vdots & \vdots & \vdots & \vdots \\[2ex]
0 & 0 & 0 & \cdots & \frac{_5L_{45}}{_5L_{40}} & 0
\end{bmatrix}
\tag{14}
$$

where $_5L_{5j}$ is the stationary population aged $5j$ to $(5j+4)$ years, and F_{5j} is the age-specific birth rate for girl children in the same age interval. Simple algebra shows that to produce the same result as the projection the value $m_{1,j}$ in the jth position of the first line must be

$$
m_{1,j} = \frac{_5L_0}{2}\left(F_{5(j-1)} + \frac{_5L_{5j}}{_5L_{5(j-1)}}F_{5j}\right),\ j = 2, 3, 4, \ldots, 9.
$$

This will generate the number of girls less than five-years old in $\{P_1\} = M\{P_0\}$. The value of $m_{i,i-1}$ in the ith row must be

$$
m_{i,i-1} = \frac{_5L_{5(i-1)}}{_5L_{5(i-2)}},\ i = 2, 3, \ldots, 10.
$$

Our program assembles the matrix, prints it out, and makes the first steps in its analysis. The input is produced by the program LIFE, or can be provided independently, and will include births by age of mother or of father. The input consists of the title card; two cards for PP, the population; two cards for BB, the births by age of mother or father; and two cards for VLL, the column of the life table giving L_x, the stationary age distribution.

For the basic analysis our matrix need only apply to ages up to the end of reproduction. (We see from (17), the equation for r, in the next section that death rates for ages beyond reproduction do not have any effect on the long-term rate of increase r.) Hence the size of matrix that we want to assemble here will be 9×9 if the highest fertile age is 40–44, 10×10 if the highest fertile age is 45–49, etc. We know that age 25–29 is always fertile in human populations, and hence that the matrix must be at least 6×6. The program adds one row and one column for each nonzero age group from 30 onward, supposing that the curve of fertility for any large population does not descend to zero until reproduction is finally terminated.

The matrix as printed out may be studied directly as providing a representation of fertility in its top row and survival in its subdiagonal. It serves to distinguish populations of various patterns of mortality and fertility.

Extension to all ages is a matter of continuing the subdiagonal beyond the end of reproductive life, so that the matrix would be a square with 18×18 elements if we recognize five-year age intervals up to 85–89, say for females. Males would be shown in another 18×18 matrix; combining the sexes would require a 36×36 matrix. Such a 36×36 matrix, arranged for female dominance, would produce results arithmetically identical to those of the program PROJECT.

A further direction in which the matrix model may be extended is birth order (Keyfitz, 1968). Rogers (1968) has shown the usefulness of the matrix approach in the study of migration. Tabah (1968) has applied it in the analysis of the labor force, and school attendance may be similarly studied.

The small Leslie matrix here programmed provides an alternative means to the projection for calculating the stable age distribution, at least to the end of the reproductive ages, along with the intrinsic rate of natural increase. The method is taking the matrix to a high power. Squaring is accomplished by a very brief program (essentially one statement within three successive loops), and seven successive squarings provide the 128th power. We have here multiple objectives; if the sole object is to find the intrinsic rate r, the program ROOT given in Chapter 9 is more efficient.

We can obtain the dominant root λ as the ratio of any one element in a high power of the matrix to the same element in the preceding power. From the 128th power of the matrix, for example, λ is the upper-left element multiplied by $_5L_5/_5L_0$ and divided by the first element of the second row.

The result may be compared with that of PROJECT, and the λ's from the two sources will be found to be identical. This is a check on the two programs, which were independently written. The distribution given by any column of the high power of the matrix is identical with that of the projection at stability, though we constructed the matrix only to the end of reproductive age and this is where the stable age distribution made from the matrix necessarily ends. An extension of the matrix to 36×36, not shown here, verified the entire stable distribution for 18 ages and two sexes given by PROJECT. In a general stable age distribution the absolute values of the elements have no meaning, but only their ratios to one another. However, a particular way of normalizing the stable ages that determines absolute values has been developed for projection, and it may be translated into matrix terms.

We can think of the matrix operator $\mathbf{M}$ carrying the population forward 375 years, or 75 periods of 5 years, by premultiplication by $\mathbf{M}^{75}$. Once this stable condition has been reached and λ obtained from it, we can go back in time by dividing by λ^{75}. This meets the condition that $\mathbf{M}^{75}\mathbf{P}_0 = \lambda^{75}\mathbf{Q}$. Hence the stable equivalent is

$$\mathbf{Q} = \frac{\mathbf{M}^{75}\mathbf{P}_0}{\lambda^{75}}, \tag{15}$$

an alternative form to the calculation described in Chapter 7.

The reader can convince himself that this stable equivalent is such that we could work forward from it either on the matrix or on λ. We could attain the same $\mathbf{M}^{75}\mathbf{P}_0 = \mathbf{P}_{75}$ by premultiplying $\mathbf{Q}$ by $\mathbf{M}^{75}$ or by multiplying $\mathbf{Q}$ by λ^{75}. That either the $\mathbf{Q}$ or the original $\mathbf{P}_0$ would project to the same ultimate population is the sense in which the former is equivalent to the latter. The preceding program PROJECT shows the stable equivalent by age and sex, that is, it in effect evaluates (15) with a 36×36 matrix $\mathbf{M}$.

The rows of the high power of the matrix also have demographic meaning. This is the reproductive value of a woman, which is discussed in the next chapter in terms of the Lotka model.

Program MATRIX

```
C
C                        MATRIX
C
C
C        ASSEMBLES A PROJECTICN MATRIX FOR ONE SEX, FOR AGES UP
C        TO THE END OF REPRODUCTION, AND CALCULATES THE INTRINSIC RATE
C        AND REPRODUCTIVE VALUES.
C
        DIMENSICN PP(20),BB(2C),VLL(20),FF(20),VALUE(15),AM(15,15),         1
       A BM(15,15),STABLE(15),IAGE(19),VALYOU(15),VALEWE(15),NAME(19)       2
C
C        INPUT CONSISTS OF 7 CARDS AS FOLLOWS
C           TITLE CARD (1 CARD IN FORMAT (19A4))
C           POPULATICN BY AGE (2 CARDS IN FORMAT (10F8.0))
C           BIRTHS BY AGE OF PARENT (2 CARDS IN FORMAT (10F8.0))
C           THE LIFE TABLE STATICNARY AGE DISTRIBUTION
C              (2 CARDS IN FORMAT (10F8.0))
C        AGE GROUPS ARE 0,1-4,5-5,10-14,... 85+, UNKNOWN (20 CATEGORIES).
C        BB(I) = BIRTHS TC MOTHERS (OR FATHERS IN THE MALE MODEL)
C        IN THE ITH AGE GROUP, I=1,17, SO THAT BIRTHS BB(5) TO WOMEN
C        15-19 ARE IN COLUMNS 33-40, ETC.
C           BB(18)=TCTAL MALE BIRTHS
C           BB(19)=TCTAL FEMALE BIRTHS
C           BB(2C)=TBB=TCTAL BIRTHS
C
C        SETS CF THE ABOVE INPUT MAY BE REPEATED INDEFINITELY.  THE
C        PROGRAM TERMINATES EXECUTION WHEN A BLANK TITLE CARD IS READ.
C
C        PP(I) IS POPULATION IN ITH AGE GROUP
C        VLL(I) IS STATICNARY POPULATION IN ITH AGE GROUP
C        AM IS LESLIE PROJECTICN MATRIX
C
C        COLUMNS 1-76 CF THE TITLE CARD ARE STORED IN 'NAME'.
C        COLUMNS 77-80 OF THE TITLE CARD MUST ALWAYS BE BLANK.
C
        READ 1,NAME,IBK                                                     3
      1 FORMAT (2CA4)                                                       4
      3 PRINT 5,NAME                                                        5
      5 FORMAT (1H1 19A4)                                                   6
C
C        MF=INCICATOR CF MALE CR FEMALE DOMINANCE
C           MF=1   MALE DCMINANT
C           MF=2 FEMALE DCMINANT.
        MF=2                                                                7
        IF (NAME(19) .NE. IBK) MF=1                                         8
C        READ THE POPULATION, BIRTHS, AND LIFE TABLE ARRAYS.
        READ 7,PF,BB,VLL                                                    9
      7 FORMAT (1CF8.C)                                                    10
C
```

```
C           SET INITIAL AGE FCR EACH AGE GROUP IN IAGE.
        IAGE(2)=C                                                          11
        DO 9 I=3,19                                                        12
      9 IAGE(I)=IAGE(I-1)+5                                                13
        IAGE(1)=0                                                          14
        IAGE(2)=1                                                          15
C
C           PRINT THE INPUT DATA.
        PRINT 11                                                           16
     11 FORMAT (1H0/34X 1CHINPUT CATA//14X 3HAGE 7X 5HPP(X) 8X 5HBB(X) 8X  17
      B 5HLL(X) 7X 3HAGE /)                                                18
        PRINT 13,(IAGE(I),PP(I),BB(I),VLL(I),IAGE(I),I=1,19)               19
     13 FORMAT (9X I7,F14.C,2F13.C,I8)                                     20
        PRINT 14,BB(2C)                                                    21
     14 FCRMAT (30X F13.0)                                                 22
C
C           F INCLUCES A FACTOR FCR THE SEX RATIO, A FACTOR FOR THE
C           PROBABILITY OF SURVIVING FROM BIRTH TO AGE 0-4, AND A
C           FACTOR CF .5 FOR TAKINC ARITHMETIC MEAN OF TWO SUCCESSIVE
C           POINTS CF TIME.
        F=.5*(VLL(1)+VLL(2))*BB(MF+17)/(BB(20)*100000.0)                   23
        KK=7                                                               24
        DO 15 I=3,15                                                       25
C           WITHIN THIS LCOP I IS THE AGE INDEX FOR INPUT, I.E.
C               I=1    AGE C
C               I=2    AGE 1-4
C               I=3    AGE 5-9, ETC.
        STABLE(I)=0.                                                       26
        VALUE(I)=C.                                                        27
        IF (I.GT.8.AND.BB(I).GT.0.) KK=KK+1                                28
     15 FF(I)=F*BB(I)/PP(I)                                                29
C
C           KK=THE NUMBER CF COLLMNS OF THE SQUARE LESLIE MATRIX WITH
C           A NON-ZERC ELEMENT IN THE UPPER RIGHT POSITION.
C
C           IN THE MATRIX, THE AGE INDEXING IS DIFFERENT...
C               I=1    AGE C-4
C               I=2    AGE 5-9, ETC.
C
C           NOW ASSEMBLE THE MATRIX, STARTING WITH SUB-DIAGONAL ELEMENTS.
        DO 18 I=1,KK                                                       30
        DO 18 J=1,KK                                                       31
     18 AM(I,J)=.C                                                         32
        SLRV=VLL(3)/(VLL(1)+VLL(2))                                        33
        IAGE(1)=0                                                          34
        AM(2,1)=SURV                                                       35
        DO 20 J=2,KK                                                       36
        AM(J+1,J)=VLL(J+2)/VLL(J+1)                                        37
        AM(1,J)=FF(J+1)+FF(J+2)*AM(J+1,J)                                  38
     20 IAGE(J)=5*(J-1)                                                    39
C
        PRINT 25, (IAGE(J),J=1,KK)                                         40
     25 FORMAT (1HO/1HC 30X 13HLESLIE MATRIX /1HO I4,11I7)                 41
        PRINT 26                                                           42
     26 FCRMAT (1X)                                                        43
        DO 28 I=1,KK                                                       44
     28 PRINT 3C, (AM(I,J),J=1,KK)                                         45
     30 FORMAT (1X 12F7.5)                                                 46
C
```

```
C          CCMPUTE THE 64-TH POWER CF THE PRCJECTION MATRIX, IN ORDER TO
C          FIND ITS REAL LATENT RCCT AND VECTORS.                            47
           DO 40 L=1,6                                                       48
           DO 35 I=1,KK                                                      49
           DO 35 J=1,KK                                                      50
           BM(I,J)=C.                                                        51
           DO 35 K=1,KK                                                      52
     35 BM(I,J)=BM(I,J)+AM(I,K)*AM(K,J)                                      53
           DO 40 I=1,KK                                                      54
           DO 40 J=1,KK                                                      55
     40 AM(I,J)=BM(I,J)                                                      56
           ALAM=SURV*AM(1,1)/AM(2,1)
C          THE NUMERATOR OF ALAM IS SURV*AM(1,1), THE FIRST ELEMENT OF THE
C          SECOND ROW OF THE MATRIX OF ONE-HIGHER POWER THAN AM.
C
C          CALCULATE STABLE AGE CISTRIBUTION ON RADIX L(0) = 1.
           SUMA=0.                                                          57
           DC 45 J=1,KK                                                     58
     45 SUMA=SUMA+AM(1,J)                                                   59
           FACTOR=(VLL(1)*ALAM**(-.1)+VLL(2)*ALAM**(-.6))/100000.0          60
           SUMB=0.                                                          61
           PP(2)=PP(2)+PP(1)                                                62
           DO 50 J=1,KK                                                     63
C
C          CALCULATE REPRODUCTIVE VALUES.
           STABLE(J)=(FACTCR*AM(J,1))/AM(1,1)                               64
           VALUE(J)=AM(1,J)/SUMA                                            65
           VALYOU(J)=VALUE(J)/(VALUE(1)*FACTOR)*5.                          66
           VALEWE(J)=VALYOU(J)*PP(J+1)                                      67
     50 SUMB=SUMB+VALEWE(J)                                                 68
           R=C.2*ALCG (ALAM)                                                69
C
C          PRINT CUT STABLE AGE CISTRIBUTION AND REPRODUCTIVE VALUES.
           PRINT 55,ALAM,R                                                  70
     55 FORMAT (1HC/1HO 6X 8HLAMBCA = F9.5,6X 16HINTRINSIC RATE = F9.5 )     71
           PRINT 57                                                         72
     57 FORMAT (1H1 22X 27HHIGH PCWER OF LESLIE MATRIX /1HO 17X 6HSTABLE     73
        C 8X 5HFIRST 9X 6FFISHER 9X 12HREPRODUCTIVE /7X 3HAGE 6X            74
        D 1CHPOPULATICN 7X 3HRCW 1CX 6HVALUES 12X 6HVALUES / 15X           75
        E 12HON CNE BIRTH /)                                               76
           DO 58 I=1,KK                                                     77
     58 PRINT 59, IAGE(I),STABLE(I),VALUE(I),VALYOU(I),VALEWE(I)            78
     59 FORMAT (8X,I2,3(7X,F7.5),7X,F11.0)                                  79
           PRINT 6C, SUMB                                                   80
     60 FORMAT (1HC 32X 26HTOTAL REPRODUCTIVE VALUE = F11.0)                81
           READ 1,NAME                                                      82
           DC 65 I=1,1C                                                     83
           IF (NAME(I) .NE. IBK) CC TO 3                                    84
     65 CONTINUE                                                            85
           PRINT 67                                                         86
     67 FORMAT (11H1END CF JCB )                                            87
           STCP                                                             88
           ENC                                                              89
```

ENGLAND AND WALES 1968
```
 393600  1631200  1882500  1633100  1681800  1838900  1500800  1426100  1443300  1522100
1644900  1488800  1585300  1483800  1280500  1033400   753600   464300   275100        0
      0        0        0      222    81853   295946   240807   125316    58083    15904
   1140        1        0        0        0        0        0   421130   398142   819272
  98581   392994   490330   489641   488871   487929   486812   485280   482970   479116
 472723   462731   447963   425638   391456   339660   265710   175219   119454        0
```

MEXICO 1966
```
 868000  3126000  3271000  2712000  2235000  1838000  1538000  1311000  1110000   938000
 777000   630000   514000   409000   304000   209000   130000    66502    42498        0
      0        0        0     3390   213986   537112   491128   328540   241290   107736
  17383        0        0        0        0        0        0  1004002   936563  1940565
  95064   366577   448818   445208   442455   438270   432511   425791   417068   406870
 395649   381523   362496   334158   293893   244831   188052   119594    44744        0
```

ENGLAND AND WALES 1968

                              INPUT DATA

AGE	PP(X)	BB(X)	LL(X)	AGE
0	393600.	0.	98581.	0
1	1631200.	0.	392994.	1
5	1882500.	0.	490330.	5
10	1633100.	222.	489641.	10
15	1681800.	81853.	488871.	15
20	1838900.	295946.	487929.	20
25	1500800.	240807.	486812.	25
30	1426100.	125316.	485280.	30
35	1443300.	58083.	482970.	35
40	1522100.	15904.	479116.	40
45	1644900.	1140.	472723.	45
50	1488800.	1.	462731.	50
55	1585300.	0.	447963.	55
60	1483800.	0.	425638.	60
65	1280500.	0.	391456.	65
70	1033400.	0.	339660.	70
75	753600.	0.	265710.	75
80	464300.	421130.	175219.	80
85	275100.	398142.	119454.	85
		819272.		

LESLIE MATRIX

	0	5	10	15	20	25	30	35	40	45	50
0.0	0.00016	0.05820	0.24999	0.38345	0.29628	0.15280	0.06045	0.01330	0.00083	0.00000	
0.997470	0.0	0.0	0.0	0.0	0.0	0.0	0.0	0.0	0.0	0.0	
0.0	0.998590	0.0	0.0	0.0	0.0	0.0	0.0	0.0	0.0	0.0	
0.0	0.0	0.998430	0.0	0.0	0.0	0.0	0.0	0.0	0.0	0.0	
0.0	0.0	0.0	0.998070	0.0	0.0	0.0	0.0	0.0	0.0	0.0	
0.0	0.0	0.0	0.0	0.997710	0.0	0.0	0.0	0.0	0.0	0.0	
0.0	0.0	0.0	0.0	0.0	0.996850	0.0	0.0	0.0	0.0	0.0	
0.0	0.0	0.0	0.0	0.0	0.0	0.995240	0.0	0.0	0.0	0.0	
0.0	0.0	0.0	0.0	0.0	0.0	0.0	0.992020	0.0	0.0	0.0	
0.0	0.0	0.0	0.0	0.0	0.0	0.0	0.0	0.986660	0.0	0.0	
0.0	0.0	0.0	0.0	0.0	0.0	0.0	0.0	0.0	0.978860	0.0	

LAMBDA = 1.03539   INTRINSIC RATE = 0.00696

HIGH POWER OF LESLIE MATRIX

AGE	STABLE POPULATION ON ONE BIRTH	FIRST ROW	FISHER VALUES	REPRODUCTIVE VALUES
0	4.83118	0.17197	1.03494	2095553.
5	4.65424	0.17851	1.07429	2022346.
10	4.48886	0.18506	1.11370	1818781.
15	4.32864	0.18189	1.09459	1840880.
20	4.17266	0.14561	0.87628	1611388.
25	4.02083	0.08501	0.51161	767829.
30	3.87117	0.03719	0.22378	319139.
35	3.72106	0.01228	0.07392	106682.
40	3.56523	0.00234	0.01408	21434.
45	3.39748	0.00014	0.00083	1364.
50	3.21202	0.00000	0.00000	1.

TOTAL REPRODUCTIVE VALUE = 10605394.

MEXICO 1966

INPUT DATA

AGE	PP(X)	BB(X)	LL(X)	AGE
0	868000.	0.	95064.	0
1	3126000.	0.	366577.	1
5	3271000.	0.	448818.	5
10	2712000.	3390.	445208.	10
15	2235000.	213986.	442455.	15
20	1838000.	537112.	438270.	20
25	1538000.	491128.	432511.	25
30	1311000.	328540.	425791.	30
35	1110000.	241250.	417068.	35
40	938000.	107736.	406870.	40
45	777000.	17383.	395649.	45
50	630000.	0.	381523.	50
55	514000.	0.	362496.	55
60	409000.	0.	334158.	60
65	304000.	0.	293893.	65
70	209000.	0.	244831.	70
75	130000.	0.	188052.	75
80	66502.	1004002.	119594.	80
85	42498.	936563.	44744.	85
		1940565.		

LESLIE MATRIX

0	5	10	15	20	25	30	35	40	45
0.0	0.00138	0.10739	0.42912	0.67659	0.63056	0.51637	0.36698	0.15219	0.02492
0.97222	0.0	0.0	0.0	0.0	0.0	0.0	0.0	0.0	0.0
0.0	0.99196	0.0	0.0	0.0	0.0	0.0	0.0	0.0	0.0
0.0	0.0	0.99382	0.0	0.0	0.0	0.0	0.0	0.0	0.0
0.0	0.0	0.0	0.99054	0.0	0.0	0.0	0.0	0.0	0.0
0.0	0.0	0.0	0.0	0.98686	0.0	0.0	0.0	0.0	0.0
0.0	0.0	0.0	0.0	0.0	0.98446	0.0	0.0	0.0	0.0
0.0	0.0	0.0	0.0	0.0	0.0	0.97951	0.0	0.0	0.0
0.0	0.0	0.0	0.0	0.0	0.0	0.0	0.97555	0.0	0.0
0.0	0.0	0.0	0.0	0.0	0.0	0.0	0.0	0.97242	0.0

LAMBDA = 1.18997   INTRINSIC RATE = 0.03479

HIGH POWER OF LESLIE MATRIX

AGE	STABLE POPULATION ON ONE BIRTH	FIRST ROW	FISHER VALUES	REPRODUCTIVE VALUES
0	4.23675	0.10588	1.18015	4713519.
5	3.46148	0.12959	1.44447	4724853.
10	2.88547	0.15531	1.73117	4694937.
15	2.40983	0.17452	1.94534	4347835.
20	2.00596	0.16380	1.82575	3355722.
25	1.66357	0.12492	1.39240	2141512.
30	1.37627	0.08318	0.92717	1215513.
35	1.13286	0.04524	0.50424	559707.
40	0.92873	0.01535	0.17113	160517.
45	0.75894	0.00222	0.02472	19205.

TOTAL REPRODUCTIVE VALUE = 25933264.

CHAPTER 9

The Lotka Equation

The greatest single contribution to population theory has been that of A. J. Lotka, contained in a series of papers extending from 1907 to 1948. Lotka emphasized the continuous model in development of the theory, and only at the point of entering data did he modify the integrals into finite sums. This is the approach followed in the discussion that follows.

In the Lotka theory the unknown function is $B(t)$, the number of births at time t. Let us again consider only women, and female births to these women. The data are the observed probability of surviving to age a, called l_a, and the chance $m_a da$ of bearing a child between ages a and $a + da$. Of the births $B(t - a)$ at time $t - a$ the proportion l_a will survive to time t on this deterministic model, and of these $m_a da$ will themselves bear children during the interval of age da. To find the total number of births at time t we need only add the products so obtained for the several ages, and find

$$B(t) = \int_{\alpha}^{\beta} B(t - a)\, l_a m_a dx, \tag{16}$$

where ages α and β are the lower and upper limits of reproduction. In this form of the equation we suppose that the birth and aging process has been going on for a long time. If the process started recently we need an additional term, say $G(t)$, to provide for the births at time t occurring to the women alive at the inception.

If now we suppose that the solution for $B(t)$ is in the form Qe^{rt}, then our first problem is to find r. Substituting $B(t) = Qe^{rt}$ in (16) gives the characteristic equation

$$\int_{\alpha}^{\beta} e^{-ra}\, l_a m_a da = 1. \tag{17}$$

To solve for r, Lotka first divided both sides by R_0, the net reproduction rate, defined as $R_0 = \int_\alpha^\beta l_a m_a da$, and thus could use not $l_a m_a$ but the distribution $l_a m_a / R_0$, which has a total of unity. After dividing he expanded the exponential under the integral up to the term in r_2, then took logarithms, and so obtained

$$\ln \left[\int_\alpha^\beta \left(1 - ra + \frac{r^2 a^2}{2} \right) \frac{l_a m_a}{R_0} \, da \right] = -\ln R_0$$

in place of (17).

If we define $R_1 = \int_\alpha^\beta a l_a m_a da$ and $R_2 = \int_\alpha^\beta a^2 l_a m_a da$, the equation may be expressed entirely in terms of these quantities along with R_0,

$$\ln \left(1 - r \frac{R_1}{R_0} + \frac{r^2}{2} \frac{R_2}{R_0} \right) = -\ln R_0.$$

Expanding the logarithm by the approximate formula $\ln(1 + x) = x - x^2/2$ gives (up to terms in r^2)

$$-r \frac{R_1}{R_0} + \frac{r^2}{2} \left(\frac{R_2}{R_0} - \left(\frac{R_1}{R_0} \right)^2 \right) = -\ln R_0.$$

Now R_1/R_0 is the mean age of childbearing, which we can call μ, in the hypothetical population described by the net maternity function $l_a m_a$, and $R_2/R_0 - (R_1/R_0)^2$ is the variance, say σ^2, in the same distribution of childbearing. Hence (17) may be written as the quadratic equation in r

$$r\mu - \frac{r^2 \sigma^2}{2} = \ln R_0. \tag{18}$$

An easy way to solve (18) is to divide both sides by $\mu - r \, \sigma^2/2$:

$$r^* = \frac{\ln R_0}{\mu - \dfrac{r\sigma^2}{2}} \tag{19}$$

and regard the r of the righthand side as an approximation to the answer, so that r^* is an improved approximation. Such a functional iteration is readily programmed, and converges in three or four cycles.

To obtain numerically the arithmetic mean μ of the net maternity function $l_a m_a$ we resort to multiplying the observed net maternity function $_5L_x \, F_x$ in each age interval by the midpoint of the interval, and then we divide the weighted total so obtained by the number of individuals:

$$\mu = \frac{\displaystyle\sum_{x=10}^{50} \left(x + 2\frac{1}{2} \right) {}_5L_x \, F_x}{\displaystyle\sum_{x=10}^{50} {}_5L_x \, F_x}, \tag{20}$$

where x is the initial value of the five-year age groups under the summation.

To establish the variance σ^2 each of the terms in the numerator of (20) must contain, instead of $x + 2\frac{1}{2}$, the square of the difference between the midpoint of the interval and μ:

$$\sigma^2 = \frac{\sum_{x=10}^{50} \left(x + 2\frac{1}{2} - \mu\right)^2 {}_5L_x F_x}{\sum_{x=10}^{50} {}_5L_x F_x}.$$

Note that we have followed Lotka in arbitrarily cutting off the expansion of the exponential under the integral in (17) at the term in r^2. This may be shown to be equivalent to supposing that the $l_a m_a / R_0$ is distributed normally. For the real root r the error so introduced is trifling, but we will nonetheless develop in ROOT and ZEROS solutions that avoid this approximation.

The Lotka continuous formulation provides a way of looking at the *reproductive value of a woman*, a concept developed by R. A. Fisher (1929). Fisher began by interpreting the characteristic equation (17) and its solution for r. If the birth of a female child is seen as the loaning to her of a life, and the birth of female children to her in turn as repayment of the debt, the method by which r is calculated shows that it is equivalent to answering the question, "At what rate of interest are the payments the just equivalent of the loan?" The value of r is the rate of interest or discount rate at which the present value of the prospective births of her female children is equal to unity at the date of birth of the female.

Suppose we go on to ask about females of any age: what is the present value of their prospective daughters? For a girl or woman now x years old, the discount back from age a is $e^{-r(a-x)}$, where as usual r is an annual rate compounded momently. The probability of living from age x to age a is l_a/l_x. If she lives, the chance of her having a female child when she is between ages a and $a + da$ is $m_a da$. The discounted expected value of the child is the product of these three factors. The woman's reproductive value is the same product added through all ages a:

$$v_x = \int_x^\beta e^{-r(a-x)} \frac{l_x}{l_a} m_a da,$$

where it is indifferent whether the upper limit of the integral is written β, the highest age of reproduction, or ω the end of life, or ∞ as Fisher writes it. The average reproductive value over a five-year age interval will be written ${}_5V_x$.

As so defined the reproductive value is one for a female child just born; it rises gradually to a peak at about age 15, since the girl is coming closer to childbearing, and the discount factor as well as the chance of survival increases; it then gradually declines to zero as her children are born and the number she has in prospect correspondingly diminishes. Reproductive value is shown age by age in Table 8 of the Main Tables (Part IV).

A way of assessing a population from the viewpoint of reproduction, then, is to assign to each woman her reproductive value. The total of the reproductive values is given in column 9 of the Summary Table (Part II). Fisher shows that as the population moves forward in time, provided the age-specific rates of birth and death remain constant, its reproductive value increases according to the intrinsic rate r. The table of $_5V_x$ also serves to answer such a question as, "What would be the effect Δr on r of a *diminution* of mortality at age x?" The answer turns out to be that it would raise the intrinsic rate by an amount equal to the reproductive value $_5V_x$ of a woman at that age, multiplied by the diminution of mortality $\Delta\mu_x$, and divided by κ, the mean age of childbearing in the stable population:

$$\Delta r = \frac{_5V_x\Delta\mu_x}{\kappa}.$$

Program LOTKA

The program LOTKA calculates means and variances of the net maternity function, as well as the gross and net reproduction rates, and the intrinsic rate of natural increase. Input consists of the deck punched out by the program LIFE. After reading the twelve cards, the program determines the age range over which a positive number of births is reported and subsequently confines itself to this range.

The only quantity printed in the output of LOTKA that still requires definition is the *total fertility rate*, the sum of the age-specific fertility rates $_5F_x$ multiplied by 5. This is, of course, related to the gross reproduction rate, obtainable by multiplying the total fertility rate by the fraction of births that are girls. (Elsewhere $_5F_x$ is defined as including girl children only.)

The mean length of generation, referred to in Part I, is defined, in Lotka's terms, as the number of years the population would have to increase at rate r in order to grow in the ratio R_0 of one generation to the preceding; in symbols it is the solution of the equation

$$e^{rT} = R_0, \quad \text{or} \quad T = \frac{\ln R_0}{r}.$$

```
C
C
C                              LOTKA
C
C
C       COMPUTES THE NET MATERNITY FUNCTION AND ITS FIRST AND
C       SECOND MOMENTS, THE TOTAL FERTILITY RATE, GROSS REPRODUCTION
C       RATE, NET REPRODUCTION RATE, MEAN AND VARIANCE OF AGE AT
C       CHILDBEARING, INTRINSIC RATE OF NATURAL INCREASE, AND
C       MEAN LENGTH OF GENERATION.
C
C       THE INPUT IS THE STANDARD DECK PRODUCED BY PROGRAM 'LIFE'.
C       'LOTKA' USES THE INPUT FOR MALES OR FOR FEMALES, NOT BOTH,
C       EVEN THOUGH BOTH ARE INCLUDED IN INPUT.
C
C       FOR MALE-DOMINANT CALCULATION (IN WHICH BIRTH DATA ARE BY AGE
C       OF FATHER) PUNCH THE WORD 'MALE' IN COLUMNS 77-80 OF THE
C       TITLE CARD.  IN THIS CASE ONLY THE MALE OBSERVED POPULATION AND
C       THE MALE STATIONARY POPULATION WILL BE READ IN.  THE FEMALE
C       POPULATION AND DEATH CARDS MAY BE REPLACED BY BLANKS WITHOUT
C       AFFECTING THE COMPUTATION.
C       READ 'MALE' FOR 'FEMALE' IN THE COMMENTS THAT FOLLOW WHENEVER
C       MALE DOMINANCE APPLIES.
C
C       IF OUTPUT OF 'LIFE' IS NOT AVAILABLE, THE INPUT
C       WOULD BE MADE UP AS FOLLOWS--
C         TITLE CARD (1 CARD IN FORMAT 19A4)
C         ONE CARD IN FORMAT (I4, 32X, 2F9.0) THAT CONTAINS
C           THE MID-YEAR FOR POPULATION, TOTAL MALE BIRTHS AND
C           TOTAL FEMALE BIRTHS
C         THE FOLLOWING FIVE DISTRIBUTIONS EACH CONTAINING 20 NUMBERS
C           PUNCHED ON TWO CARDS IN FORMAT (10F8.0) ACCORDING TO
C           AGE GROUPS (0,1-4,5-9,...,85+, UNKNOWN)--
C             OBSERVED MALE POPULATION
C             OBSERVED FEMALE POPULATION
C             BIRTHS BY AGE OF MOTHER (OR FATHER, IF THE MODEL
C               IS MALE-DOMINANT)
C             MALE STATIONARY POPULATION LL(X) FROM THE LIFE TABLE
C               WITH RADIX 100000
C             FEMALE STATIONARY POPULATION LL(X) FROM THE LIFE TABLE
C               WITH RADIX 100000
C
C       ARRAYS
C       PP=POPULATION NUMBERS IN 5-YEAR AGE GROUPS
C       BB=BIRTHS TO MOTHERS IN 5-YEAR AGE GROUPS
C       VLL=LIFE TABLE STATIONARY AGE DISTRIBUTION
C       FF=AGE-SPECIFIC BIRTH RATES
C       'NAME' IS USED TO STORE THE CONTENTS OF THE TITLE CARD
C
```

```
C          SETS OF THE ABCVE INPLT MAY BE REPEATED INDEFINITELY.  THE
C          PROGRAM TERMINATES EXECLTION WHEN A BLANK TITLE CARD IS READ.
C
      DIMENSION NAME(19),PP(2C),BB(20),VLL(20),IAGE(18),POINT(18)              1
     A ,FNM(18)                                                               2
C
C          COLUMNS 1-76 OF THE TITLE CARD ARE STORED IN 'NAME'.
C          FOR FEMALE-DOMINANT CCMPUTATIONS, LEAVE COLUMNS 73-76 BLANK.
C          FOR MALE-DCMINANT COMPUTATIONS, PUNCH 'MALE' IN COLUMNS 73-76
C          CF THE TITLE CARC.
C          COLUMNS 77-80 CF THE TITLE CARD MUST ALWAYS BE BLANK.
C
      READ 2,NAME,IBK                                                         3
    2 FORMAT (2CA4)                                                           4
    4 PRINT 6,NAME                                                            5
    6 FORMAT (1H1 19A4)                                                       6
      IF (NAME(19) .NE. IBK) GC TO 12                                         7
C
C          READ DATA FCR FEMALES.
      PRINT 8                                                                 8
    8 FORMAT (27HCTHESE DATA ARE FOR FEMALES  //)                            9
      READ 10,TBB,TSB,PP,BB,VLL                                              10
   10 FORMAT (27X F9.C,9X F9.C//4(/10F8.0)//2(/10F8.0))                      11
      GO TO 18                                                               12
C
C          READ DATA FOR MALES.
   12 PRINT 14                                                               13
   14 FORMAT (25HCTHESE CATA ARE FOR MALES  //)                             14
      READ 16,TBB,TSB,PP,BB,VLL                                              15
   16 FORMAT (27X 2F9.C,2(/1CF8.C)//4(/10F8.0)//)                           16
C
C          PRINT INPLT DATA.
   18 PRINT 2C                                                               17
   20 FORMAT (9H START CF,5X,3HMID,8X,10HPCPULATION,9X,6HBIRTHS,7X,          18
     B 1CHSTATIONARY,4X,8HSTART CF, /,18H AGE GROUP    POINT,              19
     B 39X,10HPCPLLATICN,4X,9HAGE GROUP/)                                   20
C
C          FIND THE RANGE OF PARENTAL AGES REPORTING BIRTHS
C              IS = THE INDEX OF THE YOUNGEST AGE GROUP WITH BIRTHS
C              IE = THE INDEX OF THE OLDEST AGE GROUP WITH BIRTHS.
      IS=3                                                                   21
   22 IS=IS+1                                                                22
      IF (BB(IS) .LE. C.C) GC TC 22                                         23
      IE=17                                                                  24
   24 IE=IE-1                                                                25
      IF (BB(IE) .LE. C.C) GC TC 24                                         26
C
C          SET THE START AND MID-PCINT OF EACH AGE GROUP.
C          ALSO COMPUTE THE STATIONARY POPULATICN ON RADIX L(0) = 1.0
C          AND PRINT THE TABLE.
      POINT(IS-1)=5.0*FLCAT(IS) - 12.5                                      27
      DC 26 I=IS,IE                                                         28
      PCINT(I)=PCINT(I-1)+5.C                                               29
      IAGE(I)=POINT(I)-2.5                                                  30
      VLL(I)=VLL(I)*.CCCC1                                                  31
   26 PRINT 28,IAGE(I),PCINT(I),PP(I),BB(I),VLL(I),IAGE(I)                 32
   28 FORMAT (I6,F11.1,F17.0,F16.0,F16.5,I10)                              33
C
C          PRINT THE HEACINGS FCR THE OUTPUT.
```

```
         PRINT 30
      30 FORMAT (77H- AGE    AGE SPEC.   SEX-AGE   NET MATERNITY   MOMENTS OF      34
       C NET MAT. FUNCT.   AGE / 7X,33HBIRTH RATE  SPEC. B.R.   FUNCTION          35
       D 7X,5HFIRST 1CX,6HSECOND /)                                               36
C                                                                                 37
C         SET INITIAL VALUES FCR SUMMING THE COLUMNS
C            TFR = TOTAL FERTILITY RATE
C            GRR = GRCSS REPRODUCTICN RATE
C            RO, R1, R2 = MOMENTS CF THE NET MATERNITY FUNCTION
C            SR = SEX RATIC.
         TFR=0.0                                                                  38
         GRR=0.0                                                                  39
         RO=0.0                                                                   40
         R1=0.0                                                                   41
         R2=0.0                                                                   42
         SR=TSB/TBB                                                               43
C
C         SET THE MATERNITY FUNCTICN TO ZERO FCR UPPER AGES.
         DO 32 I=IE,18
      32 FNM(I)=0.0                                                               44
C                                                                                 45
C         COMPUTE AND PRINT EACH RCW OF THE TABLE
C            F = AGE SPECIFIC BIRTH RATE
C            SF = SEX-AGE SPECIFIC BIRTH RATE
C            FNMF = NET MATERNITY FLNCTION
C            FIRSTM, SECM = MOMENTS OF THE NET MATERNITY FUNCTION.
         DO 36 I=IS,IE                                                            46
         F=BB(I)/PP(I)                                                            47
         SF=F*SR                                                                  48
         FNMF=SF*VLL(I)                                                           49
         FIRSTM=FNMF*POINT(I)                                                     50
         SECM=FIRSTM*POINT(I)                                                     51
         PRINT 34,IAGE(I),F,SF,FNMF,FIRSTM,SECM,IAGE(I)                           52
      34 FORMAT (I6,F9.5,F12.5,2F13.5,F17.5,I6)                                   53
C
C         SAVE NET MATERNITY FLNCTION FOR PUNCHING AND TOTAL THE COLUMNS.
         FNM(I)=FNMF                                                              54
         TFR=TFR+F                                                                55
         RO=RO+FNMF                                                               56
         GRR=GRR+SF                                                               57
         R1=R1+FIRSTM                                                             58
      36 R2=R2+SECM                                                               59
C
C         PUNCH THE NET MATERNITY FUNCTION AND PRINT THE TOTALS.
         PUNCH 38,(FNM(I),I=4,14)                                                 60
      38 FORMAT (11F7.5)                                                          61
         PRINT 40,TFR,GRR,RC,R1,R2                                               62
      40 FORMAT (8X 7H------- 5X 7H------- 6X 7H------- 4X 9H--------- 7X          63
       E 1CH--------- / F15.5,F12.5, 2F13.5,F17.5 ///)                            64
         TFR=5.0*TFR                                                              65
         GRR=5.0*GRR                                                              66
         PRINT 42,TFR,GRR,RC                                                      67
      42 FORMAT (9X 20HTCTAL FERTILITY RATE 11X 6HTFR  = F11.3 /                  68
       F       9X 23HGRCSS REPRODUCTION RATE 8X 6HGRR  = F11.3 /                  69
       G       9X 21HNET REPRCDUCTION RATE 1OX 6HNRR  = F11.3)                    70
         FMU=R1/RC                                                                71
         SIG2=R2/RO-FMU**2                                                        72
C         CORRECTICN FOR GROUPING (SUBTRACTION OF 25./12. FROM SIG2)
C         IS NOT APPLIED HERE.
C
```

```
      CONST=ALCG (RO)                                                      73
      R=(FMU-SQRT (FMU**2-2.C*SIG2*CONST) )/SIG2                           74
      T=CONST/R                                                            75
      PRINT 44,FMU,SIG2,R,T                                                76
   44 FORMAT (9X 22HMEAN AGE AT CHILDBIRTH 9X 6HFMU  = F11.3 /             77
     H         9X 37HVARIANCE CF AGE AT CHILDBIRTH  SIG2 = F11.3 /         78
     I         9X 27HINTRINSIC RATE (NORMAL FIT) 4X 6H R   = F11.5 /       79
     J         9X 25HMEAN LENGTH CF GENERATION 6X 6H T   = F11.3 )         80
C
C        CHECK FOR ANOTHER SET CF INPUT DATA.
      READ 2,NAME                                                          81
      DO 46 I=1,1C                                                         82
      IF (NAME(I) .NE. IBK) GC TO 4                                        83
   46 CONTINUE                                                             84
      PRINT 48                                                             85
   48 FORMAT (11H1END CF JOB )                                             86
      STCP                                                                 87
      END                                                                  88
```

```
ENGLAND ANC WALES 1968
1968        48593000    576880     819272     421130     398142    -0.
    414700 1716200 1980500 1716000 1734800 1857200 1538700 1504100 1508800 1540800
   1626400  141160C 1458300 1292800  991000  6311C0  399200  206600  101100       0
    393600 1631200 1882500 1633100 1681800 1838900 1500800 1426100 1443300 1522100
   1644900 1488800 1585300 1483800 1280500 1C334C0  753600  464300  275100       0
         0       C       C     222   81853  295946  240807  125316   58083   15904
      1140       1       C       0       0       0       0  421130  398142  819272
     98157  390908  487464  486493  484940  482653  480541  478315  475271  469932
    460751  444967  418291  376447  315914  238822  155344   81302   38039       0
     98581  392994  49C33C  489641  485871  487929  486812  485280  482970  479116
    472723  462731  447963  425638  391456  335660  265710  175219  119454       0


MEXICO 1966
1966        44145000    424141  1940565  1004002   936563    -0.
    896000 3266000 3445999 2837C00 2290000 1839000 1497000 1238000 1044000  881000
    713000  575000  484000  399000  292000  195000  122000   62439   39562       0
    868000 3126000 3271000 2712000 2235000 1838000 1538000 1311000 1110000  938000
    777000  630000  514000  409000  304000  209000  130000   66502   42498       0
         0       0       C    3390  213986  537112  491128  328540  241290  107736
     17383       C       C       0       0       0       0 1004002  936563 1940565
     94262  362518  444092  440214  436888  431577  424178  415246  403362  388803
    372482  353039  328004  295478  252790  204153  152650   98518   52533       0
     95064  366577  448818  445208  442455  438270  432511  425791  417068  406870
    395649  381523  362496  334158  293893  244831  188052  119594   44744       0
```

ENGLAND AND WALES 1968

THESE DATA ARE FOR FEMALES

START OF AGE GROUP	MID POINT	POPULATION	BIRTHS	STATIONARY POPULATION	START OF AGE GROUP
10	12.5	1633100.	222.	4.89641	10
15	17.5	1681800.	81853.	4.88871	15
20	22.5	1838900.	295946.	4.87929	20
25	27.5	1500800.	240807.	4.86812	25
30	32.5	1426100.	125316.	4.85280	30
35	37.5	1443300.	58083.	4.82970	35
40	42.5	1522100.	15904.	4.79116	40
45	47.5	1644900.	1140.	4.72723	45
50	52.5	1488800.	1.	4.62731	50

AGE	AGE SPEC. BIRTH RATE	SEX-AGE SPEC. B.R.	NET MATERNITY FUNCTION	MOMENTS OF NET MAT. FUNCT. FIRST	SECOND	AGE
10	0.00014	0.00007	0.00032	0.00404	0.05054	10
15	0.04867	0.02365	0.11563	2.02349	35.41115	15
20	0.16094	0.07821	0.38161	8.58624	193.19037	20
25	0.16045	0.07798	0.37959	10.43878	287.06641	25
30	0.08787	0.04270	0.20723	6.73507	218.88971	30
35	0.04024	0.01956	0.09445	3.54204	132.82649	35
40	0.01045	0.00508	0.02433	1.03396	43.94315	40
45	0.00069	0.00034	0.00159	0.07563	3.59227	45
50	0.00000	0.00000	0.00000	0.00008	0.00416	50
	-------	-------	-------	---------	---------	
	0.50945	0.24758	1.20476	32.43930	914.97363	

TOTAL FERTILITY RATE	TFR =	2.547
GROSS REPRODUCTION RATE	GRR =	1.238
NET REPRODUCTION RATE	NRR =	1.205
MEAN AGE AT CHILDBIRTH	FMU =	26.926
VARIANCE OF AGE AT CHILDBIRTH	SIG2 =	34.460
INTRINSIC RATE (NORMAL FIT)	R =	0.00695
MEAN LENGTH OF GENERATION	T =	26.804

MEXICO 1966

THESE DATA ARE FOR FEMALES

START OF AGE GROUP	MID POINT	POPULATION	BIRTHS	STATIONARY POPULATION	START OF AGE GROUP
10	12.5	2712000.	3390.	4.45208	10
15	17.5	2235000.	213986.	4.42455	15
20	22.5	1838000.	537112.	4.38270	20
25	27.5	1538000.	491128.	4.32511	25
30	32.5	1311000.	328540.	4.25791	30
35	37.5	1110000.	241290.	4.17068	35
40	42.5	938000.	107736.	4.06870	40
45	47.5	777000.	17383.	3.95649	45

AGE	AGE SPEC. BIRTH RATE	SEX-AGE SPEC. B.R.	NET MATERNITY FUNCTION	MOMENTS OF FIRST	NET MAT. FUNCT. SECOND	AGE
10	0.00125	0.00060	0.00269	0.03357	0.41966	10
15	0.09574	0.04621	0.20445	3.57786	62.61252	15
20	0.29223	0.14104	0.61812	13.90760	312.92090	20
25	0.31933	0.15412	0.66657	18.33060	504.09131	25
30	0.25060	0.12095	0.51498	16.73685	543.94751	30
35	0.21738	0.10491	0.43755	16.40826	615.30981	35
40	0.11486	0.05543	0.22554	9.58542	407.38037	40
45	0.02237	0.01080	0.04272	2.02916	96.38498	45
	-------	-------	-------	---------	----------	
	1.31376	0.63405	2.71261	80.60930	2543.06665	

TOTAL FERTILITY RATE	TFR	=	6.569
GROSS REPRODUCTION RATE	GRR	=	3.170
NET REPRODUCTION RATE	NRR	=	2.713
MEAN AGE AT CHILDBIRTH	FMU	=	29.717
VARIANCE OF AGE AT CHILDBIRTH	SIG2	=	54.427
INTRINSIC RATE (NORMAL FIT)	R	=	0.03468
MEAN LENGTH OF GENERATION	T	=	28.773

Program ROOT

The theory of the previous section is in terms of the continuous variables preferred by Lotka. We always have to come down to discrete elements in order to apply numbers, and Lotka did this in several ways, of which the one already exhibited in this chapter is in effect the fitting of a normal curve to the net maternity function. The discrete calculations then enter through the moments R_0, μ, and σ^2 of the net maternity function.

However we can calculate r both more easily and more precisely by a direct method. We reformulate the renewal process in order to obtain the characteristic equation in suitable form for this.

```
C
C                          ROOT
C
C
C     CALCULATES THE INTRINSIC RATE OF NATURAL INCREASE  R
C     BY THREE APPROXIMATIONS.
C
      DIMENSION A(11),NAME(19),RR(2,3)                                    1
C
C     INPUT IS OBTAINED FROM PROGRAM LOTKA OR MAY BE CALCULATED
C       DIRECTLY
C
C     INPUT CONSISTS OF
C       TITLE CARD IN FORMAT (19A4)
C       A(I), THE NET MATERNITY FUNCTION FOR FIVE-YEAR AGE GROUPS
C       10-14, 15-19,...,55-59, 60-64. (1 CARD IN FORMAT (11F7.5))
C
C     SETS OF THE ABOVE INPUT MAY BE REPEATED INDEFINITELY.   THE
C     PROGRAM TERMINATES EXECUTION WHEN A BLANK TITLE CARD IS READ.
C
C     COLUMNS 1-76 OF THE TITLE CARD ARE STORED IN 'NAME'.
C     COLUMNS 77-80 OF TITLE CARD MUST ALWAYS BE BLANK.
C
      READ 1,NAME,IBK                                                     2
    1 FORMAT (20A4)                                                       3
    3 PRINT 5,NAME                                                        4
    5 FORMAT (1H1 19A4)                                                   5
C
C     READ THE INPUT NET MATERNITY FUNCTION.
      READ 7,A                                                            6
    7 FORMAT (11F7.5)                                                     7
      PRINT 12, (I, I=10,60,5), A                                         8
   12 FORMAT (// 1X,35HINPUT DATA...NET MATERNITY FUNCTION//2X,4HAGE ,     9
     A 11(I2,5X)//3X,11F7.4//)                                           10
      DO 40 J=1,3                                                        11
C
C       J = 1 INTEGRAL EQUATION METHOD
C       J = 2 LAPLACE TRANSFORM METHOD
C       J = 3 MATRIX METHOD
C
      R=.02                                                              12
C
C       K INDEXES THE ITERATIONS.
      DO 30 K=1,50                                                       13
      SUM=0.                                                             14
      IF (J.EQ.3) SUM=.5*A(1)*(EXP(R)**20)*EXP(-2.5*R)                   15
C
C       I INDEXES THE AGE GROUPS.
      DO 25 I=1,10                                                       16
```

```
       GO TO (21,22,23),J                                                    17
C         AS J GOES THROUGH VALUES 1 TO 3 THE CALCULATION IS
C         EXECUTED BY THE THREE METHODS SPECIFIED.
C
   21 SUM=SUM+A(I)/(EXP(R)**(5*I-20))                                        18
       GO TO 25                                                              19
   22 SUM=SUM+A(I)*(EXP(R)**(-5*I-5)-EXP(R)**(-5*I-10))                      20
      B  /((5.*R)*EXP(R)**(-27.5))                                           21
       GO TO 25                                                             22
   23 SUM=SUM+.5*(A(I+1)+A(I))*(EXP(R)**(20-5*I))*EXP(-2.5*R)                23
   25 CONTINUE                                                              24
C
C         RSTAR=AN IMPROVED ESTIMATE OF R.
       RSTAR=ALOG(SUM)/27.5                                                 25
       IF (ABS(RSTAR-R).LT. .000002) GO TO 35                              26
       R=RSTAR                                                             27
   30 CONTINUE                                                             28
C         IF THE ITERATION DOES NOT CHANGE R BY .000002, THE LOOP
C         TERMINATES AND R AND K ARE STORED.
   35 RR(1,J)=R                                                            29
       RR(2,J)=K                                                           30
   40 CONTINUE                                                             31
C         END OF LOOP FOR THREE METHODS.
C
C         PRINT RESULTS.
       PRINT 45, RR                                                        32
   45 FORMAT ( 1X,6HOUTPUT// 5X,24HINTEGRAL EQUATION METHOD, 5X,4HR = ,    33
      C F9.5, 5X,3HIN F3.0,11H ITERATIONS// 5X,24HLAPLACE TRANSFORM METH   34
      DOD, 5X,4HR = ,F9.5, 5X,3HIN F3.0,11H ITERATIONS//16X,              35
      E  13HMATRIX METHOD, 5X,4HR = ,F9.5, 5X,3HIN F3.0,11H ITERATIONS)   36
C
C         CHECK FOR ANOTHER SET OF INPUT DATA.
       READ 1,NAME                                                         37
       DO 50 I=1,10                                                        38
       IF (NAME(I) .NE. IBK) GO TO 3                                       39
   50 CONTINUE                                                             40
       PRINT 55                                                            41
   55 FORMAT (11H1END OF JOB )                                             42
       STOP                                                                43
       END                                                                 44
```

```
ENGLAND AND WALES 1968
 .00032 .11563 .38161 .37959 .20723 .09445 .02433 .00159 .000000.    0.

MEXICO 1966
 .00269 .20445 .61812 .66657 .51498 .43755 .22554 .042720.    0.    0.
```

ENGLAND AND WALES 1968

INPUT DATA...NET MATERNITY FUNCTION

AGE 10	15	20	25	30	35	40	45	50	55	60
0.0003	0.1156	0.3816	0.3796	0.2072	0.0944	0.0243	0.0016	0.0	0.0	0.0

OUTPUT

    INTEGRAL EQUATION METHOD   R =   0.00695   IN 4. ITERATIONS

    LAPLACE TRANSFORM METHOD   R =   0.00695   IN 8. ITERATIONS

          MATRIX METHOD   R =   0.00695   IN 4. ITERATIONS

MEXICO 1966

INPUT DATA...NET MATERNITY FUNCTION

AGE 10	15	20	25	30	35	40	45	50	55	60
0.0027	0.2044	0.6181	0.6666	0.5150	0.4375	0.2255	0.0427	0.0	0.0	0.0

OUTPUT

    INTEGRAL EQUATION METHOD   R =   0.03465   IN 4. ITERATIONS

    LAPLACE TRANSFORM METHOD   R =   0.03470   IN 4. ITERATIONS

          MATRIX METHOD   R =   0.03479   IN 4. ITERATIONS

Birth Cohorts Spread Out Over Five Years of Time

If the births over a five-year time interval are $5l_0$, then ten years after the end of the interval, if the population is closed to migration, the individuals will be between 10 and 14 years old, and will number $_5L_{10}$. The birth rate of females 10–14 years old is called F_{10} (which is zero for some populations, and a very small quantity like 0.0002 or 0.0003 for others), and the number of births that will take place in the cohort is $_5L_{10}F_{10}$. Similar notation applies to later ages.

With this way of envisaging the cohort of mothers in a given period around time t, we can say that current births B_t will be the annual births 10–15 years earlier times $(_5L_{10}/l_0)F_{10}$, plus the number of births 15–20 years earlier times $(_5L_{15}/l_0)F_{15}$, ... If we locate the births of each period at the midpoint of its five-year time span, the renewal equation corresponding to (16) is

$$B_t = \frac{_5L_{10}}{l_0} F_{10}B_{t-12.5} + \frac{_5L_{15}}{l_0}F_{15}B_{t-17.5} + \dots . \tag{21}$$

We begin the numerical solution of (21) with the trial value $B_t = Qe^{rt}$, where Q is a constant. Cancellation gives the characteristic equation

$$1 = \frac{_5L_{10}}{l_0} F_{10}e^{-12.5r} + \frac{_5L_{15}}{l_0}F_{15}e^{-17.5r} + \dots + \frac{_5L_{45}}{l_0}F_{45}e^{-47.5r},$$

or

$$1 = \Phi_{10}e^{-12.5r} + \Phi_{15}e^{-17.5r} + \dots + \Phi_{45}e^{-47.5r}, \tag{22}$$

if $\Phi_{10} = {}_5L_{10} F_{10}/l_0$, etc. This may also be obtained as the discrete equivalent of (17).

Equation (22) can have only one real root in r. That root is the demographic measure we have frequently used in the preceding pages, designated by Lotka the intrinsic rate of natural increase. It summarizes the age-specific rates of birth and death by saying how fast the population will ultimately be increasing if these age-specific rates are allowed to continue indefinitely. We will write $e^{2.5r}$ as x.

The computation of the positive root r, if the other roots are not required, is readily carried out by an iterative formula obtained by multiplying both sides of (22) by $x^{11} = e^{27.5r}$:

$$x^{11} = \Phi_{10}x^6 + \Phi_{15}x^4 + \dots + \Phi_{45}x^{-8},$$

and taking the 11th root provides

$$x^* = \sqrt[11]{\Phi_{10}x^6 + \Phi_{15}x^4 + \dots + \Phi_{45}x^{-8}}, \tag{23}$$

where the asterisk is to remind us that the x is an improved value.

Using a loop DO 5 I = 1, 5, as in the program that follows, assumes that convergence will occur within 5 cycles. How can we be sure of this from the nature of the iterative process? Propositions concerning the rapidity of convergence appear in textbooks of numerical analysis (Scarborough, 1958). One basic theorem will serve most purposes of demography, and we will develop it here.

If the iterative process is designated for two successive iterates x and x^* as

$$x^* = f(x), \tag{24}$$

then let $x = \bar{x}$ be the value in the limit such that

$$\bar{x} = f(\bar{x}). \tag{25}$$

Subtracting (25) from (24), we have

$$x^* - \bar{x} = f(x) - f(\bar{x}). \tag{26}$$

But the mean value theorem tells us that

$$f(x) - f(\bar{x}) = (x - \bar{x})f'(\xi), \tag{27}$$

where $f'(\xi)$ is the derivative for some value of the argument between x and $\bar{x}$. Combining (26) and (27) gives

$$x^* - \bar{x} = (x - \bar{x})f'(\xi). \tag{28}$$

This is all we need. For (28) shows the departure of the improved x^* from the true value, in terms of the departure of the preceding iterate x from the true value. Thus $f'(\xi)$ measures the ratio of error in successive iterates—we clearly want it to be less than one. If it is much less than one, convergence will be rapid. The real root in r or x is unique, and (23) cannot iterate to anything other than this real root.

Applying this to our iterative process (23) requires calculating the derivative of x^* with respect to x at the point ξ. We can easily convince ourselves that the derivative is only about 0.1, and hence that the error of each successive iterate is about 0.1 of the error of the preceding iterate, so that we gain about one decimal place per cycle of (23). Five significant digits is more than enough for all purposes.

The above is only one of the ways of obtaining an equation satisfied by the intrinsic rate. Our program provides three different forms, of which the solution to (22) may be called r_B.

A second way in which an equation for r can be derived is through the Laplace transform, which translates exactly the histogram form of $p(a)m(a)$ in which births are usually expressed (Keyfitz, 1968). Call this value r_C.

The third way of securing an equation is through the projection matrix. If we carry on the projection for several generations, then we see that in any age group the number of individuals increases in one projected five-year cycle in the ratio λ, after a certain point a constant no longer changing with time and the same for all ages. (See the discussion of program **PROJECT** in Chapter 7.) The intrinsic rate of increase r, compounded continuously, gives rise to the alternative expression e^{5r}, which may be equated to λ. Then we have $r = 0.2 \ln \lambda$. Call this value r_A. In our program forms of the characteristic equation corresponding to r_A, r_B, and r_C are established and then solved, all using the same iterative sequence.

For an increasing population the reader will find that $r_A > r_C > r_B$, and that the difference $r_A - r_C$ is always twice the difference $r_C - r_B$. If a choice must be made, r_A appears somewhat too high; r_B is better known and more commonly used than r_C. But, as examination of the output of program ROOT shows, the differences among the three values are small.

Real and Complex Roots of a Regime of Fertility and Mortality

The analysis of a set of birth and death rates may be in the form of the integral equation of the preceding section, or alternatively in terms of the projection matrix developed earlier. Either way we look for a solution such as

$$B(t) = Q_1\lambda_1{}^t + Q_2\lambda_2{}^t + \ldots,$$

or what is the same,

$$B(t) = Q_1e^{r_1 t} + Q_2e^{r_2 t} + \ldots,$$

where $B(t)$ may be the births, the number at any given age, or the total population, all in the one-sex model. The values of λ or r depend only on the age-specific rates of birth and death, while the coefficients Q depend on the initial conditions, and for a given initial population will be different according to whether births, numbers at a particular age, or total population is the subject of the analysis. The λ's and r's are alternative forms of essentially the same constants, each r being one-fifth the logarithm of the corresponding λ; the unit of time for the λ's is five years, for the r's one year. This discussion and the program to which it leads are concerned with the λ's and r's; we will not bother with the Q's except to mention that Q_1, the stable equivalent of the births, resembles the stable equivalent for the several ages in the output of the program PROJECT.

We saw that the matrix operator **M** projects the population, and that after a certain number of time periods the age distribution evolves to a stable form, and does not change further. The stable form may be designated by the vector **K**, and the fact that the projection no longer changes the age distribution may be expressed as

$$\mathbf{MK} = \lambda\mathbf{K} \text{ or } \mathbf{MK} - \lambda\mathbf{K} = 0.$$

In this equation the elements k_j of the stable vector **K** and the scalar number λ are the unknowns, and the matrix **M**, of elements m_{ij}, is assumed to be known.

The form $\mathbf{MK} - \lambda\mathbf{K} = 0$ is a set of linear equations in the elements of **K**, and only for certain values of λ does it have nonzero solutions in the elements of **K**. The point may be readily illustrated for two age-groups. The $\mathbf{MK} - \lambda\mathbf{K} = 0$ becomes

$$(m_{11} - \lambda)k_1 + m_{12}k_2 = 0$$
$$m_{21}k_1 + (m_{22} - \lambda)k_2 = 0.$$

Solving the first of these for the ratio k_1/k_2 gives

$$\frac{k_1}{k_2} = -\frac{m_{12}}{m_{11} - \lambda},$$

and solving the second for the same ratio gives

$$\frac{k_1}{k_2} = -\frac{m_{22} - \lambda}{m_{21}}.$$

Unless the two solutions are equal, the equations $\mathbf{MK} - \lambda\mathbf{K} = 0$ are not consistent with one another, so the condition for consistency is

$$\frac{m_{12}}{m_{11} - \lambda} = \frac{m_{22} - \lambda}{m_{21}}$$

or

$$\lambda^2 - (m_{11} + m_{22})\lambda + m_{11}m_{22} - m_{12}m_{21} = 0.$$

This is an example of a characteristic equation in λ, of the second degree because only two age-groups were admitted.

Elsewhere (Leslie, 1945; Keyfitz, 1968) it is shown that the condition in λ that the general equation $\mathbf{MK} - \lambda\mathbf{K} = 0$ be consistent with itself, and therefore have nonzero solutions, is the vanishing of the determinant $|\mathbf{M} - \lambda\mathbf{I}|$, or more explicitly

$$\phi(\lambda) = \lambda^{11} - \frac{1}{2}\,_5L_{10}\,F_{10}\,\lambda^9 - \frac{1}{2}(_5L_{10}\,F_{10} + _5L_{15}\,F_{15})\lambda^8 - \ldots = 0,$$

if positive fertility starts in the 10–14 age group.

The program ZEROS that finds the roots λ is described in terms of the matrix analysis, but it may be adapted to the Lotka integral equation discussed in ROOT. We will suppose, as seems to be true in all demographic applications, that the roots are distinct.

Program ZEROS

The program ZEROS finds not one but all the roots, real and complex. Input is the net maternity function punched out by LOTKA, or readily obtained as $_5L_xF_x$.

The program is based on Newton-Raphson iteration, which derives from the Taylor expansion to the linear term, a simplified form of the mean-value theorem:

$$\phi(\lambda^*) \cong \phi(\lambda) + (\lambda^* - \lambda)\phi'(\lambda),$$

where ϕ is a differentiable function, and λ^* is an improved value of λ. The equation to be solved can now be expressed as $\phi(\lambda^*) = 0$, or

$$\phi(\lambda) + (\lambda^* - \lambda)\phi'(\lambda) = 0,$$

or

$$\lambda^* = \lambda - \frac{\phi(\lambda)}{\phi'(\lambda)}.$$

Each application of this last equation provides an improved λ^* given λ of the preceding application.

Each Newton-Raphson iteration starts with an arbitrary λ. Since we do not want to iterate to a root already found, we must arrange to sweep out each root in turn, and lower the polynomial by one degree.

We do this by forming the new polynomial that results from dividing $\phi(\lambda) = a_n\lambda^{n-1} + a_{n-1}\lambda^{n-2} + \ldots$ by $\lambda - \lambda_1$. The result of the division is λ^{n-2} with coefficient a_n, plus λ^{n-3} with coefficient $a_n\lambda_1 + a_{n-1}$, etc. If we were to divide $\phi(\lambda)/(\lambda - \lambda_1)$ synthetically we would have

$$\begin{array}{r} a_n\lambda^{n-2} + (a_n\lambda_1 + a_{n-1})\lambda^{n-3} + [(a_n\lambda_1 + a_{n-1})\lambda_1 + a_{n-2}]\lambda^{n-4} + \ldots \\ \hline \lambda - \lambda_1 \overline{)a_n\lambda^{n-1} + a_{n-1}\lambda^{n-2} + a_{n-2}\lambda^{n-3} + \ldots} \\ \underline{a_n\lambda^{n-1} - a_n\lambda_1\lambda^{n-2}} \\ (a_n\lambda_1 + a_{n-1})\lambda^{n-2} + a_{n-2}\lambda^{n-3} \\ \underline{(a_n\lambda_1 + a_{n-1})\lambda^{n-2} - (a_n\lambda_1 + a_{n-1})\lambda_1\,\lambda^{n-3}} \\ [(a_n\lambda_1 + a_{n-1})\lambda_1 + a_{n-2}]\lambda^{n-3} \\ \cdots\cdots\cdots\cdots\cdots\cdots \end{array}$$

What makes the procedure simple is that each coefficient (as we work our way down the new polynomial consisting of the quotient $\phi(\lambda)/(\lambda - \lambda_1)$ is the *preceding coefficient* times the root, added to the corresponding coefficient of λ one degree higher in the *preceding polynomial*. In order to sweep out of the first root we need only calculate the new coefficients of $\phi(\lambda)/(\lambda - \lambda_1)$ with the formula $\beta\lambda_1 + \alpha$, where β is the preceding coefficient in the reduced $\phi(\lambda)/(\lambda - \lambda_1)$ and α is the corresponding coefficient in $\phi(\lambda)$, and similarly for later roots.

Each element in the original array of coefficients is successively replaced by the coefficient obtained on division. The new coefficients number one fewer than the old. With these the program can repeat the Newton-Raphson iteration to find another root, and the danger of rediscovering a root already calculated has been eliminated.

The equation always has one real root and the first iteration can ascertain this root by starting with the arbitrary $\lambda = 1$. But the real initial value would never iterate to complex roots, and on later iterates the initial value is set to the complex number $0.3 + 0.7i$. However, as the first member of each new complex pair is found the next starting point is set at the conjugate of this, so that no iteration will be required to find it. Any later (necessarily negative) real roots that may turn up are found with the same complex starting point, $0.3 + 0.7i$. This device saves some computer time.

The procedure just described finds the roots in an irregular order, and since those of higher absolute value are the most easily interpreted in demographic terms, we rearrange to put these more important roots first.

Having arranged the roots in descending order of absolute value, the program prints them out. The interpretation of the roots is aided by their logarithms, and these are also shown, expressed as annual rates. For example, for the United States, 1966, the dominant root of the projection matrix is $\lambda = 1.0498$. One-fifth of its natural logarithm is 0.0097, or just less than one percent, and this is the intrinsic rate of increase of the United States, 1966, female population, that is, the rate at which it would ultimately increase if its age-specific rates of birth and death were indefinitely maintained (calculations on page 355).

The next root is $\lambda_2 = 0.3112 + 0.7442i$, and one-fifth of its logarithm is $r_2 = -0.0430 + 0.2349i$. The corresponding term in the solution of the integral equation is $Q_2 e^{(-0.0430+0.2349i)t} = Q_2 e^{-0.0430t}(\cos 0.2349t + i \sin 0.2349t)$. The value of Q_2 depends on the initial condition, including which age or ages we are concerned with. Whatever Q_2 appears in the numerical application, the total exponential diminishes with increasing t, while the exponential of $0.2349it$ is broken down into two sine waves of fixed amplitude and of wavelength $2\pi/0.2349 = 26.7$ years, about one generation. In the first three terms as a whole, $Q_1 e^{r_1 t} + Q_2 e^{r_2 t} + Q_3 e^{r_3 t}$, the imaginary parts cancel out, leaving an exponential curve on which is superimposed a pair of real sine curves of diminishing amplitude.

```
C
C
C                         ZERCS
C
C
C       FINDS ALL THE ROOTS, REAL AND COMPLEX, OF A POLYNOMIAL
C       EQUATICN, PROVIDED THERE ARE NO MULTIPLE ROOTS.
C       APPLIED IN THIS EXAMPLE TO THE ROOTS OF THE PROJECTION MATRIX.
C       WITH SLIGHT MODIFICATION IT WILL SERVE FOR THE SOLUTION
C       CF THE INTEGRAL EQUATICN.
C
C
C       INPUT IS CBTAINED FRCM FROGRAM LOTKA OR MAY BE CALCULATED
C         DIRECTLY
C
C       INPUT CONSISTS CF
C         TITLE CARD IN FORMAT (19A4)
C         A(I), THE NET MATERNITY FUNCTION FOR FIVE-YEAR AGE GROUPS
C         10-14, 15-19,...,55-59, 60-64. (1 CARD IN FORMAT (11F7.5))
C
C       SETS OF THE ABOVE INPLT MAY BE REPEATED INDEFINITELY.   THE
C       PROGRAM TERMINATES EXECLTION WHEN A BLANK TITLE CARD IS READ.
C
C       IN THE PRCGRAM WE USE FCRMAT (12D5.5) TO CONVERT THE DATA
C       FOR PHI INSTEAD OF FCRMAT (12F5.5).   THE DOUBLE PRECISION
C       IS REQUIRED IN THE CCURSE OF CALCULATION SINCE ERRORS
C       CUMULATE FRCM ONE RCCT TC THE NEXT.   BECAUSE SOME INSTALLATIONS
C       CANNOT DO CCMPLEX ARITHMETIC IN DOUBLE PRECISICN, THE
C       PROGRAM IS WRITTEN IN REAL ARITHMETIC.
C
C       THE PRCGRAM IS DESIGNED FOR NON-ZERO FERTILITY FROM AGES
C       10 TO 54.   THE COEFFICIENTS ARE OBTAINED FROM NET
C       MATERNITY FUNCTICN, WHICH IS THE PRCDUCT OF THE
C       STATICNARY POPULATICN AND THE AGE SPECIFIC FERTILITY
C       RATE FCR SUCCESSIVE FIVE-YEAR AGE INTERVALS.   THE
C       STATICNARY POPULATICN IS TAKEN WITH RADIX UNITY.
C       THE CCEFFICIENT CF THE ELEVENTH POWER IS -1,
C       THE CCEFFICIENT CF THE TENTH POWER IS 0,
C       THE COEFFICIENT CF THE NINTH POWER IS ONE-HALF THE
C           NET MATERNITY FLNCTION FOR AGE 10 TO 14
C       THE CCEFFICIENT CF THE EIGHTH POWER IS THE ARITHMETIC MEAN
C           OF THE NET MATERNITY FUNCTION FOR AGE 10 TO 14 AND
C           FCR 15 TC 19,
C       ....................
C       THE ABSCLUTE TERM IS CNE-HALF THE NET MATERNITY
C           FUNCTION FCR AGE 5C TO 54
C
        DOUBLE PRECISION PHI                                              1
        CCMPLEX RCCT(12)                                                 2
        DIMENSICN B(11),PHI(12),NAME(19),IDEG(6),SPHI(12)                3
```

```
      READ 1,NAME,IBK                                                      4
   1  FORMAT (20A4)                                                        5
   3 PRINT 5,NAME                                                          6
   5 FORMAT (1H1 19A4)                                                     7
      READ 7,B                                                             8
   7 FORMAT(11F7.5)                                                        9
      PHI(1)=-1.                                                          10
      PHI(2)=0.                                                           11
      PHI(3)=B(1)/2.                                                      12
      DO 8 I=4,11                                                         13
   8 PHI(I)=(B(I-3)+B(I-2))/2.                                            14
      PHI(12)=B(9)/2.                                                     15
      PRINT 9                                                             16
   9 FORMAT (1H0/55H THE COEFFICIENTS OF THE CHARACTERISTIC EQUATION AR   17
     AE -- )                                                              18
      J=11                                                                19
      DO 11 I=1,6                                                         20
      IDEG(I)=J                                                           21
  11 J=J-1                                                                22
      DO 12 I=1,12                                                        23
  12 SPHI(I)=PHI(I)                                                       24
      PRINT 13,IDEG,(SPHI(I),I=1,6)                                       25
  13 FORMAT (7HODEGREE 3X 6I10 /12H COEFFICIENT 6F10.4)                   26
      DO 15 I=1,6                                                         27
      IDEG(I)=J                                                           28
  15 J=J-1                                                                29
      PRINT 13,IDEG,(SPHI(I),I=7,12)                                      30
C        THE CHARACTERISTIC EQUATION HAS BEEN PRINTED
C
      N=12                                                                31
      CALL ZERO (PHI,ROOT,N)                                              32
      READ 1,NAME                                                         33
      DO 17 I=1,10                                                        34
      IF (NAME(I) .NE. IBK) GO TO 3                                       35
  17 CONTINUE                                                             36
      PRINT 19                                                            37
  19 FORMAT (11H1END OF JOB )                                             38
      STOP                                                                39
      END                                                                40


      SUBROUTINE ZERO(PHI,ROOT,N)                                         41
      DOUBLE PRECISION PHI(12),AR(12),AI(12),FLR,FLI,FUNR,FUNI,DERIVR,    42
     1DERIVI,PR(14),PI(14),FLAR,FLAI,E,ROOTR(12),ROOTI(12),ALPHAR,        43
     2ALPHAI,BETAR,BETAI                                                  44
      COMPLEX ROOT(N),Y,TEMP                                             45
      DIMENSION ITER(12),RR(12),RI(12)                                    46
C
C
C     INPUT --
C        PHI = A REAL POLYNOMIAL OF DEGREE 11, ABSOLUTE TERM = PHI(12),
C        COEFFICIENT OF FIRST POWER = PHI(11), ETC.
C        N = THE NUMBER OF TERMS OF PHI, EQUALS THE NUMBER OF
C        ROOTS PLUS ONE, AND IS SET TO 12 IN OUR PROBLEM.
C
C     OUTPUT --
```

```
C              ROOT = THE ROOTS OF THE POLYNOMIAL PHI ARRANGED IN DESCENDING
C              ORDER.
C
C              A(1) = COMPLEX VERSION OF (PHI(N), 0)
C              A(2) = COMPLEX VERSION OF (PHI(N-1),0), ETC.
C              A AND ROOT MUST BE DECLARED COMPLEX AND DIMENSION
C              N SPECIFIED IN THE MAIN PROGRAM.
C
       NN= N- 1                                                           47
       NNN=NN-1                                                           48
       DO 50 I=1,N                                                        49
       N1I=N+1-I                                                          50
C
C         A(I)=(-PHI(N+1-I), C.)
C         TRANSLATION OF COMPLEX VARIABLES FOR REAL ARITHMETIC.
       AR(I)=-PHI(N1I)                                                    51
    50 AI(I)=0.D1                                                         52
C
       KK = 0                                                             53
C
C         KK COUNTS THE ROOTS.
C         K COUNTS THE ITERATIONS FOR A GIVEN ROOT.
C
C         FL=(1.,0.)
C         TRANSLATION OF COMPLEX VARIABLES FOR REAL ARITHMETIC.
       FLR=1.DC                                                          54
       FLI=0.D1                                                          55
C
    52 KK = KK+1                                                         56
       KKK=N-KK+1                                                        57
       K =0                                                              58
    54 K=K+1                                                             59
C
C         THE METHOD IS NEWTON-RAPHSON, FUN IS THE VALUE OF THE FUNCTION
C         AT THE TRIAL ROOT, AND DERIV IS THE VALUE OF THE DERIVATIVE.
C
C         FUN=A(1)
C         DERIV=(C.,C.)
C         TRANSLATION OF COMPLEX VARIABLES FOR REAL ARITHMETIC.
       FUNR=AR(1)                                                        60
       FUNI=AI(1)                                                        61
       DERIVR=0.D1                                                       62
       DERIVI=0.D1                                                       63
C
       DO 56 I=2,KKK                                                     64
       FI=I                                                              65
C
C         FUN = FUN+A(I)*FL**(I-1)
C         DERIV = DERIV+(FI-1.)*A(I)*FL**(I-2)
C         TRANSLATION OF COMPLEX VARIABLES FOR REAL ARITHMETIC.
       PR(1)=1.DO                                                        66
       PI(1)=0.D1                                                        67
       PR(2)=FLR                                                         68
       PI(2)=FLI                                                         69
       PR(I+1)=PR(I)*FLR-PI(I)*FLI                                       70
       PI(I+1)=PR(I)*FLI+PI(I)*FLR                                       71
       FUNR=FUNR+AR(I)*PR(I)-AI(I)*PI(I)                                 72
       FUNI=FUNI+AR(I)*PI(I)+AI(I)*PR(I)                                 73
       DERIVR=DERIVR+(FI-1.)*(AR(I)*PR(I-1)-AI(I)*PI(I-1))               74
```

```
   56 DERIVI=DERIVI+(FI-1.)*(AR(I)*PI(I-1)+AI(I)*PR(I-1))                    75
C
C        FLA = FL-FUN/DERIV
C        E=CDABS(FUN)
C        TRANSLATICN CF COMPLEX VARIABLES FOR REAL ARITHMETIC.
      FLAR=FLR-(FUNR*DERIVR+FUNI*DERIVI)/(DERIVR**2+DERIVI**2)              76
      FLAI=FLI-(FUNI*DERIVR-FUNR*DERIVI)/(DERIVR**2+DERIVI**2)              77
      E=CSQRT(FUNR**2+FUNI**2)                                             78
C
      IF(E-.000C0001) 62,58,58                                             79
   58 IF (K-100) 60,72,72                                                  80
C
C        FL=FLA
C        TRANSLATICN CF CCMPLEX VARIABLES FOR REAL ARITHMETIC.
   60 FLR=FLAR                                                             81
      FLI=FLAI                                                             82
C
      GO TO 54                                                             83
C
C        ROOT(KK) = FL
C        TRANSLATICN CF CCMPLEX VARIABLES FOR REAL ARITHMETIC.
   62 ROOTR(KK)=FLR                                                        84
      ROOTI(KK)=FLI                                                        85
C
      ITER(KK) = K                                                         86
      IF (KK-NN) 63,78,78                                                  87
C
C        STATEMENT 5 ENTERS THE KK-TH ROOT IN THE KK-TH CELL OF THE
C        ARRAY ROOT, AND ITER RECORDS THE ITERATIONS THAT WERE NECESSARY.
C
C        ALPHA = A(N-KK)
C        A(N-KK)=A(N+1-KK)
C        TRANSLATICN CF CCMPLEX VARIABLES FOR REAL ARITHMETIC.
   63 NKK=N-KK                                                             88
      ALPHAR=AR(NKK)                                                       89
      ALPHAI=AI(NKK)                                                       90
      N1KK=N+1-KK                                                          91
      AR(NKK)=AR(N1KK)                                                     92
      AI(NKK)=AI(N1KK)                                                     93
      KKKK=N-KK-1                                                          94
      DO 64 I=1,KKKK                                                       95
      M=KKKK+1-I                                                           96
C
C        THE DC-LOCP TO 64 SWEEPS OUT THE ROOT WHICH HAS JUST BEEN
C        EVALUATED.
C
C        BETA = A(M)
C        A(M) = ALPHA + FL*A(M+1)
C        ALPHA = BETA
C        TRANSLATICN CF CCMPLEX VARIABLES FOR REAL ARITHMETIC.
      BETAR=AR(M)                                                          97
      BETAI=AI(M)                                                          98
      AR(M)=ALPHAR+FLR*AR(M+1)-FLI*AI(M+1)                                 99
      AI(M)=ALPHAI+FLR*AI(M+1)+FLI*AR(M+1)                                100
      ALPHAR=BETAR                                                        101
   64 ALPHAI=BETAI                                                        102
C
C        IF ROOT K IS COMPLEX FL IS SET TO ITS CONJUGATE,
```

```
C           IF NOT, FL IS SET TO (.3, .7)
C
C           SROOT=ROOT(KK)
C           IF(ABS(AIMAG(SROOT)) -.00001) 68,68,66
C           FL=DCONJG(ROOT(KK))
C           TRANSLATICN CF COMPLEX VARIABLES FOR REAL ARITHMETIC.
      IF(CABS(ROOTI(KK))-.00001) 68,68,66                               103
   66 FLR=ROOTR(KK)                                                     104
      FLI=-ROOTI(KK)                                                    105
C
      GO TO 52                                                          106
C
C           FL=(.3DO,.7DO)
C           TRANSLATICN CF COMPLEX VARIABLES FOR REAL ARITHMETIC.
   68 FLR=.3DC                                                          107
      FLI=.7DC                                                          108
      GO TO 52                                                          109
C
C
C           IF MORE THAN 100 ITERATICNS ARE NEEDED TC FIND A ROOT THE
C           PROGRAM WILL ABORT TO THIS STATEMENT AND THE ROOTS THAT HAVE
C           BEEN FOUND WILL BE PRINTED.
C
   72 PRINT 74,KK                                                       110
   74 FORMAT (34HOMORE THAN 100 ITERATIONS FOR ROOT I4,                 111
     A 17H  PROGRAM ABORTED )                                           112
      RETURN                                                            113
C
C           CONVERSION TO SINGLE PRECISION COMPLEX.
   78 DO 79 I = 1,12                                                    114
      RR(I)=ROOTR(I)                                                    115
      RI(I)=ROOTI(I)                                                    116
   79 ROOT(I)=CMPLX(RR(I),RI(I))                                        117
C
C           PUT ROOTS IN DESCENDING CRDER OF ABSOLUTE VALUE.
      DO 80 J=1,NNN                                                     118
      JJ = J + 1                                                        119
      DO 80 I=JJ,NN                                                     120
      IF(CABS(ROOT(I)).LE.CABS(ROOT(J))) GO TO 80                       121
      TEMP = ROOT(J)                                                    122
      ROOT(J)=ROOT(I)                                                   123
      ROOT(I) = TEMP                                                    124
   80 CONTINUE                                                          125
C
C           THE ROOTS, IN ORDER CF ABSOLUTE VALUE, ARE PRINTED,
C           ALONG WITH THEIR ABSOLUTE VALUE AND R = .2*LOG (LAMBDA).
      PRINT 82                                                          126
   82 FORMAT (1HO/1HO 15X 52HROOTS ARRANGED IN ORDER OF DESCENDING ABSOL 127
     BUTE VALUE /23X 4HROOT 16X 15HLOG ROOT /5 = R 5X 8HABS ROOT/17X     128
     C4FREAL 8X 7HCOMPLEX 5X 4HREAL 8X 7HCOMPLEX)                        129
      DO 84 J=1,NN                                                      130
      Y = CLOG (ROOT(J)) /5.                                            131
      Z = CABS(ROOT(J))                                                 132
      IF (Z-.0001) 88,84,84                                             133
   84 PRINT 86,J,ROOT(J),Y,Z                                            134
   86 FORMAT (7X,I4,5F12.4)                                             135
   88 CONTINUE                                                          136
      RETURN                                                            137
      END                                                               138
```

ENGLAND AND WALES 1968
.00032 .11563 .38161 .37959 .20723 .05445 .02433 .00159 .000000.   0.

MEXICO 1966
.00269 .20445 .61812 .66657 .51498 .43755 .22554 .042720.   0.   0.

ENGLAND AND WALES 1968

THE COEFFICIENTS OF THE CHARACTERISTIC EQUATION ARE --

DEGREE	11	10	9	8	7	6
COEFFICIENT	−1.0000	0.0	0.0002	0.0580	0.2486	0.3806

DEGREE	5	4	3	2	1	0
COEFFICIENT	0.2934	0.1508	0.0594	0.0130	0.0008	0.0

ROOTS ARRANGED IN ORDER OF DESCENDING ABSOLUTE VALUE

	ROOT REAL	ROOT COMPLEX	LOG ROOT /5 = R REAL	LOG ROOT /5 = R COMPLEX	ABS ROOT
1	1.0354	0.0	0.0070	0.0	1.0354
2	0.3423	0.7582	−0.0368	0.2293	0.8319
3	0.3423	−0.7582	−0.0368	−0.2293	0.8319
4	−0.3819	0.3999	−0.1185	0.4666	0.5530
5	−0.3819	−0.3999	−0.1185	−0.4666	0.5530
6	−0.0255	0.4798	−0.1466	0.3248	0.4805
7	−0.0255	−0.4798	−0.1466	−0.3248	0.4805
8	−0.4059	−0.0602	−0.1781	−0.5989	0.4104
9	−0.4059	0.0602	−0.1781	0.5989	0.4104
10	−0.0933	0.0000	−0.4744	0.6283	0.0933

MEXICO 1966

THE COEFFICIENTS OF THE CHARACTERISTIC EQUATION ARE --

DEGREE	11	10	9	8	7	6
COEFFICIENT	−1.0000	0.0	0.0013	0.1036	0.4113	0.6423

DEGREE	5	4	3	2	1	0
COEFFICIENT	0.5908	0.4763	0.3315	0.1341	0.0214	0.0

ROOTS ARRANGED IN ORDER OF DESCENDING ABSOLUTE VALUE

	ROOT		LOG ROOT /5 = R		ABS ROOT
	REAL	COMPLEX	REAL	COMPLEX	
1	1.1900	-0.0000	0.0348	-0.0000	1.1900
2	0.4506	-0.7703	-0.0228	-0.2083	0.8924
3	0.4506	0.7703	-0.0228	0.2083	0.8924
4	0.0581	-0.7446	-0.0584	-0.2986	0.7468
5	0.0581	0.7446	-0.0584	0.2986	0.7468
6	-0.4415	-0.4821	-0.0850	-0.4624	0.6538
7	-0.4415	0.4821	-0.0850	0.4624	0.6538
8	-0.4484	-0.1420	-0.1509	-0.5670	0.4703
9	-0.4484	0.1420	-0.1509	0.5670	0.4703
10	-0.4274	0.0000	-0.1700	0.6283	0.4274

CHAPTER 10

The Stable Population

In Chapter 7 we saw how projection leads ultimately to an age-distribution, or an age-sex distribution, that depends only on the age-specific rates of birth and death, assumed for such analysis to be fixed. In this ultimate condition the population will be increasing at the annual intrinsic rate r, or in the ratio $\lambda = r^{5r}$ per five-year period.

If we know r and the life table, however, there is no need to project in order to find the stable age distribution. We may more directly seek a vector $\mathbf{K}$ that satisfies the equation $\mathbf{MK} = \lambda\mathbf{K}$. From the constitution of $\mathbf{M}$ as shown in (14) the $\mathbf{K}$ of this equation must be built up on a simple relation among its successive elements $_5K_x$, $x = 0, 5, 10, \ldots$. The element for $x + 5$ is obtained from the element for x by

$$_5K_{x+5} = \frac{_5L_{x+5}\,_5K_x}{_5L_x\lambda},$$

which determines the ratios among the successive elements of the stable population. The value of the first element $_5K_0$ is at our disposal, and if we make it $_5K_0 = _5L_0/\lambda^{1/2}$, then the stable vector becomes

$$_5K_0 = \frac{_5L_0}{\lambda^{1/2}} = e^{-2.5r}\,_5L_0$$

$$_5K_5 = \frac{_5L_5}{\lambda^{3/2}} = e^{-7.5r}\,_5L_5$$

$$\cdots$$

$$_5K_x = \frac{_5L_x}{\lambda^{x/5+1/2}} = e^{-(x+2.5)r}\,_5L_x$$

$$\vdots$$

This is a commonly used approximation; it is produced in the program STABLE, which follows, along with an alternative that seems slightly preferable.

Departing somewhat further from observation, we can use a given life table along with an arbitrary value of r to see to what age distribution a population would tend if its mortality remained as observed, but its rate of increase took on a hypothetical value. This is a main subject of Coale and Demeny (1966), who apply it effectively in reverse to ascertain the rate of increase of a population whose age distribution and life table are known. (See Chapters 2 and 11 of this book.)

Our program STABLE starts with a given life table and arbitrary rates of increase r and calculates the corresponding stable age distributions.

The life table input takes the form of the l_x column. The output stable age distribution accords with the rate r applicable to the population from which the life table comes, or such arbitrary rates as $r = 0.02$, 0.03, and 0.04. Two methods of calculating the stable age distribution are employed, the conventional one implied in the preceding paragraphs being designated the L-method, and a slightly superior alternative being called the K-method.

The L-Method

A method often used on a desk calculator to find the number $_5K_x$ in the stable distribution for ages x to $x + 4$ is given above as

$$_5K_x = e^{-(x+2.5)\,r}\,_5L_x,$$

where $_5L_x$ is the number in the stationary age distribution in the same ages. As we saw in the discussion of the life table this stationary age distribution is obtained by integration of the l_x:

$$_5L_x = \int_0^5 l(x + t)\,dt,$$

and the curve for obtaining the integral numerically is a cubic through l_{x-5}, l_x, l_{x+5}, and l_{x+10}. These four values are symmetrically placed with respect to the interval from exact age x to exact age $x + 5$ over which the integral is to be calculated.

By fitting a cubic equation $l(x) = \alpha + \beta x + \gamma x^2 + \delta x^3$ through the four values of l_x, then integrating, we find $_5L_x$:

$$_5L_x = \frac{65}{24}(l_x + l_{x+5}) - \frac{5}{24}(l_{x-5} + l_{x+10}), \tag{29}$$

as in (5).

For ages younger than five years the cubic does not fit well, and we resort to the hyperbola $l_x = (ax + b)/(x + b)$, and the fitting is to l_0, l_1, and l_5. The values of the constants are

$$b = \frac{5(l_1 - l_5)}{4l_0 - 5l_1 + l_5},$$

$$a = \frac{l_1(1 + b)}{l_0} - b,$$

(30)

and the integral turns out to be

$$_1L_0 = \int_0^1 l(t)\, dt = l_0 \left[a + b(1 - a) \ln\left(\frac{1 + b}{b}\right) \right],$$

$$_4L_1 = \int_0^4 l(1 + t)\, dt = l_0 \left[4a + b(1 - a) \ln\left(\frac{5 + b}{1 + b}\right) \right].$$

We are now ready to calculate the stable age distribution. If the radix l_0 is set to 1, which is to say the several l_x are each divided by l_0, then we will obtain as the integrals the stationary age distribution per one birth. The corresponding stable age distribution will also be said to be of radix 1. If we want the stable age distribution per one person in the whole population, or as percentages of the total, these are obtained by dividing by the total or by 1/100 of the total, respectively.

With the stationary population on a radix l_0, our stable population on the same radix is

$$_1K_0 = e^{-r/2}{}_1L_0$$
$$_4K_1 = e^{-3r}{}_4L_1$$

for the first two ages, and

$$_5K_x = e^{-(x+2.5)r}{}_5L_x$$

for subsequent ages.

The K-Method

Method L above first integrates in the stationary l_x, and then uses $_5K_x = e^{-(x+2.5)r}{}_5L_x$, as an approximation to the integral of the product. Thus two approximations go into it, one of which is avoidable. Whatever method is used to find the integral $_5L_x$ can be applied to the desired integrand $k(x + t) = e^{-(x+t)r}l(x + t)$. If the cubic fits the product of the exponential and l_{x+t} as well as it fits l_{x+t} alone—and we have no reason to doubt that it does—then we have avoided the approximation

$$\int_0^5 e^{-(x+t)r}l(x + t)\, dt \cong e^{-(x+2.5)r}{}_5L_x$$

at no cost. Note that in this notation, the lower case letters k and l refer to the exact ages in the stable and stationary populations, respectively, and the upper case K and L to the integrals over intervals of age. In the L-method the primary integration is of l_x to establish $_5L_x$, while in the K-method the primary integration is of k_x to provide $_5K_x$ directly.

Hence our preferred estimate of $_5K_x$ is

$$_5K_x = \int_0^5 k(x+t)\, dt$$

$$= \frac{65}{24}\left(e^{-rx}l_x + e^{-r(x+5)}l_{x+5}\right) - \frac{5}{24}\left(e^{-r(x-5)}l_{x-5} + e^{-r(x+10)}l_{x+10}\right) \qquad (31)$$

for ages x from five years onward. For the first two age groups, the hyperbola will again be used, now fitted through $k_0 = l_0 = 1$, $k_1 = e^{-r}l_1$, $k_5 = e^{-5r}l_5$.

To avoid programming both (30) and (31) we calculate the integral for $k_x = e^{-rx}l_x$ first, and then that for l_x is obtained by simply putting $r = 0$. We are grateful to Geoffrey McNicoll for this and other devices.

A More Accurate Projection Factor and Birth Rate

One feature of the program STABLE is its calculation of the quantity $_nL'_x$ now defined (slightly differently from in the discussion of the life table in Chapter 2) as

$$_nL'_x = \int_0^5 e^{-r(t-2.5)}l_{x+t}\, dt,$$

corresponding to a cohort in which the births were increasing geometrically within the five-year period. The ratio $_nL'_{x+5}/_nL'_x$ with appropriate r is preferable in principle to $_nL_{x+5}/_nL_x$ for projection.

For the Jamaica, 1956, females with $r = 0.02782$, we have $_5L'_{40} = 424{,}041$ compared with $_5L_{40} = 423{,}600$, a difference of one part in 1000. The ratio of consecutive values will be closer yet on the two models; we find

$$\frac{_5L_{45}}{_5L_{40}} = \frac{412{,}588}{423{,}600} = 0.97400,$$

$$\frac{_5L'_{45}}{_5L'_{40}} = \frac{413{,}039}{424{,}041} = 0.97405,$$

a difference of one part in 20,000. The ratio of L' is higher, as it should be at ages of rising mortality, since with $r > 0$ $_5L'_x$ implicitly contains a slightly younger population than does $_5L_x$.

Any way of calculating the stable-population age distribution provides a way of finding the intrinsic birth rate, defined as the birth rate in the stable population:

$$b = \frac{\int_0^\omega e^{-ra} l_a m_a \, da}{\int_0^\omega e^{-ra} l_a \, da}.$$

But since the numerator of this is unity if r satisfies the characteristic equation (17), we have for the intrinsic birth rate

$$b = \frac{1}{\int_0^\omega e^{-ra} l_a \, da}$$

Thus we obtain the intrinsic birth rate corresponding to any given life table and rate of increase r simply as the reciprocal of the total stable population on radix unity. Since we have here developed two approximations for going from r and l_x to the stable age distribution, we have two intrinsic birth rates for each r. With $1000r = 27.82$ of Jamaica, 1956, and the Jamaica life table, we find an intrinsic birth rate of $1000b = 35.957$ on the K-method, and 35.964 on the L-method, a difference of about one part in 5000.

The value of the intrinsic rate of the given population may be found from ROOT or ZEROS among the programs here presented. Whether from this or other source r is included on the fourth data card; if the effect of the different approximations to r shown by ROOT is required, all of these may be incorporated.

Program STABLE

The input of the program consists of: (1) A title card describing the population to which the life table applies; (2) The life table l_x values, for age x equal to 0, 1, 5, 10, . . . , 85, in format 10F8.6—two punch cards are required for the 19 values, and the numbers are stored in the array VL(20); (3) The number of values of r for which the stable age distributions are desired, entered on a card in format (I4); (4) The values of r themselves, punched in format 10F8.6.

```
C
C
C                            STABLE
C
C
C        COMPUTES THE STABLE AGE DISTRIBUTICN, MEAN AGE
C        AND INTRINSIC BIRTH RATE OF A POPULATION SPECIFIED BY A LIFE
C        TABLE AND ARBITRARY RATE OF NATURAL INCREASE. TWO METHODS ARE
C        USED, DENOTED BY K AND L.
C
C        METHOD K COMPUTES THE SMALL K(X) BY MULTIPLYING THE LIFE
C        TABLE SMALL L(X) BY EXP(-R*X), AND THEN OBTAINS THE STABLE
C        DISTRIBUTION BY INTEGRATION.
C
C        METHOD L COMPUTES THE STATIONARY DISTRIBUTION (LARGE L(X))
C        BY THE INTEGRATION OF THE LIFE TABLE SMALL L(X), AND THEN
C        ESTIMATES THE STABLE DISTRIBUTION BY MULTIPLYING BY
C        EXP(-R(X+2.5))IF AGE GRCUPS ARE OF FIVE YEARS.
C        METHOD K IS PREFERRED IN MOST CIRCUMSTANCES.
C
C        INPUT CONSISTS CF
C          TITLE CARD IN FORMAT (19A4)
C          LIFE TABLE SURVIVORSHIPS L(X) ON RADIX L(0) = 100000.,
C            (FORMAT (10F8.0) FOR 2 CARDS)
C          THE NUMBER N LESS THAN OR EQUAL TO EIGHT FOR 1 CARD
C            IN FORMAT (I4)
C          N VALUES OF R, THE RATE OF INCREASE FOR 1 CARD
C            IN FORMAT (8F10.8)
C
C        SETS OF THE ABOVE INPUT MAY BE REPEATED INDEFINITELY.  THE
C        PROGRAM TERMINATES EXECUTION WHEN A BLANK TITLE CARD IS READ.
C
C        THE FUNCTIONS TABULATED IN THE OUTPUT ARE
C          L(X) = SURVIVORSHIPS READ IN AS DATA
C          LL(X) = COMPUTED STATIONARY POPULATION
C          LLP(X) = INTEGRAL (EXP(-R(T-5/2)).L(X+T)) DT FROM 0 TO 5, I.E.
C            STATIONARY POPULATICN BUT ALLOWING FOR INCREASE WITHIN
C            AGE INTERVALS.  THE VALUE 5 APPLIES TO AGE INTERVALS
C            BETWEEN AGES 5 AND 85, AND IS REPLACED BY 1 FOR THE FIRST
C            AGE INTERVAL AND 4 FOR THE SECOND.
C          KK(X) METHOD K = EXP(-R.X).LLP(X)
C          KK(X) METHOD L = EXP(-R(X + 5/2)).LL(X), WHERE 5 IS THE WIDTH
C            OF THE AGE INTERVAL.
C        IN THE PROGRAM, THE LAST TWO FUNCTIONS ARE DENOTED BY VKKA(I)
C        AND VKKB(I) RESPECTIVELY, AND REPRESENT THE ALTERNATIVE
C        METHODS OF CALCULATING THE STABLE POPULATION.
C
         DIMENSION VL(20), VLL(20), VK(20), VKK(20), VKKA(20), VKKB(20),   1
        AVLLP(20),X(20),J(20),R1(8),NAME(19)                               2
C
```

```
C        COLUMNS 1-76 OF THE TITLE CARD ARE STORED IN 'NAME'.
C        COLUMNS 77-80 OF THE TITLE CARD MUST ALWAYS BE BLANK.
C                                                                          3
      READ 1,NAME,IBK                                                      4
    1 FORMAT (20A4)                                                        5
    6 READ 7,VL                                                            6
    7 FORMAT (10F8.0)
C
C        N (LESS THAN OR EQUAL TO 8) IS THE NUMBER OF VALUES
C        OF R READ IN.                                                     7
      READ 9,N,(R1(I),I=1,N)                                               8
    9 FORMAT (I4/8F10.8)
C
C        LOWER BOUND OF AGE GROUP I IS GIVEN BY J(I) AND THE MID-POINT
C        BY X(I).                                                          9
      X(2)=2.5                                                            10
      DO 11 I=3,20                                                        11
      X(I)=X(I-1)+5.0                                                     12
   11 J(I)=X(I)-2.5                                                       13
      X(1)=0.5                                                            14
      X(2)=3.0                                                            15
      J(1)=0                                                              16
      J(2)=1
C
C        THIS LOOP ESTIMATES THE STABLE POPULATION FOR EACH OF THE
C        ARBITRARY RATES OF INCREASE READ IN.                             17
      DO 37 L=1,N                                                         18
      PRINT 12,NAME                                                       19
   12 FORMAT (1H1 19A4)                                                   20
      R = R1(L)                                                           21
      PRINT 13,R                                                          22
   13 FORMAT (1H0 6X 3HR = F8.5//)                                        23
      RR = 1.                                                             24
   15 DO 17 I=1,20                                                        25
   17 VK(I)=VL(I)/EXP(R*FLOAT(J(I)))
C
C        INTEGRATION IS BY A HYPERBOLA FOR THE FIRST TWO AGE GROUPS,
C        BY A PARABOLA FOR THE THIRD AGE GROUP, AND BY A THIRD DEGREE
C        POLYNOMIAL FOR THE REST OF LIFE.
C        THE SAME EXPRESSIONS, WHEN R=0, ARE USED TO COMPUTE VLL FROM
C        VL FOR METHOD L.                                                 26
      B = 5.*(VK(2) - VK(3))/(400000. + VK(3) - 5.*VK(2))                 27
      A = VK(2)*(1. + B)/100000. - B                                      28
      VKK(1) =(A + B*(1.-A)*ALOG((1.+B)/B))*100000.                       29
      VKK(2)=(4.*A+B*(1.-A)*ALOG((5.+B)/(1.+B))  )*100000.                30
      VKK(3) = (25./12.)*VK(3) + (10./3.)*VK(4) - (5./12.)*VK(5)          31
      DO 19 I=4,18                                                        32
   19 VKK(I) = (65./24.)*(VK(I)+VK(I+1)) - (5./24.)*(VK(I-1)+VK(I+2))     33
      VKK(19) = (65./24.)*(VK(19)+VK(20))-(5./24.)*(VK(18))
C
      IR=1000000*R+.5                                                     34
      IF(IR .EQ. 0) GO TO 23                                              35
      DO 21 I=1,19                                                        36
      VKKA(I) = VKK(I)                                                    37
   21 VLLP(I)=VKKA(I)*EXP (R*X(I))                                        38
      RR = R                                                              39
      R = 0.0                                                             40
      GO TO 15                                                            41
C
```

```
   23 IRR=1000000*RR+.5                                              42
      IF(IRR. NE. 1000000) R=RR                                      43
      DO 25 I=1,19                                                   44
      VLL(I) = VKK(I)                                                45
   25 VKKB(I)=VLL(I)/EXP (R*X(I))                                    46
      IF(IRR .NE. 1000000) GO TO 29                                  47
      DO 27 I=1,19                                                   48
      VKKA(I) = VKKB(I)                                              49
   27 VLLP(I)=VKKA(I)*EXP (R*X(I))                                   50
C         THE FOREGOING DEVICE WAS NECESSARY IN ORDER TO PERMIT
C         THE SAME PROGRAMMING TO CALCULATE THE STATIONARY AND THE
C         STABLE POPULATIONS.  ON THE FIRST ROUND THE GIVEN VALUE
C         OF R WAS ENTERED.  ON THE SECOND ROUND THE VALUE IN R
C         WAS SAVED IN RR, R WAS SET EQUAL TO ZERO, AND THE CONTROL
C         TRANSFERRED TO 15.  THE PROGRAM RECOGNIZED THAT IT WAS
C         ON THE SECOND ROUND BY FINDING ZERO IN R, AND IT THEN
C         TRANSFERRED TO 23, HAVING PUT THE STABLE POPULATION IN
C         THE ARRAY VKKA AND THE STATIONARY IN VKK, FROM WHERE THE
C         STATIONARY IS TRANSFERRED IN THE LOOP AT 25 TO VLL.
C
   29 PRINT 31                                                       51
   31 FORMAT (10X,1HX,7X,4HL(X),7X,5HLL(X),7X,6HLLP(X),6X,5HKK(X),7X, 52
     B  5HKK(X),7X,1HK,/ 52X,8HMETHOD K,4X,8HMETHOD L, /)            53
      PRINT 33,(J(I),VL(I),VLL(I),VLLP(I),VKKA(I),VKKB(I),J(I),I=1,19) 54
   33 FORMAT (9X I2,5F12.0,6X I2)                                    55
C
C         CALCULATION OF STABLE BIRTH RATES AND MEAN AGES FOR METHODS
C         K AND L.
      SUMA = 0.                                                      56
      SUMB = 0.                                                      57
      WA = 0.                                                        58
      WB = 0.                                                        59
      DO 35 I=1,19                                                   60
      SUMA = SUMA + VKKA(I)                                          61
      SUMB = SUMB + VKKB(I)                                          62
      WA = WA + VKKA(I)*X(I)                                         63
   35 WB = WB + VKKB(I)*X(I)                                         64
C
C      BIRTH RATES:
      BRA = 100000./SUMA                                             65
      BRB = 100000./SUMB                                             66
C
C      MEAN AGES:
      ABARA = WA/SUMA                                                67
      ABARB = WB/SUMB                                                68
C
C         DIFFERENCE BETWEEN METHODS K AND L --
      DIFFBR = (BRA - BRB)*100./BRA                                  69
      DIFFMA = (ABARA - ABARB)*100./ABARA                           70
   37 PRINT 39, BRA, ABARA, BRB, ABARB, DIFFBR, DIFFMA              71
   39 FORMAT (//42X,20HINTRINSIC BIRTH RATE, 9X,8HMEAN AGE //27X,    72
     C 9HMETHOD K ,10X,F7.6,16X,F9.4/27X,8HMETHOD L,12X,F7.6,16X,F9.4/ 73
     D 24X,17H(K - L)/K PERCENT,5X,F6.3,20X,F6.3 )                   74
C
C         CHECK FOR ANOTHER SET OF INPUT DATA.
      READ 1,NAME                                                    75
      DO 41 I=1,10                                                   76
      IF (NAME(I) .NE. IBK) GO TO 6                                  77
   41 CONTINUE                                                       78
```

```
      PRINT 43                                                        79
   43 FORMAT (11H1END CF JOB )                                        80
      STCP                                                            81
      END                                                             82
```

```
ENGLAND AND WALES 1968
   100000    98428     98141     97991     97862     97681     97484     97226     96859     96277
    95285    93684     91245     87648     82172     73827     61324     44431     25581         0
   3
.00694909         .015        .030
```

```
MEXICO 1966
   100000    94000     90231     89296     88808     88131     87127     85842     84411     82367
    80342    77820     74620     70073     63207     54053     43611     31238     16333         0
   3
.03465095         .015        .030
```

ENGLAND AND WALES 1968

   R = 0.00695

X	L(X)	LL(X)	LLP(X)	KK(X) METHOD K	KK(X) METHOD L	
0	100000.	98818.	99088.	98745.	98476.	0
1	98428.	392879.	391661.	383581.	384774.	1
5	98141.	490321.	490349.	465448.	465421.	5
10	97991.	489639.	489664.	448925.	448902.	10
15	97862.	488872.	488859.	432917.	432893.	15
20	97681.	487928.	487955.	417326.	417304.	20
25	97484.	486810.	486838.	402152.	402130.	25
30	97226.	485280.	485308.	387199.	387176.	30
35	96859.	482970.	483001.	372198.	372175.	35
40	96277.	479117.	479153.	356625.	356598.	40
45	95285.	472724.	472768.	339857.	339825.	45
50	93684.	462738.	462794.	321325.	321287.	50
55	91245.	447865.	447932.	300387.	300341.	55
60	87648.	425535.	425630.	275683.	275624.	60
65	82172.	391461.	391590.	244974.	244893.	65
70	73827.	339658.	339856.	205349.	205230.	70
75	61324.	265710.	265995.	155233.	155066.	75
80	44431.	176840.	177072.	99809.	99678.	80
85	25581.	60025.	60744.	33070.	32679.	85

	INTRINSIC BIRTH RATE	MEAN AGE
METHOD K	.017419	35.2081
METHOD L	.017420	35.1957
(K - L)/K PERCENT	-0.006	0.035

ENGLAND AND WALES 1968

R = 0.01500

X	L(X)	LL(X)	LLP(X)	KK(X) METHOD K	KK(X) METHOD L	
0	100000.	98818.	99125.	98384.	98080.	0
1	98428.	392879.	391172.	373959.	375592.	1
5	98141.	490321.	490450.	438265.	438150.	5
10	97991.	489639.	489756.	406022.	405925.	10
15	97862.	488872.	488993.	376097.	376004.	15
20	97681.	487928.	488048.	348247.	348162.	20
25	97484.	486810.	486931.	322345.	322265.	25
30	97226.	485280.	485403.	298115.	298039.	30
35	96859.	482970.	483097.	275261.	275188.	35
40	96277.	479117.	479257.	253341.	253267.	40
45	95285.	472724.	472880.	231908.	231832.	45
50	93684.	462738.	462917.	210619.	210537.	50
55	91245.	447865.	448069.	189132.	189046.	55
60	87648.	425539.	425791.	166742.	166644.	60
65	82172.	391461.	391791.	142342.	142222.	65
70	73827.	339658.	340132.	114644.	114485.	70
75	61324.	267710.	266363.	83293.	83088.	75
80	44431.	176840.	177367.	51456.	51303.	80
85	25581.	60025.	61571.	16572.	16156.	85

	INTRINSIC BIRTH RATE	MEAN AGE
METHOD K	.022744	31.1669
METHOD L	.022748	31.1461
(K - L)/K PERCENT	-0.017	0.067

ENGLAND AND WALES 1968

R = 0.03000

X	L(X)	LL(X)	LLP(X)	KK(X) METHOD K	KK(X) METHOD L	
0	100000.	98818.	99148.	97672.	97347.	0
1	98428.	392879.	390939.	357291.	359065.	1
5	98141.	490321.	490859.	391959.	391529.	5
10	97991.	489639.	490099.	336840.	336524.	10
15	97862.	488872.	489339.	289471.	289195.	15
20	97681.	487928.	488392.	248668.	248432.	20
25	97484.	486810.	487277.	213542.	213337.	25
30	97226.	485280.	485750.	183221.	183044.	30
35	96859.	482970.	483449.	156953.	156798.	35
40	96277.	479117.	479619.	134021.	133880.	40
45	95285.	472724.	473258.	113823.	113694.	45
50	93684.	462738.	463314.	95909.	95790.	50
55	91245.	447865.	448484.	79908.	79798.	55
60	87648.	425539.	426249.	65367.	65259.	60
65	82172.	391461.	392314.	51783.	51671.	65
70	73827.	339658.	340776.	38715.	38588.	70
75	61324.	265710.	267143.	26122.	25982.	75
80	44431.	176840.	177982.	14980.	14883.	80
85	25581.	60025.	63086.	4570.	4348.	85

	INTRINSIC BIRTH RATE	MEAN AGE
METHOD K	.034473	24.6223
METHOD L	.034493	24.5964
(K - L)/K PERCENT	-0.057	0.105

MEXICO 1966

   R = 0.03465

X	L(X)	LL(X)	LLP(X)	KK(X) METHOD K	KK(X) METHOD L	
0	100000.	96283.	96666.	95006.	94630.	0
1	94000.	365756.	362841.	327017.	329644.	1
5	90231.	448631.	449410.	346559.	345959.	5
10	89296.	445206.	445755.	289059.	288704.	10
15	88808.	442455.	443046.	241600.	241277.	15
20	88131.	438272.	438891.	201262.	200977.	20
25	87127.	432511.	433147.	167031.	166785.	25
30	85842.	425791.	426398.	138271.	138074.	30
35	84411.	417069.	417768.	113922.	113732.	35
40	82367.	406872.	407493.	93444.	93301.	40
45	80342.	395650.	396315.	76424.	76295.	45
50	77820.	381522.	382197.	61977.	61867.	50
55	74620.	362496.	363237.	49532.	49431.	55
60	70073.	334160.	335091.	38425.	38319.	60
65	63207.	293895.	294984.	28445.	28340.	65
70	54053.	244831.	245858.	19937.	19853.	70
75	43611.	188052.	189156.	12899.	12823.	75
80	31238.	119752.	121041.	6941.	6867.	80
85	16333.	37727.	39799.	1919.	1819.	85

	INTRINSIC BIRTH RATE	MEAN AGE
METHOD K	.043296	21.8937
METHOD L	.043315	21.8606
(K - L)/K PERCENT	-0.042	0.152

MEXICO 1966

R = 0.01500

X	L(X)	LL(X)	LLP(X)	KK(X) METHOD K	KK(X) METHOD L	
0	100000.	96283.	96552.	95831.	95564.	0
1	94000.	365756.	363880.	347868.	349661.	1
5	90231.	448631.	448796.	401043.	400896.	5
10	89296.	445206.	445310.	369175.	369089.	10
15	88808.	442455.	442577.	340398.	340304.	15
20	88131.	438272.	438407.	312826.	312730.	20
25	87127.	432511.	432656.	286415.	286320.	25
30	85842.	425791.	425925.	261586.	261503.	30
35	84411.	417069.	417245.	237739.	237639.	35
40	82367.	406872.	407019.	215155.	215078.	40
45	80342.	395650.	395918.	194116.	194033.	45
50	77820.	381522.	381697.	173665.	173585.	50
55	74620.	362496.	362704.	153099.	153012.	55
60	70073.	334160.	334458.	130976.	130859.	60
65	63207.	293895.	294276.	106914.	106775.	65
70	54053.	244831.	245202.	82647.	82522.	70
75	43611.	188052.	188473.	58936.	58805.	75
80	31238.	119752.	120275.	34893.	34741.	80
85	16333.	37727.	38643.	10401.	10154.	85

	INTRINSIC BIRTH RATE	MEAN AGE
METHOD K	.026221	29.6404
METHOD L	.026224	29.6183
(K - L)/K PERCENT	-0.011	0.074

MEXICO 1966

R = 0.03000

X	L(X)	LL(X)	LLP(X)	KK(X) METHOD K	KK(X) METHOD L	
0	100000.	96283.	96647.	95208.	94850.	0
1	94000.	365756.	362997.	331754.	334275.	1
5	90231.	448631.	449220.	358710.	358239.	5
10	89296.	445206.	445619.	306269.	305985.	10
15	88808.	442455.	442904.	262002.	261737.	15
20	88131.	438272.	438746.	223390.	223149.	20
25	87127.	432511.	433001.	189756.	189542.	25
30	85842.	425791.	426256.	160781.	160605.	30
35	84411.	417069.	417615.	135580.	135403.	35
40	82367.	406872.	407353.	113827.	113693.	40
45	80342.	395650.	396170.	95282.	95157.	45
50	77820.	381522.	382052.	79088.	78978.	50
55	74620.	362496.	363085.	64692.	64587.	55
60	70073.	334160.	334918.	51361.	51245.	60
65	63207.	293895.	294797.	38911.	38792.	65
70	54053.	244831.	245686.	27912.	27815.	70
75	43611.	188052.	188982.	18479.	18388.	75
80	31238.	119752.	120853.	10171.	10079.	80
85	16333.	37727.	39530.	2864.	2733.	85

	INTRINSIC BIRTH RATE	MEAN AGE
METHOD K	.038971	23.5064
METHOD L	.038983	23.4747
(K - L)/K PERCENT	-0.031	0.135

CHAPTER 11

Inferences From Incomplete Data

Data on birth and death suffer from many kinds of inaccuracy. Our object has been to select that part of the contemporary material that is sufficiently accurate for the purposes to which readers would be likely to put it. Where data provided by national agencies fell conspicuously short of this standard we usually omitted it altogether, though in a few instances we ventured to make corrections. All such corrected data are indicated in the notes of Part V, where the amount of alteration to official figures is shown.

The principal basis of judgment for rejection or correction was inference from an age distribution. Supposing population to be correctly given, what can we say about births independently of birth registrations?

The task of estimating birth rates from an age distribution is easiest if we can assume it to be stable and also know the deaths by age and sex. Some countries apparently have attained relatively complete registration of deaths, at least for ages beyond infancy; in some other countries the degree of incompleteness of the registration of deaths is known. Death registrations, if possible corrected for incompleteness, along with a census or estimated population permit a life table to be made, for instance using the program LIFE above. The column of the life table required as the input to the program INFER, which may be used to ascertain birth rates from an age distribution, is the stationary population $_5L_x$.

Many countries collect no information on deaths, or not enough for calculation of a reliable life table. In these we may be in a position to select a table from somewhere else. We may know the country is part of a region in which expectation of life is 50 years, and does not differ greatly from its neighbors in conditions affecting health. In that case we may use the life table from a neighboring country, or select one from the set of model tables constructed by Coale and Demeny (1966).

Another application of the program INFER is sometimes made to collections of data in which both birth and death figures are on hand, both look reasonable, and we want to check one against the other, with an open mind regarding which is right if a discrepancy occurs. We may even want to assume that both are correct and that it is the validity of the assumption of stability that is to be checked. Table 7 in each set of Main Tables (Part IV) pertains to the several ways of reconciling rates of birth and natural increase for those populations in which registrations reach acceptable standards.

The arguments by which births are inferred apply equally to males and females. Our input includes the observed age distribution and the stationary age distribution for each sex, and the output of INFER shows results calculated first from the male side and then from the female. Due to lack of space, we show, in Table 7 of the Main Tables, only certain selected results for females.

Five ways of inferring births are programmed here, and we proceed to outline the theory on which they are based.

The Bourgeois-Pichat Regression

The Bourgeois-Pichat regression supposes that the observed age distribution is stable at least within a specified range, and identifies it with the theoretical

$$c(a) = be^{-ra}l(a),$$

where the fraction of the population between ages a and $a + da$ is $c(a)da$; b is the birth rate; r the intrinsic rate of natural increase, and $l(a) = l(a)/l_0$ is the probability of a child just born living to age a, that is, the life table survivorship column on radix $l_0 = 1$. Dividing by $l(a)$ and taking logarithms gives

$$\ln \frac{c(a)}{l(a)} = \ln b - ra,$$

a linear equation in which the only unknowns are b and r. In Table 7 of the Main Tables b and r are shown as inferred from age ranges of $M = 25$ consecutive years: 5–29, 30–54, ...The program INFER contains the variable M, which the user can set to any range desired.

In the implementation of the formula we have to convert it into finite age intervals. The equation for any one five-year age interval becomes

$$\ln \frac{_5P_a}{_5L_a} = \ln b - r\left(a + 2\frac{1}{2}\right),$$

where $_5P_a$ is the fraction of the population aged a to $a + 4$, and $l_0 = 1$. Least-squares fitting to $n + 1$ of these equations taken consecutively is accomplished by solving two equations for the unknown b and r:

$$\sum_{a=x}^{x+5n} \ln\left(\frac{_5P_a}{_5L_a}\right) = (n + 1) \ln b - r \sum_{a=x}^{x+5n} \left(a + 2\frac{1}{2}\right),$$

$$\sum_{a=x}^{x+5n} \left(a + 2\frac{1}{2}\right) \ln\left(\frac{_5P_a}{_5L_a}\right) = (\ln b) \sum_{a=x}^{x+5n} \left(a + 2\frac{1}{2}\right) - r \sum_{a=x}^{x+5n} \left(a + 2\frac{1}{2}\right)^2,$$

(32)

where the summations are over points 5 years apart: $x, x + 5, \ldots$.

Three Successive Age Groups, with Assumption of Local Stability

The next section of the program infers r from three successive age groups. Here $_5P_x$, the observed number or proportion aged x to $x + 4$, is identified with the corresponding stable expression,

$$_5P_x = K e^{-r(x+2.5)} {}_5L_x,$$

where K is a constant independent of age, and we solve for r:

$$r = 0.1 \ln \frac{\dfrac{_5P_{x-5}}{_5L_{x-5}}}{\dfrac{_5P_{x+5}}{_5L_{x+5}}}$$

(33)

This is applied for $x = 10$, so that $x - 5$ is 5 and $x + 5$ is 15, and similarly through later ages. It will be recalled that this same formula was applied in each iteration of the life table.

Ratio of Girls to Women and Boys to Men: Thompson's Index

Thompson's index is the ratio of girl children less than 5 years old to women 15–45 years old, divided by the corresponding ratio from the female life table, or, in symbols,

$$Th = \frac{(_5P_0/_{30}P_{15})}{(_5L_0/_{30}L_{15})},$$

where Th is an index named after Warren R. Thompson. It may be proved to be very nearly the net reproduction rate R_0, which estimates from given assumptions the ratio of a generation to the preceding generation.

The proof consists in identifying the observed ratio $_5P_0/_{30}P_{15}$ with the corresponding ratio in the stable population:

$$\frac{_5P_0}{_{30}P_{15}} = \frac{b \displaystyle\int_0^5 e^{-ra}l(a)da}{b \displaystyle\int_{15}^{45} e^{-ra}l(a)da}.$$

If the integral in the numerator is approximated by $e^{-2.5r}{}_5L_0$ and that in the denominator by $e^{-30r}{}_{30}L_{15}$, then on multiplying up we have

$$e^{27.5r} = \frac{\dfrac{_5P_0}{_{30}P_{15}}}{\dfrac{_5L_0}{_{30}L_{15}}} = Th. \tag{34}$$

Insofar as $27\frac{1}{2}$ years is close to the length of generation for most populations, the quantity $e^{27.5r}$ is close to the net reproduction rate R_0, and from (34) so is Th. Taking logarithms in (34) shows that the inferred value of r is approximately $\ln Th/27.5$.

Iteration provides a more precise result. The equation above with $_5P_0/_{30}P_{15}$ on the left-hand side may be readily transformed into

$$e^{-27.5r} = \frac{_{30}P_{15}}{_5P_0} \times \frac{\displaystyle\int_0^5 e^{-r(a-2.5)}l(a)da}{\displaystyle\int_{15}^{45} e^{-r(a-30)}l(a)da},$$

which in finite terms may be written

$$r^* = \frac{1}{27.5} \ln \frac{\dfrac{_5P_0}{_{30}P_{15}}}{\dfrac{_5L_0}{e^{10r}{}_5L_{15} + e^{5r}{}_5L_{20} + \ldots + e^{-15r}{}_5L_{40}}}. \tag{35}$$

The iterative form (35) converges quickly for actual values of r. That it is a generalization of the expression $r = (1/27.5)\ln Th$ just obtained is seen by putting $r = 0$ in (35). We could have used a Newton-Raphson formula, but it would have been more complicated to derive and to program, and could hardly converge more rapidly. Here as elsewhere in demography we know in advance a narrow range within which the parameter must lie (r must be between -0.01 and $+0.05$ for human populations) and this fact permits the devising of simple iterative processes.

Backward Projection

If, as is necessary throughout this section, we may suppose net migration to be unimportant, the number of children younger than 5 years old, $_5P_0$, divided by $_5L_0$ provides an estimate of annual births during the preceding five years. The births are inferred by projecting back along a cohort line, for which stability is not a required condition. We similarly estimate the births of the 5–10 years preceding the date of the observation of the population by dividing $_5P_5$ by $_5L_5$, and similarly for births in earlier years.

To obtain a denominator corresponding to the births as so estimated we bring in the assumption of stability. Suppose the population to have been increasing at rate r, as obtained by any of the other methods, for instance Thompson's index; if it totals P at the time to which our data refer, then it is estimated for a date 2.5 years earlier as $Pe^{-2.5r}$. The birth rate will consist of the births divided by the total population:

$$\frac{_5P_0/_5L_0}{Pe^{-2.5r}}, \quad \frac{_5P_5/_5L_5}{Pe^{-7.5r}}, \quad \ldots,$$

from consecutive five-year age groups. In STABLE the value of r is taken from the estimate using Thompson's index for the 5–9 age group divided by the 20–49 age group.

Generalized Ratios from Pairs of Age Ranges

Coale and Demeny (1966) applied the proportion of the population younger than a given age to infer the rate of increase, on the assumption of stability. We extend and generalize their method, already introduced in Chapter 2.

Suppose that the fraction of the population between ages m and M is observed to be α, and that we have a life table fraction surviving $l(a)$ for that population; then the equation to be solved for the unknown r is readily set down as

$$\alpha = \frac{\int_m^M e^{-ra}l(a)\,da}{\int_n^N e^{-ra}l(a)\,da}, \tag{36}$$

where to begin with $n = 0$, and $N = \omega$ is the oldest possible age, so that the denominator covers the range of life.

However, we need not confine the use of (36) to this special case, and the n and N will be allowed to assume other values. If α is the observed ratio of population between m and M years to that between n and N years, and we equate α to the corresponding ratio from the stable age distribution, then we have (36), which is a generalization of Thompson's ratio of girl children to women, of the "local r" obtained earlier for the life table, and of other commonly used forms. With $m = 0$, $M = 5$, $n = 15$, $N = 45$, for example, we have the most common form of Thompson's index. These values have a special claim on our attention because they represent two successive generations, and so lean less heavily on the assumption of stability. If $m = 5$, $M = 10$, $n = 15$, $N = 20$, we have the estimate of r used in the method we call local stability for ages 10–15 years. If $m = 0$, $M = 20$, $n = 0$, $N = \omega$, we have one of the values used by Coale and Demeny (1967).

A sufficiently close approximation to (36) for the present purpose is, if now n, N, m, and M are all multiples of 5,

$$\alpha - \frac{\sum_{x=m}^{M-5} e^{-r(x+2.5)} {}_5L_x}{\sum_{x=n}^{N-5} e^{-r(x+2.5)} {}_5L_x} = 0, \tag{37}$$

or more concisely, $f(r) = 0$. Suppose r is any approximation and r^* is an improved approximation. Then the Newton-Raphson iteration is obtained from the expansion $f(r^*) = f(r) + (r - r^*)f'(r)$ by equating $f(r^*)$ to zero; $r^* = r - f(r)/f'(r)$ is the iterative form we need, the same that was used in the program ZEROS and elsewhere. The derivatives of numerator and denominator in the ratio in (37) are readily calculable for a given r and given life table. As an alternative to the Newton-Raphson form based on (37) we might use (35) in an obvious generalization.

Insofar as the population is stable and the life table value for number surviving to the given age $l(a)$ is appropriate, the different age ranges, n to M and n to N, will provide identical values of r. In practice the variation in the value of r from one pair of ranges to another will indicate the departures from stability. Even if the population is really close to being stable, variations in r will normally occur owing to inaccuracies of enumeration. Data on some ages are more complete than others; if we take an age range that is complete (or even overstated), like 5–9, and another that is notoriously underenumerated, like 15–19, and use the life table to try to find r from the ratio of the first of these to the second, we are bound to overestimate. For the Dominican Republic in 1960, for example, we obtain an increase of 0.060 for this age interval, as against numbers closer to 0.035 for most others. The narrower the interval over which the inference is made the more influence minor fluctuations have, both genuine fluctuations in birth rates and spurious ones of age misstatement. Hence we have used rather wide age intervals, especially in the denominator.

When the age range of the numerator is identical with that of the denominator, evidently no information on r can be extracted. Less obviously, when the two are different but the one is centered on the other, nothing can be said about r. In place of printing r in this case the program prints 0.88888*. Other instances of non-convergence in the table are indicated by 0.99999*.

Verification and Correction of Methods

We would like to be able to experiment and find what methods are the best for making inferences once and for all, in order to be able to apply these best methods thereafter. Unfortunately experimentation is limited by the fact that neither the age distributions nor the patterns of census error for populations in which vital statistics are good enough to provide r with accuracy are the same as for populations for which r is lacking. The developed countries have a history of fluctuations in birth rates that makes their age distributions highly unstable, and for them most of the methods of this program are not helpful. We hope that methods for inferring rates of increase will work better for those countries for which vital statistics data are lacking than for those on which they are available.

The most serious troubles with the methods of the program INFER arise from changing death rates and, especially, from changing birth rates. Coale (1963) has studied the effect of death rates alone changing; he found that under general conditions, especially if a decline in deaths takes place more or less uniformly in the several age groups, age distribution is not greatly affected. Insofar as it is affected, a correction may be made, and Table III-1 of the United Nations Manual IV provides this in convenient form.

Changing birth rates present a more serious problem. In Table 7 of the Main Tables a generalization of the Bourgeois-Pichat method is provided that can produce good estimates in some circumstances. The device is obtained from a relation first studied by Coale and Zelnik (1963) and described in Keyfitz et al. (1967).

Multiple Estimates

Where any element of arbitrariness enters the selection of the life table a sound practice is to select more than one and so obtain a range of estimates of the rates of birth and natural increase. In principle this applies to all cases in which births are to be inferred for a population on which there are no good statistics on deaths.

The technique to which the computer naturally lends itself is the production of simultaneous multiple estimates. We see that the program INFER applies a large number of methods. We can, of course, study the printout and reject those results that are grossly inconsistent with other information. Rather than deciding in advance that we will apply the Bourgeois-Pichat method here, assuming stability, and that in some other instance Thompson's index is preferable, we run the program for all methods and then examine the results for consistency. If they all give the same answer we are likely to accept it, on the ground that misstatements in the age distribution of the population, an appreciable proportion of immigrants, or changing birth and death rates would normally make different ages give different results. Where they do not agree with one another, some restraint is needed to avoid selecting those that agree with prior unsupported notions.

Program INFER

The input to INFER is the punchout of LIFE, in which the two cards for births by age of mother may be blank.

We are especially grateful to Geoffrey McNicoll for several ingenious contributions to the development of this program.

```
C
C
C                              INFER
C
C
C      THIS PROGRAM ESTIMATES THE BIRTH RATE AND RATE OF NATURAL
C      INCREASE OF A POPULATION FROM AN AGE DISTRIBUTION AND
C      A LIFE TABLE. FIVE METHODS ARE USED, EACH GIVING SEVERAL
C      ESTIMATES OF THE BIRTH RATE AND/OR NATURAL INCREASE DEPENDING
C      ON WHICH SECTION OF THE AGE DISTRIBUTION IS CONSIDERED.
C      CALCULATIONS ARE MADE FIRST FROM MALE AND THEN FROM
C      FEMALE AGE DISTRIBUTIONS.
C
C      FOR AGE GROUP I --
C         J(I) IS THE INITIAL YEAR
C         X(I) IS THE EXACT MID-POINT OF THE GROUP
C         PP(I) IS THE OBSERVED POPULATION
C         VLL(I) IS THE LIFE TABLE STATIONARY POPULATION.
C
C      INPUT CONSISTS OF--
C         TITLE CARD IN FORMAT (19A4)
C         THE FOLLOWING FOUR DISTRIBUTIONS SET UP IN FORMAT (10F8.0)
C         ACCORDING TO AGE GROUPS (0,1-4,5-9,...,85+, UNKNOWN) FOR TWO
C         CARDS EACH
C            MALE POPULATION BY AGE
C            FEMALE POPULATION BY AGE
C            MALE LIFE TABLE STATIONARY POPULATION
C            FEMALE LIFE TABLE STATIONARY POPULATION.
C
C      SETS OF THE ABOVE INPUT MAY BE REPEATED INDEFINITELY.  THE
C      PROGRAM TERMINATES EXECUTION WHEN A BLANK TITLE CARD IS READ.
C
      DIMENSION NAME(19),PP(20),VLL(20),X(20),Y(20),J(20),VKK(20),      1
     A PPF(20),VLLF(20),R1(7),LPH(6),P1(4),P2(4),T(4)                   2
C
C      IAST STORES AN ASTERISK TO BE PRINTED FOLLOWING TABLE ENTRIES
C      A) WHICH REFER TO TWO AGE RANGES WITH APPROXIMATELY THE SAME
C      MEAN IN THE FITTED STABLE POPULATION (R SET TO .88888), OR
C      B) WHICH DO NOT CONVERGE (R SET TO .99999) FOR SOME OTHER
C         REASON.
C
      DATA IAST/1H*/                                                    3
C
C      COLUMNS 1-76 OF THE TITLE CARD ARE STORED IN 'NAME'.
C      COLUMNS 77-80 OF THE TITLE CARD MUST BE BLANK.
C
      READ 1,NAME,IBK                                                   4
    1 FORMAT (20A4)                                                     5
    3 PRINT 5,NAME                                                      6
    5 FORMAT (1H1,19A4)                                                 7
```

```
C
C          READ INPUT DATA.
       READ 7,PP,PPF,VLL,VLLF                                              8
     7 FORMAT (1CF8.C)                                                     9
       PRINT 9                                                             10
     9 FORMAT (6HOMALES )                                                  11
C
C          L = 1 FOR MALE COMPUTATICNS
C          L = 2 FOR FEMALE COMPUTATIONS.
       DO 69 L=1,2                                                         12
       SUM=PP(1)+PP(2)                                                     13
       X(2)=2.5                                                            14
       DO 11 I=3,2C                                                        15
       X(I)=X(I-1)+5.0                                                     16
       J(I)=X(I)-2.5                                                       17
    11 SUM=SUM+PP(I)                                                       18
       J(1)=0                                                              19
       J(2)=1                                                              20
C
C          PRINT THE INPUT.
       PRINT 13                                                            21
    13 FORMAT (/22X,1HX,9X,5HPP(X),10X,5HLL(X)/)                           22
       PRINT 15,(J(I),PP(I),VLL(I), I = 1,19)                              23
    15 FORMAT (20X,I3,2F15.C)                                              24
C
C          COMBINE FIRST TWO AGE GRCUPS
       PP(2) = PP(2) + PP(1)                                               25
       VLL(2) = VLL(2) + VLL(1)                                            26
       J(2) = C                                                            27
C
C       THE FIRST METHOD IS DUE TO BOURGEOIS-PICHAT. IT FITS A STABLE
C       MODEL BY LEAST SQUARES REGRESSION OF THE LOGARITHM OF THE
C       RATIO CF CBSERVED TC STATIONARY POPULATION ON TO AGE. SEPARATE
C       FITS ARE GIVEN FOR DIFFERENT M-YEAR AGE INTERVALS FROM (0,M)
C       TO (70-M,70), WHERE M IS A MULTIPLE OF 5, SET AS FOLLOWS --
C       M = 30                                                             28
C
       PRINT 17                                                            29
    17 FORMAT (// 4X, 14HINFERENCE FROM, 15X, 5HBIRTH, 15X, 15HRATE OF NA  30
      BTURAL / 6X, 1CHAGE  RANGE, 18X, 4HRATE, 18X, 8HINCREASE, //21X,     31
      C 17HBOURCECIS-PICHAT , 10HREGRESSION/)                             32
       MM = M/5                                                            33
       MM1 = (75 - M)/5 + 1                                                34
       DO 21 N = 2, MM1                                                    35
       NN = N + MM - 1                                                     36
       SUMX = C.                                                           37
       SUMY = C.                                                           38
       SUMXY = C.                                                          39
       SUMX2 = C.                                                          40
       DO 19 I = N, NN                                                     41
       Y(I) = ALOG(PP(I)/VLL(I)) - ALOG(SUM) + ALOG(100000.)              42
       SUMX = SUMX + X(I)                                                  43
       SUMY = SUMY + Y(I)                                                  44
       SUMXY = SUMXY + X(I)*Y(I)                                           45
    19 SUMX2 = SUMX2 + X(I)**2                                             46
       WM=FLOAT(MM)                                                        47
       R = -((WM*SUMXY - SUMX*SUMY)/(WM*SUMX2 - SUMX**2))                  48
       B = EXP((SUMY + R*SUMX)/WM)                                         49
       L1 = J(N) + M - 1                                                   50
```

```
   21 PRINT 23,J(N),L1,B,R                                              51
   23 FORMAT (7X,I2, 3H - I2,18X,F6.5,18X,F7.5)                         52
C
C        THE SECCND METHOD INFERS THE RATE OF NATURAL INCREASE ON THE
C        ASSUMPTION OF LOCAL STABILITY WITHIN A 15-YEAR AGE INTERVAL.
      PRINT 25                                                          53
   25 FORMAT (1H0, 18X, 29HASSUMPTION OF LOCAL STABILITY /)             54
      DO 27 I=4,14                                                      55
      R = .1*ALOG(PP(I-1)*VLL(I+1)/(PP(I+1)*VLL(I-1)))                  56
      L2 = J(I+2) - 1                                                   57
   27 PRINT 29, J(I-1),L2,R                                             58
   29 FORMAT ( 7X,I2,3H - I2,42X,F7.5)                                  59
C
C        THE THIRD METHOD IS DUE TO THOMPSON, AND USES THE OBSERVED
C        RATIO OF CHILDREN TC WOMEN, DIVIDED BY THE CORRESPONDING RATIO
C        FROM THE LIFE TABLE, TC ESTIMATE THE RATE OF NATURAL INCREASE.
C        THE PRCGRAM PROVIDES FOUR ESTIMATES BASED ON THE FOLLOWING AGE
C        RANGES FCR CHILDREN AND ADULTS:  0-4/15-44, 5-9/20-49, 10-14/
C        25-54, AND 15-19/30-59.
      PRINT 31                                                          60
   31 FORMAT (1H0, 25X, 15HTHCMPSONS INDEX /)                           61
      P1(1)=PP(1)+PP(2)                                                 62
      P2(1)=PP(5)+PP(6)+PP(7)+PP(8)+PP(9)+PP(10)                        63
      T(1)=VLL(1)+VLL(2)                                                64
      DO 33 M=2,4                                                       65
      P1(M)=PP(M+1)                                                     66
      P2(M)=PP(M+4)+PP(M+5)+PP(M+6)+PP(M+7)+PP(M+8)+PP(M+9)             67
   33 T(M)=VLL(M+1)                                                     68
      DO 38 K=1,4                                                       69
      R=.025                                                            70
      K1=K                                                             71
      K2=K+5                                                            72
      DO 36 I=1,2C                                                      73
      V=C.0                                                             74
      DO 35 II=K1,K2                                                    75
      Z=-17.5-5.*(II-1)                                                 76
   35 V=V+EXP(Z*R)*VLL(II+4)                                            77
      W=EXP((-2.5-5.*(K-1))*R)*T(K)                                     78
      R2=(2./55.)*ALCG((P1(K)*EXP(27.5*R)*V)/(P2(K)*W))                 79
   36 R=R2                                                              80
      L1=J(K+2)-1                                                       81
      L2=J(K+1C)-1                                                      82
      PRINT 37,J(K+1),L1,J(K+4),L2,R                                    83
   37 FORMAT(5X,I2,1H-,I2,1H,,I2,1H-,I2,40X,F7.5)                       84
      IF(K.EQ.2) RR=R                                                   85
   38 CONTINUE                                                          86
C
C        THE FOURTH METHOD INFERS THE BIRTH RATE BY BACKWARD PROJECTION
C        OR REVERSE SURVIVAL CF THE AGE GROUPS 0 - 4, 5 - 9, AND 10 - 14.
C        STABILITY IS NCT NECESSARY, BUT AN ADJUSTMENT FCR POPULATION
C        GROWTH IS MADE USING NATURAL INCREASE ESTIMATED FROM THCMPSONS
C        INDEX.
      PRINT 39                                                          87
   39 FORMAT (1H0,23X 21H BACKWARD PROJECTICN /)                        88
      DO 41 I=2,4                                                       89
      B = PP(I)*100000.*EXP(RR*X(I))/(VLL(I)*SUM)                       90
      L1 = J(I) + 4                                                     91
   41 PRINT 43, J(I),L1,B,RR                                            92
   43 FORMAT ( 7X,I2,3H - I2, 18X,F6.5, 17X,1H( F7.5,1H) )              93
C
```

```
C         THE FIFTH METHOD INFERS THE RATE OF NATURAL INCREASE BY
C         EQUATING THE RATIO (ALPHA) OF THE OBSERVED POPULATION WITHIN
C         TWO GIVEN AGE RANGES TC THE CORRESPONDING RATIO IN A STABLE
C         POPULATION WITH THE GIVEN LIFE TABLE. THE EQUATION IS SOLVED
C         ITERATIVELY FCR R BY THE NEWTON-RAPHSON METHOD. (ONLY A FEW OF
C         THE 14,535 PCSSIBLE CCMFARISONS BETWEEN PAIRS OF AGE RANGES
C         HAVE BEEN USED TO GIVE ESTIMATES OF R.) THOMPSCNS INDEX AND
C         LOCAL STABILITY ARE SPECIAL CASES OF THIS METHCD.
          PRINT 45                                                          94
   45 FORMAT (1HC/12X 55HRATE OF NATURAL INCREASE AS ESTIMATED FROM PAIR   95
     DS CF AGE /12X 56HRANGES BY COMPARISON WITH CUMULATIVE STABLE DISTR    96
     EIBLTION //13X 8HALL AGES 2X 8H    5 +   3X 7H 0 - 69 3X 7H 5 - 69     97
     F,4X,7H1C - 69,4X,7H15 - 69 /)                                        98
C
C         THESE FOUR NESTED DC LCCPS DETERMINE THE PAIRS OF AGE RANGES
C         TO BE CCNSIDERED.
          DO 61 M = 2,8                                                     99
          M1 = M + 3                                                       100
          M2 = M + 5                                                       101
          DO 61 MM = M1,M2,2                                               102
          K = 1                                                            103
          DO 59 NN1 = 1,5,4                                                104
          NN = 20 - NN1                                                    105
          DO 59 N = 2,4                                                    106
          R = RR                                                           107
C
C         THE FOLLCWING DC LOOP PERFORMS THE ITERATIONS.
          DO 51 JJ = 1,25                                                  108
          SUM1 = C.                                                        109
          SUM2 = C.                                                        110
          SUM3 = 0.                                                        111
          SUM4 = C.                                                        112
          SUM5 = C.                                                        113
          SUM6 = 0.                                                        114
C
C         THIS LCOP GIVES THE NUMERATOR OF ALPHA AS ESTIMATED FROM
C         PREVIOUS R.
          DO 47 I = M,MM                                                   115
          VKK(I) = EXP(-R*X(I))*VLL(I)                                     116
          SUM3 = SUM3 + VKK(I)                                             117
          SUM4 = SUM4 + VKK(I)*X(I)                                        118
   47 SUM6 = SUM6 + PP(I)                                                  119
C
C         THIS LCOP GIVES THE DENCMINATOR OF ALPHA AS ESTIMATED FROM
C         PREVICLS R.
          DO 49 I = N,NN                                                   120
          VKK(I) = EXP(-R*X(I))*VLL(I)                                     121
          SUM1 = SUM1 + VKK(I)                                             122
          SUM2 = SUM2 + VKK(I)*X(I)                                        123
   49 SUM5 = SUM5 + PP(I)                                                  124
C
C         THIS LCOP SOLVES THE INTEGRAL EQUATICN TC PROVIDE
C         IMPROVED R.
          ALPHA = SUM6/SUM5                                                125
          AMEAN = SUM4/SUM3                                                126
          AAMEAN = SUM2/SUM1                                               127
          IF (ABS(AAMEAN - AMEAN).LT.0.001) GO TO 55                       128
          RSTAR = R + (ALPHA*SUM1/SUM3 - 1.)/(AAMEAN - AMEAN)              129
          IF (ABS(RSTAR).GT.C.5) GC TO 53                                  130
```

```
      IF (ABS(R - RSTAR).LT.C.CCC005) GO TC 57                    131
   51 R = RSTAR                                                   132
C
C        IF THE PROCESS DCES NCT CCNVERGE, R IS PRINTED AS .99999*.
C        IF THE FITTED STABLE PCPULATION HAS APPROXIMATELY THE SAME
C        MEAN IN BCTH AGE RANGES R IS PRINTED AS .88888*.
C
   53 R1(K) = .99999                                              133
      LPH(K) = IAST                                               134
      GC TO 59                                                    135
   55 R1(K) = .88888                                              136
      LPH(K) = IAST                                               137
      GC TO 59                                                    138
   57 R1(K) = R                                                   139
      LPH(K) = IBK                                                140
   59 K = K + 1                                                   141
      L1 = J(MM) - 1                                              142
   61 PRINT 63, J(M),L1,(R1(K),LPH(K),K = 1,6)                    143
   63 FORMAT (1X,I2,3H - ,I2,3X 6(F9.5,A1),1X)                    144
      IF (L .EC. 2) GC TC 71                                      145
      DO 65 I = 1,19                                              146
      PP(I) = PPF(I)                                              147
   65 VLL(I) = VLLF(I)                                            148
      PRINT 5,NAME                                                149
      PRINT 67                                                    150
   67 FORMAT (8HCFEMALES )                                        151
   69 CONTINUE                                                    152
   71 READ 1,NAME                                                 153
      DO 73 I = 1,10                                              154
      IF (NAME(I) .NE. IBK) GC TC 3                               155
   73 CONTINUE                                                    156
      PRINT 75                                                    157
   75 FORMAT (11H1END CF JCB )                                    158
      STCP                                                        159
      ENC                                                         160
```

```
ENGLAND AND WALES 1968
  414700 1716200 1980500 1716000 1734800 1857200 1538700 1504100 1508800 1540800
 1626400 1411600 1458300 1292800  991000  631100  399200  206600  101100       0
  393600 1631200 1882500 1633100 1681800 1838900 1500800 1426100 1443300 1522100
 1644900 1488800 1585300 1483800 1280500 1033400  753600  464300  275100       0
   98157  390908  487464  486493  484940  482693  480541  478315  475271  469932
  460751  444967  418291  376447  315914  238822  155344   81302   38039       0
   98581  392994  490330  489641  488871  487929  486812  485280  482970  479116
  472723  462731  447963  425638  391456  335660  265710  175219  119454       0


MEXICO 1966
  896000 3266000 3445999 2837000 2290000 1839000 1497000 1238000 1044000  881000
  713000  575000  484000  399000  292000  195000  122000   62439   39562       0
  868000 3126000 3271000 2712000 2235000 1838000 1538000 1311000 1110000  938000
  777000  630000  514000  409000  304000  209000  130000   66502   42498       0
   94262  362518  444092  440214  436888  431577  424178  415246  403362  388803
  372482  353039  328004  295478  252790  204153  152650   98518   52533       0
   95064  366577  448818  445208  442455  438270  432511  425791  417068  406870
  395649  381523  362496  334158  293893  244831  188052  119594   44744       0
```

ENGLAND AND WALES 1968

MALES

X	PP(X)	LL(X)
0	414700.	98157.
1	171620C.	390908.
5	198050C.	487464.
10	1716C0C.	486493.
15	173480C.	484940.
20	185720C.	482693.
25	153870C.	480541.
30	150410C.	478315.
35	15C880C.	475271.
40	154080C.	469932.
45	162640C.	460751.
50	141160C.	444967.
55	145830C.	418291.
60	129280C.	376447.
65	991C0C.	315914.
70	63110C.	238822.
75	39920C.	155344.
80	206600.	81302.
85	101100.	38039.

INFERENCE FROM AGE RANGE	BIRTH RATE	RATE OF NATURAL INCREASE
BOURGEOIS-PICHAT REGRESSION		
0 - 29	.01831	0.00965
5 - 34	.01781	0.00856
10 - 39	.01684	0.00627
15 - 44	.01697	0.00589
20 - 49	.01522	0.00200
25 - 54	.01274	-.00190
30 - 59	.01199	-.00336
35 - 64	.01237	-.00269
40 - 69	.01508	0.00120
ASSUMPTION OF LOCAL STABILITY		
5 - 19		0.01273
10 - 24		-.00869
15 - 29		0.01108
20 - 34		0.02018
25 - 39		0.00086
30 - 44		-.00418
35 - 49		-.01061
40 - 54		0.00330
45 - 59		0.00124
50 - 64		-.00793
55 - 69		0.01056

THCMPSCNS INCEX

0- 4,15-44	0.00927
5- 9,20-49	0.00697
10-14,25-54	0.00302
15-19,30-59	0.00305

BACKWARD PRCJECTICN

0 - 4	.C1876	(0.00697)
5 - 9	.C1812	(0.00697)
10 - 14	.C1629	(0.00697)

RATE OF NATURAL INCREASE AS ESTIMATED FROM PAIRS OF AGE
RANGES BY COMPARISCN WITH CUMULATIVE STABLE DISTRIBUTION

	ALL AGES	5 +	0 - 69	5 - 69	10 - 69	15 - 69
0 - 14	0.0C473	0.00501	C.CC512	C.CC449	0.00483	0.00496
0 - 24	0.00433	0.0C472	C.CC488	C.CC356	0.00445	0.00466
0 - 34	0.003C5	0.00373	C.CC4C7	C.CC226	0.00320	0.00365
0 - 44	0.0C333	0.0C419	C.CC454	0.CC218	0.00355	0.00409
5 - 19	0.00422	C.00462	C.CC48C	C.CC382	0.00434	0.00457
5 - 29	0.00212	0.00294	0.CC338	C.CC112	0.00225	0.00285
5 - 39	0.0C094	C.0C226	C.CC295	-C.CC103	0.00108	0.00212
5 - 49	0.00057	0.0C268	C.CC354	-C.CC397	0.00078	0.00248
10 - 24	0.00172	0.0026C	C.CC3C9	C.CCC63	0.00184	0.00250
10 - 34	-0.0C071	0.0C088	C.CC178	-C.CC317	-0.00068	0.00068
10 - 44	-0.00132	0.0C126	C.CC247	-C.CC671	-0.00135	0.00099
10 - 54	0.99999*	0.00152	C.CC344	C.C1368	-0.00717	0.00095
15 - 29	0.00004	0.00153	C.CC234	-C.CC220	0.00012	0.00136
15 - 39	-0.00287	C.CC001	0.00149	-C.CC860	-0.00313	-0.00036
15 - 49	0.01763	-C.CC028	C.CC237	C.C1318	0.02129	-0.00117
15 - 59	0.00509	0.99999*	C.99999*	C.CC571	0.00448	-0.00066
20 - 34	-0.CC393	-0.00092	C.CCC74	-C.CC976	-0.00437	-0.00136
20 - 44	0.01555	-C.CC063	C.CC222	C.C1218	0.01749	-0.00161
20 - 54	0.00624	0.0C469	C.99999*	C.CC639	0.00580	0.00536
20 - 64	0.00377	0.00173	C.99999*	0.CC449	0.00348	0.00212
25 - 39	0.02227	-0.CC888	-C.CC468	C.C1872	0.02547	-0.01150
25 - 49	0.01057	0.01272	C.99999*	C.CC959	0.01060	0.01399
25 - 59	0.00502	0.00397	C.CC2C4	C.CC538	0.00477	0.00419
25 - 69	0.00493	0.00420	C.CC334	C.CC523	0.00473	0.00434
30 - 44	0.00889	0.0C997	C.C1494	C.CC832	0.00874	0.01069
30 - 54	0.00482	0.00377	C.CC197	C.CC520	0.00458	0.00397
30 - 64	0.00341	0.00233	C.CCC86	0.CC396	0.00324	0.00250
30 - 74	0.00421	0.00352	C.CC278	C.CC456	0.00406	0.00363

ENGLAND AND WALES 1968

FEMALES

X	PP(X)	LL(X)
0	393600.	98581.
1	1631200.	392994.
5	1882500.	490330.
10	1633100.	489641.
15	1681800.	488871.
20	1838900.	487929.
25	1500800.	486812.
30	1426100.	485280.
35	1443300.	482970.
40	1522100.	479116.
45	1644900.	472723.
50	1488800.	462731.
55	1585300.	447963.
60	1483800.	425638.
65	1280500.	391456.
70	1033400.	339660.
75	753600.	265710.
80	464300.	175219.
85	275100.	119454.

INFERENCE FROM AGE RANGE	BIRTH RATE	RATE OF NATURAL INCREASE
BOURGEOIS-PICHAT REGRESSION		
0 - 29	.01628	0.00842
5 - 34	.01606	0.00847
10 - 39	.01549	0.00699
15 - 44	.01569	0.00653
20 - 49	.01370	0.00167
25 - 54	.01053	-.00446
30 - 59	.00936	-.00709
35 - 64	.00992	-.00580
40 - 69	.01245	-.00141
ASSUMPTION OF LOCAL STABILITY		
5 - 19		0.01098
10 - 24		-.01222
15 - 29		0.01096
20 - 34		0.02488
25 - 39		0.00311
30 - 44		-.00779
35 - 49		-.01522
40 - 54		-.00127
45 - 59		-.00169
50 - 64		-.00802
55 - 69		0.00787

THOMPSONS INDEX

0- 4,15-44	0.00873
5- 9,20-49	0.00625
10-14,25-54	0.00215
15-19,30-59	0.00245

BACKWARD PROJECTION

0 - 4	.C1676	(0.00625)
5 - 9	.C1612	(0.00625)
10 - 14	.C1445	(0.00625)

RATE OF NATURAL INCREASE AS ESTIMATED FROM PAIRS OF AGE RANGES BY COMPARISON WITH CUMULATIVE STABLE DISTRIBUTION

	ALL AGES	5 +	C - 6S	5 - 69	10 - 69	15 - 69
0 - 14	0.00350	0.00374	C.CC382	C.CC333	0.00365	0.00376
0 - 24	0.00322	0.00353	C.CC365	C.CC292	0.00338	0.00355
0 - 34	0.00163	0.00221	C.CC251	C.CCC68	0.00161	0.00207
0 - 44	0.00173	0.00247	C.CC28C	C.CCC33	0.00173	0.00233
5 - 19	0.0032C	0.00352	C.CC364	C.CC290	0.00336	0.00353
5 - 29	0.00103	0.00168	C.CC2C4	-C.CCC14	0.00092	0.00147
5 - 39	-0.00028	0.00075	C.CC132	-C.CC270	-0.00072	0.00031
5 - 49	-0.00025	0.00120	C.CC188	-C.CC5C8	-0.00101	0.00065
10 - 24	0.00111	C.00176	C.CC211	-C.CCC03	0.00101	0.00156
10 - 34	-0.00157	-0.00038	C.CCC34	-C.CC456	-0.00232	-0.00103
10 - 44	-0.00184	-0.00011	C.CCC8C	-C.CC770	-0.00322	-0.00104
10 - 54	-0.00243	0.00062	C.CC181	0.C1577	-0.00710	-0.00087
15 - 29	-0.00058	0.00050	C.CC11C	-0.CC311	-0.00109	0.00000
15 - 39	-0.00309	-0.00119	-C.CCC11	-C.CC546	-0.00492	-0.00243
15 - 49	-0.00420	-0.00081	C.CCC75	C.C1549	-0.00983	-0.00313
15 - 59	0.00637	0.00498	C.CC48C	C.CC499	0.00398	-0.00020
20 - 34	-0.00414	-0.00213	-C.CCC92	-C.C1C80	-0.00631	-0.00362
20 - 44	-0.00525	-0.00176	C.CCCCC	0.C1526	0.99999*	-0.00455
20 - 54	0.00867	-0.CC120	C.CC23C	C.CC625	0.00624	0.00847
20 - 64	0.00253	-0.00152	C.99999*	C.CC333	0.00230	0.00099
25 - 39	0.03029	-0.00839	-C.CC575	C.02259	0.99999*	-0.01397
25 - 49	0.01467	C.02038	-C.CC528	C.01C61	0.01265	0.01838
25 - 59	0.00503	0.00439	C.CC362	C.CC477	0.00430	0.00406
25 - 69	0.00352	0.00259	C.CC13C	C.CC377	0.00321	0.00276
30 - 44	0.01400	0.01887	-C.CC534	C.01C33	0.01211	0.01687
30 - 54	0.00530	0.00489	C.CC5C9	C.CC495	0.00456	0.00445
30 - 64	0.00233	0.00103	-C.0C1C9	C.CC292	0.00223	0.00156
30 - 74	0.00268	0.0C187	C.CCC97	0.00308	0.00255	0.00211

MEXICO 1966

MALES

X	PP(X)	LL(X)
0	8560CC.	94262.
1	3266CCC.	362518.
5	3445959.	444092.
10	2837CCC.	440214.
15	2290CCC.	436888.
20	1839CCC.	431577.
25	1497CCC.	424178.
30	1238CCC.	415246.
35	1C44CCC.	4C3362.
40	881CCC.	388803.
45	713CCC.	372482.
50	575CCC.	353039.
55	484CCC.	328004.
60	399CCC.	295478.
65	292CCC.	252790.
70	195CCC.	2C4153.
75	122CCC.	152650.
80	62439.	98518.
85	39562.	52533.

INFERENCE FRCM AGE RANGE	BIRTH RATE	RATE CF NATURAL INCREASE
BOURGEOIS-PICHAT REGRESSION		
0 - 29	.C4631	0.03856
5 - 34	.C4688	0.03884
10 - 39	.C45C7	0.03681
15 - 44	.C4118	0.03347
20 - 49	.C381C	0.03127
25 - 54	.C3673	0.03045
30 - 59	.C3465	0.02900
35 - 64	.C3155	0.02687
40 - 69	.C2974	0.02580
ASSUMPTION CF LOCAL STABILITY		
5 - 19		0.03923
10 - 24		0.04137
15 - 29		0.03956
20 - 34		0.03571
25 - 39		0.03101
30 - 44		0.02744
35 - 49		0.03017
40 - 54		0.03302
45 - 59		0.02602
50 - 64		0.01874
55 - 69		0.02449

THOMPSONS INDEX

0- 4,15-44	0.03714
5- 9,20-49	0.03742
10-14,25-54	0.03652
15-19,30-59	0.03419

BACKWARD PROJECTION

0 - 4	.04524	(0.03742)
5 - 9	.04645	(0.03742)
10 - 14	.04652	(0.03742)

RATE OF NATURAL INCREASE AS ESTIMATED FROM PAIRS OF AGE RANGES BY COMPARISON WITH CUMULATIVE STABLE DISTRIBUTION

	ALL AGES	5 +	0 - 69	5 - 69	10 - 69	15 - 69
0 - 14	0.03522	0.03521	0.03537	0.03556	0.03551	0.03568
0 - 24	0.03376	0.03421	0.03464	0.03407	0.03452	0.03497
0 - 34	0.03247	0.03355	0.03425	0.03271	0.03387	0.03461
0 - 44	0.03162	0.03343	0.03430	0.03177	0.03384	0.03475
5 - 19	0.03391	0.03437	0.03480	0.03431	0.03473	0.03517
5 - 29	0.03040	0.03264	0.03374	0.03020	0.03292	0.03412
5 - 39	0.02569	0.03169	0.03350	0.05216	0.03191	0.03397
5 - 49	0.04429	0.03053	0.03349	0.04056	0.03040	0.03412
10 - 24	0.02687	0.03102	0.03280	0.02556	0.03106	0.03311
10 - 34	0.04848	0.02720	0.03136	0.04550	0.02601	0.03155
10 - 44	0.04131	0.99999*	0.03054	0.03579	0.05141	0.03061
10 - 54	0.03834	0.04437	0.02956	0.03745	0.04050	0.02897
15 - 29	0.04720	0.02147	0.02829	0.04525	0.99999*	0.02783
15 - 39	0.04131	0.04890	0.02485	0.04026	0.04567	0.02232
15 - 49	0.03876	0.04181	0.05572	0.03810	0.04010	0.04778
15 - 59	0.03690	0.03804	0.04140	0.03645	0.03707	0.03795
20 - 34	0.04178	0.04719	0.06416	0.04091	0.04504	0.05825
20 - 44	0.03870	0.04077	0.04612	0.03817	0.03963	0.04281
20 - 54	0.03710	0.03798	0.03950	0.03673	0.03728	0.03789
20 - 64	0.03582	0.03608	0.03612	0.03556	0.03562	0.03524
25 - 39	0.03845	0.04001	0.04320	0.03800	0.03913	0.04106
25 - 49	0.03689	0.03752	0.03835	0.03658	0.03699	0.03729
25 - 59	0.03550	0.03560	0.03543	0.03529	0.03526	0.03485
25 - 69	0.03481	0.03471	0.03422	0.03464	0.03445	0.03382
30 - 44	0.03632	0.03670	0.03700	0.03606	0.03627	0.03624
30 - 54	0.03524	0.03525	0.03499	0.03506	0.03498	0.03455
30 - 64	0.03420	0.03397	0.03337	0.03407	0.03379	0.03311
30 - 74	0.03388	0.03360	0.03295	0.03378	0.03345	0.03275

MEXICC 1966

FEMALES

X	PP(X)	LL(X)
0	868000.	55064.
1	3126000.	366577.
5	3271000.	448818.
10	2712000.	445208.
15	2235000.	442455.
20	1838000.	438270.
25	1538000.	432511.
30	1311000.	425791.
35	1110000.	417068.
40	938000.	406870.
45	777000.	395649.
50	630000.	381523.
55	514000.	362496.
60	409000.	334158.
65	304000.	293893.
70	209000.	244831.
75	130000.	188052.
80	66502.	119594.
85	42498.	44744.

INFERENCE FROM AGE RANGE	BIRTH RATE	RATE OF NATURAL INCREASE
BOURGEOIS-PICHAT REGRESSION		
0 - 29	.04313	0.03595
5 - 34	.04256	0.03491
10 - 39	.04094	0.03309
15 - 44	.03862	0.03103
20 - 49	.03709	0.02994
25 - 54	.03764	0.03045
30 - 59	.03899	0.03125
35 - 64	.03961	0.03152
40 - 69	.04040	0.03188
ASSUMPTION OF LOCAL STABILITY		
5 - 19		0.03666
10 - 24		0.03733
15 - 29		0.03510
20 - 34		0.03090
25 - 39		0.02898
30 - 44		0.02893
35 - 49		0.03040
40 - 54		0.03337
45 - 59		0.03257
50 - 64		0.02994
55 - 69		0.03154

THOMPSONS INDEX

0- 4,15-44	0.03517
5- 9,20-49	0.03436
10-14,25-54	0.03336
15-19,30-59	0.03191

BACKWARD PROJECTION

0 - 4	.04280	(0.03436)
5 - 9	.04281	(0.03436)
10 - 14	.04249	(0.03436)

RATE OF NATURAL INCREASE AS ESTIMATED FROM PAIRS OF AGE
RANGES BY COMPARISON WITH CUMULATIVE STABLE DISTRIBUTION

	ALL AGES	5 +	0 - 69	5 - 69	10 - 69	15 - 69
0 - 14	0.03348	0.03363	0.03370	0.03358	0.03373	0.03380
0 - 24	0.03256	0.03301	0.03324	0.03257	0.03308	0.03333
0 - 34	0.03220	0.03291	0.03321	0.03215	0.03298	0.03331
0 - 44	0.03226	0.03314	0.03342	0.03219	0.03327	0.03357
5 - 19	0.03204	0.03271	0.03303	0.03198	0.03275	0.03310
5 - 29	0.03037	0.03200	0.03261	0.02983	0.03195	0.03266
5 - 39	0.02851	0.03197	0.03277	0.02595	0.03189	0.03286
5 - 49	0.04076	0.03198	0.03302	0.03735	0.03182	0.03321
10 - 24	0.02763	0.03067	0.03178	0.02615	0.03037	0.03173
10 - 34	0.04603	0.02947	0.03154	0.04276	0.02847	0.03142
10 - 44	0.03751	0.02723	0.03177	0.03645	0.04649	0.03164
10 - 54	0.03528	0.03864	0.03177	0.03484	0.03601	0.03146
15 - 29	0.04376	0.02585	0.02981	0.04179	0.02327	0.02925
15 - 39	0.03727	0.04337	0.02921	0.03657	0.04017	0.02765
15 - 49	0.03520	0.03641	0.02959	0.03490	0.03551	0.03996
15 - 59	0.03433	0.03452	0.03566	0.03415	0.03415	0.03421
20 - 34	0.03735	0.04116	0.02965	0.03678	0.03929	0.02159
20 - 44	0.03490	0.03550	0.03831	0.03468	0.03499	0.03609
20 - 54	0.03410	0.03412	0.03423	0.03397	0.03390	0.03375
20 - 64	0.03366	0.03350	0.03317	0.03358	0.03337	0.03299
25 - 39	0.03445	0.03468	0.03550	0.03429	0.03435	0.03456
25 - 49	0.03360	0.03341	0.03302	0.03352	0.03330	0.03287
25 - 59	0.03319	0.03291	0.03241	0.03315	0.03286	0.03237
25 - 69	0.03306	0.03277	0.03231	0.03303	0.03274	0.03229
30 - 44	0.03297	0.03257	0.03180	0.03293	0.03255	0.03186
30 - 54	0.03276	0.03239	0.03179	0.03274	0.03238	0.03183
30 - 64	0.03258	0.03222	0.03168	0.03257	0.03223	0.03173
30 - 74	0.03264	0.03232	0.03187	0.03263	0.03232	0.03189

CHAPTER 12

Standardization

The United States population in mid-1966 was estimated to be 195,857,000, and deaths for the year 1966 were reported to be 1,863,149. This makes an observed crude death rate M of

$$M = \frac{1,863,149}{195,857,000} = 0.00951,$$

often written as 9.51 per thousand population. The reason why this rate is termed crude is that it takes no account of the age and sex distribution. Some populations are concentrated at youthful ages where mortality is low, others contain proportionately more old people; crude rates confound the effects of age distribution with those of mortality as such.

To satisfy ourselves on this point let us compare the populations of Taiwan and the United States. Taiwan shows a crude death rate of 5.36 per thousand, or just a little more than half that of the United States. However considerable Taiwan's progress over the past few years, it is hardly as healthy as this comparison with the United States indicates, and we will not be able to trust demographic statistics at all until such a discrepancy from general knowledge and common sense is straightened up. We cannot blame the difference on defective statistics—for example, unregistered deaths in Taiwan—because we have evidence of their completeness (United Nations Demographic Yearbook, 1967).

Let us divide the population and death figures into two age groups in both countries: younger than age 50, and age 50 and older, and calculate the ratios $_{50}M_0$ and $_{50}M_{50}$. For the younger than 50's we find that Taiwan stands at $1000\,_{50}M_0 = 1000\,_{50}D_0/_{50}P_0 = 2.9$ per thousand, while the United States stands at 2.8 per thousand. For those 50 and older Taiwan shows $1000 \, _{50}M_{50} = 1000 \, _{50}D_{50}/_{50}P_{50} = 27.0$ per thousand compared with 33.0 for the United States. These age-specific rates, for very broad age intervals, deprive Taiwan of much of its apparent superiority. The age intervals can be made narrower—down to the five years used in this book and generally. The sexes can be taken separately. For most such intervals we find the United States favored: at 30–34, for example, its male $1000 \, _5M_{30}$ is 2.188 compared with Taiwan's 2.549. But this does not apply in every age-sex group, and no one can comfortably assess so many separate comparisons. We still want to answer the simple question: which country has higher mortality on the whole?

Direct Standardization

If P_x^s is the population of the standard country, say the United States, and P_x the population of the given country, distributed by age, by age and sex, or indeed by any other classification that might be related to mortality, and if D_x^s and D_x are the deaths for the standard and the given countries, respectively, similarly distributed, then the death rates for the given country are $M_x = D_x/P_x$, and the mean of these weighted by the standard population is

$$\text{SRD} = \frac{\text{SPVM}}{\text{SP}} = \frac{\sum_x (P_x^s)(M_x)}{\sum_x P_x^s},$$

where SPVM is the result of applying the given death rates to the standard population, and SP is the total size of the standard population, in the notation to be used for the FORTRAN program. This is the directly standardized death rate for any partition whatever of the population, including any partition of the span of ages, or age and sex. Equal age intervals are not required, and we will apply the method to age intervals 0, 1–4, 5–9, . . . , 85+.

The ratio of the standardized Taiwanese rate to the crude United States rate is

$$\text{DEX} = \frac{\text{SRD}}{\text{CDRST}} = \frac{\sum (P_x^s)(M_x)/P^s}{\sum (P_x^s)(M_x^s)/P^s} = \frac{\text{SPVM}}{\text{SPSM}},$$

where DEX is an index, SRD the directly standardized rate, CDRST the crude death rate of the standard population. This index associated with direct standardization is analogous to the base-weighted aggregative price index of economics, widely used in comparing consumer prices. To make the analogy, we think of the given mortality rates M_x as the prices of the several commodities in the given year, and the standard rates M_x^s as those of the base year. Then the standard population

$P_x{}^s$ is the quantities of the several commodities that the housewife put in her shopping basket in the base year. The index is the ratio of the cost of filling the basket in the given year to the cost in the base year (Duncan, Cuzzort, and Duncan, 1961; Kitagawa, 1964).

Decomposition of Mortality Differences

Of the difference in crude death rates between two countries, some is attributable to the difference in age distribution, and some to the true difference in death rates. If we call the effect of age structure on the difference in crude rates the *composition* component, and the mortality difference the *rates* component, then we have

$$\text{Difference in crude rates} = \frac{\sum (P_x{}^s)(M_x{}^s)}{P^s} - \frac{\sum (P_x)(M_x)}{P};$$

$$\text{Composition component} = \frac{\sum (P_x{}^s)(M_x)}{P^s} - \frac{\sum (P_x)(M_x)}{P} = \sum M_x \left(\frac{P_x{}^s}{P^s} - \frac{P_x}{P} \right);$$

$$\text{Rates component} = \frac{\sum (P_x{}^s)(M_x{}^s)}{P^s} - \frac{\sum (P_x{}^s)(M_x)}{P^s} = \sum \frac{P_x{}^s}{P^s} (M_x{}^s - M_x).$$

The composition component is a weighted average of the difference in age distributions (where "age" could be replaced by any social characteristic, such as income or education), and the rates component is a weighted average of the difference in age-specific death rates. The sum of the two, calculated according to the expressions just given is exactly equal to the difference in crude rates. This additivity was attained by using one weight from the standard population and the other weight from the given population.

We could take both weights from the standard population to obtain

$$\text{Composition component} = \sum M_x{}^s \left(\frac{P_x{}^s}{P^s} - \frac{P_x}{P} \right);$$

$$\text{Rates component} = \sum \frac{P_x{}^s}{P^s} (M_x{}^s - M_x).$$

The two now do not add to the difference between crude rates in standard and given populations, the discrepancy being the *interaction*:

$$\text{Interaction} = \sum \left(\frac{P_x{}^s}{P^s} - \frac{P_x}{P} \right) (M_x{}^s - M_x).$$

Let us express the interaction in words. If we add the differences between the standard and given age-specific rates, $M_x{}^s - M_x$, by weighting each such difference by the proportion of individuals in the proper age group in the standard population,

$P_x{}^s/P^s$, we get one total; if we add up the same differences with weights taken from the given population, P_x/P, we get another total; the difference between these totals is interaction. The choice of weights is unavoidably arbitrary, and interaction is the ambiguousness in the main comparison, the uncertainty in the difference we are trying to measure. It is related to the correlation between weight-differences, answering the question: Are those ages at which the standard mortality is higher than the given mortality also those at which the standard population is more heavily concentrated? The higher the interaction the more the overall comparison depends on which set of weights is selected, and the less certain is the conclusion based on an index number.

Table L shows rates directly standardized on (a) the population of England and Wales, 1961, which has a large proportion of old people, and (b) that of Mexico, 1960, which has a large proportion of young people. The death rates standardized on (a) are for some countries more than double what they are standardized on (b). We note that on standard (a) the United States has higher mortality than Italy, and on standard (b) Italy has higher mortality than the United States.

The more populations vary in age composition, the more is standardization required for meaningful comparison of mortality. Since World War II, populations around the world have increasingly differed in age structure, since some countries of high fertility no longer have high rates of infant deaths, and therefore have very large proportions of young people. We can see in the tables or by experimenting with the program STABLE what gross differences in age distribution appear when a population having a natural rate of decrease of about one-half percent per year is

TABLE L

Death rates per thousand, directly standardized for age and sex on two standard populations: (a) England and Wales, 1961, and (b) Mexico, 1960.

Population	Standard population	
	(a) England and Wales, 1961	(b) Mexico, 1960
Austria, 1966	11.94	5.21
Canada, 1966	10.14	4.46
Greece, 1966	9.51	4.39
Guatemala, 1964	21.64	16.33
Italy, 1965	11.33	5.15
Sweden, 1966	9.29	3.67
United States, 1966	11.35	4.98

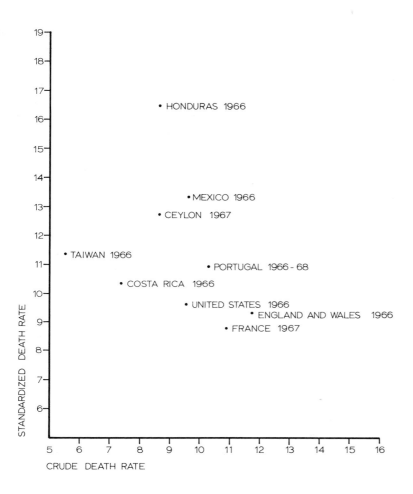

FIGURE 12

Relation of crude and standardized death rates per thousand population,
selected countries.

compared with a population having a rate of increase of about four percent per year.
Since the populations of underdeveloped countries are the ones increasing fastest,
and their younger age distributions offset their poorer health conditions, an overall
correlation of rates is approaching the paradox that the lowest crude death rates are
shown by the countries with worst health conditions. Such is our interpretation
of Figure 12.

Male and Female Mortality: Comparison by Standardization

We have already compared male and female mortality; a further example will show the use of the program DIRECT, and enable us to reiterate an important point of method.

The $\mathring{e}_0$ of Denmark, 1967, is 70.7 for males and 75.4 for females. These numbers are the reciprocals of the death rates in the stationary population, and they contain different implicit weightings of the several ages. The stationary population that has the more favorable mortality will have more old people; favorable mortality causes more individuals to live into the ages at which death rates are higher. Hence under most circumstances the expectation of life will *understate* the difference in mortality between two populations.

The ratio of female to male expectation of life for Denmark, 1967, is 75.4/70.7 = 1.067, and this is the same as the ratio of the male to the female death rate in the stationary population. Males seem to have only 7 percent higher mortality than females. The ratio of the male to the female crude rate is 10.81/8.97 = 1.205. Here as in many other instances (especially for those in which a differential has developed so recently that age distribution has not yet taken account of it), the ratio of crude rates is a better index than the ratio of expectations of life.

However, direct standardization is a clear improvement over both measures. We will weight both male and female age-specific rates by the female age distribution. According to DIRECT, taking females as the standard, we obtain 12.75 as the standardized male rate, and the ratio of this to the crude female rate of 8.97 gives 12.75/8.97 = 1.421. It now looks as if male mortality is 42 percent higher than female mortality.

This result is not independent of which sex is used as the standard age distribution. When we take males as the standard we obtain a ratio of male to female mortality of 10.81/7.51 = 1.439. We can thus say that the true difference is probably between 42 and 44 percent.

The difference between the male crude rate of 10.81 and the female crude rate of 8.97, 1.84 per thousand, is now to be thought of as containing two components that we could have suspected all along partly offset one another: lower favorable female mortality versus more favorable male age composition. The difference of standardized rates gets at the rates component, which is 12.75 − 8.97 = 3.78. A simple way of getting at the composition component is by subtracting from this the difference in crude rates: 3.78 − 1.84 = 1.94.

The composition component thus cancels out about half of the rates component, so that the difference of crude rates is only about half of the true difference in mortality.

We have obtained the striking result that male mortality is more than 40 percent higher than female mortality for Denmark, 1967, while the ratio of expectations of life would put males only 7 percent higher than females in mortality.

Program DIRECT

The program that follows will most often be used for standardizing mortality for age and sex, but it can equally well adjust for any other set of composition variables.

The input includes the number NCATS of categories of composition (38 in a typical age-sex analysis of mortality in which five-year age groups plus the group younger than one year are available).

```
C
C                              DIRECT
C
C
C       STANDARDIZES FOR AGE (OR OTHER VARIABLE) BY DIRECT METHOD,
C       APPLYING AGE-SPECIFIC RATES (FOR EXAMPLE OF DEATH) OF THE
C       GIVEN POPULATION TO STANDARD AGE DISTRIBUTION.
C       THE PROGRAM READS A STANDARD POPULATION, THEN SUCCESSIVE GIVEN
C       POPULATIONS UNTIL A BLANK TITLE CARD (FOR THE NEXT GIVEN
C       POPULATION) IS REACHED.  THE PROGRAM THEN ATTEMPTS TO READ A
C       NEW STANDARD POPULATION.  IF THE TITLE CARD FOR THE STANDARD
C       POPULATION IS ALSO BLANK, THE PROGRAM STOPS.
C
C       INPUT FOR STANDARD POPULATION CONSISTS OF
C          TITLE CARD (ONE CARD IN FORMAT (20A4))
C          NCATS = NUMBER OF AGE GROUPS OR OTHER CATEGORIES TO BE
C             STANDARDIZED (ONE CARD IN FORMAT (I5))
C          STPP = POPULATION NUMBERS (FORMAT (10F8.0) FOR AS MANY CARDS
C             AS NEEDED TO CONTAIN NCATS, I.E. NCATS/10 OR THE NEXT
C             HIGHER INTEGER)
C          STDD = NUMBER OF DEATHS FOR SAME CATEGORIES AS POPULATION
C          (FORMAT (10F8.0))
C       INPUT FOR GIVEN POPULATION IS SAME, EXCEPT NO CARD IS REQUIRED
C          FOR NCATS.
C
C       ONE BLANK CARD SIGNIFIES THAT A NEW STANDARD POPULATION
C       FOLLOWS.  TWO BLANK CARDS IN SUCCESSION TERMINATE THE
C       PROGRAM.
C
      DIMENSION STPP(100),STDD(100),STMM(100),NAMEST(19),NAMGIV(19),       1
     A VPP(100),VDD(100),VMM(100)                                          2
C
      READ 1,NAMEST,IBK                                                    3
    1 FORMAT (19A4,A4)                                                     4
    3 READ 5,NCATS                                                         5
    5 FORMAT (I5)                                                          6
C          NCATS=NUMBER OF CATEGORIES IN POPULATION COMPOSITION (WITH
C          THE ABOVE DIMENSION STATEMENTS NCATS MAY BE AS MUCH AS 100).
C
C          IN THE PRESENT APPLICATION TO MORTALITY STANDARDIZATION FOR
C          AGE AND SEX, 38 CATEGORIES ARE RECOGNIZED.
C
C          FROM HERE TO STATEMENT 7 WE READ THE POPULATION AND DEATHS OF
C          THE STANDARD POPULATION, WITH AS MANY CARDS AS ARE NEEDED TO
C          READ NCATS ENTRIES FOR POPULATION AND DEATHS, 4 IN THE
C          PRESENT EXAMPLE.
      READ 7,(STPP(I),I=1,NCATS)                                           7
      READ 7,(STDD(I),I=1,NCATS)                                           8
    7 FORMAT (10F8.0)                                                      9
```

```
C
C          NEXT WE READ THE TITLE, POPULATION, AND DEATHS OF
C          THE GIVEN POPULATION, DATA ARRANGED JUST AS FOR THE
C          STANDARD PCPULATION.
      READ 1,NAMGIV                                                          10
    9 READ 7,(VPP(I),I=1,NCATS)                                              11
      READ 7,(VDD(I),I=1,NCATS)                                              12
C
      PRINT 11,NAMEST,NAMGIV                                                 13
   11 FORMAT (24H1DIRECT STANDARDIZATION /  26H0STANDARD POPULATION IS -     14
     B- /1X 19A4 /23HCGIVEN PCPULATION IS -- /1X 19A4/1H0 13X 19HSTANDAR     15
     CD POPULATION 13X 16HGIVEN POPULATION / 9H CATEGORY 6X 3HPOP 11X 4H     16
     DRATE 13X 3HPOP 11X 4HRATE /1H0)                                        17
      SP=0.                                                                  18
      VP=0.                                                                  19
      SPSM=0.                                                                20
      VPVM=0.                                                                21
      SPVM=0.                                                                22
      DO 20 I=1,NCATS                                                        23
      SP=SP+STPP(I)                                                          24
      VP=VP+VPP(I)                                                           25
      IF (IFIX(STPP(I)).EQ.C) STPP(I)=.1                                     26
      IF (IFIX(VPP(I)).EQ.0) VPP(I)=.1                                       27
      STMM(I)=STDD(I)/STPP(I)*1000.                                          28
      VMM(I)=VDD(I)/VPP(I)*1CC0.C                                            29
      SPSM=SPSM+STDD(I)                                                      30
      VPVM=VPVM+VCD(I)                                                       31
      SPVM=SPVM+STPP(I)*VMM(I)                                               32
   20 PRINT 27, I,STPP(I),STMM(I),VPP(I),VMM(I)                              33
   27 FORMAT (1X I5,F14.C,F13.2,F18.0,F13.2)                                 34
      CRST=SPSM/SP*1CCC.                                                     35
      CRV=VPVM/VP*1C00.                                                      36
      SRD=SPVM/SP                                                            37
      RATIO=SRD/CRST                                                         38
      PRINT 28, CRST,CRV,SRD,RATIO                                           39
   28 FORMAT (11HCCRUDE RATE F22.2,F31.2 /1H0 13X 37HSTANDARDIZED RATE,      40
     EGIVEN POPULATION = F13.2 /1H0 13X 38HRATIO OF GIVEN TO STANDARD MO     41
     FRTALITY = F13.2 )                                                      42
C
C          WE NOW COMPUTE THE DECOMPOSITION OF RATES.
      CCMPA=0.                                                               43
      CCMPB=0.                                                               44
      COMPC=0.                                                               45
      RATEAB=0.                                                              46
      RATEC=0.                                                               47
      RESB =0.                                                               48
      RESAC=0.                                                               49
      DIFF=CRST-CRV                                                          50
      DO 40 I=1,NCATS                                                        51
      PDIF=STPP(I)/SP-VPP(I)/VP                                              52
      PSUM=STPP(I)/SP+VPP(I)/VP                                              53
      RDIF=STMM(I)-VMM(I)                                                    54
      RSUM=STMM(I)+VMM(I)                                                    55
      COMPA=COMPA+VMM(I)*PDIF                                                56
      RATEAB=RATEAB+(STPP(I)/SP)*RDIF                                        57
      COMPB=COMPB+STMM(I)*PDIF                                               58
      RESB=RESB-PDIF*RDIF                                                    59
      RATEC=RATEC+.5*PSUM*RDIF                                               60
   40 COMPC=COMPC+.5*RSUM*PDIF                                               61
```

```
      PRINT 50, DIFF                                                      62
      PRINT 45, COMPA,RATEAB,RESAC                                        63
      PRINT 60                                                            64
      PRINT 45, COMPB,RATEAB,RESB                                         65
      PRINT 70                                                            66
      PRINT 45, COMPC,RATEC,RESAC                                         67
   45 FORMAT (/31X, 24HCOMPOSITION COMPONENT = ,F8.2/37X, 17HRATES COMPO  68
     FNENT = ,F8.2/20X, 35HINTERACTION (RESIDUAL) COMPONENT = ,F8.2)      69
   50 FORMAT (///5X, 46HDECOMPOSITION OF DIFFERENCE IN CRUDE RATES OF ,   70
     G F8.2//10X, 38HI.   WEIGHTS FROM DIFFERENT POPULATIONS )            71
   60 FORMAT (//10X, 37HII.   WEIGHTS FROM STANDARD POPULATION )          72
   70 FORMAT (//10X, 46HIII.   WEIGHTS FROM AVERAGE OF BOTH POPULATIONS ) 73
      READ 1,NAMGIV                                                       74
      DO 75 I=1,10                                                        75
      IF (NAMGIV(I) .NE. IBK) GO TO 9                                     76
   75 CONTINUE                                                            77
      READ 1,NAMEST                                                       78
      DO 80 I=1,10                                                        79
      IF (NAMEST(I) .NE. IBK) GO TO 3                                     80
   80 CONTINUE                                                            81
      PRINT 85                                                            82
   85 FORMAT (11HIEND OF JOB )                                            83
      STOP                                                                84
      END                                                                 85
```

```
ENGLAND AND WALES 1968
   38
  414700 1716200 1980500 1716000 1734800 1857200 1538700 1504100 1508800 1540800
 1626400 1411600 1458300 1292800  991000  631100  399200  206600  101100  393600
 1631200 1882500 1633100 1681800 1838900 1500800 1426100 1443300 1522100 1644900
 1488800 1585300 1483800 1280500 1033400  753600  464300  275100
    8707    1490     869     677    1545    1712    1347    1554    2447    4653
    8275   13023   23368   34785   43710   43426   42011   32675   27037    6275
    1194     573     431     624     740     794    1077    1739    3153    5569
    7848   12601   19196   27233   37936   47724   49949   58913


MEXICO 1966
  896000 3266000 3445999 2837000 2290000 1839000 1497000 1238000 1044000  881000
  713000  575000  484000  395000  292000  195000  122000   62439   39562  868000
 3126000 3271000 2712000 2235000 1838000 1538000 1311000 1110000  938000  777000
  630000  514000  409000  304000  209000  130000   66502   42498
   68108   31788    7574    3644    4371    5477    5820    5813    7200    6809
    6796    6970    8510    9823   11098    9233    8634    6807   10773   54788
   32138    6811    2988    3404    4192    4557    4393    5428    4662    4936
    5260    6413    8357    9418    8863    8484    8288   15513
```

DIRECT STANCARCIZATION

STANDARD POPULATICN IS --
ENGLAND ANC WALES 1968

GIVEN POPULATICN IS --
MEXICO 1966

CATEGORY	STANCARC PCPULATICN		GIVEN POPULATION	
	POP	RATE	PCP	RATE
1	414700.	21.00	856CC0.	76.01
2	1716200.	0.87	3266CC0.	9.73
3	1980500.	C.44	3445999.	2.20
4	1716000.	C.35	2837CC0.	1.28
5	1734800.	C.89	2290CC0.	1.91
6	1857200.	C.92	1839CC0.	2.98
7	1538700.	C.88	1497C00.	3.89
8	15C4100.	1.C3	1238C00.	4.70
9	1508800.	1.62	1C44C00.	6.90
10	1540800.	3.02	881C00.	7.73
11	1626400.	5.C9	713CC0.	9.53
12	1411600.	9.23	575CC0.	12.12
13	145830C.	16.C2	484C00.	17.58
14	1292800.	26.91	399000.	24.62
15	991C00.	44.11	292000.	38.01
16	631100.	68.81	195000.	47.35
17	399200.	105.24	122CC0.	70.77
18	206600.	158.16	62439.	109.02
19	1C1100.	267.43	39562.	272.31
20	393600.	15.94	868CC0.	63.12
21	1631200.	C.73	3126CC0.	10.28
22	1882500.	C.3C	3271C00.	2.08
23	1633100.	C.26	2712CC0.	1.10
24	168180C.	C.37	2235C00.	1.52
25	1838900.	C.40	1838C00.	2.28
26	150080C.	C.53	1538C00.	2.96
27	14261C0.	C.76	1311000.	3.35
28	144330C.	1.20	1110C00.	4.89
29	1522100.	2.07	938000.	4.97
30	164490C.	3.39	777000.	6.35
31	1488800.	5.27	630CC0.	8.35
32	1585300.	7.95	514CC0.	12.48
33	1483800.	12.94	4C9000.	20.43
34	1280500.	21.27	3C4C00.	30.98
35	1033400.	36.71	2C9C00.	42.41
36	75360C.	63.33	130000.	65.26
37	464300.	107.58	665C2.	124.63
38	275100.	214.15	42498.	365.03

CRUDE RATE   11.87   9.61

STANDARCIZED RATE, GIVEN PCPULATICN =   15.99

RATIO OF GIVEN TC STANDARD MORTALITY =   1.35

DECOMPOSITION OF DIFFERENCE IN CRUDE RATES OF   2.26

    I.   WEIGHTS FROM DIFFERENT POPULATIONS

                        COMPOSITION COMPONENT =   6.38
                              RATES COMPONENT =   -4.11
            INTERACTION (RESIDUAL) COMPONENT =   0.0

    II. WEIGHTS FROM STANDARD POPULATION

                        COMPOSITION COMPONENT =   7.33
                              RATES COMPONENT =   -4.11
            INTERACTION (RESIDUAL) COMPONENT =   -0.95

    III. WEIGHTS FROM AVERAGE OF BOTH POPULATIONS

                        COMPOSITION COMPONENT =   6.85
                              RATES COMPONENT =   -4.59
            INTERACTION (RESIDUAL) COMPONENT =   0.0

```
                    DIRECT STANDARDIZATION

                    STANDARD POPULATICN IS --
                    MEXICO 1966

                    GIVEN POPULATICN IS --
                    ENGLAND AND WALES 1968
```

CATEGORY	STANDARD POPULATICN POP	RATE	GIVEN POPULATION PCP	RATE
1	896000.	76.C1	414700.	21.00
2	3266000.	9.73	1716200.	0.87
3	3445999.	2.20	1980500.	0.44
4	2837000.	1.28	1716000.	0.39
5	2290000.	1.91	1734800.	0.89
6	1839000.	2.98	1857200.	0.92
7	1497000.	3.89	1538700.	0.88
8	1238000.	4.70	1504100.	1.03
9	1044000.	6.90	1508800.	1.62
10	881000.	7.73	1540800.	3.02
11	713000.	9.53	1626400.	5.09
12	575000.	12.12	1411600.	9.23
13	484000.	17.58	1458300.	16.02
14	399000.	24.62	1292800.	26.91
15	292000.	38.C1	991000.	44.11
16	195000.	47.35	631100.	68.81
17	122000.	70.77	399200.	105.24
18	62439.	109.02	206600.	158.16
19	39562.	272.31	101100.	267.36
20	868000.	63.12	393600.	15.94
21	3126000.	10.28	1631200.	0.73
22	3271000.	2.C8	1882500.	0.30
23	2712000.	1.10	1633100.	0.26
24	2235000.	1.52	1681800.	0.37
25	1838000.	2.28	1838900.	0.40
26	1538000.	2.96	1500800.	0.53
27	1311000.	3.35	1426100.	0.76
28	1110000.	4.89	1443300.	1.20
29	938000.	4.97	1522100.	2.07
30	777000.	6.35	1644900.	3.39
31	630000.	8.35	1488800.	5.27
32	514000.	12.48	1585300.	7.95
33	409000.	20.43	1483800.	12.94
34	304000.	30.98	1280500.	21.27
35	209000.	42.41	1033400.	36.71
36	130000.	65.26	753600.	63.33
37	66502.	124.63	464300.	107.58
38	42498.	365.03	275100.	214.15

```
CRUDE RATE              9.61                    11.87

        STANDARDIZED RATE, GIVEN POPULATICN =      4.54

        RATIO OF GIVEN TO STANDARD MORTALITY =     0.47
```

DECOMPOSITION OF DIFFERENCE IN CRUDE RATES OF   -2.26

    I.   WEIGHTS FROM DIFFERENT POPULATIONS

                       COMPOSITION COMPONENT =   -7.33
                             RATES COMPONENT =   5.07
        INTERACTION (RESIDUAL) COMPONENT =   0.0

    II.   WEIGHTS FROM STANDARD POPULATION

                       COMPOSITION COMPONENT =   -6.38
                             RATES COMPONENT =   5.07
        INTERACTION (RESIDUAL) COMPONENT =   -0.95

    III.   WEIGHTS FROM AVERAGE OF BOTH POPULATIONS

                       COMPOSITION COMPONENT =   -6.85
                             RATES COMPONENT =   4.59
        INTERACTION (RESIDUAL) COMPONENT =   0.0

Indirect Standardization

An alternative mode of comparison is called indirect standardization. It dispenses with the rates of the given population, requiring only its age distribution and total annual number of deaths. Indirect standardization begins by asking what the (crude) mortality rate would be if the age-specific rates $M_x{}^s$ of the standard were applied to the age distribution of the given population:

$$\frac{\sum (P_x)(M_x{}^s)}{\sum P_x}.$$

This has little to do with the mortality of the given country, but is an index of its age distribution. Being a measure of the mortality of the standard country, it is a suitable denominator for judging the crude rate of the given country. The ratio of the given country's death rate to this as denominator would be

$$\frac{\sum (P_x)(M_x)}{\sum (P_x)(M_x{}^s)},$$

an index of mortality weighted by the given population distribution. To make this an indirectly standardized death rate we multiply by the crude death rate of the standard population:

$$SRI = \frac{\sum (P_x)(M_x)}{\sum (P_x)(M_x{}^s)} \times \frac{\sum (P_x{}^s)(M_x{}^s)}{\sum P_x{}^s}.$$

Program INDIR

The program INDIR implements indirect standardization. Its input, notation, and general style are very close to those of DIRECT.

```
C
C                              INDIR
C
C
C          ADJUSTS THE CRUDE RATE CF EVENTS (E.G. CRUDE DEATH RATE OF A
C          GIVEN COUNTRY) SO AS TC ELIMINATE THE EFFECTS OF DISTRIBUTION
C          AMONG THE CATEGORIES.  THE METHOD USED IS INDIRECT
C          STANDARDIZATION, IN THIS EXAMPLE APPLIED TO DEATHS BY AGE
C          CATEGORIES.
C
          DIMENSION STPP(100),STDD(100),STMM(100),NAMEST(19),VPP(100),       1
        A NAMGIV(19),ISTPP(100)                                              2
C
C          INPUT DATA
C             NAMEST=TITLE CF STANDARD POPULATION (1 CARD IN FORMAT (20A4))
C             NCATS=NUMBER CF CATEGORIES (1 CARD IN FORMAT (I5))
C             STPP=DISTRIBUTION CF THE STANDARD POPULATION (NUMBER OF CARDS
C                EQUAL TO OR JUST LARGER THAN NCATS/10 (IN FORMAT (10F8.0))
C             STDD=DISTRIBUTION CF EVENTS (E.G. DEATHS) OCCURRING TO THE
C                STANDARD POPULATION (SAME NUMBER OF CARDS AND SAME
C                FORMAT AS STPP)
C             NAMGIV=TITLE CF GIVEN POPULATION (1 CARD IN FORMAT (20A4))
C             VPP=DISTRIBUTION OF THE GIVEN POPULATION (NUMBER OF CARDS
C                EQUAL TO CR JUST LARGER THAN NCATS/10) (10F8.0)
C             VPVM=TOTAL NUMBER CF EVENTS OCCURRING TO GIVEN POPULATION,
C                ENTERED ON LAST CARD OF VPP, IN 8 COLUMNS JUST FOLLOWING
C                LAST CATEGORY OF VPP.
C
C          AGE GROUPS ARE C,1-4,5-9,10-14,...,85+, UNKNOWN
C          (38 CATEGORIES) IN THE EXAMPLE SHOWN.
C
C          READ DATA FOR STANDARD POPULATION
          READ 2,NAMEST,IBK                                                  3
        2 FORMAT (20A4)                                                      4
        4 READ 6,NCATS                                                       5
        6 FORMAT (I5)                                                        6
          READ 8,(STPP(I),I=1,NCATS)                                         7
          READ 8,(STDD(I),I=1,NCATS)                                         8
        8 FORMAT (10F8.0)                                                    9
C
C          READ TITLE, DISTRIBUTION, AND TOTAL EVENTS FOR GIVEN POPULATION.
          READ 2,NAMGIV                                                     10
       10 READ 8,(VPP(I),I=1,NCATS),VPVM                                    11
C
C          PRINT HEADINGS.
          PRINT 15,NAMEST,NAMGIV                                            12
       15 FORMAT (25H1INDIRECT STANDARDIZATION/26HOSTANDARD POPULATION IS -- 13
        B /1X 19A4 /23HOGIVEN POPULATION IS -- /1X 19A4/1HO 23X              14
        C 19HSTANDARD POPULATION 14X 16HGIVEN POPULATION /9H CATEGORY 9X     15
```

```
      D 3HPOP 9X 6HDEATHS 9X 4HRATE 15X 3HPOP /)                          16
C
C         ZEROIZE ARRAYS AND CALCULATE RATES.
      SP=0.                                                               17
      VP=0.                                                               18
      SPSM=0.                                                             19
      VPSM=0.                                                             20
      DO 20 I=1,NCATS                                                     21
      SP=SP+STPP(I)                                                       22
      SPSM=SPSM+STDD(I)                                                   23
      VP=VP+VPP(I)                                                        24
      ISTPP(I)=1000000*STPP(I)                                           25
      IF(ISTPP(I).EQ.0) STPP(I)=1.                                        26
      IF (STPP(I).EQ.C.) STPP(I)=.1                                       27
      STMM(I)=STDD(I)/STPP(I)*1000.0                                      28
      VPSM=VPSM+VPP(I)*STMM(I)                                            29
   20 PRINT 27, I,STPP(I),STDD(I),STMM(I),VPP(I)                          30
   27 FORMAT (1X I5,4X 2F13.C,F13.2,10X F10.0)                            31
C
C         CDRV, CDRST=CRUDE RATES CF EVENTS OF THE GIVEN AND STANDARD
C             POPULATIONS.
C         SRI=INDIRECTLY STANDARDIZED RATE OF EVENTS.
C
      CDRV=VPVM/VP*1CCC.C                                                 32
      CDRST=SPSM/SP*1CCC.0                                                33
      SRI=(VPVM/VPSM)*CDRST*1CCC.0                                        34
C
C         PRINT RESULTS.
      PRINT 30, CDRST,CDRV,SRI                                           35
   30 FORMAT (13HC CRUDE RATES 23X F13.2,F20.2 /52H  INDIRECTLY STANDARD  36
     EIZED RATE, GIVEN POPULATICN, IS    F10.2 )                          37
C
C         FIND IF FURTHER WORK IS TO BE DONE.
      READ 33,NAMGIV                                                      38
   33 FORMAT(19A4)                                                        39
      DO 32 I=1,1C                                                        40
      IF (NAMGIV(I) .NE. IBK) GC TO 10                                    41
   32 CONTINUE                                                            42
      READ 33,NAMEST                                                      43
      DO 34 I=1,1C                                                        44
      IF (NAMEST(I) .NE. IBK) GC TO 4                                     45
   34 CONTINUE                                                            46
      PRINT 36                                                            47
   36 FORMAT (11H1END CF JOB )                                            48
      STOP                                                                49
      END                                                                 50
```

```
ENGLAND AND WALES 1968
  38
  414700 1716200 1980500 1716000 1734800 1857200 1538700 1504100 1508800 1540800
 1626400 1411600 1458300 1292800  991000  631100  399200  206600  101100  393600
 1631200 1882500 1633100 1681800 1838900 1500800 1426100 1443300 1522100   16449
 1488800 1585300 1483800 1280500 1033400  753600  464300  275100
    8707    1490     869     677    1545    1712    1347    1554    2447    4653
    8275   13023   23368   34785   43710   43426   42011   32675   27037    6275
    1194     573     431     624     740     794    1077     173    3153    5569
    7848   12601   19196   27233   37936   47724   49949   58913


MEXICO 1966
  896000 3266000 3445999 2837000 2290000 1839000 1497000 1238000 1044000  881000
  713000  575000  484000  399000  292000  195000  122000   62439   39562  868000
 3126000 3271000 2712000 2235000 1838000 1538000 1311000 1110000  938000  777000
  630000  514000  409000  304000  209000  130000   66502   42498  424141




MEXICO 1966
  38
  896000 3266000 3445999 2837000 2290000 1839000 1497000 1238000 1044000  881000
  713000  575000  484000  399000  292000  195000  122000   62439   39562  868000
 3126000 3271000 2712000 2235000 1838000 1538000 1311000 1110000  938000  777000
  630000  514000  409000  304000  209000  130000   66502   42498
   68108   31788    7574    3644    4371    5477    5820    5813    7200    6809
    6796    6970    8510    9823   11098    9233    8634    6807   10773   54788
   32138    6811    2988    3404    4192    4557    4393    5428    4662    4936
    5260    6413    8357    9418    8863    8484    8288   15513


ENGLAND AND WALES 1968
  414700 1716200 1980500 1716000 1734800 1857200 1538700 1504100 1508800 1540800
 1626400 1411600 1458300 1292800  991000  631100  399200  206600  101100  393600
 1631200 1882500 1633100 1681800 1838900 1500800 1426100 1443300 1522100 1644900
 1488800 1585300 1483800 1280500 1033400  753600  464300  275100  576880
```

INDIRECT STANDARDIZATION

STANDARD POPULATION IS --
MEXICO 1966

GIVEN POPULATION IS --
ENGLAND AND WALES 1968

CATEGORY	POP	STANDARD POPULATION DEATHS	RATE	GIVEN POPULATION POP
1	896000.	68108.	76.01	414700.
2	3266000.	31788.	9.73	1716200.
3	3445999.	7574.	2.20	1980500.
4	2837000.	3644.	1.28	1716000.
5	2290000.	4371.	1.91	1734800.
6	1839000.	5477.	2.98	1857200.
7	1497000.	5820.	3.89	1538700.
8	1238000.	5813.	4.70	1504100.
9	1044000.	7200.	6.90	1508800.
10	881000.	6809.	7.73	1540800.
11	713000.	6756.	9.53	1626400.
12	575000.	6970.	12.12	1411600.
13	484000.	8510.	17.58	1458300.
14	399000.	9823.	24.62	1292800.
15	292000.	11098.	38.01	991000.
16	195000.	9233.	47.35	631100.
17	122000.	8634.	70.77	399200.
18	62439.	6807.	109.02	206600.
19	39562.	10773.	272.31	101100.
20	868000.	54788.	63.12	393600.
21	3126000.	32138.	10.28	1631200.
22	3271000.	6811.	2.08	1882500.
23	2712000.	2988.	1.10	1633100.
24	2235000.	3404.	1.52	1681800.
25	1838000.	4192.	2.28	1838900.
26	1538000.	4557.	2.96	1500800.
27	1311000.	4393.	3.35	1426100.
28	1110000.	5428.	4.89	1443300.
29	938000.	4662.	4.97	1522100.
30	777000.	4936.	6.35	1644900.
31	630000.	5260.	8.35	1488800.
32	514000.	6413.	12.48	1585300.
33	409000.	8357.	20.43	1483800.
34	304000.	9418.	30.98	1280500.
35	209000.	8863.	42.41	1033400.
36	130000.	8484.	65.26	753600.
37	66502.	8288.	124.63	464300.
38	42498.	15513.	365.03	275100.

CRUDE RATES   9.61   11.87
INDIRECTLY STANDARDIZED RATE, GIVEN POPULATION, IS   7.14

INDIRECT STANDARDIZATION

STANDARD POPULATION IS --
ENGLAND AND WALES 1968

GIVEN POPULATION IS --
MEXICO 1966

| CATEGORY | STANDARD POPULATION | | | GIVEN POPULATION |
	POP	DEATHS	RATE	POP
1	414700.	8707.	21.00	896000.
2	1716200.	1490.	0.87	3266000.
3	1980500.	869.	0.44	3445999.
4	1716000.	677.	0.39	2837000.
5	1734800.	1545.	0.89	2290000.
6	1857200.	1712.	0.92	1839000.
7	1538700.	1347.	0.88	1497000.
8	1504100.	1554.	1.03	1238000.
9	1508800.	2447.	1.62	1044000.
10	1540800.	4653.	3.02	881000.
11	1626400.	8275.	5.09	713000.
12	1411600.	13023.	9.23	575000.
13	1458300.	23368.	16.02	484000.
14	1292800.	34785.	26.91	399000.
15	991000.	43710.	44.11	292000.
16	631100.	43426.	68.81	195000.
17	399200.	42011.	105.24	122000.
18	206600.	32675.	158.16	62439.
19	101100.	27037.	267.43	39562.
20	393600.	6275.	15.94	868000.
21	1631200.	1194.	0.73	3126000.
22	1882500.	573.	0.30	3271000.
23	1633100.	431.	0.26	2712000.
24	1681800.	624.	0.37	2235000.
25	1838900.	740.	0.40	1838000.
26	1500800.	794.	0.53	1538000.
27	1426100.	1077.	0.76	1311000.
28	1443300.	1730.	1.20	1110000.
29	1522100.	3153.	2.07	938000.
30	1644900.	5569.	3.39	777000.
31	1488800.	7848.	5.27	630000.
32	1585300.	12601.	7.95	514000.
33	1483800.	19196.	12.94	409000.
34	1280500.	27233.	21.27	304000.
35	1033400.	37936.	36.71	209000.
36	753600.	47724.	63.33	130000.
37	464300.	49949.	107.58	66502.
38	275100.	58913.	214.15	42498.

CRUDE RATES   11.87   9.61
INDIRECTLY STANDARDIZED RATE, GIVEN POPULATION, IS   25.12

Direct and Indirect Standardization Compared

A relation exists between the standardized direct and indirect rates. We may exemplify by comparing Sweden, 1967, with Europe, 1965, noting that the crude death rates for both sexes combined are 10.14 per thousand for Sweden compared with 10.20 for Europe. It looks as if Sweden's mortality is not appreciably lower than that of Europe. Standardization will show that this is incorrect: in fact it is very much lower.

To begin with the direct comparison, we find that on the standard of Europe, the death rate of Sweden is 8.15 per thousand. If both Sweden and Europe had the age distribution of Europe their crude rates would be 8.15 and 10.20, respectively, giving a ratio of 8.15/10.20 = 0.799.

Let us check this against the reverse comparison, which is to say using the Swedish age-distribution as the standard. Now we find that the European death rate standardized on Sweden is 12.53, and this is to be compared with the crude rate for Sweden of 10.14. This time Sweden is 10.14/12.53 = 0.809 of Europe. The reverse comparison would not be expected to provide results the same as that given in the preceding paragraph, since the age distributions of Sweden and Europe constitute different weightings for the several age-sex rates.

Is the mortality of Sweden really 0.799 that of Europe, or is it 0.809 that of Europe? The answer is indeterminate between these two numbers; an investigator straining after precision could take the average of the two, as is sometimes done in price comparisons, but this is an arbitrary solution.

Now let us turn to indirect standardization. Here we find that when Europe is the standard, Sweden's crude rate adjusts to 8.25, or 8.25/10.20 = 0.809 of that of Europe. Again reversing, interchanging the standard and the given country by making Sweden the standard, we find Europe's rate to be adjusted to 12.69, so that Sweden is 10.14/12.69 = 0.799 of Europe. We do not have two new index numbers for indirect standardization, but the same 0.809 and 0.799, now obtained with Europe and Sweden, respectively, as the standards instead of vice versa.

This suggests the rule: When given population V is compared with standard population S on the direct method, the ratio is the same as the reciprocal of the ratio of given population S to standard V on the indirect method. In symbols, the index of the direct method for V in terms of S (where P is population and M mortality, and summation is over age-sex groups) is

$$\sum P_S M_V / \sum P_S M_S,$$

and the same index on the indirect method is

$$\sum P_V M_V / \sum P_V M_S.$$

The reader can show that if we interchange V and S in the indirect formula we obtain the reciprocal of the direct formula.

CHAPTER 13

Interpolation and Graduation

The first program included in this chapter, POLATE, fits a number of polynomial curves of the form $y = a + bx + cx^2 + \ldots$ to an age distribution provided as data. The curves for successive age intervals are tangential to each other, and they preserve exactly the distribution provided as input. When the input data are preserved, fitting is called *interpolation*; when some degree of smoothing occurs, so that the original data are not preserved, we have *graduation*, exemplified by the program GRAD. A number of methods of interpolation are in common use, and our program POLATE follows the one developed by Thomas Greville and expressed in the form of Greville's multipliers. The program can be adapted to any other set of multipliers by replacing the three DATA statements.

Program POLATE

The first example printed out is the female age distribution of England and Wales, 1968. The input starts with 1,681,800 for ages 15–19, and it is distributed into the first line of the second section of the table (page 272). The first entry is 309,784, which is the estimate of the number at age 15 years; 321,107 is the estimate of the number at age 16 years, etc. These in turn are broken down in the first two lines of the third section of the output, on page 273; the estimate is 61,284 between exact ages 15.0 and 15.2 years, 61,574 between 15.2 and 15.4 years, etc. Such interpolation is by no means the equivalent of exact counts, but for some purposes may be an acceptable substitute for them.

```
C
C                              POLATE
C
C
      DIMENSION PP(20),SK(1CC),SKSK(500),TITLE(20)                              1
C
C       INTERPCLATES FROM FIVE-YEAR GROUPS, FIRST TO SINGLE
C       YEARS OF AGE AND THEN TO FIFTHS OF A YEAR.  THE METHOD IS
C       OSCULATORY INTERPOLATION IN THE FORM OF GREVILLE MULTIPLIERS.
C       TO USE OTHER MULTIPLIERS ONLY THE DATA-STATEMENTS OF THE
C       SUBROUTINE NEED REPLACEMENT.
C
C       PP IS INPUT DATA, THE INTERPOLATED VALUES SK AND SKSK
C       ARE COMPUTED BY 'OSCUL'.
C       INPUT ENTERED AS FOLLOWS
C         NPOPS=NUMBER OF POPULATIONS TO BE GRADUATED, 1 CARD
C            IN FORMAT (I5)
C         TITLE=NAME OF POPULATION, 1 CARD IN FORMAT (20A4)
C         N,M=INITIAL AGE OF BEGINNING AND ENDING AGE GROUPS,
C            1 CARD IN FORMAT (2I5)
C         PP=NUMBERS IN AGE-GROUPS TO BE GRADUATED, 2 CARDS IN
C            FORMAT (10F8.0)
C
      READ 5, NPOPS                                                             2
    5 FORMAT (I5)                                                               3
      DO 145 L=1,NPOPS                                                          4
      READ 11C, TITLE,N,M,PP                                                    5
  110 FORMAT (20A4/2I5/(10F8.0))                                                6
      N=N/5+2                                                                   7
      M=M/5+2                                                                   8
      PP(2)=PP(1)+PP(2)                                                         9
      PRINT 111, TITLE                                                         10
  111 FORMAT (1H1,20A4)                                                        11
      PRINT 115                                                                12
  115 FORMAT (1H3,9X,3HAGE 16X 10HPOPULATION //)                               13
      DO 120 I=N,M                                                             14
      I2=5*I-1C                                                                15
  120 PRINT 125, I2,PP(I)                                                      16
  125 FORMAT (10X,I4,1CX,F15.C)                                                17
      CALL OSCUL (PP,20,SK,1CC,N,M,N)                                          18
C        PP IS GRADUATED FROM PP(N) TO PP(M+4).
C
      IF (SK(1).LT.C.) GO TO 145                                               19
      J=5*(M-N+1)                                                              20
      CALL OSCUL (SK,1CC,SKSK,5CC,1,J,N)                                       21
  145 CONTINUE                                                                 22
      STOP                                                                     23
      END                                                                      24
```

```
      SUBROUTINE CSCUL (VK,N,SK,M,MSTART,MSTOP,NS)                      25
      DIMENSION VK(N),SK(M),AAA(5,5),XXX(5,5),YYY(5,5),ZZZ(5,5)         26
C
C         VK IS THE VECTOR OF INPUT DATA.  EACH DATUM IS SPLIT INTO
C     FIVE NUMBERS WHICH SUM TO THE ORIGINAL DATUM, THE GRADUATION
C     BEING DONE BY GREVILLE MULTIPLIERS FROM VK(MSTART) TO VK(MSTOP).
C     THE GRADUATED VALUES ARE STORED AS OUTPUT IN SK.   THEREFORE THE
C     DIMENSION M OF SK MUST BE AT LEAST FIVE TIMES (MSTOP-MSTART+1).
C
      DATA ZZZ/+.3237,+.2586,+.1956,+.1370,+.0851,-.1252,-.0744,-.0064, 27
     1 +.0680,+.1380,-.0786,+.0076,+.0376,+.0300,+.0034,+.1180,+.0136,  28
     2 -.0384,-.0520,-.0412,-.0379,-.0054,+.0116,+.0170,+.0147/         29
C     THIS IS THE FIRST PANEL OF GREVILLE MULTIPLIERS.
C
      DATA XXX/+.0420,+.0094,-.0114,-.0205,-.0195,+.1936,+.2264,+.2296, 30
     1 +.2020,+.1484,-.0248,-.0396,-.0284,+.0130,+.0798,-.0192,+.0024,  31
     2 +.0136,+.0100,-.0068,+.0084,+.0014,-.0034,-.0045,-.0019/         32
C     THIS IS THE SECOND PANEL OF GREVILLE MULTIPLIERS.
C
      DATA YYY/-.0117,-.0019,+.0048,+.0061,+.0027,+.0804,+.0156,-.0272, 33
     1 -.0404,-.0284,+.1570,+.2206,+.2448,+.2206,+.1570,-.0284,-.0404,  34
     2 -.0272,+.0156,+.0804,+.0027,+.0061,+.0048,-.0019,-.0117/         35
C     THIS IS THE MIDDLE PANEL OF GREVILLE MULTIPLIERS.
C
      L=0                                                               36
C         THIS INDEX TELLS WHICH PANEL OF MULTIPLIERS TO USE,
C     DEPENDING ON WHETHER WE ARE AT THE BEGINNING, MIDDLE, OR
C     END OF THE AGE DISTRIBUTION.
C
      IF (MSTOP-MSTART.GE.4) GO TO 14                                   37
C
C         THE GREVILLE MULTIPLIERS ARE 5 BY 5 MATRICES, SO THERE MUST BE
C     AT LEAST FIVE AGE GROUPS FOR THE MATRIX MULTIPLICATION TO WORK.
      PRINT 12                                                          38
   12 FORMAT (1H0, 41HINTERVAL OF GRADUATION TOO SHORT -- ABORT )       39
      SK(1)=-99.                                                        40
C         IF THERE ARE FEWER THAN FIVE AGE GROUPS, SK(1) IS RETURNED
C     WITH A NEGATIVE VALUE.
      RETURN                                                            41
C
C         THE GRADUATION REQUIRES BRINGING INTO POSITION THE
C     APPROPRIATE ARRAY OF MULTIPLIERS.
                                                                        42
   14 DO 15 I=1,5                                                       43
      DO 15 J=1,5                                                       44
   15 AAA(I,J)=ZZZ(I,J)
      ISTART=MSTART                                                     45
      ISTOP=MSTART                                                      46
      INCR=0                                                            47
   24 DO 25 I=ISTART,ISTOP                                              48
      II=(I-MSTART)*5                                                   49
      DO 25 J=1,5                                                       50
      IIJ=II+J                                                          51
      SK(IIJ)=0.                                                        52
      DO 25 K=1,5                                                       53
      IKINCR=I+K-1+INCR                                                 54
   25 SK(IIJ)=SK(IIJ)+AAA(J,K)*VK(IKINCR)                               55
C         THE LOOP ENDING AT 25 IS THE GRADUATION PROPER.
C
      L=L+1                                                             56
```

```
      GO TO (30,40,30,60,50),L                                     57
   30 DO 35 I=1,3                                                  58
      I6=6-I                                                       59
      DO 35 J=I,5                                                  60
      J6=6-J                                                       61
      X=AAA(I,J)                                                   62
      AAA(I,J)=AAA(I6,J6)                                          63
   35 AAA(I6,J6)=X                                                 64
      X=AAA(4,5)                                                   65
      AAA(4,5)=AAA(2,1)                                            66
      AAA(2,1)=X                                                   67
C
C
C        NOW THE NEW AAA, TRANSPOSE OF THE PRIOR AAA, REQUIRED FOR THE
C        LAST TWO PANELS.
C
C        WITH L=1 WE CALCULATE THE LAST PANEL OF GRADUATED AGES.
C        L/2=0, AND ISTART, ISTOP, AND INCR ARE APPROPRIATELY VALUED.
C        IF L=3 WE ARE CALCULATING THE SECOND TO LAST PANEL OF GRADUATED
C        AGES. L/2=1, AND ISTART, ISTOP, AND INCR ARE APPROPRIATELY
C        VALUED.
      ISTART=MSTOP-L/2                                             68
      ISTOP=MSTOP-L/2                                              69
      INCR=-4+L/2                                                  70
      GO TO 24                                                     71
   40 DO 45 I=1,5                                                  72
      DO 45 J=1,5                                                  73
   45 AAA(I,J)=XXX(I,J)                                            74
      ISTART =MSTART+1                                             75
      ISTOP=MSTART+1                                               76
      INCR=-1                                                      77
      GO TO 24                                                     78
   60 DO 65 I=1,5                                                  79
      DO 65 J=1,5                                                  80
   65 AAA(I,J)=YYY(I,J)                                            81
      ISTART=MSTART+2                                              82
      ISTOP=MSTOP-2                                                83
      INCR=-2                                                      84
      GO TO 24                                                     85
   50 CONTINUE                                                     86
C
C        THE REMAINING STATEMENTS PRINT OUT THE RESULTS.
      IF(N.EQ.20) GO TO 54                                         87
      PRINT 53                                                     88
   53 FORMAT(1H1,23X,27HGRADUATION INTO FIFTHS OF A/5H  AGE,28X,    89
     111HYEAR OF AGE,21X,9HTOTAL FOR/13X,2HO.,8X,2H.2,9X,2H.4,9X,   90
     22H.6,9X,2H.8,7X,9HAGE GROUP/)                                91
      GO TO 56                                                     92
   54 PRINT 55, (I,I=1,4)                                          93
   55 FORMAT (1H1 22X 23HGRADUATION INTO SINGLE /5H  AGE 23X 12HYEARS OF  94
     G AGE 25X 9HTOTAL FOR /13X,1HO,4I11,7X,9HAGE GROUP/)          95
   56 DO 70 I=MSTART,MSTOP                                         96
      IF(N.EQ.20) GO TO 57                                         97
      I1=(NS-2)*5+I-1                                              98
      GO TO 58                                                     99
   57 I1=5*I-10                                                    100
   58 J=5*(I-MSTART)                                               101
      TOTAL=0.                                                     102
      DO 68 K=1,5                                                  103
      JK=J+K                                                       104
```

```
 68 TOTAL=TCTAL+SK(JK)                                                    105
    IB=J+1                                                                106
    IE=J+5                                                                107
 70 PRINT 75, I1,(SK(K),K=IB,IE),TOTAL                                    108
 75 FORMAT (1X I3,2X 5F11.C,F13.0 )                                       109
    RETURN                                                                110
    END                                                                   111
```

```
    2
ENGLAND AND WALES 1968 FEMALES
    15    45
    393600 1631200 1882500 1633100 1681800 1838900 1500800 1426100 1443300 1522100
   1644900 1488800 1585300 1483800 1280500 1033400  753600  464300  275100        0


MEXICO 1966 MALES
   10    75
   1764000 6392000 6716999 5549000 4525000 3677000 3035000 2549000 2154000 1819000
   1490000 1205000  998000  808000  596000  404000  252000  128941   82060
```

```
ENGLAND AND WALES 1968 FEMALES


        AGE                 POPULATION


        15                  1681800.
        20                  1838900.
        25                  1500800.
        30                  1426100.
        35                  1443300.
        40                  1522100.
        45                  1644900.
```

	GRADUATION INTO SINGLE					
AGE	YEARS OF AGE					TOTAL FOR
	0	1	2	3	4	AGE GROUP
15	309784.	321107.	335601.	350854.	364453.	1681799.
20	374169.	378147.	374904.	364257.	347421.	1838898.
25	327192.	307757.	293588.	286549.	285713.	1500798.
30	286167.	285492.	285162.	284806.	284473.	1426098.
35	284911.	286329.	288228.	290552.	293280.	1443298.
40	296430.	300014.	304025.	308434.	313196.	1522099.
45	318244.	323509.	328916.	334387.	339843.	1644899.

AGE	GRADUATION INTO FIFTHS OF A YEAR OF AGE					TOTAL FOR AGE GROUP
	0.	.2	.4	.6	.8	
15	61284.	61574.	61912.	62295.	62719.	309784.
16	63179.	63673.	64196.	64744.	65314.	321106.
17	65902.	66503.	67114.	67731.	68351.	335601.
18	68969.	69582.	70185.	70773.	71344.	350854.
19	71896.	72424.	72923.	73389.	73820.	364452.
20	74214.	74570.	74881.	75145.	75358.	374169.
21	75524.	75640.	75693.	75682.	75607.	378147.
22	75478.	75295.	75047.	74731.	74352.	374903.
23	73923.	73445.	72908.	72314.	71667.	364257.
24	70984.	70270.	69518.	68731.	67918.	347421.
25	67092.	66264.	65433.	64608.	63794.	327191.
26	62995.	62222.	61497.	60828.	60216.	307757.
27	59642.	59111.	58647.	58255.	57932.	293588.
28	57650.	57411.	57241.	57142.	57104.	286548.
29	57104.	57121.	57144.	57164.	57179.	285713.
30	57209.	57247.	57261.	57245.	57205.	286166.
31	57157.	57118.	57087.	57069.	57061.	285491.
32	57055.	57046.	57035.	57021.	57005.	285162.
33	56992.	56980.	56964.	56946.	56925.	284806.
34	56906.	56892.	56886.	56889.	56900.	284472.
35	56917.	56938.	56971.	57015.	57069.	284910.
36	57131.	57196.	57264.	57333.	57404.	286328.
37	57479.	57559.	57642.	57729.	57818.	288228.
38	57911.	58008.	58107.	58210.	58316.	290551.
39	58424.	58537.	58653.	58772.	58894.	293280.
40	59020.	59150.	59282.	59419.	59559.	296430.
41	59702.	59849.	59999.	60153.	60310.	300014.
42	60471.	60634.	60802.	60972.	61146.	304024.
43	61322.	61501.	61684.	61869.	62057.	308434.
44	62248.	62441.	62637.	62835.	63035.	313196.
45	63237.	63441.	63647.	63855.	64064.	318244.
46	64275.	64487.	64701.	64915.	65131.	323509.
47	65347.	65565.	65783.	66001.	66220.	328916.
48	66439.	66658.	66877.	67097.	67315.	334386.
49	67534.	67752.	67969.	68186.	68402.	339843.

MEXICO 1966 MALES

AGE	POPULATION
10	5549000.
15	4525000.
20	3677000.
25	3035000.
30	2549000.
35	2154000.
40	1819000.
45	1490000.
50	1205000.
55	998000.
60	808000.
65	596000.
70	404000.
75	252000.

GRADUATION INTO SINGLE YEARS OF AGE

AGE	0	1	2	3	4	TOTAL FOR AGE GROUP
10	1202190.	1153766.	1107703.	1063734.	1021598.	5548991.
15	981047.	941863.	903864.	866976.	831248.	4524995.
20	796864.	764128.	733368.	704688.	677952.	3676997.
25	652607.	628444.	605680.	584244.	564023.	3034997.
30	544923.	526743.	509235.	492271.	475826.	2548998.
35	459971.	444772.	430209.	416252.	402795.	2153998.
40	389879.	377185.	364193.	350753.	336989.	1818998.
45	323448.	310383.	297629.	285247.	273291.	1489998.
50	261537.	250220.	239920.	230756.	222566.	1204999.
55	214797.	207118.	199969.	192038.	184477.	997999.
60	177161.	169910.	162165.	153806.	144958.	807999.
65	136065.	127402.	118934.	110746.	102852.	595999.
70	95210.	87779.	80555.	73569.	66887.	404000.
75	60605.	54826.	49665.	45239.	41666.	252000.

GRADUATION INTO FIFTHS OF A YEAR OF AGE

AGE	0.	.2	.4	.6	.8	TOTAL FOR AGE GROUP
10	244434.	242415.	240417.	238440.	236484.	1202189.
11	234548.	232631.	230734.	228856.	226996.	1153765.
12	225155.	223331.	221524.	219734.	217960.	1107702.
13	216202.	214459.	212732.	211019.	209321.	1063733.
14	207636.	205965.	204307.	202661.	201028.	1021598.
15	199407.	197797.	196199.	194611.	193034.	981046.
16	191467.	189911.	188364.	186825.	185296.	941862.
17	183776.	182266.	180764.	179271.	177786.	903863.
18	176310.	174844.	173386.	171937.	170497.	866975.
19	169068.	167648.	166239.	164840.	163452.	831247.
20	162075.	160711.	159360.	158021.	156696.	796863.

21	155385.	154089.	152809.	151545.	150299.	764127.
22	149069.	147853.	146656.	145476.	144314.	733367.
23	143167.	142034.	140920.	139823.	138743.	704687.
24	137678.	136624.	135581.	134547.	133522.	677951.
25	132509.	131508.	130514.	129527.	128548.	652607.
26	127579.	126622.	125676.	124743.	123823.	628444.
27	122913.	122014.	121125.	120247.	119380.	605679.
28	118523.	117676.	116839.	116012.	115194.	584244.
29	114385.	113585.	112795.	112015.	111243.	564023.
30	110480.	109725.	108977.	108237.	107504.	544923.
31	106778.	106058.	105344.	104634.	103928.	526743.
32	103229.	102534.	101843.	101156.	100473.	509234.
33	99795.	99121.	98450.	97784.	97121.	492271.
34	96463.	95809.	95160.	94516.	93877.	475825.
35	93242.	92613.	91989.	91370.	90757.	459971.
36	90149.	89547.	88949.	88357.	87769.	444771.
37	87187.	86609.	86037.	85469.	84907.	430209.
38	84350.	83797.	83247.	82700.	82158.	416251.
39	81618.	81082.	80553.	80030.	79512.	402795.
40	78997.	78483.	77973.	77465.	76960.	389878.
41	76455.	75950.	75441.	74928.	74410.	377184.
42	73891.	73370.	72843.	72312.	71777.	364193.
43	71239.	70699.	70155.	69606.	69053.	350752.
44	68499.	67946.	67395.	66847.	66303.	336989.
45	65760.	65219.	64684.	64154.	63630.	323448.
46	63110.	62592.	62075.	61560.	61046.	310383.
47	60535.	60027.	59523.	59021.	58522.	297628.
48	58026.	57533.	57045.	56561.	56082.	285247.
49	55606.	55133.	54659.	54184.	53709.	273291.
50	53238.	52771.	52305.	51842.	51381.	261537.
51	50924.	50474.	50034.	49604.	49185.	250220.
52	48773.	48368.	47974.	47590.	47216.	239920.
53	46850.	46491.	46142.	45802.	45472.	230756.
54	45148.	44828.	44511.	44196.	43883.	222565.
55	43574.	43268.	42960.	42652.	42343.	214797.
56	42034.	41727.	41422.	41118.	40817.	207118.
57	40516.	40215.	39914.	39613.	39312.	199569.
58	39011.	38711.	38409.	38106.	37801.	192038.
59	37495.	37191.	36891.	36596.	36304.	184477.
60	36012.	35720.	35430.	35143.	34857.	177161.
61	34571.	34282.	33988.	33688.	33381.	169910.
62	33071.	32758.	32439.	32114.	31783.	162165.
63	31448.	31110.	30767.	30417.	30063.	153806.
64	29707.	29349.	28991.	28634.	28277.	144958.
65	27920.	27564.	27210.	26859.	26512.	136065.
66	26167.	25823.	25479.	25137.	24796.	127402.
67	24456.	24119.	23784.	23452.	23122.	118934.
68	22795.	22469.	22146.	21826.	21509.	110746.
69	21193.	20880.	20569.	20259.	19952.	102852.
70	19646.	19342.	19040.	18740.	18441.	95210.
71	18144.	17848.	17554.	17262.	16971.	87779.
72	16682.	16395.	16109.	15825.	15544.	80555.
73	15264.	14987.	14712.	14439.	14168.	73569.
74	13901.	13636.	13374.	13116.	12861.	66887.
75	12609.	12361.	12117.	11877.	11641.	60605.
76	11409.	11182.	10960.	10743.	10531.	54826.
77	10324.	10123.	9927.	9737.	9554.	49665.
78	9376.	9205.	9041.	8883.	8733.	45239.
79	8590.	8454.	8325.	8205.	8092.	41666.

Program GRAD

GRAD analyzes a bell-shaped distribution given in five-year age intervals, providing the mean, variance, and skewness, a graduation to half-years of age by a Type III curve whose moments are those of the original distribution, and a graph of the fitted curve.

Input to the program in the example shown is the array BB(20), the number of births occurring to women in five-year age intervals. The program is equally suited to the net maternity function, the number of births to women in the stable population, the number of births by age of father in the observed or stable population, or similar sets of numbers entered as BB(20)—any distribution that is approximately bell-shaped.

The format of the input is as elsewhere (10F8.0) with two cards required. The number at age 10–14 years goes into columns 25–32, the number at age 15–19 years into columns 33–40, etc. In columns 73–80 of the second card the total is punched, this serving as a check on errors of transcription.

As the program stands, the fitted curve is the Pearson Type III, or incomplete gamma function, which has the form

$$B(x) = Bc^k x^{k-1} e^{-cx} / \Gamma(k),$$

where x is age, B is total births, $\Gamma(k)$ is the gamma function, approximated for our purpose by

$$\Gamma(k) = \sqrt{2\pi}\, k^{k-1/2} e^{-k+1/12k},$$

and k and c are constants fitted by $k = \mu^2/\sigma^2$ and $c = \mu/\sigma^2$ to the mean μ and the variance σ^2 of the $B(x)$ distribution. Our $B(x)$ was introduced into demography by Wicksell (1931).

A simple extension of the same program permits the fitting of several curves to a given set of birth or other data, and their tracing on the output paper.

```
C
C
C                              GRAD
C
C
C      CALCULATES MOMENTS AND GRADUATES BIRTHS BY AGE OF
C      MOTHER OR ANY SIMILAR DISTRIBUTION.  IN THIS EXAMPLE A
C      PEARSON TYPE III CURVE IS FITTED BY MOMENTS, FOLLOWING
C      WICKSELL.
C
       DIMENSION BB(20),SUM(5),NAME(19),X(100),Y(100),YD(100)        1
C
C         INPUT --
C         TITLE CARD (19A4)
C         BB(I)=THE NUMBER OF BIRTHS TO WOMEN IN AGE GROUP I, WITH
C         BIRTHS AT AGE 10-14 PUNCHED IN COLUMNS 25-32, AT AGE 15-19
C         IN COLUMNS 33-40,...., USING TWO CARDS FOR THE DISTRIBUTION.
C         BB(20)=TOTAL NUMBER OF BIRTHS AND SHOULD EQUAL TBB.
C
C         SETS OF THE ABOVE INPUT MAY BE REPEATED INDEFINITELY.  THE
C         PROGRAM TERMINATES EXECUTION WHEN A BLANK TITLE CARD IS READ.
C
       READ 1,NAME,IBK                                                2
     1 FORMAT (20A4)                                                  3
     3 PRINT 5,NAME                                                   4
     5 FORMAT (1H1,19A4)                                              5
C
C         READ THE BIRTHS BY AGE OF MOTHER.
       READ 7,BB                                                      6
     7 FORMAT (10F8.0/10F8.0)                                         7
C
C         PRINT THE INPUT.
       PRINT 9                                                        8
     9 FORMAT (11H0INPUT DATA )                                       9
       PRINT 11,(I,I=10,35,5)                                        10
    11 FORMAT (14H0AGE OF MOTHER,I7,5I10)                            11
       PRINT 13,(BB(I),I=4,9)                                        12
    13 FORMAT (7H BIRTHS,6X,6F10.0)                                  13
       PRINT 11,(I,I=40,65,5)                                        14
       PRINT 13, (BB(I),I=10,15)                                     15
       TBB=0.                                                        16
       ABAR=0.                                                       17
       DO 17 J=1, 3                                                  18
       SUM(J)=0.                                                     19
       DO 15 I=4,13                                                  20
       IF (J.EQ.1) TBB=TBB+BB(I)                                     21
       H=I                                                           22
    15 SUM(J) = SUM(J) + BB(I)*(5.*H-7.5-ABAR)**J                    23
    17 IF (J.EQ.1) ABAR=SUM(1)/TBB                                   24
       PRINT 19,TBB,BB(20)                                           25
```

```
   19 FORMAT (/10X,14HCCMPUTED TBB =,F10.0/16X,8HBB(20) =,F10.0)           26
C         THE CCMPARISON OF TBB AND BB(20) IS A CHECK FOR
C         DATA CARD ERRORS.
C
      VAR=SUM(2)/TBB                                                       27
      THIRD=SUM(3)/TBB                                                     28
      BETA1=THIRD**2/VAR**3                                               29
      PRINT 20                                                            30
   20 FORMAT (///8X,7HMCMENTS)                                            31
      PRINT 21, ABAR, VAR, THIRD, BETA1                                   32
   21 FORMAT(/12X,6HABAR =,F10.5/13X,5HVAR =,F10.5/11X,7HTHIRD =,         33
     A F10.5/10X,8HBETA 1 =,F10.5)                                        34
                                                                          35
      WK=ABAR**2/VAR                                                      36
      WC=ABAR/VAR                                                         37
      PRINT 22
   22 FORMAT(//8X,18HWICKSELL CCNSTANTS)                                  38
      PRINT 23,WK,WC                                                      39
   23 FORMAT (/14X,4HWK =,F1C.5/14X,4HWC =,F10.5)                         40
      PRINT 25                                                            41
   25 FORMAT (1H1,19X,34HBIRTHS GRADUATED BY BIRTH FUNCTION / 1H0         42
     B 2(4X,3HAGE,5X,6HBIRTHS,4X,12HDISTRIBUTION,3X),1X /)                43
C
C         PUT AGES IN X(I).
      X(1)=10.25                                                          44
      DO 27 I=2,1CO                                                       45
   27 X(I)=X(I-1)+C.5                                                     46
C
C         COMPUTE BIRTHS AND THEIR DISTRIBUTICN.
      DO 29 I=1,1CO                                                       47
      Y(I)=BRTH (TBB,WK,WC,X(I))                                          48
   29 YD(I)=Y(I)/TBB                                                      49
C
C         PRINT THE RESULTS.
      DO 31 I=1,5C                                                        50
   31 PRINT 33,X(I),Y(I),YD(I),X(I+50),Y(I+50),YD(I+50)                   51
   33 FORMAT (1X,F8.2,F1C.0,F14.5,F13.2,F10.0,F14.5)                      52
      CALL GRAPH (YD,1,1,81,X)                                            53
C
C         CHECK FOR ANOTHER SET CF INPUT DATA.
      READ 1,NAME                                                         54
      DC 35 I=1,1C                                                        55
      IF (NAME(I) .NE. IBK) GC TC 3                                       56
   35 CONTINUE                                                            57
      PRINT 37                                                            58
   37 FORMAT (11H1END CF JOB )                                            59
      STCP                                                                60
      END                                                                 61


C
      FUNCTICN BRTH(B,K,C,X)                                              62
      REAL K                                                              63
      ZA=ALOG(B/X)+K*ALCG(C*X)-C*X                                        64
      ZB=ALOG(2.5C6)+(K-.5)*ALCG(K)-K+1.0/(12.0*K)                        65
      Z=ZA-ZB                                                             66
      BRTH=EXP(Z)                                                         67
      RETURN                                                              68
      END                                                                 69
```

```
C
      SUBROUTINE GRAPH (GGG,MC, MIN, MAX, ABCISA)                        70
C     GGG(I,J)=VARIABLES TC BE GRAPHED
C     MO=NUMBER OF VARIABLES TO BE GRAPHED LESS THAN OR EQUAL TO 5
C     MIN,MAX=LIMIT CF SUBSCRIPTS OF VARIABLES TO BE GRAPHED
C     ABCISA=VARIABLE DENCTING THE ABCISSA NUMBERS.
      DIMENSION MAY( 51),KO(5), GGG(MAX,MO),ABCISA(MAX ) ,   SCALE(2),    71
     1 L(7)                                                              72
      DATA MAY /51*1H /,L /1HI,1H ,1H1,1H2,1H3,1H4,1H5/                  73
      PRINT 63                                                          74
   63 FCRMAT (1H1)                                                      75
      VMAX = .C8                                                        76
C
C     SCALE THE ABCISSA.
      MAY(2) =L(1)                                                      77
      MAY(26)=L(1)                                                      78
      MAY(51)=L(1)                                                      79
      SCALE(1)=.5*VMAX                                                  80
      SCALE(2)=VMAX                                                     81
      IZERC=0                                                           82
      PRINT 9, IZERC, SCALE, MAY                                        83
    9 FORMAT (1H1,I9, F24.5, F25.5 / 1HX, 7X, 51A1)                     94
C
C     RESTORE BLANKS.
      MAY(2) = L(2)                                                     85
      MAY(26)=L(2)                                                      86
      MAY(51)=L(2)                                                      87
      FACTOR = 49./VMAX                                                 88
C
C     GRAPH CGG.
      DO 20 I=MIN,MAX                                                   89
      DO 30 J=1,MC                                                      90
      KE= FACTCR*CGG(I,J)+1.5                                           91
      KO(J)= KE                                                         92
      IF(KE.LE.C) KE=1                                                  93
      IF(KE.GT.126) KE=126                                              94
C
C     SET ENTRIES IN 'MAY'.
      GO TO (51,52,53,54,55),J                                          95
   51 MAY(KE)=L(3)                                                      96
      GO TO 30                                                          97
   52 MAY(KE)=L(4)                                                      98
      GO TO 3C                                                          99
   53 MAY(KE)=L(5)                                                     100
      GC TO 3C                                                         101
   54 MAY(KE)=L(6)                                                     102
      GO TO 3C                                                         103
   55 MAY(KE)=L(7)                                                     104
   30 CONTINUE                                                         105
      PRINT 21, ABCISA(I), MAY                                         106
   21 FORMAT (1X,F6.2, 2H- ,   51A1)                                   107
C
C     RESTORE BLANKS.
      DO 31 J=1,MC                                                     108
      KE=KC(J)                                                         109
   31 MAY(KE)=L(2)                                                     110
   20 CONTINUE                                                         111
C
```

```
C       SCALE THE ABCISSA AGAIN.
      MAY(2)=L(1)                                                    112
      DO 4 K=26,51,25                                                113
    4 MAY(K)= L(1)                                                   114
      PRINT 8, MAY, IZERC,  SCALE                                    115
    8 FORMAT (8X, 51A1/1HY,IS, F24.5,  F25.5//)                      116
      RETURN                                                         117
      END                                                            118
```

```
ENGLAND AND WALES 1968
        0         0         C       222     81853    295946    240807    125316     58083     15904
     1140         1         C         C         C         0         0    421130    398142    819272


MEXICO 1966
        0         0         C      339C    213986    537112    491128    328540    241290    107736
    17383         0         C         0         C         0         0   1004002    936563   1940565
```

ENGLAND AND WALES 1968

INPUT DATA

AGE CF MCTHER	10	15	2C	25	30	35
BIRTHS	222.	81853.	295946.	240807.	125316.	58083.

AGE CF MOTHER	40	45	5C	55	60	65
BIRTHS	15904.	114C.	1.	0.	0.	0.

```
        CCMPUTED TBB =    819272.
            BB(20) =      819272.


                MCMENTS

              ABAR =  26.48346
               VAR =  33.88806
             THIRC = 125.1C193
             BETA 1 =   C.4C215


            WICKSELL CONSTANTS

              WK =  2C.69676
              WC =   0.78150
```

BIRTHS GRADUATED BY BIRTH FUNCTION

AGE	BIRTHS	DISTRIBUTION	AGE	BIRTHS	DISTRIBUTION
10.25	137.	0.00017	35.25	16533.	0.02018
10.75	237.	0.00029	35.75	14761.	0.01802
11.25	393.	0.00048	36.25	13129.	0.01603
11.75	626.	0.00076	36.75	11634.	0.01420
12.25	962.	0.00117	37.25	10271.	0.01254
12.75	1432.	0.00175	37.75	9036.	0.01103
13.25	2066.	0.00252	38.25	7922.	0.00967
13.75	2899.	0.00354	38.75	6922.	0.00845
14.25	3964.	0.00484	39.25	6028.	0.00736
14.75	5290.	0.00646	39.75	5233.	0.00639
15.25	6901.	0.00842	40.25	4529.	0.00553
15.75	8814.	0.01076	40.75	3908.	0.00477
16.25	11036.	0.01347	41.25	3362.	0.00410
16.75	13563.	0.01655	41.75	2883.	0.00352
17.25	16378.	0.01999	42.25	2466.	0.00301
17.75	19453.	0.02374	42.75	2104.	0.00257
18.25	22747.	0.02776	43.25	1790.	0.00218
18.75	26208.	0.03199	43.75	1518.	0.00185
19.25	29774.	0.03634	44.25	1285.	0.00157
19.75	33380.	0.04074	44.75	1085.	0.00132
20.25	36954.	0.04511	45.25	913.	0.00111
20.75	40422.	0.04934	45.75	767.	0.00094
21.25	43712.	0.05335	46.25	643.	0.00078
21.75	46757.	0.05707	46.75	538.	0.00066
22.25	49495.	0.06041	47.25	449.	0.00055
22.75	51875.	0.06332	47.75	373.	0.00046
23.25	53856.	0.06574	48.25	310.	0.00038
23.75	55404.	0.06763	48.75	257.	0.00031
24.25	56502.	0.06897	49.25	213.	0.00026
24.75	57140.	0.06975	49.75	176.	0.00021
25.25	57324.	0.06997	50.25	145.	0.00018
25.75	57065.	0.06965	50.75	119.	0.00015
26.25	56387.	0.06883	51.25	98.	0.00012
26.75	55320.	0.06752	51.75	80.	0.00010
27.25	53901.	0.06579	52.25	65.	0.00008
27.75	52171.	0.06368	52.75	53.	0.00007
28.25	50175.	0.06124	53.25	43.	0.00005
28.75	47959.	0.05854	53.75	35.	0.00004
29.25	45567.	0.05562	54.25	29.	0.00004
29.75	43047.	0.05254	54.75	23.	0.00003
30.25	40441.	0.04936	55.25	19.	0.00002
30.75	37788.	0.04612	55.75	15.	0.00002
31.25	35126.	0.04288	56.25	12.	0.00001
31.75	32487.	0.03965	56.75	10.	0.00001
32.25	29900.	0.03650	57.25	8.	0.00001
32.75	27389.	0.03343	57.75	6.	0.00001
33.25	24974.	0.03048	58.25	5.	0.00001
33.75	22671.	0.02767	58.75	4.	0.00000
34.25	20491.	0.02501	59.25	3.	0.00000
34.75	18443.	0.02251	59.75	3.	0.00000

```
            0                    0.C4CCC                  0.08000
            I                       I                        I
   10.25-   1
   10.75-   1
   11.25-   1
   11.75-   1
   12.25-    1
   12.75-    1
   13.25-     1
   13.75-     1
   14.25-      1
   14.75-       1
   15.25-        1
   15.75-         1
   16.25-          1
   16.75-           1
   17.25-            1
   17.75-             1
   18.25-              1
   18.75-               1
   19.25-                1
   19.75-                 1
   20.25-                  1
   20.75-                   1
   21.25-                    1
   21.75-                     1
   22.25-                      1
   22.75-                       1
   23.25-                        1
   23.75-                        1
   24.25-                         1
   24.75-                          1
   25.25-                          1
   25.75-                          1
   26.25-                          1
   26.75-                         1
   27.25-                        1
   27.75-                        1
   28.25-                       1
   28.75-                      1
   29.25-                     1
   29.75-                    1
   30.25-                   1
   30.75-                  1
   31.25-                 1
   31.75-                1
   32.25-               1
   32.75-              1
   33.25-             1
   33.75-            1
   34.25-           1
   34.75-          1
   35.25-         1
   35.75-         1
   36.25-        1
   36.75-       1
   37.25-       1
   37.75-      1
   38.25-      1
```

```
38.75-        1
39.25-        1
39.75-       1
40.25-      1
40.75-      1
41.25-      1
41.75-     1
42.25-     1
42.75-     1
43.25-    1
43.75-    1
44.25-    1
44.75-    1
45.25-    1
45.75-    1
46.25- 1
46.75- 1
47.25- 1
47.75- 1
48.25- 1
48.75- 1
49.25- 1
49.75- 1
50.25- 1
       I               I                        I
       0            0.C400C                  0.08000
```


MEXICO 1966

INPUT DATA

AGE OF MOTHER	10	15	2C	25	30	35
BIRTHS	3390.	213986.	537112.	491128.	328540.	241290.

AGE OF MOTHER	40	45	5C	55	60	65
BIRTHS	107736.	17383.	0.	0.	0.	0.

```
      CCMPUTED TBB =   1940565.
            BB(20) =   1940565.
```

MOMENTS

```
       ABAR =  28.C8859
        VAR =  50.73373
      THIRC = 163.92447
     BETA 1 =   0.20578
```

WICKSELL CONSTANTS

```
         WK =  15.55161
         WC =   0.55366
```

BIRTHS GRACUATED BY BIRTH FUNCTION

AGE	BIRTHS	DISTRIBUTION	AGE	BIRTHS	DISTRIBUTION
10.25	896.	C.00046	35.25	55879.	0.02880
10.75	1359.	C.00070	35.75	52003.	0.02680
11.25	1997.	0.00103	36.25	48259.	0.02487
11.75	2851.	0.00147	36.75	44661.	0.02301
12.25	3963.	0.00204	37.25	41219.	0.02124
12.75	5378.	C.00277	37.75	37945.	0.01955
13.25	7137.	C.00368	38.25	34840.	0.01795
13.75	9276.	C.00478	38.75	31910.	0.01644
14.25	11827.	C.00609	39.25	29155.	0.01502
14.75	14812.	C.00763	39.75	26576.	0.01370
15.25	18241.	0.00940	40.25	24170.	0.01245
15.75	22116.	0.01140	40.75	21931.	0.01130
16.25	26423.	C.01362	41.25	19857.	0.01023
16.75	31137.	0.01605	41.75	17940.	0.00924
17.25	36220.	C.01866	42.25	16175.	0.00834
17.75	41619.	C.02145	42.75	14553.	0.00750
18.25	47274.	C.02436	43.25	13069.	0.00673
18.75	53114.	C.02737	43.75	11712.	0.00604
19.25	59062.	C.03044	44.25	10477.	0.00540
19.75	65034.	0.03351	44.75	9355.	C.00482
20.25	70943.	C.03656	45.25	8337.	0.00430
20.75	76708.	C.03953	45.75	7417.	0.00382
21.25	82239.	0.04238	46.25	6587.	0.00339
21.75	87464.	0.04507	46.75	5840.	0.00301
22.25	92310.	0.04757	47.25	5169.	0.00266
22.75	96708.	0.04983	47.75	4568.	0.00235
23.25	100608.	C.05184	48.25	4030.	0.00208
23.75	103961.	0.05357	48.75	3550.	0.00183
24.25	106737.	0.05500	49.25	3123.	0.00161
24.75	108909.	0.05612	49.75	2742.	0.00141
25.25	110467.	0.05693	50.25	2405.	0.00124
25.75	111412.	0.05741	50.75	2106.	0.00109
26.25	111750.	0.05759	51.25	1842.	0.00095
26.75	111498.	0.05746	51.75	1608.	0.00083
27.25	110680.	0.05703	52.25	1402.	0.00072
27.75	109333.	0.05634	52.75	1221.	0.00063
28.25	107494.	0.05539	53.25	1062.	0.00055
28.75	105204.	0.05421	53.75	923.	0.00048
29.25	102512.	0.05283	54.25	801.	0.00041
29.75	99464.	0.05126	54.75	694.	0.00036
30.25	96110.	0.04953	55.25	600.	0.00031
30.75	92502.	C.04767	55.75	519.	0.00027
31.25	88687.	0.04570	56.25	448.	0.00023
31.75	84712.	C.04365	56.75	386.	0.00020
32.25	80625.	0.04155	57.25	333.	0.00017
32.75	76467.	0.03940	57.75	286.	0.00015
33.25	72277.	0.03725	58.25	246.	0.00013
33.75	68094.	C.03509	58.75	211.	0.00011
34.25	63947.	0.03295	59.25	181.	0.00009
34.75	59867.	C.03085	59.75	155.	0.00008

```
              0                        0.C40CC                    0.08000
              I                           I                          I
    10.25-    1
    10.75-    1
    11.25-     1
    11.75-     1
    12.25-     1
    12.75-      1
    13.25-      1
    13.75-       1
    14.25-        1
    14.75-         1
    15.25-          1
    15.75-           1
    16.25-            1
    16.75-             1
    17.25-              1
    17.75-               1
    18.25-                1
    18.75-                 1
    19.25-                   1
    19.75-                    1
    20.25-                     1
    20.75-                      1
    21.25-                        1
    21.75-                         1
    22.25-                          1
    22.75-                           1
    23.25-                            1
    23.75-                             1
    24.25-                              1
    24.75-                              1
    25.25-                               1
    25.75-                               1
    26.25-                               1
    26.75-                               1
    27.25-                               1
    27.75-                               1
    28.25-                              1
    28.75-                             1
    29.25-                            1
    29.75-                           1
    30.25-                          1
    30.75-                         1
    31.25-                        1
    31.75-                       1
    32.25-                      1
    32.75-                     1
    33.25-                    1
    33.75-                   1
    34.25-                  1
    34.75-                 1
    35.25-                1
    35.75-               1
    36.25-              1
    36.75-             1
    37.25-            1
    37.75-           1
    38.25-          1
```

```
38.75-                 1
39.25-                1
39.75-               1
40.25-               1
40.75-              1
41.25-             1
41.75-             1
42.25-            1
42.75-            1
43.25-           1
43.75-           1
44.25-          1
44.75-          1
45.25-          1
45.75-         1
46.25-         1
46.75-         1
47.25-         1
47.75-        1
48.25-        1
48.75-        1
49.25-        1
49.75-        1
50.25-        1
          I                       I                       I
          0                    0.04000                 0.08000
```

CHAPTER 14

Comparison and Extension of the Programs

Relation of Programs to One Another

The results of the several programs that we have included in the preceding chapters are not independent of one another. Five of them, for instance, are different ways of approaching the stable population, and show values of the intrinsic rate r. We will compare the five programs using data on the female population of Sweden, 1967.

PROJECT takes the population forward through time and examines for stability as it proceeds; when stability is attained to the accuracy specified it calculates intrinsic rates, as well as the age-sex distribution. For the intrinsic rate of natural increase of Sweden, 1967, it finds 0.00288 or 2.88 per thousand per year.

MATRIX establishes the elements of the projection matrix, or that part of it relating to females up to the last reproductive age, takes the matrix to a high power, and ascertains the intrinsic rate from the change in a particular element from one high power to the next. This also gives 2.88 per thousand per year.

LOTKA finds the net maternity function and its zeroth, first, and second moments, then uses the quadratic form of the characteristic equation due to A. J. Lotka (1939) to ascertain the intrinsic rate, again producing 2.88 per thousand.

ROOT uses the somewhat more precise characteristic equation in five-year age groups, as punched out by LOTKA or otherwise obtained, and solves it to find $1000r = 2.88$.

Finally, the characteristic equation of the projection matrix is used as the input to ZEROS, which ascertains all roots. Among these the real root for Sweden, 1967, equal to the intrinsic rate, is 2.88 per thousand.

Each of the five different programs thus produces the same value for the intrinsic rate, and it is also the same as that shown on page 465 in the Main Tables for Sweden. The results agree to three significant figures here, but will not do so for all populations, since minor arithmetical differences exist among formulations. These differences are of the order of r^2 or r^3, and a population of rapid increase can have a high enough r that r^2 constitutes a noticeable difference. As an example we have for Guatemala, 1964, the values of $1000r$ from the several programs as follows:

PROJECT	28.51
MATRIX	28.51
LOTKA	28.44
ROOT	28.41
ZEROS	28.51

The value given in the Main Tables (page 339) is 28.44.

We would not present five programs in order merely to find these minor differences, which are submerged in errors of the data and, even if arising from perfectly accurate data, could have no demographic meaning. Each of the five programs has a different set of aims, and the fact that each produces a value for the intrinsic rate is incidental to these.

The programs DIRECT and INDIR both produce standardizations, and we saw in Chapter 12 that their results are closely related. The program STABLE of Chapter 10 produces the intrinsic birth rate as well as the stable age distribution, both part of the results of PROJECT in Chapter 7. We were able to check the program INFER by feeding into it the output of STABLE and noting that it gives back the intrinsic rate fed in.

Other Uses of the Programs

Aside from the computations for which the programs are directly designed and to which they can be applied without any alteration on most installations, they may be thought of as serving a variety of other purposes.

Some other uses of these programs require only the entry of different kinds of data. An instance is the decomposition discussed in Chapter 1, by which we found to what extent the difference in intrinsic rates between Sweden, 1803–1807, and Venezuela, 1965, was due to the difference between their birth rates and to what extent to the difference between their death rates. We simply applied the program ROOT to input consisting of the required combinations of mortality and fertility.

Another example of further uses of these programs is the preliminary adding of information for a number of countries. A short program was devised to add data on the several countries of Europe, for example, in each of our input categories of age and sex; then the totals were fed into programs such as LIFE for obtaining aggregate life tables and other functions. Period data were assembled into cohorts, and again our standard programs applied.

Other uses need small changes in the programs. One such is answering the question on the ultimate fixed number in the population that would result from imposition of stationary rates of birth and death. We found that if Canadian age-specific rates of birth and death dropped in 1968 to those that would ultimately ensure a stationary population, the ultimate population size would be 40.9 percent higher than that of 1968. In order to calculate this we modified the program PROJECT by causing the births to be divided by R_0, the net reproduction rate, at a point in the program immediately after the R_0 became available. Then we could read in the regular data for the country under study, Canada, in the standard form. The result was a complete projection by age and sex, giving not only the ultimate stationary population, but the detailed trajectory by which this would be attained.

Other uses will require putting together two or more programs. For instance, we might want to make a life table merely in order to apply it to projection; if this is the only purpose of the life table then the punchout of LIFE, which is subsequently read into PROJECT in instances in which the life table is to be put to other uses as well, could be eliminated by putting the two together. We could indeed assemble together about six of the programs listed in Part III, convert them into subroutines, and so produce all and more of the results in the Main Tables of Part IV.

The versions of the programs given in the preceding chapters are not those that produced the numbers in the tables of this book. The program that we actually used was a collection of subroutines including over 4000 statements. It required so much storage that the IBM 7094 would not handle it in a single pass, and we had to arrange a first phase to make the life table and do the matrix analysis, then punch out a deck that was the input to the second phase; the second phase did the remaining computations, printed the pages shown in Part IV, and punched out a set of 11 summary cards. With these as input a simple program printed the 42 numbers of the Summary Table of Part II.

MAIN TABLES

CHAPTER 15

Quantities Computed and Their Definitions

The Main Tables for each country include one table giving data that were used as input to the computations. We will describe, in this chapter, each of the eight tables, using tables for Canada, 1968, as examples. (Data on Newfoundland have been excluded from the input on Canada in order that the numbers might be comparable with those on Canada published earlier in our *World Population*.) Where row and column headings are self-explanatory, discussion is omitted.

Table 1 contains the whole of the data input from which all of the remaining tables were calculated. Given population and deaths by age and sex, the life tables follow on the method described in Chapter 6. From the male and female life tables and age-specific birth rates obtained from Table 1 follow the projections of Table 4, made by the methods of Chapter 7. The purpose of the computations is in part to enable the reader to judge the accuracy of the data. In Table 7, for example, birth rates are calculated by various methods (Chapter 11) relying mostly on the age distribution, independently of birth registrations. These methods generally do not give satisfactory results where past births have been subject to violent fluctuations, as is true for most of the developed countries; fortunately they are at their best for the less developed countries, for which they are most often required.

TABLE 1   DATA INPUT TO COMPUTATIONS

Age at last birthday	Population					Births, by age of mother	Deaths			Age at last birthday
	Total	Males	%	Females	%		Total	Males	Females	
0	349859	178592	1.8	171267	1.7	0	7274	4109	3165	0
1–4	1605350	824492	8.1	780858	7.7	0	1404	785	619	1–4
5–9	2264366	1156633	11.4	1107733	11.0	0	1091	674	417	5–9
10–14	2144608	1096625	10.8	1047983	10.4	251	844	530	314	10–14
15–19	1914308	973458	9.6	940850	9.3	40531	1730	1250	480	15–19
20–24	1624617	813025	8.0	811592	8.0	123158	1905	1442	463	20–24
25–29	1339750	668800	6.6	670950	6.6	98275	1405	973	432	25–29
30–34	1233592	624817	6.1	608775	6.0	52209	1543	1028	515	30–34
35–39	1261450	640325	6.3	621125	6.1	27580	2235	1433	802	35–39
40–44	1267133	633150	6.2	633983	6.3	8709	3445	2185	1260	40–44
45–49	1133467	560600	5.5	572867	5.7	774	5014	3239	1775	45–49
50–54	999717	498500	4.9	501217	5.0	3	7083	4552	2531	50–54
55–59	858391	430758	4.2	427633	4.2	0	9821	6525	3296	55–59
60–64	690509	342042	3.4	348467	3.5	0	12151	8067	4084	60–64
65–69	546275	261192	2.6	285083	2.8	0	15025	9664	5361	65–69
70–74	430000	196983	1.9	233017	2.3		17374	10287	7087	70–74
75–79	309175	138567	1.4	170608	1.7		19766	11116	8650	75–79
80–84	182225	80667	0.8	101558	1.0	180972 M	19500	10212	9288	80–84
85 +	109875	45217	0.4	64658	0.6	170518 E	21463	9629	11834	85 +
All ages	20264667	10164443		10100224		351490	150073	87700	62373	All ages

Population   The number of persons age x to $x + n$ years, written $_nP_x$ in equations, where n is 1, 4, or 5, and x is 0, 1, 5, 10, ... The data are usually based on a preceding census extrapolated to the midpoint of the period of our birth and death observations; not-stated ages were distributed. For example, 349,859 children less than one year old were estimated to live in Canada at mid-1968, and of these 178,592 were boys. The number of girls 5–9 years old was 1,107,733. The grand total of residents was 20,264,667. The last four or so digits are not significant, and are printed for the sake of consistency with subsequent ratios.

%   Percentage distribution of male and female populations. For Canada, 1968, 11.4% of the male population is estimated to be 5–9 years old.

Births, by age of mother   Registered births, by age of mother, with births to mothers whose ages were not recorded distributed. In a table showing data on a three-year period, this column gives the average per year. The table for Canada says that 40,531 babies were born during 1968 to mothers 15–19 years old, and that a total of 351,490 babies were born to mothers of all ages during that year.

M, F   Number of males and of females among the births registered. Of the total births shown for Canada 180,972 were male, 170,518 were female.

Deaths   Registered deaths, by age. In a table showing data on a three-year period, this column gives the average per year.

TABLE 2   LIFE TABLE FOR MALES

Age, x	$_nq_x$	l_x	$_nd_x$	$_nL_x$	$_nm_x$	T_x	$1000r_x$	$\overset{\circ}{e}_x$	$_nM_x$	Age, x
0	0.02261	100000	2261	98275	0.02301	6904571	0.00	69.05	0.02301	0
1	0.00380	97739	371	389876	0.00095	6806296	0.00	69.64	0.00095	1
5	0.00291	97368	283	486130	0.00058	6416420	0.00	65.90	0.00058	5
10	0.00243	97084	236	484904	0.00049	5930289	16.56	61.08	0.00048	10
15	0.00644	96849	624	482813	0.00129	5445385	28.70	56.23	0.00128	15
20	0.00884	96225	850	479015	0.00177	4962572	35.93	51.57	0.00177	20
25	0.00724	95375	691	475132	0.00145	4483557	24.76	47.01	0.00145	25
30	0.00820	94684	776	471554	0.00165	4008425	2.65	42.33	0.00165	30
35	0.01113	93908	1045	467097	0.00224	3536871	0.00	37.66	0.00224	35
40	0.01715	92863	1593	460657	0.00346	3069774	9.64	33.06	0.00345	40
45	0.02861	91270	2611	450317	0.00580	2609116	17.97	28.59	0.00578	45
50	0.04487	88658	3978	434099	0.00916	2158799	16.69	24.35	0.00913	50
55	0.07345	84681	6220	408856	0.01521	1724700	22.10	20.37	0.01515	55
60	0.11199	78461	8787	371512	0.02365	1315844	15.22	16.77	0.02358	60
65	0.17017	69674	11857	319693	0.03709	944332	15.22	13.55	0.03700	65
70	0.23195	57818	13411	256190	0.05235	624639	15.22	10.80	0.05222	70
75	0.33510	44407	14881	185004	0.08043	368449	15.22	8.30	0.08022	75
80	0.48228	29526	14240	112115	0.12701	183444	15.22	6.21	0.12659	80
85+	•1.00000	15286	15286	71330	0.21430	71330	15.22	4.67	0.21295	85+

Exact age with which interval begins.   Age, x

Probability of dying, for an individual of exact age x, before reaching age $x + n$; n is 1 for the first line, 4 for the second, and 5 for all remaining lines up to the line for age 80. The chance that a boy just born will die before his first birthday is estimated to be 0.02261 or one in forty-four; that a man exactly 70 years old will die in the next five years, 0.23195. Note that the last two or three digits here are not significant, and are carried only for consistency with the remainder of the table. $_nq_x$

Number surviving to exact age x out of 100,000 born, equal to $l_x = l_{x-n}(1 - {}_nq_{x-n})$, $x = 1, 5, 10, \ldots, 85$. This is also the probability that a boy child just born will survive at least to exact age x, multiplied by 100,000 to remove the decimal. Thus the probability of surviving to age 30 for a boy just born would be $94684/100,000 = 0.94684$, according to Canadian records of mortality in 1968. Like other elements of all the life tables of this volume, which refer to a cross section of time, l_x is synthesized from the several ages of the given period, and estimates expected values. l_x

Number dying between ages x and $x + n$ out of 100,000 born: $_nd_x = l_x \, {}_nq_x$. Like l_x, this can be interpreted as a probability: the chance that a boy just born will die between exact ages 70 and 75 is 0.13411. $_nd_x$

Total years lived between ages x and $x + n$ per 100,000 born: $_nL_x = \int_0^n l(x + t) \, dt$, which is also the stationary age distribution. If the 1968 mortality shown were to persist over a long period of time, in a population in which exactly 100,000 births occurred each year, then the number of men in the 20–24 age group in that population at any time would be 479,015. $_nL_x$

$_nm_x$ Age-specific death rate in hypothetical life table population for interval x to $x + n$: $_nm_x = {_nd_x}/{_nL_x}$. In the stationary population constructed from Canadian data on males the age-specific death rate for men 60–64 years old is 0.02365. Note that this is slightly larger than the observed death rate $_5M_x = 0.02358$ given in the last column of the table; the stationary population within any age interval is slightly older than the observed wherever the latter is increasing.

T_x Total years lived beyond age x per 100,000 born, obtained by summing the $_nL_x$ column from age x to the end of the table. The total years lived by 100,000 boys born would be 6,904,571, of which 944,332 would be lived at ages 65 and older, under the assumption that the 1968 death rates of Canadian males persist. Expressed another way, the hypothetical male stationary population having $_nL_x$ persons at age x would contain 6,904,571 persons in all, and 944,332 at age 65 and older.

$1000r_x$ Increase from an annual cohort to the next as estimated from the observed age distribution by

$$r = 0.1 \ln \frac{\dfrac{_5P_{x-5}}{_5L_{x-5}}}{\dfrac{_5P_{x+5}}{_5L_{x+5}}}.$$

Where the quantity turns out negative the program substitutes zero as a partial protection against error, and zero is used also in the first three age groups. The value $1000\, r_{20} = 35.93$ reflects the high and increasing births of the 1940's; the low values of r_{30} and r_{35} the births of the 1930's.

$\mathring{e}_x$ Expectation of life at age x—that is, average number of years lived subsequent to age x by those reaching age x: $\mathring{e}_x = T_x/l_x$. The expectation of life on the mortality of Canada, 1968, of a boy just born is shown as 69.05; that of a man of 70 as 10.80.

$_nM_x$ Observed age-specific death rate for the interval x to $x + n$. From Table 1, the deaths of boys less than one year old number 4,109; the number of boys in the age group is estimated at 178,592; from these the age-specific death rate is $M_0 = 4{,}109/178{,}592 = 0.02301$ as shown. The reader is again reminded that the last few decimal places are not to be taken seriously.

TABLE 3   LIFE TABLE FOR FEMALES

Age, x	$_nq_x$	l_x	$_nd_x$	$_nL_x$	$_nm_x$	T_x	$1000r_x$	$\overset{\circ}{e}_x$	$_nM_x$	Age, x
0	0.01822	100000	1822	98617	0.01848	7565326	0.00	75.65	0.01848	0
1	0.00316	98178	311	391808	0.00079	7466709	0.00	76.05	0.00079	1
5	0.00188	97867	184	488875	0.00038	7074901	0.00	72.29	0.00038	5
10	0.00150	97683	146	488062	0.00030	6586026	15.96	67.42	0.00030	10
15	0.00255	97536	249	487087	0.00051	6097964	25.09	62.52	0.00051	15
20	0.00285	97287	278	485756	0.00057	5610877	33.23	57.67	0.00057	20
25	0.00322	97010	313	484294	0.00065	5125122	28.09	52.83	0.00064	25
30	0.00423	96697	409	482528	0.00085	4640827	6.83	47.99	0.00085	30
35	0.00644	96288	620	480005	0.00129	4158299	0.00	43.19	0.00129	35
40	0.00990	95669	947	476151	0.00199	3678294	6.03	38.45	0.00199	40
45	0.01545	94721	1463	470238	0.00311	3202143	20.23	33.81	0.00310	45
50	0.02507	93258	2338	460862	0.00507	2731905	24.06	29.29	0.00505	50
55	0.03804	90920	3459	446512	0.00775	2271042	28.39	24.98	0.00771	55
60	0.05733	87461	5014	425606	0.01178	1824530	27.00	20.86	0.01172	60
65	0.09052	82447	7464	394762	0.01891	1398842	27.00	16.97	0.01881	65
70	0.14262	74984	10694	349675	0.03058	1004162	27.00	13.39	0.03041	70
75	0.22734	64290	14615	286557	0.05100	654488	27.00	10.18	0.05070	75
80	0.37428	49675	18592	202220	0.09194	367931	27.00	7.41	0.09146	80
85 +	1.00000	31082	31082	165711	0.18757	165711	27.00	5.33	0.18303	85 +

Table 3, the life table for females, contains symbols identical with those of Table 2.

TABLE 4   POPULATION PROJECTION, USING FIXED AGE-SPECIFIC BIRTH AND DEATH RATES, IN THOUSANDS

Age at last birthday	1973			1978			1983			Age at last birthday
	Total	Males	Females	Total	Males	Females	Total	Males	Females	
0–4	1838	944	894	2081	1069	1012	2291	1177	1114	0–4
5–9	1948	999	949	1831	940	891	2073	1064	1009	5–9
10–14	2260	1154	1106	1944	996	948	1827	938	889	10–14
15–19	2138	1092	1046	2253	1149	1104	1938	992	946	15–19
20–24	1904	966	938	2126	1083	1043	2241	1140	1101	20–24
25–29	1615	806	809	1893	958	935	2115	1075	1040	25–29
30–34	1333	664	669	1606	800	806	1883	951	932	30–34
35–39	1225	619	606	1322	657	665	1595	793	802	35–39
40–44	1247	631	616	1211	610	601	1308	648	660	40–44
45–49	1245	619	626	1225	617	608	1190	597	593	45–49
50–54	1101	540	561	1211	597	614	1191	595	596	50–54
55–59	956	470	486	1053	509	544	1157	562	595	55–59
60–64	799	391	408	890	427	463	980	462	518	60–64
65–69	617	294	323	715	337	378	796	367	429	65–69
70–74	462	209	253	522	236	286	605	270	335	70–74
75–79	333	142	191	358	151	207	405	170	235	75–79
80–84	204	84	120	221	86	135	238	92	145	80–84
85 +	134	51	83	152	53	99	165	55	110	85 +
All ages	21359	10675	10684	22614	11275	11339	23998	11948	12050	All ages

Table 4 is a projection, part of the interpretation of current mortality and fertility. It applies the age-specific rates of birth and death of the given year—in our example those of Canada, 1968—and is female dominant, in that the number of females at each point of time determines the number of boy as well as girl babies. (Details of the techniques of projection are provided in the discussion of the program PROJECT.)

On the assumptions of the projection, Canada (excluding Newfoundland) will have 23,998,000 residents by mid-1983. Note that the 10–19 age groups in the projection reflect the low birth rates of the 1960's; the population less than five years old in

1983 is more numerous than at any other age even though it was assumed that the low birth rates of 1968 persist. The reason is that by 1983 the large cohorts born in the 1950's will be at childbearing ages. Note that the table makes no claim to prediction: not only does it merely assume persistence of the 1968 rates, but it supposes the population to be closed to migration.

TABLE 5   OBSERVED AND PROJECTED VITAL RATES

Rates per thousand	Observed			Projected						Stable	
				1973		1978		1983			
	Total	Males	Females	Males	Females	Males	Females	Males	Females	Males	Females
Birth	17.34	17.80	16.88	19.28	18.15	20.58	19.29	20.93	19.55	17.28	15.97
Death	7.41	3.63	6.18	8.84	6.68	9.04	7.09	9.22	7.40	12.36	11.05
Increase	9.94	9.18	10.71	10.44	11.47	11.55	12.20	11.71	12.15		4.9164

Observed   Crude rates of birth, death, and natural increase per thousand population. The births as shown in Table 1 total 351,490, in a population of 20,264,667; the ratio of the first number to the second gives the crude birth rate 351,490/20,264,667 = 0.01734, which multiplied by 1000 is the 17.34 per thousand population shown. The crude death rate is similarly $1000 \times 150,073/20,264,667 = 7.41$. The rate of natural increase is the difference between these two: 17.34 − 7.41 = 9.94. (The three numbers are rounded independently, and hence the rounded version of the last need not be exactly the difference between the rounded versions of the first and second.)

Projected   Crude rates of birth, death, and natural increase per thousand population, as they would obtain in the years specified, taken from the projection of Table 4. Note that the crude death rate for females rises from the observed 6.18 to 6.68, 7.09, and 7.40 in successive five-year periods to 1983. This corresponds to prospective survival into higher ages because of recent low female mortality; as people become older the age-distribution becomes less favorable, and the crude death rate rises even though healthfulness as measured by age-specific rates is by hypothesis constant.

Stable   Crude rates of birth, death, and natural increase per thousand population, as they would stand ultimately if the observed age-specific rates applied; these are the intrinsic rates called *b*, *d*, and *r*. The death rate for females followed beyond the projection here shown continues rising, and ends up at 11.06, or 79 percent higher than the observed 6.18. This effect of changed age distribution results partly from the survival to older ages mentioned above, and partly from the relatively low rate of natural increase, 4.9164 per thousand, as shown in the righthand column of the table, which also tends to make the population old.

TABLE 6   RATES STANDARDIZED ON THREE STANDARD COUNTRIES

Standardized rates per thousand	England and Wales, 1961			United States, 1960			Mexico, 1960		
	Total	Males	Females	Total	Males	Females	Total	Males	Females
Birth	15.46	17.72*	14.54	15.74	16.30*	15.05	18.53	16.08*	17.94
Death	9.95	10.86*	9.20	8.17	9.62*	6.80	4.33	7.52*	3.36
Increase	5.51	6.86*	5.34	7.57	6.67*	8.24	14.21	8.56*	14.58

Directly standardized death rates, obtained by applying the given age-specific rates to the standard age distribution and calculating the overall death rate that results. Births are attributed to mothers in the female-dominant tables, and are standardized in the same way as deaths. Chapter 12 discusses standardization further.

Standardized rates per thousand

Three sets of standard rates are provided; for any particular comparison, choosing whichever of the three standards has an age distribution closest to those of the populations being compared gives the most precise result. If the age-sex distribution of Canada, 1968, were exactly that of the United States, 1960, then the Canadian birth rate would have been 15.74 per thousand instead of the observed 17.34, and the death rate would have been 8.17 instead of 7.41. The 1960 United States population had an age-sex distribution containing a smaller proportion of women of childbearing age and a larger proportion of old people.

England and Wales, 1961 United States, 1960 Mexico, 1960

Indirect standardization, in which the age-specific rates of the standard country are applied to the age distribution of the given country, is signified in Table 6 by an asterisk, which appears on the male figures. We had no choice in respect to births, and have made births and deaths uniform. If the directly standardized male death rates are required, they may be found by subtracting the female standardized rate from the total, each weighted by its standard population.

TABLE 7   VITAL STATISTICS AND RATES INFERRED FROM AGE DISTRIBUTIONS
(FEMALES)

Vital statistics		Thompson				Bourgeois-Pichat					Coale	
TFR	2.43	Age range	NRR	1000r	Interval	Age range	NRR	1000b	1000d	1000r	1000b	25.43
GRR	1.18	0–4	1.31	10.00	27.44	5–29	1.95	28.24	3.54	24.70	1000d	7.50
NRR	1.14	5–9	1.66	18.83	27.41	30–54	1.21	16.57	9.43	7.15	1000r	17.94
Generation	27.20	10–14	1.70	19.06	27.36	55–79	1.93	37.59	13.31	24.27	$1000k_1$	0.
Sex ratio	106.1	15–19	1.62	16.62	27.28	*45–69	2.05	43.14	16.54	26.59	$1000k_2$	0.

The purpose of Table 7 is to check the estimates of birth and natural increase as they are given by vital statistics. The means of checking is by inference from the age distribution and the life table. The five figures in the box on the left are calculated from birth and death registrations but all the remainder of the table is independently obtained. The theory behind these numbers is given in Chapter 11.

TFR
Total fertility rate. The sum of the age-specific fertility rates, taken in five-year age groups and multiplied by five. It is the average family size that would obtain at the fertility rates of the given year if all females born survived to the end of reproduction. Under these circumstances the average number of children born to the Canadian woman would be 2.43.

GRR
Gross reproduction rate, same as TFR but for female children only. For Canada the average number of female children that would be born per female in the absence of mortality, at 1968 fertility rates, would be 1.18.

NRR
Net reproduction rate, R_0. The same as GRR except for a factor in each term from the female life table providing for the probability of surviving from age zero to the age in question: $R_0 = \sum_{10}^{50} {}_5L_x F_x$. The NRR is the number of female children expected to be born to a female just born, and hence is the ratio of the number in one (female) generation to the number of the preceding generation, according to mortality and fertility in the given period. For Canada $R_0 = 1.14$; there would be about a 14 percent increase per generation at 1968 rates.

Generation
The number of years T that a population subject to the intrinsic rate r would take to increase in the ratio of the NRR—that is the solution in T of $e^{rT} = R_0$. The quantity T is a mean of the average age of childbearing with the stationary age distribution and with the stable age distribution. The formula is $T = \ln R_0/r = \ln 1.143/ 0.004916 = 0.1337/0.004916 = 27.20$ years.

The ratio of male to female births multiplied by 100; for Canada, $100 \times 180{,}972/$ 170,518 $= 106.1$.

Sex ratio

The first of three indirect methods of inferring rates of increase. (See page 228.)

Thompson

Estimated here from the ratio of children to women in the observed population, divided by the corresponding ratio from the life table, and with a small correction for variance; approximately,

NRR

$$\text{NRR} = \frac{\dfrac{{}_5P_x}{{}_{30}P_{x+15}}}{\dfrac{{}_5L_x}{{}_{30}L_{x+15}}}, \qquad x = 0, 5, 10, 15$$

where ${}_5P_x$ is the observed population between age x and $x + 4$ at the last birthday, and ${}_{30}P_{x+15}$ is the observed population between age $x + 15$ and $x + 44$ at last birthday.

Calculated from the ratio of numbers in successive generations, reduced to an annual value:

$1000r$

$$r = \frac{\ln\left(\dfrac{\dfrac{{}_5P_x}{{}_{30}P_{x+15}}}{\dfrac{{}_5L_x}{{}_{30}L_{x+15}}}\right)}{\text{Interval}}, \qquad x = 0, 5, 10, 15.$$

The number of years between the mean age of children x to $x + 4$, and that of women $x + 15$ to $x + 44$, $x = 0, 5, 10, 15$.

Interval

Used for the formula just given in the definition of $1000r$.

Age range

Signifies that $x = 0$ in the formulas for NRR and r above; thus children less than 5 years old are referred to women 15–44 years old.

0–4

5–9	Signifies that $x = 5$ in the formulas; children 5–9 years old are referred to women 20–49 years old.
10–14, 15–19	Signifies $x = 10$ and 15 respectively in the formulas for NRR and r.
Bourgeois-Pichat	Second indirect method of inferring rates of increase, relying on assumption of stability.
$1000b$, $1000r$	Intrinsic rates of birth and natural increase inferred by least-squares fitting to the logarithm of the age distribution of the straight line: $$\ln \frac{{}_5P_x}{{}_5L_x} = \ln b - r\left(x + 2\frac{1}{2}\right) + \ln \frac{P}{l_0},$$ where P is the female population totalled over all ages.
Age range	Twenty-five-year intervals over which b and r were separately calculated, including finally the closest-fitting interval, recognized after the computer had tried all such intervals, identified here by asterisk *.
$1000d$	$d = b - r$, where b and r are obtained from straight-line fitting. The departure of d from its value in Table 4 constitutes a check on the indirect calculation. This form of calculation leans heavily on the stability of the age distribution in the given 25-year intervals. For a country whose fertility has seen considerable variation, as has that of Canada, the results are not satisfactory, and in any case Canadian birth registrations are complete enough that such a check can tell us little. For countries whose fertility has been more nearly constant and whose registration is more in doubt, this is a useful check on the completeness of data on births.
NRR	Here calculated as $(e^r)^{27}$, after r is inferred from age distribution. The results for Canada are not very useful; for some underdeveloped countries this and Coale calculations are the best means we have for estimating birth rates.
Coale	Third indirect method of calculating rates of increase, using weaker assumptions than stability, named for Ansley J. Coale. Where the method is inappropriate, it is suppressed.

Intrinsic rates of birth, death, and natural increase as inferred by a least-squares fitting of a curve with constants b, r, k_1, and k_2 to the logarithm of age distribution from ages 5–74; does not appear for populations whose age distributions cannot be fitted by this model. The method of inference has been found effective where a smooth trend of birth rates has prevailed over the lifetimes of those now living. For Canada it gives a high estimate of births.

$1000b$, $1000d$, $1000r$

Linear component of inferred trend in births, or in births less infant deaths, multiplied by 1000.

$1000k_1$

Quadratic component of inferred trend in births, or in births less infant deaths, multiplied by 1000. The program fits with and without the linear and quadratic components k_1 and k_2, and found for Canada, 1968, that it could reproduce the given ages better with both of these constants equal to zero. For this special case the Coale model reduces to Bourgeois-Pichat.

$1000k_2$

TABLE 8 LESLIE MATRIX AND ITS ANALYSIS (FEMALES)

Start of age interval	Sub-diagonal	First row	Percent in stable population	Fisher values	Total reproductive values	Net maternity function	Matrix equation coefficient	Parameters		
									Integral	Matrix
0	0.99684	0.00000	7.739	1.032	982701	0.00000	0.00000	λ_1	1.0249	1.0249
5	0.99834	0.00028	7.527	1.061	1175490	0.00000	0.00028	λ_2	0.3397	0.3496
10	0.99800	0.05143	7.332	1.089	1141364	0.00057	0.05118		+0.7598	+0.7338 i
15	0.99727	0.23127	7.139	1.065	1002262	0.10180	0.22970	r_1	0.0049	0.0049
20	0.99699	0.35424	6.947	0.855	694267	0.35760	0.35086	r_2	-0.0367	-0.0415
25	0.99635	0.27589	6.758	0.513	343976	0.34413	0.27244		+0.2301	+0.2252 i
30	0.99477	0.15457	6.569	0.242	147060	0.20076	0.15208	c_1		128441
35	0.99197	0.06903	6.376	0.089	54980	0.10340	0.06757	c_2		1487
40	0.98758	0.01793	6.171	0.023	12442	0.03173	0.01741			354866 i
45	0.98006	0.00161	5.947	0.002	937	0.00308	0.00155	$2\pi/y$	27.310	27.898
50	0.96886	0.00001	5.686	0.000	3	0.00001	0.00001	Δ	11.546	
55	0.81144		25.813							

The first two columns of printout in Table 8 are the female matrix. All elements but those of the first row and the subdiagonal are zero and are omitted to save space on our page. This matrix, extended to allow for mortality beyond ages of reproduction and to include males, would generate Tables 4 and 5.

The elements of the subdiagonal shown are probabilities of surviving from the age group specified to the succeeding age group: ${}_5L_{x+5}/{}_5L_x$. For women in the 30–34 age group the fraction surviving to the next age group at the rates of Canada, 1968, is ${}_5L_{35}/{}_5L_{30} = 480,005/482,528 = 0.99477$.

Subdiagonal

First row	The number opposite x is the factor by which the female population x to $x + 4$ is multiplied to obtain the contribution to the female children 0–4 alive at the end of the five-year period. The expected number of female children at the end of the five-year period per female 20–24 at the start of the period is 0.35424.
Percent in stable population	The percent distribution of the stable population, calculated from a column of the first stable matrix obtained as a high power of the projection matrix. We see that 7.527 percent of the stable age distribution of females is 5–9 years old, compared with 11.0 percent of the observed female population (Table 1). The large difference is owing to the fact that the stable population has adjusted to the low birth rates of 1968, while the observed 1968 population reflects in its 5–9 age group the higher births of 1958–63.
Fisher values	Numbers proportional to the rows of the first stable matrix; may be interpreted as index of reproductive value per woman—that is, the female children expected to be born to a female on the given fertility rates and life table, discounted at the intrinsic rate. Value is arbitrarily taken as unity at birth, and is necessarily zero at the end of the reproductive period. Note that a peak of 1.089 is reached at ages 10–14; as a girl draws near the period of childbearing, her prospective children are not discounted as much as when she was younger.
Total reproductive values	Fisher value per female multiplied by observed female population at each age. The observed number of girls 10–14 in Canada, 1968, was 1,047,983 (Table 1) and these multiplied by the unit reproductive value gives 1,141,364 as shown. (The computer used an unrounded unit reproductive value rather than the 1.089 shown.) The total of the column appears in Column 4 of the Summary Table for Canada, 1966–68, as 5,695,000. (1966–68 was preferred to 1968 for the Summary Table.)
Net maternity function	Age-specific birth rate multiplied by stationary population in the five-year age group: $_5L_x \, F_x$. The NRR of Table 7 is the sum of this column.
Matrix equation coefficient	The average of two numbers under net maternity function, the one given in the same line as this coefficient, and the one below it: $\frac{1}{2}(_5L_x \, F_x + {}_5L_{x+5}F_{x+5})$. The numbers in this column are the coefficients of a polynomial equation whose roots serve to analyze the projection matrix. The real and complex roots are given by the pro-

gram ZEROS (Part III), and the first three roots appear in the last column of this table under the heading "Matrix," denoted λ_1 and λ_2.

Ratio of increase per five-year period after stability is attained if age-specific birth and death rates are held constant. The value included under the column heading "Matrix" is obtained as the real root of the polynomial equation whose coefficients are given in the column headed "Matrix equation coefficient." The value under "Integral" is obtained from intrinsic rate r_1 as $\lambda_1 = e^{5r_1}$. Numbers on same row in these two columns are different finite approximations to same parameter. If the age-specific rates of birth and death of 1968 continue, then ultimately the Canadian population will increase in the ratio 1.02489 per five-year period on the integral-equation model and 1.02490 on the matrix model, both rounded to 1.0249 on the printout. Coefficients of the integral equation are shown under "Net Maternity Function."

λ_1

Principle complex root of characteristic equation; the value under "Matrix" is obtained as λ_2 from the matrix equation; the value under "Integral" is obtained from the integral equation as $\lambda_2 = e^{5r_2}$. The i's designating the imaginary parts have been omitted in the integral model, whose λ_2 is to be read $0.3397 + 0.7598i$.

λ_2

Intrinsic rate of natural increase obtained from the integral equation is r_1 under "Integral"; under "Matrix," $r_1 = 0.2\ln\lambda_1$. This is the annual rate (compounded momently) that corresponds to the ratio of increase λ_1.

r_1

Second root of integral equation under "Integral," and $r_2 = 0.2\ln\lambda_2$ under "Matrix." For printing ease again i was omitted under "Integral;" r_2 is to be read $-0.0367 + 0.2301i$.

r_2

Factor to be applied to percent distribution of the stable population in order to obtain stable component in analysis of age distribution, as given in this table under r_1. The quantity $100c_1$ is the stable equivalent of the female population. If the 1968 rates continue, then ultimately the female population will follow the curve $12,844,100e^{0.0049t}$, where t is time measured from 1968, and 12,844,100 is the stable equivalent. The stable equivalent number of females is higher than the observed number of females (10,100,224 according to Table 1) after a downturn in the birth rate, because the downturn has left a larger number in the childbearing ages than would be in those ages after the new low rates have persisted for some time. In

c_1

general the ultimate curve followed by the female population under fixed rates of birth and death would be $100c_1e^{r_1 t}$.

---

c_2　　　Factor to be multiplied by λ^{t}_2 to give wave component of the projection to time t.

$2\pi/y$　　If y is the imaginary part of the second complex root r_2 in the solution of the integral equation, then $2\pi/y$ is the wavelength of the principal complex component. This wavelength is 27.310 for Canada, 1968, on the integral equation model; 27.898 on the matrix model. The quantity $2\pi/y$ is close to T, the length of generation in Table 7, given as 27.20 for Canada, 1968. The mean age of childbearing in the stationary population is 27.29 and that in the stable population 27.11, these numbers not being shown in this book for want of space.

Δ　　　The index of dissimilarity between the observed age distribution and the stable component; when both are expressed as percentages, Δ is the sum of the positive differences. The departure of the stable age distribution from the observed age distribution is partly due to irregularities in the latter resulting from birth fluctuations of a long past time—for example, the small numbers around age 35 at present in countries whose births were low in the 1930's; it is also due to any recent drop in births that drastically changes the parameters of the stable curve. The latter is responsible for the large value of 11.546 in Table 8 for Canada, 1968, which may be compared with 7.580 found as recently as 1966. The value of Δ tells how reliable results of applying stable theory will be for the particular population. Few of the 752 populations shown in the Summary Table show as high a Δ as does Canada, 1968.

CHAPTER 16

Countries

Following are the data and analysis described in the previous chapter for the seventy countries for which we were able to find reliable information. The arrangement is by continents in the following order:

Africa

North America

South America

Asia

Europe

Oceania

Within continents the countries are arranged alphabetically according to the name of the country in English. (Both East Germany and West Germany are alphabetized under "G.") This is the sequence fixed on by the United Nations, and we have not tried to improve on it, particularly because our readers may wish to use the *United Nations Demographic Yearbook* in conjunction with the present volume.

Examples of substantive interpretation will be found in Part I, comments on accuracy in Part V, and definitions in Chapter 15. Note again that the asterisk * in Table 6 for each population denotes indirect standardization, and is used for males in Chapters 16, 17, and 18. Because of the standard-country weighting in direct standardization, and the given-country weighting in indirect standardization, the rate shown for the total of both sexes is not in general an average of the male and female rates. The asterisk in Table 7 identifies the age interval for which the Bourgeois-Pichat fitting is closest. The inferences in Table 7 are to be used only where the age distribution is reasonably stable.

Algeria,1965

TABLE 1 DATA INPUT TO COMPUTATIONS

Age at last birthday	Population					Births, by age of mother	Deaths			Age at last birthday
	Total	Males	%	Females	%		Total	Males	Females	
0	492370	250826	4.1	241544	4.0	0	46602	25269	21333	0
1–4	1871852	948059	15.6	923793	15.3	0	25074	13017	12057	1–4
5–9	1795714	912398	15.0	883316	14.6	0	4137	2238	1899	5–9
10–14	1571331	824604	13.5	746727	12.4	772	2360	1299	1061	10–14
15–19	1099848	554190	9.1	545658	9.0	67477	2046	956	1090	15–19
20–24	824029	399595	6.6	424434	7.0	131233	2280	1014	1266	20–24
25–29	801328	387138	6.4	414190	6.9	130900	2436	1073	1363	25–29
30–34	733430	351780	5.8	381650	6.3	101147	2465	1085	1380	30–34
35–39	604765	301755	5.0	303010	5.0	62464	2288	1107	1181	35–39
40–44	473185	233248	3.8	239937	4.0	30055	2017	1041	976	40–44
45–49	396648	202107	3.3	194541	3.2	2661	2285	1318	967	45–49
50–54	361695	181817	3.0	179878	3.0	2219	2619	1584	1035	50–54
55–59	301229	157608	2.6	143621	2.4	0	3004	1910	1094	55–59
60–64	269286	134303	2.2	134983	2.2	0	3603	2211	1392	60–64
65–69	200384	102762	1.7	97622	1.6	0	3760	2244	1516	65–69
70–74	143833	65695	1.1	78138	1.3		3538	2057	1481	70–74
75–79	87083	40984	0.7	46099	0.8		3050	1731	1319	75–79
80–84	55544	23606	0.4	31938	0.5	269118 M	2436	1348	1088	80–84
85 +	50221	23305	0.4	26916	0.4	259810 F	5023	2590	2433	85 +
All ages	12133775	6095780		6037995		528928	121023	65092	55931	All ages

TABLE 2 LIFE TABLE FOR MALES

Age, x	$_nq_x$	l_x	$_nd_x$	$_nL_x$	$_nm_x$	T_x	$1000r_x$	$\overset{\circ}{e}_x$	$_nM_x$	Age, x
0	0.09463	100000	9463	93934	0.10074	6301908	0.00	63.02	0.10074	0
1	0.05291	90537	4791	348909	0.01373	6207974	0.00	68.57	0.01373	1
5	0.01185	85746	1015	426191	0.00238	5859065	32.59	68.33	0.00245	5
10	0.00781	84730	662	421935	0.00157	5432874	48.06	64.12	0.00158	10
15	0.00866	84068	728	418602	0.00174	5010939	70.58	59.61	0.00173	15
20	0.01265	83340	1054	414150	0.00254	4592337	33.46	55.10	0.00254	20
25	0.01377	82286	1133	408638	0.00277	4178187	9.95	50.78	0.00277	25
30	0.01533	81153	1244	402723	0.00309	3769550	21.78	46.45	0.00308	30
35	0.01823	79909	1457	396007	0.00368	3366826	37.40	42.13	0.00367	35
40	0.02218	78452	1740	388121	0.00448	2970819	35.34	37.87	0.00446	40
45	0.03219	76712	2469	377686	0.00654	2582698	18.39	33.67	0.00652	45
50	0.04276	74243	3175	363637	0.00873	2205012	15.90	29.70	0.00871	50
55	0.05902	71068	4195	345303	0.01215	1841374	17.98	25.91	0.01212	55
60	0.07964	66874	5326	321518	0.01657	1496072	50.92	22.37	0.01646	60
65	0.10441	61548	6425	292244	0.02199	1174554	50.92	19.08	0.02184	65
70	0.14639	55121	8069	255980	0.03152	882310	50.92	16.01	0.03131	70
75	0.19234	47052	9050	212943	0.04250	626330	50.92	13.31	0.04224	75
80	0.25120	38002	9545	166157	0.05745	413387	50.92	10.88	0.05710	80
85 +	1.00000	28456	28456	247230	0.11510	247230	50.92	8.69	0.11114	85 +

TABLE 3 LIFE TABLE FOR FEMALES

Age, x	$_nq_x$	l_x	$_nd_x$	$_nL_x$	$_nm_x$	T_x	$1000r_x$	$\overset{\circ}{e}_x$	$_nM_x$	Age, x
0	0.08365	100000	8365	94712	0.08832	6684610	0.00	66.85	0.08832	0
1	0.05040	91635	4618	353858	0.01305	6589898	0.00	71.91	0.01305	1
5	0.01029	87017	896	432844	0.00207	6236040	40.06	71.66	0.00215	5
10	0.00708	86121	609	429073	0.00142	5803196	46.47	67.38	0.00142	10
15	0.01003	85512	858	425548	0.00202	5374123	54.41	62.85	0.00200	15
20	0.01484	84654	1256	420234	0.00299	4948575	24.73	58.46	0.00298	20
25	0.01633	83398	1362	413529	0.00329	4528341	7.31	54.30	0.00329	25
30	0.01794	82036	1471	406543	0.00362	4114712	27.64	50.16	0.00362	30
35	0.01932	80565	1557	398957	0.00390	3708169	42.55	46.03	0.00390	35
40	0.02018	79008	1594	391127	0.00408	3309212	40.08	41.88	0.00407	40
45	0.02460	77414	1904	382423	0.00498	2918085	23.89	37.69	0.00497	45
50	0.02844	75509	2147	372355	0.00577	2535662	24.37	33.58	0.00575	50
55	0.03750	73362	2751	360231	0.00764	2163307	20.96	29.49	0.00762	55
60	0.05070	70611	3580	344581	0.01039	1803076	47.99	25.54	0.01031	60
65	0.07525	67031	5044	322975	0.01562	1458494	47.99	21.76	0.01553	65
70	0.09120	61987	5653	296327	0.01908	1135519	47.99	18.32	0.01895	70
75	0.13439	56334	7571	263165	0.02877	839191	47.99	14.90	0.02861	75
80	0.15766	48763	7688	224721	0.03421	576026	47.99	11.81	0.03407	80
85 +	1.00000	41075	41075	351305	0.11692	351305	47.99	8.55	0.09039	85 +

TABLE 4 POPULATION PROJECTION, USING FIXED AGE-SPECIFIC BIRTH AND DEATH RATES, IN THOUSANDS

Age at last birthday	1970 Total	Males	Females	1975 Total	Males	Females	1980 Total	Males	Females	Age at last birthday
0–4	2558	1293	1265	3042	1538	1504	3689	1865	1824	0–4
5–9	2278	1154	1124	2465	1245	1220	2931	1480	1451	5–9
10–14	1779	903	876	2257	1142	1115	2442	1232	1210	10–14
15–19	1559	818	741	1764	896	868	2239	1133	1106	15–19
20–24	1087	548	539	1540	809	731	1745	887	858	20–24
25–29	812	394	418	1071	541	530	1519	799	720	25–29
30–34	789	382	407	800	389	411	1054	533	521	30–34
35–39	721	346	375	774	375	399	785	382	403	35–39
40–44	593	296	297	706	339	367	760	368	392	40–44
45–49	462	227	235	578	288	290	689	330	359	45–49
50–54	384	195	189	447	219	228	560	277	283	50–54
55–59	347	173	174	368	185	183	429	208	221	55–59
60–64	284	147	137	327	161	166	347	172	175	60–64
65–69	249	122	127	262	133	129	302	146	156	65–69
70–74	180	90	90	223	107	116	235	117	118	70–74
75–79	124	55	69	155	75	80	192	89	103	75–79
80–84	71	32	39	102	43	59	126	58	68	80–84
85 +	85	35	50	110	48	62	156	63	93	85 +
All ages	14362	7210	7152	16991	8533	8458	20200	10139	10061	All ages

TABLE 5 OBSERVED AND PROJECTED VITAL RATES

Rates per thousand	Observed Total	Males	Females	Projected 1970 Males	Females	1975 Males	Females	1980 Males	Females	Stable Males	Females
Birth	43.59	44.15	43.03	43.69	42.52	44.50	43.33	45.63	44.40	46.21	45.19
Death	9.97	10.68	9.26	10.32	9.09	10.43	9.15	10.57	9.39	10.55	9.52
Increase	33.62	33.47	33.77	33.36	33.43	34.08	34.18	35.06	35.01		35.6615

TABLE 6 RATES STANDARDIZED ON THREE STANDARD COUNTRIES

Standardized rates per thousand	England and Wales, 1961 Total	Males	Females	United States, 1960 Total	Males	Females	Mexico, 1960 Total	Males	Females
Birth	44.34	50.27*	42.21	45.01	46.49*	43.56	48.51	47.84*	47.53
Death	9.74	18.80*	9.21	9.52	16.00*	8.69	8.62	8.99*	7.95
Increase	34.60	31.48*	33.01	35.49	30.49*	34.87	39.88	38.85*	39.58

TABLE 7 VITAL STATISTICS AND RATES INFERRED FROM AGE DISTRIBUTIONS (FEMALES)

Vital statistics		Thompson Age range	NRR	$1000r$	Interval	Bourgeois-Pichat Age range	NRR	$1000b$	$1000d$	$1000r$	Coale	
TFR	6.86	0–4	2.76	37.26	27.28	5–29	2.89	44.76	5.40	39.36	$1000b$	48.13
GRR	3.37	5–9	2.52	34.66	27.23	30–54	2.54	46.12	11.52	34.59	$1000d$	8.03
NRR	2.76	10–14	2.40	31.42	27.20	55–79	2.25	38.86	8.87	29.99	$1000r$	40.10
Generation	28.50	15–19	2.05	26.52	27.15	*30–59	2.28	38.14	7.58	30.55	$1000k_1$	28.24
Sex ratio	103.6										$1000k_2$	0.30

TABLE 8 LESLIE MATRIX AND ITS ANALYSIS (FEMALES)

Start of age interval	Sub-diagonal	First row	Percent in stable population	Fisher values	Total reproductive values	Net maternity function	Matrix equation coefficient
0	0.96494	0.00000	18.599	1.217	1418208	0.00000	0.00000
5	0.99129	0.00113	15.005	1.508	1332470	0.00000	0.00109
10	0.99178	0.13626	12.436	1.819	1358085	0.00218	0.13033
15	0.98751	0.47262	10.312	2.026	1105567	0.25849	0.44836
20	0.98428	0.68334	8.514	1.872	794356	0.63824	0.64018
25	0.98287	0.53515	7.007	1.429	592024	0.64211	0.58568
30	0.98134	0.51485	5.758	0.953	363692	0.52924	0.46561
35	0.98037	0.36240	4.724	0.523	158463	0.40398	0.32232
40	0.97775	0.15273	3.872	0.188	45144	0.24066	0.13318
45	0.97367	0.02830	3.165	0.040	7794	0.02569	0.02413
50	0.96744	0.01359	2.577	0.014	2487	0.02256	0.01128
55	0.88557		8.029				

Parameters

	Integral	Matrix
λ_1	1.1952	1.1961
λ_2	0.4246	0.4343
	+0.7767	+0.7587 i
r_1	0.0357	0.0358
r_2	-0.0244	-0.0269
	+0.2141	+0.2102 i
c_1		58085
c_2		174846
		7091 i
$2\pi/y$	29.346	29.893
Δ	3.749	

Cameroon (West), 1964

TABLE 1 DATA INPUT TO COMPUTATIONS

Age at last birthday	Population					Births, by age of mother	Deaths			Age at last birthday
	Total	Males	%	Females	%		Total	Males	Females	
0	48650	24640	4.8	24010	4.6	0	7062	3929	3133	0
1–4	161709	81059	15.9	80650	15.5	0	6358	3249	3109	1–4
5–9	159381	79176	15.5	80205	15.4	0	2476	1423	1053	5–9
10–14	130867	64892	12.7	65975	12.7	2834	1111	557	554	10–14
15–19	109062	54114	10.6	54948	10.6	13478	753	399	354	15–19
20–24	91246	45032	8.8	46214	8.9	13592	829	382	447	20–24
25–29	76156	37313	7.3	38843	7.5	10113	899	497	402	25–29
30–34	63322	30977	6.1	32345	6.2	6486	629	302	327	30–34
35–39	52477	25510	5.0	26967	5.2	3124	805	495	310	35–39
40–44	42387	20420	4.0	21967	4.2	1050	869	416	453	40–44
45–49	33050	16184	3.2	16866	3.2	524	955	407	548	45–49
50–54	24417	12113	2.4	12304	2.4	0	1062	591	471	50–54
55–59	16201	8068	1.6	8133	1.6	0	1249	697	552	55–59
60–64	10450	5244	1.0	5206	1.0	0	447	265	182	60–64
65–69	6791	3313	0.6	3478	0.7	0	450	307	143	65–69
70–74	3145	1498	0.3	1647	0.3		300	204	96	70–74
75–79	1073	500	0.1	573	0.1		145	90	55	75–79
80–84	274	125	0.0	149	0.0	27970 M	56	28	28	80–84
85+	62	28	0.0	34	0.0	23231 F	26	7	19	85+
All ages	1030720	510206		520514		51201	26481	14245	12236	All ages

TABLE 2 LIFE TABLE FOR MALES

Age, x	$_nq_x$	l_x	$_nd_x$	$_nL_x$	$_nm_x$	T_x	$1000r_x$	$\overset{\circ}{e}_x$	$_nM_x$	Age, x
0	0.14552	100000	14552	91394	0.15922	3427163	2.77	34.27	0.15946	0
1	0.14486	85448	12378	309094	0.04005	3335770	2.77	39.04	0.04008	1
5	0.08523	73070	6228	349778	0.01781	3026676	28.34	41.42	0.01797	5
10	0.04161	66842	2781	326441	0.00852	2676897	27.41	40.05	0.00858	10
15	0.03619	64060	2318	314463	0.00737	2350457	28.94	36.69	0.00737	15
20	0.04174	61742	2577	302579	0.00852	2035994	27.79	32.98	0.00848	20
25	0.06450	59165	3816	286299	0.01333	1733415	26.15	29.30	0.01332	25
30	0.04776	55349	2643	270362	0.00978	1447116	25.15	26.15	0.00975	30
35	0.09294	52706	4898	251699	0.01946	1176754	24.41	22.33	0.01940	35
40	0.09707	47807	4641	227487	0.02040	925055	24.36	19.35	0.02037	40
45	0.11927	43167	5149	203734	0.02527	697568	23.29	16.16	0.02515	45
50	0.21952	38018	8346	170349	0.04899	493835	17.75	12.99	0.04879	50
55	0.35344	29672	10488	121289	0.08647	323496	13.40	10.90	0.08639	55
60	0.22113	19185	4242	84316	0.05031	202207	50.37	10.54	0.05053	60
65	0.37956	14943	5672	60624	0.09355	117891	50.37	7.89	0.09267	65
70	0.50416	9271	4674	34067	0.13720	57267	50.37	6.18	0.13618	70
75	0.60412	4597	2777	15327	0.18119	23200	50.37	5.05	0.18000	75
80	0.68174	1820	1241	5505	0.22538	7874	50.37	4.33	0.22400	80
85+	1.00000	579	579	2369	0.24450	2369	50.37	4.09	0.25000	85+

TABLE 3 LIFE TABLE FOR FEMALES

Age, x	$_nq_x$	l_x	$_nd_x$	$_nL_x$	$_nm_x$	T_x	$1000r_x$	$\overset{\circ}{e}_x$	$_nM_x$	Age, x
0	0.12123	100000	12123	93011	0.13034	3808730	2.28	38.09	0.13049	0
1	0.14011	87877	12313	319625	0.03852	3715719	2.28	42.28	0.03855	1
5	0.06281	75564	4746	365956	0.01297	3396094	28.62	44.94	0.01313	5
10	0.04087	70818	2894	346315	0.00836	3030139	28.77	42.79	0.00840	10
15	0.03174	67924	2156	334276	0.00645	2683824	28.09	39.51	0.00644	15
20	0.04735	65768	3114	321264	0.00969	2349548	25.63	35.72	0.00967	20
25	0.05045	62654	3161	305330	0.01035	2028284	25.49	32.37	0.01035	25
30	0.04933	59493	2935	290132	0.01012	1722954	26.15	28.96	0.01011	30
35	0.05622	56558	3180	275329	0.01155	1432822	25.61	25.33	0.01150	35
40	0.09886	53378	5277	254550	0.02073	1157493	25.74	21.68	0.02062	40
45	0.15095	48101	7261	222752	0.03260	902943	27.00	18.77	0.03249	45
50	0.17587	40841	7182	186763	0.03846	680190	28.78	16.65	0.03828	50
55	0.28921	33658	9734	143239	0.06796	493428	32.19	14.66	0.06787	55
60	0.15633	23924	3740	109033	0.03430	350189	82.61	14.64	0.03496	60
65	0.18819	20184	3798	91526	0.04150	241156	82.61	11.95	0.04112	65
70	0.25822	16386	4231	71555	0.05913	149630	82.61	9.13	0.05829	70
75	0.39353	12154	4783	48918	0.09778	78075	82.61	6.42	0.09599	75
80	0.64164	7371	4730	24586	0.19237	29156	82.61	3.96	0.18792	80
85+	•1.00000	2642	2642	4570	0.57806	4570	82.61	1.73	0.55882	85+

[310]

TABLE 4 POPULATION PROJECTION, USING FIXED AGE-SPECIFIC BIRTH AND DEATH RATES, IN THOUSANDS

Age at last birthday	1969 Total	Males	Females	1974 Total	Males	Females	1979 Total	Males	Females	Age at last birthday
0–4	223	120	103	256	138	118	293	158	135	0–4
5–9	185	92	93	196	105	91	224	120	104	5–9
10–14	150	74	76	174	86	88	184	98	86	10–14
15–19	127	63	64	144	71	73	168	83	85	15–19
20–24	105	52	53	121	60	61	138	68	70	20–24
25–29	87	43	44	99	49	50	115	57	58	25–29
30–34	72	35	37	82	40	42	95	47	48	30–34
35–39	60	29	31	68	33	35	77	37	40	35–39
40–44	48	23	25	54	26	28	62	30	32	40–44
45–49	37	18	19	43	21	22	48	23	25	45–49
50–54	28	14	14	31	15	16	35	17	18	50–54
55–59	18	9	9	21	10	11	23	11	12	55–59
60–64	12	6	6	13	6	7	15	7	8	60–64
65–69	8	4	4	9	4	5	10	4	6	65–69
70–74	5	2	3	5	2	3	6	2	4	70–74
75–79	2	1	1	3	1	2	3	1	2	75–79
80–84	0	0	0	1	0	1	1	0	1	80–84
85 +	0	0	0	0	0	0	0	0	0	85 +
All ages	1167	585	582	1320	667	653	1497	763	734	All ages

TABLE 5 OBSERVED AND PROJECTED VITAL RATES

Rates per thousand	Observed Total	Males	Females	Projected 1969 Males	Females	1974 Males	Females	1979 Males	Females	Stable Males	Females
Birth	49.67	54.82	44.63	54.88	45.68	55.07	46.69	54.94	47.37	49.09	45.57
Death	25.69	27.92	23.51	27.81	22.58	27.74	22.94	27.65	23.31	27.58	24.06
Increase	23.98	26.90	21.12	27.07	23.10	27.33	23.75	27.29	24.06		21.5098

TABLE 6 RATES STANDARDIZED ON THREE STANDARD COUNTRIES

Standardized rates per thousand	England and Wales, 1961 Total	Males	Females	United States, 1960 Total	Males	Females	Mexico, 1960 Total	Males	Females
Birth	40.30	54.54*	35.44	41.52	49.50*	37.12	48.75	53.60*	44.12
Death	37.98	95.67*	36.59	34.64	69.83*	31.88	27.11	28.45*	24.51
Increase	2.32	-41.14*	-1.14	6.88	-20.33*	5.24	21.64	25.14*	19.61

TABLE 7 VITAL STATISTICS AND RATES INFERRED FROM AGE DISTRIBUTIONS (FEMALES)

Vital statistics		Thompson Age range	NRR	$1000r$	Interval	Bourgeois-Pichat Age range	NRR	$1000b$	$1000d$	$1000r$	Coale	
TFR	6.19	0–4	2.04	27.57	26.79	5–29	2.09	51.45	24.08	27.38	$1000b$	62.76
GRR	2.81	5–9	2.00	26.58	26.51	30–54	2.03	50.28	24.09	26.19	$1000d$	27.47
NRR	1.72	10–14	1.96	25.17	26.17	55–79	4.88	343.21	284.47	58.74	$1000r$	35.29
Generation	25.33	15–19	1.90	25.11	25.62	*25–59	2.01	49.73	23.85	25.88	$1000k_1$	55.77
Sex ratio	120.4										$1000k_2$	0.84

TABLE 8 LESLIE MATRIX AND ITS ANALYSIS (FEMALES)

Start of age interval	Sub-diagonal	First row	Percent in stable population	Fisher values	Total reproductive values	Net maternity function	Matrix equation coefficient	Parameters	Integral	Matrix
0	0.88687	0.00000	17.845	1.277	133627	0.00000	0.00000	λ_1	1.1135	1.1139
5	0.94633	0.03805	14.208	1.604	128614	0.00000	0.03375	λ_2	0.1351	0.3116
10	0.96524	0.26184	12.071	1.836	121139	0.06750	0.21976		+0.6221	+0.6226i
15	0.96107	0.49922	10.460	1.773	97397	0.37202	0.40036	r_1	0.0215	0.0215
20	0.95040	0.50695	9.025	1.398	64597	0.42871	0.39470	r_2	-0.0903	-0.0724
25	0.95022	0.42209	7.701	0.957	37179	0.36068	0.31233		+0.2714	+0.2214i
30	0.94898	0.29062	6.569	0.555	17947	0.26397	0.20434	c_1		5451
35	0.92453	0.14981	5.597	0.260	7018	0.14472	0.09996	c_2		13753
40	0.87508	0.07015	4.645	0.107	2343	0.05521	0.04330			8775i
45	0.83843	0.02909	3.650	0.033	564	0.03140	0.01570	$2\pi/y$	23.151	28.385
50	0.76695	0.00008	2.747	0.000	1	0.00000	0.00000	Δ	4.193	
55	0.72958		5.483							

Madagascar, 1966

TABLE 1 DATA INPUT TO COMPUTATIONS

Age at last birthday	Population					Births, by age of mother	Deaths			Age at last birthday
	Total	Males	%	Females	%		Total	Males	Females	
0	230390	115118	3.8	115272	3.7	0	29209	13503	15706	0
1–4	890670	446697	14.7	443973	14.2	0	29105	13603	15502	1–4
5–9	935036	481272	15.9	453764	14.5	0	12464	6651	5813	5–9
10–14	810691	425588	14.0	385103	12.3	1206	4666	2116	2550	10–14
15–19	567008	267484	8.8	299524	9.6	42612	6287	3023	3264	15–19
20–24	417799	191912	6.3	225887	7.2	68541	6084	2922	3162	20–24
25–29	390953	162081	5.3	228872	7.3	66329	6391	2821	3570	25–29
30–34	333243	155120	5.1	178123	5.7	51053	5880	2922	2958	30–34
35–39	332249	153132	5.1	179117	5.7	33165	5880	2922	2958	35–39
40–44	272559	132250	4.4	140309	4.5	13768	5169	2721	2448	40–44
45–49	250673	124295	4.1	126378	4.0	4120	4965	2721	2244	45–49
50–54	202922	105403	3.5	97519	3.1	1206	4758	2922	1836	50–54
55–59	172090	83526	2.8	88564	2.8	0	5164	3124	2040	55–59
60–64	113396	59661	2.0	53735	1.7	0	5364	3426	1938	60–64
65–69	96486	50712	1.7	45774	1.5	0	6885	4131	2754	65–69
70–74	68489	35723	1.2	32766	1.0		6515	3723	2792	70–74
75–79	41449	21334	0.7	20115	0.6		4984	2707	2277	75–79
80–84	21645	10935	0.4	10710	0.3	144958 M	3187	1639	1548	80–84
85 +	15636	7580	0.3	8056	0.3	137042 F	3043	1403	1640	85 +
All ages	6163384	3029823		3133561		282000	156000	79000	77000	All ages

TABLE 2 LIFE TABLE FOR MALES

Age, x	$_nq_x$	l_x	$_nd_x$	$_nL_x$	$_nm_x$	T_x	$1000r_x$	$\overset{\circ}{e}_x$	$_nM_x$	Age, x
0	0.10976	100000	10976	93577	0.11730	3757623	0.00	37.58	0.11730	0
1	0.11281	89024	10042	329775	0.03045	3664046	0.00	41.16	0.03045	1
5	0.06651	78981	5253	381774	0.01376	3334271	12.63	42.22	0.01382	5
10	0.02439	73728	1798	363887	0.00494	2952497	50.13	40.05	0.00497	10
15	0.05576	71930	4011	350291	0.01145	2588610	69.06	35.99	0.01130	15
20	0.07360	67919	4999	327358	0.01527	2238319	35.10	32.96	0.01523	20
25	0.08342	62921	5249	301520	0.01741	1910961	3.96	30.37	0.01740	25
30	0.08992	57672	5186	275296	0.01884	1609441	0.00	27.91	0.01884	30
35	0.09103	52486	4778	250378	0.01908	1334144	0.00	25.42	0.01908	35
40	0.09782	47708	4667	226811	0.02057	1083766	0.43	22.72	0.02057	40
45	0.10381	43042	4468	204111	0.02189	856955	0.00	19.91	0.02189	45
50	0.12996	38574	5013	180605	0.02776	652845	11.45	16.92	0.02772	50
55	0.17185	33560	5767	153795	0.03750	472239	17.47	14.07	0.03740	55
60	0.25155	27793	6991	121747	0.05742	318444	0.00	11.46	0.05742	60
65	0.33747	20802	7020	86177	0.08146	196697	0.00	9.46	0.08146	65
70	0.40943	13782	5643	54142	0.10422	110520	0.00	8.02	0.10422	70
75	0.47334	8139	3853	30362	0.12689	56378	0.00	6.93	0.12689	75
80	0.53085	4286	2275	15182	0.14989	26015	0.00	6.07	0.14989	80
85 +	1.00000	2011	2011	10834	0.18562	10834	0.00	5.39	0.18509	85 +

TABLE 3 LIFE TABLE FOR FEMALES

Age, x	$_nq_x$	l_x	$_nd_x$	$_nL_x$	$_nm_x$	T_x	$1000r_x$	$\overset{\circ}{e}_x$	$_nM_x$	Age, x
0	0.12615	100000	12615	92584	0.13625	3849487	0.00	38.49	0.13625	0
1	0.12792	87385	11178	320142	0.03492	3756903	0.00	42.99	0.03492	1
5	0.06154	76207	4690	369310	0.01270	3436761	21.27	45.10	0.01281	5
10	0.03248	71517	2323	351571	0.00661	3067451	32.43	42.89	0.00662	10
15	0.05342	69194	3697	337170	0.01096	2715880	42.87	39.25	0.01090	15
20	0.06772	65498	4436	316584	0.01401	2378710	13.16	36.32	0.01400	20
25	0.07509	61062	4585	293861	0.01560	2062126	8.22	33.77	0.01560	25
30	0.07970	56477	4501	271035	0.01661	1768265	8.14	31.31	0.01661	30
35	0.07927	51976	4120	249473	0.01652	1497230	7.10	28.81	0.01651	35
40	0.08358	47855	4000	229196	0.01745	1247757	17.59	26.07	0.01745	40
45	0.08500	43856	3728	209877	0.01776	1018561	18.50	23.23	0.01776	45
50	0.09001	40128	3612	191667	0.01884	808684	16.20	20.15	0.01883	50
55	0.10964	36516	4004	172944	0.02315	617017	34.88	16.90	0.02303	55
60	0.16624	32512	5405	149697	0.03611	444073	5.57	13.66	0.03507	60
65	0.26235	27107	7112	118092	0.06022	294376	5.57	10.86	0.06017	65
70	0.35039	19996	7006	82164	0.08527	176285	5.57	8.82	0.08521	70
75	0.43684	12990	5674	50095	0.11327	94121	5.57	7.25	0.11320	75
80	0.52012	7315	3805	26308	0.14462	44026	5.57	6.02	0.14454	80
85 +	1.00000	3510	3510	17717	0.19814	17717	5.57	5.05	0.20358	85 +

TABLE 4 POPULATION PROJECTION, USING FIXED AGE-SPECIFIC BIRTH AND DEATH RATES, IN THOUSANDS

Age at last birthday	1971 Total	Males	Females	1976 Total	Males	Females	1981 Total	Males	Females	Age at last birthday
0–4	1243	647	596	1393	725	668	1584	824	760	0–4
5–9	1007	507	500	1117	583	534	1252	554	598	5–9
10–14	891	459	432	959	483	476	1064	556	508	10–14
15–19	779	410	369	856	442	414	922	465	457	15–19
20–24	531	250	281	730	383	347	802	413	389	20–24
25–29	387	177	210	491	230	261	675	353	322	25–29
30–34	359	148	211	354	161	193	451	210	241	30–34
35–39	305	141	164	329	135	194	325	147	178	35–39
40–44	304	139	165	279	128	151	301	122	179	40–44
45–49	247	119	128	276	125	151	253	115	138	45–49
50–54	225	110	115	222	105	117	248	110	138	50–54
55–59	178	90	88	198	94	104	196	90	106	55–59
60–64	143	66	77	147	71	76	164	74	90	60–64
65–69	84	42	42	107	47	60	110	50	60	65–69
70–74	64	32	32	56	27	29	71	29	42	70–74
75–79	40	20	20	37	18	19	33	15	18	75–79
80–84	22	11	11	20	10	10	19	9	10	80–84
85 +	15	8	7	15	8	7	14	7	7	85 +
All ages	6824	3376	3448	7586	3775	3811	8484	4243	4241	All ages

TABLE 5 OBSERVED AND PROJECTED VITAL RATES

Rates per thousand	Observed Total	Males	Females	Projected 1971 Males	Females	1976 Males	Females	1981 Males	Females	Stable Males	Females
Birth	45.75	47.84	43.73	47.63	44.05	48.20	45.09	48.89	46.26	46.38	45.70
Death	25.31	26.07	24.57	25.34	23.96	24.78	23.89	24.37	24.01	23.85	24.17
Increase	20.44	21.77	19.16	22.29	20.09	23.42	21.20	24.52	22.25		22.5283

TABLE 6 RATES STANDARDIZED ON THREE STANDARD COUNTRIES

Standardized rates per thousand	England and Wales, 1961 Total	Males	Females	United States, 1960 Total	Males	Females	Mexico, 1960 Total	Males	Females
Birth	43.80	59.15*	41.25	44.48	54.39*	42.59	48.23	54.52*	46.75
Death	31.31	48.06*	31.21	29.10	40.46*	28.07	24.15	23.32*	23.59
Increase	12.48	11.09*	10.04	15.38	13.93*	14.52	24.07	31.19*	23.15

TABLE 7 VITAL STATISTICS AND RATES INFERRED FROM AGE DISTRIBUTIONS (FEMALES)

Vital statistics		Thompson Age range	NRR	$1000r$	Interval	Bourgeois-Pichat Age range	NRR	$1000b$	$1000d$	$1000r$	Coale	
TFR	6.77	0–4	1.84	23.72	26.44	5–29	2.06	47.01	20.20	26.81	$1000b$	49.75
GRR	3.29	5–9	1.79	22.46	26.31	30–54	1.45	35.26	21.50	13.76	$1000d$	23.04
NRR	1.88	10–14	1.67	19.13	26.26	55–79	1.44	31.45	17.98	13.47	$1000r$	26.72
Generation	27.91	15–19	1.45	13.57	26.21	*35–59	1.59	42.35	25.13	17.22	$1000k_1$	29.75
Sex ratio	105.8										$1000k_2$	0.33

TABLE 8 LESLIE MATRIX AND ITS ANALYSIS (FEMALES)

Start of age interval	Sub-diagonal	First row	Percent in stable population	Fisher values	Total reproductive values	Net maternity function	Matrix equation coefficient
0	0.89481	0.00000	18.244	1.280	715675	0.00000	0.00000
5	0.95197	0.00299	14.581	1.601	726545	0.00000	0.00268
10	0.95904	0.13997	12.399	1.879	723607	0.00535	0.11923
15	0.93895	0.42839	10.621	2.007	601063	0.23311	0.34997
20	0.92822	0.57407	8.907	1.809	408601	0.46682	0.44034
25	0.92232	0.55574	7.385	1.390	318198	0.41386	0.39569
30	0.92045	0.45835	6.084	0.917	163251	0.37751	0.30099
35	0.91872	0.27609	5.002	0.478	85529	0.22448	0.16689
40	0.91571	0.12834	4.105	0.197	27686	0.10929	0.07127
45	0.91323	0.04402	3.357	0.062	7820	0.03325	0.02238
50	0.90232	0.01240	2.739	0.014	1383	0.01152	0.00576
55	0.74379		6.575				

Parameters

	Integral	Matrix
λ_1	1.1192	1.1196
λ_2	0.3804	0.3930
	+0.7263	+0.7087 i
r_1	0.0225	0.0226
r_2	-0.0397	-0.0421
	+0.2177	+0.2129 i
c_1		29828
c_2		58425
		27266 i
$2\pi/y$	28.866	29.513
Δ	4.015	

Mauritius, 1966 (excluding dependencies)

TABLE 1 DATA INPUT TO COMPUTATIONS

Age at last birthday	Total	Males	%	Females	%	Births, by age of mother	Total	Males	Females	Age at last birthday
0	25750	12950	3.4	12800	3.4	0	1721	943	778	0
1–4	99550	50250	13.2	49300	13.0	0	729	362	367	1–4
5–9	109900	55650	14.6	54250	14.3	0	192	105	87	5–9
10–14	100000	50300	13.2	49700	13.1	32	93	57	36	10–14
15–19	85950	43150	11.3	42800	11.3	3556	121	59	62	15–19
20–24	55750	27850	7.3	27900	7.4	7866	115	36	79	20–24
25–29	45700	22700	6.0	23000	6.1	6397	107	37	70	25–29
30–34	40250	20100	5.3	20150	5.3	4445	113	43	70	30–34
35–39	39800	20250	5.3	19550	5.2	3010	168	88	80	35–39
40–44	39250	20400	5.4	18850	5.0	1097	181	109	72	40–44
45–49	29600	15500	4.1	14100	3.7	102	211	127	84	45–49
50–54	26050	13800	3.6	12250	3.2	5	306	212	94	50–54
55–59	19550	10050	2.6	9500	2.5	0	371	244	127	55–59
60–64	15850	7700	2.0	8150	2.2	0	455	295	160	60–64
65–69	11850	5350	1.4	6500	1.7	0	502	294	208	65–69
70–74	7700	2900	0.8	4800	1.3		460	239	221	70–74
75–79	4150	1400	0.4	2750	0.7		376	167	209	75–79
80–84	2000	600	0.2	1400	0.4	13346 M	256	81	175	80–84
85 +	450	100	0.0	350	0.1	13164 F	224	52	172	85 +
All ages	759100	381000		378100		26510	6701	3550	3151	All ages

TABLE 2 LIFE TABLE FOR MALES

Age, x	$_nq_x$	l_x	$_nd_x$	$_nL_x$	$_nm_x$	T_x	$1000r_x$	$\overset{\circ}{e}_x$	$_nM_x$	Age, x
0	0.06942	100000	6942	95337	0.07282	5947969	0.00	59.48	0.07282	0
1	0.02824	93058	2628	364835	0.00720	5852632	0.00	62.89	0.00720	1
5	0.00929	90429	840	450048	0.00187	5487797	19.84	60.69	0.00189	5
10	0.00564	89590	505	446638	0.00113	5037750	24.07	56.23	0.00113	10
15	0.00682	89085	608	443918	0.00137	4591112	57.84	51.54	0.00137	15
20	0.00646	88477	572	440978	0.00130	4147194	62.85	46.87	0.00129	20
25	0.00815	87905	716	437811	0.00164	3706217	30.98	42.16	0.00163	25
30	0.01067	87189	930	433858	0.00214	3268405	8.90	37.49	0.00214	30
35	0.02151	86259	1855	426928	0.00435	2834548	0.00	32.86	0.00435	35
40	0.02646	84404	2234	416741	0.00536	2407619	21.03	28.53	0.00534	40
45	0.04051	82170	3329	403287	0.00825	1990878	30.01	24.23	0.00819	45
50	0.07459	78841	5881	380564	0.01545	1587591	27.68	20.14	0.01535	50
55	0.11548	72960	8425	344884	0.02443	1207027	32.92	16.54	0.02428	55
60	0.17648	64535	11389	295142	0.03859	862143	44.40	13.35	0.03831	60
65	0.24349	53146	12941	233880	0.05533	567002	44.40	10.67	0.05495	65
70	0.34330	40205	13802	166334	0.08298	333122	44.40	8.29	0.08241	70
75	0.45652	26403	12053	100502	0.11993	166787	44.40	6.32	0.11929	75
80	0.50084	14349	7187	52761	0.13621	66285	44.40	4.62	0.13500	80
85 +	*1.00000	7163	7163	13524	0.52962	13524	44.40	1.89	0.52000	85 +

TABLE 3 LIFE TABLE FOR FEMALES

Age, x	$_nq_x$	l_x	$_nd_x$	$_nL_x$	$_nm_x$	T_x	$1000r_x$	$\overset{\circ}{e}_x$	$_nM_x$	Age, x
0	0.05848	100000	5848	96206	0.06078	6370696	0.00	63.71	0.06078	0
1	0.02917	94152	2747	368981	0.00744	6274490	0.00	66.64	0.00744	1
5	0.00787	91406	720	455229	0.00158	5905510	19.53	64.61	0.00160	5
10	0.00361	90686	328	452599	0.00072	5450280	22.62	60.10	0.00072	10
15	0.00734	90358	663	450330	0.00147	4997681	56.14	55.31	0.00145	15
20	0.01416	89695	1270	445440	0.00285	4547351	59.52	50.70	0.00283	20
25	0.01512	88425	1337	438829	0.00305	4101911	29.42	46.39	0.00304	25
30	0.01724	87088	1501	431768	0.00348	3663082	12.72	42.06	0.00347	30
35	0.02026	85587	1734	423617	0.00409	3231314	2.81	37.75	0.00409	35
40	0.01898	83853	1591	415431	0.00383	2807696	28.32	33.48	0.00382	40
45	0.02952	82262	2428	405537	0.00599	2392265	37.33	29.08	0.00596	45
50	0.03792	79833	3027	392135	0.00772	1986728	30.94	24.89	0.00767	50
55	0.06513	76806	5002	372305	0.01344	1594593	27.38	20.76	0.01337	55
60	0.09432	71804	6773	343068	0.01974	1222288	29.63	17.02	0.01963	60
65	0.14928	65031	9708	301874	0.03216	879220	29.63	13.52	0.03200	65
70	0.20811	55323	11513	248747	0.04629	577345	29.63	10.44	0.04504	70
75	0.32172	43810	14095	184388	0.07644	328599	29.63	7.50	0.07600	75
80	0.48035	29715	14274	113173	0.12613	144211	29.63	4.85	0.12500	80
85 +	*1.00000	15441	15441	31038	0.49750	31038	29.63	2.01	0.49143	85 +

[314]

TABLE 4 POPULATION PROJECTION, USING FIXED AGE-SPECIFIC BIRTH AND DEATH RATES, IN THOUSANDS

Age at last birthday	1971 Total	1971 Males	1971 Females	1976 Total	1976 Males	1976 Females	1981 Total	1981 Males	1981 Females	Age at last birthday
0–4	138	69	69	170	85	85	205	103	102	0–4
5–9	123	62	61	134	67	67	166	83	83	5–9
10–14	109	55	54	121	61	60	134	67	67	10–14
15–19	99	50	49	109	55	54	121	61	60	15–19
20–24	85	43	42	99	50	49	108	55	53	20–24
25–29	55	28	27	85	43	42	97	49	48	25–29
30–34	45	22	23	54	27	27	83	42	41	30–34
35–39	40	20	20	44	22	22	54	27	27	35–39
40–44	39	20	19	38	19	19	44	22	22	40–44
45–49	38	20	18	38	19	19	38	19	19	45–49
50–54	29	15	14	37	19	18	36	18	18	50–54
55–59	25	13	12	26	13	13	34	17	17	55–59
60–64	18	9	9	22	11	11	23	11	12	60–64
65–69	13	6	7	15	7	8	17	8	9	65–69
70–74	9	4	5	10	4	6	11	5	6	70–74
75–79	6	2	4	6	2	4	7	3	4	75–79
80–84	3	1	2	3	1	2	3	1	2	80–84
85 +	0	0	0	0	0	0	1	0	1	85 +
All ages	874	439	435	1011	505	506	1182	591	591	All ages

TABLE 5 OBSERVED AND PROJECTED VITAL RATES

Rates per thousand	Observed Total	Observed Males	Observed Females	Projected 1971 Males	Projected 1971 Females	Projected 1976 Males	Projected 1976 Females	Projected 1981 Males	Projected 1981 Females	Stable Males	Stable Females
Birth	34.92	35.03	34.82	38.07	37.70	40.32	39.79	40.87	40.22	39.87	38.83
Death	8.83	9.32	8.33	9.32	8.28	9.53	8.44	9.56	8.48	9.33	8.35
Increase	26.10	25.71	26.48	28.75	29.42	30.79	31.35	31.32	31.74		30.5371

TABLE 6 RATES STANDARDIZED ON THREE STANDARD COUNTRIES

Standardized rates per thousand	England and Wales, 1961 Total	Males	Females	United States, 1960 Total	Males	Females	Mexico, 1960 Total	Males	Females
Birth	34.78	39.28*	33.47	35.40	35.78*	34.63	39.37	36.41*	39.00
Death	17.77	22.89*	17.61	15.22	18.06*	13.90	9.27	9.84*	8.25
Increase	17.01	16.39*	15.86	20.18	17.72*	20.73	30.10	26.57*	30.75

TABLE 7 VITAL STATISTICS AND RATES INFERRED FROM AGE DISTRIBUTIONS (FEMALES)

Vital statistics		Thompson Age range	NRR	$1000r$	Interval	Bourgeois-Pichat Age range	NRR	$1000b$	$1000d$	$1000r$	Coale
TFR	5.42	0–4	2.28	30.28	27.28	5–29	3.29	47.82	3.74	44.09	$1000b$
GRR	2.69	5–9	2.47	33.96	27.23	30–54	1.80	26.82	5.10	21.72	$1000d$
NRR	2.35	10–14	2.55	33.55	27.18	55–79	1.66	20.02	1.29	18.73	$1000r$
Generation	27.97	15–19	2.46	33.19	27.09	*45–74	1.89	27.78	4.17	23.61	$1000k_1$
Sex ratio	101.38										$1000k_2$

TABLE 8 LESLIE MATRIX AND ITS ANALYSIS (FEMALES)

Start of age interval	Sub-diagonal	First row	Percent in stable population	Fisher values	Total reproductive values	Net maternity function	Matrix equation coefficient	Parameters Integral	Matrix
0	0.97859	0.00000	16.800	1.159	71989	0.00000	0.00000	λ_1 1.1650	1.1656
5	0.99422	0.00073	14.105	1.381	74906	0.00000	0.00072	λ_2 0.4010	0.4090
10	0.99498	0.09621	12.031	1.618	80408	0.00145	0.09362	+0.8175	+0.7929 i
15	0.98914	0.41803	10.270	1.783	76320	0.18579	0.40470	r_1 0.0305	0.0306
20	0.98516	0.64209	8.716	1.611	44956	0.52362	0.61484	r_2 −0.0187	−0.0228
25	0.98391	0.57195	7.367	1.151	26471	0.60607	0.53952	+0.2229	+0.2189 i
30	0.98112	0.42927	6.218	0.690	13894	0.47296	0.39842	c_1	3758
35	0.98067	0.24375	5.234	0.312	6099	0.32387	0.22196	c_2	−832
40	0.97618	0.07537	4.404	0.083	1558	0.12005	0.06731		12818 i
45	0.96695	0.00882	3.688	0.009	129	0.01457	0.00768	$2\pi/y$ 28.182	28.701
50	0.94943	0.00050	3.060	0.000	6	0.00079	0.00040	Δ 3.938	
55	0.80718		8.106						

Reunion, 1963

TABLE 1 DATA INPUT TO COMPUTATIONS

Age at last birthday	Population					Births, by age of mother	Deaths			Age at last birthday
	Total	Males	%	Females	%		Total	Males	Females	
0	15354	7711	4.3	7643	4.0	0	1158	599	559	0
1–4	52536	26201	14.5	26335	13.8	0	479	227	252	1–4
5–9	51979	26004	14.4	25975	13.6	0	56	28	28	5–9
10–14	47372	23832	13.2	23540	12.4	8	35	20	15	10–14
15–19	33979	17050	9.4	16929	8.9	1030	35	19	16	15–19
20–24	27225	12530	6.9	14695	7.7	3942	53	33	20	20–24
25–29	26359	12676	7.0	13683	7.2	4602	77	44	33	25–29
30–34	21629	10675	5.9	10954	5.7	3321	109	47	62	30–34
35–39	20455	10128	5.6	10327	5.4	2422	126	67	59	35–39
40–44	18026	9005	5.0	9021	4.7	1062	164	99	65	40–44
45–49	14504	7110	3.9	7394	3.9	86	165	108	57	45–49
50–54	12695	6329	3.5	6366	3.3	9	207	149	58	50–54
55–59	9633	4443	2.5	5190	2.7	0	236	161	75	55–59
60–64	6806	2981	1.6	3825	2.0	0	208	132	76	60–64
65–69	5347	2092	1.2	3255	1.7	0	251	132	119	65–69
70–74	3616	1240	0.7	2376	1.2		258	128	130	70–74
75–79	2142	629	0.3	1513	0.8		221	83	138	75–79
80–84	1123	275	0.2	848	0.4	8396 M	118	35	83	80–84
85 +	870	151	0.1	719	0.4	8086 F	102	27	75	85 +
All ages	371650	181062		190588		16482	4058	2138	1920	All ages

TABLE 2 LIFE TABLE FOR MALES

Age, x	$_nq_x$	l_x	$_nd_x$	$_nL_x$	$_nm_x$	T_x	$1000r_x$	$\overset{\circ}{e}_x$	$_nM_x$	Age, x
0	0.07334	100000	7334	95164	0.07707	5557875	11.28	55.58	0.07768	0
1	0.03359	92666	3113	361962	0.00860	5462711	11.28	58.95	0.00866	1
5	0.00516	89553	462	446611	0.00103	5100750	32.48	56.96	0.00108	5
10	0.00419	89091	373	444532	0.00084	4654139	41.28	52.24	0.00084	10
15	0.00568	88718	504	442495	0.00114	4209607	62.90	47.45	0.00111	15
20	0.01315	88214	1160	438379	0.00265	3767112	27.17	42.70	0.00263	20
25	0.01723	87054	1500	431667	0.00348	3328734	12.53	38.24	0.00347	25
30	0.02184	85554	1869	423353	0.00441	2897067	17.80	33.86	0.00440	30
35	0.03264	83685	2732	412112	0.00663	2473714	9.95	29.56	0.00662	35
40	0.05379	80953	4354	394484	0.01104	2061604	24.51	25.47	0.01099	40
45	0.07354	76599	5633	369659	0.01524	1667117	19.22	21.76	0.01519	45
50	0.11191	70966	7942	335996	0.02364	1297458	22.51	18.28	0.02354	50
55	0.16717	63024	10536	289314	0.03642	961462	40.13	15.25	0.03642	55
60	0.20008	52488	10502	236390	0.04443	672149	28.77	12.81	0.04428	60
65	0.27419	41986	11512	181567	0.06341	435758	28.77	10.38	0.06310	65
70	0.41015	30474	12499	120549	0.10368	254192	28.77	8.34	0.10323	70
75	0.48752	17975	8763	66261	0.13225	133643	28.77	7.43	0.13196	75
80	0.46800	9212	4311	33899	0.12718	67381	28.77	7.31	0.12727	80
85 +	1.00000	4901	4901	33483	0.14636	33483	28.77	6.83	0.17881	85 +

TABLE 3 LIFE TABLE FOR FEMALES

Age, x	$_nq_x$	l_x	$_nd_x$	$_nL_x$	$_nm_x$	T_x	$1000r_x$	$\overset{\circ}{e}_x$	$_nM_x$	Age, x
0	0.06941	100000	6941	95538	0.07265	6240280	9.69	62.40	0.07314	0
1	0.03708	93059	3451	362687	0.00951	6144742	9.69	66.03	0.00957	1
5	0.00512	89608	459	446893	0.00103	5782055	33.78	64.53	0.00108	5
10	0.00318	89149	283	445030	0.00064	5335162	42.01	59.85	0.00064	10
15	0.00475	88866	422	443341	0.00095	4890132	46.17	55.03	0.00095	15
20	0.00681	88444	603	440846	0.00137	4446792	19.83	50.28	0.00135	20
25	0.01211	87841	1064	436926	0.00244	4005946	26.44	45.60	0.00241	25
30	0.02800	86777	2430	428084	0.00568	3569020	23.21	41.13	0.00566	30
35	0.02819	84347	2378	415891	0.00572	3140936	13.30	37.24	0.00571	35
40	0.03545	81969	2906	402710	0.00722	2725045	26.45	33.24	0.00721	40
45	0.03788	79063	2995	387933	0.00772	2322335	27.00	29.37	0.00771	45
50	0.04476	76069	3405	372270	0.00915	1934402	25.44	25.43	0.00911	50
55	0.07024	72664	5104	351193	0.01453	1562132	36.68	21.50	0.01445	55
60	0.09535	67560	6442	322782	0.01996	1210939	20.45	17.92	0.01987	60
65	0.16876	61118	10315	281028	0.03670	888157	20.45	14.53	0.03656	65
70	0.24223	50804	12306	224080	0.05492	607129	20.45	11.95	0.05471	70
75	0.37098	38498	14282	156173	0.09145	383049	20.45	9.95	0.09121	75
80	0.38731	24216	9379	95794	0.09791	226876	20.45	9.37	0.09788	80
85 +	1.00000	14837	14837	131083	0.11318	131083	20.45	8.84	0.10431	85 +

TABLE 4 POPULATION PROJECTION, USING FIXED AGE-SPECIFIC BIRTH AND DEATH RATES, IN THOUSANDS

Age at last birthday	1968			1973			1978			Age at last birthday
	Total	Males	Females	Total	Males	Females	Total	Males	Females	
0–4	81	41	40	94	48	46	112	57	55	0–4
5–9	66	33	33	79	40	39	91	46	45	5–9
10–14	52	26	26	66	33	33	78	40	38	10–14
15–19	47	24	23	52	26	26	66	33	33	15–19
20–24	34	17	17	47	24	23	52	26	26	20–24
25–29	27	12	15	34	17	17	46	23	23	25–29
30–34	25	12	13	26	12	14	32	16	16	30–34
35–39	21	10	11	25	12	13	26	12	14	35–39
40–44	20	10	10	20	10	10	25	12	13	40–44
45–49	17	8	9	19	9	10	19	9	10	45–49
50–54	13	6	7	16	8	8	17	8	9	50–54
55–59	11	5	6	13	6	7	15	7	8	55–59
60–64	9	4	5	10	4	6	11	5	6	60–64
65–69	5	2	3	7	3	4	8	3	5	65–69
70–74	4	1	3	5	2	3	5	2	3	70–74
75–79	3	1	2	3	1	2	3	1	2	75–79
80–84	1	0	1	1	0	1	1	0	1	80–84
85 +	1	0	1	1	0	1	1	0	1	85 +
All ages	437	212	225	518	255	263	608	300	308	All ages

TABLE 5 OBSERVED AND PROJECTED VITAL RATES

Rates per thousand	Observed			Projected						Stable	
				1968		1973		1978			
	Total	Males	Females	Males	Females	Males	Females	Males	Females	Males	Females
Birth	44.35	46.37	42.43	44.43	41.01	44.60	41.51	45.01	42.18	45.24	43.89
Death	10.92	11.81	10.07	11.68	9.95	11.35	9.68	11.11	9.54	10.18	8.83
Increase	33.43	34.56	32.35	32.75	31.07	33.25	31.83	33.90	32.64		35.0565

TABLE 6 RATES STANDARDIZED ON THREE STANDARD COUNTRIES

Standardized rates per thousand	England and Wales, 1961			United States, 1960			Mexico, 1960		
	Total	Males	Females	Total	Males	Females	Total	Males	Females
Birth	43.01	48.71*	40.90	43.70	45.15*	42.25	45.75	45.60*	44.78
Death	18.12	28.92*	15.72	15.74	22.69*	12.85	10.37	11.41*	8.69
Increase	24.90	19.80*	25.18	27.97	22.46*	29.39	35.38	34.19*	36.09

TABLE 7 VITAL STATISTICS AND RATES INFERRED FROM AGE DISTRIBUTIONS (FEMALES)

Vital statistics		Thompson				Bourgeois-Pichat					Coale	
		Age range	NRR	1000r	Interval	Age range	NRR	1000b	1000d	1000r		
TFR	6.67	0–4	2.52	33.90	27.24	5–29	2.50	39.42	5.45	33.97	1000b	42.16
GRR	3.27	5–9	2.21	29.83	27.12	30–54	1.78	28.08	6.67	21.41	1000d	6.90
NRR	2.81	10–14	2.24	29.12	27.03	55–79	1.73	23.89	3.52	20.38	1000r	35.27
Generation	29.44	15–19	1.83	16.24	26.94	*35–59	2.03	35.08	8.93	26.16	$1000k_1$	25.15
Sex ratio	103.8										$1000k_2$	0.26

TABLE 8 LESLIE MATRIX AND ITS ANALYSIS (FEMALES)

Start of age interval	Sub-diagonal	First row	Percent in stable population	Fisher values	Total reproductive values	Net maternity function	Matrix equation coefficient	Parameters		
									Integral	Matrix
0	0.97527	0.00000	18.475	1.190	40429	0.00000	0.00000	λ_1	1.1916	1.1924
5	0.99583	0.00038	15.111	1.455	37787	0.00000	0.00037	λ_2	0.4781	0.4794
10	0.99620	0.06851	12.620	1.741	40993	0.00074	0.06654		+0.8398	+0.8178 i
15	0.99437	0.36821	10.544	2.003	33901	0.13233	0.35625	r_1	0.0351	0.0352
20	0.99111	0.57620	8.793	1.961	28813	0.58017	0.65055	r_2	-0.0068	-0.0107
25	0.97976	0.71192	7.308	1.547	21169	0.72094	0.67883		+0.2106	+0.2081 i
30	0.97152	0.59688	6.005	1.018	11154	0.63672	0.55762	c_1		1770
35	0.96831	0.39175	4.893	0.519	5357	0.47852	0.35556	c_2		2715
40	0.96331	0.14492	3.973	0.157	1420	0.23259	0.12736			-1262 i
45	0.95962	0.01460	3.210	0.015	117	0.02214	0.01236	$2\pi/y$	29.828	30.192
50	0.94338	0.00159	2.583	0.002	10	0.00258	0.00129	Δ	5.450	
55	0.81660		6.485							

Seychelles, 1960

TABLE 1 DATA INPUT TO COMPUTATIONS

Age at last birthday	Population Total	Males	%	Females	%	Births, by age of mother	Deaths Total	Males	Females	Age at last birthday
0	1508	812	4.0	696	3.3	0	89	47	42	0
1–4	5231	2687	13.2	2544	12.0	0	27	19	8	1–4
5–9	5053	2572	12.6	2481	11.7	0	5	2	3	5–9
10–14	4202	2129	10.5	2073	9.8	0	2	1	1	10–14
15–19	3456	1766	8.7	1690	8.0	125	3	2	1	15–19
20–24	3196	1479	7.3	1717	8.1	527	9	6	3	20–24
25–29	2972	1409	6.9	1563	7.4	461	6	3	3	25–29
30–34	2577	1248	6.1	1329	6.3	255	9	8	1	30–34
35–39	2390	1144	5.6	1246	5.9	238	8	2	6	35–39
40–44	1963	948	4.7	1015	4.8	87	16	11	5	40–44
45–49	1964	953	4.7	1011	4.8	21	13	11	2	45–49
50–54	1802	881	4.3	921	4.3	0	21	8	13	50–54
55–59	1474	722	3.5	752	3.5	0	13	7	6	55–59
60–64	1170	539	2.6	631	3.0	0	24	8	16	60–64
65–69	960	425	2.1	535	2.5	0	28	16	12	65–69
70–74	700	307	1.5	393	1.9		43	23	20	70–74
75–79	433	177	0.9	256	1.2		27	18	9	75–79
80–84	257	84	0.4	173	0.8	867 M	33	18	15	80–84
85 +	227	61	0.3	166	0.8	847 F	37	14	23	85 +
All ages	41535	20343		21192		1714	413	224	189	All ages

TABLE 2 LIFE TABLE FOR MALES

Age, x	nq_x	l_x	nd_x	nL_x	nm_x	T_x	$1000r_x$	$\mathring{e}_x$	nM_x	Age, x
0	0.05523	100000	5523	96418	0.05728	6191553	15.00	61.92	0.05788	0
1	0.02749	94477	2597	370697	0.00701	6095135	15.00	64.51	0.00707	1
5	0.00362	91880	332	458571	0.00072	5724438	15.00	62.30	0.00078	5
10	0.00236	91548	216	457240	0.00047	5265867	36.96	57.52	0.00047	10
15	0.00578	91332	528	455674	0.00116	4808628	34.73	52.65	0.00113	15
20	0.02011	90804	1826	449542	0.00406	4352954	19.70	47.94	0.00406	20
25	0.01062	88978	945	442726	0.00214	3903411	13.28	43.87	0.00213	25
30	0.03154	88033	2777	433183	0.00641	3460685	16.71	39.31	0.00641	30
35	0.00882	85256	752	424819	0.00177	3027502	22.32	35.51	0.00175	35
40	0.05657	84504	4781	411343	0.01162	2602684	8.98	30.80	0.01160	40
45	0.05605	79723	4469	387145	0.01154	2191340	0.00	27.49	0.01154	45
50	0.04433	75255	3336	367715	0.00907	1804196	18.06	23.97	0.00908	50
55	0.04759	71918	3423	351372	0.00974	1436480	38.82	19.97	0.00970	55
60	0.07228	68496	4951	331694	0.01493	1085108	15.61	15.84	0.01484	60
65	0.17410	63545	11063	292503	0.03782	753414	15.61	11.86	0.03765	65
70	0.31714	52482	16644	221521	0.07513	460911	15.61	8.78	0.07492	70
75	0.40546	35838	14531	142450	0.10201	239390	15.61	6.68	0.10169	75
80	0.68855	21307	14671	68212	0.21507	96940	15.61	4.55	0.21429	80
85 +	*1.00000	6636	6636	28728	0.23100	28728	15.61	4.33	0.22951	85 +

TABLE 3 LIFE TABLE FOR FEMALES

Age, x	nq_x	l_x	nd_x	nL_x	nm_x	T_x	$1000r_x$	$\mathring{e}_x$	nM_x	Age, x
0	0.05749	100000	5749	95745	0.06004	6921262	6.54	69.21	0.06034	0
1	0.01237	94251	1166	373635	0.00312	6825517	6.54	72.42	0.00314	1
5	0.00593	93085	552	464046	0.00119	6451882	43.09	69.31	0.00121	5
10	0.00239	92533	221	462057	0.00048	5987837	37.73	64.71	0.00048	10
15	0.00298	92313	275	460996	0.00060	5525780	18.03	59.86	0.00059	15
20	0.00871	92038	802	458308	0.00175	5064783	6.26	55.03	0.00175	20
25	0.00952	91236	869	453913	0.00191	4606475	24.06	50.49	0.00192	25
30	0.00382	90367	345	451240	0.00076	4152563	20.71	45.95	0.00075	30
35	0.02391	90022	2152	445101	0.00484	3701323	23.00	41.12	0.00482	35
40	0.02427	87870	2132	433745	0.00492	3256222	16.83	37.06	0.00493	40
45	0.00990	85737	849	427330	0.00199	2822477	4.19	32.92	0.00198	45
50	0.06838	84889	5805	410404	0.01414	2395147	20.02	28.22	0.01412	50
55	0.03941	79084	3117	388314	0.00803	1984743	24.13	25.10	0.00798	55
60	0.11979	75967	9100	357925	0.02542	1596429	19.77	21.01	0.02536	60
65	0.10687	66867	7146	317389	0.02251	1238505	19.77	18.52	0.02243	65
70	0.22614	59721	13505	264915	0.05098	921115	19.77	15.42	0.05089	70
75	0.16198	46216	7486	212459	0.03524	656200	19.77	14.20	0.03516	75
80	0.36028	38730	13954	160109	0.08715	443741	19.77	11.46	0.08671	80
85 +	1.00000	24776	24776	283632	0.08735	283632	19.77	11.45	0.13855	85 +

TABLE 4   POPULATION PROJECTION, USING FIXED AGE-SPECIFIC BIRTH AND DEATH RATES, IN THOUSANDS

Age at last birthday	1966 Total	1966 Males	1966 Females	1971 Total	1971 Males	1971 Females	1976 Total	1976 Males	1976 Females	Age at last birthday
0–4	8	4	4	10	5	5	10	5	5	0–4
5–9	6	3	3	8	4	4	9	5	4	5–9
10–14	5	3	2	6	3	3	8	4	4	10–14
15–19	4	2	2	5	3	2	6	3	3	15–19
20–24	4	2	2	4	2	2	5	3	2	20–24
25–29	3	1	2	4	2	2	4	2	2	25–29
30–34	3	1	2	3	1	2	4	2	2	30–34
35–39	2	1	1	3	1	2	3	1	2	35–39
40–44	2	1	1	2	1	1	2	1	1	40–44
45–49	2	1	1	2	1	1	2	1	1	45–49
50–54	2	1	1	2	1	1	2	1	1	50–54
55–59	2	1	1	2	1	1	2	1	1	55–59
60–64	2	1	1	2	1	1	2	1	1	60–64
65–69	1	0	1	2	1	1	2	1	1	65–69
70–74	0	0	0	0	0	0	1	0	1	70–74
75–79	0	0	0	0	0	0	0	0	0	75–79
80–84	0	0	0	0	0	0	0	0	0	80–84
85 +	0	0	0	0	0	0	0	0	0	85 +
All ages	46	22	24	55	27	28	62	31	31	All ages

TABLE 5   OBSERVED AND PROJECTED VITAL RATES

Rates per thousand	Observed Total	Observed Males	Observed Females	Projected 1966 Males	Projected 1966 Females	Projected 1971 Males	Projected 1971 Females	Projected 1976 Males	Projected 1976 Females	Stable Males	Stable Females
Birth	41.27	42.62	39.97	39.40	36.91	38.04	35.80	38.17	36.04	41.78	40.21
Death	9.94	11.01	8.92	10.34	9.54	9.92	9.20	9.75	9.13	8.24	6.53
Increase	31.32	31.61	31.05	29.06	27.37	28.13	26.60	28.42	26.90		33.5358

TABLE 6   RATES STANDARDIZED ON THREE STANDARD COUNTRIES

Standardized rates per thousand	England and Wales, 1961 Total	Males	Females	United States, 1960 Total	Males	Females	Mexico, 1960 Total	Males	Females
Birth	37.50	44.07*	35.92	37.98	40.80*	35.98	41.54	41.10*	40.95
Death	13.15	17.06*	12.07	11.50	14.49*	9.70	7.49	9.02*	5.28
Increase	24.34	27.01*	23.85	26.47	26.31*	27.28	34.05	32.08*	34.66

TABLE 7   VITAL STATISTICS AND RATES INFERRED FROM AGE DISTRIBUTIONS (FEMALES)

Vital statistics		Thompson Age range	NRR	1000r	Interval	Bourgeois-Pichat Age range	NRR	1000b	1000d	1000r	Coale
TFR	5.83	0–4	2.18	28.50	27.34	5–29	1.77	27.92	6.72	21.20	1000b
GRR	2.88	5–9	1.81	22.09	27.29	30–54	1.47	21.81	7.57	14.24	1000d
NRR	2.60	10–14	1.66	18.35	27.21	55–79	1.58	24.18	7.29	16.89	1000r
Generation	28.50	15–19	1.49	14.11	27.08	*45–74	1.66	27.49	8.71	18.78	1000k_1
Sex ratio	102.36										1000k_2

TABLE 8   LESLIE MATRIX AND ITS ANALYSIS (FEMALES)

Start of age interval	Sub-diagonal	First row	Percent in stable population	Fisher values	Total reproductive values	Net maternity function	Matrix equation coefficient	Parameters	Integral	Matrix
0	0.98864	0.00000	17.405	1.158	3751	0.00000	0.00000	λ_1	1.1826	1.1833
5	0.99571	0.00000	14.542	1.386	3438	0.00000	0.00000	λ_2	0.3984	0.4127
10	0.99770	0.08558	12.236	1.647	3414	0.00000	0.08425		+0.7825	+0.7625i
15	0.99417	0.43967	10.317	1.854	3133	0.16850	0.43182	r_1	0.0335	0.0337
20	0.99041	0.69475	8.668	1.694	2909	0.69514	0.67836	r_2	−0.0260	−0.0285
25	0.99411	0.56328	7.255	1.212	1895	0.66159	0.54472		+0.2200	+0.2149i
30	0.98640	0.44104	6.095	0.787	1046	0.42785	0.42399	c_1		183
35	0.97449	0.31840	5.081	0.427	532	0.42014	0.30193	c_2		−28
40	0.98521	0.12201	4.184	0.140	142	0.18372	0.11379			−849i
45	0.96039	0.02415	3.484	0.025	25	0.04386	0.02193	$2\pi/y$	28.562	29.233
50	0.94617	0.00126	2.827	0.001	1	0.00000	0.00000	Δ	10.221	
55	0.84496		7.906							

South Africa, 1961 (Colored)

TABLE 1 DATA INPUT TO COMPUTATIONS

Age at last birthday	Population					Births, by age of mother	Deaths			Age at last birthday
	Total	Males	%	Females	%		Total	Males	Females	
0	69030	34224	4.4	34806	4.5	0	9175	4842	4333	0
1–4	207092	102672	13.3	104420	13.4	0	4146	2086	2060	1–4
5–9	232284	115077	15.0	117207	15.0	0	383	200	183	5–9
10–14	190379	94366	12.3	96013	12.3	114	222	111	111	10–14
15–19	150258	74669	9.7	75589	9.7	9192	292	165	127	15–19
20–24	135692	67167	8.7	68525	8.8	22701	425	253	172	20–24
25–29	113991	55739	7.2	58252	7.5	17896	458	280	178	25–29
30–34	96291	48041	6.2	48250	6.2	11563	529	308	221	30–34
35–39	77362	39281	5.1	38081	4.9	6775	573	314	259	35–39
40–44	64856	33023	4.3	31833	4.1	2608	565	353	212	40–44
45–49	56609	28066	3.6	28543	3.7	544	588	425	263	45–49
50–54	46200	23465	3.1	22735	2.9	63	839	517	322	50–54
55–59	34890	18206	2.4	16684	2.1	0	748	471	277	55–59
60–64	25829	12354	1.6	13475	1.7	0	960	509	451	60–64
65–69	18897	8988	1.2	9909	1.3	0	899	491	408	65–69
70–74	13286	6159	0.8	7127	0.9		917	499	418	70–74
75–79	8861	4190	0.5	4671	0.6		778	392	386	75–79
80–84	4125	1921	0.2	2204	0.3	35775 M	630	309	321	80–84
85+	3510	1526	0.2	1984	0.3	35681 F	705	325	380	85+
All ages	1549442	769134		780308		71456	23932	12850	11082	All ages

TABLE 2 LIFE TABLE FOR MALES

Age, x	$_nq_x$	l_x	$_nd_x$	$_nL_x$	$_nm_x$	T_x	$1000r_x$	$\overset{\circ}{e}_x$	$_nM_x$	Age, x
0	0.12838	100000	12838	91799	0.13985	4985354	18.19	49.85	0.14148	0
1	0.07620	87162	6642	330324	0.02011	4893555	18.19	56.14	0.02032	1
5	0.00814	80521	656	400963	0.00164	4563231	31.37	56.67	0.00174	5
10	0.00589	79865	470	398195	0.00118	4162268	41.75	52.12	0.00118	10
15	0.01108	79394	880	394982	0.00223	3764073	31.69	47.41	0.00221	15
20	0.01874	78515	1471	389112	0.00378	3369092	25.53	42.91	0.00377	20
25	0.02489	77043	1918	380611	0.00504	2979980	28.44	38.68	0.00502	25
30	0.03165	75125	2378	369879	0.00643	2599369	28.55	34.60	0.00641	30
35	0.03934	72748	2862	356849	0.00802	2229490	29.27	30.65	0.00799	35
40	0.05228	69886	3653	340711	0.01072	1872641	22.60	26.80	0.01069	40
45	0.07328	66233	4853	319608	0.01519	1531930	18.47	23.13	0.01514	45
50	0.10477	61379	6431	291207	0.02208	1212323	22.05	19.75	0.02203	50
55	0.12231	54948	6720	258484	0.02600	921115	35.70	16.76	0.02587	55
60	0.18748	48228	9042	219101	0.04127	662631	10.92	13.74	0.04120	60
65	0.24088	39186	9439	172533	0.05471	443530	10.92	11.32	0.05463	65
70	0.33628	29747	10003	123311	0.08112	270997	10.92	9.11	0.08102	70
75	0.37714	19744	7446	79480	0.09368	147685	10.92	7.48	0.09356	75
80	0.57028	12298	7013	43505	0.16120	68205	10.92	5.55	0.16085	80
85+	*1.00000	5285	5285	24700	0.21394	24700	10.92	4.67	0.21298	85+

TABLE 3 LIFE TABLE FOR FEMALES

Age, x	$_nq_x$	l_x	$_nd_x$	$_nL_x$	$_nm_x$	T_x	$1000r_x$	$\overset{\circ}{e}_x$	$_nM_x$	Age, x
0	0.11419	100000	11419	92828	0.12302	5455576	18.88	54.56	0.12449	0
1	0.07415	88581	6569	336343	0.01953	5362748	18.88	60.54	0.01973	1
5	0.00728	82012	597	408568	0.00146	5026405	31.59	61.29	0.00155	5
10	0.00577	81415	470	405918	0.00116	4617837	42.52	56.72	0.00116	10
15	0.00841	80945	681	403134	0.00169	4211920	31.99	52.03	0.00168	15
20	0.01251	80264	1004	398920	0.00252	3808786	23.52	47.45	0.00251	20
25	0.01524	79260	1208	393443	0.00307	3409866	31.81	43.02	0.00305	25
30	0.02280	78052	1780	386094	0.00461	3016424	37.73	38.65	0.00458	30
35	0.03353	76273	2557	375104	0.00682	2630330	35.33	34.49	0.00680	35
40	0.03282	73716	2419	362670	0.00667	2255226	21.58	30.59	0.00665	40
45	0.04527	71297	3228	348885	0.00925	1892556	23.93	26.54	0.00921	45
50	0.06877	68069	4681	329033	0.01423	1543671	40.28	22.68	0.01416	50
55	0.08048	63388	5102	305096	0.01672	1214638	32.41	19.16	0.01660	55
60	0.15526	58286	9050	269604	0.03356	909543	15.96	15.60	0.03347	60
65	0.18719	49237	9216	223395	0.04126	639879	16.96	13.00	0.04117	65
70	0.25655	40020	10267	174641	0.05879	416483	16.96	10.41	0.05865	70
75	0.34338	29753	10217	123258	0.08289	241842	16.96	8.13	0.08264	75
80	0.53390	19537	10431	71375	0.14614	118584	16.96	6.07	0.14565	80
85+	*1.00000	9106	9106	47209	0.19289	47209	16.96	5.18	0.19153	85+

TABLE 4 POPULATION PROJECTION, USING FIXED AGE-SPECIFIC BIRTH AND DEATH RATES, IN THOUSANDS

Age at last birthday	1966 Total	Males	Females	1971 Total	Males	Females	1976 Total	Males	Females	Age at last birthday
0–4	328	163	165	386	192	194	457	227	230	0–4
5–9	263	130	133	313	155	158	367	182	185	5–9
10–14	230	114	116	261	129	132	311	154	157	10–14
15–19	189	94	95	229	113	116	259	128	131	15–19
20–24	149	74	75	186	92	94	226	112	114	20–24
25–29	134	66	68	146	72	74	183	90	93	25–29
30–34	111	54	57	130	64	66	142	70	72	30–34
35–39	93	46	47	108	52	56	126	62	64	35–39
40–44	75	38	37	89	44	45	104	50	54	40–44
45–49	62	31	31	70	35	35	86	42	44	45–49
50–54	53	26	27	57	28	29	65	32	33	50–54
55–59	42	21	21	48	23	25	52	25	27	55–59
60–64	30	15	15	37	18	19	41	19	22	60–64
65–69	21	10	11	24	12	12	29	14	15	65–69
70–74	14	6	8	16	7	9	19	9	10	70–74
75–79	9	4	5	9	4	5	10	4	6	75–79
80–84	5	2	3	5	2	3	5	2	3	80–84
85 +	2	1	1	3	1	2	3	1	2	85 +
All ages	1810	895	915	2117	1043	1074	2485	1223	1262	All ages

TABLE 5 OBSERVED AND PROJECTED VITAL RATES

Rates per thousand	Observed Total	Males	Females	Projected 1966 Males	Females	1971 Males	Females	1976 Males	Females	Stable Males	Females
Birth	46.12	46.51	45.73	46.44	45.31	47.17	45.76	47.78	46.15	48.25	46.23
Death	15.45	15.71	14.20	16.52	14.03	16.37	13.94	16.28	13.91	15.41	13.37
Increase	30.67	29.81	31.52	29.92	31.28	30.81	31.82	31.50	32.24		32.8366

TABLE 6 RATES STANDARDIZED ON THREE STANDARD COUNTRIES

Standardized rates per thousand	England and Wales, 1961 Total	Males	Females	United States, 1960 Total	Males	Females	Mexico, 1960 Total	Males	Females
Birth	41.29	45.99*	39.96	41.97	41.91*	41.29	46.61	44.58*	46.43
Death	20.72	36.00*	20.40	18.69	29.26*	17.28	14.27	15.29*	12.90
Increase	20.57	9.98*	19.56	23.28	12.65*	24.01	32.34	29.30*	33.53

TABLE 7 VITAL STATISTICS AND RATES INFERRED FROM AGE DISTRIBUTIONS (FEMALES)

Vital statistics		Thompson Age range	NRR	1000r	Interval	Bourgeois-Pichat Age range	NRR	1000b	1000d	1000r	Coale	
TFR	6.41	0–4	2.35	31.33	27.24	5–29	2.43	45.65	12.79	32.86	1000b	47.57
GRR	3.20	5–9	2.38	32.63	27.11	30–54	2.13	38.43	10.41	28.02	1000d	12.86
NRR	2.49	10–14	2.28	29.81	26.99	55–79	1.71	22.09	2.15	19.94	1000r	34.70
Generation	27.81	15–19	2.12	28.04	26.84	*20–44	2.53	48.28	13.87	34.40	$1000k_1$	4.50
Sex ratio	100.3										$1000k_2$	0.

TABLE 8 LESLIE MATRIX AND ITS ANALYSIS (FEMALES)

Start of age interval	Sub-diagonal	First row	Percent in stable population	Fisher values	Total reproductive values	Net maternity function	Matrix equation coefficient	Parameters	Integral	Matrix
0	0.95199	0.00000	18.318	1.263	175797	0.00000	0.00000	λ_1	1.1784	1.1792
5	0.99351	0.00126	14.789	1.564	183311	0.00000	0.00120	λ_2	0.3757	0.3904
10	0.99314	0.13068	12.460	1.855	178070	0.00241	0.12360		+0.7847	+0.7627 i
15	0.98955	0.48156	10.494	2.036	153891	0.24479	0.45235	r_1	0.0328	0.0330
20	0.98627	0.57962	8.807	1.812	124136	0.65990	0.63173	r_2	−0.0279	−0.0309
25	0.98132	0.58117	7.366	1.295	75481	0.60357	0.53279		+0.2248	+0.2195 i
30	0.97154	0.44200	6.130	0.809	39044	0.46202	0.39763	c_1		7570
35	0.96685	0.27552	5.051	0.408	15526	0.33324	0.24080	c_2		2275
40	0.96199	0.10743	4.141	0.137	4374	0.14837	0.09079			1059 i
45	0.94310	0.02322	3.379	0.027	782	0.03320	0.01888			
50	0.92725	0.00297	2.702	0.003	72	0.00455	0.00228	$2\pi/y$	27.944	28.619
55	0.78538		6.363					Δ	1.908	

South Africa, 1961 (White)

TABLE 1 DATA INPUT TO COMPUTATIONS

Age at last birthday	Population					Births, by age of mother	Deaths			Age at last birthday
	Total	Males	%	Females	%		Total	Males	Females	
0	89653	45364	2.9	44289	2.8	0	2127	1215	912	0
1–4	268957	136091	8.7	132866	8.5	0	383	211	172	1–4
5–9	334386	170597	10.9	163789	10.4	0	204	119	85	5–9
10–14	320722	164164	10.5	156558	10.0	31	148	91	57	10–14
15–19	282610	144275	9.3	138335	8.8	6225	248	187	61	15–19
20–24	238469	120020	7.7	118449	7.5	26097	405	316	89	20–24
25–29	207583	104477	6.7	103106	6.6	22034	336	217	119	25–29
30–34	210597	104505	6.7	106092	6.8	13060	443	295	148	30–34
35–39	196525	98721	6.3	97804	6.2	6211	529	343	185	35–39
40–44	187656	94053	6.0	93603	6.0	1878	826	523	303	40–44
45–49	185578	91879	5.9	93699	6.0	180	1145	736	409	45–49
50–54	172442	85998	5.5	86444	5.5	9	1757	1129	628	50–54
55–59	130605	64192	4.1	66413	4.2	0	2035	1321	714	55–59
60–64	94179	43731	2.8	50448	3.2	0	2203	1353	850	60–64
65–69	80037	35287	2.3	44750	2.8	0	2732	1621	1111	65–69
70–74	57113	24390	1.6	32723	2.1		3132	1701	1431	70–74
75–79	38644	16468	1.1	22176	1.4		3097	1614	1483	75–79
80–84	21750	9452	0.6	12298	0.8	38972 M	2683	1305	1378	80–84
85+	11593	4617	0.3	6976	0.4	36753 F	2575	1189	1386	85+
All ages	3129099	1558281		1570818		75725	27008	15486	11522	All ages

TABLE 2 LIFE TABLE FOR MALES

Age, x	$_nq_x$	l_x	$_nd_x$	$_nL_x$	$_nm_x$	T_x	$1000r_x$	$\overset{\circ}{e}_x$	$_nM_x$	Age, x
0	0.02573	100000	2573	98128	0.02622	6527825	27.62	65.28	0.02678	0
1	0.00601	97427	585	388023	0.00151	6429697	27.62	66.00	0.00155	1
5	0.00347	96842	336	483357	0.00070	6041674	9.14	62.39	0.00070	5
10	0.00278	96505	268	481916	0.00056	5558307	16.02	57.60	0.00055	10
15	0.00653	96237	628	479820	0.00131	5076391	29.87	52.75	0.00130	15
20	0.01310	95609	1253	474985	0.00264	4596571	30.07	48.08	0.00263	20
25	0.01033	94356	975	469354	0.00208	4121587	11.45	43.68	0.00208	25
30	0.01402	93381	1310	463759	0.00282	3652233	2.92	39.11	0.00282	30
35	0.01725	92071	1588	456631	0.00348	3188474	6.77	34.63	0.00347	35
40	0.02745	90483	2484	446596	0.00556	2731843	1.63	30.19	0.00555	40
45	0.03932	87999	3460	431953	0.00801	2285247	0.42	25.97	0.00801	45
50	0.06396	84539	5407	410084	0.01319	1853294	22.28	21.92	0.01313	50
55	0.09887	79131	7824	377114	0.02075	1443210	46.45	18.24	0.02058	55
60	0.14424	71308	10285	331827	0.03100	1066095	11.44	14.95	0.03094	60
65	0.20695	61022	12629	274397	0.04602	734269	11.44	12.03	0.04594	65
70	0.29755	48394	14400	206115	0.06986	459871	11.44	9.50	0.06974	70
75	0.39220	33994	13332	135818	0.09816	253756	11.44	7.46	0.09801	75
80	0.50630	20662	10461	75650	0.13828	117937	11.44	5.71	0.13807	80
85+	1.00000	10201	10201	42287	0.24122	42287	11.44	4.15	0.25753	85+

TABLE 3 LIFE TABLE FOR FEMALES

Age, x	$_nq_x$	l_x	$_nd_x$	$_nL_x$	$_nm_x$	T_x	$1000r_x$	$\overset{\circ}{e}_x$	$_nM_x$	Age, x
0	0.01987	100000	1987	98573	0.02016	7215506	27.84	72.16	0.02059	0
1	0.00503	98013	493	390638	0.00126	7116933	27.84	72.61	0.00129	1
5	0.00258	97520	252	486971	0.00052	6726295	11.68	68.97	0.00052	5
10	0.00182	97268	177	485892	0.00036	6239324	16.48	64.15	0.00036	10
15	0.00221	97092	215	484960	0.00044	5753432	27.41	59.26	0.00044	15
20	0.00377	96877	365	483541	0.00076	5268472	28.62	54.38	0.00075	20
25	0.00576	96511	556	481229	0.00116	4784931	9.90	49.58	0.00115	25
30	0.00695	95955	667	478180	0.00140	4303702	3.84	44.85	0.00140	30
35	0.00949	95288	904	474356	0.00191	3825521	10.45	40.15	0.00190	35
40	0.01607	94384	1515	468358	0.00324	3351165	1.15	35.51	0.00324	40
45	0.02162	92867	2008	459682	0.00437	2882807	3.22	31.04	0.00437	45
50	0.03589	90860	3261	446691	0.00730	2423125	27.08	26.67	0.00726	50
55	0.05283	87598	4628	427150	0.01083	1976434	42.54	22.56	0.01075	55
60	0.08135	82971	6749	398888	0.01692	1549284	24.90	18.67	0.01685	60
65	0.11788	76221	8985	360023	0.02496	1150396	24.90	15.09	0.02483	65
70	0.19875	67237	13364	304139	0.04394	790374	24.90	11.76	0.04373	70
75	0.28837	53874	15536	231238	0.06718	486235	24.90	9.03	0.06687	75
80	0.43769	38337	16780	149082	0.11255	254997	24.90	6.65	0.11205	80
85+	1.00000	21558	21558	105915	0.20354	105915	24.90	4.91	0.19868	85+

TABLE 4 POPULATION PROJECTION, USING FIXED AGE-SPECIFIC BIRTH AND DEATH RATES, IN THOUSANDS

Age at last birthday	1966			1971			1976			Age at last birthday
	Total	Males	Females	Total	Males	Females	Total	Males	Females	
0–4	390	200	190	435	223	212	481	247	234	0–4
5–9	356	180	176	388	199	189	433	222	211	5–9
10–14	333	170	163	356	180	176	386	198	188	10–14
15–19	319	163	156	332	169	163	355	179	176	15–19
20–24	281	143	138	318	162	156	331	168	153	20–24
25–29	237	119	118	278	141	137	315	160	155	25–29
30–34	205	103	102	234	117	117	275	139	136	30–34
35–39	208	103	105	204	102	102	231	115	116	35–39
40–44	194	97	97	205	101	104	199	99	100	40–44
45–49	183	91	92	188	93	95	199	97	102	45–49
50–54	178	87	91	175	86	89	181	89	92	50–54
55–59	162	79	83	167	80	87	164	79	85	55–59
60–64	118	56	62	147	70	77	152	71	81	60–64
65–69	82	36	46	103	47	56	128	58	70	65–69
70–74	65	27	38	65	27	38	82	35	47	70–74
75–79	41	16	25	46	17	29	47	18	29	75–79
80–84	23	9	14	25	9	16	29	10	19	80–84
85+	14	5	9	15	5	10	16	5	11	85+
All ages	3389	1684	1705	3681	1828	1853	4004	1989	2015	All ages

TABLE 5 OBSERVED AND PROJECTED VITAL RATES

Rates per thousand	Observed			Projected						Stable	
				1966		1971		1976			
	Total	Males	Females	Males	Females	Males	Females	Males	Females	Males	Females
Birth	24.20	25.01	23.40	25.68	23.93	26.51	24.67	26.73	24.86	26.53	24.99
Death	8.63	9.94	7.34	9.95	7.66	9.94	7.88	9.95	8.04	9.15	7.61
Increase	15.57	15.07	16.06	15.72	16.27	16.58	16.79	16.77	16.82		17.3827

TABLE 6 RATES STANDARDIZED ON THREE STANDARD COUNTRIES

Standardized rates per thousand	England and Wales, 1961			United States, 1960			Mexico, 1960		
	Total	Males	Females	Total	Males	Females	Total	Males	Females
Birth	21.81	24.43*	20.51	22.15	22.64*	21.19	25.97	22.08*	25.14
Death	12.88	14.21*	11.97	10.55	12.18*	8.87	5.63	8.62*	4.41
Increase	8.93	10.22*	8.54	11.60	10.46*	12.32	20.34	13.45*	20.73

TABLE 7 VITAL STATISTICS AND RATES INFERRED FROM AGE DISTRIBUTIONS (FEMALES)

Vital statistics		Thompson				Bourgeois-Pichat				Coale	
TFR	3.44	Age range	NRR	1000r	Interval	Age range	NRR	1000b	1000d	1000r	1000b 24.12
GRR	1.67	0–4	1.58	17.08	27.40	5–29	1.89	26.59	3.07	23.52	1000d 8.04
NRR	1.60	5–9	1.56	16.48	27.36	30–54	1.17	16.61	10.92	5.70	1000r 16.08
Generation	27.20	10–14	1.56	16.04	27.29	55–79	1.83	34.85	12.41	22.44	1000k_1 0.
Sex ratio	106.0	15–19	1.44	12.93	27.19	*30–54	1.17	16.61	10.92	5.70	1000k_2 0.

TABLE 8 LESLIE MATRIX AND ITS ANALYSIS (FEMALES)

Start of age interval	Sub-diagonal	First row	Percent in stable population	Fisher values	Total reproductive values	Net maternity function	Matrix equation coefficient	Parameters		
									Integral	Matrix
0	0.99542	0.00000	11.717	1.067	189079	0.00000	0.00000	λ_1	1.0908	1.0910
5	0.99778	0.00023	10.690	1.170	191598	0.00000	0.00023	λ_2	0.3476	0.3537
10	0.99808	0.05355	9.777	1.279	200208	0.00047	0.05319		+0.8318	+0.7998 i
15	0.99707	0.31422	8.944	1.341	185450	0.10592	0.31149	r_1	0.0174	0.0174
20	0.99522	0.51406	8.174	1.131	133907	0.51707	0.50810	r_2	-0.0207	-0.0268
25	0.99366	0.39892	7.457	0.688	70938	0.49913	0.39241		+0.2350	+0.2309 i
30	0.99200	0.22093	6.792	0.327	34683	0.28570	0.21595	c_1		15229
35	0.98736	0.09891	6.175	0.122	11916	0.14621	0.09591	c_2		-2362
40	0.98147	0.32606	5.589	0.028	2593	0.04561	0.02495			12549 i
45	0.97174	0.00240	5.028	0.002	230	0.00429	0.00226	$2\pi/y$	26.738	27.214
50	0.95625	0.00012	4.478	0.000	11	0.00023	0.00011	Δ	3.311	
55	0.80889		15.179							

Tunisia, 1960

TABLE 1   DATA INPUT TO COMPUTATIONS

Age at last birthday	Population					Births, by age of mother	Deaths			Age at last birthday
	Total	Males	%	Females	%		Total	Males	Females	
0	133763	68563	3.3	65200	3.1	0	16194	8754	7440	0
1–4	555829	279674	13.5	276155	13.1	0	11374	5877	5497	1–4
5–9	568996	286131	13.8	282865	13.4	0	1225	674	551	5–9
10–14	449825	226328	10.9	223497	10.6	115	704	428	276	10–14
15–19	384803	193324	9.3	191479	9.1	10665	620	342	278	15–19
20–24	342891	170809	8.2	172082	8.2	46000	998	458	540	20–24
25–29	308997	154085	7.4	154912	7.4	49523	1000	460	540	25–29
30–34	272068	136045	6.6	136023	6.5	38955	1007	444	563	30–34
35–39	234960	117528	5.7	117432	5.6	23208	951	445	505	35–39
40–44	205553	102193	4.9	103360	4.9	10206	1046	561	485	40–44
45–49	174351	86380	4.2	87971	4.2	2551	1078	665	413	45–49
50–54	144985	71384	3.4	73601	3.5	898	1628	936	692	50–54
55–59	118896	57258	2.8	61638	2.9	0	1369	883	486	55–59
60–64	92165	43238	2.1	48927	2.3	0	2205	1312	893	60–64
65–69	67755	30833	1.5	36922	1.8	0	1666	1044	622	65–69
70–74	47355	20810	1.0	26545	1.3		2370	1361	1009	70–74
75–79	31526	13315	0.6	18211	0.9		1647	1027	620	75–79
80–84	20022	8086	0.4	11936	0.6	95268 M	1107	716	391	80–84
85 +	27213	9784	0.5	17429	0.8	86953 F	2157	1047	1110	85 +
All ages	4181953	2075768		2106185		182221	50346	27434	22912	All ages

TABLE 2   LIFE TABLE FOR MALES

Age, x	$_nq_x$	l_x	$_nd_x$	$_nL_x$	$_nm_x$	T_x	$1000r_x$	$\overset{\circ}{e}_x$	$_nM_x$	Age, x
0	0.11824	100000	11824	92609	0.12768	5565513	0.00	55.66	0.12768	0
1	0.07949	88176	7009	333562	0.02101	5472904	0.00	62.07	0.02101	1
5	0.01111	81166	902	403578	0.00223	5139342	35.60	63.32	0.00236	5
10	0.00939	80265	754	399397	0.00189	4735765	37.28	59.00	0.00189	10
15	0.00883	79511	702	395861	0.00177	4336367	26.15	54.54	0.00177	15
20	0.01335	78809	1052	391509	0.00269	3940506	20.15	50.00	0.00268	20
25	0.01483	77757	1153	385942	0.00299	3548998	19.76	45.64	0.00299	25
30	0.01621	76604	1242	379971	0.00327	3163056	23.79	41.29	0.00326	30
35	0.01882	75362	1418	373427	0.00380	2783085	24.58	36.93	0.00379	35
40	0.02720	73944	2011	364968	0.00551	2409658	25.26	32.59	0.00549	40
45	0.03802	71933	2735	353328	0.00774	2044691	27.43	28.42	0.00770	45
50	0.06378	69198	4414	335397	0.01316	1691362	28.88	24.44	0.01311	50
55	0.07493	64784	4854	312637	0.01553	1355965	31.75	20.93	0.01542	55
60	0.14178	59930	8497	279082	0.03046	1043329	24.72	17.41	0.03034	60
65	0.15720	51433	8085	237735	0.03401	764247	24.72	14.86	0.03386	65
70	0.28249	43348	12246	186527	0.06565	526512	24.72	12.15	0.06540	70
75	0.32173	31103	10007	129525	0.07726	339984	24.72	10.93	0.07713	75
80	0.35952	21096	7585	85536	0.08867	210459	24.72	9.98	0.08855	80
85 +	1.00000	13511	13511	124923	0.10816	124923	24.72	9.25	0.10701	85 +

TABLE 3   LIFE TABLE FOR FEMALES

Age, x	$_nq_x$	l_x	$_nd_x$	$_nL_x$	$_nm_x$	T_x	$1000r_x$	$\overset{\circ}{e}_x$	$_nM_x$	Age, x
0	0.10659	100000	10659	93406	0.11411	6323331	0.00	63.23	0.11411	0
1	0.07554	89341	6749	339035	0.01991	6229925	0.00	69.73	0.01991	1
5	0.00911	82593	752	411083	0.00183	5890890	36.51	71.32	0.00195	5
10	0.00614	81840	503	407913	0.00123	5479807	37.62	66.96	0.00123	10
15	0.00728	81338	592	405366	0.00146	5071895	24.37	62.35	0.00145	15
20	0.01561	80745	1261	400739	0.00315	4666528	18.36	57.79	0.00314	20
25	0.01730	79485	1375	394057	0.00349	4265789	19.92	53.67	0.00349	25
30	0.02051	78110	1602	386597	0.00414	3871732	23.67	49.57	0.00414	30
35	0.02133	76508	1632	378488	0.00431	3485135	23.09	45.55	0.00431	35
40	0.02320	74876	1737	370053	0.00469	3106648	24.36	41.49	0.00469	40
45	0.02335	73139	1708	361747	0.00472	2736595	28.14	37.42	0.00469	45
50	0.04605	71431	3289	349128	0.00942	2374847	27.77	33.25	0.00940	50
55	0.03897	68141	2655	334581	0.00794	2025719	30.08	29.73	0.00788	55
60	0.08780	65486	5750	313520	0.01834	1691138	42.71	25.82	0.01825	60
65	0.08174	59736	4883	287271	0.01700	1377618	42.71	23.06	0.01685	65
70	0.17462	54853	9579	250775	0.03820	1090347	42.71	19.88	0.03801	70
75	0.15609	45275	7067	207912	0.03399	839572	42.71	18.54	0.03405	75
80	0.15107	38208	5772	176204	0.03276	631660	42.71	16.53	0.03276	80
85 +	1.00000	32436	32436	455456	0.07122	455456	42.71	14.04	0.06369	85 +

[324]

TABLE 4 POPULATION PROJECTION, USING FIXED AGE-SPECIFIC BIRTH AND DEATH RATES, IN THOUSANDS

Age at last birthday	1965 Total	Males	Females	1970 Total	Males	Females	1975 Total	Males	Females	Age at last birthday
0–4	826	429	397	924	480	444	1058	549	509	0–4
5–9	654	330	324	783	406	377	876	454	422	5–9
10–14	564	283	281	648	326	322	776	402	374	10–14
15–19	446	224	222	560	281	279	643	323	320	15–19
20–24	380	191	189	442	222	220	554	278	276	20–24
25–29	337	168	169	374	188	186	435	219	216	25–29
30–34	304	152	152	332	166	166	369	186	183	30–34
35–39	267	134	133	298	149	149	326	163	163	35–39
40–44	230	115	115	261	131	130	291	146	145	40–44
45–49	200	99	101	223	111	112	254	127	127	45–49
50–54	167	82	85	192	94	98	214	106	108	50–54
55–59	138	67	71	157	76	81	181	88	93	55–59
60–64	109	51	58	125	59	66	144	68	75	60–64
65–69	82	37	45	97	44	53	112	51	61	65–69
70–74	56	24	32	68	29	39	80	34	46	70–74
75–79	36	14	22	44	17	27	52	20	32	75–79
80–84	24	9	15	29	10	19	34	11	23	80–84
85 +	43	12	31	53	13	40	62	14	48	85 +
All ages	4863	2421	2442	5610	2802	2808	6461	3239	3222	All ages

TABLE 5 OBSERVED AND PROJECTED VITAL RATES

Rates per thousand	Observed Total	Males	Females	Projected 1965 Males	Females	1970 Males	Females	1975 Males	Females	Stable Males	Females
Birth	43.57	45.90	41.28	43.73	39.56	42.60	38.79	42.75	39.19	42.44	40.54
Death	12.04	13.22	10.88	13.54	11.20	13.27	11.18	13.17	11.24	13.54	11.64
Increase	31.53	32.68	30.41	30.20	28.36	29.34	27.61	29.58	27.95		28.9013

TABLE 6 RATES STANDARDIZED ON THREE STANDARD COUNTRIES

Standardized rates per thousand	England and Wales, 1961 Total	Males	Females	United States, 1960 Total	Males	Females	Mexico, 1960 Total	Males	Females
Birth	40.85	44.32*	37.79	41.32	40.82*	38.85	43.44	42.08*	41.35
Death	13.17	23.31*	11.51	12.84	19.80*	10.93	11.43	11.58*	10.17
Increase	27.69	21.02*	26.28	28.48	21.02*	27.92	32.01	30.51*	31.17

TABLE 7 VITAL STATISTICS AND RATES INFERRED FROM AGE DISTRIBUTIONS (FEMALES)

Vital statistics		Thompson Age range	NRR	$1000r$	Interval	Bourgeois-Pichat Age range	NRR	$1000b$	$1000d$	$1000r$	Coale	
TFR	6.34	0–4	2.11	28.27	27.27	5–29	2.09	37.96	10.69	27.27	$1000b$	41.80
GRR	3.02	5–9	2.04	26.75	27.20	30–54	1.98	38.32	12.96	25.36	$1000d$	11.54
NRR	2.35	10–14	1.82	21.72	27.16	55–79	2.73	74.59	37.46	37.13	$1000r$	30.25
Generation	29.60	15–19	1.78	16.49	27.09	*25–49	1.90	36.10	12.27	23.83	$1000k_1$	31.29
Sex ratio	109.6										$1000k_2$	0.45

TABLE 8 LESLIE MATRIX AND ITS ANALYSIS (FEMALES)

Start of age interval	Sub-diagonal	First row	Percent in stable population	Fisher values	Total reproductive values	Net maternity function	Matrix equation coefficient
0	0.95061	0.00000	16.346	1.241	423670	0.00000	0.00000
5	0.99229	0.00053	13.442	1.509	426925	0.00000	0.00050
10	0.99376	0.05764	11.538	1.758	392827	0.00100	0.05437
15	0.98859	0.33013	9.919	1.973	377711	0.10774	0.30946
20	0.98333	0.60081	8.482	1.892	325607	0.51118	0.55676
25	0.98108	0.62040	7.215	1.466	227114	0.60234	0.56533
30	0.97903	0.49512	6.124	0.943	128217	0.52832	0.44263
35	0.97771	0.30352	5.186	0.485	56992	0.35694	0.26565
40	0.97756	0.13113	4.386	0.189	19485	0.17436	0.11221
45	0.96512	0.04207	3.709	0.056	4966	0.05006	0.03519
50	0.95834	0.01259	3.097	0.014	995	0.02033	0.01016
55	0.87483		10.556				

Parameters

	Integral	Matrix
λ_1	1.1555	1.1560
λ_2	0.4459	0.4495
	+0.8114 i	+0.7877 i
r_1	0.0289	0.0290
r_2	-0.0154	-0.0195
	+0.2137 i	+0.2104 i
c_1		20483
c_2		24101
		-23596 i
$2\pi/y$	29.407	29.857
Δ	3.442	

Canada, 1966-68 (excluding Newfoundland)

TABLE 1 DATA INPUT TO COMPUTATIONS

Age at last birthday	Population					Births, by age of mother	Deaths			Age at last birthday
	Total	Males	%	Females	%		Total	Males	Females	
0	359959	184692	1.8	175267	1.8	0	7875	4467	3408	0
1–4	1687550	866592	8.7	820958	8.3	0	1572	891	681	1–4
5–9	2253966	1150233	11.5	1103733	11.1	0	1125	674	451	5–9
10–14	2090508	1069925	10.7	1020583	10.3	228	893	574	319	10–14
15–19	1856608	941558	9.4	915050	9.2	41317	1677	1211	466	15–19
20–24	1529617	763525	7.6	766092	7.7	122338	1829	1402	427	20–24
25–29	1276750	637600	6.4	639150	6.4	98055	1366	960	406	25–29
30–34	1226492	622217	6.2	604275	6.1	56420	1544	1011	533	30–34
35–39	1263250	640025	6.4	623225	6.3	31573	2221	1410	811	35–39
40–44	1255933	625350	6.3	630583	6.4	10186	3459	2181	1278	40–44
45–49	1099067	545000	5.4	554067	5.6	832	4914	3144	1770	45–49
50–54	987517	494900	4.9	492617	5.0	6	7144	4684	2460	50–54
55–59	829691	418058	4.2	411633	4.1	0	9566	6381	3185	55–59
60–64	671209	333142	3.3	338067	3.4	0	11999	7958	4041	60–64
65–69	533375	255292	2.6	278083	2.8	0	14614	9319	5295	65–69
70–74	425200	195983	2.0	229217	2.3		17263	10284	6979	70–74
75–79	302275	137767	1.4	164508	1.7		19578	11034	8544	75–79
80–84	178325	79867	0.8	98458	1.0	185343 M	18950	9892	9058	80–84
85 +	105375	43817	0.4	61558	0.6	175712 F	20419	9277	11142	85 +
All ages	19932667	10005543		9927124		361055	148008	86754	61254	All ages

TABLE 2 LIFE TABLE FOR MALES

Age, x	$_nq_x$	l_x	$_nd_x$	$_nL_x$	$_nm_x$	T_x	$1000r_x$	$\overset{\circ}{e}_x$	$_nM_x$	Age, x
0	0.02375	100000	2375	98194	0.02419	6888509	0.00	68.89	0.02419	0
1	0.00410	97625	400	389337	0.00103	6790315	0.00	69.56	0.00103	1
5	0.00293	97225	284	485413	0.00059	6400978	0.00	65.84	0.00059	5
10	0.00269	96940	261	484120	0.00054	5915565	19.31	61.02	0.00054	10
15	0.00646	96679	624	481964	0.00129	5431446	32.49	56.18	0.00129	15
20	0.00915	96055	879	478097	0.00184	4949481	37.33	51.53	0.00184	20
25	0.00750	95176	713	474075	0.00151	4471384	18.86	46.98	0.00151	25
30	0.00809	94463	764	470469	0.00162	3997309	0.00	42.32	0.00162	30
35	0.01096	93699	1027	466101	0.00220	3526840	0.00	37.64	0.00220	35
40	0.01734	92672	1607	459668	0.00350	3060739	12.41	33.03	0.00349	40
45	0.02857	91064	2602	449339	0.00579	2601071	17.37	28.56	0.00577	45
50	0.04646	88463	4110	432796	0.00950	2151732	16.66	24.32	0.00946	50
55	0.07401	84352	6243	407143	0.01533	1718936	23.78	20.38	0.01526	55
60	0.11333	78110	8852	369543	0.02395	1311793	15.48	16.79	0.02389	60
65	0.16809	69258	11641	318138	0.03659	942250	15.48	13.60	0.03650	65
70	0.23297	57616	13423	255180	0.05260	624112	15.48	10.83	0.05247	70
75	0.33455	44193	14785	184115	0.08030	368932	15.48	8.35	0.08009	75
80	0.47452	29409	13955	112294	0.12427	184817	15.48	6.28	0.12386	80
85 +	•1.00000	15454	15454	72522	0.21309	72522	15.48	4.69	0.21172	85 +

TABLE 3 LIFE TABLE FOR FEMALES

Age, x	$_nq_x$	l_x	$_nd_x$	$_nL_x$	$_nm_x$	T_x	$1000r_x$	$\overset{\circ}{e}_x$	$_nM_x$	Age, x
0	0.01916	100000	1916	98544	0.01944	7546510	0.00	75.47	0.01944	0
1	0.00331	98084	325	391392	0.00083	7447966	0.00	75.93	0.00083	1
5	0.00204	97759	200	488297	0.00041	7056574	0.00	72.18	0.00041	5
10	0.00156	97560	153	487427	0.00031	6568277	18.37	67.33	0.00031	10
15	0.00255	97407	248	486439	0.00051	6080850	28.21	62.43	0.00051	15
20	0.00279	97159	271	485129	0.00056	5594411	35.32	57.58	0.00056	20
25	0.00318	96888	308	483701	0.00064	5109282	23.06	52.73	0.00064	25
30	0.00440	96580	425	481902	0.00088	4625581	1.61	47.89	0.00088	30
35	0.00649	96155	624	479326	0.00130	4143679	0.00	43.09	0.00130	35
40	0.01011	95531	965	475425	0.00203	3664352	9.66	38.35	0.00203	40
45	0.01592	94566	1506	469343	0.00321	3188927	21.38	33.72	0.00319	45
50	0.02480	93060	2307	459940	0.00502	2719584	24.54	29.22	0.00499	50
55	0.03821	90753	3467	445676	0.00778	2259644	29.64	24.90	0.00774	55
60	0.05843	87285	5100	424521	0.01201	1813968	26.56	20.78	0.01195	60
65	0.09159	82185	7527	393265	0.01914	1389447	26.56	16.91	0.01904	65
70	0.14278	74658	10660	348168	0.03062	996182	26.56	13.34	0.03045	70
75	0.23220	63998	14860	284466	0.05224	648014	26.56	10.13	0.05194	75
80	0.37584	49138	18468	199724	0.09247	363548	26.56	7.40	0.09200	80
85 +	1.00000	30670	30670	163824	0.18721	163824	26.56	5.34	0.18100	85 +

[326]

TABLE 4 POPULATION PROJECTION, USING FIXED AGE-SPECIFIC BIRTH AND DEATH RATES, IN THOUSANDS

Age at last birthday	1972			1977			1982			Age at last birthday
	Total	Males	Females	Total	Males	Females	Total	Males	Females	
0–4	1884	965	919	2140	1096	1044	2382	1220	1152	0–4
5–9	2040	1047	993	1877	961	916	2131	1091	1040	5–9
10–14	2249	1147	1102	2035	1044	991	1873	958	915	10–14
15–19	2084	1065	1019	2242	1142	1100	2028	1039	989	15–19
20–24	1847	934	913	2073	1057	1016	2230	1133	1097	20–24
25–29	1521	757	764	1836	926	910	2061	1048	1013	25–29
30–34	1270	633	637	1512	751	761	1826	919	907	30–34
35–39	1217	616	601	1260	627	633	1501	744	757	35–39
40–44	1249	631	618	1204	608	596	1246	518	528	40–44
45–49	1234	611	623	1227	617	610	1183	594	589	45–49
50–54	1068	525	543	1199	589	610	1192	594	598	50–54
55–59	943	466	477	1020	494	526	1145	554	591	55–59
60–64	771	379	392	878	423	455	949	448	501	60–64
65–69	600	287	313	690	327	363	785	364	421	65–69
70–74	451	205	246	507	230	277	584	262	322	70–74
75–79	328	141	187	349	148	201	393	166	227	75–79
80–84	200	84	116	217	86	131	231	90	141	80–84
85 +	133	52	81	149	54	95	164	56	108	85 +
All ages	21089	10545	10544	22415	11180	11235	23904	11898	12006	All ages

TABLE 5 OBSERVED AND PROJECTED VITAL RATES

Rates per thousand	Observed			Projected						Stable	
				1972		1977		1982			
	Total	Males	Females	Males	Females	Males	Females	Males	Females	Males	Females
Birth	18.11	18.52	17.70	19.96	18.93	21.38	20.16	21.98	20.65	18.84	17.52
Death	7.43	8.67	6.17	8.87	6.65	9.03	7.02	9.17	7.32	11.45	10.12
Increase	10.69	9.85	11.53	11.10	12.28	12.34	13.14	12.81	13.34	7.3975	

TABLE 6 RATES STANDARDIZED ON THREE STANDARD COUNTRIES

Standardized rates per thousand	England and Wales, 1961			United States, 1960			Mexico, 1960		
	Total	Males	Females	Total	Males	Females	Total	Males	Females
Birth	16.55	18.74*	15.61	16.84	17.30*	16.15	19.71	16.89*	19.13
Death	10.02	10.89*	9.29	8.23	9.66*	6.88	4.40	7.49*	3.42
Increase	6.53	7.84*	6.32	8.62	7.65*	9.28	15.31	9.40*	15.71

TABLE 7 VITAL STATISTICS AND RATES INFERRED FROM AGE DISTRIBUTIONS (FEMALES)

Vital statistics		Thompson				Bourgeois-Pichat					Coale	
		Age range	NRR	1000r	Interval	Age range	NRR	1000b	1000d	1000r		
TFR	2.60	0–4	1.41	12.65	27.44	5–29	2.08	29.04	1.93	27.12	1000b	25.26
GRR	1.27	5–9	1.70	19.67	27.41	30–54	1.25	17.48	9.24	8.24	1000d	7.38
NRR	1.22	10–14	1.68	18.75	27.36	55–79	1.85	33.68	10.99	22.69	1000r	17.88
Generation	27.32	15–19	1.59	16.18	27.28	*45–69	2.04	42.34	15.91	26.43	$1000k_1$	0.
Sex ratio	105.5										$1000k_2$	0.

TABLE 8 LESLIE MATRIX AND ITS ANALYSIS (FEMALES)

Start of age interval	Sub-diagonal	First row	Percent in stable population	Fisher values	Total reproductive values	Net maternity function	Matrix equation coefficient	Parameters	Integral	Matrix
0	0.99665	0.00000	8.429	1.040	1035632	0.00000	0.00000	λ_1	1.0377	1.0377
5	0.99822	0.00027	8.096	1.082	1194663	0.00026	0.00026	λ_2	0.3466	0.3565
10	0.99797	0.05399	7.788	1.125	1148088	0.00053	0.05371		+0.7526	+0.7370 i
15	0.99731	0.24369	7.489	1.113	1018898	0.10689	0.24196	r_1	0.0074	0.0074
20	0.99706	0.37274	7.198	0.905	692995	0.37702	0.36908	r_2	-0.0354	-0.0400
25	0.99628	0.29379	6.916	0.553	353349	0.36114	0.29005		+0.2289	+0.2240 i
30	0.99465	0.17157	6.640	0.269	162719	0.21897	0.16876	c_1		119578
35	0.99186	0.07969	6.364	0.102	63331	0.11855	0.07796	c_2		50659
40	0.98721	0.02102	6.083	0.023	14375	0.03737	0.02040			343262 i
45	0.97996	0.00180	5.787	0.002	1009	0.00343	0.00173	$2\pi/y$	27.455	28.045
50	0.96899	0.00001	5.465	0.000	6	0.00003	0.00001	Δ	9.645	
55	0.81472		23.747							

Costa Rica, 1966

TABLE 1 DATA INPUT TO COMPUTATIONS

Age at last birthday	Population					Births, by age of mother	Deaths			Age at last birthday
	Total	Males	%	Females	%		Total	Males	Females	
0	61266	31164	4.0	30102	3.9	0	4118	2274	1844	0
1–4	236769	120386	15.6	116383	15.2	0	1327	624	703	1–4
5–9	248300	126170	16.3	122130	15.9	0	286	165	121	5–9
10–14	196970	99665	12.9	97305	12.7	72	136	83	53	10–14
15–19	151470	75435	9.8	76035	9.9	8568	154	96	58	15–19
20–24	118945	58285	7.5	60660	7.9	18001	178	131	47	20–24
25–29	98235	48200	6.2	50035	6.5	15462	165	98	67	25–29
30–34	86155	42785	5.5	43370	5.7	10897	174	86	88	30–34
35–39	75310	37485	4.8	37825	4.9	8163	206	101	105	35–39
40–44	61915	30905	4.0	31010	4.0	2760	248	124	124	40–44
45–49	52160	26210	3.4	25950	3.4	409	242	135	107	45–49
50–54	44050	22175	2.9	21875	2.9	0	306	176	130	50–54
55–59	34045	17190	2.2	16855	2.2	0	362	208	154	55–59
60–64	26145	13175	1.7	12970	1.7	0	466	270	196	60–64
65–69	19080	9500	1.2	9580	1.2	0	603	333	270	65–69
70–74	12910	6435	0.8	6475	0.8		605	298	307	70–74
75–79	8390	4190	0.5	4200	0.5		559	279	280	75–79
80–84	5000	2390	0.3	2610	0.3	32941 M	532	282	250	80–84
85 +	3645	1560	0.2	2085	0.3	31391 F	712	312	400	85 +
All ages	1540760	773305		767455		64332	11379	6075	5304	All ages

TABLE 2 LIFE TABLE FOR MALES

Age, x	$_nq_x$	l_x	$_nd_x$	$_nL_x$	$_nm_x$	T_x	$1000r_x$	$\overset{\circ}{e}_x$	$_nM_x$	Age, x
0	0.06939	100000	6939	95094	0.07297	6501601	0.00	65.02	0.07297	0
1	0.02043	93061	1901	366810	0.00518	6406507	0.00	68.84	0.00518	1
5	0.00637	91160	581	454348	0.00128	6039697	39.73	66.25	0.00131	5
10	0.00416	90579	376	451955	0.00083	5585350	50.41	61.66	0.00083	10
15	0.00642	90203	579	449697	0.00129	5133395	52.25	56.91	0.00127	15
20	0.01121	89624	1005	445672	0.00225	4683699	42.80	52.26	0.00225	20
25	0.01011	88619	896	440829	0.00203	4238027	28.83	47.82	0.00203	25
30	0.01002	87723	879	436476	0.00201	3797198	23.00	43.29	0.00201	30
35	0.01345	86844	1168	431476	0.00271	3360722	29.70	38.70	0.00269	35
40	0.01995	85677	1709	424313	0.00403	2929246	31.83	34.19	0.00401	40
45	0.02555	83967	2146	414784	0.00517	2504933	27.70	29.83	0.00515	45
50	0.03920	81821	3207	401614	0.00799	2090150	34.02	25.55	0.00794	50
55	0.05932	78614	4663	382261	0.01220	1688536	39.12	21.48	0.01210	55
60	0.09845	73951	7280	352836	0.02063	1306275	30.81	17.66	0.02049	60
65	0.16229	66671	10820	307213	0.03522	953439	30.81	14.30	0.03505	65
70	0.20857	55851	11649	250526	0.04650	646226	30.81	11.57	0.04631	70
75	0.28762	44202	12713	189822	0.06697	395700	30.81	8.95	0.06659	75
80	0.46078	31489	14509	122058	0.11887	205878	30.81	6.54	0.11799	80
85 +	*1.00000	16979	16979	83820	0.20257	83820	30.81	4.94	0.20000	85 +

TABLE 3 LIFE TABLE FOR FEMALES

Age, x	$_nq_x$	l_x	$_nd_x$	$_nL_x$	$_nm_x$	T_x	$1000r_x$	$\overset{\circ}{e}_x$	$_nM_x$	Age, x
0	0.05884	100000	5884	96050	0.06126	6774267	0.00	67.74	0.06126	0
1	0.02376	94116	2236	370174	0.00604	6678216	0.00	70.96	0.00604	1
5	0.00476	91880	437	458307	0.00095	6308043	38.82	68.66	0.00099	5
10	0.00271	91443	248	456576	0.00054	5849736	46.69	63.97	0.00054	10
15	0.00382	91195	348	455126	0.00077	5393160	46.56	59.14	0.00076	15
20	0.00389	90847	354	453404	0.00078	4938034	40.95	54.36	0.00077	20
25	0.00672	90493	608	451063	0.00135	4484630	32.19	49.56	0.00134	25
30	0.01014	89885	911	447280	0.00204	4033567	25.94	44.87	0.00203	30
35	0.01385	88974	1232	441964	0.00279	3586288	30.64	40.31	0.00278	35
40	0.01985	87742	1741	434466	0.00401	3144324	33.94	35.84	0.00400	40
45	0.02047	86000	1761	425755	0.00414	2709858	30.41	31.51	0.00412	45
50	0.02949	84240	2485	415389	0.00598	2284103	36.97	27.11	0.00594	50
55	0.04512	81755	3689	400232	0.00922	1868714	42.63	22.86	0.00914	55
60	0.07358	78066	5744	377207	0.01523	1468481	30.63	18.81	0.01511	60
65	0.13308	72322	9624	339142	0.02838	1091274	30.63	15.09	0.02818	65
70	0.21355	62698	13389	280957	0.04765	752132	30.63	12.00	0.04741	70
75	0.28682	49309	14143	211226	0.06696	471175	30.63	9.56	0.06667	75
80	0.38602	35166	13575	141130	0.09619	259949	30.63	7.39	0.09579	80
85 +	1.00000	21591	21591	118819	0.18172	118819	30.63	5.50	0.19185	85 +

TABLE 4 POPULATION PROJECTION, USING FIXED AGE-SPECIFIC BIRTH AND DEATH RATES, IN THOUSANDS

Age at last birthday	1971 Total	1971 Males	1971 Females	1976 Total	1976 Males	1976 Females	1981 Total	1981 Males	1981 Females	Age at last birthday
0–4	330	168	162	402	205	197	496	253	243	0–4
5–9	293	149	144	324	165	159	396	202	194	5–9
10–14	248	126	122	291	148	143	322	164	158	10–14
15–19	196	99	97	246	125	121	291	148	143	15–19
20–24	151	75	76	195	98	97	245	124	121	20–24
25–29	118	58	60	149	74	75	193	97	96	25–29
30–34	98	48	50	117	57	60	148	73	75	30–34
35–39	85	42	43	96	47	49	115	56	59	35–39
40–44	74	37	37	84	42	42	94	46	48	40–44
45–49	60	30	30	72	36	36	82	41	41	45–49
50–54	50	25	25	59	29	30	71	35	36	50–54
55–59	42	21	21	48	24	24	57	28	29	55–59
60–64	32	16	16	39	19	20	45	22	23	60–64
65–69	23	11	12	28	14	14	35	17	18	65–69
70–74	16	8	8	19	9	10	23	11	12	70–74
75–79	10	5	5	12	6	6	14	7	7	75–79
80–84	6	3	3	6	3	3	8	4	4	80–84
85 +	4	2	2	4	2	2	5	2	3	85 +
All ages	1836	923	913	2191	1103	1088	2640	1330	1310	All ages

TABLE 5 OBSERVED AND PROJECTED VITAL RATES

Rates per thousand	Observed			Projected						Stable	
				1971		1976		1981			
	Total	Males	Females	Males	Females	Males	Females	Males	Females	Males	Females
Birth	41.75	42.60	40.90	43.13	41.54	44.36	42.85	45.52	44.07	44.31	43.44
Death	7.39	7.86	6.91	7.54	6.61	7.57	6.64	7.62	6.72	7.70	6.84
Increase	34.37	34.74	33.99	35.59	34.93	36.80	36.21	37.90	37.36		36.6018

TABLE 6 RATES STANDARDIZED ON THREE STANDARD COUNTRIES

Standardized rates per thousand	England and Wales, 1961			United States, 1960			Mexico, 1960		
	Total	Males	Females	Total	Males	Females	Total	Males	Females
Birth	41.67	47.73*	39.41	42.40	43.50*	40.77	45.10	45.79*	44.87
Death	11.98	16.93*	12.79	10.36	13.94*	10.22	6.97	7.32*	6.48
Increase	29.69	30.80*	26.62	32.04	29.56*	30.55	39.12	38.47*	38.39

TABLE 7 VITAL STATISTICS AND RATES INFERRED FROM AGE DISTRIBUTIONS (FEMALES)

Vital statistics		Thompson				Bourgeois-Pichat					Coale	
		Age range	NRR	1000r	Interval	Age range	NRR	1000b	1000d	1000r		
TFR	6.46										1000b	53.92
GRR	3.15	0–4	2.82	37.86	27.38	5–29	3.31	48.07	3.70	44.37	1000d	6.98
NRR	2.82	5–9	2.84	39.22	27.32	30–54	2.32	35.22	4.01	31.21	1000r	46.94
Generation	28.36	10–14	2.65	34.83	27.26	55–79	2.95	55.03	14.93	40.10	$1000k_1$	43.70
Sex ratio	104.9	15–19	2.42	32.55	27.18	*50–74	3.03	58.63	17.59	41.04	$1000k_2$	0.54

TABLE 8 LESLIE MATRIX AND ITS ANALYSIS (FEMALES)

Start of age interval	Sub-diagonal	First row	Percent in stable population	Fisher values	Total reproductive values	Net maternity function	Matrix equation coefficient	Parameters	Integral	Matrix
0	0.98301	0.00000	18.542	1.174	172000	0.00000	0.00000	λ_1	1.2008	1.2017
5	0.99621	0.00084	15.167	1.435	175313	0.00000	0.00082	λ_2	0.4365	0.4437
10	0.99681	0.12861	12.573	1.731	168400	0.00165	0.12595		+0.8042	+0.7845 i
15	0.99620	0.46445	10.429	1.935	147124	0.25025	0.45339	r_1	0.0366	0.0368
20	0.99482	0.68723	8.645	1.787	108385	0.65653	0.66834	r_2	-0.0178	-0.0208
25	0.99158	0.63489	7.156	1.347	67411	0.68015	0.61426		+0.2147	+0.2112 i
30	0.98807	0.52834	5.905	0.881	38211	0.54837	0.50689	c_1		7579
35	0.98297	0.34498	4.855	0.444	16784	0.46541	0.32705	c_2		17510
40	0.97986	0.11877	3.971	0.130	4043	0.18869	0.11072			15291 i
45	0.97567	0.01795	3.238	0.018	456	0.03274	0.01637	$2\pi/y$	29.265	29.748
50	0.96363	0.00005	2.629	0.000	1	0.00000	0.00000	Δ	2.346	
55	0.83413		6.891							

Dominican Republic, 1966

TABLE 1   DATA INPUT TO COMPUTATIONS

Age at last birthday	Population					Births, by age of mother	Deaths			Age at last birthday
	Total	Males	%	Females	%		Total	Males	Females	
0	108378	55098	3.1	53280	3.1	0	10550	5753	4797	0
1–4	428622	218902	12.4	209720	12.1	0	4138	2146	1992	1–4
5–9	540000	273000	15.5	267000	15.4	0	702	358	344	5–9
10–14	482000	244000	13.8	238000	13.7	146	409	239	170	10–14
15–19	390000	201000	11.4	189000	10.9	15901	488	269	219	15–19
20–24	283000	132000	7.5	151000	8.7	33242	542	303	239	20–24
25–29	253000	120000	6.8	133000	7.7	29542	552	297	255	25–29
30–34	209000	102000	5.8	107000	6.2	21021	546	284	262	30–34
35–39	184000	93000	5.3	91000	5.3	14818	603	318	285	35–39
40–44	148000	76000	4.3	72000	4.2	6614	484	246	238	40–44
45–49	121000	64000	3.6	57000	3.3	3955	530	292	238	45–49
50–54	93000	50000	2.8	43000	2.5	1028	743	435	308	50–54
55–59	85000	45000	2.5	40000	2.3	0	566	328	238	55–59
60–64	48000	27000	1.5	21000	1.2	0	981	613	368	60–64
65–69	56000	29000	1.6	27000	1.6	0	803	479	324	65–69
70–74	23000	12000	0.7	11000	0.6		1082	601	481	70–74
75–79	23000	12000	0.7	11000	0.6		602	318	284	75–79
80–84	17000	8000	0.5	9000	0.5	63874 M	851	450	401	80–84
85 +	6000	3000	0.2	3000	0.2	62393 F	1554	696	858	85 +
All ages	3498000	1765000		1733000		126267	26726	14425	12301	All ages

TABLE 2   LIFE TABLE FOR MALES

Age, x	$_nq_x$	l_x	$_nd_x$	$_nL_x$	$_nm_x$	T_x	$1000r_x$	$\overset{\circ}{e}_x$	$_nM_x$	Age, x
0	0.09750	100000	9750	93378	0.10441	6360797	0.00	63.61	0.10441	0
1	0.03816	90250	3444	351273	0.00980	6267419	0.00	69.45	0.00980	1
5	0.00647	86806	562	432627	0.00130	5916146	8.29	68.15	0.00131	5
10	0.00489	86244	421	430172	0.00098	5483519	29.49	63.58	0.00098	10
15	0.00675	85823	580	427782	0.00135	5053347	59.96	58.88	0.00134	15
20	0.01147	85243	978	423867	0.00231	4625566	49.45	54.26	0.00230	20
25	0.01231	84265	1037	418770	0.00248	4201698	23.27	49.86	0.00247	25
30	0.01385	83228	1153	413332	0.00279	3782928	22.62	45.45	0.00278	30
35	0.01697	82075	1392	406926	0.00342	3369596	26.21	41.05	0.00342	35
40	0.01610	80683	1299	400254	0.00324	2962669	33.84	36.72	0.00324	40
45	0.02278	79384	1808	392819	0.00460	2562415	36.62	32.28	0.00456	45
50	0.04268	77576	3311	379790	0.00872	2169597	28.00	27.97	0.00870	50
55	0.03653	74265	2713	365452	0.00742	1789806	50.24	24.10	0.00729	55
60	0.10803	71552	7730	338939	0.02281	1424344	44.66	19.91	0.02270	60
65	0.08053	63822	5139	307380	0.01672	1085406	44.66	17.01	0.01652	65
70	0.22337	58682	13108	260747	0.05027	778025	44.66	13.26	0.05008	70
75	0.12383	45575	5644	213184	0.02647	517278	44.66	11.35	0.02650	75
80	0.25864	39931	10328	178826	0.05775	304094	44.66	7.62	0.05625	80
85 +	*1.00000	29603	29603	125258	0.23632	125268	44.66	4.23	0.23200	85 +

TABLE 3   LIFE TABLE FOR FEMALES

Age, x	$_nq_x$	l_x	$_nd_x$	$_nL_x$	$_nm_x$	T_x	$1000r_x$	$\overset{\circ}{e}_x$	$_nM_x$	Age, x
0	0.08494	100000	8494	94342	0.09003	6606015	0.00	66.06	0.09003	0
1	0.03701	91506	3386	356522	0.00950	6511673	0.00	71.16	0.00950	1
5	0.00637	88120	561	439195	0.00128	6155151	6.87	69.85	0.00129	5
10	0.00356	87558	312	437001	0.00071	5715956	33.60	65.28	0.00071	10
15	0.00582	87247	508	435042	0.00117	5278955	44.36	60.51	0.00116	15
20	0.00791	86739	686	432045	0.00159	4843913	33.57	55.84	0.00158	20
25	0.00957	86053	824	428279	0.00192	4411868	32.48	51.27	0.00192	25
30	0.01222	85229	1041	423645	0.00246	3983589	35.45	46.74	0.00245	30
35	0.01557	84188	1311	417730	0.00314	3559945	36.60	42.29	0.00313	35
40	0.01644	82877	1363	411059	0.00332	3142215	43.35	37.91	0.00331	40
45	0.02086	81514	1700	403623	0.00421	2731156	46.84	33.51	0.00418	45
50	0.03525	79814	2814	392163	0.00717	2327533	29.37	29.16	0.00715	50
55	0.02998	77000	2309	379955	0.00608	1935370	62.58	25.13	0.00595	55
60	0.08429	74691	6295	358083	0.01758	1555415	38.32	20.82	0.01752	60
65	0.05931	68396	4056	333183	0.01217	1197332	38.32	17.51	0.01200	65
70	0.19806	64340	12743	290294	0.04390	864150	38.32	13.43	0.04373	70
75	0.12080	51597	6233	241744	0.02578	573856	38.32	11.12	0.02582	75
80	0.21141	45364	9590	208996	0.04589	332112	38.32	7.32	0.04455	80
85 +	*1.00000	35773	35773	123116	0.29057	123116	38.32	3.44	0.28600	85 +

Age at last birthday	1971 Total	Males	Females	1976 Total	Males	Females	1981 Total	Males	Females	Age at last birthday
0–4	623	313	310	750	377	373	884	444	440	0–4
5–9	523	267	256	607	305	302	731	367	364	5–9
10–14	537	271	266	520	265	255	604	303	301	10–14
15–19	480	243	237	534	270	264	518	264	254	15–19
20–24	387	199	188	475	240	235	530	267	263	20–24
25–29	280	130	150	383	197	186	471	238	233	25–29
30–34	250	118	132	277	129	148	378	194	184	30–34
35–39	206	100	106	247	117	130	273	127	146	35–39
40–44	181	91	90	203	99	104	243	115	128	40–44
45–49	146	75	71	178	90	88	199	97	102	45–49
50–54	117	62	55	141	72	69	172	87	85	50–54
55–59	90	48	42	114	60	54	136	69	67	55–59
60–64	80	42	38	84	45	39	106	55	51	60–64
65–69	44	24	20	73	38	35	77	40	37	65–69
70–74	49	25	24	38	21	17	63	32	31	70–74
75–79	19	10	9	40	20	20	31	17	14	75–79
80–84	20	10	10	16	8	8	34	17	17	80–84
85 +	11	6	5	13	7	6	11	6	5	85 +
All ages	4043	2034	2009	4693	2360	2333	5461	2739	2722	All ages

TABLE 5 OBSERVED AND PROJECTED VITAL RATES

Rates per thousand	Observed Total	Males	Females	Projected 1971 Males	Females	1976 Males	Females	1981 Males	Females	Stable Males	Females
Birth	36.10	36.19	36.00	37.83	37.49	39.27	38.77	39.15	38.52	36.82	35.91
Death	7.64	9.17	7.10	8.68	7.67	8.81	7.65	8.93	7.75	9.98	9.07
Increase	28.46	28.02	28.90	29.15	29.82	30.45	31.12	30.22	30.76		26.8411

TABLE 6 RATES STANDARDIZED ON THREE STANDARD COUNTRIES

Standardized rates per thousand	England and Wales, 1961 Total	Males	Females	United States, 1960 Total	Males	Females	Mexico, 1960 Total	Males	Females
Birth	34.91	38.38*	33.43	34.98	35.12*	34.06	36.25	36.73*	35.73
Death	10.83	17.12*	11.45	10.06	14.29*	9.95	8.07	8.31*	7.53
Increase	24.07	21.27*	21.98	24.92	20.83*	24.11	28.18	28.41*	28.20

TABLE 7 VITAL STATISTICS AND RATES INFERRED FROM AGE DISTRIBUTIONS (FEMALES)

Vital statistics		Thompson Age range	NRR	$1000r$	Interval	Bourgeois-Pichat Age range	NRR	$1000b$	$1000d$	$1000r$	Coale
TFR	5.36	0–4	2.00	26.16	27.36	5–29	2.62	46.94	11.20	35.74	$1000b$
GRR	2.65	5–9	2.50	34.39	27.30	30–54	3.11	59.16	17.11	42.05	$1000d$
NRR	2.24	10–14	2.68	35.20	27.25	55–79	4.40	134.52	79.68	54.84	$1000r$
Generation	30.06	15–19	2.57	34.76	27.19	*25–49	2.85	52.35	13.51	38.84	$1000k_1$
Sex ratio	102.37										$1000k_2$

TABLE 8 LESLIE MATRIX AND ITS ANALYSIS (FEMALES)

Start of age interval	Sub-diagonal	First row	Percent in stable population	Fisher values	Total reproductive values	Net maternity function	Matrix equation coefficient	Parameters	Integral	Matrix
0	0.97412	0.00000	15.168	1.185	311653	0.00000	0.00000	λ_1	1.1436	1.1441
5	0.99500	0.00068	12.915	1.392	371594	0.00000	0.00066	λ_2	0.4573	0.4611
10	0.99552	0.09398	11.232	1.599	380666	0.00132	0.09109		+0.5510	+0.6329 i
15	0.99311	0.33724	9.774	1.725	326261	0.18086	0.32542	r_1	0.0268	0.0269
20	0.99129	0.49049	8.484	1.586	239522	0.46999	0.47003	r_2	-0.0457	-0.0489
25	0.98920	0.46391	7.351	1.244	165504	0.47007	0.44066		+0.1917	+0.1882 i
30	0.98603	0.39770	6.355	0.883	94533	0.41126	0.37369	c_1		18933
35	0.98402	0.28208	5.478	0.547	49790	0.33612	0.26135	c_2		925
40	0.98190	0.17823	4.712	0.296	21344	0.18659	0.16249			21483 i
45	0.97161	0.10318	4.044	0.130	7427	0.13839	0.09236			
50	0.96887	0.02664	3.434	0.028	1187	0.04633	0.02316	$2\pi/y$	32.781	33.377
55	0.84305		11.053					Δ	7.013	

El Salvador, 1961

TABLE 1   DATA INPUT TO COMPUTATIONS

Age at last birthday	Population					Births, by age of mother	Deaths			Age at last birthday
	Total	Males	%	Females	%		Total	Males	Females	
0	97887	49476	4.0	48411	3.8	0	8822	4906	3916	0
1–4	336618	169616	13.6	167002	13.0	0	5561	2837	2724	1–4
5–9	386083	194673	15.6	191410	14.9	0	1288	640	648	5–9
10–14	311347	160884	12.9	150463	11.7	150	456	240	215	10–14
15–19	243844	118031	9.5	125813	9.8	17811	578	309	269	15–19
20–24	216243	102052	8.2	114191	8.9	36773	758	477	281	20–24
25–29	173639	81409	6.5	92230	7.2	30040	693	451	242	25–29
30–34	151723	73531	5.9	78192	6.1	21234	754	438	315	30–34
35–39	139937	66550	5.3	73387	5.7	13766	778	445	333	35–39
40–44	112533	55239	4.4	57294	4.5	4155	764	414	350	40–44
45–49	90498	44008	3.5	46490	3.6	772	761	410	351	45–49
50–54	76344	37489	3.0	38855	3.0	170	878	471	407	50–54
55–59	51248	24933	2.0	26315	2.1	0	822	432	390	55–59
60–64	58458	29004	2.3	29454	2.3	0	1268	608	660	60–64
65–69	29349	14292	1.1	15057	1.2	0	938	515	423	65–69
70–74	21610	10335	0.8	11275	0.9		968	501	467	70–74
75–79	13243	6298	0.5	6945	0.5		750	392	358	75–79
80–84	8756	3855	0.3	4901	0.4	63495 M	678	307	371	80–84
85 +	7390	2943	0.2	4447	0.3	61376 F	976	440	536	85 +
All ages	2526750	1244618		1282132		124871	28491	15233	13258	All ages

TABLE 2   LIFE TABLE FOR MALES

Age, x	$_nq_x$	l_x	$_nd_x$	$_nL_x$	$_nm_x$	T_x	$1000r_x$	$\overset{\circ}{e}_x$	$_nM_x$	Age, x
0	0.09301	100000	9301	94230	0.09871	5635214	7.17	56.35	0.09915	0
1	0.06378	90699	5785	347059	0.01667	5540985	7.17	61.09	0.01673	1
5	0.01598	84914	1357	421178	0.00322	5193925	25.02	61.17	0.00329	5
10	0.00740	83557	618	416186	0.00149	4772747	47.89	57.12	0.00149	10
15	0.01315	82939	1091	412235	0.00265	4356562	42.73	52.53	0.00262	15
20	0.02321	81848	1900	404720	0.03469	3944327	32.71	48.19	0.00467	20
25	0.02736	79948	2188	394353	0.00555	3539607	27.30	44.27	0.00554	25
30	0.02937	77761	2284	383157	0.00596	3145254	14.12	40.45	0.00596	30
35	0.03293	75477	2485	371258	0.00669	2762097	21.92	36.60	0.00669	35
40	0.03689	72992	2693	358381	0.00751	2390839	33.66	32.75	0.00749	40
45	0.04571	70300	3213	343761	0.00935	2032458	29.16	28.91	0.00932	45
50	0.06132	67086	4114	325570	0.01264	1688697	43.90	25.17	0.01256	50
55	0.08320	62973	5239	302117	0.01734	1363127	8.73	21.65	0.01733	55
60	0.10050	57733	5802	274874	0.02111	1061010	40.62	18.38	0.02096	60
65	0.16674	51931	8659	238757	0.03627	786135	40.62	15.14	0.03603	65
70	0.21715	43272	9397	192970	0.04869	547379	40.62	12.65	0.04848	70
75	0.26987	33876	9142	146275	0.06250	354409	40.62	10.46	0.06224	75
80	0.33189	24733	8209	102646	0.07997	208134	40.62	8.42	0.07964	80
85 +	1.00000	16525	16525	105489	0.15665	105489	40.62	6.38	0.14951	85 +

TABLE 3   LIFE TABLE FOR FEMALES

Age, x	$_nq_x$	l_x	$_nd_x$	$_nL_x$	$_nm_x$	T_x	$1000r_x$	$\overset{\circ}{e}_x$	$_nM_x$	Age, x
0	0.07680	100000	7680	95371	0.08053	6065221	7.29	60.65	0.08089	0
1	0.06233	92320	5755	353884	0.01626	5969850	7.29	64.66	0.01631	1
5	0.01640	86565	1420	429278	0.00331	5615966	30.12	64.88	0.00339	5
10	0.00710	85146	605	424110	0.00143	5186687	39.91	60.92	0.00144	10
15	0.01066	84541	901	420540	0.00214	4762577	25.58	56.33	0.00214	15
20	0.01224	83640	1024	415676	0.00246	4342037	28.64	51.91	0.00245	20
25	0.01309	82616	1082	410501	0.00264	3926361	34.95	47.53	0.00262	25
30	0.02005	81534	1635	403732	0.00405	3515860	19.04	43.12	0.00404	30
35	0.02250	79899	1797	395154	0.00455	3112128	26.30	38.95	0.00454	35
40	0.03022	78102	2360	384820	0.00613	2716974	39.60	34.79	0.00611	40
45	0.03721	75741	2819	371950	0.00758	2332154	30.96	30.79	0.00755	45
50	0.05143	72923	3750	355684	0.01054	1960204	46.18	26.88	0.01047	50
55	0.07172	69173	4961	334105	0.01485	1604520	12.15	23.20	0.01482	55
60	0.10672	64211	6852	304469	0.02251	1270414	34.98	19.78	0.02241	60
65	0.13206	57359	7575	268387	0.02822	965945	34.98	16.84	0.02809	65
70	0.18865	49784	9392	225794	0.04159	697558	34.98	14.01	0.04142	70
75	0.22932	40393	9263	178921	0.05177	471754	34.98	11.68	0.05155	75
80	0.31936	31130	9942	130684	0.07607	292843	34.98	9.41	0.07570	80
85 +	1.00000	21188	21188	162159	0.13066	162159	34.98	7.65	0.12053	85 +

TABLE 4 POPULATION PROJECTION, USING FIXED AGE-SPECIFIC BIRTH AND DEATH RATES, IN THOUSANDS

Age at last birthday	1966			1971			1976			Age at last birthday
	Total	Males	Females	Total	Males	Females	Total	Males	Females	
0–4	597	301	296	693	349	344	812	409	403	0–4
5–9	415	209	206	570	287	283	661	333	328	5–9
10–14	381	192	189	410	207	203	564	284	280	10–14
15–19	308	159	149	379	191	188	407	205	202	15–19
20–24	240	116	124	303	156	147	372	187	185	20–24
25–29	212	99	113	236	113	123	298	152	146	25–29
30–34	170	79	91	208	97	111	231	110	121	30–34
35–39	148	71	77	166	77	89	203	94	109	35–39
40–44	135	64	71	144	69	75	160	74	86	40–44
45–49	108	53	55	131	62	69	138	66	72	45–49
50–54	86	42	44	103	50	53	124	58	66	50–54
55–59	71	35	36	81	39	42	97	47	50	55–59
60–64	47	23	24	65	32	33	73	35	38	60–64
65–69	51	25	26	41	20	21	56	27	29	65–69
70–74	25	12	13	42	20	22	34	16	18	70–74
75–79	17	8	9	19	9	10	32	15	17	75–79
80–84	9	4	5	12	5	7	13	6	7	80–84
85 +	10	4	6	11	5	6	14	6	8	85 +
All ages	3030	1496	1534	3614	1788	1826	4289	2124	2165	All ages

TABLE 5 OBSERVED AND PROJECTED VITAL RATES

Rates per thousand	Observed			Projected						Stable	
				1966		1971		1976			
	Total	Males	Females	Males	Females	Males	Females	Males	Females	Males	Females
Birth	49.42	51.02	47.87	48.71	45.90	47.77	45.20	47.12	44.70	48.19	46.39
Death	11.28	12.24	10.34	13.06	11.05	12.85	10.93	12.72	10.86	12.49	10.68
Increase	38.14	38.78	37.53	35.65	34.85	34.93	34.27	34.40	33.84		35.7045

TABLE 6 RATES STANDARDIZED ON THREE STANDARD COUNTRIES

Standardized rates per thousand	England and Wales, 1961			United States, 1960			Mexico, 1960		
	Total	Males	Females	Total	Males	Females	Total	Males	Females
Birth	43.25	53.44*	41.20	44.05	48.74*	42.67	48.93	51.08*	47.98
Death	14.27	25.59*	14.29	13.21	21.08*	12.46	10.75	11.40*	9.80
Increase	28.98	27.86*	26.91	30.85	27.67*	30.20	38.18	39.68*	38.17

TABLE 7 VITAL STATISTICS AND RATES INFERRED FROM AGE DISTRIBUTIONS (FEMALES)

Vital statistics		Thompson				Bourgeois-Pichat					Coale	
		Age range	NRR	1000r	Interval	Age range	NRR	1000b	1000d	1000r		
TFR	6.71	0–4	2.15	28.13	27.28	5–29	2.41	42.67	10.36	32.53	1000b	39.35
GRR	3.30	5–9	2.30	31.29	27.18	30–54	2.30	43.04	12.21	30.82	1000d	11.74
NRR	2.69	10–14	2.13	27.33	27.09	55–79	2.81	63.66	25.42	38.24	1000r	27.62
Generation	27.70	15–19	2.10	27.44	26.97	*10–34	2.24	40.30	10.36	29.94	$1000k_1$	-4.45
Sex ratio	103.5										$1000k_2$	0.

TABLE 8 LESLIE MATRIX AND ITS ANALYSIS (FEMALES)

Start of age interval	Sub-diagonal	First row	Percent in stable population	Fisher values	Total reproductive values	Net maternity function	Matrix equation coefficient	Parameters	Integral	Matrix
0	0.95553	0.00000	19.121	1.215	261759	0.00000	0.00000	λ_1	1.1954	1.1963
5	0.98796	0.00109	15.272	1.521	291209	0.00000	0.00104	λ_2	0.3942	0.4037
10	0.99158	0.15609	12.612	1.841	276995	0.00208	0.14735		+0.8132	+0.7898 i
15	0.98843	0.50774	10.454	2.030	255379	0.29262	0.47528	r_1	0.0357	0.0359
20	0.98755	0.71068	8.637	1.833	209266	0.65794	0.65756	r_2	-0.0202	-0.0240
25	0.98351	0.65449	7.130	1.346	124103	0.65717	0.59803		+0.2239	+0.2197 i
30	0.97875	0.50253	5.861	0.828	64754	0.53889	0.45161	c_1		12299
35	0.97385	0.28508	4.795	0.388	28499	0.36433	0.25075	c_2		-21326
40	0.96655	0.09779	3.903	0.121	6951	0.13717	0.08376			-21439 i
45	0.95627	0.02295	3.154	0.027	1266	0.03036	0.01900	$2\pi/y$	28.064	28.605
50	0.93933	0.00483	2.521	0.005	191	0.00765	0.00382	Δ	4.087	
55	0.83428		6.540							

Greenland, 1960

TABLE 1 DATA INPUT TO COMPUTATIONS

Age at last birthday	Population					Births, by age of mother	Deaths			Age at last birthday
	Total	Males	%	Females	%		Total	Males	Females	
0	1452	761	4.6	691	4.3	0	102	58	44	0
1–4	4882	2490	15.2	2392	14.9	0	19	14	5	1–4
5–9	4607	2341	14.3	2266	14.1	0	6	5	1	5–9
10–14	3425	1747	10.6	1678	10.5	0	4	3	1	10–14
15–19	2984	1446	8.8	1538	9.6	173	10	9	1	15–19
20–24	2705	1392	8.5	1313	8.2	424	3	1	2	20–24
25–29	2739	1441	8.8	1298	8.1	430	6	5	1	25–29
30–34	2430	1271	7.7	1159	7.2	322	4	2	2	30–34
35–39	1641	846	5.2	795	5.0	151	12	6	6	35–39
40–44	1388	713	4.3	675	4.2	71	10	3	7	40–44
45–49	1197	603	3.7	594	3.7	12	7	2	5	45–49
50–54	985	457	2.8	528	3.3	3	8	5	3	50–54
55–59	783	375	2.3	408	2.5	0	13	7	6	55–59
60–64	569	262	1.6	307	1.9	0	7	1	6	60–64
65–69	378	172	1.0	206	1.3	0	18	10	8	65–69
70–74	175	65	0.4	110	0.7		12	6	6	70–74
75–79	96	36	0.2	60	0.4		9	4	5	75–79
80–84	28	7	0.0	21	0.1	843 M	2	1	1	80–84
85 +	5	2	0.0	3	0.0	743 F	3	2	1	85 +
All ages	32469	16427		16042		1586	255	144	111	All ages

TABLE 2 LIFE TABLE FOR MALES

Age, x	nq_x	l_x	nd_x	nL_x	nm_x	T_x	$1000r_x$	$\mathring{e}_x$	nM_x	Age, x
0	0.07152	100000	7152	94970	0.07531	6023282	16.26	60.23	0.07622	0
1	0.02184	92848	2028	365605	0.00555	5928312	16.26	63.85	0.00562	1
5	0.01043	90820	947	451733	0.00210	5562707	59.29	61.25	0.00214	5
10	0.00874	89873	786	447771	0.00176	5110974	45.21	56.87	0.00172	10
15	0.03062	89087	2728	438516	0.00622	4663203	18.84	52.34	0.00622	15
20	0.00358	86359	309	430752	0.00072	4224587	0.00	48.92	0.00072	20
25	0.01721	86050	1481	426623	0.00347	3793925	6.91	44.09	0.00347	25
30	0.00802	84569	679	421451	0.00161	3367302	49.85	39.82	0.00157	30
35	0.03501	83890	2937	412317	0.00712	2945851	52.65	35.12	0.00709	35
40	0.02069	80953	1675	400245	0.00418	2533534	29.22	31.30	0.00421	40
45	0.01674	79279	1327	393603	0.00337	2133290	39.38	26.91	0.00332	45
50	0.05393	77952	4204	380337	0.01105	1739686	36.27	22.32	0.01094	50
55	0.08881	73748	6550	351787	0.01862	1359349	42.83	18.43	0.01867	55
60	0.02131	67198	1432	334625	0.00428	1007552	68.25	14.99	0.00382	60
65	0.26125	65766	17181	289389	0.05937	672936	68.25	10.23	0.05814	65
70	0.37652	48585	18293	196333	0.09317	383547	68.25	7.89	0.09231	70
75	0.43138	30291	13067	116868	0.11181	187214	68.25	6.18	0.11111	75
80	0.52668	17224	9072	62419	0.14534	70346	68.25	4.08	0.14286	80
85 +	*1.00000	8153	8153	7927	1.02844	7927	68.25	0.97	1.00000	85 +

TABLE 3 LIFE TABLE FOR FEMALES

Age, x	nq_x	l_x	nd_x	nL_x	nm_x	T_x	$1000r_x$	$\mathring{e}_x$	nM_x	Age, x
0	0.06006	100000	6006	95257	0.06305	6489700	12.52	64.90	0.06368	0
1	0.00813	93994	764	373741	0.00204	6394443	12.52	68.03	0.00209	1
5	0.00213	93230	199	465652	0.00043	6020703	59.86	64.58	0.00044	5
10	0.00298	93031	278	464482	0.00060	5555051	38.20	59.71	0.00060	10
15	0.00327	92753	303	463097	0.00065	5090569	23.67	54.88	0.00065	15
20	0.00759	92450	702	460506	0.00152	4627472	15.83	50.05	0.00152	20
25	0.00385	91748	353	457883	0.00077	4166966	11.40	45.42	0.00077	25
30	0.00892	91395	816	455572	0.00179	3709083	46.20	40.58	0.00173	30
35	0.03750	90580	3397	445154	0.00763	3253511	47.09	35.92	0.00755	35
40	0.05056	87182	4408	424893	0.01037	2808357	19.67	32.21	0.01037	40
45	0.04110	82774	3402	404916	0.00840	2383464	16.43	28.79	0.00842	45
50	0.02822	79373	2240	391706	0.00572	1978548	29.30	24.93	0.00568	50
55	0.07166	77133	5528	372803	0.01483	1586842	40.72	20.57	0.01471	55
60	0.09552	71605	6840	342210	0.01999	1214039	94.64	16.95	0.01954	60
65	0.18056	64765	11694	295857	0.03953	871828	94.64	13.46	0.03883	65
70	0.24345	53071	12920	233490	0.05533	575971	94.64	10.85	0.05455	70
75	0.34335	40151	13786	164822	0.08364	342481	94.64	8.53	0.08333	75
80	0.22292	26365	5877	118528	0.04959	177659	94.64	6.74	0.04762	80
85 +	*1.00000	20488	20488	59131	0.34648	59131	94.64	2.89	0.33333	85 +

TABLE 4 POPULATION PROJECTION, USING FIXED AGE-SPECIFIC BIRTH AND DEATH RATES, IN THOUSANDS

Age at last birthday	1965			1970			1975			Age at last birthday
	Total	Males	Females	Total	Males	Females	Total	Males	Females	
0–4	8	4	4	9	5	4	10	5	5	0–4
5–9	6	3	3	8	4	4	9	5	4	5–9
10–14	4	2	2	6	3	3	8	4	4	10–14
15–19	4	2	2	4	2	2	6	3	3	15–19
20–24	3	1	2	4	2	2	4	2	2	20–24
25–29	2	1	1	3	1	2	4	2	2	25–29
30–34	2	1	1	2	1	1	3	1	2	30–34
35–39	2	1	1	2	1	1	2	1	1	35–39
40–44	2	1	1	2	1	1	2	1	1	40–44
45–49	2	1	1	2	1	1	2	1	1	45–49
50–54	2	1	1	2	1	1	2	1	1	50–54
55–59	1	0	1	2	1	1	2	1	1	55–59
60–64	0	0	0	0	0	0	2	1	1	60–64
65–69	0	0	0	0	0	0	0	0	0	65–69
70–74	0	0	0	0	0	0	0	0	0	70–74
75–79	0	0	0	0	0	0	0	0	0	75–79
80–84	0	0	0	0	0	0	0	0	0	80–84
85 +	0	0	0	0	0	0	0	0	0	85 +
All ages	38	18	20	46	23	23	56	28	28	All ages

TABLE 5 OBSERVED AND PROJECTED VITAL RATES

Rates per thousand	Observed			Projected						Stable	
				1965		1970		1975			
	Total	Males	Females	Males	Females	Males	Females	Males	Females	Males	Females
Birth	48.85	51.32	46.32	47.19	43.16	44.56	41.15	44.64	41.53	45.58	44.41
Death	7.85	8.77	6.92	9.10	7.19	9.17	7.29	9.17	7.28	8.99	5.83
Increase	40.99	42.55	39.40	38.09	35.98	35.40	33.86	35.46	34.25		37.5875

TABLE 6 RATES STANDARDIZED ON THREE STANDARD COUNTRIES

Standardized rates per thousand	England and Wales, 1961			United States, 1960			Mexico, 1960		
	Total	Males	Females	Total	Males	Females	Total	Males	Females
Birth	43.97	45.30*	39.92	44.65	42.09*	41.22	48.60	44.24*	45.42
Death	16.93	25.12*	15.88	14.89	18.88*	12.60	8.83	8.61*	7.19
Increase	27.04	20.18*	24.05	29.76	23.21*	28.62	39.77	35.63*	38.23

TABLE 7 VITAL STATISTICS AND RATES INFERRED FROM AGE DISTRIBUTIONS (FEMALES)

Vital statistics		Thompson				Bourgeois-Pichat					Coale	
TFR	6.83	Age range	NRR	1000r	Interval	Age range	NRR	1000b	1000d	1000r		
GRR	3.20	0–4	2.63	35.37	27.29	5–29	2.04	33.87	7.52	26.35	1000b	41.00
NRR	2.90	5–9	2.21	29.81	27.13	30–54	2.21	36.92	7.57	29.34	1000d	5.35
Generation	28.31	10–14	1.85	22.29	27.01	55–79	4.49	174.75	119.11	55.64	1000r	34.65
Sex ratio	113.5	15–19	1.99	25.62	26.90	*10–34	1.59	27.62	10.42	17.19	$1000k_1$	44.07
											$1000k_2$	0.58

TABLE 8 LESLIE MATRIX AND ITS ANALYSIS (FEMALES)

Start of age interval	Sub-diagonal	First row	Percent in stable population	Fisher values	Total reproductive values	Net maternity function	Matrix equation coefficient	Parameters		
									Integral	Matrix
0	0.99287	0.00000	19.022	1.170	3608	0.00000	0.00000	λ_1	1.2068	1.2077
5	0.99749	0.00000	15.638	1.424	3226	0.00000	0.00000	λ_2	0.4071	0.4169
10	0.99702	0.12320	12.915	1.724	2893	0.00000	0.12202		+0.8190	+0.7947i
15	0.99441	0.47634	10.662	1.944	2989	0.24403	0.47035	r_1	0.0376	0.0377
20	0.99430	0.71661	8.779	1.800	2363	0.69666	0.70364	r_2	-0.0179	-0.0215
25	0.99495	0.66760	7.227	1.343	1743	0.71061	0.65178		+0.2219	+0.2175i
30	0.97713	0.50910	5.954	0.844	979	0.59295	0.49452	c_1		151
35	0.95449	0.31895	4.817	0.434	345	0.39610	0.30274	c_2		243
40	0.95298	0.13670	3.807	0.158	107	0.20937	0.12385			-579i
45	0.96738	0.02823	3.004	0.032	19	0.03832	0.02437	$2\pi/y$	28.316	28.884
50	0.95174	0.00624	2.406	0.006	3	0.01043	0.00521	Δ	5.781	
55	0.81075		5.769							

Grenada, 1961

TABLE 1 DATA INPUT TO COMPUTATIONS

Age at last birthday	Population					Births, by age of mother	Deaths			Age at last birthday
	Total	Males	%	Females	%		Total	Males	Females	
0	3952	1939	4.6	2013	4.0	0	266	137	129	0
1–4	14368	7180	16.9	7188	14.4	0	189	100	89	1–4
5–9	14517	7284	17.1	7233	14.5	0	16	9	7	5–9
10–14	11173	5591	13.2	5582	11.2	4	10	3	7	10–14
15–19	8114	3906	9.2	4208	8.4	732	7	5	2	15–19
20–24	6512	2874	6.8	3638	7.3	1137	8	5	3	20–24
25–29	5233	2144	5.0	3089	6.2	999	8	2	6	25–29
30–34	4433	1955	4.6	2478	5.0	686	16	9	7	30–34
35–39	3914	1615	3.8	2299	4.6	395	11	3	8	35–39
40–44	3507	1485	3.5	2022	4.1	138	16	3	13	40–44
45–49	3501	1533	3.6	1968	4.0	25	17	9	8	45–49
50–54	3481	1505	3.5	1976	4.0	1	39	25	14	50–54
55–59	2493	1034	2.4	1459	2.9	0	31	21	10	55–59
60–64	2315	851	2.0	1464	2.9	0	67	32	35	60–64
65–69	1592	588	1.4	1004	2.0	0	51	26	25	65–69
70–74	1337	438	1.0	899	1.8		60	23	37	70–74
75–79	840	257	0.6	583	1.2		48	19	29	75–79
80–84	577	192	0.5	385	0.8	2099 M	68	26	42	80–84
85+	445	120	0.3	325	0.7	2018 F	94	25	69	85+
All ages	92304	42491		49813		4117	1022	482	540	All ages

TABLE 2 LIFE TABLE FOR MALES

Age, x	$_nq_x$	l_x	$_nd_x$	$_nL_x$	$_nm_x$	T_x	$1000r_x$	$\overset{\circ}{e}_x$	$_nM_x$	Age, x
0	0.06771	100000	6771	95910	0.07060	6054420	1.22	60.54	0.07065	0
1	0.05368	93229	5004	359509	0.01392	5958510	1.22	63.91	0.01393	1
5	0.00564	88224	498	439877	0.00113	5599002	45.03	63.46	0.00124	5
10	0.00269	87726	236	438057	0.00054	5159125	61.46	58.81	0.00054	10
15	0.00646	87491	565	436146	0.00130	4721068	65.32	53.96	0.00128	15
20	0.00864	86925	751	432716	0.00174	4284922	58.59	49.29	0.00174	20
25	0.00476	86174	410	430095	0.00095	3852206	36.50	44.70	0.00093	25
30	0.02279	85764	1954	424007	0.00461	3422111	25.22	39.90	0.00460	30
35	0.00917	83809	769	416893	0.00184	2998104	24.98	35.77	0.00186	35
40	0.01007	83041	836	413450	0.00202	2581211	2.62	31.08	0.00202	40
45	0.02901	82205	2385	406222	0.00587	2167761	0.00	26.37	0.00587	45
50	0.08029	79820	6409	384071	0.01669	1761538	24.54	22.07	0.01661	50
55	0.09752	73411	7159	350203	0.02044	1377468	33.45	18.75	0.02031	55
60	0.17258	66252	11434	303456	0.03768	1027265	14.53	15.51	0.03760	60
65	0.19907	54818	10913	246550	0.04426	723809	14.53	13.20	0.04422	65
70	0.23232	43905	10200	193951	0.05259	477259	14.53	10.87	0.05251	70
75	0.31331	33705	10560	142448	0.07413	283308	14.53	8.41	0.07393	75
80	0.50784	23145	11754	86513	0.13586	140861	14.53	6.09	0.13542	80
85+	*1.00000	11391	11391	54348	0.20959	54348	14.53	4.77	0.20833	85+

TABLE 3 LIFE TABLE FOR FEMALES

Age, x	$_nq_x$	l_x	$_nd_x$	$_nL_x$	$_nm_x$	T_x	$1000r_x$	$\overset{\circ}{e}_x$	$_nM_x$	Age, x
0	0.06148	100000	6148	96279	0.06386	6501911	5.54	65.02	0.06408	0
1	0.04782	93852	4488	363371	0.01235	6405532	5.54	68.25	0.01238	1
5	0.00440	89364	393	445839	0.00088	6042261	46.38	67.61	0.00097	5
10	0.00623	88971	554	443433	0.00125	5596423	53.19	62.90	0.00125	10
15	0.00236	88417	208	441527	0.00047	5152989	42.09	58.28	0.00048	15
20	0.00416	88209	367	440252	0.00083	4711463	29.94	53.41	0.00082	20
25	0.00974	87842	856	437248	0.00196	4271200	36.50	48.62	0.00194	25
30	0.01407	86986	1224	432001	0.00283	3833952	26.79	44.08	0.00282	30
35	0.01732	85762	1485	425397	0.00349	3401951	16.26	39.67	0.00348	35
40	0.03165	84277	2667	414748	0.00643	2976554	10.38	35.32	0.00643	40
45	0.02012	81609	1642	403967	0.00407	2561806	0.00	31.39	0.00407	45
50	0.03490	79967	2791	393066	0.00710	2157839	23.94	26.98	0.00709	50
55	0.03410	77177	2632	380484	0.00692	1764773	19.14	22.87	0.00685	55
60	0.11340	74545	8453	352663	0.02397	1384289	15.72	18.57	0.02391	60
65	0.11761	66092	7773	311541	0.02495	1031626	15.72	15.61	0.02490	65
70	0.18731	58319	10924	264867	0.04124	720085	15.72	12.35	0.04115	70
75	0.22288	47395	10563	211631	0.04991	455219	15.72	9.60	0.04974	75
80	0.43512	36832	16025	146228	0.10960	243588	15.72	6.61	0.10909	80
85+	*1.00000	20806	20806	97360	0.21370	97360	15.72	4.68	0.21231	85+

TABLE 4 POPULATION PROJECTION, USING FIXED AGE-SPECIFIC BIRTH AND DEATH RATES, IN THOUSANDS

Age at last birthday	1966 Total	Males	Females	1971 Total	Males	Females	1976 Total	Males	Females	Age at last birthday
0–4	20	10	10	25	13	12	31	16	15	0–4
5–9	18	9	9	20	10	10	24	12	12	5–9
10–14	14	7	7	18	9	9	20	10	10	10–14
15–19	12	6	6	14	7	7	18	9	9	15–19
20–24	8	4	4	12	6	6	14	7	7	20–24
25–29	7	3	4	8	4	4	11	5	6	25–29
30–34	5	2	3	7	3	4	8	4	4	30–34
35–39	4	2	2	5	2	3	7	3	4	35–39
40–44	4	2	2	4	2	2	5	2	3	40–44
45–49	3	1	2	4	2	2	4	2	2	45–49
50–54	3	1	2	3	1	2	3	1	2	50–54
55–59	3	1	2	3	1	2	3	1	2	55–59
60–64	2	1	1	3	1	2	3	1	2	60–64
65–69	2	1	1	2	1	1	3	1	2	65–69
70–74	1	0	1	2	1	1	2	1	1	70–74
75–79	1	0	1	1	0	1	1	0	1	75–79
80–84	0	0	0	0	0	0	1	0	1	80–84
85 +	0	0	0	0	0	0	0	0	0	85 +
All ages	107	50	57	131	63	68	157	75	82	All ages

TABLE 5 OBSERVED AND PROJECTED VITAL RATES

Rates per thousand	Observed Total	Males	Females	Projected 1966 Males	Females	1971 Males	Females	1976 Males	Females	Stable Males	Females
Birth	44.60	49.40	40.51	48.56	41.34	49.31	43.25	50.46	45.39	47.77	46.65
Death	11.07	11.34	10.84	10.49	9.84	10.05	9.68	9.79	9.51	9.28	8.17
Increase	33.53	38.06	29.67	38.08	31.49	39.26	33.56	40.66	35.88		38.4965

TABLE 6 RATES STANDARDIZED ON THREE STANDARD COUNTRIES

Standardized rates per thousand	England and Wales, 1961 Total	Males	Females	United States, 1960 Total	Males	Females	Mexico, 1960 Total	Males	Females
Birth	43.17	65.59*	41.02	44.13	59.18*	42.62	49.59	52.41*	48.49
Death	13.89	20.90*	13.47	12.26	17.61*	11.14	8.64	9.54*	7.71
Increase	29.28	44.68*	27.55	31.87	41.57*	31.48	40.95	52.87*	40.78

TABLE 7 VITAL STATISTICS AND RATES INFERRED FROM AGE DISTRIBUTIONS (FEMALES)

Vital statistics		Thompson Age range	NRR	$1000r$	Interval	Bourgeois-Pichat Age range	NRR	$1000b$	$1000d$	$1000r$	Coale
TFR	6.70	0–4	2.92	39.25	27.35	5–29	3.08	42.70	1.03	41.67	$1000b$
GRR	3.29	5–9	2.67	36.98	27.25	30–54	1.22	14.19	6.84	7.35	$1000d$
NRR	2.85	10–14	2.28	29.62	27.19	55–79	1.40	16.31	3.93	12.38	$1000r$
Generation	27.25	15–19	1.91	23.92	27.13	*15–39	2.25	32.23	2.23	29.99	$1000k_1$
Sex ratio	104.01										$1000k_2$

TABLE 8 LESLIE MATRIX AND ITS ANALYSIS (FEMALES)

Start of age interval	Sub-diagonal	First row	Percent in stable population	Fisher values	Total reproductive values	Net maternity function	Matrix equation coefficient	Parameters Integral	Matrix
0	0.96984	0.00000	19.553	1.196	11006	0.00000	0.00000	λ_1 1.2123	1.2133
5	0.99458	0.00071	15.629	1.496	10824	0.00000	0.00078	λ_2 0.3894	0.3994
10	0.99568	0.19574	12.812	1.825	10186	0.00156	0.18901	+0.8170	+0.7943i
15	0.99713	0.54696	10.513	1.988	8368	0.37647	0.52546	r_1 0.0385	0.0387
20	0.99313	0.71384	8.640	1.763	6416	0.67445	0.68379	r_2 -0.0200	-0.0235
25	0.98795	0.57215	7.072	1.295	3999	0.69313	0.63967	+0.2252	+0.2210i
30	0.98466	0.50214	5.758	0.776	1924	0.58620	0.47223	c_1	441
35	0.97487	0.26856	4.673	0.347	797	0.35826	0.24850	c_2	1331
40	0.97391	0.39089	3.755	0.102	206	0.13875	0.08195		363i
45	0.97291	0.01486	3.014	0.015	30	0.02515	0.01306	$2\pi/y$ 27.901	28.435
50	0.96787	0.00067	2.417	0.001	1	0.00098	0.00049	Δ 8.828	
55	0.83384		6.164						

Guatemala, 1964

TABLE 1 DATA INPUT TO COMPUTATIONS

Age at last birthday	Population					Births, by age of mother	Deaths			Age at last birthday
	Total	Males	%	Females	%		Total	Males	Females	
0	165360	82942	3.7	82418	3.7	0	17278	9454	7824	0
1–4	617548	313202	14.1	304346	13.7	0	16124	7916	8208	1–4
5–9	696089	354519	16.0	341570	15.4	0	4501	2250	2251	5–9
10–14	565909	290562	13.1	275347	12.4	353	1752	942	810	10–14
15–19	446232	215047	9.7	231185	10.4	32148	1817	977	840	15–19
20–24	355548	171371	7.7	184177	8.3	53378	1890	896	994	20–24
25–29	304267	146895	6.6	157372	7.1	45322	1918	948	970	25–29
30–34	273577	137211	6.2	136366	6.1	33081	1983	1034	949	30–34
35–39	248853	122673	5.5	126180	5.7	22937	2023	1060	963	35–39
40–44	191814	96784	4.4	95030	4.3	7602	1821	1002	819	40–44
45–49	150005	77752	3.5	72253	3.3	1278	1786	1066	720	45–49
50–54	125090	60914	2.7	64176	2.9	287	1908	1043	865	50–54
55–59	89061	44815	2.0	44246	2.0	0	1790	950	840	55–59
60–64	87775	44414	2.0	43361	2.0	0	2913	1540	1373	60–64
65–69	50332	25974	1.2	24358	1.1	0	2204	1160	1044	65–69
70–74	34236	17027	0.8	17209	0.8		2149	1091	1058	70–74
75–79	18732	10022	0.5	8710	0.4		1498	773	725	75–79
80–84	11391	5296	0.2	6095	0.3	100392 M	1431	614	817	80–84
85+	8417	4136	0.2	4281	0.2	95994 F	1492	641	851	85+
All ages	4440236	2221556		2218680		196386	68278	35357	32921	All ages

TABLE 2 LIFE TABLE FOR MALES

Age, x	$_nq_x$	l_x	$_nd_x$	$_nL_x$	$_nm_x$	T_x	$1000r_x$	$\overset{\circ}{e}_x$	$_nM_x$	Age, x
0	0.10671	100000	10671	93622	0.11398	4925156	0.00	49.25	0.11398	0
1	0.09473	89329	8462	334801	0.02527	4831534	0.00	54.09	0.02527	1
5	0.03083	80867	2493	398101	0.00626	4496733	21.23	55.61	0.00635	5
10	0.01599	78374	1253	388578	0.00322	4098632	45.70	52.30	0.00324	10
15	0.02257	77120	1741	381396	0.00456	3710054	48.48	48.11	0.00454	15
20	0.02588	75380	1951	372147	0.00524	3328658	32.74	44.16	0.00523	20
25	0.03180	73429	2335	361450	0.00646	2956512	15.81	40.26	0.00645	25
30	0.03702	71094	2632	349008	0.00754	2595062	10.48	36.50	0.00754	30
35	0.04238	68462	2902	335201	0.00866	2246053	26.15	32.81	0.00864	35
40	0.05067	65561	3322	319757	0.01039	1910852	34.89	29.15	0.01035	40
45	0.06656	62239	4143	301142	0.01376	1591096	32.58	25.56	0.01371	45
50	0.08244	58096	4789	278766	0.01718	1289953	37.95	22.20	0.01712	50
55	0.10101	53307	5385	253677	0.02123	1011188	8.34	18.97	0.02120	55
60	0.16059	47922	7696	220940	0.03483	757511	31.76	15.81	0.03467	60
65	0.20185	40226	8120	181081	0.04484	536570	31.76	13.34	0.04466	65
70	0.27677	32107	8886	138191	0.06430	355489	31.76	11.07	0.06407	70
75	0.32323	23221	7506	96954	0.07742	217299	31.76	9.36	0.07713	75
80	0.44794	15715	7039	60424	0.11650	120345	31.76	7.66	0.11594	80
85+	1.00000	8676	8676	59921	0.14478	59921	31.76	6.91	0.15498	85+

TABLE 3 LIFE TABLE FOR FEMALES

Age, x	$_nq_x$	l_x	$_nd_x$	$_nL_x$	$_nm_x$	T_x	$1000r_x$	$\overset{\circ}{e}_x$	$_nM_x$	Age, x
0	0.09001	100000	9001	94814	0.09493	5086999	0.00	50.87	0.09493	0
1	0.10084	90999	9176	340246	0.02697	4992186	0.00	54.86	0.02697	1
5	0.03192	81823	2612	402586	0.00649	4651939	23.80	56.85	0.00659	5
10	0.01449	79211	1148	392939	0.00292	4249353	35.08	53.65	0.00294	10
15	0.01810	78064	1413	386974	0.00365	3856415	36.42	49.40	0.00363	15
20	0.02672	76651	2048	378310	0.00541	3469440	33.28	45.26	0.00540	20
25	0.03040	74602	2268	367431	0.00617	3091130	23.85	41.43	0.00616	25
30	0.03423	72335	2476	355557	0.00696	2723699	15.16	37.65	0.00696	30
35	0.03750	69859	2620	342821	0.00764	2368142	28.41	33.90	0.00763	35
40	0.04231	67239	2845	329192	0.00864	2025322	47.09	30.12	0.00862	40
45	0.04879	64394	3142	314362	0.00999	1696130	28.85	26.34	0.00996	45
50	0.06559	61253	4018	296652	0.01354	1381768	35.26	22.56	0.01348	50
55	0.09117	57235	5218	273893	0.01905	1085117	18.68	18.96	0.01898	55
60	0.14767	52017	7682	241590	0.03180	811224	26.57	15.60	0.03166	60
65	0.19453	44335	8625	200503	0.04302	569635	26.57	12.85	0.04286	65
70	0.26739	35711	9549	154765	0.06170	369131	26.57	10.34	0.06148	70
75	0.34516	26162	9030	108041	0.08358	214366	26.57	8.19	0.08324	75
80	0.50336	17132	8623	63992	0.13476	106325	26.57	6.21	0.13404	80
85+	*1.00000	8508	8508	42333	0.20099	42333	26.57	4.98	0.19879	85+

TABLE 4 POPULATION PROJECTION, USING FIXED AGE-SPECIFIC BIRTH AND DEATH RATES, IN THOUSANDS

Age at last birthday	1969			1974			1979			Age at last birthday
	Total	Males	Females	Total	Males	Females	Total	Males	Females	
0–4	915	464	451	1068	542	526	1249	634	615	0–4
5–9	726	368	358	848	431	417	991	504	487	5–9
10–14	679	346	333	708	359	349	828	421	407	10–14
15–19	556	285	271	668	340	328	697	353	344	15–19
20–24	436	210	226	543	278	265	652	331	321	20–24
25–29	345	166	179	424	204	220	527	270	257	25–29
30–34	294	142	152	334	161	173	409	197	212	30–34
35–39	263	132	131	283	136	147	321	154	167	35–39
40–44	238	117	121	252	126	126	271	130	141	40–44
45–49	182	91	91	226	110	116	239	118	121	45–49
50–54	140	72	68	170	84	86	211	102	109	50–54
55–59	114	55	59	128	65	63	156	77	79	55–59
60–64	78	39	39	100	48	52	113	57	56	60–64
65–69	72	36	36	64	32	32	83	40	43	65–69
70–74	39	20	19	56	28	28	49	24	25	70–74
75–79	24	12	12	27	14	13	38	19	19	75–79
80–84	11	6	5	14	7	7	17	9	8	80–84
85 +	9	5	4	9	6	3	12	7	5	85 +
All ages	5121	2566	2555	5922	2971	2951	6863	3447	3416	All ages

TABLE 5 OBSERVED AND PROJECTED VITAL RATES

Rates per thousand	Observed			Projected						Stable	
				1969		1974		1979			
	Total	Males	Females	Males	Females	Males	Females	Males	Females	Males	Females
Birth	44.23	45.19	43.27	45.31	43.52	45.98	44.27	46.16	44.53	44.85	43.86
Death	15.38	15.92	14.84	15.99	14.79	16.08	14.89	16.11	15.03	16.41	15.43
Increase	28.85	29.27	28.43	29.32	28.73	29.90	29.38	30.05	29.50		28.4385

TABLE 6 RATES STANDARDIZED ON THREE STANDARD COUNTRIES

Standardized rates per thousand	England and Wales, 1961			United States, 1960			Mexico, 1960		
	Total	Males	Females	Total	Males	Females	Total	Males	Females
Birth	40.19	47.23*	33.07	40.92	43.39*	39.42	45.12	45.01*	44.00
Death	20.45	36.35*	21.77	18.80	29.58*	18.91	15.35	15.57*	14.86
Increase	19.74	10.88*	16.30	22.12	13.81*	20.51	29.77	29.44*	29.13

TABLE 7 VITAL STATISTICS AND RATES INFERRED FROM AGE DISTRIBUTIONS (FEMALES)

Vital statistics		Thompson				Bourgeois-Pichat					Coale	
		Age range	NRR	1000r	Interval	Age range	NRR	1000b	1000d	1000r		
TFR	6.22	0–4	2.06	27.70	27.07	5–29	2.55	49.09	14.46	34.63	1000b	46.52
GRR	3.04	5–9	2.30	31.49	26.96	30–54	2.39	51.50	19.18	32.32	1000d	16.00
NRR	2.21	10–14	2.16	27.97	26.89	55–79	2.26	45.20	14.98	30.22	1000r	30.52
Generation	27.84	15–19	2.12	28.12	26.77	*5–29	2.55	49.09	14.46	34.63	$1000k_1$	0.
Sex ratio	104.6										$1000k_2$	0.

TABLE 8 LESLIE MATRIX AND ITS ANALYSIS (FEMALES)

Start of age interval	Sub-diagonal	First row	Percent in stable population	Fisher values	Total reproductive values	Net maternity function	Matrix equation coefficient	Parameters	Integral	Matrix
0	0.92536	0.00000	17.813	1.232	476539	0.00000	0.00000	λ_1	1.1528	1.1533
5	0.97603	0.00133	14.292	1.536	524544	0.00000	0.00123	λ_2	0.4001	0.4105
10	0.98482	0.14698	12.094	1.813	499199	0.00246	0.13275		+0.7570	+0.7391 i
15	0.97762	0.44913	10.327	1.939	448345	0.26303	0.39948	r_1	0.0284	0.0285
20	0.97125	0.60559	8.754	1.722	317126	0.53593	0.52658	r_2	-0.0310	-0.0336
25	0.96770	0.55583	7.372	1.276	200871	0.51724	0.46943		+0.2169	+0.2128 i
30	0.96420	0.44431	6.185	0.814	110943	0.42161	0.36311	c_1		22376
35	0.96024	0.27496	5.171	0.405	51152	0.30461	0.21667	c_2		9031
40	0.95492	0.10302	4.305	0.134	12744	0.12872	0.07795			32381 i
45	0.94367	0.02329	3.564	0.029	2098	0.02718	0.01683	$2\pi/y$	28.966	29.530
50	0.92333	0.00475	2.916	0.005	325	0.00648	0.00324	Δ	2.291	
55	0.77965		7.206							

Honduras, 1966

TABLE 1   DATA INPUT TO COMPUTATIONS

Age at last birthday	Population Total	Males	%	Females	%	Births, by age of mother	Deaths Total	Males	Females	Age at last birthday
0	121159	61412	5.2	59747	5.0	0	3889	2073	1815	0
1–4	363476	184233	15.7	179243	15.1	0	4467	2280	2187	1–4
5–9	423085	215040	18.3	208045	17.5	0	1597	788	809	5–9
10–14	308723	156505	13.3	152218	12.8	202	558	313	245	10–14
15–19	227928	110496	9.4	117432	9.9	16268	542	281	261	15–19
20–24	186962	87826	7.5	99136	8.3	27731	587	340	247	20–24
25–29	158744	75300	6.4	83444	7.0	23995	581	340	241	25–29
30–34	135623	65696	5.6	69927	5.9	18318	656	346	310	30–34
35–39	111298	54555	4.6	56743	4.8	12104	649	327	322	35–39
40–44	86303	42780	3.6	43523	3.7	4244	573	302	271	40–44
45–49	68800	34562	2.9	34238	2.9	1566	590	295	295	45–49
50–54	53241	26861	2.3	26380	2.2	0	623	329	294	50–54
55–59	41464	20885	1.8	20579	1.7	0	742	402	340	55–59
60–64	34329	17234	1.5	17095	1.4	0	890	449	441	60–64
65–69	21522	10977	0.9	10545	0.9	0	928	440	488	65–69
70–74	10691	5424	0.5	5267	0.4		728	354	374	70–74
75–79	5120	2488	0.2	2632	0.2		560	276	284	75–79
80–84	2377	1061	0.1	1316	0.1	53951 M	416	207	209	80–84
85+	1972	654	0.1	1318	0.1	50477 F	917	447	470	85+
All ages	2362817	1173989		1188828		104428	20493	10589	9904	All ages

TABLE 2   LIFE TABLE FOR MALES

Age, x	$_nq_x$	l_x	$_nd_x$	$_nL_x$	$_nm_x$	T_x	$1000r_x$	$\overset{\circ}{e}_x$	$_nM_x$	Age, x
0	0.03275	100000	3275	98192	0.03335	5923873	24.26	59.24	0.03375	0
1	0.04772	96725	4615	375452	0.01229	5825680	24.26	60.23	0.01238	1
5	0.01780	92109	1639	456448	0.00359	5450218	39.96	59.17	0.00366	5
10	0.00988	90470	894	450012	0.00199	4993770	64.09	55.20	0.00200	10
15	0.01275	89576	1142	445195	0.00256	4543758	55.09	50.72	0.00254	15
20	0.01925	88435	1702	438083	0.00389	4098562	34.63	46.35	0.00387	20
25	0.02236	86732	1940	428918	0.00452	3660479	24.47	42.20	0.00452	25
30	0.02604	84793	2208	418549	0.00528	3231561	26.97	38.11	0.00527	30
35	0.02960	82585	2445	406933	0.00601	2813013	36.83	34.05	0.00599	35
40	0.03480	80140	2789	393896	0.00708	2406080	38.53	30.02	0.00706	40
45	0.04201	77351	3250	378976	0.00858	2012183	37.56	26.01	0.00854	45
50	0.05991	74101	4439	360072	0.01233	1633207	37.42	22.04	0.01225	50
55	0.09234	69662	6432	332930	0.01932	1273136	25.26	18.28	0.01925	55
60	0.12346	63230	7806	297420	0.02625	940206	46.88	14.87	0.02605	60
65	0.18432	55423	10216	252624	0.04044	642785	46.88	11.60	0.04008	65
70	0.28384	45208	12832	194777	0.06588	390161	46.88	8.63	0.06527	70
75	0.43701	32376	14149	126300	0.11202	195384	46.88	6.03	0.11093	75
80	0.64958	18227	11840	59918	0.19760	69084	46.88	3.79	0.19510	80
85+	*1.00000	6387	6387	9166	0.69684	9166	46.88	1.44	0.68349	85+

TABLE 3   LIFE TABLE FOR FEMALES

Age, x	$_nq_x$	l_x	$_nd_x$	$_nL_x$	$_nm_x$	T_x	$1000r_x$	$\overset{\circ}{e}_x$	$_nM_x$	Age, x
0	0.02956	100000	2956	98387	0.03004	6069541	24.47	60.70	0.03039	0
1	0.04711	97044	4572	377007	0.01213	5971155	24.47	61.53	0.01220	1
5	0.01889	92472	1746	457996	0.00381	5594148	39.99	60.50	0.00389	5
10	0.00792	90726	719	451677	0.00159	5136152	54.90	56.61	0.00161	10
15	0.01109	90007	998	447621	0.00223	4684475	40.79	52.05	0.00222	15
20	0.01240	89009	1104	442341	0.00250	4236854	31.66	47.60	0.00249	20
25	0.01441	87905	1266	436526	0.00290	3794513	31.76	43.17	0.00289	25
30	0.02203	86639	1909	428652	0.00445	3357986	34.19	38.76	0.00443	30
35	0.02806	84730	2378	417835	0.00569	2929334	41.90	34.57	0.00567	35
40	0.03080	82352	2536	405629	0.00625	2511499	43.87	30.50	0.00623	40
45	0.04241	79816	3385	390956	0.00866	2105869	41.47	26.38	0.00862	45
50	0.05458	76430	4172	372220	0.01121	1714913	39.18	22.44	0.01114	50
55	0.07987	72259	5772	347695	0.01660	1342693	26.18	18.58	0.01552	55
60	0.12270	66487	8158	313388	0.02603	994998	40.49	14.97	0.02580	60
65	0.20973	58329	12233	262280	0.04664	681611	40.49	11.69	0.04628	65
70	0.30364	46096	13997	195783	0.07149	419331	40.49	9.10	0.07101	70
75	0.42507	32100	13644	125624	0.10861	223547	40.49	6.96	0.10790	75
80	0.56006	18455	10336	64683	0.15979	97923	40.49	5.31	0.15881	80
85+	1.00000	8119	8119	33240	0.24425	33240	40.49	4.09	0.35660	85+

TABLE 4 POPULATION PROJECTION, USING FIXED AGE-SPECIFIC BIRTH AND DEATH RATES, IN THOUSANDS

Age at last birthday	1971			1976			1981			Age at last birthday
	Total	Males	Females	Total	Males	Females	Total	Males	Females	
0–4	545	281	264	663	342	321	816	421	395	0–4
5–9	467	237	230	525	271	254	638	329	309	5–9
10–14	417	212	205	460	233	227	518	267	251	10–14
15–19	306	155	151	413	210	203	456	231	225	15–19
20–24	225	109	116	301	152	149	407	206	201	20–24
25–29	184	86	98	221	106	115	296	149	147	25–29
30–34	155	73	82	180	84	96	216	104	112	30–34
35–39	132	64	68	151	71	80	176	82	94	35–39
40–44	108	53	55	128	62	66	147	69	78	40–44
45–49	83	41	42	104	51	53	123	59	64	45–49
50–54	66	33	33	79	39	40	99	48	51	50–54
55–59	50	25	25	60	30	30	73	36	37	55–59
60–64	38	19	19	44	22	22	54	27	27	60–64
65–69	29	15	14	32	16	16	38	19	19	65–69
70–74	16	8	8	22	11	11	24	12	12	70–74
75–79	7	4	3	10	5	5	14	7	7	75–79
80–84	2	1	1	4	2	2	6	3	3	80–84
85 +	1	0	1	1	0	1	1	0	1	85 +
All ages	2831	1416	1415	3398	1707	1691	4102	2069	2033	All ages

TABLE 5 OBSERVED AND PROJECTED VITAL RATES

Rates per thousand	Observed			Projected						Stable	
				1971		1976		1981			
	Total	Males	Females	Males	Females	Males	Females	Males	Females	Males	Females
Birth	44.20	45.96	42.46	45.67	42.74	46.63	44.09	47.39	45.20	44.61	44.05
Death	8.67	9.02	8.33	8.62	7.99	8.74	8.10	8.86	8.25	8.97	8.41
Increase	35.52	36.94	34.13	37.05	34.75	37.89	35.99	38.54	36.95		35.6405

TABLE 6 RATES STANDARDIZED ON THREE STANDARD COUNTRIES

Standardized rates per thousand	England and Wales, 1961			United States, 1960			Mexico, 1960		
	Total	Males	Females	Total	Males	Females	Total	Males	Females
Birth	43.00	51.53*	40.28	43.68	47.04*	41.60	46.85	50.15*	45.19
Death	19.34	25.42*	20.96	16.44	19.50*	16.39	10.05	9.53*	9.63
Increase	23.67	26.11*	19.32	27.24	27.54*	25.21	36.82	41.61*	35.55

TABLE 7 VITAL STATISTICS AND RATES INFERRED FROM AGE DISTRIBUTIONS (FEMALES)

Vital statistics		Thompson				Bourgeois-Pichat					Coale	
		Age range	NRR	1000r	Interval	Age range	NRR	1000b	1000d	1000r		
TFR	6.63	0–4	2.76	37.24	27.23	5–29	3.17	49.79	7.01	42.78	1000b	45.11
GRR	3.20	5–9	2.96	39.98	27.14	30–54	3.12	54.46	12.34	42.12	1000d	8.38
NRR	2.76	10–14	2.63	34.77	27.04	55–79	4.23	117.06	63.65	53.41	1000r	36.73
Generation	28.47	15–19	2.47	33.54	26.91	*15–39	2.42	39.31	6.62	32.69	$1000k_1$	−3.18
Sex ratio	106.9										$1000k_2$	0.

TABLE 8 LESLIE MATRIX AND ITS ANALYSIS (FEMALES)

Start of age interval	Sub-diagonal	First row	Percent in stable population	Fisher values	Total reproductive values	Net maternity function	Matrix equation coefficient	Parameters	Integral	Matrix
0	0.96340	0.00000	19.213	1.149	274530	0.00000	0.00000	λ_1	1.1951	1.1959
5	0.98620	0.00150	15.477	1.426	296665	0.00000	0.00145	λ_2	0.4373	0.4462
10	0.99102	0.15926	12.763	1.727	262952	0.00290	0.15132		+0.7598	+0.7441 i
15	0.98820	0.47675	10.576	1.900	223129	0.29973	0.44891	r_1	0.0356	0.0358
20	0.98686	0.54742	8.739	1.745	173023	0.59809	0.60242	r_2	−0.0263	−0.0284
25	0.98196	0.52594	7.211	1.361	113607	0.60675	0.57476		+0.2097	+0.2061 i
30	0.97476	0.53989	5.921	0.925	64746	0.54277	0.48680	c_1		12043
35	0.97079	0.35386	4.826	0.500	28359	0.43082	0.31101	c_2		33973
40	0.96383	0.16267	3.917	0.197	8573	0.19119	0.13881			25405 i
45	0.95208	0.05257	3.157	0.051	1730	0.08643	0.04322	$2\pi/y$	29.961	30.481
50	0.93411	0.00004	2.513	0.000	1	0.00000	0.00000	Δ	3.084	
55	0.78292		5.684							

Jamaica, 1963

TABLE 1 DATA INPUT TO COMPUTATIONS

Age at last birthday	Population					Births, by age of mother	Deaths			Age at last birthday
	Total	Males	%	Females	%		Total	Males	Females	
0	63200	31950	3.9	31250	3.5	0	3387	1846	1541	0
1–4	243400	122550	15.0	120850	13.7	0	1653	866	787	1–4
5–9	257050	129700	15.9	127350	14.5	0	195	121	74	5–9
10–14	201650	101500	12.4	100150	11.4	167	112	60	52	10–14
15–19	159600	78400	9.6	81200	9.2	12351	149	83	66	15–19
20–24	123300	57100	7.0	66200	7.5	19432	168	75	93	20–24
25–29	98250	42650	5.2	55600	6.3	15361	195	96	99	25–29
30–34	83150	35700	4.4	47450	5.4	10978	226	108	118	30–34
35–39	77900	34000	4.2	43900	5.0	6729	248	111	137	35–39
40–44	75150	34450	4.2	40700	4.6	2174	341	181	160	40–44
45–49	72750	35450	4.3	37300	4.2	292	464	255	209	45–49
50–54	68900	33950	4.2	34950	4.0	13	721	391	330	50–54
55–59	54950	26950	3.3	28000	3.2	0	732	439	293	55–59
60–64	41650	20000	2.5	21650	2.5	0	1103	622	481	60–64
65–69	28450	13050	1.6	15400	1.7	0	907	516	391	65–69
70–74	19050	8050	1.0	11000	1.2		1008	557	451	70–74
75–79	13050	5150	0.6	7900	0.9		916	428	488	75–79
80–84	7734	2833	0.3	4901	0.6	34332 M	1043	470	573	80–84
85 +	6967	2218	0.3	4749	0.5	33165 F	1541	549	992	85 +
All ages	1696151	815651		880500		67497	15109	7774	7335	All ages

TABLE 2 LIFE TABLE FOR MALES

Age, x	$_nq_x$	l_x	$_nd_x$	$_nL_x$	$_nm_x$	T_x	$1000r_x$	$\overset{\circ}{e}_x$	$_nM_x$	Age, x
0	0.05568	100000	5568	96388	0.05777	6288735	0.20	62.89	0.05778	0
1	0.02772	94432	2618	370457	0.00707	6192347	0.20	65.57	0.00707	1
5	0.00444	91814	407	458053	0.00089	5821890	39.75	63.41	0.00093	5
10	0.00296	91407	271	456374	0.00059	5363837	49.57	58.68	0.00059	10
15	0.00532	91136	485	454537	0.00107	4907463	56.53	53.85	0.00106	15
20	0.00662	90651	600	451866	0.00133	4452926	59.40	49.12	0.00131	20
25	0.01127	90051	1015	447871	0.00227	4001060	44.74	44.43	0.00225	25
30	0.01504	89036	1339	441917	0.00303	3553189	19.78	39.91	0.00303	30
35	0.01620	87697	1421	435122	0.00326	3111272	0.00	35.48	0.00326	35
40	0.02595	86277	2239	426109	0.00525	2676151	0.00	31.02	0.00525	40
45	0.03537	84038	2973	413240	0.00719	2250042	0.00	26.77	0.00719	45
50	0.05621	81065	4556	394577	0.01155	1836802	15.98	22.66	0.01152	50
55	0.07911	76509	6053	368595	0.01642	1442225	34.35	18.85	0.01629	55
60	0.14523	70456	10233	327712	0.03122	1073924	25.07	15.24	0.03110	60
65	0.18117	60224	10911	274752	0.03971	745917	25.07	12.39	0.03954	65
70	0.29612	49313	14603	210277	0.06945	471165	25.07	9.55	0.06919	70
75	0.34472	34710	11965	143372	0.08346	260888	25.07	7.52	0.08311	75
80	0.58603	22745	13329	79870	0.16688	117517	25.07	5.17	0.16590	80
85 +	*1.00000	9416	9416	37647	0.25011	37647	25.07	4.00	0.24752	85 +

TABLE 3 LIFE TABLE FOR FEMALES

Age, x	$_nq_x$	l_x	$_nd_x$	$_nL_x$	$_nm_x$	T_x	$1000r_x$	$\overset{\circ}{e}_x$	$_nM_x$	Age, x
0	0.04780	100000	4780	96939	0.04931	6714657	0.00	67.15	0.04931	0
1	0.02559	95220	2437	374149	0.00651	6617718	0.00	69.50	0.00651	1
5	0.00270	92783	251	463290	0.00054	6243568	39.86	67.29	0.00058	5
10	0.00261	92533	241	462087	0.00052	5780279	44.42	62.47	0.00052	10
15	0.00409	92292	378	460597	0.00082	5318192	40.52	57.62	0.00081	15
20	0.00704	91914	647	458042	0.00141	4857595	35.52	52.85	0.00140	20
25	0.00890	91267	812	454402	0.00179	4399553	31.44	48.21	0.00178	25
30	0.01239	90455	1121	449590	0.00249	3945151	21.16	43.61	0.00249	30
35	0.01551	89334	1385	443330	0.00312	3495561	12.20	39.13	0.00312	35
40	0.01950	87949	1715	435664	0.00394	3052231	12.22	34.70	0.00393	40
45	0.02771	86233	2389	425644	0.00561	2616567	9.13	30.34	0.00560	45
50	0.04626	83844	3879	409883	0.00946	2190923	20.03	26.13	0.00944	50
55	0.05151	79965	4119	390392	0.01055	1781040	34.92	22.27	0.01046	55
60	0.10581	75846	8026	360003	0.02229	1390648	23.50	18.34	0.02222	60
65	0.11997	67820	8136	319418	0.02547	1030645	23.50	15.20	0.02539	65
70	0.18729	59684	11178	271507	0.04117	711228	23.50	11.92	0.04100	70
75	0.26987	48506	13090	210854	0.06208	439720	23.50	9.07	0.06177	75
80	0.45776	35416	16212	137823	0.11763	228867	23.50	6.45	0.11692	80
85 +	*1.00000	19204	19204	91043	0.21093	91043	23.50	4.74	0.20889	85 +

TABLE 4 POPULATION PROJECTION, USING FIXED AGE-SPECIFIC BIRTH AND DEATH RATES, IN THOUSANDS

Age at last birthday	1968			1973			1978			Age at last birthday
	Total	Males	Females	Total	Males	Females	Total	Males	Females	
0–4	345	175	170	415	210	205	505	256	249	0–4
5–9	302	152	150	340	172	168	407	206	201	5–9
10–14	256	129	127	300	151	149	338	171	167	10–14
15–19	201	101	100	256	129	127	299	150	149	15–19
20–24	159	78	81	199	100	99	254	128	126	20–24
25–29	123	57	66	157	77	80	198	100	98	25–29
30–34	97	42	55	121	56	65	155	76	79	30–34
35–39	82	35	47	95	41	54	119	55	64	35–39
40–44	76	33	43	80	34	46	94	41	53	40–44
45–49	73	33	40	74	32	42	78	33	45	45–49
50–54	70	34	36	70	32	38	72	31	41	50–54
55–59	65	32	33	66	32	34	66	30	36	55–59
60–64	50	24	26	59	28	31	60	28	32	60–64
65–69	36	17	19	43	20	23	51	24	27	65–69
70–74	23	10	13	29	13	16	34	15	19	70–74
75–79	14	5	9	17	7	10	22	9	13	75–79
80–84	8	3	5	9	3	6	11	4	7	80–84
85 +	4	1	3	4	1	3	5	1	4	85 +
All ages	1984	961	1023	2334	1138	1196	2768	1358	1410	All ages

TABLE 5 OBSERVED AND PROJECTED VITAL RATES

Rates per thousand	Observed			Projected						Stable	
				1968		1973		1978			
	Total	Males	Females	Males	Females	Males	Females	Males	Females	Males	Females
Birth	39.79	42.09	37.67	42.21	38.34	43.30	39.81	44.38	41.26	43.04	42.01
Death	8.91	9.53	8.33	8.89	7.67	8.73	7.59	8.56	7.54	7.73	6.71
Increase	30.89	32.56	29.34	33.32	30.67	34.57	32.22	35.82	33.72	35.3023	

TABLE 6 RATES STANDARDIZED ON THREE STANDARD COUNTRIES

Standardized rates per thousand	England and Wales, 1961			United States, 1960			Mexico, 1960		
	Total	Males	Females	Total	Males	Females	Total	Males	Females
Birth	37.66	54.04*	35.86	38.49	48.66*	37.27	43.65	50.45*	42.79
Death	13.72	17.29*	13.52	11.73	14.45*	10.65	7.41	8.33*	6.54
Increase	23.94	36.75*	22.34	26.77	34.22*	26.62	36.24	42.12*	36.25

TABLE 7 VITAL STATISTICS AND RATES INFERRED FROM AGE DISTRIBUTIONS (FEMALES)

Vital statistics		Thompson				Bourgeois-Pichat					Coale
		Age range	NRR	$1000r$	Interval	Age range	NRR	$1000b$	$1000d$	$1000r$	
TFR	5.85	0–4	2.60	34.98	27.35	5–29	2.98	41.37	0.89	40.48	$1000b$
GRR	2.87	5–9	2.52	34.61	27.29	30–54	1.34	17.00	6.02	10.98	$1000d$
NRR	2.60	10–14	2.18	28.06	27.21	55–79	2.84	75.65	36.97	38.69	$1000r$
Generation	27.09	15–19	1.94	24.43	27.10	*30–54	1.34	17.00	6.02	10.98	$1000k_1$
Sex ratio	103.52										$1000k_2$

TABLE 8 LESLIE MATRIX AND ITS ANALYSIS (FEMALES)

Start of age interval	Sub-diagonal	First row	Percent in stable population	Fisher values	Total reproductive values	Net maternity function	Matrix equation coefficient	Parameters	Integral	Matrix
0	0.98344	0.00000	18.176	1.158	176190	0.00000	0.00000	λ_1	1.1931	1.1939
5	0.99740	0.00193	14.971	1.406	179096	0.00000	0.00189	λ_2	0.3817	0.3929
10	0.99678	0.17741	12.507	1.681	168372	0.00379	0.17401		+0.8000	+0.7789i
15	0.99445	0.51388	10.441	1.808	146775	0.34424	0.50244	r_1	0.0353	0.0355
20	0.99205	0.65692	8.697	1.572	104040	0.66063	0.63874	r_2	-0.0241	-0.0273
25	0.98941	0.58467	7.226	1.124	62515	0.61685	0.56397		+0.2251	+0.2207i
30	0.98608	0.44270	5.988	0.672	31899	0.51109	0.42249	c_1		8075
35	0.98271	0.23817	4.946	0.294	12903	0.33389	0.22412	c_2		15671
40	0.97700	0.07067	4.071	0.076	3108	0.11434	0.06536			8833i
45	0.96297	0.00947	3.331	0.010	356	0.01637	0.00856	$2\pi/y$	27.910	28.466
50	0.95245	0.00044	2.687	0.000	15	0.00075	0.00037	Δ	6.361	
55	0.82621		6.959							

[343]

Mexico, 1966

TABLE 1   DATA INPUT TO COMPUTATIONS

Age at last birthday	Population					Births, by age of mother	Deaths			Age at last birthday
	Total	Males	%	Females	%		Total	Males	Females	
0	1764000	896000	4.1	868000	3.9	0	122896	68108	54788	0
1–4	6392000	3266000	14.8	3126000	14.2	0	63926	31788	32138	1–4
5–9	6716999	3445999	15.6	3271000	14.8	0	14385	7574	6811	5–9
10–14	5549000	2837000	12.8	2712000	12.3	3390	6632	3644	2988	10–14
15–19	4525000	2290000	10.4	2235000	10.1	213986	7775	4371	3404	15–19
20–24	3677000	1839000	8.3	1838000	8.3	537112	9669	5477	4192	20–24
25–29	3035000	1497000	6.8	1538000	7.0	491128	10377	5820	4557	25–29
30–34	2549000	1238000	5.6	1311000	6.0	328540	10206	5813	4393	30–34
35–39	2154000	1044000	4.7	1110000	5.0	241290	12628	7200	5428	35–39
40–44	1819000	881000	4.0	938000	4.3	107736	11471	6809	4662	40–44
45–49	1490000	713000	3.2	777000	3.5	17383	11732	6796	4935	45–49
50–54	1205000	575000	2.6	630000	2.9	0	12230	6970	5260	50–54
55–59	998000	484000	2.2	514000	2.3	0	14923	8510	6413	55–59
60–64	808000	399000	1.8	409000	1.9	0	18180	9823	8357	60–64
65–69	596000	292000	1.3	304000	1.4	0	20516	11098	9418	65–69
70–74	404000	195000	0.9	209000	0.9		18096	9233	8863	70–74
75–79	252000	122000	0.6	130000	0.6		17118	8634	8484	75–79
80–84	128941	62439	0.3	66502	0.3	1004002 M	15095	6807	8288	80–84
85+	82060	39562	0.2	42498	0.2	936563 F	26286	10773	15513	85+
All ages	44145000	22116000		22029000		1940565	424141	225248	198893	All ages

TABLE 2   LIFE TABLE FOR MALES

Age, x	$_nq_x$	l_x	$_nd_x$	$_nL_x$	$_nm_x$	T_x	$1000r_x$	$\overset{\circ}{e}_x$	$_nM_x$	Age, x
0	0.07227	100000	7227	95336	0.07581	5948730	3.91	59.49	0.07601	0
1	0.03783	92773	3509	361365	0.00971	5853394	3.91	63.09	0.00973	1
5	0.01068	89263	953	443934	0.00215	5492029	34.63	61.53	0.00220	5
10	0.00639	88310	564	440116	0.00128	5048096	39.24	57.16	0.00128	10
15	0.00957	87746	840	436779	0.00192	4607980	41.37	52.52	0.00191	15
20	0.01487	86906	1292	431467	0.00299	4171201	39.56	48.00	0.00298	20
25	0.01932	85613	1654	424071	0.00390	3739734	35.71	43.68	0.00389	25
30	0.02331	83959	1957	415140	0.00471	3315663	31.01	39.49	0.00470	30
35	0.03400	82002	2788	403250	0.00691	2900523	27.44	35.37	0.00690	35
40	0.03801	79214	3011	388704	0.00775	2497264	30.17	31.53	0.00773	40
45	0.04672	76203	3561	372383	0.00956	2108560	33.02	27.67	0.00953	45
50	0.05910	72643	4293	352944	0.01216	1736177	26.02	23.90	0.01212	50
55	0.08459	68350	5781	327922	0.01763	1383233	18.74	20.24	0.01758	55
60	0.11677	62568	7306	295380	0.02473	1055311	28.52	16.87	0.02462	60
65	0.17443	55262	9640	252711	0.03814	759932	28.52	13.75	0.03801	65
70	0.21262	45623	9700	204116	0.04752	507221	28.52	11.12	0.04735	70
75	0.30228	35922	10859	152708	0.07111	303105	28.52	8.44	0.07077	75
80	0.43341	25064	10863	98858	0.10988	150397	28.52	6.00	0.10902	80
85+	•1.00000	14201	14201	51538	0.27554	51538	28.52	3.63	0.27231	85+

TABLE 3   LIFE TABLE FOR FEMALES

Age, x	$_nq_x$	l_x	$_nd_x$	$_nL_x$	$_nm_x$	T_x	$1000r_x$	$\overset{\circ}{e}_x$	$_nM_x$	Age, x
0	0.06053	100000	6053	96242	0.06290	6282339	5.33	62.82	0.06312	0
1	0.03990	93947	3749	365585	0.01025	6186097	5.33	65.85	0.01028	1
5	0.01008	90198	909	448716	0.00203	5820512	35.04	64.53	0.00208	5
10	0.00547	89288	489	445172	0.00110	5371796	36.67	60.16	0.00110	10
15	0.00763	88800	678	442411	0.00153	4926624	37.33	55.48	0.00152	15
20	0.01139	88122	1004	438225	0.00229	4484213	35.10	50.89	0.00228	20
25	0.01474	87118	1284	432467	0.00297	4045988	30.90	46.44	0.00295	25
30	0.01668	85833	1432	425746	0.00336	3613522	28.98	42.10	0.00335	30
35	0.02421	84402	2043	417024	0.00490	3187776	28.93	37.77	0.00489	35
40	0.02460	82358	2026	406827	0.00498	2770751	30.39	33.64	0.00497	40
45	0.03140	80333	2522	395602	0.00638	2363924	33.37	29.43	0.00635	45
50	0.04113	77810	3201	381472	0.00839	1968322	32.57	25.30	0.00835	50
55	0.06097	74610	4549	362440	0.01255	1586820	29.94	21.27	0.01248	55
60	0.09798	70061	6864	334102	0.02055	1224410	30.15	17.48	0.02043	60
65	0.14469	63197	9144	293867	0.03112	890308	30.15	14.09	0.03098	65
70	0.19300	54053	10432	244854	0.04260	596441	30.15	11.03	0.04241	70
75	0.28336	43621	12360	188162	0.06569	351587	30.15	8.06	0.06526	75
80	0.48092	31260	15034	119523	0.12578	163425	30.15	5.23	0.12463	80
85+	•1.00000	16227	16227	43902	0.36962	43902	30.15	2.71	0.36503	85+

TABLE 4 POPULATION PROJECTION, USING FIXED AGE-SPECIFIC BIRTH AND DEATH RATES, IN THOUSANDS

Age at last birthday	1971			1976			1981			Age at last birthday
	Total	Males	Females	Total	Males	Females	Total	Males	Females	
0–4	9717	5000	4717	11526	5931	5595	13749	7075	6674	0–4
5–9	7927	4046	3881	9443	4860	4583	11201	5765	5436	5–9
10–14	6661	3416	3245	7861	4011	3850	9364	4818	4546	10–14
15–19	5510	2815	2695	6615	3390	3225	7806	3980	3826	15–19
20–24	4476	2262	2214	5451	2781	2670	6544	3349	3195	20–24
25–29	3621	1807	1814	4408	2223	2185	5369	2734	2635	25–29
30–34	2979	1465	1514	3555	1769	1786	4328	2177	2151	30–34
35–39	2487	1203	1284	2907	1424	1483	3468	1719	1749	35–39
40–44	2089	1006	1083	2412	1159	1253	2819	1372	1447	40–44
45–49	1756	844	912	2017	964	1053	2328	1110	1218	45–49
50–54	1425	676	749	1680	800	880	1929	914	1015	50–54
55–59	1133	534	599	1340	628	712	1579	743	836	55–59
60–64	910	436	474	1033	481	552	1222	566	656	60–64
65–69	701	341	360	790	373	417	897	412	485	65–69
70–74	489	236	253	576	276	300	648	301	347	70–74
75–79	307	146	161	371	176	195	436	206	230	75–79
80–84	162	79	83	196	94	102	238	114	124	80–84
85 +	57	33	24	71	41	30	86	49	37	85 +
All ages	52407	26345	26062	62252	31381	30871	74011	37404	36607	All ages

TABLE 5 OBSERVED AND PROJECTED VITAL RATES

Rates per thousand	Observed			Projected						Stable	
				1971		1976		1981			
	Total	Males	Females	Males	Females	Males	Females	Males	Females	Males	Females
Birth	43.96	45.40	42.52	45.00	42.44	44.98	42.66	45.08	42.97	44.49	43.31
Death	9.61	10.18	9.03	10.01	8.69	9.93	8.71	9.85	8.72	9.84	8.66
Increase	34.35	35.21	33.49	34.99	33.75	35.05	33.96	35.23	34.25		34.6470

TABLE 6 RATES STANDARDIZED ON THREE STANDARD COUNTRIES

Standardized rates per thousand	England and Wales, 1961			United States, 1960			Mexico, 1960		
	Total	Males*	Females	Total	Males*	Females	Total	Males*	Females
Birth	42.42	48.25*	39.68	43.07	43.71*	40.95	46.09	47.10*	44.38
Death	15.30	22.01*	16.43	13.33	18.11*	13.29	9.18	9.59*	8.55
Increase	27.12	26.24*	23.25	29.74	25.60*	27.67	36.92	37.51*	35.81

TABLE 7 VITAL STATISTICS AND RATES INFERRED FROM AGE DISTRIBUTIONS (FEMALES)

Vital statistics		Thompson				Bourgeois-Pichat					Coale	
TFR	6.57	Age range	NRR	1000r	Interval	Age range	NRR	1000b	1000d	1000r		
GRR	3.17	0–4	2.47	33.16	27.28	5–29	2.66	43.34	7.15	36.17	1000b	45.71
NRR	2.71	5–9	2.44	33.55	27.20	30–54	2.31	38.61	7.61	31.00	1000d	8.20
Generation	28.80	10–14	2.38	31.11	27.14	55–79	2.49	45.54	11.71	33.83	1000r	37.50
Sex ratio	107.2	15–19	2.29	30.57	27.05	*25–49	2.22	36.49	6.95	29.53	$1000k_1$	18.86
											$1000k_2$	0.22

TABLE 8 LESLIE MATRIX AND ITS ANALYSIS (FEMALES)

Start of age interval	Sub-diagonal	First row	Percent in stable population	Fisher values	Total reproductive values	Net maternity function	Matrix equation coefficient	Parameters		
									Integral	Matrix
0	0.97161	0.00000	18.395	1.179	4710535	0.00000	0.00000	λ_1	1.1891	1.1899
5	0.99210	0.00138	15.020	1.444	4724737	0.00000	0.00134	λ_2	0.4428	0.4506
10	0.99380	0.10743	12.523	1.731	4694056	0.00269	0.10356		+0.7890	+0.7703 i
15	0.99054	0.42929	10.458	1.945	4347031	0.20443	0.41124	r_1	0.0346	0.0348
20	0.98686	0.67687	8.706	1.825	3355072	0.61805	0.64228	r_2	-0.0200	-0.0228
25	0.98446	0.63082	7.220	1.392	2141083	0.66650	0.59071		+0.2119	+0.2083 i
30	0.97951	0.51658	5.973	0.927	1215268	0.51493	0.47522	c_1		215816
35	0.97555	0.36713	4.917	0.504	559592	0.43751	0.33151	c_2		104170
40	0.97241	0.15224	4.031	0.171	160488	0.22552	0.13411			18075 i
45	0.96428	0.02493	3.294	0.025	19206	0.04271	0.02136	$2\pi/y$	29.655	30.163
50	0.95011	0.00000	2.669	0.000	0	0.00000	0.00000	Δ	1.503	
55	0.81669		6.795							

Nicaragua, 1965

TABLE 1 DATA INPUT TO COMPUTATIONS

Age at last birthday	Population					Births, by age of mother	Deaths			Age at last birthday
	Total	Males	%	Females	%		Total	Males	Females	
0	66620	34356	4.2	32264	3.9	0	3686	2006	1680	0
1–4	225448	114994	14.0	110454	13.2	0	1892	946	945	1–4
5–9	286279	145355	17.7	140924	16.9	0	460	239	221	5–9
10–14	221690	113655	13.9	108035	12.9	88	202	115	87	10–14
15–19	160172	78165	9.5	82007	9.8	11735	285	143	142	15–19
20–24	136611	65190	8.0	71421	8.5	21011	354	217	137	20–24
25–29	114079	53800	6.6	60279	7.2	18421	391	249	142	25–29
30–34	93955	44969	5.5	48986	5.9	10009	376	240	136	30–34
35–39	79984	39210	4.8	40774	4.9	7527	356	209	147	35–39
40–44	72572	35273	4.3	37299	4.5	2117	311	184	127	40–44
45–49	45525	22200	2.7	23325	2.8	348	329	173	156	45–49
50–54	46967	22561	2.8	24406	2.9	0	392	212	180	50–54
55–59	27003	13323	1.6	13580	1.6	0	378	214	164	55–59
60–64	30140	14242	1.7	15898	1.9	0	544	276	268	60–64
65–69	17358	8495	1.0	8863	1.1	0	495	244	251	65–69
70–74	12953	5769	0.7	7184	0.9		562	288	274	70–74
75–79	8462	3570	0.4	4892	0.6		346	163	183	75–79
80–84	4872	2021	0.2	2851	0.3	36754 M	278	128	150	80–84
85+	4327	1909	0.2	2418	0.3	34502 F	471	194	277	85+
All ages	1655017	819057		835960		71256	12108	6440	5668	All ages

TABLE 2 LIFE TABLE FOR MALES

Age, x	$_nq_x$	l_x	$_nd_x$	$_nL_x$	$_nm_x$	T_x	$1000r_x$	$\overset{\circ}{e}_x$	$_nM_x$	Age, x
0	0.05581	100000	5581	96460	0.05786	6454701	13.46	64.55	0.05839	0
1	0.03195	94419	3017	369380	0.00817	6358241	13.46	67.34	0.00823	1
5	0.00804	91402	735	455175	0.00161	5988861	24.34	65.52	0.00164	5
10	0.00506	90668	459	452211	0.00101	5533686	60.71	61.03	0.00101	10
15	0.00924	90209	833	449174	0.00186	5081475	53.62	56.33	0.00183	15
20	0.01661	89375	1485	443411	0.00335	4632301	34.05	51.83	0.00333	20
25	0.02295	87891	2017	434572	0.00464	4188889	32.60	47.65	0.00463	25
30	0.02635	85874	2263	423747	0.00534	3754317	26.43	43.72	0.00534	30
35	0.02630	83610	2199	412522	0.00533	3330571	19.01	39.83	0.00533	35
40	0.02588	81411	2107	401966	0.00524	2918049	51.07	35.84	0.00522	40
45	0.03841	79304	3045	389204	0.00783	2516080	37.21	31.73	0.00779	45
50	0.04629	76259	3530	373009	0.00946	2126879	40.47	27.89	0.00940	50
55	0.07763	72728	5646	350093	0.01613	1753870	30.78	24.12	0.01606	55
60	0.09311	67082	6246	320339	0.01950	1403777	47.21	20.93	0.01938	60
65	0.13570	60836	8255	284681	0.02900	1083438	47.21	17.81	0.02872	65
70	0.22280	52581	11715	233639	0.05014	798757	47.21	15.19	0.04992	70
75	0.20465	40866	8363	182844	0.04574	565118	47.21	13.83	0.04566	75
80	0.27530	32503	8948	140293	0.06378	382274	47.21	11.76	0.06334	80
85+	1.00000	23555	23555	241981	0.09734	241981	47.21	10.27	0.10162	85+

TABLE 3 LIFE TABLE FOR FEMALES

Age, x	$_nq_x$	l_x	$_nd_x$	$_nL_x$	$_nm_x$	T_x	$1000r_x$	$\overset{\circ}{e}_x$	$_nM_x$	Age, x
0	0.05008	100000	5008	96901	0.05168	6788476	11.29	67.88	0.05207	0
1	0.03330	94992	3163	371374	0.00852	6691575	11.29	70.44	0.00856	1
5	0.00765	91829	702	457388	0.00154	6320201	24.91	68.83	0.00157	5
10	0.00403	91127	367	454733	0.00081	5862813	52.94	64.34	0.00081	10
15	0.00867	90759	787	451933	0.00174	5408080	39.84	59.59	0.00173	15
20	0.00956	89973	861	447766	0.00192	4956147	28.79	55.09	0.00192	20
25	0.01174	89112	1046	443019	0.00236	4508381	35.36	50.59	0.00236	25
30	0.01384	88066	1218	437388	0.00279	4065362	36.20	46.16	0.00278	30
35	0.01788	86847	1553	430403	0.00361	3627975	23.93	41.77	0.00361	35
40	0.01705	85294	1454	423089	0.00344	3197572	51.62	37.49	0.00344	40
45	0.03306	83840	2772	412582	0.00672	2774484	36.38	33.09	0.00669	45
50	0.03647	81068	2957	398322	0.00742	2361902	45.07	29.13	0.00738	50
55	0.05858	78111	4576	379751	0.01205	1963580	30.95	25.14	0.01199	55
60	0.08174	73535	6011	353572	0.01700	1583829	43.77	21.54	0.01686	60
65	0.13342	67524	9009	315973	0.02851	1230257	43.77	18.22	0.02832	65
70	0.17442	58515	10207	266908	0.03824	914284	43.77	15.62	0.03814	70
75	0.17136	48309	8278	220677	0.03751	647376	43.77	13.40	0.03741	75
80	0.23447	40030	9386	177153	0.05298	426699	43.77	10.66	0.05261	80
85+	1.00000	30644	30644	249546	0.12280	249546	43.77	8.14	0.11455	85+

TABLE 4 POPULATION PROJECTION, USING FIXED AGE-SPECIFIC BIRTH AND DEATH RATES, IN THOUSANDS

Age at last birthday	1970 Total	1970 Males	1970 Females	1975 Total	1975 Males	1975 Females	1980 Total	1980 Males	1980 Females	Age at last birthday
0–4	365	188	177	441	227	214	536	276	260	0–4
5–9	285	146	139	356	183	173	431	222	209	5–9
10–14	284	144	140	284	145	139	354	182	172	10–14
15–19	220	113	107	282	143	139	282	144	138	15–19
20–24	158	77	81	217	111	106	280	142	138	20–24
25–29	135	64	71	156	76	80	214	109	105	25–29
30–34	112	52	60	132	62	70	153	74	79	30–34
35–39	92	44	48	110	51	59	130	61	69	35–39
40–44	78	38	40	90	43	47	108	50	58	40–44
45–49	70	34	36	76	37	39	87	41	46	45–49
50–54	44	21	23	68	33	35	73	35	38	50–54
55–59	44	21	23	41	20	21	64	31	33	55–59
60–64	25	12	13	41	19	22	38	18	20	60–64
65–69	27	13	14	22	11	11	36	17	19	65–69
70–74	14	7	7	22	10	12	19	9	10	70–74
75–79	11	5	6	11	5	6	18	8	10	75–79
80–84	7	3	4	8	3	5	9	4	5	80–84
85 +	7	3	4	11	5	6	13	6	7	85 +
All ages	1978	985	993	2368	1184	1184	2845	1429	1416	All ages

TABLE 5 OBSERVED AND PROJECTED VITAL RATES

Rates per thousand	Observed Total	Observed Males	Observed Females	Projected 1970 Males	Projected 1970 Females	Projected 1975 Males	Projected 1975 Females	Projected 1980 Males	Projected 1980 Females	Stable Males	Stable Females
Birth	43.05	44.87	41.27	44.41	41.33	45.34	42.60	45.28	42.89	42.76	41.79
Death	7.32	7.86	6.78	8.17	7.09	8.28	7.23	8.33	7.28	8.31	7.34
Increase	35.74	37.01	34.49	36.24	34.24	37.06	35.37	36.95	35.61		34.4555

TABLE 6 RATES STANDARDIZED ON THREE STANDARD COUNTRIES

Standardized rates per thousand	England and Wales, 1961 Total	Males	Females	United States, 1960 Total	Males	Females	Mexico, 1960 Total	Males	Females
Birth	38.81	48.87*	36.42	39.56	44.44*	37.74	44.51	47.32*	42.99
Death	11.01	18.15*	11.07	9.82	14.81*	9.30	7.27	7.47*	6.64
Increase	27.81	30.72*	25.36	29.74	29.63*	28.44	37.24	39.85*	36.36

TABLE 7 VITAL STATISTICS AND RATES INFERRED FROM AGE DISTRIBUTIONS (FEMALES)

Vital statistics:

TFR	6.02
GRR	2.92
NRR	2.57
Generation	27.41
Sex ratio	106.5

Thompson:

Age range	NRR	$1000r$	Interval
0–4	2.36	31.35	27.33
5–9	2.83	39.19	27.27
10–14	2.57	33.81	27.20
15–19	2.39	32.14	27.10

Bourgeois-Pichat:

Age range	NRR	$1000b$	$1000d$	$1000r$
5–29	3.00	47.73	7.07	40.66
30–54	2.53	41.29	6.83	34.45
55–79	2.07	22.90	-4.03	26.93
*15–39	2.44	39.53	6.46	33.07

Coale:

$1000b$	45.09
$1000d$	8.04
$1000r$	37.04
$1000k_1$	0.
$1000k_2$	0.

TABLE 8 LESLIE MATRIX AND ITS ANALYSIS (FEMALES)

Start of age interval	Sub-diagonal	First row	Percent in stable population	Fisher values	Total reproductive values	Net maternity function	Matrix equation coefficient
0	0.97675	0.00000	18.010	1.163	165950	0.00000	0.00000
5	0.99419	0.00092	14.797	1.415	199446	0.00000	0.00090
10	0.99384	0.16215	12.374	1.691	182718	0.00179	0.15746
15	0.99078	0.49267	10.345	1.833	150353	0.31313	0.47547
20	0.98940	0.67629	8.621	1.622	115825	0.63781	0.54413
25	0.98729	0.57514	7.175	1.154	69552	0.65553	0.54413
30	0.98403	0.43758	5.959	0.712	34878	0.43272	0.40872
35	0.98301	0.27253	4.932	0.343	13991	0.38471	0.25049
40	0.97517	0.08079	4.078	0.093	3454	0.11627	0.07304
45	0.96544	0.01691	3.345	0.017	387	0.02981	0.01490
50	0.95338	0.00005	2.716	0.000	1	0.00000	0.00000
55	0.85017		7.647				

Parameters:

	Integral	Matrix
λ_1	1.1880	1.1888
λ_2	0.3828	0.3955
	+0.7867	+0.7666i
r_1	0.0345	0.0346
r_2	-0.0267	-0.0296
	+0.2236	+0.2189i
c_1		8483
c_2		1233
		17490i
$2\pi/y$	28.101	28.703
Δ	3.448	

Panama, 1966

TABLE 1 DATA INPUT TO COMPUTATIONS

Age at last birthday	Population					Births, by age of mother	Deaths			Age at last birthday
	Total	Males	%	Females	%		Total	Males	Females	
0	47510	24310	3.9	23200	3.9	0	2243	1258	985	0
1–4	163550	83240	13.4	80310	13.4	0	1385	703	682	1–4
5–9	171730	87230	14.0	84500	14.1	0	310	156	154	5–9
10–14	147910	75440	12.1	72470	12.1	167	167	101	65	10–14
15–19	122390	60980	9.8	61410	10.3	9006	205	100	105	15–19
20–24	102350	51630	8.3	50720	8.5	16033	216	105	111	20–24
25–29	84770	42960	6.9	41810	7.0	11825	173	80	93	25–29
30–34	74260	38100	6.1	36160	6.0	6844	204	110	94	30–34
35–39	66690	34360	5.5	32330	5.4	4178	198	106	92	35–39
40–44	57890	30550	4.9	27340	4.6	1155	245	121	124	40–44
45–49	50080	26440	4.2	23640	4.0	169	249	149	100	45–49
50–54	36400	19450	3.1	16950	2.8	17	319	178	141	50–54
55–59	28090	14280	2.3	13810	2.3	0	344	204	140	55–59
60–64	24180	12530	2.0	11650	1.9	0	449	247	202	60–64
65–69	16120	8290	1.3	7830	1.3	0	494	287	207	65–69
70–74	12700	6730	1.1	5970	1.0		469	272	197	70–74
75–79	7330	3680	0.6	3650	0.6		538	287	251	75–79
80–84	4030	1870	0.3	2160	0.4	25071 M	445	221	224	80–84
85 +	3420	1430	0.2	1990	0.3	24323 F	531	229	302	85 +
All ages	1221400	623500		597900		49394	9184	4914	4270	All ages

TABLE 2 LIFE TABLE FOR MALES

Age, x	$_nq_x$	l_x	$_nd_x$	$_nL_x$	$_nm_x$	T_x	$1000r_x$	$\overset{\circ}{e}_x$	$_nM_x$	Age, x
0	0.04978	100000	4978	96916	0.05136	6499338	11.31	64.99	0.05175	0
1	0.03285	95022	3121	371605	0.00840	6402422	11.31	67.38	0.00845	1
5	0.00871	91901	800	457504	0.00175	6030817	32.31	65.62	0.00179	5
10	0.00667	91101	607	453973	0.00134	5573313	34.30	61.18	0.00134	10
15	0.00819	90493	741	450676	0.00165	5119340	36.26	56.57	0.00164	15
20	0.01013	89752	909	446505	0.00204	4668665	33.13	52.02	0.00203	20
25	0.00929	88843	825	442225	0.00187	4222160	28.24	47.52	0.00186	25
30	0.01436	88017	1264	437032	0.00289	3779934	19.66	42.95	0.00289	30
35	0.01533	86753	1330	430529	0.00309	3342902	18.85	38.53	0.00308	35
40	0.01968	85423	1681	423127	0.00397	2912373	22.11	34.09	0.00396	40
45	0.02802	83743	2346	413264	0.00568	2489247	39.13	29.72	0.00564	45
50	0.04525	81396	3683	398408	0.00924	2075983	52.08	25.50	0.00915	50
55	0.06939	77713	5392	375747	0.01435	1677575	29.73	21.59	0.01429	55
60	0.09484	72321	6859	345522	0.01985	1301827	34.74	18.00	0.01971	60
65	0.16032	65462	10495	301766	0.03478	956305	34.74	14.61	0.03462	65
70	0.18519	54967	10179	250274	0.04067	654540	34.74	11.91	0.04042	70
75	0.32928	44788	14748	187791	0.07853	404266	34.74	9.03	0.07799	75
80	0.45406	30040	13640	114844	0.11877	216475	34.74	7.21	0.11818	80
85 +	1.00000	16400	16400	101632	0.16137	101632	34.74	6.20	0.16014	85 +

TABLE 3 LIFE TABLE FOR FEMALES

Age, x	$_nq_x$	l_x	$_nd_x$	$_nL_x$	$_nm_x$	T_x	$1000r_x$	$\overset{\circ}{e}_x$	$_nM_x$	Age, x
0	0.04113	100000	4113	97531	0.04217	6720901	10.52	67.21	0.04245	0
1	0.03307	95887	3171	375086	0.00845	6623370	10.52	69.07	0.00849	1
5	0.00886	92716	821	461524	0.00178	6248283	32.60	67.39	0.00182	5
10	0.00454	91894	417	458419	0.00091	5786759	30.61	62.97	0.00091	10
15	0.00856	91477	783	455546	0.00172	5328340	34.06	58.25	0.00171	15
20	0.01090	90694	989	451041	0.00219	4872794	36.34	53.73	0.00219	20
25	0.01107	89705	993	446074	0.00223	4421753	31.53	49.29	0.00222	25
30	0.01293	88712	1147	440742	0.00260	3975679	23.17	44.82	0.00260	30
35	0.01418	87564	1242	434883	0.00286	3534937	24.76	40.37	0.00285	35
40	0.02247	86323	1940	426877	0.00454	3100054	27.29	35.91	0.00454	40
45	0.02110	84383	1781	417756	0.00426	2673178	42.54	31.68	0.00423	45
50	0.04107	82602	3392	404980	0.00838	2255412	46.06	27.30	0.00832	50
55	0.04974	79210	3940	386809	0.01018	1850432	26.15	23.35	0.01014	55
60	0.08380	75270	6308	361553	0.01745	1463623	32.54	19.44	0.01734	60
65	0.12469	68962	8599	323939	0.02654	1102070	32.54	15.98	0.02644	65
70	0.15415	60364	9305	279917	0.03324	778131	32.54	12.89	0.03300	70
75	0.29640	51059	15134	218595	0.06923	498214	32.54	9.76	0.06877	75
80	0.41087	35925	14760	141698	0.10417	279618	32.54	7.78	0.10370	80
85 +	1.00000	21164	21164	137921	0.15345	137921	32.54	6.52	0.15175	85 +

TABLE 4   POPULATION PROJECTION, USING FIXED AGE-SPECIFIC BIRTH AND DEATH RATES, IN THOUSANDS

Age at last birthday	1971			1976			1981			Age at last birthday
	Total	Males	Females	Total	Males	Females	Total	Males	Females	
0–4	253	128	125	297	150	147	350	177	173	0–4
5–9	206	105	101	247	125	122	291	147	144	5–9
10–14	171	87	84	204	104	100	245	124	121	10–14
15–19	147	75	72	169	86	83	203	103	100	15–19
20–24	121	60	61	145	74	71	168	85	83	20–24
25–29	101	51	50	120	60	60	144	73	71	25–29
30–34	83	42	41	101	51	50	118	59	59	30–34
35–39	74	38	36	83	42	41	99	50	49	35–39
40–44	66	34	32	72	37	35	81	41	40	40–44
45–49	57	30	27	64	33	31	70	36	34	45–49
50–54	48	25	23	55	29	26	62	32	30	50–54
55–59	34	18	16	46	24	22	52	27	25	55–59
60–64	26	13	13	32	17	15	42	22	20	60–64
65–69	21	11	10	23	11	12	29	15	14	65–69
70–74	14	7	7	18	9	9	20	10	10	70–74
75–79	10	5	5	10	5	5	14	7	7	75–79
80–84	4	2	2	6	3	3	6	3	3	80–84
85 +	4	2	2	4	2	2	6	3	3	85 +
All ages	1440	733	707	1696	862	834	2000	1014	986	All ages

TABLE 5   OBSERVED AND PROJECTED VITAL RATES

Rates per thousand	Observed			Projected						Stable	
				1971		1976		1981			
	Total	Males	Females	Males	Females	Males	Females	Males	Females	Males	Females
Birth	40.44	40.21	40.68	40.25	40.50	40.26	40.32	40.29	40.19	41.45	40.85
Death	7.52	7.88	7.14	7.98	7.18	8.01	7.16	8.06	7.22	7.73	7.12
Increase	32.92	32.33	33.54	32.27	33.33	32.25	33.16	32.23	32.97		33.7295

TABLE 6   RATES STANDARDIZED ON THREE STANDARD COUNTRIES

Standardized rates per thousand	England and Wales, 1961			United States, 1960			Mexico, 1960		
	Total	Males	Females	Total	Males	Females	Total	Males	Females
Birth	35.83	40.53*	34.20	36.57	37.07*	35.48	42.51	38.43*	41.76
Death	11.89	15.69*	12.55	10.30	12.97*	10.09	7.06	7.24*	6.67
Increase	23.94	24.84*	21.65	26.27	24.10*	25.39	35.45	31.19*	35.09

TABLE 7   VITAL STATISTICS AND RATES INFERRED FROM AGE DISTRIBUTIONS (FEMALES)

Vital statistics		Thompson				Bourgeois-Pichat					Coale	
		Age range	NRR	$1000r$	Interval	Age range	NRR	$1000b$	$1000d$	$1000r$		
TFR	5.58	0–4	2.33	30.92	27.33	5–29	2.48	39.95	6.36	33.60	$1000b$	39.73
GRR	2.75	5–9	2.26	30.51	27.28	30–54	2.40	41.14	8.76	32.38	$1000d$	7.48
NRR	2.45	10–14	2.28	29.57	27.23	55–79	2.69	50.30	13.64	36.66	$1000r$	32.25
Generation	26.57	15–19	2.25	29.95	27.13	*25–49	1.97	31.34	6.20	25.14	$1000k_1$	10.18
Sex ratio	103.1										$1000k_2$	0.18

TABLE 8   LESLIE MATRIX AND ITS ANALYSIS (FEMALES)

Start of age interval	Sub-diagonal	First row	Percent in stable population	Fisher values	Total reproductive values	Net maternity function	Matrix equation coefficient	Parameters		
									Integral	Matrix
0	0.97653	0.00000	17.798	1.150	119048	0.00000	0.00000	λ_1	1.1837	1.1845
5	0.99330	0.00266	14.673	1.395	117883	0.00000	0.00260	λ_2	0.3193	0.3381
10	0.99374	0.17226	12.304	1.661	120340	0.00520	0.16709		+0.8113	+0.7829 i
15	0.99010	0.53485	10.323	1.780	109310	0.32898	0.51554	r_1	0.0337	0.0339
20	0.98898	0.59331	8.628	1.508	76499	0.70239	0.66167	r_2	−0.0274	−0.0318
25	0.98805	0.54671	7.204	1.000	41819	0.52126	0.51602		+0.2392	+0.2326 i
30	0.98671	0.36863	6.009	0.563	20348	0.41078	0.34376	c_1		5866
35	0.98156	0.19861	5.005	0.246	7949	0.27674	0.18277	c_2		−2114
40	0.97862	0.05727	4.148	0.064	1749	0.08880	0.05175			−2565 i
45	0.96932	0.00947	3.427	0.010	240	0.01471	0.00835	$2\pi/y$	26.270	27.010
50	0.95497	0.00119	2.804	0.001	20	0.00200	0.00100	Δ	1.615	
55	0.83566		7.676							

Trinidad and Tobago, 1962

TABLE 1   DATA INPUT TO COMPUTATIONS

Age at last birthday	Population					Births, by age of mother	Deaths			Age at last birthday
	Total	Males	%	Females	%		Total	Males	Females	
0	31800	16150	3.6	15650	3.5	0	1313	728	585	0
1–4	117300	59450	13.2	57850	12.8	0	226	122	104	1–4
5–9	128150	64500	14.4	63650	14.1	0	70	36	34	5–9
10–14	106050	53150	11.8	52900	11.7	42	69	42	27	10–14
15–19	91650	45200	10.1	46450	10.3	5871	87	50	37	15–19
20–24	72650	35650	7.9	37000	8.2	10628	98	57	41	20–24
25–29	61200	30250	6.7	30950	6.9	8323	107	56	51	25–29
30–34	52600	25700	5.7	26900	6.0	5195	106	49	57	30–34
35–39	48300	23950	5.3	24350	5.4	3073	146	73	73	35–39
40–44	45800	23050	5.1	22750	5.0	884	207	115	92	40–44
45–49	37700	19600	4.4	18100	4.0	91	317	185	132	45–49
50–54	32100	16700	3.7	15400	3.4	0	406	248	158	50–54
55–59	23750	12450	2.8	11300	2.5	0	426	247	179	55–59
60–64	19100	9500	2.1	9500	2.1	0	496	292	204	60–64
65–69	12850	5850	1.3	7000	1.6	0	619	335	284	65–69
70–74	10100	4250	0.9	5850	1.3		546	302	244	70–74
75–79	5050	2100	0.5	2950	0.7		435	225	210	75–79
80–84	2750	1050	0.2	1700	0.4	17420 M	356	163	193	80–84
85 +	1600	500	0.1	1100	0.2	16687 F	435	166	269	85 +
All ages	900500	449050		451450		34107	6465	3491	2974	All ages

TABLE 2   LIFE TABLE FOR MALES

Age, x	$_nq_x$	l_x	$_nd_x$	$_nL_x$	$_nm_x$	T_x	$1000r_x$	$\mathring{e}_x$	$_nM_x$	Age, x
0	0.04338	100000	4338	96729	0.04485	6373260	6.61	63.73	0.04508	0
1	0.00809	95662	774	380403	0.00203	6276532	6.61	65.61	0.00205	1
5	0.00275	94888	261	473788	0.00055	5896128	34.21	62.14	0.00055	5
10	0.00396	94627	375	472251	0.00079	5422341	34.76	57.30	0.00079	10
15	0.00555	94252	523	470030	0.00111	4950089	38.78	52.52	0.00111	15
20	0.00799	93729	749	466841	0.00160	4480060	38.61	47.80	0.00160	20
25	0.00922	92980	858	462781	0.00185	4013219	30.93	43.16	0.00185	25
30	0.00952	92122	877	458528	0.00191	3550438	21.23	38.54	0.00191	30
35	0.01516	91245	1383	453050	0.00305	3091911	7.73	33.89	0.00305	35
40	0.02476	89862	2225	444307	0.00501	2638861	14.54	29.37	0.00499	40
45	0.04641	87637	4067	428807	0.00948	2194554	22.59	25.04	0.00944	45
50	0.07202	83570	6019	403494	0.01492	1765746	30.67	21.13	0.01485	50
55	0.09523	77551	7385	370146	0.01995	1362253	35.44	17.57	0.01984	55
60	0.14414	70166	10114	327160	0.03091	992107	25.11	14.14	0.03074	60
65	0.25193	60052	15129	263159	0.05749	664947	25.11	11.07	0.05725	65
70	0.30197	44923	13565	190308	0.07128	401788	25.11	8.94	0.07106	70
75	0.42188	31358	13229	122985	0.10757	211480	25.11	6.74	0.10714	75
80	0.55468	18129	10056	64430	0.15607	88494	25.11	4.88	0.15524	80
85 +	*1.00000	8073	8073	24065	0.33547	24065	25.11	2.98	0.33200	85 +

TABLE 3   LIFE TABLE FOR FEMALES

Age, x	$_nq_x$	l_x	$_nd_x$	$_nL_x$	$_nm_x$	T_x	$1000r_x$	$\mathring{e}_x$	$_nM_x$	Age, x
0	0.03619	100000	3619	97294	0.03719	6782366	6.43	67.82	0.03738	0
1	0.00710	96381	684	383544	0.00178	6685072	6.43	69.35	0.00180	1
5	0.00263	95697	252	477856	0.00053	6301528	32.01	65.85	0.00053	5
10	0.00256	95445	244	476643	0.00051	5823672	30.93	61.02	0.00051	10
15	0.00400	95201	381	475113	0.00080	5347029	34.95	56.17	0.00080	15
20	0.00556	94821	527	472857	0.00112	4871916	39.44	51.38	0.00111	20
25	0.00824	94293	777	469621	0.00165	4399048	30.25	46.65	0.00165	25
30	0.01057	93516	989	465236	0.00213	3929428	21.78	42.02	0.00212	30
35	0.01491	92528	1380	459366	0.00300	3464191	13.77	37.44	0.00300	35
40	0.02014	91148	1835	451534	0.00407	3004825	25.13	32.97	0.00404	40
45	0.03605	89312	3220	439032	0.00733	2553291	31.84	28.59	0.00729	45
50	0.05039	86092	4338	420250	0.01032	2114260	36.24	24.56	0.01026	50
55	0.07665	81754	6267	393800	0.01591	1694009	31.66	20.72	0.01584	55
60	0.10178	75487	7683	359538	0.02137	1300209	25.31	17.22	0.02125	60
65	0.18500	67805	12544	308244	0.04070	940671	25.31	13.87	0.04057	65
70	0.18953	55261	10473	250346	0.04184	632427	25.31	11.44	0.04171	70
75	0.30439	44787	13633	190570	0.07154	382082	25.31	8.53	0.07119	75
80	0.44657	31154	13913	121742	0.11428	191511	25.31	6.15	0.11353	80
85 +	*1.00000	17242	17242	69769	0.24712	69769	25.31	4.05	0.24455	85 +

TABLE 4 POPULATION PROJECTION, USING FIXED AGE-SPECIFIC BIRTH AND DEATH RATES, IN THOUSANDS

Age at last birthday	1967 Total	1967 Males	1967 Females	1972 Total	1972 Males	1972 Females	1977 Total	1977 Males	1977 Females	Age at last birthday
0–4	178	91	87	210	107	103	248	126	122	0–4
5–9	148	75	73	177	90	87	208	106	102	5–9
10–14	127	64	63	148	75	73	177	90	87	10–14
15–19	106	53	53	127	64	63	147	74	73	15–19
20–24	91	45	46	105	53	52	127	64	63	20–24
25–29	72	35	37	91	45	46	104	52	52	25–29
30–34	61	30	31	71	35	36	89	44	45	30–34
35–39	52	25	27	60	30	30	71	35	36	35–39
40–44	47	23	24	51	25	26	59	29	30	40–44
45–49	44	22	22	46	23	23	49	24	25	45–49
50–54	35	18	17	42	21	21	43	21	22	50–54
55–59	29	15	14	33	17	16	39	19	20	55–59
60–64	21	11	10	27	14	13	30	15	15	60–64
65–69	16	8	8	18	9	9	22	11	11	65–69
70–74	10	4	6	13	6	7	13	6	7	70–74
75–79	7	3	4	7	3	4	9	4	5	75–79
80–84	3	1	2	4	1	3	4	1	3	80–84
85 +	1	0	1	1	0	1	3	1	2	85 +
All ages	1048	523	525	1231	618	613	1442	722	720	All ages

TABLE 5 OBSERVED AND PROJECTED VITAL RATES

Rates per thousand	Observed Total	Observed Males	Observed Females	Projected 1967 Males	Projected 1967 Females	Projected 1972 Males	Projected 1972 Females	Projected 1977 Males	Projected 1977 Females	Stable Males	Stable Females
Birth	37.88	38.79	36.96	39.10	37.37	39.41	37.76	39.59	38.03	39.41	38.50
Death	7.18	7.77	6.59	7.65	6.49	7.57	6.45	7.49	6.46	6.88	5.97
Increase	30.70	31.02	30.38	31.45	30.88	31.84	31.31	32.10	31.57		32.5311

TABLE 6 RATES STANDARDIZED ON THREE STANDARD COUNTRIES

Standardized rates per thousand	England and Wales, 1961 Total	England and Wales, 1961 Males	England and Wales, 1961 Females	United States, 1960 Total	United States, 1960 Males	United States, 1960 Females	Mexico, 1960 Total	Mexico, 1960 Males	Mexico, 1960 Females
Birth	33.55	40.36*	31.81	34.25	36.88*	33.02	39.49	37.93*	38.54
Death	14.99	16.95*	14.76	12.43	13.67*	11.21	6.86	7.64*	5.95
Increase	18.57	23.42*	17.06	21.82	23.21*	21.81	32.63	30.29*	32.58

TABLE 7 VITAL STATISTICS AND RATES INFERRED FROM AGE DISTRIBUTIONS (FEMALES)

Vital statistics		Thompson Age range	NRR	1000r	Interval	Bourgeois-Pichat Age range	NRR	1000b	1000d	1000r	Coale
TFR	5.23	0–4	2.27	29.91	27.36	5–29	2.58	38.63	3.49	35.14	1000b
GRR	2.56	5–9	2.30	31.07	27.29	30–54	1.87	28.08	4.82	23.27	1000d
NRR	2.40	10–14	2.17	27.83	27.19	55–79	1.52	15.38	−0.18	15.55	1000r
Generation	26.89	15–19	2.16	28.55	27.04	*5–29	2.58	38.63	3.49	35.14	$1000k_1$
Sex ratio	104.39										$1000k_2$

TABLE 8 LESLIE MATRIX AND ITS ANALYSIS (FEMALES)

Start of age interval	Sub-diagonal	First row	Percent in stable population	Fisher values	Total reproductive values	Net maternity function	Matrix equation coefficient	Parameters	Integral	Matrix
0	0.99380	0.00000	17.112	1.127	82870	0.00000	0.00000	λ_1	1.1766	1.1774
5	0.99746	0.00094	14.444	1.336	85021	0.00000	0.00093	λ_2	0.3539	0.3667
10	0.99679	0.14914	12.237	1.576	83351	0.00185	0.14783		+0.8183	+0.7919 i
15	0.99527	0.48497	10.360	1.692	78612	0.29380	0.47917	r_1	0.0325	0.0327
20	0.99313	0.65204	8.758	1.453	53749	0.66454	0.64121	r_2	−0.0230	−0.0272
25	0.99066	0.54135	7.387	0.982	30391	0.61788	0.52873		+0.2325	+0.2274 i
30	0.98738	0.37371	6.216	0.551	14819	0.43958	0.36161	c_1		4345
35	0.98295	0.19334	5.213	0.230	5604	0.28363	0.18474	c_2		−324
40	0.97231	0.05136	4.352	0.054	1226	0.08584	0.04832			1303 i
45	0.95722	0.00590	3.594	0.006	103	0.01080	0.00540	$2\pi/y$	27.022	27.627
50	0.93706	0.00008	2.922	0.000	1	0.00000	0.00000	Δ	3.037	
55	0.80767		7.406							

Trinidad and Tobago, 1967

TABLE 1 DATA INPUT TO COMPUTATIONS

Age at last birthday	Population					Births, by age of mother	Deaths			Age at last birthday
	Total	Males	%	Females	%		Total	Males	Females	
0	28000	14150	2.8	13850	2.7	0	1018	561	457	0
1–4	125100	63500	12.6	61600	12.2	0	266	143	123	1–4
5–9	147300	74900	14.9	72400	14.3	0	89	57	32	5–9
10–14	127400	64100	12.7	63300	12.5	53	59	44	15	10–14
15–19	103200	51750	10.3	51450	10.2	4871	103	70	33	15–19
20–24	85700	42500	8.4	43200	8.5	9833	121	72	49	20–24
25–29	68350	33150	6.6	35200	7.0	6485	104	57	47	25–29
30–34	57800	28700	5.7	29100	5.8	4132	108	57	51	30–34
35–39	51350	25600	5.1	25750	5.1	2336	171	96	75	35–39
40–44	46200	22200	4.4	24000	4.7	641	189	98	91	40–44
45–49	44100	22050	4.4	22050	4.4	111	311	169	142	45–49
50–54	36800	19050	3.8	17750	3.5	0	416	241	175	50–54
55–59	31250	16350	3.2	14900	2.9	0	496	297	199	55–59
60–64	21250	11200	2.2	10050	2.0	0	563	341	222	60–64
65–69	15500	7200	1.4	8300	1.6	0	678	370	308	65–69
70–74	9800	4050	0.8	5750	1.1		625	320	305	70–74
75–79	7550	2950	0.6	4600	0.9		559	308	251	75–79
80–84	2650	900	0.2	1750	0.3	14542 M	395	185	210	80–84
85+	750	50	0.0	700	0.1	13920 F	504	192	312	85+
All ages	1010050	504350		505700		28462	6775	3678	3097	All ages

TABLE 2 LIFE TABLE FOR MALES

Age, x	$_nq_x$	l_x	$_nd_x$	$_nL_x$	$_nm_x$	T_x	$1000r_x$	$\overset{\circ}{e}_x$	$_nM_x$	Age, x
0	0.03853	100000	3853	97189	0.03965	6410508	0.00	64.11	0.03965	0
1	0.00895	96147	860	382108	0.00225	6313320	0.00	65.66	0.00225	1
5	0.00377	95286	360	475532	0.00076	5931211	18.04	62.25	0.00075	5
10	0.00345	94927	327	473874	0.00069	5455679	36.12	57.47	0.00069	10
15	0.00678	94599	642	471489	0.00136	4981805	39.81	52.66	0.00135	15
20	0.00845	93958	794	467835	0.00170	4510316	42.90	48.00	0.00169	20
25	0.00857	93163	799	463846	0.00172	4042481	37.51	43.39	0.00172	25
30	0.00993	92365	918	459719	0.00200	3578634	23.52	38.74	0.00199	30
35	0.01864	91447	1705	453193	0.00376	3118915	22.23	34.11	0.00375	35
40	0.02189	89743	1964	444138	0.00442	2665723	9.97	29.70	0.00441	40
45	0.03772	87779	3311	431290	0.00768	2221585	7.33	25.31	0.00765	45
50	0.06160	84468	5203	410087	0.01269	1790295	17.25	21.20	0.01265	50
55	0.08766	79264	6948	380019	0.01828	1380208	33.57	17.41	0.01817	55
60	0.14285	72316	10331	337271	0.03063	1000189	28.31	13.83	0.03045	60
65	0.22959	61985	14231	275487	0.05166	662919	28.31	10.69	0.05139	65
70	0.33073	47754	15794	199078	0.07933	387432	28.31	8.11	0.07901	70
75	0.41391	31961	13229	126064	0.10494	188354	28.31	5.89	0.10441	75
80	0.67209	18732	12590	60709	0.20737	62290	28.31	3.33	0.20555	80
85+	*1.00000	6142	6142	1581	3.88530	1581	28.31	0.26	3.84000	85+

TABLE 3 LIFE TABLE FOR FEMALES

Age, x	$_nq_x$	l_x	$_nd_x$	$_nL_x$	$_nm_x$	T_x	$1000r_x$	$\overset{\circ}{e}_x$	$_nM_x$	Age, x
0	0.03223	100000	3223	97672	0.03300	6836737	0.00	68.37	0.03300	0
1	0.00794	96777	769	384900	0.00200	6739066	0.00	69.63	0.00200	1
5	0.00218	96009	210	479519	0.00044	6354166	16.76	66.18	0.00044	5
10	0.00119	95799	114	478731	0.00024	5874646	33.79	61.32	0.00024	10
15	0.00324	95685	310	477739	0.00065	5395915	37.55	56.39	0.00064	15
20	0.00568	95375	542	475588	0.00114	4918176	36.88	51.57	0.00113	20
25	0.00668	94833	633	472642	0.00134	4442587	38.13	46.85	0.00134	25
30	0.00878	94200	827	469083	0.00176	3969946	29.34	42.14	0.00175	30
35	0.01450	93373	1354	463670	0.00292	3500863	16.46	37.49	0.00291	35
40	0.01883	92019	1733	456082	0.00380	3037193	11.35	33.01	0.00379	40
45	0.03187	90286	2877	444758	0.00647	2581111	23.58	28.59	0.00644	45
50	0.04837	87409	4228	427006	0.00990	2136353	29.38	24.44	0.00986	50
55	0.06524	83181	5427	403168	0.01346	1709347	42.44	20.55	0.01336	55
60	0.10564	77754	8214	369584	0.02223	1306178	28.87	16.80	0.02209	60
65	0.17109	69540	11898	319061	0.03729	936594	28.87	13.47	0.03711	65
70	0.23445	57643	13514	254169	0.05317	617533	28.87	10.71	0.05304	70
75	0.24165	44128	10664	194437	0.05484	363364	28.87	8.23	0.05457	75
80	0.46919	33464	15701	129548	0.12120	168927	28.87	5.05	0.12000	80
85+	*1.00000	17763	17763	39379	0.45108	39379	28.87	2.22	0.44571	85+

TABLE 4 POPULATION PROJECTION, USING FIXED AGE-SPECIFIC BIRTH AND DEATH RATES, IN THOUSANDS

Age at last birthday	1972 Total	Males	Females	1977 Total	Males	Females	1982 Total	Males	Females	Age at last birthday
0–4	150	76	74	179	91	88	210	107	103	0–4
5–9	152	77	75	149	76	73	178	91	87	5–9
10–14	147	75	72	152	77	75	149	76	73	10–14
15–19	127	64	63	146	74	72	151	76	75	15–19
20–24	102	51	51	126	63	63	146	74	72	20–24
25–29	85	42	43	102	51	51	125	63	62	25–29
30–34	68	33	35	85	42	43	101	50	51	30–34
35–39	57	28	29	67	32	35	83	41	42	35–39
40–44	50	25	25	56	28	28	66	32	34	40–44
45–49	45	22	23	49	24	25	55	27	28	45–49
50–54	42	21	21	42	20	22	47	23	24	50–54
55–59	35	18	17	39	19	20	40	19	21	55–59
60–64	29	15	14	31	16	15	35	17	18	60–64
65–69	18	9	9	24	12	12	26	13	13	65–69
70–74	12	5	7	14	7	7	18	9	9	70–74
75–79	7	3	4	8	3	5	9	4	5	75–79
80–84	4	1	3	4	1	3	5	2	3	80–84
85 +	1	0	1	1	0	1	1	0	1	85 +
All ages	1131	565	566	1274	636	638	1445	724	721	All ages

TABLE 5 OBSERVED AND PROJECTED VITAL RATES

Rates per thousand	Observed Total	Males	Females	Projected 1972 Males	Females	1977 Males	Females	1982 Males	Females	Stable Males	Females
Birth	28.18	28.83	27.53	30.74	29.38	32.59	31.18	33.22	31.83	29.98	28.97
Death	6.71	7.29	6.12	7.18	6.04	7.39	6.32	7.49	6.34	8.59	7.57
Increase	21.47	21.54	21.40	23.56	23.34	25.20	24.86	25.74	25.48		21.3924

TABLE 6 RATES STANDARDIZED ON THREE STANDARD COUNTRIES

Standardized rates per thousand	England and Wales, 1961 Total	Males	Females	United States, 1960 Total	Males	Females	Mexico, 1960 Total	Males	Females
Birth	24.75	30.21*	23.46	25.26	27.39*	24.34	29.29	28.80*	28.57
Death	22.61	17.02*	16.04	20.00	13.63*	12.08	8.89	8.03*	5.92
Increase	2.14	13.19*	7.43	5.26	13.76*	12.27	20.40	20.80*	22.66

TABLE 7 VITAL STATISTICS AND RATES INFERRED FROM AGE DISTRIBUTIONS (FEMALES)

Vital statistics		Thompson Age range	NRR	$1000r$	Interval	Bourgeois-Pichat Age range	NRR	$1000b$	$1000d$	$1000r$	Coale	
TFR	3.86	0–4	2.11	28.20	27.37	5–29	2.63	39.86	4.08	35.78	$1000b$	34.84
GRR	1.89	5–9	2.34	31.83	27.31	30–54	1.64	22.29	4.00	18.28	$1000d$	6.32
NRR	1.78	10–14	2.35	30.61	27.22	55–79	2.27	39.39	9.06	30.33	$1000r$	28.52
Generation	26.97	15–19	2.15	28.24	27.08	*10–34	2.76	41.92	3.97	37.65	$1000k_1$	0.
Sex ratio	104.5										$1000k_2$	0.

TABLE 8 LESLIE MATRIX AND ITS ANALYSIS (FEMALES)

Start of age interval	Sub-diagonal	First row	Percent in stable population	Fisher values	Total reproductive values	Net maternity function	Matrix equation coefficient	Parameters	Integral	Matrix
0	0.99367	0.00000	13.269	1.093	82451	0.00000	0.00000	λ_1	1.1129	1.1132
5	0.99836	0.00099	11.844	1.224	88634	0.00000	0.00098	λ_2	0.3498	0.3637
10	0.99793	0.11248	10.622	1.364	86339	0.00196	0.11158		+0.7622	+0.7407 i
15	0.99550	0.37911	9.522	1.398	71944	0.22121	0.37532	r_1	0.0214	0.0214
20	0.99380	0.48467	8.516	1.147	49572	0.52943	0.47765	r_2	-0.0352	-0.0384
25	0.99247	0.38373	7.602	0.752	26485	0.42587	0.37581		+0.2281	+0.2229 i
30	0.98846	0.27339	6.778	0.421	12263	0.32575	0.26574	c_1		5537
35	0.98363	0.13803	6.018	0.172	4438	0.20572	0.13265	c_2		7564
40	0.97517	0.03723	5.318	0.042	1001	0.05957	0.03526			19293 i
45	0.96009	0.00593	4.659	0.006	130	0.01095	0.00547	$2\pi/y$	27.546	28.191
50	0.94417	0.00007	4.018	0.000	1	0.00000	0.00000	Δ	6.801	
55	0.79262		11.834							

United States, 1966

TABLE 1 DATA INPUT TO COMPUTATIONS

Age at last birthday	Population					Births, by age of mother	Deaths			Age at last birthday
	Total	Males	%	Females	%		Total	Males	Females	
0	3665000	1872000	2.0	1793000	1.8	0	85545	49192	36353	0
1–4	16185000	8263000	8.6	7922000	7.9	0	15094	8388	6705	1–4
5–9	20807000	10581000	11.0	10226000	10.2	0	9124	5372	3752	5–9
10–14	19403000	9861000	10.3	9542000	9.5	8128	8015	5109	2905	10–14
15–19	17756000	8950000	9.3	8806000	8.8	621426	18177	13006	5171	15–19
20–24	13606000	6625000	6.9	6981000	7.0	1297990	18161	13180	4981	20–24
25–29	11472000	5632000	5.9	5840000	5.8	872786	15747	10610	5137	25–29
30–34	10853000	5326000	5.6	5527000	5.5	474542	18662	11652	7010	30–34
35–39	11704000	5717000	6.0	5987000	6.0	252526	28467	17509	10958	35–39
40–44	12392000	6021000	6.3	6371000	6.4	74440	46395	28554	17841	40–44
45–49	11611000	5633000	5.9	5978000	6.0	4436	67903	42540	25363	45–49
50–54	10687000	5189000	5.4	5498000	5.5	0	97765	63457	34308	50–54
55–59	9329000	4490000	4.7	4839000	4.8	0	130727	86359	44368	55–59
60–64	7931000	3757000	3.9	4174000	4.2	0	162738	106146	56592	60–64
65–69	6377000	2901000	3.0	3476000	3.5	0	202538	124753	77775	65–69
70–74	5190000	2261000	2.4	2929000	2.9		241451	139410	102041	70–74
75–79	3688000	1564000	1.6	2124000	2.1		251451	133137	118314	75–79
80–84	2077000	847000	0.9	1230000	1.2	1845862 M	219728	104393	115335	80–84
85 +	1124000	430000	0.4	694000	0.7	1760412 F	225461	90050	135411	85 +
All ages	195857000	95920000		99937000		3606274	1863149	1052827	810322	All ages

TABLE 2 LIFE TABLE FOR MALES

Age, x	$_nq_x$	l_x	$_nd_x$	$_nL_x$	$_nm_x$	T_x	$1000r_x$	$\overset{\circ}{e}_x$	$_nM_x$	Age, x
0	0.02576	100000	2576	98016	0.02628	6674967	0.00	66.75	0.02628	0
1	0.00405	97424	394	388549	0.00102	6576951	0.00	67.51	0.00102	1
5	0.00253	97030	246	484535	0.00051	6188403	2.09	63.78	0.00051	5
10	0.00260	96784	252	483386	0.00052	5703868	16.02	58.93	0.00052	10
15	0.00730	96532	705	481044	0.00146	5220482	38.40	54.08	0.00145	15
20	0.00992	95827	950	476799	0.00199	4739438	44.46	49.46	0.00199	20
25	0.00938	94877	890	472175	0.00188	4262639	19.85	44.93	0.00188	25
30	0.01088	93987	1023	467487	0.00219	3790464	0.00	40.33	0.00219	30
35	0.01520	92964	1413	461522	0.00306	3322977	0.00	35.74	0.00306	35
40	0.02345	91551	2147	452783	0.00474	2861455	0.00	31.26	0.00474	40
45	0.03716	89404	3323	439332	0.00756	2408672	6.99	26.94	0.00755	45
50	0.05956	86081	5127	418449	0.01225	1969340	10.02	22.88	0.01223	50
55	0.09216	80954	7461	387078	0.01928	1550891	12.74	19.16	0.01923	55
60	0.13260	73493	9745	344136	0.02832	1163813	13.93	15.84	0.02825	60
65	0.19505	63747	12434	288485	0.04310	819676	13.93	12.86	0.04301	65
70	0.26772	51314	13738	222379	0.06178	531192	13.93	10.35	0.06165	70
75	0.35064	37576	13176	154478	0.08529	308813	13.93	8.22	0.08513	75
80	0.47188	24400	11514	93156	0.12360	154335	13.93	6.33	0.12325	80
85 +	*1.00000	12886	12885	61178	0.21063	61178	13.93	4.75	0.20942	85 +

TABLE 3 LIFE TABLE FOR FEMALES

Age, x	$_nq_x$	l_x	$_nd_x$	$_nL_x$	$_nm_x$	T_x	$1000r_x$	$\overset{\circ}{e}_x$	$_nM_x$	Age, x
0	0.01997	100000	1997	98479	0.02027	7386389	0.00	73.86	0.02027	0
1	0.00338	98003	331	391051	0.00085	7287911	0.00	74.36	0.00085	1
5	0.00183	97672	179	487914	0.00037	6896860	1.30	70.61	0.00037	5
10	0.00153	97493	149	487118	0.00031	6408946	14.57	65.74	0.00030	10
15	0.00295	97345	287	486048	0.00059	5921828	30.70	60.83	0.00059	15
20	0.00357	97058	347	484452	0.00072	5435780	40.35	56.01	0.00071	20
25	0.00440	96711	426	482546	0.00088	4951328	22.43	51.20	0.00088	25
30	0.00632	96285	609	479998	0.00127	4468782	0.00	46.41	0.00127	30
35	0.00911	95677	872	476352	0.00183	3988784	0.00	41.69	0.00183	35
40	0.01391	94805	1319	470955	0.00280	3512433	0.00	37.05	0.00280	40
45	0.02104	93486	1967	462825	0.00425	3041478	10.40	32.53	0.00424	45
50	0.03082	91519	2821	450964	0.00626	2578653	14.73	28.18	0.00624	50
55	0.04501	88698	3992	434087	0.00920	2127689	18.14	23.99	0.00917	55
60	0.06601	84706	5591	410480	0.01362	1693601	23.61	19.99	0.01355	60
65	0.10673	79115	8444	375678	0.02248	1283121	23.61	16.22	0.02237	65
70	0.16147	70671	11411	326111	0.03499	907444	23.61	12.84	0.03484	70
75	0.24644	59260	14604	260958	0.05596	581332	23.61	9.81	0.05570	75
80	0.38102	44656	17015	180684	0.09417	320374	23.61	7.17	0.09377	80
85 +	1.00000	27641	27641	139690	0.19788	139690	23.61	5.05	0.19512	85 +

[354]

TABLE 4   POPULATION PROJECTION, USING FIXED AGE-SPECIFIC
BIRTH AND DEATH RATES, IN THOUSANDS

Age at last birthday	1971 Total	1971 Males	1971 Females	1976 Total	1976 Males	1976 Females	1981 Total	1981 Males	1981 Females	Age at last birthday
0–4	18939	9665	9274	21515	11031	10584	23910	12202	11708	0–4
5–9	19776	10093	9683	18869	9625	9244	21534	10985	10549	5–9
10–14	20765	10556	10209	19736	10069	9667	18830	9502	9228	10–14
15–19	19334	9813	9521	20592	10505	10187	19666	10020	9646	15–19
20–24	17648	8871	8777	19217	9727	9490	20565	10412	10153	20–24
25–29	13515	6561	6954	17528	8785	8743	19084	9632	9452	25–29
30–34	11385	5576	5809	13413	6496	6917	17394	8698	8696	30–34
35–39	10743	5258	5485	11270	5505	5765	13277	6413	6864	35–39
40–44	11528	5609	5919	10581	5158	5423	11101	5401	5700	40–44
45–49	12103	5842	6261	11259	5442	5817	10334	5005	5329	45–49
50–54	11190	5365	5825	11665	5564	6101	10851	5183	5668	50–54
55–59	10092	4800	5292	10570	4963	5607	11019	5147	5872	55–59
60–64	8568	3992	4576	9271	4267	5004	9714	4412	5302	60–64
65–69	6969	3149	3820	7534	3346	4188	8157	3577	4580	65–69
70–74	5253	2236	3017	5744	2428	3316	6215	2580	3635	70–74
75–79	3915	1571	2344	3968	1553	2415	4340	1686	2654	75–79
80–84	2414	943	1471	2570	947	1623	2609	937	1672	80–84
85 +	1507	556	951	1756	619	1137	1877	522	1255	85 +
All ages	205644	100456	105188	217258	106030	111228	230477	112514	117963	All ages

TABLE 5   OBSERVED AND PROJECTED VITAL RATES

Rates per thousand	Observed Total	Observed Males	Observed Females	Projected 1971 Males	Projected 1971 Females	Projected 1976 Males	Projected 1976 Females	Projected 1981 Males	Projected 1981 Females	Stable Males	Stable Females
Birth	18.41	19.24	17.62	21.17	19.29	22.70	20.64	23.18	21.09	20.81	19.30
Death	9.51	10.98	8.11	11.14	8.73	11.10	9.06	10.88	9.17	11.11	9.60
Increase	8.90	8.27	9.51	10.03	10.56	11.60	11.58	12.30	11.92		9.6994

TABLE 6   RATES STANDARDIZED ON THREE STANDARD COUNTRIES

Standardized rates per thousand	England and Wales, 1961 Total	Males	Females	United States, 1960 Total	Males	Females	Mexico, 1960 Total	Males	Females
Birth	17.42	21.09*	16.48	17.77	19.47*	17.09	21.50	18.69*	20.94
Death	11.36	12.29*	10.38	9.33	10.99*	7.72	4.99	8.87*	3.85
Increase	6.06	8.80*	6.10	8.44	8.47*	9.37	16.51	9.82*	17.09

TABLE 7   VITAL STATISTICS AND RATES INFERRED FROM AGE DISTRIBUTIONS
(FEMALES)

Vital statistics		Thompson Age range	NRR	1000r	Interval	Bourgeois-Pichat Age range	NRR	1000b	1000d	1000r	Coale 1000b
TFR	2.74	0–4	1.45	13.70	27.41	5–29	2.14	27.32	-0.79	28.11	1000d
GRR	1.34	5–9	1.63	18.12	27.37	30–54	0.93	11.11	13.94	-2.83	1000r
NRR	1.29	10–14	1.57	16.33	27.31	55–79	1.49	25.88	11.03	14.85	$1000k_1$
Generation	26.17	15–19	1.47	13.52	27.22	*45–69	1.58	29.36	12.38	16.97	$1000k_2$
Sex ratio	104.85										

TABLE 8   LESLIE MATRIX AND ITS ANALYSIS (FEMALES)

Start of age interval	Sub-diagonal	First row	Percent in stable population	Fisher values	Total reproductive values	Net maternity function	Matrix equation coefficient	Parameters	Integral	Matrix
0	0.99670	0.00000	9.225	1.046	10165867	0.00000	0.00000	λ_1	1.0497	1.0498
5	0.99837	0.00102	8.759	1.102	11270176	0.00000	0.00101	λ_2	0.2967	0.3112
10	0.99780	0.08515	8.330	1.158	11047419	0.00203	0.08473		+0.7737	+0.7442 i
15	0.99672	0.30574	7.918	1.129	9939733	0.16743	0.30357	r_1	0.0097	0.0097
20	0.99607	0.40002	7.518	0.868	6058268	0.43970	0.39587	r_2	-0.0376	-0.0430
25	0.99472	0.28061	7.133	0.494	2887072	0.35204	0.27661		+0.2409	+0.2349 i
30	0.99240	0.15260	6.759	0.227	1251956	0.20118	0.14963	c_1		1052433
35	0.98867	0.05420	6.390	0.079	471150	0.09808	0.06247	c_2		264745
40	0.98274	0.01483	6.018	0.016	99447	0.02686	0.01427			2538719 i
45	0.97437	0.00089	5.634	0.001	5267	0.00168	0.00084	$2\pi/y$	26.079	25.743
50	0.96258	0.00000	5.229	0.000	0	0.00000	0.00000	Δ	5.208	
55	0.81104		21.087							

[355]

United States, 1966 (Nonwhite)

TABLE 1 DATA INPUT TO COMPUTATIONS

Age at last birthday	Population Total	Males	%	Females	%	Births, by age of mother	Deaths Total	Males	Females	Age at last birthday
0	612000	309000	2.7	303000	2.5	0	23793	13179	10614	0
1–4	2610000	1315000	11.6	1295000	10.7	0	4005	2164	1841	1–4
5–9	3068000	1532000	13.5	1536000	12.7	0	1833	1054	779	5–9
10–14	2713000	1355000	11.9	1358000	11.2	5462	1504	944	560	10–14
15–19	2297000	1143000	10.1	1154000	9.5	156314	2985	2070	915	15–19
20–24	1656000	796000	7.0	860000	7.1	196870	3666	2511	1155	20–24
25–29	1377000	647000	5.7	730000	6.0	123560	4008	2595	1413	25–29
30–34	1299000	602000	5.3	697000	5.8	75174	5259	3139	2120	30–34
35–39	1335000	610000	5.4	725000	6.0	41820	7460	4254	3206	35–39
40–44	1320000	615000	5.4	705000	5.8	12988	10537	6110	4427	40–44
45–49	1159000	544000	4.8	615000	5.1	856	13050	7518	5532	45–49
50–54	1042000	495000	4.4	547000	4.5	0	16014	9450	6564	50–54
55–59	854000	410000	3.6	444000	3.7	0	19268	11446	7822	55–59
60–64	716000	347000	3.1	369000	3.0	0	22209	12630	9579	60–64
65–69	496000	233000	2.0	263000	2.2	0	26154	14519	11635	65–69
70–74	399000	178000	1.6	221000	1.8		23284	13016	10268	70–74
75–79	272000	122000	1.1	150000	1.2		18208	9633	8575	75–79
80–84	162000	73000	0.6	89000	0.7	310376 M	12716	6402	6314	80–84
85 +	106000	46000	0.4	60000	0.5	302668 F	12735	5851	6884	85 +
All ages	23493000	11372000		12121000		613044	228688	128485	100203	All ages

TABLE 2 LIFE TABLE FOR MALES

Age, x	$_nq_x$	l_x	$_nd_x$	$_nL_x$	$_nm_x$	T_x	$1000r_x$	$\overset{\circ}{e}_x$	$_nM_x$	Age, x
0	0.04129	100000	4129	96816	0.04265	6077243	0.00	60.77	0.04265	0
1	0.00655	95871	628	381653	0.00165	5980428	0.00	62.38	0.00165	1
5	0.00342	95243	326	475399	0.00069	5598774	17.14	58.78	0.00069	5
10	0.00351	94917	333	473864	0.00070	5123375	28.36	53.98	0.00070	10
15	0.00915	94584	865	470993	0.00184	4649512	51.33	49.16	0.00181	15
20	0.01578	93718	1479	465097	0.00318	4178519	53.84	44.59	0.00315	20
25	0.01991	92240	1837	456783	0.00402	3713422	23.84	40.26	0.00401	25
30	0.02575	90403	2328	446441	0.00521	3256638	0.59	36.02	0.00521	30
35	0.03430	88075	3021	433197	0.00697	2810197	0.00	31.91	0.00697	35
40	0.04854	85054	4128	415448	0.00994	2377000	1.37	27.95	0.00993	40
45	0.06695	80926	5418	391660	0.01383	1961552	7.67	24.24	0.01382	45
50	0.09139	75507	6901	361026	0.01911	1569892	8.46	20.79	0.01909	50
55	0.13085	68606	8977	321235	0.02795	1208866	7.97	17.62	0.02792	55
60	0.16773	59629	10001	274067	0.03649	887631	14.94	14.89	0.03640	60
65	0.27030	49628	13415	214839	0.06244	613564	14.94	12.36	0.06231	65
70	0.30747	36213	11134	152145	0.07318	398724	14.94	11.01	0.07312	70
75	0.32706	25079	8202	103823	0.07900	246580	14.94	9.83	0.07896	75
80	0.35653	16877	6017	68554	0.08777	142757	14.94	8.46	0.08770	80
85 +	1.00000	10860	10860	74203	0.14635	74203	14.94	6.83	0.12720	85 +

TABLE 3 LIFE TABLE FOR FEMALES

Age, x	$_nq_x$	l_x	$_nd_x$	$_nL_x$	$_nm_x$	T_x	$1000r_x$	$\overset{\circ}{e}_x$	$_nM_x$	Age, x
0	0.03411	100000	3411	97388	0.03503	6748818	0.00	67.49	0.03503	0
1	0.00566	96589	547	384763	0.00142	6651430	0.00	68.86	0.00142	1
5	0.00252	96042	242	479603	0.00050	6266667	15.52	65.25	0.00051	5
10	0.00207	95800	198	478532	0.00041	5787064	28.08	60.41	0.00041	10
15	0.00400	95601	383	477143	0.00080	5308533	44.86	55.53	0.00079	15
20	0.00675	95219	642	474599	0.00135	4831389	44.45	50.74	0.00134	20
25	0.00967	94577	914	470758	0.00194	4356790	18.97	46.07	0.00194	25
30	0.01510	93662	1414	465005	0.00304	3886033	0.00	41.49	0.00304	30
35	0.02188	92248	2019	456480	0.00442	3421028	0.00	37.09	0.00442	35
40	0.03098	90229	2796	444540	0.00629	2964547	10.00	32.86	0.00628	40
45	0.04412	87434	3858	427959	0.00901	2520007	16.37	28.82	0.00900	45
50	0.05850	83576	4889	406242	0.01204	2092048	20.05	25.03	0.01200	50
55	0.08482	78686	6675	377571	0.01768	1685806	21.32	21.42	0.01762	55
60	0.12290	72012	8851	339173	0.02609	1308234	26.29	18.17	0.02596	60
65	0.19991	63161	12627	284585	0.04437	969061	26.29	15.34	0.04424	65
70	0.20793	50535	10508	225861	0.04652	684476	26.29	13.54	0.04545	70
75	0.25021	40027	10015	174791	0.05730	458615	26.29	11.46	0.05717	75
80	0.30095	30012	9032	126998	0.07112	283824	26.29	9.46	0.07094	80
85 +	1.00000	20980	20980	156826	0.13378	156826	26.29	7.48	0.11473	85 +

TABLE 4 POPULATION PROJECTION, USING FIXED AGE-SPECIFIC BIRTH AND DEATH RATES, IN THOUSANDS

Age at last birthday	1971			1976			1981			Age at last birthday
	Total	Males	Females	Total	Males	Females	Total	Males	Females	
0–4	3220	1624	1596	3811	1922	1889	4410	2224	2186	0–4
5–9	3204	1614	1590	3202	1614	1588	3789	1910	1879	5–9
10–14	3060	1527	1533	3194	1608	1586	3193	1509	1584	10–14
15–19	2701	1347	1354	3046	1518	1528	3180	1599	1581	15–19
20–24	2277	1129	1148	2677	1330	1347	3019	1499	1520	20–24
25–29	1635	782	853	2248	1109	1139	2642	1306	1336	25–29
30–34	1353	632	721	1607	764	843	2208	1083	1125	30–34
35–39	1268	584	684	1322	614	708	1568	741	827	35–39
40–44	1291	585	706	1226	560	666	1277	588	689	40–44
45–49	1259	580	679	1232	552	580	1169	528	641	45–49
50–54	1085	501	584	1178	534	644	1153	508	645	50–54
55–59	948	440	508	989	446	543	1075	476	599	55–59
60–64	749	350	399	833	376	457	868	381	487	60–64
65–69	582	272	310	609	274	335	678	295	383	65–69
70–74	374	165	209	439	193	246	450	194	266	70–74
75–79	292	121	171	275	113	162	321	131	190	75–79
80–84	190	81	109	204	80	124	191	74	117	80–84
85 +	189	79	110	222	87	135	240	87	153	85 +
All ages	25677	12413	13264	28314	13694	14620	31441	15233	16208	All ages

TABLE 5 OBSERVED AND PROJECTED VITAL RATES

Rates per thousand	Observed			Projected						Stable	
				1971		1976		1981			
	Total	Males	Females	Males	Females	Males	Females	Males	Females	Males	Females
Birth	26.09	27.29	24.97	29.69	27.10	31.77	29.03	32.48	29.76	30.27	28.55
Death	9.73	11.30	8.27	11.13	8.58	10.79	8.64	10.35	8.56	9.86	8.13
Increase	16.36	15.99	16.70	18.56	18.52	20.98	20.39	22.13	21.21	20.4117	

TABLE 6 RATES STANDARDIZED ON THREE STANDARD COUNTRIES

Standardized rates per thousand	England and Wales, 1961			United States, 1960			Mexico, 1960		
	Total	Males	Females	Total	Males	Females	Total	Males	Females
Birth	23.19	31.27*	22.19	23.78	28.62*	23.14	28.92	28.47*	28.48
Death	14.84	16.15*	13.77	12.41	14.11*	10.69	7.29	9.74*	5.98
Increase	8.35	15.11*	8.43	11.37	14.51*	12.45	21.63	18.73*	22.50

TABLE 7 VITAL STATISTICS AND RATES INFERRED FROM AGE DISTRIBUTIONS (FEMALES)

Vital statistics		Thompson				Bourgeois-Pichat					Coale
		Age range	NRR	$1000r$	Interval	Age range	NRR	$1000b$	$1000d$	$1000r$	$1000b$
TFR	3.62	0–4	1.90	24.16	27.30	5–29	2.79	36.58	-1.40	37.98	$1000d$
GRR	1.78	5–9	2.03	26.40	27.21	30–54	1.19	16.04	9.75	6.29	$1000r$
NRR	1.68	10–14	1.89	22.99	27.08	55–79	1.47	21.66	7.37	14.29	$1000k_1$
Generation	25.40	15–19	1.67	15.97	26.91	*40–64	1.67	29.54	10.45	19.09	$1000k_2$
Sex ratio	102.55										

TABLE 8 LESLIE MATRIX AND ITS ANALYSIS (FEMALES)

Start of age interval	Sub-diagonal	First row	Percent in stable population	Fisher values	Total reproductive values	Net maternity function	Matrix equation coefficient	Parameters		
									Integral	Matrix
0	0.99472	0.00000	13.096	1.091	1743595	0.00000	0.00000	λ_1	1.1074	1.1077
5	0.99777	0.00478	11.760	1.215	1866373	0.00000	0.00475	λ_2	0.2510	0.2798
10	0.99710	0.16554	10.592	1.344	1824863	0.00950	0.16430		+0.7520	+0.7261 i
15	0.99467	0.43223	9.534	1.312	1513755	0.31909	0.42774	r_1	0.0204	0.0205
20	0.99190	0.47229	8.561	0.987	848574	0.53639	0.46489	r_2	-0.0464	-0.0502
25	0.98778	0.32826	7.666	0.582	425165	0.39339	0.32050		+0.2497	+0.2406 i
30	0.98167	0.19577	6.836	0.291	202512	0.24761	0.18880	c_1		120004
35	0.97384	0.09001	6.058	0.110	79950	0.13000	0.08522	c_2		143441
40	0.96270	0.02352	5.326	0.025	17335	0.04043	0.02169			331069 i
45	0.94925	0.00166	4.628	0.002	1006	0.00294	0.00147	$2\pi/y$	25.159	26.114
50	0.92942	0.00000	3.966	0.000	0	0.00000	0.00000	Δ	4.789	
55	0.79996		11.977							

United States, 1966 (White)

TABLE 1 DATA INPUT TO COMPUTATIONS

Age at last birthday	Population					Births, by age of mother	Deaths			Age at last birthday
	Total	Males	%	Females	%		Total	Males	Females	
0	3054000	1564000	1.8	1490000	1.7	0	61764	35020	25744	0
1–4	13575000	6948000	8.2	6627000	7.5	0	11092	6226	4866	1–4
5–9	17738000	9047000	10.7	8691000	9.9	0	7292	4318	2974	5–9
10–14	16689000	8505000	10.1	8184000	9.3	2666	6511	4165	2346	10–14
15–19	15459000	7807000	9.2	7652000	8.7	465112	15193	10936	4257	15–19
20–24	11951000	5830000	6.9	6121000	7.0	1101120	14497	10670	3827	20–24
25–29	10095000	4985000	5.9	5110000	5.8	749226	11741	8016	3725	25–29
30–34	9552000	4723000	5.6	4829000	5.5	399368	13406	8515	4891	30–34
35–39	10369000	5107000	6.0	5262000	6.0	210706	21010	13257	7753	35–39
40–44	11072000	5406000	6.4	5666000	6.5	61452	35862	22446	13416	40–44
45–49	10452000	5089000	6.0	5363000	6.1	3580	54858	35025	19833	45–49
50–54	9644000	4694000	5.6	4950000	5.6	0	81754	54009	27745	50–54
55–59	8475000	4080000	4.8	4395000	5.0	0	111461	74914	36547	55–59
60–64	7215000	3410000	4.0	3805000	4.3	0	140530	93515	47015	60–64
65–69	5882000	2668000	3.2	3214000	3.7	0	176385	110243	66142	65–69
70–74	4791000	2083000	2.5	2708000	3.1		218157	126389	91768	70–74
75–79	3417000	1443000	1.7	1974000	2.2		233233	123498	109735	75–79
80–84	1915000	774000	0.9	1141000	1.3	1535486 M	207001	97986	109015	80–84
85 +	1019000	385000	0.5	634000	0.7	1457744 F	212714	84194	128520	85 +
All ages	172364000	84548000		87816000		2993230	1634461	924342	710119	All ages

TABLE 2 LIFE TABLE FOR MALES

Age, x	$_nq_x$	l_x	$_nd_x$	$_nL_x$	$_nm_x$	T_x	$1000r_x$	$\overset{\circ}{e}_x$	$_nM_x$	Age, x
0	0.02263	100000	2263	98258	0.02303	6760966	0.00	67.61	0.02303	0
1	0.00358	97737	349	389931	0.00090	6662707	0.00	68.17	0.00090	1
5	0.00238	97388	232	486358	0.00048	6272777	0.00	64.41	0.00048	5
10	0.00246	97155	239	485274	0.00049	5786419	14.05	59.56	0.00049	10
15	0.00703	96917	682	483012	0.00141	5301145	36.46	54.70	0.00140	15
20	0.00912	96235	878	478998	0.00183	4818134	43.16	50.07	0.00183	20
25	0.00801	95357	764	474873	0.00161	4339135	19.36	45.50	0.00161	25
30	0.00898	94594	849	470940	0.00180	3864263	0.00	40.85	0.00180	30
35	0.01290	93745	1209	465920	0.00260	3393323	0.00	36.20	0.00260	35
40	0.02056	92535	1903	458308	0.00415	2927402	0.00	31.64	0.00415	40
45	0.03393	90633	3075	446103	0.00689	2469094	6.90	27.24	0.00688	45
50	0.05615	87558	4916	426375	0.01153	2022991	10.18	23.10	0.01151	50
55	0.08819	82642	7288	395988	0.01840	1596616	13.22	19.32	0.01835	55
60	0.12895	75354	9717	353532	0.02748	1200627	13.21	15.93	0.02742	60
65	0.18813	65637	12349	298223	0.04141	847005	13.21	12.91	0.04132	65
70	0.26417	53289	14077	231557	0.06079	548872	13.21	10.30	0.06068	70
75	0.35237	39212	13817	161129	0.08575	317315	13.21	8.09	0.08558	75
80	0.48130	25395	12223	96283	0.12694	156186	13.21	6.15	0.12660	80
85 +	*1.00000	13172	13172	59903	0.21989	59903	13.21	4.55	0.21869	85 +

TABLE 3 LIFE TABLE FOR FEMALES

Age, x	$_nq_x$	l_x	$_nd_x$	$_nL_x$	$_nm_x$	T_x	$1000r_x$	$\overset{\circ}{e}_x$	$_nM_x$	Age, x
0	0.01705	100000	1705	98704	0.01728	7480149	0.00	74.80	0.01728	0
1	0.00293	98295	288	392341	0.00073	7381445	0.00	75.10	0.00073	1
5	0.00171	98007	168	489614	0.00034	6989104	0.00	71.31	0.00034	5
10	0.00144	97839	140	488866	0.00029	6499490	12.37	66.43	0.00029	10
15	0.00279	97699	272	487846	0.00056	6010625	28.54	61.52	0.00055	15
20	0.00313	97426	305	486386	0.00063	5522778	39.74	56.69	0.00063	20
25	0.00365	97121	354	484760	0.00073	5036393	22.95	51.86	0.00073	25
30	0.00505	96767	489	482697	0.00101	4551633	0.00	47.04	0.00101	30
35	0.00734	96278	707	479757	0.00147	4068946	0.00	42.26	0.00147	35
40	0.01177	95571	1125	475258	0.00237	3589189	0.00	37.55	0.00237	40
45	0.01836	94446	1734	468195	0.00370	3113932	9.71	32.97	0.00370	45
50	0.02773	92712	2571	457538	0.00562	2645737	14.16	28.54	0.00561	50
55	0.04090	90141	3687	442038	0.00834	2188199	17.78	24.28	0.00832	55
60	0.06033	86454	5215	420133	0.01241	1746161	23.42	20.20	0.01235	60
65	0.09864	81238	8013	387475	0.02068	1326028	23.42	16.32	0.02058	65
70	0.15752	73225	11535	338784	0.03405	938552	23.42	12.82	0.03389	70
75	0.24614	61691	15184	271838	0.05586	599768	23.42	9.72	0.05559	75
80	0.38692	46506	17994	187517	0.09596	327930	23.42	7.05	0.09554	80
85 +	1.00000	28512	28512	140413	0.20306	140413	23.42	4.92	0.20271	85 +

[358]

TABLE 4 POPULATION PROJECTION, USING FIXED AGE-SPECIFIC BIRTH AND DEATH RATES, IN THOUSANDS

Age at last birthday	1971 Total	Males	Females	1976 Total	Males	Females	1981 Total	Males	Females	Age at last birthday
0–4	15747	8055	7692	17889	9151	8738	19655	10054	9601	0–4
5–9	16573	8480	8093	15693	8024	7669	17829	9116	8713	5–9
10–14	17705	9027	8678	16542	8461	8081	15664	8007	7557	10–14
15–19	16632	8465	8167	17645	8985	8660	16486	8422	8064	15–19
20–24	15371	7742	7629	16537	8395	8142	17544	8910	8634	20–24
25–29	11881	5780	6101	15279	7675	7604	16438	8323	8115	25–29
30–34	10032	4944	5088	11806	5732	6074	15183	7512	7571	30–34
35–39	9473	4673	4800	9948	4891	5057	11709	5671	6038	35–39
40–44	10237	5024	5213	9351	4596	4755	9821	4811	5010	40–44
45–49	10844	5262	5582	10025	4890	5135	9158	4474	4684	45–49
50–54	10105	4864	5241	10484	5029	5455	9692	4674	5018	50–54
55–59	9141	4359	4782	9580	4517	5063	9941	4671	5270	55–59
60–64	7820	3643	4177	8437	3892	4545	8845	4033	4812	60–64
65–69	6386	2877	3509	6926	3073	3853	7475	3283	4192	65–69
70–74	4882	2072	2810	5301	2233	3068	5754	2386	3368	70–74
75–79	3622	1449	2173	3697	1442	2255	4016	1554	2462	75–79
80–84	2224	862	1362	2365	866	1499	2416	861	1555	80–84
85 +	1336	482	854	1556	536	1020	1661	539	1122	85 +
All ages	180011	88060	91951	189061	92388	96673	199287	97401	101886	All ages

TABLE 5 OBSERVED AND PROJECTED VITAL RATES

Rates per thousand	Observed Total	Males	Females	Projected 1971 Males	Females	1976 Males	Females	1981 Males	Females	Stable Males	Females
Birth	17.37	18.16	16.60	20.04	18.22	21.48	19.49	21.92	19.89	19.44	17.95
Death	9.48	10.93	8.09	11.14	8.76	11.15	9.15	10.98	9.30	11.52	10.03
Increase	7.88	7.23	8.51	8.90	9.46	10.33	10.34	10.94	10.59		7.9268

TABLE 6 RATES STANDARDIZED ON THREE STANDARD COUNTRIES

Standardized rates per thousand	England and Wales, 1961 Total	Males	Females	United States, 1960 Total	Males	Females	Mexico, 1960 Total	Males	Females
Birth	16.58	19.79*	15.65	16.90	18.28*	16.21	20.42	17.48*	19.84
Death	10.96	11.89*	9.99	8.97	10.66*	7.37	4.68	8.76*	3.56
Increase	5.62	7.90*	5.66	7.93	7.62*	8.85	15.74	8.72*	16.28

TABLE 7 VITAL STATISTICS AND RATES INFERRED FROM AGE DISTRIBUTIONS (FEMALES)

Vital statistics		Thompson Age range	NRR	1000r	Interval	Bourgeois-Pichat Age range	NRR	1000b	1000d	1000r	Coale	
TFR	2.61	0–4	1.38	11.98	27.43	5–29	2.05	26.09	−0.46	26.55	1000b	
GRR	1.27	5–9	1.58	16.86	27.39	30–54	0.90	10.58	14.58	−4.00	1000d	
NRR	1.23	10–14	1.53	15.34	27.34	55–79	1.49	26.28	11.43	14.85	1000r	
Generation	26.33	15–19	1.44	12.91	27.25	*45–69	1.56	28.90	12.43	16.47	$1000k_1$	
Sex ratio	105.33										$1000k_2$	

TABLE 8 LESLIE MATRIX AND ITS ANALYSIS (FEMALES)

Start of age interval	Sub-diagonal	First row	Percent in stable population	Fisher values	Total reproductive values	Net maternity function	Matrix equation coefficient	Parameters Integral	Matrix
0	0.99708	0.00000	8.649	1.039	8430160	0.00000	0.00000	λ_1 1.0404	1.0405
5	0.99847	0.00039	8.289	1.084	9419040	0.00000	0.00039	λ_2 0.3026	0.3157
10	0.99791	0.07292	7.954	1.129	9239345	0.00078	0.07259	+0.7757	+0.7461 i
15	0.99701	0.28714	7.629	1.101	8426403	0.14441	0.28527	r_1 0.0079	0.0079
20	0.99666	0.38983	7.310	0.850	5203447	0.42612	0.38613	r_2 −0.0366	−0.0421
25	0.99572	0.27378	7.002	0.481	2459119	0.34615	0.27028	+0.2398	+0.2341 i
30	0.99393	0.14648	6.701	0.217	1049308	0.19441	0.14399	c_1	952073
35	0.99062	0.36073	6.401	0.074	391524	0.09356	0.05933	c_2	117339
40	0.98514	0.01375	6.095	0.014	82077	0.02510	0.01331		2257079 i
45	0.97724	0.00080	5.771	0.001	4273	0.00152	0.00076	$2\pi/y$ 26.206	26.839
50	0.96612	0.00000	5.420	0.000	0	0.00000	0.00000	Δ 5.638	
55	0.81061		22.780						

United States, 1967

TABLE 1 DATA INPUT TO COMPUTATIONS

Age at last birthday	Population					Births, by age of mother	Deaths			Age at last birthday
	Total	Males	%	Females	%		Total	Males	Females	
0	3539000	1806000	1.9	1733000	1.7	0	79053	45457	33596	0
1–4	15652000	7988000	8.3	7664000	7.6	0	13511	7654	5857	1–4
5–9	20910000	10642000	11.0	10268000	10.1	0	8812	5193	3619	5–9
10–14	19885000	10101000	10.4	9784000	9.7	8593	8087	5172	2915	10–14
15–19	17693000	8909000	9.2	8784000	8.7	596445	18174	13051	5123	15–19
20–24	14572000	7042000	7.3	7530000	7.4	1310588	19545	14143	5402	20–24
25–29	11958000	5875000	6.1	6083000	6.0	867426	16361	11221	5140	25–29
30–34	10861000	5323000	5.5	5538000	5.5	439373	18437	11705	6732	30–34
35–39	11506000	5609000	5.8	5897000	5.8	227323	28391	17478	10913	35–39
40–44	12332000	5992000	6.2	6340000	6.3	67053	45671	28282	17389	40–44
45–49	11815000	5719000	5.9	6096000	6.0	4158	68269	42785	25484	45–49
50–54	10773000	5217000	5.4	5556000	5.5	0	96825	62613	34212	50–54
55–59	9523000	4572000	4.7	4951000	4.9	-0	130979	86022	44957	55–59
60–64	8048000	3798000	3.9	4250000	4.2	-0	163277	106527	56750	60–64
65–69	6501000	2958000	3.1	3543000	3.5	-0	199678	122672	77006	65–69
70–74	5177000	2236000	2.3	2941000	2.9		238376	138293	100083	70–74
75–79	3785000	1587000	1.6	2198000	2.2		250632	132788	117844	75–79
80–84	2160000	874000	0.9	1286000	1.3	1803388 M	219186	103953	115233	80–84
85 +	1173000	446000	0.5	727000	0.7	1717571 F	228059	90936	137123	85 +
All ages	197863000	96694000		101169000		3520959	1851323	1045945	805378	All ages

TABLE 2 LIFE TABLE FOR MALES

Age, x	$_nq_x$	l_x	$_nd_x$	$_nL_x$	$_nm_x$	T_x	$1000r_x$	$\overset{\circ}{e}_x$	$_nM_x$	Age, x
0	0.02469	100000	2469	98094	0.02517	6698012	0.00	66.98	0.02517	0
1	0.00382	97531	373	389038	0.00096	6599918	0.00	67.67	0.00096	1
5	0.00244	97158	237	485199	0.00049	6210880	0.00	63.93	0.00049	5
10	0.00257	96921	250	484082	0.00052	5725681	17.06	59.08	0.00051	10
15	0.00735	96672	711	481730	0.00148	5241599	34.69	54.22	0.00146	15
20	0.01001	95961	961	477443	0.00201	4759869	39.76	49.60	0.00201	20
25	0.00951	95000	903	472758	0.00191	4282426	25.99	45.08	0.00191	25
30	0.01094	94097	1029	468023	0.00220	3809668	2.33	40.49	0.00220	30
35	0.01547	93067	1440	461970	0.00312	3341645	0.00	35.91	0.00312	35
40	0.02334	91628	2139	453179	0.00472	2879676	0.00	31.43	0.00472	40
45	0.03681	89489	3294	439814	0.00749	2426497	6.06	27.12	0.00748	45
50	0.05848	86195	5041	419211	0.01202	1986683	9.96	23.05	0.01200	50
55	0.09025	81154	7324	388433	0.01886	1567472	12.51	19.31	0.01881	55
60	0.13167	73830	9721	345840	0.02811	1179039	13.38	15.97	0.02805	60
65	0.18876	64108	12101	291173	0.04156	833199	13.38	13.00	0.04147	65
70	0.26849	52007	13963	225346	0.06196	542025	13.38	10.42	0.06185	70
75	0.34549	38044	13144	156811	0.08382	316680	13.38	8.32	0.08367	75
80	0.45481	24900	11325	95039	0.11916	159869	13.38	6.42	0.11894	80
85 +	1.00000	13575	13575	64829	0.20940	64829	13.38	4.78	0.20389	85 +

TABLE 3 LIFE TABLE FOR FEMALES

Age, x	$_nq_x$	l_x	$_nd_x$	$_nL_x$	$_nm_x$	T_x	$1000r_x$	$\overset{\circ}{e}_x$	$_nM_x$	Age, x
0	0.01910	100000	1910	98533	0.01939	7422270	0.00	74.22	0.01939	0
1	0.00305	98090	299	391488	0.00076	7323737	0.00	74.66	0.00076	1
5	0.00176	97791	172	488523	0.00035	6932249	0.00	70.89	0.00035	5
10	0.00149	97618	146	487752	0.00030	6443726	15.23	66.01	0.00030	10
15	0.00292	97473	285	486694	0.00059	5955975	25.64	61.10	0.00058	15
20	0.00359	97188	349	485093	0.00072	5469281	36.03	56.28	0.00072	20
25	0.00423	96839	410	483219	0.00085	4984188	29.83	51.47	0.00084	25
30	0.00606	96429	585	480782	0.00122	4500969	1.84	46.68	0.00122	30
35	0.00921	95844	883	477163	0.00185	4020186	0.00	41.94	0.00185	35
40	0.01363	94961	1294	471793	0.00274	3543024	0.00	37.31	0.00274	40
45	0.02073	93667	1942	463794	0.00419	3071231	8.93	32.79	0.00418	45
50	0.03042	91726	2790	452074	0.00617	2607437	14.47	28.43	0.00616	50
55	0.04458	88935	3964	435335	0.00911	2155363	17.50	24.24	0.00908	55
60	0.06503	84971	5526	411932	0.01341	1720028	24.24	20.24	0.01335	60
65	0.10384	79445	8249	377794	0.02184	1308096	24.24	16.47	0.02173	65
70	0.15801	71196	11250	329111	0.03418	930302	24.24	13.07	0.03403	70
75	0.23828	59946	14284	265172	0.05387	601191	24.24	10.03	0.05361	75
80	0.36743	45662	16778	186422	0.09000	336018	24.24	7.36	0.08961	80
85 +	1.00000	28885	28885	149597	0.19308	149597	24.24	5.18	0.18861	85 +

TABLE 4 POPULATION PROJECTION, USING FIXED AGE-SPECIFIC BIRTH AND DEATH RATES, IN THOUSANDS

Age at last birthday	1972 Total	Males	Females	1977 Total	Males	Females	1982 Total	Males	Females	Age at last birthday
0–4	18429	9412	9017	20881	10664	10217	22874	11682	11192	0–4
5–9	19123	9755	9368	18363	9374	8989	20808	10622	10186	5–9
10–14	20869	10617	10252	19086	9733	9353	18328	9353	8975	10–14
15–19	19815	10052	9763	20796	10566	10230	19018	9685	9333	15–19
20–24	17585	8830	8755	19693	9962	9731	20668	10472	10196	20–24
25–29	14474	6973	7501	17464	8743	8721	19558	9865	9693	25–29
30–34	11868	5816	6052	14366	6903	7463	17332	8655	8677	30–34
35–39	10750	5254	5496	11748	5741	6007	14221	6814	7407	35–39
40–44	11333	5502	5831	10588	5154	5434	11571	5632	5939	40–44
45–49	12048	5815	6233	11072	5340	5732	10344	5002	5342	45–49
50–54	11393	5451	5942	11618	5543	6075	10677	5090	5587	50–54
55–59	10184	4834	5350	10773	5051	5722	10986	5136	5850	55–59
60–64	8756	4071	4685	9367	4304	5063	9911	4497	5414	60–64
65–69	7096	3198	3898	7724	3427	4297	8267	3624	4643	65–69
70–74	5375	2289	3086	5871	2475	3396	6395	2652	3743	70–74
75–79	3926	1556	2370	4080	1593	2487	4458	1722	2736	75–79
80–84	2507	962	1545	2609	943	1666	2713	965	1748	80–84
85+	1628	596	1032	1896	656	1240	1980	643	1337	85+
All ages	207159	100983	106176	217995	106172	111823	230109	112111	117998	All ages

TABLE 5 OBSERVED AND PROJECTED VITAL RATES

Rates per thousand	Observed Total	Males	Females	Projected 1972 Males	Females	1977 Males	Females	1982 Males	Females	Stable Males	Females
Birth	17.79	18.65	16.98	20.41	18.48	21.83	19.74	22.11	20.00	19.26	17.75
Death	9.36	10.82	7.96	11.06	8.66	11.05	9.04	10.88	9.16	11.88	10.36
Increase	8.44	7.83	9.02	9.35	9.82	10.78	10.70	11.23	10.85		7.3848

TABLE 6 RATES STANDARDIZED ON THREE STANDARD COUNTRIES

Standardized rates per thousand	England and Wales, 1961 Total	Males	Females	United States, 1960 Total	Males	Females	Mexico, 1960 Total	Males	Females
Birth	16.37	20.11*	15.48	16.71	18.49*	16.06	20.27	17.98*	19.72
Death	11.10	12.06*	10.07	9.12	10.80*	7.49	4.88	8.78*	3.74
Increase	5.28	8.05*	5.41	7.59	7.70*	8.56	15.39	9.20*	15.99

TABLE 7 VITAL STATISTICS AND RATES INFERRED FROM AGE DISTRIBUTIONS (FEMALES)

Vital statistics		Thompson Age range	NRR	1000r	Interval	Bourgeois-Pichat Age range	NRR	1000b	1000d	1000r	Coale
TFR	2.57	0–4	1.38	11.85	27.42	5–29	2.00	26.56	0.93	25.63	1000b
GRR	1.26	5–9	1.60	17.48	27.37	30–54	0.90	10.53	14.35	−3.82	1000d
NRR	1.21	10–14	1.60	16.93	27.31	55–79	1.56	28.54	12.16	16.38	1000r
Generation	26.15	15–19	1.46	13.28	27.22	*45–69	1.58	29.48	12.48	17.00	$1000k_1$
Sex ratio	105.00										$1000k_2$

TABLE 8 LESLIE MATRIX AND ITS ANALYSIS (FEMALES)

Start of age interval	Sub-diagonal	First row	Percent in stable population	Fisher values	Total reproductive values	Net maternity function	Matrix equation coefficient	Parameters Integral	Matrix
0	0.99694	0.00000	8.539	1.039	9766713	0.00000	0.00000	λ_1 1.0376	1.0376
5	0.99842	0.00105	8.204	1.082	11107699	0.00000	0.00104	λ_2 0.2954	0.3098
10	0.99783	0.08203	7.894	1.123	10989283	0.00209	0.08165	+0.7664	+0.7374i
15	0.99671	0.28849	7.591	1.083	9509304	0.16121	0.28653	r_1 0.0074	0.0074
20	0.99614	0.37780	7.292	0.826	6221292	0.41186	0.37400	r_2 −0.0394	−0.0447
25	0.99496	0.26478	7.000	0.466	2837405	0.33613	0.26110	+0.2406	+0.2346i
30	0.99247	0.14055	6.712	0.210	1162265	0.18607	0.13790	c_1	1130784
35	0.98875	0.05857	6.420	0.072	425981	0.08973	0.05703	c_2	35782
40	0.98305	0.01344	6.117	0.014	90253	0.02434	0.01294		2699705i
45	0.97473	0.00081	5.795	0.001	4977	0.00154	0.00077	$2\pi/y$ 26.118	26.781
50	0.96297	0.00000	5.444	0.000	0	0.00000	0.00000	Δ 6.176	
55	0.80966		22.993						

Argentina, 1964

TABLE 1 DATA INPUT TO COMPUTATIONS

Age at last birthday	Population					Births, by age of mother	Deaths			Age at last birthday
	Total	Males	%	Females	%		Total	Males	Females	
0	469531	238800	2.1	230731	2.1	0	25552	14163	11389	0
1–4	1766345	898355	8.1	867990	8.0	0	5490	2765	2725	1–4
5–9	2231585	1135863	10.2	1095722	10.1	0	1541	877	664	5–9
10–14	2112453	1072970	9.6	1039483	9.5	0	1177	696	481	10–14
15–19	1927589	979281	8.8	948308	8.7	1182	1916	1114	802	15–19
20–24	1758557	890173	8.0	868384	8.0	51726	2320	1404	916	20–24
25–29	1684109	859517	7.7	824592	7.6	132129	2519	1465	1054	25–29
30–34	1640279	834412	7.5	805867	7.4	130097	3300	1903	1397	30–34
35–39	1557789	786335	7.1	771454	7.1	93539	4133	2532	1501	35–39
40–44	1446998	727807	6.5	719191	6.6	52020	5307	3402	1905	40–44
45–49	1247901	624143	5.6	623758	5.7	17442	6896	4522	2374	45–49
50–54	1122214	570175	5.1	552039	5.1	2720	10072	6754	3318	50–54
55–59	974949	490141	4.4	484808	4.5	784	12898	8866	4032	55–59
60–64	764113	392165	3.5	371948	3.4	0	16330	11030	5300	60–64
65–69	571726	287181	2.6	284545	2.6	0	16690	10807	5883	65–69
70–74	370562	181012	1.6	189550	1.7		17646	10588	7058	70–74
75–79	210505	99327	0.9	111178	1.0		16145	8930	7215	75–79
80–84	105584	47779	0.4	57805	0.5	255774 M	12147	5122	5025	80–84
85 +	75126	31303	0.3	43823	0.4	225865 F	10641	4324	6317	85 +
All ages	22037915	11146739		10891176		481639	172720	102264	70455	All ages

TABLE 2 LIFE TABLE FOR MALES

Age, x	$_nq_x$	l_x	$_nd_x$	$_nL_x$	$_nm_x$	T_x	$1000r_x$	$\overset{\circ}{e}_x$	$_nM_x$	Age, x
0	0.05666	100000	5666	95805	0.05914	6497041	3.71	64.97	0.05931	0
1	0.01215	94334	1146	374024	0.00306	6401236	3.71	67.86	0.00308	1
5	0.00384	93188	358	465044	0.00077	6027213	4.44	64.68	0.00077	5
10	0.00324	92830	301	463431	0.00065	5562169	14.05	59.92	0.00065	10
15	0.00569	92529	526	461415	0.00114	5098738	17.55	55.10	0.00114	15
20	0.00786	92002	723	458254	0.00158	4637323	11.54	50.40	0.00158	20
25	0.00849	91279	775	454519	0.00171	4179070	4.67	45.78	0.00170	25
30	0.01135	90504	1027	450087	0.00228	3724550	6.56	41.15	0.00228	30
35	0.01600	89476	1432	444013	0.00323	3274463	10.36	36.60	0.00322	35
40	0.02319	88044	2042	435458	0.00469	2830450	18.23	32.15	0.00466	40
45	0.03575	86002	3074	422897	0.00727	2394992	16.77	27.85	0.00725	45
50	0.05776	82928	4790	403441	0.01187	1972095	12.06	23.78	0.01185	50
55	0.08702	78138	6800	374660	0.01815	1568654	18.51	20.08	0.01809	55
60	0.13234	71338	9441	333906	0.02827	1193994	36.63	16.74	0.02813	60
65	0.17330	61897	10727	283444	0.03784	860088	36.63	13.90	0.03763	65
70	0.25724	51170	13163	223624	0.05886	576643	36.63	11.27	0.05849	70
75	0.36810	38007	13990	154723	0.09042	353019	36.63	9.29	0.08991	75
80	0.48075	24017	11545	89696	0.12872	198296	36.63	8.26	0.12813	80
85 +	1.00000	12471	12471	108600	0.11483	108600	36.63	8.71	0.13813	85 +

TABLE 3 LIFE TABLE FOR FEMALES

Age, x	$_nq_x$	l_x	$_nd_x$	$_nL_x$	$_nm_x$	T_x	$1000r_x$	$\overset{\circ}{e}_x$	$_nM_x$	Age, x
0	0.04754	100000	4754	96587	0.04922	7095229	3.85	70.95	0.04935	0
1	0.01240	95246	1181	377597	0.00313	6998642	3.85	73.48	0.00314	1
5	0.00302	94065	284	469618	0.00060	6621045	4.31	70.39	0.00061	5
10	0.00231	93782	217	468389	0.00046	6151427	13.87	65.59	0.00046	10
15	0.00423	93565	396	466891	0.00085	5683038	17.18	60.74	0.00085	15
20	0.00527	93169	491	464658	0.00106	5216147	12.92	55.99	0.00105	20
25	0.00638	92678	591	461977	0.00128	4751489	6.14	51.27	0.00128	25
30	0.00864	92087	795	458522	0.00173	4289512	4.96	46.58	0.00173	30
35	0.01033	91292	943	454184	0.00208	3830990	9.26	41.96	0.00208	35
40	0.01319	90349	1192	448918	0.00266	3376806	18.50	37.38	0.00265	40
45	0.01894	89157	1689	441854	0.00382	2927888	22.43	32.84	0.00381	45
50	0.02972	87468	2600	431215	0.00603	2486034	19.24	28.42	0.00601	50
55	0.04104	84868	3483	416270	0.00837	2054819	30.37	24.21	0.00832	55
60	0.06949	81385	5655	393633	0.01437	1638549	45.59	20.13	0.01425	60
65	0.09956	75730	7540	361078	0.02088	1244916	45.59	16.44	0.02068	65
70	0.17283	68190	11785	313237	0.03762	883838	45.59	12.96	0.03724	70
75	0.28239	56405	15928	243243	0.06548	570601	45.59	10.12	0.06490	75
80	0.41420	40477	16765	159689	0.10499	327358	45.59	8.09	0.10423	80
85 +	1.00000	23711	23711	167670	0.14142	167670	45.59	7.07	0.14415	85 +

TABLE 4 POPULATION PROJECTION, USING FIXED AGE-SPECIFIC BIRTH AND DEATH RATES, IN THOUSANDS

Age at last birthday	1969 Total	1969 Males	1969 Females	1974 Total	1974 Males	1974 Females	1979 Total	1979 Males	1979 Females	Age at last birthday
0–4	2324	1229	1095	2444	1292	1152	2595	1372	1223	0–4
5–9	2214	1126	1088	2302	1217	1085	2420	1279	1141	5–9
10–14	2225	1132	1093	2207	1122	1085	2294	1212	1082	10–14
15–19	2104	1068	1036	2216	1127	1089	2199	1117	1082	15–19
20–24	1917	973	944	2092	1061	1031	2203	1119	1084	20–24
25–29	1746	883	863	1903	965	938	2077	1052	1025	25–29
30–34	1669	851	818	1731	874	857	1886	955	931	30–34
35–39	1621	823	798	1651	840	811	1712	863	849	35–39
40–44	1534	771	763	1596	807	789	1624	823	801	40–44
45–49	1415	707	708	1500	749	751	1561	784	777	45–49
50–54	1204	595	609	1365	674	691	1446	714	732	50–54
55–59	1062	529	533	1141	553	588	1293	626	667	55–59
60–64	895	437	458	976	472	504	1049	493	556	60–64
65–69	674	333	341	792	371	421	853	401	452	65–69
70–74	474	227	247	559	263	296	658	293	365	70–74
75–79	272	125	147	349	157	192	412	182	230	75–79
80–84	131	58	73	170	73	97	217	91	126	80–84
85 +	119	58	61	147	70	77	189	88	101	85 +
All ages	23600	11925	11675	25141	12687	12454	26698	13464	13234	All ages

TABLE 5 OBSERVED AND PROJECTED VITAL RATES

Rates per thousand	Observed Total	Observed Males	Observed Females	Projected 1969 Males	Projected 1969 Females	Projected 1974 Males	Projected 1974 Females	Projected 1979 Males	Projected 1979 Females	Stable Males	Stable Females
Birth	21.86	22.95	20.74	22.43	20.23	22.28	20.04	22.40	20.12	20.43	19.05
Death	7.84	9.17	6.47	9.96	7.09	10.49	7.77	10.95	8.49	12.28	10.91
Increase	14.02	13.77	14.27	12.46	13.14	11.79	12.27	11.44	11.63		8.1488

TABLE 6 RATES STANDARDIZED ON THREE STANDARD COUNTRIES

Standardized rates per thousand	England and Wales, 1961 Total	Males	Females	United States, 1960 Total	Males	Females	Mexico, 1960 Total	Males	Females
Birth	19.84	20.38*	18.03	19.98	19.05*	18.46	18.92	18.54*	17.70
Death	11.78	13.57*	11.05	10.00	11.56*	8.62	6.31	8.48*	5.27
Increase	8.07	6.81*	6.98	9.98	7.49*	9.84	12.61	10.05*	12.42

TABLE 7 VITAL STATISTICS AND RATES INFERRED FROM AGE DISTRIBUTIONS (FEMALES)

Vital statistics		Thompson Age range	NRR	1000r	Interval	Bourgeois-Pichat Age range	NRR	1000b	1000d	1000r	Coale	
TFR	3.05	0–4	1.29	9.49	27.40	5–29	1.47	23.96	9.81	14.15	1000b	25.95
GRR	1.43	5–9	1.38	11.89	27.36	30–54	1.56	28.35	11.97	16.38	1000d	9.95
NRR	1.31	10–14	1.39	12.01	27.31	55–79	3.19	127.16	84.25	42.91	1000r	15.99
Generation	32.99	15–19	1.36	10.90	27.23	*20–44	1.21	20.16	13.01	7.15	$1000k_1$	37.83
Sex ratio	113.2										$1000k_2$	0.65

TABLE 8 LESLIE MATRIX AND ITS ANALYSIS (FEMALES)

Start of age interval	Sub-diagonal	First row	Percent in stable population	Fisher values	Total reproductive values	Net maternity function	Matrix equation coefficient
0	0.99037	0.00000	8.903	1.076	1182439	0.00000	0.00000
5	0.99738	0.00000	8.458	1.133	1241215	0.00000	0.00000
10	0.99680	0.00138	8.093	1.184	1230715	0.00000	0.00136
15	0.99522	0.06730	7.738	1.237	1172763	0.00273	0.06526
20	0.99423	0.24336	7.388	1.223	1061696	0.12979	0.23847
25	0.99252	0.35631	7.045	1.018	839832	0.34714	0.34714
30	0.99054	0.31303	6.708	0.683	550708	0.34713	0.30269
35	0.98840	0.21430	6.374	0.379	292448	0.25825	0.20526
40	0.98426	0.11102	6.044	0.166	119728	0.15227	0.10511
45	0.97592	0.03798	5.707	0.055	34262	0.05794	0.03395
50	0.96534	0.00879	5.342	0.017	9270	0.00996	0.00656
55	0.81012		22.198				

Parameters

	Integral	Matrix
λ_1	1.0416	1.0419
λ_2	0.5269	0.5262
	+0.7342	+0.7169i
r_1	0.0081	0.0082
r_2	-0.0202	-0.0235
	+0.1897	+0.1875i
c_1		122911
c_2		55036
		140512i
$2\pi/y$	33.128	33.507
Δ	8.449	

Chile, 1967

TABLE 1   DATA INPUT TO COMPUTATIONS

Age at last birthday	Population					Births, by age of mother	Deaths			Age at last birthday
	Total	Males	%	Females	%		Total	Males	Females	
0	284103	144991	3.2	139112	3.0	0	25953	14155	11798	0
1–4	1059661	537547	11.9	522114	11.3	0	4160	2153	2007	1–4
5–9	1225203	616408	13.7	608795	13.1	0	1174	664	510	5–9
10–14	1071038	536373	11.9	534665	11.5	771	867	507	360	10–14
15–19	908408	452706	10.1	455702	9.8	32850	1175	698	477	15–19
20–24	767791	379914	8.4	387877	8.4	76109	1509	906	603	20–24
25–29	661314	327415	7.3	333899	7.2	63779	1742	1068	674	25–29
30–34	577791	285636	6.3	292155	6.3	42828	1980	1181	799	30–34
35–39	514067	250226	5.6	263841	5.7	30433	2581	1694	987	35–39
40–44	454667	217646	4.8	237021	5.1	11249	2876	1841	1035	40–44
45–49	388701	184823	4.1	203878	4.4	1502	3089	1922	1167	45–49
50–54	326290	154741	3.4	171549	3.7	208	3978	2451	1527	50–54
55–59	271629	129465	2.9	142164	3.1	0	4603	2792	1811	55–59
60–64	218048	104020	2.3	114028	2.5	0	5271	3163	2108	60–64
65–69	159331	74802	1.7	84529	1.8	0	6021	3416	2605	65–69
70–74	106769	48570	1.1	58199	1.3		6001	3218	2783	70–74
75–79	65977	28634	0.6	37343	0.8		5567	2753	2814	75–79
80–84	37766	15384	0.3	22382	0.5	132027 M	4201	1788	2413	80–84
85 +	38131	13140	0.3	24991	0.5	127702 F	3992	1487	2505	85 +
All ages	9136685	4502441		4634244		259729	86840	47857	38983	All ages

TABLE 2   LIFE TABLE FOR MALES

Age, x	$_nq_x$	l_x	$_nd_x$	$_nL_x$	$_nm_x$	T_x	$1000r_x$	$\overset{\circ}{e}_x$	$_nM_x$	Age, x
0	0.09056	100000	9056	93054	0.09731	5923593	4.15	59.24	0.09763	0
1	0.01574	90944	1432	359611	0.00398	5830639	4.15	64.11	0.00401	1
5	0.00531	89513	476	446375	0.00107	5471028	22.21	61.12	0.00108	5
10	0.00473	89037	421	444176	0.00095	5024653	29.77	56.43	0.00095	10
15	0.00773	88616	685	441497	0.00155	4580477	32.90	51.69	0.00154	15
20	0.01191	87931	1047	437187	0.00240	4138980	30.00	47.07	0.00238	20
25	0.01623	86884	1410	431040	0.00327	3701794	25.29	42.61	0.00325	25
30	0.02055	85474	1757	423264	0.00415	3270753	22.35	38.27	0.00413	30
35	0.03340	83717	2796	411926	0.00679	2847489	20.64	34.01	0.00677	35
40	0.04152	80920	3360	396442	0.00848	2435563	21.81	30.10	0.00846	40
45	0.05090	77560	3948	378405	0.01043	2039121	22.96	26.29	0.01040	45
50	0.07652	73612	5633	354612	0.01588	1660716	19.79	22.56	0.01584	50
55	0.10274	67979	6984	323070	0.02162	1306104	17.54	19.21	0.02157	55
60	0.14216	60995	8671	284092	0.03052	983034	23.98	16.12	0.03041	60
65	0.20615	52325	10786	235319	0.04584	598942	23.98	13.36	0.04567	65
70	0.28526	41538	11849	178210	0.06649	463623	23.98	11.16	0.06625	70
75	0.38643	29689	11473	118978	0.09643	285413	23.98	9.61	0.09614	75
80	0.44383	18216	8085	69449	0.11641	166435	23.98	9.14	0.11622	80
85 +	1.00000	10131	10131	96987	0.10446	96987	23.98	9.57	0.11317	85 +

TABLE 3   LIFE TABLE FOR FEMALES

Age, x	$_nq_x$	l_x	$_nd_x$	$_nL_x$	$_nm_x$	T_x	$1000r_x$	$\overset{\circ}{e}_x$	$_nM_x$	Age, x
0	0.07952	100000	7952	93988	0.08460	6615723	3.18	66.16	0.08481	0
1	0.01514	92048	1394	364148	0.00383	6521735	3.18	70.85	0.00384	1
5	0.00413	90655	374	452337	0.00083	6157587	19.60	67.92	0.00084	5
10	0.00337	90280	304	450662	0.00067	5705250	28.18	63.19	0.00067	10
15	0.00525	89976	472	448782	0.00105	5254588	31.03	58.40	0.00105	15
20	0.00777	89504	696	445858	0.00156	4805806	29.56	53.69	0.00155	20
25	0.01008	88808	895	441908	0.00203	4359937	26.27	49.09	0.00202	25
30	0.01362	87913	1198	436721	0.00274	3918029	20.74	44.57	0.00273	30
35	0.01857	86716	1610	429688	0.00375	3481308	17.27	40.15	0.00374	35
40	0.02165	85106	1842	421079	0.00438	3051620	21.28	35.86	0.00437	40
45	0.02836	83263	2361	410757	0.00575	2630540	26.23	31.59	0.00572	45
50	0.04378	80902	3542	396164	0.00894	2219773	27.05	27.44	0.00890	50
55	0.06208	77360	4803	375401	0.01279	1823609	27.77	23.57	0.01274	55
60	0.08899	72557	6457	347630	0.01857	1448208	24.48	19.95	0.01849	60
65	0.14420	66100	9532	307863	0.03096	1100578	24.48	16.65	0.03082	65
70	0.21512	56569	12169	253379	0.04803	792714	24.48	14.01	0.04782	70
75	0.31828	44399	14131	186795	0.07565	539336	24.48	12.15	0.07535	75
80	0.42210	30268	12775	118164	0.10812	352540	24.48	11.65	0.10781	80
85 +	1.00000	17492	17492	234376	0.07463	234376	24.48	13.40	0.10024	85 +

TABLE 4 POPULATION PROJECTION, USING FIXED AGE-SPECIFIC BIRTH AND DEATH RATES, IN THOUSANDS

Age at last birthday	1972 Total	Males	Females	1977 Total	Males	Females	1982 Total	Males	Females	Age at last birthday
0–4	1268	641	627	1457	736	721	1570	844	826	0–4
5–9	1326	673	653	1251	632	619	1438	726	712	5–9
10–14	1220	613	607	1320	670	650	1246	529	517	10–14
15–19	1065	533	532	1214	610	604	1314	666	648	15–19
20–24	901	448	453	1057	528	529	1204	604	600	20–24
25–29	759	375	384	891	442	449	1045	521	524	25–29
30–34	652	322	330	748	368	380	877	434	443	30–34
35–39	565	278	287	638	313	325	732	358	374	35–39
40–44	500	241	259	550	268	282	519	301	318	40–44
45–49	439	208	231	482	230	252	530	255	275	45–49
50–54	370	173	197	418	195	223	458	215	243	50–54
55–59	304	141	163	344	158	186	388	177	211	55–59
60–64	246	114	132	275	124	151	312	139	173	60–64
65–69	187	86	101	211	94	117	236	103	133	65–69
70–74	127	57	70	148	65	83	167	71	96	70–74
75–79	75	32	43	89	38	51	105	44	61	75–79
80–84	41	17	24	46	19	27	54	22	32	80–84
85 +	65	21	44	70	23	47	80	26	54	85 +
All ages	10110	4973	5137	11209	5513	5696	12475	6135	6340	All ages

TABLE 5 OBSERVED AND PROJECTED VITAL RATES

Rates per thousand	Observed Total	Males	Females	Projected 1972 Males	Females	1977 Males	Females	1982 Males	Females	Stable Males	Females
Birth	28.43	29.32	27.56	30.39	28.46	31.60	29.58	32.40	30.32	29.95	28.03
Death	9.50	10.63	8.41	10.37	8.46	10.56	8.69	10.72	8.95	11.57	9.69
Increase	18.92	18.69	19.14	20.02	20.00	21.04	20.89	21.68	21.37		18.3908

TABLE 6 RATES STANDARDIZED ON THREE STANDARD COUNTRIES

Standardized rates per thousand	England and Wales, 1961 Total	Males	Females	United States, 1960 Total	Males	Females	Mexico, 1960 Total	Males	Females
Birth	25.01	28.62*	23.89	25.51	26.21*	24.72	28.31	27.27*	27.77
Death	14.59	19.75*	13.83	12.70	16.57*	11.17	8.77	9.96*	7.52
Increase	10.47	8.86*	10.06	12.82	9.64*	13.55	19.54	17.31*	20.25

TABLE 7 VITAL STATISTICS AND RATES INFERRED FROM AGE DISTRIBUTIONS (FEMALES)

Vital statistics		Thompson Age range	NRR	$1000r$	Interval	Bourgeois-Pichat Age range	NRR	$1000b$	$1000d$	$1000r$	Coale	
TFR	3.89	0–4	1.92	24.64	27.33	5–29	2.21	36.49	7.20	29.30	$1000b$	34.81
GRR	1.91	5–9	2.03	26.34	27.26	30–54	1.79	29.71	8.06	21.65	$1000d$	8.95
NRR	1.68	10–14	2.00	25.03	27.19	55–79	2.47	56.86	23.30	33.55	$1000r$	25.86
Generation	28.25	15–19	1.91	23.97	27.08	*40–64	2.07	38.48	11.47	27.01	$1000k_1$	0.
Sex ratio	103.4										$1000k_2$	0.

TABLE 8 LESLIE MATRIX AND ITS ANALYSIS (FEMALES)

Start of age interval	Sub-diagonal	First row	Percent in stable population	Fisher values	Total reproductive values	Net maternity function	Matrix equation coefficient	Parameters Integral	Matrix
0	0.98734	0.00000	12.299	1.142	755363	0.00000	0.00000	λ_1 1.0963	1.0965
5	0.99630	0.00162	11.075	1.269	772373	0.00000	0.00160	λ_2 0.4097	0.4183
10	0.99583	0.08247	10.062	1.394	745576	0.00320	0.08113	+0.7375	+0.7202 i
15	0.99351	0.30075	9.138	1.441	656603	0.15906	0.29461	r_1 0.0184	0.0184
20	0.99112	0.43422	8.280	1.244	482694	0.43015	0.42259	r_2 -0.0340	-0.0366
25	0.98826	0.37830	7.484	0.876	292602	0.41502	0.36490	+0.2128	+0.2089 i
30	0.98389	0.29292	6.745	0.535	156312	0.31477	0.27923	c_1	50773
35	0.97996	0.18229	6.052	0.256	67591	0.24369	0.17097	c_2	87840
40	0.97551	0.06155	5.409	0.074	17573	0.09826	0.05657		133924 i
45	0.96445	0.00961	4.812	0.011	2298	0.01488	0.00862	$2\pi/y$ 29.532	30.074
50	0.94759	0.00137	4.232	0.001	245	0.00235	0.00118	Δ 6.323	
55	0.81825		14.412						

Colombia, 1965

TABLE 1 DATA INPUT TO COMPUTATIONS

Age at last birthday	Population					Births, by age of mother	Deaths			Age at last birthday
	Total	Males	%	Females	%		Total	Males	Females	
0	648845	328166	3.7	320679	3.5	0	55340	30549	24791	0
1–4	2526718	1280146	14.4	1246572	13.7	0	31087	15447	15640	1–4
5–9	2882260	1460340	16.5	1421920	15.6	0	6313	3359	2954	5–9
10–14	2335087	1182351	13.3	1152736	12.6	442	2788	1644	1144	10–14
15–19	1817400	860938	9.7	956462	10.5	73864	3185	1815	1370	15–19
20–24	1458595	691061	7.8	767534	8.4	191481	3852	2361	1491	20–24
25–29	1199722	565871	6.4	633851	6.9	179244	3921	2240	1681	25–29
30–34	1060270	514953	5.8	545307	6.0	120701	3731	2011	1720	30–34
35–39	951304	456227	5.1	495077	5.4	90594	4484	2276	2208	35–39
40–44	739594	370547	4.2	369047	4.0	26416	4028	2106	1922	40–44
45–49	609455	299837	3.4	309618	3.4	6453	4788	2553	2235	45–49
50–54	533384	269982	3.0	263402	2.9	1432	5378	2943	2435	50–54
55–59	341253	172054	1.9	169199	1.9	0	5814	3192	2622	55–59
60–64	349856	168647	1.9	181209	2.0	0	7775	4297	3478	60–64
65–69	195063	94929	1.1	100134	1.1	0	7968	4278	3690	65–69
70–74	153318	70309	0.8	83009	0.9		7556	3914	3642	70–74
75–79	86131	40545	0.5	45586	0.5		6762	3467	3295	75–79
80–84	58791	24349	0.3	34442	0.4	349605 M	5676	2553	3123	80–84
85+	46199	17347	0.2	28852	0.3	341122 F	7926	2996	4930	85+
All ages	17993245	8868609		9124636		690727	178372	94001	84371	All ages

TABLE 2 LIFE TABLE FOR MALES

Age, x	$_nq_x$	l_x	$_nd_x$	$_nL_x$	$_nm_x$	T_x	$1000r_x$	$\mathring{e}_x$	$_nM_x$	Age, x
0	0.08781	100000	8781	94332	0.09309	5823490	0.00	58.23	0.09309	0
1	0.04670	91219	4260	353067	0.01207	5729158	0.00	62.81	0.01207	1
5	0.01119	86958	973	432358	0.00225	5376091	25.43	61.82	0.00230	5
10	0.00692	85985	595	428423	0.00139	4943733	51.09	57.50	0.00139	10
15	0.01060	85390	905	424862	0.00213	4515311	51.47	52.88	0.00211	15
20	0.01702	84485	1438	418981	0.00343	4090449	38.70	48.42	0.00342	20
25	0.01961	83047	1629	411193	0.00396	3671468	25.58	44.21	0.00396	25
30	0.01936	81418	1576	403223	0.00391	3260275	17.37	40.04	0.00391	30
35	0.02470	79842	1972	394411	0.00500	2857051	28.06	35.78	0.00499	35
40	0.02816	77871	2193	384119	0.00571	2462640	35.81	31.62	0.00568	40
45	0.04185	75677	3167	370822	0.00854	2078521	23.34	27.47	0.00851	45
50	0.05356	72511	3884	353459	0.01099	1707699	43.45	23.55	0.01090	50
55	0.08925	68627	6125	328585	0.01864	1354240	28.87	19.73	0.01855	55
60	0.12080	62502	7550	294691	0.02562	1025654	27.85	16.41	0.02548	60
65	0.20374	54952	11196	247432	0.04525	730963	27.85	13.30	0.04507	65
70	0.24522	43756	10730	192048	0.05587	483531	27.85	11.05	0.05567	70
75	0.35246	33026	11640	135628	0.08583	291483	27.85	8.83	0.08551	75
80	0.41138	21386	8798	83720	0.10509	155855	27.85	7.29	0.10485	80
85+	1.00000	12588	12588	72136	0.17450	72136	27.85	5.73	0.17271	85+

TABLE 3 LIFE TABLE FOR FEMALES

Age, x	$_nq_x$	l_x	$_nd_x$	$_nL_x$	$_nm_x$	T_x	$1000r_x$	$\mathring{e}_x$	$_nM_x$	Age, x
0	0.07376	100000	7376	95409	0.07731	6170867	0.00	61.71	0.07731	0
1	0.04853	92624	4495	358249	0.01255	6075457	0.00	65.59	0.01255	1
5	0.01007	88129	887	438428	0.00202	5717208	26.54	64.87	0.00208	5
10	0.00493	87242	430	435080	0.00099	5278780	38.31	60.51	0.00099	10
15	0.00718	86812	623	432588	0.00144	4843700	39.25	55.80	0.00143	15
20	0.00972	86189	838	428957	0.00195	4411112	39.15	51.18	0.00194	20
25	0.01322	85352	1128	424039	0.00266	3982155	31.59	46.66	0.00265	25
30	0.01569	84224	1322	417961	0.00316	3558116	21.36	42.25	0.00315	30
35	0.02214	82902	1835	410083	0.00447	3140155	34.73	37.88	0.00446	35
40	0.02583	81067	2094	400302	0.00523	2730072	41.43	33.68	0.00521	40
45	0.03559	78973	2810	388125	0.00724	2329769	26.57	29.50	0.00722	45
50	0.04564	76162	3475	372669	0.00933	1941644	50.20	25.49	0.00924	50
55	0.07493	72686	5445	350382	0.01554	1568975	22.70	21.59	0.01550	55
60	0.09230	67239	6206	321705	0.01929	1218593	24.41	18.12	0.01919	60
65	0.16971	61033	10358	280074	0.03698	896888	24.41	14.70	0.03685	65
70	0.19865	50675	10067	228648	0.04403	616814	24.41	12.17	0.04387	70
75	0.30709	40608	12470	171922	0.07254	388166	24.41	9.56	0.07228	75
80	0.36752	28138	10341	113805	0.09087	216244	24.41	7.69	0.09067	80
85+	1.00000	17796	17796	102439	0.17373	102439	24.41	5.76	0.17087	85+

TABLE 4   POPULATION PROJECTION, USING FIXED AGE-SPECIFIC BIRTH AND DEATH RATES, IN THOUSANDS

Age at last birthday	1970			1975			1980			Age at last birthday
	Total	Males	Females	Total	Males	Females	Total	Males	Females	
0–4	3404	1711	1693	4065	2043	2022	4866	2446	2420	0–4
5–9	3069	1554	1515	3289	1653	1536	3929	1975	1954	5–9
10–14	2858	1447	1411	3043	1540	1503	3261	1638	1623	10–14
15–19	2319	1173	1146	2838	1435	1403	3021	1527	1494	15–19
20–24	1797	849	948	2293	1156	1137	2806	1415	1391	20–24
25–29	1437	678	759	1771	833	938	2258	1135	1123	25–29
30–34	1180	555	625	1413	665	748	1741	817	924	30–34
35–39	1039	504	535	1156	543	613	1385	651	734	35–39
40–44	927	444	483	1013	491	522	1127	529	598	40–44
45–49	716	358	358	898	429	469	980	474	506	45–49
50–54	583	286	297	685	341	344	859	409	450	50–54
55–59	499	251	248	546	266	280	640	317	323	55–59
60–64	309	154	155	452	225	227	495	238	257	60–64
65–69	300	142	158	265	130	135	387	189	198	65–69
70–74	156	74	82	239	110	129	211	101	110	70–74
75–79	112	50	62	113	52	61	175	78	97	75–79
80–84	55	25	30	72	31	41	73	32	41	80–84
85 +	52	21	31	49	22	27	63	26	37	85 +
All ages	20812	10276	10536	24200	11965	12235	28277	13997	14280	All ages

TABLE 5   OBSERVED AND PROJECTED VITAL RATES

Rates per thousand	Observed			Projected						Stable	
				1970		1975		1980			
	Total	Males	Females	Males	Females	Males	Females	Males	Females	Males	Females
Birth	38.39	39.42	37.38	40.40	38.45	41.65	39.74	42.52	40.65	40.10	38.82
Death	9.91	10.60	9.25	10.27	8.99	10.37	9.01	10.57	9.25	11.15	9.88
Increase	28.47	28.82	28.14	30.14	29.46	31.27	30.73	31.95	31.40		28.9452

TABLE 6   RATES STANDARDIZED ON THREE STANDARD COUNTRIES

Standardized rates per thousand	England and Wales, 1961			United States, 1960			Mexico, 1960		
	Total	Males	Females	Total	Males	Females	Total	Males	Females
Birth	35.85	42.62*	34.32	36.37	38.91*	35.39	39.21	40.79*	38.62
Death	14.91	24.10*	15.26	13.32	19.69*	12.73	9.84	10.37*	9.04
Increase	20.95	18.52*	19.06	23.05	19.23*	22.66	29.36	30.42*	29.58

TABLE 7   VITAL STATISTICS AND RATES INFERRED FROM AGE DISTRIBUTIONS (FEMALES)

Vital statistics		Thompson				Bourgeois-Pichat					Coale	
		Age range	NRR	1000r	Interval	Age range	NRR	1000b	1000d	1000r		
TFR	5.56	0–4	2.31	30.59	27.30	5–29	2.85	47.44	8.60	38.83	1000b	43.98
GRR	2.75	5–9	2.57	35.46	27.21	30–54	2.42	42.45	9.65	32.81	1000d	9.93
NRR	2.31	10–14	2.44	32.10	27.13	55–79	2.03	26.10	-0.11	26.21	1000r	34.05
Generation	28.86	15–19	2.40	32.48	27.01	*5–29	2.85	47.44	8.60	38.83	$1000k_1$	0.
Sex ratio	102.5										$1000k_2$	0.

TABLE 8   LESLIE MATRIX AND ITS ANALYSIS (FEMALES)

Start of age interval	Sub-diagonal	First row	Percent in stable population	Fisher values	Total reproductive values	Net maternity function	Matrix equation coefficient	Parameters		
									Integral	Matrix
0	0.96643	0.00000	16.418	1.184	1855198	0.00000	0.00000	λ_1	1.1557	1.1563
5	0.99236	0.00043	13.723	1.415	2013708	0.00000	0.00341	λ_2	0.4303	0.4366
10	0.99427	0.08644	11.778	1.650	1901612	0.00082	0.08290		+0.7945	+0.7728 i
15	0.99161	0.36363	10.128	1.816	1736464	0.16498	0.34674	r_1	0.0289	0.0290
20	0.98854	0.59262	8.685	1.683	1291673	0.52850	0.56035	r_2	-0.0203	-0.0239
25	0.98567	0.56118	7.425	1.259	797886	0.59220	0.52454		+0.2149	+0.2113 i
30	0.98115	0.44930	6.330	0.803	437721	0.45689	0.41395	c_1		94757
35	0.97614	0.28349	5.371	0.404	199966	0.37101	0.25626	c_2		122930
40	0.96958	0.10282	4.534	0.135	49699	0.14151	0.09073			270801 i
45	0.96018	0.02920	3.802	0.035	10857	0.03995	0.02498	$2\pi/y$	29.240	29.736
50	0.94020	0.00609	3.158	0.005	1642	0.01001	0.00500	Δ	4.077	
55	0.81297		8.648							

Ecuador, 1965

TABLE 1 DATA INPUT TO COMPUTATIONS

Age at last birthday	Population Total	Males	%	Females	%	Births, by age of mother	Deaths Total	Males	Females	Age at last birthday
0	195115	98467	3.9	96648	3.8	0	21184	11598	9586	0
1–4	759808	384110	15.1	375598	14.7	0	13492	5620	6872	1–4
5–9	803054	406177	15.9	396877	15.5	0	2109	1074	1035	5–9
10–14	642200	328310	12.9	313890	12.3	173	1029	579	450	10–14
15–19	502838	254350	10.0	248488	9.7	25383	1023	555	468	15–19
20–24	409858	202748	7.9	207110	8.1	64383	1159	602	567	20–24
25–29	349097	169369	6.5	179728	7.0	57984	1159	619	540	25–29
30–34	296890	145260	5.7	151630	5.9	38244	1096	541	555	30–34
35–39	255438	125729	4.9	129709	5.1	28481	1255	624	631	35–39
40–44	212146	105694	4.1	106452	4.2	9314	1136	583	553	40–44
45–49	175677	87516	3.4	88161	3.4	2019	1108	593	515	45–49
50–54	144554	72700	2.8	71854	2.8	455	1319	717	602	50–54
55–59	108330	54448	2.1	53882	2.1	0	1318	746	572	55–59
60–64	92112	45520	1.8	46592	1.8	0	1690	925	765	60–64
65–69	61043	29085	1.1	31958	1.3	0	1858	986	872	65–69
70–74	39392	17999	0.7	21393	0.8		1829	939	890	70–74
75–79	24770	10791	0.4	13979	0.5		1658	822	836	75–79
80–84	15188	6269	0.2	8919	0.3	115033 M	1393	663	730	80–84
85 +	21052	7496	0.3	13556	0.5	111403 F	3368	1382	1985	85 +
All ages	5108562	2552038		2556524		226436	60193	31168	29025	All ages

TABLE 2 LIFE TABLE FOR MALES

Age, x	$_nq_x$	l_x	$_nd_x$	$_nL_x$	$_nm_x$	T_x	$1000r_x$	$\mathring{e}_x$	$_nM_x$	Age, x
0	0.10958	100000	10958	93037	0.11779	5708922	0.00	57.09	0.11779	0
1	0.06582	89042	5860	340036	0.01723	5615985	0.00	63.07	0.01723	1
5	0.01270	83181	1056	413265	0.00256	5275850	32.75	63.43	0.00264	5
10	0.00876	82125	720	408790	0.00176	4862585	44.76	59.21	0.00175	10
15	0.01091	81405	888	404904	0.00219	4453795	45.96	54.71	0.00218	15
20	0.01480	80517	1191	399721	0.00298	4048891	37.07	50.29	0.00297	20
25	0.01813	79326	1438	393083	0.00366	3649170	29.83	46.00	0.00365	25
30	0.01849	77887	1440	385927	0.00373	3256087	25.79	41.81	0.00372	30
35	0.02457	76447	1878	377663	0.00497	2870160	27.01	37.54	0.00495	35
40	0.02727	74569	2033	367875	0.00553	2492497	30.57	33.43	0.00552	40
45	0.03347	72535	2428	356891	0.00680	2124621	30.26	29.29	0.00678	45
50	0.04844	70108	3396	342458	0.00992	1767730	37.48	25.21	0.00985	50
55	0.06667	66712	4448	322997	0.01377	1425262	32.59	21.36	0.01370	55
60	0.09763	62264	6079	297042	0.02046	1102265	35.75	17.70	0.02032	60
65	0.15780	56185	8866	259786	0.03413	805223	35.75	14.33	0.03390	65
70	0.23249	47319	11001	209675	0.05247	545437	35.75	11.53	0.05217	70
75	0.32104	36318	11659	152288	0.07656	335762	35.75	9.25	0.07617	75
80	0.41646	24658	10269	96676	0.10622	183474	35.75	7.44	0.10576	80
85 +	1.00000	14389	14389	86799	0.16578	86799	35.75	6.03	0.18436	85 +

TABLE 3 LIFE TABLE FOR FEMALES

Age, x	$_nq_x$	l_x	$_nd_x$	$_nL_x$	$_nm_x$	T_x	$1000r_x$	$\mathring{e}_x$	$_nM_x$	Age, x
0	0.09351	100000	9351	94274	0.09918	6016037	0.00	50.16	0.09918	0
1	0.06972	90649	6320	345528	0.01829	5921763	0.00	65.33	0.01829	1
5	0.01245	84329	1050	419022	0.00251	5576236	35.03	66.12	0.00261	5
10	0.00711	83280	592	414861	0.00143	5157213	45.04	61.93	0.00143	10
15	0.00943	82687	780	411597	0.00189	4742352	39.63	57.35	0.00188	15
20	0.01363	81908	1117	406836	0.00274	4330755	29.79	52.87	0.00274	20
25	0.01494	80791	1207	401007	0.00301	3923919	28.09	48.57	0.00300	25
30	0.01820	79584	1448	394441	0.00367	3522913	28.82	44.27	0.00366	30
35	0.02409	78136	1882	386081	0.00487	3128472	30.70	40.04	0.00486	35
40	0.02568	76254	1958	376430	0.00520	2742391	33.36	35.96	0.00519	40
45	0.02891	74296	2148	366322	0.00586	2365961	33.05	31.85	0.00584	45
50	0.04126	72148	2977	353600	0.00842	1999639	40.99	27.72	0.00838	50
55	0.05202	69171	3599	337326	0.01067	1646039	31.98	23.80	0.01062	55
60	0.07957	65572	5218	315689	0.01653	1308714	32.40	19.96	0.01642	60
65	0.12886	60355	7777	283324	0.02745	993025	32.40	16.45	0.02729	65
70	0.18978	52578	9978	238642	0.04181	709701	32.40	13.50	0.04160	70
75	0.26130	42599	11131	185316	0.06007	471059	32.40	11.06	0.05980	75
80	0.33961	31468	10687	130082	0.08215	285743	32.40	9.08	0.08185	80
85 +	1.00000	20781	20781	155662	0.13350	155662	32.40	7.49	0.14650	85 +

TABLE 4 POPULATION PROJECTION, USING FIXED AGE-SPECIFIC BIRTH AND DEATH RATES, IN THOUSANDS

Age at last birthday	1970 Total	Males	Females	1975 Total	Males	Females	1980 Total	Males	Females	Age at last birthday
0–4	1073	541	532	1274	642	632	1535	774	761	0–4
5–9	911	461	450	1023	516	507	1215	613	602	5–9
10–14	795	402	393	902	456	446	1013	511	502	10–14
15–19	636	325	311	788	398	390	893	451	442	15–19
20–24	497	251	246	629	321	308	778	393	385	20–24
25–29	403	199	204	489	247	242	619	316	303	25–29
30–34	343	166	177	397	196	201	480	242	238	30–34
35–39	290	142	148	336	163	173	389	192	197	35–39
40–44	248	122	126	283	138	145	328	159	169	40–44
45–49	207	103	104	242	119	123	275	134	141	45–49
50–54	169	84	85	198	98	100	233	114	119	50–54
55–59	138	69	69	160	79	81	188	93	95	55–59
60–64	100	50	50	127	63	64	149	73	76	60–64
65–69	82	40	42	89	44	45	113	55	58	65–69
70–74	50	23	27	67	32	35	73	35	38	70–74
75–79	30	13	17	38	17	21	50	23	27	75–79
80–84	17	7	10	20	8	12	26	11	15	80–84
85 +	17	6	11	18	6	12	21	7	14	85 +
All ages	6006	3004	3002	7080	3543	3537	8378	4195	4182	All ages

TABLE 5 OBSERVED AND PROJECTED VITAL RATES

Rates per thousand	Observed Total	Males	Females	Projected 1970 Males	Females	1975 Males	Females	1980 Males	Females	Stable Males	Females
Birth	45.32	45.07	43.58	44.88	43.50	45.67	44.33	46.62	45.30	45.93	44.82
Death	11.78	12.21	11.35	11.77	10.88	11.87	10.95	12.05	11.10	12.62	11.50
Increase	32.54	32.86	32.22	33.12	32.62	33.80	33.39	34.57	34.20		33.3128

TABLE 6 RATES STANDARDIZED ON THREE STANDARD COUNTRIES

Standardized rates per thousand	England and Wales, 1961 Total	Males	Females	United States, 1960 Total	Males	Females	Mexico, 1960 Total	Males	Females
Birth	42.75	48.30*	40.76	43.36	43.99*	42.04	47.00	46.58*	46.13
Death	14.11	26.97*	14.27	13.23	22.13*	12.61	10.99	11.43*	10.28
Increase	28.64	21.33*	26.49	30.14	21.86*	29.42	36.02	35.15*	35.85

TABLE 7 VITAL STATISTICS AND RATES INFERRED FROM AGE DISTRIBUTIONS (FEMALES)

Vital statistics		Thompson Age range	NRR	$1000r$	Interval	Bourgeois-Pichat Age range	NRR	$1000b$	$1000d$	$1000r$	Coale	
TFR	6.62	0–4	2.49	33.51	27.28	5–29	2.78	47.74	9.89	37.85	$1000b$	45.75
GRR	3.26	5–9	2.56	35.37	27.19	30–54	2.38	43.31	11.13	32.17	$1000d$	11.50
NRR	2.59	10–14	2.37	31.00	27.14	55–79	2.95	65.59	25.55	40.04	$1000r$	34.25
Generation	28.54	15–19	2.22	29.50	27.06	*25–49	2.31	41.35	10.34	31.01	$1000k_1$	0.
Sex ratio	103.3										$1000k_2$	0.

TABLE 8 LESLIE MATRIX AND ITS ANALYSIS (FEMALES)

Start of age interval	Sub-diagonal	First row	Percent in stable population	Fisher values	Total reproductive values	Net maternity function	Matrix equation coefficient
0	0.95275	0.00000	18.187	1.234	582772	0.00000	0.00000
5	0.99007	0.00059	14.660	1.531	607470	0.00000	0.00056
10	0.99213	0.11024	12.280	1.827	573346	0.00112	0.10399
15	0.98843	0.44294	10.307	2.039	506672	0.20685	0.41453
20	0.98567	0.58035	8.619	1.885	390486	0.62222	0.62936
25	0.98363	0.61744	7.188	1.409	253294	0.63650	0.56297
30	0.97881	0.50539	5.982	0.919	139356	0.48945	0.45326
35	0.97500	0.32985	4.953	0.473	61324	0.41708	0.28956
40	0.97315	0.11877	4.086	0.156	16581	0.16204	0.10166
45	0.96527	0.03139	3.364	0.039	3404	0.04127	0.02614
50	0.95397	0.00685	2.747	0.007	514	0.01102	0.00551
55	0.83830		7.625				

Parameters

	Integral	Matrix
λ_1	1.1812	1.1820
λ_2	0.4202	0.4287
	+0.7965	+0.7752 i
r_1	0.0333	0.0334
r_2	-0.0210	-0.0242
	+0.2171	+0.2131 i
c_1		25421
c_2		42974
		30644 i
$2\pi/y$	28.944	29.481
Δ	2.118	

Guyana, 1961

TABLE 1 DATA INPUT TO COMPUTATIONS

Age at last birthday	Population					Births, by age of mother	Deaths			Age at last birthday
	Total	Males	%	Females	%		Total	Males	Females	
0	21587	10985	3.9	10602	3.7	-0	1175	638	537	0
1–4	76919	38705	13.7	38214	13.4	-0	362	194	168	1–4
5–9	92887	47154	16.7	45733	16.0	-0	90	49	41	5–9
10–14	71545	35990	12.8	35555	12.5	-0	54	38	16	10–14
15–19	52512	25629	9.1	26883	9.4	3982	73	38	35	15–19
20–24	42329	20691	7.3	21638	7.6	7264	114	64	50	20–24
25–29	36093	17297	6.1	18796	6.6	5758	94	44	50	25–29
30–34	32741	16251	5.8	16490	5.8	3924	119	48	71	30–34
35–39	29316	14573	5.2	14743	5.2	2244	130	70	60	35–39
40–44	23812	11970	4.2	11842	4.2	563	131	67	64	40–44
45–49	23887	11987	4.2	11900	4.2	62	220	137	83	45–49
50–54	18024	9438	3.3	8586	3.0	0	267	164	103	50–54
55–59	15207	7900	2.8	7307	2.6	-0	298	184	114	55–59
60–64	11291	5669	2.0	5642	2.0	-0	383	230	153	60–64
65–69	8193	3837	1.4	4356	1.5	-0	407	230	177	65–69
70–74	5130	2126	0.8	3004	1.1		329	172	157	70–74
75–79	3170	1194	0.4	1976	0.7		309	153	155	75–79
80–84	1825	560	0.2	1265	0.4	12252 M	219	96	123	80–84
85+	1133	324	0.1	809	0.3	11545 F	208	70	138	85+
All ages	567601	282260		285341		23797	4982	2686	2295	All ages

TABLE 2 LIFE TABLE FOR MALES

Age, x	$_nq_x$	l_x	$_nd_x$	$_nL_x$	$_nm_x$	T_x	$1000r_x$	$\overset{\circ}{e}_x$	$_nM_x$	Age, x
0	0.05548	100000	5548	96198	0.05768	5987391	9.45	59.87	0.05808	0
1	0.01963	94452	1854	372555	0.00498	5891194	9.45	62.37	0.00501	1
5	0.00508	92598	471	461812	0.00102	5518638	30.25	59.60	0.00104	5
10	0.00530	92127	488	459451	0.00106	5056826	59.85	54.89	0.00105	10
15	0.00750	91639	687	456667	0.00151	4597365	53.57	50.17	0.00149	15
20	0.01539	90952	1400	451352	0.00310	4140698	36.71	45.53	0.00309	20
25	0.01263	89552	1131	444911	0.00254	3689346	21.39	41.20	0.00254	25
30	0.01470	88421	1300	439050	0.00296	3244435	13.88	36.69	0.00295	30
35	0.02381	87121	2075	430638	0.00482	2805385	26.11	32.20	0.00480	35
40	0.02772	85046	2357	419867	0.00561	2374747	12.85	27.92	0.00560	40
45	0.05582	82689	4615	402775	0.01146	1954881	12.39	23.64	0.01143	45
50	0.08369	78073	6534	374723	0.01744	1552105	24.45	19.88	0.01738	50
55	0.11090	71539	7934	338967	0.02341	1177382	25.56	16.46	0.02329	55
60	0.18609	63606	11837	289604	0.04087	838415	21.19	13.18	0.04072	60
65	0.26153	51769	13539	225214	0.06012	548811	21.19	10.60	0.05994	65
70	0.33687	38230	12878	158679	0.08116	323597	21.19	8.46	0.08090	70
75	0.48235	25351	12228	95101	0.12858	164918	21.19	6.51	0.12814	75
80	0.58444	13123	7670	44620	0.17189	69817	21.19	5.32	0.17143	80
85+	1.00000	5454	5454	25196	0.21644	25196	21.19	4.62	0.21605	85+

TABLE 3 LIFE TABLE FOR FEMALES

Age, x	$_nq_x$	l_x	$_nd_x$	$_nL_x$	$_nm_x$	T_x	$1000r_x$	$\overset{\circ}{e}_x$	$_nM_x$	Age, x
0	0.04869	100000	4869	96669	0.05037	6446400	7.58	54.46	0.05065	0
1	0.01727	95131	1643	375873	0.00437	6349732	7.58	66.75	0.00440	1
5	0.00437	93488	409	466419	0.00088	5973859	30.07	63.90	0.00090	5
10	0.00227	93079	211	464911	0.00045	5507440	52.39	59.17	0.00045	10
15	0.00658	92868	611	462989	0.00132	5042530	48.33	54.30	0.00130	15
20	0.01154	92257	1064	458746	0.00232	4579541	33.63	49.64	0.00231	20
25	0.01327	91192	1210	453114	0.00267	4120794	24.18	45.19	0.00266	25
30	0.02133	89982	1920	445230	0.00431	3667680	20.43	40.76	0.00431	30
35	0.02018	88063	1777	435951	0.00408	3222450	28.67	36.59	0.00407	35
40	0.02672	86286	2306	425896	0.00541	2786499	16.06	32.29	0.00540	40
45	0.03448	83980	2895	413170	0.00701	2360603	24.40	28.11	0.00697	45
50	0.05864	81084	4755	394134	0.01206	1947433	37.22	24.02	0.01200	50
55	0.07559	76330	5770	368112	0.01567	1553299	24.66	20.35	0.01560	55
60	0.12785	70560	9021	331417	0.02722	1185187	20.26	16.80	0.02712	60
65	0.18520	61538	11397	279743	0.04074	853770	20.26	13.87	0.04063	65
70	0.23193	50141	11629	221906	0.05241	574028	20.26	11.45	0.05226	70
75	0.32981	38512	12702	160470	0.07915	352122	20.26	9.14	0.07895	75
80	0.38810	25810	10017	102842	0.09740	191652	20.26	7.43	0.09723	80
85+	1.00000	15793	15793	88810	0.17783	88810	20.26	5.62	0.17058	85+

TABLE 4 POPULATION PROJECTION, USING FIXED AGE-SPECIFIC BIRTH AND DEATH RATES, IN THOUSANDS

Age at last birthday	1966 Total	Males	Females	1971 Total	Males	Females	1976 Total	Males	Females	Age at last birthday
0–4	123	63	60	150	77	73	184	94	90	0–4
5–9	97	49	48	121	62	59	147	75	72	5–9
10–14	93	47	46	97	49	48	121	62	59	10–14
15–19	71	36	35	92	47	45	96	48	48	15–19
20–24	52	25	27	70	35	35	91	46	45	20–24
25–29	41	20	21	51	25	26	70	35	35	25–29
30–34	35	17	18	41	20	21	51	25	26	30–34
35–39	32	16	16	35	17	18	41	20	21	35–39
40–44	28	14	14	32	16	16	34	16	18	40–44
45–49	22	11	11	28	14	14	30	15	15	45–49
50–54	22	11	11	22	11	11	26	13	13	50–54
55–59	17	9	8	21	10	11	20	10	10	55–59
60–64	14	7	7	14	7	7	19	9	10	60–64
65–69	9	4	5	11	5	6	12	6	6	65–69
70–74	6	3	3	7	3	4	8	4	4	70–74
75–79	3	1	2	4	2	2	5	2	3	75–79
80–84	2	1	1	2	1	1	3	1	2	80–84
85 +	1	0	1	1	0	1	1	0	1	85 +
All ages	668	334	334	799	401	398	959	481	478	All ages

TABLE 5 OBSERVED AND PROJECTED VITAL RATES

Rates per thousand	Observed Total	Males	Females	Projected 1966 Males	Females	1971 Males	Females	1976 Males	Females	Stable Males	Females
Birth	41.93	43.41	40.46	43.59	40.89	45.31	42.78	46.16	43.81	45.02	43.95
Death	8.78	9.52	8.05	9.42	8.00	9.23	7.82	9.03	7.71	8.05	6.97
Increase	33.15	33.89	32.41	34.17	32.89	36.09	34.95	37.13	36.10		36.9763

TABLE 6 RATES STANDARDIZED ON THREE STANDARD COUNTRIES

Standardized rates per thousand	England and Wales, 1961 Total	Males	Females	United States, 1960 Total	Males	Females	Mexico, 1960 Total	Males	Females
Birth	39.55	48.20*	37.19	40.39	44.21*	38.61	46.34	45.36*	44.85
Death	16.63	21.60*	15.76	14.07	17.33*	12.36	8.57	9.27*	7.41
Increase	22.93	26.59*	21.44	26.32	26.87*	25.25	37.78	36.09*	37.44

TABLE 7 VITAL STATISTICS AND RATES INFERRED FROM AGE DISTRIBUTIONS (FEMALES)

Vital statistics		Thompson Age range	NRR	1000r	Interval	Bourgeois-Pichat Age range	NRR	1000b	1000d	1000r	Coale
TFR	6.17	0–4	2.51	33.75	27.27	5–29	3.29	46.31	2.24	44.08	1000b
GRR	2.99	5–9	2.71	37.50	27.20	30–54	1.93	29.08	4.64	24.44	1000d
NRR	2.70	10–14	2.38	31.25	27.11	55–79	1.95	28.60	3.86	24.75	1000r
Generation	26.84	15–19	2.03	26.32	26.97	*50–74	1.91	26.99	3.10	23.89	$1000k_1$
Sex ratio	106.12										$1000k_2$

TABLE 8 LESLIE MATRIX AND ITS ANALYSIS (FEMALES)

Start of age interval	Sub-diagonal	First row	Percent in stable population	Fisher values	Total reproductive values	Net maternity function	Matrix equation coefficient	Parameters	Integral	Matrix
0	0.98702	0.00000	18.999	1.160	56614	0.00000	0.00000	λ_1	1.2031	1.2041
5	0.99674	0.00000	15.574	1.415	64702	0.00000	0.00000	λ_2	0.3564	0.3691
10	0.99584	0.16907	12.893	1.709	60765	0.00000	0.16635		+0.8341	+0.8071 i
15	0.99078	0.55111	10.663	1.870	50258	0.33271	0.53993	r_1	0.0370	0.0371
20	0.98764	0.73170	8.774	1.627	35202	0.74714	0.71028	r_2	−0.0195	−0.0239
25	0.98249	0.61915	7.197	1.124	21130	0.67342	0.59371		+0.2334	+0.2284 i
30	0.97902	0.44358	5.873	0.647	10667	0.51400	0.41796	c_1		2674
35	0.97677	0.22765	4.775	0.270	3982	0.32192	0.21008	c_2		1934
40	0.97012	0.06015	3.874	0.063	742	0.09823	0.05434			4928 i
45	0.95413	0.00599	3.121	0.006	70	0.01044	0.00522	$2\pi/y$	26.920	27.513
50	0.93415	0.00013	2.473	0.000	1	0.00000	0.00000	Δ	5.403	
55	0.80475		5.785							

Peru, 1963

TABLE 1 DATA INPUT TO COMPUTATIONS

Age at last birthday	Population					Births, by age of mother	Deaths			Age at last birthday
	Total	Males	%	Females	%		Total	Males	Females	
0	418384	210896	3.8	207488	3.8	0	34063	18236	15827	0
1–4	1496822	756632	13.8	740190	13.5	0	22014	10929	11085	1–4
5–9	1627460	817307	14.9	810153	14.8	0	3564	1807	1757	5–9
10–14	1304963	666897	12.1	638066	11.6	452	1875	959	915	10–14
15–19	1106721	560839	10.2	545882	10.0	42827	2241	1153	1088	15–19
20–24	934639	468221	8.5	466418	8.5	109665	2765	1360	1405	20–24
25–29	803317	398138	7.2	405179	7.4	101763	2651	1292	1359	25–29
30–34	673028	338977	6.2	334051	6.1	68943	2813	1434	1379	30–34
35–39	579667	286173	5.2	293494	5.4	47815	2804	1355	1449	35–39
40–44	468481	234242	4.3	234239	4.3	16345	2596	1389	1207	40–44
45–49	397127	195582	3.6	201545	3.7	18929	2809	1554	1255	45–49
50–54	320176	157615	2.9	162561	3.0	7648	2854	1640	1214	50–54
55–59	251434	123003	2.2	128431	2.3	6826	2900	1723	1177	55–59
60–64	221528	110179	2.0	111349	2.0	0	4713	2622	2091	60–64
65–69	143113	66810	1.2	76303	1.4	0	3587	1897	1690	65–69
70–74	104574	46304	0.8	58270	1.1		3468	1782	1685	70–74
75–79	65292	28786	0.5	36506	0.7		3110	1540	1570	75–79
80–84	35276	16142	0.3	19134	0.3	217196 M	2610	1235	1375	80–84
85 +	27553	14467	0.3	13086	0.2	204017 F	6651	2595	4056	85 +
All ages	10979555	5497210		5482345		421213	110088	56502	53585	All ages

TABLE 2 LIFE TABLE FOR MALES

Age, x	$_nq_x$	l_x	$_nd_x$	$_nL_x$	$_nm_x$	T_x	$1000r_x$	$\overset{\circ}{e}_x$	$_nM_x$	Age, x
0	0.08188	100000	8188	94921	0.08626	6052586	3.70	60.53	0.08647	0
1	0.05549	91812	5095	353388	0.01442	5957665	3.70	64.89	0.01444	1
5	0.01063	86717	922	431279	0.00214	5604277	32.44	64.63	0.00221	5
10	0.00716	85795	614	427427	0.00144	5172998	35.92	60.30	0.00144	10
15	0.01028	85180	876	423838	0.00207	4745571	33.28	55.71	0.00206	15
20	0.01446	84305	1219	418572	0.00291	4321733	31.47	51.26	0.00290	20
25	0.01614	83086	1341	412179	0.00325	3903151	28.89	46.98	0.00325	25
30	0.02098	81745	1715	404548	0.00424	3490982	28.91	42.71	0.00423	30
35	0.02346	80030	1877	395575	0.00475	3086434	32.07	38.57	0.00473	35
40	0.02934	78152	2293	385256	0.00595	2690859	31.96	34.43	0.00593	40
45	0.03913	75859	2968	372174	0.00797	2305603	31.59	30.39	0.00795	45
50	0.05097	72891	3715	355532	0.01045	1933429	35.81	26.52	0.01041	50
55	0.06807	69176	4709	334855	0.01406	1577898	20.38	22.81	0.01401	55
60	0.11318	64467	7296	304703	0.02395	1243042	47.66	19.28	0.02380	60
65	0.13330	57171	7621	267109	0.02853	938339	47.66	16.41	0.02839	65
70	0.17684	49550	8762	226276	0.03872	671231	47.66	13.55	0.03848	70
75	0.23762	40788	9692	179973	0.05385	444954	47.66	10.91	0.05350	75
80	0.32250	31096	10028	130221	0.07701	264982	47.66	8.52	0.07651	80
85 +	1.00000	21067	21067	134761	0.15633	134761	47.66	6.40	0.17937	85 +

TABLE 3 LIFE TABLE FOR FEMALES

Age, x	$_nq_x$	l_x	$_nd_x$	$_nL_x$	$_nm_x$	T_x	$1000r_x$	$\overset{\circ}{e}_x$	$_nM_x$	Age, x
0	0.07272	100000	7272	95602	0.07607	6277673	4.47	62.78	0.07628	0
1	0.05748	92728	5330	356621	0.01495	6182071	4.47	66.67	0.01498	1
5	0.01038	87398	908	434720	0.00209	5825449	34.73	66.65	0.00217	5
10	0.00715	86490	618	430895	0.00143	5390730	37.77	62.33	0.00144	10
15	0.00997	85872	856	427357	0.00200	4959835	29.25	57.76	0.00199	15
20	0.01499	85016	1274	422007	0.00302	4532478	26.95	53.31	0.00301	20
25	0.01667	83742	1396	415304	0.00336	4110472	29.91	49.09	0.00335	25
30	0.02048	82346	1687	407632	0.00414	3695168	28.10	44.87	0.00413	30
35	0.02442	80659	1970	398438	0.00494	3287536	30.69	40.76	0.00494	35
40	0.02548	78689	2005	388515	0.00516	2889097	32.23	36.72	0.00515	40
45	0.03074	76684	2357	377680	0.00624	2500582	30.28	32.61	0.00623	45
50	0.03679	74327	2734	364982	0.00749	2122903	37.62	28.56	0.00747	50
55	0.04518	71593	3234	350598	0.00923	1757921	26.85	24.55	0.00916	55
60	0.09052	68358	6188	327015	0.01892	1407323	51.59	20.59	0.01878	60
65	0.10550	62170	6559	294742	0.02225	1380308	51.59	17.38	0.02215	65
70	0.13613	55611	7570	259732	0.02915	785566	51.59	14.13	0.02893	70
75	0.19660	48041	9445	217491	0.04343	525834	51.59	10.95	0.04301	75
80	0.30777	38596	11879	163747	0.07254	308343	51.59	7.99	0.07185	80
85 +	1.00000	26718	26718	144596	0.18477	144596	51.59	5.41	0.30995	85 +

TABLE 4 POPULATION PROJECTION, USING FIXED AGE-SPECIFIC BIRTH AND DEATH RATES, IN THOUSANDS

Age at last birthday	1968 Total	Males	Females	1973 Total	Males	Females	1978 Total	Males	Females	Age at last birthday
0–4	2043	1049	994	2374	1219	1155	2785	1430	1355	0–4
5–9	1842	931	911	1964	1009	955	2283	1173	1110	5–9
10–14	1613	810	803	1825	922	903	1947	1000	947	10–14
15–19	1294	661	633	1599	803	796	1811	915	896	15–19
20–24	1093	554	539	1278	653	625	1579	793	786	20–24
25–29	920	461	459	1075	545	530	1258	643	615	25–29
30–34	789	391	398	904	453	451	1056	535	521	30–34
35–39	658	331	327	771	382	389	882	442	440	35–39
40–44	565	279	286	641	323	318	751	372	379	40–44
45–49	454	226	228	547	269	278	622	312	310	45–49
50–54	382	187	195	436	216	220	526	257	259	50–54
55–59	304	148	156	363	176	187	415	204	211	55–59
60–64	232	112	120	281	135	146	335	160	175	60–64
65–69	197	97	100	206	98	108	249	118	131	65–69
70–74	124	57	67	170	82	88	178	83	95	70–74
75–79	86	37	49	101	45	56	139	65	74	75–79
80–84	48	21	27	64	27	37	75	33	42	80–84
85 +	34	17	17	46	22	24	60	28	32	85 +
All ages	12678	6369	6309	14645	7379	7266	16951	8563	8388	All ages

TABLE 5 OBSERVED AND PROJECTED VITAL RATES

Rates per thousand	Observed Total	Males	Females	Projected 1968 Males	Females	1973 Males	Females	1978 Males	Females	Stable Males	Females
Birth	38.36	39.51	37.21	39.38	37.34	39.71	37.87	40.28	38.62	38.40	37.73
Death	10.03	10.28	9.77	10.07	9.60	10.24	9.93	10.42	10.23	10.84	10.17
Increase	28.34	29.23	27.44	29.31	27.74	29.47	27.94	29.85	28.39		27.5595

TABLE 6 RATES STANDARDIZED ON THREE STANDARD COUNTRIES

Standardized rates per thousand	England and Wales, 1961 Total	Males	Females	United States, 1960 Total	Males	Females	Mexico, 1960 Total	Males	Females
Birth	39.11	39.34*	36.72	38.39	35.88*	36.64	38.97	38.14*	37.65
Death	13.00	21.47*	13.76	11.92	17.73*	11.92	9.42	9.59*	9.02
Increase	26.11	17.87*	22.96	26.47	18.15*	24.72	29.56	28.54*	28.64

TABLE 7 VITAL STATISTICS AND RATES INFERRED FROM AGE DISTRIBUTIONS (FEMALES)

Vital statistics		Thompson Age range	NRR	$1000r$	Interval	Bourgeois-Pichat Age range	NRR	$1000b$	$1000d$	$1000r$	Coale	
TFR	5.99	0–4	2.26	29.94	27.25	5–29	2.36	41.52	9.78	31.74	$1000b$	41.83
GRR	2.90	5–9	2.32	31.64	27.18	30–54	2.30	41.46	10.62	30.84	$1000d$	10.30
NRR	2.35	10–14	2.14	27.36	27.13	55–79	2.57	51.43	16.53	34.90	$1000r$	31.54
Generation	30.97	15–19	2.16	28.41	27.07	*10–34	2.19	38.87	9.81	29.06	$1000k_1$	0.
Sex ratio	106.5										$1000k_2$	0.

TABLE 8 LESLIE MATRIX AND ITS ANALYSIS (FEMALES)

Start of age interval	Sub-diagonal	First row	Percent in stable population	Fisher values	Total reproductive values	Net maternity function	Matrix equation coefficient	Parameters	Integral	Matrix
0	0.96129	0.00000	16.423	1.185	1123009	0.00000	0.00000	λ_1	1.1477	1.1515
5	0.99120	0.00077	13.661	1.425	1154144	0.00000	0.00074	λ_2	0.3560	0.3341
10	0.99179	0.08599	11.717	1.660	1059215	0.00148	0.08194		+0.8301	+0.8375i
15	0.98748	0.34020	10.056	1.832	999815	0.16240	0.32149	r_1	0.0276	0.0282
20	0.98412	0.52820	8.592	1.735	809339	0.48059	0.49290	r_2	-0.0204	-0.0207
25	0.98153	0.49691	7.317	1.402	567920	0.50521	0.45635		+0.2331	+0.2382i
30	0.97745	0.40043	6.215	1.050	350876	0.40748	0.36094	c_1		55766
35	0.97509	0.25294	5.256	0.756	222003	0.31441	0.22286	c_2		58778
40	0.97211	0.17641	4.435	0.589	137985	0.13131	0.15156			74412i
45	0.96638	0.19709	3.731	0.485	97801	0.17181	0.12749	$2\pi/y$	26.951	26.373
50	0.96059	0.15342	3.120	0.339	55046	0.08317	0.08671	Δ	2.951	
55	0.83942		9.476							

[373]

Uruguay, 1963

TABLE 1 DATA INPUT TO COMPUTATIONS

Age at last birthday	Population Total	Males	%	Females	%	Births, by age of mother	Deaths Total	Males	Females	Age at last birthday
0	51286	25764	2.0	25522	1.9	0	3533	2051	1482	0
1–4	209966	109114	8.3	100852	7.6	0	378	190	188	1–4
5–9	250878	126974	9.6	123904	9.3	0	151	77	74	5–9
10–14	229395	117120	8.9	112275	8.5	124	126	79	47	10–14
15–19	212446	105316	8.0	107130	8.1	6309	230	152	78	15–19
20–24	197951	99054	7.5	98897	7.4	15755	318	197	121	20–24
25–29	191585	93614	7.1	97971	7.4	15131	319	197	122	25–29
30–34	207100	102749	7.8	104351	7.9	11465	463	258	205	30–34
35–39	192918	95359	7.2	97559	7.3	6069	588	359	229	35–39
40–44	173387	86839	6.6	86548	6.5	2004	807	506	301	40–44
45–49	152938	75035	5.7	77903	5.9	253	1013	651	362	45–49
50–54	145837	74932	5.7	70905	5.3	31	1607	1052	555	50–54
55–59	120451	62512	4.7	57939	4.4	0	2003	1361	642	55–59
60–64	104940	51529	3.9	53411	4.0	0	2783	1843	940	60–64
65–69	79556	37774	2.9	41782	3.1	0	3091	1914	1177	65–69
70–74	58587	28023	2.1	30564	2.3		3307	1847	1460	70–74
75–79	36184	15808	1.2	20376	1.5		3283	1739	1544	75–79
80–84	19739	7801	0.6	11938	0.9	29464 M	2717	1249	1468	80–84
85 +	12750	4106	0.3	8644	0.7	27677 F	3163	1196	1967	85 +
All ages	2647894	1319423		1328471		57141	29880	16918	12962	All ages

TABLE 2 LIFE TABLE FOR MALES

Age, x	$_nq_x$	l_x	$_nd_x$	$_nL_x$	$_nm_x$	T_x	$1000r_x$	$\overset{\circ}{e}_x$	$_nM_x$	Age, x
0	0.07468	100000	7468	93816	0.07961	6137219	0.00	61.37	0.07961	0
1	0.00693	92532	641	368238	0.00174	6043403	0.00	65.31	0.00174	1
5	0.00302	91890	277	458759	0.00060	5675165	13.10	61.76	0.00061	5
10	0.00338	91613	310	457371	0.00068	5216406	17.88	56.94	0.00067	10
15	0.00721	91303	659	454992	0.00145	4759036	15.36	52.12	0.00144	15
20	0.00990	90645	898	451038	0.00199	4304044	9.88	47.48	0.00199	20
25	0.01047	89747	939	446430	0.00210	3853006	0.00	42.93	0.00210	25
30	0.01248	88808	1108	441413	0.00251	3406575	0.00	38.36	0.00251	30
35	0.01870	87699	1640	434681	0.00377	2965152	12.91	33.81	0.00375	35
40	0.02883	86059	2481	424491	0.00585	2530481	18.03	29.40	0.00583	40
45	0.04257	83578	3558	409611	0.00869	2105991	5.60	25.20	0.00868	45
50	0.06801	80020	5442	387367	0.01405	1696379	3.86	21.20	0.01404	50
55	0.10384	74578	7744	354691	0.02183	1309013	14.39	17.55	0.02177	55
60	0.16497	66833	11025	307611	0.03584	954322	12.85	14.28	0.03577	60
65	0.22539	55808	12578	247852	0.05075	646710	12.85	11.59	0.05067	65
70	0.28362	43230	12261	185655	0.06604	398858	12.85	9.23	0.06591	70
75	0.43079	30969	13341	120997	0.11026	213204	12.85	6.88	0.11001	75
80	0.56112	17628	9891	61652	0.16041	92206	12.85	5.23	0.16011	80
85 +	1.00000	7736	7736	30544	0.25328	30544	12.85	3.95	0.29128	85 +

TABLE 3 LIFE TABLE FOR FEMALES

Age, x	$_nq_x$	l_x	$_nd_x$	$_nL_x$	$_nm_x$	T_x	$1000r_x$	$\overset{\circ}{e}_x$	$_nM_x$	Age, x
0	0.05552	100000	5552	95611	0.05807	6816039	0.00	68.16	0.05807	0
1	0.00742	94448	700	375743	0.00186	6720428	0.00	71.15	0.00186	1
5	0.00297	93748	278	468043	0.00059	6344685	10.87	67.68	0.00060	5
10	0.00209	93469	196	466871	0.00042	5876642	14.02	62.87	0.00042	10
15	0.00364	93274	340	465597	0.00073	5409771	11.92	58.00	0.00073	15
20	0.00610	92934	567	463300	0.00122	4944175	7.83	53.20	0.00122	20
25	0.00621	92367	573	460468	0.00125	4480875	0.00	48.51	0.00125	25
30	0.00978	91793	897	456825	0.00196	4020406	0.00	43.80	0.00195	30
35	0.01170	90896	1063	451958	0.00235	3563582	16.19	39.21	0.00235	35
40	0.01729	89833	1553	445482	0.00349	3111624	19.06	34.64	0.00348	40
45	0.02305	88279	2035	436678	0.00466	2666142	14.86	30.20	0.00465	45
50	0.03857	86244	3327	423416	0.00786	2229464	21.84	25.85	0.00783	50
55	0.05416	82918	4490	404054	0.01111	1806048	16.61	21.78	0.01108	55
60	0.08476	78427	6648	376563	0.01765	1401994	15.69	17.88	0.01760	60
65	0.13250	71780	9511	336523	0.02826	1025431	15.69	14.29	0.02817	65
70	0.21482	62269	13377	279180	0.04791	688908	15.69	11.05	0.04777	70
75	0.31995	48892	15643	205841	0.07600	409728	15.69	8.38	0.07578	75
80	0.47272	33249	15718	127345	0.12343	203887	15.69	6.13	0.12297	80
85 +	*1.00000	17531	17531	76542	0.22904	76542	15.69	4.37	0.22756	85 +

TABLE 4   POPULATION PROJECTION, USING FIXED AGE-SPECIFIC BIRTH AND DEATH RATES, IN THOUSANDS

Age at last birthday	1968			1973			1978			Age at last birthday
	Total	Males	Females	Total	Males	Females	Total	Males	Females	
0–4	270	138	132	278	142	136	292	149	143	0–4
5–9	259	134	125	268	137	131	276	141	135	5–9
10–14	251	127	124	259	134	125	267	136	131	10–14
15–19	229	117	112	249	126	123	258	133	125	15–19
20–24	211	104	107	226	115	111	248	125	123	20–24
25–29	196	98	98	209	103	106	225	114	111	25–29
30–34	190	93	97	195	97	98	207	102	105	30–34
35–39	204	101	103	187	91	96	191	95	96	35–39
40–44	189	93	96	201	99	102	184	89	95	40–44
45–49	169	84	85	184	90	94	195	95	100	45–49
50–54	147	71	76	161	79	82	176	85	91	50–54
55–59	137	69	68	137	65	72	151	73	78	55–59
60–64	108	54	54	123	60	63	123	55	67	60–64
65–69	90	42	48	92	44	48	104	48	56	65–69
70–74	63	28	35	71	31	40	73	33	40	70–74
75–79	41	18	23	44	18	26	49	20	29	75–79
80–84	21	8	13	23	9	14	25	9	16	80–84
85 +	11	4	7	12	4	8	13	5	8	85 +
All ages	2786	1383	1403	2919	1444	1475	3057	1508	1549	All ages

TABLE 5   OBSERVED AND PROJECTED VITAL RATES

Rates per thousand	Observed			Projected						Stable	
				1968		1973		1978			
	Total	Males	Females	Males	Females	Males	Females	Males	Females	Males	Females
Birth	21.58	22.33	20.83	21.84	20.23	21.74	20.00	21.95	20.07	21.82	20.07
Death	11.28	12.82	9.76	12.84	9.67	12.95	9.95	13.08	10.29	13.02	11.27
Increase	10.30	9.51	11.08	9.00	10.56	8.79	10.05	8.86	9.78		8.7941

TABLE 6   RATES STANDARDIZED ON THREE STANDARD COUNTRIES

Standardized rates per thousand	England and Wales, 1961			United States, 1960			Mexico, 1960		
	Total	Males	Females	Total	Males	Females	Total	Males	Females
Birth	18.31	20.35*	17.19	18.67	19.15*	17.82	21.48	18.23*	20.75
Death	14.83	16.46*	13.89	12.53	14.31*	10.69	7.58	11.16*	5.14
Increase	3.48	3.89*	3.30	6.14	4.84*	7.13	13.90	7.07*	14.61

TABLE 7   VITAL STATISTICS AND RATES INFERRED FROM AGE DISTRIBUTIONS (FEMALES)

Vital statistics		Thompson				Bourgeois-Pichat				Coale	
		Age range	NRR	$1000r$	Interval	Age range	NRR	$1000b$	$1000d$	$1000r$	
TFR	2.86	0–4	1.24	7.98	27.38	5–29	1.35	21.17	10.05	11.12	$1000b$ 20.56
GRR	1.39	5–9	1.28	8.97	27.33	30–54	1.55	29.35	13.12	16.23	$1000d$ 12.62
NRR	1.27	10–14	1.20	6.71	27.26	55–79	1.66	33.06	14.21	18.86	$1000r$ 7.94
Generation	27.56	15–19	1.22	7.05	27.16	*30–54	1.55	29.35	13.12	16.23	$1000k_1$ 9.51
Sex ratio	106.5										$1000k_2$ 0.23

TABLE 8   LESLIE MATRIX AND ITS ANALYSIS (FEMALES)

Start of age interval	Sub-diagonal	First row	Percent in stable population	Fisher values	Total reproductive values	Net maternity function	Matrix equation coefficient	Parameters		
									Integral	Matrix
0	0.99298	0.00000	9.255	1.084	137023	0.00000	0.00000	λ_1	1.0450	1.0450
5	0.99750	0.00126	8.795	1.141	141383	0.00000	0.00125	λ_2	0.3642	0.3745
10	0.99728	0.06830	8.395	1.194	134060	0.00250	0.06765		+0.7376	+0.7162 i
15	0.99509	0.24819	8.011	1.177	126081	0.13281	0.24515	r_1	0.0088	0.0088
20	0.99389	0.35708	7.629	0.966	95485	0.35749	0.35098	r_2	-0.0390	-0.0426
25	0.99209	0.30073	7.256	0.626	61291	0.34446	0.29378		+0.2224	+0.2178 i
30	0.98936	0.19568	6.888	0.330	34466	0.24311	0.18964	c_1		13613
35	0.98567	0.09707	6.522	0.134	13113	0.13618	0.09307	c_2		6054
40	0.98022	0.03007	6.151	0.036	3092	0.04996	0.02842			-6 i
45	0.96961	0.00419	5.770	0.005	376	0.00687	0.00388	$2\pi/y$	28.247	28.848
50	0.95427	0.00050	5.354	0.001	37	0.00090	0.00045	Δ	3.270	
55	0.78921		19.974							

Venezuela, 1965

TABLE 1 DATA INPUT TO COMPUTATIONS

Age at last birthday	Population					Births, by age of mother	Deaths			Age at last birthday
	Total	Males	%	Females	%		Total	Males	Females	
0	355511	180723	4.1	174788	4.1	0	18096	10044	8052	0
1–4	1234094	627729	14.2	606365	14.1	0	6894	3422	3472	1–4
5–9	1276640	651426	14.7	625214	14.6	0	1630	897	733	5–9
10–14	1094445	561572	12.7	532873	12.4	1011	903	516	387	10–14
15–19	862490	436961	9.9	425529	9.9	54133	1148	685	463	15–19
20–24	685281	338539	7.6	346742	8.1	107945	1344	891	453	20–24
25–29	598937	304681	6.9	294256	6.9	95344	1310	802	508	25–29
30–34	539245	278551	6.3	260694	6.1	62628	1438	869	569	30–34
35–39	486913	253721	5.7	233192	5.4	43426	1696	931	765	35–39
40–44	385840	201617	4.6	184223	4.3	12291	1811	1034	777	40–44
45–49	317102	167123	3.8	149979	3.5	2495	2061	1230	831	45–49
50–54	274119	140309	3.2	133810	3.1	257	2648	1539	1109	50–54
55–59	198714	99727	2.3	98987	2.3	0	2676	1574	1102	55–59
60–64	151829	76602	1.7	75227	1.8	0	3795	2061	1734	60–64
65–69	114331	52258	1.2	62073	1.4	0	2950	1623	1327	65–69
70–74	73506	30920	0.7	42586	1.0		2979	1540	1439	70–74
75–79	40810	16007	0.4	24803	0.6		2359	1155	1204	75–79
80–84	19694	7291	0.2	12403	0.3	193557 M	2346	936	1410	80–84
85+	12711	4429	0.1	8282	0.2	185973 F	3484	1175	2309	85+
All ages	8722212	4430186		4292026		379530	61568	32924	28644	All ages

TABLE 2 LIFE TABLE FOR MALES

Age, x	$_nq_x$	l_x	$_nd_x$	$_nL_x$	$_nm_x$	T_x	$1000r_x$	$\overset{\circ}{e}_x$	$_nM_x$	Age, x
0	0.05318	100000	5318	96430	0.05514	6389719	10.78	63.90	0.05558	0
1	0.02132	94682	2019	373050	0.00541	6293289	10.78	66.47	0.00545	1
5	0.00673	92664	624	461760	0.00135	5920239	34.22	63.89	0.00138	5
10	0.00459	92040	423	459164	0.00092	5458480	38.77	59.31	0.00092	10
15	0.00790	91617	723	456438	0.00159	4999315	48.95	54.57	0.00157	15
20	0.01311	90894	1192	451583	0.00264	4542877	33.66	49.98	0.00263	20
25	0.01308	89702	1174	445613	0.00263	4091294	16.75	45.61	0.00263	25
30	0.01550	88528	1372	439298	0.00312	3645681	15.19	41.18	0.00312	30
35	0.01825	87156	1590	431974	0.00368	3206382	28.47	36.79	0.00367	35
40	0.02547	85566	2180	422682	0.00516	2774408	36.48	32.42	0.00513	40
45	0.03634	83387	3030	409804	0.00739	2351727	28.60	28.20	0.00736	45
50	0.05379	80356	4323	391560	0.01104	1941923	40.47	24.17	0.01097	50
55	0.07675	76034	5835	366538	0.01592	1550364	43.22	20.39	0.01578	55
60	0.12707	70198	8920	329332	0.02708	1183826	53.69	16.86	0.02691	60
65	0.14536	61278	8907	284708	0.03129	854494	53.69	13.94	0.03106	65
70	0.22386	52371	11724	233306	0.05025	569786	53.69	10.88	0.04981	70
75	0.30889	40647	12556	172257	0.07289	336480	53.69	8.28	0.07216	75
80	0.48751	28092	13695	105543	0.12976	164223	53.69	5.85	0.12838	80
85+	1.00000	14397	14397	58680	0.24534	58680	53.69	4.08	0.26530	85+

TABLE 3 LIFE TABLE FOR FEMALES

Age, x	$_nq_x$	l_x	$_nd_x$	$_nL_x$	$_nm_x$	T_x	$1000r_x$	$\overset{\circ}{e}_x$	$_nM_x$	Age, x
0	0.04440	100000	4440	97132	0.04571	6770180	11.04	67.70	0.04607	0
1	0.02240	95560	2141	376304	0.00569	6673048	11.04	69.83	0.00573	1
5	0.00569	93419	532	465767	0.00114	6296744	36.15	67.40	0.00117	5
10	0.00362	92887	336	463590	0.00073	5830977	37.57	62.77	0.00073	10
15	0.00545	92551	505	461549	0.00109	5367387	41.93	57.99	0.00109	15
20	0.00654	92046	602	458787	0.00131	4905838	35.53	53.30	0.00131	20
25	0.00862	91445	788	455334	0.00173	4447051	26.80	48.63	0.00173	25
30	0.01089	90657	987	450956	0.00219	3991717	20.93	44.03	0.00218	30
35	0.01634	89669	1465	444862	0.00329	3540762	31.48	39.49	0.00328	35
40	0.02097	88204	1850	436584	0.00424	3095899	39.84	35.10	0.00422	40
45	0.02745	86354	2371	426174	0.00556	2659315	26.12	30.80	0.00554	45
50	0.04083	83984	3429	411773	0.00833	2233141	33.38	26.59	0.00829	50
55	0.05491	80555	4423	392739	0.01126	1821368	44.25	22.61	0.01113	55
60	0.10951	76132	8337	360333	0.02314	1428629	36.94	18.77	0.02305	60
65	0.10186	67794	6905	321964	0.02145	1068296	36.94	15.76	0.02138	65
70	0.15713	60889	9568	281438	0.03400	746332	36.94	12.26	0.03379	70
75	0.21990	51321	11285	230168	0.04903	464894	36.94	9.06	0.04854	75
80	0.45173	40036	18086	157188	0.11506	234726	36.94	5.86	0.11368	80
85+	*1.00000	21950	21950	77539	0.28309	77539	36.94	3.53	0.27880	85+

TABLE 4 POPULATION PROJECTION, USING FIXED AGE-SPECIFIC BIRTH AND DEATH RATES, IN THOUSANDS

Age at last birthday	1970			1975			1980			Age at last birthday
	Total	Males	Females	Total	Males	Females	Total	Males	Females	
0–4	1951	991	960	2322	1179	1143	2788	1416	1372	0–4
5–9	1563	795	768	1920	975	945	2284	1160	1124	5–9
10–14	1270	648	622	1556	791	765	1909	969	940	10–14
15–19	1089	558	531	1264	644	620	1548	786	762	15–19
20–24	855	432	423	1079	552	527	1253	637	516	20–24
25–29	678	334	344	847	427	420	1068	545	523	25–29
30–34	591	300	291	670	329	341	837	421	416	30–34
35–39	531	274	257	582	295	287	660	324	336	35–39
40–44	477	248	229	520	268	252	571	289	282	40–44
45–49	375	195	180	464	241	223	506	260	246	45–49
50–54	305	160	145	361	187	174	446	230	216	50–54
55–59	259	131	128	287	149	138	341	175	166	55–59
60–64	181	90	91	235	118	117	251	134	127	60–64
65–69	133	66	67	158	77	81	207	102	105	65–69
70–74	97	43	54	113	54	59	134	63	71	70–74
75–79	58	23	35	76	32	44	88	40	48	75–79
80–84	27	10	17	38	14	24	49	19	30	80–84
85 +	10	4	6	13	5	8	20	8	12	85 +
All ages	10450	5302	5148	12505	6337	6168	14970	7578	7392	All ages

TABLE 5   OBSERVED AND PROJECTED VITAL RATES

Rates per thousand	Observed			Projected						Stable	
				1970		1975		1980			
	Total	Males	Females	Males	Females	Males	Females	Males	Females	Males	Females
Birth	43.51	43.69	43.33	43.11	42.67	43.19	42.64	43.46	42.81	44.98	43.95
Death	7.06	7.43	6.67	7.57	6.60	7.69	6.68	7.78	6.71	7.39	6.35
Increase	36.45	36.26	36.66	35.54	36.06	35.50	35.96	35.68	36.11		37.5941

TABLE 6   RATES STANDARDIZED ON THREE STANDARD COUNTRIES

Standardized rates per thousand	England and Wales, 1961			United States, 1960			Mexico, 1960		
	Total	Males	Females	Total	Males	Females	Total	Males	Females
Birth	41.08	44.60*	39.01	41.82	41.10*	40.38	45.58	42.25*	45.53
Death	12.83	18.18*	13.19	10.97	14.37*	10.41	7.02	7.29*	6.33
Increase	28.25	26.42*	25.82	30.85	26.73*	29.96	39.56	34.97*	39.21

TABLE 7   VITAL STATISTICS AND RATES INFERRED FROM AGE DISTRIBUTIONS (FEMALES)

Vital statistics		Thompson				Bourgeois-Pichat					Coale	
		Age range	NRR	$1000r$	Interval	Age range	NRR	$1000b$	$1000d$	$1000r$		
TFR	6.38	0–4	2.56	34.38	27.36	5–29	2.76	41.85	4.22	37.63	$1000b$	
GRR	3.13	5–9	2.44	33.45	27.29	30–54	2.31	37.39	6.38	31.01	$1000d$	
NRR	2.83	10–14	2.40	31.41	27.21	55–79	2.39	37.41	5.21	32.21	$1000r$	
Generation	27.70	15–19	2.23	29.54	27.11	*5–29	2.76	41.85	4.22	37.63	$1000k_1$	
Sex ratio	104.08										$1000k_2$	

TABLE 8   LESLIE MATRIX AND ITS ANALYSIS (FEMALES)

Start of age interval	Sub-diagonal	First row	Percent in stable population	Fisher values	Total reproductive values	Net maternity function	Matrix equation coefficient	Parameters		
									Integral	Matrix
0	0.98380	0.00000	19.008	1.159	905543	0.00000	0.00300	λ_1	1.2068	1.2078
5	0.99533	0.00219	15.482	1.423	889799	0.00000	0.00215	λ_2	0.3904	0.4010
10	0.99560	0.14911	12.759	1.724	918911	0.00431	0.14601		+0.8222	+0.7975 i
15	0.99402	0.50650	10.517	1.918	816328	0.28771	0.49378	r_1	0.0376	0.0378
20	0.99247	0.73411	8.656	1.740	603427	0.69986	0.71140	r_2	−0.0188	−0.0227
25	0.99038	0.55182	7.112	1.260	370871	0.72294	0.62690		+0.2255	+0.2210 i
30	0.98649	0.49175	5.832	0.774	201804	0.53085	0.46840	c_1		41152
35	0.98139	0.29196	4.763	0.370	86258	0.40594	0.27434	c_2		3642
40	0.97615	0.09622	3.871	0.110	20333	0.14273	0.08873			−30586 i
45	0.96621	0.02145	3.128	0.022	3345	0.03474	0.01931	$2\pi/y$	27.864	28.432
50	0.95377	0.00223	2.502	0.002	287	0.00388	0.00194	Δ	3.419	
55	0.83306		6.369							

Ceylon, 1963

TABLE 1 DATA INPUT TO COMPUTATIONS

Age at last birthday	Population					Births, by age of mother	Deaths			Age at last birthday
	Total	Males	%	Females	%		Total	Males	Females	
0	338734	171867	3.1	166867	3.3	0	20406	11318	9088	0
1–4	1270308	648791	11.8	621517	12.2	0	11886	5442	6444	1–4
5–9	1469736	740814	13.5	728922	14.3	0	2952	1430	1522	5–9
10–14	1340469	686122	12.5	654347	12.9	174	1491	800	691	10–14
15–19	1028981	524105	9.5	504876	9.9	26198	1536	759	777	15–19
20–24	889995	443022	8.1	446973	8.8	100946	2085	908	1177	20–24
25–29	752440	378632	6.9	373808	7.4	102961	2106	935	1171	25–29
30–34	674956	356555	6.5	318401	6.3	75615	1919	881	1038	30–34
35–39	653301	341702	6.2	311599	6.1	48877	2380	1190	1190	35–39
40–44	472952	259914	4.7	213038	4.2	9768	2208	1203	1005	40–44
45–49	447345	248846	4.5	198499	3.9	1303	2865	1687	1178	45–49
50–54	347602	193643	3.5	153959	3.0	0	2823	1741	1082	50–54
55–59	271794	157035	2.9	114759	2.3	0	3507	2148	1359	55–59
60–64	245433	141600	2.6	103833	2.0	0	4396	2718	1678	60–64
65–69	150668	84656	1.5	66012	1.3	0	5157	2959	2198	65–69
70–74	103830	55525	1.0	48305	1.0		5515	3090	2425	70–74
75–79	63335	33174	0.6	30161	0.6		4685	2541	2144	75–79
80–84	34390	18118	0.3	16272	0.3	186431 M	4967	2663	2304	80–84
85+	28451	16046	0.3	12405	0.2	179411 F	8789	4232	4557	85+
All ages	10584720	5500167		5084553		365842	91673	48645	43028	All ages

TABLE 2 LIFE TABLE FOR MALES

Age, x	$_nq_x$	l_x	$_nd_x$	$_nL_x$	$_nm_x$	T_x	$1000r_x$	$\overset{\circ}{e}_x$	$_nM_x$	Age, x
0	0.06312	100000	6312	95928	0.06580	6303692	1.13	63.04	0.06585	0
1	0.03277	93688	3070	366244	0.00838	6207764	1.13	66.26	0.00839	1
5	0.00951	90618	862	450933	0.00191	5841520	14.66	64.46	0.00193	5
10	0.00580	89756	520	447433	0.00116	5390587	33.20	60.06	0.00117	10
15	0.00725	89235	647	444639	0.00146	4943154	42.24	55.39	0.00145	15
20	0.01023	88588	906	440764	0.00206	4498516	30.49	50.78	0.00205	20
25	0.01228	87682	1077	435750	0.00247	4057752	19.35	46.28	0.00247	25
30	0.01229	86605	1064	430449	0.00247	3622003	7.57	41.82	0.00247	30
35	0.01733	85541	1483	424177	0.00350	3191554	28.13	37.31	0.00348	35
40	0.02298	84058	1932	415724	0.00465	2767377	26.86	32.92	0.00463	40
45	0.03346	82126	2748	404091	0.00680	2351652	22.68	28.63	0.00678	45
50	0.04426	79378	3514	388586	0.00904	1947561	36.51	24.54	0.00899	50
55	0.06642	75865	5039	367360	0.01372	1558975	17.61	20.55	0.01368	55
60	0.09249	70826	6550	338880	0.01933	1191615	32.37	16.82	0.01919	60
65	0.16241	64276	10439	296674	0.03519	852735	32.37	13.27	0.03495	65
70	0.24585	53837	13236	236657	0.05593	556060	32.37	10.33	0.05565	70
75	0.32361	40601	13139	170471	0.07707	319403	32.37	7.87	0.07660	75
80	0.53681	27462	14742	99593	0.14802	148932	32.37	5.42	0.14698	80
85+	1.00000	12720	12720	49339	0.25781	49339	32.37	3.88	0.26374	85+

TABLE 3 LIFE TABLE FOR FEMALES

Age, x	$_nq_x$	l_x	$_nd_x$	$_nL_x$	$_nm_x$	T_x	$1000r_x$	$\overset{\circ}{e}_x$	$_nM_x$	Age, x
0	0.05265	100000	5265	96811	0.05438	6344223	2.22	63.44	0.05446	0
1	0.04031	94735	3819	368691	0.01036	6247413	2.22	65.95	0.01037	1
5	0.01027	90916	933	452247	0.00206	5878721	14.95	64.66	0.00209	5
10	0.00525	89983	472	448683	0.00105	5426475	35.33	60.31	0.00106	10
15	0.00773	89511	692	445968	0.00155	4977792	36.46	55.61	0.00154	15
20	0.01313	88819	1166	441319	0.00264	4531824	27.54	51.02	0.00263	20
25	0.01556	87653	1364	434901	0.00314	4090505	30.86	46.67	0.00313	25
30	0.01618	86289	1396	428004	0.00326	3655603	14.85	42.35	0.00325	30
35	0.01897	84892	1611	420550	0.00383	3227599	36.30	38.02	0.00382	35
40	0.02341	83282	1949	411696	0.00474	2807049	40.30	33.71	0.00472	40
45	0.02931	81332	2384	400868	0.00595	2395353	26.62	29.45	0.00593	45
50	0.03484	78948	2751	388285	0.00708	1994486	46.94	25.26	0.00703	50
55	0.05785	76197	4408	370557	0.01190	1606201	27.89	21.08	0.01184	55
60	0.07845	71789	5632	346087	0.01627	1235634	27.16	17.21	0.01616	60
65	0.15516	66157	10265	306563	0.03348	889547	27.16	13.45	0.03330	65
70	0.22432	55892	12538	248726	0.05041	582984	27.16	10.43	0.05020	70
75	0.30422	43354	13189	184496	0.07149	334258	27.16	7.71	0.07109	75
80	0.52669	30165	15888	111332	0.14271	149762	27.16	4.95	0.14159	80
85+	*1.00000	14277	14277	38430	0.37151	38430	27.16	2.69	0.36735	85+

TABLE 4   POPULATION PROJECTION, USING FIXED AGE-SPECIFIC BIRTH AND DEATH RATES, IN THOUSANDS

Age at last birthday	1968 Total	Males	Females	1973 Total	Males	Females	1978 Total	Males	Females	Age at last birthday
0–4	1822	925	897	2119	1076	1043	2479	1259	1220	0–4
5–9	1567	801	766	1774	903	871	2064	1050	1014	5–9
10–14	1458	735	723	1554	794	760	1760	896	864	10–14
15–19	1332	682	650	1449	730	719	1545	790	755	15–19
20–24	1020	520	500	1320	676	644	1435	724	711	20–24
25–29	878	438	440	1006	514	492	1302	668	634	25–29
30–34	742	374	368	866	433	433	992	507	485	30–34
35–39	664	351	313	730	369	361	852	426	426	35–39
40–44	640	335	305	650	344	306	715	361	354	40–44
45–49	460	253	207	523	326	297	633	335	298	45–49
50–54	431	239	192	444	243	201	501	313	288	50–54
55–59	330	183	147	409	226	183	422	230	192	55–59
60–64	252	145	107	306	169	137	380	209	171	60–64
65–69	216	124	92	222	127	95	270	148	122	65–69
70–74	122	68	54	174	99	75	178	101	77	70–74
75–79	76	40	36	89	49	40	126	71	55	75–79
80–84	37	19	18	45	23	22	52	28	24	80–84
85 +	15	9	6	16	10	6	19	12	7	85 +
All ages	12062	6241	5821	13796	7111	6685	15825	8128	7697	All ages

TABLE 5   OBSERVED AND PROJECTED VITAL RATES

Rates per thousand	Observed Total	Males	Females	Projected 1968 Males	Females	Projected 1973 Males	Females	Projected 1978 Males	Females	Stable Males	Females
Birth	34.56	33.90	35.29	34.29	35.37	35.41	36.24	36.04	36.62	35.25	35.14
Death	8.66	8.84	8.46	8.60	8.00	8.81	8.14	9.00	8.29	9.15	9.04
Increase	25.90	25.05	26.82	25.69	27.38	26.60	28.10	27.04	28.34		25.0941

TABLE 6   RATES STANDARDIZED ON THREE STANDARD COUNTRIES

Standardized rates per thousand	England and Wales, 1961 Total	Males	Females	United States, 1960 Total	Males	Females	Mexico, 1960 Total	Males	Females
Birth	32.05	33.48*	30.47	32.65	30.84*	31.55	35.48	31.42*	34.71
Death	14.72	16.64*	16.72	12.65	13.90*	13.34	8.34	8.37*	8.33
Increase	17.34	16.84*	13.75	20.00	16.94*	18.21	27.14	23.06*	26.39

TABLE 7   VITAL STATISTICS AND RATES INFERRED FROM AGE DISTRIBUTIONS (FEMALES)

Vital statistics		Thompson Age range	NRR	1000r	Interval	Bourgeois-Pichat Age range	NRR	1000b	1000d	1000r	Coale	
TFR	5.00	0–4	2.02	26.56	27.29	5–29	2.40	41.05	8.61	32.44	1000b	38.22
GRR	2.45	5–9	2.20	29.47	27.22	30–54	2.45	45.36	12.14	33.23	1000d	9.97
NRR	2.12	10–14	2.31	30.05	27.17	55–79	2.55	46.63	12.00	34.63	1000r	28.26
Generation	28.76	15–19	2.09	27.23	27.09	*5–34	2.36	40.67	8.88	31.79	1000k_1	–4.45
Sex ratio	103.9										1000k_2	0.

TABLE 8   LESLIE MATRIX AND ITS ANALYSIS (FEMALES)

Start of age interval	Sub-diagonal	First row	Percent in stable population	Fisher values	Total reproductive values	Net maternity function	Matrix equation coefficient	Parameters	Integral	Matrix
0	0.97152	0.00000	15.352	1.146	903272	0.00000	0.00000	λ_1	1.1394	1.1398
5	0.99212	0.00030	13.086	1.344	979793	0.00000	0.00029	λ_2	0.4465	0.4477
10	0.99395	0.05917	11.390	1.544	1010247	0.00059	0.05704		+0.8316	+0.8081i
15	0.98957	0.31432	9.933	1.702	859420	0.11349	0.30113	r_1	0.0261	0.0262
20	0.98546	0.56760	8.624	1.597	713689	0.48878	0.53812	r_2	-0.0116	-0.0158
25	0.98414	0.58116	7.456	1.187	443662	0.58745	0.54296		+0.2156	+0.2130i
30	0.98258	0.44699	6.438	0.698	222248	0.49847	0.41099	c_1		53052
35	0.97894	0.23028	5.550	0.288	89891	0.32351	0.20804	c_2		-1166
40	0.97370	0.05962	4.767	0.066	14141	0.09257	0.05274			107287i
45	0.96861	0.00749	4.072	0.008	1497	0.01290	0.00545	$2\pi/y$	29.141	29.501
50	0.95437	0.00001	3.460	0.000	1	0.00000	0.00000	Δ	3.859	
55	0.80534		9.874							

Ceylon, 1967

TABLE 1 DATA INPUT TO COMPUTATIONS

Age at last birthday	Population					Births, by age of mother	Deaths			Age at last birthday
	Total	Males	%	Females	%		Total	Males	Females	
0	406000	214000	3.5	192000	3.4	0	17555	9854	7801	0
1–4	1440000	723000	11.9	717000	12.8	0	9051	4234	4817	1–4
5–9	1589999	802999	13.2	787000	14.0	0	2807	1402	1405	5–9
10–14	1462000	748000	12.3	714000	12.7	137	1484	780	704	10–14
15–19	1135000	575000	9.5	560000	10.0	26175	1597	853	734	15–19
20–24	985000	494000	8.1	491000	8.7	102819	1920	1013	907	20–24
25–29	827000	417000	6.9	410000	7.3	105719	1874	936	938	25–29
30–34	743000	393000	6.5	350000	6.2	72455	1580	839	841	30–34
35–39	726000	381000	6.3	345000	6.1	50194	2351	1264	1097	35–39
40–44	523000	287000	4.7	236000	4.2	10396	2042	1250	792	40–44
45–49	492000	274000	4.5	218000	3.9	1413	2850	1856	994	45–49
50–54	384000	215000	3.5	169000	3.0	223	2979	1890	1089	50–54
55–59	298000	172000	2.8	126000	2.2	0	3747	2424	1323	55–59
60–64	268000	154000	2.5	114000	2.0	0	4342	2703	1639	60–64
65–69	167000	94000	1.5	73000	1.3	0	5873	3555	2318	65–69
70–74	114000	62000	1.0	52000	0.9		6019	3443	2576	70–74
75–79	63000	34000	0.6	29000	0.5		4782	2723	2059	75–79
80–84	34829	18619	0.3	16210	0.3	187575 M	5231	2798	2433	80–84
85+	43172	22382	0.4	20790	0.4	181956 F	9583	4783	4800	85+
All ages	11701000	6081000		5620000		369531	87877	43610	39267	All ages

TABLE 2 LIFE TABLE FOR MALES

Age, x	$_nq_x$	l_x	$_nd_x$	$_nL_x$	$_nm_x$	T_x	$1000r_x$	$\overset{\circ}{e}_x$	$_nM_x$	Age, x
0	0.04431	100000	4431	97148	0.04561	6514480	13.65	65.14	0.04605	0
1	0.02288	95569	2187	376223	0.00581	6417332	13.65	67.15	0.00586	1
5	0.00861	93382	804	464902	0.00173	6041109	20.02	54.69	0.00175	5
10	0.00519	92578	481	461667	0.00104	5576207	32.09	60.23	0.00104	10
15	0.00752	92098	693	458852	0.00151	5114540	39.98	55.53	0.00150	15
20	0.01023	91405	935	454755	0.00206	4655688	30.14	50.93	0.00205	20
25	0.01116	90471	1010	449831	0.00224	4200933	20.71	46.43	0.00224	25
30	0.01063	89461	951	445021	0.00214	3751101	6.61	41.93	0.00213	30
35	0.01652	88510	1462	439088	0.00333	3306080	28.19	37.35	0.00332	35
40	0.02166	87047	1885	430813	0.00438	2866992	28.29	32.94	0.00436	40
45	0.03343	85162	2847	419045	0.00679	2436179	22.26	28.61	0.00677	45
50	0.04333	82315	3566	403188	0.00885	2017134	37.01	24.50	0.00879	50
55	0.06834	78749	5381	380848	0.01413	1613946	19.95	20.49	0.01409	55
60	0.08508	73367	6242	352554	0.01770	1233098	33.82	16.81	0.01755	60
65	0.17465	67126	11724	307850	0.03808	880544	33.82	13.12	0.03782	65
70	0.24533	55402	13592	243514	0.05582	572694	33.82	10.34	0.05553	70
75	0.33599	41810	14048	174251	0.08062	329179	33.82	7.87	0.08009	75
80	0.54482	27762	15125	99927	0.15136	154929	33.82	5.58	0.15028	80
85+	1.00000	12637	12637	55002	0.22975	55002	33.82	4.35	0.21370	85+

TABLE 3 LIFE TABLE FOR FEMALES

Age, x	$_nq_x$	l_x	$_nd_x$	$_nL_x$	$_nm_x$	T_x	$1000r_x$	$\overset{\circ}{e}_x$	$_nM_x$	Age, x
0	0.03954	100000	3954	97558	0.04053	6680500	3.51	66.81	0.04063	0
1	0.02635	96046	2531	377314	0.00671	6582943	3.51	68.54	0.00672	1
5	0.00878	93515	821	465521	0.00176	6205628	21.46	66.36	0.00179	5
10	0.00490	92694	454	462287	0.00098	5740108	32.78	61.93	0.00099	10
15	0.00657	92239	606	459764	0.00132	5277820	36.11	57.22	0.00131	15
20	0.00923	91634	845	456144	0.00185	4818057	29.34	52.58	0.00185	20
25	0.01139	90788	1034	451403	0.00229	4361913	31.64	48.04	0.00229	25
30	0.01196	89754	1073	446163	0.00241	3910510	14.70	43.57	0.00240	30
35	0.01581	88681	1402	439978	0.00319	3464347	36.38	39.07	0.00318	35
40	0.01670	87278	1458	432860	0.00337	3024370	42.32	34.65	0.00336	40
45	0.02265	85821	1943	424500	0.00458	2591510	28.73	30.20	0.00456	45
50	0.03203	83877	2686	413135	0.00650	2167000	47.89	25.84	0.00644	50
55	0.05146	81191	4178	396077	0.01055	1753875	29.12	21.60	0.01050	55
60	0.07025	77013	5410	372887	0.01451	1357798	32.10	17.63	0.01438	60
65	0.14877	71602	10652	333073	0.03198	984912	32.10	13.76	0.03175	65
70	0.22198	60950	13529	271717	0.04979	651839	32.10	10.69	0.04954	70
75	0.30452	47421	14441	201938	0.07151	380122	32.10	8.02	0.07100	75
80	0.54630	32980	18017	119134	0.15123	178184	32.10	5.40	0.15009	80
85+	1.00000	14963	14963	59050	0.25340	59050	32.10	3.95	0.23088	85+

TABLE 4 POPULATION PROJECTION, USING FIXED AGE-SPECIFIC BIRTH AND DEATH RATES, IN THOUSANDS

Age at last birthday	1972 Total	1972 Males	1972 Females	1977 Total	1977 Males	1977 Females	1982 Total	1982 Males	1982 Females	Age at last birthday
0–4	1886	956	930	2196	1113	1083	2571	1303	1268	0–4
5–9	1811	920	891	1850	938	912	2155	1093	1062	5–9
10–14	1579	797	782	1799	914	885	1837	932	905	10–14
15–19	1453	743	710	1570	793	777	1788	908	880	15–19
20–24	1126	570	556	1442	737	705	1556	785	771	20–24
25–29	975	489	486	1114	564	550	1426	729	697	25–29
30–34	818	413	405	963	483	480	1101	558	543	30–34
35–39	733	388	345	807	407	400	951	477	474	35–39
40–44	713	374	339	720	380	340	792	399	393	40–44
45–49	510	279	231	697	364	333	703	370	333	45–49
50–54	476	264	212	494	269	225	674	350	324	50–54
55–59	365	203	162	452	249	203	470	254	216	55–59
60–64	278	159	119	341	188	153	422	231	191	60–64
65–69	236	134	102	245	139	106	300	164	136	65–69
70–74	134	74	60	189	106	83	196	110	86	70–74
75–79	83	44	39	97	53	44	138	76	52	75–79
80–84	36	19	17	48	25	23	57	31	26	80–84
85 +	18	10	8	19	11	8	25	14	11	85 +
All ages	13230	6836	6394	15043	7733	7310	17152	8784	8378	All ages

TABLE 5 OBSERVED AND PROJECTED VITAL RATES

Rates per thousand	Observed Total	Observed Males	Observed Females	Projected 1972 Males	Projected 1972 Females	Projected 1977 Males	Projected 1977 Females	Projected 1982 Males	Projected 1982 Females	Stable Males	Stable Females
Birth	31.58	30.85	32.38	31.61	32.80	32.87	33.73	33.74	34.31	32.85	32.47
Death	7.51	7.99	6.99	7.57	6.37	7.82	6.56	8.06	6.78	8.30	7.92
Increase	24.07	22.85	25.39	24.05	26.42	25.04	27.17	25.68	27.52	24.5508	

TABLE 6 RATES STANDARDIZED ON THREE STANDARD COUNTRIES

Standardized rates per thousand	England and Wales, 1961 Total	England and Wales, 1961 Males	England and Wales, 1961 Females	United States, 1960 Total	United States, 1960 Males	United States, 1960 Females	Mexico, 1960 Total	Mexico, 1960 Males	Mexico, 1960 Females
Birth	29.44	30.44*	28.10	29.95	28.02*	29.06	32.58	28.58*	32.00
Death	13.24	14.59*	14.50	11.16	12.20*	11.27	6.97	7.18*	6.73
Increase	16.20	15.86*	13.60	18.79	15.82*	17.79	25.61	21.40*	25.28

TABLE 7 VITAL STATISTICS AND RATES INFERRED FROM AGE DISTRIBUTIONS (FEMALES)

Vital statistics		Thompson Age range	NRR	1000r	Interval	Bourgeois-Pichat Age range	NRR	1000b	1000d	1000r	Coale	
TFR	4.59	0–4	2.15	28.00	27.34	5–29	2.38	39.13	7.06	32.07	1000b	35.25
GRR	2.26	5–9	2.19	29.22	27.29	30–54	2.54	45.37	10.86	34.51	1000d	8.45
NRR	2.03	10–14	2.33	30.31	27.25	55–79	2.73	50.30	13.15	37.15	1000r	27.80
Generation	28.84	15–19	2.15	28.23	27.17	*10–34	2.44	40.20	7.24	32.97	$1000k_1$	−5.89
Sex ratio	103.1										$1000k_2$	0.

TABLE 8 LESLIE MATRIX AND ITS ANALYSIS (FEMALES)

Start of age interval	Sub-diagonal	First row	Percent in stable population	Fisher values	Total reproductive values	Net maternity function	Matrix equation coefficient	Parameters		
0	0.98031	0.00000	14.527	1.119	1017196	0.00000	0.00000	λ_1	1.1306	1.1310
5	0.99305	0.00022	12.591	1.291	1016040	0.00000	0.00022	λ_2	0.4416	0.4436
10	0.99454	0.05457	11.056	1.470	1049064	0.00044	0.05313		+0.8220	+0.7987i
15	0.99213	0.29754	9.722	1.610	901812	0.10582	0.28808	r_1	0.0246	0.0245
20	0.98961	0.54315	8.528	1.500	736579	0.47034	0.52173	r_2	−0.0138	−0.0181
25	0.98839	0.54068	7.462	1.100	451121	0.57312	0.51396		+0.2156	+0.2128i
30	0.98614	0.40976	6.521	0.647	226412	0.45479	0.38499	c_1		60182
35	0.98382	0.22076	5.686	0.277	95537	0.31519	0.20454	c_2		70590
40	0.98069	0.05893	4.945	0.067	15869	0.09389	0.05372			137310i
45	0.97323	0.00908	4.289	0.010	2244	0.01355	0.00812	$2\pi/y$	29.148	29.531
50	0.95871	0.00154	3.691	0.002	258	0.00268	0.00134	Δ	5.806	
55	0.80871		10.980							

China (Taiwan), 1966

TABLE 1 DATA INPUT TO COMPUTATIONS

Age at last birthday	Population					Births, by age of mother	Deaths			Age at last birthday
	Total	Males	%	Females	%		Total	Males	Females	
0	379218	195400	2.9	183818	3.0	0	8380	4541	3839	0
1–4	1602667	824482	12.1	778185	12.5	0	6830	3431	3399	1–4
5–9	1931672	991494	14.6	940178	15.1	0	1535	911	624	5–9
10–14	1775971	911017	13.4	864954	13.9	0	1073	629	444	10–14
15–19	1293730	664565	9.8	629165	10.1	25266	1435	841	594	15–19
20–24	935252	485077	7.1	450175	7.2	123481	1556	982	574	20–24
25–29	929845	476755	7.0	453090	7.3	147935	1708	1094	614	25–29
30–34	829161	433161	6.4	396000	6.4	74465	1846	1104	742	30–34
35–39	783669	434123	6.4	349546	5.6	31705	2318	1491	827	35–39
40–44	660474	372002	5.5	288472	4.6	10904	2816	1818	998	40–44
45–49	524544	297318	4.4	227226	3.7	1352	3194	2187	1007	45–49
50–54	452389	257721	3.8	194668	3.1	0	4082	2757	1325	50–54
55–59	338831	181438	2.7	157393	2.5	0	4807	3185	1622	55–59
60–64	240185	123556	1.8	116529	1.9	0	5578	3563	2115	60–64
65–69	160047	76722	1.1	83325	1.3	0	5977	3544	2433	65–69
70–74	94822	41847	0.6	52975	0.9		5515	2944	2571	70–74
75–79	53214	20567	0.3	32647	0.5		4738	2198	2540	75–79
80–84	23705	7817	0.1	15888	0.3	213327 M	3207	1271	1936	80–84
85+	11819	2997	0.0	8822	0.1	201781 F	3085	890	2195	85+
All ages	13021215	6798059		6223156		415108	69780	39381	30399	All ages

TABLE 2 LIFE TABLE FOR MALES

Age, x	$_nq_x$	l_x	$_nd_x$	$_nL_x$	$_nm_x$	T_x	$1000r_x$	$\overset{\circ}{e}_x$	$_nM_x$	Age, x
0	0.02292	100000	2292	98605	0.02324	6518643	0.00	65.19	0.02324	0
1	0.01646	97708	1608	386504	0.00416	6420038	0.00	65.71	0.00416	1
5	0.00455	96100	438	479406	0.00091	6033534	9.71	62.78	0.00092	5
10	0.00346	95662	331	477520	0.00069	5554128	39.14	58.06	0.00069	10
15	0.00639	95331	610	475253	0.00128	5076608	61.72	53.25	0.00127	15
20	0.01011	94722	957	471311	0.00203	4601346	31.29	48.58	0.00202	20
25	0.01141	93764	1070	466192	0.00230	4130035	9.03	44.05	0.00229	25
30	0.01267	92694	1175	460636	0.00255	3663843	6.70	39.53	0.00255	30
35	0.01706	91519	1562	453904	0.00344	3203207	11.69	35.00	0.00343	35
40	0.02429	89958	2185	444666	0.00491	2749303	32.76	30.56	0.00489	40
45	0.03632	87773	3188	431365	0.00739	2304638	29.21	26.26	0.00735	45
50	0.05257	84585	4445	412567	0.01078	1873273	37.96	22.15	0.01070	50
55	0.08525	80138	6832	384767	0.01776	1460706	55.02	18.23	0.01755	55
60	0.13632	73306	9993	342890	0.02914	1075938	53.84	14.68	0.02884	60
65	0.20952	63313	13266	284468	0.04663	733048	53.84	11.58	0.04619	65
70	0.30180	50048	15105	212792	0.07098	448581	53.84	8.96	0.07035	70
75	0.42292	34943	14778	137040	0.10784	235788	53.84	6.75	0.10687	75
80	0.57518	20165	11598	70534	0.16444	98749	53.84	4.90	0.16260	80
85+	•1.00000	8566	8566	28214	0.30362	28214	53.84	3.29	0.29696	85+

TABLE 3 LIFE TABLE FOR FEMALES

Age, x	$_nq_x$	l_x	$_nd_x$	$_nL_x$	$_nm_x$	T_x	$1000r_x$	$\overset{\circ}{e}_x$	$_nM_x$	Age, x
0	0.02063	100000	2063	98773	0.02088	6983194	0.00	69.83	0.02088	0
1	0.01727	97937	1692	387263	0.00437	6884421	0.00	70.29	0.00437	1
5	0.00328	96246	315	480438	0.00066	6497157	9.19	67.51	0.00066	5
10	0.00258	95930	247	479060	0.00052	6016719	39.52	62.72	0.00051	10
15	0.00476	95683	456	477349	0.00095	5537660	64.38	57.88	0.00094	15
20	0.00637	95227	605	474657	0.00128	5060311	31.61	53.14	0.00128	20
25	0.00676	94621	640	471560	0.00136	4585654	11.37	48.46	0.00136	25
30	0.00935	93981	879	467803	0.00188	4114093	24.09	43.78	0.00187	30
35	0.01181	93102	1100	462908	0.00238	3646291	29.18	39.16	0.00237	35
40	0.01724	92002	1586	456232	0.00348	3183383	39.66	34.60	0.00346	40
45	0.02205	90416	1993	447387	0.00446	2727151	34.60	30.16	0.00443	45
50	0.03368	88423	2978	435157	0.00684	2279765	29.74	25.78	0.00681	50
55	0.05077	85445	4338	417240	0.01040	1844607	40.01	21.59	0.01031	55
60	0.08770	81107	7113	388968	0.01829	1427367	39.94	17.60	0.01813	60
65	0.13762	73993	10183	345935	0.02944	1038399	39.94	14.03	0.02920	65
70	0.21878	63810	13960	285437	0.04891	692463	39.94	10.85	0.04853	70
75	0.32814	49850	16358	208736	0.07837	407027	39.94	8.17	0.07780	75
80	0.47127	33492	15784	128283	0.12304	198291	39.94	5.92	0.12185	80
85+	•1.00000	17708	17708	70007	0.25295	70007	39.94	3.95	0.24881	85+

TABLE 4 POPULATION PROJECTION, USING FIXED AGE-SPECIFIC BIRTH AND DEATH RATES, IN THOUSANDS

Age at last birthday	1971			1976			1981			Age at last birthday
	Total	Males	Females	Total	Males	Females	Total	Males	Females	
0–4	2190	1124	1066	2678	1375	1303	3305	1597	1508	0–4
5–9	1959	1008	951	2164	1111	1053	2547	1359	1288	5–9
10–14	1925	988	937	1952	1004	948	2157	1107	1050	10–14
15–19	1769	907	862	1917	983	934	1944	999	945	15–19
20–24	1285	659	626	1756	899	857	1904	975	929	20–24
25–29	927	480	447	1274	652	622	1740	889	851	25–29
30–34	920	471	449	918	474	444	1261	644	617	30–34
35–39	819	427	392	909	464	445	906	467	439	35–39
40–44	770	425	345	804	418	386	893	455	438	40–44
45–49	644	361	283	751	413	338	785	406	379	45–49
50–54	505	284	221	620	345	275	724	395	329	50–54
55–59	427	240	187	477	265	212	586	322	264	55–59
60–64	309	162	147	388	214	174	434	235	198	60–64
65–69	207	103	104	264	134	130	333	178	155	65–69
70–74	126	57	69	163	77	86	208	100	108	70–74
75–79	66	27	39	87	37	50	112	49	63	75–79
80–84	31	11	20	38	14	24	50	19	31	80–84
85 +	12	3	9	15	4	11	19	6	13	85 +
All ages	14891	7737	7154	17175	8883	8292	20008	10303	9705	All ages

TABLE 5 OBSERVED AND PROJECTED VITAL RATES

Rates per thousand	Observed			Projected						Stable	
				1971		1976		1981			
	Total	Males	Females	Males	Females	Males	Females	Males	Females	Males	Females
Birth	31.88	31.38	32.42	32.35	33.10	35.63	36.11	37.18	37.34	35.41	34.48
Death	5.36	5.79	4.88	6.15	4.98	6.58	5.21	6.89	5.39	6.93	6.00
Increase	26.52	25.59	27.54	26.20	28.12	29.05	30.89	30.29	31.95		28.4788

TABLE 6 RATES STANDARDIZED ON THREE STANDARD COUNTRIES

Standardized rates per thousand	England and Wales, 1961			United States, 1960			Mexico, 1960		
	Total	Males	Females	Total	Males	Females	Total	Males	Females
Birth	30.51	31.40*	28.74	30.95	29.20*	29.65	35.45	28.98*	34.37
Death	13.80	15.59*	13.67	11.37	12.08*	10.26	6.18	6.54*	5.34
Increase	16.71	15.81*	15.07	19.58	17.12*	19.39	29.25	22.44*	29.04

TABLE 7 VITAL STATISTICS AND RATES INFERRED FROM AGE DISTRIBUTIONS (FEMALES)

Vital statistics		Thompson				Bourgeois-Pichat				Coale	
		Age range	NRR	$1000r$	Interval	Age range	NRR	$1000b$	$1000d$	$1000r$	
TFR	4.82	0–4	2.17	28.25	27.38	5–29	3.05	44.22	2.89	41.33	$1000b$ 37.14
GRR	2.34	5–9	2.51	34.50	27.33	30–54	2.47	41.29	7.85	33.44	$1000d$ 6.82
NRR	2.20	10–14	2.59	34.00	27.27	55–79	3.55	90.56	43.62	46.94	$1000r$ 30.32
Generation	27.73	15–19	2.20	28.93	27.18	*35–59	2.55	44.04	9.36	34.68	$1000k_1$ -4.08
Sex ratio	105.7										$1000k_2$ 0.

TABLE 8 LESLIE MATRIX AND ITS ANALYSIS (FEMALES)

Start of age interval	Sub-diagonal	First row	Percent in stable population	Fisher values	Total reproductive values	Net maternity function	Matrix equation coefficient	Parameters		
									Integral	Matrix
0	0.98848	0.00000	15.640	1.104	1062227	0.00000	0.00000	λ_1	1.1530	1.1536
5	0.99713	0.00000	13.402	1.289	1211508	0.00000	0.00000	λ_2	0.3831	0.3822
10	0.99643	0.04727	11.584	1.491	1289441	0.00000	0.04659		+0.8980	+0.8636i
15	0.99436	0.36963	10.005	1.673	1052897	0.09318	0.36303	r_1	0.0285	0.0286
20	0.99347	0.70720	8.625	1.531	689205	0.63288	0.69065	r_2	-0.0048	-0.0114
25	0.99203	0.50606	7.428	0.992	449314	0.74842	0.58801		+0.2335	+0.2308i
30	0.98954	0.32816	6.388	0.479	189516	0.42760	0.31585	c_1		64465
35	0.98558	0.15115	5.480	0.192	67017	0.20410	0.14396	c_2		-21459
40	0.98061	0.05154	4.682	0.055	15882	0.38383	0.04838			267379i
45	0.97267	0.00703	3.980	0.007	1530	0.01294	0.00647	$2\pi/y$	26.906	27.221
50	0.95883	-0.00001	3.356	0.000	2	0.00000	0.00000	Δ	4.546	
55	0.81238		9.430							

[383]

China (Taiwan), 1966 (cities)

TABLE 1 DATA INPUT TO COMPUTATIONS

Age at last birthday	Population					Births, by age of mother	Deaths			Age at last birthday
	Total	Males	%	Females	%		Total	Males	Females	
0	100892	52354	2.6	48538	2.7	0	1778	952	826	0
1–4	445247	229980	11.4	215267	11.9	0	1381	698	683	1–4
5–9	551459	285011	14.1	266448	14.7	0	344	210	134	5–9
10–14	506495	261796	13.0	244699	13.5	0	250	154	95	10–14
15–19	371722	190710	9.4	181012	10.0	7261	342	204	138	15–19
20–24	270498	132458	6.6	138040	7.6	34661	340	203	137	20–24
25–29	286186	139217	6.9	146969	8.1	42497	467	299	168	25–29
30–34	258455	132723	6.6	125732	6.9	19944	492	288	204	30–34
35–39	252999	142837	7.1	110162	6.1	7102	655	445	210	35–39
40–44	228320	135388	6.7	92932	5.1	2201	856	556	300	40–44
45–49	174724	105601	5.2	69123	3.8	315	991	692	299	45–49
50–54	141696	86156	4.3	55540	3.1	0	1230	858	372	50–54
55–59	95021	54075	2.7	40946	2.3	0	1373	924	449	55–59
60–64	64803	34769	1.7	30034	1.7	0	1552	1032	520	60–64
65–69	40906	19796	1.0	21110	1.2	0	1559	948	611	65–69
70–74	23511	10215	0.5	13296	0.7		1332	724	608	70–74
75–79	12291	4428	0.2	7863	0.4		981	427	554	75–79
80–84	5127	1507	0.1	3620	0.2	58657 M	627	221	406	80–84
85+	2328	512	0.0	1816	0.1	55324 F	620	162	458	85+
All ages	3832680	2019533		1813147		113981	17170	9997	7173	All ages

TABLE 2 LIFE TABLE FOR MALES

Age, x	$_nq_x$	l_x	$_nd_x$	$_nL_x$	$_nm_x$	T_x	$1000r_x$	$\overset{\circ}{e}_x$	$_nM_x$	Age, x
0	0.01798	100000	1798	98894	0.01818	6644973	0.00	66.45	0.01818	0
1	0.01204	98202	1182	389605	0.00304	6546079	0.00	66.66	0.00304	1
5	0.00366	97019	355	484208	0.00073	6156073	6.35	63.46	0.00074	5
10	0.00295	96664	285	482640	0.00059	5672266	39.45	58.68	0.00059	10
15	0.00540	96378	521	480685	0.00108	5189626	67.07	53.85	0.00107	15
20	0.00767	95858	735	477555	0.00154	4708941	29.89	49.12	0.00153	20
25	0.01068	95123	1016	473132	0.00215	4231386	0.00	44.48	0.00215	25
30	0.01079	94107	1016	468083	0.00217	3758254	0.00	39.94	0.00217	30
35	0.01546	93091	1439	462035	0.00312	3290171	0.00	35.34	0.00312	35
40	0.02043	91652	1872	453885	0.00413	2828136	25.79	30.86	0.00411	40
45	0.03250	89779	2918	442103	0.00660	2374251	38.49	26.45	0.00655	45
50	0.04926	86861	4279	424439	0.01008	1932149	56.17	22.24	0.00996	50
55	0.08353	82583	6898	396994	0.01738	1507710	72.40	18.26	0.01709	55
60	0.14071	75684	10649	353300	0.03014	1110716	75.11	14.68	0.02968	60
65	0.21697	65035	14110	290901	0.04851	757416	75.11	11.65	0.04789	65
70	0.30369	50924	15465	215902	0.07163	466515	75.11	9.16	0.07088	70
75	0.39018	35459	13836	141915	0.09749	250613	75.11	7.07	0.09643	75
80	0.53921	21624	11660	78163	0.14917	108698	75.11	5.03	0.14665	80
85+	•1.00000	9964	9964	30536	0.32631	30536	75.11	3.06	0.31541	85+

TABLE 3 LIFE TABLE FOR FEMALES

Age, x	$_nq_x$	l_x	$_nd_x$	$_nL_x$	$_nm_x$	T_x	$1000r_x$	$\overset{\circ}{e}_x$	$_nM_x$	Age, x
0	0.01684	100000	1684	98982	0.01702	7110214	0.00	71.10	0.01702	0
1	0.01258	98316	1237	389946	0.00317	7011233	0.00	71.31	0.00317	1
5	0.00250	97078	242	484786	0.00050	6621287	6.45	68.21	0.00050	5
10	0.00197	96836	191	483730	0.00039	6136501	38.16	63.37	0.00039	10
15	0.00384	96645	371	482358	0.00077	5652771	56.52	58.49	0.00076	15
20	0.00496	96274	477	480213	0.00099	5170413	19.86	53.71	0.00099	20
25	0.00571	95797	547	477679	0.00114	4690200	8.12	48.96	0.00114	25
30	0.00810	95250	772	474395	0.00163	4212521	27.27	44.23	0.00162	30
35	0.00954	94478	901	470293	0.00192	3738126	28.09	39.57	0.00191	35
40	0.01613	93577	1509	464340	0.00325	3267833	43.45	34.92	0.00323	40
45	0.02158	92068	1987	455685	0.00436	2803493	46.88	30.45	0.00433	45
50	0.03328	90082	2998	443479	0.00676	2347808	45.27	26.06	0.00670	50
55	0.05399	87084	4701	424483	0.01108	1904329	50.10	21.87	0.01097	55
60	0.08405	82382	6924	395771	0.01750	1479845	50.42	17.96	0.01731	60
65	0.13669	75458	10314	352878	0.02923	1084074	50.42	14.37	0.02894	65
70	0.20754	65144	13520	293023	0.04614	731196	50.42	11.22	0.04573	70
75	0.30243	51624	15613	219609	0.07109	438173	50.42	8.49	0.07046	75
80	0.44482	36011	16019	140922	0.11367	218563	50.42	6.07	0.11215	80
85+	•1.00000	19993	19993	77641	0.25750	77641	50.42	3.88	0.25220	85+

TABLE 4   POPULATION PROJECTION, USING FIXED AGE-SPECIFIC BIRTH AND DEATH RATES, IN THOUSANDS

Age at last birthday	1971			1976			1981			Age at last birthday
	Total	Males	Females	Total	Males	Females	Total	Males	Females	
0–4	593	305	288	700	360	340	844	434	410	0–4
5–9	542	280	262	589	303	286	694	357	337	5–9
10–14	550	284	266	540	279	261	587	302	285	10–14
15–19	505	261	244	548	283	265	538	278	260	15–19
20–24	369	189	180	502	259	243	545	281	264	20–24
25–29	268	131	137	367	188	179	499	257	242	25–29
30–34	284	138	146	266	130	136	364	185	178	30–34
35–39	256	131	125	281	136	145	263	128	135	35–39
40–44	249	140	109	252	129	123	277	134	143	40–44
45–49	223	132	91	244	137	107	246	125	121	45–49
50–54	168	101	67	216	127	89	235	131	104	50–54
55–59	134	81	53	159	95	64	203	118	85	55–59
60–64	86	48	38	122	72	50	144	84	60	60–64
65–69	56	29	27	74	40	34	103	59	44	65–69
70–74	33	15	18	43	21	22	57	29	28	70–74
75–79	17	7	10	23	10	13	31	14	17	75–79
80–84	7	2	5	10	4	6	13	5	8	80–84
85 +	3	1	2	4	1	3	5	1	4	85 +
All ages	4343	2275	2068	4940	2574	2366	5648	2923	2725	All ages

TABLE 5   OBSERVED AND PROJECTED VITAL RATES

Rates per thousand	Observed			Projected						Stable	
				1971		1976		1981			
	Total	Males	Females	Males	Females	Males	Females	Males	Females	Males	Females
Birth	29.74	29.04	30.51	29.17	30.26	31.59	32.37	32.99	33.39	31.22	30.32
Death	4.48	4.95	3.96	5.53	4.19	6.19	4.52	6.76	4.82	7.25	5.35
Increase	25.26	24.09	26.56	23.64	26.07	25.40	27.85	26.23	28.57		23.9634

TABLE 6   RATES STANDARDIZED ON THREE STANDARD COUNTRIES

Standardized rates per thousand	England and Wales, 1961			United States, 1960			Mexico, 1960		
	Total	Males	Females	Total	Males	Females	Total	Males	Females
Birth	26.26	28.68*	24.70	26.66	26.95*	25.49	31.11	25.61*	30.12
Death	13.12	14.30*	12.92	10.74	10.79*	9.61	5.60	5.83*	4.78
Increase	13.15	14.39*	11.78	15.92	16.16*	15.88	25.51	19.78*	25.34

TABLE 7   VITAL STATISTICS AND RATES INFERRED FROM AGE DISTRIBUTIONS (FEMALES)

Vital statistics		Thompson				Bourgeois-Pichat					Coale	
		Age range	NRR	1000r	Interval	Age range	NRR	1000b	1000d	1000r	1000b	
TFR	4.16	0–4	1.93	24.82	27.40	5–29	2.54	39.53	5.01	34.51	1000d	
GRR	2.02	5–9	2.27	30.61	27.35	30–54	2.53	53.71	15.03	38.68	1000r	
NRR	1.93	10–14	2.35	30.50	27.29	55–79	3.86	95.01	45.01	50.01	$1000k_1$	
Generation	27.34	15–19	2.07	26.83	27.19	*50–74	3.87	96.03	45.86	50.15	$1000k_2$	
Sex ratio	106.02											

TABLE 8   LESLIE MATRIX AND ITS ANALYSIS (FEMALES)

Start of age interval	Sub-diagonal	First row	Percent in stable population	Fisher values	Total reproductive values	Net maternity function	Matrix equation coefficient	Parameters	Integral	Matrix
0	0.99153	0.00000	13.986	1.085	286356	0.00000	0.00000	λ_1	1.1273	1.1277
5	0.99782	0.00000	12.298	1.235	328936	0.00000	0.00000	λ_2	0.3699	0.3693
10	0.99716	0.04746	10.882	1.395	341397	0.00000	0.04696		+0.8905	+0.8564 i
15	0.99555	0.34421	9.622	1.525	276241	0.09392	0.33959	r_1	0.0240	0.0240
20	0.99472	0.63924	8.495	1.353	186810	0.58525	0.62784	r_2	-0.0073	-0.0140
25	0.99313	0.53003	7.494	0.837	122957	0.67042	0.51784		+0.2354	+0.2327 i
30	0.99135	0.26405	6.600	0.371	46600	0.36525	0.25621	c_1		19745
35	0.98734	0.10424	5.802	0.132	14593	0.14716	0.10027	c_2		-2124
40	0.98136	0.03339	5.080	0.037	3410	0.05338	0.03173			69133 i
45	0.97321	0.00541	4.421	0.005	361	0.01008	0.00504	$2\pi/y$	26.689	25.997
50	0.95717	0.00002	3.815	0.000	1	0.00000	0.00000	Δ	7.530	
55	0.81027		11.506							

China (Taiwan), 1966 (townships)

TABLE 1 DATA INPUT TO COMPUTATIONS

Age at last birthday	Population					Births, by age of mother		Deaths			Age at last birthday
	Total	Males	%	Females	%			Total	Males	Females	
0	112116	57682	2.9	54434	2.9	0		2419	1337	1082	0
1–4	473466	243489	12.2	229977	12.5	0		1995	981	1014	1–4
5–9	570160	292633	14.6	277527	15.0	0		438	243	195	5–9
10–14	529818	271439	13.5	258379	14.0	0		320	188	132	10–14
15–19	385777	197734	9.9	188043	10.2	6782		437	263	174	15–19
20–24	279374	144464	7.2	134910	7.3	36182		485	300	185	20–24
25–29	275108	140598	7.0	134510	7.3	44249		476	300	176	25–29
30–34	242901	127265	6.4	115636	6.3	21600		505	309	196	30–34
35–39	229097	127290	6.4	101807	5.5	9126		661	424	237	35–39
40–44	190088	106968	5.3	83120	4.5	3075		844	561	283	40–44
45–49	151420	85015	4.2	66405	3.6	359		934	661	273	45–49
50–54	131652	73958	3.7	57694	3.1	0		1219	826	393	50–54
55–59	100800	53023	2.6	47777	2.6	0		1415	960	455	55–59
60–64	72440	36695	1.8	35745	1.9	0		1704	1061	643	60–64
65–69	49077	23094	1.2	25983	1.4	0		1842	1098	744	65–69
70–74	28531	12408	0.6	16123	0.9			1729	928	801	70–74
75–79	16337	6224	0.3	10113	0.5			1495	679	816	75–79
80–84	7457	2451	0.1	5006	0.3	62273 M		1032	401	631	80–84
85+	3852	1006	0.1	2846	0.2	59100 F		1029	313	716	85+
All ages	3849471	2003436		1846035		121373		20979	11833	9146	All ages

TABLE 2 LIFE TABLE FOR MALES

Age, x	$_nq_x$	l_x	$_nd_x$	$_nL_x$	$_nm_x$	T_x	$1000r_x$	$\overset{\circ}{e}_x$	$_nM_x$	Age, x
0	0.02285	100000	2285	98602	0.02318	6498401	0.00	64.98	0.02318	0
1	0.01594	97715	1558	386654	0.00403	6399798	0.00	65.49	0.00403	1
5	0.00412	96157	396	479794	0.00083	6013145	8.89	62.53	0.00083	5
10	0.00348	95761	333	478022	0.00070	5533351	38.34	57.78	0.00069	10
15	0.00672	95428	641	475671	0.00135	5055329	61.71	52.98	0.00133	15
20	0.01036	94787	982	471552	0.00208	4579659	32.17	48.32	0.00208	20
25	0.01062	93805	995	466553	0.00213	4108106	10.49	43.79	0.00213	25
30	0.01208	92809	1121	461351	0.00243	3641543	7.41	39.24	0.00243	30
35	0.01657	91688	1519	454898	0.00334	3180192	13.85	34.68	0.00333	35
40	0.02606	90169	2350	445355	0.00528	2725294	35.00	30.22	0.00524	40
45	0.03835	87819	3368	431149	0.00781	2279940	28.98	25.96	0.00778	45
50	0.05478	84451	4625	411448	0.01124	1848790	35.30	21.89	0.01117	50
55	0.08769	79825	7000	382734	0.01829	1437342	51.20	18.01	0.01811	55
60	0.13652	72825	9942	340629	0.02919	1054608	47.32	14.48	0.02891	60
65	0.21497	62883	13518	281813	0.04797	713980	47.32	11.35	0.04754	65
70	0.31736	49365	15666	207853	0.07537	432167	47.32	8.75	0.07479	70
75	0.42867	33699	14446	131429	0.10991	224314	47.32	6.66	0.10909	75
80	0.57669	19253	11103	67197	0.16523	92885	47.32	4.82	0.16361	80
85+	*1.00000	8150	8150	25688	0.31727	25688	47.32	3.15	0.31113	85+

TABLE 3 LIFE TABLE FOR FEMALES

Age, x	$_nq_x$	l_x	$_nd_x$	$_nL_x$	$_nm_x$	T_x	$1000r_x$	$\overset{\circ}{e}_x$	$_nM_x$	Age, x
0	0.01965	100000	1965	98842	0.01988	6995486	0.00	69.95	0.01988	0
1	0.01743	98035	1709	387637	0.00441	6896644	0.00	70.35	0.00441	1
5	0.00348	96326	335	480793	0.00070	6509007	8.13	67.57	0.00070	5
10	0.00256	95991	245	479363	0.00051	6028214	38.28	62.80	0.00051	10
15	0.00467	95745	447	477691	0.00094	5548851	64.04	57.95	0.00093	15
20	0.00685	95298	652	474892	0.00137	5071159	32.24	53.21	0.00137	20
25	0.00653	94645	618	471712	0.00131	4596267	14.01	48.56	0.00131	25
30	0.00847	94028	795	468244	0.00170	4124555	25.12	43.87	0.00169	30
35	0.01163	93231	1084	463605	0.00234	3656311	30.58	39.22	0.00233	35
40	0.01696	92147	1563	456989	0.00342	3192706	39.44	34.65	0.00340	40
45	0.02047	90584	1854	448583	0.00413	2735717	31.96	30.20	0.00411	45
50	0.03367	88730	2987	436636	0.00684	2287134	26.22	25.78	0.00681	50
55	0.04700	85743	4030	419497	0.00961	1850499	37.10	21.58	0.00952	55
60	0.08699	81713	7108	392053	0.01813	1431002	36.68	17.51	0.01799	60
65	0.13514	74604	10082	349339	0.02886	1038949	36.68	13.93	0.02863	65
70	0.22340	64522	14414	288004	0.05005	689610	36.68	10.69	0.04968	70
75	0.33804	50108	16938	208525	0.08123	401606	36.68	8.01	0.08069	75
80	0.48253	33170	16005	125882	0.12714	193081	36.68	5.82	0.12605	80
85+	*1.00000	17164	17164	67199	0.25543	67199	36.68	3.92	0.25158	85+

TABLE 4 POPULATION PROJECTION, USING FIXED AGE-SPECIFIC BIRTH AND DEATH RATES, IN THOUSANDS

Age at last birthday	1971 Total	Males	Females	1976 Total	Males	Females	1981 Total	Males	Females	Age at last birthday
0–4	642	329	313	787	403	384	972	498	474	0–4
5–9	579	298	281	634	325	309	778	399	379	5–9
10–14	569	292	277	577	297	280	632	324	308	10–14
15–19	527	270	257	566	290	276	574	295	279	15–19
20–24	383	196	187	524	268	256	562	288	274	20–24
25–29	277	143	134	380	194	186	519	265	254	25–29
30–34	273	139	134	274	141	133	376	192	184	30–34
35–39	239	125	114	269	137	132	271	139	132	35–39
40–44	225	125	100	236	123	113	264	134	130	40–44
45–49	186	104	82	220	121	99	230	119	111	45–49
50–54	146	81	65	178	99	79	211	115	96	50–54
55–59	124	69	55	137	75	62	168	92	76	55–59
60–64	92	47	45	113	61	52	125	67	58	60–64
65–69	62	30	32	79	39	40	97	51	46	65–69
70–74	38	17	21	48	22	26	62	29	33	70–74
75–79	20	8	12	27	11	16	33	14	19	75–79
80–84	9	3	6	11	4	7	15	6	9	80–84
85 +	4	1	3	4	1	3	6	2	4	85 +
All ages	4395	2277	2118	5064	2611	2453	5895	3029	2866	All ages

TABLE 5 OBSERVED AND PROJECTED VITAL RATES

Rates per thousand	Observed Total	Males	Females	Projected 1971 Males	Females	1976 Males	Females	1981 Males	Females	Stable Males	Females
Birth	31.53	31.08	32.01	32.20	32.85	35.57	35.95	37.09	37.17	35.08	34.09
Death	5.45	5.91	4.95	6.22	5.01	6.62	5.23	6.90	5.38	7.01	6.02
Increase	26.08	25.18	27.06	25.97	27.84	28.95	30.72	30.20	31.79	28.0713	

TABLE 6 RATES STANDARDIZED ON THREE STANDARD COUNTRIES

Standardized rates per thousand	England and Wales, 1961 Total	Males	Females	United States, 1960 Total	Males	Females	Mexico, 1960 Total	Males	Females
Birth	30.13	31.12*	28.43	30.56	28.90*	29.32	34.97	28.83*	33.96
Death	14.02	15.78*	13.76	11.54	12.28*	10.29	6.23	6.65*	5.32
Increase	16.11	15.34*	14.68	19.02	16.63*	19.04	28.74	22.18*	28.65

TABLE 7 VITAL STATISTICS AND RATES INFERRED FROM AGE DISTRIBUTIONS (FEMALES)

Vital statistics		Thompson Age range	NRR	1000r	Interval	Bourgeois-Pichat Age range	NRR	1000b	1000d	1000r	Coale	
TFR	4.76	0–4	2.17	28.29	27.38	5–29	3.03	44.14	3.12	41.02	1000b	40.13
GRR	2.32	5–9	2.53	34.66	27.34	30–54	2.43	39.64	6.74	32.90	1000d	5.18
NRR	2.18	10–14	2.65	34.71	27.28	55–79	3.53	91.33	44.64	46.69	1000r	33.95
Generation	27.80	15–19	2.24	29.73	27.19	*25–59	2.34	37.19	5.77	31.42	$1000k_1$	0.
Sex ratio	105.4										$1000k_2$	0.

TABLE 8 LESLIE MATRIX AND ITS ANALYSIS (FEMALES)

Start of age interval	Sub-diagonal	First row	Percent in stable population	Fisher values	Total reproductive values	Net maternity function	Matrix equation coefficient
0	0.98831	0.00000	15.492	1.102	313440	0.00000	0.00000
5	0.99703	0.00000	13.300	1.284	356266	0.00000	0.00000
10	0.99651	0.04257	11.518	1.482	382974	0.00000	0.04195
15	0.99414	0.35850	9.971	1.665	313136	0.08389	0.35203
20	0.99330	0.70467	8.610	1.531	206535	0.62017	0.68788
25	0.99265	0.60924	7.429	0.992	133494	0.75560	0.59074
30	0.99009	0.32536	6.406	0.475	54877	0.42589	0.31412
35	0.98573	0.14936	5.509	0.189	19194	0.20236	0.14234
40	0.98161	0.05008	4.718	0.053	4421	0.08232	0.04706
45	0.97337	0.00640	4.023	0.006	408	0.01181	0.00590
50	0.96075	0.00002	3.401	0.000	1	0.00000	0.00000
55	0.81166		9.624				

Parameters

	Integral	Matrix
λ_1	1.1507	1.1512
λ_2	0.3873	0.3859
	+0.8994	+0.8553 i
r_1	0.0281	0.0282
r_2	-0.0042	-0.0108
	+0.2328	+0.2303 i
c_1		19245
c_2		-8817
		81865 i
$2\pi/y$	26.986	27.288
Δ	4.783	

China (Taiwan), 1966 (rural)

TABLE 1 DATA INPUT TO COMPUTATIONS

Age at last birthday	Population					Births, by age of mother	Deaths			Age at last birthday
	Total	Males	%	Females	%		Total	Males	Females	
0	166210	85364	3.1	80846	3.2	0	4183	2252	1931	0
1–4	683955	351013	12.6	332942	13.0	0	3454	1752	1702	1–4
5–9	810053	413850	14.9	396203	15.5	0	753	458	295	5–9
10–14	739658	377782	13.6	361876	14.1	0	503	287	215	10–14
15–19	536231	276121	9.9	260110	10.1	11224	656	374	282	15–19
20–24	385380	208155	7.5	177225	6.9	52640	731	479	252	20–24
25–29	368551	196940	7.1	171511	6.7	61189	765	495	270	25–29
30–34	327805	173173	6.2	154632	6.0	32920	849	507	342	30–34
35–39	301573	163996	5.9	137577	5.4	15476	1002	622	380	35–39
40–44	242066	129646	4.7	112420	4.4	5627	1116	701	415	40–44
45–49	198400	106702	3.8	91698	3.6	678	1269	834	435	45–49
50–54	179041	97607	3.5	81434	3.2	0	1633	1073	560	50–54
55–59	143009	74340	2.7	68669	2.7	0	2019	1301	718	55–59
60–64	102942	52092	1.9	50850	2.0	0	2422	1470	952	60–64
65–69	70064	33832	1.2	36232	1.4	0	2576	1498	1078	65–69
70–74	42780	19224	0.7	23556	0.9		2454	1292	1162	70–74
75–79	24586	9915	0.4	14571	0.6		2262	1092	1170	75–79
80–84	11117	3860	0.1	7257	0.3	92397 M	1550	650	900	80–84
85 +	5643	1478	0.1	4165	0.2	87357 F	1434	414	1020	85 +
All ages	5339064	2775090		2563974		179754	31631	17551	14080	All ages

TABLE 2 LIFE TABLE FOR MALES

Age, x	$_nq_x$	l_x	$_nd_x$	$_nL_x$	$_nm_x$	T_x	$1000r_x$	$\overset{\circ}{e}_x$	$_nM_x$	Age, x
0	0.02597	100000	2597	98431	0.02638	6446677	0.00	64.47	0.02638	0
1	0.01970	97403	1919	384472	0.00499	6348245	0.00	65.17	0.00499	1
5	0.00547	95484	523	476115	0.00110	5963773	12.54	62.45	0.00111	5
10	0.00380	94962	361	473932	0.00076	5487658	39.50	57.79	0.00076	10
15	0.00684	94601	647	471534	0.00137	5013727	58.17	53.00	0.00135	15
20	0.01148	93953	1079	467176	0.00231	4542193	31.65	48.35	0.00230	20
25	0.01250	92874	1161	461523	0.00252	4075017	15.83	43.88	0.00251	25
30	0.01456	91714	1335	455343	0.00293	3613494	15.30	39.40	0.00293	30
35	0.01886	90379	1704	447850	0.00381	3158150	25.01	34.94	0.00379	35
40	0.02685	88674	2381	437756	0.00544	2710301	37.41	30.55	0.00541	40
45	0.03848	86294	3321	423600	0.00784	2272544	20.46	26.34	0.00782	45
50	0.05381	82973	4465	404395	0.01104	1848944	24.48	22.28	0.01099	50
55	0.08478	78507	6655	376965	0.01766	1444549	44.42	18.40	0.01750	55
60	0.13341	71852	9585	336523	0.02848	1067584	49.62	14.86	0.02822	60
65	0.20152	62266	12548	280974	0.04466	731061	49.62	11.74	0.04428	65
70	0.29058	49718	14447	213044	0.06781	450088	49.62	9.05	0.06721	70
75	0.43342	35271	15287	137559	0.11113	237044	49.62	6.72	0.11014	75
80	0.58415	19984	11673	68741	0.16982	99484	49.62	4.98	0.16839	80
85 +	1.00000	8310	8310	30744	0.27031	30744	49.62	3.70	0.28011	85 +

TABLE 3 LIFE TABLE FOR FEMALES

Age, x	$_nq_x$	l_x	$_nd_x$	$_nL_x$	$_nm_x$	T_x	$1000r_x$	$\overset{\circ}{e}_x$	$_nM_x$	Age, x
0	0.02355	100000	2355	98604	0.02388	6893059	0.00	68.93	0.02388	0
1	0.02018	97645	1970	385366	0.00511	6794456	0.00	69.58	0.00511	1
5	0.00367	95675	351	477496	0.00074	6409089	11.73	66.99	0.00074	5
10	0.00300	95324	286	475939	0.00060	5931593	41.34	62.23	0.00060	10
15	0.00547	95038	520	473972	0.00110	5455654	70.34	57.40	0.00108	15
20	0.00711	94518	672	470959	0.00143	4981682	40.21	52.71	0.00142	20
25	0.00785	93847	736	467467	0.00158	4510724	11.95	48.06	0.00157	25
30	0.01102	93111	1027	463097	0.00222	4043256	19.92	43.42	0.00221	30
35	0.01376	92084	1267	457385	0.00277	3580159	29.03	38.88	0.00275	35
40	0.01837	90817	1668	450085	0.00371	3122774	36.87	34.39	0.00369	40
45	0.02354	89148	2099	440762	0.00476	2672689	27.29	29.98	0.00474	45
50	0.03396	87049	2957	428320	0.00690	2231927	21.81	25.64	0.00688	50
55	0.05146	84093	4328	410531	0.01054	1803607	35.65	21.45	0.01046	55
60	0.09035	79765	7207	382022	0.01887	1393077	36.68	17.45	0.01872	60
65	0.13995	72558	10154	338788	0.02997	1011054	36.68	13.93	0.02975	65
70	0.22187	62404	13845	278677	0.04968	672266	36.68	10.77	0.04933	70
75	0.33475	48559	16255	202480	0.08028	393589	36.68	8.11	0.07975	75
80	0.47686	32304	15404	123142	0.12509	191108	36.68	5.92	0.12402	80
85 +	*1.00000	16899	16899	67957	0.24864	67957	36.68	4.02	0.24490	85 +

TABLE 4 POPULATION PROJECTION, USING FIXED AGE-SPECIFIC BIRTH AND DEATH RATES, IN THOUSANDS

Age at last birthday	1971 Total	Males	Females	1976 Total	Males	Females	1981 Total	Males	Females	Age at last birthday
0–4	956	491	465	1197	615	582	1504	772	732	0–4
5–9	838	430	408	943	484	459	1181	605	575	5–9
10–14	807	412	395	835	428	407	940	482	458	10–14
15–19	736	376	360	803	410	393	831	426	405	15–19
20–24	532	274	258	730	372	358	797	406	391	20–24
25–29	382	206	176	527	270	257	723	368	355	25–29
30–34	364	194	170	377	203	174	521	267	254	30–34
35–39	323	170	153	359	191	168	372	200	172	35–39
40–44	295	160	135	316	166	150	352	187	165	40–44
45–49	235	125	110	288	155	133	308	151	147	45–49
50–54	191	102	89	227	120	107	277	148	129	50–54
55–59	169	91	78	180	95	85	215	112	103	55–59
60–64	130	66	64	154	81	73	164	85	79	60–64
65–69	88	43	45	112	55	57	132	68	54	65–69
70–74	56	26	30	70	33	37	89	42	47	70–74
75–79	29	12	17	39	17	22	48	21	27	75–79
80–84	14	5	9	16	6	10	21	8	13	80–84
85 +	6	2	4	7	2	5	9	3	6	85 +
All ages	6151	3185	2966	7180	3703	3477	8484	4362	4122	All ages

TABLE 5 OBSERVED AND PROJECTED VITAL RATES

Rates per thousand	Observed Total	Males	Females	Projected 1971 Males	Females	1976 Males	Females	1981 Males	Females	Stable Males	Females
Birth	33.67	33.30	34.07	34.85	35.37	38.75	39.03	40.44	40.45	38.76	37.85
Death	5.92	5.32	5.49	6.57	5.52	6.87	5.69	7.04	5.79	6.76	5.85
Increase	27.74	26.97	28.58	28.28	29.86	31.88	33.34	33.40	34.66		31.9959

TABLE 6 RATES STANDARDIZED ON THREE STANDARD COUNTRIES

Standardized rates per thousand	England and Wales, 1961 Total	Males	Females	United States, 1960 Total	Males	Females	Mexico, 1960 Total	Males	Females
Birth	34.25	33.63*	32.26	34.75	31.06*	33.27	39.35	31.74*	38.15
Death	14.07	16.29*	14.05	11.66	12.82*	10.63	5.54	6.94*	5.71
Increase	20.18	17.34*	18.21	23.09	18.24*	22.64	32.81	24.80*	32.44

TABLE 7 VITAL STATISTICS AND RATES INFERRED FROM AGE DISTRIBUTIONS (FEMALES)

Vital statistics		Thompson Age range	NRR	1000r	Interval	Bourgeois-Pichat Age range	NRR	1000b	1000d	1000r	Coale
TFR	5.40	0–4	2.35	31.19	27.36	5–29	3.53	48.07	1.38	46.69	1000b
GRR	2.62	5–9	2.70	37.26	27.31	30–54	2.24	34.86	4.96	29.90	1000d
NRR	2.44	10–14	2.75	35.04	27.25	55–79	3.40	88.43	43.10	45.33	1000r
Generation	27.93	15–19	2.25	29.85	27.16	*30–54	2.24	34.86	4.96	29.90	$1000k_1$
Sex ratio	105.77										$1000k_2$

TABLE 8 LESLIE MATRIX AND ITS ANALYSIS (FEMALES)

Start of age interval	Sub-diagonal	First row	Percent in stable population	Fisher values	Total reproductive values	Net maternity function	Matrix equation coefficient
0	0.98662	0.00000	16.952	1.119	462845	0.00000	0.00000
5	0.99674	0.00000	14.244	1.331	527421	0.00000	0.00000
10	0.99587	0.05054	12.091	1.568	567480	0.00000	0.04970
15	0.99364	0.39782	10.255	1.792	466164	0.09939	0.38961
20	0.99259	0.76550	8.678	1.670	295959	0.67982	0.74492
25	0.99065	0.56733	7.335	1.113	190974	0.81003	0.64458
30	0.98767	0.38102	6.190	0.566	87445	0.47913	0.36459
35	0.98404	0.19021	5.206	0.241	33126	0.25004	0.17976
40	0.97929	0.06736	4.363	0.071	7992	0.10948	0.06266
45	0.97177	0.00870	3.639	0.008	761	0.01584	0.00792
50	0.95847	0.00001	3.012	0.000	1	0.00000	0.00000
55	0.81482		8.033				

Parameters

	Integral	Matrix
λ_1	1.1735	1.1742
λ_2	0.3902	0.3894
	+0.9049	+0.8701 i
r_1	0.0320	0.0321
r_2	-0.0029	-0.0096
	+0.2327	+0.2300 i
c_1		25629
c_2		-11147
		118222 i
$2\pi/y$	26.998	27.319
Δ	3.836	

Hong Kong, 1966

TABLE 1 DATA INPUT TO COMPUTATIONS

Age at last birthday	Population					Births, by age of mother	Deaths			Age at last birthday
	Total	Males	%	Females	%		Total	Males	Females	
0	97700	50100	2.6	47600	2.6	0	2298	1302	996	0
1–4	435500	224000	11.8	211500	11.5	0	969	511	458	1–4
5–9	528300	275100	14.5	253200	13.8	0	256	147	109	5–9
10–14	448400	233600	12.3	214800	11.7	48	233	139	94	10–14
15–19	385300	204100	10.8	181200	9.9	5246	242	160	82	15–19
20–24	201100	106900	5.6	94200	5.1	20078	210	141	69	20–24
25–29	211300	114200	6.0	97100	5.3	28275	267	172	95	25–29
30–34	245000	129200	6.8	115800	6.3	23473	428	275	153	30–34
35–39	260000	132100	7.0	127900	7.0	14224	501	354	237	35–39
40–44	233600	118600	6.3	115000	6.3	4783	826	513	313	40–44
45–49	192000	98300	5.2	93700	5.1	309	1067	686	381	45–49
50–54	165900	83400	4.4	82500	4.5	0	1404	920	484	50–54
55–59	116600	53100	2.8	63500	3.5	0	1584	1032	552	55–59
60–64	90500	35400	1.9	55100	3.0	0	1755	1075	680	60–64
65–69	56900	18200	1.0	38700	2.1	0	1737	915	822	65–69
70–74	37900	11300	0.6	26600	1.4		1715	800	915	70–74
75–79	16800	3900	0.2	12900	0.7		1371	518	853	75–79
80–84	6437	1461	0.1	4976	0.3	49630 M	962	315	647	80–84
85+	3163	1139	0.1	2024	0.1	46806 F	772	206	566	85+
All ages	3732400	1894100		1838300		96436	18697	10191	8506	All ages

TABLE 2 LIFE TABLE FOR MALES

Age, x	$_nq_x$	l_x	$_nd_x$	$_nL_x$	$_nm_x$	T_x	$1000r_x$	$\overset{\circ}{e}_x$	$_nM_x$	Age, x
0	0.02554	100000	2554	98260	0.02599	6589799	0.00	65.90	0.02599	0
1	0.00907	97446	883	387288	0.00228	6491539	0.00	66.62	0.00228	1
5	0.00265	96563	256	482176	0.00053	6104252	15.02	63.22	0.00053	5
10	0.00298	96307	287	480845	0.00060	5622076	29.24	58.38	0.00060	10
15	0.00397	96020	381	479221	0.00080	5141231	77.30	53.54	0.00078	15
20	0.00662	95639	633	476683	0.00133	4662010	56.83	48.75	0.00132	20
25	0.00750	95006	713	473326	0.00151	4185327	0.00	44.05	0.00151	25
30	0.01059	94293	998	469089	0.00213	3712002	0.00	39.37	0.00213	30
35	0.01370	93295	1278	463484	0.00276	3242913	5.62	34.76	0.00276	35
40	0.02152	92017	1980	455514	0.00435	2779429	25.03	30.21	0.00433	40
45	0.03453	90036	3109	442982	0.00702	2323915	27.99	25.81	0.00698	45
50	0.05439	86928	4728	423781	0.01116	1880933	49.58	21.64	0.01103	50
55	0.09413	82199	7738	392887	0.01969	1457151	65.72	17.73	0.01944	55
60	0.14311	74462	10656	347056	0.03071	1064254	56.24	14.29	0.03037	60
65	0.22579	63805	14407	283920	0.05074	717208	56.24	11.24	0.05027	65
70	0.30428	49398	15031	210001	0.07158	433288	56.24	8.77	0.07080	70
75	0.50108	34367	17221	128093	0.13444	223287	56.24	6.50	0.13282	75
80	0.68283	17147	11708	53690	0.21808	95194	56.24	5.55	0.21561	80
85+	1.00000	5438	5438	41504	0.13103	41504	56.24	7.63	0.18086	85+

TABLE 3 LIFE TABLE FOR FEMALES

Age, x	$_nq_x$	l_x	$_nd_x$	$_nL_x$	$_nm_x$	T_x	$1000r_x$	$\overset{\circ}{e}_x$	$_nM_x$	Age, x
0	0.02064	100000	2064	98631	0.02092	7268807	0.00	72.69	0.02092	0
1	0.00861	97936	843	389382	0.00217	7170177	0.00	73.21	0.00217	1
5	0.00212	97093	206	484949	0.00043	6780794	17.91	69.84	0.00043	5
10	0.00219	96887	212	483907	0.00044	6295845	33.02	64.98	0.00044	10
15	0.00229	96675	221	482852	0.00046	5811938	81.92	60.12	0.00045	15
20	0.00369	96454	356	481431	0.00074	5329086	61.66	55.25	0.00073	20
25	0.00488	96098	469	479375	0.00098	4847655	0.00	50.44	0.00098	25
30	0.00659	95629	630	476656	0.00132	4368280	0.00	45.68	0.00132	30
35	0.00922	94999	876	472941	0.00185	3891624	0.00	40.96	0.00185	35
40	0.01359	94123	1279	467626	0.00273	3418684	28.30	36.32	0.00272	40
45	0.02023	92844	1878	459809	0.00409	2951058	29.06	31.79	0.00407	45
50	0.02909	90966	2646	448609	0.00590	2491249	32.82	27.39	0.00587	50
55	0.04280	88320	3780	432668	0.00874	2042640	31.55	23.13	0.00869	55
60	0.06075	84540	5136	410758	0.01250	1509972	63.39	19.04	0.01234	60
65	0.10247	79404	8136	378007	0.02152	1199204	63.39	15.10	0.02124	65
70	0.16151	71268	11510	329474	0.03493	821197	63.39	11.52	0.03440	70
75	0.28963	59758	17307	257536	0.06720	491723	63.39	8.23	0.06612	75
80	0.49911	42450	21187	160107	0.13233	234187	63.39	5.52	0.13002	80
85+	•1.00000	21263	21263	74080	0.28703	74080	63.39	3.48	0.27964	85+

TABLE 4 POPULATION PROJECTION, USING FIXED AGE-SPECIFIC BIRTH AND DEATH RATES, IN THOUSANDS

Age at last birthday	1971 Total	Males	Females	1976 Total	Males	Females	1981 Total	Males	Females	Age at last birthday
0–4	503	258	245	608	312	296	764	392	372	0–4
5–9	529	272	257	499	256	243	604	310	294	5–9
10–14	527	274	253	528	271	257	499	256	243	10–14
15–19	447	233	214	525	273	252	527	271	256	15–19
20–24	384	203	181	446	232	214	523	272	251	20–24
25–29	200	106	94	382	202	180	443	230	213	25–29
30–34	210	113	97	198	105	93	379	200	179	30–34
35–39	243	128	115	208	112	96	197	104	93	35–39
40–44	256	130	126	239	125	114	205	110	95	40–44
45–49	228	115	113	250	126	124	234	122	112	45–49
50–54	185	94	91	220	110	110	242	121	121	50–54
55–59	157	77	80	175	87	88	208	102	106	55–59
60–64	107	47	60	144	68	76	161	77	84	60–64
65–69	80	29	51	93	38	55	126	56	70	65–69
70–74	47	13	34	65	21	44	76	28	48	70–74
75–79	28	7	21	34	8	26	48	13	35	75–79
80–84	10	2	8	16	3	13	19	3	16	80–84
85 +	3	1	2	5	1	4	8	2	6	85 +
All ages	4144	2102	2042	4635	2350	2285	5263	2669	2594	All ages

TABLE 5 OBSERVED AND PROJECTED VITAL RATES

Rates per thousand	Observed Total	Males	Females	Projected 1971 Males	Females	1976 Males	Females	1981 Males	Females	Stable Males	Females
Birth	25.84	26.20	25.46	26.94	26.17	30.61	29.73	33.53	32.54	32.53	31.20
Death	5.01	5.38	4.63	5.91	5.06	6.59	5.67	7.20	6.11	7.12	5.80
Increase	20.83	20.82	20.83	21.03	21.11	24.02	24.06	26.32	26.43		25.4082

TABLE 6 RATES STANDARDIZED ON THREE STANDARD COUNTRIES

Standardized rates per thousand	England and Wales, 1961 Total	Males	Females	United States, 1960 Total	Males	Females	Mexico, 1960 Total	Males	Females
Birth	28.38	27.57*	26.70	28.85	26.05*	27.59	31.88	24.29*	30.87
Death	13.11	14.84*	11.90	10.74	11.33*	8.80	5.61	6.15*	4.33
Increase	15.27	12.74*	14.79	18.11	14.72*	18.79	26.28	18.13*	26.54

TABLE 7 VITAL STATISTICS AND RATES INFERRED FROM AGE DISTRIBUTIONS (FEMALES)

Vital statistics		Thompson Age range	NRR	$1000r$	Interval	Bourgeois-Pichat Age range	NRR	$1000b$	$1000d$	$1000r$	Coale
TFR	4.46	0–4	2.08	27.57	27.41	5–29	4.33	45.23	−9.03	54.25	$1000b$
GRR	2.17	5–9	2.30	31.09	27.37	30–54	1.57	25.24	8.44	16.80	$1000d$
NRR	2.07	10–14	1.97	24.34	27.31	55–79	3.05	89.80	48.54	41.26	$1000r$
Generation	28.63	15–19	1.73	16.74	27.23	*40–64	2.30	48.96	18.15	30.81	$1000k_1$
Sex ratio	106.03										$1000k_2$

TABLE 8 LESLIE MATRIX AND ITS ANALYSIS (FEMALES)

Start of age interval	Sub-diagonal	First row	Percent in stable population	Fisher values	Total reproductive values	Net maternity function	Matrix equation coefficient	Parameters	Integral	Matrix
0	0.99372	0.00000	14.316	1.091	282793	0.00000	0.00000	λ_1	1.1355	1.1359
5	0.99785	0.00026	12.524	1.248	315885	0.00000	0.00026	λ_2	0.4291	0.4285
10	0.99782	0.03448	11.002	1.420	304980	0.00052	0.03419			+0.8618	+0.8340 i
15	0.99706	0.28597	9.665	1.579	286037	0.06785	0.28295	r_1	0.0254	0.0255
20	0.99573	0.59582	8.484	1.485	139915	0.49804	0.58778	r_2	−0.0076	−0.0129
25	0.99433	0.58356	7.437	1.041	101107	0.67752	0.57323		+0.2218	+0.2192 i
30	0.99221	0.37074	6.510	0.549	63566	0.46895	0.36212	c_1		17458
35	0.98876	0.18041	5.687	0.221	28214	0.25528	0.17484	c_2		39853
40	0.98328	0.05308	4.950	0.054	6241	0.09440	0.05088			102515 i
45	0.97564	0.00391	4.285	0.004	353	0.00736	0.00368	$2\pi/y$	28.332	28.662
50	0.96446	0.00001	3.681	0.000	1	0.00000	0.00000	Δ	7.278	
55	0.82600		11.457							

Indonesia, 1961 (including West Irian)

TABLE 1 DATA INPUT TO COMPUTATIONS

Age at last birthday	Population					Births, by age of mother	Deaths			Age at last birthday
	Total	Males	%	Females	%		Total	Males	Females	
0	3176525	1505915	3.2	1670510	3.4	0	474199	245239	228960	0
1–4	13895763	6969412	14.7	6926351	14.2	0	363067	197080	165987	1–4
5–9	15349882	7695680	16.2	7654202	15.7	0	56937	29070	27867	5–9
10–14	8193708	4325370	9.1	3868338	7.9	0	31798	16794	15004	10–14
15–19	7721731	3840178	8.1	3881553	7.9	536346	37856	19571	18285	15–19
20–24	7804816	3457820	7.3	4346996	8.9	1240764	48978	22422	26556	20–24
25–29	8228414	3770673	7.9	4457741	9.1	1221766	61581	28636	32945	25–29
30–34	7675424	3574537	7.5	4100887	8.4	738359	62922	30255	32667	30–34
35–39	6104370	3100735	6.5	3003635	6.1	419010	55877	30480	25397	35–39
40–44	4998238	2628163	5.5	2370075	4.9	148192	55951	33236	22715	40–44
45–49	3986643	2021627	4.3	1965016	4.0	29910	55579	32726	22853	45–49
50–54	3068054	1543006	3.2	1525048	3.1	0	55778	32202	23576	50–54
55–59	2216435	1123233	2.4	1093202	2.2	0	58687	32688	25999	55–59
60–64	1538051	777277	1.6	760774	1.6	0	61986	32937	29049	60–64
65–69	1010324	498965	1.1	511359	1.0	0	59758	30717	29041	65–69
70–74	617306	298024	0.6	319282	0.7		52320	26297	26023	70–74
75–79	369489	190972	0.4	178517	0.4		44687	23635	21052	75–79
80–84	240862	102017	0.2	138845	0.3	2232189 M	47971	20384	27587	80–84
85 +	175386	85356	0.2	90030	0.2	2102158 F	84620	41197	43423	85 +
All ages	96371421	47508960		48862461		4334347	1770552	925566	844986	All ages

TABLE 2 LIFE TABLE FOR MALES

Age, x	nq_x	l_x	nd_x	nL_x	nm_x	T_x	$1000r_x$	$\overset{\circ}{e}_x$	nM_x	Age, x
0	0.14785	100000	14785	90788	0.16285	4413481	0.00	44.13	0.15285	0
1	0.10502	85215	8949	316463	0.02828	4322693	0.00	50.73	0.02828	1
5	0.01750	76266	1335	377994	0.00353	4006230	57.98	52.53	0.00378	5
10	0.01934	74931	1449	371142	0.00390	3628236	65.45	48.42	0.00388	10
15	0.02522	73482	1853	362954	0.00511	3257094	17.26	44.32	0.00510	15
20	0.03192	71629	2286	352583	0.00648	2894140	0.00	40.40	0.00648	20
25	0.03728	69343	2585	340354	0.00759	2541557	0.00	36.65	0.00759	25
30	0.04148	66758	2769	326971	0.00847	2201204	11.01	32.97	0.00846	30
35	0.04809	63989	3077	312457	0.00985	1874233	20.63	29.29	0.00983	35
40	0.06154	60912	3748	295479	0.01269	1561776	29.99	25.64	0.01265	40
45	0.07817	57164	4468	274963	0.01625	1266297	36.84	22.15	0.01619	45
50	0.09977	52696	5257	250754	0.02097	991335	37.16	18.81	0.02087	50
55	0.13667	47438	6483	221529	0.02927	740581	38.46	15.61	0.02910	55
60	0.19244	40955	7881	185564	0.04247	519052	15.41	12.67	0.04237	60
65	0.26757	33073	8849	143424	0.06170	333488	15.41	10.08	0.06156	65
70	0.36111	24224	8748	98921	0.08843	190064	15.41	7.85	0.08824	70
75	0.46917	15477	7261	58525	0.12407	91143	15.41	5.89	0.12376	75
80	0.65294	8215	5364	26748	0.20055	32618	15.41	3.97	0.19981	80
85 +	*1.00000	2851	2851	5870	0.48575	5870	15.41	2.06	0.48265	85 +

TABLE 3 LIFE TABLE FOR FEMALES

Age, x	nq_x	l_x	nd_x	nL_x	nm_x	T_x	$1000r_x$	$\overset{\circ}{e}_x$	nM_x	Age, x
0	0.12631	100000	12631	92165	0.13705	4753404	0.00	47.53	0.13705	0
1	0.08999	87369	7862	328089	0.02396	4661239	0.00	53.35	0.02396	1
5	0.01682	79506	1337	394188	0.00339	4333151	71.66	54.50	0.00364	5
10	0.01930	78169	1508	387157	0.00390	3938963	63.97	50.39	0.00388	10
15	0.02329	76660	1785	378994	0.00471	3551796	0.00	46.33	0.00471	15
20	0.03010	74875	2254	368918	0.00611	3172802	0.00	42.37	0.00611	20
25	0.03629	72621	2636	356618	0.00739	2803884	0.00	38.61	0.00739	25
30	0.03909	69986	2736	343122	0.00797	2447266	31.52	34.97	0.00797	30
35	0.04148	67250	2790	329336	0.00847	2104144	46.24	31.29	0.00846	35
40	0.04692	64460	3025	314885	0.00961	1774808	32.68	27.53	0.00958	40
45	0.05674	61436	3485	298739	0.01167	1459923	32.14	23.76	0.01163	45
50	0.07504	57950	4349	279418	0.01556	1161183	42.27	20.04	0.01546	50
55	0.11348	53601	6083	253629	0.02398	881765	44.51	16.45	0.02378	55
60	0.17533	47519	8331	217536	0.03830	628137	17.54	13.22	0.03818	60
65	0.24966	39187	9784	171817	0.05694	410601	17.54	10.48	0.05679	65
70	0.33880	29404	9962	121912	0.08171	238784	17.54	8.12	0.08150	70
75	0.45348	19442	8816	74536	0.11828	116872	17.54	6.01	0.11793	75
80	0.65230	10625	6931	34732	0.19955	42336	17.54	3.98	0.19869	80
85 +	*1.00000	3694	3694	7504	0.48584	7504	17.54	2.05	0.48232	85 +

TABLE 4 POPULATION PROJECTION, USING FIXED AGE-SPECIFIC BIRTH AND DEATH RATES, IN THOUSANDS

Age at last birthday	1966			1971			1976			Age at last birthday
	Total	Males	Females	Total	Males	Females	Total	Males	Females	
0–4	17831	9043	8788	18481	9373	9108	21124	10713	10411	0–4
5–9	15930	7866	8064	16536	8393	8243	17242	8599	8543	5–9
10–14	15074	7556	7518	15544	7724	7920	16337	8241	8096	10–14
15–19	8017	4230	3787	14748	7389	7359	15306	7553	7753	15–19
20–24	7508	3730	3778	7795	4109	3686	14342	7178	7164	20–24
25–29	7540	3338	4202	7253	3601	3652	7530	3967	3563	25–29
30–34	7911	3622	4289	7250	3207	4043	6973	3459	3514	30–34
35–39	7352	3416	3936	7579	3462	4117	6945	3064	3881	35–39
40–44	5804	2932	2872	6993	3230	3763	7210	3274	3936	40–44
45–49	4695	2446	2249	5454	2729	2725	5576	3006	3570	45–49
50–54	3682	1844	1838	4333	2230	2103	5036	2488	2548	50–54
55–59	2747	1363	1384	3297	1529	1668	3879	1970	1909	55–59
60–64	1879	941	938	2329	1142	1187	2795	1364	1431	60–64
65–69	1202	601	601	1468	727	741	1821	883	938	65–69
70–74	707	344	363	840	414	426	1027	502	525	70–74
75–79	371	176	195	426	204	222	506	245	261	75–79
80–84	170	87	83	172	81	91	196	93	103	80–84
85 +	52	22	30	37	19	18	38	18	20	85 +
All ages	108472	53557	54915	120735	59663	61072	134883	66717	68166	All ages

TABLE 5 OBSERVED AND PROJECTED VITAL RATES

Rates per thousand	Observed			Projected						Stable	
				1966		1971		1976			
	Total	Males	Females	Males	Females	Males	Females	Males	Females	Males	Females
Birth	44.98	46.98	43.02	41.24	37.88	40.13	36.92	42.97	39.61	42.80	40.45
Death	18.37	19.48	17.29	18.27	15.85	17.82	15.48	18.16	15.90	19.50	17.25
Increase	26.60	27.50	25.73	22.97	22.03	22.32	21.44	24.81	23.71		23.1994

TABLE 6 RATES STANDARDIZED ON THREE STANDARD COUNTRIES

Standardized rates per thousand	England and Wales, 1961			United States, 1960			Mexico, 1960		
	Total	Males	Females	Total	Males	Females	Total	Males	Females
Birth	35.23	43.11*	33.12	35.88	40.58*	34.29	40.78	40.18*	39.45
Death	27.79	47.07*	29.45	24.94	37.60*	24.60	18.78	19.70*	17.55
Increase	7.44	-3.96*	3.66	10.95	2.98*	9.69	22.00	20.49*	21.90

TABLE 7 VITAL STATISTICS AND RATES INFERRED FROM AGE DISTRIBUTIONS (FEMALES)

Vital statistics		Thompson				Bourgeois-Pichat					Coale
		Age range	NRR	1000r	Interval	Age range	NRR	1000b	1000d	1000r	
TFR	5.47	0–4	1.93	25.14	27.01	5–29	1.47	32.59	18.27	14.32	1000b
GRR	2.66	5–9	1.93	24.86	26.89	30–54	2.78	80.20	42.31	37.89	1000d
NRR	1.88	10–14	1.10	3.62	26.81	55–79	2.45	58.01	24.89	33.12	1000r
Generation	27.18	15–19	1.33	10.20	26.66	*45–69	2.99	92.66	52.03	40.62	$1000k_1$
Sex ratio	106.19										$1000k_2$

TABLE 8 LESLIE MATRIX AND ITS ANALYSIS (FEMALES)

Start of age interval	Sub-diagonal	First row	Percent in stable population	Fisher values	Total reproductive values	Net maternity function	Matrix equation coefficient	Parameters		
									Integral	Matrix
0	0.93798	0.00000	16.071	1.259	10825469	0.00000	0.00000	λ_1	1.1230	1.1233
5	0.98219	0.00000	13.419	1.508	11543130	0.00000	0.00000	λ_2	0.3385	0.3587
10	0.97889	0.13785	11.732	1.725	6672221	0.00000	0.12699		+0.7216	+0.7061 i
15	0.97341	0.42397	10.224	1.802	6994705	0.25399	0.38235	r_1	0.0232	0.0233
20	0.96666	0.56089	8.859	1.531	6655906	0.51071	0.49238	r_2	-0.0454	-0.0466
25	0.96215	0.45586	7.623	1.049	4674831	0.47404	0.38683		+0.2264	+0.2201 i
30	0.95982	0.31994	6.529	0.628	2574483	0.29963	0.26122	c_1		477701
35	0.95612	0.20309	5.579	0.315	946134	0.22282	0.15916	c_2		2217972
40	0.94872	0.07844	4.748	0.103	243187	0.09549	0.05877			-1188671 i
45	0.93532	0.01551	4.010	0.017	34170	0.02205	0.01103	$2\pi/y$	27.749	28.541
50	0.90770	0.00000	3.339	0.000	0	0.00000	0.00000	Δ	8.346	
55	0.73804		7.866							

Israel, 1967 (Jewish population)

TABLE 1 DATA INPUT TO COMPUTATIONS

Age at last birthday	Population					Births, by age of mother	Deaths			Age at last birthday
	Total	Males	%	Females	%		Total	Males	Females	
0	50564	25885	2.2	24679	2.1	0	1052	582	470	0
1–4	196163	100779	8.5	95384	8.1	0	175	101	74	1–4
5–9	240701	123271	10.4	117430	10.0	0	91	54	37	5–9
10–14	252728	129715	10.9	123013	10.5	0	96	54	42	10–14
15–19	255499	132065	11.1	123434	10.5	3678	190	128	62	15–19
20–24	194317	100321	8.4	93996	8.0	17349	193	151	42	20–24
25–29	137124	68591	5.8	68533	5.8	14175	110	87	23	25–29
30–34	138965	68039	5.7	70926	6.1	9612	145	82	63	30–34
35–39	133782	64100	5.4	69682	5.9	4534	184	110	74	35–39
40–44	140282	65785	5.5	74497	6.4	1138	317	181	136	40–44
45–49	126039	63566	5.3	62473	5.3	195	463	255	208	45–49
50–54	122518	59053	5.0	63465	5.4	0	765	422	343	50–54
55–59	125779	64596	5.4	61183	5.2	0	1284	722	562	55–59
60–64	92772	49513	4.2	43259	3.7	0	1642	995	647	60–64
65–69	69654	34654	2.9	35000	3.0	0	2113	1216	897	65–69
70–74	41576	20570	1.7	21006	1.8		2132	1177	955	70–74
75–79	22889	11057	0.9	11832	1.0		2008	1055	953	75–79
80–84	11661	5399	0.5	6262	0.5	26067 M	1378	634	744	80–84
85+	9561	3907	0.3	5654	0.5	24514 F	1318	593	725	85+
All ages	2362574	1190866		1171708		50681	15656	8599	7057	All ages

TABLE 2 LIFE TABLE FOR MALES

Age, x	$_nq_x$	l_x	$_nd_x$	$_nL_x$	$_nm_x$	T_x	$1000r_x$	$\overset{\circ}{e}_x$	$_nM_x$	Age, x
0	0.02208	100000	2208	98333	0.02245	7058555	1.86	70.59	0.02248	0
1	0.00399	97792	390	390038	0.00100	6960322	1.86	71.17	0.00100	1
5	0.00219	97402	213	486479	0.00044	6570285	0.00	67.46	0.00044	5
10	0.00208	97189	202	485495	0.00042	6083806	0.00	62.60	0.00042	10
15	0.00486	96987	472	483866	0.00097	5598311	24.72	57.72	0.00097	15
20	0.00752	96515	726	480791	0.00151	5114445	64.17	52.99	0.00151	20
25	0.00631	95790	604	477406	0.00127	4633654	37.52	48.37	0.00127	25
30	0.00601	95185	572	474540	0.00121	4156248	5.46	43.66	0.00121	30
35	0.00855	94613	809	471192	0.00172	3681708	1.56	38.91	0.00172	35
40	0.01367	93804	1282	466032	0.00275	3210516	0.00	34.23	0.00275	40
45	0.01990	92522	1842	458404	0.00402	2744484	6.41	29.66	0.00401	45
50	0.03515	90681	3187	446045	0.00715	2286080	0.00	25.21	0.00715	50
55	0.05456	87493	4774	426539	0.01119	1840034	5.49	21.03	0.01118	55
60	0.09700	82719	8024	395085	0.02031	1413495	44.67	17.09	0.02010	60
65	0.16338	74695	12204	344591	0.03542	1018410	44.67	13.63	0.03509	65
70	0.25320	62491	15823	274112	0.05772	673819	44.67	10.78	0.05722	70
75	0.38624	46668	18025	187657	0.09605	399707	44.67	8.56	0.09541	75
80	0.44813	28643	12836	108935	0.11783	212050	44.67	7.40	0.11743	80
85+	1.00000	15807	15807	103115	0.15330	103115	44.67	6.52	0.15178	85+

TABLE 3 LIFE TABLE FOR FEMALES

Age, x	$_nq_x$	l_x	$_nd_x$	$_nL_x$	$_nm_x$	T_x	$1000r_x$	$\overset{\circ}{e}_x$	$_nM_x$	Age, x
0	0.01873	100000	1873	98568	0.01900	7413606	2.76	74.14	0.01904	0
1	0.00308	98127	303	391627	0.00077	7315038	2.76	74.55	0.00078	1
5	0.00157	97824	154	488736	0.00032	6923411	0.00	70.77	0.00032	5
10	0.00171	97670	167	487954	0.00034	6434675	0.00	65.88	0.00034	10
15	0.00251	97504	245	486917	0.00050	5946721	25.45	60.99	0.00050	15
20	0.00222	97259	216	485737	0.00044	5459805	58.41	56.14	0.00045	20
25	0.00169	97043	164	484848	0.00034	4974067	27.68	51.26	0.00034	25
30	0.00443	96879	429	483393	0.00089	4489219	0.00	46.34	0.00089	30
35	0.00530	96449	511	481063	0.00106	4005826	0.00	41.53	0.00106	35
40	0.00911	95939	874	477729	0.00183	3524764	8.96	36.74	0.00183	40
45	0.01657	95064	1575	471722	0.00334	3047035	12.62	32.05	0.00333	45
50	0.02669	93489	2495	461738	0.00540	2575312	0.00	27.55	0.00540	50
55	0.04525	90994	4117	445476	0.00924	2113574	28.79	23.23	0.00919	55
60	0.07291	86877	6334	419738	0.01509	1668093	40.17	19.20	0.01495	60
65	0.12201	80543	9827	379875	0.02587	1248360	40.17	15.50	0.02563	65
70	0.20690	70716	14631	318903	0.04588	868485	40.17	12.28	0.04546	70
75	0.33786	56085	18949	233529	0.08114	549582	40.17	9.80	0.08054	75
80	0.45548	37136	16915	141615	0.11944	316054	40.17	8.51	0.11881	80
85+	1.00000	20221	20221	174439	0.11592	174439	40.17	8.63	0.12823	85+

TABLE 4 POPULATION PROJECTION, USING FIXED AGE-SPECIFIC BIRTH AND DEATH RATES, IN THOUSANDS

Age at last birthday	1972 Total	1972 Males	1972 Females	1977 Total	1977 Males	1977 Females	1982 Total	1982 Males	1982 Females	Age at last birthday
0–4	273	140	133	320	164	156	353	181	172	0–4
5–9	246	126	120	272	140	132	319	164	155	5–9
10–14	240	123	117	246	126	120	271	139	132	10–14
15–19	252	129	123	240	123	117	244	125	119	15–19
20–24	254	131	123	250	128	122	239	122	117	20–24
25–29	194	100	94	253	130	123	250	128	122	25–29
30–34	136	68	68	193	99	94	253	130	123	30–34
35–39	139	68	71	136	68	68	191	98	93	35–39
40–44	132	63	69	137	67	70	135	67	68	40–44
45–49	139	65	74	130	62	68	135	66	69	45–49
50–54	123	62	61	135	63	72	128	61	67	50–54
55–59	117	56	61	118	59	59	129	60	69	55–59
60–64	118	60	58	110	52	58	111	55	56	60–64
65–69	82	43	39	104	52	52	98	46	52	65–69
70–74	57	28	29	67	34	33	86	42	44	70–74
75–79	29	14	15	41	19	22	48	24	24	75–79
80–84	13	6	7	17	8	9	24	11	13	80–84
85 +	13	5	8	15	6	9	19	8	11	85 +
All ages	2557	1287	1270	2784	1400	1384	3033	1527	1506	All ages

TABLE 5 OBSERVED AND PROJECTED VITAL RATES

Rates per thousand	Observed Total	Observed Males	Observed Females	Projected 1972 Males	Projected 1972 Females	Projected 1977 Males	Projected 1977 Females	Projected 1982 Males	Projected 1982 Females	Stable Males	Stable Females
Birth	21.45	21.89	21.01	24.33	23.30	25.66	24.54	25.06	23.95	23.35	22.62
Death	6.63	7.22	6.02	7.91	6.70	8.41	7.27	8.68	7.77	8.65	7.92
Increase	14.82	14.67	14.98	16.43	16.60	17.24	17.27	16.38	16.18		14.6931

TABLE 6 RATES STANDARDIZED ON THREE STANDARD COUNTRIES

Standardized rates per thousand	England and Wales, 1961 Total	England and Wales, 1961 Males	England and Wales, 1961 Females	United States, 1960 Total	United States, 1960 Males	United States, 1960 Females	Mexico, 1960 Total	Mexico, 1960 Males	Mexico, 1960 Females
Birth	20.29	23.32*	19.10	20.62	21.08*	19.73	23.68	21.42*	22.94
Death	10.59	9.88*	11.26	8.49	8.52*	8.16	4.39	6.43*	3.93
Increase	9.70	13.44*	7.83	12.13	12.56*	11.57	19.29	14.99*	19.01

TABLE 7 VITAL STATISTICS AND RATES INFERRED FROM AGE DISTRIBUTIONS (FEMALES)

Vital statistics		Thompson Age range	NRR	1000r	Interval	Bourgeois-Pichat Age range	NRR	1000b	1000d	1000r	Coale
TFR	3.20	0–4	1.42	12.92	27.45	5–29	2.05	28.66	2.15	26.51	1000b
GRR	1.55	5–9	1.57	16.75	27.42	30–54	1.13	14.74	10.34	4.40	1000d
NRR	1.51	10–14	1.76	20.33	27.37	55–79	3.49	166.93	120.60	46.33	1000r
Generation	27.85	15–19	1.78	16.45	27.28	*30–59	1.11	14.35	10.63	3.72	1000k_1
Sex ratio	105.90										1000k_2

TABLE 8 LESLIE MATRIX AND ITS ANALYSIS (FEMALES)

Start of age interval	Sub-diagonal	First row	Percent in stable population	Fisher values	Total reproductive values	Net maternity function	Matrix equation coefficient	Parameters	Integral	Matrix
0	0.99702	0.00000	10.694	1.058	127036	0.00000	0.00000	λ_1	1.0762	1.0764
5	0.99840	0.00000	9.906	1.142	134137	0.00000	0.00000	λ_2	0.3862	0.3888
10	0.99787	0.03539	9.188	1.231	151487	0.00000	0.03523		+0.8260	+0.7980 i
15	0.99758	0.25464	8.518	1.291	159330	0.07046	0.25294	r_1	0.0147	0.0147
20	0.99817	0.45546	7.895	1.123	105526	0.43541	0.46123	r_2	−0.0185	−0.0238
25	0.99700	0.40704	7.321	0.717	49153	0.48704	0.40260		+0.2267	+0.2235 i
30	0.99518	0.23840	6.781	0.342	24280	0.31816	0.23509	c_1		12223
35	0.99307	0.09551	6.270	0.117	8138	0.15202	0.09373	c_2		−27992
40	0.98743	0.02183	5.785	0.025	1850	0.03544	0.02130			19337 i
45	0.97883	0.00371	5.307	0.004	229	0.00715	0.00358	$2\pi/y$	27.717	28.115
50	0.96478	0.00002	4.826	0.000	1	0.00000	0.00000	Δ	5.662	
55	0.81045		17.509							

Japan, 1964

TABLE 1 DATA INPUT TO COMPUTATIONS

Age at last birthday	Population					Births, by age of mother	Deaths			Age at last birthday
	Total	Males	%	Females	%		Total	Males	Females	
0	1649367	847592	1.8	801775	1.6	0	34956	19917	15039	0
1–4	6259762	3212513	6.7	3047249	6.2	0	9230	5241	3989	1–4
5–9	7956427	4069997	8.5	3886430	7.9	0	4991	3097	1894	5–9
10–14	9832899	5022458	10.5	4810441	9.8	15	4032	2489	1543	10–14
15–19	10237028	5220415	11.0	5016513	10.2	16777	7480	5155	2325	15–19
20–24	9479078	4754676	10.0	4724402	9.6	478711	11256	7271	3985	20–24
25–29	8164043	4036993	8.5	4127050	8.4	809500	11910	7315	4595	25–29
30–34	7969418	3968187	8.3	4001231	8.1	332438	13514	8175	5339	30–34
35–39	7219116	3556873	7.5	3662243	7.4	68502	16162	9641	6521	35–39
40–44	5667150	2517584	5.3	3149566	6.4	10230	17334	9525	7809	40–44
45–49	4733298	2165102	4.5	2568196	5.2	469	22282	12423	9859	45–49
50–54	4613000	2161774	4.5	2451226	5.0	18	33323	19438	13885	50–54
55–59	3843248	1856133	3.9	1987115	4.0	1	44982	27967	17015	55–59
60–64	3317636	1612478	3.4	1705158	3.5	0	62229	39080	23149	60–64
65–69	2471922	1172783	2.5	1299139	2.6	0	76600	46123	30477	65–69
70–74	1682610	755252	1.6	927358	1.9		87940	48964	38976	70–74
75–79	1054771	430782	0.9	623989	1.3		90529	44521	46008	75–79
80–84	526722	185764	0.4	340958	0.7	882968 M	72527	30079	42448	80–84
85 +	238769	70286	0.1	168483	0.3	833793 F	51583	17077	34506	85 +
All ages	96916264	47617642		49298622		1716761	672860	363498	309362	All ages

TABLE 2 LIFE TABLE FOR MALES

Age, x	$_nq_x$	l_x	$_nd_x$	$_nL_x$	$_nm_x$	T_x	$1000r_x$	$\overset{\circ}{e}_x$	$_nM_x$	Age, x
0	0.02304	100000	2304	98371	0.02342	6771682	4.24	67.72	0.02350	0
1	0.00647	97696	632	388976	0.00163	6673311	4.24	68.31	0.00163	1
5	0.00380	97064	369	484396	0.00076	6284334	0.00	64.74	0.00075	5
10	0.00247	96695	239	482899	0.00050	5799938	0.00	59.98	0.00050	10
15	0.00493	96456	476	481192	0.00099	5317039	4.49	55.12	0.00099	15
20	0.00764	95980	733	478147	0.00153	4835847	24.23	50.38	0.00153	20
25	0.00903	95247	860	474133	0.00181	4357699	16.28	45.75	0.00181	25
30	0.01026	94387	968	469598	0.00206	3883566	10.52	41.15	0.00205	30
35	0.01354	93419	1265	464091	0.00273	3413958	42.71	36.54	0.00271	35
40	0.01889	92153	1741	456686	0.00381	2949877	45.69	32.01	0.00378	40
45	0.02836	90413	2564	446097	0.00575	2493192	9.29	27.58	0.00574	45
50	0.04410	87849	3874	430300	0.00900	2047095	5.88	23.30	0.00899	50
55	0.07298	83975	6129	405614	0.01511	1616794	13.70	19.25	0.01507	55
60	0.11534	77846	8979	368100	0.02439	1211180	32.19	15.56	0.02424	60
65	0.18083	68867	12453	314638	0.03958	843080	32.19	12.24	0.03933	65
70	0.28128	56414	15868	243281	0.06523	528442	32.19	9.37	0.06483	70
75	0.41156	40546	16687	160533	0.10395	285161	32.19	7.03	0.10335	75
80	0.56884	23859	13572	83350	0.16283	124628	32.19	5.22	0.16192	80
85 +	1.00000	10287	10287	41278	0.24921	41278	32.19	4.01	0.24297	85 +

TABLE 3 LIFE TABLE FOR FEMALES

Age, x	$_nq_x$	l_x	$_nd_x$	$_nL_x$	$_nm_x$	T_x	$1000r_x$	$\overset{\circ}{e}_x$	$_nM_x$	Age, x
0	0.01845	100000	1845	98697	0.01870	7294064	4.19	72.94	0.01875	0
1	0.00520	98155	510	391161	0.00130	7195367	4.19	73.31	0.00131	1
5	0.00243	97644	238	487628	0.00049	6804206	0.00	69.68	0.00049	5
10	0.00160	97407	156	486641	0.00032	6316578	0.00	64.85	0.00032	10
15	0.00232	97251	225	485743	0.00046	5829936	1.30	59.95	0.00046	15
20	0.00422	97026	410	484169	0.00085	5344193	18.70	55.08	0.00084	20
25	0.00556	96616	537	481785	0.00111	4860024	15.51	50.30	0.00111	25
30	0.00666	96079	640	478859	0.00134	4378240	10.57	45.57	0.00133	30
35	0.00889	95439	849	475185	0.00179	3899381	22.11	40.85	0.00178	35
40	0.01240	94590	1172	470216	0.00249	3424196	32.87	36.20	0.00248	40
45	0.01909	93418	1784	462922	0.00385	2953980	21.15	31.62	0.00384	45
50	0.02805	91634	2570	452158	0.00568	2491058	19.79	27.18	0.00566	50
55	0.04219	89064	3758	436570	0.00861	2038900	27.35	22.89	0.00856	55
60	0.06626	85307	5653	413478	0.01367	1602330	31.67	18.78	0.01358	60
65	0.11205	79654	8925	377614	0.02364	1188851	31.67	14.93	0.02346	65
70	0.19242	70729	13610	321498	0.04233	811237	31.67	11.47	0.04203	70
75	0.31419	57119	17946	241798	0.07422	489740	31.67	8.57	0.07373	75
80	0.47858	39172	18747	149510	0.12539	247941	31.67	6.33	0.12450	80
85 +	*1.00000	20425	20425	98431	0.20751	98431	31.67	4.82	0.20480	85 +

TABLE 4 POPULATION PROJECTION, USING FIXED AGE-SPECIFIC BIRTH AND DEATH RATES, IN THOUSANDS

Age at last birthday	1969			1974			1979			Age at last birthday
	Total	Males	Females	Total	Males	Females	Total	Males	Females	
0–4	8768	4498	4270	9342	4793	4549	9286	4764	4522	0–4
5–9	7868	4036	3832	8721	4471	4250	9292	4764	4528	5–9
10–14	7936	4057	3879	7847	4023	3824	8699	4457	4242	10–14
15–19	9807	5005	4802	7914	4043	3871	7826	4009	3817	15–19
20–24	10187	5187	5000	9759	4973	4786	7876	4017	3859	20–24
25–29	9416	4715	4701	10120	5144	4976	9693	4931	4762	25–29
30–34	8100	3998	4102	9343	4670	4573	10041	5095	4946	30–34
35–39	7893	3922	3971	8022	3951	4071	9252	4515	4537	35–39
40–44	7124	3500	3624	7788	3859	3929	7916	3888	4028	40–44
45–49	5560	2459	3101	6987	3419	3568	7638	3770	3868	45–49
50–54	4596	2088	2508	5401	2372	3029	5783	3298	3485	50–54
55–59	4405	2038	2367	4391	1969	2422	5150	2236	2924	55–59
60–64	3566	1684	1882	4091	1849	2242	4081	1787	2294	60–64
65–69	2935	1378	1557	3159	1440	1719	3628	1581	2047	65–69
70–74	2013	907	1106	2392	1066	1326	2576	1113	1463	70–74
75–79	1195	498	697	1430	598	832	1700	703	997	75–79
80–84	610	224	386	690	259	431	825	311	514	80–84
85 +	316	92	224	365	111	254	412	128	284	85 +
All ages	102295	50286	52009	107762	53010	54752	112684	55467	57217	All ages

TABLE 5 OBSERVED AND PROJECTED VITAL RATES

Rates per thousand	Observed			Projected						Stable	
				1969		1974		1979			
	Total	Males	Females	Males	Females	Males	Females	Males	Females	Males	Females
Birth	17.71	18.54	16.91	19.15	17.49	18.94	17.31	17.15	15.70	13.78	12.74
Death	6.94	7.63	6.28	8.23	6.88	8.73	7.41	9.17	7.99	15.65	14.61
Increase	10.77	10.91	10.64	10.92	10.61	10.21	9.91	7.98	7.71		-1.8681

TABLE 6 RATES STANDARDIZED ON THREE STANDARD COUNTRIES

Standardized rates per thousand	England and Wales, 1961			United States, 1960			Mexico, 1960		
	Total	Males	Females	Total	Males	Females	Total	Males	Females
Birth	12.65	14.85*	11.91	12.84	13.70*	12.29	15.09	14.09*	14.62
Death	11.95	12.42*	11.73	9.73	10.52*	8.60	5.07	7.91*	4.19
Increase	0.70	2.43*	0.18	3.11	3.18*	3.68	10.02	6.17*	10.43

TABLE 7 VITAL STATISTICS AND RATES INFERRED FROM AGE DISTRIBUTIONS (FEMALES)

Vital statistics		Thompson				Bourgeois-Pichat					Coale
		Age range	NRR	1000r	Interval	Age range	NRR	1000b	1000d	1000r	
TFR	2.03	0–4	0.92	-3.20	27.41	5–29	0.93	17.94	20.55	-2.63	1000b
GRR	0.99	5–9	1.02	0.82	27.37	30–54	1.91	37.20	13.32	23.88	1000d
NRR	0.95	10–14	1.40	12.12	27.32	55–79	2.31	56.18	25.19	30.99	$1000r$
Generation	27.78	15–19	1.61	16.49	27.24	*50–74	2.30	55.59	24.76	30.84	$1000k_1$
Sex ratio	105.90										$1000k_2$

TABLE 8 LESLIE MATRIX AND ITS ANALYSIS (FEMALES)

Start of age interval	Sub-diagonal	First row	Percent in stable population	Fisher values	Total reproductive values	Net maternity function	Matrix equation coefficient	Parameters		Integral	Matrix
0	0.99545	0.00000	6.271	1.016	3910430	0.00000	0.00000	λ_1		0.9907	0.9907
5	0.99798	0.00000	6.301	1.011	3929623	0.00000	0.00000	λ_2		0.3849	0.3832
10	0.99815	0.00397	6.347	1.004	4828458	0.00001	0.00395			+0.8242	+0.7966i
15	0.99676	0.12412	6.395	0.992	4977539	0.00789	0.12308	r_1		-0.0019	-0.0019
20	0.99508	0.35274	6.434	0.860	4061445	0.23827	0.34865	r_2		-0.0189	-0.0247
25	0.99393	0.33159	6.463	0.496	2045993	0.45902	0.32612			+0.2268	+0.2245i
30	0.99233	0.12091	6.484	0.155	621011	0.19323	0.11820	c_1			691539
35	0.98954	0.02607	6.494	0.031	114100	0.04317	0.02529	c_2			-1389688
40	0.98449	0.00408	5.487	0.004	13928	0.00742	0.00391				-122926i
45	0.97675	0.00023	6.446	0.000	629	0.00041	0.00021	$2\pi/y$		27.708	27.989
50	0.96552	0.00001	6.355	0.000	27	0.00002	0.00001	Δ		17.936	
55	0.78287		29.523								

TABLE 1   DATA INPUT TO COMPUTATIONS

Age at last birthday	Population					Births, by age of mother	Deaths			Age at last birthday
	Total	Males	%	Females	%		Total	Males	Females	
0	1508133	772908	1.6	735225	1.5	0	26213	15025	11188	0
1–4	6525238	3328237	6.9	3197001	6.4	0	8366	4746	3620	1–4
5–9	7804073	3972503	8.2	3831570	7.6	0	4433	2791	1642	5–9
10–14	8844852	4499043	9.3	4345809	8.6	16	3411	2064	1347	10–14
15–19	11295972	5709835	11.8	5586137	11.1	20014	8145	5569	2576	15–19
20–24	8742672	4339324	8.9	4403348	8.7	394061	9849	6313	3536	20–24
25–29	8458457	4197507	8.6	4260950	8.5	617830	10928	6864	4064	25–29
30–34	8338083	4182314	8.6	4155769	8.3	258490	13100	8029	5071	30–34
35–39	7624135	3820627	7.9	3803508	7.6	61114	16233	10188	6045	35–39
40–44	6235601	2908417	6.0	3327184	6.6	8958	18028	10444	7584	40–44
45–49	4963203	2223399	4.6	2739804	5.4	471	21510	12042	9468	45–49
50–54	4702250	2183476	4.5	2518774	5.0	18	32035	18602	13433	50–54
55–59	4124252	1972867	4.1	2151385	4.3	2	45680	28056	17624	55–59
60–64	3333615	1617522	3.3	1716093	3.4	0	61301	38531	22770	60–64
65–69	2641578	1256467	2.6	1385111	2.8	0	79152	47883	31269	65–69
70–74	1807141	816749	1.7	990392	2.0		90638	51123	39515	70–74
75–79	1118479	462468	1.0	656011	1.3		92928	46437	46491	75–79
80–84	531030	189237	0.4	341793	0.7	705463 M	72741	30247	42494	80–84
85 +	260481	77714	0.2	182767	0.4	655511 F	55444	18255	37189	85 +
All ages	98859245	48530614		50328631		1360974	670135	363209	306926	All ages

TABLE 2   LIFE TABLE FOR MALES

Age, x	$_nq_x$	l_x	$_nd_x$	$_nL_x$	$_nm_x$	T_x	$1000r_x$	$\overset{\circ}{e}_x$	$_nM_x$	Age, x
0	0.01918	100000	1918	98656	0.01944	6849168	0.00	68.49	0.01944	0
1	0.00568	98082	557	390740	0.00143	6750511	0.00	68.83	0.00143	1
5	0.00351	97525	342	486770	0.00070	6359771	0.00	65.21	0.00070	5
10	0.00229	97183	223	485385	0.00046	5873001	0.00	60.43	0.00046	10
15	0.00487	96960	472	483721	0.00098	5387616	2.66	55.57	0.00098	15
20	0.00727	96488	701	480752	0.00146	4903395	29.38	50.82	0.00145	20
25	0.00814	95787	780	477027	0.00164	4423143	2.03	46.18	0.00164	25
30	0.00956	95007	909	472861	0.00192	3946116	7.39	41.54	0.00192	30
35	0.01331	94098	1252	467518	0.00268	3473255	33.64	36.91	0.00267	35
40	0.01795	92846	1666	460314	0.00362	3005737	50.36	32.37	0.00359	40
45	0.02686	91180	2449	450203	0.00544	2545423	23.03	27.92	0.00542	45
50	0.04180	88731	3709	435095	0.00852	2095221	2.97	23.61	0.00852	50
55	0.06906	85022	5872	411530	0.01427	1660125	15.04	19.53	0.01422	55
60	0.11352	79150	8985	374634	0.02398	1248595	34.06	15.77	0.02382	60
65	0.17574	70165	12331	321416	0.03836	873961	34.06	12.46	0.03811	65
70	0.27303	57834	15791	250652	0.06300	552545	34.06	9.55	0.06259	70
75	0.40267	42044	16930	167557	0.10104	301893	34.06	7.18	0.10041	75
80	0.56444	25114	14175	88153	0.16080	134336	34.06	5.35	0.15984	80
85 +	1.00000	10939	10939	46183	0.23685	46183	34.06	4.22	0.23490	85 +

TABLE 3   LIFE TABLE FOR FEMALES

Age, x	$_nq_x$	l_x	$_nd_x$	$_nL_x$	$_nm_x$	T_x	$1000r_x$	$\overset{\circ}{e}_x$	$_nM_x$	Age, x
0	0.01506	100000	1506	98948	0.01522	7372496	0.00	73.72	0.01522	0
1	0.00451	98494	445	392710	0.00113	7273548	0.00	73.85	0.00113	1
5	0.00214	98050	210	489723	0.00043	6880838	0.00	70.18	0.00043	5
10	0.00155	97840	152	488823	0.00031	6391115	0.00	65.32	0.00031	10
15	0.00230	97688	225	487929	0.00046	5902292	0.00	60.42	0.00046	15
20	0.00402	97463	392	486386	0.00081	5414363	26.32	55.55	0.00080	20
25	0.00476	97071	462	484242	0.00095	4927977	4.81	50.77	0.00095	25
30	0.00609	96609	588	481638	0.00122	4443735	10.12	46.00	0.00122	30
35	0.00794	96021	762	478302	0.00159	3962097	20.59	41.26	0.00159	35
40	0.01140	95259	1085	473758	0.00229	3483794	30.43	36.57	0.00228	40
45	0.01722	94173	1621	467095	0.00347	3010036	24.25	31.96	0.00345	45
50	0.02643	92552	2446	457065	0.00535	2542941	18.67	27.48	0.00533	50
55	0.04043	90106	3643	442079	0.00824	2085876	29.76	23.15	0.00819	55
60	0.06482	86463	5605	419363	0.01337	1643796	33.11	19.01	0.01327	60
65	0.10805	80858	8737	384040	0.02275	1224434	33.11	15.14	0.02258	65
70	0.18362	72121	13243	329411	0.04020	840094	33.11	11.65	0.03990	70
75	0.30423	58878	17913	250936	0.07138	510983	33.11	8.68	0.07087	75
80	0.47869	40966	19610	156521	0.12528	260047	33.11	6.35	0.12433	80
85 +	*1.00000	21356	21356	103526	0.20629	103526	33.11	4.85	0.20348	85 +

TABLE 4 POPULATION PROJECTION, USING FIXED AGE-SPECIFIC BIRTH AND DEATH RATES, IN THOUSANDS

Age at last birthday	1971 Total	Males	Females	1976 Total	Males	Females	1981 Total	Males	Females	Age at last birthday
0–4	6992	3616	3376	7469	3863	3606	7255	3752	3503	0–4
5–9	7996	4079	3917	6960	3597	3363	7433	3842	3591	5–9
10–14	7786	3961	3825	7978	4068	3910	6943	3587	3356	10–14
15–19	8822	4484	4338	7766	3948	3818	7956	4054	3902	15–19
20–24	11243	5675	5568	8780	4456	4324	7728	3923	3805	20–24
25–29	8690	4306	4384	11175	5631	5544	8727	4422	4305	25–29
30–34	8399	4161	4238	8628	4268	4360	11096	5582	5514	30–34
35–39	8262	4135	4127	8323	4114	4209	8550	4220	4330	35–39
40–44	7529	3762	3767	8159	4071	4088	8219	4050	4169	40–44
45–49	6125	2845	3280	7393	3679	3714	8012	3982	4030	45–49
50–54	4830	2149	2681	5959	2749	3210	7191	3556	3635	50–54
55–59	4501	2065	2436	4625	2032	2593	5705	2600	3105	55–59
60–64	3837	1796	2041	4191	1880	2311	4310	1850	2450	60–64
65–69	2960	1388	1572	3410	1541	1869	3729	1513	2116	65–69
70–74	2168	980	1188	2430	1082	1348	2805	1202	1603	70–74
75–79	1300	546	754	1560	655	905	1750	723	1027	75–79
80–84	652	243	409	758	287	471	910	345	565	80–84
85 +	325	99	226	398	127	271	461	150	311	85 +
All ages	102417	50290	52127	105962	52048	53914	108780	53453	55327	All ages

TABLE 5 OBSERVED AND PROJECTED VITAL RATES

Rates per thousand	Observed Total	Males	Females	Projected 1971 Males	Females	1976 Males	Females	1981 Males	Females	Stable Males	Females
Birth	13.77	14.54	13.02	15.36	13.77	15.49	13.89	13.61	12.22	9.59	8.68
Death	6.78	7.48	6.10	8.18	6.76	8.87	7.49	9.51	8.26	20.26	19.35
Increase	6.99	7.05	6.93	7.18	7.01	6.62	6.41	4.10	3.95		10.5744

TABLE 6 RATES STANDARDIZED ON THREE STANDARD COUNTRIES

Standardized rates per thousand	England and Wales, 1961 Total	Males	Females	United States, 1960 Total	Males	Females	Mexico, 1960 Total	Males	Females
Birth	9.95	11.59*	9.30	10.10	10.81*	9.58	11.95	10.83*	11.48
Death	11.50	11.89*	11.30	9.31	10.10*	8.23	4.75	7.72*	3.91
Increase	-1.54	-0.29*	-2.00	0.79	0.71*	1.35	7.20	3.11*	7.57

TABLE 7 VITAL STATISTICS AND RATES INFERRED FROM AGE DISTRIBUTIONS (FEMALES)

Vital statistics		Thompson Age range	NRR	1000r	Interval	Bourgeois-Pichat Age range	NRR	1000b	1000d	1000r	Coale
TFR	1.60	0–4	0.91	-3.59	27.42	5–29	0.87	16.60	21.66	-5.05	1000b
GRR	0.77	5–9	0.99	-0.36	27.39	30–54	1.91	38.02	14.00	24.02	1000d
NRR	0.74	10–14	1.21	7.07	27.34	55–79	2.34	58.71	27.29	31.42	1000r
Generation	27.69	15–19	1.71	16.50	27.26	*50–74	2.26	54.17	23.95	30.23	1000k₁
Sex ratio	107.62										1000k₂

Note: In the Coale column the labels are $1000b$, $1000d$, $1000r$, $1000k_1$, $1000k_2$.

TABLE 8 LESLIE MATRIX AND ITS ANALYSIS (FEMALES)

Start of age interval	Sub-diagonal	First row	Percent in stable population	Fisher values	Total reproductive values	Net maternity function	Matrix equation coefficient
0	0.99606	0.00000	4.386	0.990	3893669	0.00000	0.00000
5	0.99816	0.00000	4.608	0.943	3611276	0.00000	0.00000
10	0.99817	0.00424	4.851	0.895	3890452	0.00001	0.00421
15	0.99684	0.10987	5.107	0.845	4726434	0.00842	0.10903
20	0.99559	0.27689	5.370	0.695	3062906	0.20955	0.27392
25	0.99462	0.24493	5.639	0.387	1649029	0.33819	0.24124
30	0.99307	0.09254	5.916	0.125	519727	0.14429	0.09355
35	0.99050	0.02218	6.197	0.027	103166	0.03702	0.02158
40	0.98594	0.00339	6.474	0.004	12603	0.00614	0.00327
45	0.97853	0.00021	6.732	0.000	660	0.00039	0.00020
50	0.96721	0.00001	6.948	0.000	37	0.00002	0.00001
55	0.77016		37.771				

Parameters:

	Integral	Matrix
λ_1	0.9480	0.9481
λ_2	0.3638	0.3652
	+0.7808	+0.7543 i
r_1	-0.0107	-0.0107
r_2	-0.0298	-0.0353
	+0.2270	+0.2240 i
c_1		887108
c_2		-654301
		320828 i
$2\pi/y$	27.684	28.053
Δ	26.266	

Kuwait, 1966

TABLE 1 DATA INPUT TO COMPUTATIONS

Age at last birthday	Population					Births, by age of mother	Deaths			Age at last birthday
	Total	Males	%	Females	%		Total	Males	Females	
0	17978	9313	3.1	8665	4.6	0	957	504	453	0
1–4	66527	33579	11.2	32948	17.3	0	260	136	124	1–4
5–9	62212	31766	10.6	30446	16.0	0	61	34	27	5–9
10–14	40003	21630	7.2	18373	9.7	0	37	28	9	10–14
15–19	41415	24336	8.1	17079	9.0	3157	39	26	13	15–19
20–24	59192	39736	13.2	19456	10.2	7614	71	46	25	20–24
25–29	62279	43326	14.4	18953	10.0	7906	111	70	41	25–29
30–34	43837	32044	10.7	11793	6.2	3920	95	70	25	30–34
35–39	31627	22831	7.6	8796	4.6	2228	89	65	24	35–39
40–44	20564	14775	4.9	5789	3.0	364	86	59	27	40–44
45–49	14006	9718	3.2	4288	2.3	80	96	70	26	45–49
50–54	11274	6939	2.3	4335	2.3	0	112	67	45	50–54
55–59	5592	3472	1.2	2120	1.1	0	59	45	14	55–59
60–64	6198	3176	1.1	3022	1.6	0	163	104	59	60–64
65–69	2886	1536	0.5	1350	0.7	0	77	48	29	65–69
70–74	2766	1351	0.4	1415	0.7		148	88	60	70–74
75–79	1010	540	0.2	470	0.2		146	81	65	75–79
80–84	815	381	0.1	434	0.2	13003 M	105	51	54	80–84
85 +	819	358	0.1	461	0.2	12266 F	101	34	67	85 +
All ages	491000	300807		190193		25269	2813	1626	1187	All ages

TABLE 2 LIFE TABLE FOR MALES

Age, x	$_nq_x$	l_x	$_nd_x$	$_nL_x$	$_nm_x$	T_x	$1000r_x$	$\overset{\circ}{e}_x$	$_nM_x$	Age, x
0	0.05186	100000	5186	96368	0.05381	6468717	7.61	64.69	0.05412	0
1	0.01591	94814	1509	374956	0.00402	6372349	7.61	67.21	0.00405	1
5	0.00519	93306	484	465318	0.00104	5997393	66.59	64.28	0.00107	5
10	0.00645	92821	599	462611	0.00129	5532076	25.47	59.60	0.00129	10
15	0.00533	92223	491	459870	0.00107	5069464	0.00	54.97	0.00107	15
20	0.00577	91731	529	457383	0.00116	4609595	0.00	50.25	0.00115	20
25	0.00807	91202	736	454265	0.00162	4152211	19.88	45.53	0.00162	25
30	0.01095	90466	990	449966	0.00220	3697947	61.86	40.88	0.00218	30
35	0.01428	89476	1278	444347	0.00288	3247980	74.48	36.30	0.00285	35
40	0.02014	88198	1777	436925	0.00407	2803633	80.92	31.79	0.00399	40
45	0.03581	86421	3095	424827	0.00728	2366708	68.51	27.39	0.00720	45
50	0.04773	83326	3977	407107	0.00977	1941881	93.22	23.30	0.00966	50
55	0.06428	79349	5101	385519	0.01323	1534774	61.27	19.34	0.01296	55
60	0.15217	74248	11298	353847	0.03286	1149254	26.08	15.48	0.03275	60
65	0.14591	62950	9185	292621	0.03139	805407	26.08	12.79	0.03125	65
70	0.28452	53765	15297	233024	0.06565	512786	26.08	9.54	0.06514	70
75	0.54332	38468	20901	138658	0.15073	279762	26.08	7.27	0.15000	75
80	0.47969	17568	8427	63111	0.13353	141105	25.08	8.03	0.13386	80
85 +	1.00000	9141	9141	77994	0.11720	77994	26.08	8.53	0.09497	85 +

TABLE 3 LIFE TABLE FOR FEMALES

Age, x	$_nq_x$	l_x	$_nd_x$	$_nL_x$	$_nm_x$	T_x	$1000r_x$	$\overset{\circ}{e}_x$	$_nM_x$	Age, x
0	0.05033	100000	5033	96454	0.05218	6705024	2.45	67.05	0.05228	0
1	0.01486	94967	1411	375837	0.00376	6608570	2.45	69.59	0.00376	1
5	0.00420	93555	393	466794	0.00084	6232734	80.25	66.62	0.00089	5
10	0.00244	93162	227	465235	0.00049	5765939	57.18	61.89	0.00049	10
15	0.00380	92935	353	463868	0.00076	5300704	0.00	57.04	0.00076	15
20	0.00641	92582	593	461560	0.00128	4836836	0.00	52.24	0.00128	20
25	0.01080	91989	994	457537	0.00217	4375275	48.11	47.56	0.00215	25
30	0.01059	90995	964	452617	0.00213	3917738	74.50	43.05	0.00212	30
35	0.01374	90032	1237	447296	0.00276	3465121	68.12	38.49	0.00273	35
40	0.02329	88795	2068	439088	0.00471	3017825	67.34	33.99	0.00465	40
45	0.03002	86726	2603	427580	0.00609	2578737	22.06	29.73	0.00606	45
50	0.05065	84123	4260	409966	0.01039	2151156	62.11	25.57	0.01038	50
55	0.03275	79863	2615	393395	0.00665	1741190	25.58	21.80	0.00660	55
60	0.09369	77247	7237	369098	0.01961	1347795	25.87	17.45	0.01952	60
65	0.10274	70010	7193	333126	0.02159	978698	25.87	13.98	0.02148	65
70	0.19604	62817	12314	287225	0.04287	645571	25.87	10.28	0.04240	70
75	0.51544	50503	26031	187200	0.13905	358346	25.87	7.10	0.13830	75
80	0.45679	24472	11178	90030	0.12416	171146	25.87	6.99	0.12442	80
85 +	1.00000	13293	13293	81116	0.16388	81116	25.87	6.10	0.14534	85 +

TABLE 4 POPULATION PROJECTION, USING FIXED AGE-SPECIFIC BIRTH AND DEATH RATES, IN THOUSANDS

Age at last birthday	1971			1976			1981			Age at last birthday
	Total	Males	Females	Total	Males	Females	Total	Males	Females	
0–4	125	64	61	140	72	68	165	85	80	0–4
5–9	83	42	41	124	64	60	138	71	67	5–9
10–14	62	32	30	83	42	41	123	63	60	10–14
15–19	40	22	18	61	31	30	83	42	41	15–19
20–24	41	24	17	39	21	18	61	31	30	20–24
25–29	58	39	19	41	24	17	39	21	18	25–29
30–34	62	43	19	58	39	19	41	24	17	30–34
35–39	44	32	12	61	42	19	58	39	19	35–39
40–44	31	22	9	42	31	11	60	42	18	40–44
45–49	20	14	6	30	22	8	41	30	11	45–49
50–54	13	9	4	19	14	5	29	21	8	50–54
55–59	11	7	4	13	9	4	18	13	5	55–59
60–64	5	3	2	10	6	4	12	8	4	60–64
65–69	6	3	3	5	3	2	9	5	4	65–69
70–74	2	1	1	4	2	2	4	2	2	70–74
75–79	2	1	1	2	1	1	3	1	2	75–79
80–84	0	0	0	0	0	0	0	0	0	80–84
85 +	0	0	0	0	0	0	0	0	0	85 +
All ages	605	358	247	732	423	309	884	498	386	All ages

TABLE 5 OBSERVED AND PROJECTED VITAL RATES

Rates per thousand	Observed			Projected						Stable	
				1971		1976		1981			
	Total	Males	Females	Males	Females	Males	Females	Males	Females	Males	Females
Birth	51.46	43.23	64.49	39.97	54.77	38.44	49.40	39.71	48.44	54.02	53.55
Death	5.73	5.41	6.24	6.06	6.26	6.21	5.74	6.59	5.70	6.37	5.91
Increase	45.74	37.82	58.25	33.90	48.51	32.23	43.66	33.12	42.74		47.6430

TABLE 6 RATES STANDARDIZED ON THREE STANDARD COUNTRIES

Standardized rates per thousand	England and Wales, 1961			United States, 1960			Mexico, 1960		
	Total	Males	Females	Total	Males	Females	Total	Males	Females
Birth	53.47	25.42*	50.30	54.56	23.63*	52.19	61.01	25.69*	59.08
Death	13.97	17.48*	14.79	11.62	13.11*	11.30	7.13	6.16*	6.65
Increase	39.50	7.94*	35.52	42.95	10.52*	40.88	53.89	19.53*	52.42

TABLE 7 VITAL STATISTICS AND RATES INFERRED FROM AGE DISTRIBUTIONS (FEMALES)

Vital statistics		Thompson				Bourgeois-Pichat					Coale	
TFR	8.30	Age range	NRR	1000r	Interval	Age range	NRR	1000b	1000d	1000r	1000b	
GRR	4.03	0–4	2.93	39.30	27.35	5–29	1.58	31.10	14.24	16.85	1000d	
NRR	3.67	5–9	2.54	34.90	27.29	30–54	3.81	64.01	14.47	49.54	1000r	
Generation	27.30	10–14	1.93	23.68	27.20	55–79	1.69	10.14	-9.31	19.45	$1000k_1$	
Sex ratio	106.01	15–19	2.55	34.54	27.09	*25–49	6.68	143.33	72.97	70.36	$1000k_2$	

TABLE 8 LESLIE MATRIX AND ITS ANALYSIS (FEMALES)

Start of age interval	Sub-diagonal	First row	Percent in stable population	Fisher values	Total reproductive values	Net maternity function	Matrix equation coefficient	Parameters		
									Integral	Matrix
0	0.98836	0.00000	22.556	1.191	49576	0.00000	0.00000	λ_1	1.2690	1.2707
5	0.99666	0.00000	17.544	1.532	46635	0.00000	0.00000	λ_2	0.3988	0.4069
10	0.99706	0.21126	13.760	1.953	35881	0.00000	0.20811		+0.8732	+0.8466 i
15	0.99502	0.55825	10.797	2.236	38196	0.41622	0.64651	r_1	0.0476	0.0479
20	0.99128	0.92259	8.455	2.068	40234	0.87680	0.90163	r_2	-0.0082	-0.0125
25	0.98925	0.85509	6.595	1.542	29227	0.92645	0.82838		+0.2285	+0.2246 i
30	0.98824	0.66796	5.135	0.951	11216	0.73031	0.64014	c_1		1832
35	0.98165	0.36110	3.993	0.418	3673	0.54997	0.34199	c_2		-844
40	0.97379	0.09264	3.085	0.102	593	0.13402	0.08637			-20437 i
45	0.95880	0.02137	2.364	0.020	87	0.03872	0.01936	$2\pi/y$	27.500	27.981
50	0.95958	0.00026	1.784	0.000	1	0.00000	0.00000	Δ	8.413	
55	0.83542		3.932							

[401]

Malaysia (West), 1966 (all races)

TABLE 1 DATA INPUT TO COMPUTATIONS

Age at last birthday	Population					Births, by age of mother	Deaths			Age at last birthday
	Total	Males	%	Females	%		Total	Males	Females	
0	291009	148836	3.4	142173	3.4	0	14865	8386	6479	0
1–4	1103115	560831	12.9	542284	12.9	0	5705	2915	2790	1–4
5–9	1272090	645404	14.8	626686	15.0	0	2152	1117	1035	5–9
10–14	1106640	563606	13.0	543034	13.0	343	1086	578	508	10–14
15–19	896014	456607	10.5	439407	10.5	33021	1180	633	547	15–19
20–24	646736	332091	7.6	314645	7.5	80869	1174	616	558	20–24
25–29	595557	295493	6.8	300064	7.2	87200	1279	577	702	25–29
30–34	476688	229949	5.3	246739	5.9	60324	1313	589	724	30–34
35–39	414882	198173	4.6	216709	5.2	33167	1547	706	841	35–39
40–44	344899	170360	3.9	174539	4.2	11602	1752	961	791	40–44
45–49	328271	167471	3.8	160800	3.8	2364	2503	1385	1118	45–49
50–54	285363	152645	3.5	132718	3.2	426	3135	1947	1188	50–54
55–59	280285	152052	3.5	128233	3.1	0	4698	2907	1791	55–59
60–64	185482	108491	2.5	76991	1.8	0	4760	3162	1598	60–64
65–69	145706	81804	1.9	63902	1.5	0	5236	3283	1953	65–69
70–74	91346	48937	1.1	42409	1.0		4466	2652	1814	70–74
75–79	46940	23798	0.5	23142	0.6		3128	1752	1376	75–79
80–84	20063	9530	0.2	10533	0.3	159163 M	1848	968	880	80–84
85+	10096	4295	0.1	5801	0.1	150153 F	1571	720	851	85+
All ages	8541182	4350373		4190809		309316	63398	35854	27544	All ages

TABLE 2 LIFE TABLE FOR MALES

Age, x	$_nq_x$	l_x	$_nd_x$	$_nL_x$	$_nm_x$	T_x	$1000r_x$	$\overset{\circ}{e}_x$	$_nM_x$	Age, x
0	0.05417	100000	5417	96327	0.05623	6351503	2.69	63.52	0.05634	0
1	0.02045	94583	1934	372872	0.00519	6255175	2.69	66.13	0.00520	1
5	0.00854	92649	791	461266	0.00172	5882303	20.65	63.49	0.00173	5
10	0.00510	91857	469	458083	0.00102	5421038	33.33	59.02	0.00103	10
15	0.00695	91389	635	455432	0.00140	4962955	51.50	54.31	0.00139	15
20	0.00926	90753	840	451716	0.00186	4507523	41.75	49.67	0.00185	20
25	0.00974	89913	876	447438	0.00196	4055807	34.69	45.11	0.00195	25
30	0.01279	89037	1139	442481	0.00257	3608369	37.33	40.53	0.00256	30
35	0.01775	87898	1560	435855	0.00358	3165888	26.21	36.02	0.00356	35
40	0.02789	86338	2408	426056	0.00565	2730033	11.12	31.62	0.00564	40
45	0.04058	83930	3406	411673	0.00827	2303977	2.37	27.45	0.00827	45
50	0.06192	80524	4986	390890	0.01276	1892304	0.00	23.50	0.01275	50
55	0.09167	75538	6925	361305	0.01917	1501415	14.24	19.88	0.01912	55
60	0.13739	68614	9427	320328	0.02943	1140109	65.15	16.62	0.02915	60
65	0.18401	59187	10891	269162	0.04046	819782	65.15	13.85	0.04013	65
70	0.24044	48296	11612	212568	0.05463	550619	65.15	11.40	0.05419	70
75	0.31257	36684	11466	154461	0.07423	338051	65.15	9.22	0.07362	75
80	0.40507	25217	10215	99731	0.10242	183590	65.15	7.28	0.10157	80
85+	1.00000	15003	15003	83858	0.17890	83858	65.15	5.59	0.16764	85+

TABLE 3 LIFE TABLE FOR FEMALES

Age, x	$_nq_x$	l_x	$_nd_x$	$_nL_x$	$_nm_x$	T_x	$1000r_x$	$\overset{\circ}{e}_x$	$_nM_x$	Age, x
0	0.04419	100000	4419	97101	0.04551	6675518	1.75	66.76	0.04557	0
1	0.02027	95581	1937	376918	0.00514	6578417	1.75	68.83	0.00514	1
5	0.00815	93643	763	466309	0.00164	6201500	20.85	66.22	0.00165	5
10	0.00465	92880	432	463283	0.00093	5735190	34.33	61.75	0.00094	10
15	0.00625	92448	578	460876	0.00125	5271907	53.30	57.03	0.00124	15
20	0.00887	91870	815	457414	0.00178	4811031	36.36	52.37	0.00177	20
25	0.01166	91055	1062	452727	0.00234	4353617	21.97	47.81	0.00234	25
30	0.01462	89994	1315	446815	0.00294	3900890	29.52	43.35	0.00293	30
35	0.01927	88678	1709	439253	0.00389	3454075	30.83	38.95	0.00388	35
40	0.02250	86969	1956	430206	0.00455	3014822	24.91	34.67	0.00453	40
45	0.03429	85013	2915	418120	0.00697	2584616	20.61	30.40	0.00695	45
50	0.04392	82098	3606	401980	0.00895	2166496	13.04	26.39	0.00895	50
55	0.06807	78492	5343	379873	0.01406	1764515	40.13	22.48	0.01397	55
60	0.09981	73149	7301	348348	0.02096	1384642	60.45	18.93	0.02076	60
65	0.14347	65848	9447	306392	0.03083	1036294	60.45	15.74	0.03056	65
70	0.19498	56401	10997	255012	0.04312	729902	60.45	12.94	0.04277	70
75	0.26082	45404	11842	197548	0.05995	474891	60.45	10.46	0.05946	75
80	0.34692	33562	11643	138251	0.08422	277342	60.45	8.26	0.08355	80
85+	1.00000	21918	21918	139091	0.15758	139091	60.45	6.35	0.14670	85+

TABLE 4 POPULATION PROJECTION, USING FIXED AGE-SPECIFIC BIRTH AND DEATH RATES, IN THOUSANDS

Age at last birthday	1971 Total	1971 Males	1971 Females	1976 Total	1976 Males	1976 Females	1981 Total	1981 Males	1981 Females	Age at last birthday
0–4	1602	820	782	1932	989	943	2323	1189	1134	0–4
5–9	1371	698	673	1575	806	769	1899	972	927	5–9
10–14	1264	641	623	1362	693	669	1565	801	764	10–14
15–19	1100	560	540	1256	637	619	1354	689	665	15–19
20–24	889	453	436	1092	556	536	1247	632	615	20–24
25–29	640	329	311	881	449	432	1082	551	531	25–29
30–34	588	292	296	632	325	307	870	444	426	30–34
35–39	470	227	243	579	288	291	622	320	302	35–39
40–44	406	194	212	459	221	238	566	281	285	40–44
45–49	335	165	170	393	187	206	445	214	231	45–49
50–54	314	159	155	319	156	163	376	178	198	50–54
55–59	266	141	125	293	147	146	298	144	154	55–59
60–64	253	135	118	240	125	115	264	130	134	60–64
65–69	159	91	68	216	113	103	206	105	101	65–69
70–74	118	65	53	128	72	56	175	89	86	70–74
75–79	69	36	33	88	47	41	96	52	44	75–79
80–84	31	15	16	46	23	23	59	30	29	80–84
85 +	19	8	11	29	13	16	42	19	23	85 +
All ages	9894	5029	4865	11520	5847	5673	13489	6840	6549	All ages

TABLE 5 OBSERVED AND PROJECTED VITAL RATES

Rates per thousand	Observed Total	Observed Males	Observed Females	Projected 1971 Males	Projected 1971 Females	Projected 1976 Males	Projected 1976 Females	Projected 1981 Males	Projected 1981 Females	Stable Males	Stable Females
Birth	36.21	36.59	35.83	37.89	36.95	39.53	38.43	40.31	39.14	38.87	38.05
Death	7.42	8.24	6.57	8.46	6.82	8.58	7.08	8.53	7.21	8.01	7.20
Increase	28.79	28.34	29.26	29.43	30.12	30.95	31.35	31.79	31.92		30.8565

TABLE 6 RATES STANDARDIZED ON THREE STANDARD COUNTRIES

Standardized rates per thousand	England and Wales, 1961 Total	Males	Females	United States, 1960 Total	Males	Females	Mexico, 1960 Total	Males	Females
Birth	35.49	40.17*	33.39	36.07	36.51*	34.50	39.36	38.76*	38.11
Death	12.89	16.56*	13.05	11.05	13.61*	10.43	7.20	8.08*	6.59
Increase	22.60	23.61*	20.34	25.02	22.90*	24.07	32.16	30.69*	31.52

TABLE 7 VITAL STATISTICS AND RATES INFERRED FROM AGE DISTRIBUTIONS (FEMALES)

Vital statistics		Thompson Age range	NRR	1000r	Interval	Bourgeois-Pichat Age range	NRR	1000b	1000d	1000r	Coale	
TFR	5.53	0–4	2.29	30.39	27.31	5–29	2.86	43.72	4.79	38.94	1000b	37.68
GRR	2.68	5–9	2.51	34.63	27.24	30–54	1.99	30.12	4.55	25.56	1000d	7.33
NRR	2.41	10–14	2.46	32.35	27.16	55–79	3.25	91.79	48.15	43.64	1000r	30.35
Generation	28.51	15–19	2.26	30.21	27.04	*30–54	1.99	30.12	4.56	25.56	$1000k_1$	0.
Sex ratio	106.0										$1000k_2$	0.

TABLE 8 LESLIE MATRIX AND ITS ANALYSIS (FEMALES)

Start of age interval	Sub-diagonal	First row	Percent in stable population	Fisher values	Total reproductive values	Net maternity function	Matrix equation coefficient	Parameters	Integral	Matrix
0	0.98374	0.00000	16.740	1.139	779402	0.00000	0.00000	λ_1	1.1668	1.1674
5	0.99351	0.00072	14.106	1.351	846886	0.00000	0.00071	λ_2	0.4209	0.4256
10	0.99480	0.08674	12.004	1.587	861867	0.00142	0.08477		+0.8287	+0.8034 i
15	0.99249	0.37994	10.229	1.763	774804	0.16813	0.36941	r_1	0.0309	0.0310
20	0.98975	0.62663	8.696	1.638	515453	0.57069	0.63468	r_2	-0.0146	-0.0190
25	0.98694	0.51196	7.372	1.211	363494	0.63866	0.58447		+0.2202	+0.2167 i
30	0.98307	0.45439	6.232	0.727	179348	0.53029	0.42832	c_1		41966
35	0.97940	0.25099	5.248	0.337	73000	0.32634	0.23258	c_2		7468
40	0.97191	0.39292	4.403	0.110	19151	0.13882	0.08433			111375 i
45	0.96140	0.02046	3.665	0.023	3686	0.02984	0.01805	$2\pi/y$	28.539	28.991
50	0.94500	0.00369	3.018	0.004	478	0.00626	0.00313	Δ	3.091	
55	0.82323		8.287							

Malaysia (West), 1966 (Malays)

TABLE 1 DATA INPUT TO COMPUTATIONS

Age at last birthday	Population					Births, by age of mother	Deaths			Age at last birthday
	Total	Males	%	Females	%		Total	Males	Females	
0	159727	81167	3.8	78560	3.7	0	9919	5616	4303	0
1–4	581011	293937	13.9	287074	13.4	0	4018	2062	1956	1–4
5–9	649177	326697	15.5	322480	15.1	0	1531	774	757	5–9
10–14	549827	277420	13.1	272407	12.7	257	677	355	322	10–14
15–19	429934	216747	10.3	213187	10.0	22332	693	350	343	15–19
20–24	323907	164835	7.8	159072	7.4	46147	726	331	395	20–24
25–29	297065	143551	6.8	153514	7.2	45240	796	291	505	25–29
30–34	228023	105697	5.0	122326	5.7	31209	786	294	492	30–34
35–39	218610	98552	4.7	120058	5.6	18584	967	370	597	35–39
40–44	186548	87407	4.1	99141	4.6	6462	1033	515	518	40–44
45–49	174661	85832	4.1	88829	4.2	1369	1440	724	716	45–49
50–54	125446	64630	3.1	60816	2.8	241	1506	838	668	50–54
55–59	124883	61185	2.9	63698	3.0	0	2303	1204	1099	55–59
60–64	70521	38466	1.8	32055	1.5	0	1999	1161	838	60–64
65–69	63042	32741	1.5	30301	1.4	0	2513	1378	1135	65–69
70–74	40556	20451	1.0	20105	0.9		2181	1151	1030	70–74
75–79	19808	9816	0.5	9992	0.5		1446	739	707	75–79
80–84	7520	3698	0.2	3822	0.2	88016 M	764	379	385	80–84
85 +	2898	1430	0.1	1468	0.1	83825 F	486	231	255	85 +
All ages	4253164	2114259		2138905		171841	35784	18763	17021	All ages

TABLE 2 LIFE TABLE FOR MALES

Age, x	$_nq_x$	l_x	$_nd_x$	$_nL_x$	$_nm_x$	T_x	$1000r_x$	$\overset{\circ}{e}_x$	$_nM_x$	Age, x
0	0.06587	100000	6587	95594	0.06891	6161451	5.69	61.61	0.06919	0
1	0.02742	93413	2561	366454	0.00699	6065856	5.69	64.94	0.00702	1
5	0.01164	90851	1058	451613	0.00234	5699402	26.96	62.73	0.00237	5
10	0.00635	89794	570	447474	0.00127	5247789	39.42	58.44	0.00128	10
15	0.00808	89224	721	444382	0.00162	4800316	50.45	53.80	0.00161	15
20	0.01001	88503	885	440334	0.00201	4355933	39.28	49.22	0.00201	20
25	0.01012	87617	887	435935	0.00203	3915599	42.25	44.69	0.00203	25
30	0.01388	86730	1204	430791	0.00279	3479664	34.81	40.12	0.00278	30
35	0.01866	85527	1596	423903	0.00376	3048873	15.01	35.65	0.00375	35
40	0.02910	83931	2442	413923	0.00590	2624970	7.89	31.28	0.00589	40
45	0.04151	81489	3382	399509	0.00847	2211047	21.36	27.13	0.00844	45
50	0.06313	78107	4931	378943	0.01301	1811538	20.48	23.19	0.01297	50
55	0.09452	73176	6916	349520	0.01979	1432595	31.36	19.58	0.01968	55
60	0.14197	66259	9407	308615	0.03048	1083075	64.67	16.35	0.03018	60
65	0.19209	56853	10921	257379	0.04243	774460	64.67	13.62	0.04209	65
70	0.24837	45932	11408	201153	0.05671	517081	64.67	11.26	0.05628	70
75	0.31821	34524	10986	144778	0.07588	315928	64.67	9.15	0.07529	75
80	0.40766	23538	9596	92876	0.10332	171150	64.67	7.27	0.10249	80
85 +	1.00000	13943	13943	78274	0.17812	78274	64.67	5.61	0.15154	85 +

TABLE 3 LIFE TABLE FOR FEMALES

Age, x	$_nq_x$	l_x	$_nd_x$	$_nL_x$	$_nm_x$	T_x	$1000r_x$	$\overset{\circ}{e}_x$	$_nM_x$	Age, x
0	0.05271	100000	5271	96591	0.05457	6275990	5.23	62.76	0.05477	0
1	0.02667	94729	2527	371906	0.00679	6179399	5.23	65.23	0.00681	1
5	0.01154	92202	1064	458350	0.00232	5807493	26.35	62.99	0.00235	5
10	0.00586	91138	534	454285	0.00118	5349143	39.84	58.69	0.00118	10
15	0.00809	90604	733	451308	0.00162	4894858	52.11	54.02	0.00161	15
20	0.01240	89871	1114	446721	0.00249	4443550	30.37	49.44	0.00248	20
25	0.01635	88757	1452	440288	0.00330	3996829	22.99	45.03	0.00329	25
30	0.01995	87306	1742	432309	0.00403	3556542	20.49	40.74	0.00402	30
35	0.02458	85564	2103	422647	0.00498	3124233	16.24	36.51	0.00497	35
40	0.02588	83460	2160	412138	0.00524	2701586	24.33	32.37	0.00522	40
45	0.03978	81301	3234	398841	0.00811	2289448	40.87	28.15	0.00805	45
50	0.05373	78066	4194	380457	0.01102	1890607	21.56	24.22	0.01098	50
55	0.08356	73872	6173	354806	0.01740	1510150	46.21	20.44	0.01725	55
60	0.12417	67699	8406	318332	0.02641	1155344	64.33	17.07	0.02614	60
65	0.17296	59293	10255	271415	0.03779	837012	64.33	14.12	0.03746	65
70	0.22898	49038	11229	217364	0.05166	565597	64.33	11.53	0.05123	70
75	0.30265	37809	11443	160312	0.07138	348233	64.33	9.21	0.07076	75
80	0.40307	26366	10627	104560	0.10164	187921	64.33	7.13	0.10073	80
85 +	1.00000	15739	15739	83360	0.18880	83360	64.33	5.30	0.17371	85 +

TABLE 4 POPULATION PROJECTION, USING FIXED AGE-SPECIFIC BIRTH AND DEATH RATES, IN THOUSANDS

Age at last birthday	1971			1976			1981			Age at last birthday
	Total	Males	Females	Total	Males	Females	Total	Males	Females	
0–4	871	443	428	1040	529	511	1250	636	614	0–4
5–9	725	367	358	851	433	418	1017	517	500	5–9
10–14	644	324	320	718	363	355	844	429	415	10–14
15–19	547	276	271	639	321	318	713	361	352	15–19
20–24	426	215	211	541	273	268	633	319	314	20–24
25–29	320	163	157	421	213	208	534	270	264	25–29
30–34	293	142	151	315	161	154	414	210	204	30–34
35–39	224	104	120	287	140	147	309	159	150	35–39
40–44	213	96	117	219	102	117	280	136	144	40–44
45–49	180	84	96	206	93	113	211	98	113	45–49
50–54	166	81	85	172	80	92	196	88	108	50–54
55–59	117	60	57	154	75	79	159	74	85	55–59
60–64	111	54	57	104	53	51	137	66	71	60–64
65–69	59	32	27	94	45	49	87	44	43	65–69
70–74	50	26	24	47	25	22	74	35	39	70–74
75–79	30	15	15	36	18	18	34	18	16	75–79
80–84	13	6	7	19	9	10	24	12	12	80–84
85 +	6	3	3	10	5	5	16	8	8	85 +
All ages	4995	2491	2504	5873	2938	2935	6932	3480	3452	All ages

TABLE 5 OBSERVED AND PROJECTED VITAL RATES

Rates per thousand	Observed			Projected 1971		1976		1981		Stable	
	Total	Males	Females	Males	Females	Males	Females	Males	Females	Males	Females
Birth	40.40	41.63	39.19	41.65	39.49	42.60	40.65	43.16	41.42	41.93	41.39
Death	8.41	8.87	7.96	9.05	8.20	9.12	8.41	9.10	8.52	8.80	8.25
Increase	31.99	32.76	31.23	32.60	31.29	33.48	32.24	34.06	32.90		33.1307

TABLE 6 RATES STANDARDIZED ON THREE STANDARD COUNTRIES

Standardized rates per thousand	England and Wales, 1961			United States, 1960			Mexico, 1960		
	Total	Males	Females	Total	Males	Females	Total	Males	Females
Birth	38.07	45.83*	36.00	38.75	41.54*	37.24	42.89	44.15*	41.73
Death	14.74	20.05*	15.92	12.66	16.15*	12.79	8.51	8.75*	8.22
Increase	23.34	25.77*	20.07	26.08	25.39*	24.45	34.38	35.39*	33.51

TABLE 7 VITAL STATISTICS AND RATES INFERRED FROM AGE DISTRIBUTIONS (FEMALES)

Vital statistics		Thompson				Bourgeois-Pichat					Coale	
		Age range	NRR	1000r	Interval	Age range	NRR	1000b	1000d	1000r		
TFR	5.92	0–4	2.34	31.27	27.25	5–29	2.83	43.77	5.26	38.50	1000b	39.44
GRR	2.89	5–9	2.42	33.21	27.17	30–54	2.11	35.38	7.68	27.71	1000d	8.39
NRR	2.52	10–14	2.31	30.21	27.09	55–79	2.77	63.48	25.75	37.73	1000r	30.05
Generation	27.94	15–19	2.04	26.53	26.95	*20–49	1.70	26.59	6.84	19.75	1000k_1	0.
Sex ratio	105.0										1000k_2	0.

TABLE 8 LESLIE MATRIX AND ITS ANALYSIS (FEMALES)

Start of age interval	Sub-diagonal	First row	Percent in stable population	Fisher values	Total reproductive values	Net maternity function	Matrix equation coefficient	Parameters	Integral	Matrix
0	0.97834	0.00000	17.897	1.159	423590	0.00000	0.00000	λ_1	1.1802	1.1809
5	0.99113	0.00107	14.827	1.398	450952	0.00000	0.00105	λ_2	0.3970	0.4045
10	0.99345	0.11999	12.444	1.665	453530	0.00209	0.11635		+0.8251	+0.7993i
15	0.98984	0.44782	10.469	1.839	392081	0.23061	0.43139	r_1	0.0331	0.0333
20	0.98560	0.66339	8.775	1.670	265657	0.63217	0.63255	r_2	-0.0176	-0.0220
25	0.98188	0.62299	7.323	1.221	187476	0.63293	0.58548		+0.2245	+0.2205i
30	0.97765	0.46445	6.089	0.734	89754	0.53802	0.42858	c_1		20731
35	0.97513	0.24950	5.041	0.335	40327	0.31913	0.22509	c_2		13707
40	0.96774	0.09152	4.163	0.110	10941	0.13104	0.08051			33462i
45	0.95391	0.02193	3.411	0.025	2230	0.02998	0.01867	$2\pi/y$	27.991	28.500
50	0.93258	0.00453	2.755	0.004	270	0.00735	0.00368	Δ	3.559	
55	0.80333		6.806							

Malaysia (West), 1966 (Chinese)

TABLE 1 DATA INPUT TO COMPUTATIONS

Age at last birthday	Total	Males	%	Females	%	Births, by age of mother	Total	Males	Females	Age at last birthday
0	96765	49976	3.1	46789	3.0	0	3124	1784	1340	0
1–4	382615	196164	12.0	186451	12.1	0	1007	543	464	1–4
5–9	451423	231755	14.2	219668	14.2	0	372	214	158	5–9
10–14	412263	212249	13.0	200014	12.9	24	282	163	119	10–14
15–19	353298	182354	11.2	170944	11.1	5066	318	201	117	15–19
20–24	253413	131942	8.1	121471	7.9	25102	298	213	85	20–24
25–29	225408	116986	7.2	108422	7.0	32232	315	207	108	25–29
30–34	182336	91958	5.6	90378	5.8	22005	327	197	130	30–34
35–39	138437	67267	4.1	71170	4.6	11433	372	223	149	35–39
40–44	103574	49204	3.0	54370	3.5	4149	411	242	169	40–44
45–49	99698	46573	2.9	53125	3.4	816	570	332	238	45–49
50–54	113281	55970	3.4	57311	3.7	151	1027	685	342	50–54
55–59	118019	64617	4.0	53402	3.5	0	1652	1191	461	55–59
60–64	91220	51915	3.2	39305	2.5	0	2049	1470	579	60–64
65–69	67260	37946	2.3	29314	1.9	0	2098	1481	617	65–69
70–74	42678	23136	1.4	19542	1.3		1812	1225	587	70–74
75–79	23681	11952	0.7	11729	0.8		1356	853	503	75–79
80–84	11646	5278	0.3	6368	0.4	52196 M	912	514	398	80–84
85 +	8340	2903	0.2	5437	0.4	48782 F	1243	471	772	85 +
All ages	3175355	1630145		1545210		100978	19545	12209	7336	All ages

TABLE 2 LIFE TABLE FOR MALES

Age, x	$_nq_x$	l_x	$_nd_x$	$_nL_x$	$_nm_x$	T_x	$1000r_x$	$\overset{\circ}{e}_x$	$_nM_x$	Age, x
0	0.03483	100000	3483	97577	0.03570	6653343	0.00	66.53	0.03570	0
1	0.01099	96517	1060	383050	0.00277	6555766	0.00	67.92	0.00277	1
5	0.00458	95456	438	476189	0.00092	6172715	13.47	64.67	0.00092	5
10	0.00384	95019	365	474201	0.00077	5696527	23.10	59.95	0.00077	10
15	0.00554	94654	524	472044	0.00111	5222325	46.40	55.17	0.00110	15
20	0.00807	94130	760	468814	0.00162	4750282	42.85	50.47	0.00161	20
25	0.00883	93371	824	464841	0.00177	4281457	34.29	45.85	0.00177	25
30	0.01074	92546	994	460391	0.00216	3816627	53.02	41.24	0.00214	30
35	0.01662	91552	1521	454208	0.00335	3356236	59.13	36.66	0.00332	35
40	0.02443	90031	2200	444980	0.00494	2902028	31.76	32.23	0.00492	40
45	0.03507	87831	3080	432048	0.00713	2457048	0.00	27.97	0.00713	45
50	0.05949	84751	5042	411976	0.01224	2024999	0.00	23.89	0.01224	50
55	0.08831	79709	7039	381920	0.01843	1613023	0.00	20.24	0.01843	55
60	0.13359	72670	9708	339964	0.02856	1231104	56.37	16.94	0.02832	60
65	0.17925	62962	11286	287106	0.03931	891140	56.37	14.15	0.03903	65
70	0.23536	51676	12162	228126	0.05331	604034	56.37	11.69	0.05295	70
75	0.30416	39513	12018	167230	0.07187	375908	56.37	9.51	0.07137	75
80	0.39141	27495	10762	109747	0.09806	208678	56.37	7.59	0.09739	80
85 +	1.00000	16733	16733	98931	0.16914	98931	56.37	5.91	0.16225	85 +

TABLE 3 LIFE TABLE FOR FEMALES

Age, x	$_nq_x$	l_x	$_nd_x$	$_nL_x$	$_nm_x$	T_x	$1000r_x$	$\overset{\circ}{e}_x$	$_nM_x$	Age, x
0	0.02809	100000	2809	98082	0.02864	7404260	0.00	74.04	0.02864	0
1	0.00988	97191	961	386046	0.00249	7306178	0.00	75.17	0.00249	1
5	0.00357	96230	343	480293	0.00071	6920132	14.24	71.91	0.00072	5
10	0.00297	95887	285	478720	0.00059	6439839	24.43	67.16	0.00059	10
15	0.00342	95602	327	477204	0.00069	5961119	49.21	62.35	0.00068	15
20	0.00351	95275	334	475571	0.00070	5483915	44.77	57.56	0.00070	20
25	0.00499	94941	474	473593	0.00100	5008344	28.55	52.75	0.00100	25
30	0.00721	94467	682	470738	0.00145	4534752	40.61	48.00	0.00144	30
35	0.01050	93786	985	466624	0.00211	4064014	48.65	43.33	0.00209	35
40	0.01549	92801	1438	460627	0.00312	3597390	26.06	38.76	0.00311	40
45	0.02216	91363	2025	452001	0.00448	3136763	0.00	34.33	0.00448	45
50	0.02942	89338	2628	440467	0.00597	2684762	0.00	30.05	0.00597	50
55	0.04256	86710	3691	425017	0.00868	2244295	28.33	25.88	0.00863	55
60	0.07188	83019	5967	401029	0.01488	1819278	57.96	21.91	0.01473	60
65	0.10100	77052	7782	366596	0.02123	1418250	57.96	18.41	0.02105	65
70	0.14113	69269	9776	322711	0.03029	1051654	57.96	15.18	0.03004	70
75	0.19562	59494	11638	269052	0.04326	728943	57.96	12.25	0.04289	75
80	0.27249	47855	13040	206894	0.06303	459891	57.96	9.61	0.06250	80
85 +	1.00000	34815	34815	252997	0.13761	252997	57.96	7.27	0.14199	85 +

TABLE 4 POPULATION PROJECTION, USING FIXED AGE-SPECIFIC BIRTH AND DEATH RATES, IN THOUSANDS

Age at last birthday	1971			1976			1981			Age at last birthday
	Total	Males	Females	Total	Males	Females	Total	Males	Females	
0–4	543	280	263	666	343	323	802	413	389	0–4
5–9	475	244	231	538	277	261	661	340	321	5–9
10–14	450	231	219	474	243	231	536	276	260	10–14
15–19	410	211	199	448	230	218	472	242	230	15–19
20–24	351	181	170	409	210	199	446	228	218	20–24
25–29	252	131	121	350	180	170	406	208	198	25–29
30–34	224	116	108	250	130	120	347	178	169	30–34
35–39	181	91	90	221	114	107	247	128	119	35–39
40–44	136	66	70	177	89	88	217	112	105	40–44
45–49	101	48	53	133	64	69	173	86	87	45–49
50–54	96	44	52	98	46	52	128	61	67	50–54
55–59	107	52	55	91	41	50	92	42	50	55–59
60–64	108	58	50	98	46	52	84	37	47	60–64
65–69	80	44	36	95	49	46	87	39	48	65–69
70–74	56	30	26	67	35	32	80	39	41	70–74
75–79	33	17	16	44	22	22	52	26	26	75–79
80–84	17	8	9	24	11	13	32	15	17	80–84
85 +	13	5	8	18	7	11	25	10	15	85 +
All ages	3633	1857	1776	4201	2137	2064	4887	2480	2407	All ages

TABLE 5 OBSERVED AND PROJECTED VITAL RATES

Rates per thousand	Observed			Projected						Stable	
				1971		1976		1981			
	Total	Males	Females	Males	Females	Males	Females	Males	Females	Males	Females
Birth	31.80	32.02	31.57	34.57	33.72	36.88	35.58	37.61	35.21	35.60	34.15
Death	6.16	7.49	4.75	7.65	5.03	7.64	5.32	7.42	5.49	6.87	5.43
Increase	25.65	24.53	26.82	26.91	28.69	29.24	30.37	30.19	30.73		28.7217

TABLE 6 RATES STANDARDIZED ON THREE STANDARD COUNTRIES

Standardized rates per thousand	England and Wales, 1961			United States, 1960			Mexico, 1960		
	Total	Males	Females	Total	Males	Females	Total	Males	Females
Birth	33.11	34.18*	31.00	33.58	30.94*	31.96	35.38	34.07*	34.10
Death	10.32	12.86*	9.13	8.74	10.93*	7.12	5.24	7.10*	4.14
Increase	22.79	21.32*	21.87	24.84	20.01*	24.84	30.14	26.96*	29.96

TABLE 7 VITAL STATISTICS AND RATES INFERRED FROM AGE DISTRIBUTIONS (FEMALES)

Vital statistics		Thompson				Bourgeois-Pichat					Coale	
		Age range	NRR	$1000r$	Interval	Age range	NRR	$1000b$	$1000d$	$1000r$	$1000b$	
TFR	5.16	0–4	2.21	28.87	27.41	5–29	2.75	41.37	3.84	37.52	$1000d$	
GRR	2.49	5–9	2.57	35.25	27.36	30–54	1.75	21.83	1.06	20.77	$1000r$	
NRR	2.35	10–14	2.66	34.81	27.29	55–79	3.64	127.66	79.80	47.86	$1000k_1$	
Generation	29.72	15–19	2.56	34.57	27.21	*10–44	3.05	45.60	4.27	41.32	$1000k_2$	
Sex ratio	107.00											

TABLE 8 LESLIE MATRIX AND ITS ANALYSIS (FEMALES)

Start of age interval	Sub-diagonal	First row	Percent in stable population	Fisher values	Total reproductive values	Net maternity function	Matrix equation coefficient	Parameters		
									Integral	Matrix
0	0.99208	0.00000	15.421	1.109	258719	0.00000	0.00000	λ_1	1.1544	1.1549
5	0.99672	0.00014	13.246	1.291	283664	0.00000	0.00014	λ_2	0.4656	0.4656
10	0.99683	0.03469	11.431	1.496	299255	0.00028	0.03430		+0.8412	+0.8168i
15	0.99658	0.27548	9.866	1.695	289731	0.06832	0.27155	r_1	0.0287	0.0288
20	0.99584	0.58785	8.514	1.658	201350	0.47477	0.57746	r_2	-0.0079	-0.0123
25	0.99397	0.63065	7.341	1.268	137440	0.68015	0.61692		+0.2131	+0.2105i
30	0.99126	0.47094	6.318	0.769	69515	0.55370	0.45791	c_1		15902
35	0.98715	0.27595	5.422	0.369	26274	0.36213	0.26597	c_2		-17701
40	0.98127	0.10686	4.634	0.122	6626	0.16981	0.10168			53398i
45	0.97448	0.02096	3.938	0.023	1202	0.03354	0.01957	$2\pi/y$	29.491	29.842
50	0.96492	0.00308	3.322	0.003	170	0.00561	0.00280	Δ	5.139	
55	0.85101		10.547							

MAIN TABLES — Countries of Asia

Malaysia (West), 1966 (Indians and Pakistanis)

TABLE 1 DATA INPUT TO COMPUTATIONS

Age at last birthday	Population Total	Males	%	Females	%	Births, by age of mother	Deaths Total	Males	Females	Age at last birthday
0	31468	16152	3.0	15316	3.6	0	1721	923	798	0
1–4	125056	63340	11.6	61716	14.3	0	650	294	355	1–4
5–9	153149	77571	14.2	75578	17.5	0	231	118	113	5–9
10–14	130588	66611	12.2	63977	14.8	56	121	58	63	10–14
15–19	102006	52499	9.6	49507	11.5	5373	160	79	81	15–19
20–24	58315	31988	5.8	26327	6.1	8762	133	59	74	20–24
25–29	59174	31353	5.7	27821	6.4	8831	154	70	84	25–29
30–34	55991	28996	5.3	26995	6.3	6566	191	93	98	30–34
35–39	48518	28975	5.3	19543	4.5	2877	194	103	91	35–39
40–44	47429	30441	5.6	16988	3.9	907	290	191	99	40–44
45–49	48132	32384	5.9	15748	3.7	171	476	317	159	45–49
50–54	41778	29431	5.4	12347	2.9	33	568	402	166	50–54
55–59	33873	24397	4.5	9476	2.2	0	700	485	215	55–59
60–64	20893	16410	3.0	4483	1.0	0	654	493	161	60–64
65–69	13074	9830	1.8	3244	0.8	0	577	392	185	65–69
70–74	6070	4485	0.8	1585	0.4		384	253	131	70–74
75–79	2141	1592	0.3	549	0.1		195	131	64	75–79
80–84	583	445	0.1	138	0.0	17198 M	81	58	23	80–84
85+	147	118	0.0	29	0.0	16378 F	37	30	7	85+
All ages	978385	547018		431367		33576	7517	4549	2968	All ages

TABLE 2 LIFE TABLE FOR MALES

Age, x	$_nq_x$	l_x	$_nd_x$	$_nL_x$	$_nm_x$	T_x	$1000r_x$	$\overset{\circ}{e}_x$	$_nM_x$	Age, x
0	0.05497	100000	5497	96198	0.05714	6255142	0.00	62.55	0.05714	0
1	0.01832	94503	1732	373092	0.00464	6158945	0.00	65.17	0.00464	1
5	0.00753	92771	698	462110	0.00151	5785853	15.54	62.37	0.00152	5
10	0.00434	92073	400	459363	0.00087	5323743	37.87	57.82	0.00087	10
15	0.00757	91673	694	456721	0.00152	4864380	71.93	53.06	0.00150	15
20	0.00922	90979	839	452852	0.00185	4407659	49.69	48.45	0.00184	20
25	0.01111	90140	1002	448318	0.00223	3954797	7.45	43.87	0.00223	25
30	0.01592	89138	1419	442258	0.00321	3506480	4.87	39.34	0.00321	30
35	0.01763	87719	1546	434990	0.00355	3064222	0.00	34.93	0.00355	35
40	0.03092	86173	2665	424713	0.00627	2629232	0.00	30.51	0.00627	40
45	0.04784	83508	3995	408097	0.00979	2204518	0.00	26.40	0.00979	45
50	0.06629	79513	5271	385035	0.01369	1796422	14.21	22.59	0.01365	50
55	0.09549	74243	7090	354380	0.02001	1411386	37.59	19.01	0.01988	55
60	0.14207	67153	9540	312647	0.03052	1057007	112.03	15.74	0.03004	60
65	0.18404	57613	10603	262028	0.04046	744360	112.03	12.92	0.03988	65
70	0.25114	47010	11806	205865	0.05735	482332	112.03	10.26	0.05641	70
75	0.34637	35204	12194	145446	0.08384	276666	112.03	7.85	0.08229	75
80	0.49449	23010	11378	85607	0.13291	131021	112.03	5.69	0.13034	80
85+	1.00000	11632	11632	45414	0.25613	45414	112.03	3.90	0.25424	85+

TABLE 3 LIFE TABLE FOR FEMALES

Age, x	$_nq_x$	l_x	$_nd_x$	$_nL_x$	$_nm_x$	T_x	$1000r_x$	$\overset{\circ}{e}_x$	$_nM_x$	Age, x
0	0.05037	100000	5037	96683	0.05210	6033976	0.00	60.34	0.05210	0
1	0.02271	94963	2156	373825	0.00577	5937293	0.00	62.52	0.00577	1
5	0.00738	92806	685	462319	0.00148	5563468	16.20	59.95	0.00150	5
10	0.00492	92121	453	459489	0.00099	5101149	41.06	55.37	0.00098	10
15	0.00832	91668	762	456606	0.00167	4641660	87.03	50.64	0.00164	15
20	0.01404	90906	1276	451460	0.00283	4185054	55.03	46.04	0.00281	20
25	0.01499	89630	1343	444857	0.00302	3733595	0.00	41.66	0.00302	25
30	0.01805	88287	1593	437587	0.00364	3288738	31.60	37.25	0.00363	30
35	0.02312	86693	2004	428633	0.00468	2851150	41.68	32.89	0.00466	35
40	0.02883	84689	2442	417772	0.00584	2422517	15.08	28.60	0.00583	40
45	0.04948	82248	4069	401625	0.01013	2004745	22.14	24.37	0.01010	45
50	0.06561	78178	5129	378885	0.01354	1603120	36.03	20.51	0.01344	50
55	0.10931	73049	7985	346495	0.02305	1224234	77.69	16.76	0.02269	55
60	0.16816	65064	10941	299164	0.03657	877740	96.93	13.49	0.03591	60
65	0.25364	54123	13728	236928	0.05794	578575	96.93	10.69	0.05703	65
70	0.34584	40395	13970	166682	0.08381	341648	96.93	8.46	0.08265	70
75	0.45233	26425	11953	101097	0.11823	174966	96.93	6.62	0.11658	75
80	0.58503	14472	8467	49955	0.16949	73869	96.93	5.10	0.16667	80
85+	•1.00000	6006	6006	23914	0.25113	23914	96.93	3.98	0.24138	85+

TABLE 4 POPULATION PROJECTION, USING FIXED AGE-SPECIFIC BIRTH AND DEATH RATES, IN THOUSANDS

Age at last birthday	1971 Total	Males	Females	1976 Total	Males	Females	1981 Total	Males	Females	Age at last birthday
0–4	180	92	88	234	120	114	295	151	144	0–4
5–9	154	78	76	178	91	87	230	118	112	5–9
10–14	152	77	75	153	78	75	176	90	85	10–14
15–19	130	66	64	152	77	75	152	77	75	15–19
20–24	101	52	49	129	66	63	150	76	74	20–24
25–29	58	32	26	100	52	48	127	65	62	25–29
30–34	58	31	27	57	31	26	98	51	47	30–34
35–39	55	29	26	57	30	27	56	31	25	35–39
40–44	47	28	19	54	28	26	56	30	26	40–44
45–49	45	29	16	45	27	18	52	27	25	45–49
50–54	46	31	15	43	28	15	43	25	17	50–54
55–59	38	27	11	42	28	14	39	25	14	55–59
60–64	30	22	8	34	24	10	37	25	12	60–64
65–69	18	14	4	24	18	6	28	20	8	65–69
70–74	10	8	2	13	11	2	19	14	5	70–74
75–79	4	3	1	6	5	1	10	8	2	75–79
80–84	1	1	0	2	2	0	4	3	1	80–84
85 +	0	0	0	0	0	0	1	1	0	85 +
All ages	1127	620	507	1323	716	607	1573	838	735	All ages

TABLE 5 OBSERVED AND PROJECTED VITAL RATES

Rates per thousand	Observed Total	Males	Females	Projected 1971 Males	Females	1976 Males	Females	1981 Males	Females	Stable Males	Females
Birth	34.32	31.44	37.97	35.77	41.54	40.23	45.07	42.42	45.09	42.98	43.37
Death	7.68	8.32	6.88	8.97	7.17	9.56	7.61	9.78	7.84	7.70	8.09
Increase	26.63	23.12	31.09	26.80	34.38	30.67	37.47	32.64	38.25		35.2814

TABLE 6 RATES STANDARDIZED ON THREE STANDARD COUNTRIES

Standardized rates per thousand	England and Wales, 1961 Total	Males	Females	United States, 1960 Total	Males	Females	Mexico, 1960 Total	Males	Females
Birth	38.97	37.13*	36.84	39.66	34.46*	38.12	44.92	32.88*	43.71
Death	18.15	18.03*	22.19	14.88	14.15*	17.00	8.88	8.63*	9.57
Increase	20.81	19.10*	14.65	24.78	20.31*	21.12	36.04	24.25*	34.14

TABLE 7 VITAL STATISTICS AND RATES INFERRED FROM AGE DISTRIBUTIONS (FEMALES)

Vital statistics		Thompson Age range	NRR	1000r	Interval	Bourgeois-Pichat Age range	NRR	1000b	1000d	1000r	Coale
TFR	6.09	0–4	2.58	34.80	27.26	5–29	4.52	60.31	4.47	55.84	1000b
GRR	2.97	5–9	3.16	42.39	27.17	30–54	2.16	33.49	4.95	28.54	1000d
NRR	2.63	10–14	2.93	34.33	27.05	55–79	5.81	243.88	178.69	55.19	$1000k_1$
Generation	27.38	15–19	2.59	35.37	26.86	*35–59	1.96	27.58	2.70	24.87	$1000k_2$
Sex ratio	105.01										

TABLE 8 LESLIE MATRIX AND ITS ANALYSIS (FEMALES)

Start of age interval	Sub-diagonal	First row	Percent in stable population	Fisher values	Total reproductive values	Net maternity function	Matrix equation coefficient	Parameters	Integral	Matrix
0	0.98259	0.00000	18.740	1.160	89340	0.00000	0.00000	λ_1	1.1929	1.1938
5	0.99388	0.00100	15.425	1.409	106494	0.00000	0.00098	λ_2	0.3667	0.3754
10	0.99372	0.12477	12.841	1.691	108207	0.00196	0.12184		+0.8545	+0.8237i
15	0.98873	0.50216	10.689	1.886	93383	0.24173	0.48732	r_1	0.0353	0.0354
20	0.98537	0.74085	8.853	1.688	44452	0.73291	0.71085	r_2	−0.0145	−0.0199
25	0.98366	0.53881	7.307	1.174	32652	0.68879	0.60398		+0.2331	+0.2286i
30	0.97954	0.44459	6.021	0.671	18118	0.51918	0.41349	c_1		4358
35	0.97466	0.22865	4.940	0.292	5698	0.30780	0.20830	c_2		858
40	0.96135	0.07325	4.034	0.085	1445	0.10880	0.06504			24776i
45	0.94338	0.01535	3.248	0.017	272	0.02127	0.01311	$2\pi/y$	26.957	27.482
50	0.91451	0.00307	2.567	−0.003	37	0.00494	0.00247	Δ	6.056	
55	0.75373		5.334							

Philippines, 1960

TABLE 1 DATA INPUT TO COMPUTATIONS

Age at last birthday	Population					Births, by age of mother	Deaths			Age at last birthday
	Total	Males	%	Females	%		Total	Males	Females	
0	796101	409376	3.0	386725	2.8	0	83078	47726	35352	0
1–4	3832346	1973682	14.3	1858664	13.7	0	54882	29298	25584	1–4
5–9	4422943	2282360	16.5	2140583	15.8	0	12730	7200	5530	5–9
10–14	3477526	1787763	12.9	1689763	12.4	1067	5785	3402	2383	10–14
15–19	2848784	1401830	10.1	1446954	10.6	85913	5704	3320	2384	15–19
20–24	2488741	1208904	8.7	1279837	9.4	398562	7426	4211	3215	20–24
25–29	1977278	964109	7.0	1013169	7.5	344582	7712	4197	3515	25–29
30–34	1575519	774409	5.6	801110	5.9	238262	7866	4012	3854	30–34
35–39	1445974	711229	5.1	734745	5.4	154724	8715	4333	4382	35–39
40–44	1112443	553129	4.0	559314	4.1	55641	8157	4365	3792	40–44
45–49	1045337	531106	3.8	514231	3.8	12288	9439	5170	4269	45–49
50–54	718801	369858	2.7	348943	2.6	0	8740	4915	3825	50–54
55–59	493909	255505	1.8	238404	1.8	0	8771	4805	3966	55–59
60–64	436186	234643	1.7	201543	1.5	0	9940	5556	4384	60–64
65–69	228594	114091	0.8	114503	0.8	0	7711	4203	3508	65–69
70–74	211501	108116	0.8	103385	0.8		10668	5507	5161	70–74
75–79	111359	56418	0.4	54941	0.4		8450	4484	3966	75–79
80–84	100563	49082	0.4	51481	0.4	666687 M	10457	5195	5262	80–84
85+	95680	45693	0.3	49987	0.4	624352 F	21734	9910	11824	85+
All ages	27419585	13831303		13588282		1291039	297965	161809	136156	All ages

TABLE 2 LIFE TABLE FOR MALES

Age, x	$_nq_x$	l_x	$_nd_x$	$_nL_x$	$_nm_x$	T_x	$1000r_x$	$\overset{\circ}{e}_x$	$_nM_x$	Age, x
0	0.10838	100000	10838	92957	0.11658	5539755	0.00	55.40	0.11658	0
1	0.05703	89162	5085	342523	0.01484	5446789	0.00	61.09	0.01484	1
5	0.01539	84077	1294	417150	0.00310	5104266	23.17	60.71	0.00315	5
10	0.00943	82783	781	411896	0.00190	4687115	46.46	56.62	0.00190	10
15	0.01184	82002	971	407714	0.00238	4275220	36.64	52.14	0.00237	15
20	0.01734	81032	1405	401801	0.00350	3867505	34.00	47.73	0.00348	20
25	0.02161	79626	1721	393953	0.00437	3465704	40.18	43.52	0.00435	25
30	0.02562	77906	1996	384656	0.00519	3071751	25.23	39.43	0.00518	30
35	0.03009	75909	2284	374016	0.00611	2687095	27.36	35.40	0.00609	35
40	0.03880	73625	2856	361213	0.00791	2313079	21.34	31.42	0.00789	40
45	0.04772	70769	3377	345718	0.00977	1951857	30.14	27.58	0.00973	45
50	0.06492	67392	4375	326503	0.01340	1606149	59.42	23.83	0.01329	50
55	0.09019	63017	5684	301306	0.01886	1279646	25.94	20.31	0.01881	55
60	0.11237	57333	6442	271174	0.02376	978340	22.50	17.06	0.02368	60
65	0.16962	50891	8632	233531	0.03696	707166	22.50	13.90	0.03684	65
70	0.22711	42259	9598	187751	0.05112	473635	22.50	11.21	0.05094	70
75	0.33221	32661	10850	136058	0.07974	285874	22.50	8.75	0.07948	75
80	0.41546	21811	9062	85410	0.10610	149806	22.50	6.87	0.10584	80
85+	1.00000	12749	12749	64396	0.19798	64396	22.50	5.05	0.21688	85+

TABLE 3 LIFE TABLE FOR FEMALES

Age, x	$_nq_x$	l_x	$_nd_x$	$_nL_x$	$_nm_x$	T_x	$1000r_x$	$\overset{\circ}{e}_x$	$_nM_x$	Age, x
0	0.08643	100000	8643	94549	0.09141	5867611	0.00	58.68	0.09141	0
1	0.05306	91357	4847	352133	0.01376	5773061	0.00	63.19	0.01376	1
5	0.01258	86510	1089	429828	0.00253	5420928	23.58	62.66	0.00258	5
10	0.00699	85421	597	425532	0.00140	4991100	37.44	58.43	0.00141	10
15	0.00824	84824	699	422459	0.00165	4565568	25.03	53.82	0.00165	15
20	0.01255	84125	1056	418142	0.00252	4143099	33.11	49.25	0.00251	20
25	0.01731	83070	1438	411940	0.00349	3724957	43.28	44.84	0.00347	25
30	0.02385	81632	1947	403483	0.00482	3313016	27.35	40.58	0.00481	30
35	0.02945	79685	2347	392692	0.00598	2909533	30.03	36.51	0.00595	35
40	0.03341	77338	2584	380379	0.00679	2516841	28.76	32.54	0.00678	40
45	0.04086	74754	3054	366403	0.00834	2136462	38.67	28.58	0.00830	45
50	0.05395	71700	3868	349330	0.01107	1770058	65.21	24.69	0.01096	50
55	0.08038	67832	5452	326071	0.01672	1420728	38.42	20.94	0.01664	55
60	0.10360	62380	6463	296276	0.02181	1094657	21.60	17.55	0.02175	60
65	0.14324	55917	8010	260445	0.03075	798381	21.60	14.28	0.03064	65
70	0.22328	47908	10697	213504	0.05010	537936	21.60	11.23	0.04992	70
75	0.30654	37211	11407	157522	0.07241	324432	21.60	8.72	0.07219	75
80	0.41139	25804	10616	103271	0.10279	166910	21.60	6.47	0.10221	80
85+	*1.00000	15189	15189	63639	0.23867	63639	21.60	4.19	0.23654	85+

TABLE 4 POPULATION PROJECTION, USING FIXED AGE-SPECIFIC BIRTH AND DEATH RATES, IN THOUSANDS

Age at last birthday	1965 Total	1965 Males	1965 Females	1970 Total	1970 Males	1970 Females	1975 Total	1975 Males	1975 Females	Age at last birthday
0–4	6194	3159	3035	7284	3715	3569	8581	4377	4204	0–4
5–9	4444	2283	2161	5946	3026	2920	6993	3559	3434	5–9
10–14	4373	2254	2119	4393	2254	2139	5879	2988	2891	10–14
15–19	3448	1770	1678	4335	2231	2104	4355	2231	2124	15–19
20–24	2813	1381	1432	3404	1744	1660	4280	2198	2082	20–24
25–29	2446	1185	1261	2766	1355	1411	3346	1710	1636	25–29
30–34	1933	941	992	2392	1157	1235	2705	1323	1382	30–34
35–39	1533	753	780	1881	915	966	2327	1125	1202	35–39
40–44	1399	687	712	1482	727	755	1820	884	936	40–44
45–49	1068	529	539	1343	657	686	1423	696	727	45–49
50–54	992	502	490	1014	500	514	1275	621	654	50–54
55–59	667	341	326	921	463	458	940	461	479	55–59
60–64	447	230	217	603	307	296	833	417	416	60–64
65–69	379	202	177	388	198	190	525	265	260	65–69
70–74	186	92	94	307	162	145	315	159	156	70–74
75–79	154	78	76	135	66	69	225	118	107	75–79
80–84	71	35	36	99	49	50	87	42	45	80–84
85 +	69	37	32	49	27	22	68	37	31	85 +
All ages	32616	16459	16157	38742	19553	19189	45977	23211	22766	All ages

TABLE 5 OBSERVED AND PROJECTED VITAL RATES

Rates per thousand	Observed Total	Observed Males	Observed Females	Projected 1965 Males	Projected 1965 Females	Projected 1970 Males	Projected 1970 Females	Projected 1975 Males	Projected 1975 Females	Stable Males	Stable Females
Birth	47.08	43.20	45.95	47.65	45.46	47.15	45.00	46.88	44.75	46.25	44.37
Death	10.87	11.70	10.02	11.94	10.07	11.73	9.93	11.75	9.98	12.88	11.00
Increase	36.22	35.50	35.93	35.71	35.39	35.42	35.06	35.14	34.78		33.3687

TABLE 6 RATES STANDARDIZED ON THREE STANDARD COUNTRIES

Standardized rates per thousand	England and Wales, 1961 Total	Males	Females	United States, 1960 Total	Males	Females	Mexico, 1960 Total	Males	Females
Birth	43.18	49.53*	40.47	43.80	44.82*	41.74	46.75	48.18*	45.10
Death	16.32	26.38*	17.13	14.76	21.95*	14.45	11.36	11.79*	10.46
Increase	26.85	23.16*	23.34	29.04	22.87*	27.29	35.39	36.39*	34.64

TABLE 7 VITAL STATISTICS AND RATES INFERRED FROM AGE DISTRIBUTIONS (FEMALES)

Vital statistics		Thompson Age range	NRR	1000r	Interval	Bourgeois-Pichat Age range	NRR	1000b	1000d	1000r	Coale	
TFR	6.71	0–4	2.09	28.07	27.23	5–29	2.47	45.96	12.53	33.43	1000b	43.64
GRR	3.25	5–9	2.41	33.17	27.12	30–54	2.45	45.39	12.16	33.23	1000d	12.66
NRR	2.64	10–14	2.30	30.14	27.03	55–79	2.47	36.93	3.48	33.45	1000r	30.98
Generation	29.04	15–19	2.38	32.18	26.90	*5–29	2.47	45.96	12.53	33.43	$1000k_1$	−6.44
Sex ratio	106.8										$1000k_2$	0.

TABLE 8 LESLIE MATRIX AND ITS ANALYSIS (FEMALES)

Start of age interval	Sub-diagonal	First row	Percent in stable population	Fisher values	Total reproductive values	Net maternity function	Matrix equation coefficient	Parameters	Integral	Matrix
0	0.96227	0.00000	18.283	1.215	2728628	0.00000	0.00000	λ_1	1.1816	1.1823
5	0.99001	0.00067	14.880	1.493	3196087	0.00000	0.00065	λ_2	0.4406	0.4450
10	0.99280	0.06435	12.460	1.782	3011620	0.00130	0.06130		+0.8345	+0.8097i
15	0.98976	0.39704	10.463	2.044	2957138	0.12131	0.37552	r_1	0.0334	0.0335
20	0.98517	0.59825	8.759	1.954	2500530	0.62973	0.65364	r_2	−0.0116	−0.0158
25	0.97947	0.58198	7.299	1.483	1502978	0.67754	0.62894		+0.2170	+0.2137i
30	0.97326	0.54260	6.047	0.945	756656	0.58033	0.49012	c_1		137081
35	0.96864	0.33153	4.977	0.470	345244	0.39991	0.29145	c_2		−275902
40	0.96326	0.13231	4.078	0.158	88152	0.18300	0.11267			−4429i
45	0.95340	0.02581	3.322	0.027	13643	0.04234	0.02117	$2\pi/y$	28.955	29.407
50	0.93342	0.00000	2.679	0.000	0	0.00000	0.00000	Δ	3.119	
55	0.81190		6.752							

Ryukyu Islands, 1965

TABLE 1 DATA INPUT TO COMPUTATIONS

Age at last birthday	Population					Births, by age of mother	Deaths			Age at last birthday
	Total	Males	%	Females	%		Total	Males	Females	
0	20909	10579	2.4	10330	2.1	0	309	168	141	0
1–4	86775	44368	10.0	42407	8.8	0	222	106	116	1–4
5–9	120337	60913	13.7	59424	12.3	0	113	68	45	5–9
10–14	133550	67854	15.2	65696	13.6	0	139	76	63	10–14
15–19	95717	48798	10.9	46919	9.7	393	125	80	45	15–19
20–24	58592	27550	6.2	31042	6.4	4050	127	82	45	20–24
25–29	71109	34381	7.7	36728	7.6	8593	189	101	88	25–29
30–34	67312	33566	7.5	33746	7.0	6113	197	106	91	30–34
35–39	55233	25848	5.8	29385	6.1	2262	195	103	92	35–39
40–44	43444	18892	4.2	24552	5.1	599	221	147	74	40–44
45–49	37371	16075	3.6	21296	4.4	42	251	148	103	45–49
50–54	33339	14520	3.3	18819	3.9	5	319	200	119	50–54
55–59	28012	12021	2.7	15991	3.3	0	459	269	190	55–59
60–64	24072	9913	2.2	14159	2.9	0	564	343	221	60–64
65–69	19078	7839	1.8	11239	2.3	0	659	378	281	65–69
70–74	15993	6350	1.4	9643	2.0		908	485	423	70–74
75–79	10182	3524	0.8	6658	1.4		866	423	443	75–79
80–84	5775	1796	0.4	3979	0.8	11436 M	785	283	502	80–84
85 +	3542	906	0.2	2636	0.5	10521 F	796	225	571	85 +
All ages	930342	445693		484649		22057	7444	3791	3653	All ages

TABLE 2 LIFE TABLE FOR MALES

Age, x	nq_x	l_x	nd_x	nL_x	nm_x	T_x	$1000r_x$	$\overset{\circ}{e}_x$	nM_x	Age, x
0	0.01572	100000	1572	99017	0.01588	6388222	0.00	63.88	0.01588	0
1	0.00949	98428	935	391159	0.00239	6289204	0.00	63.90	0.00239	1
5	0.00557	97493	543	486108	0.00112	5898046	0.00	60.50	0.00112	5
10	0.00560	96950	543	483450	0.00112	5411937	20.96	55.82	0.00112	10
15	0.00834	96408	804	480212	0.00167	4928488	88.29	51.12	0.00164	15
20	0.01482	95604	1417	474597	0.00299	4448276	32.34	46.53	0.00298	20
25	0.01458	94187	1373	467512	0.00294	3973679	0.00	42.19	0.00294	25
30	0.01570	92814	1457	460522	0.00316	3506167	25.29	37.78	0.00316	30
35	0.01999	91357	1826	452632	0.00404	3045645	52.80	33.34	0.00398	35
40	0.03841	89531	3439	439485	0.00783	2593013	40.29	28.96	0.00778	40
45	0.04514	86092	3886	421172	0.00923	2153528	16.45	25.01	0.00921	45
50	0.06690	82206	5500	398172	0.01381	1732355	14.54	21.07	0.01377	50
55	0.10656	76706	8174	364230	0.02244	1334184	15.11	17.39	0.02238	55
60	0.15974	68532	10947	316179	0.03462	969954	4.43	14.15	0.03460	60
65	0.21586	57585	12430	257591	0.04826	653774	4.43	11.35	0.04822	65
70	0.32135	45155	14511	189835	0.07644	396183	4.43	8.77	0.07638	70
75	0.45852	30644	14051	116978	0.12012	206348	4.43	6.73	0.12003	75
80	0.55194	16593	9158	58092	0.15765	89370	4.43	5.39	0.15757	80
85 +	1.00000	7435	7435	31278	0.23770	31278	4.43	4.21	0.24834	85 +

TABLE 3 LIFE TABLE FOR FEMALES

Age, x	nq_x	l_x	nd_x	nL_x	nm_x	T_x	$1000r_x$	$\overset{\circ}{e}_x$	nM_x	Age, x
0	0.01354	100000	1354	99191	0.01365	7078352	0.00	70.78	0.01365	0
1	0.01086	98646	1072	391733	0.00274	6979161	0.00	70.75	0.00274	1
5	0.00378	97575	369	486951	0.00076	6587428	0.00	67.51	0.00075	5
10	0.00479	97206	465	484886	0.00096	6100477	22.73	62.76	0.00096	10
15	0.00482	96740	467	482584	0.00097	5615592	73.91	58.05	0.00096	15
20	0.00726	96274	699	479762	0.00146	5133008	22.94	53.32	0.00145	20
25	0.01191	95575	1138	475147	0.00240	4653246	0.00	48.69	0.00240	25
30	0.01341	94437	1256	469082	0.00270	4178098	19.55	44.24	0.00270	30
35	0.01554	93170	1448	462254	0.00313	3709017	28.83	39.81	0.00313	35
40	0.01501	91722	1377	455318	0.00302	3246763	28.75	35.40	0.00301	40
45	0.02398	90345	2167	446597	0.00485	2791445	21.93	30.90	0.00484	45
50	0.03131	88178	2761	434569	0.00635	2344848	21.41	26.59	0.00632	50
55	0.05794	85417	4949	415401	0.01191	1910279	17.11	22.36	0.01188	55
60	0.07539	80468	6067	387976	0.01564	1494878	10.94	18.58	0.01561	60
65	0.11838	74401	8808	351438	0.02506	1106903	10.94	14.88	0.02500	65
70	0.19881	65593	13041	296670	0.04396	755465	10.94	11.52	0.04387	70
75	0.28691	52553	15078	226090	0.06669	458794	10.94	8.73	0.06654	75
80	0.47897	37475	17949	141948	0.12645	232704	10.94	6.21	0.12616	80
85 +	1.00000	19525	19525	90756	0.21514	90756	10.94	4.65	0.21662	85 +

TABLE 4 POPULATION PROJECTION, USING FIXED AGE-SPECIFIC BIRTH AND DEATH RATES, IN THOUSANDS

Age at last birthday	1970			1975			1980			Age at last birthday
	Total	Males	Females	Total	Males	Females	Total	Males	Females	
0–4	112	58	54	129	67	62	156	81	75	0–4
5–9	106	54	52	112	58	54	128	66	62	5–9
10–14	120	61	59	106	54	52	110	57	53	10–14
15–19	132	67	65	119	60	59	106	54	52	15–19
20–24	95	48	47	132	67	65	118	59	59	20–24
25–29	58	27	31	94	48	46	130	66	64	25–29
30–34	70	34	36	57	27	30	93	47	45	30–34
35–39	66	33	33	69	33	36	56	26	30	35–39
40–44	54	25	29	65	32	33	67	32	35	40–44
45–49	42	18	24	52	24	28	63	31	32	45–49
50–54	36	15	21	40	17	23	51	23	28	50–54
55–59	31	13	18	34	14	20	38	16	22	55–59
60–64	25	10	15	29	12	17	31	12	19	60–64
65–69	21	8	13	23	9	14	24	9	15	65–69
70–74	15	6	9	17	6	11	17	5	11	70–74
75–79	11	4	7	11	4	7	12	4	8	75–79
80–84	6	2	4	7	2	5	7	2	5	80–84
85 +	4	1	3	4	1	3	4	1	3	85 +
All ages	1004	484	520	1100	535	565	1211	592	619	All ages

TABLE 5 OBSERVED AND PROJECTED VITAL RATES

Rates per thousand	Observed			Projected						Stable	
				1970		1975		1980			
	Total	Males	Females	Males	Females	Males	Females	Males	Females	Males	Females
Birth	23.71	25.66	21.91	25.33	21.92	28.13	24.66	30.33	26.95	24.22	22.69
Death	8.00	8.51	7.54	8.32	7.39	8.19	7.42	8.07	7.44	10.48	8.96
Increase	15.71	17.15	14.38	17.01	14.53	19.94	17.24	22.26	19.51		13.7322

TABLE 6 RATES STANDARDIZED ON THREE STANDARD COUNTRIES

Standardized rates per thousand	England and Wales, 1961			United States, 1960			Mexico, 1960		
	Total	Males	Females	Total	Males	Females	Total	Males	Females
Birth	20.85	25.03*	19.46	21.23	23.61*	20.14	23.06	23.70*	22.15
Death	13.95	15.85*	12.67	11.47	13.51*	9.47	5.18	8.87*	4.90
Increase	6.90	9.19*	6.78	9.76	10.10*	10.67	15.88	14.83*	17.25

TABLE 7 VITAL STATISTICS AND RATES INFERRED FROM AGE DISTRIBUTIONS (FEMALES)

Vital statistics		Thompson				Bourgeois-Pichat					Coale	
		Age range	NRR	$1000r$	Interval	Age range	NRR	$1000b$	$1000d$	$1000r$	$1000b$	
TFR	3.29	0–4	1.50	15.10	27.33	5–29	2.44	35.22	2.17	33.05	$1000d$	
GRR	1.58	5–9	1.93	24.40	27.29	30–54	2.02	34.42	8.37	26.05	$1000r$	
NRR	1.49	10–14	2.26	29.21	27.25	55–79	1.41	16.47	3.68	12.79	$1000k_1$	
Generation	29.28	15–19	1.81	16.03	27.16	*45–69	1.69	24.69	5.29	19.40	$1000k_2$	
Sex ratio	107.67											

TABLE 8 LESLIE MATRIX AND ITS ANALYSIS (FEMALES)

Start of age interval	Sub-diagonal	First row	Percent in stable population	Fisher values	Total reproductive values	Net maternity function	Matrix equation coefficient	Parameters	Integral	Matrix
0	0.99187	0.00000	10.772	1.054	55582	0.00000	0.00000	λ_1	1.0711	1.0712
5	0.99573	0.00000	9.974	1.138	67637	0.00000	0.00000	λ_2	0.4493	0.4466
10	0.99522	0.00984	9.272	1.224	80442	0.00000	0.00973		+0.8344	+0.8100i
15	0.99410	0.16320	8.614	1.308	61347	0.01945	0.16043	r_1	0.0137	0.0138
20	0.99038	0.42810	7.994	1.236	38364	0.30140	0.41835	r_2	-0.0107	-0.0156
25	0.98729	0.48791	7.391	0.881	32362	0.53530	0.47223		+0.2154	+0.2134i
30	0.98545	0.30378	6.812	0.435	14684	0.40917	0.29025	c_1		5404
35	0.98497	0.11942	6.267	0.148	4352	0.17134	0.11242	c_2		-4549
40	0.98087	0.03111	5.763	0.033	817	0.05349	0.02887			28512i
45	0.97304	0.00264	5.277	0.003	62	0.00424	0.00240	$2\pi/y$	29.172	29.445
50	0.95576	0.00034	4.793	0.000	6	0.00056	0.00028	Δ	8.207	
55	0.80281		17.071							

Sarawak, 1961

TABLE 1   DATA INPUT TO COMPUTATIONS

Age at last birthday	Population					Births, by age of mother	Deaths			Age at last birthday
	Total	Males	%	Females	%		Total	Males	Females	
0	21257	10744	2.9	10513	2.8	0	1376	815	561	0
1–4	106757	53573	14.2	53184	14.4	0	629	335	294	1–4
5–9	124411	63694	16.9	60717	16.5	0	184	98	86	5–9
10–14	78959	41696	11.1	37263	10.1	11	84	51	33	10–14
15–19	66538	31807	8.5	34731	9.4	3060	87	27	60	15–19
20–24	53929	25096	6.7	28833	7.8	7599	125	57	68	20–24
25–29	53804	24406	6.5	29398	8.0	7497	181	71	110	25–29
30–34	47667	23947	6.4	23720	6.4	5148	182	52	120	30–34
35–39	42267	21292	5.7	20975	5.7	2804	224	92	132	35–39
40–44	37948	19533	5.2	18415	5.0	1212	256	134	122	40–44
45–49	29300	15919	4.2	13381	3.6	218	308	198	110	45–49
50–54	27393	14979	4.0	12414	3.4	0	366	234	132	50–54
55–59	16135	9317	2.5	6818	1.8	0	305	203	102	55–59
60–64	16300	8675	2.3	7625	2.1	0	486	297	189	60–64
65–69	7860	4165	1.1	3695	1.0	0	259	161	98	65–69
70–74	7448	3817	1.0	3631	1.0		397	246	151	70–74
75–79	4528	2247	0.6	2281	0.6		198	114	84	75–79
80–84	1925	922	0.2	1003	0.3	14104 M	189	105	84	80–84
85 +	751	341	0.1	410	0.1	13445 F	143	63	80	85 +
All ages	745177	376170		369007		27549	5979	3363	2615	All ages

TABLE 2   LIFE TABLE FOR MALES

Age, x	$_nq_x$	l_x	$_nd_x$	$_nL_x$	$_nm_x$	T_x	$1000r_x$	$\overset{\circ}{e}_x$	$_nM_x$	Age, x
0	0.07208	100000	7208	95018	0.07586	6062981	0.00	60.63	0.07586	0
1	0.02458	92792	2280	364693	0.00625	5967964	0.00	64.32	0.00625	1
5	0.00749	90512	678	450864	0.00150	5603271	40.71	61.91	0.00154	5
10	0.00605	89834	544	447749	0.00121	5152407	68.26	57.35	0.00122	10
15	0.00429	89290	383	445591	0.00086	4704658	49.52	52.69	0.00085	15
20	0.01135	88907	1009	442198	0.00228	4259067	24.39	47.90	0.00227	20
25	0.01444	87898	1269	436340	0.00291	3816868	2.00	43.42	0.00291	25
30	0.01288	86629	1115	430473	0.00259	3380528	10.62	39.02	0.00259	30
35	0.02146	85513	1835	423336	0.00434	2950055	15.97	34.50	0.00432	35
40	0.03395	83678	2841	411925	0.00690	2526719	21.53	30.20	0.00685	40
45	0.06053	80837	4893	392558	0.01247	2114794	14.69	26.16	0.01244	45
50	0.07560	75944	5742	365869	0.01569	1722237	37.30	22.68	0.01562	50
55	0.10410	70203	7308	333628	0.02190	1356367	31.36	19.32	0.02179	55
60	0.15884	62895	9990	289936	0.03446	1022739	58.04	16.26	0.03424	60
65	0.17781	52905	9407	241443	0.03896	732803	58.04	13.85	0.03866	65
70	0.27795	43498	12090	186782	0.06473	491360	58.04	11.30	0.06445	70
75	0.22603	31408	7099	139067	0.05105	304579	58.04	9.70	0.05073	75
80	0.45333	24309	11020	95282	0.11565	165512	58.04	6.81	0.11383	80
85 +	*1.00000	13289	13289	70229	0.18922	70229	58.04	5.28	0.18475	85 +

TABLE 3   LIFE TABLE FOR FEMALES

Age, x'	$_nq_x$	l_x	$_nd_x$	$_nL_x$	$_nm_x$	T_x	$1000r_x$	$\overset{\circ}{e}_x$	$_nM_x$	Age, x
0	0.05153	100000	5153	96570	0.05336	6437756	0.00	64.38	0.05336	0
1	0.02177	94847	2065	373594	0.00553	6341186	0.00	66.86	0.00553	1
5	0.00685	92782	636	462318	0.00138	5967592	51.37	64.32	0.00142	5
10	0.00444	92146	409	459739	0.00089	5505274	54.67	59.75	0.00089	10
15	0.00864	91737	793	456840	0.00173	5045535	24.00	55.00	0.00173	15
20	0.01176	90944	1069	452231	0.00236	4588695	14.14	50.46	0.00235	20
25	0.01859	89875	1671	445436	0.00375	4136465	15.80	46.02	0.00374	25
30	0.02507	88204	2211	435702	0.00507	3691029	28.69	41.85	0.00506	30
35	0.03102	85993	2667	423405	0.00630	3255327	19.22	37.86	0.00629	35
40	0.03267	83326	2722	409949	0.00664	2831922	38.04	33.99	0.00663	40
45	0.04043	80604	3259	395148	0.00825	2421973	31.07	30.05	0.00822	45
50	0.05222	77345	4039	377061	0.01071	2026826	56.44	26.20	0.01063	50
55	0.07269	73307	5329	354033	0.01505	1649764	32.45	22.51	0.01496	55
60	0.11754	67978	7990	320369	0.02494	1295731	59.02	19.06	0.02479	60
65	0.12533	59987	7518	281544	0.02670	975362	59.02	16.26	0.02652	65
70	0.18902	52469	9918	237499	0.04176	693819	59.02	13.22	0.04159	70
75	0.17067	42551	7262	195174	0.03721	456320	59.02	10.72	0.03683	75
80	0.35891	35289	12665	147982	0.08559	261145	59.02	7.40	0.08375	80
85 +	*1.00000	22624	22624	113163	0.19992	113163	59.02	5.00	0.19512	85 +

TABLE 4 POPULATION PROJECTION, USING FIXED AGE-SPECIFIC BIRTH AND DEATH RATES, IN THOUSANDS

Age at last birthday	1966 Total	Males	Females	1971 Total	Males	Females	1976 Total	Males	Females	Age at last birthday
0–4	135	68	67	152	77	75	182	92	90	0–4
5–9	126	63	63	133	67	66	150	76	74	5–9
10–14	123	63	60	125	63	62	132	67	65	10–14
15–19	78	41	37	123	63	60	124	62	62	15–19
20–24	66	32	34	78	41	37	121	62	59	20–24
25–29	53	25	28	65	31	34	77	41	36	25–29
30–34	53	24	29	52	24	28	64	31	33	30–34
35–39	47	24	23	52	24	28	51	24	27	35–39
40–44	41	21	20	45	23	22	50	23	27	40–44
45–49	37	19	18	40	20	20	44	22	22	45–49
50–54	28	15	13	34	17	17	37	18	19	50–54
55–59	26	14	12	26	14	12	32	16	16	55–59
60–64	14	8	6	23	12	11	23	12	11	60–64
65–69	14	7	7	12	7	5	19	10	9	65–69
70–74	6	3	3	12	6	6	10	5	5	70–74
75–79	6	3	3	5	2	3	9	4	5	75–79
80–84	4	2	2	4	2	2	4	2	2	80–84
85 +	2	1	1	2	1	1	3	1	2	85 +
All ages	859	433	426	983	494	489	1132	568	564	All ages

TABLE 5 OBSERVED AND PROJECTED VITAL RATES

Rates per thousand	Observed Total	Males	Females	Projected 1966 Males	Females	1971 Males	Females	1976 Males	Females	Stable Males	Females
Birth	36.97	37.49	36.44	36.22	35.04	36.46	35.16	38.99	37.51	38.11	36.93
Death	8.02	8.94	7.09	8.93	7.13	9.15	7.47	9.14	7.57	9.46	8.27
Increase	28.95	28.55	29.35	27.29	27.91	27.32	27.69	29.85	29.94		28.6595

TABLE 6 RATES STANDARDIZED ON THREE STANDARD COUNTRIES

Standardized rates per thousand	England and Wales, 1961 Total	Males	Females	United States, 1960 Total	Males	Females	Mexico, 1960 Total	Males	Females
Birth	33.40	39.87*	31.59	33.97	37.19*	32.67	37.57	36.68*	36.58
Death	14.00	19.84*	13.78	12.21	16.15*	11.29	8.30	9.29*	7.46
Increase	19.40	20.03*	17.82	21.76	21.04*	21.38	29.27	27.39*	29.12

TABLE 7 VITAL STATISTICS AND RATES INFERRED FROM AGE DISTRIBUTIONS (FEMALES)

Vital statistics		Thompson Age range	NRR	$1000r$	Interval	Bourgeois-Pichat Age range	NRR	$1000b$	$1000d$	$1000r$	Coale
TFR	5.20	0–4	2.28	30.26	27.20	5–29	2.39	38.46	6.14	32.32	$1000b$
GRR	2.54	5–9	2.50	34.55	27.11	30–54	2.11	37.22	9.50	27.73	$1000d$
NRR	2.23	10–14	1.70	19.41	27.02	55–79	2.00	25.17	-0.58	25.75	$1000r$
Generation	28.05	15–19	1.90	23.90	26.91	*10–44	1.71	28.57	8.67	19.89	$1000k_1$
Sex ratio	104.90										$1000k_2$

TABLE 8 LESLIE MATRIX AND ITS ANALYSIS (FEMALES)

Start of age interval	Sub-diagonal	First row	Percent in stable population	Fisher values	Total reproductive values	Net maternity function	Matrix equation coefficient	Parameters	Integral	Matrix
0	0.98333	0.00000	16.198	1.142	72728	0.00000	0.00000	λ_1	1.1541	1.1546
5	0.99444	0.00034	13.795	1.341	81402	0.00000	0.00033	λ_2	0.3895	0.4001
10	0.99369	0.10080	11.881	1.556	57989	0.00066	0.09855		+0.7933	+0.7694i
15	0.98995	0.40038	10.225	1.692	58780	0.19644	0.38906	r_1	0.0287	0.0288
20	0.98507	0.59053	8.767	1.512	43600	0.58168	0.56803	r_2	-0.0247	-0.0285
25	0.97819	0.53613	7.480	1.088	31983	0.55438	0.50794		+0.2229	+0.2183i
30	0.97177	0.39804	6.337	0.658	15616	0.46150	0.36887	c_1		3688
35	0.96828	0.22652	5.333	0.315	6598	0.27624	0.20396	c_2		14800
40	0.96406	0.09350	4.473	0.108	1989	0.13168	0.08155			3819i
45	0.95432	0.01873	3.734	0.019	249	0.03142	0.01571	$2\pi/y$	28.192	28.788
50	0.93892	0.00009	3.087	0.000	1	0.00000	0.00000	Δ	6.228	
55	0.82115		8.691							

Singapore, 1966-68

TABLE 1   DATA INPUT TO COMPUTATIONS

Age at last birthday	Population Total	Males	%	Females	%	Births, by age of mother	Deaths Total	Males	Females	Age at last birthday
0	51800	26300	2.6	25500	2.7	0	1259	709	550	0
1–4	226700	115500	11.4	111200	11.8	0	410	212	198	1–4
5–9	297100	151900	15.0	145200	15.4	0	173	98	75	5–9
10–14	261000	133700	13.2	127300	13.5	23	141	83	58	10–14
15–19	218900	112400	11.1	106500	11.3	3622	153	93	60	15–19
20–24	136900	70900	7.0	66000	7.0	12912	162	105	57	20–24
25–29	135900	69900	6.9	66000	7.0	16661	162	97	65	25–29
30–34	119200	60800	6.0	58400	6.2	10249	187	110	77	30–34
35–39	110700	58800	5.8	51900	5.5	5337	253	164	89	35–39
40–44	88200	48600	4.8	39600	4.2	1770	319	205	114	40–44
45–49	80400	44600	4.4	35800	3.8	253	481	323	158	45–49
50–54	71600	39500	3.9	32100	3.4	0	727	497	230	50–54
55–59	58800	32400	3.2	26400	2.8	0	1040	715	325	55–59
60–64	43100	23300	2.3	19800	2.1	0	1224	861	363	60–64
65–69	28300	14200	1.4	14100	1.5	0	1220	786	434	65–69
70–74	16500	7100	0.7	9400	1.0		1027	592	435	70–74
75–79	6700	2000	0.2	4700	0.5		808	382	425	75–79
80–84	2547	626	0.1	1921	0.2	26045 M	500	192	308	80–84
85+	1253	374	0.0	879	0.1	24782 F	404	112	292	85+
All ages	1955600	1012900		942700		50827	10650	6336	4314	All ages

TABLE 2   LIFE TABLE FOR MALES

Age, x	nq_x	l_x	nd_x	nL_x	nm_x	T_x	$1000r_x$	$\overset{\circ}{e}_x$	nM_x	Age, x
0	0.02645	100000	2645	98124	0.02696	6444629	0.00	64.45	0.02696	0
1	0.00730	97355	711	387385	0.00184	6346505	0.00	65.19	0.00184	1
5	0.00322	96644	311	482442	0.00064	5959120	4.94	61.66	0.00065	5
10	0.00311	96333	299	480936	0.00062	5476679	29.45	56.85	0.00062	10
15	0.00419	96034	402	479249	0.00084	4995743	62.49	52.02	0.00083	15
20	0.00740	95632	708	476442	0.00149	4516493	46.19	47.23	0.00148	20
25	0.00692	94924	657	473007	0.00139	4040051	13.87	42.56	0.00139	25
30	0.00903	94267	851	469340	0.00181	3567045	15.38	37.84	0.00181	30
35	0.01390	93416	1299	464057	0.00280	3097704	19.55	33.16	0.00279	35
40	0.02099	92117	1934	456150	0.00424	2633647	23.13	28.59	0.00422	40
45	0.03573	90183	3222	443569	0.00726	2177497	13.09	24.15	0.00724	45
50	0.06141	86961	5341	422576	0.01264	1733928	18.58	19.94	0.01258	50
55	0.10560	81620	8619	388043	0.02221	1311352	29.58	16.07	0.02207	55
60	0.17117	73001	12496	335064	0.03729	923309	50.77	12.65	0.03695	60
65	0.24548	60505	14853	266118	0.05581	588245	50.77	9.72	0.05535	65
70	0.34987	45652	15972	189226	0.08441	322128	50.77	7.05	0.08338	70
75	0.64542	29680	19156	98969	0.19355	132902	50.77	4.48	0.19100	75
80	0.81541	10524	8581	27580	0.31114	33932	50.77	3.22	0.30671	80
85+	*1.00000	1943	1943	6352	0.30580	6352	50.77	3.27	0.29947	85+

TABLE 3   LIFE TABLE FOR FEMALES

Age, x	nq_x	l_x	nd_x	nL_x	nm_x	T_x	$1000r_x$	$\overset{\circ}{e}_x$	nM_x	Age, x
0	0.02125	100000	2125	98538	0.02157	7037706	0.00	70.38	0.02157	0
1	0.00709	97875	694	389532	0.00178	6939168	0.00	70.90	0.00178	1
5	0.00257	97181	250	485280	0.00052	6549637	6.31	67.40	0.00052	5
10	0.00228	96931	221	484109	0.00046	6064356	30.51	62.55	0.00046	10
15	0.00284	96710	275	482906	0.00057	5580247	65.08	57.70	0.00055	15
20	0.00433	96436	418	481175	0.00087	5097341	47.03	52.86	0.00086	20
25	0.00492	96018	472	478954	0.00099	4616166	11.20	48.08	0.00098	25
30	0.00659	95546	630	476227	0.00132	4137212	22.72	43.30	0.00132	30
35	0.00860	94916	816	472692	0.00173	3660985	36.97	38.57	0.00171	35
40	0.01439	94100	1354	467357	0.00290	3188293	34.21	33.88	0.00288	40
45	0.02192	92746	2033	459034	0.00443	2720925	16.36	29.34	0.00441	45
50	0.03543	90713	3214	446206	0.00720	2261891	22.80	24.93	0.00717	50
55	0.06022	87499	5269	425172	0.01239	1815686	35.90	20.75	0.01231	55
60	0.08862	82230	7287	394090	0.01849	1390514	42.67	16.91	0.01833	60
65	0.14444	74943	10825	348945	0.03102	996424	42.67	13.30	0.03078	65
70	0.21031	64118	13485	288568	0.04673	647479	42.67	10.10	0.04628	70
75	0.37387	50633	18930	206813	0.09153	358911	42.67	7.09	0.09064	75
80	0.57254	31703	18151	112016	0.16204	152098	42.67	4.80	0.16033	80
85+	*1.00000	13552	13552	40082	0.33810	40082	42.67	2.96	0.33220	85+

TABLE 4 POPULATION PROJECTION, USING FIXED AGE-SPECIFIC BIRTH AND DEATH RATES, IN THOUSANDS

Age at last birthday	1972			1977			1982			Age at last birthday
	Total	Males	Females	Total	Males	Females	Total	Males	Females	
0–4	274	140	134	339	173	166	415	212	203	0–4
5–9	277	141	136	272	139	133	337	172	165	5–9
10–14	296	151	145	276	140	136	272	139	133	10–14
15–19	260	133	127	295	151	144	275	140	135	15–19
20–24	218	112	106	259	132	127	294	150	144	20–24
25–29	136	70	66	217	111	106	257	131	126	25–29
30–34	135	69	66	135	70	65	215	110	105	30–34
35–39	118	60	58	134	69	65	134	69	65	35–39
40–44	109	58	51	116	59	57	131	67	64	40–44
45–49	86	47	39	106	56	50	113	57	56	45–49
50–54	77	42	35	83	45	38	103	54	49	50–54
55–59	67	36	31	72	39	33	77	41	36	55–59
60–64	52	28	24	59	31	28	65	34	31	60–64
65–69	37	19	18	44	22	22	50	25	25	65–69
70–74	22	10	12	27	13	14	34	16	18	70–74
75–79	11	4	7	13	5	8	17	7	10	75–79
80–84	4	1	3	5	1	4	6	1	5	80–84
85 +	1	0	1	1	0	1	1	0	1	85 +
All ages	2180	1121	1059	2453	1256	1197	2796	1425	1371	All ages

TABLE 5 OBSERVED AND PROJECTED VITAL RATES

Rates per thousand	Observed			Projected						Stable	
				1972		1977		1982			
	Total	Males	Females	Males	Females	Males	Females	Males	Females	Males	Females
Birth	25.99	25.71	26.29	28.20	28.50	31.54	31.53	33.40	33.06	30.21	28.97
Death	5.45	6.26	4.58	6.69	4.74	7.18	5.09	7.40	5.34	8.02	6.78
Increase	20.54	19.46	21.71	21.51	23.76	24.37	26.44	26.01	27.72		22.1855

TABLE 6 RATES STANDARDIZED ON THREE STANDARD COUNTRIES

Standardized rates per thousand	England and Wales, 1961			United States, 1960			Mexico, 1960		
	Total	Males	Females	Total	Males	Females	Total	Males	Females
Birth	25.90	26.75*	24.48	26.31	24.71*	25.27	29.00	24.96*	28.20
Death	16.49	16.48*	15.21	13.39	12.79*	11.10	6.67	7.24*	5.21
Increase	9.41	10.27*	9.26	12.92	11.92*	14.18	22.33	17.72*	23.00

TABLE 7 VITAL STATISTICS AND RATES INFERRED FROM AGE DISTRIBUTIONS (FEMALES)

Vital statistics		Thompson				Bourgeois-Pichat					Coale
		Age range	NRR	$1000r$	Interval	Age range	NRR	$1000b$	$1000d$	$1000r$	$1000b$
TFR	4.06	0–4	2.06	27.29	27.41	5–29	3.28	46.07	2.04	44.03	$1000d$
GRR	1.98	5–9	2.67	36.76	27.37	30–54	2.14	32.13	3.96	28.17	$1000r$
NRR	1.89	10–14	2.59	33.99	27.30	55–79	3.20	78.45	35.39	43.06	$1000k_1$
Generation	28.72	15–19	2.48	33.42	27.19	*50–74	2.97	65.04	24.75	40.28	$1000k_2$
Sex ratio	105.10										

TABLE 8 LESLIE MATRIX AND ITS ANALYSIS (FEMALES)

Start of age interval	Sub-diagonal	First row	Percent in stable population	Fisher values	Total reproductive values	Net maternity function	Matrix equation coefficient	Parameters		
									Integral	Matrix
0	0.99428	0.00000	13.395	1.083	147995	0.00000	0.00000	λ_1	1.1173	1.1176
5	0.99759	0.00021	11.917	1.217	176697	0.00000	0.00021	λ_2	0.4169	0.4197
10	0.99751	0.04058	10.637	1.363	173524	0.00043	0.04025		+0.3269	+0.8002 i
15	0.99642	0.27241	9.494	1.483	157960	0.08008	0.26953	r_1	0.0222	0.0222
20	0.99538	0.53176	8.464	1.368	90263	0.45898	0.52425	r_2	-0.0154	-0.0203
25	0.99431	0.50799	7.539	0.957	63176	0.58951	0.49850		+0.2208	+0.2175 i
30	0.99258	0.33026	6.707	0.523	30532	0.40750	0.32225	c_1		10473
35	0.98874	0.17494	5.956	0.228	11856	0.23700	0.16943	c_2		6524
40	0.98217	0.06141	5.269	0.067	2640	0.10195	0.05884			6000 3 i
45	0.97205	0.00841	4.631	0.008	293	0.01582	0.00791	$2\pi/y$	28.462	28.882
50	0.95286	0.00004	4.028	0.000	1	0.00000	0.00000	Δ	9.421	
55	0.79682		11.963							

TABLE 1 DATA INPUT TO COMPUTATIONS

Age at last birthday	Population Total	Males	%	Females	%	Births, by age of mother	Deaths Total	Males	Females	Age at last birthday
0	124985	63820	1.9	61165	1.6	0	3400	1984	1416	0
1–4	512307	260932	7.6	251375	6.5	0	536	297	239	1–4
5–9	601080	307368	9.0	293712	7.5	0	308	194	114	5–9
10–14	508321	258929	7.6	249392	6.4	26	195	120	75	10–14
15–19	496755	253255	7.4	243500	6.3	15646	492	374	118	15–19
20–24	495005	251494	7.3	243511	6.3	40436	502	455	147	20–24
25–29	563148	287126	8.4	276022	7.1	38323	664	491	173	25–29
30–34	395225	199783	5.8	195442	5.0	18520	539	450	189	30–34
35–39	448462	225477	6.6	222985	5.7	10531	963	645	318	35–39
40–44	475100	208317	6.1	266783	6.8	3621	1447	851	595	40–44
45–49	396195	165723	4.8	230472	5.9	262	1755	989	766	45–49
50–54	378363	161310	4.7	217053	5.6	0	2714	1571	1143	50–54
55–59	474549	205764	6.0	268785	6.9	0	5444	3297	2147	55–59
60–64	453749	199031	5.8	254718	6.5	0	8877	5517	3360	60–64
65–69	386964	161647	4.7	225317	5.8	0	12285	7230	5055	65–69
70–74	279816	103895	3.0	175921	4.5		14120	5955	7165	70–74
75–79	182859	64195	1.9	118664	3.0		14920	6498	8422	75–79
80–84	101112	34044	1.0	67068	1.7	65387 M	13669	5373	8296	80–84
85 +	48825	15551	0.5	33274	0.9	61978 F	11269	3874	7395	85 +
All ages	7322820	3427661		3895159		127365	94299	47165	47134	All ages

TABLE 2 LIFE TABLE FOR MALES

Age, x	$_nq_x$	l_x	$_nd_x$	$_nL_x$	$_nm_x$	T_x	$1000r_x$	$\overset{\circ}{e}_x$	$_nM_x$	Age, x
0	0.03035	100000	3035	97644	0.03109	6662928	0.00	66.63	0.03109	0
1	0.00454	96965	440	386575	0.00114	6565285	0.00	67.71	0.00114	1
5	0.00314	96524	303	481855	0.00063	6178710	21.91	64.01	0.00063	5
10	0.00233	96222	224	480631	0.00047	5696845	18.63	59.21	0.00046	10
15	0.00736	95997	707	478352	0.00148	5216214	1.59	54.34	0.00148	15
20	0.00901	95291	858	474328	0.00181	4737862	0.00	49.72	0.00181	20
25	0.00852	94433	805	470190	0.00171	4263533	21.16	45.15	0.00171	25
30	0.01123	93628	1051	465616	0.00226	3793343	21.93	40.52	0.00225	30
35	0.01421	92576	1315	459761	0.00286	3327727	0.00	35.95	0.00286	35
40	0.02032	91261	1854	451947	0.00410	2867966	25.60	31.43	0.00409	40
45	0.02954	89407	2641	440907	0.00599	2416019	19.26	27.02	0.00597	45
50	0.04762	86766	4132	424280	0.00974	1975112	0.00	22.76	0.00974	50
55	0.07726	82634	6384	398420	0.01602	1550832	0.00	18.77	0.01602	55
60	0.13039	76250	9942	357858	0.02778	1152411	11.03	15.11	0.02772	60
65	0.20216	66308	13405	299126	0.04481	794554	11.03	11.98	0.04473	65
70	0.28757	52903	15214	226857	0.06706	495427	11.03	9.36	0.06694	70
75	0.40331	37690	15201	149891	0.10141	268570	11.03	7.13	0.10122	75
80	0.55768	22489	12542	79316	0.15812	118680	11.03	5.28	0.15783	80
85 +	1.00000	9947	9947	39363	0.25271	39363	11.03	3.96	0.24911	85 +

TABLE 3 LIFE TABLE FOR FEMALES

Age, x	$_nq_x$	l_x	$_nd_x$	$_nL_x$	$_nm_x$	T_x	$1000r_x$	$\overset{\circ}{e}_x$	$_nM_x$	Age, x
0	0.02275	100000	2275	98262	0.02315	7341072	0.00	73.41	0.02315	0
1	0.00379	97725	371	389823	0.00095	7242810	0.00	74.11	0.00095	1
5	0.00193	97355	188	486304	0.00039	6852987	22.04	70.39	0.00039	5
10	0.00150	97167	146	485479	0.00030	6366683	18.39	65.52	0.00030	10
15	0.00242	97021	235	484547	0.00048	5881204	1.92	60.62	0.00048	15
20	0.00301	96786	292	483215	0.00060	5396657	0.00	55.75	0.00060	20
25	0.00314	96494	303	481751	0.00063	4913442	21.30	50.92	0.00063	25
30	0.00484	96192	466	479872	0.00097	4431692	20.36	46.07	0.00097	30
35	0.00711	95726	680	477051	0.00143	3951820	0.00	41.28	0.00143	35
40	0.01111	95046	1056	472769	0.00223	3474768	0.00	36.56	0.00223	40
45	0.01654	93989	1555	466340	0.00333	3001999	17.14	31.94	0.00332	45
50	0.02601	92434	2404	456573	0.00527	2535659	0.00	27.43	0.00527	50
55	0.03921	90030	3530	441981	0.00799	2079086	0.00	23.09	0.00799	55
60	0.06426	86500	5558	419672	0.01324	1637105	18.36	18.93	0.01319	60
65	0.10710	80941	8668	384685	0.02253	1217432	18.36	15.04	0.02244	65
70	0.18651	72273	13479	329579	0.04090	832748	18.36	11.52	0.04073	70
75	0.30368	58793	17855	250580	0.07125	503169	18.36	8.56	0.07097	75
80	0.47575	40939	19477	156753	0.12425	252589	18.36	6.17	0.12370	80
85 +	*1.00000	21462	21462	95836	0.22395	95836	18.36	4.47	0.22225	85 +

TABLE 4 POPULATION PROJECTION, USING FIXED AGE-SPECIFIC BIRTH AND DEATH RATES, IN THOUSANDS

Age at last birthday	1972			1977			1982			Age at last birthday
	Total	Males	Females	Total	Males	Females	Total	Males	Females	
0–4	622	318	304	634	324	310	664	340	324	0–4
5–9	634	323	311	620	317	303	632	323	309	5–9
10–14	600	307	293	633	322	311	618	316	302	10–14
15–19	507	258	249	598	305	293	631	321	310	15–19
20–24	494	251	243	504	256	248	595	303	292	20–24
25–29	492	249	243	491	249	242	500	253	247	25–29
30–34	559	284	275	489	247	242	488	247	241	30–34
35–39	391	197	194	554	281	273	484	244	240	35–39
40–44	443	222	221	387	194	193	547	276	271	40–44
45–49	466	203	263	434	216	218	379	189	190	45–49
50–54	385	159	226	454	196	258	421	208	213	50–54
55–59	361	151	210	368	150	218	433	184	249	55–59
60–64	440	185	255	336	136	200	342	135	207	60–64
65–69	399	166	233	388	154	234	297	114	183	65–69
70–74	316	123	193	326	126	200	317	117	200	70–74
75–79	203	69	134	228	81	147	235	83	152	75–79
80–84	108	34	74	120	36	84	135	43	92	80–84
85 +	58	17	41	62	17	45	69	18	51	85 +
All ages	7478	3516	3962	7626	3607	4019	7787	3714	4073	All ages

TABLE 5   OBSERVED AND PROJECTED VITAL RATES

Rates per thousand	Observed			Projected						Stable	
	Total	Males	Females	1972		1977		1982		Males	Females
				Males	Females	Males	Females	Males	Females		
Birth	17.39	19.08	15.91	18.77	15.79	18.84	16.03	19.49	16.82	19.62	18.15
Death	12.88	13.76	12.10	13.77	12.94	13.58	13.45	13.21	13.70	11.81	10.34
Increase	4.52	5.32	3.81	5.00	2.85	5.26	2.58	6.28	3.12		7.8154

TABLE 6   RATES STANDARDIZED ON THREE STANDARD COUNTRIES

Standardized rates per thousand	England and Wales, 1961			United States, 1960			Mexico, 1960		
	Total	Males	Females	Total	Males	Females	Total	Males	Females
Birth	16.77	18.01*	15.82	17.12	16.82*	16.41	20.30	16.61*	19.71
Death	12.17	12.82*	11.50	9.95	11.61*	8.43	5.24	10.11*	4.09
Increase	4.60	5.19*	4.31	7.17	5.21*	7.98	15.06	6.50*	15.62

TABLE 7   VITAL STATISTICS AND RATES INFERRED FROM AGE DISTRIBUTIONS (FEMALES)

Vital statistics		Thompson				Bourgeois-Pichat					Coale	
		Age range	NRR	1000r	Interval	Age range	NRR	1000b	1000d	1000r		
TFR	2.63	0–4	1.27	8.90	27.43	5–29	1.07	14.42	11.93	2.49	1000b	
GRR	1.28	5–9	1.20	6.81	27.40	30–54	0.82	9.02	16.32	−7.30	1000d	
NRR	1.23	10–14	1.03	1.21	27.35	55–79	1.26	26.06	17.53	8.54	1000r	
Generation	26.74	15–19	1.00	0.07	27.27	*45–69	0.73	7.23	18.91	−11.68	$1000k_1$	
Sex ratio	105.50										$1000k_2$	

TABLE 8   LESLIE MATRIX AND ITS ANALYSIS (FEMALES)

Start of age interval	Sub-diagonal	First row	Percent in stable population	Fisher values	Total reproductive values	Net maternity function	Matrix equation coefficient	Parameters		
									Integral	Matrix
0	0.99635	0.00000	8.694	1.045	326474	0.00000	0.00000	λ_1	1.0399	1.0399
5	0.99830	0.00012	8.330	1.090	320213	0.00000	0.00012	λ_2	0.3307	0.3432
10	0.99808	0.07628	7.997	1.136	283188	0.00025	0.07588		+0.7483	+0.7245 i
15	0.99725	0.27296	7.675	1.103	268640	0.15151	0.27098	r_1	0.0078	0.0078
20	0.99697	0.36158	7.361	0.864	210514	0.39046	0.35797	r_2	−0.0402	−0.0442
25	0.99610	0.27697	7.057	0.523	144321	0.32548	0.27338		+0.2309	+0.2257 i
30	0.99412	0.16829	6.760	0.255	49914	0.22128	0.16546	c_1		33793
35	0.99102	0.07206	6.462	0.090	20139	0.10963	0.07043	c_2		37839
40	0.98640	0.01744	6.158	0.019	5020	0.03123	0.01690			−6586 i
45	0.97905	0.00135	5.842	0.001	313	0.00258	0.00129	$2\pi/y$	27.208	27.841
50	0.96804	0.00000	5.500	0.000	1	0.00000	0.00000	Δ	8.084	
55	0.79968		22.165							

[419]

Belgium, 1966

TABLE 1   DATA INPUT TO COMPUTATIONS

Age at last birthday	Population					Births, by age of mother	Deaths			Age at last birthday
	Total	Males	%	Females	%		Total	Males	Females	
0	151466	77606	1.7	73860	1.5	0	3737	2116	1621	0
1–4	625207	320683	6.9	304524	6.3	0	584	338	246	1–4
5–9	771293	394631	8.4	376662	7.8	0	380	235	145	5–9
10–14	728126	371747	8.0	356379	7.3	20	279	180	99	10–14
15–19	710235	362023	7.7	348212	7.2	11036	519	363	155	15–19
20–24	606671	311026	6.7	295645	6.1	47152	579	417	162	20–24
25–29	584669	299013	6.4	285656	5.9	45394	629	425	204	25–29
30–34	628327	318754	6.8	309573	6.4	28434	738	481	257	30–34
35–39	659108	331455	7.1	327653	6.8	14581	1170	736	434	35–39
40–44	666721	332376	7.1	334345	6.9	4209	1826	1087	739	40–44
45–49	494121	244273	5.2	249848	5.1	263	2281	1433	848	45–49
50–54	553167	270902	5.8	282265	5.8	7	4121	2638	1483	50–54
55–59	578641	277449	5.9	301192	6.2	0	7064	4685	2379	55–59
60–64	547026	254584	5.4	292442	6.0	0	11032	7186	3845	60–64
65–69	459422	202403	4.3	257019	5.3	0	14415	8603	5812	65–69
70–74	338379	139394	3.0	198985	4.1		16429	8769	7660	70–74
75–79	225787	90321	1.9	135466	2.8		17914	8557	9357	75–79
80–84	129232	50169	1.1	79063	1.6	77503 M	16852	7394	9458	80–84
85 +	67879	24431	0.5	43448	0.9	73593 F	15064	5883	9181	85 +
All ages	9525477	4673240		4852237		151096	115613	61526	54087	All ages

TABLE 2   LIFE TABLE FOR MALES

Age, x	$_nq_x$	l_x	$_nd_x$	$_nL_x$	$_nm_x$	T_x	$1000r_x$	$\overset{\circ}{e}_x$	$_nM_x$	Age, x
0	0.02670	100000	2670	97943	0.02727	6773900	0.00	67.74	0.02727	0
1	0.00420	97330	409	388126	0.00105	6675957	0.00	68.59	0.00105	1
5	0.00297	96920	288	483882	0.00059	6287831	6.18	64.88	0.00060	5
10	0.00242	96633	234	482619	0.00048	5803949	8.00	60.06	0.00048	10
15	0.00502	96399	484	480859	0.00101	5321330	16.87	55.20	0.00100	15
20	0.00669	95915	642	478010	0.00134	4840461	17.83	50.47	0.00134	20
25	0.00708	95273	675	474694	0.00142	4362451	0.00	45.79	0.00142	25
30	0.00752	94599	711	471291	0.00151	3887757	0.00	41.10	0.00151	30
35	0.01105	93887	1037	467012	0.00222	3416666	0.00	36.39	0.00222	35
40	0.01633	92850	1516	460798	0.00329	2949454	25.94	31.77	0.00327	40
45	0.02904	91334	2652	450604	0.00589	2488656	14.40	27.25	0.00587	45
50	0.04763	88682	4224	433728	0.00974	2038052	0.00	22.98	0.00974	50
55	0.08125	84458	6862	406398	0.01689	1604323	0.00	19.00	0.01689	55
60	0.13247	77596	10279	363558	0.02827	1197925	9.19	15.44	0.02823	60
65	0.19290	67317	12986	305064	0.04257	834367	9.19	12.39	0.04250	65
70	0.27259	54331	14810	235077	0.06300	529303	9.19	9.74	0.06291	70
75	0.38272	39521	15126	159411	0.09489	294226	9.19	7.44	0.09474	75
80	0.53198	24396	12978	87922	0.14761	134816	9.19	5.53	0.14738	80
85 +	1.00000	11418	11418	46893	0.24348	46893	9.19	4.11	0.24080	85 +

TABLE 3   LIFE TABLE FOR FEMALES

Age, x	$_nq_x$	l_x	$_nd_x$	$_nL_x$	$_nm_x$	T_x	$1000r_x$	$\overset{\circ}{e}_x$	$_nM_x$	Age, x
0	0.02158	100000	2158	98327	0.02195	7379480	0.00	73.79	0.02195	0
1	0.00322	97842	315	390448	0.00081	7281153	0.00	74.42	0.00081	1
5	0.00192	97527	187	487165	0.00038	6890704	5.50	70.65	0.00038	5
10	0.00139	97339	135	486365	0.00028	6403540	7.51	65.79	0.00028	10
15	0.00224	97204	218	485503	0.00045	5917175	18.26	60.87	0.00045	15
20	0.00274	96986	266	484292	0.00055	5431672	19.24	56.00	0.00055	20
25	0.00356	96720	345	482767	0.00071	4947379	0.00	51.15	0.00071	25
30	0.00414	96376	399	480940	0.00083	4464612	0.00	46.33	0.00083	30
35	0.00660	95976	634	478433	0.00132	3983672	0.00	41.51	0.00132	35
40	0.01105	95343	1053	474279	0.00222	3505239	24.85	36.76	0.00221	40
45	0.01688	94289	1592	467749	0.00340	3030960	13.41	32.15	0.00339	45
50	0.02595	92698	2406	457872	0.00525	2563212	0.00	27.65	0.00525	50
55	0.03878	90292	3502	443362	0.00790	2105340	0.00	23.32	0.00790	55
60	0.06406	86790	5560	421145	0.01320	1661977	17.23	19.15	0.01315	60
65	0.10780	81230	8757	385773	0.02270	1240833	17.23	15.28	0.02261	65
70	0.17711	72473	12836	332138	0.03865	855060	17.23	11.80	0.03850	70
75	0.29682	59637	17701	255313	0.06933	522921	17.23	8.77	0.06907	75
80	0.46411	41936	19463	162016	0.12013	267609	17.23	6.38	0.11963	80
85 +	*1.00000	22473	22473	105593	0.21283	105593	17.23	4.70	0.21131	85 +

TABLE 4 POPULATION PROJECTION, USING FIXED AGE-SPECIFIC BIRTH AND DEATH RATES, IN THOUSANDS

Age at last birthday	1971 Total	1971 Males	1971 Females	1976 Total	1976 Males	1976 Females	1981 Total	1981 Males	1981 Females	Age at last birthday
0–4	753	385	368	792	405	387	837	428	409	0–4
5–9	773	396	377	749	383	366	789	403	386	5–9
10–14	770	394	376	772	395	377	748	382	366	10–14
15–19	726	370	356	767	392	375	770	394	376	15–19
20–24	707	360	347	723	368	355	764	390	374	20–24
25–29	604	309	295	703	357	346	720	366	354	25–29
30–34	582	297	285	601	307	294	700	355	345	30–34
35–39	624	316	308	577	294	283	596	304	292	35–39
40–44	652	327	325	617	312	305	571	290	281	40–44
45–49	655	325	330	640	320	320	606	305	301	45–49
50–54	480	235	245	636	313	323	622	308	314	50–54
55–59	527	254	273	457	220	237	606	293	313	55–59
60–64	534	248	286	487	227	260	422	197	225	60–64
65–69	482	214	268	470	208	262	429	191	238	65–69
70–74	377	156	221	396	165	231	386	160	225	70–74
75–79	248	95	153	276	106	170	289	112	177	75–79
80–84	136	50	86	149	52	97	166	58	108	80–84
85 +	79	27	52	83	27	56	91	28	63	85 +
All ages	9709	4758	4951	9895	4851	5044	10112	4964	5148	All ages

TABLE 5 OBSERVED AND PROJECTED VITAL RATES

Rates per thousand	Observed Total	Observed Males	Observed Females	Projected 1971 Males	Projected 1971 Females	Projected 1976 Males	Projected 1976 Females	Projected 1981 Males	Projected 1981 Females	Stable Males	Stable Females
Birth	15.86	16.58	15.17	17.02	15.53	17.69	16.15	18.23	16.69	18.15	16.90
Death	12.14	13.17	11.15	13.33	11.84	13.36	12.32	13.30	12.61	12.25	11.00
Increase	3.73	3.42	4.02	3.68	3.69	4.33	3.84	4.93	4.09		5.9022

TABLE 6 RATES STANDARDIZED ON THREE STANDARD COUNTRIES

Standardized rates per thousand	England and Wales, 1961 Total	Males	Females	United States, 1960 Total	Males	Females	Mexico, 1960 Total	Males	Females
Birth	15.84	16.52*	14.95	16.09	15.57*	15.45	18.90	14.50*	18.37
Death	11.66	12.14*	11.16	9.49	10.99*	8.17	4.93	9.64*	3.94
Increase	4.17	4.39*	3.79	6.60	4.57*	7.28	13.98	4.85*	14.42

TABLE 7 VITAL STATISTICS AND RATES INFERRED FROM AGE DISTRIBUTIONS (FEMALES)

Vital statistics		Thompson Age range	NRR	1000r	Interval	Bourgeois-Pichat Age range	NRR	1000b	1000d	1000r	Coale
TFR	2.50	0–4	1.18	5.93	27.44	5–29	1.47	18.05	3.70	14.35	1000b
GRR	1.22	5–9	1.23	7.60	27.40	30–54	1.20	17.37	10.67	6.70	1000d
NRR	1.18	10–14	1.16	5.52	27.35	55–79	1.25	23.39	15.02	8.37	1000r
Generation	27.37	15–19	1.11	3.90	27.27	*20–44	0.79	10.04	18.72	-8.68	$1000k_1$
Sex ratio	105.31										$1000k_2$

TABLE 8 LESLIE MATRIX AND ITS ANALYSIS (FEMALES)

Start of age interval	Sub-diagonal	First row	Percent in stable population	Fisher values	Total reproductive values	Net maternity function	Matrix equation coefficient	Parameters	Integral	Matrix
0	0.99671	0.00000	8.140	1.038	392818	0.00000	0.00000	λ_1	1.0300	1.0300
5	0.99836	0.00007	7.877	1.073	404082	0.00000	0.00007	λ_2	0.3497	0.3568
10	0.99823	0.03772	7.636	1.107	394405	0.00013	0.03754		+0.7843	+0.7565 i
15	0.99751	0.22709	7.400	1.103	383958	0.07495	0.22557	r_1	0.0059	0.0059
20	0.99685	0.37840	7.167	0.902	266730	0.37620	0.37493	r_2	-0.0305	-0.0357
25	0.99621	0.29807	6.937	0.538	153711	0.37366	0.29441		+0.2303	+0.2260 i
30	0.99479	0.16202	6.709	0.246	76066	0.21515	0.15943	c_1		45752
35	0.99132	0.06782	6.480	0.085	27954	0.10370	0.06639	c_2		17928
40	0.98623	0.01622	6.237	0.018	5888	0.02908	0.01574			40880 i
45	0.97888	0.00128	5.972	0.001	330	0.00240	0.00123	$2\pi/y$	27.287	27.798
50	0.96831	0.00003	5.676	0.000	9	0.00006	0.00003	Δ	4.466	
55	0.79875		23.769							

Bulgaria, 1966-68

TABLE 1 DATA INPUT TO COMPUTATIONS

Age at last birthday	Population Total	Males	%	Females	%	Births, by age of mother	Deaths Total	Males	Females	Age at last birthday
0	120694	62027	1.5	58667	1.4	0	4032	2275	1757	0
1–4	499770	256336	6.2	243434	5.9	0	718	385	333	1–4
5–9	648284	332059	8.0	316225	7.6	0	364	232	132	5–9
10–14	679827	347220	8.4	332607	8.0	161	303	190	113	10–14
15–19	696956	354215	8.5	342741	8.2	23715	508	332	176	15–19
20–24	619447	313342	7.5	306105	7.4	56102	601	417	184	20–24
25–29	561463	281844	6.8	279619	6.7	30095	607	411	196	25–29
30–34	637301	320476	7.7	316825	7.6	13354	831	542	289	30–34
35–39	642355	324039	7.8	318316	7.7	4837	1152	722	430	35–39
40–44	662693	332104	8.0	330589	8.0	1274	1673	1012	661	40–44
45–49	492188	245704	5.9	246484	5.9	138	1867	1151	716	45–49
50–54	429351	215906	5.2	213445	5.1	16	2637	1636	1001	50–54
55–59	475111	237405	5.7	237706	5.7	0	4606	2818	1788	55–59
60–64	408620	201140	4.8	207480	5.0	0	6787	4097	2690	60–64
65–69	298680	142589	3.4	156091	3.8	0	8606	4854	3742	65–69
70–74	197876	89151	2.1	108725	2.6		9468	4807	4661	70–74
75–79	125635	51886	1.2	73749	1.8		9776	4373	5403	75–79
80–84	75616	32094	0.8	43522	1.0	66747 M	9720	4347	5373	80–84
85 +	38359	16028	0.4	22331	0.5	62945 F	7437	3288	4199	85 +
All ages	8310226	4155565		4154661		129692	71743	37899	33844	All ages

TABLE 2 LIFE TABLE FOR MALES

Age, x	$_nq_x$	l_x	$_nd_x$	$_nL_x$	$_nm_x$	T_x	$1000r_x$	$\overset{\circ}{e}_x$	$_nM_x$	Age, x
0	0.03568	100000	3568	97272	0.03668	6885880	0.00	68.86	0.03668	0
1	0.00598	96432	577	384051	0.00150	6788609	0.00	70.40	0.00150	1
5	0.00349	95855	334	478442	0.00070	6404557	0.00	66.81	0.00070	5
10	0.00273	95521	261	476977	0.00055	5926116	0.00	62.04	0.00055	10
15	0.00468	95260	445	475252	0.00094	5449139	9.33	57.20	0.00094	15
20	0.00664	94814	630	472545	0.00133	4973876	21.58	52.46	0.00133	20
25	0.00727	94184	684	469242	0.00146	4501332	0.00	47.79	0.00146	25
30	0.00842	93500	787	465602	0.00169	4032089	0.00	43.12	0.00169	30
35	0.01108	92712	1027	461119	0.00223	3566687	0.00	38.47	0.00223	35
40	0.01519	91685	1393	455168	0.00306	3105368	24.47	33.87	0.00305	40
45	0.02334	90292	2108	446585	0.00472	2650201	38.14	29.35	0.00468	45
50	0.03723	88184	3283	433296	0.00758	2203616	0.00	24.99	0.00758	50
55	0.05777	84901	4905	413191	0.01187	1770320	0.00	20.85	0.01187	55
60	0.09787	79996	7829	381773	0.02051	1357129	31.12	16.96	0.02037	60
65	0.15865	72167	11449	333612	0.03432	975356	31.12	13.52	0.03411	65
70	0.23951	60718	14543	268215	0.05422	641744	31.12	10.57	0.05392	70
75	0.34990	46175	16157	190628	0.08476	373530	31.12	8.09	0.08428	75
80	0.50734	30019	15230	111734	0.13630	182902	31.12	6.09	0.13545	80
85 +	*1.00000	14789	14789	71158	0.20780	71168	31.12	4.81	0.20514	85 +

TABLE 3 LIFE TABLE FOR FEMALES

Age, x	$_nq_x$	l_x	$_nd_x$	$_nL_x$	$_nm_x$	T_x	$1000r_x$	$\overset{\circ}{e}_x$	$_nM_x$	Age, x
0	0.02929	100000	2929	97795	0.02995	7292750	0.00	72.93	0.02995	0
1	0.00545	97071	529	386750	0.00137	7194955	0.00	74.12	0.00137	1
5	0.00208	96542	201	482207	0.00042	6808204	0.00	70.52	0.00042	5
10	0.00170	96341	164	481305	0.00034	6325997	0.00	65.66	0.00034	10
15	0.00257	96177	247	480295	0.00051	5844692	7.81	60.77	0.00051	15
20	0.00300	95930	288	478950	0.00060	5364397	19.75	55.92	0.00060	20
25	0.00350	95642	335	477405	0.00070	4885447	0.00	51.08	0.00070	25
30	0.00455	95308	434	475517	0.00091	4408042	0.00	46.25	0.00091	30
35	0.00673	94874	639	472878	0.00135	3932526	0.00	41.45	0.00135	35
40	0.00999	94235	941	468971	0.00201	3459648	23.53	36.71	0.00200	40
45	0.01454	93294	1356	463326	0.00293	2990676	40.67	32.06	0.00290	45
50	0.02320	91937	2133	454764	0.00469	2527351	0.00	27.49	0.00469	50
55	0.03697	89805	3320	441420	0.00752	2072586	0.00	23.08	0.00752	55
60	0.06338	86484	5481	419955	0.01305	1631166	26.31	18.86	0.01297	60
65	0.11428	81003	9257	383654	0.02413	1211211	26.31	14.95	0.02397	65
70	0.19560	71746	14034	325470	0.04312	827557	26.31	11.53	0.04287	70
75	0.31205	57713	18009	244508	0.07365	502087	26.31	8.70	0.07326	75
80	0.47059	39703	18684	150640	0.12403	257579	26.31	6.49	0.12345	80
85 +	1.00000	21019	21019	106939	0.19655	106939	26.31	5.09	0.18803	85 +

TABLE 4 POPULATION PROJECTION, USING FIXED AGE-SPECIFIC BIRTH AND DEATH RATES, IN THOUSANDS

Age at last birthday	1972 Total	Males	Females	1977 Total	Males	Females	1982 Total	Males	Females	Age at last birthday
0–4	643	330	313	662	340	322	657	337	320	0–4
5–9	617	316	301	640	328	312	659	338	321	5–9
10–14	647	331	316	615	315	300	638	327	311	10–14
15–19	678	346	332	645	330	315	613	314	299	15–19
20–24	694	352	342	675	344	331	642	328	314	20–24
25–29	616	311	305	691	350	341	572	342	330	25–29
30–34	559	280	279	613	309	304	686	347	339	30–34
35–39	632	317	315	554	277	277	608	306	302	35–39
40–44	636	320	316	525	313	312	548	273	275	40–44
45–49	653	326	327	626	314	312	616	307	309	45–49
50–54	480	238	242	637	316	321	610	304	306	50–54
55–59	413	206	207	462	227	235	612	301	311	55–59
60–64	445	219	226	387	190	197	433	210	223	60–64
65–69	366	176	190	399	192	207	346	166	180	65–69
70–74	247	115	132	302	141	161	329	154	175	70–74
75–79	145	63	82	180	81	99	221	100	121	75–79
80–84	75	30	45	87	37	50	109	48	61	80–84
85 +	51	20	31	51	19	32	60	24	36	85 +
All ages	8597	4296	4301	8851	4423	4428	9059	4526	4533	All ages

TABLE 5 OBSERVED AND PROJECTED VITAL RATES

Rates per thousand	Observed Total	Males	Females	Projected 1972 Males	Females	1977 Males	Females	1982 Males	Females	Stable Males	Females
Birth	15.61	15.06	15.15	16.35	15.41	16.02	15.09	15.25	14.36	14.09	13.28
Death	8.63	9.12	8.15	9.92	8.95	10.64	9.59	11.47	10.33	14.90	14.09
Increase	6.97	5.94	7.00	6.43	6.46	5.38	5.50	3.77	4.03		-0.8105

TABLE 6 RATES STANDARDIZED ON THREE STANDARD COUNTRIES

Standardized rates per thousand	England and Wales, 1961 Total	Males	Females	United States, 1960 Total	Males	Females	Mexico, 1960 Total	Males	Females
Birth	13.39	14.53*	12.60	13.64	13.67*	13.04	17.51	12.76*	16.95
Death	10.98	10.52*	11.44	8.98	9.24*	8.46	4.95	7.72*	4.32
Increase	2.41	4.01*	1.16	4.66	4.42*	4.58	12.56	5.04*	12.53

TABLE 7 VITAL STATISTICS AND RATES INFERRED FROM AGE DISTRIBUTIONS (FEMALES)

Vital statistics		Thompson Age range	NRR	$1000r$	Interval	Bourgeois-Pichat Age range	NRR	$1000b$	$1000d$	$1000r$	Coale	
TFR	2.11	0–4	0.94	-2.27	27.44	5–29	1.18	17.55	11.47	6.08	$1000b$	
GRR	1.03	5–9	1.03	1.25	27.41	30–54	1.66	32.10	13.38	18.72	$1000d$	
NRR	0.98	10–14	1.14	4.77	27.36	55–79	2.41	86.98	54.44	32.53	$1000r$	
Generation	24.69	15–19	1.19	6.28	27.29	*20–44	0.83	12.63	19.34	-6.70	$1000k_1$	
Sex ratio	106.04										$1000k_2$	

TABLE 8 LESLIE MATRIX AND ITS ANALYSIS (FEMALES)

Start of age interval	Sub-diagonal	First row	Percent in stable population	Fisher values	Total reproductive values	Net maternity function	Matrix equation coefficient	Parameters	Integral	Matrix
0	0.99517	0.00000	6.450	1.030	311107	0.00000	0.00000	λ_1	0.9960	0.9960
5	0.99813	0.00057	6.445	1.031	325907	0.00000	0.00057	λ_2	0.2205	0.2347
10	0.99790	0.08176	6.459	1.028	341850	0.00113	0.08121		+0.7970	+0.7586i
15	0.99720	0.29626	6.471	0.941	322661	0.16129	0.29366	r_1	-0.0008	-0.0008
20	0.99677	0.34165	6.479	0.634	194158	0.42604	0.33771	r_2	-0.0380	-0.0461
25	0.99604	0.17592	6.485	0.281	78514	0.24938	0.17333		+0.2602	+0.2541i
30	0.99445	0.06733	6.485	0.099	31329	0.09728	0.06608	c_1		49270
35	0.99174	0.02236	6.475	0.029	9329	0.03488	0.02182	c_2		-30691
40	0.98796	0.00518	6.448	0.006	2054	0.00877	0.00502			11947i
45	0.98152	0.00074	6.396	0.001	212	0.00125	0.00071	$2\pi/y$	24.149	24.723
50	0.97066	0.00009	6.304	0.000	20	0.00017	0.00008	Δ	10.283	
55	0.78571		29.103							

Czechoslovakia, 1967

TABLE 1 DATA INPUT TO COMPUTATIONS

Age at last birthday	Total	Males	%	Females	%	Births, by age of mother	Total	Males	Females	Age at last birthday
0	214927	110144	1.6	104783	1.4	0	4937	2838	2099	0
1–4	904889	463546	6.6	441343	6.0	0	935	544	391	1–4
5–9	1090830	558213	8.0	532617	7.3	0	458	284	174	5–9
10–14	1274525	651177	9.3	623348	8.5	53	478	299	179	10–14
15–19	1300843	663424	9.5	637419	8.7	28549	1028	738	290	15–19
20–24	1136570	575379	8.2	561191	7.7	99430	1266	951	315	20–24
25–29	914274	461825	6.6	452449	6.2	51908	1061	809	252	25–29
30–34	854409	427918	6.1	426491	5.8	22822	1196	854	342	30–34
35–39	955612	473593	6.8	482019	6.6	10412	1831	1203	628	35–39
40–44	993568	483307	6.9	510261	7.0	2637	2874	1891	983	40–44
45–49	774703	374410	5.4	400293	5.5	169	3380	2122	1258	45–49
50–54	723941	348701	5.0	375240	5.1	5	5245	3383	1862	50–54
55–59	899765	431973	6.2	467792	6.4	0	10443	6708	3735	55–59
60–64	777836	361344	5.2	416492	5.7	0	15539	10038	5501	60–64
65–69	625143	271695	3.9	353448	4.8	0	20242	11954	8288	65–69
70–74	421694	165378	2.4	256316	3.5		21699	10883	10815	70–74
75–79	249990	92474	1.3	157516	2.2		20500	9170	11330	75–79
80–84	130228	46176	0.7	84052	1.1	111149 M	17543	7082	10461	80–84
85+	61374	20696	0.3	40678	0.6	104836 F	13770	5090	8680	85+
All ages	14305121	6981373		7323748		215985	144425	76841	67584	All ages

TABLE 2 LIFE TABLE FOR MALES

Age, x	$_nq_x$	l_x	$_nd_x$	$_nL_x$	$_nm_x$	T_x	$1000r_x$	$\overset{\circ}{e}_x$	$_nM_x$	Age, x
0	0.02528	100000	2528	98097	0.02577	6738194	0.00	67.38	0.02577	0
1	0.00468	97472	456	388557	0.00117	6640097	0.00	68.12	0.00117	1
5	0.00254	97016	246	484466	0.00051	6251530	0.00	64.44	0.00051	5
10	0.00229	96770	222	483355	0.00046	5767065	0.00	59.60	0.00046	10
15	0.00556	96548	537	481516	0.00112	5283709	11.29	54.73	0.00111	15
20	0.00825	96011	792	478135	0.00166	4802193	34.66	50.02	0.00165	20
25	0.00873	95218	831	474044	0.00175	4324058	27.82	45.41	0.00175	25
30	0.00993	94387	937	469665	0.00200	3850014	0.00	40.79	0.00200	30
35	0.01263	93450	1180	464478	0.00254	3380349	0.00	36.17	0.00254	35
40	0.01945	92270	1794	457148	0.00393	2915871	19.55	31.60	0.00391	40
45	0.02813	90475	2545	446511	0.00570	2458722	26.52	27.18	0.00567	45
50	0.04744	87931	4172	430003	0.00970	2012211	0.00	22.88	0.00970	50
55	0.07496	83759	6279	404344	0.01553	1582208	0.00	18.89	0.01553	55
60	0.13105	77480	10153	363509	0.02793	1177864	26.67	15.20	0.02778	60
65	0.19964	67327	13441	304104	0.04420	814355	26.67	12.10	0.04400	65
70	0.28401	53886	15304	231564	0.06609	510251	26.67	9.47	0.06581	70
75	0.39763	38582	15341	154019	0.09961	278687	26.67	7.22	0.09915	75
80	0.54775	23240	12730	82631	0.15406	124668	26.67	5.36	0.15337	80
85+	1.00000	10511	10511	42037	0.25003	42037	26.67	4.00	0.24594	85+

TABLE 3 LIFE TABLE FOR FEMALES

Age, x	$_nq_x$	l_x	$_nd_x$	$_nL_x$	$_nm_x$	T_x	$1000r_x$	$\overset{\circ}{e}_x$	$_nM_x$	Age, x
0	0.01973	100000	1973	98508	0.02003	7377369	0.00	73.77	0.02003	0
1	0.00353	98027	346	391101	0.00089	7278860	0.00	74.25	0.00089	1
5	0.00163	97680	159	488002	0.00033	6887759	0.00	70.51	0.00033	5
10	0.00143	97521	140	487267	0.00029	6399757	0.00	65.62	0.00029	10
15	0.00228	97381	222	486378	0.00046	5912490	10.06	60.72	0.00045	15
20	0.00281	97159	273	485125	0.00056	5426112	33.74	55.85	0.00056	20
25	0.00279	96887	270	483782	0.00056	4940987	26.84	51.00	0.00056	25
30	0.00400	96617	387	482190	0.00080	4457205	0.00	46.13	0.00080	30
35	0.00649	96230	625	479698	0.00130	3975015	0.00	41.31	0.00130	35
40	0.00962	95605	920	475904	0.00193	3495317	16.54	36.56	0.00193	40
45	0.01569	94685	1485	469997	0.00316	3019413	27.49	31.89	0.00314	45
50	0.02453	93200	2286	460717	0.00496	2549416	0.00	27.35	0.00496	50
55	0.03920	90914	3564	446357	0.00798	2088699	0.00	22.97	0.00798	55
60	0.06455	87350	5638	423818	0.01330	1642342	30.60	18.80	0.01321	60
65	0.11201	81711	9152	387420	0.02362	1218524	30.60	14.91	0.02345	65
70	0.19300	72559	14004	329634	0.04248	831104	30.60	11.45	0.04220	70
75	0.30767	58555	18016	248864	0.07239	501470	30.60	8.56	0.07193	75
80	0.47876	40540	19409	154825	0.12536	252606	30.60	6.23	0.12445	80
85+	*1.00000	21131	21131	97781	0.21610	97781	30.60	4.63	0.21338	85+

TABLE 4 POPULATION PROJECTION, USING FIXED AGE-SPECIFIC BIRTH AND DEATH RATES, IN THOUSANDS

Age at last birthday	1972 Total	Males	Females	1977 Total	Males	Females	1982 Total	Males	Females	Age at last birthday
0–4	1115	572	543	1194	613	581	1185	608	577	0–4
5–9	1115	571	544	1110	569	541	1189	610	579	5–9
10–14	1089	557	532	1114	570	544	1108	568	540	10–14
15–19	1271	649	622	1086	555	531	1111	568	543	15–19
20–24	1295	659	636	1265	644	621	1080	551	529	20–24
25–29	1130	570	560	1287	653	634	1258	639	519	25–29
30–34	909	458	451	1123	565	558	1279	647	632	30–34
35–39	847	423	424	902	453	449	1114	559	555	35–39
40–44	944	466	478	838	417	421	890	445	445	40–44
45–49	976	472	504	927	455	472	823	407	415	45–49
50–54	753	361	392	949	455	494	901	438	463	50–54
55–59	692	328	364	719	339	380	906	427	479	55–59
60–64	832	388	444	640	295	345	666	305	361	60–64
65–69	683	302	381	731	325	406	563	247	316	65–69
70–74	508	207	301	554	230	324	592	247	345	70–74
75–79	304	110	194	365	138	227	398	153	245	75–79
80–84	148	50	98	179	59	120	215	74	141	80–84
85 +	76	23	53	87	25	62	106	30	76	85 +
All ages	14687	7166	7521	15070	7360	7710	15384	7523	7861	All ages

TABLE 5 OBSERVED AND PROJECTED VITAL RATES

Rates per thousand	Observed Total	Males	Females	Projected 1972 Males	Females	1977 Males	Females	1982 Males	Females	Stable Males	Females
Birth	15.10	15.92	14.31	17.29	15.54	17.37	15.64	16.24	14.66	14.44	13.15
Death	10.10	11.01	9.23	11.69	10.23	12.19	11.03	12.49	11.64	15.19	13.91
Increase	5.00	4.91	5.09	5.59	5.31	5.19	4.61	3.75	3.02		-0.7473

TABLE 6 RATES STANDARDIZED ON THREE STANDARD COUNTRIES

Standardized rates per thousand	England and Wales, 1961 Total	Males	Females	United States, 1960 Total	Males	Females	Mexico, 1960 Total	Males	Females
Birth	13.19	15.48*	12.41	13.40	14.24*	12.81	16.77	13.94*	16.23
Death	11.95	12.55*	11.44	9.70	11.04*	8.32	4.99	9.38*	3.94
Increase	1.25	2.93*	0.97	3.70	3.20*	4.49	11.78	4.55*	12.30

TABLE 7 VITAL STATISTICS AND RATES INFERRED FROM AGE DISTRIBUTIONS (FEMALES)

Vital statistics		Thompson Age range	NRR	1000r	Interval	Bourgeois-Pichat Age range	NRR	1000b	1000d	1000r	Coale
TFR	2.09	0–4	1.05	1.82	27.44	5–29	1.25	18.06	9.87	8.19	1000b
GRR	1.01	5–9	1.11	3.76	27.41	30–54	1.20	16.64	10.04	6.61	1000d
NRR	0.98	10–14	1.38	11.62	27.36	55–79	1.69	44.53	25.14	19.40	1000r
Generation	25.66	15–19	1.39	11.50	27.29	*10–34	1.79	24.35	2.84	21.51	1000k_1
Sex ratio	106.02										1000k_2

TABLE 8 LESLIE MATRIX AND ITS ANALYSIS (FEMALES)

Start of age interval	Sub-diagonal	First row	Percent in stable population	Fisher values	Total reproductive values	Net maternity function	Matrix equation coefficient	Parameters	Integral	Matrix
0	0.99672	0.00000	6.458	1.019	556676	0.00000	0.00000	λ_1	0.9963	0.9963
5	0.99849	0.00010	6.461	1.019	542665	0.00000	0.00010	λ_2 0.2606		0.2732
10	0.99818	0.05322	6.475	1.016	633627	0.00020	0.05297		+0.7852	+0.7501 i
15	0.99742	0.26321	6.487	0.960	612049	0.10574	0.26147	r_1 -0.0007		-0.0007
20	0.99723	0.34648	6.495	0.690	387282	0.41720	0.34330	r_2 -0.0379		-0.0451
25	0.99671	0.19970	6.501	0.335	151702	0.25940	0.19732		+0.2501	+0.24437
30	0.99483	0.08912	6.504	0.131	55834	0.12524	0.08777	c_1		87666
35	0.99209	0.03176	6.495	0.040	19181	0.05029	0.03112	c_2		-79791
40	0.98759	0.00664	6.467	0.007	3741	0.01194	0.00645			39142 i
45	0.98025	0.00052	6.411	0.001	217	0.00096	0.00050	$2\pi/y$	25.126	25.718
50	0.96883	0.00002	6.308	0.000	6	0.00003	0.00001	Δ	8.072	
55	0.78509		28.939							

Denmark, 1967

TABLE 1 DATA INPUT TO COMPUTATIONS

Age at last birthday	Population					Births, by age of mother	Deaths			Age at last birthday
	Total	Males	%	Females	%		Total	Males	Females	
0	85672	44030	1.8	41642	1.7	0	1287	794	493	0
1–4	328104	168174	7.0	159930	6.6	0	231	129	102	1–4
5–9	368785	188420	7.9	180365	7.4	0	166	95	71	5–9
10–14	371062	190154	7.9	180908	7.4	0	131	83	48	10–14
15–19	386434	197698	8.2	188736	7.7	9290	238	166	72	15–19
20–24	418746	214833	9.0	203913	8.4	32879	289	218	71	20–24
25–29	318006	161650	6.7	156356	6.4	22788	229	159	70	25–29
30–34	284363	142427	5.9	141936	5.8	10839	271	168	103	30–34
35–39	280727	139511	5.8	141216	5.8	4484	428	229	199	35–39
40–44	297736	146947	6.1	150789	6.2	1052	753	391	362	40–44
45–49	306154	151222	6.3	154932	6.4	78	1196	652	544	45–49
50–54	291378	143266	6.0	148112	6.1	0	1872	1147	725	50–54
55–59	288183	140727	5.9	147456	6.0	0	2997	1893	1104	55–59
60–64	248759	118289	4.9	130470	5.3	0	4223	2634	1589	60–64
65–69	207575	95224	4.0	112351	4.6	0	5591	3348	2243	65–69
70–74	159458	70939	3.0	88519	3.6		6978	3838	3140	70–74
75–79	106604	46538	1.9	60066	2.5		7447	3785	3662	75–79
80–84	60349	25936	1.1	34413	1.4	41791 M	7021	3313	3708	80–84
85 +	30677	12918	0.5	17759	0.7	39619 F	6488	2899	3589	85 +
All ages	4838772	2398903		2439869		81410	47836	25941	21895	All ages

TABLE 2 LIFE TABLE FOR MALES

Age, x	$_nq_x$	l_x	$_nd_x$	$_nL_x$	$_nm_x$	T_x	$1000r_x$	$\overset{\circ}{e}_x$	$_nM_x$	Age, x
0	0.01773	100000	1773	98652	0.01798	7066025	3.96	70.66	0.01803	0
1	0.00305	98227	299	392037	0.00076	6967373	3.96	70.93	0.00077	1
5	0.00251	97927	246	489021	0.00050	6575336	10.40	67.15	0.00050	5
10	0.00218	97681	213	487907	0.00044	6086315	0.00	62.31	0.00044	10
15	0.00419	97468	408	486378	0.00084	5598408	0.00	57.44	0.00084	15
20	0.00506	97060	492	484084	0.00102	5112031	19.16	52.67	0.00101	20
25	0.00491	96568	474	481671	0.00098	4627947	40.07	47.92	0.00098	25
30	0.00589	96094	566	479118	0.00118	4146277	13.51	43.15	0.00118	30
35	0.00818	95528	781	475829	0.00164	3667159	0.00	38.39	0.00164	35
40	0.01322	94747	1253	470855	0.00266	3191330	0.00	33.68	0.00266	40
45	0.02135	93494	1996	462967	0.00431	2720475	0.00	29.10	0.00431	45
50	0.03931	91498	3597	449276	0.00801	2257508	0.00	24.67	0.00801	50
55	0.06530	87901	5740	426223	0.01347	1808232	5.08	20.57	0.01345	55
60	0.10615	82161	8722	390294	0.02235	1382009	18.15	16.82	0.02227	60
65	0.16263	73439	11943	338591	0.03527	991715	18.15	13.50	0.03516	65
70	0.23955	61496	14731	271466	0.05427	653124	18.15	10.62	0.05410	70
75	0.33889	46765	15848	194262	0.08158	381657	18.15	8.16	0.08133	75
80	0.48560	30917	15013	117061	0.12825	187395	18.15	6.06	0.12774	80
85 +	*1.00000	15903	15903	70334	0.22611	70334	18.15	4.42	0.22442	85 +

TABLE 3 LIFE TABLE FOR FEMALES

Age, x	$_nq_x$	l_x	$_nd_x$	$_nL_x$	$_nm_x$	T_x	$1000r_x$	$\overset{\circ}{e}_x$	$_nM_x$	Age, x
0	0.01170	100000	1170	99141	0.01181	7541451	3.57	75.41	0.01184	0
1	0.00254	98830	251	394595	0.00064	7442310	3.57	75.30	0.00064	1
5	0.00196	98579	193	492410	0.00039	7047716	10.38	71.49	0.00039	5
10	0.00133	98385	130	491599	0.00027	6555305	0.00	66.63	0.00027	10
15	0.00191	98255	187	490815	0.00038	6063706	0.00	61.71	0.00038	15
20	0.00174	98068	171	489918	0.00035	5572892	18.45	56.83	0.00035	20
25	0.00225	97897	220	488972	0.00045	5082974	35.76	51.92	0.00045	25
30	0.00363	97677	355	487593	0.00073	4594001	9.38	47.03	0.00073	30
35	0.00702	97322	684	485067	0.00141	4106409	0.00	42.19	0.00141	35
40	0.01194	96638	1154	480512	0.00240	3621342	0.00	37.47	0.00240	40
45	0.01741	95485	1663	473500	0.00351	3140830	0.00	32.89	0.00351	45
50	0.02420	93822	2270	463792	0.00489	2667330	0.00	28.43	0.00489	50
55	0.03683	91552	3372	449951	0.00749	2203538	4.82	24.07	0.00749	55
60	0.05955	88180	5251	428728	0.01225	1753588	26.92	19.89	0.01218	60
65	0.09598	82929	7959	396224	0.02009	1324860	26.92	15.98	0.01996	65
70	0.16462	74970	12341	345823	0.03569	928636	26.92	12.39	0.03547	70
75	0.26718	62628	16733	272855	0.06133	582813	26.92	9.31	0.06097	75
80	0.43045	45896	19756	182048	0.10852	309958	26.92	6.75	0.10775	80
85 +	*1.00000	26140	26140	127910	0.20436	127910	26.92	4.89	0.20209	85 +

TABLE 4 POPULATION PROJECTION, USING FIXED AGE-SPECIFIC BIRTH AND DEATH RATES, IN THOUSANDS

Age at last birthday	1972 Total	Males	Females	1977 Total	Males	Females	1982 Total	Males	Females	Age at last birthday
0–4	413	211	202	426	218	208	428	219	209	0–4
5–9	412	211	201	412	211	201	424	217	207	5–9
10–14	368	188	180	412	211	201	411	210	201	10–14
15–19	371	190	181	367	187	180	410	210	200	15–19
20–24	335	197	188	369	189	180	366	187	179	20–24
25–29	418	214	204	384	196	188	368	188	180	25–29
30–34	317	161	156	416	213	203	382	195	187	30–34
35–39	282	141	141	315	160	155	413	211	202	35–39
40–44	278	138	140	280	140	140	312	158	154	40–44
45–49	293	144	149	274	136	138	276	138	138	45–49
50–54	299	147	152	286	140	146	267	132	135	50–54
55–59	280	136	144	286	139	147	274	133	141	55–59
60–64	270	129	141	261	124	137	267	127	140	60–64
65–69	224	103	121	242	112	130	235	108	127	65–69
70–74	174	76	98	187	82	105	203	90	113	70–74
75–79	121	51	70	132	55	77	142	59	83	75–79
80–84	68	28	40	78	31	47	85	33	52	80–84
85 +	40	16	24	45	17	28	51	18	33	85 +
All ages	5013	2481	2532	5172	2561	2611	5314	2633	2681	All ages

TABLE 5 OBSERVED AND PROJECTED VITAL RATES

Rates per thousand	Observed Total	Males	Females	Projected 1972 Males	Females	1977 Males	Females	1982 Males	Females	Stable Males	Females
Birth	16.82	17.42	16.24	17.87	16.62	17.41	16.18	16.95	15.77	16.60	15.67
Death	9.89	10.81	8.97	11.25	9.88	11.50	10.49	11.68	10.99	12.22	11.30
Increase	6.94	6.61	7.26	6.62	6.74	5.90	5.69	5.27	4.79		4.3788

TABLE 6 RATES STANDARDIZED ON THREE STANDARD COUNTRIES

Standardized rates per thousand	England and Wales, 1961 Total	Males	Females	United States, 1960 Total	Males	Females	Mexico, 1960 Total	Males	Females
Birth	14.94	17.03*	14.09	15.21	15.53*	14.59	18.45	15.53*	17.91
Death	10.11	10.11*	10.10	8.14	9.15*	7.32	4.03	7.91*	3.34
Increase	4.83	6.92*	3.99	7.07	6.38*	7.26	14.42	7.62*	14.57

TABLE 7 VITAL STATISTICS AND RATES INFERRED FROM AGE DISTRIBUTIONS (FEMALES)

Vital statistics		Thompson Age range	NRR	$1000r$	Interval	Bourgeois-Pichat Age range	NRR	$1000b$	$1000d$	$1000r$	Coale	
TFR	2.36	0–4	1.21	7.13	27.44	5–29	1.08	15.96	12.99	2.97	$1000b$	18.16
GRR	1.15	5–9	1.12	4.19	27.41	30–54	0.85	9.77	15.81	−6.04	$1000d$	7.90
NRR	1.12	10–14	1.19	6.21	27.35	55–79	1.55	34.35	18.11	16.24	$1000r$	10.25
Generation	26.38	15–19	1.23	7.55	27.27	*30–59	0.87	10.09	15.30	−5.21	$1000k_1$	22.17
Sex ratio	105.5										$1000k_2$	0.27

TABLE 8 LESLIE MATRIX AND ITS ANALYSIS (FEMALES)

Start of age interval	Sub-diagonal	First row	Percent in stable population	Fisher values	Total reproductive values	Net maternity function	Matrix equation coefficient	Parameters	Integral	Matrix
0	0.99732	0.00000	7.655	1.024	206374	0.00000	0.00000	λ_1	1.0221	1.0221
5	0.99835	0.00000	7.469	1.049	189260	0.00000	0.00000	λ_2	0.3149	0.3240
10	0.99840	0.05904	7.296	1.074	194354	0.00000	0.05879		+0.7858	+0.7563 i
15	0.99817	0.25250	7.126	1.039	196158	0.11757	0.25100	r_1	0.0044	0.0044
20	0.99807	0.36847	6.959	0.805	164212	0.34444	0.36563	r_2	−0.0333	−0.0390
25	0.99718	0.26658	6.795	0.447	69851	0.34682	0.26401		+0.2379	+0.2332 i
30	0.99482	0.12970	6.629	0.184	26148	0.18121	0.12808	c_1		25623
35	0.99061	0.04645	6.452	0.056	7881	0.07496	0.04564	c_2		−5352
40	0.98541	0.00897	6.253	0.010	1444	0.01631	0.00874			−11804 i
45	0.97950	0.00060	6.028	0.001	95	0.00116	0.00058	$2\pi/y$	26.408	26.942
50	0.97016	0.00001	5.776	0.000	1	0.00000	0.00000	Δ	4.147	
55	0.80290		25.561							

Finland, 1966

TABLE 1 DATA INPUT TO COMPUTATIONS

Age at last birthday	Population Total	Males	%	Females	%	Births, by age of mother	Deaths Total	Males	Females	Age at last birthday
0	76586	39018	1.7	37568	1.6	0	1154	651	513	0
1–4	316343	161527	7.2	154816	6.5	0	268	141	127	1–4
5–9	402165	205178	9.2	196987	8.2	0	215	134	81	5–9
10–14	436059	222120	9.9	213939	8.9	7	196	121	65	10–14
15–19	484050	246764	11.0	237286	9.9	8317	366	260	106	15–19
20–24	377401	191823	8.6	185578	7.7	25624	359	268	91	20–24
25–29	318676	161899	7.2	156777	6.5	21439	365	255	110	25–29
30–34	284503	145245	6.5	139258	5.8	12319	449	318	131	30–34
35–39	303379	152527	6.8	150852	6.3	7152	730	518	212	35–39
40–44	290154	138097	6.2	152057	6.3	2592	1101	761	340	40–44
45–49	252999	114678	5.1	138321	5.8	247	1464	1013	451	45–49
50–54	259158	117482	5.2	141676	5.9	0	2265	1564	701	50–54
55–59	256409	115171	5.1	141238	5.9	0	3659	2505	1154	55–59
60–64	206223	88837	4.0	117386	4.9	0	4544	2845	1699	60–64
65–69	157427	63249	2.8	94178	3.9	0	5511	3068	2443	65–69
70–74	105534	39481	1.8	66053	2.8		6038	2915	3123	70–74
75–79	66365	22929	1.0	43436	1.8		6361	2606	3755	75–79
80–84	32617	10420	0.5	22197	0.9	39551 M	4909	1741	3168	80–84
85 +	13140	4014	0.2	9126	0.4	38146 F	3594	1153	2441	85 +
All ages	4639188	2240459		2398729		77697	43548	22837	20711	All ages

TABLE 2 LIFE TABLE FOR MALES

Age, x	$_nq_x$	l_x	$_nd_x$	$_nL_x$	$_nm_x$	T_x	$1000r_x$	$\mathring{e}_x$	$_nM_x$	Age, x
0	0.01648	100000	1648	98784	0.01668	6598322	0.00	65.98	0.01668	0
1	0.00348	98352	343	392418	0.00087	6499537	0.00	66.08	0.00087	1
5	0.00326	98009	320	489248	0.00065	6107119	0.00	62.31	0.00065	5
10	0.00272	97690	266	487825	0.00054	5617872	0.00	57.51	0.00054	10
15	0.00527	97424	513	485923	0.00106	5130047	13.65	52.66	0.00105	15
20	0.00698	96911	677	482913	0.00140	4644124	40.78	47.92	0.00140	20
25	0.00787	96234	757	479353	0.00158	4161211	26.15	43.24	0.00158	25
30	0.01090	95477	1041	474957	0.00219	3681858	3.68	38.56	0.00219	30
35	0.01685	94436	1592	468515	0.00340	3206901	1.49	33.96	0.00340	35
40	0.02733	92845	2538	458364	0.00554	2738386	22.78	29.49	0.00551	40
45	0.04333	90307	3913	442387	0.00884	2280023	7.18	25.25	0.00883	45
50	0.06456	86394	5577	418956	0.01331	1837636	0.00	21.27	0.01331	50
55	0.10352	80817	8365	384259	0.02177	1418680	5.96	17.55	0.02175	55
60	0.14923	72450	10811	336276	0.03215	1034421	23.69	14.28	0.03202	60
65	0.21770	61639	13419	275541	0.04870	698144	23.69	11.33	0.04851	65
70	0.31301	48220	15094	203619	0.07413	422604	23.69	8.76	0.07383	70
75	0.44147	33127	14625	128171	0.11410	218984	23.69	6.61	0.11365	75
80	0.58203	18502	10769	64153	0.15786	90813	23.69	4.91	0.15708	80
85 +	*1.00000	7733	7733	26650	0.29008	26650	23.69	3.45	0.28724	85 +

TABLE 3 LIFE TABLE FOR FEMALES

Age, x	$_nq_x$	l_x	$_nd_x$	$_nL_x$	$_nm_x$	T_x	$1000r_x$	$\mathring{e}_x$	$_nM_x$	Age, x
0	0.01352	100000	1352	99023	0.01366	7316538	0.00	73.17	0.01365	0
1	0.00327	98648	323	393653	0.00082	7217514	0.00	73.15	0.00082	1
5	0.00205	98325	202	491120	0.00041	6823851	0.00	69.40	0.00041	5
10	0.00152	98123	149	490246	0.00030	6332732	0.00	54.54	0.00030	10
15	0.00223	97974	219	489342	0.00045	5842486	13.80	59.63	0.00045	15
20	0.00246	97755	240	488200	0.00049	5353144	40.92	54.76	0.00049	20
25	0.00352	97515	343	486751	0.00070	4864944	28.01	49.89	0.00070	25
30	0.00470	97172	456	484788	0.00094	4378183	2.87	45.06	0.00094	30
35	0.00700	96716	677	482012	0.00141	3893394	0.00	40.25	0.00141	35
40	0.01113	96038	1069	477697	0.00224	3411382	6.41	35.52	0.00224	40
45	0.01619	94969	1538	471254	0.00326	2933685	3.71	30.89	0.00326	45
50	0.02446	93431	2285	461887	0.00495	2462431	0.00	26.36	0.00495	50
55	0.04020	91146	3664	447378	0.00819	2000545	10.09	21.95	0.00817	55
60	0.07048	87482	6166	423316	0.01457	1553167	25.81	17.75	0.01447	60
65	0.12310	81316	10010	383446	0.02611	1129850	25.81	13.89	0.02594	65
70	0.21382	71306	15247	320508	0.04757	746604	25.81	10.47	0.04728	70
75	0.35799	56059	20069	230895	0.08692	425897	25.81	7.60	0.08545	75
80	0.52642	35990	18946	131957	0.14358	195002	25.81	5.42	0.14272	80
85 +	*1.00000	17044	17044	63045	0.27035	63045	25.81	3.70	0.26748	85 +

[428]

TABLE 4 POPULATION PROJECTION, USING FIXED AGE-SPECIFIC BIRTH AND DEATH RATES, IN THOUSANDS

Age at last birthday	1971 Total	Males	Females	1976 Total	Males	Females	1981 Total	Males	Females	Age at last birthday
0–4	409	208	201	451	229	222	468	238	230	0–4
5–9	392	200	192	408	207	201	450	229	221	5–9
10–14	402	205	197	390	199	191	407	207	200	10–14
15–19	435	221	214	400	204	196	389	198	191	15–19
20–24	482	245	237	433	220	213	399	203	196	20–24
25–29	375	190	185	479	243	236	430	218	212	25–29
30–34	316	160	156	373	189	184	476	241	235	30–34
35–39	281	143	138	313	158	155	369	186	183	35–39
40–44	299	149	150	277	140	137	309	155	154	40–44
45–49	283	133	150	291	144	147	270	135	135	45–49
50–54	245	109	136	273	126	147	281	136	145	50–54
55–59	245	108	137	231	100	131	258	116	142	55–59
60–64	235	101	134	224	94	130	211	87	124	60–64
65–69	179	73	106	204	83	121	195	77	118	65–69
70–74	126	47	79	143	54	89	162	61	101	70–74
75–79	73	25	48	86	29	57	98	34	64	75–79
80–84	36	11	25	39	12	27	47	15	32	80–84
85 +	15	4	11	17	5	12	18	5	13	85 +
All ages	4828	2332	2496	5032	2436	2596	5237	2541	2696	All ages

TABLE 5 OBSERVED AND PROJECTED VITAL RATES

Rates per thousand	Observed Total	Males	Females	Projected 1971 Males	Females	1976 Males	Females	1981 Males	Females	Stable Males	Females
Birth	16.75	17.65	15.90	19.35	17.46	19.81	17.93	19.36	17.32	17.23	15.71
Death	9.39	10.19	8.63	10.61	9.23	10.95	9.78	11.19	10.25	13.51	11.98
Increase	7.36	7.46	7.27	8.74	8.23	8.86	8.15	7.88	7.06	3.7245	

TABLE 6 RATES STANDARDIZED ON THREE STANDARD COUNTRIES

Standardized rates per thousand	England and Wales, 1961 Total	Males	Females	United States, 1960 Total	Males	Females	Mexico, 1960 Total	Males	Females
Birth	14.78	16.40*	14.06	15.04	15.06*	14.55	17.38	15.07*	17.02
Death	13.71	14.63*	12.98	11.00	12.52*	9.32	5.36	9.85*	4.14
Increase	1.07	1.77*	1.08	4.03	2.54*	5.22	12.01	5.22*	12.88

TABLE 7 VITAL STATISTICS AND RATES INFERRED FROM AGE DISTRIBUTIONS (FEMALES)

Vital statistics		Thompson Age range	NRR	1000r	Interval	Bourgeois-Pichat Age range	NRR	1000b	1000d	1000r	Coale
TFR	2.32	0–4	1.11	3.88	27.43	5–29	1.37	20.47	8.93	11.54	1000b
GRR	1.14	5–9	1.26	8.38	27.40	30–54	0.96	11.95	13.29	-1.34	1000d
NRR	1.11	10–14	1.42	12.74	27.35	55–79	2.13	56.46	38.44	28.02	1000r
Generation	27.75	15–19	1.59	16.02	27.28	*35–59	1.01	13.14	12.75	0.39	$1000k_1$
Sex ratio	103.68										$1000k_2$

TABLE 8 LESLIE MATRIX AND ITS ANALYSIS (FEMALES)

Start of age interval	Sub-diagonal	First row	Percent in stable population	Fisher values	Total reproductive values	Net maternity function	Matrix equation coefficient	Parameters	Integral	Matrix
0	0.99682	0.00000	7.667	1.024	197064	0.00000	0.00000	λ_1	1.0188	1.0188
5	0.99822	0.00004	7.502	1.047	206229	0.00000	0.00004	λ_2	0.3600	0.3693
10	0.99816	0.04235	7.350	1.068	228587	0.00008	0.04214		+0.7440	+0.7205i
15	0.99767	0.20900	7.201	1.047	248464	0.08421	0.20758	r_1	0.0037	0.0037
20	0.99705	0.33190	7.052	0.855	158616	0.33095	0.32888	r_2	-0.0381	-0.0422
25	0.99595	0.27194	6.901	0.532	83465	0.32680	0.26867		+0.2240	+0.2194i
30	0.99427	0.16400	6.747	0.265	36891	0.21055	0.16137	c_1		27139
35	0.99105	0.07777	6.584	0.102	15460	0.11220	0.07609	c_2		-40928
40	0.98651	0.02274	6.405	0.025	3797	0.03998	0.02205			30610i
45	0.98012	0.00216	6.202	0.002	301	0.00413	0.00207	$2\pi/y$	28.046	28.633
50	0.96859	0.00001	5.965	0.000	1	0.00000	0.00000	Δ	6.224	
55	0.78219		24.423							

Finland, 1966 (urban communes)

TABLE 1   DATA INPUT TO COMPUTATIONS

Age at last birthday	Population					Births, by age of mother	Deaths			Age at last birthday
	Total	Males	%	Females	%		Total	Males	Females	
0	38086	19393	2.0	18693	1.7	0	563	307	256	0
1–4	147387	75479	7.7	71908	6.4	0	106	55	51	1–4
5–9	166166	84832	8.7	81334	7.2	0	80	52	28	5–9
10–14	165773	84006	8.6	81767	7.3	6	58	40	18	10–14
15–19	196173	95797	9.8	100376	8.9	4367	138	100	38	15–19
20–24	201696	93931	9.6	107765	9.6	14431	181	127	54	20–24
25–29	177152	87180	8.9	89972	8.0	11518	171	119	52	25–29
30–34	144384	71572	7.3	72812	6.5	5604	198	136	62	30–34
35–39	142791	69063	7.1	73728	6.5	2749	336	236	100	35–39
40–44	133404	60862	6.2	72542	6.4	749	518	333	185	40–44
45–49	116255	50587	5.2	65668	5.8	50	689	465	224	45–49
50–54	117142	50608	5.2	66534	5.9	0	1056	705	351	50–54
55–59	114178	47651	4.9	66527	5.9	0	1719	1144	575	55–59
60–64	89845	35522	3.6	54323	4.8	0	2036	1237	799	60–64
65–69	65660	23436	2.4	42224	3.7	0	2361	1252	1109	65–69
70–74	42601	13368	1.4	29233	2.6		2515	1104	1411	70–74
75–79	26033	7200	0.7	18833	1.7		2332	827	1505	75–79
80–84	12545	3018	0.3	9527	0.8	20045 M	1775	500	1275	80–84
85 +	5077	1071	0.1	4006	0.4	19429 F	1317	292	1025	85 +
All ages	2102348	974576		1127772		39474	18149	9031	9118	All ages

TABLE 2   LIFE TABLE FOR MALES

Age, x	$_nq_x$	l_x	$_nd_x$	$_nL_x$	$_nm_x$	T_x	$1000r_x$	$\overset{\circ}{e}_x$	$_nM_x$	Age, x
0	0.01562	100000	1562	98826	0.01580	6560333	2.13	65.60	0.01583	0
1	0.00290	98438	286	392925	0.00073	6461507	2.13	65.64	0.00073	1
5	0.00306	98153	300	490012	0.00061	6068582	11.55	61.83	0.00061	5
10	0.00238	97852	233	488724	0.00048	5578570	0.00	57.01	0.00048	10
15	0.00521	97620	508	486916	0.00104	5089846	0.00	52.14	0.00104	15
20	0.00674	97111	655	483952	0.00135	4602930	8.14	47.40	0.00135	20
25	0.00682	96457	658	480694	0.00137	4118978	25.72	42.70	0.00136	25
30	0.00950	95799	911	476919	0.00191	3638285	21.21	37.98	0.00190	30
35	0.01700	94889	1613	470749	0.00343	3161365	12.72	33.32	0.00342	35
40	0.02716	93276	2534	460560	0.00550	2690616	25.32	28.85	0.00547	40
45	0.04507	90742	4090	444175	0.00921	2230056	9.16	24.58	0.00919	45
50	0.06747	86652	5847	419707	0.01393	1785881	0.00	20.61	0.01393	50
55	0.11380	80805	9195	382230	0.02406	1366175	11.41	16.91	0.02401	55
60	0.16154	71610	11568	330187	0.03503	983945	36.49	13.74	0.03482	60
65	0.23763	60042	14268	265407	0.05376	653758	36.49	10.89	0.05342	65
70	0.34356	45774	15726	189364	0.08305	388351	36.49	8.48	0.08259	70
75	0.44423	30048	13348	115609	0.11546	198987	36.49	6.62	0.11485	75
80	0.57930	16700	9674	57996	0.16681	83379	36.49	4.99	0.15567	80
85 +	*1.00000	7026	7025	25382	0.27679	25382	36.49	3.61	0.27264	85 +

TABLE 3   LIFE TABLE FOR FEMALES

Age, x	$_nq_x$	l_x	$_nd_x$	$_nL_x$	$_nm_x$	T_x	$1000r_x$	$\overset{\circ}{e}_x$	$_nM_x$	Age, x
0	0.01352	100000	1352	99001	0.01366	7330515	3.34	73.31	0.01369	0
1	0.00282	98648	278	393787	0.00071	7231514	3.34	73.31	0.00071	1
5	0.00172	98369	169	491425	0.00034	6837727	9.84	69.51	0.00034	5
10	0.00110	98201	108	490737	0.00022	6346302	0.00	64.63	0.00022	10
15	0.00189	98093	186	490028	0.00038	5855565	0.00	59.69	0.00038	15
20	0.00250	97907	245	488943	0.00050	5365537	10.45	54.80	0.00050	20
25	0.00290	97662	283	487637	0.00058	4876594	38.59	49.93	0.00058	25
30	0.00426	97379	415	485933	0.00085	4388957	19.03	45.07	0.00085	30
35	0.00676	96963	656	483347	0.00136	3903024	0.00	40.25	0.00136	35
40	0.01269	96308	1223	478682	0.00255	3419677	9.13	35.51	0.00255	40
45	0.01693	95085	1610	471654	0.00341	2940995	5.05	30.93	0.00341	45
50	0.02606	93475	2436	461756	0.00528	2469342	0.00	26.42	0.00528	50
55	0.04248	91039	3867	446321	0.00866	2007586	11.16	22.05	0.00864	55
60	0.07169	87172	6249	421534	0.01482	1561265	32.66	17.91	0.01471	60
65	0.12476	80923	10096	381287	0.02648	1139731	32.66	14.08	0.02626	65
70	0.21778	70827	15425	317344	0.04861	758444	32.66	10.71	0.04827	70
75	0.33557	55402	18591	231153	0.08043	441100	32.66	7.96	0.07991	75
80	0.49969	36811	18394	136629	0.13463	209948	32.66	5.70	0.13383	80
85 +	1.00000	18417	18417	73318	0.25119	73318	32.66	3.98	0.25587	85 +

TABLE 4 POPULATION PROJECTION, USING FIXED AGE-SPECIFIC BIRTH AND DEATH RATES, IN THOUSANDS

Age at last birthday	1971 Total	Males	Females	1976 Total	Males	Females	1981 Total	Males	Females	Age at last birthday
0–4	199	101	98	199	101	98	191	97	94	0–4
5–9	185	95	90	197	100	97	198	100	98	5–9
10–14	166	85	81	184	94	90	197	100	97	10–14
15–19	166	84	82	165	84	81	184	94	90	15–19
20–24	195	95	100	164	83	81	165	84	81	20–24
25–29	200	93	107	195	95	100	164	83	81	25–29
30–34	176	86	90	200	93	107	194	94	100	30–34
35–39	143	71	72	174	85	89	198	91	107	35–39
40–44	141	68	73	141	69	72	172	84	88	40–44
45–49	130	59	71	137	65	72	138	67	71	45–49
50–54	112	48	64	125	55	70	132	62	70	50–54
55–59	110	46	64	106	44	62	119	51	68	55–59
60–64	104	41	63	101	40	61	97	38	59	60–64
65–69	78	29	49	90	33	57	87	32	55	65–69
70–74	52	17	35	61	20	41	71	24	47	70–74
75–79	29	8	21	36	10	26	42	12	30	75–79
80–84	15	4	11	17	4	13	20	5	15	80–84
85 +	6	1	5	8	2	6	9	2	7	85 +
All ages	2207	1031	1176	2300	1077	1223	2378	1120	1258	All ages

TABLE 5 OBSERVED AND PROJECTED VITAL RATES

Rates per thousand	Observed Total	Males	Females	Projected 1971 Males	Females	1976 Males	Females	1981 Males	Females	Stable Males	Females
Birth	18.78	20.57	17.23	20.30	17.18	18.66	15.94	17.16	14.79	15.90	14.29
Death	8.63	9.27	8.08	9.86	8.85	10.39	9.55	10.89	10.24	14.58	13.07
Increase	10.14	11.30	9.14	10.44	8.33	8.26	6.39	6.27	4.55		1.2193

TABLE 6 RATES STANDARDIZED ON THREE STANDARD COUNTRIES

Standardized rates per thousand	England and Wales, 1961 Total	Males	Females	United States, 1960 Total	Males	Females	Mexico, 1960 Total	Males	Females
Birth	13.69	16.76*	13.06	13.95	15.47*	13.53	15.53	15.72*	15.23
Death	13.85	15.44*	12.66	11.15	12.81*	9.11	5.41	9.39*	4.04
Increase	-0.17	1.32*	0.40	2.80	2.66*	4.42	11.12	6.34*	12.19

TABLE 7 VITAL STATISTICS AND RATES INFERRED FROM AGE DISTRIBUTIONS (FEMALES)

Vital statistics		Thompson Age range	NRR	$1000r$	Interval	Bourgeois-Pichat Age range	NRR	$1000b$	$1000d$	$1000r$	Coale
TFR	2.15	0–4	1.04	1.29	27.44	5–29	0.76	13.95	23.89	-9.94	$1000b$
GRR	1.06	5–9	0.99	-0.24	27.40	30–54	1.10	15.09	11.70	3.39	$1000d$
NRR	1.03	10–14	1.08	2.92	27.35	55–79	2.37	83.47	51.56	31.91	$1000r$
Generation	27.04	15–19	1.39	11.52	27.26	*30–54	1.10	15.09	11.70	3.39	$1000k_1$
Sex ratio	103.17										$1000k_2$

TABLE 8 LESLIE MATRIX AND ITS ANALYSIS (FEMALES)

Start of age interval	Sub-diagonal	First row	Percent in stable population	Fisher values	Total reproductive values	Net maternity function	Matrix equation coefficient
0	0.99723	0.00000	7.020	1.018	92207	0.00000	0.00000
5	0.99860	0.00009	6.958	1.027	83513	0.00000	0.00009
10	0.99856	0.05277	6.906	1.034	84582	0.00018	0.05256
15	0.99779	0.21480	6.854	0.988	99219	0.10493	0.21360
20	0.99733	0.31724	6.798	0.778	83802	0.32227	0.31476
25	0.99650	0.24827	6.738	0.461	41455	0.30726	0.24567
30	0.99468	0.13832	6.674	0.212	15410	0.18408	0.13639
35	0.99035	0.05762	6.598	0.073	5350	0.08870	0.05651
40	0.98532	0.01341	6.495	0.015	1052	0.02433	0.01305
45	0.97901	0.00092	6.360	0.001	63	0.00177	0.00088
50	0.96657	0.00002	6.189	0.000	1	0.00000	0.00000
55	0.77959		26.409				

Parameters

	Integral	Matrix
λ_1	1.0061	1.0061
λ_2	0.3378	0.3478
	+0.7455	+0.7210 i
r_1	0.0012	0.0012
r_2	-0.0401	-0.0445
	+0.2291	+0.2243 i
c_1		13129
c_2		-13701
		-17188 i
$2\pi/y$	27.428	28.015
Δ	7.655	

Finland, 1966 (rural communes)

TABLE 1 DATA INPUT TO COMPUTATIONS

Age at last birthday	Population					Births, by age of mother	Deaths			Age at last birthday
	Total	Males	%	Females	%		Total	Males	Females	
0	38500	19625	1.6	18875	1.5	0	601	344	257	0
1–4	168956	86048	6.8	82908	6.5	0	162	86	76	1–4
5–9	235999	120346	9.5	115653	9.1	0	135	82	53	5–9
10–14	270286	138114	10.9	132172	10.4	1	128	81	47	10–14
15–19	287877	150967	11.9	136910	10.8	3950	228	160	68	15–19
20–24	175705	97892	7.7	77813	6.1	11193	178	141	37	20–24
25–29	141524	74719	5.9	66805	5.3	9921	194	136	58	25–29
30–34	140119	73673	5.8	66446	5.2	6715	251	182	69	30–34
35–39	160588	83464	6.6	77124	6.1	4403	394	282	112	35–39
40–44	156750	77235	6.1	79515	6.3	1843	583	428	155	40–44
45–49	136744	64091	5.1	72653	5.7	197	775	548	227	45–49
50–54	142016	66874	5.3	75142	5.9	0	1209	859	350	50–54
55–59	142231	67520	5.3	74711	5.9	0	1940	1361	579	55–59
60–64	116378	53315	4.2	63063	5.0	0	2508	1608	900	60–64
65–69	91767	39813	3.1	51954	4.1	0	3150	1816	1334	65–69
70–74	62933	26113	2.1	36820	2.9		3523	1811	1712	70–74
75–79	40332	15729	1.2	24603	1.9		4029	1779	2250	75–79
80–84	20072	7402	0.6	12670	1.0	19506 M	3134	1241	1893	80–84
85 +	8063	2943	0.2	5120	0.4	18717 F	2277	861	1416	85 +
All ages	2536840	1265883		1270957		38223	25399	13806	11593	All ages

TABLE 2 LIFE TABLE FOR MALES

Age, x	$_nq_x$	l_x	$_nd_x$	$_nL_x$	$_nm_x$	T_x	$1000r_x$	$\overset{\circ}{e}_x$	$_nM_x$	Age, x
0	0.01731	100000	1731	98740	0.01753	6617327	0.00	66.17	0.01753	0
1	0.00399	98269	392	391949	0.00100	6518587	0.00	66.33	0.00100	1
5	0.00340	97877	333	488555	0.00068	6126638	0.00	62.59	0.00068	5
10	0.00293	97545	286	487047	0.00059	5638083	0.00	57.80	0.00059	10
15	0.00532	97259	517	485088	0.00107	5151036	33.39	52.96	0.00106	15
20	0.00723	96742	700	482035	0.00145	4665947	68.89	48.23	0.00144	20
25	0.00909	96042	873	478127	0.00183	4183912	26.55	43.56	0.00182	25
30	0.01228	95169	1159	473072	0.00247	3705785	0.00	38.94	0.00247	30
35	0.01676	94001	1576	466350	0.00338	3232713	0.00	34.39	0.00338	35
40	0.02746	92425	2538	456237	0.00556	2766363	20.73	29.93	0.00554	40
45	0.04195	89887	3771	440596	0.00856	2310126	5.65	25.70	0.00855	45
50	0.06235	86116	5369	417989	0.01285	1869530	0.00	21.71	0.01285	50
55	0.09623	80747	7770	385334	0.02016	1451541	2.07	17.98	0.02016	55
60	0.14102	72977	10291	340225	0.03025	1066207	17.43	14.61	0.03016	60
65	0.20587	62685	12905	282100	0.04575	725982	17.43	11.58	0.04561	65
70	0.29693	49780	14781	212470	0.06957	443882	17.43	8.92	0.06935	70
75	0.44015	34999	15405	135784	0.11345	231412	17.43	6.61	0.11310	75
80	0.58303	19594	11424	67903	0.16824	95628	17.43	4.88	0.16765	80
85 +	*1.00000	8170	8170	27725	0.29468	27725	17.43	3.39	0.29255	85 +

TABLE 3 LIFE TABLE FOR FEMALES

Age, x	$_nq_x$	l_x	$_nd_x$	$_nL_x$	$_nm_x$	T_x	$1000r_x$	$\overset{\circ}{e}_x$	$_nM_x$	Age, x
0	0.01349	100000	1349	99043	0.01362	7308677	0.00	73.09	0.01362	0
1	0.00366	98651	361	393574	0.00092	7209634	0.00	73.08	0.00092	1
5	0.00229	98291	225	490891	0.00046	6816060	0.00	69.35	0.00046	5
10	0.00178	98066	174	489897	0.00036	6325169	0.00	64.50	0.00035	10
15	0.00249	97891	243	488851	0.00050	5835272	52.53	59.61	0.00050	15
20	0.00240	97648	235	487691	0.00048	5346411	71.18	54.75	0.00048	20
25	0.00434	97413	423	486066	0.00087	4858720	14.98	49.88	0.00087	25
30	0.00518	96991	502	483754	0.00104	4372654	0.00	45.08	0.00104	30
35	0.00724	96488	698	480785	0.00145	3888900	0.00	40.30	0.00145	35
40	0.00971	95790	930	476786	0.00195	3408115	3.89	35.58	0.00195	40
45	0.01552	94860	1472	470875	0.00313	2931329	2.50	30.90	0.00312	45
50	0.02304	93388	2152	461980	0.00466	2460454	0.00	26.35	0.00465	50
55	0.03817	91236	3482	448297	0.00777	1998474	9.15	21.90	0.00775	55
60	0.06946	87754	6096	424877	0.01435	1550177	20.99	17.67	0.01427	60
65	0.12178	81658	9944	385307	0.02581	1125301	20.99	13.78	0.02568	65
70	0.21065	71714	15106	323151	0.04675	739993	20.99	10.32	0.04650	70
75	0.37468	56608	21210	230868	0.09187	416842	20.99	7.36	0.09145	75
80	0.54255	35398	19205	127932	0.15012	185974	20.99	5.25	0.14941	80
85 +	*1.00000	16193	16193	58043	0.27898	58043	20.99	3.58	0.27655	85 +

TABLE 4 POPULATION PROJECTION, USING FIXED AGE-SPECIFIC BIRTH AND DEATH RATES, IN THOUSANDS

Age at last birthday	1971 Total	Males	Females	1976 Total	Males	Females	1981 Total	Males	Females	Age at last birthday
0–4	210	107	103	253	129	124	281	143	138	0–4
5–9	206	105	101	210	107	103	253	129	124	5–9
10–14	235	120	115	206	105	101	209	106	103	10–14
15–19	270	138	132	234	119	115	205	104	101	15–19
20–24	287	150	137	269	137	132	234	119	115	20–24
25–29	175	97	78	285	149	136	267	135	131	25–29
30–34	140	74	66	173	96	77	282	147	135	30–34
35–39	139	73	66	139	73	66	172	95	77	35–39
40–44	158	82	76	136	71	65	137	71	66	40–44
45–49	154	75	79	155	79	76	134	69	65	45–49
50–54	132	61	71	148	71	77	149	75	74	50–54
55–59	135	62	73	125	56	69	140	65	75	55–59
60–64	131	60	71	123	54	69	115	49	66	60–64
65–69	101	44	57	113	49	64	108	45	63	65–69
70–74	74	30	44	81	33	48	91	37	54	70–74
75–79	43	17	26	50	19	31	55	21	34	75–79
80–84	22	8	14	23	8	15	27	10	17	80–84
85 +	9	3	6	9	3	6	10	3	7	85 +
All ages	2621	1306	1315	2732	1358	1374	2869	1424	1445	All ages

TABLE 5 OBSERVED AND PROJECTED VITAL RATES

Rates per thousand	Observed Total	Males	Females	Projected 1971 Males	Females	1976 Males	Females	1981 Males	Females	Stable Males	Females
Birth	15.07	15.41	14.73	18.57	17.66	20.93	19.86	21.01	19.91	18.82	17.33
Death	10.01	10.91	9.12	11.23	9.59	11.44	10.01	11.47	10.29	12.35	10.87
Increase	5.06	4.50	5.61	7.34	8.07	9.49	9.85	9.54	9.61		6.4584

TABLE 6 RATES STANDARDIZED ON THREE STANDARD COUNTRIES

Standardized rates per thousand	England and Wales, 1961 Total	Males	Females	United States, 1960 Total	Males	Females	Mexico, 1960 Total	Males	Females
Birth	16.09	16.04*	15.27	16.34	14.66*	15.77	18.53	14.44*	18.10
Death	13.65	14.14*	13.22	10.93	12.34*	9.48	5.36	10.17*	4.21
Increase	2.44	1.90*	2.04	5.41	2.33*	6.29	13.17	4.27*	13.89

TABLE 7 VITAL STATISTICS AND RATES INFERRED FROM AGE DISTRIBUTIONS (FEMALES)

Vital statistics		Thompson Age range	NRR	$1000r$	Interval	Bourgeois-Pichat Age range	NRR	$1000b$	$1000d$	$1000r$	Coale
TFR	2.53	0–4	1.19	6.36	27.43	5–29	2.38	28.70	−3.37	32.06	$1000b$
GRR	1.24	5–9	1.54	16.03	27.40	30–54	0.85	9.51	15.53	−5.98	$1000d$
NRR	1.20	10–14	1.76	20.39	27.36	55–79	1.95	54.84	30.10	24.74	$1000r$
Generation	28.26	15–19	1.77	16.40	27.29	*35–59	0.97	12.15	13.17	−1.03	$1000k_1$
Sex ratio	104.22										$1000k_2$

TABLE 8 LESLIE MATRIX AND ITS ANALYSIS (FEMALES)

Start of age interval	Sub-diagonal	First row	Percent in stable population	Fisher values	Total reproductive values	Net maternity function	Matrix equation coefficient	Parameters	Integral	Matrix
0	0.99650	0.00000	8.403	1.031	104987	0.00000	0.00000	λ_1	1.0328	1.0328
5	0.99797	0.00001	8.107	1.069	123646	0.00000	0.00001	λ_2	0.3791	0.3873
10	0.99789	0.03473	7.833	1.106	146242	0.00002	0.03454		+0.7507	+0.7276i
15	0.99761	0.20788	7.568	1.109	151875	0.06907	0.20629	r_1	0.0065	0.0065
20	0.99667	0.35201	7.310	0.934	72642	0.34352	0.34849	r_2	−0.0346	−0.0387
25	0.99524	0.30043	7.054	0.603	40292	0.35347	0.29643		+0.2206	+0.2163i
30	0.99386	0.19032	6.797	0.315	20900	0.23939	0.18690	c_1		13832
35	0.99168	0.09658	6.541	0.129	9976	0.13441	0.09426	c_2		−26463
40	0.98760	0.03117	6.280	0.034	2724	0.05411	0.03018			49937i
45	0.98111	0.00327	6.005	0.003	238	0.00625	0.00313	$2\pi/y$	28.479	29.044
50	0.97038	0.00002	5.704	0.000	1	0.00000	0.00000	Δ	7.536	
55	0.78572		22.399							

France, 1967

TABLE 1   DATA INPUT TO COMPUTATIONS

Age at last birthday	Population					Births, by age of mother	Deaths			Age at last birthday
	Total	Males	%	Females	%		Total	Males	Females	
0	837781	427988	1.8	409793	1.6	0	14350	8292	6058	0
1–4	3409657	1739524	7.2	1670133	6.6	0	2924	1631	1293	1–4
5–9	4157501	2117961	8.8	2039540	8.0	0	1581	962	619	5–9
10–14	4119626	2097350	8.7	2022276	8.0	211	1478	929	549	10–14
15–19	4276838	2181540	9.0	2095298	8.2	75871	3507	2419	1088	15–19
20–24	3390550	1741753	7.2	1648797	6.5	287697	3972	2819	1153	20–24
25–29	2877889	1483175	6.1	1394714	5.5	225879	3448	2373	1075	25–29
30–34	3183952	1626809	6.7	1557143	6.1	148887	4803	3221	1582	30–34
35–39	3382752	1720069	7.1	1662683	6.5	76380	7280	4814	2466	35–39
40–44	3314116	1659108	6.9	1655008	6.5	21168	10893	7291	3602	40–44
45–49	2654393	1310344	5.4	1344049	5.3	1359	13488	9025	4463	45–49
50–54	2315512	1123367	4.7	1192145	4.7	29	18198	12071	6127	50–54
55–59	2813037	1346331	5.6	1466706	5.8	0	33422	22900	10522	55–59
60–64	2630462	1223622	5.1	1406840	5.5	0	47735	32039	15695	60–64
65–69	2257161	982257	4.1	1274904	5.0	0	62558	39283	23275	65–69
70–74	1663876	620603	2.6	1043273	4.1		69307	35861	33446	70–74
75–79	1169579	398354	1.7	771225	3.0		79487	35791	43696	75–79
80–84	701147	220009	0.9	481138	1.9	428864 M	79920	31387	48533	80–84
85+	392466	107601	0.4	284865	1.1	408617 F	81595	25965	55630	85+
All ages	49548295	24127765		25420530		837481	539946	279073	260873	All ages

TABLE 2   LIFE TABLE FOR MALES

Age, x	$_nq_x$	l_x	$_nd_x$	$_nL_x$	$_nm_x$	T_x	$1000r_x$	$\overset{\circ}{e}_x$	$_nM_x$	Age, x
0	0.01910	100000	1910	98575	0.01937	6803833	0.00	68.04	0.01937	0
1	0.00374	98090	367	391299	0.00094	6705258	0.00	68.36	0.00094	1
5	0.00227	97723	222	488062	0.00045	6313959	2.71	64.61	0.00045	5
10	0.00221	97502	216	487036	0.00044	5825897	0.00	59.75	0.00044	10
15	0.00555	97286	540	485198	0.00111	5338861	17.50	54.88	0.00111	15
20	0.00808	96746	782	481822	0.00162	4853664	37.08	50.17	0.00162	20
25	0.00797	95964	765	477942	0.00160	4371841	5.14	45.56	0.00160	25
30	0.00985	95199	938	473765	0.00198	3893900	0.00	40.90	0.00198	30
35	0.01390	94261	1311	468258	0.00280	3420134	0.00	36.28	0.00280	35
40	0.02185	92951	2031	460050	0.00441	2951876	22.65	31.76	0.00439	40
45	0.03409	90920	3100	447387	0.00693	2491825	31.86	27.41	0.00689	45
50	0.05241	87820	4603	428366	0.01075	2044439	0.00	23.28	0.01075	50
55	0.08177	83217	6805	400082	0.01701	1616073	0.00	19.42	0.01701	55
60	0.12358	76412	9443	359586	0.02626	1215990	16.70	15.91	0.02618	60
65	0.18273	66969	12237	305179	0.04010	856404	16.70	12.79	0.03999	65
70	0.25359	54732	13879	239542	0.05794	551226	16.70	10.07	0.05778	70
75	0.36756	40853	15016	166637	0.09011	311683	16.70	7.63	0.08985	75
80	0.52087	25837	13458	94065	0.14307	145046	16.70	5.61	0.14265	80
85+	1.00000	12379	12379	50981	0.24282	50981	16.70	4.12	0.24131	85+

TABLE 3   LIFE TABLE FOR FEMALES

Age, x	$_nq_x$	l_x	$_nd_x$	$_nL_x$	$_nm_x$	T_x	$1000r_x$	$\overset{\circ}{e}_x$	$_nM_x$	Age, x
0	0.01462	100000	1462	98922	0.01478	7546676	0.00	75.47	0.01473	0
1	0.00309	98538	304	393271	0.00077	7447755	0.00	75.58	0.00077	1
5	0.00152	98233	149	490794	0.00030	7054483	2.39	71.81	0.00030	5
10	0.00136	98084	133	490111	0.00027	6563690	0.00	66.92	0.00027	10
15	0.00260	97951	255	489163	0.00052	6073579	19.91	62.01	0.00052	15
20	0.00350	97696	342	487652	0.00070	5584416	40.02	57.16	0.00070	20
25	0.00385	97354	375	485866	0.00077	5096764	4.91	52.35	0.00077	25
30	0.00507	96980	491	483740	0.00102	4610898	0.00	47.54	0.00102	30
35	0.00739	96488	713	480773	0.00148	4127158	0.00	42.77	0.00148	35
40	0.01086	95775	1040	476453	0.00218	3646385	19.01	38.07	0.00218	40
45	0.01656	94735	1569	470027	0.00334	3169932	29.35	33.46	0.00332	45
50	0.02539	93166	2365	460254	0.00514	2699905	0.00	28.98	0.00514	50
55	0.03528	90800	3203	446495	0.00717	2239651	0.00	24.67	0.00717	55
60	0.05453	87597	4777	426891	0.01119	1793156	14.59	20.47	0.01115	60
65	0.08786	82820	7277	397268	0.01832	1366264	14.59	16.50	0.01825	65
70	0.14958	75543	11300	351239	0.03217	968996	14.59	12.83	0.03206	70
75	0.25016	64243	16071	282734	0.05684	617697	14.59	9.61	0.05666	75
80	0.40353	48172	19439	192173	0.10115	334964	14.59	6.95	0.10087	80
85+	1.00000	28733	28733	142791	0.20123	142791	14.59	4.97	0.19529	85+

TABLE 4 POPULATION PROJECTION, USING FIXED AGE-SPECIFIC BIRTH AND DEATH RATES, IN THOUSANDS

Age at last birthday	1972 Total	Males	Females	1977 Total	Males	Females	1982 Total	Males	Females	Age at last birthday
0–4	4341	2218	2123	4747	2425	2322	5028	2569	2459	0–4
5–9	4233	2159	2074	4326	2209	2117	4731	2416	2315	5–9
10–14	4151	2114	2037	4226	2155	2071	4319	2205	2114	10–14
15–19	4107	2089	2018	4139	2106	2033	4214	2147	2067	15–19
20–24	4255	2166	2089	4087	2075	2012	4117	2091	2026	20–24
25–29	3371	1728	1643	4230	2149	2081	4063	2058	2005	25–29
30–34	2859	1470	1389	3349	1713	1636	4202	2130	2072	30–34
35–39	3156	1608	1548	2833	1453	1380	3319	1693	1626	35–39
40–44	3338	1690	1648	3114	1580	1534	2796	1428	1368	40–44
45–49	3246	1613	1633	3269	1643	1626	3049	1536	1513	45–49
50–54	2571	1255	1316	3144	1545	1599	3166	1574	1592	50–54
55–59	2206	1049	1157	2449	1172	1277	2994	1443	1551	55–59
60–64	2612	1210	1402	2049	943	1106	2274	1053	1221	60–64
65–69	2347	1038	1309	2332	1027	1305	1829	800	1029	65–69
70–74	1898	771	1127	1973	815	1158	1960	806	1154	70–74
75–79	1272	432	840	1443	536	907	1499	567	932	75–79
80–84	749	225	524	815	244	571	920	303	517	80–84
85 +	477	119	358	511	122	389	556	132	424	85 +
All ages	51189	24954	26235	53036	25912	27124	55036	26951	28085	All ages

TABLE 5 OBSERVED AND PROJECTED VITAL RATES

Rates per thousand	Observed Total	Males	Females	Projected 1972 Males	Females	1977 Males	Females	1982 Males	Females	Stable Males	Females
Birth	16.90	17.77	16.07	19.09	17.31	19.82	18.04	19.86	18.16	19.53	18.04
Death	10.90	11.57	10.26	11.84	10.91	11.95	11.12	11.96	11.15	11.28	9.78
Increase	6.00	6.21	5.81	7.26	6.40	7.87	6.92	7.90	7.01		8.2530

TABLE 6 RATES STANDARDIZED ON THREE STANDARD COUNTRIES

Standardized rates per thousand	England and Wales, 1961 Total	Males	Females	United States, 1960 Total	Males	Females	Mexico, 1960 Total	Males	Females
Birth	16.73	17.69*	15.82	17.00	16.51*	16.35	20.07	15.67*	19.54
Death	10.73	11.85*	9.62	8.77	10.63*	7.04	4.51	9.02*	3.37
Increase	6.00	5.84*	6.20	8.24	5.88*	9.30	15.57	6.65*	16.17

TABLE 7 VITAL STATISTICS AND RATES INFERRED FROM AGE DISTRIBUTIONS (FEMALES)

Vital statistics		Thompson Age range	NRR	1000r	Interval	Bourgeois-Pichat Age range	NRR	1000b	1000d	1000r	Coale
TFR	2.64	0–4	1.23	7.48	27.43	5–29	1.66	20.33	1.55	18.78	1000b
GRR	1.29	5–9	1.29	9.47	27.40	30–54	1.40	20.74	8.25	12.50	1000d
NRR	1.25	10–14	1.34	10.58	27.35	55–79	1.19	19.23	12.65	6.58	1000r
Generation	27.16	15–19	1.36	10.85	27.27	*20–44	0.88	11.01	15.82	-4.81	$1000k_1$
Sex ratio	104.96										$1000k_2$

TABLE 8 LESLIE MATRIX AND ITS ANALYSIS (FEMALES)

Start of age interval	Sub-diagonal	First row	Percent in stable population	Fisher values	Total reproductive values	Net maternity function	Matrix equation coefficient	Parameters	Integral	Matrix
0	0.99716	0.00000	8.698	1.037	2156889	0.00000	0.00000	λ_1	1.0421	1.0422
5	0.99861	0.00012	8.322	1.084	2210479	0.00000	0.00012	λ_2	0.3423	0.3500
10	0.99806	0.04352	7.975	1.131	2287110	0.00025	0.04334		+0.7925	+0.7637i
15	0.99691	0.25235	7.637	1.136	2379673	0.08642	0.25079	r_1	0.0083	0.0083
20	0.99634	0.40327	7.305	0.925	1524777	0.41515	0.39955	r_2	-0.0294	-0.0348
25	0.99562	0.30877	6.984	0.548	763743	0.38393	0.30480		+0.2326	+0.2282i
30	0.99387	0.16963	6.672	0.252	391768	0.22567	0.15672	c_1		244354
35	0.99101	0.07038	6.363	0.087	144371	0.10776	0.06875	c_2		-131583
40	0.98651	0.01655	5.051	0.018	29243	0.02973	0.01603			223284i
45	0.97921	0.00124	5.727	0.001	1696	0.00232	0.00119	$2\pi/y$	27.011	27.532
50	0.97010	0.00003	5.381	0.000	37	0.00005	0.00003	Δ	4.955	
55	0.81403		22.884							

East Germany, 1967 (including East Berlin)

TABLE 1 DATA INPUT TO COMPUTATIONS

Age at last birthday	Population					Births, by age of mother	Deaths			Age at last birthday
	Total	Males	%	Females	%		Total	Males	Females	
0	260891	133565	1.7	127326	1.4	0	5400	3135	2265	0
1–4	1124401	576736	7.4	547665	5.9	0	1204	700	504	1–4
5–9	1374052	703776	9.0	670276	7.2	0	661	408	253	5–9
10–14	1307666	670437	8.6	637229	6.9	92	573	382	191	10–14
15–19	1135528	581923	7.4	553605	6.0	37652	839	597	242	15–19
20–24	938600	472495	6.0	466105	5.0	84528	1018	709	309	20–24
25–29	1352274	681001	8.7	671273	7.2	79227	1505	993	512	25–29
30–34	1156525	582595	7.5	573930	6.2	35225	1546	1006	540	30–34
35–39	1035070	505254	6.5	529816	5.7	13483	1899	1084	815	35–39
40–44	893862	360090	4.6	533772	5.8	2506	2368	1184	1184	40–44
45–49	804555	306309	3.9	498246	5.4	104	3172	1434	1738	45–49
50–54	827025	313310	4.0	513715	5.5	0	5411	2714	2697	50–54
55–59	1144667	453081	5.8	691586	7.5	0	11910	6386	5524	55–59
60–64	1156187	493054	6.3	663133	7.2	0	20807	12050	8757	60–64
65–69	993559	409425	5.2	584134	6.3	0	30049	16747	13302	65–69
70–74	722632	266110	3.4	456522	4.9		35234	16650	18584	70–74
75–79	485141	175832	2.2	309309	3.3		40240	16904	23336	75–79
80–84	255193	93531	1.2	161662	1.7	130015 M	35486	14573	20913	80–84
85+	114425	41536	0.5	72889	0.8	122802 F	27746	10885	16861	85+
All ages	17082253	7820060		9262193		252817	227068	108541	118527	All ages

TABLE 2 LIFE TABLE FOR MALES

Age, x	$_nq_x$	l_x	$_nd_x$	$_nL_x$	$_nm_x$	T_x	$1000r_x$	$\overset{\circ}{e}_x$	$_nM_x$	Age, x
0	0.02307	100000	2307	98295	0.02347	6845424	0.00	68.45	0.02347	0
1	0.00484	97693	473	389406	0.00121	6747129	0.00	69.06	0.00121	1
5	0.00289	97220	281	485398	0.00058	6357723	5.02	65.40	0.00058	5
10	0.00285	96939	277	484049	0.00057	5872325	18.34	60.58	0.00057	10
15	0.00515	96662	498	482160	0.00103	5388276	33.96	55.74	0.00103	15
20	0.00748	96165	719	479067	0.00150	4906116	0.00	51.02	0.00150	20
25	0.00726	95446	693	475516	0.00146	4427049	0.00	46.38	0.00146	25
30	0.00862	94752	817	471786	0.00173	3951533	28.11	41.70	0.00173	30
35	0.01075	93936	1010	467303	0.00216	3479747	45.81	37.04	0.00215	35
40	0.01644	92926	1527	461045	0.00331	3012444	46.75	32.42	0.00329	40
45	0.02321	91399	2121	452164	0.00469	2551399	8.72	27.91	0.00468	45
50	0.04247	89278	3791	437684	0.00865	2099236	0.00	23.51	0.00866	50
55	0.06925	85486	5835	413978	0.01409	1661551	0.00	19.44	0.01409	55
60	0.11585	79652	9228	376710	0.02450	1247064	10.54	15.66	0.02444	60
65	0.18657	70424	13139	320591	0.04098	870363	10.54	12.37	0.04090	65
70	0.27154	57285	15555	248170	0.06268	550273	10.54	9.61	0.06257	70
75	0.38762	41730	16175	167937	0.09632	302103	10.54	7.24	0.09614	75
80	0.55712	25555	14237	91168	0.15616	134166	10.54	5.25	0.15581	80
85+	*1.00000	11318	11318	42998	0.26321	42998	10.54	3.80	0.26206	85+

TABLE 3 LIFE TABLE FOR FEMALES

Age, x	$_nq_x$	l_x	$_nd_x$	$_nL_x$	$_nm_x$	T_x	$1000r_x$	$\overset{\circ}{e}_x$	$_nM_x$	Age, x
0	0.01756	100000	1756	98703	0.01779	7354873	0.00	73.55	0.01779	0
1	0.00367	98244	361	391935	0.00092	7256170	0.00	73.86	0.00092	1
5	0.00188	97883	184	488957	0.00038	6864235	5.25	70.13	0.00038	5
10	0.00150	97699	146	488136	0.00030	6375278	18.78	65.25	0.00030	10
15	0.00220	97553	214	487265	0.00044	5887142	30.82	60.35	0.00044	15
20	0.00331	97339	322	485920	0.00066	5399877	0.00	55.48	0.00066	20
25	0.00381	97017	369	484187	0.00076	4913957	0.00	50.65	0.00076	25
30	0.00471	96647	455	482174	0.00094	4429770	22.64	45.83	0.00094	30
35	0.00767	96192	738	479239	0.00154	3947596	5.72	41.04	0.00154	35
40	0.01104	95454	1054	474821	0.00222	3468357	3.81	36.34	0.00222	40
45	0.01730	94400	1633	468198	0.00349	2993536	0.27	31.71	0.00349	45
50	0.02593	92767	2406	458217	0.00525	2525339	0.00	27.22	0.00525	50
55	0.03921	90361	3543	443609	0.00799	2067122	0.00	22.88	0.00799	55
60	0.06436	86818	5587	421221	0.01326	1623512	19.72	18.70	0.01321	60
65	0.10864	81230	8825	385740	0.02288	1202292	19.72	14.80	0.02277	65
70	0.18661	72405	13511	330334	0.04090	816552	19.72	11.28	0.04071	70
75	0.31987	58894	18838	248623	0.07577	486218	19.72	8.26	0.07545	75
80	0.48702	40056	19508	150248	0.12984	237595	19.72	5.93	0.12936	80
85+	1.00000	20548	20548	87347	0.23524	87347	19.72	4.25	0.23132	85+

TABLE 4 POPULATION PROJECTION, USING FIXED AGE-SPECIFIC BIRTH AND DEATH RATES, IN THOUSANDS

Age at last birthday	1972 Total	1972 Males	1972 Females	1977 Total	1977 Males	1977 Females	1982 Total	1982 Males	1982 Females	Age at last birthday
0–4	1246	639	607	1296	665	631	1377	706	671	0–4
5–9	1380	707	673	1241	636	605	1290	661	629	5–9
10–14	1371	702	669	1377	705	672	1238	634	604	10–14
15–19	1304	668	636	1367	699	668	1372	702	670	15–19
20–24	1130	578	552	1298	664	634	1361	695	666	20–24
25–29	933	469	464	1124	574	550	1291	659	632	25–29
30–34	1344	676	668	928	465	463	1117	569	548	30–34
35–39	1147	577	570	1333	669	664	921	461	460	35–39
40–44	1023	498	525	1134	569	565	1318	660	658	40–44
45–49	879	353	526	1007	489	518	1115	558	557	45–49
50–54	785	297	488	857	342	515	980	473	507	50–54
55–59	793	296	497	752	280	472	822	323	499	55–59
60–64	1069	412	657	742	270	472	703	255	448	60–64
65–69	1027	420	607	952	351	601	661	229	432	65–69
70–74	817	317	500	845	325	520	787	272	515	70–74
75–79	524	180	344	590	214	376	611	220	391	75–79
80–84	282	95	187	306	98	208	344	116	228	80–84
85 +	138	44	94	154	45	109	167	46	121	85 +
All ages	17192	7928	9264	17303	8060	9243	17475	8239	9236	All ages

TABLE 5 OBSERVED AND PROJECTED VITAL RATES

Rates per thousand	Observed Total	Observed Males	Observed Females	Projected 1972 Males	Projected 1972 Females	Projected 1977 Males	Projected 1977 Females	Projected 1982 Males	Projected 1982 Females	Stable Males	Stable Females
Birth	14.80	16.63	13.26	16.63	13.44	17.45	14.37	18.07	15.23	16.32	15.28
Death	13.29	13.88	12.80	13.84	14.00	13.54	14.78	12.94	15.08	13.24	12.20
Increase	1.51	2.75	0.46	2.79	-0.55	3.91	-0.41	5.13	0.15	3.0804	

TABLE 6 RATES STANDARDIZED ON THREE STANDARD COUNTRIES

Standardized rates per thousand	England and Wales, 1961 Total	Males	Females	United States, 1960 Total	Males	Females	Mexico, 1960 Total	Males	Females
Birth	14.58	15.42*	13.73	14.87	14.71*	14.23	18.60	14.46*	18.03
Death	11.77	11.78*	11.76	9.51	10.85*	8.54	4.83	9.76*	4.00
Increase	2.81	3.64*	1.97	5.35	3.86*	5.69	13.77	4.70*	14.03

TABLE 7 VITAL STATISTICS AND RATES INFERRED FROM AGE DISTRIBUTIONS (FEMALES)

Vital statistics		Thompson Age range	NRR	1000r	Interval	Bourgeois-Pichat Age range	NRR	1000b	1000d	1000r	Coale
TFR	2.30	0–4	1.20	6.58	27.43	5–29	1.17	14.56	8.85	5.71	1000b
GRR	1.12	5–9	1.20	6.81	27.40	30–54	1.09	13.83	10.68	3.16	1000d
NRR	1.08	10–14	1.12	4.10	27.35	55–79	1.24	27.35	19.35	8.01	1000r
Generation	25.35	15–19	0.95	-1.73	27.27	*30–54	1.09	13.83	10.68	3.16	$1000k_1$
Sex ratio	105.87										$1000k_2$

TABLE 8 LESLIE MATRIX AND ITS ANALYSIS (FEMALES)

Start of age interval	Sub-diagonal	First row	Percent in stable population	Fisher values	Total reproductive values	Net maternity function	Matrix equation coefficient		Parameters Integral	Matrix
0	0.99657	0.00000	7.440	1.027	693182	0.00000	0.00000	λ_1	1.0155	1.0155
5	0.99832	0.00017	7.301	1.046	701432	0.00000	0.00017	λ_2	0.2544	0.2707
10	0.99822	0.08107	7.178	1.064	678227	0.00034	0.08066		+0.7753	+0.7420 i
15	0.99724	0.29654	7.055	0.999	553271	0.16097	0.29450	r_1	0.0031	0.0031
20	0.99643	0.35623	6.928	0.712	332027	0.42804	0.35281	r_2	-0.0407	-0.0472
25	0.99584	0.21347	6.798	0.359	240887	0.27758	0.21066		+0.2507	+0.2442 i
30	0.99391	0.10327	6.666	0.146	83683	0.14375	0.10149	c_1		85633
35	0.99078	0.03587	6.524	0.042	22396	0.05924	0.03503	c_2		88671
40	0.98605	0.00584	6.365	0.006	3282	0.01093	0.00565			85516 i
45	0.97868	0.00025	6.181	0.000	127	0.00047	0.00024	$2\pi/y$	25.059	25.731
50	0.96812	0.00000	5.956	0.000	0	0.00000	0.00000	Δ	6.845	
55	0.79032		25.605							

West Germany, 1967 (including West Berlin)

TABLE 1 DATA INPUT TO COMPUTATIONS

Age at last birthday	Population					Births, by age of mother	Deaths			Age at last birthday
	Total	Males	%	Females	%		Total	Males	Females	
0	1011194	517743	1.8	493451	1.6	0	23303	13480	9823	0
1–4	4083152	2091451	7.4	1991701	6.3	0	4095	2342	1753	1–4
5–9	4656731	2386263	8.4	2270468	7.2	0	2438	1539	899	5–9
10–14	4028522	2063082	7.3	1965440	6.2	40	1513	980	533	10–14
15–19	3928578	2015039	7.1	1913539	6.1	49248	3605	2630	975	15–19
20–24	3707126	1902327	6.7	1804799	5.7	257459	4195	3110	1085	20–24
25–29	4981987	2604663	9.2	2377324	7.6	359275	5769	4104	1665	25–29
30–34	4248538	2212374	7.8	2036164	6.5	225492	5800	3892	1908	30–34
35–39	3928322	2023133	7.1	1905189	6.1	93239	7572	4881	2691	35–39
40–44	3800857	1703080	6.0	2097777	6.7	31422	10586	5953	4633	40–44
45–49	3287019	1383418	4.9	1903601	6.1	3272	14135	7641	6494	45–49
50–54	3196967	1345589	4.7	1851378	5.9	12	22088	12499	9589	50–54
55–59	3912852	1674712	5.9	2238140	7.1	0	43582	25244	17338	55–59
60–64	3631381	1599405	5.6	2031976	6.5	0	67997	41674	26323	60–64
65–69	2973623	1246682	4.4	1726941	5.5	0	91434	53136	38298	65–69
70–74	2088121	767812	2.7	1320309	4.2		100388	49115	51773	70–74
75–79	1354434	489763	1.7	864671	2.7		107622	47327	60295	75–79
80–84	711068	261004	0.9	450064	1.4	523634 M	93499	38930	54569	80–84
85+	342345	125020	0.4	217325	0.7	495825 F	77228	31040	46188	85+
All ages	59872817	28412560		31460257		1019459	687349	350517	336832	All ages

TABLE 2 LIFE TABLE FOR MALES

Age, x	$_nq_x$	l_x	$_nd_x$	$_nL_x$	$_nm_x$	T_x	$1000r_x$	$\overset{\circ}{e}_x$	$_nM_x$	Age, x
0	0.02553	100000	2553	98062	0.02604	6771402	0.00	67.71	0.02504	0
1	0.00446	97447	435	388524	0.00112	6673340	0.00	68.48	0.00112	1
5	0.00321	97012	311	484281	0.00064	6284817	22.74	64.78	0.00064	5
10	0.00238	96701	231	482993	0.00048	5800536	16.21	59.98	0.00048	10
15	0.00651	96470	628	480894	0.00131	5317542	6.92	55.12	0.00131	15
20	0.00814	95842	780	477282	0.00163	4836648	0.00	50.45	0.00163	20
25	0.00785	95061	745	473452	0.00158	4359365	0.00	45.86	0.00158	25
30	0.00878	94315	828	469586	0.00176	3885913	23.42	41.20	0.00176	30
35	0.01204	93487	1125	464787	0.00242	3416327	23.68	36.54	0.00241	35
40	0.01745	92362	1611	458065	0.00352	2951540	34.34	31.96	0.00350	40
45	0.02737	90751	2484	448044	0.00554	2493475	17.73	27.48	0.00552	45
50	0.04547	88267	4014	432109	0.00929	2045430	0.00	23.17	0.00929	50
55	0.07561	84253	6370	406501	0.01567	1613321	0.00	19.15	0.01567	55
60	0.12313	77883	9590	366868	0.02614	1206820	15.75	15.50	0.02606	60
65	0.19374	68293	13231	309555	0.04274	839952	15.75	12.30	0.04262	65
70	0.27682	55062	15242	237675	0.06413	530388	15.75	9.63	0.06397	70
75	0.38908	39820	15493	159909	0.09689	292713	15.75	7.35	0.09663	75
80	0.53664	24326	13055	87296	0.14954	132803	15.75	5.46	0.14915	80
85+	1.00000	11272	11272	45507	0.24769	45507	15.75	4.04	0.24828	85+

TABLE 3 LIFE TABLE FOR FEMALES

Age, x	$_nq_x$	l_x	$_nd_x$	$_nL_x$	$_nm_x$	T_x	$1000r_x$	$\overset{\circ}{e}_x$	$_nM_x$	Age, x
0	0.01961	100000	1961	98518	0.01991	7383623	0.00	73.84	0.01991	0
1	0.00351	98039	344	391156	0.00088	7285105	0.00	74.31	0.00088	1
5	0.00197	97695	192	487993	0.00039	6893949	22.95	70.57	0.00040	5
10	0.00136	97503	132	487194	0.00027	6405957	16.75	65.70	0.00027	10
15	0.00255	97370	248	486254	0.00051	5918763	8.06	60.79	0.00051	15
20	0.00300	97122	292	484901	0.00060	5432499	0.00	55.93	0.00060	20
25	0.00350	96831	339	483341	0.00070	4947598	0.00	51.10	0.00070	25
30	0.00469	96492	453	481400	0.00094	4464258	21.16	46.27	0.00094	30
35	0.00704	96040	675	478632	0.00141	3982858	0.00	41.47	0.00141	35
40	0.01099	95363	1048	474390	0.00221	3504226	0.00	36.75	0.00221	40
45	0.01695	94316	1599	467858	0.00342	3029836	8.99	32.12	0.00341	45
50	0.02559	92717	2372	458038	0.00518	2561978	0.00	27.63	0.00518	50
55	0.03805	90345	3438	443781	0.00775	2103940	0.00	23.29	0.00775	55
60	0.06329	86907	5500	421858	0.01304	1560159	28.49	19.10	0.01295	60
65	0.10613	81407	8640	387025	0.02232	1238291	28.49	15.21	0.02218	65
70	0.18058	72767	13140	332937	0.03947	851266	28.49	11.70	0.03921	70
75	0.29982	59627	17877	254788	0.07016	518359	28.49	8.69	0.06973	75
80	0.46967	41750	19609	160615	0.12209	263571	28.49	6.31	0.12125	80
85+	*1.00000	22141	22141	102956	0.21505	102956	28.49	4.65	0.21253	85+

[438]

TABLE 4 POPULATION PROJECTION, USING FIXED AGE-SPECIFIC BIRTH AND DEATH RATES, IN THOUSANDS

Age at last birthday	1972 Total	Males	Females	1977 Total	Males	Females	1982 Total	Males	Females	Age at last birthday
0–4	4898	2508	2390	4782	2449	2333	4849	2483	2366	0–4
5–9	5074	2597	2477	4878	2496	2382	4762	2437	2325	5–9
10–14	4647	2380	2267	5063	2590	2473	4868	2490	2378	10–14
15–19	4016	2054	1962	4632	2370	2262	5047	2579	2468	15–19
20–24	3908	2000	1908	3995	2039	1956	4608	2352	2256	20–24
25–29	3686	1887	1799	3886	1984	1902	3972	2022	1950	25–29
30–34	4951	2583	2368	3664	1872	1792	3862	1968	1894	30–34
35–39	4214	2190	2024	4911	2557	2354	3634	1853	1781	35–39
40–44	3882	1994	1888	4165	2158	2007	4853	2520	2333	40–44
45–49	3735	1666	2069	3812	1950	1862	4090	2111	1979	45–49
50–54	3198	1334	1864	3532	1607	2025	3704	1881	1823	50–54
55–59	3060	1266	1794	3061	1255	1806	3473	1511	1962	55–59
60–64	3639	1511	2128	2847	1142	1705	2849	1133	1716	60–64
65–69	3214	1350	1864	3227	1275	1952	2528	964	1564	65–69
70–74	2442	957	1485	2639	1036	1603	2658	979	1679	70–74
75–79	1527	517	1010	1781	644	1137	1924	697	1227	75–79
80–84	812	267	545	919	282	637	1069	352	717	80–84
85 +	424	136	288	488	139	349	555	147	408	85 +
All ages	61327	29197	32130	62382	29845	32537	63305	30479	32826	All ages

TABLE 5 OBSERVED AND PROJECTED VITAL RATES

Rates per thousand	Observed Total	Males	Females	Projected 1972 Males	Females	1977 Males	Females	1982 Males	Females	Stable Males	Females
Birth	17.03	18.43	15.76	17.38	14.95	16.72	14.52	17.11	15.04	17.87	15.50
Death	11.48	12.34	10.71	12.57	11.86	12.70	12.77	12.71	13.39	12.45	11.18
Increase	5.55	6.09	5.05	4.81	3.09	4.03	1.76	4.40	1.65		5.4251

TABLE 6 RATES STANDARDIZED ON THREE STANDARD COUNTRIES

Standardized rates per thousand	England and Wales, 1961 Total	Males	Females	United States, 1960 Total	Males	Females	Mexico, 1960 Total	Males	Females
Birth	15.74	15.87*	14.83	16.01	15.13*	15.34	18.30	14.62*	17.75
Death	11.65	12.16*	11.19	9.49	10.93*	8.17	4.92	9.35*	3.91
Increase	4.08	3.71*	3.65	6.52	4.20*	7.17	13.39	5.27*	13.84

TABLE 7 VITAL STATISTICS AND RATES INFERRED FROM AGE DISTRIBUTIONS (FEMALES)

Vital statistics		Thompson Age range	NRR	1000r	Interval	Bourgeois-Pichat Age range	NRR	1000b	1000d	1000r	Coale	
TFR	2.48	0–4	1.21	6.96	27.43	5–29	0.98	13.30	13.91	-0.61	1000b	16.60
GRR	1.21	5–9	1.10	3.54	27.40	30–54	1.04	13.97	12.59	1.38	1000d	7.10
NRR	1.16	10–14	0.94	-2.17	27.35	55–79	1.54	40.81	24.86	15.95	1000r	9.50
Generation	28.04	15–19	0.92	-3.21	27.27	*30–54	1.04	13.97	12.59	1.38	$1000k_1$	41.48
Sex ratio	105.6										$1000k_2$	0.51

TABLE 8 LESLIE MATRIX AND ITS ANALYSIS (FEMALES)

Start of age interval	Sub-diagonal	First row	Percent in stable population	Fisher values	Total reproductive values	Net maternity function	Matrix equation coefficient	Parameters		Integral	Matrix
0	0.99657	0.00000	8.020	1.035	2572149	0.00000	0.00000	λ_1		1.0275	1.0275
5	0.99836	0.00002	7.779	1.067	2422917	0.00000	0.00002	λ_2		0.3833	0.3881
10	0.99809	0.03061	7.558	1.098	2158603	0.00005	0.03046			+0.7750	+0.7505i
15	0.99720	0.20004	7.341	1.099	2102804	0.06087	0.19865	r_1		0.0054	0.0054
20	0.99678	0.34925	7.125	0.925	1668887	0.33643	0.34585	r_2		-0.0291	-0.0337
25	0.99598	0.31130	6.912	0.591	1403962	0.35526	0.30728			+0.2223	+0.2187i
30	0.99425	0.18981	6.700	0.286	581852	0.25929	0.18661	c_1			283728
35	0.99114	0.07595	6.483	0.098	186185	0.11393	0.07424	c_2			455955
40	0.98623	0.01985	6.253	0.022	46141	0.03455	0.01924				-137325i
45	0.97901	0.00205	6.002	0.002	3956	0.00391	0.00196				
50	0.96887	0.00001	5.719	0.000	12	0.00001	0.00001	$2\pi/y$	28.265		28.730
55	0.79769		24.109					Δ	5.967		

Greece, 1966-68

TABLE 1   DATA INPUT TO COMPUTATIONS

Age at last birthday	Population Total	Males	%	Females	%	Births, by age of mother	Deaths Total	Males	Females	Age at last birthday
0	160041	82815	2.0	77226	1.7	0	5457	2993	2464	0
1–4	586182	302040	7.1	284142	6.4	0	680	366	314	1–4
5–9	735308	377717	8.9	357591	8.0	0	331	199	132	5–9
10–14	719712	369997	8.7	349715	7.8	43	274	176	98	10–14
15–19	706338	361451	8.5	344887	7.7	10589	403	273	130	15–19
20–24	669243	338187	8.0	331056	7.4	42856	536	377	159	20–24
25–29	623544	302533	7.1	321011	7.2	50589	558	345	213	25–29
30–34	674391	312844	7.4	361547	8.1	36179	678	398	280	30–34
35–39	671613	317123	7.5	354490	7.9	15578	868	483	385	35–39
40–44	566412	267813	6.3	298599	6.7	3015	1108	647	461	40–44
45–49	445247	210352	5.0	234895	5.3	276	1421	831	590	45–49
50–54	479581	228468	5.4	251113	5.6	39	2444	1494	950	50–54
55–59	460786	222695	5.2	238091	5.3	0	3886	2409	1477	55–59
60–64	398125	192121	4.5	206004	4.6	0	5485	3372	2113	60–64
65–69	309860	141180	3.3	168680	3.8	0	7344	4108	3236	65–69
70–74	217034	93886	2.2	123148	2.8		8221	4158	4053	70–74
75–79	157226	65407	1.5	91819	2.1		9982	4518	5464	75–79
80–84	88066	37797	0.9	50269	1.1	82235 M	9537	4310	5227	80–84
85 +	47732	18563	0.4	29169	0.7	77029 F	11853	4941	6912	85 +
All ages	8716441	4242989		4473452		159264	71066	36408	34658	All ages

TABLE 2   LIFE TABLE FOR MALES

Age, x	$_nq_x$	l_x	$_nd_x$	$_nL_x$	$_nm_x$	T_x	$1000r_x$	$\overset{\circ}{e}_x$	$_nM_x$	Age, x
0	0.03492	100000	3492	97254	0.03591	7064536	8.11	70.65	0.03614	0
1	0.00477	96508	460	384687	0.00120	6967282	8.11	72.19	0.00121	1
5	0.00263	96048	252	479608	0.00053	6582595	3.21	68.53	0.00053	5
10	0.00238	95795	228	478430	0.00048	6102988	3.86	63.71	0.00048	10
15	0.00378	95568	361	476999	0.00076	5624558	8.22	58.85	0.00076	15
20	0.00557	95207	530	474747	0.00112	5147558	16.75	54.07	0.00111	20
25	0.00569	94677	538	472053	0.00114	4672812	6.62	49.35	0.00114	25
30	0.00634	94139	597	469237	0.00127	4200759	0.00	44.62	0.00127	30
35	0.00760	93542	711	466039	0.00153	3731522	13.89	39.89	0.00152	35
40	0.01211	92830	1124	461568	0.00244	3265483	38.52	35.18	0.00242	40
45	0.01962	91706	1800	454401	0.00396	2803915	11.76	30.57	0.00395	45
50	0.03221	89907	2896	442875	0.00654	2349514	0.00	26.13	0.00654	50
55	0.05283	87011	4597	424412	0.01083	1906638	6.09	21.91	0.01082	55
60	0.08477	82414	6987	395792	0.01765	1482226	27.37	17.99	0.01755	60
65	0.13672	75427	10313	352629	0.02924	1086434	27.37	14.40	0.02910	65
70	0.20131	65114	13108	293867	0.04461	733804	27.37	11.27	0.04439	70
75	0.29659	52006	15424	222159	0.06943	439938	27.37	8.46	0.06908	75
80	0.44869	36582	16414	142863	0.11489	217779	27.37	5.95	0.11403	80
85 +	*1.00000	20168	20168	74916	0.26921	74916	27.37	3.71	0.26617	85 +

TABLE 3   LIFE TABLE FOR FEMALES

Age, x	$_nq_x$	l_x	$_nd_x$	$_nL_x$	$_nm_x$	T_x	$1000r_x$	$\overset{\circ}{e}_x$	$_nM_x$	Age, x
0	0.03095	100000	3095	97578	0.03172	7449622	7.35	74.50	0.03191	0
1	0.00435	96905	422	386387	0.00109	7352044	7.35	75.87	0.00111	1
5	0.00184	96483	178	481970	0.00037	6965658	2.70	72.20	0.00037	5
10	0.00140	96305	135	481189	0.00028	6483688	3.29	67.32	0.00028	10
15	0.00188	96170	181	480418	0.00038	6002498	5.11	62.42	0.00038	15
20	0.00240	95989	230	479398	0.00048	5522080	6.68	57.53	0.00048	20
25	0.00331	95759	317	478029	0.00066	5042682	0.00	52.66	0.00065	25
30	0.00387	95441	369	476327	0.00077	4564653	0.00	47.83	0.00077	30
35	0.00543	95073	516	474148	0.00109	4088326	18.02	43.00	0.00109	35
40	0.00775	94556	733	471086	0.00156	3614178	39.50	38.22	0.00154	40
45	0.01252	93823	1175	466390	0.00252	3143092	14.77	33.50	0.00251	45
50	0.01875	92649	1737	459237	0.00378	2676702	0.00	28.89	0.00378	50
55	0.03067	90911	2788	448151	0.00622	2217465	13.35	24.39	0.00620	55
60	0.05046	88123	4446	430531	0.01033	1769314	26.84	20.08	0.01025	60
65	0.09242	83677	7733	400557	0.01931	1338783	26.84	16.00	0.01918	65
70	0.15369	75944	11672	352432	0.03312	938226	26.84	12.35	0.03291	70
75	0.26175	64272	16823	281012	0.05987	585794	26.84	9.11	0.05951	75
80	0.41915	47449	19888	189761	0.10481	304782	26.84	6.42	0.10398	80
85 +	*1.00000	27561	27561	115022	0.23961	115022	26.84	4.17	0.23696	85 +

TABLE 4 POPULATION PROJECTION, USING FIXED AGE-SPECIFIC BIRTH AND DEATH RATES, IN THOUSANDS

Age at last birthday	1972 Total	1972 Males	1972 Females	1977 Total	1977 Males	1977 Females	1982 Total	1982 Males	1982 Females	Age at last birthday
0–4	769	396	373	774	399	375	786	405	381	0–4
5–9	743	383	360	765	394	371	771	397	374	5–9
10–14	734	377	357	741	382	359	764	393	371	10–14
15–19	718	369	349	732	376	356	740	381	359	15–19
20–24	704	360	344	715	367	348	730	374	356	20–24
25–29	666	336	330	701	358	343	712	365	347	25–29
30–34	621	301	320	663	334	329	698	356	342	30–34
35–39	671	311	360	617	299	318	659	332	327	35–39
40–44	666	314	352	666	308	358	612	296	316	40–44
45–49	560	264	296	658	309	349	557	303	354	45–49
50–54	436	205	231	548	257	291	644	301	343	50–54
55–59	464	219	245	422	196	226	530	246	284	55–59
60–64	437	208	229	439	204	235	400	183	217	60–64
65–69	363	171	192	398	185	213	401	182	219	65–69
70–74	266	118	148	312	143	169	341	154	187	70–74
75–79	169	71	98	207	89	118	242	108	134	75–79
80–84	104	42	62	112	46	66	137	57	80	80–84
85 +	50	20	30	60	22	38	64	24	40	85 +
All ages	9141	4465	4676	9530	4668	4862	9888	4857	5031	All ages

TABLE 5 OBSERVED AND PROJECTED VITAL RATES

Rates per thousand	Observed Total	Observed Males	Observed Females	Projected 1972 Males	Projected 1972 Females	Projected 1977 Males	Projected 1977 Females	Projected 1982 Males	Projected 1982 Females	Stable Males	Stable Females
Birth	18.27	19.38	17.22	18.42	16.47	17.84	16.04	17.46	15.79	15.98	15.22
Death	8.15	8.58	7.75	8.98	8.20	9.46	8.86	9.93	9.38	12.73	11.93
Increase	10.12	10.80	9.47	9.44	8.26	8.38	7.18	7.52	6.41		3.2413

TABLE 6 RATES STANDARDIZED ON THREE STANDARD COUNTRIES

Standardized rates per thousand	England and Wales, 1961 Total	Males	Females	United States, 1960 Total	Males	Females	Mexico, 1960 Total	Males	Females
Birth	15.01	17.66*	14.07	15.29	16.50*	14.57	17.68	16.00*	17.05
Death	9.71	9.45*	10.11	8.00	8.41*	7.54	4.41	6.89*	3.87
Increase	5.30	8.21*	3.96	7.28	8.08*	7.02	13.27	9.11*	13.18

TABLE 7 VITAL STATISTICS AND RATES INFERRED FROM AGE DISTRIBUTIONS (FEMALES)

Vital statistics		Thompson Age range	NRR	1000r	Interval	Bourgeois-Pichat Age range	NRR	1000b	1000d	1000r	Coale
TFR	2.37	0–4	1.06	2.18	27.45	5–29	1.14	17.31	12.30	5.01	1000b
GRR	1.15	5–9	1.11	3.82	27.42	30–54	1.76	34.39	13.38	21.02	1000d
NRR	1.09	10–14	1.13	4.36	27.39	55–79	2.11	59.48	31.79	27.69	1000r
Generation	27.76	15–19	1.15	5.16	27.33	*5–29	1.14	17.31	12.30	5.01	$1000k_1$
Sex ratio	106.76										$1000k_2$

TABLE 8 LESLIE MATRIX AND ITS ANALYSIS (FEMALES)

Start of age interval	Sub-diagonal	First row	Percent in stable population	Fisher values	Total reproductive values	Net maternity function	Matrix equation coefficient	Parameters Integral	Parameters Matrix
0	0.99588	0.00000	7.307	1.042	376374	0.00000	0.00000	λ_1 1.0163	1.0163
5	0.99838	0.00014	7.160	1.063	380095	0.00000	0.00014	λ_2 0.3775	0.3817
10	0.99840	0.03602	7.033	1.082	378360	0.00029	0.03581	+0.7769	+0.7521i
15	0.99787	0.18712	6.909	1.064	366883	0.07134	0.18575	r_1 0.0032	0.0032
20	0.99714	0.33578	6.784	0.888	294033	0.30015	0.33262	r_2 −0.0293	−0.0340
25	0.99644	0.30150	6.655	0.555	178013	0.36508	0.29781	+0.2237	+0.2202i
30	0.99543	0.16831	6.525	0.250	90558	0.23053	0.16555	c_1	49769
35	0.99354	0.06317	6.391	0.080	28227	0.10078	0.06189	c_2	2095
40	0.99003	0.01318	6.247	0.015	4549	0.02301	0.01283		−2765i
45	0.98466	0.00155	6.086	0.002	417	0.00265	0.00150	$2\pi/y$ 28.088	28.531
50	0.97586	0.00018	5.896	0.000	47	0.00034	0.00017	Δ 7.846	
55	0.80330		27.007						

Hungary, 1967

TABLE 1   DATA INPUT TO COMPUTATIONS

Age at last birthday	Population					Births, by age of mother	Deaths			Age at last birthday
	Total	Males	%	Females	%		Total	Males	Females	
0	136469	70941	1.4	65528	1.2	0	5508	3146	2362	0
1–4	501018	257129	5.2	243889	4.6	0	592	332	260	1–4
5–9	697398	358018	7.2	339380	6.4	0	281	169	112	5–9
10–14	942436	482387	9.8	460049	8.7	115	343	225	118	10–14
15–19	862359	438231	8.9	424128	8.0	21089	623	439	184	15–19
20–24	742275	374361	7.6	367914	7.0	59598	782	569	213	20–24
25–29	699501	344873	7.0	354528	6.7	40155	779	523	255	25–29
30–34	684390	331560	6.7	352830	6.7	18655	1006	666	340	30–34
35–39	727451	356276	7.2	371175	7.0	7373	1393	911	482	35–39
40–44	747391	358076	7.3	389315	7.4	1895	2200	1338	862	40–44
45–49	602892	282665	5.7	320227	6.1	6	2685	1530	1155	45–49
50–54	555035	257816	5.2	297219	5.6	0	3770	2222	1548	50–54
55–59	653889	306560	6.2	347329	6.6	0	7242	4432	2810	55–59
60–64	547376	253912	5.1	293464	5.6	0	10273	5242	4031	60–64
65–69	459142	207263	4.2	251879	4.8	0	14336	8139	6197	65–69
70–74	320728	128891	2.6	191837	3.6		16659	8238	8421	70–74
75–79	189463	74547	1.5	114916	2.2		16343	7301	9042	75–79
80–84	103451	39343	0.8	64108	1.2	76910 M	14673	6168	8505	80–84
85 +	42188	15973	0.3	26215	0.5	71976 F	10042	3888	6154	85 +
All ages	10214852	4938822		5276030		148886	109530	56478	53052	All ages

TABLE 2   LIFE TABLE FOR MALES

Age, x	$_nq_x$	l_x	$_nd_x$	$_nL_x$	$_nm_x$	T_x	$1000r_x$	$\overset{\circ}{e}_x$	$_nM_x$	Age, x
0	0.04254	100000	4254	96593	0.04404	6686354	8.60	66.86	0.04435	0
1	0.00506	95746	485	381562	0.00127	6589751	8.60	68.83	0.00129	1
5	0.00236	95261	225	475744	0.00047	6208199	0.00	65.17	0.00047	5
10	0.00233	95037	221	474682	0.00047	5732455	0.00	60.32	0.00047	10
15	0.00502	94815	476	472988	0.00101	5257774	24.35	55.45	0.00100	15
20	0.00758	94339	715	469954	0.00152	4784786	22.55	50.72	0.00152	20
25	0.00756	93623	708	466392	0.00152	4314832	10.51	46.09	0.00152	25
30	0.01000	92916	929	462352	0.00201	3848441	0.00	41.42	0.00201	30
35	0.01271	91987	1169	457170	0.00256	3386089	0.00	36.81	0.00255	35
40	0.01858	90818	1687	450127	0.00375	2928919	19.33	32.25	0.00374	40
45	0.02686	89131	2394	440081	0.00544	2478792	27.16	27.81	0.00541	45
50	0.04225	86737	3665	425233	0.00862	2038712	0.00	23.50	0.00862	50
55	0.06995	83072	5811	401947	0.01446	1613479	0.00	19.42	0.01445	55
60	0.11673	77261	9018	365110	0.02470	1211532	23.61	15.68	0.02458	60
65	0.18025	68242	12300	311813	0.03945	846422	23.61	12.40	0.03927	65
70	0.27729	55942	15512	241684	0.06418	534609	23.61	9.55	0.06391	70
75	0.39396	40430	15928	161956	0.09835	292925	23.61	7.25	0.09794	75
80	0.56015	24502	13725	87124	0.15753	130968	23.61	5.35	0.15678	80
85 +	*1.00000	10777	10777	43844	0.24581	43844	23.61	4.07	0.24341	85 +

TABLE 3   LIFE TABLE FOR FEMALES

Age, x	$_nq_x$	l_x	$_nd_x$	$_nL_x$	$_nm_x$	T_x	$1000r_x$	$\overset{\circ}{e}_x$	$_nM_x$	Age, x
0	0.03487	100000	3487	97215	0.03587	7194774	6.17	71.95	0.03605	0
1	0.00420	96513	405	384864	0.00105	7097559	6.17	73.54	0.00107	1
5	0.00165	96108	158	480142	0.00033	6712695	0.00	69.85	0.00033	5
10	0.00128	95949	123	479449	0.00026	6232553	0.00	64.96	0.00025	10
15	0.00217	95826	208	478642	0.00044	5753105	21.93	60.04	0.00043	15
20	0.00290	95618	277	477425	0.00058	5274463	17.32	55.16	0.00058	20
25	0.00360	95341	344	475883	0.00072	4797038	3.45	50.31	0.00072	25
30	0.00481	94997	457	473900	0.00096	4321155	0.00	45.49	0.00095	30
35	0.00647	94541	612	471294	0.00130	3847255	0.00	40.69	0.00130	35
40	0.01104	93929	1037	467259	0.00222	3375961	12.46	35.94	0.00221	40
45	0.01795	92891	1668	460559	0.00362	2908692	23.37	31.31	0.00361	45
50	0.02573	91223	2347	450637	0.00521	2448133	0.00	26.84	0.00521	50
55	0.03971	88876	3529	436260	0.00809	1997496	0.00	22.48	0.00809	55
60	0.06698	85347	5715	413650	0.01382	1561236	24.85	18.29	0.01374	60
65	0.11705	79631	9321	376589	0.02475	1147586	24.85	14.41	0.02460	65
70	0.19990	70310	14055	318354	0.04415	770997	24.85	10.97	0.04390	70
75	0.33131	56255	18638	235640	0.07909	452643	24.85	8.05	0.07868	75
80	0.49608	37617	18661	140026	0.13327	217004	24.85	5.77	0.13267	80
85 +	1.00000	18956	18956	76977	0.24625	76977	24.85	4.06	0.23475	85 +

TABLE 4

TABLE 4 POPULATION PROJECTION, USING FIXED AGE-SPECIFIC BIRTH AND DEATH RATES, IN THOUSANDS

Age at last birthday	1972			1977			1982			Age at last birthday
	Total	Males	Females	Total	Males	Females	Total	Males	Females	
0–4	742	382	360	785	404	381	768	395	373	0–4
5–9	634	326	308	739	380	359	782	402	380	5–9
10–14	696	357	339	634	326	308	737	379	358	10–14
15–19	940	481	459	694	356	338	632	325	307	15–19
20–24	858	435	423	936	478	458	591	354	337	20–24
25–29	739	372	367	854	432	422	931	474	457	25–29
30–34	695	342	353	733	368	365	848	428	420	30–34
35–39	679	328	351	689	338	351	727	364	363	35–39
40–44	719	351	368	671	323	348	681	333	348	40–44
45–49	734	350	384	706	343	363	659	316	343	45–49
50–54	586	273	313	713	338	375	686	331	355	50–54
55–59	532	244	288	561	258	303	683	320	363	55–59
60–64	607	278	329	494	221	273	523	235	288	60–64
65–69	484	217	267	538	238	300	437	189	248	65–69
70–74	374	161	213	394	168	226	437	184	253	70–74
75–79	228	86	142	266	108	158	280	113	167	75–79
80–84	108	40	68	130	46	84	152	58	94	80–84
85 +	55	20	35	58	20	38	69	23	46	85 +
All ages	10410	5043	5367	10595	5145	5450	10723	5223	5500	All ages

TABLE 5 OBSERVED AND PROJECTED VITAL RATES

Rates per thousand	Observed			Projected						Stable	
				1972		1977		1982			
	Total	Males	Females	Males	Females	Males	Females	Males	Females	Males	Females
Birth	14.58	15.57	13.64	16.43	14.45	16.75	14.80	15.12	13.43	13.40	12.38
Death	10.72	11.44	10.06	12.27	11.15	12.81	11.91	13.24	12.61	16.34	15.32
Increase	3.85	4.14	3.59	4.16	3.30	3.94	2.89	1.88	0.82		-2.9432

TABLE 6 RATES STANDARDIZED ON THREE STANDARD COUNTRIES

Standardized rates per thousand	England and Wales, 1961			United States, 1960			Mexico, 1960		
	Total	Males	Females	Total	Males	Females	Total	Males	Females
Birth	12.74	14.67*	11.94	12.97	13.69*	12.35	16.22	13.07*	15.64
Death	12.36	12.18*	12.47	10.14	10.80*	9.23	5.56	9.52*	4.68
Increase	0.38	2.50*	-0.53	2.83	2.89*	3.12	10.65	3.55*	10.95

TABLE 7 VITAL STATISTICS AND RATES INFERRED FROM AGE DISTRIBUTIONS (FEMALES)

Vital statistics		Thompson				Bourgeois-Pichat					Coale
		Age range	NRR	$1000r$	Interval	Age range	NRR	$1000b$	$1000d$	$1000r$	$1000b$
TFR	2.01	0–4	0.81	-7.70	27.44	5–29	1.06	15.94	13.67	2.27	$1000d$
GRR	0.97	5–9	0.93	-2.78	27.40	30–54	1.22	19.20	11.86	7.34	$1000r$
NRR	0.93	10–14	1.29	9.19	27.35	55–79	1.62	41.89	24.00	17.89	$1000k_1$
Generation	25.60	15–19	1.18	5.86	27.27	*20–44	0.89	12.81	17.04	-4.23	$1000k_2$
Sex ratio	106.86										

TABLE 8 LESLIE MATRIX AND ITS ANALYSIS (FEMALES)

Start of age interval	Sub-diagonal	First row	Percent in stable population	Fisher values	Total reproductive values	Net maternity function	Matrix equation coefficient	Parameters	Integral	Matrix
0	0.99598	0.00000	6.012	1.030	318570	0.00000	0.00000	λ_1	0.9854	0.9854
5	0.99856	0.00029	6.076	1.019	345706	0.00000	0.00029	λ_2	0.2650	0.2783
10	0.99832	0.05813	6.158	1.005	462312	0.00058	0.05782		+0.7690	+0.7365i
15	0.99746	0.24622	6.238	0.932	395269	0.11505	0.24446	r_1	-0.0029	-0.0029
20	0.99677	0.32028	6.315	0.667	245229	0.37387	0.31718	r_2	-0.0413	-0.0478
25	0.99583	0.19330	6.388	0.328	116359	0.26050	0.19081		+0.2478	+0.2419i
30	0.99450	0.08463	6.455	0.125	44043	0.12113	0.08319	c_1		61172
35	0.99146	0.02877	6.515	0.035	13387	0.04526	0.02813	c_2		-120954
40	0.98564	0.00569	6.555	0.006	2324	0.01100	0.00552			25027i
45	0.97846	0.00002	6.557	0.000	8	0.00004	0.00002	$2\pi/y$	25.358	25.974
50	0.96810	0.00000	6.510	0.000	2	0.00000	0.00000	Δ	7.512	
55	0.77684		30.221							

Iceland, 1965

TABLE 1 DATA INPUT TO COMPUTATIONS

Age at last birthday	Population					Births, by age of mother	Deaths			Age at last birthday
	Total	Males	%	Females	%		Total	Males	Females	
0	4708	2383	2.5	2325	2.4	0	71	36	35	0
1–4	18604	9489	9.8	9115	9.6	0	26	15	11	1–4
5–9	22793	11730	12.1	11063	11.6	0	4	3	1	5–9
10–14	20304	10438	10.7	9866	10.4	0	4	3	1	10–14
15–19	17806	9189	9.5	8617	9.1	747	18	17	1	15–19
20–24	14133	7148	7.4	6985	7.3	1500	13	10	3	20–24
25–29	11339	5800	6.0	5539	5.8	990	14	11	3	25–29
30–34	11792	6011	6.2	5781	6.1	773	21	11	10	30–34
35–39	11572	5906	6.1	5666	6.0	516	20	13	7	35–39
40–44	10719	5479	5.6	5240	5.5	180	26	17	9	40–44
45–49	9418	4778	4.9	4640	4.9	14	42	32	10	45–49
50–54	8615	4282	4.4	4333	4.6	1	53	25	28	50–54
55–59	7629	3824	3.9	3805	4.0	0	82	57	25	55–59
60–64	6692	3323	3.4	3369	3.5	0	89	64	25	60–64
65–69	5806	2765	2.8	3041	3.2	0	122	71	51	65–69
70–74	4809	2262	2.3	2547	2.7		156	74	82	70–74
75–79	2968	1343	1.4	1625	1.7		157	83	74	75–79
80–84	1597	655	0.7	942	1.0	2344 M	159	77	82	80–84
85 +	1036	379	0.4	657	0.7	2377 F	214	74	140	85 +
All ages	192340	97184		95156		4721	1291	693	598	All ages

TABLE 2 LIFE TABLE FOR MALES

Age, x	$_nq_x$	l_x	$_nd_x$	$_nL_x$	$_nm_x$	T_x	$1000r_x$	$\mathring{e}_x$	$_nM_x$	Age, x
0	0.01496	100000	1496	99010	0.01511	7140924	0.00	71.41	0.01511	0
1	0.00630	98504	620	392281	0.00158	7041914	0.00	71.49	0.00158	1
5	0.00126	97884	124	489111	0.00025	6649633	12.32	67.93	0.00026	5
10	0.00148	97760	144	488603	0.00030	6160522	23.76	63.02	0.00029	10
15	0.00925	97616	903	485933	0.00186	5671919	36.48	58.10	0.00185	15
20	0.00697	96713	674	481880	0.00140	5185986	44.36	53.62	0.00140	20
25	0.00945	96039	907	477955	0.00190	4704106	15.57	48.98	0.00190	25
30	0.00911	95131	867	473517	0.00183	4226141	0.00	44.42	0.00183	30
35	0.01096	94265	1033	468863	0.00220	3752524	7.01	39.81	0.00220	35
40	0.01549	93232	1444	462966	0.00312	3283761	17.44	35.22	0.00310	40
45	0.03301	91788	3030	451600	0.00671	2820794	19.12	30.73	0.00670	45
50	0.02893	88758	2567	438038	0.00586	2369194	14.16	26.69	0.00584	50
55	0.07217	86191	6221	416407	0.01494	1931156	11.65	22.41	0.01491	55
60	0.09233	79970	7384	381929	0.01933	1514749	33.57	18.94	0.01926	60
65	0.12122	72586	8799	341425	0.02577	1132820	33.57	15.61	0.02568	65
70	0.15273	63787	9742	295802	0.03294	791395	33.57	12.41	0.03271	70
75	0.27132	54045	14664	235312	0.06232	495593	33.57	9.17	0.06180	75
80	0.46041	39381	18131	152949	0.11854	260281	33.57	6.61	0.11756	80
85 +	*1.00000	21250	21250	107332	0.19798	107332	33.57	5.05	0.19525	85 +

TABLE 3 LIFE TABLE FOR FEMALES

Age, x	$_nq_x$	l_x	$_nd_x$	$_nL_x$	$_nm_x$	T_x	$1000r_x$	$\mathring{e}_x$	$_nM_x$	Age, x
0	0.01489	100000	1489	98972	0.01504	7655202	1.20	76.55	0.01505	0
1	0.00481	98511	473	392702	0.00121	7556230	1.20	76.70	0.00121	1
5	0.00044	98038	43	490083	0.00009	7163529	14.43	73.07	0.00009	5
10	0.00051	97995	50	489854	0.00010	6673446	24.89	68.10	0.00010	10
15	0.00059	97945	58	489615	0.00012	6183592	34.35	63.13	0.00012	15
20	0.00216	97887	212	488950	0.00043	5693977	43.83	58.17	0.00043	20
25	0.00273	97675	267	487841	0.00055	5205027	18.11	53.29	0.00054	25
30	0.00861	97409	839	485015	0.00173	4717185	0.00	48.43	0.00173	30
35	0.00616	96570	595	481359	0.00124	4232171	8.35	43.82	0.00124	35
40	0.00857	95975	823	477910	0.00172	3750812	18.36	39.08	0.00172	40
45	0.01081	95153	1028	473647	0.00217	3272902	15.95	34.40	0.00216	45
50	0.03189	94124	3001	463518	0.00648	2799255	14.34	29.74	0.00646	50
55	0.03234	91123	2947	448297	0.00657	2335737	18.49	25.63	0.00657	55
60	0.03678	88176	3243	433599	0.00748	1887440	28.47	21.41	0.00742	60
65	0.08146	84933	6919	409134	0.01691	1453840	28.47	17.12	0.01677	65
70	0.15025	78014	11722	362176	0.03236	1044706	28.47	13.39	0.03219	70
75	0.20647	66293	13687	298752	0.04581	682530	28.47	10.30	0.04554	75
80	0.36042	52605	18960	216478	0.08758	383777	28.47	7.30	0.08705	80
85 +	1.00000	33645	33645	167299	0.20111	167299	28.47	4.97	0.21309	85 +

TABLE 4   POPULATION PROJECTION, USING FIXED AGE-SPECIFIC BIRTH AND DEATH RATES, IN THOUSANDS

Age at last birthday	1970 Total	1970 Males	1970 Females	1975 Total	1975 Males	1975 Females	1980 Total	1980 Males	1980 Females	Age at last birthday
0–4	25	12	13	28	14	14	33	16	17	0–4
5–9	23	12	11	25	12	13	28	14	14	5–9
10–14	23	12	11	23	12	11	25	12	13	10–14
15–19	20	10	10	23	12	11	23	12	11	15–19
20–24	18	9	9	20	10	10	23	12	11	20–24
25–29	14	7	7	18	9	9	20	10	10	25–29
30–34	12	6	6	14	7	7	18	9	9	30–34
35–39	12	6	6	11	6	5	14	7	7	35–39
40–44	12	6	6	12	6	6	11	6	5	40–44
45–49	10	5	5	12	6	6	12	6	6	45–49
50–54	10	5	5	10	5	5	11	6	5	50–54
55–59	8	4	4	8	4	4	10	5	5	55–59
60–64	8	4	4	8	4	4	8	4	4	60–64
65–69	6	3	3	6	3	3	7	3	4	65–69
70–74	5	2	3	6	3	3	6	3	3	70–74
75–79	4	2	2	4	2	2	4	2	2	75–79
80–84	2	1	1	3	1	2	3	1	2	80–84
85 +	1	0	1	2	1	1	2	1	1	85 +
All ages	213	106	107	233	117	116	258	129	129	All ages

TABLE 5   OBSERVED AND PROJECTED VITAL RATES

Rates per thousand	Observed Total	Observed Males	Observed Females	Projected 1970 Males	Projected 1970 Females	Projected 1975 Males	Projected 1975 Females	Projected 1980 Males	Projected 1980 Females	Stable Males	Stable Females
Birth	24.55	24.12	24.98	25.36	26.03	26.66	27.12	27.46	27.71	28.55	27.63
Death	6.71	7.13	6.28	7.50	6.45	7.82	6.72	7.90	6.86	6.59	5.67
Increase	17.83	16.99	18.70	17.85	19.57	18.83	20.40	19.56	20.85		21.9635

TABLE 6   RATES STANDARDIZED ON THREE STANDARD COUNTRIES

Standardized rates per thousand	England and Wales, 1961 Total	Males	Females	United States, 1960 Total	Males	Females	Mexico, 1960 Total	Males	Females
Birth	23.82	25.52*	23.24	24.29	23.55*	24.10	27.93	23.17*	28.05
Death	8.84	8.87*	8.85	7.17	7.86*	6.52	3.76	5.93*	3.09
Increase	14.98	16.65*	14.40	17.12	15.69*	17.58	24.17	17.24*	24.95

TABLE 7   VITAL STATISTICS AND RATES INFERRED FROM AGE DISTRIBUTIONS (FEMALES)

Vital statistics		Thompson Age range	NRR	$1000r$	Interval	Bourgeois-Pichat Age range	NRR	$1000b$	$1000d$	$1000r$	Coale
TFR	3.71	0–4	1.79	21.81	27.43	5–29	2.53	32.01	-2.34	34.36	$1000b$
GRR	1.87	5–9	1.93	24.40	27.41	30–54	1.44	19.88	6.49	13.39	$1000d$
NRR	1.82	10–14	1.85	22.13	27.36	55–79	1.39	17.76	5.59	12.17	$1000r$
Generation	27.24	15–19	1.69	16.12	27.29	*35–64	1.56	23.03	6.51	16.52	$1000k_1$
Sex ratio	98.61										$1000k_2$

TABLE 8   LESLIE MATRIX AND ITS ANALYSIS (FEMALES)

Start of age interval	Sub-diagonal	First row	Percent in stable population	Fisher values	Total reproductive values	Net maternity function	Matrix equation coefficient	Parameters	Integral	Matrix
0	0.99676	0.00000	12.879	1.074	12288	0.00000	0.00000	λ_1	1.1161	1.1164
5	0.99953	0.00000	11.499	1.203	13309	0.00000	0.00000	λ_2	0.3612	0.3751
10	0.99951	0.10725	10.295	1.344	13257	0.00000	0.10685		+0.7521	+0.7328i
15	0.99864	0.37275	9.217	1.386	11940	0.21370	0.37119	r_1	0.0220	0.0220
20	0.99773	0.48654	8.245	1.148	8019	0.52867	0.48384	r_2	-0.0352	-0.0389
25	0.99421	0.38578	7.369	0.761	4214	0.43901	0.38277		+0.2246	+0.2195i
30	0.99246	0.27738	6.562	0.437	2529	0.32653	0.27363	c_1		909
35	0.99283	0.15494	5.834	0.192	1087	0.22072	0.15169	c_2		295
40	0.99108	0.04622	5.188	0.048	252	0.08266	0.04493			1548i
45	0.97862	0.00401	4.605	0.004	19	0.00720	0.00387	$2\pi/y$	27.972	28.621
50	0.96716	0.00029	4.037	0.000	1	0.00054	0.00027	Δ	3.933	
55	0.84273		14.269							

Ireland, 1968

TABLE 1 DATA INPUT TO COMPUTATIONS

Age at last birthday	Population Total	Males	%	Females	%	Births, by age of mother	Deaths Total	Males	Females	Age at last birthday
0	62193	32053	2.2	30140	2.1	0	1280	700	580	0
1–4	255401	130262	8.9	125139	8.6	0	200	118	82	1–4
5–9	304923	155509	10.6	149414	10.3	0	130	91	39	5–9
10–14	289501	147593	10.1	141908	9.8	5	87	44	43	10–14
15–19	256706	131476	9.0	125230	8.6	1790	156	108	48	15–19
20–24	194734	99174	6.8	95560	6.6	12943	185	137	48	20–24
25–29	158415	79731	5.5	78684	5.4	17424	141	100	41	25–29
30–34	148131	74798	5.1	73333	5.1	14476	171	103	68	30–34
35–39	151628	75899	5.2	75729	5.2	10166	236	141	95	35–39
40–44	158688	78965	5.4	79723	5.5	3866	492	280	212	40–44
45–49	163453	81929	5.6	81524	5.6	334	836	462	374	45–49
50–54	162244	82433	5.6	79811	5.5	0	1200	711	489	50–54
55–59	149553	76597	5.2	72956	5.0	0	1804	1146	658	55–59
60–64	127823	64146	4.4	63677	4.4	0	2730	1728	1002	60–64
65–69	112549	54349	3.7	58200	4.0	0	3603	2207	1396	65–69
70–74	93585	43489	3.0	50096	3.5		4831	2689	2142	70–74
75–79	64368	29176	2.0	35192	2.4		5077	2695	2382	75–79
80–84	36180	15865	1.1	20315	1.4	31469 M	4792	2306	2486	80–84
85 +	19613	7688	0.5	11925	0.8	29535 F	5206	2265	2941	85 +
All ages	2909688	1461132		1448556		61004	33157	18031	15126	All ages

TABLE 2 LIFE TABLE FOR MALES

Age, x	$_nq_x$	l_x	$_nd_x$	$_nL_x$	$_nm_x$	T_x	$1000r_x$	$\mathring{e}_x$	$_nM_x$	Age, x
0	0.02148	100000	2148	98361	0.02184	6869267	0.00	68.69	0.02184	0
1	0.00361	97852	354	390379	0.00091	6770905	0.00	69.20	0.00091	1
5	0.00292	97498	284	486780	0.00058	6380526	8.89	65.44	0.00059	5
10	0.00149	97214	145	485731	0.00030	5893746	16.31	60.63	0.00030	10
15	0.00414	97069	402	484447	0.00083	5408015	38.93	55.71	0.00082	15
20	0.00691	96666	668	481705	0.00139	4923568	48.78	50.93	0.00138	20
25	0.00625	95999	600	478492	0.00125	4441863	26.89	46.27	0.00125	25
30	0.00686	95399	655	475415	0.00138	3963371	3.50	41.55	0.00138	30
35	0.00925	94744	876	471736	0.00186	3487957	0.00	36.81	0.00186	35
40	0.01759	93868	1651	465563	0.00355	3016220	0.00	32.13	0.00355	40
45	0.02783	92217	2566	455114	0.00564	2550657	0.00	27.66	0.00564	45
50	0.04229	89650	3791	439536	0.00863	2095543	0.00	23.37	0.00863	50
55	0.07248	85859	6223	415050	0.01499	1656007	9.03	19.29	0.01496	55
60	0.12669	79636	10089	373340	0.02695	1240957	2.50	15.58	0.02694	60
65	0.18496	69547	12864	316643	0.04062	866617	2.50	12.46	0.04061	65
70	0.26839	56683	15213	245941	0.06186	549974	2.50	9.70	0.06183	70
75	0.37478	41470	15542	168190	0.09241	304032	2.50	7.33	0.09237	75
80	0.53040	25928	13752	94557	0.14544	135842	2.50	5.24	0.14535	80
85 +	*1.00000	12176	12176	41285	0.29492	41285	2.50	3.39	0.29461	85 +

TABLE 3 LIFE TABLE FOR FEMALES

Age, x	$_nq_x$	l_x	$_nd_x$	$_nL_x$	$_nm_x$	T_x	$1000r_x$	$\mathring{e}_x$	$_nM_x$	Age, x
0	0.01896	100000	1896	98515	0.01924	7321178	0.00	73.21	0.01924	0
1	0.00262	98104	257	391667	0.00066	7222663	0.00	73.62	0.00066	1
5	0.00130	97848	127	488919	0.00026	6830996	8.61	69.81	0.00026	5
10	0.00152	97720	148	488243	0.00030	6342077	17.35	64.90	0.00030	10
15	0.00192	97572	188	487411	0.00038	5853833	39.15	59.99	0.00038	15
20	0.00252	97384	245	486324	0.00050	5366422	46.00	55.11	0.00050	20
25	0.00261	97139	254	485105	0.00052	4880099	25.87	50.24	0.00052	25
30	0.00463	96886	448	483380	0.00093	4394994	2.95	45.36	0.00093	30
35	0.00625	96437	603	480848	0.00125	3911614	0.00	40.56	0.00125	35
40	0.01322	95834	1267	476325	0.00266	3430766	0.00	35.80	0.00266	40
45	0.02269	94567	2146	467789	0.00459	2954441	0.00	31.24	0.00459	45
50	0.03022	92421	2793	455504	0.00613	2486652	4.75	26.91	0.00613	50
55	0.04430	89628	3970	438991	0.00904	2031147	12.80	22.66	0.00902	55
60	0.07602	85658	6512	413061	0.01576	1592156	9.46	18.59	0.01574	60
65	0.11379	79146	9006	374700	0.02404	1179096	9.46	14.90	0.02399	65
70	0.19433	70140	13630	318175	0.04284	804396	9.46	11.47	0.04276	70
75	0.29103	56510	16446	242498	0.06782	486220	9.46	8.60	0.06769	75
80	0.46760	40064	18734	152805	0.12260	243722	9.46	6.08	0.12237	80
85 +	1.00000	21330	21330	90917	0.23461	90917	9.46	4.26	0.24663	85 +

TABLE 4 POPULATION PROJECTION, USING FIXED AGE-SPECIFIC BIRTH AND DEATH RATES, IN THOUSANDS

Age at last birthday	1973 Total	1973 Males	1973 Females	1978 Total	1978 Males	1978 Females	1983 Total	1983 Males	1983 Females	Age at last birthday
0–4	319	164	155	370	191	179	433	223	210	0–4
5–9	317	162	155	318	164	154	369	190	179	5–9
10–14	304	155	149	316	161	155	317	163	154	10–14
15–19	289	147	142	304	155	149	315	161	154	15–19
20–24	256	131	125	287	146	141	303	154	149	20–24
25–29	194	99	95	255	130	125	286	145	141	25–29
30–34	157	79	78	193	98	95	253	129	124	30–34
35–39	147	74	73	157	79	78	191	97	94	35–39
40–44	150	75	75	145	73	72	155	78	77	40–44
45–49	155	77	78	147	73	74	143	72	71	45–49
50–54	158	79	79	151	75	76	143	71	72	50–54
55–59	155	78	77	152	75	77	143	70	73	55–59
60–64	138	69	69	142	70	72	139	67	72	60–64
65–69	112	54	58	120	58	62	125	59	66	65–69
70–74	91	42	49	91	42	49	98	45	53	70–74
75–79	68	30	38	67	29	38	66	29	37	75–79
80–84	38	16	22	41	17	24	40	16	24	80–84
85 +	19	7	12	20	7	13	21	7	14	85 +
All ages	3067	1538	1529	3276	1643	1633	3540	1776	1764	All ages

TABLE 5 OBSERVED AND PROJECTED VITAL RATES

Rates per thousand	Observed Total	Observed Males	Observed Females	Projected 1973 Males	Projected 1973 Females	Projected 1978 Males	Projected 1978 Females	Projected 1983 Males	Projected 1983 Females	Stable Males	Stable Females
Birth	20.97	21.54	20.39	23.23	21.93	25.73	24.28	27.52	26.01	26.74	25.83
Death	11.40	12.34	10.44	11.72	10.24	11.20	10.04	10.53	9.63	7.85	6.94
Increase	9.57	9.20	9.95	11.51	11.68	14.53	14.24	16.99	16.38		18.8889

TABLE 6 RATES STANDARDIZED ON THREE STANDARD COUNTRIES

Standardized rates per thousand	England and Wales, 1961 Total	Males	Females	United States, 1960 Total	Males	Females	Mexico, 1960 Total	Males	Females
Birth	24.24	25.39*	22.74	24.66	23.27*	23.52	25.69	22.71*	24.81
Death	11.93	11.83*	12.02	9.63	10.76*	8.77	4.81	9.00*	4.08
Increase	12.31	13.56*	10.72	15.02	12.51*	14.76	20.88	13.71*	20.73

TABLE 7 VITAL STATISTICS AND RATES INFERRED FROM AGE DISTRIBUTIONS (FEMALES)

Vital statistics		Thompson Age range	NRR	$1000r$	Interval	Bourgeois-Pichat Age range	NRR	$1000b$	$1000d$	$1000r$	Coale
TFR	3.78	0–4	1.74	20.68	27.44	5–29	2.45	29.07	−4.09	33.17	$1000b$
GRR	1.83	5–9	1.82	22.11	27.39	30–54	0.81	8.18	15.97	−7.79	$1000d$
NRR	1.77	10–14	1.77	20.48	27.33	55–79	1.09	13.35	10.26	3.09	$1000r$
Generation	30.18	15–19	1.56	15.38	27.23	*30–54	0.81	8.18	15.97	−7.79	$1000k_1$
Sex ratio	106.55										$1000k_2$

TABLE 8 LESLIE MATRIX AND ITS ANALYSIS (FEMALES)

Start of age interval	Sub-diagonal	First row	Percent in stable population	Fisher values	Total reproductive values	Net maternity function	Matrix equation coefficient	Parameters	Integral	Matrix
0	0.99742	0.00000	12.088	1.069	166026	0.00000	0.00000	λ_1	1.0990	1.0993
5	0.99862	0.00004	10.968	1.178	176064	0.00000	0.00004	λ_2	0.4885	0.4868
10	0.99830	0.01697	9.964	1.297	184065	0.00008	0.01691		+0.8138	+0.7931i
15	0.99777	0.17732	9.049	1.410	176583	0.03373	0.17632	r_1	0.0189	0.0189
20	0.99749	0.42282	8.213	1.363	130293	0.31891	0.41950	r_2	−0.0104	−0.0144
25	0.99644	0.49617	7.453	1.049	82567	0.52009	0.49103		+0.2060	+0.2041i
30	0.99476	0.39269	6.756	0.625	45849	0.46197	0.38725	c_1		12856
35	0.99059	0.21629	6.114	0.269	20356	0.31252	0.21217	c_2		1310
40	0.98208	0.06230	5.509	0.065	5169	0.11183	0.06055			46043i
45	0.97374	0.00486	4.922	0.005	386	0.00928	0.00464	$2\pi/y$	30.496	30.791
50	0.96375	0.00001	4.360	0.000	1	0.00000	0.00000	Δ	8.787	
55	0.81153		14.605							

Italy, 1966

TABLE 1 DATA INPUT TO COMPUTATIONS

Age at last birthday	Population Total	Males	%	Females	%	Births, by age of mother	Deaths Total	Males	Females	Age at last birthday
0	976500	499500	1.9	477000	1.8	0	34207	19244	14963	0
1–4	3783500	1935000	7.4	1848500	6.8	0	4655	2477	2178	1–4
5–9	4202499	2151500	8.3	2050999	7.6	0	1949	1174	775	5–9
10–14	3976000	2027000	7.8	1949000	7.2	307	1604	999	605	10–14
15–19	4245500	2168500	8.3	2077000	7.7	78139	3116	2236	880	15–19
20–24	3736000	1893000	7.3	1843000	6.8	207248	3107	2132	975	20–24
25–29	4052500	2033500	7.8	2019000	7.4	320901	3695	2373	1322	25–29
30–34	3796000	1893500	7.3	1902500	7.0	216243	4495	2746	1749	30–34
35–39	3848500	1907500	7.3	1941000	7.2	118381	6434	3990	2444	35–39
40–44	3759500	1831000	7.0	1928500	7.1	35825	6094	6094	-0	40–44
45–49	2653000	1273500	4.9	1379500	5.1	2855	10642	6495	4147	45–49
50–54	3248000	1569000	6.0	1679000	6.2	41	21185	13266	7919	50–54
55–59	3041000	1463500	5.6	1577500	5.8	0	32399	20950	11449	55–59
60–64	2460000	1149000	4.4	1311000	4.8	0	42592	27037	15555	60–64
65–69	1982500	869000	3.3	1113500	4.1	0	54004	31470	22534	65–69
70–74	1478000	605000	2.3	873000	3.2		64967	33149	31818	70–74
75–79	1033000	417000	1.6	616000	2.3		72401	34641	37760	75–79
80–84	542839	216131	0.8	326708	1.2	502724 M	68700	30503	38197	80–84
85 +	313662	122369	0.5	191293	0.7	477216 F	58035	24080	33955	85 +
All ages	53128500	26024500		27104000		979940	494281	265056	229225	All ages

TABLE 2 LIFE TABLE FOR MALES

Age, x	nq_x	l_x	nd_x	nL_x	nm_x	T_x	$1000r_x$	$\mathring{e}_x$	nM_x	Age, x
0	0.03734	100000	3734	97063	0.03847	6844056	2.01	68.44	0.03853	0
1	0.00508	96266	489	383635	0.00128	6746993	2.01	70.09	0.00128	1
5	0.00271	95777	260	478236	0.00054	6363358	17.56	66.44	0.00055	5
10	0.00246	95517	235	477046	0.00049	5885123	0.00	61.61	0.00049	10
15	0.00515	95282	490	475246	0.00103	5408076	5.91	56.76	0.00103	15
20	0.00562	94792	532	472639	0.00113	4932830	5.31	52.04	0.00113	20
25	0.00582	94259	548	469956	0.00117	4460191	0.00	47.32	0.00117	25
30	0.00723	93711	678	466948	0.00145	3990235	4.89	42.58	0.00145	30
35	0.01041	93033	969	462923	0.00209	3523287	1.15	37.87	0.00209	35
40	0.01663	92065	1531	456771	0.00335	3060365	36.99	33.24	0.00333	40
45	0.02526	90534	2286	447397	0.00511	2603594	10.06	28.76	0.00510	45
50	0.04147	88247	3660	432837	0.00846	2156197	0.00	24.43	0.00846	50
55	0.06951	84588	5880	409312	0.01436	1723360	16.21	20.37	0.01431	55
60	0.11186	78708	8804	372738	0.02362	1314048	20.48	16.70	0.02353	60
65	0.16710	69904	11681	321422	0.03634	941310	20.48	13.47	0.03621	65
70	0.24229	58223	14107	256589	0.05498	619888	20.48	10.65	0.05479	70
75	0.34529	44116	15233	182680	0.08339	363299	20.48	8.24	0.08307	75
80	0.51833	28884	14971	105679	0.14167	180619	20.48	6.25	0.14113	80
85 +	1.00000	13912	13912	74941	0.18564	74941	20.48	5.39	0.19678	85 +

TABLE 3 LIFE TABLE FOR FEMALES

Age, x	nq_x	l_x	nd_x	nL_x	nm_x	T_x	$1000r_x$	$\mathring{e}_x$	nM_x	Age, x
0	0.03058	100000	3058	97634	0.03132	7424081	2.12	74.24	0.03137	0
1	0.00468	96942	454	386447	0.00117	7326447	2.12	75.58	0.00118	1
5	0.00188	96489	181	481991	0.00038	6940000	17.06	71.93	0.00038	5
10	0.00155	96308	149	481170	0.00031	6458010	0.00	67.06	0.00031	10
15	0.00212	96158	204	480304	0.00042	5976840	5.17	62.16	0.00042	15
20	0.00264	95955	254	479162	0.00053	5496536	2.30	57.28	0.00053	20
25	0.00327	95701	313	477762	0.00065	5017374	0.00	52.43	0.00065	25
30	0.00459	95388	438	475906	0.00092	4539612	2.97	47.59	0.00092	30
35	0.00627	94951	596	473172	0.00126	4063705	0.00	42.80	0.00126	35
40	-0.	94355	-0	471945	-0.	3590533	33.20	38.05	-0.	40
45	0.01499	94355	1414	468691	0.00302	3118588	11.22	33.05	0.00301	45
50	0.02333	92941	2168	459666	0.00472	2649898	0.00	28.51	0.00472	50
55	0.03581	90773	3251	446345	0.00728	2190232	17.11	24.13	0.00726	55
60	0.05811	87522	5086	425890	0.01194	1743887	28.85	19.93	0.01186	60
65	0.09731	82436	8022	393684	0.02038	1317997	28.85	15.99	0.02024	65
70	0.16879	74414	12561	342462	0.03668	924313	28.85	12.42	0.03645	70
75	0.26878	61854	16625	269404	0.06171	581852	28.85	9.41	0.06130	75
80	0.45804	45229	20717	175994	0.11771	312447	28.85	6.91	0.11692	80
85 +	*1.00000	24512	24512	136453	0.17964	136453	28.85	5.57	0.17750	85 +

TABLE 4 POPULATION PROJECTION, USING FIXED AGE-SPECIFIC BIRTH AND DEATH RATES, IN THOUSANDS

Age at last birthday	1971 Total	Males	Females	1976 Total	Males	Females	1981 Total	Males	Females	Age at last birthday
0–4	4733	2420	2313	4764	2436	2328	4831	2470	2361	0–4
5–9	4737	2422	2315	4710	2407	2303	4741	2423	2318	5–9
10–14	4194	2146	2048	4728	2416	2312	4700	2401	2299	10–14
15–19	3964	2019	1945	4182	2138	2044	4714	2407	2307	15–19
20–24	4229	2157	2072	3949	2008	1941	4165	2126	2039	20–24
25–29	3720	1882	1838	4210	2144	2066	3932	1997	1935	25–29
30–34	4031	2020	2011	3700	1870	1830	4189	2131	2058	30–34
35–39	3769	1877	1892	4003	2003	2000	3674	1854	1820	35–39
40–44	3818	1882	1936	3739	1852	1887	3970	1976	1994	40–44
45–49	3708	1793	1915	3767	1844	1923	3688	1814	1874	45–49
50–54	2585	1232	1353	3613	1735	1878	3670	1784	1886	50–54
55–59	3114	1484	1630	2479	1165	1314	3465	1641	1824	55–59
60–64	2838	1333	1505	2907	1351	1556	2315	1061	1254	60–64
65–69	2203	991	1212	2540	1149	1391	2603	1165	1438	65–69
70–74	1663	694	969	1845	791	1054	2127	917	1210	70–74
75–79	1118	431	687	1256	494	762	1392	563	829	75–79
80–84	643	241	402	698	249	449	784	286	498	80–84
85 +	406	153	253	483	171	312	525	177	348	85 +
All ages	55473	27177	28296	57573	28223	29350	59485	29193	30292	All ages

TABLE 5 OBSERVED AND PROJECTED VITAL RATES

Rates per thousand	Observed Total	Males	Females	Projected 1971 Males	Females	1976 Males	Females	1981 Males	Females	Stable Males	Females
Birth	18.44	19.32	17.61	18.55	16.91	18.05	16.48	17.75	16.24	17.84	16.65
Death	9.30	10.18	8.46	10.66	9.25	11.04	9.88	11.39	10.34	12.27	11.08
Increase	9.14	9.13	9.15	7.88	7.66	7.01	6.60	6.36	5.90		5.5752

TABLE 6 RATES STANDARDIZED ON THREE STANDARD COUNTRIES

Standardized rates per thousand	England and Wales, 1961 Total	Males	Females	United States, 1960 Total	Males	Females	Mexico, 1960 Total	Males	Females
Birth	16.09	17.38*	15.19	16.42	16.37*	15.75	18.38	15.62*	17.86
Death	10.58	11.01*	10.24	8.71	9.78*	7.59	4.85	8.01*	3.97
Increase	5.51	6.37*	4.95	7.70	6.59*	8.16	13.53	7.62*	13.89

TABLE 7 VITAL STATISTICS AND RATES INFERRED FROM AGE DISTRIBUTIONS (FEMALES)

Vital statistics		Thompson Age range	NRR	1000r	Interval	Bourgeois-Pichat Age range	NRR	1000b	1000d	1000r	Coale
TFR	2.52	0–4	1.17	5.84	27.45	5–29	1.04	15.62	14.31	1.31	1000b
GRR	1.23	5–9	1.10	3.48	27.44	30–54	1.32	21.26	11.02	10.25	1000d
NRR	1.17	10–14	1.06	1.97	27.40	55–79	1.78	43.83	22.54	21.30	1000r
Generation	28.47	15–19	1.16	5.38	27.33	*50–74	1.66	37.14	18.30	18.84	1000k_1
Sex ratio	105.35										1000k_2

TABLE 8 LESLIE MATRIX AND ITS ANALYSIS (FEMALES)

Start of age interval	Sub-diagonal	First row	Percent in stable population	Fisher values	Total reproductive values	Net maternity function	Matrix equation coefficient	Parameters Integral	Matrix
0	0.99568	0.00000	7.950	1.047	2435615	0.00000	0.00000	λ_1 1.0283	1.0283
5	0.99830	0.00018	7.698	1.082	2218460	0.00000	0.00018	λ_2 0.4099	0.4137
10	0.99820	0.04445	7.473	1.114	2171078	0.00037	0.04418	+0.7587	+0.7373 i
15	0.99762	0.17657	7.255	1.101	2286533	0.08800	0.17520	r_1 0.0056	0.0056
20	0.99708	0.31934	7.038	0.949	1749635	0.26240	0.31610	r_2 −0.0296	−0.0336
25	0.99612	0.32080	6.825	0.644	1299044	0.36980	0.31661	+0.2151	+0.2119 i
30	0.99426	0.20545	6.611	0.327	622302	0.26342	0.20198	c_1	277243
35	0.99740	0.09373	6.392	0.122	236549	0.14054	0.09162	c_2	127889
40	0.99310	0.02432	6.200	0.027	52496	0.04269	0.02371		−199987 i
45	0.98075	0.00247	5.988	0.003	3505	0.00472	0.00239	$2\pi/y$ 29.212	29.653
50	0.97102	0.00003	5.711	0.000	54	0.00005	0.00003	Δ 4.666	
55	0.80519		24.859						

Luxembourg, 1966

TABLE 1 DATA INPUT TO COMPUTATIONS

Age at last birthday	Population					Births, by age of mother	Deaths			Age at last birthday
	Total	Males	%	Females	%		Total	Males	Females	
0	5073	2554	1.6	2519	1.5	0	139	77	62	0
1–4	20743	10619	6.5	10124	6.0	0	27	11	16	1–4
5–9	25549	13049	7.9	12500	7.4	0	11	6	5	5–9
10–14	23957	12108	7.4	11849	7.0	2	5	4	1	10–14
15–19	22349	11319	6.9	11030	6.5	317	12	11	1	15–19
20–24	22007	11438	7.0	10569	6.2	1634	26	24	2	20–24
25–29	22910	11823	7.2	11087	6.5	1693	29	20	9	25–29
30–34	23292	12043	7.3	11249	6.6	946	36	26	10	30–34
35–39	25852	13379	8.1	12473	7.3	484	45	30	15	35–39
40–44	22135	10291	6.3	11844	7.0	113	82	49	33	40–44
45–49	18890	8991	5.5	9899	5.8	5	107	57	50	45–49
50–54	20803	10231	6.2	10572	6.2	0	196	125	71	50–54
55–59	21781	10577	6.4	11204	6.6	0	320	221	99	55–59
60–64	19683	9146	5.6	10537	6.2	0	403	264	139	60–64
65–69	15831	7151	4.4	8680	5.1	0	537	312	225	65–69
70–74	10984	4687	2.9	6297	3.7		582	318	264	70–74
75–79	6860	2811	1.7	4049	2.4		589	289	300	75–79
80–84	3715	1476	0.9	2239	1.3	2518 M	514	225	289	80–84
85+	1803	692	0.4	1111	0.7	2576 F	390	168	222	85+
All ages	334217	164385		169832		5194	4050	2237	1813	All ages

TABLE 2 LIFE TABLE FOR MALES

Age, x	$_nq_x$	l_x	$_nd_x$	$_nL_x$	$_nm_x$	T_x	$1000r_x$	$\overset{\circ}{e}_x$	$_nM_x$	Age, x
0	0.02945	100000	2945	97694	0.03015	6629096	0.00	66.29	0.03015	0
1	0.00413	97055	401	387047	0.00104	6531401	0.00	67.30	0.00104	1
5	0.00229	96654	221	482715	0.00046	6144354	7.82	63.57	0.00046	5
10	0.00166	96432	160	481813	0.00033	5661639	13.74	58.71	0.00033	10
15	0.00486	96272	468	480358	0.00097	5179827	4.60	53.80	0.00097	15
20	0.01044	95805	1000	476592	0.00210	4699459	0.00	49.05	0.00210	20
25	0.00842	94805	798	472029	0.00169	4222867	0.00	44.54	0.00169	25
30	0.01074	94006	1009	467558	0.00216	3750838	0.00	39.90	0.00216	30
35	0.01119	92997	1041	462626	0.00225	3283280	12.93	35.31	0.00224	35
40	0.02369	91956	2179	454702	0.00479	2820654	35.30	30.67	0.00476	40
45	0.03125	89777	2805	442497	0.00634	2365953	0.00	26.35	0.00634	45
50	0.05943	86972	5169	423051	0.01222	1923456	0.00	22.12	0.01222	50
55	0.09953	81803	8142	389661	0.02089	1500405	0.00	18.34	0.02089	55
60	0.13524	73662	9962	344331	0.02893	1110744	15.00	15.08	0.02887	60
65	0.19779	63699	12599	288024	0.04374	766412	15.00	12.03	0.04363	65
70	0.29119	51100	14880	218758	0.06802	478388	15.00	9.36	0.06785	70
75	0.40821	36221	14786	143467	0.10306	259631	15.00	7.17	0.10281	75
80	0.54371	21435	11654	76275	0.15279	116164	15.00	5.42	0.15244	80
85+	1.00000	9781	9781	39888	0.24520	39888	15.00	4.08	0.24278	85+

TABLE 3 LIFE TABLE FOR FEMALES

Age, x	$_nq_x$	l_x	$_nd_x$	$_nL_x$	$_nm_x$	T_x	$1000r_x$	$\overset{\circ}{e}_x$	$_nM_x$	Age, x
0	0.02419	100000	2419	98269	0.02461	7262598	0.00	72.63	0.02461	0
1	0.00629	97581	614	388555	0.00158	7164328	0.00	73.42	0.00158	1
5	0.00199	96967	193	484354	0.00040	6775754	5.85	69.88	0.00040	5
10	0.00042	96774	40	483739	0.00008	6291410	12.35	65.01	0.00008	10
15	0.00045	96734	44	483570	0.00009	5807671	11.34	60.04	0.00009	15
20	0.00095	96690	91	483293	0.00019	5324102	0.00	55.06	0.00019	20
25	0.00405	96598	391	482083	0.00081	4840809	0.00	50.11	0.00081	25
30	0.00444	96207	427	480006	0.00089	4358726	0.00	45.31	0.00089	30
35	0.00600	95780	574	477653	0.00120	3878719	0.00	40.50	0.00120	35
40	0.01392	95206	1325	473084	0.00280	3401067	20.19	35.72	0.00279	40
45	0.02498	93880	2346	463891	0.00506	2927983	6.45	31.19	0.00505	45
50	0.03305	91535	3025	450420	0.00672	2464092	0.00	26.92	0.00672	50
55	0.04328	88510	3830	433480	0.00884	2013672	0.00	22.75	0.00884	55
60	0.06446	84679	5459	410980	0.01328	1580192	26.67	18.65	0.01319	60
65	0.12290	79221	9737	373399	0.02608	1169212	26.67	14.76	0.02592	65
70	0.19164	69484	13316	315793	0.04217	795813	26.67	11.45	0.04192	70
75	0.31538	56168	17714	237716	0.07452	480020	26.67	8.55	0.07409	75
80	0.49109	38454	18884	145445	0.12984	242304	26.67	6.30	0.12907	80
85+	*1.00000	19569	19569	96859	0.20204	96859	26.67	4.95	0.19982	85+

TABLE 4 POPULATION PROJECTION, USING FIXED AGE-SPECIFIC BIRTH AND DEATH RATES, IN THOUSANDS

Age at last birthday	1971			1976			1981			Age at last birthday
	Total	Males	Females	Total	Males	Females	Total	Males	Females	
0–4	25	13	12	26	13	13	26	13	13	0–4
5–9	26	13	13	25	13	12	26	13	13	5–9
10–14	25	13	12	26	13	13	25	13	12	10–14
15–19	24	12	12	25	13	12	26	13	13	15–19
20–24	22	11	11	24	12	12	25	13	12	20–24
25–29	22	11	11	22	11	11	24	12	12	25–29
30–34	23	12	11	21	11	10	22	11	11	30–34
35–39	23	12	11	23	12	11	21	11	10	35–39
40–44	25	13	12	23	12	11	22	11	11	40–44
45–49	22	10	12	25	13	12	22	11	11	45–49
50–54	19	9	10	21	10	11	24	12	12	50–54
55–59	19	9	10	17	8	9	20	9	11	55–59
60–64	20	9	11	18	8	10	16	7	9	60–64
65–69	18	8	10	18	8	10	16	7	9	65–69
70–74	12	5	7	14	6	8	14	6	8	70–74
75–79	8	3	5	10	4	6	10	4	6	75–79
80–84	3	1	2	5	2	3	5	2	3	80–84
85 +	2	1	1	3	1	2	3	1	2	85 +
All ages	338	165	173	346	170	176	347	169	178	All ages

TABLE 5 OBSERVED AND PROJECTED VITAL RATES

Rates per thousand	Observed			Projected						Stable	
				1971		1976		1981			
	Total	Males	Females	Males	Females	Males	Females	Males	Females	Males	Females
Birth	15.54	15.93	15.17	15.62	14.73	15.95	14.95	16.52	15.43	17.45	16.11
Death	12.12	13.61	10.68	14.05	11.72	14.36	12.52	14.61	13.17	13.27	11.92
Increase	3.42	2.32	4.49	1.57	3.00	1.58	2.42	1.92	2.26		4.1889

TABLE 6 RATES STANDARDIZED ON THREE STANDARD COUNTRIES

Standardized rates per thousand	England and Wales, 1961			United States, 1960			Mexico, 1960		
	Total	Males	Females	Total	Males	Females	Total	Males	Females
Birth	14.83	14.72*	14.25	15.07	13.94*	14.72	17.85	13.07*	17.65
Death	12.64	13.25*	12.00	10.29	11.85*	8.83	5.40	10.41*	4.32
Increase	2.19	1.47*	2.25	4.78	2.08*	5.90	12.45	2.65*	13.33

TABLE 7 VITAL STATISTICS AND RATES INFERRED FROM AGE DISTRIBUTIONS (FEMALES)

Vital statistics		Thompson				Bourgeois-Pichat					Coale	
		Age range	NRR	$1000r$	Interval	Age range	NRR	$1000b$	$1000d$	$1000r$		
TFR	2.35	0–4	1.10	3.35	27.44	5–29	1.20	15.64	8.77	6.88	$1000b$	18.14
GRR	1.16	5–9	1.10	3.48	27.39	30–54	1.11	16.61	12.63	3.98	$1000d$	6.97
NRR	1.12	10–14	1.03	1.14	27.31	55–79	1.61	43.31	25.78	17.53	$1000r$	11.18
Generation	27.20	15–19	0.94	-2.19	27.21	*20–44	0.81	10.84	18.79	-7.95	$1000k_1$	48.19
Sex ratio	101.6										$1000k_2$	0.62

TABLE 8 LESLIE MATRIX AND ITS ANALYSIS (FEMALES)

Start of age interval	Sub-diagonal	First row	Percent in stable population	Fisher values	Total reproductive values	Net maternity function	Matrix equation coefficient	Parameters		
									Integral	Matrix
0	0.99490	0.00000	7.762	1.038	13121	0.00000	0.00000	λ_1	1.0212	1.0212
5	0.99873	0.00020	7.562	1.065	13315	0.00000	0.00020	λ_2	0.3447	0.3513
10	0.99965	0.03489	7.396	1.089	12903	0.00040	0.03467		+0.7877i	+0.7594i
15	0.99943	0.22123	7.240	1.076	11870	0.06893	0.21975	r_1	0.0042	0.0042
20	0.99750	0.37053	7.086	0.870	9194	0.37057	0.36783	r_2	-0.0302	-0.0357
25	0.99569	0.28543	6.922	0.505	5599	0.36510	0.28265		+0.2317i	+0.2275i
30	0.99510	0.14814	6.749	0.220	2480	0.20020	0.14606	c_1		1593
35	0.99043	0.05825	6.576	0.072	894	0.09192	0.05715	c_2		975
40	0.98057	0.01200	6.379	0.013	153	0.02239	0.01177			523i
45	0.97096	0.00060	6.125	0.001	7	0.00115	0.00058	$2\pi/y$	27.123	27.518
50	0.96239	0.00011	5.824	0.000	1	0.00000	0.00000	Δ	4.558	
55	0.79129		24.380							

Malta (and Gozo), 1966

TABLE 1 DATA INPUT TO COMPUTATIONS

Age at last birthday	Population					Births, by age of mother	Deaths			Age at last birthday
	Total	Males	%	Females	%		Total	Males	Females	
0	5292	2764	1.8	2528	1.5	0	161	85	76	0
1–4	24915	13009	8.6	11906	7.2	0	25	14	11	1–4
5–9	36518	18945	12.5	17573	10.6	0	11	9	2	5–9
10–14	35161	18372	12.1	16789	10.1	81	7	5	2	10–14
15–19	36026	18144	12.0	17882	10.8	162	9	6	3	15–19
20–24	24702	11442	7.5	13260	8.0	1562	15	10	5	20–24
25–29	17795	7359	4.9	10436	6.3	1648	8	4	4	25–29
30–34	19303	7679	5.1	11624	7.0	900	20	9	11	30–34
35–39	18079	7644	5.0	10435	6.3	753	34	20	14	35–39
40–44	17466	7978	5.3	9488	5.7	134	40	23	17	40–44
45–49	15569	7275	4.8	8294	5.0	99	59	35	24	45–49
50–54	13840	6648	4.4	7192	4.3	1	102	56	46	50–54
55–59	15019	7166	4.7	7853	4.7	0	212	138	74	55–59
60–64	12004	5817	3.8	6187	3.7	0	288	154	124	60–64
65–69	9861	4482	3.0	5379	3.2	0	381	205	176	65–69
70–74	8332	3635	2.4	4697	2.8		462	234	228	70–74
75–79	4417	1924	1.3	2493	1.5		442	213	229	75–79
80–84	2217	972	0.6	1245	0.8	2803 M	330	136	194	80–84
85 +	966	469	0.3	497	0.3	2537 F	259	97	162	85 +
All ages	317482	151724		165758		5340	2865	1463	1402	All ages

TABLE 2 LIFE TABLE FOR MALES

Age, x	$_nq_x$	l_x	$_nd_x$	$_nL_x$	$_nm_x$	T_x	$1000r_x$	$\overset{\circ}{e}_x$	$_nM_x$	Age, x
0	0.03003	100000	3003	97655	0.03075	6797405	0.00	67.97	0.03075	0
1	0.00429	96997	416	386772	0.00108	6699750	0.00	69.07	0.00108	1
5	0.00237	96581	229	482330	0.00048	6312978	0.00	65.36	0.00048	5
10	0.00136	96351	131	481416	0.00027	5830548	3.99	60.51	0.00027	10
15	0.00168	96221	162	480758	0.00034	5349232	46.91	55.59	0.00033	15
20	0.00438	96059	421	479262	0.00088	4868473	89.58	50.68	0.00087	20
25	0.00273	95638	261	477566	0.00055	4389211	39.13	45.89	0.00054	25
30	0.00585	95377	558	475695	0.00117	3911645	0.00	41.01	0.00117	30
35	0.01300	94820	1233	471180	0.00262	3435950	0.00	36.24	0.00262	35
40	0.01432	93587	1340	464786	0.00288	2964770	1.72	31.68	0.00288	40
45	0.02387	92247	2202	456225	0.00483	2499985	13.24	27.10	0.00481	45
50	0.04136	90045	3724	442112	0.00842	2043760	0.00	22.70	0.00842	50
55	0.09216	86321	7955	413102	0.01926	1601647	0.00	18.55	0.01925	55
60	0.13249	78365	10382	367135	0.02828	1188545	16.69	15.17	0.02819	60
65	0.20631	67983	14025	305820	0.04586	821410	16.69	12.08	0.04574	65
70	0.27856	53958	15031	232799	0.06456	515591	16.69	9.55	0.06437	70
75	0.43270	38927	16844	151733	0.11101	282792	16.69	7.26	0.11071	75
80	0.50837	22083	11226	80107	0.14014	131058	16.69	5.93	0.13992	80
85 +	1.00000	10857	10857	50952	0.21308	50952	16.69	4.69	0.20682	85 +

TABLE 3 LIFE TABLE FOR FEMALES

Age, x	$_nq_x$	l_x	$_nd_x$	$_nL_x$	$_nm_x$	T_x	$1000r_x$	$\overset{\circ}{e}_x$	$_nM_x$	Age, x
0	0.02936	100000	2936	97668	0.03006	7123537	0.00	71.24	0.03006	0
1	0.00369	97064	358	387208	0.00092	7025869	0.00	72.38	0.00092	1
5	0.00057	96706	55	483393	0.00011	6638661	0.00	68.65	0.00011	5
10	0.00060	96651	58	483117	0.00012	6155268	0.00	63.69	0.00012	10
15	0.00084	96593	82	482789	0.00017	5672152	23.39	58.72	0.00017	15
20	0.00190	96512	183	482123	0.00038	5189362	53.53	53.77	0.00038	20
25	0.00192	96329	185	481238	0.00038	4707239	12.66	48.87	0.00038	25
30	0.00472	96144	454	479679	0.00095	4226001	0.00	43.95	0.00095	30
35	0.00670	95690	641	476928	0.00134	3746322	18.96	39.15	0.00134	35
40	0.00896	95048	851	473264	0.00180	3269394	21.07	34.40	0.00179	40
45	0.01449	94197	1365	468005	0.00292	2796130	24.30	29.68	0.00289	45
50	0.03152	92832	2926	457427	0.00640	2328125	0.00	25.08	0.00640	50
55	0.04620	89906	4153	440256	0.00943	1870697	4.04	20.81	0.00942	55
60	0.09614	85753	8244	409746	0.02012	1430441	16.56	16.68	0.02004	60
65	0.15213	77509	11791	359335	0.03281	1020695	16.56	13.17	0.03272	65
70	0.21817	65717	14337	294309	0.04872	661360	16.56	10.05	0.04854	70
75	0.37570	51380	19303	209388	0.09219	367052	16.56	7.14	0.09186	75
80	0.55856	32077	17917	114520	0.15645	157664	16.56	4.92	0.15582	80
85 +	*1.00000	14160	14160	43144	0.32820	43144	16.56	3.05	0.32596	85 +

TABLE 4   POPULATION PROJECTION, USING FIXED AGE-SPECIFIC
BIRTH AND DEATH RATES, IN THOUSANDS

Age at last birthday	1971			1976			1981			Age at last birthday
	Total	Males	Females	Total	Males	Females	Total	Males	Females	
0–4	28	15	13	32	17	15	36	19	17	0–4
5–9	30	16	14	28	15	13	32	17	15	5–9
10–14	37	19	18	30	16	14	28	15	13	10–14
15–19	35	18	17	37	19	18	30	16	14	15–19
20–24	36	18	18	35	18	17	37	19	18	20–24
25–29	24	11	13	36	18	18	35	18	17	25–29
30–34	17	7	10	24	11	13	36	18	18	30–34
35–39	20	8	12	17	7	10	24	11	13	35–39
40–44	18	8	10	19	8	11	17	7	10	40–44
45–49	17	8	9	17	7	10	18	7	11	45–49
50–54	15	7	8	17	8	9	17	7	10	50–54
55–59	13	6	7	15	7	8	16	7	9	55–59
60–64	13	6	7	12	6	6	13	5	7	60–64
65–69	10	5	5	11	5	6	11	5	6	65–69
70–74	7	3	4	8	4	4	9	4	5	70–74
75–79	5	2	3	5	2	3	5	2	3	75–79
80–84	2	1	1	3	1	2	3	1	2	80–84
85 +	1	1	0	2	1	1	2	1	1	85 +
All ages	328	159	169	348	170	178	369	180	189	All ages

TABLE 5   OBSERVED AND PROJECTED VITAL RATES

Rates per thousand	Observed			Projected						Stable	
				1971		1976		1981			
	Total	Males	Females	Males	Females	Males	Females	Males	Females	Males	Females
Birth	16.82	18.47	15.31	20.83	17.45	21.96	18.63	21.91	18.84	15.83	15.15
Death	9.02	9.64	8.46	9.74	8.69	9.59	8.96	9.42	9.09	13.79	13.11
Increase	7.80	8.83	6.85	11.09	8.76	12.37	9.67	12.49	9.75		2.0394

TABLE 6   RATES STANDARDIZED ON THREE STANDARD COUNTRIES

Standardized rates per thousand	England and Wales, 1961			United States, 1960			Mexico, 1960		
	Total	Males	Females	Total	Males	Females	Total	Males	Females
Birth	14.87	22.13*	13.69	15.05	19.90*	14.08	16.70	20.18*	15.83
Death	13.63	12.28*	14.88	10.86	10.88*	10.80	5.43	8.68*	4.98
Increase	1.24	9.85*	-1.19	4.19	9.03*	3.29	11.28	11.50*	10.85

TABLE 7   VITAL STATISTICS AND RATES INFERRED FROM AGE DISTRIBUTIONS
(FEMALES)

Vital statistics		Thompson				Bourgeois-Pichat					Coale	
		Age range	NRR	1000r	Interval	Age range	NRR	1000b	1000d	1000r	1000b	
TFR	2.33	0–4	1.17	5.79	27.45	5–29	1.98	28.99	3.65	25.34	1000d	
GRR	1.11	5–9	1.64	18.20	27.42	30–54	1.79	29.65	8.13	21.52	1000r	
NRR	1.06	10–14	1.72	19.41	27.36	55–79	1.20	15.00	8.15	6.85	1000k_1	
Generation	29.16	15–19	1.89	16.75	27.27	*30–54	1.79	29.65	8.13	21.52	1000k_2	
Sex ratio	110.48											

TABLE 8   LESLIE MATRIX AND ITS ANALYSIS (FEMALES)

Start of age interval	Sub-diagonal	First row	Percent in stable population	Fisher values	Total reproductive values	Net maternity function	Matrix equation coefficient	Parameters		
									Integral	Matrix
0	0.99694	0.00000	7.307	1.036	14960	0.00000	0.00000	λ_1	1.0102	1.0103
5	0.99943	0.00555	7.211	1.050	18457	0.00000	0.00554	λ_2	0.3895	0.3965
10	0.99932	0.01598	7.133	1.056	17728	0.01107	0.01593		+0.7346	+0.7112i
15	0.99862	0.14593	7.056	1.051	18792	0.02078	0.14530	r_1	0.0020	0.0020
20	0.99816	0.31723	6.975	0.912	12089	0.26982	0.31543	r_2	-0.0369	-0.0411
25	0.99676	0.27078	6.892	0.593	6192	0.36105	0.26875		+0.2167	+0.2124i
30	0.99426	0.17182	6.800	0.320	3717	0.17645	0.16998	c_1		2133
35	0.99232	0.09926	6.692	0.146	1521	0.16351	0.09763	c_2		-1151
40	0.98889	0.02986	6.573	0.045	425	0.03176	0.02915			5456i
45	0.97740	0.01390	5.434	0.014	120	0.02654	0.01342	$2\pi/y$	28.999	29.575
50	0.96246	0.00016	6.225	0.000	1	0.00030	0.00015	Δ	12.757	
55	0.76771		24.702							

Netherlands, 1967

TABLE 1 DATA INPUT TO COMPUTATIONS

Age at last birthday	Population					Births, by age of mother		Deaths			Age at last birthday
	Total	Males	%	Females	%			Total	Males	Females	
0	235946	120841	1.9	115105	1.8	0		3191	1811	1380	0
1–4	971629	498025	7.9	473504	7.5	0		900	547	353	1–4
5–9	1180907	603706	9.6	577201	9.1	0		544	349	195	5–9
10–14	1119782	573770	9.1	546012	8.7	25		429	272	157	10–14
15–19	1141592	584998	9.3	556594	8.8	12501		764	560	204	15–19
20–24	1053999	541667	8.6	512332	8.1	71661		775	579	196	20–24
25–29	840154	436470	6.9	403684	6.4	78359		661	453	208	25–29
30–34	774559	399129	6.3	375430	6.0	45223		749	471	278	30–34
35–39	772627	390391	6.2	382236	6.1	22953		985	595	390	35–39
40–44	754217	372263	5.9	381954	6.1	7355		1635	973	662	40–44
45–49	703905	345305	5.5	358600	5.7	601		2456	1500	955	45–49
50–54	653906	318522	5.1	335384	5.3	0		3805	2444	1361	50–54
55–59	611776	292998	4.7	318778	5.1	0		5773	3833	1940	55–59
60–64	547720	257062	4.1	290658	4.6	0		8469	5421	3048	60–64
65–69	447727	204215	3.2	243512	3.9	0		11005	6811	4194	65–69
70–74	348108	155903	2.5	192205	3.0			13972	7952	6020	70–74
75–79	235356	104972	1.7	130384	2.1			15520	8055	7465	75–79
80–84	133610	58963	0.9	74647	1.2	122529 M		14316	6895	7421	80–84
85+	70681	30338	0.5	40343	0.6	116149 F		13843	6264	7579	85+
All ages	12598201	6289538		6308663		238678		99792	55785	44007	All ages

TABLE 2 LIFE TABLE FOR MALES

Age, x	$_nq_x$	l_x	$_nd_x$	$_nL_x$	$_nm_x$	T_x	$1000r_x$	$\overset{\circ}{e}_x$	$_nM_x$	Age, x
0	0.01483	100000	1483	98961	0.01499	7120004	0.00	71.20	0.01499	0
1	0.00438	98517	431	392838	0.00110	7021043	0.00	71.27	0.00110	1
5	0.00288	98085	283	489720	0.00058	6528206	6.89	67.58	0.00058	5
10	0.00237	97803	232	488473	0.00047	6138485	2.54	62.76	0.00047	10
15	0.00478	97571	466	486749	0.00096	5650013	4.89	57.91	0.00096	15
20	0.00533	97105	518	484236	0.00107	5163264	28.24	53.17	0.00107	20
25	0.00518	96587	500	481694	0.00104	4579027	29.46	48.44	0.00104	25
30	0.00589	96087	566	479066	0.00118	4197333	9.95	43.68	0.00118	30
35	0.00760	95521	726	475928	0.00153	3718267	5.30	38.93	0.00152	35
40	0.01302	94795	1234	471157	0.00262	3242339	9.57	34.20	0.00261	40
45	0.02156	93561	2018	463223	0.00436	2771182	10.96	29.62	0.00434	45
50	0.03778	91543	3458	449817	0.00769	2307959	8.39	25.21	0.00767	50
55	0.06359	88085	5601	427435	0.01310	1858142	7.90	21.09	0.01308	55
60	0.10083	82484	8317	392855	0.02117	1430708	20.27	17.35	0.02109	60
65	0.15495	74167	11492	343342	0.03347	1037853	20.27	13.99	0.03335	65
70	0.22749	62675	14258	278593	0.05118	694511	20.27	11.08	0.05101	70
75	0.32300	48417	15639	203126	0.07699	415919	20.27	8.59	0.07673	75
80	0.45529	32778	14923	127043	0.11747	212793	20.27	6.49	0.11694	80
85+	•1.00000	17855	17855	85750	0.20822	85750	20.27	4.80	0.20647	85+

TABLE 3 LIFE TABLE FOR FEMALES

Age, x	$_nq_x$	l_x	$_nd_x$	$_nL_x$	$_nm_x$	T_x	$1000r_x$	$\overset{\circ}{e}_x$	$_nM_x$	Age, x
0	0.01189	100000	1189	99146	0.01199	7659016	0.00	76.59	0.01199	0
1	0.00298	98811	294	394402	0.00075	7559870	0.00	76.51	0.00075	1
5	0.00168	98517	166	492172	0.00034	7165469	7.09	72.73	0.00034	5
10	0.00144	98351	141	491406	0.00029	6673297	3.32	67.85	0.00029	10
15	0.00183	98210	180	490610	0.00037	6181890	6.02	62.95	0.00037	15
20	0.00192	98030	188	489697	0.00038	5691280	31.71	58.06	0.00038	20
25	0.00258	97842	253	488616	0.00052	5201584	30.56	53.16	0.00052	25
30	0.00370	97589	361	487095	0.00074	4712968	4.72	48.29	0.00074	30
35	0.00509	97229	495	485005	0.00102	4225873	0.00	43.46	0.00102	35
40	0.00864	96734	836	481741	0.00173	3740868	4.62	38.67	0.00173	40
45	0.01327	95898	1273	476531	0.00267	3259127	10.25	33.99	0.00267	45
50	0.02013	94625	1904	468681	0.00406	2782596	7.63	29.41	0.00406	50
55	0.03006	92721	2787	457204	0.00610	2313916	7.77	24.95	0.00609	55
60	0.05151	89934	4633	438988	0.01055	1856711	29.18	20.65	0.01049	60
65	0.08339	85301	7114	410149	0.01734	1417724	29.18	16.62	0.01722	65
70	0.14696	78187	11490	364246	0.03155	1007575	29.18	12.89	0.03132	70
75	0.25317	66697	16886	293023	0.05763	643328	29.18	9.65	0.05725	75
80	0.39956	49811	19902	199118	0.09995	350305	29.18	7.03	0.09941	80
85+	1.00000	29909	29909	151188	0.19783	151188	29.18	5.05	0.18786	85+

[454]

TABLE 4 POPULATION PROJECTION, USING FIXED AGE-SPECIFIC BIRTH AND DEATH RATES, IN THOUSANDS

Age at last birthday	1972 Total	Males	Females	1977 Total	Males	Females	1982 Total	Males	Females	Age at last birthday
0–4	1249	640	609	1374	704	670	1463	750	713	0–4
5–9	1203	616	587	1244	637	607	1369	701	668	5–9
10–14	1178	602	575	1201	615	586	1241	635	606	10–14
15–19	1117	572	545	1175	600	575	1198	613	585	15–19
20–24	1138	582	556	1113	569	544	1171	597	574	20–24
25–29	1050	539	511	1133	579	554	1109	565	543	25–29
30–34	836	434	402	1046	536	510	1129	575	553	30–34
35–39	771	397	374	832	431	401	1039	532	507	35–39
40–44	766	386	380	764	393	371	825	427	398	40–44
45–49	744	366	378	756	380	376	753	385	367	45–49
50–54	688	335	353	727	355	372	738	369	369	50–54
55–59	630	303	327	663	319	344	700	338	362	55–59
60–64	575	269	306	592	278	314	623	293	330	60–64
65–69	497	225	272	521	235	286	536	243	293	65–69
70–74	382	166	216	423	182	241	445	191	254	70–74
75–79	269	114	155	295	121	174	327	133	194	75–79
80–84	155	66	89	176	71	105	194	76	118	80–84
85 +	97	40	57	111	44	67	128	48	80	85 +
All ages	13345	6652	6693	14146	7049	7097	14988	7474	7514	All ages

TABLE 5 OBSERVED AND PROJECTED VITAL RATES

Rates per thousand	Observed Total	Males	Females	Projected 1972 Males	Females	1977 Males	Females	1982 Males	Females	Stable Males	Females
Birth	18.95	19.48	18.41	20.69	19.50	21.11	19.88	20.90	19.69	19.91	18.87
Death	7.92	8.87	6.98	9.22	7.71	9.32	8.16	9.35	8.49	10.00	8.96
Increase	11.02	10.61	11.44	11.48	11.79	11.79	11.72	11.55	11.20		9.9109

TABLE 6 RATES STANDARDIZED ON THREE STANDARD COUNTRIES

Standardized rates per thousand	England and Wales, 1961 Total	Males	Females	United States, 1960 Total	Males	Females	Mexico, 1960 Total	Males	Females
Birth	17.68	18.69*	16.68	17.98	17.14*	17.24	20.31	17.19*	19.71
Death	9.32	9.59*	9.07	7.53	8.62*	6.57	3.77	7.05*	3.03
Increase	8.37	9.10*	7.61	10.46	8.53*	10.67	16.54	10.14*	16.68

TABLE 7 VITAL STATISTICS AND RATES INFERRED FROM AGE DISTRIBUTIONS (FEMALES)

Vital statistics		Thompson Age range	NRR	$1000r$	Interval	Bourgeois-Pichat Age range	NRR	$1000b$	$1000d$	$1000r$	Coale	
TFR	2.79	0–4	1.33	10.66	27.45	5–29	1.51	21.73	6.51	15.22	$1000b$	20.06
GRR	1.36	5–9	1.41	12.72	27.42	30–54	1.11	14.28	10.39	3.89	$1000d$	8.75
NRR	1.32	10–14	1.43	13.03	27.38	55–79	1.67	33.39	14.49	18.90	$1000r$	11.32
Generation	28.39	15–19	1.51	14.26	27.32	*40–64	1.27	18.12	9.39	8.73	$1000k_1$	0.
Sex ratio	105.5										$1000k_2$	0.

TABLE 8 LESLIE MATRIX AND ITS ANALYSIS (FEMALES)

Start of age interval	Sub-diagonal	First row	Percent in stable population	Fisher values	Total reproductive values	Net maternity function	Matrix equation coefficient	Parameters	Integral	Matrix
0	0.99721	0.00000	9.090	1.038	611340	0.00000	0.00000	λ_1	1.0508	1.0509
5	0.99844	0.00005	8.626	1.094	631635	0.00000	0.00005	λ_2	0.4014	0.4036
10	0.99838	0.32698	8.195	1.152	628842	0.00011	0.02687		+0.8032	+0.7775 i
15	0.99814	0.19463	7.786	1.184	659103	0.05362	0.19347	r_1	0.0099	0.0099
20	0.99779	0.40056	7.396	1.044	534994	0.33332	0.39743	r_2	−0.0215	−0.0265
25	0.99689	0.37731	7.022	0.683	275673	0.46155	0.37354		+0.2215	+0.2184 i
30	0.99571	0.21646	6.662	0.327	122703	0.28553	0.21363	c_1		56233
35	0.99327	0.09508	6.312	0.119	45558	0.14173	0.09344	c_2		−44534
40	0.98918	0.02511	5.966	0.027	10194	0.04514	0.02451			49014 i
45	0.98353	0.00201	5.616	0.002	715	0.00389	0.00194	$2\pi/y$	28.369	28.770
50	0.97551	0.00000	5.256	0.000	2	0.00000	0.00000	Δ	3.567	
55	0.81855		22.071							

[455]

Norway, 1967

TABLE 1   DATA INPUT TO COMPUTATIONS

Age at last birthday	Total	Males	%	Females	%	Births, by age of mother	Total	Males	Females	Age at last birthday
		Population						Deaths		
0	66067	34015	1.8	32052	1.7	0	985	563	422	0
1–4	255258	131331	7.0	123927	6.5	0	226	137	89	1–4
5–9	305590	156606	8.3	148984	7.8	0	117	81	36	5–9
10–14	306990	156957	8.3	150033	7.9	0	113	75	38	10–14
15–19	303906	156384	8.3	147522	7.8	6244	200	143	57	15–19
20–24	295879	152557	8.1	143322	7.5	25552	203	162	41	20–24
25–29	215044	109623	5.8	105421	5.6	17704	156	113	43	25–29
30–34	193232	98052	5.2	95180	5.0	9796	191	134	57	30–34
35–39	214100	108473	5.8	105627	5.6	5503	303	196	107	35–39
40–44	242559	122808	6.5	119751	6.3	1821	524	357	167	40–44
45–49	258541	128992	6.8	129549	6.8	158	884	607	277	45–49
50–54	240205	119331	6.3	120874	6.4	1	1315	855	460	50–54
55–59	223693	109924	5.8	113769	6.0	0	1938	1266	672	55–59
60–64	195649	92559	4.9	103090	5.4	0	2795	1777	1018	60–64
65–69	169967	78152	4.1	91815	4.8	0	4144	2538	1606	65–69
70–74	131530	59328	3.1	72202	3.8		5127	2845	2282	70–74
75–79	86928	37667	2.0	49261	2.6		5709	2859	2840	75–79
80–84	50062	20890	1.1	29172	1.5	34358 M	5344	2500	2844	80–84
85+	29062	11896	0.6	17166	0.9	32421 F	5942	2512	3430	85+
All ages	3784262	1885545		1898717		66779	36216	19730	16486	All ages

TABLE 2   LIFE TABLE FOR MALES

Age, x	$_nq_x$	l_x	$_nd_x$	$_nL_x$	$_nm_x$	T_x	$1000r_x$	$\overset{\circ}{e}_x$	$_nM_x$	Age, x
0	0.01632	100000	1632	98829	0.01652	7135956	2.77	71.36	0.01655	0
1	0.00415	98368	408	392300	0.00104	7037126	2.77	71.54	0.00104	1
5	0.00258	97960	253	489166	0.00052	6644827	4.57	67.83	0.00052	5
10	0.00239	97707	233	487991	0.00048	6155661	0.00	63.00	0.00048	10
15	0.00456	97474	445	486314	0.00091	5667670	2.00	58.15	0.00091	15
20	0.00530	97029	514	483869	0.00106	5181356	34.50	53.40	0.00105	20
25	0.00515	96515	497	481358	0.00103	4697487	43.09	48.67	0.00103	25
30	0.00681	96017	654	478525	0.00137	4216129	0.00	43.91	0.00137	30
35	0.00900	95363	858	474818	0.00181	3737604	0.00	39.19	0.00181	35
40	0.01444	94505	1364	469387	0.00291	3262785	0.00	34.52	0.00291	40
45	0.02327	93141	2168	460668	0.00471	2793398	0.00	29.99	0.00471	45
50	0.03530	90973	3211	447413	0.00718	2332730	8.50	25.64	0.00716	50
55	0.05625	87762	4936	427392	0.01155	1885317	13.29	21.48	0.01152	55
60	0.09228	82826	7643	396351	0.01928	1457925	20.11	17.60	0.01920	60
65	0.15119	75183	11367	348768	0.03259	1061564	20.11	14.12	0.03248	65
70	0.21543	63816	13748	285694	0.04812	712796	20.11	11.17	0.04795	70
75	0.32142	50068	16093	210524	0.07644	427102	20.11	8.53	0.07617	75
80	0.46340	33975	15744	130960	0.12022	216578	20.11	6.37	0.11968	80
85+	•1.00000	18231	18231	85618	0.21293	85618	20.11	4.70	0.21115	85+

TABLE 3   LIFE TABLE FOR FEMALES

Age, x	$_nq_x$	l_x	$_nd_x$	$_nL_x$	$_nm_x$	T_x	$1000r_x$	$\overset{\circ}{e}_x$	$_nM_x$	Age, x
0	0.01301	100000	1301	99046	0.01314	7685116	2.84	76.85	0.01317	0
1	0.00286	98699	282	393982	0.00072	7586059	2.84	76.86	0.00072	1
5	0.00121	98417	119	491787	0.00024	7192087	3.51	73.08	0.00024	5
10	0.00127	98298	124	491194	0.00025	6700300	0.70	68.16	0.00025	10
15	0.00193	98174	189	490398	0.00039	6209106	4.25	63.25	0.00039	15
20	0.00143	97984	140	489573	0.00029	5718709	33.26	58.36	0.00029	20
25	0.00205	97844	201	488750	0.00041	5229135	40.52	53.44	0.00041	25
30	0.00299	97643	292	487548	0.00060	4740386	0.00	48.55	0.00060	30
35	0.00505	97351	492	485637	0.00101	4252839	0.00	43.69	0.00101	35
40	0.00695	96859	673	482725	0.00139	3767232	0.00	38.89	0.00139	40
45	0.01064	96186	1023	478607	0.00214	3284507	0.00	34.15	0.00214	45
50	0.01890	95163	1798	471673	0.00381	2805900	9.14	29.49	0.00381	50
55	0.02920	93365	2726	460550	0.00592	2334226	9.67	25.00	0.00591	55
60	0.04856	90639	4402	443140	0.00993	1873676	24.72	20.67	0.00987	60
65	0.08458	86237	7294	414466	0.01760	1430536	24.72	16.59	0.01749	65
70	0.14804	78943	11687	367542	0.03180	1016069	24.72	12.87	0.03161	70
75	0.25438	67256	17109	295179	0.05796	648528	24.72	9.64	0.05765	75
80	0.39291	50148	19703	201218	0.09792	353348	24.72	7.05	0.09749	80
85+	1.00000	30444	30444	152130	0.20012	152130	24.72	5.00	0.19981	85+

TABLE 4 POPULATION PROJECTION, USING FIXED AGE-SPECIFIC BIRTH AND DEATH RATES, IN THOUSANDS

Age at last birthday	1972			1977			1982			Age at last birthday
	Total	Males	Females	Total	Males	Females	Total	Males	Females	
0–4	347	178	169	378	194	184	397	204	193	0–4
5–9	321	165	156	345	177	168	376	193	183	5–9
10–14	305	156	149	319	164	155	345	177	168	10–14
15–19	306	156	150	305	156	149	319	164	155	15–19
20–24	303	156	147	306	156	150	303	155	148	20–24
25–29	295	152	143	302	155	147	304	155	149	25–29
30–34	214	109	105	294	151	143	301	154	147	30–34
35–39	192	97	95	213	108	105	292	150	142	35–39
40–44	212	107	105	190	96	94	211	107	104	40–44
45–49	240	121	119	209	105	104	187	94	93	45–49
50–54	253	125	128	234	117	117	205	102	103	50–54
55–59	232	114	118	245	120	125	226	112	114	55–59
60–64	211	102	109	220	106	114	231	111	120	60–64
65–69	177	81	96	192	90	102	199	93	106	65–69
70–74	145	64	81	153	67	86	164	73	91	70–74
75–79	102	44	58	112	47	65	118	49	69	75–79
80–84	57	23	34	67	27	40	74	29	45	80–84
85 +	36	14	22	40	15	25	48	18	30	85 +
All ages	3948	1964	1984	4124	2051	2073	4300	2140	2160	All ages

TABLE 5 OBSERVED AND PROJECTED VITAL RATES

Rates per thousand	Observed			Projected						Stable	
				1972		1977		1982			
	Total	Males	Females	Males	Females	Males	Females	Males	Females	Males	Females
Birth	17.65	18.22	17.08	19.42	18.14	19.91	18.60	19.78	18.49	20.22	19.15
Death	9.57	10.46	8.68	10.94	9.53	11.25	10.08	11.43	10.51	9.81	8.74
Increase	8.08	7.76	8.39	8.48	8.62	8.66	8.52	8.35	7.98		10.4101

TABLE 6 RATES STANDARDIZED ON THREE STANDARD COUNTRIES

Standardized rates per thousand	England and Wales, 1961			United States, 1960			Mexico, 1960		
	Total	Males	Females	Total	Males	Females	Total	Males	Females
Birth	17.77	19.57*	16.72	18.08	17.82*	17.29	21.21	17.33*	20.54
Death	9.20	9.38*	9.04	7.44	8.52*	6.54	3.73	7.40*	2.99
Increase	8.57	10.19*	7.68	10.64	9.30*	10.75	17.48	9.94*	17.55

TABLE 7 VITAL STATISTICS AND RATES INFERRED FROM AGE DISTRIBUTIONS (FEMALES)

Vital statistics		Thompson				Bourgeois-Pichat					Coale
		Age range	NRR	1000r	Interval	Age range	NRR	1000b	1000d	1000r	
TFR	2.80	0–4	1.29	9.41	27.46	5–29	1.48	19.07	4.63	14.44	1000b
GRR	1.36	5–9	1.26	8.55	27.44	30–54	0.66	6.50	21.75	-15.26	1000d
NRR	1.33	10–14	1.31	9.70	27.40	55–79	1.49	30.67	15.95	14.73	1000r
Generation	27.25	15–19	1.26	8.21	27.34	*45–69	1.31	22.87	12.92	9.95	1000k_1
Sex ratio	105.97										1000k_2

TABLE 8 LESLIE MATRIX AND ITS ANALYSIS (FEMALES)

Start of age interval	Sub-diagonal	First row	Percent in stable population	Fisher values	Total reproductive values	Net maternity function	Matrix equation coefficient	Parameters		
									Integral	Matrix
0	0.99748	0.00000	9.203	1.041	162348	0.00000	0.00000	λ_1	1.0534	1.0535
5	0.99879	0.00000	8.714	1.099	163775	0.00000	0.00000	λ_2	0.3480	0.3561
10	0.99838	0.05057	8.262	1.159	173961	0.00000	0.05039		+0.7903	+0.7623i
15	0.99832	0.26367	7.829	1.171	172715	0.10077	0.25226	r_1	0.0104	0.0104
20	0.99832	0.41402	7.419	0.961	137672	0.42375	0.41112	r_2	-0.0294	-0.0345
25	0.99754	0.32386	7.031	0.582	61356	0.39849	0.32105		+0.2312	+0.2267i
30	0.99602	0.18528	6.657	0.277	26340	0.24362	0.18322	c_1		17620
35	0.99407	0.08044	6.294	0.099	10466	0.12283	0.07923	c_2		-17693
40	0.99147	0.01965	5.939	0.021	2489	0.03564	0.01924			5752i
45	0.98551	0.00147	5.589	0.001	189	0.00283	0.00143	$2\pi/y$	27.175	27.710
50	0.97642	0.00001	5.229	0.000	2	0.00002	0.00001	Δ	6.482	
55	0.81966		21.834							

Poland, 1965

TABLE 1 DATA INPUT TO COMPUTATIONS

Age at last birthday	Population					Births, by age of mother	Deaths			Age at last birthday
	Total	Males	%	Females	%		Total	Males	Females	
0	556771	285781	1.9	270990	1.7	0	22811	13240	9571	0
1–4	2296788	1178392	7.8	1118396	7.0	0	2918	1620	1298	1–4
5–9	3494321	1785456	11.8	1708865	10.6	0	1578	932	646	5–9
10–14	3446565	1756610	11.6	1689955	10.5	150	1291	784	507	10–14
15–19	2739146	1391561	9.2	1347585	8.4	44542	1949	1339	610	15–19
20–24	1949145	984736	6.5	964409	6.0	176017	2210	1595	615	20–24
25–29	2219783	1111061	7.3	1108722	6.9	158774	2936	2049	887	25–29
30–34	2344158	1166763	7.7	1177395	7.3	97901	3867	2584	1283	30–34
35–39	2275529	1092162	7.2	1183367	7.4	51781	5129	3256	1873	35–39
40–44	1946208	900188	6.0	1046020	6.5	15950	5981	3637	2344	40–44
45–49	1253694	576916	3.8	676778	4.2	1027	5833	3423	2410	45–49
50–54	1682539	770879	5.1	911660	5.7	120	11261	6730	4531	50–54
55–59	1600943	745018	4.9	855925	5.3	0	18005	11065	6940	55–59
60–64	1300470	579900	3.8	720570	4.5	0	23613	14177	9436	60–64
65–69	905470	374995	2.5	530475	3.3	0	28378	15356	13022	65–69
70–74	575364	222456	1.5	352908	2.2		28365	13778	14587	70–74
75–79	347593	123771	0.8	223822	1.4		28287	11921	16366	75–79
80–84	168704	55729	0.4	112975	0.7	282381 M	21066	7996	13070	80–84
85+	78520	22773	0.2	55747	0.3	263981 F	16943	5555	11388	85+
All ages	31181711	15125147		16056564		546362	232421	121037	111384	All ages

TABLE 2 LIFE TABLE FOR MALES

Age, x	$_nq_x$	l_x	$_nd_x$	$_nL_x$	$_nm_x$	T_x	$1000r_x$	$\overset{\circ}{e}_x$	$_nM_x$	Age, x
0	0.04468	100000	4458	96434	0.04633	6639207	0.00	66.39	0.04633	0
1	0.00548	95532	523	380596	0.00137	6542773	0.00	68.49	0.00137	1
5	0.00261	95009	248	474426	0.00052	6162177	0.00	64.86	0.00052	5
10	0.00224	94761	212	473321	0.00045	5687751	24.35	60.02	0.00045	10
15	0.00487	94549	460	471708	0.00098	5214431	56.88	55.15	0.00098	15
20	0.00809	94089	761	468624	0.00162	4742722	20.98	50.41	0.00162	20
25	0.00918	93328	857	464551	0.00184	4274099	0.00	45.80	0.00184	25
30	0.01101	92471	1019	459913	0.00221	3809548	0.00	41.20	0.00221	30
35	0.01484	91453	1358	454035	0.00299	3349634	22.91	36.63	0.00298	35
40	0.02019	90095	1819	446183	0.00408	2895599	59.61	32.14	0.00404	40
45	0.02930	88276	2587	435298	0.00594	2449416	9.45	27.75	0.00593	45
50	0.04279	85689	3666	419972	0.00873	2014118	0.00	23.50	0.00873	50
55	0.07199	82023	5904	396642	0.01489	1594146	13.00	19.44	0.01485	55
60	0.11668	76118	8882	359789	0.02469	1197706	45.92	15.73	0.02445	60
65	0.18783	67237	12629	305839	0.04129	837918	45.92	12.46	0.04095	65
70	0.27057	54608	14775	236703	0.06242	532079	45.92	9.74	0.06194	70
75	0.38968	39832	15522	159930	0.09706	295375	45.92	7.42	0.09631	75
80	0.52331	24310	12722	88038	0.14451	135446	45.92	5.57	0.14348	80
85+	1.00000	11589	11589	47407	0.24445	47407	45.92	4.09	0.24393	85+

TABLE 3 LIFE TABLE FOR FEMALES

Age, x	$_nq_x$	l_x	$_nd_x$	$_nL_x$	$_nm_x$	T_x	$1000r_x$	$\overset{\circ}{e}_x$	$_nM_x$	Age, x
0	0.03436	100000	3435	97294	0.03532	7232278	0.00	72.32	0.03532	0
1	0.00463	96564	447	384949	0.00116	7134985	0.00	73.89	0.00115	1
5	0.00189	96117	182	480131	0.00038	6750036	0.00	70.23	0.00038	5
10	0.00150	95935	144	479325	0.00030	6269905	23.40	65.36	0.00030	10
15	0.00228	95791	218	478445	0.00046	5790580	55.64	60.45	0.00045	15
20	0.00319	95573	305	477136	0.00064	5312136	18.88	55.58	0.00064	20
25	0.00399	95268	380	475433	0.00080	4834999	0.00	50.75	0.00080	25
30	0.00543	94888	515	473226	0.00109	4359566	0.00	45.94	0.00109	30
35	0.00790	94372	745	470109	0.00159	3886340	10.23	41.18	0.00158	35
40	0.01125	93627	1054	465685	0.00226	3416231	53.49	36.49	0.00224	40
45	0.01769	92573	1637	459018	0.00357	2950545	10.21	31.87	0.00356	45
50	0.02457	90936	2234	449491	0.00497	2491527	0.00	27.40	0.00497	50
55	0.03992	88702	3541	435332	0.00813	2042036	15.14	23.02	0.00811	55
60	0.06425	85161	5472	413333	0.01324	1506705	43.22	18.87	0.01310	60
65	0.11720	79689	9340	376739	0.02479	1193371	43.22	14.98	0.02455	65
70	0.18989	70349	13358	320112	0.04173	816633	43.22	11.61	0.04133	70
75	0.31235	56991	17801	241374	0.07375	496520	43.22	8.71	0.07312	75
80	0.45388	39190	17788	152231	0.11685	255146	43.22	6.51	0.11569	80
85+	*1.00000	21402	21402	102916	0.20796	102916	43.22	4.81	0.20428	85+

TABLE 4 POPULATION PROJECTION, USING FIXED AGE-SPECIFIC BIRTH AND DEATH RATES, IN THOUSANDS

Age at last birthday	1970			1975			1980			Age at last birthday
	Total	Males	Females	Total	Males	Females	Total	Males	Females	
0–4	2752	1415	1337	3126	1607	1519	3522	1811	1711	0–4
5–9	2839	1456	1383	2738	1407	1331	3110	1598	1512	5–9
10–14	3487	1781	1706	2834	1453	1381	2733	1404	1329	10–14
15–19	3438	1751	1687	3478	1775	1703	2826	1448	1378	15–19
20–24	2726	1382	1344	3421	1739	1682	3462	1764	1698	20–24
25–29	1937	976	961	2709	1370	1339	3400	1724	1676	25–29
30–34	2204	1100	1104	1923	966	957	2690	1357	1333	30–34
35–39	2322	1152	1170	2182	1086	1096	1904	954	950	35–39
40–44	2245	1073	1172	2291	1132	1159	2153	1067	1086	40–44
45–49	1909	878	1031	2202	1047	1155	2246	1104	1142	45–49
50–54	1220	557	663	1857	847	1010	2141	1010	1131	50–54
55–59	1611	728	883	1167	525	642	1778	800	978	55–59
60–64	1489	676	813	1498	660	838	1086	477	609	60–64
65–69	1150	493	657	1316	575	741	1325	561	764	65–69
70–74	741	290	451	940	382	558	1074	445	629	70–74
75–79	416	150	266	536	196	340	679	258	421	75–79
80–84	209	68	141	251	83	168	322	108	214	80–84
85 +	106	30	76	132	37	95	158	45	113	85 +
All ages	32801	15956	16845	34601	16887	17714	36609	17935	18674	All ages

TABLE 5 OBSERVED AND PROJECTED VITAL RATES

Rates per thousand	Observed			Projected							Stable	
				1970		1975		1980				
	Total	Males	Females	Males	Females	Males	Females	Males	Females		Males	Females
Birth	17.52	18.67	16.44	19.48	17.25	21.50	19.16	22.09	19.83		18.15	16.85
Death	7.45	8.00	6.94	8.71	7.75	9.42	8.55	9.93	9.20		12.86	11.57
Increase	10.07	10.67	9.50	10.77	9.50	12.07	10.61	12.16	10.63			5.2822

TABLE 6 RATES STANDARDIZED ON THREE STANDARD COUNTRIES

Standardized rates per thousand	England and Wales, 1961			United States, 1960			Mexico, 1960		
	Total	Males	Females	Total	Males	Females	Total	Males	Females
Birth	15.93	17.49*	14.92	16.16	16.57*	15.39	19.19	15.89*	18.50
Death	11.96	12.82*	11.64	9.90	10.83*	8.69	5.54	8.07*	4.52
Increase	3.97	4.67*	3.28	6.26	5.75*	6.70	13.65	7.81*	13.97

TABLE 7 VITAL STATISTICS AND RATES INFERRED FROM AGE DISTRIBUTIONS (FEMALES)

Vital statistics		Thompson				Bourgeois-Pichat				Coale	
		Age range	NRR	1000r	Interval	Age range	NRR	1000b	1000d	1000r	1000b
TFR	2.51	0–4	1.20	6.66	27.43	5–29	2.13	28.30	0.26	28.04	1000d
GRR	1.21	5–9	1.63	18.07	27.39	30–54	1.66	29.34	10.47	18.87	1000r
NRR	1.15	10–14	1.61	17.25	27.34	55–79	2.86	119.21	80.23	38.98	$1000k_1$
Generation	27.11	15–19	1.33	9.98	27.27	*50–74	2.31	69.84	38.78	31.06	$1000k_2$
Sex ratio	106.97										

TABLE 8 LESLIE MATRIX AND ITS ANALYSIS (FEMALES)

Start of age interval	Sub-diagonal	First row	Percent in stable population	Fisher values	Total reproductive values	Net maternity function	Matrix equation coefficient	Parameters		
									Integral	Matrix
0	0.99562	0.00000	8.019	1.051	1459652	0.00000	0.00000	λ_1	1.0268	1.0268
5	0.99832	0.00010	7.776	1.083	1851465	0.00000	0.00010	λ_2	0.3148	0.3270
10	0.99816	0.03863	7.561	1.114	1882994	0.00021	0.03839		+0.7695	+0.7392i
15	0.99727	0.25064	7.350	1.106	1489775	0.07658	0.24867	r_1	0.0053	0.0053
20	0.99643	0.37887	7.139	0.874	843083	0.42075	0.37486	r_2	−0.0369	−0.0426
25	0.99536	0.26325	6.928	0.501	555879	0.32896	0.25954		+0.2365	+0.2309i
30	0.99341	0.14751	6.716	0.239	281795	0.19012	0.14475	c_1		186895
35	0.99059	0.06857	6.497	0.091	108129	0.09939	0.06585	c_2		5876
40	0.98568	0.01951	6.268	0.022	23001	0.03431	0.01884			593221i
45	0.97924	0.00192	6.017	0.002	1429	0.00337	0.00183	$2\pi/y$	26.567	27.217
50	0.96850	0.00015	5.739	0.000	144	0.00029	0.00014	Δ	9.246	
55	0.79510		23.990							

Portugal, 1966-68

TABLE 1 DATA INPUT TO COMPUTATIONS

Age at last birthday	Population					Births, by age of mother	Deaths			Age at last birthday
	Total	Males	%	Females	%		Total	Males	Females	
0	199555	104019	2.3	95536	2.0	0	12426	6990	5436	0
1–4	729545	376781	8.3	352764	7.2	0	3048	1627	1421	1–4
5–9	904600	464900	10.3	439700	9.0	0	763	449	314	5–9
10–14	884100	447800	9.9	436300	8.9	60	493	291	202	10–14
15–19	721600	352200	7.8	369400	7.6	11366	694	482	212	15–19
20–24	682700	318200	7.0	364500	7.5	51595	747	489	258	20–24
25–29	681100	326600	7.2	354500	7.3	56270	827	537	290	25–29
30–34	724300	346400	7.6	377900	7.7	42106	1097	716	381	30–34
35–39	620000	300800	6.6	319200	6.5	27509	1499	949	550	35–39
40–44	487400	238400	5.3	249000	5.1	11417	1992	1295	697	40–44
45–49	560000	275600	6.1	284400	5.8	981	2462	1560	902	45–49
50–54	561700	268400	5.9	293300	6.0	18	3679	2373	1306	50–54
55–59	476600	219200	4.8	257400	5.3	0	5343	3384	1959	55–59
60–64	371000	164700	3.6	206300	4.2	0	7107	4254	2853	60–64
65–69	295600	127800	2.8	167800	3.4	0	9021	5061	3960	65–69
70–74	238600	97600	2.2	141000	2.9		11257	5695	5562	70–74
75–79	150974	57825	1.3	93149	1.9		20128	8408	11720	75–79
80–84	77290	27351	0.6	49939	1.0	104080 M	7650	3054	4596	80–84
85+	48336	14824	0.3	33512	0.7	97242 F	6622	2049	4573	85+
All ages	9415000	4529400		4885600		201322	96855	49663	47192	All ages

TABLE 2 LIFE TABLE FOR MALES

Age, x	$_nq_x$	l_x	$_nd_x$	$_nL_x$	$_nm_x$	T_x	$1000r_x$	$\overset{\circ}{e}_x$	$_nM_x$	Age, x
0	0.06379	100000	6379	95421	0.06686	6396528	6.79	63.97	0.06720	0
1	0.01695	93621	1587	369929	0.00429	6301107	6.79	67.30	0.00432	1
5	0.00480	92034	442	459064	0.00096	5931178	5.35	64.45	0.00097	5
10	0.00326	91592	298	457252	0.00065	5472114	26.87	59.74	0.00065	10
15	0.00685	91294	625	454987	0.00137	5014861	32.93	54.93	0.00137	15
20	0.00766	90668	694	451629	0.00154	4559874	6.02	50.29	0.00154	20
25	0.00819	89974	737	448075	0.00164	4108245	0.00	45.66	0.00164	25
30	0.01029	89237	919	444027	0.00207	3660170	6.05	41.02	0.00207	30
35	0.01578	88319	1393	438404	0.00318	3216143	33.92	36.42	0.00315	35
40	0.02682	86925	2331	429000	0.00543	2777739	3.82	31.96	0.00543	40
45	0.02792	84594	2362	417323	0.00566	2348739	0.00	27.76	0.00566	45
50	0.04346	82232	3574	402963	0.00887	1931416	13.43	23.49	0.00884	50
55	0.07505	78658	5903	379641	0.01555	1528453	32.64	19.43	0.01544	55
60	0.12225	72755	8894	342721	0.02595	1148811	25.53	15.79	0.02583	60
65	0.18140	63860	11584	291299	0.03977	806090	25.53	12.62	0.03960	65
70	0.25803	52276	13489	229542	0.05876	514791	25.53	9.85	0.05835	70
75	0.53167	38787	20622	141182	0.14607	285249	25.53	7.35	0.14540	75
80	0.42561	18165	7731	69375	0.11144	144068	25.53	7.93	0.11166	80
85+	*1.00000	10434	10434	74692	0.13969	74692	25.53	7.16	0.13822	85+

TABLE 3 LIFE TABLE FOR FEMALES

Age, x	$_nq_x$	l_x	$_nd_x$	$_nL_x$	$_nm_x$	T_x	$1000r_x$	$\overset{\circ}{e}_x$	$_nM_x$	Age, x
0	0.05450	100000	5450	96149	0.05668	6973151	5.18	69.73	0.05690	0
1	0.01585	94550	1499	373917	0.00401	6877002	5.18	72.73	0.00403	1
5	0.00356	93051	331	464428	0.00071	6503084	1.21	69.89	0.00071	5
10	0.00231	92720	214	463051	0.00046	6038656	16.87	65.13	0.00046	10
15	0.00287	92506	265	461889	0.00057	5575605	17.41	60.27	0.00057	15
20	0.00353	92240	326	460410	0.00071	5113717	3.42	55.44	0.00071	20
25	0.00408	91914	375	458662	0.00082	4653307	0.00	50.63	0.00082	25
30	0.00504	91539	461	456629	0.00101	4194645	9.38	45.82	0.00101	30
35	0.00866	91078	788	453585	0.00174	3738017	39.91	41.04	0.00172	35
40	0.01392	90290	1256	448435	0.00280	3284432	8.91	36.38	0.00280	40
45	0.01574	89033	1401	441804	0.00317	2835997	0.00	31.85	0.00317	45
50	0.02206	87632	1933	433707	0.00446	2394193	5.19	27.32	0.00445	50
55	0.03766	85699	3227	421180	0.00766	1960486	27.00	22.88	0.00761	55
60	0.06735	82471	5554	399599	0.01390	1539306	21.65	18.66	0.01383	60
65	0.11234	76917	8641	364430	0.02371	1139707	21.65	14.82	0.02360	65
70	0.18297	68276	12492	313922	0.03979	775277	21.65	11.35	0.03945	70
75	0.47936	55784	26741	211701	0.12631	461355	21.65	8.27	0.12582	75
80	0.36941	29043	10729	116639	0.09198	249653	21.65	8.60	0.09203	80
85+	*1.00000	18315	18315	133014	0.13769	133014	21.65	7.25	0.13646	85+

[460]

TABLE 4 POPULATION PROJECTION, USING FIXED AGE-SPECIFIC BIRTH AND DEATH RATES, IN THOUSANDS

Age at last birthday	1972			1977			1982			Age at last birthday
	Total	Males	Females	Total	Males	Females	Total	Males	Females	
0–4	962	495	467	1010	520	490	1063	547	516	0–4
5–9	917	474	443	950	488	462	998	513	485	5–9
10–14	901	463	438	914	472	442	946	486	460	10–14
15–19	881	446	435	898	461	437	911	470	441	15–19
20–24	718	350	368	876	442	434	893	457	436	20–24
25–29	679	316	363	714	347	367	871	439	432	25–29
30–34	677	324	353	675	313	362	709	344	365	30–34
35–39	717	342	375	671	320	351	668	309	359	35–39
40–44	610	294	316	706	335	371	660	313	347	40–44
45–49	477	232	245	597	286	311	592	326	366	45–49
50–54	545	266	279	465	224	241	581	276	305	50–54
55–59	538	253	285	522	251	271	445	211	234	55–59
60–64	442	198	244	498	228	270	483	226	257	60–64
65–69	328	140	188	391	168	223	440	194	246	65–69
70–74	246	101	145	272	110	162	325	133	192	70–74
75–79	155	60	95	159	62	97	177	68	109	75–79
80–84	79	28	51	81	29	52	84	30	54	80–84
85 +	86	29	57	90	31	59	92	32	60	85 +
All ages	9958	4811	5147	10489	5087	5402	11038	5374	5664	All ages

TABLE 5 OBSERVED AND PROJECTED VITAL RATES

Rates per thousand	Observed			Projected							Stable	
				1972		1977		1982				
	Total	Males	Females	Males	Females	Males	Females	Males	Females		Males	Females
Birth	21.38	22.98	19.90	22.59	19.72	22.53	19.83	22.39	19.85		20.85	19.45
Death	10.29	10.96	9.66	11.37	10.20	11.49	10.27	11.64	10.49		12.50	11.10
Increase	11.10	12.01	10.24	11.22	9.52	11.05	9.56	10.76	9.36			8.3514

TABLE 6 RATES STANDARDIZED ON THREE STANDARD COUNTRIES

Standardized rates per thousand	England and Wales, 1961			United States, 1960			Mexico, 1960		
	Total	Males	Females	Total	Males	Females	Total	Males	Females
Birth	18.54	21.66*	17.36	18.82	20.41*	17.91	20.50	19.61*	19.75
Death	12.85	13.84*	12.61	10.89	12.06*	9.71	6.87	9.28*	5.84
Increase	5.68	7.82*	4.74	7.93	8.36*	8.20	13.62	10.33*	13.91

TABLE 7 VITAL STATISTICS AND RATES INFERRED FROM AGE DISTRIBUTIONS (FEMALES)

Vital statistics		Thompson				Bourgeois-Pichat					Coale	
		Age range	NRR	$1000r$	Interval	Age range	NRR	$1000b$	$1000d$	$1000r$		
TFR	2.89	0–4	1.28	9.23	27.43	5–29	1.37	21.24	9.65	11.60	$1000b$	19.98
GRR	1.40	5–9	1.32	10.23	27.38	30–54	1.31	21.03	11.17	9.86	$1000d$	12.07
NRR	1.28	10–14	1.35	10.90	27.34	55–79	1.75	39.90	19.13	20.77	$1000r$	7.91
Generation	29.26	15–19	1.19	6.31	27.27	*50–74	1.81	43.45	21.42	22.03	$1000k_1$	-3.13
Sex ratio	107.0										$1000k_2$	0.

TABLE 8 LESLIE MATRIX AND ITS ANALYSIS (FEMALES)

Start of age interval	Sub-diagonal	First row	Percent in stable population	Fisher values	Total reproductive values	Net maternity function	Matrix equation coefficient	Parameters		
									Integral	Matrix
0	0.98800	0.00000	8.959	1.086	486854	0.00000	0.00000	λ_1	1.0426	1.0427
5	0.99703	0.00016	8.489	1.145	503938	0.00000	0.00015	λ_2	0.4297	0.4363
10	0.99749	0.03500	8.117	1.198	522861	0.00031	0.03448		+0.7190	+0.7022 i
15	0.99680	0.19511	7.766	1.215	448669	0.06865	0.19172	r_1	0.0084	0.0084
20	0.99620	0.34021	7.424	1.058	385612	0.31479	0.33322	r_2	-0.0354	-0.0381
25	0.99557	0.30613	7.093	0.736	261054	0.35165	0.29870		+0.2064	+0.2030 i
30	0.99333	0.22368	6.772	0.437	165262	0.24575	0.21728	c_1		50657
35	0.98865	0.14930	6.452	0.214	68467	0.18881	0.14406	c_2		8369
40	0.98521	0.05591	6.118	0.062	15493	0.09931	0.05334			19068 i
45	0.98167	0.00398	5.780	0.004	1199	0.00735	0.00374	$2\pi/y$	30.438	30.957
50	0.97111	0.00007	5.442	0.000	21	0.00013	0.00006	Δ	3.590	
55	0.79786		21.588							

Spain, 1967

TABLE 1 DATA INPUT TO COMPUTATIONS

Age at last birthday	Population					Births, by age of mother	Deaths			Age at last birthday
	Total	Males	%	Females	%		Total	Males	Females	
0	683650	349368	2.2	334282	2.0	0	17563	10019	7544	0
1–4	2571830	1314293	8.4	1257537	7.5	0	2535	1407	1128	1–4
5–9	3044302	1552349	9.9	1491953	8.9	0	1375	823	552	5–9
10–14	2775936	1434083	9.2	1341853	8.0	108	1089	659	430	10–14
15–19	2590908	1310897	8.4	1280011	7.6	15221	1574	1143	531	15–19
20–24	2369886	1152385	7.4	1217501	7.2	132620	2193	1511	682	20–24
25–29	2133066	1022715	6.5	1110351	6.6	200028	2074	1324	750	25–29
30–34	2235585	1056123	6.8	1179462	7.0	178403	3071	1850	1221	30–34
35–39	2278467	1096025	7.0	1182442	7.0	104778	4284	2623	1661	35–39
40–44	2195068	1050003	6.7	1145065	6.8	35364	5845	3631	2214	40–44
45–49	1882867	882993	5.6	999874	6.0	4534	7454	4535	2919	45–49
50–54	1705670	791205	5.1	914465	5.4	983	10359	6227	4132	50–54
55–59	1603436	743258	4.8	860178	5.1	0	15614	9639	5975	55–59
60–64	1403324	647950	4.1	755374	4.5	0	23133	14065	9068	60–64
65–69	1154170	513775	3.3	640395	3.8	0	29016	16729	12287	65–69
70–74	828569	346681	2.2	481888	2.9		36460	19282	17178	70–74
75–79	507599	200905	1.3	306694	1.8		39961	19037	20924	75–79
80–84	268474	100962	0.6	167512	1.0	344791 M	35051	14754	20297	80–84
85 +	197851	69330	0.4	128521	0.8	327248 F	35270	12303	22967	85 +
All ages	32430658	15635300		16795358		672039	274021	141561	132460	All ages

TABLE 2 LIFE TABLE FOR MALES

Age, x	$_nq_x$	l_x	$_nd_x$	$_nL_x$	$_nm_x$	T_x	$1000r_x$	$\overset{\circ}{e}_x$	$_nM_x$	Age, x
0	0.02794	100000	2794	97836	0.02856	6924450	5.18	69.24	0.02868	0
1	0.00424	97206	412	387623	0.00106	6826514	5.18	70.23	0.00107	1
5	0.00264	96794	256	483331	0.00053	6438991	14.17	66.52	0.00053	5
10	0.00230	96538	222	482172	0.00046	5955660	16.34	61.69	0.00046	10
15	0.00437	96316	421	480614	0.00088	5473489	20.99	56.83	0.00087	15
20	0.00655	95896	628	477949	0.00131	4992874	23.62	52.07	0.00131	20
25	0.00646	95268	615	474843	0.00130	4514926	7.32	47.39	0.00129	25
30	0.00872	94653	825	471304	0.00175	4040083	0.00	42.68	0.00175	30
35	0.01190	93827	1116	466505	0.00239	3568778	0.00	38.04	0.00239	35
40	0.01720	92711	1595	459818	0.00347	3102273	18.05	33.45	0.00345	40
45	0.02548	91116	2321	450160	0.00516	2642455	22.98	29.00	0.00514	45
50	0.03872	88795	3438	436016	0.00788	2192295	8.94	24.69	0.00787	50
55	0.06304	85357	5381	414343	0.01299	1756280	6.30	20.58	0.01297	55
60	0.10367	79976	8292	380297	0.02180	1341937	24.01	16.78	0.02171	60
65	0.15180	71684	10882	332611	0.03272	961640	24.01	13.41	0.03255	65
70	0.24636	60803	14979	267968	0.05590	629029	24.01	10.35	0.05562	70
75	0.38446	45824	17617	185087	0.09518	361061	24.01	7.88	0.09476	75
80	0.53317	28206	15039	102507	0.14671	175974	24.01	6.24	0.14613	80
85 +	*1.00000	13167	13167	73466	0.17923	73466	24.01	5.58	0.17745	85 +

TABLE 3 LIFE TABLE FOR FEMALES

Age, x	$_nq_x$	l_x	$_nd_x$	$_nL_x$	$_nm_x$	T_x	$1000r_x$	$\overset{\circ}{e}_x$	$_nM_x$	Age, x
0	0.02209	100000	2209	98304	0.02247	7455483	5.35	74.55	0.02257	0
1	0.00355	97791	347	390153	0.00089	7357179	5.35	75.23	0.00090	1
5	0.00184	97444	179	486770	0.00037	6967026	16.57	71.50	0.00037	5
10	0.00160	97264	156	485936	0.00032	6480257	14.97	66.63	0.00032	10
15	0.00207	97108	201	485053	0.00042	5994320	9.30	61.73	0.00041	15
20	0.00280	96907	271	483882	0.00056	5509257	13.67	56.85	0.00056	20
25	0.00337	96636	326	482410	0.00068	5025375	2.45	52.00	0.00068	25
30	0.00516	96310	497	480377	0.00104	4542955	0.00	47.17	0.00104	30
35	0.00700	95812	671	477472	0.00141	4062588	1.53	42.40	0.00140	35
40	0.00965	95141	918	473559	0.00194	3585116	14.75	37.68	0.00193	40
45	0.01455	94224	1371	467933	0.00293	3111557	19.46	33.02	0.00292	45
50	0.02240	92853	2080	459426	0.00453	2643624	10.41	28.47	0.00452	50
55	0.03427	90773	3111	446725	0.00696	2184198	11.65	24.06	0.00695	55
60	0.05869	87662	5145	426386	0.01207	1737473	24.91	19.82	0.01200	60
65	0.09241	82516	7625	395032	0.01930	1311087	24.91	15.89	0.01919	65
70	0.16561	74891	12403	345695	0.03588	916055	24.91	12.23	0.03565	70
75	0.29443	62489	18398	268133	0.06862	570360	24.91	9.13	0.06822	75
80	0.46468	44091	20488	168300	0.12173	302228	24.91	6.85	0.12117	80
85 +	1.00000	23603	23603	133927	0.17623	133927	24.91	5.67	0.17870	85 +

[462]

TABLE 4 POPULATION PROJECTION, USING FIXED AGE-SPECIFIC BIRTH AND DEATH RATES, IN THOUSANDS

Age at last birthday	1972			1977			1982			Age at last birthday
	Total	Males	Females	Total	Males	Females	Total	Males	Females	
0–4	3310	1693	1617	3415	1747	1668	3589	1836	1753	0–4
5–9	3242	1656	1586	3296	1685	1511	3401	1739	1662	5–9
10–14	3038	1549	1489	3236	1652	1584	3289	1681	1608	10–14
15–19	2768	1429	1339	3031	1544	1487	3228	1647	1581	15–19
20–24	2581	1304	1277	2758	1422	1336	3018	1535	1483	20–24
25–29	2359	1145	1214	2568	1295	1273	2744	1412	1332	25–29
30–34	2121	1015	1106	2345	1136	1209	2554	1286	1258	30–34
35–39	2217	1045	1172	2104	1005	1099	2326	1125	1201	35–39
40–44	2253	1080	1173	2193	1030	1163	208C	990	1090	40–44
45–49	2159	1028	1131	2217	1058	1159	2158	1009	1149	45–49
50–54	1837	855	982	2107	996	1111	2152	1024	1138	50–54
55–59	1641	752	889	1768	813	955	2026	946	1080	55–59
60–64	1503	682	821	1539	690	849	1657	746	911	60–64
65–69	1267	567	700	1358	597	761	1390	604	786	65–69
70–74	974	414	560	1069	457	612	1147	481	666	70–74
75–79	613	239	374	721	286	435	790	315	475	75–79
80–84	304	111	193	368	133	235	431	158	273	80–84
85 +	205	72	133	233	80	153	282	95	187	85 +
All ages	34392	16636	17756	36326	17626	18700	38272	18629	19643	All ages

TABLE 5 OBSERVED AND PROJECTED VITAL RATES

Rates per thousand	Observed			Projected						Stable	
				1972		1977		1982			
	Total	Males	Females	Males	Females	Males	Females	Males	Females	Males	Females
Birth	20.72	22.05	19.48	21.20	18.85	20.82	18.63	20.90	18.81	20.49	19.40
Death	8.45	9.05	7.89	9.35	8.27	9.69	8.80	9.98	9.30	10.43	9.34
Increase	12.27	13.00	11.60	11.85	10.58	11.13	9.83	10.92	9.51		10.0599

TABLE 6 RATES STANDARDIZED ON THREE STANDARD COUNTRIES

Standardized rates per thousand	England and Wales, 1961			United States, 1960			Mexico, 1960		
	Total	Males	Females	Total	Males	Females	Total	Males	Females
Birth	18.45	21.52*	17.42	18.77	20.09*	18.01	19.88	19.16*	19.31
Death	10.52	10.71*	10.40	8.57	9.43*	7.62	4.57	7.32*	3.77
Increase	7.93	10.81*	7.02	10.20	10.67*	10.39	15.31	11.84*	15.54

TABLE 7 VITAL STATISTICS AND RATES INFERRED FROM AGE DISTRIBUTIONS (FEMALES)

Vital statistics		Thompson				Bourgeois-Pichat					Coale	
		Age range	NRR	1000r	Interval	Age range	NRR	1000b	1000d	1000r		
TFR	2.89	0–4	1.32	10.26	27.43	5–29	1.43	19.88	6.56	13.32	1000b	20.83
GRR	1.41	5–9	1.29	9.21	27.40	30–54	1.36	22.05	10.71	11.35	1000d	7.93
NRR	1.35	10–14	1.20	6.66	27.36	55–79	1.77	39.25	18.09	21.15	1000r	12.90
Generation	29.97	15–19	1.18	5.90	27.30	*45–69	1.44	24.16	10.79	13.38	1000k_1	31.33
Sex ratio	105.4										1000k_2	0.47

TABLE 8 LESLIE MATRIX AND ITS ANALYSIS (FEMALES)

Start of age interval	Sub-diagonal	First row	Percent in stable population	Fisher values	Total reproductive values	Net maternity function	Matrix equation coefficient	Parameters		
									Integral	Matrix
0	0.99655	0.00000	9.243	1.050	1670845	0.00000	0.00000	λ_1	1.0516	1.0515
5	0.99829	0.00010	8.759	1.108	1652598	0.00000	0.00010	λ_2	0.4602	0.4601
10	0.99820	0.01421	8.314	1.167	1565644	0.00019	0.01414		+0.7851	+0.7640i
15	0.99757	0.14337	7.892	1.214	1554309	0.02809	0.14237	r_1	0.0101	0.0101
20	0.99696	0.34314	7.485	1.129	1374879	0.25666	0.33992	r_2	-0.0189	-0.0229
25	0.99578	0.39337	7.097	0.830	921520	0.42318	0.38850		+0.2081	+0.2058i
30	0.99395	0.28463	6.720	0.462	544726	0.35332	0.27992	c_1		165973
35	0.99180	0.14181	6.351	0.188	222379	0.20603	0.13862	c_2		145606
40	0.98812	0.04206	5.990	0.049	56488	0.07122	0.04078			-345i
45	0.98182	0.00665	5.628	0.008	7825	0.01033	0.00637	$2\pi/y$	30.192	30.538
50	0.97235	0.00128	5.254	0.001	1166	0.00240	0.00120	Δ	3.047	
55	0.81142		21.263							

Sweden, 1967

TABLE 1 DATA INPUT TO COMPUTATIONS

Age at last birthday	Population					Births, by age of mother	Deaths			Age at last birthday
	Total	Males	%	Females	%		Total	Males	Females	
0	120904	62236	1.6	58668	1.5	0	1560	892	668	0
1–4	471120	242062	6.2	229058	5.8	0	250	145	105	1–4
5–9	522261	268137	6.8	254124	6.5	0	171	106	65	5–9
10–14	534756	274948	7.0	259808	6.6	18	148	87	61	10–14
15–19	589158	301014	7.7	288144	7.3	13805	318	227	91	15–19
20–24	656338	337101	8.6	319237	8.1	43254	508	360	148	20–24
25–29	511055	264761	6.7	246294	6.3	35956	476	326	150	25–29
30–34	445412	227626	5.8	217786	5.5	17855	517	338	179	30–34
35–39	462977	233063	5.9	229914	5.8	8133	683	442	241	35–39
40–44	506480	254672	6.5	251808	6.4	2177	1157	727	430	40–44
45–49	543670	273362	7.0	270308	6.9	161	1853	1138	715	45–49
50–54	516154	258546	6.6	257608	6.5	1	2724	1732	992	50–54
55–59	511489	254566	6.5	256923	6.5	0	4266	2708	1558	55–59
60–64	446800	216052	5.5	230748	5.9	0	6189	3948	2241	60–64
65–69	373773	175534	4.5	198239	5.0	0	8770	5283	3487	65–69
70–74	286391	129615	3.3	156776	4.0		11339	6323	5016	70–74
75–79	196498	85154	2.2	111344	2.8		13715	6868	6847	75–79
80–84	113212	48094	1.2	65118	1.7	62617 M	12766	6073	6693	80–84
85+	59483	24423	0.6	35060	0.9	58743 F	12373	5388	6985	85+
All ages	7867931	3930966		3936965		121360	79783	43111	36672	All ages

TABLE 2 LIFE TABLE FOR MALES

Age, x	$_nq_x$	l_x	$_nd_x$	$_nL_x$	$_nm_x$	T_x	$1000r_x$	$\overset{\circ}{e}_x$	$_nM_x$	Age, x
0	0.01415	100000	1415	98922	0.01431	7187432	2.29	71.87	0.01433	0
1	0.00238	98585	235	393656	0.00060	7088510	2.29	71.90	0.00060	1
5	0.00197	98350	194	491263	0.00039	6694854	9.70	68.07	0.00040	5
10	0.00158	98156	155	490427	0.00032	6203591	0.00	63.20	0.00032	10
15	0.00376	98001	369	489156	0.00075	5713164	0.00	58.30	0.00075	15
20	0.00533	97632	521	486904	0.00107	5224008	11.79	53.51	0.00107	20
25	0.00615	97111	598	484102	0.00123	4737103	38.02	48.78	0.00123	25
30	0.00741	96513	715	480844	0.00148	4253002	11.25	44.07	0.00148	30
35	0.00944	95799	904	476864	0.00190	3772158	0.00	39.38	0.00190	35
40	0.01418	94894	1345	471321	0.00285	3295294	0.00	34.73	0.00285	40
45	0.02062	93549	1929	463272	0.00416	2823973	0.00	30.19	0.00416	45
50	0.03298	91620	3022	451104	0.00670	2360701	0.22	25.77	0.00670	50
55	0.05199	88598	4606	432385	0.01065	1909597	6.62	21.55	0.01064	55
60	0.08801	83992	7392	402769	0.01835	1477212	20.47	17.59	0.01827	60
65	0.14102	76600	10802	357456	0.03022	1074442	20.47	14.03	0.03010	65
70	0.21908	65797	14415	294309	0.04898	716987	20.47	10.90	0.04878	70
75	0.33720	51382	17326	214011	0.08096	422678	20.47	8.23	0.08065	75
80	0.48172	34056	16405	129335	0.12684	208667	20.47	6.13	0.12627	80
85+	*1.00000	17651	17651	79332	0.22249	79332	20.47	4.49	0.22061	85+

TABLE 3 LIFE TABLE FOR FEMALES

Age, x	$_nq_x$	l_x	$_nd_x$	$_nL_x$	$_nm_x$	T_x	$1000r_x$	$\overset{\circ}{e}_x$	$_nM_x$	Age, x
0	0.01127	100000	1127	99137	0.01137	7658221	2.02	76.58	0.01139	0
1	0.00183	98873	181	394967	0.00046	7559084	2.02	76.45	0.00046	1
5	0.00128	98692	126	493147	0.00026	7164118	9.89	72.59	0.00026	5
10	0.00117	98567	116	492550	0.00023	6670970	0.00	67.68	0.00023	10
15	0.00158	98451	155	491889	0.00032	6178421	0.00	62.76	0.00032	15
20	0.00232	98296	228	490938	0.00046	5686531	15.23	57.85	0.00046	20
25	0.00305	98067	300	489624	0.00061	5195594	37.62	52.98	0.00061	25
30	0.00410	97768	401	487880	0.00082	4705969	6.07	48.13	0.00082	30
35	0.00523	97367	509	485649	0.00105	4218089	0.00	43.32	0.00105	35
40	0.00850	96858	824	482385	0.00171	3732441	0.00	38.54	0.00171	40
45	0.01314	96034	1262	477219	0.00265	3250055	0.00	33.84	0.00265	45
50	0.01909	94772	1809	469652	0.00385	2772837	1.05	29.26	0.00385	50
55	0.02993	92963	2782	458378	0.00607	2303185	4.73	24.78	0.00606	55
60	0.04778	90180	4309	441072	0.00977	1844807	24.27	20.46	0.00971	60
65	0.08505	85872	7303	412655	0.01770	1403735	24.27	16.35	0.01759	65
70	0.14983	78569	11772	365636	0.03220	991080	24.27	12.61	0.03199	70
75	0.26910	66796	17975	290755	0.06182	625444	24.27	9.36	0.06149	75
80	0.40934	48821	19985	193614	0.10322	334689	24.27	6.86	0.10278	80
85+	1.00000	28837	28837	141075	0.20441	141075	24.27	4.89	0.19923	85+

TABLE 4 POPULATION PROJECTION, USING FIXED AGE-SPECIFIC BIRTH AND DEATH RATES, IN THOUSANDS

Age at last birthday	1972 Total	Males	Females	1977 Total	Males	Females	1982 Total	Males	Females	Age at last birthday
0–4	615	317	298	625	322	303	613	316	297	0–4
5–9	590	303	287	613	316	297	624	321	303	5–9
10–14	522	268	254	590	303	287	612	315	297	10–14
15–19	533	274	259	520	267	253	588	302	286	15–19
20–24	588	300	288	532	273	259	519	266	253	20–24
25–29	653	335	318	585	298	287	529	271	258	25–29
30–34	508	263	245	650	333	317	582	296	286	30–34
35–39	443	226	217	505	261	244	646	330	316	35–39
40–44	458	230	228	438	223	215	501	258	243	40–44
45–49	499	250	249	452	226	226	432	219	213	45–49
50–54	532	266	266	489	244	245	442	220	222	50–54
55–59	499	248	251	515	255	260	473	234	239	55–59
60–64	484	237	247	473	231	242	488	238	250	60–64
65–69	408	192	216	441	210	231	431	205	226	65–69
70–74	321	145	176	349	158	191	378	173	205	70–74
75–79	219	94	125	245	105	140	267	115	152	75–79
80–84	125	51	74	140	57	83	157	64	93	80–84
85 +	77	30	47	86	32	54	95	35	60	85 +
All ages	8074	4029	4045	8248	4114	4134	8377	4178	4199	All ages

TABLE 5 OBSERVED AND PROJECTED VITAL RATES

Rates per thousand	Observed Total	Males	Females	Projected 1972 Males	Females	1977 Males	Females	1982 Males	Females	Stable Males	Females
Birth	15.42	15.93	14.92	16.37	15.29	15.77	14.72	15.14	14.12	15.49	14.61
Death	10.14	10.97	9.31	11.65	10.36	12.15	11.06	12.63	11.69	12.61	11.73
Increase	5.28	4.96	5.61	4.72	4.93	3.63	3.66	2.50	2.44		2.8821

TABLE 6 RATES STANDARDIZED ON THREE STANDARD COUNTRIES

Standardized rates per thousand	England and Wales, 1961 Total	Males	Females	United States, 1960 Total	Males	Females	Mexico, 1960 Total	Males	Females
Birth	14.47	15.71*	13.57	14.75	14.38*	14.07	17.56	14.11*	16.96
Death	9.27	9.28*	9.31	7.45	8.45*	6.71	3.65	7.60*	3.02
Increase	5.20	6.42*	4.26	7.31	5.93*	7.36	13.91	6.51*	13.94

TABLE 7 VITAL STATISTICS AND RATES INFERRED FROM AGE DISTRIBUTIONS (FEMALES)

Vital statistics		Thompson Age range	NRR	1000r	Interval	Bourgeois-Pichat Age range	NRR	1000b	1000d	1000r	Coale	
TFR	2.28	0–4	1.10	3.42	27.45	5–29	0.92	13.30	16.52	−3.22	1000b	15.37
GRR	1.10	5–9	0.98	−0.81	27.42	30–54	0.73	7.83	19.65	−11.83	1000d	10.10
NRR	1.08	10–14	1.04	1.26	27.38	55–79	1.62	39.99	22.21	17.78	1000r	5.27
Generation	26.87	15–19	1.13	4.38	27.32	*45–69	1.23	20.95	13.42	7.54	1000k₁	24.80
Sex ratio	106.6										1000k₂	0.35

TABLE 8 LESLIE MATRIX AND ITS ANALYSIS (FEMALES)

Start of age interval	Sub-diagonal	First row	Percent in stable population	Fisher values	Total reproductive values	Net maternity function	Matrix equation coefficient	Parameters	Integral	Matrix
0	0.99806	0.00000	7.169	1.019	293263	0.00000	0.00000	λ_1	1.0145	1.0145
5	0.99879	0.00008	7.053	1.036	263286	0.00000	0.00008	λ_2	0.3409	0.3487
10	0.99866	0.05730	6.943	1.052	273392	0.00017	0.05712		+0.7681	+0.7421 i
15	0.99806	0.21900	6.835	1.011	291175	0.21802	0.21900	r_1	0.0029	0.0029
20	0.99732	0.33613	6.724	0.804	256515	0.32197	0.33393	r_2	−0.0348	−0.0397
25	0.99644	0.27227	6.610	0.474	116708	0.34599	0.26980		+0.2306	+0.2263 i
30	0.99543	0.14015	6.492	0.204	44419	0.19361	0.13838	c_1		39739
35	0.99328	0.05257	6.370	0.064	14799	0.08315	0.05167	c_2		−25083
40	0.98929	0.01104	6.236	0.012	2972	0.02019	0.01078			−38899 i
45	0.98414	0.00072	6.081	0.001	196	0.00138	0.00069	$2\pi/y$	27.246	27.764
50	0.97599	0.00000	5.899	0.000	1	0.00001	0.00000	Δ	4.997	
55	0.80582		27.588							

Switzerland, 1967

TABLE 1 DATA INPUT TO COMPUTATIONS

Age at last birthday	Population					Births, by age of mother	Deaths			Age at last birthday
	Total	Males	%	Females	%		Total	Males	Females	
0	101740	51808	1.8	49932	1.6	0	1878	1113	765	0
1–4	398910	204592	7.0	194318	6.3	0	372	209	163	1–4
5–9	459650	233950	8.0	225700	7.3	0	258	167	91	5–9
10–14	436900	222400	7.6	214500	7.0	9	164	105	59	10–14
15–19	470150	235700	8.1	234450	7.6	5249	356	255	101	15–19
20–24	565400	284550	9.8	280850	9.1	34259	503	388	115	20–24
25–29	442150	226700	7.8	215450	7.0	35706	414	292	122	25–29
30–34	398800	199400	6.8	199400	6.5	20333	450	321	129	30–34
35–39	378400	184300	6.3	194100	6.3	8967	585	374	211	35–39
40–44	356300	172100	5.9	184200	6.0	2689	850	527	323	40–44
45–49	346300	171000	5.9	175300	5.7	203	1214	761	453	45–49
50–54	332750	162750	5.6	170000	5.5	1	1960	1289	671	50–54
55–59	336900	158650	5.4	178250	5.8	1	3265	2113	1152	55–59
60–64	301450	136800	4.7	164650	5.4	0	4839	2999	1840	60–64
65–69	251200	107300	3.7	143900	4.7	0	6575	3913	2662	65–69
70–74	186750	76400	2.6	110350	3.6		7839	4248	3591	70–74
75–79	122650	47950	1.6	74700	2.4		8376	3951	4425	75–79
80–84	68412	25749	0.9	42663	1.4	55015 M	8065	3375	4690	80–84
85 +	34838	11901	0.4	22937	0.7	52402 F	7179	2613	4565	85 +
All ages	5989650	2914000		3075650		107417	55142	29013	26129	All ages

TABLE 2 LIFE TABLE FOR MALES

Age, x	$_nq_x$	l_x	$_nd_x$	$_nL_x$	$_nm_x$	T_x	$1000r_x$	$\overset{\circ}{e}_x$	$_nM_x$	Age, x
0	0.02114	100000	2114	98419	0.02148	6972975	0.44	69.73	0.02148	0
1	0.00407	97886	399	390391	0.00102	6874557	0.44	70.23	0.00102	1
5	0.00356	97488	347	486572	0.00071	6484166	13.48	66.51	0.00071	5
10	0.00236	97141	229	485170	0.00047	5997593	0.00	61.74	0.00047	10
15	0.00540	96912	523	483342	0.00108	5512424	0.00	56.88	0.00108	15
20	0.00680	96389	655	480327	0.00136	5029082	2.60	52.17	0.00136	20
25	0.00643	95734	615	477155	0.00129	4548754	34.18	47.51	0.00129	25
30	0.00803	95119	764	473754	0.00161	4071600	19.09	42.81	0.00161	30
35	0.01012	94355	955	469524	0.00203	3597846	12.57	38.13	0.00203	35
40	0.01521	93400	1421	463671	0.00306	3128322	4.41	33.49	0.00306	40
45	0.02203	91979	2025	455253	0.00445	2664651	0.74	28.97	0.00445	45
50	0.03890	89953	3499	441759	0.00792	2209388	0.00	24.56	0.00792	50
55	0.06465	86454	5589	419333	0.01334	1767628	3.49	20.45	0.01332	55
60	0.10474	80865	8470	384525	0.02203	1348296	22.47	16.67	0.02192	60
65	0.16834	72395	12187	332822	0.03662	963770	22.47	13.31	0.03647	65
70	0.24543	60208	14777	264801	0.05580	630948	22.47	10.48	0.05560	70
75	0.34266	45431	15567	188211	0.08271	366147	22.47	8.06	0.08240	75
80	0.49078	29864	14657	111393	0.13158	177936	22.47	5.96	0.13107	80
85 +	1.00000	15207	15207	66542	0.22853	66542	22.47	4.38	0.21956	85 +

TABLE 3 LIFE TABLE FOR FEMALES

Age, x	$_nq_x$	l_x	$_nd_x$	$_nL_x$	$_nm_x$	T_x	$1000r_x$	$\overset{\circ}{e}_x$	$_nM_x$	Age, x
0	0.01513	100000	1513	98892	0.01530	7588367	2.10	75.88	0.01532	0
1	0.00334	98487	329	393001	0.00084	7489475	2.10	76.05	0.00084	1
5	0.00201	98158	197	490299	0.00040	7096474	12.50	72.30	0.00040	5
10	0.00137	97961	135	489473	0.00028	6606175	0.00	67.44	0.00028	10
15	0.00215	97827	210	488621	0.00043	6116702	0.00	62.53	0.00043	15
20	0.00205	97616	200	487595	0.00041	5628081	8.00	57.66	0.00041	20
25	0.00284	97416	276	486415	0.00057	5140486	33.71	52.77	0.00057	25
30	0.00324	97140	314	484967	0.00065	4654070	9.72	47.91	0.00065	30
35	0.00543	96826	526	482925	0.00109	4169103	6.80	43.05	0.00109	35
40	0.00874	96300	842	479542	0.00176	3686177	8.41	38.28	0.00175	40
45	0.01286	95458	1227	474431	0.00259	3206636	5.35	33.59	0.00258	45
50	0.01956	94231	1843	466905	0.00395	2732205	0.00	28.99	0.00395	50
55	0.03184	92388	2942	455222	0.00646	2265300	0.00	24.52	0.00645	55
60	0.05479	89446	4901	435936	0.01124	1810078	27.36	20.24	0.01118	60
65	0.08924	84545	7544	405283	0.01862	1374142	27.36	16.25	0.01850	65
70	0.15216	77000	11715	357689	0.03276	968859	27.36	12.58	0.03254	70
75	0.26100	65284	17039	285778	0.05962	611169	27.36	9.35	0.05924	75
80	0.43739	48245	21102	190576	0.11073	325391	27.36	6.74	0.10993	80
85 +	*1.00000	27143	27143	134815	0.20134	134815	27.36	4.97	0.19907	85 +

TABLE 4   POPULATION PROJECTION, USING FIXED AGE-SPECIFIC BIRTH AND DEATH RATES, IN THOUSANDS

Age at last birthday	1972			1977			1982			Age at last birthday
	Total	Males	Females	Total	Males	Females	Total	Males	Females	
0–4	543	277	266	552	282	270	538	275	263	0–4
5–9	498	255	243	541	276	265	550	281	269	5–9
10–14	458	233	225	497	254	243	539	275	264	10–14
15–19	436	222	214	457	232	225	497	254	243	15–19
20–24	468	234	234	434	220	214	455	231	224	20–24
25–29	563	283	280	466	233	233	432	219	213	25–29
30–34	440	225	215	560	281	279	464	231	233	30–34
35–39	397	198	199	437	223	214	556	278	278	35–39
40–44	375	182	193	392	195	197	432	220	212	40–44
45–49	351	169	182	370	179	191	387	192	195	45–49
50–54	339	166	173	343	164	179	361	173	188	50–54
55–59	320	154	166	326	158	168	331	156	175	55–59
60–64	316	145	171	301	142	159	305	144	161	60–64
65–69	271	118	153	285	126	159	271	123	148	65–69
70–74	212	85	127	229	94	135	240	100	140	70–74
75–79	142	54	88	152	61	101	175	67	108	75–79
80–84	78	28	50	91	32	59	104	36	68	80–84
85 +	45	15	30	52	17	35	61	19	42	85 +
All ages	6252	3043	3209	6495	3169	3326	6698	3274	3424	All ages

TABLE 5   OBSERVED AND PROJECTED VITAL RATES

Rates per thousand	Observed			Projected						Stable	
				1972		1977		1982			
	Total	Males	Females	Males	Females	Males	Females	Males	Females	Males	Females
Birth	17.93	18.88	17.04	19.15	17.32	17.99	16.32	16.91	15.40	16.55	15.45
Death	9.21	9.96	8.50	10.48	9.35	10.79	9.97	11.05	10.49	12.53	11.32
Increase	8.73	8.92	8.54	8.67	7.96	7.20	6.35	5.86	4.91		4.1382

TABLE 6   RATES STANDARDIZED ON THREE STANDARD COUNTRIES

Standardized rates per thousand	England and Wales, 1961			United States, 1960			Mexico, 1960		
	Total	Males	Females	Total	Males	Females	Total	Males	Females
Birth	15.01	16.62*	14.19	15.27	15.22*	14.68	17.41	15.47*	16.94
Death	10.03	10.48*	9.64	8.15	9.35*	7.00	4.19	7.91*	3.29
Increase	4.98	6.14*	4.56	7.12	5.87*	7.68	13.23	7.55*	13.55

TABLE 7   VITAL STATISTICS AND RATES INFERRED FROM AGE DISTRIBUTIONS (FEMALES)

Vital statistics		Thompson				Bourgeois-Pichat					Coale	
		Age range	NRR	$1000r$	Interval	Age range	NRR	$1000b$	$1000d$	$1000r$		
TFR	2.37	0–4	1.10	3.63	27.45	5–29	0.90	14.48	18.41	−3.93	$1000b$	16.84
GRR	1.16	5–9	1.07	2.37	27.42	30–54	1.19	16.56	10.02	6.54	$1000d$	10.81
NRR	1.12	10–14	1.11	3.69	27.38	55–79	1.52	31.85	16.31	15.54	$1000r$	5.03
Generation	28.21	15–19	1.24	7.65	27.32	*30–54	1.19	16.56	10.02	6.54	$1000k_1$	0.
Sex ratio	105.0										$1000k_2$	0.

TABLE 8   LESLIE MATRIX AND ITS ANALYSIS (FEMALES)

Start of age interval	Sub-diagonal	First row	Percent in stable population	Fisher values	Total reproductive values	Net maternity function	Matrix equation coefficient	Parameters		
									Integral	Matrix
0	0.99676	0.00000	7.527	1.027	250854	0.00000	0.00000	λ_1	1.0209	1.0209
5	0.99831	0.00005	7.349	1.052	237421	0.00000	0.00005	λ_2	0.3895	0.3928
10	0.99826	0.32687	7.185	1.076	230738	0.00010	0.02673		+0.7819	+0.7570i
15	0.99790	0.17291	7.027	1.072	251444	0.05337	0.17176	r_1	0.0041	0.0041
20	0.99758	0.34472	6.868	0.919	258174	0.29016	0.34171	r_2	−0.0270	−0.0318
25	0.99702	0.32082	6.711	0.586	126226	0.39326	0.31725		+0.2217	+0.2184i
30	0.99579	0.17754	5.554	0.269	53725	0.24125	0.17504	c_1		32912
35	0.99299	0.07282	6.393	0.093	18074	0.10884	0.07149	c_2		−22781
40	0.98934	0.01889	6.218	0.020	3761	0.03415	0.01842			−45451i
45	0.98414	0.00140	6.025	0.001	256	0.00268	0.00135	$2\pi/y$	28.338	23.766
50	0.97498	0.00002	5.808	0.000	8	0.00001	0.00001	Δ	3.968	
55	0.80588		26.334							

U. K.: England and Wales, 1964

TABLE 1 DATA INPUT TO COMPUTATIONS

Age at last birthday	Population					Births, by age of mother	Deaths			Age at last birthday
	Total	Males	%	Females	%		Total	Males	Females	
0	829797	425947	1.8	403850	1.7	0	17445	10011	7434	0
1–4	3179703	1631253	7.1	1548450	6.4	0	2552	1414	1138	1–4
5–9	3439600	1763500	7.7	1676100	6.9	0	1345	808	537	5–9
10–14	3312200	1695300	7.4	1616900	6.6	187	1089	687	402	10–14
15–19	3708000	1894600	8.2	1813400	7.4	76547	2582	1859	723	15–19
20–24	3080100	1542800	6.7	1537300	6.3	276103	2396	1591	705	20–24
25–29	2977900	1515500	6.6	1462400	6.0	270700	2375	1509	866	25–29
30–34	2945200	1511900	6.6	1433300	5.9	153513	2974	1800	1174	30–34
35–39	3049300	1542100	6.7	1507200	6.2	75371	4756	2859	1897	35–39
40–44	3412900	1707000	7.4	1705900	7.0	22313	8984	5158	3816	40–44
45–49	2875200	1416000	6.1	1459200	6.0	1237	12484	7452	5032	45–49
50–54	3195200	1552900	6.7	1642300	6.7	1	22868	14311	8557	50–54
55–59	3029700	1455800	6.3	1573900	6.5	0	36064	23656	12408	55–59
60–64	2650700	1231400	5.3	1419300	5.8	0	52055	33677	18378	60–64
65–69	2059300	852600	3.7	1206700	5.0	0	62183	36448	25735	65–69
70–74	1588800	613700	2.7	975100	4.0		75590	39808	35782	70–74
75–79	1104100	390000	1.7	714100	2.9		82636	38597	44039	75–79
80–84	624900	203900	0.9	421000	1.7	451072 M	75636	30203	45433	80–84
85 +	338700	97500	0.4	241200	1.0	424900 F	68723	22815	45908	85 +
All ages	47401300	23043700		24357600		875972	534737	274773	259964	All ages

TABLE 2 LIFE TABLE FOR MALES

Age, x	$_nq_x$	l_x	$_nd_x$	$_nL_x$	$_nm_x$	T_x	$1000r_x$	$\overset{\circ}{e}_x$	$_nM_x$	Age, x
0	0.02302	100000	2302	98215	0.02344	6853014	3.57	68.53	0.02350	0
1	0.00344	97698	336	389813	0.00086	6754799	3.57	69.14	0.00087	1
5	0.00228	97362	222	486255	0.00046	6364986	18.78	65.37	0.00046	5
10	0.00202	97140	197	485251	0.00041	5878731	0.00	60.52	0.00041	10
15	0.00490	96943	475	483598	0.00098	5393470	8.55	55.64	0.00098	15
20	0.00547	96468	527	481024	0.00110	4909872	21.27	50.90	0.00110	20
25	0.00497	95941	476	478522	0.00100	4428848	0.97	46.16	0.00100	25
30	0.00594	95465	567	475989	0.00119	3950326	0.00	41.38	0.00119	30
35	0.00923	94898	876	472476	0.00185	3474337	0.00	36.61	0.00185	35
40	0.01505	94022	1415	466891	0.00303	3001861	5.32	31.93	0.00303	40
45	0.02603	92607	2410	457561	0.00527	2534970	3.92	27.37	0.00526	45
50	0.04513	90196	4071	441710	0.00922	2077409	0.00	23.03	0.00922	50
55	0.07841	86126	6753	415027	0.01627	1635700	6.21	18.99	0.01625	55
60	0.12884	79372	10226	372687	0.02744	1220672	17.17	15.38	0.02735	60
65	0.19425	69146	13432	313273	0.04288	847985	17.17	12.26	0.04275	65
70	0.28027	55714	15615	240047	0.06505	534712	17.17	9.60	0.06487	70
75	0.39646	40099	15898	160187	0.09925	294666	17.17	7.35	0.09897	75
80	0.53345	24201	12910	86922	0.14853	134479	17.17	5.56	0.14813	80
85 +	1.00000	11291	11291	47557	0.23742	47557	17.17	4.21	0.23400	85 +

TABLE 3 LIFE TABLE FOR FEMALES

Age, x	$_nq_x$	l_x	$_nd_x$	$_nL_x$	$_nm_x$	T_x	$1000r_x$	$\overset{\circ}{e}_x$	$_nM_x$	Age, x
0	0.01810	100000	1810	98612	0.01836	7468328	3.59	74.68	0.01841	0
1	0.00292	98190	287	391926	0.00073	7369716	3.59	75.06	0.00073	1
5	0.00159	97903	156	489127	0.00032	6977791	18.42	71.27	0.00032	5
10	0.00124	97747	121	488441	0.00025	6488664	0.00	66.38	0.00025	10
15	0.00199	97626	195	487665	0.00040	6000223	4.67	61.45	0.00040	15
20	0.00229	97431	224	486618	0.00046	5512558	21.04	56.58	0.00046	20
25	0.00296	97208	288	485356	0.00059	5025940	6.40	51.70	0.00059	25
30	0.00409	96920	395	483677	0.00082	4540584	0.00	46.85	0.00082	30
35	0.00628	96524	606	481246	0.00126	4056907	0.00	42.03	0.00126	35
40	0.01113	95918	1068	477135	0.00224	3575652	0.97	37.28	0.00224	40
45	0.01711	94851	1622	470475	0.00345	3098527	0.26	32.67	0.00345	45
50	0.02574	93228	2400	460538	0.00521	2628052	0.00	28.19	0.00521	50
55	0.03876	90829	3520	445990	0.00789	2167514	6.27	23.85	0.00788	55
60	0.06309	87308	5508	423775	0.01300	1721524	17.95	19.72	0.01295	60
65	0.10197	81800	8342	389592	0.02141	1297749	17.95	15.86	0.02133	65
70	0.16942	73459	12446	337854	0.03684	908156	17.95	12.36	0.03670	70
75	0.26923	61013	16427	265356	0.06190	570293	17.95	9.35	0.06167	75
80	0.42529	44586	18962	175119	0.10828	304936	17.95	6.84	0.10792	80
85 +	1.00000	25624	25624	129817	0.19739	129817	17.95	5.07	0.19033	85 +

TABLE 4 POPULATION PROJECTION, USING FIXED AGE-SPECIFIC BIRTH AND DEATH RATES, IN THOUSANDS

Age at last birthday	1969 Total	Males	Females	1974 Total	Males	Females	1979 Total	Males	Females	Age at last birthday
0–4	4407	2264	2143	4588	2357	2231	4692	2410	2282	0–4
5–9	3997	2050	1947	4392	2255	2137	4573	2348	2225	5–9
10–14	3434	1760	1674	3990	2046	1944	4385	2251	2134	10–14
15–19	3303	1689	1614	3425	1754	1671	3980	2039	1941	15–19
20–24	3695	1885	1810	3291	1680	1511	3413	1745	1668	20–24
25–29	3068	1535	1533	3680	1875	1805	3279	1672	1607	25–29
30–34	2964	1507	1457	3055	1527	1528	3564	1865	1799	30–34
35–39	2927	1501	1426	2946	1496	1450	3035	1515	1520	35–39
40–44	3018	1524	1494	2897	1483	1414	2917	1479	1438	40–44
45–49	3355	1673	1582	2966	1493	1473	2847	1453	1394	45–49
50–54	2795	1367	1428	3262	1615	1647	2884	1442	1442	50–54
55–59	3049	1459	1590	2567	1284	1383	3112	1517	1595	55–59
60–64	2803	1307	1496	2821	1310	1511	2467	1153	1314	60–64
65–69	2340	1035	1305	2474	1099	1375	2490	1101	1389	65–69
70–74	1699	653	1046	1925	793	1132	2034	842	1192	70–74
75–79	1176	410	766	1258	436	822	1418	529	889	75–79
80–84	683	212	471	727	222	505	779	237	542	80–84
85 +	424	112	312	465	116	349	497	122	375	85 +
All ages	49137	23943	25194	50829	24841	25988	52456	25720	26745	All ages

TABLE 5 OBSERVED AND PROJECTED VITAL RATES

Rates per thousand	Observed Total	Males	Females	Projected 1969 Males	Females	1974 Males	Females	1979 Males	Females	Stable Males	Females
Birth	18.48	19.57	17.44	19.91	17.82	19.69	17.73	19.38	17.55	21.41	20.13
Death	11.28	11.92	10.67	12.29	11.43	12.50	11.79	12.64	11.98	10.09	8.85
Increase	7.20	7.65	6.77	7.62	6.39	7.20	5.94	6.73	5.57	11.3237	

TABLE 6 RATES STANDARDIZED ON THREE STANDARD COUNTRIES

Standardized rates per thousand	England and Wales, 1961 Total	Males	Females	United States, 1960 Total	Males	Females	Mexico, 1960 Total	Males	Females
Birth	18.31	19.50*	17.21	18.63	18.30*	17.80	21.94	16.99*	21.23
Death	11.12	11.95*	10.33	9.05	10.62*	7.56	4.61	9.08*	3.61
Increase	7.19	7.55*	6.88	9.57	7.68*	10.25	17.33	7.91*	17.61

TABLE 7 VITAL STATISTICS AND RATES INFERRED FROM AGE DISTRIBUTIONS (FEMALES)

Vital statistics		Thompson Age range	NRR	$1000r$	Interval	Bourgeois-Pichat Age range	NRR	$1000b$	$1000d$	$1000r$	Coale
TFR	2.89	0–4	1.22	7.34	27.44	5–29	1.18	15.15	9.07	6.08	$1000b$
GRR	1.40	5–9	1.09	3.00	27.41	30–54	0.82	9.84	17.06	-7.21	$1000d$
NRR	1.36	10–14	1.03	0.99	27.35	55–79	1.44	31.92	18.29	13.63	$1000r$
Generation	27.16	15–19	1.12	4.24	27.21	*50–74	1.35	26.86	15.79	11.07	$1000k_1$
Sex ratio	106.16										$1000k_2$

TABLE 8 LESLIE MATRIX AND ITS ANALYSIS (FEMALES)

Start of age interval	Sub-diagonal	First row	Percent in stable population	Fisher values	Total reproductive values	Net maternity function	Matrix equation coefficient	Parameters	Integral	Matrix
0	0.99712	0.00000	9.628	1.048	2046985	0.00000	0.00000	λ_1	1.0583	1.0583
5	0.99860	0.00014	9.071	1.113	1865267	0.00000	0.00014	λ_2	0.3531	0.3589
10	0.99841	0.05028	8.559	1.179	1906789	0.00027	0.05006		+0.8095	+0.7805i
15	0.99785	0.25343	8.075	1.197	2171114	0.09985	0.25189	r_1	0.0113	0.0113
20	0.99741	0.43332	7.613	0.993	1526570	0.42393	0.42986	r_2	-0.0249	-0.0304
25	0.99654	0.34720	7.175	0.598	874738	0.43579	0.34354		+0.2319	+0.2280i
30	0.99497	0.18662	5.756	0.270	386892	0.25128	0.18401	c_1		201537
35	0.99146	0.07492	5.352	0.090	136349	0.11673	0.07350	c_2		-108612
40	0.98604	0.01656	5.950	0.017	29575	0.03027	0.01610			-272770i
45	0.97888	0.00101	5.544	0.001	1462	0.00193	0.00097	$2\pi/y$	27.095	27.563
50	0.96841	0.00000	5.128	0.000	0	0.00000	0.00000	Δ	9.850	
55	0.81186		20.147							

[469]

U. K.: England and Wales, 1966-68

TABLE 1   DATA INPUT TO COMPUTATIONS

Age at last birthday	Population Total	Males	%	Females	%	Births, by age of mother	Deaths Total	Males	Females	Age at last birthday
0	828300	425400	1.8	402900	1.6	0	15455	8912	6553	0
1–4	3345900	1715600	7.3	1630300	6.6	0	2680	1493	1187	1–4
5–9	3747000	1921600	8.2	1825400	7.3	0	1390	848	542	5–9
10–14	3283900	1682100	7.2	1601800	6.4	223	1119	697	422	10–14
15–19	3532500	1791100	7.6	1741400	7.0	84232	2455	1765	690	15–19
20–24	3540300	1777400	7.5	1762900	7.1	291137	2464	1718	746	20–24
25–29	2990900	1512600	6.4	1478300	6.0	246117	2210	1400	810	25–29
30–34	2909000	1493300	6.4	1415700	5.7	130667	2720	1632	1088	30–34
35–39	2968300	1513100	6.4	1455200	5.9	62735	4370	2569	1801	35–39
40–44	3124900	1567000	6.7	1557900	6.3	17380	7962	4710	3252	40–44
45–49	3144800	1559200	6.6	1585600	6.4	1261	13347	7994	5353	45–49
50–54	3044600	1477900	6.3	1566700	6.3	2	21636	13445	8191	50–54
55–59	3053500	1464900	6.2	1588600	6.4	0	35905	23344	12561	55–59
60–64	2750500	1277400	5.4	1473100	5.9	0	53182	34475	18707	60–64
65–69	2213300	954700	4.1	1258600	5.1	0	68468	41707	26761	65–69
70–74	1646700	626400	2.7	1020300	4.1		79022	42075	36947	70–74
75–79	1141300	397100	1.7	744200	3.0		86522	40267	45255	75–79
80–84	662000	206900	0.9	455100	1.8	428765 M	79645	31564	48081	80–84
85 +	373100	101600	0.4	271500	1.1	404989 F	80442	25754	54688	85 +
All ages	48300800	23465300		24835500		833754	561004	286369	274635	All ages

TABLE 2   LIFE TABLE FOR MALES

Age, x	nq_x	l_x	nd_x	nL_x	nm_x	T_x	$1000r_x$	$\overset{\circ}{e}_x$	nM_x	Age, x
0	0.02062	100000	2062	98428	0.02095	6871842	0.00	68.72	0.02095	0
1	0.00347	97938	340	390763	0.00087	6773414	0.00	69.16	0.00087	1
5	0.00220	97598	214	487454	0.00044	6382651	23.56	65.40	0.00044	5
10	0.00207	97384	202	486458	0.00042	5895197	6.48	60.54	0.00041	10
15	0.00492	97182	478	484770	0.00099	5408729	0.00	55.66	0.00099	15
20	0.00482	96704	466	482348	0.00097	4923959	15.93	50.92	0.00097	20
25	0.00462	96238	445	480090	0.00093	4441611	16.46	46.15	0.00093	25
30	0.00545	95793	522	477737	0.00109	3961521	0.00	41.35	0.00109	30
35	0.00846	95271	806	474527	0.00170	3483785	0.00	36.57	0.00170	35
40	0.01493	94466	1410	469126	0.00301	3009258	0.00	31.86	0.00301	40
45	0.02534	93055	2358	459930	0.00513	2540132	0.41	27.30	0.00513	45
50	0.04456	90697	4042	444278	0.00910	2080202	0.00	22.94	0.00910	50
55	0.07685	86655	6660	417907	0.01594	1635924	0.00	18.88	0.01594	55
60	0.12725	79996	10180	376024	0.02707	1218017	15.20	15.23	0.02699	60
65	0.19811	69816	13832	315748	0.04381	841993	15.20	12.06	0.04369	65
70	0.28866	55985	16161	239990	0.06734	526045	15.20	9.40	0.06717	70
75	0.40390	39824	16085	158232	0.10165	286255	15.20	7.19	0.10140	75
80	0.54437	23739	12923	84502	0.15293	128023	15.20	5.39	0.15256	80
85 +	1.00000	10816	10815	43520	0.24853	43520	15.20	4.02	0.25348	85 +

TABLE 3   LIFE TABLE FOR FEMALES

Age, x	nq_x	l_x	nd_x	nL_x	nm_x	T_x	$1000r_x$	$\overset{\circ}{e}_x$	nM_x	Age, x
0	0.01607	100000	1607	98788	0.01626	7492059	0.00	74.92	0.01626	0
1	0.00291	98393	286	392743	0.00073	7393271	0.00	75.14	0.00073	1
5	0.00147	98107	145	490175	0.00030	7000527	23.43	71.36	0.00030	5
10	0.00132	97963	129	489501	0.00026	6510352	4.41	66.46	0.00026	10
15	0.00198	97834	194	488700	0.00040	6020851	0.00	61.54	0.00040	15
20	0.00212	97640	207	487649	0.00042	5532151	15.94	56.66	0.00042	20
25	0.00274	97433	267	486533	0.00055	5044452	21.37	51.77	0.00055	25
30	0.00384	97166	373	484967	0.00077	4557919	0.76	46.91	0.00077	30
35	0.00617	96793	597	482604	0.00124	4072952	0.00	42.08	0.00124	35
40	0.01039	96196	999	478690	0.00209	3590348	0.00	37.32	0.00209	40
45	0.01675	95197	1594	472293	0.00338	3111658	0.00	32.69	0.00338	45
50	0.02583	93602	2417	462373	0.00523	2639365	0.00	28.20	0.00523	50
55	0.03882	91185	3540	447701	0.00791	2176992	0.00	23.87	0.00791	55
60	0.06188	87645	5424	425659	0.01274	1729291	15.69	19.73	0.01270	60
65	0.10163	82221	8355	391661	0.02134	1303622	15.69	15.86	0.02126	65
70	0.16733	73865	12360	340156	0.03634	911961	15.69	12.35	0.03621	70
75	0.27090	61505	16662	267202	0.06236	571805	15.69	9.30	0.06215	75
80	0.41792	44844	18741	176887	0.10595	304603	15.69	6.79	0.10565	80
85 +	1.00000	26103	26103	127715	0.20438	127715	15.69	4.89	0.20143	85 +

TABLE 4 POPULATION PROJECTION, USING FIXED AGE-SPECIFIC BIRTH AND DEATH RATES, IN THOUSANDS

Age at last birthday	1972 Total	Males	Females	1977 Total	Males	Females	1982 Total	Males	Females	Age at last birthday
0–4	4181	2145	2036	4300	2206	2094	4407	2261	2146	0–4
5–9	4161	2133	2028	4167	2137	2030	4286	2198	2088	5–9
10–14	3741	1918	1823	4154	2129	2025	4160	2133	2027	10–14
15–19	3275	1676	1599	3731	1911	1820	4143	2122	2021	15–19
20–24	3520	1782	1738	3264	1668	1596	3717	1901	1816	20–24
25–29	3528	1769	1759	3508	1774	1734	3252	1660	1592	25–29
30–34	2979	1505	1474	3513	1760	1753	3493	1765	1728	30–34
35–39	2892	1483	1409	2961	1495	1466	3493	1749	1744	35–39
40–44	2939	1496	1443	2863	1466	1397	2932	1478	1454	40–44
45–49	3073	1536	1537	2891	1467	1424	2817	1438	1379	45–49
50–54	3058	1506	1552	2989	1484	1505	2811	1417	1394	50–54
55–59	2907	1390	1517	2920	1417	1503	2853	1396	1457	55–59
60–64	2828	1318	1510	2693	1251	1442	2704	1275	1429	60–64
65–69	2428	1073	1355	2497	1107	1390	2377	1050	1327	65–69
70–74	1819	726	1093	1992	815	1177	2048	841	1207	70–74
75–79	1214	413	801	1337	478	859	1463	538	925	75–79
80–84	705	212	493	752	221	531	824	255	558	80–84
85 +	436	107	329	465	109	356	497	114	383	85 +
All ages	49684	24188	25496	50997	24895	26102	52277	25592	26685	All ages

TABLE 5 OBSERVED AND PROJECTED VITAL RATES

Rates per thousand	Observed Total	Males	Females	Projected 1972 Males	Females	1977 Males	Females	1982 Males	Females	Stable Males	Females
Birth	17.26	18.27	16.31	18.53	16.60	18.22	16.42	18.39	16.65	19.31	18.08
Death	11.61	12.20	11.06	12.48	11.69	12.73	12.02	12.87	12.24	11.13	9.90
Increase	5.65	6.07	5.25	6.04	4.92	5.50	4.40	5.52	4.42		8.1821

TABLE 6 RATES STANDARDIZED ON THREE STANDARD COUNTRIES

Standardized rates per thousand	England and Wales, 1961 Total	Males	Females	United States, 1960 Total	Males	Females	Mexico, 1960 Total	Males	Females
Birth	16.72	18.21*	15.74	17.03	16.91*	16.30	20.24	16.10*	19.62
Death	11.17	12.08*	10.31	9.08	10.76*	7.52	4.54	9.23*	3.52
Increase	5.56	6.13*	5.43	7.95	6.15*	8.78	15.71	6.87*	16.09

TABLE 7 VITAL STATISTICS AND RATES INFERRED FROM AGE DISTRIBUTIONS (FEMALES)

Vital statistics		Thompson Age range	NRR	$1000r$	Interval	Bourgeois-Pichat Age range	NRR	$1000b$	$1000d$	$1000r$	Coale
TFR	2.64	0–4	1.28	9.06	27.44	5–29	1.18	15.39	9.25	6.15	$1000b$
GRR	1.28	5–9	1.16	5.56	27.41	30–54	0.80	9.07	17.19	-8.11	$1000d$
NRR	1.25	10–14	1.04	1.28	27.36	55–79	1.37	28.16	16.60	11.56	$1000r$
Generation	26.89	15–19	1.10	3.43	27.28	*30–59	0.81	9.20	16.96	-7.75	$1000k_1$
Sex ratio	105.87										$1000k_2$

TABLE 8 LESLIE MATRIX AND ITS ANALYSIS (FEMALES)

Start of age interval	Sub-diagonal	First row	Percent in stable population	Fisher values	Total reproductive values	Net maternity function	Matrix equation coefficient	Parameters Integral	Matrix
0	0.99724	0.00000	8.709	1.038	2110900	0.00000	0.00000	λ_1 1.0418	1.0418
5	0.99862	0.00017	8.337	1.085	1979834	0.00000	0.00017	λ_2 0.3386	0.3464
10	0.99836	0.05781	7.991	1.131	1812150	0.00033	0.05758	+0.7911	+0.7627i
15	0.99795	0.25449	7.658	1.120	1951103	0.11482	0.25302	r_1 0.0082	0.0382
20	0.99761	0.39542	7.336	0.905	1595235	0.39123	0.39234	r_2 -0.0300	-0.0354
25	0.99678	0.30858	7.025	0.533	788614	0.39346	0.30544	+0.2333	+0.2289i
30	0.99513	0.16140	6.721	0.236	334307	0.21743	0.15924	c_1	221857
35	0.99189	0.06467	6.420	0.079	114718	0.10106	0.06350	c_2	109892
40	0.98664	0.01425	6.113	0.015	23527	0.02594	0.01388		-141737i
45	0.97900	0.00095	5.789	0.001	1500	0.00182	0.00091	$2\pi/y$ 26.935	27.449
50	0.96827	0.00000	5.440	0.000	0	0.00000	0.00000	Δ 6.618	
55	0.80728		22.460						

U. K.: England and Wales, 1967

TABLE 1 DATA INPUT TO COMPUTATIONS

Age at last birthday	Population					Births, by age of mother	Deaths			Age at last birthday
	Total	Males	%	Females	%		Total	Males	Females	
0	828300	425400	1.8	402900	1.6	0	15266	8673	6593	0
1–4	3345900	1715600	7.3	1630300	6.6	0	2574	1427	1147	1–4
5–9	3747000	1921600	8.2	1825400	7.3	0	1386	851	535	5–9
10–14	3283900	1682100	7.2	1601800	6.4	228	1146	708	438	10–14
15–19	3532500	1791100	7.6	1741400	7.0	84314	2459	1749	710	15–19
20–24	3540300	1777400	7.6	1762900	7.1	291656	2473	1718	755	20–24
25–29	2990900	1512600	6.4	1478300	6.0	243802	2192	1408	784	25–29
30–34	2909000	1493300	6.4	1415700	5.7	130279	2654	1595	1059	30–34
35–39	2968300	1513100	6.4	1455200	5.9	63085	4347	2538	1809	35–39
40–44	3124900	1567000	6.7	1557900	6.3	17522	7803	4580	3223	40–44
45–49	3144800	1559200	6.6	1585600	6.4	1276	13151	7906	5245	45–49
50–54	3044600	1477900	6.3	1566700	6.3	2	21158	13075	8083	50–54
55–59	3053500	1464900	6.2	1588600	6.4	0	35278	22902	12375	55–59
60–64	2750500	1277400	5.4	1473100	5.9	0	52011	33730	18281	60–64
65–69	2213300	954700	4.1	1258600	5.1	0	66759	40682	26077	65–69
70–74	1646700	626400	2.7	1020300	4.1		76503	40748	35755	70–74
75–79	1141300	397100	1.7	744200	3.0		82634	38380	44254	75–79
80–84	662000	206900	0.9	455100	1.8	427901 M	76118	30048	46070	80–84
85+	373100	101600	0.4	271500	1.1	404263 F	76504	24460	52144	85+
All ages	48300800	23465300		24835500		832164	542516	277178	265338	All ages

TABLE 2 LIFE TABLE FOR MALES

Age, x	$_nq_x$	l_x	$_nd_x$	$_nL_x$	$_nm_x$	T_x	$1000r_x$	$\overset{\circ}{e}_x$	$_nM_x$	Age, x
0	0.02007	100000	2007	98465	0.02039	6904130	0.00	69.04	0.02039	0
1	0.00332	97993	325	391024	0.00083	6805665	0.00	69.45	0.00083	1
5	0.00220	97667	215	487798	0.00044	6414641	23.57	65.68	0.00044	5
10	0.00211	97452	205	486801	0.00042	5926843	6.48	60.82	0.00042	10
15	0.00487	97247	474	485104	0.00098	5440042	0.00	55.94	0.00098	15
20	0.00482	96773	466	482694	0.00097	4954938	15.93	51.20	0.00097	20
25	0.00465	96307	447	480424	0.00093	4472244	16.46	46.44	0.00093	25
30	0.00533	95859	511	478092	0.00107	3991820	0.00	41.64	0.00107	30
35	0.00835	95349	797	474931	0.00168	3513728	0.00	36.85	0.00168	35
40	0.01452	94552	1373	469649	0.00292	3038797	0.00	32.14	0.00292	40
45	0.02507	93179	2336	460592	0.00507	2569149	0.52	27.57	0.00507	45
50	0.04336	90844	3939	445249	0.00885	2108557	0.00	23.21	0.00885	50
55	0.07545	86904	6557	419397	0.01563	1663308	0.00	19.14	0.01563	55
60	0.12474	80348	10022	378155	0.02650	1243911	18.35	15.48	0.02541	60
65	0.19379	70325	13629	318784	0.04275	865756	18.35	12.31	0.04261	65
70	0.28093	56696	15928	244127	0.06524	546971	18.35	9.65	0.06505	70
75	0.38901	40768	15859	163608	0.09693	302844	18.35	7.43	0.09665	75
80	0.52639	24909	13112	90025	0.14565	139236	18.35	5.59	0.14523	80
85+	1.00000	11797	11797	49211	0.23973	49211	18.35	4.17	0.24075	85+

TABLE 3 LIFE TABLE FOR FEMALES

Age, x	$_nq_x$	l_x	$_nd_x$	$_nL_x$	$_nm_x$	T_x	$1000r_x$	$\overset{\circ}{e}_x$	$_nM_x$	Age, x
0	0.01616	100000	1616	98774	0.01636	7519740	0.00	75.20	0.01635	0
1	0.00281	98384	276	392732	0.00070	7420967	0.00	75.43	0.00070	1
5	0.00146	98107	143	490180	0.00029	7028234	23.44	71.66	0.00029	5
10	0.00137	97965	134	489500	0.00027	6538055	4.40	66.74	0.00027	10
15	0.00204	97831	199	488671	0.00041	6048555	0.00	61.83	0.00041	15
20	0.00214	97631	209	487647	0.00043	5559884	15.93	56.95	0.00043	20
25	0.00266	97422	259	486497	0.00053	5072237	21.39	52.06	0.00053	25
30	0.00373	97164	363	484982	0.00075	4585740	0.78	47.20	0.00075	30
35	0.00620	96801	600	482635	0.00124	4100758	0.00	42.36	0.00124	35
40	0.01030	96201	990	478729	0.00207	3618123	0.00	37.61	0.00207	40
45	0.01641	95210	1563	472436	0.00331	3139395	0.00	32.97	0.00331	45
50	0.02549	93648	2387	462673	0.00516	2666958	0.00	28.44	0.00516	50
55	0.03826	91261	3492	448184	0.00779	2204286	0.00	24.15	0.00779	55
60	0.06053	87769	5313	426539	0.01246	1756102	17.50	20.01	0.01241	60
65	0.09919	82456	8179	393240	0.02080	1329563	17.50	16.12	0.02072	65
70	0.16239	74278	12062	342910	0.03517	936322	17.50	12.61	0.03504	70
75	0.26080	62216	16225	271877	0.05968	593412	17.50	9.54	0.05947	75
80	0.40440	45990	18598	183142	0.10155	321535	17.50	6.99	0.10123	80
85+	1.00000	27392	27392	138393	0.19793	138393	17.50	5.05	0.19206	85+

TABLE 4 POPULATION PROJECTION, USING FIXED AGE-SPECIFIC BIRTH AND DEATH RATES, IN THOUSANDS

Age at last birthday	1972			1977			1982			Age at last birthday
	Total	Males	Females	Total	Males	Females	Total	Males	Females	
0–4	4172	2141	2031	4291	2202	2089	4398	2257	2141	0–4
5–9	4162	2134	2028	4160	2134	2026	4277	2194	2083	5–9
10–14	3741	1918	1823	4154	2129	2025	4153	2130	2023	10–14
15–19	3275	1676	1599	3731	1911	1820	4143	2122	2021	15–19
20–24	3520	1782	1738	3264	1668	1596	3717	1901	1816	20–24
25–29	3528	1769	1759	3508	1774	1734	3252	1660	1592	25–29
30–34	2979	1505	1474	3513	1760	1753	3493	1765	1728	30–34
35–39	2892	1483	1409	2962	1495	1467	3494	1749	1745	35–39
40–44	2939	1496	1443	2864	1467	1397	2934	1479	1455	40–44
45–49	3074	1537	1537	2891	1467	1424	2818	1439	1379	45–49
50–54	3060	1507	1553	2992	1486	1506	2814	1419	1395	50–54
55–59	2910	1392	1518	2924	1420	1504	2857	1399	1458	55–59
60–64	2833	1321	1512	2699	1255	1444	2712	1280	1432	60–64
65–69	2435	1077	1358	2507	1113	1394	2390	1058	1332	65–69
70–74	1829	731	1098	2009	825	1184	2068	853	1215	70–74
75–79	1229	420	809	1360	490	870	1492	553	939	75–79
80–84	720	219	501	776	231	545	856	270	586	80–84
85 +	457	113	344	498	119	379	538	126	412	85 +
All ages	49755	24221	25534	51103	24946	26157	52406	25654	26752	All ages

TABLE 5 OBSERVED AND PROJECTED VITAL RATES

Rates per thousand	Observed			Projected						Stable	
				1972		1977		1982			
	Total	Males	Females	Males	Females	Males	Females	Males	Females	Males	Females
Birth	17.23	18.24	16.28	18.46	16.54	18.14	16.35	18.31	16.58	19.19	17.98
Death	11.23	11.81	10.68	12.22	11.44	12.53	11.84	12.71	12.09	11.09	9.88
Increase	6.00	5.42	5.59	6.23	5.10	5.61	4.51	5.59	4.49		8.1025

TABLE 6 RATES STANDARDIZED ON THREE STANDARD COUNTRIES

Standardized rates per thousand	England and Wales, 1961			United States, 1960			Mexico, 1960		
	Total	Males	Females	Total	Males	Females	Total	Males	Females
Birth	16.69	18.17*	15.71	17.00	16.88*	16.27	20.20	15.07*	19.58
Death	10.80	11.69*	9.97	8.79	10.42*	7.28	4.41	8.94*	3.44
Increase	5.89	6.48*	5.75	8.20	6.46*	8.99	15.79	7.13*	16.14

TABLE 7 VITAL STATISTICS AND RATES INFERRED FROM AGE DISTRIBUTIONS (FEMALES)

Vital statistics		Thompson				Bourgeois-Pichat				Coale	
		Age range	NRR	1000r	Interval	Age range	NRR	1000b	1000d	1000r	1000b
TFR	2.63	0–4	1.28	9.06	27.45	5–29	1.18	9.08	17.17	6.14	1000d
GRR	1.28	5–9	1.16	5.56	27.41	30–54	0.80	9.08	17.17	-8.08	1000r
NRR	1.24	10–14	1.04	1.29	27.36	55–79	1.38	28.91	16.88	12.02	1000k_1
Generation	26.89	15–19	1.10	3.44	27.28	*30–59	0.81	9.22	16.93	-7.71	1000k_2
Sex ratio	105.85										

TABLE 8 LESLIE MATRIX AND ITS ANALYSIS (FEMALES)

Start of age interval	Sub-diagonal	First row	Percent in stable population	Fisher values	Total reproductive values	Net maternity function	Matrix equation coefficient	Parameters		
									Integral	Matrix
0	0.99730	0.00000	8.664	1.038	2110590	0.00000	0.00000	λ_1	1.0413	1.0414
5	0.99861	0.00017	8.297	1.084	1978640	0.00000	0.00017	λ_2	0.3380	0.3459
10	0.99831	0.05788	7.956	1.130	1810348	0.00034	0.05764		+0.7894	+0.7611 i
15	0.99790	0.25490	7.627	1.119	1948254	0.11494	0.25343	r_1	0.0081	0.0081
20	0.99764	0.39394	7.309	0.902	1590790	0.39193	0.39085	r_2	-0.0305	-0.0358
25	0.99689	0.30641	7.002	0.532	786506	0.38977	0.30329		+0.2333	+0.2288 i
30	0.99516	0.16137	6.703	0.237	335114	0.21681	0.15923	c_1		222811
35	0.99191	0.06507	6.405	0.079	115521	0.10164	0.06390	c_2		112598
40	0.98686	0.01438	5.101	0.015	23742	0.02616	0.01400			-138002 i
45	0.97933	0.00096	5.781	0.001	1528	0.00185	0.00092	$2\pi/y$	26.937	27.457
50	0.96868	0.00000	5.437	0.000	0	0.00000	0.00000	Δ	6.480	
55	0.80955		22.717							

U. K.: England and Wales, 1967 (urban districts)

TABLE 1   DATA INPUT TO COMPUTATIONS

Age at last birthday	Population					Births, by age of mother	Deaths			Age at last birthday
	Total	Males	%	Females	%		Total	Males	Females	
0	650100	333400	1.8	316700	1.6	0	12489	7067	5422	0
1–4	2617900	1340600	7.3	1277300	6.5	0	2024	1100	924	1–4
5–9	2904598	1488799	8.1	1415799	7.2	0	1056	621	435	5–9
10–14	2559500	1307800	7.1	1251700	6.4	0	904	573	331	10–14
15–19	2797900	1405600	7.6	1392300	7.1	69540	1739	1221	518	15–19
20–24	2832400	1412500	7.7	1419900	7.2	232240	1976	1369	607	20–24
25–29	2343800	1187000	6.5	1156800	5.9	189272	1540	988	552	25–29
30–34	2256100	1157500	6.3	1098600	5.6	102111	2313	1385	928	30–34
35–39	2312800	1175300	6.4	1137500	5.8	50115	3406	1961	1445	35–39
40–44	2468300	1234000	6.7	1234300	6.3	14092	6428	3815	2613	40–44
45–49	2494700	1232700	6.7	1262300	6.4	1025	10211	6090	4121	45–49
50–54	2431100	1172200	6.4	1258900	6.4	0	17830	11122	6708	50–54
55–59	2442700	1165500	6.3	1277200	6.5	0	30115	20197	9918	55–59
60–64	2192300	1010000	5.5	1182300	6.0	0	40841	26001	14840	60–64
65–69	1752700	743800	4.0	1008900	5.1	0	51830	30994	20836	65–69
70–74	1308100	486100	2.6	822000	4.2		63728	34356	29372	70–74
75–79	846815	282088	1.5	564727	2.9		60880	29411	31469	75–79
80–84	479254	146180	0.8	333074	1.7	338445 M	48769	20611	28158	80–84
85 +	402533	112033	0.6	290500	1.5	319950 F	76925	22187	54738	85 +
All ages	38093600	18393100		19700500		658395	435004	221069	213935	All ages

TABLE 2   LIFE TABLE FOR MALES

Age, x	$_nq_x$	l_x	$_nd_x$	$_nL_x$	$_nm_x$	T_x	$1000r_x$	$\overset{\circ}{e}_x$	$_nM_x$	Age, x
0	0.02086	100000	2086	98394	0.02120	6882807	0.00	68.83	0.02120	0
1	0.00327	97914	321	390724	0.00082	6784413	0.00	69.29	0.00082	1
5	0.00208	97594	203	487462	0.00042	6393690	24.14	65.51	0.00042	5
10	0.00219	97391	213	486468	0.00044	5906227	5.22	60.64	0.00044	10
15	0.00433	97178	421	484889	0.00087	5419759	0.00	55.77	0.00087	15
20	0.00483	96757	468	482609	0.00097	4934870	15.99	51.00	0.00097	20
25	0.00416	96289	400	480465	0.00083	4452261	18.97	46.24	0.00083	25
30	0.00597	95889	572	478094	0.00120	3971796	0.00	41.42	0.00120	30
35	0.00831	95316	792	474785	0.00167	3493702	0.00	36.65	0.00167	35
40	0.01535	94524	1451	469303	0.00309	3018916	0.00	31.94	0.00309	40
45	0.02443	93073	2274	460259	0.00494	2549613	0.00	27.39	0.00494	45
50	0.04645	90800	4217	444483	0.00949	2089355	0.00	23.01	0.00949	50
55	0.08326	86582	7209	416022	0.01733	1644872	0.00	19.00	0.01733	55
60	0.12170	79373	9660	373976	0.02583	1228860	17.92	15.48	0.02574	60
65	0.19015	69713	13256	316954	0.04182	854874	17.92	12.26	0.04167	65
70	0.30179	56457	17038	240312	0.07090	537911	17.92	9.53	0.07068	70
75	0.41211	39419	16245	155409	0.10453	297598	17.92	7.55	0.10426	75
80	0.51301	23174	11888	84134	0.14130	142190	17.92	6.14	0.14100	80
85 +	1.00000	11285	11285	58056	0.19439	58056	17.92	5.14	0.19804	85 +

TABLE 3   LIFE TABLE FOR FEMALES

Age, x	$_nq_x$	l_x	$_nd_x$	$_nL_x$	$_nm_x$	T_x	$1000r_x$	$\overset{\circ}{e}_x$	$_nM_x$	Age, x
0	0.01690	100000	1690	98715	0.01712	7562510	0.00	75.63	0.01712	0
1	0.00289	98310	284	392415	0.00072	7463795	0.00	75.92	0.00072	1
5	0.00153	98026	150	489757	0.00031	7071380	23.75	72.14	0.00031	5
10	0.00132	97877	129	489066	0.00026	6581624	1.38	67.24	0.00026	10
15	0.00186	97747	182	488298	0.00037	6092558	0.00	62.33	0.00037	15
20	0.00214	97566	209	487317	0.00043	5604260	18.11	57.44	0.00043	20
25	0.00239	97357	233	486244	0.00048	5116943	25.11	52.56	0.00048	25
30	0.00422	97124	409	484675	0.00084	4630698	0.84	47.68	0.00084	30
35	0.00633	96714	613	482167	0.00127	4146024	0.00	42.87	0.00127	35
40	0.01053	96102	1012	478172	0.00212	3663857	0.00	38.12	0.00212	40
45	0.01621	95090	1541	471898	0.00327	3185685	0.00	33.50	0.00327	45
50	0.02631	93549	2462	461992	0.00533	2713787	0.00	29.01	0.00533	50
55	0.03814	91087	3474	447356	0.00777	2251795	0.00	24.72	0.00777	55
60	0.06127	87613	5368	425619	0.01261	1804440	22.77	20.60	0.01255	60
65	0.09901	82245	8143	392304	0.02076	1378821	22.77	16.76	0.02065	65
70	0.16533	74102	12252	341358	0.03589	986517	22.77	13.31	0.03573	70
75	0.24605	61851	15219	272051	0.05594	645160	22.77	10.43	0.05572	75
80	0.34948	46632	16297	192115	0.08483	373109	22.77	8.00	0.08454	80
85 +	1.00000	30335	30335	180993	0.16760	180993	22.77	5.97	0.18843	85 +

TABLE 4 POPULATION PROJECTION, USING FIXED AGE-SPECIFIC BIRTH AND DEATH RATES, IN THOUSANDS

Age at last birthday	1972			1977			1982			Age at last birthday
	Total	Males	Females	Total	Males	Females	Total	Males	Females	
0–4	3306	1696	1610	3399	1744	1655	3464	1777	1687	0–4
5–9	3258	1668	1590	3295	1690	1605	3389	1738	1551	5–9
10–14	2900	1486	1414	3252	1665	1587	3290	1687	1603	10–14
15–19	2554	1304	1250	2893	1481	1412	3245	1660	1585	15–19
20–24	2789	1399	1390	2544	1297	1247	2883	1474	1409	20–24
25–29	2823	1406	1417	2779	1393	1386	2536	1292	1244	25–29
30–34	2334	1181	1153	2811	1399	1412	2768	1386	1382	30–34
35–39	2242	1149	1093	2320	1173	1147	2795	1390	1405	35–39
40–44	2290	1162	1128	2220	1136	1084	2297	1159	1138	40–44
45–49	2428	1210	1218	2252	1139	1113	2184	1114	1070	45–49
50–54	2426	1190	1236	2362	1169	1193	2190	1100	1090	50–54
55–59	2316	1097	1219	2310	1114	1196	2249	1094	1155	55–59
60–64	2263	1048	1215	2146	986	1160	2140	1002	1138	60–64
65–69	1946	856	1090	2008	888	1120	1905	835	1069	65–69
70–74	1442	564	878	1597	649	948	1648	673	975	70–74
75–79	969	314	655	1065	365	700	1176	420	756	75–79
80–84	552	153	399	633	170	463	691	197	494	80–84
85 +	415	101	314	481	105	376	553	117	436	85 +
All ages	39253	18984	20269	40367	19563	20804	41403	20116	21287	All ages

TABLE 5 OBSERVED AND PROJECTED VITAL RATES

Rates per thousand	Observed			Projected						Stable	
				1972		1977		1982			
	Total	Males	Females	Males	Females	Males	Females	Males	Females	Males	Females
Birth	17.28	18.40	16.24	18.70	16.56	18.30	16.27	18.33	16.38	19.23	17.91
Death	11.42	12.02	10.86	12.29	11.46	12.67	12.20	12.90	12.70	11.15	9.83
Increase	5.86	6.38	5.38	6.41	5.10	5.62	4.06	5.43	3.68		8.0842

TABLE 6 RATES STANDARDIZED ON THREE STANDARD COUNTRIES

Standardized rates per thousand	England and Wales, 1961			United States, 1960			Mexico, 1960		
	Total	Males	Females	Total	Males	Females	Total	Males	Females
Birth	16.70	18.33*	15.73	17.01	17.00*	16.29	20.19	16.22*	19.57
Death	10.70	11.75*	9.61	8.75	10.49*	7.07	4.43	8.79*	3.39
Increase	6.00	6.58*	6.12	8.26	6.51*	9.21	15.76	7.42*	16.18

TABLE 7 VITAL STATISTICS AND RATES INFERRED FROM AGE DISTRIBUTIONS (FEMALES)

Vital statistics		Thompson				Bourgeois-Pichat					Coale
		Age range	NRR	1000r	Interval	Age range	NRR	1000b	1000d	1000r	
TFR	2.63	0–4	1.27	8.75	27.44	5–29	1.15	15.07	9.87	5.20	1000b
GRR	1.28	5–9	1.14	4.90	27.41	30–54	0.77	8.39	18.26	-9.87	1000d
NRR	1.24	10–14	1.03	0.93	27.36	55–79	1.37	28.86	17.10	11.76	1000r
Generation	26.91	15–19	1.11	3.74	27.28	*30–59	0.78	8.59	17.86	-9.27	$1000k_1$
Sex ratio	105.78										$1000k_2$

TABLE 8 LESLIE MATRIX AND ITS ANALYSIS (FEMALES)

Start of age interval	Sub-diagonal	First row	Percent in stable population	Fisher values	Total reproductive values	Net maternity function	Matrix equation coefficient	Parameters		
									Integral	Matrix
0	0.99720	0.00000	8.622	1.039	1655865	0.00000	0.00000	λ_1	1.0412	1.0413
5	0.99859	0.00000	8.257	1.085	1535761	0.00000	0.00000	λ_2	0.3395	0.3476
10	0.99843	0.05951	7.918	1.131	1415820	0.00000	0.05926		+0.7862	+0.7584i
15	0.99799	0.25439	7.593	1.118	1556244	0.11852	0.25293	r_1	0.0081	0.0081
20	0.99780	0.39000	7.277	0.901	1279972	0.38733	0.38697	r_2	-0.0310	-0.0362
25	0.99677	0.30581	6.973	0.535	618554	0.38661	0.30277		+0.2326	+0.2282i
30	0.99482	0.16322	6.675	0.240	263538	0.21892	0.16107	c_1		176303
35	0.99172	0.06609	6.377	0.081	91744	0.10323	0.06488	c_2		54597
40	0.98688	0.01458	6.073	0.015	19085	0.02653	0.01420			-140701i
45	0.97901	0.00097	5.756	0.001	1218	0.00186	0.00093	$2\pi/y$	27.010	27.534
50	0.96832	0.00000	5.412	0.000	0	0.00000	0.00000	Δ	6.754	
55	0.81412		23.068							

U. K.: England and Wales, 1967 (rural districts)

TABLE 1 DATA INPUT TO COMPUTATIONS

Age at last birthday	Population					Births, by age of mother	Deaths			Age at last birthday
	Total	Males	%	Females	%		Total	Males	Females	
0	178200	92000	1.8	86200	1.7	0	2777	1606	1171	0
1–4	728000	375000	7.4	353000	6.9	0	550	327	223	1–4
5–9	842400	432800	8.5	409600	8.0	0	304	194	110	5–9
10–14	724400	374300	7.4	350100	6.8	0	268	171	97	10–14
15–19	734600	385500	7.6	349100	6.8	15002	582	421	161	15–19
20–24	707900	364900	7.2	343000	6.7	59416	635	456	179	20–24
25–29	647100	325600	6.4	321500	6.3	54530	429	286	143	25–29
30–34	652900	335800	6.6	317100	6.2	28168	564	344	220	30–34
35–39	655500	337800	6.7	317700	6.2	12970	829	475	354	35–39
40–44	656600	333000	6.6	323600	6.3	3430	1487	857	620	40–44
45–49	650100	326500	6.4	323600	6.3	253	2258	1317	941	45–49
50–54	613500	305700	6.0	307800	6.0	0	4010	2452	1558	50–54
55–59	610800	299400	5.9	311400	6.1	0	6828	4448	2380	55–59
60–64	558200	267400	5.3	290800	5.7	0	9505	5986	3519	60–64
65–69	460600	210900	4.2	249700	4.9	0	12073	7075	4998	65–69
70–74	338600	140300	2.8	198300	3.9		15631	9005	6626	70–74
75–79	217884	83561	1.6	134323	2.6		15303	8251	7052	75–79
80–84	123582	44788	0.9	78794	1.5	89456 M	12440	5985	6455	80–84
85 +	106334	36951	0.7	69383	1.4	84313 F	21039	6443	14596	85 +
All ages	10207200	5072200		5135000		173769	107512	56109	51403	All ages

TABLE 2 LIFE TABLE FOR MALES

Age, x	$_nq_x$	l_x	$_nd_x$	$_nL_x$	$_nm_x$	T_x	$1000r_x$	$\overset{\circ}{e}_x$	$_nM_x$	Age, x
0	0.01723	100000	1723	98720	0.01746	7030901	0.00	70.31	0.01745	0
1	0.00348	98277	342	392118	0.00087	6932181	0.00	70.54	0.00087	1
5	0.00223	97935	219	489127	0.00045	6540063	21.57	66.78	0.00045	5
10	0.00229	97716	224	488087	0.00046	6050936	10.98	61.92	0.00045	10
15	0.00545	97493	531	486214	0.00109	5562849	1.55	57.06	0.00109	15
20	0.00623	96961	604	483275	0.00125	5076635	15.75	52.36	0.00125	20
25	0.00438	96358	422	480710	0.00088	4593360	7.32	47.67	0.00088	25
30	0.00511	95936	490	478505	0.00102	4112649	0.00	42.87	0.00102	30
35	0.00701	95446	669	475709	0.00141	3634145	0.00	38.08	0.00141	35
40	0.01294	94777	1227	471067	0.00260	3158436	0.82	33.33	0.00260	40
45	0.02001	93550	1872	463567	0.00404	2687369	4.04	28.73	0.00403	45
50	0.03940	91678	3612	450288	0.00802	2223802	0.12	24.26	0.00802	50
55	0.07179	88066	6323	425586	0.01486	1773514	0.00	20.14	0.01486	55
60	0.10656	81743	8711	387998	0.02245	1347928	16.95	16.49	0.02239	60
65	0.15606	73033	11398	338432	0.03368	959930	16.95	13.14	0.03355	65
70	0.27852	61635	17167	266548	0.06440	621497	16.95	10.08	0.06418	70
75	0.39533	44469	17580	177584	0.09899	354949	16.95	7.98	0.09874	75
80	0.49381	26889	13278	99167	0.13389	177365	16.95	6.60	0.13363	80
85 +	1.00000	13611	13611	78198	0.17406	78198	16.95	5.75	0.17437	85 +

TABLE 3 LIFE TABLE FOR FEMALES

Age, x	$_nq_x$	l_x	$_nd_x$	$_nL_x$	$_nm_x$	T_x	$1000r_x$	$\overset{\circ}{e}_x$	$_nM_x$	Age, x
0	0.01345	100000	1345	98991	0.01358	7631762	0.00	76.32	0.01358	0
1	0.00252	98655	249	393900	0.00063	7532770	0.00	76.35	0.00063	1
5	0.00134	98406	131	491703	0.00027	7138871	22.30	72.54	0.00027	5
10	0.00139	98275	136	491054	0.00028	6647167	15.67	67.64	0.00028	10
15	0.00230	98139	226	490153	0.00046	6156114	1.61	62.73	0.00046	15
20	0.00261	97913	255	488923	0.00052	5665961	7.75	57.87	0.00052	20
25	0.00222	97657	217	487761	0.00045	5177038	7.34	53.01	0.00044	25
30	0.00346	97440	338	486425	0.00069	4689277	0.47	48.12	0.00069	30
35	0.00556	97103	540	484287	0.00111	4202852	0.00	43.28	0.00111	35
40	0.00954	96563	921	480689	0.00192	3718565	0.00	38.51	0.00192	40
45	0.01445	95642	1382	475055	0.00291	3237876	1.87	33.85	0.00291	45
50	0.02502	94260	2358	465837	0.00506	2762821	0.00	29.31	0.00506	50
55	0.03755	91902	3451	451484	0.00764	2296984	0.00	24.99	0.00764	55
60	0.05916	88452	5233	430123	0.01217	1845500	25.88	20.86	0.01210	60
65	0.09612	83219	7999	397442	0.02013	1415377	25.88	17.01	0.02002	65
70	0.15549	75220	11696	348286	0.03358	1017935	25.88	13.53	0.03341	70
75	0.23374	63524	14848	281522	0.05274	669648	25.88	10.54	0.05250	75
80	0.34104	48676	16601	201806	0.08226	388126	25.88	7.97	0.08192	80
85 +	1.00000	32075	32075	186321	0.17215	186321	25.88	5.81	0.21037	85 +

TABLE 4 POPULATION PROJECTION, USING FIXED AGE-SPECIFIC BIRTH AND DEATH RATES, IN THOUSANDS

Age at last birthday	1972			1977			1982			Age at last birthday
	Total	Males	Females	Total	Males	Females	Total	Males	Females	
0–4	866	445	421	890	457	433	935	480	455	0–4
5–9	903	465	438	863	443	420	888	456	432	5–9
10–14	841	432	409	902	464	438	861	442	419	10–14
15–19	722	373	349	838	430	408	900	463	437	15–19
20–24	731	383	348	720	371	349	835	428	407	20–24
25–29	705	363	342	728	381	347	717	369	348	25–29
30–34	645	324	321	702	361	341	725	379	345	30–34
35–39	650	334	316	641	322	319	599	359	340	35–39
40–44	650	335	315	644	331	313	636	319	317	40–44
45–49	648	328	320	641	329	312	635	325	310	45–49
50–54	634	317	317	632	318	314	626	320	306	50–54
55–59	587	289	298	608	300	308	605	301	304	55–59
60–64	570	273	297	547	263	284	566	273	293	60–64
65–69	502	233	269	512	238	274	493	230	263	65–69
70–74	385	166	219	419	184	235	428	188	240	70–74
75–79	253	93	160	288	111	177	312	122	190	75–79
80–84	143	47	96	167	52	115	189	62	127	80–84
85 +	108	35	73	126	37	89	147	41	106	85 +
All ages	10543	5235	5308	10868	5392	5476	11197	5557	5640	All ages

TABLE 5 OBSERVED AND PROJECTED VITAL RATES

Rates per thousand	Observed			Projected						Stable	
				1972		1977		1982			
	Total	Males	Females	Males	Females	Males	Females	Males	Females	Males	Females
Birth	17.02	17.64	16.42	17.54	16.30	17.54	16.28	18.21	16.91	19.00	17.85
Death	10.53	11.06	10.01	11.37	10.54	11.79	11.39	12.09	12.02	10.78	9.64
Increase	6.49	5.57	6.41	6.17	5.76	5.75	4.89	6.11	4.89		8.2155

TABLE 6 RATES STANDARDIZED ON THREE STANDARD COUNTRIES

Standardized rates per thousand	England and Wales, 1961			United States, 1960			Mexico, 1960		
	Total	Males	Females	Total	Males	Females	Total	Males	Females
Birth	16.67	17.59*	15.68	16.95	16.43*	16.21	20.25	15.52*	19.60
Death	9.94	10.39*	9.37	8.07	9.37*	6.86	4.05	7.83*	3.18
Increase	6.73	7.19*	6.30	8.88	7.07*	9.34	15.21	7.70*	16.42

TABLE 7 VITAL STATISTICS AND RATES INFERRED FROM AGE DISTRIBUTIONS (FEMALES)

Vital statistics		Thompson				Bourgeois-Pichat					Coale
TFR	2.63	Age range	NRR	1000r	Interval	Age range	NRR	1000b	1000d	1000r	1000b
GRR	1.28	0–4	1.32	10.21	27.45	5–29	1.30	16.65	6.95	9.69	1000d
NRR	1.25	5–9	1.24	7.96	27.42	30–54	0.97	12.25	13.54	−1.29	1000r
Generation	26.83	10–14	1.07	2.61	27.37	55–79	1.42	28.92	15.95	12.97	$1000k_1$
Sex ratio	106.10	15–19	1.07	2.30	27.29	*25–49	0.95	12.02	13.98	−1.95	$1000k_2$

TABLE 8 LESLIE MATRIX AND ITS ANALYSIS (FEMALES)

Start of age interval	Sub-diagonal	First row	Percent in stable population	Fisher values	Total reproductive values	Net maternity function	Matrix equation coefficient
0	0.99759	0.00000	8.623	1.035	454765	0.00000	0.00000
5	0.99868	0.00000	8.256	1.082	442816	0.00000	0.00000
10	0.99816	0.05129	7.913	1.128	395050	0.00000	0.05110
15	0.99749	0.25800	7.580	1.125	392636	0.10220	0.25657
20	0.99762	0.40947	7.256	0.907	311117	0.41093	0.40617
25	0.99726	0.30874	6.948	0.522	167947	0.40141	0.30553
30	0.99560	0.15482	6.649	0.225	71427	0.20965	0.15279
35	0.99257	0.36140	6.353	0.075	23739	0.09593	0.06032
40	0.98828	0.01359	6.052	0.014	4658	0.02472	0.01326
45	0.98059	0.00093	5.740	0.001	303	0.00180	0.00090
50	0.96919	0.00000	5.402	0.000	2	0.00000	0.00000
55	0.81655		23.227				

Parameters

	Integral	Matrix
λ_1	1.0419	1.0420
λ_2	0.3327	0.3398
	+0.8021	+0.7720i
r_1	0.0082	0.0082
r_2	−0.0282	−0.0340
	+0.2355	+0.2312i
c_1		47589
c_2		56603
		4513i
$2\pi/y$	26.677	27.174
Δ	4.743	

[477]

U. K.: Northern Ireland, 1966

TABLE 1 DATA INPUT TO COMPUTATIONS

Age at last birthday	Population Total	Males	%	Females	%	Births, by age of mother	Deaths Total	Males	Females	Age at last birthday
0	30767	15874	2.3	14893	2.0	0	849	465	384	0
1–4	115752	59480	8.6	56272	7.7	0	139	83	56	1–4
5–9	132444	68096	9.8	64348	8.8	0	59	40	19	5–9
10–14	133171	68130	9.8	65041	8.9	11	43	24	19	10–14
15–19	120237	60287	8.7	59950	8.2	526	91	59	32	15–19
20–24	93752	46875	6.8	46877	6.4	4159	92	65	27	20–24
25–29	85239	41618	6.0	43621	6.0	10028	72	47	25	25–29
30–34	86481	41582	6.0	44899	6.1	10402	82	47	35	30–34
35–39	90938	43912	6.3	47026	6.4	5762	141	82	59	35–39
40–44	85067	41633	6.0	43434	5.9	1972	270	158	112	40–44
45–49	87025	42098	6.1	44927	6.1	461	380	213	167	45–49
50–54	82043	39593	5.7	42450	5.8	79	643	390	253	50–54
55–59	72542	34357	4.9	38185	5.2	0	1015	677	338	55–59
60–64	65725	29435	4.2	36290	5.0	0	1414	889	525	60–64
65–69	52209	23004	3.3	29205	4.0	0	1947	1138	809	65–69
70–74	40062	16982	2.4	23080	3.2		2311	1195	1116	70–74
75–79	27034	11337	1.6	15697	2.1		2477	1173	1304	75–79
80–84	16166	6730	1.0	9436	1.3	17200 M	2150	972	1178	80–84
85 +	8388	3201	0.5	5187	0.7	16200 F	2266	942	1324	85 +
All ages	1425042	694224		730818		33400	16441	8659	7782	All ages

TABLE 2 LIFE TABLE FOR MALES

Age, x	$_nq_x$	l_x	$_nd_x$	$_nL_x$	$_nm_x$	T_x	$1000r_x$	$\overset{\circ}{e}_x$	$_nM_x$	Age, x
0	0.02855	100000	2855	97863	0.02917	6695710	5.40	66.96	0.02929	0
1	0.00552	97145	537	387027	0.00139	6597847	5.40	67.92	0.00140	1
5	0.00292	96609	283	482338	0.00059	6210820	9.32	64.29	0.00059	5
10	0.00176	96326	170	481246	0.00035	5728482	11.63	59.47	0.00035	10
15	0.00492	96156	473	479701	0.00099	5247236	36.46	54.57	0.00098	15
20	0.00691	95683	662	476774	0.00139	4767535	35.81	49.83	0.00139	20
25	0.00563	95021	535	473743	0.00113	4290761	10.80	45.16	0.00113	25
30	0.00564	94487	533	471173	0.00113	3817018	0.00	40.40	0.00113	30
35	0.00930	93954	874	467840	0.00187	3345846	0.00	35.61	0.00187	35
40	0.01881	93080	1751	461319	0.00380	2878005	0.66	30.92	0.00380	40
45	0.02501	91330	2284	451469	0.00506	2416686	0.00	26.46	0.00505	45
50	0.04833	89045	4304	435658	0.00988	1965218	9.47	22.07	0.00985	50
55	0.09439	84742	7999	405070	0.01975	1529559	10.02	18.05	0.01970	55
60	0.14098	76743	10819	358035	0.03022	1124490	2.74	14.65	0.03020	60
65	0.22085	65924	14559	294172	0.04949	766455	2.74	11.63	0.04947	65
70	0.29935	51365	15376	218419	0.07040	472283	2.74	9.19	0.07037	70
75	0.40915	35989	14725	142259	0.10351	253864	2.74	7.05	0.10347	75
80	0.52596	21264	11184	77392	0.14451	111606	2.74	5.25	0.14443	80
85 +	*1.00000	10080	10080	34214	0.29462	34214	2.74	3.39	0.29428	85 +

TABLE 3 LIFE TABLE FOR FEMALES

Age, x	$_nq_x$	l_x	$_nd_x$	$_nL_x$	$_nm_x$	T_x	$1000r_x$	$\overset{\circ}{e}_x$	$_nM_x$	Age, x
0	0.02519	100000	2519	98058	0.02569	7216677	4.82	72.17	0.02578	0
1	0.00394	97481	384	388806	0.00099	7118618	4.82	73.03	0.00100	1
5	0.00147	97097	143	485129	0.00029	6729812	8.50	69.31	0.00030	5
10	0.00146	96954	142	484442	0.00029	6244683	6.73	64.41	0.00029	10
15	0.00268	96813	259	483444	0.00054	5760242	32.26	59.50	0.00053	15
20	0.00288	96554	278	482078	0.00058	5276797	31.23	54.65	0.00058	20
25	0.00286	96276	276	480711	0.00057	4794719	3.70	49.80	0.00057	25
30	0.00389	96000	373	479135	0.00078	4314009	0.00	44.94	0.00078	30
35	0.00626	95627	599	476814	0.00126	3834873	1.89	40.10	0.00125	35
40	0.01282	95028	1218	472331	0.00258	3358059	2.07	35.34	0.00258	40
45	0.01843	93810	1729	465039	0.00372	2885729	0.00	30.76	0.00372	45
50	0.02944	92081	2711	454076	0.00597	2420690	10.23	26.29	0.00596	50
55	0.04342	89370	3880	437834	0.00886	1966613	6.39	22.01	0.00885	55
60	0.07019	85490	6000	413799	0.01450	1528779	8.94	17.88	0.01447	60
65	0.13041	79489	10366	373410	0.02776	1114980	8.94	14.03	0.02770	65
70	0.21715	69124	15010	309822	0.04845	741571	8.94	10.73	0.04835	70
75	0.34490	54114	18664	224300	0.08321	431749	8.94	7.98	0.08307	75
80	0.47643	35450	16889	135004	0.12510	207449	8.94	5.85	0.12484	80
85 +	*1.00000	18561	18561	72444	0.25620	72444	8.94	3.90	0.25525	85 +

TABLE 4 POPULATION PROJECTION, USING FIXED AGE-SPECIFIC BIRTH AND DEATH RATES, IN THOUSANDS

Age at last birthday	1971			1976			1981			Age at last birthday
	Total	Males	Females	Total	Males	Females	Total	Males	Females	
0–4	166	85	81	179	92	87	199	102	97	0–4
5–9	146	75	71	165	85	80	177	91	86	5–9
10–14	132	68	64	146	75	71	165	85	80	10–14
15–19	133	68	65	132	68	64	146	75	71	15–19
20–24	120	60	60	132	67	65	131	67	64	20–24
25–29	94	47	47	120	60	60	132	67	65	25–29
30–34	84	41	43	93	46	47	118	59	59	30–34
35–39	86	41	45	84	41	43	92	46	46	35–39
40–44	90	43	47	85	41	44	84	41	43	40–44
45–49	84	41	43	88	42	46	84	40	44	45–49
50–54	85	41	44	81	39	42	86	41	45	50–54
55–59	78	37	41	80	38	42	77	37	40	55–59
60–64	66	30	36	72	33	39	73	33	40	60–64
65–69	57	24	33	58	25	33	62	27	35	65–69
70–74	41	17	24	45	18	27	46	19	27	70–74
75–79	28	11	17	29	11	18	32	12	20	75–79
80–84	15	6	9	16	6	10	17	6	11	80–84
85 +	8	3	5	8	3	5	8	3	5	85 +
All ages	1513	738	775	1613	790	823	1729	851	878	All ages

TABLE 5 OBSERVED AND PROJECTED VITAL RATES

Rates per thousand	Observed			Projected						Stable	
				1971		1976		1981			
	Total	Males	Females	Males	Females	Males	Females	Males	Females	Males	Females
Birth	23.44	24.78	22.17	24.28	21.82	25.24	22.84	26.13	23.82	26.15	25.04
Death	11.54	12.47	10.65	11.83	10.45	11.29	10.31	10.84	10.19	8.65	7.55
Increase	11.90	12.30	11.52	12.45	11.37	13.96	12.53	15.29	13.62		17.4894

TABLE 6 RATES STANDARDIZED ON THREE STANDARD COUNTRIES

Standardized rates per thousand	England and Wales, 1961			United States, 1960			Mexico, 1960		
	Total	Males	Females	Total	Males	Females	Total	Males	Females
Birth	23.72	26.51*	22.30	24.15	24.65*	23.08	24.44	23.45*	23.65
Death	13.10	13.24*	12.96	10.63	11.84*	9.49	5.42	9.57*	4.52
Increase	10.62	13.27*	9.34	13.53	12.80*	13.60	19.02	13.88*	19.13

TABLE 7 VITAL STATISTICS AND RATES INFERRED FROM AGE DISTRIBUTIONS (FEMALES)

Vital statistics		Thompson				Bourgeois-Pichat					Coale	
		Age range	NRR	$1000r$	Interval	Age range	NRR	$1000b$	$1000d$	$1000r$		
TFR	3.70	0–4	1.47	14.30	27.44	5–29	1.79	22.83	1.20	21.64	$1000b$	19.82
GRR	1.79	5–9	1.40	12.36	27.40	30–54	1.01	13.26	12.75	0.51	$1000d$	7.93
NRR	1.72	10–14	1.43	12.83	27.34	55–79	1.37	23.99	12.24	11.75	$1000r$	11.88
Generation	30.92	15–19	1.32	9.95	27.25	*45–74	1.33	22.01	11.56	10.45	$1000k_1$	4.43
Sex ratio	106.2										$1000k_2$	0.

TABLE 8 LESLIE MATRIX AND ITS ANALYSIS (FEMALES)

Start of age interval	Sub-diagonal	First row	Percent in stable population	Fisher values	Total reproductive values	Net maternity function	Matrix equation coefficient	Parameters		
									Integral	Matrix
0	0.99643	0.00000	11.682	1.073	76341	0.00000	0.00000	λ_1	1.0914	1.0916
5	0.99858	0.00020	10.664	1.175	75618	0.00000	0.00020	λ_2	0.5094	0.5047
10	0.99794	0.01054	9.756	1.284	83534	0.00040	0.01049		+0.8268	+0.8062 i
15	0.99717	0.11482	8.919	1.393	83539	0.02057	0.11401	r_1	0.0175	0.0175
20	0.99716	0.37542	8.148	1.402	65715	0.20745	0.37173	r_2	−0.0059	−0.0100
25	0.99672	0.54408	7.443	1.131	49321	0.53601	0.53721		+0.2037	+0.2023 i
30	0.99515	0.41751	6.797	0.653	29305	0.53840	0.41089	c_1		6278
35	0.99060	0.19777	6.195	0.266	12502	0.28337	0.19369	c_2		−4293
40	0.98456	0.06553	5.623	0.079	3422	0.10401	0.06358			2789 i
45	0.97642	0.01426	5.072	0.016	716	0.02314	0.01362	$2\pi/y$	30.843	31.061
50	0.96423	0.00220	4.537	0.002	92	0.00410	0.00205	Δ	9.209	
55	0.80304		15.163							

Yugoslavia, 1966

TABLE 1 DATA INPUT TO COMPUTATIONS

Age at last birthday	Population					Births, by age of mother	Deaths			Age at last birthday
	Total	Males	%	Females	%		Total	Males	Females	
0	383000	197000	2.0	186000	1.8	0	24843	13249	11594	0
1–4	1496000	769000	8.0	727000	7.2	0	3878	1966	1912	1–4
5–9	1890000	966000	10.0	924000	9.2	0	1113	646	467	5–9
10–14	2008000	1026000	10.6	982000	9.8	151	887	533	354	10–14
15–19	1817000	927000	9.6	890000	8.8	48440	1330	843	487	15–19
20–24	1382000	697000	7.2	685000	6.8	125686	1468	878	590	20–24
25–29	1560000	786000	8.1	774000	7.7	114276	2007	1240	767	25–29
30–34	1636000	817000	8.5	819000	8.1	67642	2504	1570	1034	30–34
35–39	1546000	763000	7.9	783000	7.8	32290	3258	1963	1295	35–39
40–44	1247000	562000	5.8	685000	6.8	9244	3514	1902	1612	40–44
45–49	768000	347000	3.6	421000	4.2	1657	3148	1591	1457	45–49
50–54	866000	397000	4.1	469000	4.7	416	6005	3444	2561	50–54
55–59	949000	455000	4.7	494000	4.9	0	10379	6175	4204	55–59
60–64	791000	374000	3.9	417000	4.1	0	13987	8179	5808	60–64
65–69	610000	271000	2.8	339000	3.4	0	17739	9464	8275	65–69
70–74	351000	145000	1.5	206000	2.0		17480	8508	8972	70–74
75–79	238000	92000	1.0	146000	1.4		18534	8234	10300	75–79
80–84	122000	47000	0.5	75000	0.7	206658 M	15250	5391	8869	80–84
85+	75000	27000	0.3	48000	0.5	193144 F	12136	4718	7418	85+
All ages	19735000	9665000		10070000		399802	159570	81594	77976	All ages

TABLE 2 LIFE TABLE FOR MALES

Age, x	$_nq_x$	l_x	$_nd_x$	$_nL_x$	$_nm_x$	T_x	$1000r_x$	$\overset{\circ}{e}_x$	$_nM_x$	Age, x
0	0.06392	100000	6392	95055	0.06725	6604919	0.16	66.05	0.06725	0
1	0.01015	93608	950	371663	0.00256	6509864	0.16	69.54	0.00256	1
5	0.00334	92658	309	462517	0.00067	6138201	0.00	66.25	0.00067	5
10	0.00260	92349	240	461158	0.00052	5675684	3.48	61.46	0.00052	10
15	0.00457	92109	421	459564	0.00092	5214516	37.77	56.61	0.00091	15
20	0.00629	91689	577	457052	0.00126	4754952	15.24	51.86	0.00125	20
25	0.00786	91112	716	453829	0.00158	4297889	0.00	47.17	0.00158	25
30	0.00957	90396	865	449908	0.00192	3844060	0.99	42.52	0.00192	30
35	0.01284	89531	1149	444914	0.00258	3394152	34.81	37.91	0.00257	35
40	0.01697	88382	1499	438359	0.00342	2949238	75.29	33.37	0.00338	40
45	0.02425	86882	2107	429583	0.00490	2510879	29.41	28.90	0.00487	45
50	0.04252	84775	3605	415538	0.00868	2081296	0.00	24.55	0.00868	50
55	0.06578	81170	5339	393407	0.01357	1665758	0.00	20.52	0.01357	55
60	0.10469	75831	7938	360494	0.02202	1272351	35.34	16.78	0.02187	60
65	0.16232	67893	11020	313318	0.03517	911857	35.34	13.43	0.03492	65
70	0.25813	56872	14681	248591	0.05906	598539	35.34	10.52	0.05868	70
75	0.36699	42192	15484	171992	0.09003	349948	35.34	8.29	0.08950	75
80	0.50340	26708	13445	98343	0.13671	177956	35.34	6.66	0.13598	80
85+	1.00000	13263	13263	79613	0.16660	79613	35.34	6.00	0.17474	85+

TABLE 3 LIFE TABLE FOR FEMALES

Age, x	$_nq_x$	l_x	$_nd_x$	$_nL_x$	$_nm_x$	T_x	$1000r_x$	$\overset{\circ}{e}_x$	$_nM_x$	Age, x
0	0.05950	100000	5950	95463	0.06233	7016773	0.06	70.17	0.06233	0
1	0.01044	94050	982	373345	0.00263	6921310	0.06	73.59	0.00263	1
5	0.00252	93068	235	464753	0.00051	6547966	0.00	70.36	0.00051	5
10	0.00180	92833	167	463751	0.00036	6083213	3.32	65.53	0.00036	10
15	0.00275	92666	255	462740	0.00055	5619462	35.44	60.64	0.00055	15
20	0.00430	92411	398	461102	0.00086	5156722	13.15	55.80	0.00086	20
25	0.00494	92013	455	458966	0.00099	4695620	0.00	51.03	0.00099	25
30	0.00629	91558	576	456413	0.00126	4236653	0.00	46.27	0.00126	30
35	0.00826	90982	751	453135	0.00166	3780240	16.15	41.55	0.00165	35
40	0.01181	90231	1066	448655	0.00238	3327105	59.52	36.87	0.00235	40
45	0.01727	89165	1540	442245	0.00348	2878450	34.25	32.28	0.00346	45
50	0.02696	87625	2362	432639	0.00546	2436205	0.00	27.80	0.00546	50
55	0.04175	85262	3560	418078	0.00852	2003565	2.83	23.50	0.00851	55
60	0.06799	81703	5555	395730	0.01404	1585488	33.88	19.41	0.01393	60
65	0.11640	76148	8864	360205	0.02461	1189758	33.88	15.62	0.02441	65
70	0.19854	67284	13358	304576	0.04386	829553	33.88	12.33	0.04355	70
75	0.30242	53926	16308	229649	0.07101	524977	33.88	9.74	0.07055	75
80	0.45606	37617	17156	144225	0.11895	295328	33.88	7.85	0.11825	80
85+	1.00000	20462	20462	151103	0.13542	151103	33.88	7.38	0.15454	85+

TABLE 4 POPULATION PROJECTION, USING FIXED AGE-SPECIFIC BIRTH AND DEATH RATES, IN THOUSANDS

Age at last birthday	1971			1976			1981			Age at last birthday
	Total	Males	Females	Total	Males	Females	Total	Males	Females	
0–4	1935	998	937	2079	1072	1007	2191	1130	1061	0–4
5–9	1862	957	905	1918	989	929	2061	1063	998	5–9
10–14	1885	963	922	1858	955	903	1913	986	927	10–14
15–19	2002	1022	980	1880	960	920	1852	951	901	15–19
20–24	1809	922	887	1993	1017	976	1872	955	917	20–24
25–29	1374	692	682	1798	915	883	1982	1010	972	25–29
30–34	1549	779	770	1364	686	678	1786	908	878	30–34
35–39	1621	808	813	1535	771	764	1351	578	573	35–39
40–44	1527	752	775	1601	796	805	1516	759	757	40–44
45–49	1226	551	675	1501	737	764	1574	780	794	45–49
50–54	748	336	412	1194	533	661	1461	713	748	50–54
55–59	829	376	453	716	318	398	1142	504	638	55–59
60–64	885	417	468	773	344	429	668	291	377	60–64
65–69	705	325	380	788	362	426	689	299	390	65–69
70–74	502	215	287	579	258	321	648	288	360	70–74
75–79	255	100	155	365	149	216	420	178	242	75–79
80–84	145	53	92	155	57	98	221	85	136	80–84
85 +	117	38	79	139	43	96	148	46	102	85 +
All ages	20976	10304	10672	22236	10962	11274	23495	11624	11871	All ages

TABLE 5 OBSERVED AND PROJECTED VITAL RATES

Rates per thousand	Observed			Projected						Stable	
				1971		1976		1981			
	Total	Males	Females	Males	Females	Males	Females	Males	Females	Males	Females
Birth	20.26	21.38	19.18	21.44	19.35	21.77	19.78	21.13	19.34	18.68	17.75
Death	8.09	8.44	7.74	9.00	8.57	9.49	9.18	9.89	9.64	12.80	11.88
Increase	12.17	12.94	11.44	12.44	10.79	12.28	10.60	11.24	9.70		5.8796

TABLE 6 RATES STANDARDIZED ON THREE STANDARD COUNTRIES

Standardized rates per thousand	England and Wales, 1961			United States, 1960			Mexico, 1960		
	Total	Males	Females	Total	Males	Females	Total	Males	Females
Birth	16.78	18.37*	15.71	17.05	17.41*	16.23	20.43	16.96*	19.69
Death	11.76	12.33*	11.95	9.98	10.62*	9.28	6.31	7.90*	5.65
Increase	5.01	6.04*	3.76	7.07	6.79*	6.94	14.12	9.07*	14.04

TABLE 7 VITAL STATISTICS AND RATES INFERRED FROM AGE DISTRIBUTIONS (FEMALES)

Vital statistics		Thompson				Bourgeois-Pichat					Coale
		Age range	NRR	1000r	Interval	Age range	NRR	1000b	1000d	1000r	
TFR	2.64	0–4	1.15	5.18	27.42	5–29	1.45	23.03	9.36	13.67	1000b
GRR	1.28	5–9	1.30	9.59	27.38	30–54	2.38	53.32	21.24	32.08	1000d
NRR	1.17	10–14	1.44	13.27	27.33	55–79	2.62	95.61	59.87	35.74	1000r
Generation	26.70	15–19	1.39	11.59	27.26	*20–44	0.96	15.47	17.05	-1.58	$1000k_1$
Sex ratio	107.00										$1000k_2$

TABLE 8 LESLIE MATRIX AND ITS ANALYSIS (FEMALES)

Start of age interval	Sub-diagonal	First row	Percent in stable population	Fisher values	Total reproductive values	Net maternity function	Matrix equation coefficient	Parameters		
									Integral	Matrix
0	0.99135	0.00000	8.207	1.082	988107	0.00000	0.00000	λ_1	1.0298	1.0299
5	0.99784	0.00017	7.900	1.124	1038858	0.00000	0.00017	λ_2	0.2945	0.3070
10	0.99782	0.06167	7.655	1.160	1139303	0.00034	0.06101		+0.7706	+0.7391 i
15	0.99646	0.26867	7.417	1.131	1006180	0.12167	0.26520	r_1	0.0059	0.0059
20	0.99537	0.37419	7.176	0.877	600487	0.40872	0.36804	r_2	-0.0385	-0.0445
25	0.99444	0.26020	6.936	0.500	387107	0.32736	0.25474		+0.2412	+0.2354 i
30	0.99282	0.13989	6.697	0.235	192276	0.18211	0.13619	c_1		115459
35	0.99011	0.06183	6.456	0.091	71284	0.09028	0.05976	c_2		-51261
40	0.98571	0.01967	6.207	0.027	18569	0.02925	0.01883			113895 i
45	0.97828	0.00544	5.941	0.007	2827	0.00841	0.00513	$2\pi/y$	26.054	26.689
50	0.96634	0.00100	5.644	0.001	494	0.00185	0.00093	Δ	9.757	
55	0.80036		23.764							

Australia, 1967

TABLE 1 DATA INPUT TO COMPUTATIONS

Age at last birthday	Population					Births, by age of mother	Deaths			Age at last birthday
	Total	Males	%	Females	%		Total	Males	Females	
0	225600	115900	1.9	109700	1.9	0	4188	2422	1765	0
1–4	925500	474900	8.0	450600	7.7	0	845	462	383	1–4
5–9	1198500	613300	10.3	585200	10.0	0	457	268	189	5–9
10–14	1110100	568200	9.6	541900	9.2	127	364	236	128	10–14
15–19	1051500	538300	9.1	513200	8.8	24701	952	698	264	15–19
20–24	930500	477000	8.0	453500	7.7	77448	1081	806	275	20–24
25–29	773000	399400	6.7	373600	6.4	69111	871	609	262	25–29
30–34	705800	364300	6.1	341500	5.8	35099	903	597	305	30–34
35–39	754200	392200	6.6	362000	6.2	17322	1393	907	485	35–39
40–44	778300	399700	6.7	378500	6.5	5110	2461	1560	901	40–44
45–49	701300	355300	6.0	346000	5.9	377	3543	2232	1311	45–49
50–54	648300	325300	5.5	323000	5.5	1	5185	3280	1905	50–54
55–59	560300	283800	4.8	276500	4.7	0	7240	4851	2379	55–59
60–64	446400	222000	3.7	224400	3.8	0	9087	6056	3031	60–64
65–69	361400	165400	2.8	196000	3.3	0	11371	7229	4142	65–69
70–74	277700	115100	1.9	162600	2.8		13500	7578	5922	70–74
75–79	200700	80100	1.3	120600	2.1		15119	7819	7300	75–79
80–84	105300	39100	0.7	66200	1.1	117680 M	12587	5684	6903	80–84
85+	55800	18200	0.3	37500	0.6	111616 F	11546	4204	7342	85+
All ages	11810200	5947500		5862700		229296	102703	57508	45195	All ages

TABLE 2 LIFE TABLE FOR MALES

Age, x	$_nq_x$	l_x	$_nd_x$	$_nL_x$	$_nm_x$	T_x	$1000r_x$	$\overset{\circ}{e}_x$	$_nM_x$	Age, x
0	0.02057	100000	2057	98456	0.02090	6779166	0.00	67.79	0.02090	0
1	0.00388	97943	380	390659	0.00097	6680710	0.00	68.21	0.00097	1
5	0.00218	97562	213	487280	0.00044	6290041	3.33	64.47	0.00044	5
10	0.00209	97350	203	486328	0.00042	5802761	12.43	59.61	0.00042	10
15	0.00649	97147	630	484285	0.00130	5316433	16.30	54.73	0.00130	15
20	0.00842	96517	813	480571	0.00169	4832148	28.27	50.07	0.00169	20
25	0.00759	95704	727	476695	0.00152	4351577	25.37	45.47	0.00152	25
30	0.00816	94977	775	473022	0.00164	3874882	0.09	40.80	0.00164	30
35	0.01150	94202	1083	468515	0.00231	3401860	0.00	36.11	0.00231	35
40	0.01936	93118	1803	461449	0.00391	2933345	5.85	31.50	0.00390	40
45	0.03105	91315	2835	450023	0.00630	2471895	14.08	27.07	0.00628	45
50	0.04939	88480	4370	432333	0.01011	2021872	11.76	22.85	0.01008	50
55	0.08268	84110	6954	404319	0.01720	1589539	20.54	18.90	0.01713	55
60	0.12854	77156	9917	362312	0.02737	1185220	17.78	15.35	0.02728	60
65	0.19821	67238	13328	303993	0.04384	822909	17.78	12.24	0.04371	65
70	0.28375	53911	15297	231687	0.06603	518916	17.78	9.63	0.06584	70
75	0.39197	38613	15135	154617	0.09789	287229	17.78	7.44	0.09762	75
80	0.52654	23478	12362	84804	0.14577	132611	17.78	5.65	0.14537	80
85+	1.00000	11116	11116	47807	0.23251	47807	17.78	4.30	0.23099	85+

TABLE 3 LIFE TABLE FOR FEMALES

Age, x	$_nq_x$	l_x	$_nd_x$	$_nL_x$	$_nm_x$	T_x	$1000r_x$	$\overset{\circ}{e}_x$	$_nM_x$	Age, x
0	0.01591	100000	1591	98828	0.01610	7448424	0.00	74.48	0.01610	0
1	0.00339	98409	334	392673	0.00085	7349596	0.00	74.68	0.00085	1
5	0.00161	98075	158	489981	0.00032	6956923	2.89	70.93	0.00032	5
10	0.00118	97917	116	489316	0.00024	6466942	12.81	66.05	0.00024	10
15	0.00258	97801	252	488414	0.00052	5977627	17.34	61.12	0.00051	15
20	0.00303	97549	295	487026	0.00061	5489212	31.14	56.27	0.00061	20
25	0.00351	97253	341	485443	0.00070	5002186	27.65	51.43	0.00070	25
30	0.00447	96912	433	483541	0.00090	4516743	2.22	46.61	0.00090	30
35	0.00669	96479	646	480926	0.00134	4033202	0.00	41.80	0.00134	35
40	0.01184	95833	1135	476566	0.00238	3552276	2.09	37.07	0.00238	40
45	0.01882	94699	1783	469355	0.00380	3075710	11.96	32.48	0.00379	45
50	0.02917	92916	2710	458230	0.00591	2606346	16.44	28.05	0.00590	50
55	0.04238	90206	3823	442091	0.00865	2148116	27.38	23.81	0.00860	55
60	0.06573	86383	5678	418626	0.01356	1706025	22.03	19.75	0.01351	60
65	0.10115	80705	8163	384480	0.02123	1287399	22.03	15.95	0.02113	65
70	0.16837	72542	12214	333806	0.03659	902919	22.03	12.45	0.03642	70
75	0.26503	60328	15989	262951	0.06081	569113	22.03	9.43	0.06053	75
80	0.41430	44339	18370	175447	0.10470	306162	22.03	6.91	0.10427	80
85+	1.00000	25969	25969	130715	0.19867	130715	22.03	5.03	0.19527	85+

TABLE 4 POPULATION PROJECTION, USING FIXED AGE-SPECIFIC BIRTH AND DEATH RATES, IN THOUSANDS

Age at last birthday	1972 Total	Males	Females	1977 Total	Males	Females	1982 Total	Males	Females	Age at last birthday
0–4	1192	610	582	1325	678	647	1442	738	704	0–4
5–9	1148	589	559	1188	608	580	1321	675	645	5–9
10–14	1196	612	584	1145	587	558	1186	607	579	10–14
15–19	1107	566	541	1193	610	583	1142	585	557	15–19
20–24	1046	534	512	1100	561	539	1187	605	582	20–24
25–29	925	473	452	1040	530	510	1095	557	538	25–29
30–34	768	396	372	920	470	450	1034	526	508	30–34
35–39	701	361	340	763	393	370	913	465	448	35–39
40–44	745	386	359	692	355	337	754	387	367	40–44
45–49	763	390	373	730	377	353	678	347	331	45–49
50–54	679	341	338	738	374	364	707	362	345	50–54
55–59	616	304	312	645	319	326	701	350	351	55–59
60–64	516	254	262	568	273	295	595	286	309	60–64
65–69	392	186	206	453	213	240	500	229	271	65–69
70–74	296	126	170	321	142	179	372	163	209	70–74
75–79	205	77	128	218	84	134	236	95	141	75–79
80–84	124	44	80	127	42	85	135	46	89	80–84
85 +	71	22	49	85	25	60	88	24	64	85 +
All ages	12490	6271	6219	13251	6641	6610	14086	7048	7038	All ages

TABLE 5 OBSERVED AND PROJECTED VITAL RATES

Rates per thousand	Observed Total	Males	Females	Projected 1972 Males	Females	1977 Males	Females	1982 Males	Females	Stable Males	Females
Birth	19.42	19.79	19.04	21.02	20.11	21.91	20.88	22.19	21.08	21.33	19.95
Death	8.70	9.67	7.71	9.93	8.21	10.12	8.48	10.22	8.54	10.39	9.02
Increase	10.72	10.12	11.33	11.09	11.90	11.79	12.40	11.97	12.54		10.9425

TABLE 6 RATES STANDARDIZED ON THREE STANDARD COUNTRIES

Standardized rates per thousand	England and Wales, 1961 Total	Males	Females	United States, 1960 Total	Males	Females	Mexico, 1960 Total	Males	Females
Birth	18.05	19.34*	17.03	18.37	17.84*	17.62	21.68	17.35*	21.05
Death	11.34	12.39*	10.42	9.24	10.81*	7.63	4.73	8.50*	3.64
Increase	6.71	6.95*	6.61	9.13	7.03*	9.99	16.95	8.86*	17.41

TABLE 7 VITAL STATISTICS AND RATES INFERRED FROM AGE DISTRIBUTIONS (FEMALES)

Vital statistics		Thompson Age range	NRR	1000r	Interval	Bourgeois-Pichat Age range	NRR	1000b	1000d	1000r	Coale	
TFR	2.85	0–4	1.37	11.52	27.43	5–29	1.77	24.63	3.59	21.05	1000b	21.44
GRR	1.39	5–9	1.53	15.61	27.40	30–54	1.01	12.86	12.37	0.49	1000d	8.57
NRR	1.34	10–14	1.49	14.36	27.34	55–79	1.54	25.93	9.92	16.00	1000r	12.88
Generation	27.07	15–19	1.46	13.19	27.25	*45–69	1.73	33.63	13.40	20.23	$1000k_1$	0.
Sex ratio	105.4										$1000k_2$	0.

TABLE 8 LESLIE MATRIX AND ITS ANALYSIS (FEMALES)

Start of age interval	Sub-diagonal	First row	Percent in stable population	Fisher values	Total reproductive values	Net maternity function	Matrix equation coefficient	Parameters	Integral	Matrix
0	0.99691	0.00000	9.551	1.045	585765	0.00000	0.00000	λ_1	1.0562	1.0563
5	0.99864	0.00028	9.014	1.108	648253	0.00000	0.00028	λ_2	0.3493	0.3555
10	0.99816	0.05775	8.522	1.171	634793	0.00056	0.05749		+0.8049	+0.7761i
15	0.99716	0.26129	8.052	1.179	605155	0.11443	0.25965	r_1	0.0109	0.0110
20	0.99675	0.42487	7.601	0.975	442248	0.40487	0.42100	r_2	-0.0262	-0.0317
25	0.99608	0.34376	7.173	0.588	219614	0.43713	0.33952		+0.2323	+0.2282i
30	0.99459	0.17988	6.764	0.263	89671	0.24192	0.17597	c_1		60989
35	0.99093	0.07324	6.369	0.090	32509	0.11202	0.07167	c_2		-24271
40	0.98489	0.01743	5.974	0.018	6989	0.03131	0.01590			93428i
45	0.97627	0.00131	5.570	0.001	448	0.00249	0.00125	$2\pi/y$	27.051	27.529
50	0.96477	0.00000	5.148	0.000	2	0.00001	0.00000	Δ	3.819	
55	0.81117		20.262							

Fiji Islands, 1966

TABLE 1   DATA INPUT TO COMPUTATIONS

Age at last birthday	Population					Births, by age of mother	Deaths			Age at last birthday
	Total	Males	%	Females	%		Total	Males	Females	
0	16248	8361	3.4	7887	3.4	0	421	226	195	0
1–4	64243	33206	13.6	31037	13.3	0	166	84	82	1–4
5–9	68851	35188	14.4	33663	14.5	0	61	34	27	5–9
10–14	59536	30290	12.4	29246	12.6	0	90	52	38	10–14
15–19	50736	25689	10.5	25047	10.8	1615	52	25	27	15–19
20–24	42675	21436	8.8	21239	9.1	5835	70	33	37	20–24
25–29	35801	18043	7.4	17758	7.6	4673	56	33	23	25–29
30–34	29614	14937	6.1	14677	6.3	2402	71	42	29	30–34
35–39	24674	12553	5.1	12121	5.2	1495	77	41	36	35–39
40–44	20639	10614	4.4	10025	4.3	492	90	45	45	40–44
45–49	16869	8688	3.6	8181	3.5	141	108	73	35	45–49
50–54	13339	6955	2.9	6384	2.7	0	135	75	60	50–54
55–59	10141	5313	2.2	4828	2.1	0	163	107	56	55–59
60–64	7444	3893	1.6	3551	1.5	0	186	111	75	60–64
65–69	5756	3042	1.2	2714	1.2	0	148	106	42	65–69
70–74	4066	2171	0.9	1895	0.8		164	106	58	70–74
75–79	2642	1443	0.6	1199	0.5		149	91	58	75–79
80–84	1586	895	0.4	691	0.3	8583 M	115	70	45	80–84
85 +	1731	1066	0.4	665	0.3	8070 F	162	108	54	85 +
All ages	476591	243783		232808		16653	2484	1462	1022	All ages

TABLE 2   LIFE TABLE FOR MALES

Age, x	$_nq_x$	l_x	$_nd_x$	$_nL_x$	$_nm_x$	T_x	$1000r_x$	$\overset{\circ}{e}_x$	$_nM_x$	Age, x
0	0.02655	100000	2655	98209	0.02703	6808712	0.00	68.09	0.02703	0
1	0.01005	97345	978	386625	0.00253	6710503	0.00	68.93	0.00253	1
5	0.00480	96367	463	480679	0.00096	6323877	30.12	65.62	0.00097	5
10	0.00855	95904	820	477472	0.00172	5843198	30.12	60.93	0.00172	10
15	0.00485	95085	461	474252	0.00097	5365728	33.29	56.43	0.00097	15
20	0.00770	94624	729	471380	0.00155	4891474	33.89	51.69	0.00154	20
25	0.00915	93895	859	467448	0.00184	4420093	34.12	47.07	0.00183	25
30	0.01401	93036	1304	462052	0.00282	3952645	33.59	42.49	0.00281	30
35	0.01625	91732	1491	455061	0.00328	3490593	30.83	38.05	0.00327	35
40	0.02116	90242	1910	446886	0.00427	3035533	31.84	33.64	0.00424	40
45	0.04143	88332	3659	433049	0.00845	2588647	34.38	29.31	0.00840	45
50	0.05302	84673	4489	412995	0.01087	2155597	36.79	25.46	0.01078	50
55	0.09676	80184	7759	382602	0.02028	1742602	38.11	21.73	0.02014	55
60	0.13359	72425	9675	338424	0.02859	1360000	24.93	18.78	0.02851	60
65	0.16087	62750	10095	288891	0.03494	1021577	24.93	16.28	0.03485	65
70	0.21834	52655	11497	234766	0.04897	732686	24.93	13.91	0.04883	70
75	0.27247	41158	11214	177394	0.06322	497920	24.93	12.10	0.06306	75
80	0.32597	29944	9761	124545	0.07837	320527	24.93	10.70	0.07821	80
85 +	1.00000	20183	20183	195982	0.10299	195982	24.93	9.71	0.10131	85 +

TABLE 3   LIFE TABLE FOR FEMALES

Age, x	$_nq_x$	l_x	$_nd_x$	$_nL_x$	$_nm_x$	T_x	$1000r_x$	$\overset{\circ}{e}_x$	$_nM_x$	Age, x
0	0.02433	100000	2433	98394	0.02472	7356569	0.05	73.57	0.02472	0
1	0.01049	97567	1023	387407	0.00264	7258176	0.05	74.39	0.00264	1
5	0.00397	96544	384	481760	0.00080	6870769	27.23	71.17	0.00080	5
10	0.00648	96160	624	479259	0.00130	6389009	28.45	66.44	0.00130	10
15	0.00539	95537	515	476438	0.00108	5909739	30.69	61.85	0.00108	15
20	0.00868	95022	825	473066	0.00174	5433302	32.92	57.18	0.00174	20
25	0.00646	94197	609	469483	0.00130	4960236	35.40	52.66	0.00130	25
30	0.00990	93588	926	465784	0.00199	4490752	36.17	47.98	0.00198	30
35	0.01484	92662	1375	460102	0.00299	4024969	35.00	43.44	0.00297	35
40	0.02225	91287	2031	451468	0.00450	3564867	35.28	39.05	0.00449	40
45	0.02138	89256	1908	441928	0.00432	3113399	39.61	34.88	0.00428	45
50	0.04630	87348	4044	427218	0.00947	2671472	44.12	30.58	0.00940	50
55	0.05696	83303	4745	405457	0.01170	2244253	45.13	26.94	0.01160	55
60	0.10057	78558	7901	373153	0.02117	1838797	48.09	23.41	0.02112	60
65	0.07491	70657	5293	340371	0.01555	1465644	48.09	20.74	0.01548	65
70	0.14416	65364	9423	304697	0.03093	1125272	48.09	17.22	0.03061	70
75	0.21760	55941	12173	249871	0.04872	820575	48.09	14.67	0.04837	75
80	0.28067	43769	12284	187731	0.06544	570704	48.09	13.04	0.06512	80
85 +	1.00000	31484	31484	382973	0.08221	382973	48.09	12.16	0.08120	85 +

[484]

TABLE 4 POPULATION PROJECTION, USING FIXED AGE-SPECIFIC BIRTH AND DEATH RATES, IN THOUSANDS

Age at last birthday	1971			1976			1981			Age at last birthday
	Total	Males	Females	Total	Males	Females	Total	Males	Females	
0–4	88	45	43	103	53	50	121	62	59	0–4
5–9	80	41	39	87	45	42	103	53	50	5–9
10–14	68	35	33	79	41	38	87	45	42	10–14
15–19	59	30	29	68	35	33	79	41	38	15–19
20–24	51	26	25	59	30	29	68	35	33	20–24
25–29	42	21	21	50	25	25	59	30	29	25–29
30–34	36	18	18	42	21	21	49	25	24	30–34
35–39	29	15	14	35	18	17	42	21	21	35–39
40–44	24	12	12	28	14	14	34	17	17	40–44
45–49	20	10	10	24	12	12	28	14	14	45–49
50–54	16	8	8	19	10	9	22	11	11	50–54
55–59	12	6	6	16	8	8	18	9	9	55–59
60–64	9	5	4	12	6	6	14	7	7	60–64
65–69	6	3	3	8	4	4	10	5	5	65–69
70–74	4	2	2	6	3	3	7	3	4	70–74
75–79	4	2	2	4	2	2	4	2	2	75–79
80–84	2	1	1	2	1	1	2	1	1	80–84
85 +	2	1	1	4	2	2	4	2	2	85 +
All ages	552	281	271	646	330	316	751	383	368	All ages

TABLE 5 OBSERVED AND PROJECTED VITAL RATES

Rates per thousand	Observed			Projected						Stable	
				1971		1976		1981			
	Total	Males	Females	Males	Females	Males	Females	Males	Females	Males	Females
Birth	34.94	35.21	34.66	35.85	35.10	36.12	35.26	36.03	35.10	34.37	33.49
Death	5.21	6.00	4.39	6.00	4.66	6.02	4.84	6.05	5.00	6.70	5.82
Increase	29.73	29.21	30.27	29.85	30.45	30.10	30.42	29.99	30.10		27.6761

TABLE 6 RATES STANDARDIZED ON THREE STANDARD COUNTRIES

Standardized rates per thousand	England and Wales, 1961			United States, 1960			Mexico, 1960		
	Total	Males	Females	Total	Males	Females	Total	Males	Females
Birth	30.57	34.56*	28.72	30.98	31.43*	29.58	34.93	33.62*	33.77
Death	10.18	11.64*	9.64	8.55	9.85*	7.55	5.26	5.47*	4.62
Increase	20.40	22.92*	19.08	22.43	21.58*	22.03	29.68	28.15*	29.15

TABLE 7 VITAL STATISTICS AND RATES INFERRED FROM AGE DISTRIBUTIONS (FEMALES)

Vital statistics		Thompson				Bourgeois-Pichat					Coale	
TFR	4.78	Age range	NRR	1000r	Interval	Age range	NRR	1000b	1000d	1000r	1000b	37.04
GRR	2.32	0–4	2.22	29.17	27.36	5–29	2.29	38.22	7.54	30.69	1000d	7.13
NRR	2.17	5–9	2.30	31.10	27.31	30–54	2.71	45.24	8.35	36.90	1000r	29.91
Generation	27.93	10–14	2.40	31.31	27.23	55–79	3.15	58.94	16.43	42.51	$1000k_1$	-7.55
Sex ratio	106.4	15–19	2.48	33.50	27.11	*20–49	2.61	42.92	7.45	35.47	$1000k_2$	0.

TABLE 8 LESLIE MATRIX AND ITS ANALYSIS (FEMALES)

Start of age interval	Sub-diagonal	First row	Percent in stable population	Fisher values	Total reproductive values	Net maternity function	Matrix equation coefficient	Parameters		
									Integral	Matrix
0	0.99168	0.00000	15.215	1.103	42917	0.00000	0.00000	λ_1	1.1484	1.1489
5	0.99483	0.00000	13.133	1.277	43001	0.00000	0.00000	λ_2	0.3458	0.3597
10	0.99409	0.07545	11.372	1.475	43145	0.00000	0.07443		+0.8161	+0.7825 i
15	0.99292	0.39699	9.839	1.621	40610	0.14887	0.38934	r_1	0.0277	0.0278
20	0.99243	0.63079	8.503	1.435	30483	0.62981	0.61425	r_2	-0.0241	-0.0299
25	0.99212	0.50087	7.345	0.961	17061	0.59869	0.48405		+0.2340	+0.2280 i
30	0.98780	0.33605	6.343	0.556	8160	0.36940	0.32220	c_1		2523
35	0.98123	0.20187	5.453	0.272	3291	0.27500	0.19119	c_2		785
40	0.97887	0.07749	4.657	0.091	913	0.10737	0.07214			2642 i
45	0.96671	0.02032	3.968	0.020	161	0.03691	0.01846	$2\pi/y$	26.851	27.559
50	0.94906	0.00018	3.339	0.000	1	0.00000	0.00000	Δ	5.914	
55	0.85643		10.833							

New Zealand, 1966-68

TABLE 1 DATA INPUT TO COMPUTATIONS

Age at last birthday	Population Total	Males	%	Females	%	Births, by age of mother	Deaths Total	Males	Females	Age at last birthday
0	62168	31927	2.3	30241	2.2	0	1110	649	461	0
1–4	243580	124800	9.1	118780	8.7	0	262	144	118	1–4
5–9	309240	157790	11.5	151450	11.1	0	132	83	49	5–9
10–14	274510	140430	10.3	134080	9.9	55	106	70	35	10–14
15–19	248130	126970	9.3	121160	8.9	7965	237	174	63	15–19
20–24	201510	102340	7.5	99170	7.3	21685	228	176	52	20–24
25–29	175360	88940	6.5	86420	6.3	17980	180	117	63	25–29
30–34	150740	76740	5.6	74000	5.4	8065	200	129	71	30–34
35–39	160840	82890	6.1	77950	5.7	4091	303	193	110	35–39
40–44	162340	83140	6.1	79200	5.8	1267	453	268	185	40–44
45–49	148210	73700	5.4	74510	5.5	107	726	438	288	45–49
50–54	139470	68930	5.0	70540	5.2	0	1072	662	410	50–54
55–59	124520	62390	4.6	62130	4.6	0	1558	1015	543	55–59
60–64	102720	50760	3.7	51960	3.8	0	2032	1317	715	60–64
65–69	82050	38350	2.8	43700	3.2	0	2525	1548	977	65–69
70–74	59255	24655	1.8	34600	2.5		2800	1561	1239	70–74
75–79	43385	17560	1.3	25825	1.9		3255	1690	1565	75–79
80–84	26040	10235	0.7	15805	1.2	31312 M	3158	1495	1663	80–84
85 +	15120	5625	0.4	9495	0.7	29903 F	3414	1416	1998	85 +
All ages	2729188	1368172		1361016		61215	23751	13145	10606	All ages

TABLE 2 LIFE TABLE FOR MALES

Age, x	$_nq_x$	l_x	$_nd_x$	$_nL_x$	$_nm_x$	T_x	$1000r_x$	$\mathring{e}_x$	$_nM_x$	Age, x
0	0.02001	100000	2001	98542	0.02031	6820538	1.42	68.21	0.02033	0
1	0.00459	97999	450	390700	0.00115	6721997	1.42	68.59	0.00115	1
5	0.00262	97549	256	487105	0.00052	6331297	10.30	64.90	0.00053	5
10	0.00251	97293	244	485942	0.00050	5844192	21.03	60.07	0.00050	10
15	0.00687	97049	667	483701	0.00138	5358250	30.38	55.21	0.00137	15
20	0.00856	96383	825	479842	0.00172	4874549	34.04	50.57	0.00172	20
25	0.00655	95558	626	476216	0.00132	4394707	27.30	45.99	0.00132	25
30	0.00838	94931	795	472765	0.00168	3918491	5.33	41.28	0.00168	30
35	0.01158	94136	1090	468100	0.00233	3445726	0.00	36.60	0.00233	35
40	0.01603	93046	1492	461835	0.00323	2977626	8.16	32.00	0.00322	40
45	0.02940	91555	2691	451605	0.00596	2515790	12.69	27.48	0.00594	45
50	0.04705	88863	4181	434690	0.00962	2064186	6.48	23.23	0.00960	50
55	0.07858	84682	6655	407896	0.01631	1629496	13.80	19.24	0.01627	55
60	0.12249	78028	9558	367489	0.02601	1221600	13.04	15.66	0.02595	60
65	0.18436	68470	12623	311995	0.04046	854111	13.04	12.47	0.04037	65
70	0.27446	55847	15328	241558	0.06345	542116	13.04	9.71	0.06331	70
75	0.38767	40519	15708	162863	0.09645	300558	13.04	7.42	0.09624	75
80	0.52835	24811	13109	89559	0.14637	137695	13.04	5.55	0.14607	80
85 +	1.00000	11702	11702	48136	0.24311	48136	13.04	4.11	0.25173	85 +

TABLE 3 LIFE TABLE FOR FEMALES

Age, x	$_nq_x$	l_x	$_nd_x$	$_nL_x$	$_nm_x$	T_x	$1000r_x$	$\mathring{e}_x$	$_nM_x$	Age, x
0	0.01507	100000	1507	98925	0.01523	7433455	1.10	74.33	0.01524	0
1	0.00396	98493	390	392856	0.00099	7334530	1.10	74.47	0.00099	1
5	0.00161	98103	158	490122	0.00032	6941674	10.08	70.76	0.00032	5
10	0.00135	97945	132	489418	0.00027	6451553	21.97	65.87	0.00027	10
15	0.00260	97814	255	488457	0.00052	5962135	29.70	60.95	0.00052	15
20	0.00263	97559	256	487174	0.00053	5473678	33.22	56.11	0.00052	20
25	0.00365	97303	355	485668	0.00073	4986504	28.55	51.25	0.00073	25
30	0.00479	96947	465	483642	0.00096	4500836	9.32	46.43	0.00096	30
35	0.00703	96483	679	480852	0.00141	4017193	0.00	41.64	0.00141	35
40	0.01162	95804	1113	476474	0.00234	3536341	2.07	36.91	0.00234	40
45	0.01918	94691	1816	469236	0.00387	3059868	7.65	32.31	0.00387	45
50	0.02873	92874	2668	458130	0.00582	2590631	12.19	27.89	0.00581	50
55	0.04299	90206	3878	441981	0.00877	2132501	21.45	23.64	0.00874	55
60	0.06690	86328	5775	418180	0.01381	1690520	18.19	19.58	0.01376	60
65	0.10656	80552	8584	382581	0.02244	1272340	18.19	15.80	0.02236	65
70	0.16560	71968	11918	331577	0.03594	889759	18.19	12.36	0.03581	70
75	0.26525	60050	15928	261828	0.06083	558182	18.19	9.30	0.06060	75
80	0.42196	44122	18618	176062	0.10575	296354	18.19	6.72	0.10522	80
85 +	•1.00000	25505	25505	120292	0.21202	120292	18.19	4.72	0.21043	85 +

TABLE 4 POPULATION PROJECTION, USING FIXED AGE-SPECIFIC BIRTH AND DEATH RATES, IN THOUSANDS

Age at last birthday	1972 Total	Males	Females	1977 Total	Males	Females	1982 Total	Males	Females	Age at last birthday
0–4	323	165	158	371	189	182	419	214	205	0–4
5–9	305	156	149	322	164	158	369	188	181	5–9
10–14	308	157	151	304	156	148	321	164	157	10–14
15–19	274	140	134	308	157	151	303	155	148	15–19
20–24	247	126	121	272	139	133	306	155	151	20–24
25–29	201	102	99	245	125	120	271	138	133	25–29
30–34	174	88	86	199	101	98	244	124	120	30–34
35–39	150	76	74	173	87	86	198	100	98	35–39
40–44	159	82	77	148	75	73	171	86	85	40–44
45–49	159	81	78	156	80	76	145	73	72	45–49
50–54	144	71	73	154	78	76	151	77	74	50–54
55–59	133	65	68	137	67	70	146	73	73	55–59
60–64	115	56	59	122	58	64	126	60	66	60–64
65–69	91	43	48	102	48	54	108	49	59	65–69
70–74	68	30	38	74	33	41	84	37	47	70–74
75–79	44	17	27	50	20	30	55	22	33	75–79
80–84	27	10	17	27	9	18	31	11	20	80–84
85 +	17	6	11	17	5	12	18	5	13	85 +
All ages	2939	1471	1468	3181	1591	1590	3466	1731	1735	All ages

TABLE 5 OBSERVED AND PROJECTED VITAL RATES

Rates per thousand	Observed Total	Males	Females	Projected 1972 Males	Females	1977 Males	Females	1982 Males	Females	Stable Males	Females
Birth	22.43	22.89	21.97	24.52	23.46	25.96	24.78	26.59	25.37	25.88	24.62
Death	8.70	9.61	7.79	9.40	7.89	9.29	7.90	9.19	7.83	8.33	7.08
Increase	13.73	13.28	14.18	15.12	15.57	16.66	16.88	17.41	17.54		17.5460

TABLE 6 RATES STANDARDIZED ON THREE STANDARD COUNTRIES

Standardized rates per thousand	England and Wales, 1961 Total	Males	Females	United States, 1960 Total	Males	Females	Mexico, 1960 Total	Males	Females
Birth	21.30	23.86*	20.17	21.69	21.96*	20.87	25.95	21.59*	25.29
Death	11.28	12.02*	10.63	9.19	10.58*	7.78	4.68	8.02*	3.68
Increase	10.02	11.83*	9.54	12.50	11.38*	13.09	21.26	13.57*	21.60

TABLE 7 VITAL STATISTICS AND RATES INFERRED FROM AGE DISTRIBUTIONS (FEMALES)

Vital statistics		Thompson Age range	NRR	$1000r$	Interval	Bourgeois-Pichat Age range	NRR	$1000b$	$1000d$	$1000r$	Coale	
TFR	3.36	0–4	1.63	18.33	27.43	5–29	2.13	28.53	0.51	28.02	$1000b$	22.28
GRR	1.64	5–9	1.81	22.05	27.40	30–54	1.00	11.74	11.58	0.16	$1000d$	7.72
NRR	1.59	10–14	1.69	18.90	27.34	55–79	1.70	31.47	11.91	19.55	$1000r$	14.57
Generation	26.54	15–19	1.59	16.11	27.25	*50–74	1.70	31.80	12.08	19.71	$1000k_1$	0.
Sex ratio	104.7										$1000k_2$	0.

TABLE 8 LESLIE MATRIX AND ITS ANALYSIS (FEMALES)

Start of age interval	Sub-diagonal	First row	Percent in stable population	Fisher values	Total reproductive values	Net maternity function	Matrix equation coefficient	Parameters	Integral	Matrix
0	0.99663	0.00000	11.602	1.062	158287	0.00000	0.00000	λ_1	1.0917	1.0919
5	0.99856	0.00049	10.590	1.164	176244	0.00000	0.00049	λ_2	0.3223	0.3299
10	0.99804	0.07930	9.685	1.272	170544	0.00098	0.07892		+0.8340	+0.8004i
15	0.99737	0.34092	8.852	1.307	158378	0.15686	0.33862	r_1	0.0175	0.0176
20	0.99691	0.51178	8.085	1.068	105912	0.52038	0.50699	r_2	−0.0224	−0.0288
25	0.99583	0.38027	7.383	0.624	53965	0.49360	0.37554		+0.2404	+0.2360i
30	0.99423	0.19358	6.733	0.279	20652	0.25749	0.19038	c_1		13254
35	0.99089	0.08208	6.131	0.100	7770	0.12328	0.08026	c_2		−2066
40	0.98481	0.02090	5.564	0.022	1731	0.03723	0.02026			26039i
45	0.97633	0.00172	5.018	0.002	126	0.00329	0.00165	$2\pi/y$	26.135	26.628
50	0.96475	0.00002	4.487	0.000	1	0.00000	0.00000	Δ	4.174	
55	0.81912		15.869							

CHAPTER 17

Cities

With rapidly increasing proportions of the world's population living in cities, both in rich and poor countries, it becomes of increasing interest to obtain separate demographic data for cities. If urban mortality is different from rural, separate life tables and other calculations bearing on population dynamics will be valuable.

Most of the problems of securing and interpreting national population data apply to cities, and some additional ones as well. To ensure that the area effectively covered for purposes of the birth and death counts is the same as that of the population count is difficult in the measure that the city boundary is especially permeable to migration. The 15 cities here shown are the harvest of an extensive search.

Here as elsewhere in the book Europe is relatively well represented, with data on six countries included. Canada had a census in 1966, and we could obtain resulting data on as many Canadian cities as we wanted. We were fortunate enough to find apparently reliable material from Taiwan and Indonesia.

United States city results can be had for the years close to a census, but seldom at other times. It is a measure of the genuine difficulty of demographic statistics that between censuses we often do not know whether the population is increasing or decreasing. Such information as is available consists of uncertain postcensal estimates based on school attendance or householders' paying electric bills, estimates not easily broken down by age. Some sample censuses are available locally giving age breakdowns, but we did not gain access to them for any of the large cities.

A brief substantive analysis of the statistics of these pages appears in Part I, beginning on page 17.

Montreal, 1966

TABLE 1 DATA INPUT TO COMPUTATIONS

Age at last birthday	Population					Births, by age of mother	Deaths			Age at last birthday
	Total	Males	%	Females	%		Total	Males	Females	
0	22503	11758	2.0	10745	1.7	0	555	306	249	0
1–4	83500	42597	7.1	40903	6.5	0	75	38	37	1–4
5–9	105098	53182	8.9	51916	8.3	0	47	27	20	5–9
10–14	99353	50590	8.5	48763	7.8	0	38	25	13	10–14
15–19	103918	51678	8.6	52240	8.4	4601	69	43	26	15–19
20–24	115388	56394	9.4	58994	9.4	7107	123	85	38	20–24
25–29	93367	46997	7.9	46370	7.4	6187	115	76	39	25–29
30–34	86363	44044	7.4	42319	6.8	3237	102	50	42	30–34
35–39	85675	42347	7.1	43328	6.9	1170	170	114	56	35–39
40–44	82952	39947	6.7	43005	6.9	319	269	175	94	40–44
45–49	72414	34101	5.7	38313	6.1	70	402	237	165	45–49
50–54	70422	33285	5.6	37137	5.9	13	632	415	217	50–54
55–59	60145	28524	4.8	31621	5.1	0	880	568	312	55–59
60–64	49399	23109	3.9	26290	4.2	0	1072	699	373	60–64
65–69	37000	16421	2.7	20579	3.3	0	1265	793	472	65–69
70–74	26790	11604	1.9	15186	2.4		1319	783	535	70–74
75–79	16426	6711	1.1	9715	1.6		1293	673	620	75–79
80–84	8331	3254	0.5	5077	0.8	11743 M	1066	484	582	80–84
85+	4495	1546	0.3	2949	0.5	10961 F	999	367	632	85+
All ages	1223539	598089		625450		22704	10491	5968	4523	All ages

TABLE 2 LIFE TABLE FOR MALES

Age, x	$_nq_x$	l_x	$_nd_x$	$_nL_x$	$_nm_x$	T_x	$1000r_x$	$\overset{\circ}{e}_x$	$_nM_x$	Age, x
0	0.02532	100000	2532	98015	0.02584	6666961	9.09	66.67	0.02602	0
1	0.00351	97468	342	388871	0.00088	6568946	9.09	67.40	0.00089	1
5	0.00253	97126	246	485013	0.00051	6180074	6.55	63.63	0.00051	5
10	0.00247	96880	239	483832	0.00049	5695061	2.31	58.78	0.00049	10
15	0.00415	96640	401	482300	0.00083	5211229	0.00	53.92	0.00083	15
20	0.00752	96239	723	479464	0.00151	4728930	8.10	49.14	0.00151	20
25	0.00805	95516	769	475640	0.00162	4249466	23.20	44.49	0.00162	25
30	0.00680	94747	644	472227	0.00136	3773826	8.72	39.83	0.00136	30
35	0.01340	94103	1261	467648	0.00270	3301599	7.04	35.09	0.00269	35
40	0.02176	92842	2020	459544	0.00440	2833951	17.14	30.52	0.00440	40
45	0.03429	90822	3115	447009	0.00697	2374407	10.72	26.14	0.00695	45
50	0.06066	87707	5320	426223	0.01248	1927398	5.08	21.98	0.01247	50
55	0.09536	82387	7856	393385	0.01997	1501175	16.07	18.22	0.01991	55
60	0.14162	74531	10555	347518	0.03037	1107789	22.28	14.86	0.03025	60
65	0.21668	63976	13862	286050	0.04846	760271	22.28	11.88	0.04829	65
70	0.28959	50114	14512	214372	0.06770	474221	22.28	9.46	0.06748	70
75	0.40058	35602	14261	141711	0.10064	259849	22.28	7.30	0.10028	75
80	0.53508	21340	11419	76507	0.14925	118139	22.28	5.54	0.14874	80
85+	1.00000	9921	9921	41632	0.23831	41632	22.28	4.20	0.23739	85+

TABLE 3 LIFE TABLE FOR FEMALES

Age, x	$_nq_x$	l_x	$_nd_x$	$_nL_x$	$_nm_x$	T_x	$1000r_x$	$\overset{\circ}{e}_x$	$_nM_x$	Age, x
0	0.02269	100000	2269	98254	0.02310	7333541	4.16	73.34	0.02317	0
1	0.00359	97731	351	389901	0.00090	7235288	4.16	74.03	0.00090	1
5	0.00192	97380	187	486432	0.00038	6845386	5.23	70.30	0.00039	5
10	0.00133	97193	129	485652	0.00027	6358954	0.00	65.43	0.00027	10
15	0.00249	97063	241	484752	0.00050	5873302	0.00	60.51	0.00050	15
20	0.00322	96822	312	483396	0.00064	5388550	11.26	55.65	0.00064	20
25	0.00421	96510	406	481571	0.00084	4905184	32.39	50.83	0.00084	25
30	0.00495	96104	476	479375	0.00099	4423613	5.77	46.03	0.00099	30
35	0.00644	95628	615	476718	0.00129	3944238	0.00	41.25	0.00129	35
40	0.01091	95012	1036	472760	0.00219	3467521	9.86	36.50	0.00219	40
45	0.02136	93976	2007	465199	0.00431	2994761	10.55	31.87	0.00431	45
50	0.02890	91969	2658	453682	0.00586	2529562	12.81	27.50	0.00584	50
55	0.04842	89311	4325	436413	0.00991	2075880	24.70	23.24	0.00987	55
60	0.06908	84986	5871	411158	0.01428	1639467	34.39	19.29	0.01419	60
65	0.10944	79116	8659	375116	0.02308	1228309	34.39	15.53	0.02294	65
70	0.16403	70457	11557	325005	0.03556	853194	34.39	12.11	0.03530	70
75	0.27855	58900	16406	255072	0.06432	528189	34.39	8.97	0.06382	75
80	0.45163	42493	19191	165924	0.11566	273117	34.39	6.43	0.11464	80
85+	*1.00000	23302	23302	107193	0.21738	107193	34.39	4.60	0.21431	85+

TABLE 4 POPULATION PROJECTION, USING FIXED AGE-SPECIFIC BIRTH AND DEATH RATES, IN THOUSANDS

Age at last birthday	1971			1976			1981			Age at last birthday
	Total	Males	Females	Total	Males	Females	Total	Males	Females	
0–4	112	58	54	114	59	55	114	59	55	0–4
5–9	105	54	51	112	58	54	114	59	55	5–9
10–14	105	53	52	105	54	51	112	58	54	10–14
15–19	99	50	49	105	53	52	105	54	51	15–19
20–24	103	51	52	99	50	49	105	53	52	20–24
25–29	115	56	59	103	51	52	98	50	48	25–29
30–34	93	47	46	115	56	59	103	51	52	30–34
35–39	86	44	42	92	46	46	113	55	58	35–39
40–44	85	42	43	85	43	42	91	45	46	40–44
45–49	81	39	42	82	40	42	83	42	41	45–49
50–54	70	33	37	78	37	41	80	39	41	50–54
55–59	67	31	36	66	30	36	74	34	40	55–59
60–64	55	25	30	61	27	34	61	27	34	60–64
65–69	43	19	24	48	21	27	53	22	31	65–69
70–74	30	12	18	35	14	21	40	16	24	70–74
75–79	20	8	12	22	8	14	25	9	16	75–79
80–84	10	4	6	12	4	8	13	4	9	80–84
85 +	5	2	3	6	2	4	7	2	5	85 +
All ages	1284	628	656	1340	653	687	1391	679	712	All ages

TABLE 5 OBSERVED AND PROJECTED VITAL RATES

Rates per thousand	Observed			Projected						Stable	
				1971		1976		1981			
	Total	Males	Females	Males	Females	Males	Females	Males	Females	Males	Females
Birth	18.56	19.63	17.52	19.38	17.25	18.55	16.50	17.66	15.70	16.21	14.83
Death	8.57	9.98	7.23	10.41	7.88	10.78	8.63	11.17	9.35	14.02	12.54
Increase	9.98	9.66	10.29	8.97	9.37	7.77	7.87	6.50	6.36		2.1888

TABLE 6 RATES STANDARDIZED ON THREE STANDARD COUNTRIES

Standardized rates per thousand	England and Wales, 1961			United States, 1960			Mexico, 1960		
	Total	Males	Females	Total	Males	Females	Total	Males	Females
Birth	14.53	16.74*	13.60	14.91	15.46*	14.18	18.10	15.38*	17.43
Death	12.19	13.45*	11.17	9.96	11.58*	8.24	5.17	9.03*	4.05
Increase	2.34	3.29*	2.42	4.96	3.88*	5.95	12.92	6.35*	13.37

TABLE 7 VITAL STATISTICS AND RATES INFERRED FROM AGE DISTRIBUTIONS (FEMALES)

Vital statistics		Thompson				Bourgeois-Pichat					Coale
		Age range	NRR	1000r	Interval	Age range	NRR	1000b	1000d	1000r	
TFR	2.28	0–4	1.06	2.27	27.43	5–29	1.01	17.06	16.85	0.21	1000b
GRR	1.10	5–9	1.12	4.16	27.40	30–54	1.14	17.15	12.16	4.99	1000d
NRR	1.06	10–14	1.13	4.59	27.34	55–79	2.21	63.39	34.00	29.39	1000r
Generation	25.94	15–19	1.27	8.60	27.24	*50–74	2.13	57.69	29.70	27.99	$1000k_1$
Sex ratio	107.13										$1000k_2$

TABLE 8 LESLIE MATRIX AND ITS ANALYSIS (FEMALES)

Start of age interval	Sub-diagonal	First row	Percent in stable population	Fisher values	Total reproductive values	Net maternity function	Matrix equation coefficient	Parameters	Integral	Matrix
0	0.99647	0.00000	7.200	1.030	53191	0.00000	0.00000	λ_1	1.0110	1.0110
5	0.99840	0.00000	7.096	1.045	54247	0.00000	0.00000	λ_2	0.3092	0.3206
10	0.99815	0.10359	7.008	1.058	51596	0.00000	0.10306		+0.7402	+0.7161i
15	0.99714	0.24533	6.919	0.965	50404	0.20612	0.24362	r_1	0.0022	0.0022
20	0.99629	0.29860	6.824	0.725	42764	0.28113	0.29567	r_2	-0.0441	-0.0485
25	0.99544	0.24695	6.724	0.427	19797	0.31021	0.24361		+0.2350	+0.2300i
30	0.99446	0.12178	6.621	0.178	7538	0.17702	0.11959	c_1		7364
35	0.99170	0.04049	6.512	0.055	2382	0.06215	0.03954	c_2		-3648
40	0.98401	0.01086	6.388	0.014	602	0.01693	0.01052			-3039i
45	0.97524	0.00255	6.217	0.003	115	0.00410	0.00244	$2\pi/y$	26.735	27.315
50	0.96193	0.00041	5.997	0.000	16	0.00077	0.00038	Δ	8.832	
55	0.79325		26.494							

[491]

Toronto, 1966

TABLE 1 DATA INPUT TO COMPUTATIONS

Age at last birthday	Population					Births, by age of mother	Deaths			Age at last birthday
	Total	Males	%	Females	%		Total	Males	Females	
0	13635	6890	2.1	6745	2.0	0	291	156	135	0
1–4	43681	22559	6.9	21122	6.2	0	32	14	18	1–4
5–9	54960	27990	8.6	26970	7.9	0	16	13	3	5–9
10–14	47527	24139	7.4	23388	6.9	0	13	8	5	10–14
15–19	47258	23398	7.2	23860	7.0	2814	35	27	8	15–19
20–24	55451	25787	7.9	29664	8.7	4347	39	27	12	20–24
25–29	50979	25591	7.9	25388	7.5	3785	50	30	20	25–29
30–34	47884	24997	7.7	22887	6.7	1980	51	34	17	30–34
35–39	48058	24944	7.7	23114	6.8	715	78	53	25	35–39
40–44	45926	23347	7.2	22579	6.6	196	155	105	50	40–44
45–49	36644	18306	5.6	18338	5.4	43	209	128	81	45–49
50–54	36514	17670	5.4	18844	5.5	8	305	201	104	50–54
55–59	33228	15629	4.8	17599	5.2	0	466	298	168	55–59
60–64	30279	14018	4.3	16261	4.8	0	628	418	210	60–64
65–69	25223	11051	3.4	14172	4.2	0	751	498	253	65–69
70–74	20950	8574	2.6	12376	3.6		917	557	360	70–74
75–79	14042	5444	1.7	8598	2.5		958	512	446	75–79
80–84	8197	3071	0.9	5126	1.5	7026 M	880	424	456	80–84
85 +	4741	1598	0.5	3143	0.9	6862 F	863	344	519	85 +
All ages	665177	325003		340174		13888	6737	3847	2890	All ages

TABLE 2 LIFE TABLE FOR MALES

Age, x	$_nq_x$	l_x	$_nd_x$	$_nL_x$	$_nm_x$	T_x	$1000r_x$	$\overset{\circ}{e}_x$	$_nM_x$	Age, x
0	0.02190	100000	2190	98232	0.02229	6770832	19.42	67.71	0.02264	0
1	0.00239	97810	233	390555	0.00060	6672600	19.42	68.22	0.00062	1
5	0.00231	97577	226	487319	0.00046	6282045	19.40	64.38	0.00046	5
10	0.00167	97351	162	486417	0.00033	5794726	17.36	59.52	0.00033	10
15	0.00575	97188	559	484615	0.00115	5308309	0.00	54.62	0.00115	15
20	0.00522	96629	505	481885	0.00105	4823694	0.00	49.92	0.00105	20
25	0.00585	96125	562	479248	0.00117	4341839	1.94	45.17	0.00117	25
30	0.00678	95563	648	476286	0.00136	3862560	1.11	40.42	0.00136	30
35	0.01059	94915	1005	472365	0.00213	3386274	4.38	35.68	0.00212	35
40	0.02239	93910	2103	464744	0.00452	2913910	26.47	31.03	0.00450	40
45	0.03454	91807	3171	451694	0.00702	2449166	20.51	26.68	0.00699	45
50	0.05546	88636	4915	431821	0.01138	1997472	3.82	22.54	0.01138	50
55	0.09132	83720	7645	400671	0.01908	1565651	3.58	18.70	0.01907	55
60	0.13934	76075	10600	355052	0.02986	1164981	7.15	15.31	0.02982	60
65	0.20322	65474	13306	294941	0.04511	809928	7.15	12.37	0.04506	65
70	0.27990	52169	14602	224538	0.06503	514987	7.15	9.87	0.06496	70
75	0.37992	37566	14272	151589	0.09415	290449	7.15	7.73	0.09405	75
80	0.51106	23294	11905	86109	0.13825	138859	7.15	5.96	0.13807	80
85 +	*1.00000	11389	11389	52751	0.21591	52751	7.15	4.63	0.21527	85 +

TABLE 3 LIFE TABLE FOR FEMALES

Age, x	$_nq_x$	l_x	$_nd_x$	$_nL_x$	$_nm_x$	T_x	$1000r_x$	$\overset{\circ}{e}_x$	$_nM_x$	Age, x
0	0.01936	100000	1936	98526	0.01964	7545802	23.77	75.46	0.02001	0
1	0.00329	98064	323	391320	0.00082	7447276	23.77	75.94	0.00085	1
5	0.00055	97742	54	488576	0.00011	7055955	17.19	72.19	0.00011	5
10	0.00107	97688	105	488203	0.00021	6567379	12.04	67.23	0.00021	10
15	0.00168	97584	163	487529	0.00034	6079176	0.00	62.30	0.00034	15
20	0.00202	97420	197	486655	0.00040	5591647	0.00	57.40	0.00040	20
25	0.00394	97223	383	485193	0.00079	5104992	25.25	52.51	0.00079	25
30	0.00371	96840	359	483332	0.00074	4619799	8.57	47.71	0.00074	30
35	0.00540	96481	521	481251	0.00108	4136467	0.13	42.87	0.00108	35
40	0.01109	95961	1064	477467	0.00223	3655216	20.69	38.09	0.00221	40
45	0.02191	94896	2079	469590	0.00443	3177749	13.97	33.49	0.00442	45
50	0.02725	92818	2529	458212	0.00552	2708159	0.00	29.18	0.00552	50
55	0.04672	90289	4218	441498	0.00955	2249947	5.41	24.92	0.00955	55
60	0.06281	86071	5406	417403	0.01295	1808450	22.28	21.01	0.01291	60
65	0.08598	80664	6936	386957	0.01792	1391047	22.28	17.24	0.01785	65
70	0.13682	73728	10087	345051	0.02923	1004090	22.28	13.62	0.02909	70
75	0.23175	63641	14749	282952	0.05212	659039	22.28	10.36	0.05187	75
80	0.36525	48892	17858	199935	0.08932	376086	22.28	7.69	0.08895	80
85 +	1.00000	31034	31034	176151	0.17618	176151	22.28	5.68	0.16513	85 +

TABLE 4 POPULATION PROJECTION, USING FIXED AGE-SPECIFIC BIRTH AND DEATH RATES, IN THOUSANDS

Age at last birthday	1971			1976			1981			Age at last birthday
	Total	Males	Females	Total	Males	Females	Total	Males	Females	
0–4	68	34	34	67	34	33	67	34	33	0–4
5–9	57	29	28	67	34	33	67	34	33	5–9
10–14	55	28	27	57	29	28	67	34	33	10–14
15–19	47	24	23	55	28	27	57	29	28	15–19
20–24	47	23	24	47	24	23	55	28	27	20–24
25–29	56	26	30	47	23	24	47	24	23	25–29
30–34	50	25	25	54	25	29	47	23	24	30–34
35–39	48	25	23	50	25	25	54	25	29	35–39
40–44	48	25	23	47	24	23	50	25	25	40–44
45–49	45	23	22	47	24	23	46	24	22	45–49
50–54	36	18	18	44	22	22	45	23	22	50–54
55–59	34	16	18	33	16	17	41	20	21	55–59
60–64	31	14	17	32	15	17	30	14	16	60–64
65–69	27	12	15	27	12	15	28	12	16	65–69
70–74	21	8	13	22	9	13	23	9	14	70–74
75–79	16	6	10	16	6	10	17	6	11	75–79
80–84	9	3	6	10	3	7	10	3	7	80–84
85 +	7	2	5	7	2	5	8	2	6	85 +
All ages	702	341	361	729	355	374	759	369	390	All ages

TABLE 5 OBSERVED AND PROJECTED VITAL RATES

Rates per thousand	Observed			Projected						Stable	
				1971		1976		1981			
	Total	Males	Females	Males	Females	Males	Females	Males	Females	Males	Females
Birth	20.88	21.62	20.17	20.51	18.98	19.55	18.02	19.07	17.54	20.34	19.41
Death	10.13	11.84	8.50	11.84	9.36	11.69	9.73	11.69	10.00	10.60	9.08
Increase	10.75	9.78	11.68	8.67	9.63	7.85	8.29	7.40	7.54		10.3351

TABLE 6 RATES STANDARDIZED ON THREE STANDARD COUNTRIES

Standardized rates per thousand	England and Wales, 1961			United States, 1960			Mexico, 1960		
	Total	Males	Females	Total	Males	Females	Total	Males	Females
Birth	17.36	18.70*	16.62	17.84	17.60*	17.36	21.82	16.81*	21.51
Death	10.80	12.33*	9.24	8.88	11.03*	6.84	4.62	9.04*	3.41
Increase	6.55	6.37*	7.39	8.95	6.57*	10.52	17.20	7.77*	18.10

TABLE 7 VITAL STATISTICS AND RATES INFERRED FROM AGE DISTRIBUTIONS (FEMALES)

Vital statistics		Thompson				Bourgeois-Pichat					Coale
		Age range	NRR	$1000r$	Interval	Age range	NRR	$1000b$	$1000d$	$1000r$	
TFR	2.71	0–4	1.12	4.12	27.44	5–29	0.93	14.83	17.51	−2.68	$1000b$
GRR	1.34	5–9	1.12	4.19	27.40	30–54	1.30	19.78	10.00	9.78	$1000d$
NRR	1.30	10–14	1.04	1.53	27.34	55–79	1.23	18.17	10.60	7.57	$1000r$
Generation	25.45	15–19	1.12	3.95	27.25	*50–74	1.21	17.68	10.52	7.17	$1000k_1$
Sex ratio	102.39										$1000k_2$

TABLE 8 LESLIE MATRIX AND ITS ANALYSIS (FEMALES)

Start of age interval	Sub-diagonal	First row	Percent in stable population	Fisher values	Total reproductive values	Net maternity function	Matrix equation coefficient	Parameters	Integral	Matrix
0	0.99741	0.00000	9.270	1.047	29188	0.00000	0.00000	λ_1	1.0530	1.0531
5	0.99924	0.00000	8.780	1.106	29826	0.00000	0.00000	λ_2	0.2887	0.3026
10	0.99862	0.14253	8.331	1.165	27259	0.00000	0.14205		+0.7581	+0.7326i
15	0.99821	0.31974	7.900	1.080	25759	0.28410	0.31823	r_1	0.0103	0.0103
20	0.99700	0.35721	7.488	0.803	23834	0.35236	0.35489	r_2	−0.0418	−0.0465
25	0.99616	0.28471	7.089	0.473	12019	0.35741	0.28200		+0.2414	+0.2358i
30	0.99569	0.14197	6.706	0.201	4603	0.20660	0.14008	c_1		3157
35	0.99214	0.04786	6.340	0.063	1465	0.07356	0.04702	c_2		−2152
40	0.98350	0.01330	5.973	0.017	379	0.02048	0.01296			−6546i
45	0.97577	0.00334	5.578	0.004	70	0.00544	0.00320	$2\pi/y$	26.029	25.645
50	0.96352	0.00051	5.169	0.001	10	0.00096	0.00048	Δ	5.136	
55	0.82014		21.377							

Vancouver, 1966

TABLE 1 DATA INPUT TO COMPUTATIONS

Age at last birthday	Population					Births, by age of mother	Deaths			Age at last birthday
	Total	Males	%	Females	%		Total	Males	Females	
0	6283	3229	1.6	3054	1.5	0	138	74	64	0
1–4	23926	12267	6.1	11659	5.6	0	18	12	5	1–4
5–9	31332	15761	7.8	15571	7.4	0	16	12	4	5–9
10–14	29441	14970	7.4	14471	6.9	0	10	4	6	10–14
15–19	31496	15360	7.6	16136	7.7	1299	24	14	10	15–19
20–24	33505	15699	7.8	17806	8.5	2007	38	21	17	20–24
25–29	26770	13491	6.7	13279	6.3	1747	27	19	8	25–29
30–34	24205	12796	6.4	11409	5.4	913	38	26	12	30–34
35–39	25497	12981	6.5	12516	6.0	330	66	39	27	35–39
40–44	26849	12881	6.4	13968	6.7	90	90	54	35	40–44
45–49	26481	12289	6.1	14192	6.8	20	159	101	58	45–49
50–54	27218	12902	6.4	14316	6.8	4	221	145	76	50–54
55–59	23207	11409	5.7	11798	5.6	0	299	207	92	55–59
60–64	19027	9514	4.7	9513	4.5	0	340	239	101	60–64
65–69	16358	7743	3.9	8615	4.1	0	446	289	157	65–69
70–74	14822	6664	3.3	8158	3.9		522	394	228	70–74
75–79	12050	5595	2.8	6455	3.1		797	506	291	75–79
80–84	7791	3637	1.8	4154	2.0	3297 M	833	477	356	80–84
85+	4237	1863	0.9	2374	1.1	3113 F	778	371	407	85+
All ages	410495	201051		209444		6410	4960	3004	1955	All ages

TABLE 2 LIFE TABLE FOR MALES

Age, x	$_nq_x$	l_x	$_nd_x$	$_nL_x$	$_nm_x$	T_x	$1000r_x$	$\overset{\circ}{e}_x$	$_nM_x$	Age, x
0	0.02245	100000	2245	98294	0.02284	6791959	4.32	67.92	0.02292	0
1	0.00388	97755	379	389918	0.00097	6693665	4.32	68.47	0.00098	1
5	0.00380	97376	370	485954	0.00076	6303747	2.74	64.74	0.00076	5
10	0.00134	97006	130	484720	0.00027	5817793	2.05	59.97	0.00027	10
15	0.00455	96876	441	483387	0.00091	5333073	0.00	55.05	0.00091	15
20	0.00667	96436	643	480618	0.00134	4849686	11.72	50.29	0.00134	20
25	0.00703	95792	674	477343	0.00141	4369068	18.92	45.61	0.00141	25
30	0.01011	95119	962	473340	0.00203	3891725	1.76	40.91	0.00203	30
35	0.01492	94157	1404	467473	0.00300	3418384	0.00	36.31	0.00300	35
40	0.02077	92752	1926	459415	0.00419	2950912	0.68	31.82	0.00419	40
45	0.04032	90826	3662	445567	0.00822	2491496	0.00	27.43	0.00822	45
50	0.05475	87164	4772	424621	0.01124	2045929	0.00	23.47	0.01124	50
55	0.08713	82392	7179	394876	0.01814	1621308	12.45	19.68	0.01814	55
60	0.11856	75213	8917	354645	0.02514	1226432	5.96	16.31	0.02512	60
65	0.17142	66296	11365	304169	0.03736	871787	5.96	13.15	0.03732	65
70	0.25850	54931	14200	239918	0.05918	567648	5.96	10.33	0.05912	70
75	0.36851	40732	15010	165816	0.09052	327700	5.96	8.05	0.09044	75
80	0.49268	25722	12672	96519	0.13130	161884	5.96	6.29	0.13115	80
85+	*1.00000	13049	13049	65365	0.19964	65365	5.96	5.01	0.19914	85+

TABLE 3 LIFE TABLE FOR FEMALES

Age, x	$_nq_x$	l_x	$_nd_x$	$_nL_x$	$_nm_x$	T_x	$1000r_x$	$\overset{\circ}{e}_x$	$_nM_x$	Age, x
0	0.02054	100000	2054	98323	0.02089	7542606	4.13	75.43	0.02096	0
1	0.00204	97946	199	391199	0.00051	7444283	4.13	76.00	0.00051	1
5	0.00128	97747	125	488421	0.00026	7053084	1.27	72.16	0.00025	5
10	0.00207	97621	202	487638	0.00041	6564663	0.00	67.25	0.00041	10
15	0.00309	97419	301	486397	0.00062	6077025	0.00	62.38	0.00062	15
20	0.00476	97118	462	484431	0.00095	5590628	18.69	57.57	0.00095	20
25	0.00301	96655	291	482558	0.00060	5106197	43.74	52.83	0.00060	25
30	0.00525	96364	506	480709	0.00105	4623639	4.73	47.98	0.00105	30
35	0.01073	95858	1029	476855	0.00216	4142930	0.00	43.22	0.00216	35
40	0.01281	94829	1215	471289	0.00258	3666065	0.00	38.66	0.00258	40
45	0.02024	93614	1895	463585	0.00409	3194776	0.00	34.13	0.00409	45
50	0.02626	91720	2409	452898	0.00532	2731191	12.89	29.78	0.00531	50
55	0.03846	89311	3435	438397	0.00783	2278293	33.09	25.51	0.00780	55
60	0.05196	85876	4462	418998	0.01065	1839897	15.43	21.42	0.01062	60
65	0.08763	81414	7135	390339	0.01828	1420898	15.43	17.45	0.01822	65
70	0.13141	74280	9761	348255	0.02803	1030559	15.43	13.87	0.02795	70
75	0.20434	64518	13183	291395	0.04524	582304	15.43	10.58	0.04508	75
80	0.35491	51335	18219	211906	0.08598	390909	15.43	7.61	0.08570	80
85+	1.00000	33116	33116	179003	0.18500	179003	15.43	5.41	0.17144	85+

TABLE 4   POPULATION PROJECTION, USING FIXED AGE-SPECIFIC BIRTH AND DEATH RATES, IN THOUSANDS

Age at last birthday	1971			1976			1981			Age at last birthday
	Total	Males	Females	Total	Males	Females	Total	Males	Females	
0–4	33	17	16	33	17	16	33	17	16	0–4
5–9	30	15	15	32	16	16	33	17	16	5–9
10–14	32	16	16	30	15	15	32	16	16	10–14
15–19	29	15	14	32	16	16	30	15	15	15–19
20–24	31	15	16	29	15	14	31	16	15	20–24
25–29	34	16	18	31	15	16	29	15	14	25–29
30–34	26	13	13	33	15	18	31	15	16	30–34
35–39	24	13	11	26	13	13	33	15	18	35–39
40–44	25	13	12	23	12	11	26	13	13	40–44
45–49	26	12	14	24	12	12	23	12	11	45–49
50–54	26	12	14	25	12	13	24	12	12	50–54
55–59	26	12	14	24	11	13	24	11	13	55–59
60–64	21	10	11	24	11	13	23	10	13	60–64
65–69	17	8	9	20	9	11	21	9	12	65–69
70–74	14	6	8	14	6	8	16	7	9	70–74
75–79	12	5	7	10	4	6	11	4	7	75–79
80–84	8	3	5	8	3	5	7	2	5	80–84
85 +	6	2	4	6	2	4	6	2	4	85 +
All ages	420	203	217	424	204	220	433	208	225	All ages

TABLE 5   OBSERVED AND PROJECTED VITAL RATES

Rates per thousand	Observed			Projected						Stable	
				1971		1976		1981			
	Total	Males	Females	Males	Females	Males	Females	Males	Females	Males	Females
Birth	15.62	15.40	14.86	17.12	15.26	17.05	15.05	16.36	14.37	15.34	13.87
Death	12.08	14.94	9.34	14.72	10.38	13.96	10.75	13.48	10.95	14.21	12.73
Increase	3.53	1.46	5.52	2.41	4.88	3.09	4.30	2.87	3.42		1.1337

TABLE 6   RATES STANDARDIZED ON THREE STANDARD COUNTRIES

Standardized rates per thousand	England and Wales, 1961			United States, 1960			Mexico, 1960		
	Total	Males	Females	Total	Males	Females	Total	Males	Females
Birth	14.02	16.09*	13.19	14.38	14.92*	13.76	17.35	14.39*	16.81
Death	10.30	11.33*	8.91	8.52	10.58*	6.68	4.57	9.47*	3.43
Increase	3.72	4.76*	4.28	5.86	4.34*	7.08	12.78	4.92*	13.38

TABLE 7   VITAL STATISTICS AND RATES INFERRED FROM AGE DISTRIBUTIONS (FEMALES)

Vital statistics		Thompson				Bourgeois-Pichat				Coale
		Age range	NRR	1000r	Interval	Age range	NRR	1000b	1000d	1000r	
TFR	2.20	0–4	1.02	0.64	27.42	5–29	1.04	15.54	13.93	1.61	1000b
GRR	1.07	5–9	1.10	3.36	27.38	30–54	0.68	7.26	21.80	−14.54	1000d
NRR	1.03	10–14	1.05	1.89	27.32	55–79	1.27	20.17	11.28	8.89	1000r
Generation	26.14	15–19	1.18	5.99	27.24	*30–54	0.68	7.26	21.80	−14.54	$1000k_1$
Sex ratio	105.91										$1000k_2$

TABLE 8   LESLIE MATRIX AND ITS ANALYSIS (FEMALES)

Start of age interval	Sub-diagonal	First row	Percent in stable population	Fisher values	Total reproductive values	Net maternity function	Matrix equation coefficient	Parameters		
									Integral	Matrix
0	0.99775	0.00000	6.769	1.024	15071	0.00000	0.00000	λ_1	1.0057	1.0057
5	0.99840	0.00000	6.716	1.032	16076	0.00000	0.00000	λ_2	0.3254	0.3347
10	0.99745	0.39545	6.667	1.040	15050	0.00000	0.09508		+0.7425	+0.7192 i
15	0.99596	0.22913	6.613	0.951	15338	0.19016	0.22767	r_1	0.0011	0.0011
20	0.99613	0.28976	6.549	0.724	12895	0.26518	0.28675	r_2	−0.0420	−0.0463
25	0.99617	0.25114	6.487	0.433	5752	0.30832	0.24757		+0.2316	+0.2271 i
30	0.99200	0.12621	6.425	0.179	2043	0.18682	0.12394	c_1		2294
35	0.98831	0.03891	6.338	0.051	641	0.06106	0.03790	c_2		−1847
40	0.98365	0.00931	6.228	0.012	165	0.01475	0.00896			−350 i
45	0.97695	0.00200	6.092	0.002	34	0.00317	0.00189	$2\pi/y$	27.135	27.672
50	0.96798	0.00033	5.918	0.000	5	0.00061	0.00031	Δ	6.302	
55	0.80949		29.197							

Kaohsiung, 1966

TABLE 1 DATA INPUT TO COMPUTATIONS

Age at last birthday	Population					Births, by age of mother	Deaths			Age at last birthday
	Total	Males	%	Females	%		Total	Males	Females	
0	18388	9486	2.9	8902	3.0	0	338	179	159	0
1–4	78053	40372	12.4	37581	12.8	0	240	114	126	1–4
5–9	93440	48440	14.9	45000	15.3	0	56	35	21	5–9
10–14	83636	43250	13.3	40386	13.7	-0	44	25	19	10–14
15–19	59488	30374	9.3	29114	9.9	1458	54	32	22	15–19
20–24	42737	20336	6.2	22401	7.6	6054	57	32	25	20–24
25–29	46861	22264	6.8	24597	8.4	7349	94	54	40	25–29
30–34	42708	21946	6.7	20762	7.1	3342	87	46	41	30–34
35–39	41917	24367	7.5	17550	6.0	1108	128	96	32	35–39
40–44	35928	21328	6.5	14600	5.0	345	142	99	43	40–44
45–49	25969	15586	4.8	10383	3.5	42	161	125	36	45–49
50–54	20334	12256	3.8	8078	2.7	0	181	137	44	50–54
55–59	12550	7133	2.2	5417	1.8	0	209	147	62	55–59
60–64	7947	4223	1.3	3724	1.3	0	189	120	69	60–64
65–69	4950	2336	0.7	2614	0.9	0	228	152	76	65–69
70–74	2855	1168	0.4	1687	0.6		170	84	86	70–74
75–79	1545	576	0.2	969	0.3		98	38	60	75–79
80–84	612	187	0.1	425	0.1	9998 M	58	18	40	80–84
85+	244	49	0.0	195	0.1	9700 F	97	34	63	85+
All ages	620162	325677		294485		19698	2631	1567	1064	All ages

TABLE 2 LIFE TABLE FOR MALES

Age, x	$_nq_x$	l_x	$_nd_x$	$_nL_x$	$_nm_x$	T_x	$1000r_x$	$\overset{\circ}{e}_x$	$_nM_x$	Age, x
0	0.01865	100000	1865	98833	0.01887	6550319	0.00	65.50	0.01887	0
1	0.01121	98135	1100	389535	0.00282	6451486	0.00	65.74	0.00282	1
5	0.00358	97035	348	484307	0.00072	6061951	13.07	62.47	0.00072	5
10	0.00290	96688	281	482771	0.00058	5577644	45.96	57.69	0.00058	10
15	0.00533	96407	514	480848	0.00107	5094874	74.41	52.85	0.00105	15
20	0.00788	95893	756	477707	0.00158	4614025	29.39	48.12	0.00157	20
25	0.01206	95137	1147	472865	0.00243	4136318	0.00	43.48	0.00243	25
30	0.01043	93990	980	467640	0.00210	3663453	0.00	38.98	0.00210	30
35	0.01952	93010	1815	460747	0.00394	3195813	0.00	34.36	0.00394	35
40	0.02312	91195	2109	451061	0.00468	2735065	39.43	29.99	0.00464	40
45	0.03968	89086	3535	437140	0.00809	2284005	47.52	25.64	0.00802	45
50	0.05528	85552	4730	416876	0.01135	1846865	65.47	21.59	0.01118	50
55	0.09969	80822	8057	385044	0.02092	1429989	86.49	17.69	0.02061	55
60	0.13605	72765	9900	341110	0.02902	1044945	75.89	14.36	0.02842	60
65	0.28348	62865	17821	270549	0.06587	703835	75.89	11.20	0.05507	65
70	0.30253	45044	13627	189287	0.07199	433286	75.89	9.62	0.07192	70
75	0.28225	31417	8867	133957	0.06620	243999	75.89	7.77	0.06597	75
80	0.40030	22549	9027	91151	0.09903	110042	75.89	4.88	0.09626	80
85+	*1.00000	13523	13523	18891	0.71582	18891	75.89	1.40	0.59388	85+

TABLE 3 LIFE TABLE FOR FEMALES

Age, x	$_nq_x$	l_x	$_nd_x$	$_nL_x$	$_nm_x$	T_x	$1000r_x$	$\overset{\circ}{e}_x$	$_nM_x$	Age, x
0	0.01767	100000	1767	98932	0.01786	7087661	0.00	70.88	0.01785	0
1	0.01326	98233	1302	389442	0.00334	6988729	0.00	71.14	0.00334	1
5	0.00230	96931	223	484096	0.00046	6599287	13.17	68.08	0.00047	5
10	0.00236	96708	229	482998	0.00047	6115190	43.02	63.23	0.00047	10
15	0.00381	96479	368	481542	0.00076	5632192	58.17	58.38	0.00076	15
20	0.00558	96112	536	479303	0.00112	5150650	15.71	53.59	0.00112	20
25	0.00810	95575	775	476023	0.00163	4671348	6.00	48.88	0.00163	25
30	0.00983	94801	932	471690	0.00198	4195325	31.91	44.25	0.00197	30
35	0.00911	93869	855	467296	0.00183	3723634	33.09	39.67	0.00182	35
40	0.01471	93013	1368	461800	0.00296	3256338	49.71	35.01	0.00295	40
45	0.01734	91645	1589	454483	0.00350	2794538	55.44	30.49	0.00347	45
50	0.02738	90056	2466	444818	0.00554	2340055	58.73	25.98	0.00545	50
55	0.05660	87590	4958	426586	0.01162	1895237	65.75	21.64	0.01145	55
60	0.08966	82632	7409	395761	0.01872	1468651	53.93	17.77	0.01853	60
65	0.13755	75223	10347	351789	0.02941	1072890	53.93	14.26	0.02907	65
70	0.22809	64877	14798	288046	0.05137	721101	53.93	11.11	0.05098	70
75	0.26957	50079	13500	216539	0.06234	433056	53.93	8.65	0.06192	75
80	0.39048	36579	14283	149021	0.09585	216516	53.93	5.92	0.09412	80
85+	*1.00000	22296	22296	67495	0.33034	67495	53.93	3.03	0.32308	85+

TABLE 4 POPULATION PROJECTION, USING FIXED AGE-SPECIFIC BIRTH AND DEATH RATES, IN THOUSANDS

Age at last birthday	1971 Total	Males	Females	1976 Total	Males	Females	1981 Total	Males	Females	Age at last birthday
0–4	102	52	50	120	61	59	147	75	72	0–4
5–9	95	49	46	101	51	50	120	61	59	5–9
10–14	93	48	45	95	49	46	101	51	50	10–14
15–19	83	43	40	93	48	45	95	49	46	15–19
20–24	59	30	29	83	43	40	93	48	45	20–24
25–29	42	20	22	59	30	29	82	42	40	25–29
30–34	46	22	24	42	20	22	59	30	29	30–34
35–39	43	22	21	46	22	24	42	20	22	35–39
40–44	41	24	17	41	21	20	45	21	24	40–44
45–49	35	21	14	40	23	17	41	21	20	45–49
50–54	25	15	10	34	20	14	39	22	17	50–54
55–59	19	11	8	24	14	10	31	18	13	55–59
60–64	11	6	5	17	10	7	21	12	9	60–64
65–69	6	3	3	9	5	4	14	8	6	65–69
70–74	4	2	2	5	2	3	8	4	4	70–74
75–79	2	1	1	3	1	2	4	2	2	75–79
80–84	1	0	1	2	1	1	2	1	1	80–84
85 +	0	0	0	0	0	0	0	0	0	85 +
All ages	707	369	338	814	421	393	944	485	459	All ages

TABLE 5 OBSERVED AND PROJECTED VITAL RATES

Rates per thousand	Observed Total	Males	Females	Projected 1971 Males	Females	1976 Males	Females	1981 Males	Females	Stable Males	Females
Birth	31.76	30.70	32.94	30.44	32.12	32.88	34.14	34.50	35.28	33.34	32.34
Death	4.24	4.81	3.61	5.28	3.77	5.93	4.09	6.51	4.41	6.99	6.00
Increase	27.52	25.89	29.33	25.16	28.35	26.95	30.05	27.99	30.87	26.3422	

TABLE 6 RATES STANDARDIZED ON THREE STANDARD COUNTRIES

Standardized rates per thousand	England and Wales, 1961 Total	Males	Females	United States, 1960 Total	Males	Females	Mexico, 1960 Total	Males	Females
Birth	27.50	30.36*	26.24	27.92	28.68*	27.09	32.85	27.09*	32.27
Death	14.08	15.67*	13.21	11.70	11.56*	9.89	5.91	5.68*	4.89
Increase	13.42	14.69*	13.03	16.22	17.12*	17.20	26.94	21.41*	27.39

TABLE 7 VITAL STATISTICS AND RATES INFERRED FROM AGE DISTRIBUTIONS (FEMALES)

Vital statistics		Thompson Age range	NRR	1000r	Interval	Bourgeois-Pichat Age range	NRR	1000b	1000d	1000r	Coale	
TFR	4.35	0–4	2.10	27.99	27.38	5–29	2.58	40.63	5.51	35.12	$1000b$	
GRR	2.14	5–9	2.37	32.21	27.35	30–54	3.40	68.44	23.08	45.35	$1000d$	
NRR	2.04	10–14	2.42	31.54	27.31	55–79	3.98	80.18	29.02	51.15	$1000r$	
Generation	27.05	15–19	2.15	28.06	27.22	*40–64	5.08	139.01	78.79	50.22	$1000k_1$	
Sex ratio	103.07										$1000k_2$	

TABLE 8 LESLIE MATRIX AND ITS ANALYSIS (FEMALES)

Start of age interval	Sub-diagonal	First row	Percent in stable population	Fisher values	Total reproductive values	Net maternity function	Matrix equation coefficient
0	0.99124	0.00000	14.815	1.093	50922	0.00000	0.00000
5	0.99773	0.00000	12.868	1.259	56636	0.00000	0.00000
10	0.99698	0.06004	11.250	1.440	58140	0.00000	0.05938
15	0.99535	0.38368	9.828	1.582	46061	0.11875	0.37831
20	0.99316	0.58178	8.571	1.393	31196	0.63787	0.65912
25	0.99090	0.55106	7.459	0.850	20903	0.70035	0.53713
30	0.99068	0.26877	6.477	0.371	7700	0.37389	0.25958
35	0.98824	0.10400	5.622	0.131	2293	0.14528	0.09951
40	0.98415	0.03309	4.868	0.035	523	0.05374	0.03139
45	0.97873	0.00489	4.198	0.005	50	0.00905	0.00453
50	0.95901	0.00015	3.600	0.000	1	0.00000	0.00000
55	0.81061		10.443				

Parameters

	Integral	Matrix
λ_1	1.1408	1.1412
λ_2	0.3609	0.3603
	+0.9032	+0.8676 i
r_1	0.0263	0.0264
r_2	-0.0056	-0.0125
	+0.2381	+0.2354 i
c_1		3201
c_2		1728
		13729 i
$2\pi/y$	26.386	25.686
Δ	8.014	

Taipei, 1966

TABLE 1 DATA INPUT TO COMPUTATIONS

Age at last birthday	Population					Births, by age of mother	Deaths			Age at last birthday
	Total	Males	%	Females	%		Total	Males	Females	
0	27025	14096	2.3	12929	2.4	0	314	166	148	0
1–4	125664	65180	10.5	60484	11.2	0	372	199	173	1–4
5–9	159689	82910	13.3	76779	14.2	0	91	53	38	5–9
10–14	145455	75338	12.1	70117	13.0	0	68	39	29	10–14
15–19	110149	56219	9.0	53930	10.0	2243	76	50	26	15–19
20–24	84067	41029	6.6	43038	8.0	10027	83	47	36	20–24
25–29	90471	43932	7.0	46539	8.6	11906	118	73	45	25–29
30–34	81306	42203	6.8	39103	7.2	5694	131	76	55	30–34
35–39	80239	46201	7.4	34038	6.3	1954	192	123	69	35–39
40–44	77307	47545	7.6	29762	5.5	522	274	173	101	40–44
45–49	59700	37848	6.1	21852	4.0	119	292	203	89	45–49
50–54	47979	30662	4.9	17317	3.2	0	379	268	111	50–54
55–59	30308	18360	2.9	11948	2.2	0	393	249	144	55–59
60–64	20017	11326	1.8	8691	1.6	0	438	293	145	60–64
65–69	11785	5736	0.9	6049	1.1	0	392	229	163	65–69
70–74	6813	2928	0.5	3885	0.7		349	188	161	70–74
75–79	3540	1229	0.2	2311	0.4		274	117	157	75–79
80–84	1574	447	0.1	1127	0.2	16747 M	178	50	118	80–84
85 +	861	193	0.0	668	0.1	15818 F	172	40	132	85 +
All ages	1163949	623382		540567		32565	4586	2646	1940	All ages

TABLE 2 LIFE TABLE FOR MALES

Age, x	$_nq_x$	l_x	$_nd_x$	$_nL_x$	$_nm_x$	T_x	$1000r_x$	$\overset{\circ}{e}_x$	$_nM_x$	Age, x
0	0.01170	100000	1170	99326	0.01178	6866044	0.00	68.66	0.01178	0
1	0.01212	98830	1197	392223	0.00305	6766718	0.00	68.47	0.00305	1
5	0.00318	97633	311	487387	0.00064	6374495	3.96	65.29	0.00064	5
10	0.00260	97322	253	486005	0.00052	5887107	38.22	60.49	0.00052	10
15	0.00448	97069	435	484324	0.00090	5401103	59.92	55.64	0.00089	15
20	0.00573	96635	554	481865	0.00115	4916779	23.45	50.88	0.00115	20
25	0.00827	96081	795	478481	0.00166	4434914	0.00	46.15	0.00166	25
30	0.00897	95286	854	474389	0.00180	3956433	0.00	41.52	0.00180	30
35	0.01323	94432	1249	469209	0.00266	3482044	0.00	36.87	0.00266	35
40	0.01808	93183	1685	461949	0.00365	3012835	16.17	32.33	0.00364	40
45	0.02669	91498	2442	451836	0.00540	2550886	38.15	27.88	0.00536	45
50	0.04336	89056	3861	436308	0.00885	2099050	63.33	23.57	0.00874	50
55	0.06715	85194	5720	412920	0.01385	1662742	84.24	19.52	0.01355	55
60	0.12407	79474	9860	374209	0.02635	1249822	89.13	15.73	0.02587	60
65	0.18491	69614	12872	317153	0.04059	875613	89.13	12.58	0.03992	65
70	0.28088	56741	15937	244474	0.06519	558460	89.13	9.84	0.06421	70
75	0.38737	40804	15806	163817	0.09649	313986	89.13	7.69	0.09520	75
80	0.50561	24998	12639	92673	0.13638	150169	89.13	6.01	0.13423	80
85 +	*1.00000	12359	12359	57496	0.21495	57496	89.13	4.65	0.20725	85 +

TABLE 3 LIFE TABLE FOR FEMALES

Age, x	$_nq_x$	l_x	$_nd_x$	$_nL_x$	$_nm_x$	T_x	$1000r_x$	$\overset{\circ}{e}_x$	$_nM_x$	Age, x
0	0.01137	100000	1137	99342	0.01145	7234520	0.00	72.35	0.01145	0
1	0.01136	98863	1123	392534	0.00286	7135179	0.00	72.17	0.00285	1
5	0.00246	97740	241	488098	0.00049	6742644	3.60	68.99	0.00049	5
10	0.00207	97499	201	486992	0.00041	6254546	34.88	64.15	0.00041	10
15	0.00243	97298	236	485941	0.00049	5767555	48.26	59.28	0.00048	15
20	0.00418	97061	405	484341	0.00084	5281614	13.96	54.42	0.00084	20
25	0.00483	96656	467	482168	0.00097	4797273	8.55	49.63	0.00097	25
30	0.00704	96189	677	479356	0.00141	4315105	29.85	44.86	0.00141	30
35	0.01014	95512	968	475329	0.00204	3835749	25.09	40.16	0.00203	35
40	0.01692	94543	1600	468908	0.00341	3360420	41.10	35.54	0.00339	40
45	0.02033	92943	1889	460269	0.00410	2891512	49.74	31.11	0.00407	45
50	0.03202	91054	2915	448677	0.00650	2431244	53.21	26.70	0.00641	50
55	0.05918	88139	5216	428447	0.01217	1982567	57.15	22.49	0.01205	55
60	0.08099	82923	6716	398767	0.01684	1554120	53.07	18.74	0.01668	60
65	0.12780	76207	9739	357920	0.02721	1155353	53.07	15.15	0.02695	65
70	0.19019	66467	12641	301996	0.04186	797433	53.07	12.00	0.04144	70
75	0.29347	53826	15796	230301	0.06859	495436	53.07	9.20	0.06794	75
80	0.41577	38030	15812	149772	0.10557	265135	53.07	6.97	0.10470	80
85 +	1.00000	22218	22218	115363	0.19260	115363	53.07	5.19	0.19761	85 +

TABLE 4 POPULATION PROJECTION, USING FIXED AGE-SPECIFIC BIRTH AND DEATH RATES, IN THOUSANDS

Age at last birthday	1971			1976			1981			Age at last birthday
	Total	Males	Females	Total	Males	Females	Total	Males	Females	
0–4	169	87	82	195	100	95	228	117	111	0–4
5–9	152	79	73	168	86	82	193	99	94	5–9
10–14	160	83	77	151	78	73	167	86	81	10–14
15–19	145	75	70	158	82	76	151	78	73	15–19
20–24	110	56	54	145	75	70	158	82	76	20–24
25–29	84	41	43	110	56	54	143	74	69	25–29
30–34	90	44	46	83	40	43	108	55	53	30–34
35–39	81	42	39	89	43	46	82	40	42	35–39
40–44	79	45	34	79	41	38	87	42	45	40–44
45–49	76	47	29	77	44	33	78	40	38	45–49
50–54	58	37	21	73	45	28	75	43	32	50–54
55–59	46	29	17	55	35	20	69	42	27	55–59
60–64	28	17	11	41	26	15	50	31	19	60–64
65–69	18	10	8	24	14	10	36	22	14	65–69
70–74	9	4	5	14	7	7	19	11	8	70–74
75–79	5	2	3	7	3	4	10	5	5	75–79
80–84	3	1	2	3	1	2	5	2	3	80–84
85 +	1	0	1	1	0	1	2	1	1	85 +
All ages	1314	699	615	1473	776	697	1661	870	791	All ages

TABLE 5 OBSERVED AND PROJECTED VITAL RATES

Rates per thousand	Observed			Projected						Stable	
				1971		1976		1981			
	Total	Males	Females	Males	Females	Males	Females	Males	Females	Males	Females
Birth	27.98	26.86	29.26	26.75	28.69	28.37	29.97	29.41	30.58	28.40	27.71
Death	3.94	4.24	3.59	4.95	3.91	5.76	4.27	6.54	4.63	7.34	6.65
Increase	24.04	22.62	25.67	21.80	24.78	22.61	25.70	22.87	25.94		21.0610

TABLE 6 RATES STANDARDIZED ON THREE STANDARD COUNTRIES

Standardized rates per thousand	England and Wales, 1961			United States, 1960			Mexico, 1960		
	Total	Males	Females	Total	Males	Females	Total	Males	Females
Birth	24.01	25.67*	22.60	24.38	24.21*	23.33	28.51	22.53*	27.62
Death	11.63	12.13*	11.85	9.44	9.08*	8.76	4.87	5.09*	4.30
Increase	12.38	13.54*	10.76	14.94	15.14*	14.57	23.64	17.43*	23.32

TABLE 7 VITAL STATISTICS AND RATES INFERRED FROM AGE DISTRIBUTIONS (FEMALES)

Vital statistics		Thompson				Bourgeois-Pichat					Coale	
		Age range	NRR	1000r	Interval	Age range	NRR	1000b	1000d	1000r		
TFR	3.80	0–4	1.74	20.78	27.40	5–29	2.20	35.95	6.76	29.19	1000b	
GRR	1.85	5–9	2.09	27.48	27.36	30–54	2.80	54.68	16.52	38.15	1000d	
NRR	1.78	10–14	2.15	27.41	27.29	55–79	4.02	100.33	48.82	51.51	1000r	
Generation	27.29	15–19	1.99	25.30	27.19	*40–74	4.19	111.40	58.36	53.04	$1000k_1$	
Sex ratio	105.87										$1000k_2$	

TABLE 8 LESLIE MATRIX AND ITS ANALYSIS (FEMALES)

Start of age interval	Sub-diagonal	First row	Percent in stable population	Fisher values	Total reproductive values	Net maternity function	Matrix equation coefficient	Parameters		
									Integral	Matrix
0	0.99232	0.00000	12.949	1.071	78644	0.00000	0.00000	λ_1	1.1110	1.1113
5	0.99773	0.00000	11.562	1.200	92115	0.00000	0.00000	λ_2	0.3619	0.3628
10	0.99784	0.04958	10.380	1.336	93701	0.00000	0.04909		+0.8722	+0.8388i
15	0.99671	0.32709	9.320	1.435	77396	0.09817	0.32314	r_1	0.0211	0.0211
20	0.99551	0.58256	8.359	1.249	53738	0.54811	0.57364	r_2	-0.0115	-0.0180
25	0.99417	0.47855	7.487	0.767	35695	0.59917	0.46911		+0.2355	+0.2325i
30	0.99160	0.24196	6.698	0.342	13363	0.33905	0.23580	c_1		6048
35	0.98649	0.09321	5.976	0.122	4139	0.13254	0.09007	c_2		-1970
40	0.98157	0.03130	5.305	0.036	1065	0.04760	0.02989			16616i
45	0.97482	0.00652	4.686	0.006	139	0.01217	0.00609	$2\pi/y$	26.680	27.024
50	0.95491	0.00007	4.110	0.000	1	0.00000	0.00000	Δ	9.065	
55	0.81330		13.169							

TABLE 1 DATA INPUT TO COMPUTATIONS

Age at last birthday	Population					Births, by age of mother	Deaths			Age at last birthday
	Total	Males	%	Females	%		Total	Males	Females	
0	104886	52144	3.5	52742	3.7	0	14469	7474	6995	0
1–4	403167	203911	13.9	199256	14.1	0	11488	5993	5495	1–4
5–9	398351	199507	13.6	198844	14.0	0	1716	815	901	5–9
10–14	255742	127740	8.7	128002	9.0	0	849	424	425	10–14
15–19	287017	142500	9.7	144517	10.2	25600	1244	673	571	15–19
20–24	344841	172730	11.8	172111	12.2	45558	1804	886	918	20–24
25–29	305304	150094	10.2	155210	11.0	33430	1951	982	969	25–29
30–34	238371	128249	8.7	110122	7.8	17401	2032	1201	831	30–34
35–39	181095	101070	6.9	80025	5.7	8135	1870	1069	801	35–39
40–44	120842	66809	4.5	54033	3.8	2338	1538	885	653	40–44
45–49	78531	43226	2.9	35305	2.5	178	1392	795	597	45–49
50–54	63742	32551	2.2	31191	2.2	0	1453	731	722	50–54
55–59	33282	17550	1.2	15732	1.1	0	934	542	392	55–59
60–64	34285	16414	1.1	17871	1.3	0	1563	777	786	60–64
65–69	13733	6420	0.4	7313	0.5	0	907	450	457	65–69
70–74	11693	4953	0.3	6740	0.5		952	428	524	70–74
75–79	4088	1618	0.1	2470	0.2		560	211	349	75–79
80–84	3434	1284	0.1	2150	0.2	68310 M	667	252	415	80–84
85 +	2817	1041	0.1	1776	0.1	64330 F	867	328	539	85 +
All ages	2885221	1469811		1415410		132640	48256	24916	23340	All ages

TABLE 2 LIFE TABLE FOR MALES

Age, x	$_nq_x$	l_x	$_nd_x$	$_nL_x$	$_nm_x$	T_x	$1000r_x$	$\overset{\circ}{e}_x$	$_nM_x$	Age, x
0	0.13186	100000	13186	91998	0.14333	4453613	0.00	44.54	0.14333	0
1	0.10896	86814	9459	321843	0.02939	4361614	0.00	50.24	0.02939	1
5	0.01887	77354	1460	383123	0.00381	4039771	60.06	52.22	0.00409	5
10	0.01649	75895	1251	376404	0.00332	3656648	29.89	48.18	0.00332	10
15	0.02335	74643	1743	368984	0.00472	3280245	0.00	43.95	0.00472	15
20	0.02533	72900	1847	360002	0.00513	2911261	0.00	39.93	0.00513	20
25	0.03231	71054	2295	349804	0.00656	2551259	22.91	35.91	0.00654	25
30	0.04591	68758	3157	336130	0.00939	2201455	30.55	32.02	0.00936	30
35	0.05176	65602	3395	319702	0.01062	1865326	54.29	28.43	0.01058	35
40	0.06472	62206	4026	301333	0.01336	1545624	71.10	24.85	0.01325	40
45	0.08850	58181	5149	278377	0.01850	1244291	53.75	21.39	0.01839	45
50	0.10720	53032	5685	251299	0.02262	965914	66.72	18.21	0.02246	50
55	0.14447	47347	6840	220247	0.03106	714616	35.93	15.09	0.03088	55
60	0.21315	40506	8634	181506	0.04757	494369	30.03	12.20	0.04734	60
65	0.29888	31872	9526	135399	0.07035	312862	30.03	9.82	0.07009	65
70	0.35473	22346	7927	91400	0.08673	177463	30.03	7.94	0.08641	70
75	0.48906	14420	7052	53806	0.13106	86063	30.03	5.97	0.13041	75
80	0.64440	7368	4748	24045	0.19744	32258	30.03	4.38	0.19625	80
85 +	*1.00000	2620	2620	8212	0.31902	8212	30.03	3.13	0.31508	85 +

TABLE 3 LIFE TABLE FOR FEMALES

Age, x	$_nq_x$	l_x	$_nd_x$	$_nL_x$	$_nm_x$	T_x	$1000r_x$	$\overset{\circ}{e}_x$	$_nM_x$	Age, x
0	0.12278	100000	12278	92576	0.13263	4512550	0.00	46.13	0.13263	0
1	0.10272	87722	9011	326734	0.02758	4519984	0.00	51.53	0.02758	1
5	0.02118	78711	1667	389389	0.00428	4193251	58.42	53.27	0.00453	5
10	0.01645	77044	1268	382014	0.00332	3803861	28.23	49.37	0.00332	10
15	0.01957	75777	1483	375319	0.00395	3421848	0.00	45.15	0.00395	15
20	0.02633	74294	1956	366734	0.00533	3046529	0.00	41.01	0.00533	20
25	0.03083	72338	2230	356249	0.00626	2679795	38.32	37.05	0.00624	25
30	0.03728	70107	2613	344229	0.00759	2323546	58.42	33.14	0.00755	30
35	0.04914	67494	3317	329424	0.01007	1979317	61.28	29.33	0.01001	35
40	0.05917	64177	3797	311728	0.01218	1649893	69.10	25.71	0.01209	40
45	0.08164	60380	4929	290054	0.01699	1338164	37.64	22.16	0.01691	45
50	0.10995	55450	6097	262197	0.02325	1048110	58.82	18.90	0.02315	50
55	0.11799	49354	5823	232749	0.02502	785913	25.96	15.92	0.02492	55
60	0.19937	43531	8679	196708	0.04412	553164	18.01	12.71	0.04398	60
65	0.27060	34852	9431	150600	0.06262	356456	18.01	10.23	0.06249	65
70	0.32596	25421	8286	106278	0.07797	205856	18.01	8.10	0.07774	70
75	0.51948	17135	8901	62780	0.14178	99577	18.01	5.81	0.14130	75
80	0.63295	8233	5211	26914	0.19363	36798	18.01	4.47	0.19302	80
85 +	*1.00000	3022	3022	9884	0.30577	9884	18.01	3.27	0.30349	85 +

TABLE 4 POPULATION PROJECTION, USING FIXED AGE-SPECIFIC BIRTH AND DEATH RATES, IN THOUSANDS

Age at last birthday	1966 Total	Males	Females	1971 Total	Males	Females	1976 Total	Males	Females	Age at last birthday
0–4	555	284	271	571	292	279	623	319	304	0–4
5–9	471	237	234	514	263	251	530	271	259	5–9
10–14	391	196	195	463	233	230	505	258	247	10–14
15–19	251	125	126	384	192	192	454	228	226	15–19
20–24	280	139	141	245	122	123	374	187	187	20–24
25–29	335	168	167	272	135	137	238	119	119	25–29
30–34	294	144	150	323	161	162	263	130	133	30–34
35–39	227	122	105	281	137	144	308	153	155	35–39
40–44	171	95	76	215	115	100	265	129	136	40–44
45–49	112	62	50	158	88	70	199	106	93	45–49
50–54	71	39	32	101	56	45	143	79	64	50–54
55–59	57	29	28	62	34	28	89	49	40	55–59
60–64	27	14	13	47	24	23	52	28	24	60–64
65–69	26	12	14	21	11	10	36	18	18	65–69
70–74	9	4	5	18	8	10	14	7	7	70–74
75–79	7	3	4	6	3	3	11	5	6	75–79
80–84	2	1	1	3	1	2	2	1	1	80–84
85 +	1	0	1	0	0	0	1	0	1	85 +
All ages	3287	1674	1613	3684	1875	1809	4107	2087	2020	All ages

TABLE 5 OBSERVED AND PROJECTED VITAL RATES

Rates per thousand	Observed Total	Males	Females	Projected 1966 Males	Females	1971 Males	Females	1976 Males	Females	Stable Males	Females
Birth	45.97	45.48	45.45	41.09	40.18	38.67	37.75	39.02	38.02	38.67	37.67
Death	16.73	16.95	16.49	16.91	15.90	16.69	15.53	17.01	15.81	19.17	18.17
Increase	29.25	29.52	28.96	24.18	24.27	21.98	22.21	22.01	22.21		19.5007

TABLE 6 RATES STANDARDIZED ON THREE STANDARD COUNTRIES

Standardized rates per thousand	England and Wales, 1961 Total	Males	Females	United States, 1960 Total	Males	Females	Mexico, 1960 Total	Males	Females
Birth	31.09	33.98*	29.23	31.84	31.17*	30.43	37.41	33.86*	36.19
Death	28.13	59.39*	30.16	25.16	43.80*	25.32	18.96	18.99*	18.37
Increase	2.96	-25.42*	-0.94	6.69	-12.63*	5.11	18.44	14.87*	17.82

TABLE 7 VITAL STATISTICS AND RATES INFERRED FROM AGE DISTRIBUTIONS (FEMALES)

Vital statistics		Thompson Age range	NRR	$1000r$	Interval	Bourgeois-Pichat Age range	NRR	$1000b$	$1000d$	$1000r$	Coale
TFR	4.83	0–4	1.75	21.25	27.02	5–29	0.99	29.65	30.04	-0.39	$1000b$
GRR	2.34	5–9	1.68	19.64	26.83	30–54	4.23	123.77	70.38	53.39	$1000d$
NRR	1.66	10–14	1.36	11.49	26.64	55–79	1.56	13.49	-2.87	16.35	$1000r$
Generation	26.12	15–19	2.09	27.90	26.40	*25–49	5.52	177.92	114.65	53.25	$1000k_1$
Sex ratio	106.19										$1000k_2$

TABLE 8 LESLIE MATRIX AND ITS ANALYSIS (FEMALES)

Start of age interval	Sub-diagonal	First row	Percent in stable population	Fisher values	Total reproductive values	Net maternity function	Matrix equation coefficient	Parameters	Integral	Matrix
0	0.92864	0.00000	15.061	1.251	315155	0.00000	0.00000	λ_1	1.1024	1.1027
5	0.98106	0.00000	12.684	1.485	295283	0.00000	0.00000	λ_2	0.0353	0.3364
10	0.98248	0.17696	11.285	1.669	213645	0.00000	0.16122		+0.7097	+0.6774i
15	0.97713	0.44312	10.055	1.648	238166	0.32245	0.39663	r_1	0.0195	0.0195
20	0.97141	0.48190	8.910	1.293	222471	0.47081	0.42148	r_2	-0.0683	-0.0559
25	0.96626	0.37426	7.849	0.847	131440	0.37214	0.31797		+0.3042	+0.2220i
30	0.95699	0.25959	6.878	0.482	53078	0.26381	0.21311	c_1		15492
35	0.94628	0.14500	5.970	0.216	17296	0.16242	0.11392	c_2		10680
40	0.93047	0.04874	5.123	0.060	3254	0.06542	0.03626			-53895i
45	0.90396	0.00513	4.323	0.006	206	0.00709	0.00355	$2\pi/y$	20.654	28.308
50	0.88769	0.00003	3.544	0.000	1	0.00000	0.00000	Δ	11.609	
55	0.72455		8.320							

Copenhagen, 1966

TABLE 1 DATA INPUT TO COMPUTATIONS

Age at last birthday	Population					Births, by age of mother	Deaths			Age at last birthday
	Total	Males	%	Females	%		Total	Males	Females	
0	9852	5015	1.6	4837	1.4	0	183	113	70	0
1–4	33268	16994	5.4	16274	4.6	0	19	12	7	1–4
5–9	34761	17611	5.6	17150	4.8	0	6	4	2	5–9
10–14	35125	17850	5.7	17275	4.9	0	12	7	5	10–14
15–19	46281	23293	7.4	22988	6.5	1571	17	14	3	15–19
20–24	64263	32750	10.5	31513	8.9	4956	40	28	12	20–24
25–29	41913	22461	7.2	19452	5.5	2478	36	22	14	25–29
30–34	32403	16449	5.3	15954	4.5	1062	51	29	22	30–34
35–39	32778	16032	5.1	16746	4.7	441	67	39	28	35–39
40–44	38988	18167	5.8	20821	5.9	79	133	72	61	40–44
45–49	46508	21115	6.7	25393	7.2	6	251	140	111	45–49
50–54	50136	22781	7.3	27355	7.7	0	376	229	147	50–54
55–59	52319	23525	7.5	28794	8.1	0	628	388	240	55–59
60–64	45579	19596	6.3	25983	7.3	0	889	540	349	60–64
65–69	38495	15583	5.0	22912	6.5	0	1143	655	488	65–69
70–74	29027	11327	3.6	17700	5.0		1464	797	667	70–74
75–79	19226	6982	2.2	12244	3.5		1388	633	755	75–79
80–84	10690	3642	1.2	7048	2.0	5372 M	1271	539	732	80–84
85+	5462	1776	0.6	3686	1.0	5221 F	1136	419	717	85+
All ages	667074	312949		354125		10593	9110	4680	4430	All ages

TABLE 2 LIFE TABLE FOR MALES

Age, x	$_nq_x$	l_x	$_nd_x$	$_nL_x$	$_nm_x$	T_x	$1000r_x$	$\overset{\circ}{e}_x$	$_nM_x$	Age, x
0	0.02186	100000	2186	98265	0.02225	6830121	15.93	68.30	0.02253	0
1	0.00274	97814	268	390471	0.00069	6731855	15.93	68.82	0.00071	1
5	0.00113	97546	110	487453	0.00023	6341385	20.54	65.01	0.00023	5
10	0.00196	97436	191	486738	0.00039	5853931	0.00	60.08	0.00039	10
15	0.00300	97245	292	485540	0.00060	5367184	0.00	55.19	0.00060	15
20	0.00427	96953	414	483769	0.00086	4881653	2.82	50.35	0.00085	20
25	0.00495	96539	478	481591	0.00099	4397884	67.73	45.56	0.00098	25
30	0.00883	96061	848	478327	0.00177	3916293	32.00	40.77	0.00175	30
35	0.01209	95213	1152	473396	0.00243	3437966	0.00	36.11	0.00243	35
40	0.01964	94062	1847	466078	0.00396	2964571	0.00	31.52	0.00396	40
45	0.03265	92215	3011	454074	0.00663	2498493	0.00	27.09	0.00663	45
50	0.04911	89204	4381	435843	0.01005	2044419	0.00	22.92	0.01005	50
55	0.07942	84823	6737	408467	0.01649	1508576	0.00	18.96	0.01649	55
60	0.12962	78086	10122	366431	0.02762	1200109	12.79	15.37	0.02756	60
65	0.19135	67964	13005	308635	0.04214	833678	12.79	12.27	0.04203	65
70	0.29995	54959	16485	233831	0.07050	525044	12.79	9.55	0.07035	70
75	0.36870	38475	14186	156181	0.09083	291213	12.79	7.57	0.09066	75
80	0.53493	24289	12993	87589	0.14834	135031	12.79	5.56	0.14800	80
85+	1.00000	11296	11296	47442	0.23810	47442	12.79	4.20	0.23592	85+

TABLE 3 LIFE TABLE FOR FEMALES

Age, x	$_nq_x$	l_x	$_nd_x$	$_nL_x$	$_nm_x$	T_x	$1000r_x$	$\overset{\circ}{e}_x$	$_nM_x$	Age, x
0	0.01412	100000	1412	98872	0.01428	7460896	16.89	74.61	0.01447	0
1	0.00166	98588	164	393873	0.00042	7362024	16.89	74.67	0.00043	1
5	0.00058	98424	57	491978	0.00012	6968152	19.80	70.80	0.00012	5
10	0.00145	98367	142	491481	0.00029	6476173	0.00	65.84	0.00029	10
15	0.00065	98225	64	490973	0.00013	5984692	0.00	60.93	0.00013	15
20	0.00191	98161	188	490396	0.00038	5493719	16.31	55.97	0.00038	20
25	0.00366	97973	359	489069	0.00073	5003324	67.27	51.07	0.00072	25
30	0.00689	97614	672	486484	0.00138	4514255	13.70	46.25	0.00138	30
35	0.00833	96942	807	482843	0.00167	4027771	0.00	41.55	0.00167	35
40	0.01455	96135	1399	477435	0.00293	3544928	0.00	36.87	0.00293	40
45	0.02163	94736	2049	468778	0.00437	3067493	0.00	32.38	0.00437	45
50	0.02653	92687	2459	457627	0.00537	2598715	0.00	28.04	0.00537	50
55	0.04089	90228	3689	442582	0.00834	2141088	0.00	23.73	0.00834	55
60	0.06541	86539	5660	419492	0.01349	1698506	23.16	19.63	0.01343	60
65	0.10197	80878	8247	385223	0.02141	1279014	23.16	15.81	0.02130	65
70	0.17374	72631	12619	333255	0.03787	893791	23.16	12.31	0.03768	70
75	0.26922	60012	16157	260811	0.06195	560535	23.16	9.34	0.06166	75
80	0.41283	43855	18105	173594	0.10429	299725	23.16	6.83	0.10386	80
85+	1.00000	25751	25751	126131	0.20416	126131	23.16	4.90	0.19452	85+

TABLE 4 POPULATION PROJECTION, USING FIXED AGE-SPECIFIC BIRTH AND DEATH RATES, IN THOUSANDS

Age at last birthday	1971 Total	Males	Females	1976 Total	Males	Females	1981 Total	Males	Females	Age at last birthday
0–4	52	26	26	49	25	24	45	23	22	0–4
5–9	43	22	21	52	26	26	49	25	24	5–9
10–14	35	18	17	43	22	21	52	26	26	10–14
15–19	35	18	17	35	18	17	43	22	21	15–19
20–24	46	23	23	35	18	17	34	17	17	20–24
25–29	64	33	31	46	23	23	35	18	17	25–29
30–34	41	22	19	63	32	31	46	23	23	30–34
35–39	32	16	16	41	22	19	63	32	31	35–39
40–44	33	16	17	32	16	16	41	22	19	40–44
45–49	38	18	20	31	15	16	31	16	15	45–49
50–54	45	20	25	37	17	20	31	15	15	50–54
55–59	47	21	26	43	19	24	35	16	19	55–59
60–64	48	21	27	44	19	25	40	17	23	60–64
65–69	41	17	24	43	18	25	39	16	23	65–69
70–74	32	12	20	34	13	21	35	13	22	70–74
75–79	22	8	14	24	8	16	24	8	16	75–79
80–84	12	4	8	13	4	9	14	4	10	80–84
85 +	7	2	5	8	2	6	9	2	7	85 +
All ages	673	317	356	673	317	356	666	315	351	All ages

TABLE 5 OBSERVED AND PROJECTED VITAL RATES

Rates per thousand	Observed Total	Males	Females	Projected 1971 Males	Females	1976 Males	Females	1981 Males	Females	Stable Males	Females
Birth	15.88	17.17	14.74	16.96	14.59	15.12	13.08	14.04	12.24	16.39	15.13
Death	13.66	14.95	12.51	15.43	14.00	15.66	14.99	15.73	15.80	13.23	11.97
Increase	2.22	2.21	2.23	1.53	0.59	-0.54	-1.91	-1.59	-3.56		3.1597

TABLE 6 RATES STANDARDIZED ON THREE STANDARD COUNTRIES

Standardized rates per thousand	England and Wales, 1961 Total	Males	Females	United States, 1960 Total	Males	Females	Mexico, 1960 Total	Males	Females
Birth	14.29	16.39*	13.65	14.60	14.69*	14.17	18.06	15.23*	17.76
Death	11.29	12.09*	10.47	9.18	10.99*	7.64	4.59	10.15*	3.54
Increase	3.00	4.30*	3.18	5.42	3.70*	6.54	13.47	5.08*	14.22

TABLE 7 VITAL STATISTICS AND RATES INFERRED FROM AGE DISTRIBUTIONS (FEMALES)

Vital statistics		Thompson Age range	NRR	1000r	Interval	Bourgeois-Pichat Age range	NRR	1000b	1000d	1000r	Coale
TFR	2.25	0–4	0.98	-0.72	27.42	5–29	0.63	8.96	26.30	-17.34	1000b
GRR	1.11	5–9	0.78	-9.16	27.37	30–54	0.41	3.05	35.98	-32.93	1000d
NRR	1.08	10–14	0.80	-8.21	27.31	55–79	1.42	39.23	26.24	12.98	1000r
Generation	25.62	15–19	0.98	-0.89	27.23	*30–54	0.41	3.05	35.98	-32.93	$1000k_1$
Sex ratio	102.89										$1000k_2$

TABLE 8 LESLIE MATRIX AND ITS ANALYSIS (FEMALES)

Start of age interval	Sub-diagonal	First row	Percent in stable population	Fisher values	Total reproductive values	Net maternity function	Matrix equation coefficient	Parameters	Integral	Matrix
0	0.99844	0.00000	7.395	1.023	21592	0.00000	0.00000	λ_1	1.0159	1.0159
5	0.99899	0.00000	7.268	1.041	17848	0.00000	0.00000	λ_2	0.2867	0.2994
10	0.99897	0.08290	7.146	1.058	18283	0.00000	0.08269		+0.7712	+0.7422 i
15	0.99882	0.27373	7.027	0.991	22791	0.16537	0.27275	r_1	0.0032	0.0032
20	0.99729	0.34524	6.909	0.728	22945	0.38012	0.34360	r_2	-0.0390	-0.0445
25	0.99471	0.23509	6.782	0.388	7541	0.30707	0.23334		+0.2430	+0.2375 i
30	0.99252	0.11257	6.640	0.154	2460	0.15961	0.11114	c_1		2957
35	0.98880	0.03653	6.487	0.042	701	0.06257	0.03580	c_2		-4627
40	0.98187	0.00484	6.314	0.005	108	0.00893	0.00474			-9738 i
45	0.97621	0.00028	6.102	0.000	8	0.00055	0.00027	$2\pi/y$	25.860	26.459
50	0.96712	0.00004	5.864	0.000	1	0.00000	0.00000	Δ	12.718	
55	0.79835		26.064							

Helsinki, 1966

TABLE 1 DATA INPUT TO COMPUTATIONS

Age at last birthday	Population					Births, by age of mother	Deaths			Age at last birthday
	Total	Males	%	Females	%		Total	Males	Females	
0	8809	4461	2.0	4348	1.5	0	132	62	70	0
1–4	31585	16079	7.1	15506	5.4	0	20	7	13	1–4
5–9	32969	16771	7.4	16198	5.7	0	16	11	5	5–9
10–14	31069	15591	6.9	15478	5.4	0	12	7	5	10–14
15–19	41359	19554	8.6	21805	7.6	861	22	16	5	15–19
20–24	53537	23755	10.4	29782	10.4	3346	44	32	12	20–24
25–29	47848	22766	10.0	25082	8.8	2970	51	33	18	25–29
30–34	36279	18087	8.0	18192	6.4	1297	50	40	10	30–34
35–39	34135	16494	7.3	17641	6.2	544	86	55	31	35–39
40–44	32252	14194	6.2	18058	6.3	129	142	89	53	40–44
45–49	29779	12418	5.5	17361	6.1	9	187	130	57	45–49
50–54	31205	12638	5.6	18567	6.5	0	279	184	95	50–54
55–59	31347	12299	5.4	19048	6.7	0	478	311	167	55–59
60–64	24896	9302	4.1	15594	5.5	0	536	315	221	60–64
65–69	18589	6056	2.7	12533	4.4	0	649	320	329	65–69
70–74	13232	3800	1.7	9432	3.3		720	300	420	70–74
75–79	8238	2055	0.9	6183	2.2		671	234	437	75–79
80–84	3739	795	0.3	2944	1.0	4608 M	509	120	389	80–84
85 +	1690	282	0.1	1408	0.5	4548 F	411	89	322	85 +
All ages	512557	227397		285160		9156	5015	2355	2660	All ages

TABLE 2 LIFE TABLE FOR MALES

Age, x	$_nq_x$	l_x	$_nd_x$	$_nL_x$	$_nm_x$	T_x	$1000r_x$	$\overset{\circ}{e}_x$	$_nM_x$	Age, x
0	0.01364	100000	1364	98919	0.01379	6563372	10.00	65.63	0.01390	0
1	0.00171	98636	169	394050	0.00043	6464453	10.00	65.54	0.00044	1
5	0.00327	98467	322	491530	0.00066	6070403	27.00	61.65	0.00066	5
10	0.00224	98145	220	490190	0.00045	5578873	0.00	56.84	0.00045	10
15	0.00408	97925	400	488714	0.00082	5088683	0.00	51.97	0.00082	15
20	0.00671	97525	655	486050	0.00135	4599969	0.00	47.17	0.00135	20
25	0.00725	96870	702	482681	0.00145	4113918	25.67	42.47	0.00145	25
30	0.01106	96168	1064	478365	0.00222	3631238	29.98	37.76	0.00221	30
35	0.01663	95105	1582	471952	0.00335	3152872	20.54	33.15	0.00333	35
40	0.03106	93523	2905	460986	0.00630	2680920	21.87	28.67	0.00627	40
45	0.05109	90618	4630	442159	0.01047	2219935	1.30	24.50	0.01047	45
50	0.07041	85988	6054	415825	0.01456	1777766	0.00	20.67	0.01456	50
55	0.11934	79933	9539	376868	0.02531	1361941	6.06	17.04	0.02529	55
60	0.15746	70395	11084	325184	0.03409	985073	41.78	13.99	0.03386	60
65	0.23547	59310	13966	262457	0.05321	659889	41.78	11.13	0.05284	65
70	0.33126	45345	15021	189051	0.07945	397432	41.78	8.76	0.07895	70
75	0.44157	30324	13390	116914	0.11453	208381	41.78	6.87	0.11387	75
80	0.53834	16934	9116	60092	0.15170	91467	41.78	5.40	0.15094	80
85 +	1.00000	7818	7818	31375	0.24917	31375	41.78	4.01	0.31560	85 +

TABLE 3 LIFE TABLE FOR FEMALES

Age, x	$_nq_x$	l_x	$_nd_x$	$_nL_x$	$_nm_x$	T_x	$1000r_x$	$\overset{\circ}{e}_x$	$_nM_x$	Age, x
0	0.01578	100000	1578	98835	0.01596	7345010	10.82	73.45	0.01610	0
1	0.00331	98422	325	392749	0.00083	7246175	10.82	73.62	0.00084	1
5	0.00153	98097	150	490109	0.00031	6853425	24.44	69.86	0.00031	5
10	0.00161	97947	158	489335	0.00032	6363317	0.00	64.97	0.00032	10
15	0.00137	97789	134	488615	0.00028	5873982	0.00	60.07	0.00028	15
20	0.00201	97654	197	487824	0.00040	5385368	0.00	55.15	0.00040	20
25	0.00359	97458	350	486428	0.00072	4897544	48.70	50.25	0.00072	25
30	0.00278	97108	270	484967	0.00056	4411115	34.34	45.42	0.00055	30
35	0.00875	96838	848	482304	0.00176	3926149	0.00	40.54	0.00175	35
40	0.01457	95990	1399	476597	0.00293	3443845	0.00	35.88	0.00293	40
45	0.01629	94591	1541	469303	0.00328	2967248	0.00	31.37	0.00328	45
50	0.02529	93050	2353	459862	0.00512	2497945	0.00	26.85	0.00512	50
55	0.04304	90697	3904	444487	0.00878	2038083	8.44	22.47	0.00877	55
60	0.06915	86793	6002	420245	0.01428	1593596	31.25	18.36	0.01417	60
65	0.12453	80792	10061	380536	0.02644	1173351	31.25	14.52	0.02625	65
70	0.20228	70731	14307	319354	0.04480	792815	31.25	11.21	0.04453	70
75	0.30320	56423	17108	240438	0.07115	473461	31.25	8.39	0.07068	75
80	0.49695	39316	19538	146901	0.13300	233022	31.25	5.93	0.13213	80
85 +	1.00000	19778	19778	86122	0.22965	86122	31.25	4.35	0.22869	85 +

TABLE 4 POPULATION PROJECTION, USING FIXED AGE-SPECIFIC BIRTH AND DEATH RATES, IN THOUSANDS

Age at last birthday	1971			1976			1981			Age at last birthday
	Total	Males	Females	Total	Males	Females	Total	Males	Females	
0–4	45	23	22	42	21	21	37	19	18	0–4
5–9	40	20	20	45	23	22	42	21	21	5–9
10–14	33	17	16	40	20	20	44	22	22	10–14
15–19	31	16	15	33	17	16	40	20	20	15–19
20–24	41	19	22	30	15	15	33	17	16	20–24
25–29	54	24	30	41	19	22	30	15	15	25–29
30–34	48	23	25	53	23	30	41	19	22	30–34
35–39	36	18	18	47	22	25	52	23	29	35–39
40–44	33	16	17	35	17	18	47	22	25	40–44
45–49	32	14	18	32	15	17	35	17	18	45–49
50–54	29	12	17	30	13	17	32	15	17	50–54
55–59	29	11	18	27	11	16	29	12	17	55–59
60–64	29	11	18	27	10	17	25	9	15	60–64
65–69	22	8	14	25	9	16	23	8	15	65–69
70–74	15	4	11	17	5	12	20	6	14	70–74
75–79	9	2	7	11	3	8	12	3	9	75–79
80–84	5	1	4	5	1	4	6	1	5	80–84
85 +	2	0	2	3	1	2	4	1	3	85 +
All ages	533	239	294	543	245	298	552	250	302	All ages

TABLE 5 OBSERVED AND PROJECTED VITAL RATES

Rates per thousand	Observed			Projected						Stable	
				1971		1976		1981			
	Total	Males	Females	Males	Females	Males	Females	Males	Females	Males	Females
Birth	17.86	20.26	15.95	19.14	15.30	16.30	13.22	14.20	11.66	13.61	12.02
Death	9.78	10.36	9.33	11.10	10.31	11.75	11.25	12.37	12.07	16.77	15.18
Increase	8.08	9.91	6.62	8.04	4.99	4.55	1.97	1.83	-0.41		-3.1639

TABLE 6 RATES STANDARDIZED ON THREE STANDARD COUNTRIES

Standardized rates per thousand	England and Wales, 1961			United States, 1960			Mexico, 1960		
	Total	Males	Females	Total	Males	Females	Total	Males	Females
Birth	12.06	15.27*	11.61	12.31	14.13*	12.05	14.59	14.45*	14.45
Death	13.57	15.52*	12.02	10.98	13.01*	8.71	5.35	9.97*	3.99
Increase	-1.51	-0.25*	-0.41	1.33	1.11*	3.33	9.23	4.49*	10.47

TABLE 7 VITAL STATISTICS AND RATES INFERRED FROM AGE DISTRIBUTIONS (FEMALES)

Vital statistics		Thompson				Bourgeois-Pichat					Coale
		Age range	NRR	$1000r$	Interval	Age range	NRR	$1000b$	$1000d$	$1000r$	$1000b$
TFR	1.90	0–4	0.90	-3.85	27.44	5–29	0.43	8.77	39.72	-30.94	
GRR	0.94	5–9	0.76	-10.11	27.39	30–54	0.92	11.60	14.77	-3.17	$1000r$
NRR	0.92	10–14	0.79	-8.82	27.34	55–79	1.95	61.67	36.95	24.72	$1000k_1$
Generation	27.07	15–19	1.15	5.20	27.25	*35–59	0.81	9.50	17.10	-7.61	$1000k_2$
Sex ratio	101.32										

TABLE 8 LESLIE MATRIX AND ITS ANALYSIS (FEMALES)

Start of age interval	Sub-diagonal	First row	Percent in stable population	Fisher values	Total reproductive values	Net maternity function	Matrix equation coefficient	Parameters		
									Integral	Matrix
0	0.99700	0.00000	5.955	1.009	20035	0.00000	0.00000	λ_1	0.9843	0.9843
5	0.99842	0.00000	6.032	0.996	16138	0.00000	0.00000	λ_2	0.3451	0.3533
10	0.99853	0.04814	6.118	0.982	15202	0.00000	0.04792		+0.7395	+0.7160i
15	0.99838	0.18516	5.206	0.920	20051	0.09584	0.18404	r_1	-0.0032	-0.0032
20	0.99714	0.28132	6.295	0.719	21427	0.27224	0.27917	r_2	-0.0407	-0.0450
25	0.99699	0.23135	6.377	0.425	10672	0.28611	0.22393		+0.2268	+0.2225i
30	0.99451	0.12449	6.459	0.186	3382	0.17175	0.12281	c_1		3314
35	0.98817	0.04627	6.525	0.058	1018	0.07388	0.04539	c_2		-3221
40	0.98469	0.00928	6.552	0.010	185	0.01691	0.00906			-9683i
45	0.97988	0.00063	6.554	0.001	12	0.00121	0.00060	$2\pi/y$	27.701	28.242
50	0.96657	0.00007	6.525	0.000	1	0.00000	0.00000	Δ	9.288	
55	0.77685		30.400							

East Berlin, 1961

TABLE 1 DATA INPUT TO COMPUTATIONS

Age at last birthday	Population					Births, by age of mother	Deaths			Age at last birthday
	Total	Males	%	Females	%		Total	Males	Females	
0	16069	8280	1.8	7789	1.3	0	545	318	227	0
1–4	53842	27753	6.1	26089	4.3	0	74	35	39	1–4
5–9	58364	29625	6.5	28739	4.8	0	33	18	15	5–9
10–14	50294	25523	5.6	24771	4.1	4	18	11	7	10–14
15–19	55503	27102	6.0	28401	4.7	2229	52	36	16	15–19
20–24	88685	43352	9.6	45333	7.5	6826	103	65	38	20–24
25–29	75572	37664	8.3	37908	6.3	4406	105	54	41	25–29
30–34	61499	29982	6.6	31517	5.2	2014	104	55	49	30–34
35–39	48204	18747	4.1	29457	4.9	791	91	37	54	35–39
40–44	45514	17097	3.8	28417	4.7	197	136	50	86	40–44
45–49	59037	21502	4.7	37535	6.2	16	326	148	178	45–49
50–54	86917	33514	7.4	53403	8.9	0	686	353	333	50–54
55–59	92735	38929	8.6	53806	8.9	0	1243	739	504	55–59
60–64	80401	31342	6.9	49059	8.1	0	1742	946	796	60–64
65–69	67062	22751	5.0	44311	7.4	0	2287	1081	1205	65–69
70–74	54623	18659	4.1	35964	6.0		2949	1344	1605	70–74
75–79	35558	12590	2.8	22968	3.8		3049	1306	1743	75–79
80–84	18317	6479	1.4	11838	2.0	8562 M	2552	976	1576	80–84
85+	7686	2445	0.5	5241	0.9	7921 F	1591	571	1020	85+
All ages	1055882	453336		602546		16483	17686	8153	9533	All ages

TABLE 2 LIFE TABLE FOR MALES

Age, x	$_nq_x$	l_x	$_nd_x$	$_nL_x$	$_nm_x$	T_x	$1000r_x$	$\mathring{e}_x$	$_nM_x$	Age, x
0	0.03681	100000	3681	97095	0.03791	6600875	16.52	66.01	0.03841	0
1	0.00489	96319	471	383901	0.00123	6503779	16.52	67.52	0.00125	1
5	0.00301	95849	288	478522	0.00060	6119879	33.73	63.85	0.00061	5
10	0.00216	95560	206	477356	0.00043	5641357	8.22	59.03	0.00043	10
15	0.00662	95354	631	475295	0.00133	5164001	0.00	54.16	0.00133	15
20	0.00747	94722	708	471878	0.00150	4688707	0.00	49.50	0.00150	20
25	0.00847	94015	797	468113	0.00170	4216829	35.19	44.85	0.00170	25
30	0.00915	93218	853	463983	0.00184	3748716	67.94	40.21	0.00183	30
35	0.00988	92365	913	459644	0.00199	3284732	54.08	35.55	0.00197	35
40	0.01453	91453	1329	454387	0.00292	2825089	0.00	30.89	0.00292	40
45	0.03388	90124	3054	443640	0.00688	2370702	0.00	26.30	0.00688	45
50	0.05142	87070	4477	425085	0.01053	1927062	0.00	22.13	0.01053	50
55	0.09090	82593	7507	395459	0.01898	1501977	0.00	18.19	0.01898	55
60	0.14108	75085	10593	350247	0.03025	1106508	11.02	14.74	0.03018	60
65	0.21338	64492	13762	289082	0.04760	756261	11.02	11.73	0.04751	65
70	0.30580	50730	15514	215012	0.07215	467180	11.02	9.21	0.07203	70
75	0.41028	35217	14449	139061	0.10390	252168	11.02	7.16	0.10373	75
80	0.53874	20768	11189	74150	0.15089	113107	11.02	5.45	0.15064	80
85+	1.00000	9579	9579	38957	0.24590	38957	11.02	4.07	0.23354	85+

TABLE 3 LIFE TABLE FOR FEMALES

Age, x	$_nq_x$	l_x	$_nd_x$	$_nL_x$	$_nm_x$	T_x	$1000r_x$	$\mathring{e}_x$	$_nM_x$	Age, x
0	0.02817	100000	2817	97913	0.02877	7129392	16.58	71.29	0.02914	0
1	0.00584	97183	568	387091	0.00147	7031479	16.58	72.35	0.00149	1
5	0.00257	96615	249	482454	0.00052	6644388	30.58	68.77	0.00052	5
10	0.00141	96366	136	481496	0.00028	6161934	0.78	63.94	0.00028	10
15	0.00281	96230	271	480530	0.00056	5680438	0.00	59.03	0.00056	15
20	0.00418	95960	401	478846	0.00084	5199908	0.00	54.19	0.00084	20
25	0.00542	95558	518	476566	0.00109	4721062	35.21	49.41	0.00108	25
30	0.00776	95040	738	473428	0.00156	4244496	23.73	44.66	0.00155	30
35	0.00914	94302	862	469496	0.00184	3771068	8.33	39.99	0.00183	35
40	0.01503	93441	1404	463963·	0.00303	3301571	0.00	35.33	0.00303	40
45	0.02345	92036	2158	455070	0.00474	2837609	0.00	30.83	0.00474	45
50	0.03073	89878	2762	442871	0.00624	2382539	0.00	26.51	0.00624	50
55	0.04585	87117	3994	426385	0.00937	1939668	0.00	22.27	0.00937	55
60	0.07857	83123	6531	400504	0.01631	1513283	22.77	18.21	0.01623	60
65	0.12846	76592	9839	359817	0.02734	1112779	22.77	14.53	0.02722	65
70	0.20251	66753	13518	301483	0.04484	752962	22.77	11.28	0.04463	70
75	0.32138	53235	17108	224363	0.07625	451479	22.77	8.48	0.07589	75
80	0.50177	36126	18127	135500	0.13378	227116	22.77	6.29	0.13313	80
85+	*1.00000	17999	17999	91616	0.19647	91616	22.77	5.09	0.19462	85+

[507]

TABLE 4 POPULATION PROJECTION, USING FIXED AGE-SPECIFIC BIRTH AND DEATH RATES, IN THOUSANDS

Age at last birthday	1966 Total	Males	Females	1971 Total	Males	Females	1976 Total	Males	Females	Age at last birthday
0–4	76	39	37	68	35	33	64	33	31	0–4
5–9	70	36	34	75	39	36	68	35	33	5–9
10–14	59	30	29	70	36	34	75	39	36	10–14
15–19	50	25	25	58	29	29	70	36	34	15–19
20–24	55	27	28	50	25	25	58	29	29	20–24
25–29	88	43	45	55	27	28	50	25	25	25–29
30–34	75	37	38	88	43	45	54	26	28	30–34
35–39	61	30	31	74	37	37	86	42	44	35–39
40–44	48	19	29	60	29	31	74	37	37	40–44
45–49	45	17	28	47	18	29	59	29	30	45–49
50–54	58	21	37	43	16	27	45	17	28	50–54
55–59	82	31	51	54	19	35	41	15	26	55–59
60–64	85	34	51	76	28	48	50	17	33	60–64
65–69	70	26	44	73	28	45	66	23	43	65–69
70–74	54	17	37	56	19	37	59	21	38	70–74
75–79	39	12	27	39	11	28	39	12	27	75–79
80–84	21	7	14	22	6	16	23	6	17	80–84
85 +	11	3	8	13	4	9	14	3	11	85 +
All ages	1047	454	593	1021	449	572	995	445	550	All ages

TABLE 5 OBSERVED AND PROJECTED VITAL RATES

Rates per thousand	Observed Total	Males	Females	Projected 1966 Males	Females	1971 Males	Females	1976 Males	Females	Stable Males	Females
Birth	15.61	18.89	13.15	17.08	12.12	15.39	11.20	15.20	11.40	15.50	14.38
Death	16.75	17.98	15.82	18.12	17.85	17.56	19.16	16.78	19.99	14.85	13.73
Increase	-1.14	0.90	-2.68	-1.04	-5.74	-2.17	-7.96	-1.58	-8.59		0.6450

TABLE 6 RATES STANDARDIZED ON THREE STANDARD COUNTRIES

Standardized rates per thousand	England and Wales, 1961 Total	Males	Females	United States, 1960 Total	Males	Females	Mexico, 1960 Total	Males	Females
Birth	14.14	17.51*	13.17	14.47	15.99*	13.70	17.88	16.99*	17.14
Death	13.03	13.22*	12.68	10.67	12.17*	9.42	5.78	11.51*	4.83
Increase	1.11	4.28*	0.49	3.79	3.82*	4.28	12.10	5.48*	12.31

TABLE 7 VITAL STATISTICS AND RATES INFERRED FROM AGE DISTRIBUTIONS (FEMALES)

Vital statistics		Thompson Age range	NRR	$1000r$	Interval	Bourgeois-Pichat Age range	NRR	$1000b$	$1000d$	$1000r$	Coale
TFR	2.22	0–4	0.99	-0.45	27.40	5–29	0.53	7.35	31.12	-23.77	$1000b$
GRR	1.07	5–9	0.80	-8.18	27.36	30–54	0.45	3.64	32.88	-29.23	$1000d$
NRR	1.02	10–14	0.66	-15.66	27.29	55–79	1.09	25.19	21.93	3.27	$1000r$
Generation	25.58	15–19	0.69	-14.27	27.20	*50–74	1.03	21.50	20.58	0.92	$1000k_1$
Sex ratio	108.09										$1000k_2$

TABLE 8 LESLIE MATRIX AND ITS ANALYSIS (FEMALES)

Start of age interval	Sub-diagonal	First row	Percent in stable population	Fisher values	Total reproductive values	Net maternity function	Matrix equation coefficient
0	0.99474	0.00000	6.961	1.033	34982	0.00000	0.00000
5	0.99801	0.00019	6.902	1.041	29928	0.00000	0.00019
10	0.99799	0.09146	6.866	1.047	25926	0.00037	0.09080
15	0.99649	0.26632	6.830	0.957	27194	0.18123	0.26386
20	0.99524	0.31028	6.785	0.688	31189	0.34649	0.30634
25	0.99342	0.20943	6.730	0.372	14087	0.26618	0.20578
30	0.99169	0.10550	6.665	0.158	4967	0.14538	0.10298
35	0.98821	0.03928	6.588	0.050	1461	0.06058	0.03802
40	0.98083	0.00854	6.489	0.009	264	0.01546	0.00819
45	0.97319	0.00049	6.345	0.001	20	0.00093	0.00047
50	0.96277	0.00002	6.155	0.000	1	0.00000	0.00000
55	0.78117		26.684				

Parameters

	Integral	Matrix
λ_1	1.0032	1.0032
λ_2	0.2695	0.2870
	+0.7340	+0.7073 i
r_1	0.0006	0.0005
r_2	-0.0492	-0.0540
	+0.2438	+0.2371 i
c_1	4631	
c_2	631	
		-12461 i
$2\pi/y$	25.775	25.505
Δ	14.179	

West Berlin, 1961

TABLE 1 DATA INPUT TO COMPUTATIONS

Age at last birthday	Total	Males	%	Females	%	Births, by age of mother	Total	Males	Females	Age at last birthday
0	21840	11286	1.2	10554	0.8	0	758	411	347	0
1–4	74100	38008	4.1	36092	2.8	0	90	55	35	1–4
5–9	86911	44698	4.8	42213	3.3	0	37	21	16	5–9
10–14	104546	53379	5.7	51167	4.0	6	26	15	11	10–14
15–19	141742	71290	7.7	70452	5.5	2746	91	59	32	15–19
20–24	164308	82448	8.9	81860	6.4	8672	167	95	72	20–24
25–29	122875	60822	6.5	62053	4.9	6394	164	109	55	25–29
30–34	114314	53314	5.7	61000	4.8	3367	202	112	90	30–34
35–39	115159	43596	4.7	71563	5.6	1585	277	122	155	35–39
40–44	111152	41330	4.4	69822	5.5	414	350	141	209	40–44
45–49	160571	60845	6.5	99726	7.8	19	814	399	415	45–49
50–54	206291	81701	8.8	124590	9.8	0	1513	833	680	50–54
55–59	203962	85158	9.1	118804	9.3	0	2543	1502	1041	55–59
60–64	178204	68660	7.4	109544	8.6	0	3675	2090	1585	60–64
65–69	149457	50911	5.5	98546	7.7	0	4614	2319	2295	65–69
70–74	118974	40420	4.3	78554	6.2		5826	2719	3107	70–74
75–79	76002	26224	2.8	49778	3.9		6132	2647	3485	75–79
80–84	38334	12863	1.4	25471	2.0	11850 M	5063	1955	3108	80–84
85+	14911	4455	0.5	10456	0.8	11353 F	3369	1058	2311	85+
All ages	2203653	931408		1272245		23203	35711	16652	19049	All ages

TABLE 2 LIFE TABLE FOR MALES

Age, x	$_nq_x$	l_x	$_nd_x$	$_nL_x$	$_nm_x$	T_x	$1000r_x$	$\mathring{e}_x$	$_nM_x$	Age, x
0	0.03500	100000	3500	97309	0.03596	6540471	15.96	66.40	0.03642	0
1	0.00563	96500	544	384419	0.00141	6543162	15.96	67.80	0.00145	1
5	0.00235	95957	225	479222	0.00047	6158743	0.00	64.18	0.00047	5
10	0.00140	95732	134	478358	0.00028	5679522	0.00	59.33	0.00028	10
15	0.00413	95597	395	477086	0.00083	5201164	0.00	54.41	0.00083	15
20	0.00576	95202	548	474736	0.00116	4724078	14.65	49.62	0.00115	20
25	0.00896	94654	848	471240	0.00180	4249342	41.88	44.89	0.00179	25
30	0.01048	93806	983	466652	0.00211	3778102	31.10	40.28	0.00210	30
35	0.01393	92822	1293	460997	0.00280	3311440	22.73	35.68	0.00280	35
40	0.01693	91529	1549	454110	0.00341	2850443	0.00	31.14	0.00341	40
45	0.03230	89980	2906	443215	0.00656	2396334	0.00	26.63	0.00655	45
50	0.04981	87074	4337	425381	0.01020	1953118	0.00	22.43	0.01020	50
55	0.08474	82737	7011	397497	0.01764	1527737	0.00	18.47	0.01764	55
60	0.14231	75726	10776	353007	0.03053	1130240	15.46	14.93	0.03044	60
65	0.20546	64949	13345	292246	0.04566	777233	15.46	11.97	0.04555	65
70	0.28886	51605	14905	221055	0.06743	484987	15.46	9.40	0.06727	70
75	0.40243	36698	14769	145947	0.10119	263932	15.46	7.19	0.10094	75
80	0.54313	21930	11911	78172	0.15237	117986	15.46	5.38	0.15199	80
85+	1.00000	10019	10019	39813	0.25165	39813	15.46	3.97	0.23749	85+

TABLE 3 LIFE TABLE FOR FEMALES

Age, x	$_nq_x$	l_x	$_nd_x$	$_nL_x$	$_nm_x$	T_x	$1000r_x$	$\mathring{e}_x$	$_nM_x$	Age, x
0	0.03167	100000	3167	97467	0.03249	7201333	14.74	72.01	0.03288	0
1	0.00376	96833	364	386264	0.00094	7103866	14.74	73.36	0.00097	1
5	0.00189	96469	183	481886	0.00038	6717603	0.00	69.64	0.00038	5
10	0.00107	96286	103	481178	0.00021	6235716	0.00	64.75	0.00021	10
15	0.00227	96182	218	480433	0.00045	5754538	0.00	59.83	0.00045	15
20	0.00439	95964	422	478810	0.00088	5274105	11.92	54.96	0.00088	20
25	0.00444	95543	424	476710	0.00089	4795295	28.40	50.19	0.00089	25
30	0.00735	95118	699	473967	0.00148	4318584	0.00	45.40	0.00148	30
35	0.01077	94419	1017	469696	0.00217	3844617	0.00	40.72	0.00217	35
40	0.01486	93402	1388	463722	0.00299	3374921	0.00	36.13	0.00299	40
45	0.02060	92014	1896	455546	0.00416	2911200	0.00	31.64	0.00416	45
50	0.02695	90118	2428	444910	0.00546	2455654	0.00	27.25	0.00545	50
55	0.04298	87690	3769	429752	0.00877	2010744	3.68	22.93	0.00876	55
60	0.07038	83921	5905	405861	0.01455	1580992	27.96	18.84	0.01447	60
65	0.11105	78015	8664	369814	0.02343	1175132	27.96	15.06	0.02329	65
70	0.18191	69351	12615	316969	0.03980	805317	27.96	11.61	0.03955	70
75	0.30079	56736	17066	242288	0.07044	488348	27.96	8.61	0.07001	75
80	0.47188	39670	18720	152362	0.12286	246060	27.96	6.20	0.12202	80
85+	*1.00000	20951	20951	93699	0.22360	93699	27.96	4.47	0.22102	85+

TABLE 4 POPULATION PROJECTION, USING FIXED AGE-SPECIFIC BIRTH AND DEATH RATES, IN THOUSANDS

Age at last birthday	1966			1971			1976			Age at last birthday
	Total	Males	Females	Total	Males	Females	Total	Males	Females	
0–4	112	57	55	104	53	51	92	47	45	0–4
5–9	95	49	46	111	57	54	104	53	51	5–9
10–14	87	45	42	95	49	46	110	55	54	10–14
15–19	104	53	51	86	44	42	95	49	46	15–19
20–24	141	71	70	104	53	51	86	44	42	20–24
25–29	164	82	82	140	70	70	104	53	51	25–29
30–34	122	60	62	162	81	81	140	70	70	30–34
35–39	113	53	60	120	59	61	160	80	80	35–39
40–44	114	43	71	112	52	60	119	59	60	40–44
45–49	109	40	69	111	42	69	110	51	59	45–49
50–54	155	58	97	106	39	67	108	40	68	50–54
55–59	196	76	120	149	55	94	101	36	65	55–59
60–64	188	76	112	182	68	114	137	48	89	60–64
65–69	157	57	100	165	63	102	160	56	104	65–69
70–74	123	39	84	129	43	86	135	47	88	70–74
75–79	87	27	60	90	25	65	93	28	65	75–79
80–84	45	14	31	52	14	38	55	14	41	80–84
85 +	23	7	16	26	7	19	30	7	23	85 +
All ages	2135	907	1228	2044	874	1170	1939	838	1101	All ages

TABLE 5 OBSERVED AND PROJECTED VITAL RATES

Rates per thousand	Observed			Projected						Stable	
				1966		1971		1976			
	Total	Males	Females	Males	Females	Males	Females	Males	Females	Males	Females
Birth	10.53	12.72	8.92	12.97	9.16	11.93	8.54	10.63	7.77	10.38	9.32
Death	16.21	17.89	14.97	19.14	17.67	19.62	19.89	19.68	21.79	20.04	18.98
Increase	-5.68	-5.17	-6.05	-6.17	-8.51	-7.69	-11.34	-9.04	-14.02		-9.6595

TABLE 6 RATES STANDARDIZED ON THREE STANDARD COUNTRIES

Standardized rates per thousand	England and Wales, 1961			United States, 1960			Mexico, 1960		
	Total	Males	Females	Total	Males	Females	Total	Males	Females
Birth	10.51	13.15*	9.97	10.72	11.91*	10.34	12.95	12.13*	12.64
Death	12.48	12.83*	11.94	10.27	11.76*	8.91	5.55	11.72*	4.60
Increase	-1.97	0.32*	-1.97	0.45	0.16*	1.43	7.39	0.40*	8.05

TABLE 7 VITAL STATISTICS AND RATES INFERRED FROM AGE DISTRIBUTIONS (FEMALES)

Vital statistics		Thompson				Bourgeois-Pichat					Coale
		Age range	NRR	1000r	Interval	Age range	NRR	1000b	1000d	1000r	1000b
TFR	1.66	0–4	0.66	-14.98	27.40	5–29	0.50	6.30	31.64	-25.34	1000b
GRR	0.81	5–9	0.55	-21.29	27.36	30–54	0.36	2.75	41.09	-38.35	1000r
NRR	0.77	10–14	0.61	-18.62	27.30	55–79	1.20	32.43	25.61	6.81	$1000k_1$
Generation	26.63	15–19	0.74	-11.67	27.22	*50–74	1.16	29.92	24.30	5.62	$1000k_2$
Sex ratio	104.38										

TABLE 8 LESLIE MATRIX AND ITS ANALYSIS (FEMALES)

Start of age interval	Sub-diagonal	First row	Percent in stable population	Fisher values	Total reproductive values	Net maternity function	Matrix equation coefficient	Parameters	Integral	Matrix
0	0.99619	0.00000	4.619	1.009	47065	0.00000	0.00000	λ_1	0.9528	0.9529
5	0.99853	0.00014	4.829	0.965	40742	0.00000	0.00014	λ_2	0.3164	0.3271
10	0.99845	0.04619	5.061	0.921	47120	0.00028	0.04595		+0.7189	+0.6949i
15	0.99662	0.17107	5.302	0.832	58631	0.09152	0.16990	r_1	-0.0097	-0.0096
20	0.99561	0.24677	5.546	0.623	50958	0.24819	0.24426	r_2	-0.0483	-0.0528
25	0.99425	0.18689	5.794	0.346	21452	0.24034	0.18417		+0.2312	+0.2262i
30	0.99099	0.09130	6.045	0.142	8643	0.12801	0.08945	c_1		11117
35	0.98728	0.03314	6.287	0.043	3097	0.05090	0.03218	c_2		-17108
40	0.98237	0.00723	6.514	0.008	552	0.01345	0.00694			-17716i
45	0.97665	0.00022	6.716	0.000	24	0.00042	0.00021	$2\pi/y$	27.172	27.781
50	0.96593	0.00001	6.883	0.000	1	0.00000	0.00000	Δ	10.570	
55	0.77026		35.403							

West Berlin, 1967

TABLE 1 DATA INPUT TO COMPUTATIONS

Age at last birthday	Population					Births, by age of mother	Deaths			Age at last birthday
	Total	Males	%	Females	%		Total	Males	Females	
0	24987	12704	1.4	12283	1.0	0	645	358	287	0
1–4	100478	51408	5.5	49070	4.0	0	88	52	36	1–4
5–9	101490	51925	5.6	49565	4.0	0	40	21	19	5–9
10–14	84144	43359	4.6	40785	3.3	2	28	15	13	10–14
15–19	105565	54107	5.8	51458	4.2	1581	68	42	26	15–19
20–24	148995	78887	8.4	70108	5.7	6854	140	92	48	20–24
25–29	181992	96227	10.3	85765	6.9	9402	239	163	76	25–29
30–34	132807	67518	7.2	65289	5.3	5221	200	126	74	30–34
35–39	109259	52801	5.7	56458	4.6	1642	266	160	105	35–39
40–44	108821	43129	4.6	65692	5.3	478	397	190	207	40–44
45–49	114163	41945	4.5	72218	5.8	35	551	269	292	45–49
50–54	132211	48916	5.2	83295	6.7	0	1006	527	479	50–54
55–59	187839	71195	7.6	116644	9.4	0	2331	1275	1056	55–59
60–64	190445	75097	8.0	115348	9.3	0	3867	2162	1705	60–64
65–69	162061	58697	6.3	103364	8.3	0	5339	2835	2504	65–69
70–74	127713	38834	4.2	88879	7.2		6238	2721	3517	70–74
75–79	90551	26617	2.8	63934	5.2		7163	2710	4453	75–79
80–84	48258	14411	1.5	33847	2.7	12898 M	6203	2219	3984	80–84
85 +	21898	6300	0.7	15598	1.3	12317 F	4985	1550	3435	85 +
All ages	2173677	934077		1239600		25215	39804	17487	22317	All ages

TABLE 2 LIFE TABLE FOR MALES

Age, x	$_nq_x$	l_x	$_nd_x$	$_nL_x$	$_nm_x$	T_x	$1000r_x$	$\overset{\circ}{e}_x$	$_nM_x$	Age, x
0	0.02758	100000	2758	97854	0.02818	6680342	0.00	66.80	0.02818	0
1	0.00403	97242	392	387825	0.00101	6582487	0.00	67.69	0.00101	1
5	0.00200	96850	194	483767	0.00040	6194662	38.54	63.96	0.00040	5
10	0.00173	96657	167	482903	0.00035	5710895	0.00	59.08	0.00035	10
15	0.00387	96490	374	481595	0.00078	5227992	0.00	54.18	0.00078	15
20	0.00582	96116	559	479272	0.00117	4746397	0.00	49.38	0.00117	20
25	0.00845	95557	807	475835	0.00170	4267126	13.96	44.66	0.00169	25
30	0.00937	94750	888	471657	0.00188	3791291	57.93	40.01	0.00187	30
35	0.01515	93862	1422	465990	0.00305	3319633	41.76	35.37	0.00303	35
40	0.02186	92440	2021	457444	0.00442	2853643	18.52	30.87	0.00441	40
45	0.03160	90419	2857	445488	0.00641	2396199	0.00	26.50	0.00641	45
50	0.05256	87562	4602	427192	0.01077	1950711	0.00	22.28	0.01077	50
55	0.08595	82959	7130	398144	0.01791	1523519	0.00	18.36	0.01791	55
60	0.13499	75829	10236	355027	0.02883	1125375	7.08	14.84	0.02879	60
65	0.21641	65593	14195	293542	0.04836	770348	7.08	11.74	0.04830	65
70	0.29848	51398	15341	218718	0.07014	476807	7.08	9.28	0.07007	70
75	0.40446	36057	14584	143079	0.10193	258088	7.08	7.16	0.10181	75
80	0.54755	21473	11758	76271	0.15416	115009	7.08	5.36	0.15398	80
85 +	1.00000	9716	9716	38739	0.25080	38739	7.08	3.99	0.24603	85 +

TABLE 3 LIFE TABLE FOR FEMALES

Age, x	$_nq_x$	l_x	$_nd_x$	$_nL_x$	$_nm_x$	T_x	$1000r_x$	$\overset{\circ}{e}_x$	$_nM_x$	Age, x
0	0.02294	100000	2294	98184	0.02337	7277463	0.00	72.77	0.02337	0
1	0.00293	97706	286	389986	0.00073	7179279	0.00	73.48	0.00073	1
5	0.00190	97420	185	486636	0.00038	6789293	40.35	69.69	0.00038	5
10	0.00159	97235	155	485799	0.00032	6302657	0.00	64.82	0.00032	10
15	0.00252	97080	245	484823	0.00051	5816858	0.00	59.92	0.00051	15
20	0.00342	96835	331	483385	0.00068	5332035	0.00	55.06	0.00068	20
25	0.00442	96504	427	481497	0.00089	4848651	6.23	50.24	0.00089	25
30	0.00569	96077	547	479114	0.00114	4367154	40.58	45.45	0.00113	30
35	0.00935	95530	893	475611	0.00188	3888040	0.00	40.70	0.00188	35
40	0.01564	94637	1480	469687	0.00315	3412428	0.00	36.06	0.00315	40
45	0.02002	93157	1865	461352	0.00404	2942741	0.00	31.59	0.00404	45
50	0.02837	91291	2590	450413	0.00575	2481389	0.00	27.18	0.00575	50
55	0.04434	88701	3933	434401	0.00905	2030976	0.00	22.90	0.00905	55
60	0.07169	84769	6077	409717	0.01483	1596575	16.29	18.83	0.01478	60
65	0.11496	78692	9047	372210	0.02431	1186858	16.29	15.08	0.02423	65
70	0.18148	69645	12639	318291	0.03971	814648	16.29	11.70	0.03957	70
75	0.29870	57006	17028	243644	0.06989	496357	16.29	8.71	0.06965	75
80	0.45835	39978	18324	155045	0.11818	252712	16.29	6.32	0.11771	80
85 +	*1.00000	21654	21654	97667	0.22171	97667	16.29	4.51	0.22022	85 +

TABLE 4   POPULATION PROJECTION, USING FIXED AGE-SPECIFIC BIRTH AND DEATH RATES, IN THOUSANDS

Age at last birthday	1972 Total	Males	Females	1977 Total	Males	Females	1982 Total	Males	Females	Age at last birthday
0–4	118	60	58	104	53	51	92	47	45	0–4
5–9	125	64	61	117	60	57	104	53	51	5–9
10–14	101	52	49	125	64	61	117	60	57	10–14
15–19	84	43	41	101	52	49	125	64	61	15–19
20–24	105	54	51	84	43	41	100	51	49	20–24
25–29	148	78	70	104	53	51	83	43	40	25–29
30–34	180	95	85	147	78	69	104	53	51	30–34
35–39	132	67	65	179	94	85	146	77	59	35–39
40–44	108	52	56	129	65	64	177	93	84	40–44
45–49	107	42	65	105	50	55	127	64	63	45–49
50–54	111	40	71	103	40	63	101	48	53	50–54
55–59	126	46	80	105	37	68	99	38	61	55–59
60–64	173	63	110	117	41	76	97	33	64	60–64
65–69	167	62	105	152	52	100	103	34	69	65–69
70–74	132	44	88	136	46	90	124	39	85	70–74
75–79	93	25	68	97	29	68	99	30	69	75–79
80–84	55	14	41	57	14	43	58	15	43	80–84
85 +	28	7	21	33	7	26	34	7	27	85 +
All ages	2093	908	1185	1995	878	1117	1890	849	1041	All ages

TABLE 5   OBSERVED AND PROJECTED VITAL RATES

Rates per thousand	Observed Total	Males	Females	Projected 1972 Males	Females	1977 Males	Females	1982 Males	Females	Stable Males	Females
Birth	11.60	13.81	9.94	12.98	9.51	11.41	8.58	10.77	8.37	11.69	10.53
Death	18.31	18.72	18.00	18.97	20.37	18.69	22.02	18.07	22.84	18.26	17.10
Increase	-6.71	-4.91	-8.07	-5.99	-10.86	-7.29	-13.45	-7.31	-14.48		-6.5708

TABLE 6   RATES STANDARDIZED ON THREE STANDARD COUNTRIES

Standardized rates per thousand	England and Wales, 1961 Total	Males	Females	United States, 1960 Total	Males	Females	Mexico, 1960 Total	Males	Females
Birth	11.26	11.50*	10.66	11.50	10.77*	11.07	13.38	11.11*	13.03
Death	12.43	12.96*	11.75	10.15	12.04*	8.66	5.26	11.63*	4.24
Increase	-1.17	-1.45*	-1.08	1.35	-1.27*	2.41	8.11	-0.52*	8.79

TABLE 7   VITAL STATISTICS AND RATES INFERRED FROM AGE DISTRIBUTIONS (FEMALES)

Vital statistics		Thompson Age range	NRR	$1000r$	Interval	Bourgeois-Pichat Age range	NRR	$1000b$	$1000d$	$1000r$	Coale
TFR	1.77	0–4	0.92	-3.23	27.41	5–29	0.41	5.34	38.63	-33.29	$1000b$
GRR	0.87	5–9	0.70	-12.98	27.37	30–54	0.62	5.53	23.27	-17.75	$1000d$
NRR	0.83	10–14	0.55	-22.15	27.31	55–79	0.95	19.51	21.58	-2.08	$1000r$
Generation	27.61	15–19	0.64	-17.26	27.22	*35–64	0.37	2.33	39.14	-36.81	$1000k_1$
Sex ratio	104.72										$1000k_2$

TABLE 8   LESLIE MATRIX AND ITS ANALYSIS (FEMALES)

Start of age interval	Sub-diagonal	First row	Percent in stable population	Fisher values	Total reproductive values	Net maternity function	Matrix equation coefficient	Parameters	Integral	Matrix
0	0.99686	0.00000	5.228	1.008	61817	0.00000	0.00000	λ_1	0.9677	0.9677
5	0.99828	0.00006	5.385	0.978	48479	0.00000	0.00006	λ_2	0.3684	0.3743
10	0.99799	0.03662	5.555	0.948	38667	0.00012	0.03544		+0.7314	+0.7096 i
15	0.99703	0.15285	5.729	0.882	45403	0.07276	0.15180	r_1	-0.0066	-0.0365
20	0.99609	0.24676	5.903	0.702	49209	0.23084	0.24434	r_2	-0.0399	-0.0441
25	0.99505	0.22558	6.076	0.432	37077	0.25784	0.22250		+0.2208	+0.2171 i
30	0.99269	0.12977	6.248	0.192	12536	0.18715	0.12736	c_1		10154
35	0.98754	0.04324	6.409	0.055	3132	0.06757	0.04213	c_2		10720
40	0.98225	0.00923	6.540	0.010	672	0.01669	0.00889			-24885 i
45	0.97629	0.00057	6.639	0.001	44	0.00109	0.00055	$2\pi/y$	28.452	28.943
50	0.96445	0.00001	6.698	0.000	1	0.00000	0.00000	Δ	11.287	
55	0.77540		33.590							

Düsseldorf, 1966

TABLE 1   DATA INPUT TO COMPUTATIONS

Age at last birthday	Population					Births, by age of mother		Deaths			Age at last birthday
	Total	Males	%	Females	%			Total	Males	Females	
0	10242	5246	1.6	4996	1.3	0		206	129	77	0
1–4	38297	19551	6.0	18746	5.0	0		40	22	18	1–4
5–9	42381	21662	6.7	20719	5.6	0		30	15	15	5–9
10–14	35985	18162	5.6	17823	4.8	0		18	11	7	10–14
15–19	38469	19177	5.9	19292	5.2	659		22	13	9	15–19
20–24	49597	23688	7.3	25909	7.0	3064		43	25	18	20–24
25–29	63475	31982	9.9	31493	8.5	3883		61	36	25	25–29
30–34	52444	27442	8.5	25002	6.7	2044		72	44	28	30–34
35–39	50196	25727	8.0	24469	6.6	759		96	59	37	35–39
40–44	46821	20218	6.3	26503	7.1	234		110	63	47	40–44
45–49	38374	16011	4.9	22363	6.0	10		168	94	74	45–49
50–54	46022	19525	6.0	26497	7.1	1		356	209	147	50–54
55–59	51649	22159	6.9	29490	7.9	0		596	357	239	55–59
60–64	46550	20883	6.5	25667	6.9	0		941	615	325	60–64
65–69	34386	14010	4.3	20376	5.5	0		1198	691	507	65–69
70–74	23664	8212	2.5	15452	4.1			1223	640	583	70–74
75–79	15553	5433	1.7	10120	2.7			1066	507	559	75–79
80–84	8015	2946	0.9	5069	1.4	5491 M		820	353	467	80–84
85+	4003	1443	0.4	2560	0.7	5163 F		1295	441	854	85+
All ages	696123	323477		372646		10654		8361	4324	4037	All ages

TABLE 2   LIFE TABLE FOR MALES

Age, x	$_nq_x$	l_x	$_nd_x$	$_nL_x$	$_nm_x$	T_x	$1000r_x$	$\overset{\circ}{e}_x$	$_nM_x$	Age, x
0	0.02403	100000	2403	98191	0.02447	6745660	6.14	67.46	0.02459	0
1	0.00445	97597	435	389128	0.00112	6647469	6.14	68.11	0.00113	1
5	0.00344	97162	335	484976	0.00069	6258341	30.33	64.41	0.00069	5
10	0.00302	96828	293	483406	0.00061	5773365	11.55	59.63	0.00061	10
15	0.00338	96535	327	481903	0.00068	5289959	0.00	54.80	0.00068	15
20	0.00526	96208	506	479820	0.00106	4808056	0.00	49.98	0.00106	20
25	0.00561	95702	537	477221	0.00113	4328236	0.00	45.23	0.00113	25
30	0.00801	95165	762	474032	0.00161	3851015	20.12	40.47	0.00160	30
35	0.01145	94402	1081	469455	0.00230	3376983	28.26	35.77	0.00229	35
40	0.01563	93322	1459	463291	0.00315	2907528	43.93	31.16	0.00312	40
45	0.02897	91863	2661	453328	0.00587	2444237	0.00	26.61	0.00587	45
50	0.05222	89202	4658	435176	0.01070	1990909	0.00	22.32	0.01070	50
55	0.07767	84543	6566	407576	0.01611	1555733	0.00	18.40	0.01611	55
60	0.13826	77977	10781	364659	0.02956	1148156	17.50	14.72	0.02945	60
65	0.22105	67196	14854	300159	0.04949	783497	17.50	11.66	0.04932	65
70	0.32634	52342	17082	218673	0.07811	483338	17.50	9.23	0.07793	70
75	0.37570	35261	13248	141742	0.09346	264665	17.50	7.51	0.09332	75
80	0.46121	22013	10153	84395	0.12030	122923	17.50	5.58	0.11982	80
85+	*1.00000	11861	11861	38528	0.30784	38528	17.50	3.25	0.30561	85+

TABLE 3   LIFE TABLE FOR FEMALES

Age, x	$_nq_x$	l_x	$_nd_x$	$_nL_x$	$_nm_x$	T_x	$1000r_x$	$\overset{\circ}{e}_x$	$_nM_x$	Age, x
0	0.01518	100000	1518	98910	0.01534	7395741	5.69	73.96	0.01541	0
1	0.00381	98482	375	392852	0.00096	7296832	5.69	74.09	0.00096	1
5	0.00360	98107	353	489652	0.00072	6903980	27.96	70.37	0.00072	5
10	0.00196	97754	192	488254	0.00039	6414328	6.65	65.62	0.00039	10
15	0.00233	97562	227	487273	0.00047	5926054	0.00	60.74	0.00047	15
20	0.00347	97335	338	485854	0.00069	5438791	0.00	55.88	0.00069	20
25	0.00396	96997	384	484068	0.00079	4952927	2.72	51.06	0.00079	25
30	0.00560	96613	541	481782	0.00112	4468859	24.10	46.26	0.00112	30
35	0.00753	96072	724	478612	0.00151	3987076	0.00	41.50	0.00151	35
40	0.00881	95348	840	474812	0.00177	3508465	6.97	36.80	0.00177	40
45	0.01642	94508	1552	469015	0.00331	3033653	0.00	32.10	0.00331	45
50	0.02738	92956	2546	458841	0.00555	2564638	0.00	27.59	0.00555	50
55	0.03977	90410	3596	443658	0.00810	2105796	0.00	23.29	0.00810	55
60	0.06222	86815	5402	421826	0.01281	1662138	31.18	19.15	0.01270	60
65	0.11825	81413	9627	384468	0.02504	1240312	31.18	15.23	0.02488	65
70	0.17367	71786	12467	328779	0.03792	855844	31.18	11.92	0.03773	70
75	0.24469	59319	14515	261279	0.05555	527065	31.18	8.89	0.05524	75
80	0.38250	44804	17137	183915	0.09318	265786	31.18	5.93	0.09213	80
85+	*1.00000	27666	27666	81871	0.33793	81871	31.18	2.96	0.33359	85+

TABLE 4 POPULATION PROJECTION, USING FIXED AGE-SPECIFIC BIRTH AND DEATH RATES, IN THOUSANDS

Age at last birthday	1971 Total	Males	Females	1976 Total	Males	Females	1981 Total	Males	Females	Age at last birthday
0–4	49	25	24	45	23	22	41	21	20	0–4
5–9	49	25	24	49	25	24	44	23	21	5–9
10–14	43	22	21	49	25	24	49	25	24	10–14
15–19	36	18	18	43	22	21	49	25	24	15–19
20–24	38	19	19	36	18	18	42	21	21	20–24
25–29	50	24	26	38	19	19	36	18	18	25–29
30–34	63	32	31	49	23	26	38	19	19	30–34
35–39	52	27	25	62	31	31	49	23	26	35–39
40–44	49	25	24	52	27	25	62	31	31	40–44
45–49	46	20	26	49	25	24	50	26	24	45–49
50–54	37	15	22	45	19	26	47	24	23	50–54
55–59	44	18	26	35	14	21	43	18	25	55–59
60–64	48	20	28	40	16	24	33	13	20	60–64
65–69	40	17	23	42	16	26	35	13	22	65–69
70–74	27	10	17	33	13	20	34	12	22	70–74
75–79	17	5	12	21	7	14	24	8	15	75–79
80–84	10	3	7	12	3	9	14	4	10	80–84
85 +	3	1	2	4	1	3	5	1	4	85 +
All ages	701	326	375	704	327	377	695	325	370	All ages

TABLE 5 OBSERVED AND PROJECTED VITAL RATES

Rates per thousand	Observed Total	Males	Females	Projected 1971 Males	Females	1976 Males	Females	1981 Males	Females	Stable Males	Females
Birth	15.30	16.97	13.85	15.15	12.40	13.31	10.94	12.76	10.58	13.49	12.22
Death	12.01	13.37	10.83	13.85	11.64	14.38	13.30	14.56	14.54	16.05	14.77
Increase	3.29	3.61	3.02	1.30	0.76	-1.07	-2.36	-1.80	-3.96		-2.5570

TABLE 6 RATES STANDARDIZED ON THREE STANDARD COUNTRIES

Standardized rates per thousand	England and Wales, 1961 Total	Males	Females	United States, 1960 Total	Males	Females	Mexico, 1960 Total	Males	Females
Birth	12.61	13.48*	11.84	12.86	12.89*	12.28	15.11	12.40*	14.60
Death	12.09	12.87*	11.38	9.90	11.48*	8.39	4.94	10.05*	3.84
Increase	0.52	0.61*	0.46	2.95	1.41*	3.89	10.17	2.35*	10.75

TABLE 7 VITAL STATISTICS AND RATES INFERRED FROM AGE DISTRIBUTIONS (FEMALES)

Vital statistics		Thompson Age range	NRR	$1000r$	Interval	Bourgeois-Pichat Age range	NRR	$1000b$	$1000d$	$1000r$	Coale
TFR	1.99	0–4	0.91	-3.26	27.43	5–29	0.51	8.05	32.84	-24.79	$1000b$
GRR	0.96	5–9	0.78	-8.99	27.40	30–54	0.93	12.53	15.41	-2.88	$1000d$
NRR	0.93	10–14	0.66	-15.13	27.35	55–79	1.89	69.92	46.36	23.56	$1000r$
Generation	27.33	15–19	0.72	-12.53	27.27	*30–54	0.93	12.53	15.41	-2.88	$1000k_1$
Sex ratio	106.35										$1000k_2$

TABLE 8 LESLIE MATRIX AND ITS ANALYSIS (FEMALES)

Start of age interval	Sub-diagonal	First row	Percent in stable population	Fisher values	Total reproductive values	Net maternity function	Matrix equation coefficient
0	0.99571	0.00000	6.047	1.010	23986	0.00000	0.00000
5	0.99717	0.00000	6.098	1.002	20755	0.00000	0.00000
10	0.99797	0.04062	6.159	0.992	17678	0.00000	0.04033
15	0.99711	0.18121	6.226	0.940	18137	0.08066	0.17955
20	0.99630	0.28729	6.287	0.747	19361	0.27845	0.28384
25	0.99528	0.24387	6.345	0.449	14146	0.28923	0.24005
30	0.99342	0.13413	6.396	0.198	4951	0.19087	0.13141
35	0.99206	0.04736	6.436	0.060	1478	0.07194	0.04609
40	0.98779	0.01101	6.467	0.012	317	0.02024	0.01063
45	0.97831	0.00058	6.470	0.001	14	0.00102	0.00055
50	0.96691	0.00004	6.411	0.000	1	0.00008	0.00004
55	0.78511		30.659				

Parameters

	Integral	Matrix
λ_1	0.9873	0.9873
λ_2	0.3546	0.3615
	+0.7471	+0.7233 i
r_1	-0.0026	-0.0025
r_2	-0.0380	-0.0425
	+0.2255	+0.2214 i
c_1		3611
c_2		3332
		-8261 i
$2\pi/y$	27.859	28.373
Δ	7.388	

Hamburg, 1966

TABLE 1 DATA INPUT TO COMPUTATIONS

Age at last birthday	Population					Births, by age of mother	Deaths			Age at last birthday
	Total	Males	%	Females	%		Total	Males	Females	
0	26299	13479	1.6	12820	1.3	0	505	284	221	0
1–4	101026	51651	6.0	49375	5.0	0	73	33	40	1–4
5–9	104294	53334	6.2	50960	5.1	0	53	30	23	5–9
10–14	87267	44735	5.2	42532	4.3	1	32	20	12	10–14
15–19	101473	51655	6.0	49818	5.0	1118	65	44	21	15–19
20–24	134908	68687	8.0	66221	6.7	7332	115	77	38	20–24
25–29	165260	87227	10.1	78033	7.9	10464	176	119	57	25–29
30–34	124385	63919	7.4	60466	6.1	5714	179	117	62	30–34
35–39	116342	56893	6.6	59449	6.0	2105	208	132	76	35–39
40–44	117818	50405	5.9	67413	6.8	635	309	158	151	40–44
45–49	96669	40417	4.7	56252	5.7	53	409	234	175	45–49
50–54	120082	51416	6.0	68666	6.9	1	844	467	377	50–54
55–59	138574	60023	7.0	78551	7.9	0	1573	986	587	55–59
60–64	130282	58138	6.8	72144	7.3	0	2628	1641	987	60–64
65–69	107647	43260	5.0	64387	6.5	0	3360	1923	1437	65–69
70–74	81755	29256	3.4	52499	5.3		4104	2008	2095	70–74
75–79	54946	20397	2.4	34549	3.5		4321	2008	2313	75–79
80–84	28772	10792	1.3	17980	1.8	14047 M	3870	1635	2235	80–84
85 +	13665	4761	0.6	8904	0.9	13376 F	3290	1248	2042	85 +
All ages	1851464	860445		991019		27423	26114	13164	12950	All ages

TABLE 2 LIFE TABLE FOR MALES

Age, x	$_nq_x$	l_x	$_nd_x$	$_nL_x$	$_nm_x$	T_x	$1000r_x$	$\overset{\circ}{e}_x$	$_nM_x$	Age, x
0	0.02066	100000	2066	98356	0.02101	6816983	3.68	68.17	0.02107	0
1	0.00253	97934	248	391008	0.00063	6718627	3.68	68.60	0.00064	1
5	0.00280	97685	274	487743	0.00056	6327619	36.98	64.78	0.00055	5
10	0.00223	97412	218	486544	0.00045	5839876	2.64	59.95	0.00045	10
15	0.00425	97194	413	485006	0.00085	5353332	0.00	55.08	0.00085	15
20	0.00559	96781	541	482603	0.00112	4868326	0.00	50.30	0.00112	20
25	0.00680	96240	655	479533	0.00137	4385723	5.78	45.57	0.00136	25
30	0.00915	95585	875	475831	0.00184	3906090	40.90	40.86	0.00183	30
35	0.01157	94710	1095	470937	0.00233	3430259	21.39	36.22	0.00232	35
40	0.01567	93615	1467	464728	0.00316	2959322	30.68	31.61	0.00313	40
45	0.02857	92148	2632	454684	0.00579	2494594	0.00	27.07	0.00579	45
50	0.04449	89516	3983	438484	0.00908	2039911	0.00	22.79	0.00908	50
55	0.07914	85533	6769	412087	0.01643	1601427	0.00	18.72	0.01543	55
60	0.13253	78764	10433	369173	0.02828	1189340	8.84	15.10	0.02823	60
65	0.20100	68325	13733	308458	0.04452	820167	8.84	12.00	0.04445	65
70	0.29359	54592	16028	233196	0.06873	511710	8.84	9.37	0.06864	70
75	0.39405	38564	15196	154148	0.09858	278513	8.84	7.22	0.09845	75
80	0.54565	23368	12751	84009	0.15178	124365	8.84	5.32	0.15150	80
85 +	*1.00000	10617	10617	40355	0.26309	40355	8.84	3.80	0.26213	85 +

TABLE 3 LIFE TABLE FOR FEMALES

Age, x	$_nq_x$	l_x	$_nd_x$	$_nL_x$	$_nm_x$	T_x	$1000r_x$	$\overset{\circ}{e}_x$	$_nM_x$	Age, x
0	0.01698	100000	1698	98728	0.01720	7396678	3.12	73.97	0.01724	0
1	0.00322	98302	317	392292	0.00081	7297950	3.12	74.24	0.00081	1
5	0.00224	97986	219	489380	0.00045	6905659	37.48	70.48	0.00045	5
10	0.00141	97766	138	488485	0.00028	6416279	1.91	65.63	0.00028	10
15	0.00211	97629	206	487659	0.00042	5927794	0.00	60.72	0.00042	15
20	0.00287	97423	279	486449	0.00057	5440135	0.00	55.84	0.00057	20
25	0.00365	97144	355	484879	0.00073	4953686	8.33	50.99	0.00073	25
30	0.00513	96789	496	482760	0.00103	4468808	26.20	46.17	0.00103	30
35	0.00637	96293	614	480049	0.00128	3986048	0.00	41.40	0.00128	35
40	0.01115	95679	1067	475936	0.00224	3505999	3.35	36.64	0.00224	40
45	0.01544	94613	1461	469714	0.00311	3030093	0.00	32.03	0.00311	45
50	0.02710	93151	2525	459834	0.00549	2560379	0.00	27.49	0.00549	50
55	0.03673	90627	3329	445496	0.00747	2100545	0.00	23.18	0.00747	55
60	0.06661	87298	5815	423066	0.01375	1655049	21.17	18.95	0.01368	60
65	0.10659	81482	8685	387256	0.02243	1231983	21.17	15.12	0.02232	65
70	0.18315	72797	13333	332428	0.04011	844718	21.17	11.60	0.03992	70
75	0.28926	59464	17201	255719	0.06726	512289	21.17	8.62	0.06695	75
80	0.47428	42264	20045	160557	0.12484	256570	21.17	6.07	0.12430	80
85 +	1.00000	22219	22219	96013	0.23142	96013	21.17	4.32	0.22934	85 +

TABLE 4 POPULATION PROJECTION, USING FIXED AGE-SPECIFIC BIRTH AND DEATH RATES, IN THOUSANDS

Age at last birthday	1971 Total	Males	Females	1976 Total	Males	Females	1981 Total	Males	Females	Age at last birthday
0–4	129	66	63	116	59	57	104	53	51	0–4
5–9	127	65	62	129	66	63	116	59	57	5–9
10–14	104	53	51	127	65	62	129	66	63	10–14
15–19	87	45	42	104	53	51	127	65	62	15–19
20–24	101	51	50	86	44	42	104	53	51	20–24
25–29	134	68	66	101	51	50	86	44	42	25–29
30–34	165	87	78	134	68	66	100	51	49	30–34
35–39	123	63	60	163	86	77	132	67	65	35–39
40–44	115	56	59	122	62	60	162	85	77	40–44
45–49	116	49	67	113	55	58	120	61	59	45–49
50–54	94	39	55	113	48	65	110	53	57	50–54
55–59	115	48	67	90	37	53	108	45	63	55–59
60–64	129	54	75	106	43	63	84	33	51	60–64
65–69	115	49	66	113	45	68	94	36	58	65–69
70–74	88	33	55	94	37	57	93	34	59	70–74
75–79	59	19	40	65	22	43	68	24	44	75–79
80–84	33	11	22	36	11	25	39	12	27	80–84
85 +	16	5	11	18	5	13	20	5	15	85 +
All ages	1850	861	989	1830	857	973	1796	846	950	All ages

TABLE 5 OBSERVED AND PROJECTED VITAL RATES

Rates per thousand	Observed Total	Males	Females	Projected 1971 Males	Females	1976 Males	Females	1981 Males	Females	Stable Males	Females
Birth	14.81	16.33	13.50	15.10	12.54	13.19	11.05	12.38	10.50	13.96	12.82
Death	14.10	15.30	13.07	15.50	14.44	15.48	15.56	15.32	16.52	15.31	14.17
Increase	0.71	1.03	0.43	-0.40	-1.90	-2.30	-4.61	-2.95	-6.01		-1.3543

TABLE 6 RATES STANDARDIZED ON THREE STANDARD COUNTRIES

Standardized rates per thousand	England and Wales, 1961 Total	Males	Females	United States, 1960 Total	Males	Females	Mexico, 1960 Total	Males	Females
Birth	12.90	13.38*	12.20	13.14	12.62*	12.63	15.10	12.57*	14.69
Death	11.83	12.38*	11.31	9.58	11.32*	8.23	4.79	10.41*	3.85
Increase	1.07	1.00*	0.89	3.56	1.30*	4.40	10.31	2.16*	10.84

TABLE 7 VITAL STATISTICS AND RATES INFERRED FROM AGE DISTRIBUTIONS (FEMALES)

Vital statistics		Thompson Age range	NRR	$1000r$	Interval	Bourgeois-Pichat Age range	NRR	$1000b$	$1000d$	$1000r$	Coale
TFR	2.04	0–4	0.96	-1.40	27.43	5–29	0.49	7.33	33.68	-26.35	$1000b$
GRR	0.99	5–9	0.77	-9.33	27.40	30–54	0.84	10.12	16.49	-6.36	$1000d$
NRR	0.96	10–14	0.64	-16.73	27.35	55–79	1.21	26.87	19.75	7.12	$1000r$
Generation	28.01	15–19	0.74	-11.67	27.28	*50–74	0.97	15.46	16.53	-1.06	$1000k_1$
Sex ratio	105.02										$1000k_2$

TABLE 8 LESLIE MATRIX AND ITS ANALYSIS (FEMALES)

Start of age interval	Sub-diagonal	First row	Percent in stable population	Fisher values	Total reproductive values	Net maternity function	Matrix equation coefficient	Parameters Integral	Matrix
0	0.99666	0.00000	6.316	1.015	63119	0.00000	0.00000	λ_1 0.9933	0.9933
5	0.99817	0.00003	6.337	1.011	51540	0.00003	0.00003	λ_2 0.3824	0.3863
10	0.99831	0.02686	6.369	1.006	42803	0.00005	0.02672	+0.7620	+0.7384i
15	0.99752	0.15913	6.401	0.974	48521	0.05338	0.15804	r_1 -0.0014	-0.0014
20	0.99677	0.29265	6.429	0.808	53500	0.26271	0.28993	r_2 -0.0319	-0.0365
25	0.99563	0.27325	6.451	0.507	39570	0.31715	0.26984	+0.2211	+0.2178i
30	0.99438	0.15533	6.467	0.227	13747	0.22252	0.15272	c_1	8845
35	0.99137	0.05358	6.474	0.069	4076	0.08291	0.05239	c_2	9422
40	0.98699	0.01239	6.462	0.014	933	0.02187	0.01201		-25833i
45	0.97897	0.00114	6.421	0.001	67	0.00216	0.00110	$2\pi/y$ 28.412	28.854
50	0.96882	0.00002	6.329	0.000	1	0.00003	0.00002	Δ 7.428	
55	0.78571		29.544						

Stockholm, 1960

TABLE 1 DATA INPUT TO COMPUTATIONS

Age at last birthday	Population					Births, by age of mother	Deaths			Age at last birthday
	Total	Males	%	Females	%		Total	Males	Females	
0	9871	5092	1.3	4779	1.1	0	181	106	75	0
1–4	39860	20550	5.4	19310	4.5	0	22	12	10	1–4
5–9	49052	25132	6.6	23920	5.6	0	18	8	10	5–9
10–14	57792	29638	7.8	28154	6.5	0	18	12	6	10–14
15–19	57859	28379	7.5	29480	6.9	842	36	30	6	15–19
20–24	50530	24346	6.4	26184	6.1	2822	34	26	8	20–24
25–29	48402	24161	6.4	24241	5.6	3078	43	20	23	25–29
30–34	52996	26019	6.9	26977	6.3	2068	67	37	30	30–34
35–39	64543	31661	8.4	32882	7.6	1116	111	61	50	35–39
40–44	62294	29748	7.9	32546	7.6	284	173	95	78	40–44
45–49	63092	29476	7.8	33616	7.8	25	274	157	117	45–49
50–54	61374	27486	7.3	33888	7.9	0	418	241	177	50–54
55–59	52455	22834	6.0	29621	6.9	0	550	325	225	55–59
60–64	43964	18395	4.9	25569	5.9	0	744	468	276	60–64
65–69	36250	14359	3.8	21891	5.1	0	1049	627	422	65–69
70–74	27505	10428	2.8	17077	4.0		1319	669	650	70–74
75–79	17506	6325	1.7	11181	2.6		1323	597	726	75–79
80–84	8884	2948	0.8	5936	1.4	5244 M	968	393	575	80–84
85 +	3819	1050	0.3	2769	0.6	4991 F	925	314	611	85 +
All ages	808048	378027		430021		10235	8273	4198	4075	All ages

TABLE 2 LIFE TABLE FOR MALES

Age, x	nq_x	l_x	nd_x	nL_x	nm_x	T_x	$1000r_x$	$\overset{\circ}{e}_x$	nM_x	Age, x
0	0.02047	100000	2047	98356	0.02082	6902076	0.00	69.02	0.02082	0
1	0.00233	97953	228	391140	0.00058	6803720	0.00	69.46	0.00058	1
5	0.00159	97724	155	488232	0.00032	6412580	0.00	65.62	0.00032	5
10	0.00202	97569	197	487425	0.00040	5924348	0.00	60.72	0.00040	10
15	0.00529	97371	515	485636	0.00106	5436923	18.75	55.84	0.00105	15
20	0.00532	96857	515	482971	0.00107	4951286	15.08	51.12	0.00107	20
25	0.00413	96341	398	480745	0.00083	4468316	0.00	46.38	0.00083	25
30	0.00709	95943	680	478124	0.00142	3987570	0.00	41.56	0.00142	30
35	0.00959	95263	914	474203	0.00193	3509446	0.00	36.84	0.00193	35
40	0.01586	94350	1497	468326	0.00320	3035242	3.82	32.17	0.00319	40
45	0.02632	92853	2444	458654	0.00533	2566917	2.36	27.64	0.00533	45
50	0.04311	90409	3898	443039	0.00880	2108262	16.44	23.32	0.00877	50
55	0.06930	86511	5995	418779	0.01432	1665224	24.80	19.25	0.01423	55
60	0.12073	80515	9721	379952	0.02558	1246445	24.57	15.48	0.02544	60
65	0.19832	70795	14040	320131	0.04386	866494	24.57	12.24	0.04367	65
70	0.27766	56755	15759	244712	0.06440	546362	24.57	9.63	0.06415	70
75	0.38176	40996	15651	165208	0.09473	301650	24.57	7.36	0.09439	75
80	0.49954	25345	12661	94456	0.13404	136442	24.57	5.38	0.13331	80
85 +	*1.00000	12684	12684	41986	0.30211	41985	24.57	3.31	0.29905	85 +

TABLE 3 LIFE TABLE FOR FEMALES

Age, x	nq_x	l_x	nd_x	nL_x	nm_x	T_x	$1000r_x$	$\overset{\circ}{e}_x$	nM_x	Age, x
0	0.01550	100000	1550	98781	0.01569	7491046	0.00	74.91	0.01569	0
1	0.00207	98450	204	393204	0.00052	7392265	0.00	75.09	0.00052	1
5	0.00209	98246	205	490718	0.00042	6999062	0.00	71.24	0.00042	5
10	0.00106	98041	104	489922	0.00021	6508344	0.00	66.38	0.00021	10
15	0.00102	97937	100	489443	0.00020	6018422	7.04	61.45	0.00020	15
20	0.00154	97837	151	488883	0.00031	5528978	19.14	56.51	0.00031	20
25	0.00473	97686	462	487355	0.00095	5040096	0.00	51.59	0.00095	25
30	0.00555	97224	539	484827	0.00111	4552740	0.00	46.83	0.00111	30
35	0.00758	96685	732	481717	0.00152	4067914	0.00	42.07	0.00152	35
40	0.01192	95952	1143	477090	0.00240	3586196	0.00	37.37	0.00240	40
45	0.01726	94809	1637	470215	0.00348	3109106	0.00	32.79	0.00348	45
50	0.02583	93172	2407	460210	0.00523	2638892	7.32	28.32	0.00522	50
55	0.03742	90765	3397	445799	0.00762	2178681	20.48	24.00	0.00760	55
60	0.05304	87369	4634	426156	0.01087	1732882	33.38	19.83	0.01079	60
65	0.09317	82735	7708	396188	0.01946	1306726	33.38	15.79	0.01928	65
70	0.17596	75027	13201	344151	0.03836	910537	33.38	12.14	0.03806	70
75	0.28161	61825	17410	266517	0.06533	566386	33.38	9.15	0.06493	75
80	0.39632	44415	17603	180026	0.09778	299870	33.38	6.75	0.09687	80
85 +	*1.00000	26812	26812	119844	0.22373	119844	33.38	4.47	0.22066	85 +

TABLE 4 POPULATION PROJECTION, USING FIXED AGE-SPECIFIC BIRTH AND DEATH RATES, IN THOUSANDS

Age at last birthday	1965 Total	1965 Males	1965 Females	1970 Total	1970 Males	1970 Females	1975 Total	1975 Males	1975 Females	Age at last birthday
0–4	51	26	25	51	26	25	51	26	25	0–4
5–9	50	26	24	51	26	25	51	26	25	5–9
10–14	49	25	24	50	26	24	51	26	25	10–14
15–19	58	30	28	49	25	24	49	25	24	15–19
20–24	57	28	29	57	29	28	49	25	24	20–24
25–29	50	24	26	57	28	29	57	29	28	25–29
30–34	48	24	24	50	24	26	57	28	29	30–34
35–39	53	26	27	48	24	24	50	24	26	35–39
40–44	64	31	33	52	25	27	48	24	24	40–44
45–49	61	29	32	63	31	32	51	25	26	45–49
50–54	61	28	33	59	28	31	61	30	31	50–54
55–59	59	26	33	59	27	32	57	27	30	55–59
60–64	49	21	28	55	24	31	54	24	30	60–64
65–69	39	15	24	43	17	26	49	20	29	65–69
70–74	30	11	19	33	12	21	36	13	23	70–74
75–79	20	7	13	22	7	15	24	8	16	75–79
80–84	12	4	8	13	4	9	14	4	10	80–84
85 +	5	1	4	7	2	5	8	2	6	85 +
All ages	816	382	434	819	385	434	817	386	431	All ages

TABLE 5 OBSERVED AND PROJECTED VITAL RATES

Rates per thousand	Observed Total	Observed Males	Observed Females	Projected 1965 Males	Projected 1965 Females	Projected 1970 Males	Projected 1970 Females	Projected 1975 Males	Projected 1975 Females	Stable Males	Stable Females
Birth	12.67	13.87	11.61	13.88	11.65	13.97	11.30	13.49	11.48	12.74	11.63
Death	10.24	11.11	9.48	12.09	11.01	13.02	12.34	13.87	13.52	16.16	15.05
Increase	2.43	2.77	2.13	1.79	0.65	0.95	-0.55	-0.38	-2.05		-3.4185

TABLE 6 RATES STANDARDIZED ON THREE STANDARD COUNTRIES

Standardized rates per thousand	England and Wales, 1961 Total	Males	Females	United States, 1960 Total	Males	Females	Mexico, 1960 Total	Males	Females
Birth	12.15	13.31*	11.48	12.38	12.62*	11.89	14.42	11.25*	14.03
Death	10.99	11.70*	10.31	8.96	10.29*	7.53	4.44	9.15*	3.50
Increase	1.15	1.61*	1.17	3.42	2.33*	4.36	9.99	2.11*	10.53

TABLE 7 VITAL STATISTICS AND RATES INFERRED FROM AGE DISTRIBUTIONS (FEMALES)

Vital statistics		Thompson Age range	NRR	$1000r$	Interval	Bourgeois-Pichat Age range	NRR	$1000b$	$1000d$	$1000r$	Coale	
TFR	1.92	0–4	0.83	-6.88	27.43	5–29	1.02	12.64	12.04	0.60	$1000b$	13.64
GRR	0.93	5–9	0.80	-8.17	27.39	30–54	0.72	9.32	21.45	-12.13	$1000d$	12.69
NRR	0.91	10–14	0.89	-4.16	27.34	55–79	1.68	46.47	27.31	19.17	$1000r$	0.95
Generation	27.64	15–19	0.90	-4.07	27.26	*50–74	1.69	47.46	27.98	19.48	$1000k_1$	51.54
Sex ratio	105.1										$1000k_2$	0.81

TABLE 8 LESLIE MATRIX AND ITS ANALYSIS (FEMALES)

Start of age interval	Sub-diagonal	First row	Percent in stable population	Fisher values	Total reproductive values	Net maternity function	Matrix equation coefficient	Parameters	Integral	Matrix
0	0.99742	0.00000	5.772	1.008	24273	0.00000	0.00000	λ_1	0.9831	0.9831
5	0.99838	0.00000	5.857	0.993	23756	0.00000	0.00000	λ_2	0.3630	0.3592
10	0.99902	0.03423	5.948	0.978	27532	0.00000	0.03408		+0.7460	+0.7224i
15	0.99885	0.16340	6.045	0.928	27350	0.06817	0.16255	r_1	-0.0034	-0.0034
20	0.99687	0.28112	6.142	0.748	19592	0.25694	0.27935	r_2	-0.0374	-0.0418
25	0.99481	0.24379	6.228	0.454	10998	0.30176	0.24150		+0.2236	+0.2197i
30	0.99359	0.13241	6.302	0.201	5433	0.18124	0.13048	c_1		4388
35	0.99039	0.05108	6.370	0.065	2137	0.07973	0.05001	c_2		-3771
40	0.98559	0.01131	6.417	0.013	408	0.02030	0.01100			838i
45	0.97872	0.00089	6.434	0.001	32	0.00171	0.00085	$2\pi/y$	28.102	28.605
50	0.96868	0.00003	6.406	0.000	1	0.00000	0.00000	Δ	7.273	
55	0.78964		32.080							

Greater London, 1967

TABLE 1 DATA INPUT TO COMPUTATIONS

Age at last birthday	Population					Births, by age of mother	Deaths			Age at last birthday
	Total	Males	%	Females	%		Total	Males	Females	
0	135500	69500	1.9	66000	1.6	0	2470	1386	1084	0
1–4	501500	257200	6.9	244300	6.0	0	368	198	170	1–4
5–9	499399	255399	6.8	244000	6.0	0	177	115	62	5–9
10–14	465400	239800	6.4	225600	5.6	0	137	86	51	10–14
15–19	546800	270600	7.2	276200	6.8	12566	331	218	113	15–19
20–24	649900	315200	8.4	334900	8.2	45968	400	264	136	20–24
25–29	521800	267100	7.1	254700	6.3	40244	340	222	118	25–29
30–34	469300	242900	6.5	226400	5.6	22084	498	304	194	30–34
35–39	475000	240300	6.4	234700	5.8	10521	689	379	310	35–39
40–44	503100	248900	6.6	254200	6.3	2730	1301	755	546	40–44
45–49	525600	254400	6.8	271200	6.7	224	2056	1207	849	45–49
50–54	537300	256800	6.9	280500	6.9	0	3596	2242	1354	50–54
55–59	547100	262900	7.0	284200	7.0	0	6178	4161	2017	55–59
60–64	468500	218900	5.8	249600	6.1	0	8159	5269	2890	60–64
65–69	349200	146800	3.9	202400	5.0	0	9775	5418	4357	65–69
70–74	253400	91900	2.5	161500	4.0	0	11731	6895	4835	70–74
75–79	165311	52895	1.4	112416	2.8	0	10917	6073	4844	75–79
80–84	97153	28062	0.7	69091	1.7	68739 M	8585	4117	4468	80–84
85+	93237	24144	0.6	69093	1.7	65598 F	17579	3723	13855	85+
All ages	7804500	3743700		4060800		134337	85287	43032	42255	All ages

TABLE 2 LIFE TABLE FOR MALES

Age, x	$_nq_x$	l_x	$_nd_x$	$_nL_x$	$_nm_x$	T_x	$1000r_x$	$\overset{\circ}{e}_x$	$_nM_x$	Age, x
0	0.01953	100000	1953	98495	0.01983	6939057	7.10	69.39	0.01994	0
1	0.00304	98047	298	391318	0.00076	6840562	7.10	69.77	0.00077	1
5	0.00224	97749	219	488196	0.00045	6449244	30.40	65.98	0.00045	5
10	0.00179	97530	175	487248	0.00036	5961048	0.00	61.12	0.00036	10
15	0.00402	97355	391	485845	0.00081	5473800	0.00	56.23	0.00081	15
20	0.00418	96964	405	483807	0.00084	4987955	0.47	51.44	0.00084	20
25	0.00416	96558	402	481829	0.00083	4504148	25.13	46.65	0.00083	25
30	0.00625	96157	601	479356	0.00125	4022319	9.37	41.83	0.00125	30
35	0.00786	95556	751	476077	0.00158	3542963	0.00	37.08	0.00158	35
40	0.01506	94805	1428	470757	0.00303	3066887	0.00	32.35	0.00303	40
45	0.02347	93377	2192	461924	0.00474	2596129	0.00	27.80	0.00474	45
50	0.04281	91186	3903	447102	0.00873	2134205	0.00	23.41	0.00873	50
55	0.07632	87282	6661	420865	0.01583	1687103	0.00	19.33	0.01583	55
60	0.11426	80621	9212	381229	0.02416	1266238	22.08	15.71	0.02407	60
65	0.17075	71409	12193	328571	0.03711	885010	22.08	12.39	0.03691	65
70	0.31839	59216	18853	250138	0.07537	556439	22.08	9.40	0.07503	70
75	0.44389	40362	17917	155550	0.11518	306301	22.08	7.59	0.11481	75
80	0.52561	22446	11798	80240	0.14703	150751	22.08	6.72	0.14671	80
85+	1.00000	10648	10648	70510	0.15101	70510	22.08	6.62	0.15420	85+

TABLE 3 LIFE TABLE FOR FEMALES

Age, x	$_nq_x$	l_x	$_nd_x$	$_nL_x$	$_nm_x$	T_x	$1000r_x$	$\overset{\circ}{e}_x$	$_nM_x$	Age, x
0	0.01613	100000	1613	98773	0.01633	7698423	7.16	76.98	0.01642	0
1	0.00275	98387	271	392761	0.00069	7599650	7.16	77.24	0.00070	1
5	0.00126	98116	123	490273	0.00025	7206889	31.50	73.45	0.00025	5
10	0.00113	97993	111	489703	0.00023	6716617	0.00	68.54	0.00023	10
15	0.00204	97882	200	488929	0.00041	6226913	0.00	63.62	0.00041	15
20	0.00203	97682	198	487920	0.00041	5737984	7.69	58.74	0.00041	20
25	0.00233	97484	227	486896	0.00047	5250064	38.56	53.86	0.00046	25
30	0.00428	97256	417	485327	0.00086	4763168	7.32	48.98	0.00086	30
35	0.00658	96840	638	482733	0.00132	4277841	0.00	44.17	0.00132	35
40	0.01069	96202	1028	478617	0.00215	3795108	0.00	39.45	0.00215	40
45	0.01554	95174	1479	472426	0.00313	3316491	0.00	34.85	0.00313	45
50	0.02387	93695	2236	463244	0.00483	2844065	0.00	30.35	0.00483	50
55	0.03494	91459	3196	449887	0.00710	2380821	4.20	26.03	0.00710	55
60	0.05683	88264	5016	429897	0.01167	1930934	30.97	21.88	0.01158	60
65	0.10295	83247	8570	395948	0.02164	1501037	30.97	18.03	0.02153	65
70	0.14018	74677	10468	348050	0.03008	1105089	30.97	14.80	0.02994	70
75	0.19585	64209	12576	290435	0.04330	757039	30.97	11.79	0.04309	75
80	0.27985	51633	14449	222373	0.06498	466604	30.97	9.04	0.06467	80
85+	1.00000	37184	37184	244231	0.15225	244231	30.97	6.57	0.20054	85+

TABLE 4 POPULATION PROJECTION, USING FIXED AGE-SPECIFIC BIRTH AND DEATH RATES, IN THOUSANDS

Age at last birthday	1972			1977			1982			Age at last birthday
	Total	Males	Females	Total	Males	Females	Total	Males	Females	
0–4	669	342	327	663	339	324	636	325	311	0–4
5–9	636	326	310	668	341	327	661	338	323	5–9
10–14	499	255	244	534	325	309	666	340	326	10–14
15–19	464	239	225	497	254	243	633	324	309	15–19
20–24	545	269	276	463	238	225	496	253	243	20–24
25–29	648	314	334	543	268	275	461	237	224	25–29
30–34	520	266	254	645	312	333	541	267	274	30–34
35–39	466	241	225	517	264	253	641	310	331	35–39
40–44	471	238	233	462	239	223	511	261	250	40–44
45–49	495	244	251	463	233	230	454	234	220	45–49
50–54	512	246	266	482	236	246	451	226	225	50–54
55–59	514	242	272	490	232	258	462	223	239	55–59
60–64	510	238	272	479	219	260	457	210	247	60–64
65–69	419	189	230	455	205	250	429	189	240	65–69
70–74	290	112	178	346	144	202	376	156	220	70–74
75–79	192	57	135	217	69	148	258	89	169	75–79
80–84	113	27	86	132	29	103	150	35	114	80–84
85 +	101	25	76	119	24	95	139	26	113	85 +
All ages	8064	3870	4194	8275	3971	4304	8422	4044	4378	All ages

TABLE 5 OBSERVED AND PROJECTED VITAL RATES

Rates per thousand	Observed			Projected						Stable	
				1972		1977		1982			
	Total	Males	Females	Males	Females	Males	Females	Males	Females	Males	Females
Birth	17.21	18.36	16.15	18.31	16.12	16.98	14.95	16.11	14.20	17.77	15.34
Death	10.93	11.49	10.41	12.04	11.17	12.72	12.34	13.35	13.33	11.85	10.42
Increase	6.28	6.87	5.75	6.27	4.95	4.26	2.61	2.76	0.87		5.9152

TABLE 6 RATES STANDARDIZED ON THREE STANDARD COUNTRIES

Standardized rates per thousand	England and Wales, 1961			United States, 1960			Mexico, 1960		
	Total	Males	Females	Total	Males	Females	Total	Males	Females
Birth	15.71	17.23*	14.87	16.03	15.94*	15.42	18.74	15.45*	18.25
Death	10.07	11.25*	8.67	8.30	9.97*	6.45	4.21	8.32*	3.10
Increase	5.64	5.98*	6.20	7.73	5.96*	8.97	14.52	7.13*	15.15

TABLE 7 VITAL STATISTICS AND RATES INFERRED FROM AGE DISTRIBUTIONS (FEMALES)

Vital statistics		Thompson				Bourgeois-Pichat					Coale
		Age range	NRR	1000r	Interval	Age range	NRR	1000b	1000d	1000r	
TFR	2.47	0–4	1.16	5.52	27.44	5–29	0.76	11.20	21.15	−9.96	1000b
GRR	1.21	5–9	0.91	−3.28	27.41	30–54	0.69	7.28	21.03	−13.76	1000d
NRR	1.18	10–14	0.87	−5.17	27.36	55–79	1.77	52.57	31.51	21.06	1000r
Generation	27.31	15–19	1.03	1.13	27.29	*30–54	0.69	7.28	21.03	−13.76	$1000k_1$
Sex ratio	104.79										$1000k_2$

TABLE 8 LESLIE MATRIX AND ITS ANALYSIS (FEMALES)

Start of age interval	Sub-diagonal	First row	Percent in stable population	Fisher values	Total reproductive values	Net maternity function	Matrix equation coefficient	Parameters		
									Integral	Matrix
0	0.99743	0.00000	7.914	1.032	320340	0.00000	0.00000	λ_1	1.0300	1.0300
5	0.99884	0.00000	7.663	1.066	260128	0.00000	0.00000	λ_2	0.3647	0.3707
10	0.99842	0.05451	7.431	1.099	248024	0.00000	0.05431		+0.7758	+0.7508i
15	0.99794	0.21908	7.203	1.078	297703	0.10862	0.21792	r_1	0.0059	0.0059
20	0.99790	0.35405	6.979	0.886	296505	0.32722	0.35145	r_2	−0.0308	−0.0355
25	0.99678	0.30631	6.761	0.548	139611	0.37567	0.30342		+0.2263	+0.2224i
30	0.99466	0.17057	6.543	0.249	56417	0.23117	0.16842	c_1		36977
35	0.99147	0.06658	6.318	0.081	19016	0.10567	0.06538	c_2		−10821
40	0.98706	0.01386	6.081	0.015	3775	0.02510	0.01350			−96971i
45	0.98056	0.00099	5.828	0.001	271	0.00191	0.00095	$2\pi/y$	27.769	28.248
50	0.97116	0.00000	5.548	0.000	2	0.00000	0.00000	Δ	7.649	
55	0.82066		25.732							

Sydney Metropolitan Area, 1966

TABLE 1 DATA INPUT TO COMPUTATIONS

Age at last birthday	Population					Births, by age of mother	Deaths			Age at last birthday
	Total	Males	%	Females	%		Total	Males	Females	
0	41320	21302	1.8	20018	1.6	0	838	496	342	0
1–4	173161	88715	7.4	84446	6.8	0	163	100	63	1–4
5–9	214552	109513	9.1	105039	8.5	0	96	50	46	5–9
10–14	203802	103999	8.6	99803	8.0	20	82	47	35	10–14
15–19	217985	109619	9.1	108366	8.7	4971	172	116	56	15–19
20–24	193524	96523	8.0	97001	7.8	13909	198	139	59	20–24
25–29	164278	83405	6.9	80873	6.5	14156	161	111	50	25–29
30–34	148984	76793	6.4	72191	5.8	7624	205	127	78	30–34
35–39	168669	86624	7.2	82045	6.6	3780	408	248	160	35–39
40–44	176885	89224	7.4	87661	7.1	997	609	370	239	40–44
45–49	156956	78175	6.5	78781	6.3	57	858	533	325	45–49
50–54	146461	72481	6.0	73980	6.0	0	1363	831	532	50–54
55–59	121238	59519	4.9	61719	5.0	0	1747	1124	623	55–59
60–64	95289	44696	3.7	50593	4.1	0	2154	1410	744	60–64
65–69	78108	32690	2.7	45418	3.7	0	2748	1654	1094	65–69
70–74	62252	23706	2.0	38546	3.1		3325	1765	1560	70–74
75–79	46139	16985	1.4	29154	2.3		3894	1915	1979	75–79
80–84	24346	8236	0.7	16110	1.3	23464 M	3230	1340	1890	80–84
85 +	12396	3457	0.3	8939	0.7	22050 F	2863	864	1999	85 +
All ages	2446345	1205662		1240683		45514	25114	13240	11874	All ages

TABLE 2 LIFE TABLE FOR MALES

Age, x	nq_x	l_x	nd_x	nL_x	nm_x	T_x	$1000r_x$	$\overset{\circ}{e}_x$	nM_x	Age, x
0	0.02289	100000	2289	98292	0.02328	6651579	0.00	66.52	0.02328	0
1	0.00449	97711	439	389574	0.00113	6553287	0.00	67.07	0.00113	1
5	0.00228	97272	222	485807	0.00046	6163713	4.99	63.37	0.00046	5
10	0.00226	97051	219	484766	0.00045	5677906	0.00	58.50	0.00045	10
15	0.00528	96832	512	482977	0.00106	5193140	6.45	53.63	0.00106	15
20	0.00718	96320	692	479895	0.00144	4710162	26.00	48.90	0.00144	20
25	0.00664	95628	635	476573	0.00133	4230267	21.45	44.24	0.00133	25
30	0.00824	94993	783	473157	0.00165	3753694	0.00	39.52	0.00165	30
35	0.01422	94211	1340	467940	0.00286	3280537	0.00	34.82	0.00286	35
40	0.02056	92871	1910	459941	0.00415	2812597	5.86	30.28	0.00415	40
45	0.03366	90962	3062	447781	0.00684	2352656	13.61	25.86	0.00682	45
50	0.05603	87900	4925	428121	0.01150	1904875	15.30	21.67	0.01147	50
55	0.09097	82975	7548	397290	0.01900	1476755	28.44	17.80	0.01888	55
60	0.14708	75427	11094	350852	0.03162	1079465	11.83	14.31	0.03155	60
65	0.22564	64333	14516	286327	0.05070	728613	11.83	11.33	0.05060	65
70	0.31446	49817	15666	210012	0.07459	442285	11.83	8.88	0.07445	70
75	0.43785	34151	14953	132379	0.11296	232273	11.83	6.80	0.11275	75
80	0.56717	19198	10889	66804	0.16299	99895	11.83	5.20	0.16270	80
85 +	1.00000	8310	8310	33090	0.25112	33090	11.83	3.98	0.24993	85 +

TABLE 3 LIFE TABLE FOR FEMALES

Age, x	nq_x	l_x	nd_x	nL_x	nm_x	T_x	$1000r_x$	$\overset{\circ}{e}_x$	nM_x	Age, x
0	0.01687	100000	1687	98723	0.01708	7307309	0.00	73.07	0.01708	0
1	0.00298	98313	293	392403	0.00075	7208586	0.00	73.32	0.00075	1
5	0.00219	98021	214	489567	0.00044	6816183	4.05	69.54	0.00044	5
10	0.00175	97806	171	488611	0.00035	6326615	0.00	64.69	0.00035	10
15	0.00258	97635	252	487571	0.00052	5838004	2.35	59.79	0.00052	15
20	0.00304	97383	296	486185	0.00061	5350433	28.68	54.94	0.00061	20
25	0.00310	97087	301	484729	0.00062	4864248	28.83	50.10	0.00062	25
30	0.00539	96786	522	482757	0.00108	4379519	0.00	45.25	0.00108	30
35	0.00971	96264	934	479146	0.00195	3896762	0.00	40.48	0.00195	35
40	0.01355	95330	1292	473627	0.00273	3417616	1.23	35.85	0.00273	40
45	0.02049	94038	1927	465786	0.00414	2943989	12.49	31.31	0.00413	45
50	0.03546	92111	3267	452905	0.00721	2478203	17.29	26.90	0.00719	50
55	0.04949	88845	4397	433804	0.01014	2025298	27.59	22.80	0.01009	55
60	0.07124	84447	6016	408148	0.01474	1591494	12.36	18.85	0.01471	60
65	0.11429	78431	8964	371171	0.02415	1183346	12.36	15.09	0.02409	65
70	0.18503	69467	12853	316780	0.04057	812175	12.36	11.69	0.04047	70
75	0.29197	56614	16530	242886	0.06806	495395	12.36	8.75	0.06788	75
80	0.45714	40084	18324	155701	0.11769	252508	12.36	6.30	0.11732	80
85 +	*1.00000	21760	21760	96807	0.22478	96807	12.36	4.45	0.22363	85 +

TABLE 4 POPULATION PROJECTION, USING FIXED AGE-SPECIFIC BIRTH AND DEATH RATES, IN THOUSANDS

Age at last birthday	1971 Total	1971 Males	1971 Females	1976 Total	1976 Males	1976 Females	1981 Total	1981 Males	1981 Females	Age at last birthday
0–4	233	120	113	251	129	122	261	134	127	0–4
5–9	214	110	104	232	119	113	249	128	121	5–9
10–14	214	109	105	213	109	104	232	119	113	10–14
15–19	204	104	100	214	109	105	213	109	104	15–19
20–24	217	109	108	202	103	99	212	108	104	20–24
25–29	193	96	97	216	108	108	201	102	99	25–29
30–34	164	83	81	191	95	96	214	107	107	30–34
35–39	148	76	72	162	82	80	190	94	96	35–39
40–44	166	85	81	146	75	71	159	80	79	40–44
45–49	173	87	86	163	83	80	143	73	70	45–49
50–54	152	75	77	167	83	84	157	79	78	50–54
55–59	138	67	71	142	69	73	157	77	80	55–59
60–64	111	53	58	126	59	67	130	61	69	60–64
65–69	82	36	46	96	43	53	109	48	61	65–69
70–74	63	24	39	66	27	39	76	31	45	70–74
75–79	45	15	30	45	15	30	47	17	30	75–79
80–84	28	9	19	27	8	19	27	8	19	80–84
85 +	14	4	10	16	4	12	16	4	12	85 +
All ages	2559	1262	1297	2675	1320	1355	2793	1379	1414	All ages

TABLE 5 OBSERVED AND PROJECTED VITAL RATES

Rates per thousand	Observed Total	Observed Males	Observed Females	Projected 1971 Males	Projected 1971 Females	Projected 1976 Males	Projected 1976 Females	Projected 1981 Males	Projected 1981 Females	Stable Males	Stable Females
Birth	18.60	19.46	17.77	20.37	18.64	20.55	18.84	20.07	18.43	19.61	18.23
Death	10.27	10.98	9.57	11.07	9.84	11.18	10.01	11.36	10.01	11.76	10.38
Increase	8.34	8.48	8.20	9.30	8.80	9.37	8.83	8.71	8.42		7.8519

TABLE 6 RATES STANDARDIZED ON THREE STANDARD COUNTRIES

Standardized rates per thousand	England and Wales, 1961 Total	Males	Females	United States, 1960 Total	Males	Females	Mexico, 1960 Total	Males	Females
Birth	16.76	18.32*	15.73	17.09	16.97*	16.31	19.96	16.22*	19.29
Death	12.77	13.90*	11.78	10.39	12.09*	8.62	5.26	9.71*	4.08
Increase	3.99	4.42*	3.96	6.70	4.88*	7.70	14.70	6.51*	15.21

TABLE 7 VITAL STATISTICS AND RATES INFERRED FROM AGE DISTRIBUTIONS (FEMALES)

Vital statistics		Thompson Age range	NRR	1000r	Interval	Bourgeois-Pichat Age range	NRR	1000b	1000d	1000r	Coale	
TFR	2.64	0–4	1.17	5.63	27.42	5–29	1.33	19.43	8.90	10.53	1000b	17.85
GRR	1.28	5–9	1.24	7.78	27.38	30–54	0.92	11.72	15.01	−3.29	1000d	11.71
NRR	1.24	10–14	1.22	7.22	27.31	55–79	1.30	19.20	9.56	9.64	1000r	6.14
Generation	27.32	15–19	1.36	10.84	27.20	*40–64	1.69	34.82	15.33	19.49	$1000k_1$	−2.83
Sex ratio	106.4										$1000k_2$	0.

TABLE 8 LESLIE MATRIX AND ITS ANALYSIS (FEMALES)

Start of age interval	Sub-diagonal	First row	Percent in stable population	Fisher values	Total reproductive values	Net maternity function	Matrix equation coefficient	Parameters Integral	Parameters Matrix
0	0.99682	0.00000	8.780	1.038	108456	0.00000	0.00000	λ_1 1.0400	1.0401
5	0.99805	0.00024	8.415	1.083	113785	0.00000	0.00024	λ_2 0.3689	0.3737
10	0.99787	0.05469	8.075	1.129	112641	0.00047	0.05442	+0.7912	+0.7653i
15	0.99716	0.22467	7.747	1.119	121312	0.10836	0.22305	r_1 0.0079	0.0079
20	0.99700	0.37820	7.428	0.934	90572	0.33774	0.37440	r_2 −0.0272	−0.0321
25	0.99593	0.33337	7.120	0.580	46925	0.41105	0.32903	+0.2269	+0.2233i
30	0.99252	0.18004	6.818	0.258	18656	0.24700	0.17697	c_1	12540
35	0.98848	0.06819	6.506	0.082	6767	0.10695	0.06652	c_2	−13375
40	0.98344	0.01436	6.183	0.015	1329	0.02610	0.01386		2592i
45	0.97235	0.00086	5.847	0.001	69	0.00163	0.00082	$2\pi/y$ 27.692	28.138
50	0.95782	0.00002	5.466	0.000	1	0.00000	0.00000	Δ 3.420	
55	0.79787		21.615						

CHAPTER 18

Continents and Other Pooled Data

The following pages offer a start for supranational demographic computations. Data on population, births, and deaths for groups of countries were added in the same categories of age and sex as shown in Table 1 of the preceding Main Tables. The same program that served for individual countries was applied here to the totals, and results represent a continent or other region. Such pooling is useful in the degree in which the areas combined are demographically homogeneous.

Lists are provided below of the countries within each of the regions. Footnotes on sources will be found for individual countries in the tabulations at the end of Part V.

Central America, 1964–66
    Costa Rica, 1966
    Guatemala, 1964
    Honduras, 1966
    Nicaragua, 1965
    Panama, 1966 (excluding Canal Zone)
West Indies, 1963–64
    Barbados, 1963
    Guadaloupe, 1964
    Jamaica, 1963
    Martinique, 1963
    Puerto Rico, 1964
    St. Lucia, 1963
    Trinidad and Tobago, 1964
European Common Market, 1965
    Belgium, 1965

France, 1965
West Germany, 1965
Italy, 1965
Luxembourg, 1965
Netherlands, 1965
(Same countries for 1955 and 1960)
European Free Trade Association, 1965
  Austria, 1965
  Denmark, 1965
  Norway, 1965
  Portugal, 1965
  Sweden, 1965
  Switzerland, 1965
  United Kingdom,
    England and Wales, 1965
    Scotland, 1965
  (Same countries for 1955 and 1960)
Comecon, 1965
  Bulgaria, 1965
  Czechoslovakia, 1965
  East Germany, 1965
  Hungary, 1965
  Poland, 1965
  Romania, 1965
  (Same countries for 1955 and 1960)
Europe, 1965
  Countries of Common Market, EFTA, and COMECON shown above, plus
  Finland, 1965
  Greece, 1965
  Iceland, 1965
  Ireland, 1965
  Malta and Gozo, 1965
  Spain, 1965
  Yugoslavia, 1965
  (Same countries for 1955 and 1960)

Other Supranational Groupings

Other groups of countries seemed too incomplete, or consisting of data too uncertain, to include in the Main Tables, but we do show them in the Summary Table of Part I. These include:

Subsaharan Africa, 1960–61
   Cameroon (West), 1964
   Central African Republic (African Population), 1960
   South Africa (Colored Population), 1961
   Southwest Africa, 1960
   Togo, 1961
   Reunion, 1961
South America, 1963–65
   Chile, 1965
   Colombia, 1965
   Ecuador, 1965
   French Guiana, 1964
   Peru, 1963
   Venezuela, 1964
Southeast Asia, 1960–61
   China (Taiwan), 1960
   Indonesia, 1961
   Philippines, 1960
   Sarawak, 1961
   Thailand, 1960

See Part I for substantive analysis of some of the results for Europe and the West Indies. The three groups of states are taken from *World Population*, which reports how they were selected.

Central America, 1964-66

TABLE 1 DATA INPUT TO COMPUTATIONS

Age at last birthday	Population					Births, by age of mother	Deaths			Age at last birthday
	Total	Males	%	Females	%		Total	Males	Females	
0	462898	234684	4.2	228214	4.1	0	31210	17062	14148	0
1–4	1610459	817941	14.5	792518	14.1	0	25203	12473	12730	1–4
5–9	1829615	930446	16.5	899169	16.0	0	7158	3600	3558	5–9
10–14	1444564	737577	13.1	706987	12.6	881	2816	1555	1261	10–14
15–19	1110840	541418	9.6	569422	10.1	77765	3004	1597	1407	15–19
20–24	902526	435334	7.7	467192	8.3	136165	3226	1689	1537	20–24
25–29	761901	368040	6.5	393861	7.0	115045	3229	1715	1514	25–29
30–34	665194	329587	5.9	335607	6.0	79113	3395	1817	1578	30–34
35–39	583612	289021	5.1	294591	5.2	54905	3433	1803	1630	35–39
40–44	471632	236874	4.2	234758	4.2	17866	3199	1733	1466	40–44
45–49	367461	187632	3.3	179829	3.2	3748	3197	1818	1379	45–49
50–54	306491	152328	2.7	154163	2.7	308	3548	1938	1610	50–54
55–59	220192	110763	2.0	109429	1.9	0	3616	1978	1638	55–59
60–64	203090	101863	1.8	101227	1.8	0	5261	2781	2480	60–64
65–69	124711	63392	1.1	61319	1.1	0	4723	2463	2260	65–69
70–74	83694	41488	0.7	42206	0.8		4507	2304	2203	70–74
75–79	48146	24011	0.4	24135	0.4		3497	1776	1721	75–79
80–84	27738	12670	0.2	15068	0.3	249109 M	3100	1451	1649	80–84
85 +	21831	9714	0.2	12117	0.2	236687 F	4120	1822	2298	85 +
All ages	11246595	5624783		5621812		485796	121442	63375	58067	All ages

TABLE 2 LIFE TABLE FOR MALES

Age, x	$_nq_x$	l_x	$_nd_x$	$_nL_x$	$_nm_x$	T_x	$1000r_x$	$\overset{\circ}{e}_x$	$_nM_x$	Age, x
0	0.06939	100000	6939	95846	0.07240	5709372	6.85	57.09	0.07270	0
1	0.05846	93061	5441	357753	0.01521	5613526	6.85	60.32	0.01525	1
5	0.01882	87620	1649	433979	0.00380	5255773	29.65	59.98	0.00387	5
10	0.01044	85971	897	427529	0.00210	4821794	51.44	56.09	0.00211	10
15	0.01474	85074	1254	422384	0.00297	4394265	49.80	51.65	0.00295	15
20	0.01928	83820	1616	415194	0.00389	3971881	34.74	47.39	0.00388	20
25	0.02308	82204	1897	406397	0.00467	3556687	23.14	43.27	0.00465	25
30	0.02723	80307	2187	396175	0.00552	3150291	18.68	39.23	0.00551	30
35	0.03077	78121	2404	384707	0.00625	2754116	26.73	35.25	0.00624	35
40	0.03607	75717	2731	371978	0.00734	2369410	35.61	31.29	0.00732	40
45	0.04753	72986	3469	356587	0.00973	1997431	34.35	27.37	0.00969	45
50	0.06204	69517	4313	337248	0.01279	1640844	39.58	23.60	0.01272	50
55	0.08595	65204	5604	312712	0.01792	1303596	21.48	19.99	0.01786	55
60	0.12880	59600	7676	279571	0.02746	990884	36.53	16.63	0.02730	60
65	0.17832	51924	9259	237051	0.03906	711313	36.53	13.70	0.03885	65
70	0.24503	42665	10454	187362	0.05580	474262	36.53	11.12	0.05553	70
75	0.31325	32211	10090	135699	0.07436	286900	35.53	8.91	0.07397	75
80	0.44458	22121	9834	85369	0.11520	151201	36.53	6.84	0.11452	80
85 +	1.00000	12286	12286	65832	0.18663	65832	36.53	5.36	0.18757	85 +

TABLE 3 LIFE TABLE FOR FEMALES

Age, x	$_nq_x$	l_x	$_nd_x$	$_nL_x$	$_nm_x$	T_x	$1000r_x$	$\overset{\circ}{e}_x$	$_nM_x$	Age, x
0	0.05960	100000	5960	96542	0.06173	5911649	7.42	59.12	0.06199	0
1	0.06152	94040	5785	361101	0.01602	5815107	7.42	61.84	0.01606	1
5	0.01921	88255	1696	437037	0.00388	5454006	30.67	61.80	0.00396	5
10	0.00881	86560	763	430759	0.00177	5016968	43.24	57.96	0.00178	10
15	0.01234	85797	1059	426467	0.00248	4586210	38.98	53.45	0.00247	15
20	0.01637	84738	1387	420333	0.00330	4159742	33.63	49.09	0.00329	20
25	0.01908	83351	1591	412886	0.00385	3739410	29.16	44.86	0.00384	25
30	0.02329	81760	1904	404166	0.00471	3326523	24.34	40.69	0.00470	30
35	0.02734	79857	2183	393926	0.00554	2922358	30.23	36.60	0.00553	35
40	0.03085	77673	2396	382513	0.00626	2528431	42.97	32.55	0.00624	40
45	0.03779	75277	2845	369547	0.00770	2145918	34.12	28.51	0.00767	45
50	0.05123	72432	3711	353332	0.01050	1776371	38.93	24.52	0.01044	50
55	0.07265	68722	4992	331899	0.01504	1423039	25.05	20.71	0.01497	55
60	0.11637	63729	7415	301059	0.02463	1091140	30.20	17.12	0.02450	60
65	0.16987	56313	9566	258366	0.03702	790081	30.20	14.03	0.03686	65
70	0.23195	46747	10843	206907	0.05241	531715	30.20	11.37	0.05220	70
75	0.30370	35904	10904	152236	0.07163	324808	30.20	9.05	0.07131	75
80	0.42896	25000	10724	97532	0.10995	172572	30.20	6.90	0.10944	80
85 +	1.00000	14276	14276	75040	0.19025	75040	30.20	5.26	0.18965	85 +

TABLE 4 POPULATION PROJECTION, USING FIXED AGE-SPECIFIC BIRTH AND DEATH RATES, IN THOUSANDS

Age at last birthday	1970 Total	Males	Females	1975 Total	Males	Females	1980 Total	Males	Females	Age at last birthday
0–4	2411	1231	1180	2875	1468	1407	3449	1761	1688	0–4
5–9	1982	1007	975	2305	1178	1127	2749	1405	1344	5–9
10–14	1803	917	886	1953	992	961	2272	1161	1111	10–14
15–19	1429	729	700	1783	906	877	1931	980	951	15–19
20–24	1093	532	561	1406	716	690	1755	890	855	20–24
25–29	885	426	459	1072	521	551	1379	701	678	25–29
30–34	745	359	386	864	415	449	1048	508	540	30–34
35–39	647	320	327	724	348	376	841	403	438	35–39
40–44	565	279	286	627	309	318	702	337	365	40–44
45–49	454	227	227	544	268	276	604	297	307	45–49
50–54	349	177	172	432	215	217	517	253	264	50–54
55–59	286	141	145	327	165	162	403	199	204	55–59
60–64	198	99	99	257	126	131	294	147	147	60–64
65–69	173	86	87	169	84	85	220	107	113	65–69
70–74	99	50	49	138	68	70	134	66	68	70–74
75–79	61	30	31	72	36	36	100	49	51	75–79
80–84	30	15	15	39	19	20	46	23	23	80–84
85 +	22	10	12	24	12	12	30	15	15	85 +
All ages	13232	6635	6597	15611	7846	7765	18474	9302	9172	All ages

TABLE 5 OBSERVED AND PROJECTED VITAL RATES

Rates per thousand	Observed Total	Males	Females	Projected 1970 Males	Females	1975 Males	Females	1980 Males	Females	Stable Males	Females
Birth	43.19	44.29	42.10	44.27	42.32	45.05	43.26	45.47	43.82	43.89	43.10
Death	10.80	11.27	10.33	11.18	10.20	11.25	10.27	11.31	10.40	11.34	10.54
Increase	32.40	33.02	31.77	33.09	32.12	33.81	32.98	34.16	33.42		32.5568

TABLE 6 RATES STANDARDIZED ON THREE STANDARD COUNTRIES

Standardized rates per thousand	England and Wales, 1961 Total	Males	Females	United States, 1960 Total	Males	Females	Mexico, 1960 Total	Males	Females
Birth	40.11	47.48*	37.88	40.84	43.44*	39.21	45.08	45.55*	43.81
Death	16.03	26.17*	17.02	14.30	21.16*	14.25	10.69	10.75*	10.23
Increase	24.08	21.32*	20.85	26.54	22.28*	24.96	34.39	34.81*	33.58

TABLE 7 VITAL STATISTICS AND RATES INFERRED FROM AGE DISTRIBUTIONS (FEMALES)

Vital statistics		Thompson Age range	NRR	1000r	Interval	Bourgeois-Pichat Age range	NRR	1000b	1000d	1000r	Coale	
TFR	6.21	0–4	2.37	31.73	27.21	5–29	2.83	47.75	9.20	38.54	1000b	45.05
GRR	3.03	5–9	2.57	35.67	27.13	30–54	2.53	46.29	11.95	34.33	1000d	10.79
NRR	2.48	10–14	2.39	31.35	27.05	55–79	2.63	49.26	13.48	35.78	1000r	34.26
Generation	27.84	15–19	2.28	30.61	26.95	*20–44	2.17	37.62	9.00	28.62	1000k_1	0.
Sex ratio	105.2										1000k_2	0.

TABLE 8 LESLIE MATRIX AND ITS ANALYSIS (FEMALES)

Start of age interval	Sub-diagonal	First row	Percent in stable population	Fisher values	Total reproductive values	Net maternity function	Matrix equation coefficient
0	0.95497	0.00000	18.230	1.184	1208377	0.00000	0.00000
5	0.98563	0.00137	14.785	1.460	1312515	0.00000	0.00131
10	0.99004	0.15213	12.375	1.742	1231729	0.00262	0.14319
15	0.98562	0.47251	10.405	1.890	1076339	0.28376	0.44032
20	0.98229	0.54480	8.709	1.691	789880	0.59688	0.59223
25	0.97888	0.58290	7.265	1.250	492173	0.58759	0.52589
30	0.97467	0.46532	6.040	0.798	267891	0.46419	0.41095
35	0.97103	0.29017	4.999	0.399	117589	0.35771	0.24977
40	0.96611	0.10729	4.123	0.130	30586	0.14183	0.08968
45	0.95613	0.02537	3.383	0.027	4913	0.03753	0.02048
50	0.93934	0.00223	2.747	0.002	346	0.00344	0.00172
55	0.80567		6.939				

Parameters

	Integral	Matrix
λ_1	1.1768	1.1775
λ_2	0.4015	0.4124
	+0.7716	+0.7531i
r_1	0.0326	0.0327
r_2	-0.0279	-0.0305
	+0.2182	+0.2140i
c_1		56485
c_2		59363
		86656i
$2\pi/y$	28.795	29.366
Δ	1.868	

West Indies, 1963-64

TABLE 1 DATA INPUT TO COMPUTATIONS

Age at last birthday	Population Total	Males	%	Females	%	Births, by age of mother	Deaths Total	Males	Females	Age at last birthday
0	203315	103232	3.4	100083	3.2	0	10143	5693	4450	0
1–4	769130	389196	12.9	379934	12.0	0	3391	1727	1664	1–4
5–9	851928	429804	14.3	422124	13.3	0	644	384	260	5–9
10–14	748921	377896	12.6	371025	11.7	372	407	245	162	10–14
15–19	606755	298705	9.9	308050	9.7	34980	609	370	239	15–19
20–24	479763	228178	7.6	251585	7.9	64897	645	381	264	20–24
25–29	394753	180402	6.0	214351	6.8	49423	692	378	314	25–29
30–34	343987	153251	5.1	190736	6.0	32295	777	417	360	30–34
35–39	314484	142927	4.8	171557	5.4	20778	977	499	478	35–39
40–44	300308	143813	4.8	156495	4.9	7063	1251	724	527	40–44
45–49	272265	134406	4.5	137859	4.4	960	1512	933	679	45–49
50–54	245168	122136	4.1	123032	3.9	18	2292	1367	925	50–54
55–59	189652	94671	3.1	94981	3.0	0	2454	1468	986	55–59
60–64	150514	73479	2.4	77035	2.4	0	3326	1916	1410	60–64
65–69	112398	53162	1.8	59236	1.9	0	3467	1964	1503	65–69
70–74	90554	40840	1.4	49714	1.6		4147	2214	1933	70–74
75–79	76324	33894	1.1	42430	1.3		3157	1602	1555	75–79
80–84	13325	4642	0.2	8683	0.3	107785 M	3260	1493	1767	80–84
85+	8305	2564	0.1	5741	0.2	103001 F	5117	1973	3144	85+
All ages	6171849	3007198		3164651		210786	48368	25748	22620	All ages

TABLE 2 LIFE TABLE FOR MALES

Age, x	$_nq_x$	l_x	$_nd_x$	$_nL_x$	$_nm_x$	T_x	$1000r_x$	$\overset{\circ}{e}_x$	$_nM_x$	Age, x
0	0.05301	100000	5301	96329	0.05503	6406391	2.96	64.06	0.05515	0
1	0.01749	94699	1656	374092	0.00443	6310062	2.96	66.63	0.00444	1
5	0.00438	93043	407	464199	0.00088	5935970	24.77	63.80	0.00089	5
10	0.00325	92636	301	462453	0.00065	5471772	35.55	59.07	0.00065	10
15	0.00623	92335	575	460334	0.00125	5009309	49.25	54.25	0.00124	15
20	0.00836	91760	767	456951	0.00168	4548974	48.75	49.57	0.00167	20
25	0.01046	90993	952	452679	0.00210	4092014	37.66	44.97	0.00210	25
30	0.01355	90041	1220	447277	0.00273	3639335	20.55	40.42	0.00272	30
35	0.01732	88821	1538	440458	0.00349	3192058	2.71	35.94	0.00349	35
40	0.02488	87283	2171	431271	0.00504	2751601	1.10	31.53	0.00503	40
45	0.03421	85111	2912	418762	0.00695	2320330	8.90	27.26	0.00694	45
50	0.05472	82200	4498	400365	0.01124	1901558	23.95	23.13	0.01119	50
55	0.07528	77701	5849	374794	0.01561	1501203	33.91	19.32	0.01551	55
60	0.12340	71852	8867	338109	0.02622	1126410	33.97	15.68	0.02608	60
65	0.17029	62985	10725	288864	0.03713	788301	33.97	12.52	0.03694	65
70	0.23878	52259	12478	229676	0.05433	499435	33.97	9.56	0.05421	70
75	0.21826	39781	8683	180376	0.04814	269761	33.97	6.78	0.04727	75
80	0.89162	31098	27728	85056	0.32596	89385	33.97	2.87	0.32163	80
85+	•1.00000	3371	3371	4319	0.78039	4319	33.97	1.28	0.76950	85+

TABLE 3 LIFE TABLE FOR FEMALES

Age, x	$_nq_x$	l_x	$_nd_x$	$_nL_x$	$_nm_x$	T_x	$1000r_x$	$\overset{\circ}{e}_x$	$_nM_x$	Age, x
0	0.04310	100000	4310	97111	0.04438	6841408	2.53	68.41	0.04445	0
1	0.01727	95690	1653	378112	0.00437	6744297	2.53	70.48	0.00438	1
5	0.00299	94037	282	469482	0.00060	6366185	24.28	67.70	0.00062	5
10	0.00219	93756	205	468282	0.00044	5896703	30.95	62.89	0.00044	10
15	0.00390	93551	365	466901	0.00078	5428421	38.10	58.03	0.00078	15
20	0.00526	93186	490	464770	0.00105	4961520	35.18	53.24	0.00105	20
25	0.00732	92696	679	461851	0.00147	4496750	26.23	48.51	0.00146	25
30	0.00942	92017	867	458040	0.00189	4034889	20.27	43.85	0.00189	30
35	0.01386	91150	1264	452724	0.00279	3576848	17.09	39.24	0.00279	35
40	0.01674	89886	1505	445856	0.00338	3124124	18.30	34.76	0.00337	40
45	0.02443	88381	2159	436853	0.00494	2678268	18.93	30.30	0.00493	45
50	0.03710	86223	3199	423549	0.00755	2241406	29.76	26.00	0.00752	50
55	0.05105	83024	4239	405303	0.01046	1817857	35.30	21.90	0.01038	55
60	0.08814	78785	6944	377480	0.01840	1412554	30.03	17.93	0.01830	60
65	0.12013	71841	8630	338521	0.02549	1035074	30.03	14.41	0.02537	65
70	0.17760	63211	11226	288061	0.03897	696553	30.03	11.02	0.03888	70
75	0.17289	51984	8988	241223	0.03726	408492	30.03	7.85	0.03665	75
80	0.68220	42996	29332	142626	0.20566	167269	30.03	3.89	0.20350	80
85+	•1.00000	13664	13664	24643	0.55449	24643	30.03	1.80	0.54764	85+

TABLE 4 POPULATION PROJECTION, USING FIXED AGE-SPECIFIC BIRTH AND DEATH RATES, IN THOUSANDS

Age at last birthday	1968 Total	1968 Males	1968 Females	1973 Total	1973 Males	1973 Females	1978 Total	1978 Males	1978 Females	Age at last birthday
0–4	1081	550	531	1270	646	624	1484	755	729	0–4
5–9	960	486	474	1068	543	525	1253	637	516	5–9
10–14	849	428	421	957	484	473	1064	541	523	10–14
15–19	746	376	370	846	426	420	954	482	472	15–19
20–24	604	297	307	741	373	368	841	423	418	20–24
25–29	476	226	250	599	294	305	736	370	366	25–29
30–34	391	178	213	471	223	248	592	290	302	30–34
35–39	340	151	189	386	176	210	455	220	245	35–39
40–44	309	140	169	334	148	186	379	172	207	40–44
45–49	293	140	153	302	136	166	325	143	182	45–49
50–54	263	129	134	283	134	149	291	130	151	50–54
55–59	232	114	118	248	120	128	267	125	142	55–59
60–64	173	85	88	213	103	110	228	109	119	60–64
65–69	132	63	69	152	73	79	186	88	98	65–69
70–74	92	42	50	109	50	59	126	58	68	70–74
75–79	74	32	42	75	33	42	88	39	49	75–79
80–84	41	16	25	40	15	25	41	16	25	80–84
85 +	2	0	2	5	1	4	5	1	4	85 +
All ages	7058	3453	3605	8099	3978	4121	9325	4599	4726	All ages

TABLE 5 OBSERVED AND PROJECTED VITAL RATES

Rates per thousand	Observed Total	Observed Males	Observed Females	Projected 1968 Males	Projected 1968 Females	Projected 1973 Males	Projected 1973 Females	Projected 1978 Males	Projected 1978 Females	Stable Males	Stable Females
Birth	34.15	35.84	32.55	36.53	33.45	37.33	34.45	37.55	34.92	35.74	34.61
Death	7.84	8.56	7.15	8.69	7.07	8.48	7.24	8.24	7.04	7.99	6.85
Increase	26.32	27.28	25.40	27.84	26.38	28.85	27.21	29.31	27.87		27.7545

TABLE 6 RATES STANDARDIZED ON THREE STANDARD COUNTRIES

Standardized rates per thousand	England and Wales, 1961 Total	Males	Females	United States, 1960 Total	Males	Females	Mexico, 1960 Total	Males	Females
Birth	30.39	40.84*	28.78	31.00	37.04*	29.84	35.41	38.21*	34.52
Death	16.05	15.71*	16.33	13.47	13.10*	12.37	7.43	8.13*	5.41
Increase	14.33	25.13*	12.46	17.52	23.94*	17.47	27.98	30.08*	28.10

TABLE 7 VITAL STATISTICS AND RATES INFERRED FROM AGE DISTRIBUTIONS (FEMALES)

Vital statistics		Thompson Age range	NRR	$1000r$	Interval	Bourgeois-Pichat Age range	NRR	$1000b$	$1000d$	$1000r$	Coale
TFR	4.73	0–4	2.15	28.93	27.38	5–29	2.51	37.42	3.34	34.07	$1000b$
GRR	2.31	5–9	2.18	29.06	27.32	30–54	1.63	23.67	5.61	18.07	$1000d$
NRR	2.13	10–14	2.14	27.23	27.26	55–79	1.78	24.81	3.38	21.43	$1000r$
Generation	27.21	15–19	1.98	25.12	27.16	*30–54	1.63	23.67	5.61	18.07	$1000k_1$
Sex ratio	104.64										$1000k_2$

TABLE 8 LESLIE MATRIX AND ITS ANALYSIS (FEMALES)

Start of age interval	Sub-diagonal	First row	Percent in stable population	Fisher values	Total reproductive values	Net maternity function	Matrix equation coefficient	Parameters		Integral	Matrix
0	0.98792	0.00000	15.376	1.127	541075	0.00000	0.00000	λ_1	1.1489	1.1494	
5	0.99744	0.00116	13.216	1.311	553590	0.00000	0.00115	λ_2	0.3626	0.3771	
10	0.99705	0.13262	11.469	1.510	560208	0.00229	0.13068		+0.7682	+0.7479i	
15	0.99543	0.42999	9.949	1.591	490005	0.25907	0.42246	r_1	0.0278	0.0278	
20	0.99374	0.56555	8.616	1.350	339580	0.58584	0.55311	r_2	−0.0326	−0.0354	
25	0.99172	0.46268	7.449	0.920	197132	0.52037	0.44967		+0.2259	+0.2208i	
30	0.98839	0.33559	6.428	0.540	102996	0.37897	0.32345	c_1		31032	
35	0.98482	0.19223	5.527	0.245	42071	0.26793	0.18313	c_2		18713	
40	0.97982	0.06032	4.736	0.066	10356	0.09833	0.05660			42596i	
45	0.96951	0.00825	4.037	0.008	1135	0.01487	0.00758	$2\pi/y$	27.808	28.461	
50	0.95690	0.00017	3.405	0.000	20	0.00030	0.00015	Δ	2.475		
55	0.81657		9.791								

Europe, 1955

TABLE 1 DATA INPUT TO COMPUTATIONS

Age at last birthday	Population					Births, by age of mother	Deaths			Age at last birthday
	Total	Males	%	Females	%		Total	Males	Females	
0	73599	37731	1.9	35868	1.7	0	4113	2308	1805	0
1–4	291652	149250	7.6	142402	6.8	0	874	456	418	1–4
5–9	347691	177575	9.1	170116	8.1	0	259	147	112	5–9
10–14	309556	157738	8.1	151818	7.2	10	173	103	70	10–14
15–19	314673	159166	8.1	155507	7.4	4174	291	187	104	15–19
20–24	312424	157145	8.0	155279	7.4	21865	407	259	148	20–24
25–29	310740	153555	7.9	157185	7.5	24377	452	275	187	25–29
30–34	297042	141379	7.2	155663	7.4	16850	522	291	231	30–34
35–39	229684	108442	5.6	121242	5.8	7376	485	261	224	35–39
40–44	271866	127892	6.5	143974	6.9	3094	874	486	388	40–44
45–49	277577	132584	6.8	144993	6.9	312	1364	800	564	45–49
50–54	254395	121589	6.2	132806	6.3	21	1992	1211	781	50–54
55–59	215314	98066	5.0	117248	5.6	0	2615	1565	1050	55–59
60–64	174425	75235	3.9	99190	4.7	0	3296	1846	1450	60–64
65–69	142772	61001	3.1	81771	3.9	0	4398	2316	2082	65–69
70–74	107731	45562	2.3	62169	3.0		5517	2736	2781	70–74
75–79	70893	29500	1.5	41393	2.0		6055	2852	3203	75–79
80–84	35200	14108	0.7	21092	1.0	40190 M	4895	2171	2724	80–84
85+	17570	5824	0.3	11746	0.6	37889 F	3697	1427	2270	85+
All ages	4054804	1953342		2101462		78079	42289	21697	20592	All ages

TABLE 2 LIFE TABLE FOR MALES

Age, x	$_nq_x$	l_x	$_nd_x$	$_nL_x$	$_nm_x$	T_x	$1000r_x$	$\mathring{e}_x$	$_nM_x$	Age, x
0	0.05851	100000	5851	95644	0.06117	6488437	0.00	64.88	0.06117	0
1	0.01211	94149	1141	373298	0.00306	6392793	0.00	67.90	0.00306	1
5	0.00410	93009	381	464092	0.00082	6019496	15.61	64.72	0.00083	5
10	0.00326	92628	302	462416	0.00065	5555404	10.14	59.98	0.00065	10
15	0.00586	92325	541	460369	0.00117	5092988	0.00	55.16	0.00117	15
20	0.00821	91785	753	457095	0.00165	4632619	2.01	50.47	0.00165	20
25	0.00892	91031	812	453161	0.00179	4175524	8.75	45.87	0.00179	25
30	0.01026	90219	926	448835	0.00206	3722362	32.73	41.26	0.00206	30
35	0.01198	89293	1070	443946	0.00241	3273527	7.42	36.66	0.00241	35
40	0.01883	88224	1662	437278	0.00380	2829581	0.00	32.07	0.00380	40
45	0.02976	86562	2576	426880	0.00603	2392303	0.00	27.64	0.00603	45
50	0.04887	83986	4104	410421	0.01000	1965423	19.80	23.40	0.00995	50
55	0.07734	79882	6178	384895	0.01605	1555001	31.55	19.47	0.01596	55
60	0.11628	73704	8570	348173	0.02462	1170107	17.97	15.88	0.02454	60
65	0.17451	65133	11367	298407	0.03809	821933	17.97	12.62	0.03797	65
70	0.26264	53766	14121	234384	0.06025	523526	17.97	9.74	0.06005	70
75	0.38998	39645	15461	159399	0.09700	289143	17.97	7.29	0.09668	75
80	0.54909	24184	13279	86023	0.15437	129744	17.97	5.36	0.15388	80
85+	1.00000	10905	10905	43721	0.24942	43721	17.97	4.01	0.24502	85+

TABLE 3 LIFE TABLE FOR FEMALES

Age, x	$_nq_x$	l_x	$_nd_x$	$_nL_x$	$_nm_x$	T_x	$1000r_x$	$\mathring{e}_x$	$_nM_x$	Age, x
0	0.04855	100000	4855	96469	0.05032	6966304	0.00	69.66	0.05032	0
1	0.01164	95145	1108	377393	0.00294	6869835	0.00	72.20	0.00294	1
5	0.00326	94038	306	469422	0.00065	6492442	14.84	69.04	0.00066	5
10	0.00230	93731	216	468119	0.00046	6023020	8.43	64.26	0.00046	10
15	0.00334	93516	312	466845	0.00067	5554901	0.00	59.40	0.00067	15
20	0.00475	93203	443	464959	0.00095	5088056	0.00	54.59	0.00095	20
25	0.00593	92760	550	462476	0.00119	4523098	0.00	49.84	0.00119	25
30	0.00741	92210	683	459403	0.00149	4160622	24.47	45.12	0.00148	30
35	0.00920	91527	842	455638	0.00185	3701220	5.86	40.44	0.00185	35
40	0.01339	90684	1214	450570	0.00269	3245582	0.00	35.79	0.00269	40
45	0.01929	89470	1726	443315	0.00389	2795012	4.04	31.24	0.00389	45
50	0.02908	87744	2552	432764	0.00590	2351698	15.18	26.80	0.00588	50
55	0.04404	85193	3751	417259	0.00899	1918933	19.76	22.52	0.00895	55
60	0.07111	81441	5791	393851	0.01470	1501675	25.74	18.44	0.01462	60
65	0.12087	75650	9144	356999	0.02561	1107824	25.74	14.64	0.02546	65
70	0.20323	66506	13516	300441	0.04499	750825	25.74	11.29	0.04473	70
75	0.32664	52990	17308	222511	0.07779	450384	25.74	8.50	0.07738	75
80	0.49062	35682	17506	134823	0.12985	227873	25.74	6.39	0.12915	80
85+	•1.00000	18175	18175	93050	0.19533	93050	25.74	5.12	0.19326	85+

TABLE 4 POPULATION PROJECTION, USING FIXED AGE-SPECIFIC BIRTH AND DEATH RATES, IN THOUSANDS

Age at last birthday	1960				1965				1970			Age at last birthday
	Total	Males	Females		Total	Males	Females		Total	Males	Females	
0–4	371	190	181		373	191	182		378	194	184	0–4
5–9	362	185	177		367	188	179		369	189	180	5–9
10–14	347	177	170		360	184	176		365	187	178	10–14
15–19	308	157	151		345	176	169		360	184	176	15–19
20–24	313	158	155		307	156	151		343	175	168	20–24
25–29	310	156	154		311	157	154		305	155	150	25–29
30–34	308	152	156		307	154	153		308	155	153	30–34
35–39	294	140	154		305	150	155		305	153	152	35–39
40–44	227	107	120		291	138	153		301	148	153	40–44
45–49	267	125	142		222	104	118		284	134	150	45–49
50–54	269	127	142		258	120	138		215	100	115	50–54
55–59	242	114	128		256	120	136		246	113	133	55–59
60–64	200	89	111		224	103	121		237	108	129	60–64
65–69	154	64	90		176	76	100		198	88	110	65–69
70–74	117	48	69		127	51	76		144	60	84	70–74
75–79	77	31	46		84	33	51		90	34	56	75–79
80–84	41	16	25		45	17	28		49	18	31	80–84
85 +	22	7	15		25	8	17		27	8	19	85 +
All ages	4229	2043	2186		4383	2126	2257		4524	2203	2321	All ages

TABLE 5 OBSERVED AND PROJECTED VITAL RATES

Rates per thousand	Observed			Projected						Stable	
				1960		1965		1970			
	Total	Males	Females	Males	Females	Males	Females	Males	Females	Males	Females
Birth	19.26	20.57	18.03	19.92	17.56	19.20	17.04	18.97	15.95	18.42	17.32
Death	10.43	11.11	9.80	11.45	10.46	11.74	11.04	12.03	11.55	13.37	12.26
Increase	8.83	9.47	8.23	8.46	7.10	7.46	6.00	6.94	5.41		5.0575

TABLE 6 RATES STANDARDIZED ON THREE STANDARD COUNTRIES

Standardized rates per thousand	England and Wales, 1961			United States, 1960			Mexico, 1960		
	Total	Males	Females	Total	Males	Females	Total	Males	Females
Birth	16.42	18.70*	15.44	16.69	17.40*	15.96	18.82	17.02*	18.22
Death	12.79	13.11*	12.80	10.75	11.50*	9.80	6.52	9.36*	5.64
Increase	3.63	5.59*	2.64	5.94	5.91*	6.16	12.31	7.66*	12.58

TABLE 7 VITAL STATISTICS AND RATES INFERRED FROM AGE DISTRIBUTIONS (FEMALES)

Vital statistics		Thompson				Bourgeois-Pichat				Coale	
		Age range	NRR	1000r	Interval	Age range	NRR	1000b	1000d	1000r	
TFR	2.58	0–4	1.17	5.71	27.41	5–29	1.05	16.68	14.70	1.98	1000b 18.72
GRR	1.25	5–9	1.13	4.45	27.37	30–54	1.00	14.68	14.84	−0.16	1000d 11.51
NRR	1.15	10–14	1.02	0.89	27.31	55–79	1.73	42.73	22.47	20.25	1000r 7.21
Generation	28.41	15–19	1.09	2.98	27.23	*50–74	1.71	41.57	21.72	19.85	1000k_1 27.92
Sex ratio	106.1										1000k_2 0.45

TABLE 8 LESLIE MATRIX AND ITS ANALYSIS (FEMALES)

Start of age interval	Sub-diagonal	First row	Percent in stable population	Fisher values	Total reproductive values	Net maternity function	Matrix equation coefficient	Parameters		
									Integral	Matrix
0	0.99063	0.00000	8.104	1.069	190487	0.00000	0.00000	λ_1	1.0256	1.0256
5	0.99722	0.00008	7.827	1.106	188196	0.00000	0.00007	λ_2	0.3908	0.3970
10	0.99728	0.03085	7.610	1.138	172725	0.00015	0.03048		+0.7539	+0.7313i
15	0.99596	0.19211	7.400	1.137	176810	0.06081	0.18926	r_1	0.0051	0.0051
20	0.99466	0.33926	7.186	0.965	149806	0.31771	0.33288	r_2	−0.0327	−0.0368
25	0.99335	0.30194	6.969	0.630	99079	0.34805	0.29468		+0.2185	+0.2147i
30	0.99180	0.19383	6.750	0.326	50749	0.24132	0.18792	c_1		21408
35	0.98887	0.09438	6.527	0.128	15557	0.13451	0.09075	c_2		9504
40	0.98389	0.02714	6.293	0.031	4477	0.04699	0.02581			−10416i
45	0.97619	0.00265	6.037	0.003	426	0.00463	0.00248	$2\pi/y$	28.754	29.266
50	0.96416	0.00018	5.746	0.000	25	0.00033	0.00017	Δ	4.191	
55	0.79036		23.549							

Europe, 1960

TABLE 1 DATA INPUT TO COMPUTATIONS

Age at last birthday	Population					Births, by age of mother	Deaths			Age at last birthday
	Total	Males	%	Females	%		Total	Males	Females	
0	75759	38827	1.9	36932	1.7	0	3125	1764	1361	0
1–4	297211	152264	7.4	144947	6.6	0	592	317	275	1–4
5–9	368103	188547	9.2	179556	8.2	0	202	120	82	5–9
10–14	351223	179069	8.8	172154	7.9	24	152	94	58	10–14
15–19	304137	154014	7.5	150123	6.9	4573	241	165	76	15–19
20–24	311448	156286	7.6	155162	7.1	22799	337	228	109	20–24
25–29	305961	153682	7.5	152279	7.0	24389	381	240	141	25–29
30–34	306476	151717	7.4	154759	7.1	15808	456	275	181	30–34
35–39	297567	141116	6.9	156451	7.2	8425	593	336	257	35–39
40–44	218533	103674	5.1	114859	5.3	2278	609	346	263	40–44
45–49	272378	128636	6.3	143742	6.6	229	1218	706	512	45–49
50–54	269357	127801	6.3	141556	6.5	15	1947	1194	753	50–54
55–59	240893	113791	5.6	127102	5.8	0	2831	1784	1047	55–59
60–64	199583	88605	4.3	110978	5.1	0	3682	2195	1487	60–64
65–69	153171	63953	3.1	89218	4.1	0	4505	2439	2066	65–69
70–74	117870	47960	2.3	69910	3.2		5709	2851	2858	70–74
75–79	80212	31961	1.6	48251	2.2		6369	2955	3414	75–79
80–84	39849	15448	0.8	24401	1.1	40461 M	5671	2478	3193	80–84
85 +	18134	6520	0.3	11614	0.5	38179 F	4507	1747	2760	85 +
All ages	4227865	2043871		2183994		78640	43127	22234	20893	All ages

TABLE 2 LIFE TABLE FOR MALES

Age, x	$_nq_x$	l_x	$_nd_x$	$_nL_x$	$_nm_x$	T_x	$1000r_x$	$\mathring{e}_x$	$_nM_x$	Age, x
0	0.04392	100000	4392	96692	0.04542	6656650	0.25	66.57	0.04543	0
1	0.00828	95608	791	380137	0.00208	6559958	0.25	68.61	0.00208	1
5	0.00317	94817	301	473332	0.00063	6179821	5.48	65.18	0.00064	5
10	0.00263	94516	249	472002	0.00053	5706488	19.56	60.38	0.00052	10
15	0.00536	94268	505	470156	0.00107	5234486	12.58	55.53	0.00107	15
20	0.00727	93763	682	467155	0.00146	4764321	0.00	50.81	0.00146	20
25	0.00778	93081	724	463628	0.00156	4297165	1.37	46.17	0.00156	25
30	0.00903	92357	834	459777	0.00181	3833538	6.66	41.51	0.00181	30
35	0.01189	91523	1089	455033	0.00239	3373761	35.64	36.85	0.00238	35
40	0.01658	90435	1499	448701	0.00334	2918728	5.71	32.27	0.00334	40
45	0.02710	88936	2410	439164	0.00549	2470027	0.00	27.77	0.00549	45
50	0.04576	86525	3959	423532	0.00935	2030863	2.47	23.47	0.00934	50
55	0.07592	82566	6268	398200	0.01574	1607331	20.45	19.47	0.01568	55
60	0.11737	76298	8955	360252	0.02486	1209130	19.10	15.85	0.02477	60
65	0.17522	67342	11800	308358	0.03827	848878	19.10	12.61	0.03814	65
70	0.26024	55542	14454	242342	0.05964	540521	19.10	9.73	0.05945	70
75	0.37667	41088	15476	166780	0.09280	298178	19.10	7.26	0.09245	75
80	0.57007	25612	14600	90627	0.16110	131398	19.10	5.13	0.16041	80
85 +	•1.00000	11011	11011	40771	0.27008	40771	19.10	3.70	0.26794	85 +

TABLE 3 LIFE TABLE FOR FEMALES

Age, x	$_nq_x$	l_x	$_nd_x$	$_nL_x$	$_nm_x$	T_x	$1000r_x$	$\mathring{e}_x$	$_nM_x$	Age, x
0	0.03586	100000	3586	97345	0.03684	7170162	0.39	71.70	0.03685	0
1	0.00754	96414	727	383553	0.00190	7072816	0.39	73.36	0.00190	1
5	0.00227	95686	218	477888	0.00046	6689263	4.67	69.91	0.00046	5
10	0.00168	95469	161	476947	0.00034	6211375	17.50	65.06	0.00034	10
15	0.00253	95308	241	475973	0.00051	5734429	9.89	60.17	0.00051	15
20	0.00351	95067	333	474541	0.00070	5258456	0.00	55.31	0.00070	20
25	0.00462	94733	438	472618	0.00093	4783915	0.00	50.50	0.00093	25
30	0.00583	94296	550	470173	0.00117	4311298	0.00	45.72	0.00117	30
35	0.00821	93746	770	466910	0.00165	3841125	28.15	40.97	0.00164	35
40	0.01140	92976	1060	462407	0.00229	3374215	6.06	36.29	0.00229	40
45	0.01766	91916	1624	455794	0.00356	2911808	0.00	31.68	0.00356	45
50	0.02630	90292	2375	445928	0.00533	2456014	6.79	27.20	0.00532	50
55	0.04054	87917	3564	431329	0.00826	2010085	15.71	22.85	0.00824	55
60	0.06535	84353	5512	409056	0.01348	1578756	25.46	18.72	0.01340	60
65	0.11051	78841	8712	374011	0.02329	1169700	25.46	14.84	0.02316	65
70	0.18736	70128	13139	319582	0.04111	795689	25.46	11.35	0.04088	70
75	0.30348	56989	17295	243046	0.07116	476107	25.46	8.35	0.07075	75
80	0.49277	39694	19560	148698	0.13154	233061	25.46	5.87	0.13086	80
85 +	1.00000	20134	20134	84353	0.23866	84363	25.46	4.19	0.23765	85 +

TABLE 4 POPULATION PROJECTION, USING FIXED AGE-SPECIFIC BIRTH AND DEATH RATES, IN THOUSANDS

Age at last birthday	1965			1970			1975			Age at last birthday
	Total	Males	Females	Total	Males	Females	Total	Males	Females	
0–4	378	194	184	385	197	188	400	205	195	0–4
5–9	371	190	181	375	192	183	383	195	187	5–9
10–14	367	188	179	369	189	180	375	192	183	10–14
15–19	350	178	172	366	187	179	368	188	180	15–19
20–24	303	153	150	348	177	171	364	185	178	20–24
25–29	310	155	155	301	152	149	347	175	171	25–29
30–34	303	152	151	308	154	154	299	151	148	30–34
35–39	304	150	154	301	151	150	305	152	153	35–39
40–44	294	139	155	300	148	152	298	149	149	40–44
45–49	214	101	113	289	136	153	295	145	150	45–49
50–54	265	124	141	209	98	111	280	131	149	50–54
55–59	257	120	137	253	117	136	199	92	107	55–59
60–64	224	103	121	239	109	130	235	106	129	60–64
65–69	177	76	101	198	88	110	212	93	119	65–69
70–74	126	50	76	147	60	87	163	69	94	70–74
75–79	86	33	53	93	35	58	107	41	66	75–79
80–84	47	17	30	51	18	33	54	19	35	80–84
85 +	21	7	14	25	8	17	26	8	18	85 +
All ages	4397	2130	2267	4557	2216	2341	4710	2299	2411	All ages

TABLE 5 OBSERVED AND PROJECTED VITAL RATES

Rates per thousand	Observed			Projected						Stable	
				1965		1970		1975			
	Total	Males	Females	Males	Females	Males	Females	Males	Females	Males	Females
Birth	18.60	19.80	17.48	19.10	16.96	18.98	16.95	19.19	17.26	18.53	17.40
Death	10.20	10.88	9.57	11.17	10.24	11.49	10.85	11.77	11.31	12.57	11.44
Increase	8.40	8.92	7.91	7.93	6.72	7.49	6.10	7.42	5.95		5.9663

TABLE 6 RATES STANDARDIZED ON THREE STANDARD COUNTRIES

Standardized rates per thousand	England and Wales, 1961			United States, 1960			Mexico, 1960		
	Total	Males	Females	Total	Males	Females	Total	Males	Females
Birth	16.39	18.17*	15.42	16.67	17.03*	15.94	19.09	16.56*	18.49
Death	12.24	12.43*	12.18	10.12	10.95*	9.12	5.69	9.03*	4.80
Increase	4.15	5.74*	3.24	6.54	6.08*	6.82	13.40	7.53*	13.68

TABLE 7 VITAL STATISTICS AND RATES INFERRED FROM AGE DISTRIBUTIONS (FEMALES)

Vital statistics		Thompson				Bourgeois-Pichat					Coale	
TFR	2.58	Age range	NRR	$1000r$	Interval	Age range	NRR	$1000b$	$1000d$	$1000r$	$1000b$	20.61
GRR	1.25	0–4	1.21	6.96	27.42	5–29	1.25	17.92	9.79	8.12	$1000d$	7.59
NRR	1.18	5–9	1.20	6.70	27.39	30–54	1.07	15.76	13.10	2.66	$1000r$	13.02
Generation	27.99	10–14	1.16	5.38	27.34	55–79	1.74	43.96	23.51	20.45	$1000k_1$	40.64
Sex ratio	106.0	15–19	1.03	1.01	27.26	*15–39	0.93	13.90	16.45	-2.55	$1000k_2$	0.56

TABLE 8 LESLIE MATRIX AND ITS ANALYSIS (FEMALES)

Start of age interval	Sub-diagonal	First row	Percent in stable population	Fisher values	Total reproductive values	Net maternity function	Matrix equation coefficient	Parameters		
									Integral	Matrix
0	0.99374	0.00000	8.246	1.055	191936	0.00000	0.00000	λ_1	1.0303	1.0303
5	0.99803	0.00016	7.954	1.094	196457	0.00000	0.00016	λ_2	0.3731	0.3801
10	0.99796	0.03643	7.704	1.129	194419	0.00032	0.03613		+0.7642	+0.7396 i
15	0.99699	0.20735	7.463	1.127	169251	0.07193	0.20523	r_1	0.0060	0.0060
20	0.99595	0.35773	7.221	0.946	146722	0.33852	0.35300	r_2	-0.0324	-0.0369
25	0.99483	0.30559	6.980	0.599	91241	0.36749	0.30033		+0.2233	+0.2192 i
30	0.99306	0.18166	6.740	0.295	45866	0.23316	0.17762	c_1		21819
35	0.99035	0.08578	6.497	0.114	17905	0.12207	0.08330	c_2		11266
40	0.98570	0.02498	6.245	0.028	3175	0.04452	0.02402			5562 i
45	0.97835	0.00198	5.974	0.002	309	0.00353	0.00188	$2\pi/y$	28.135	28.664
50	0.96726	0.00012	5.673	0.000	18	0.00023	0.00011	Δ	3.630	
55	0.79482		23.303							

Europe, 1965

TABLE 1 DATA INPUT TO COMPUTATIONS

Age at last birthday	Population					Births, by age of mother	Deaths			Age at last birthday
	Total	Males	%	Females	%		Total	Males	Females	
0	78883	40458	1.9	38425	1.7	0	2465	1399	1066	0
1–4	306454	156922	7.3	149532	6.6	0	413	226	187	1–4
5–9	368228	188333	8.8	179895	7.9	0	184	110	74	5–9
10–14	361022	184627	8.6	176395	7.8	18	144	89	55	10–14
15–19	351472	178938	8.4	172534	7.6	6062	261	181	80	15–19
20–24	307331	155533	7.3	151798	6.7	22791	301	212	89	20–24
25–29	313391	158887	7.4	154504	6.8	24807	339	225	114	25–29
30–34	305483	153618	7.2	151865	6.7	15405	420	267	153	30–34
35–39	304574	150661	7.0	153913	6.8	7883	589	363	226	35–39
40–44	294944	139685	6.5	155259	6.8	2506	818	479	339	40–44
45–49	213047	100175	4.7	112872	5.0	200	913	539	374	45–49
50–54	266030	124299	5.8	141731	6.2	16	1836	1120	716	50–54
55–59	258054	120739	5.6	137315	6.0	0	2890	1825	1065	55–59
60–64	225085	103783	4.8	121302	5.3	0	4135	2588	1547	60–64
65–69	177882	76125	3.6	101757	4.5	0	5162	2961	2201	65–69
70–74	127692	50530	2.4	77162	3.4		5910	2994	2916	70–74
75–79	89237	34023	1.6	55214	2.4		6575	3032	3543	75–79
80–84	45148	16726	0.8	28422	1.2	40940 M	5873	2510	3363	80–84
85 +	23953	8280	0.4	15673	0.7	38748 F	5817	2179	3638	85 +
All ages	4417910	2142342		2275568		79688	45045	23299	21746	All ages

TABLE 2 LIFE TABLE FOR MALES

Age, x	nq_x	l_x	nd_x	nL_x	nm_x	T_x	$1000r_x$	$\overset{\circ}{e}_x$	nM_x	Age, x
0	0.03364	100000	3364	97433	0.03453	6769242	1.84	67.69	0.03458	0
1	0.00572	96636	553	384935	0.00144	6671808	1.84	69.04	0.00144	1
5	0.00291	96083	280	479714	0.00058	6286873	5.87	65.43	0.00058	5
10	0.00241	95803	231	478480	0.00048	5807159	4.49	60.62	0.00048	10
15	0.00506	95572	484	476738	0.00101	5328679	16.18	55.76	0.00101	15
20	0.00680	95089	646	473865	0.00136	4851940	10.58	51.03	0.00136	20
25	0.00706	94442	666	470580	0.00142	4378075	0.00	46.36	0.00142	25
30	0.00866	93776	812	466943	0.00174	3907496	3.52	41.67	0.00174	30
35	0.01199	92964	1115	462191	0.00241	3440553	7.04	37.01	0.00241	35
40	0.01712	91849	1573	455582	0.00345	2978362	37.21	32.43	0.00343	40
45	0.02661	90276	2402	445858	0.00539	2522780	6.00	27.95	0.00538	45
50	0.04414	87874	3879	430454	0.00901	2076922	0.00	23.64	0.00900	50
55	0.07305	83996	6136	405749	0.01512	1646469	2.24	19.60	0.01512	55
60	0.11821	77860	9204	367564	0.02504	1240720	21.62	15.94	0.02494	60
65	0.17844	68656	12251	313784	0.03904	873156	21.62	12.72	0.03890	65
70	0.25941	56405	14632	246074	0.05946	559372	21.62	9.92	0.05925	70
75	0.36546	41773	15266	170640	0.08946	313298	21.62	7.50	0.08912	75
80	0.54123	26507	14346	95210	0.15068	142658	21.62	5.38	0.15007	80
85 +	1.00000	12160	12160	47449	0.25629	47449	21.62	3.90	0.26316	85 +

TABLE 3 LIFE TABLE FOR FEMALES

Age, x	nq_x	l_x	nd_x	nL_x	nm_x	T_x	$1000r_x$	$\overset{\circ}{e}_x$	nM_x	Age, x
0	0.02714	100000	2714	97953	0.02771	7333068	1.70	73.33	0.02774	0
1	0.00497	97286	484	387741	0.00125	7235114	1.70	74.37	0.00125	1
5	0.00205	96802	198	483516	0.00041	6847373	5.72	70.74	0.00041	5
10	0.00156	96604	151	482649	0.00031	6363858	3.81	65.88	0.00031	10
15	0.00232	96453	224	481735	0.00046	5881209	14.57	60.97	0.00046	15
20	0.00293	96230	282	480470	0.00059	5399474	10.45	56.11	0.00059	20
25	0.00368	95948	353	478896	0.00074	4919004	0.00	51.27	0.00074	25
30	0.00503	95594	480	476842	0.00101	4440108	0.00	46.45	0.00101	30
35	0.00732	95114	696	473944	0.00147	3963266	0.00	41.67	0.00147	35
40	0.01092	94418	1031	469688	0.00219	3489322	28.75	36.96	0.00218	40
45	0.01646	93387	1537	463357	0.00332	3019634	5.70	32.33	0.00331	45
50	0.02497	91850	2293	453911	0.00505	2556277	0.00	27.83	0.00505	50
55	0.03815	89557	3417	439884	0.00777	2102366	7.40	23.48	0.00776	55
60	0.06229	86140	5366	418318	0.01283	1662482	26.23	19.30	0.01275	60
65	0.10357	80775	8366	384470	0.02176	1244164	26.23	15.40	0.02163	65
70	0.17437	72409	12626	332213	0.03801	859693	26.23	11.87	0.03779	70
75	0.27926	59782	16695	258651	0.06455	527481	26.23	8.82	0.06417	75
80	0.45743	43088	19710	165690	0.11896	268830	26.23	6.24	0.11832	80
85 +	1.00000	23378	23378	103140	0.22666	103140	26.23	4.41	0.23212	85 +

TABLE 4 POPULATION PROJECTION, USING FIXED AGE-SPECIFIC BIRTH AND DEATH RATES, IN THOUSANDS

Age at last birthday	1970			1975			1980			Age at last birthday
	Total	Males	Females	Total	Males	Females	Total	Males	Females	
0–4	392	201	191	408	209	199	424	217	207	0–4
5–9	383	196	187	391	200	191	406	208	198	5–9
10–14	368	188	180	383	196	187	389	199	190	10–14
15–19	360	184	176	366	187	179	381	195	186	15–19
20–24	350	178	172	359	183	176	365	186	179	20–24
25–29	305	154	151	349	177	172	357	182	175	25–29
30–34	312	158	154	304	153	151	346	175	171	30–34
35–39	303	152	151	309	156	153	302	152	150	35–39
40–44	302	149	153	300	150	150	306	154	152	40–44
45–49	290	137	153	295	145	150	295	147	148	45–49
50–54	208	97	111	282	132	150	287	140	147	50–54
55–59	254	117	137	198	91	107	269	124	145	55–59
60–64	240	109	131	237	106	131	185	83	102	60–64
65–69	200	89	111	213	93	120	211	91	120	65–69
70–74	148	60	88	165	69	96	177	73	104	70–74
75–79	95	35	60	109	41	68	123	48	75	75–79
80–84	54	19	35	58	20	38	67	23	44	80–84
85 +	26	8	18	31	9	22	34	10	24	85 +
All ages	4590	2231	2359	4757	2317	2440	4924	2407	2517	All ages

TABLE 5 OBSERVED AND PROJECTED VITAL RATES

Rates per thousand	Observed			Projected						Stable	
				1970		1975		1980			
	Total	Males	Females	Males	Females	Males	Females	Males	Females	Males	Females
Birth	18.04	19.11	17.03	18.99	16.99	19.07	17.15	19.05	17.24	18.64	17.46
Death	10.20	10.88	9.56	11.17	10.21	11.49	10.87	11.67	11.25	12.02	10.83
Increase	7.84	8.23	7.47	7.82	6.78	7.58	6.28	7.38	5.99		6.6222

TABLE 6 RATES STANDARDIZED ON THREE STANDARD COUNTRIES

Standardized rates per thousand	England and Wales, 1961			United States, 1960			Mexico, 1960		
	Total	Males	Females	Total	Males	Females	Total	Males	Females
Birth	16.41	17.76*	15.46	16.69	16.68*	15.99	19.29	16.04*	18.71
Death	11.50	11.89*	11.19	9.45	10.55*	8.29	5.09	8.76*	4.17
Increase	4.91	5.87*	4.27	7.24	6.13*	7.70	14.20	7.28*	14.54

TABLE 7 VITAL STATISTICS AND RATES INFERRED FROM AGE DISTRIBUTIONS (FEMALES)

Vital statistics		Thompson				Bourgeois-Pichat				Coale	
		Age range	NRR	1000r	Interval	Age range	NRR	1000b	1000d	1000r	Coale
TFR	2.58	0–4	1.18	6.02	27.43	5–29	1.26	17.68	9.07	8.62	$1000b$ 19.50
GRR	1.26	5–9	1.20	6.74	27.40	30–54	1.19	17.65	11.10	6.54	$1000d$ 7.66
NRR	1.20	10–14	1.18	6.12	27.35	55–79	1.70	42.81	23.25	19.56	$1000r$ 11.83
Generation	27.72	15–19	1.17	5.54	27.27	*20–44	0.95	13.30	15.24	-1.94	$1000k_1$ 29.98
Sex ratio	105.7										$1000k_2$ 0.39

TABLE 8 LESLIE MATRIX AND ITS ANALYSIS (FEMALES)

Start of age interval	Sub-diagonal	First row	Percent in stable population	Fisher values	Total reproductive values	Net maternity function	Matrix equation coefficient	Parameters	Integral	Matrix
0	0.99551	0.00000	8.340	1.047	196716	0.00000	0.00000	λ_1	1.0337	1.0337
5	0.99821	0.00012	8.032	1.087	195499	0.00000	0.00012	λ_2	0.3667	0.3734
10	0.99811	0.04153	7.756	1.125	198487	0.00024	0.04127		+0.7727	+0.7472i
15	0.99737	0.21831	7.489	1.122	193550	0.08230	0.21653	r_1	0.0066	0.0066
20	0.99672	0.36626	7.226	0.934	141714	0.35077	0.36232	r_2	-0.0313	-0.0360
25	0.99571	0.30886	6.968	0.584	90170	0.37388	0.30454		+0.2255	+0.2215i
30	0.99392	0.17989	6.712	0.281	42707	0.23520	0.17662	c_1		22419
35	0.99102	0.07937	6.454	0.103	15859	0.11803	0.07745	c_2		1315
40	0.98652	0.02113	6.187	0.024	3674	0.03686	0.02043			4978i
45	0.97961	0.00222	5.905	0.002	268	0.00399	0.00212	$2\pi/y$	27.857	28.370
50	0.96910	0.00013	5.596	0.000	19	0.00025	0.00012	Δ	3.142	
55	0.80130		23.336							

European Common Market, 1955

TABLE 1 DATA INPUT TO COMPUTATIONS

Age at last birthday	Population					Births, by age of mother	Deaths			Age at last birthday
	Total	Males	%	Females	%		Total	Males	Females	
0	2788916	1427483	1.8	1361433	1.6	0	114732	64810	49922	0
1–4	11042852	5649216	7.1	5393636	6.3	0	21043	11419	9624	1–4
5–9	13240112	6763712	8.5	6476400	7.5	0	8028	4692	3336	5–9
10–14	12285681	6264437	7.9	6021244	7.1	212	5742	3526	2216	10–14
15–19	12711934	6450358	8.2	6261576	7.3	110083	10912	7415	3497	15–19
20–24	12332035	6255438	7.9	6076597	7.1	724422	14845	10105	4740	20–24
25–29	12298412	6128069	7.7	6170343	7.2	918228	17107	10759	6348	25–29
30–34	11735662	5568010	7.0	6167652	7.2	684217	20315	11623	8692	30–34
35–39	9313010	4404749	5.6	4908261	5.8	286129	18084	9924	8160	35–39
40–44	11070970	5211037	6.6	5859933	6.9	122647	35336	20119	15217	40–44
45–49	11421902	5435693	6.9	5986209	7.0	10579	57130	34337	22793	45–49
50–54	10806790	5195832	6.6	5610958	6.6	53	84226	52586	31640	50–54
55–59	9170573	4182067	5.3	4988506	5.9	0	109766	66860	42906	55–59
60–64	7513815	3219310	4.1	4294505	5.0	0	135971	75254	59717	60–64
65–69	6229030	2648151	3.3	3580879	4.2	0	181434	95715	85719	65–69
70–74	4803288	2034679	2.6	2768609	3.2		235063	117870	119193	70–74
75–79	3251174	1370248	1.7	1880926	2.2		273421	131200	142221	75–79
80–84	1608878	656693	0.8	952185	1.1	1466341 M	224568	102086	122482	80–84
85+	679258	247534	0.3	431724	0.5	1390229 F	164881	65734	99147	85+
All ages	164304292	79112716		85191576		2856570	1733604	897034	836570	All ages

TABLE 2 LIFE TABLE FOR MALES

Age, x	$_nq_x$	l_x	$_nd_x$	$_nL_x$	$_nm_x$	T_x	$1000r_x$	$\overset{\circ}{e}_x$	$_nM_x$	Age, x
0	0.04389	100000	4389	96681	0.04540	6632472	0.00	66.32	0.04540	0
1	0.00804	95611	769	380211	0.00202	6535791	0.00	68.35	0.00202	1
5	0.00345	94842	327	473392	0.00069	6155580	11.15	64.90	0.00069	5
10	0.00281	94515	266	471954	0.00056	5682188	4.02	60.12	0.00055	10
15	0.00573	94249	540	469996	0.00115	5210233	0.00	55.28	0.00115	15
20	0.00805	93709	754	466716	0.00162	4740237	3.58	50.58	0.00162	20
25	0.00875	92955	813	462783	0.00176	4273521	9.83	45.97	0.00176	25
30	0.01040	92142	958	458357	0.00209	3810738	31.00	41.35	0.00209	30
35	0.01121	91183	1022	453521	0.00225	3352381	4.08	36.77	0.00225	35
40	0.01913	90161	1725	446852	0.00386	2898861	0.00	32.15	0.00386	40
45	0.03113	88436	2753	435822	0.00632	2452008	0.00	27.73	0.00632	45
50	0.04959	85683	4249	418531	0.01015	2016186	15.69	23.53	0.01012	50
55	0.07743	81434	6306	392279	0.01607	1597655	31.56	19.62	0.01599	55
60	0.11241	75128	8445	355532	0.02375	1205377	16.46	16.04	0.02369	60
65	0.16680	66683	11122	306798	0.03625	849845	16.46	12.74	0.03614	65
70	0.25465	55561	14148	243457	0.05811	543047	16.46	9.77	0.05793	70
75	0.38725	41412	16037	166965	0.09605	299590	16.46	7.23	0.09575	75
80	0.55676	25375	14128	90559	0.15601	132624	16.46	5.23	0.15545	80
85+	*1.00000	11247	11247	42065	0.26738	42065	16.46	3.74	0.26556	85+

TABLE 3 LIFE TABLE FOR FEMALES

Age, x	$_nq_x$	l_x	$_nd_x$	$_nL_x$	$_nm_x$	T_x	$1000r_x$	$\overset{\circ}{e}_x$	$_nM_x$	Age, x
0	0.03569	100000	3569	97336	0.03667	7128514	0.00	71.29	0.03667	0
1	0.00710	96431	685	383741	0.00178	7031178	0.00	72.91	0.00178	1
5	0.00256	95746	245	478118	0.00051	6647437	10.66	69.43	0.00052	5
10	0.00184	95501	176	477071	0.00037	6169319	2.93	64.60	0.00037	10
15	0.00279	95325	266	476003	0.00056	5692249	0.00	59.71	0.00056	15
20	0.00389	95060	370	474419	0.00078	5216246	0.59	54.87	0.00078	20
25	0.00513	94690	486	472294	0.00103	4741827	0.00	50.08	0.00103	25
30	0.00704	94204	663	469421	0.00141	4269533	21.52	45.32	0.00141	30
35	0.00828	93541	775	465878	0.00166	3800112	3.32	40.63	0.00166	35
40	0.01291	92766	1197	461035	0.00260	3334234	0.00	35.94	0.00260	40
45	0.01887	91569	1728	453796	0.00381	2873200	0.43	31.38	0.00381	45
50	0.02789	89841	2505	443349	0.00565	2419404	12.40	26.93	0.00564	50
55	0.04231	87335	3695	428097	0.00863	1976055	17.72	22.63	0.00860	55
60	0.06773	83640	5665	405122	0.01398	1547958	25.12	18.51	0.01391	60
65	0.11404	77975	8892	369272	0.02408	1142837	25.12	14.66	0.02394	65
70	0.19491	69083	13465	313615	0.04294	773565	25.12	11.20	0.04269	70
75	0.32054	55618	17828	234536	0.07601	459950	25.12	8.27	0.07561	75
80	0.48529	37790	18339	141911	0.12923	225414	25.12	5.96	0.12863	80
85+	1.00000	19451	19451	83503	0.23294	83503	25.12	4.29	0.22965	85+

[536]

TABLE 4 POPULATION PROJECTION, USING FIXED AGE-SPECIFIC BIRTH AND DEATH RATES, IN THOUSANDS

Age at last birthday	1960 Total	Males	Females	1965 Total	Males	Females	1970 Total	Males	Females	Age at last birthday
0–4	13783	7045	6738	13908	7109	6799	14008	7160	6848	0–4
5–9	13739	7025	6714	13689	6993	6596	13815	7057	6758	5–9
10–14	13205	6743	6462	13702	7003	6699	13654	6972	6582	10–14
15–19	12246	6238	6008	13163	6715	6448	13558	6974	6584	15–19
20–24	12646	6405	6241	12183	6195	5988	13394	6658	6426	20–24
25–29	12252	6203	6049	12564	6351	6213	12104	6143	5961	25–29
30–34	12202	6069	6133	12156	6143	6013	12466	6291	6175	30–34
35–39	11630	5509	6121	12092	6005	6087	12046	6079	5957	35–39
40–44	9197	4340	4857	11485	5428	6057	11940	5917	6023	40–44
45–49	10850	5082	5768	9014	4233	4781	11256	5294	5962	45–49
50–54	11068	5220	5848	10516	4881	5635	8736	4065	4671	50–54
55–59	10288	4870	5418	10540	4893	5647	10016	4575	5441	55–59
60–64	8511	3790	4721	9541	4414	5127	9778	4434	5344	60–64
65–69	6692	2778	3914	7574	3271	4303	8482	3809	4673	65–69
70–74	5142	2101	3041	5528	2204	3324	6249	2595	3554	70–74
75–79	3465	1395	2070	3715	1441	2274	3998	1512	2486	75–79
80–84	1881	743	1138	2010	757	1253	2158	782	1376	80–84
85 +	865	305	560	1015	345	570	1089	352	737	85 +
All ages	169662	81861	87801	174395	84381	90014	178547	86679	91868	All ages

TABLE 5 OBSERVED AND PROJECTED VITAL RATES

Rates per thousand	Observed Total	Males	Females	Projected 1960 Males	Females	1965 Males	Females	1970 Males	Females	Stable Males	Females
Birth	17.39	18.53	16.32	18.18	16.07	17.70	15.73	17.41	15.58	16.87	15.78
Death	10.55	11.34	9.82	11.72	10.63	12.01	11.29	12.29	11.84	13.74	12.66
Increase	6.83	7.20	6.50	6.46	5.44	5.68	4.44	5.12	3.74		3.1290

TABLE 6 RATES STANDARDIZED ON THREE STANDARD COUNTRIES

Standardized rates per thousand	England and Wales, 1961 Total	Males	Females	United States, 1960 Total	Males	Females	Mexico, 1960 Total	Males	Females
Birth	15.19	17.08*	14.33	15.45	15.90*	14.82	17.14	15.47*	16.64
Death	12.40	12.44*	12.46	10.25	11.01*	9.33	5.79	9.29*	4.92
Increase	2.79	4.64*	1.87	5.20	4.89*	5.48	11.35	6.19*	11.72

TABLE 7 VITAL STATISTICS AND RATES INFERRED FROM AGE DISTRIBUTIONS (FEMALES)

Vital statistics		Thompson Age range	NRR	$1000r$	Interval	Bourgeois-Pichat Age range	NRR	$1000b$	$1000d$	$1000r$	Coale	
TFR	2.39	0–4	1.12	4.05	27.41	5–29	1.03	15.61	14.46	1.15	$1000b$	17.61
GRR	1.16	5–9	1.08	2.72	27.37	30–54	0.92	12.82	15.82	-3.00	$1000d$	11.10
NRR	1.09	10–14	1.01	0.21	27.32	55–79	1.65	39.46	21.02	18.44	$1000r$	6.50
Generation	28.89	15–19	1.07	2.40	27.24	*50–74	1.63	38.52	20.44	18.08	$1000k_1$	30.08
Sex ratio	105.5										$1000k_2$	0.47

TABLE 8 LESLIE MATRIX AND ITS ANALYSIS (FEMALES)

Start of age interval	Sub-diagonal	First row	Percent in stable population	Fisher values	Total reproductive values	Net maternity function	Matrix equation coefficient	Parameters Integral	Matrix
0	0.99385	0.00000	7.535	1.047	7075761	0.00000	0.00000	λ_1 1.0158	1.0158
5	0.99781	0.00004	7.372	1.071	6933513	0.00000	0.00004	λ_2 0.4109	0.4148
10	0.99776	0.02058	7.242	1.090	6562049	0.00008	0.02040	+0.7560	+0.7341i
15	0.99667	0.15967	7.113	1.088	6811882	0.04073	0.15799	r_1 0.0031	0.0031
20	0.99552	0.31299	6.979	0.941	5717600	0.27525	0.30865	r_2 -0.0301	-0.0341
25	0.99392	0.30328	6.840	0.631	3891886	0.34205	0.29775	+0.2146	+0.2113i
30	0.99245	0.19760	6.693	0.325	2004391	0.25344	0.19281	c_1	874850
35	0.98960	0.09249	6.539	0.124	608085	0.13217	0.08957	c_2	232972
40	0.98430	0.02654	6.371	0.029	172605	0.04696	0.02543		-255502i
45	0.97698	0.00208	6.174	0.002	12920	0.00390	0.00196	$2\pi/y$ 29.280	29.735
50	0.96560	0.00001	5.938	0.000	71	0.00002	0.00001	Δ 4.186	
55	0.78829		25.204						

European Common Market, 1960

TABLE 1   DATA INPUT TO COMPUTATIONS

Age at last birthday	Population					Births, by age of mother	Deaths			Age at last birthday
	Total	Males	%	Females	%		Total	Males	Females	
0	3001146	1535156	1.8	1465990	1.6	0	99439	56564	42875	0
1–4	11418888	5839375	7.0	5579513	6.3	0	16980	9310	7670	1–4
5–9	13679716	6984621	8.4	6695095	7.5	0	6821	4083	2738	5–9
10–14	13831681	7059730	8.5	6771951	7.6	285	5516	3466	2050	10–14
15–19	11933327	6083640	7.3	5849687	6.6	112593	9384	6596	2788	15–19
20–24	13162648	6699168	8.1	6463480	7.3	811657	13827	9767	4060	20–24
25–29	12309237	6244037	7.5	6065200	6.8	1000109	14786	9696	5090	25–29
30–34	12485164	6234640	7.5	6250524	7.0	680635	17909	11099	6810	30–34
35–39	12407240	5871456	7.1	6535784	7.3	376556	24264	13868	10395	35–39
40–44	8261215	3872800	4.7	4388415	4.9	101149	23919	13913	10006	40–44
45–49	11492114	5393785	6.5	6098329	6.8	9387	51586	30496	21090	45–49
50–54	11384348	5378471	6.5	6005877	6.7	113	83667	52682	30985	50–54
55–59	10297459	4880091	5.9	5417368	6.1	0	122499	79078	43421	55–59
60–64	8563834	3786222	4.6	4777612	5.4	0	160116	97528	62588	60–64
65–69	6655125	2734529	3.3	3920596	4.4	0	194259	105272	88987	65–69
70–74	5168039	2102447	2.5	3065592	3.4		247835	124712	123123	70–74
75–79	3494086	1412785	1.7	2081301	2.3		285299	134276	151023	75–79
80–84	1866684	739307	0.9	1127377	1.3	1587430 M	260462	116689	143773	80–84
85+	815313	294586	0.4	520727	0.6	1505154 F	206778	82242	124536	85+
All ages	172227264	83146846		89080418		3092584	1845346	961337	884009	All ages

TABLE 2   LIFE TABLE FOR MALES

Age, x	$_nq_x$	l_x	$_nd_x$	$_nL_x$	$_nm_x$	T_x	$1000r_x$	$\overset{\circ}{e}_x$	$_nM_x$	Age, x
0	0.03574	100000	3574	97287	0.03674	6707485	3.68	67.07	0.03685	0
1	0.00632	96426	609	383934	0.00159	6610199	3.68	68.55	0.00159	1
5	0.00292	95817	279	478385	0.00058	6226265	3.51	64.98	0.00058	5
10	0.00246	95537	235	477148	0.00049	5747880	13.17	60.16	0.00049	10
15	0.00541	95302	516	475317	0.00109	5270732	4.21	55.31	0.00108	15
20	0.00726	94787	689	472256	0.00146	4795415	0.00	50.59	0.00146	20
25	0.00774	94098	728	468699	0.00155	4323159	5.61	45.94	0.00155	25
30	0.00887	93370	828	464857	0.00178	3854460	4.31	41.28	0.00178	30
35	0.01183	92542	1095	460142	0.00238	3389603	45.13	36.63	0.00236	35
40	0.01783	91448	1630	453456	0.00360	2929461	4.77	32.03	0.00359	40
45	0.02791	89817	2507	443350	0.00565	2476005	0.00	27.57	0.00565	45
50	0.04790	87310	4182	426932	0.00979	2032655	0.00	23.28	0.00979	50
55	0.07834	83129	6512	400433	0.01626	1605723	18.30	19.32	0.01620	55
60	0.12165	76616	9320	360900	0.02582	1205290	14.66	15.73	0.02576	60
65	0.17654	67296	11880	307836	0.03859	844391	14.66	12.55	0.03850	65
70	0.25964	55416	14388	241923	0.05947	536555	14.66	9.68	0.05932	70
75	0.38477	41028	15786	165635	0.09531	294632	14.66	7.18	0.09504	75
80	0.56277	25242	14205	89705	0.15835	128996	14.66	5.11	0.15784	80
85+	*1.00000	11036	11036	39291	0.28088	39291	14.66	3.56	0.27918	85+

TABLE 3   LIFE TABLE FOR FEMALES

Age, x	$_nq_x$	l_x	$_nd_x$	$_nL_x$	$_nm_x$	T_x	$1000r_x$	$\overset{\circ}{e}_x$	$_nM_x$	Age, x
0	0.02853	100000	2853	97860	0.02916	7260318	3.84	72.60	0.02925	0
1	0.00545	97147	530	387052	0.00137	7162457	3.84	73.73	0.00137	1
5	0.00204	96617	197	482592	0.00041	6775406	3.30	70.13	0.00041	5
10	0.00151	96420	146	481742	0.00030	6292813	13.13	65.26	0.00030	10
15	0.00238	96274	229	480829	0.00048	5811072	4.20	60.36	0.00048	15
20	0.00314	96045	301	479506	0.00063	5330242	0.00	55.50	0.00063	20
25	0.00419	95744	401	477760	0.00084	4850736	2.51	50.66	0.00084	25
30	0.00543	95342	518	475491	0.00109	4372976	0.00	45.87	0.00109	30
35	0.00797	94824	755	472348	0.00160	3897485	33.75	41.10	0.00159	35
40	0.01135	94069	1068	467852	0.00228	3425136	4.56	36.41	0.00228	40
45	0.01715	93002	1595	461283	0.00346	2957284	0.00	31.80	0.00346	45
50	0.02552	91406	2333	451600	0.00517	2496001	6.49	27.31	0.00516	50
55	0.03946	89074	3515	437235	0.00804	2044401	14.48	22.95	0.00802	55
60	0.06391	85559	5468	415201	0.01317	1607167	23.14	18.78	0.01310	60
65	0.10838	80091	8680	380360	0.02282	1191966	23.14	14.88	0.02270	65
70	0.18439	71411	13168	326087	0.04038	811636	23.14	11.37	0.04016	70
75	0.30980	58243	18044	247406	0.07293	485519	23.14	8.34	0.07256	75
80	0.48257	40200	19399	151445	0.12809	238113	23.14	5.92	0.12753	80
85+	1.00000	20800	20800	86668	0.24000	86668	23.14	4.17	0.23916	85+

TABLE 4 POPULATION PROJECTION, USING FIXED AGE-SPECIFIC BIRTH AND DEATH RATES, IN THOUSANDS

Age at last birthday	1965			1970			1975			Age at last birthday
	Total	Males	Females	Total	Males	Females	Total	Males	Females	
0–4	14946	7643	7303	15033	7688	7345	15335	7842	7493	0–4
5–9	14343	7331	7012	14866	7598	7268	14953	7643	7310	5–9
10–14	13650	6967	6683	14311	7312	6999	14834	7579	7255	10–14
15–19	13792	7033	6759	13611	6940	6671	14270	7284	6986	15–19
20–24	11878	6044	5834	13728	6987	6741	13547	6895	6652	20–24
25–29	13089	6649	6440	11811	5999	5812	13651	6935	6716	25–29
30–34	12229	6193	6036	13003	6594	6409	11735	5950	5785	30–34
35–39	12380	6171	6209	12126	6130	5996	12894	6527	6357	35–39
40–44	12260	5786	6474	12232	6082	6150	11980	6041	5939	40–44
45–49	8113	3786	4327	12040	5657	6383	12010	5946	6064	45–49
50–54	11164	5194	5970	7882	3646	4236	11597	5448	6249	50–54
55–59	10860	5045	5815	10652	4872	5780	7521	3420	4101	55–59
60–64	9542	4398	5144	10069	4547	5522	9880	4391	5489	60–64
65–69	7607	3230	4377	8465	3752	4713	8936	3878	5058	65–69
70–74	5510	2149	3361	6290	2538	3752	6988	2948	4040	70–74
75–79	3765	1439	2326	4021	1471	2550	4585	1738	2847	75–79
80–84	2039	765	1274	2204	780	1424	2358	797	1561	80–84
85 +	969	324	645	1064	335	729	1156	341	815	85 +
All ages	178136	86147	91989	183408	88928	94480	188330	91503	96727	All ages

TABLE 5 OBSERVED AND PROJECTED VITAL RATES

Rates per thousand	Observed			Projected 1965		1970		1975		Stable	
	Total	Males	Females	Males	Females	Males	Females	Males	Females	Males	Females
Birth	17.96	19.09	16.90	18.45	16.38	18.06	16.12	18.05	16.21	17.93	15.75
Death	10.71	11.56	9.92	11.80	10.66	12.00	11.24	12.23	11.76	12.70	11.52
Increase	7.24	7.53	6.97	6.65	5.72	6.06	4.88	5.81	4.44		5.2312

TABLE 6 RATES STANDARDIZED ON THREE STANDARD COUNTRIES

Standardized rates per thousand	England and Wales, 1961			United States, 1960			Mexico, 1960		
	Total	Males	Females	Total	Males	Females	Total	Males	Females
Birth	15.91	17.31*	15.01	16.17	16.17*	15.51	18.07	15.84*	17.55
Death	12.11	12.36*	11.91	9.93	10.98*	8.81	5.35	9.27*	4.42
Increase	3.80	4.94*	3.10	6.24	5.19*	6.70	12.71	6.57*	13.12

TABLE 7 VITAL STATISTICS AND RATES INFERRED FROM AGE DISTRIBUTIONS (FEMALES)

Vital statistics		Thompson				Bourgeois-Pichat					Coale	
		Age range	NRR	$1000r$	Interval	Age range	NRR	$1000b$	$1000d$	$1000r$		
TFR	2.50	0–4	1.17	5.65	27.43	5–29	1.13	16.04	11.65	4.39	$1000b$	18.18
GRR	1.22	5–9	1.10	3.43	27.39	30–54	1.01	14.25	13.81	0.45	$1000d$	8.98
NRR	1.16	10–14	1.12	4.01	27.34	55–79	1.66	41.21	22.45	18.75	$1000r$	9.20
Generation	28.72	15–19	0.97	-1.13	27.26	*50–74	1.61	37.98	20.43	17.55	$1000k_1$	33.57
Sex ratio	105.5										$1000k_2$	0.47

TABLE 8 LESLIE MATRIX AND ITS ANALYSIS (FEMALES)

Start of age interval	Sub-diagonal	First row	Percent in stable population	Fisher values	Total reproductive values	Net maternity function	Matrix equation coefficient
0	0.99522	0.00000	8.016	1.045	7360131	0.00000	0.00000
5	0.99824	0.00005	7.772	1.078	7214050	0.00000	0.00005
10	0.99811	0.02274	7.558	1.108	7503231	0.00010	0.02259
15	0.99725	0.17051	7.349	1.116	6526647	0.04508	0.16907
20	0.99636	0.34205	7.139	0.970	6268625	0.29306	0.33824
25	0.99525	0.32246	6.929	0.641	3885224	0.38342	0.31771
30	0.99339	0.19603	6.718	0.322	2014083	0.25200	0.19223
35	0.99048	0.39493	6.501	0.127	828875	0.13245	0.09247
40	0.98596	0.32899	6.273	0.031	137434	0.05248	0.02797
45	0.97901	0.00184	6.025	0.002	11544	0.00346	0.00175
50	0.96819	0.00002	5.746	0.000	155	0.00004	0.00002
55	0.79443		23.973				

Parameters

	Integral	Matrix
λ_1	1.0265	1.0265
λ_2	0.4024	0.4066
	+0.7675	+0.7441 i
r_1	0.0052	0.0052
r_2	-0.0286	-0.0330
	+0.2176	+0.2141 i
c_1		871950
c_2		214713
		-256424 i
$2\pi/y$	28.877	29.343
Δ	4.133	

European Common Market, 1965

TABLE 1 DATA INPUT TO COMPUTATIONS

Age at last birthday	Total	Males	%	Females	%	Births, by age of mother	Total	Males	Females	Age at last birthday
		Population						Deaths		
0	3292589	1686574	1.9	1606015	1.7	0	83718	47799	35919	0
1–4	12629549	6459111	7.3	6170438	6.6	0	13922	7813	6109	1–4
5–9	14173730	7247562	8.2	6926168	7.4	0	6636	3968	2668	5–9
10–14	13849253	7069997	8.0	6779256	7.2	508	5312	3227	2085	10–14
15–19	14136857	7228734	8.2	6908123	7.3	202804	10703	7541	3162	15–19
20–24	12522901	6443556	7.3	6079345	6.5	832194	12570	8870	3700	20–24
25–29	13403356	6933164	7.8	6470192	6.9	1103579	14270	9617	4653	25–29
30–34	12508070	6406096	7.2	6101974	6.5	689711	17059	11032	6027	30–34
35–39	12617099	6316633	7.1	6300466	6.7	351242	24721	15548	9173	35–39
40–44	12444439	5878883	6.6	6565556	7.0	114083	35686	21581	14105	40–44
45–49	8439229	3946542	4.5	4492687	4.8	8853	37080	22263	14817	45–49
50–54	11158900	5193536	5.9	5965364	6.3	154	79307	49282	30025	50–54
55–59	10987034	5107819	5.8	5879215	6.3	0	125157	80868	44289	55–59
60–64	9725225	4475911	5.0	5249314	5.6	0	181112	115383	65729	60–64
65–69	7817368	3331316	3.8	4486052	4.8	0	226239	131852	94387	65–69
70–74	5705961	2221540	2.5	3484421	3.7		261395	131829	129566	70–74
75–79	3947232	1512954	1.7	2434278	2.6		297127	138074	159053	75–79
80–84	2206248	825540	0.9	1380708	1.5	1696095 M	274041	118019	156022	80–84
85 +	1140612	400393	0.5	740219	0.8	1607033 F	247050	95961	151089	85 +
All ages	182705652	88685861		94019791		3303128	1953105	1020527	932578	All ages

TABLE 2 LIFE TABLE FOR MALES

Age, x	$_nq_x$	l_x	$_nd_x$	$_nL_x$	$_nm_x$	T_x	$1000r_x$	$\overset{\circ}{e}_x$	$_nM_x$	Age, x
0	0.02767	100000	2767	97896	0.02827	6799233	3.32	67.99	0.02834	0
1	0.00480	97233	467	387575	0.00120	6701337	3.32	68.92	0.00121	1
5	0.00273	96766	264	483171	0.00055	6313762	13.45	65.25	0.00055	5
10	0.00228	96502	220	482011	0.00046	5830591	0.00	60.42	0.00046	10
15	0.00521	96282	502	480248	0.00104	5348580	8.29	55.55	0.00104	15
20	0.00686	95781	657	477292	0.00138	4868331	2.87	50.83	0.00138	20
25	0.00691	95123	657	474005	0.00139	4391039	0.00	46.16	0.00139	25
30	0.00858	94466	811	470405	0.00172	3917034	7.52	41.47	0.00172	30
35	0.01225	93655	1147	465592	0.00246	3446629	6.04	36.80	0.00246	35
40	0.01834	92508	1696	458587	0.00370	2981037	43.23	32.22	0.00367	40
45	0.02788	90811	2532	448228	0.00565	2522451	6.41	27.78	0.00564	45
50	0.04643	88279	4099	431961	0.00949	2074223	0.00	23.50	0.00949	50
55	0.07635	84181	6427	405954	0.01583	1642261	0.00	19.51	0.01583	55
60	0.12182	77753	9472	366324	0.02586	1236307	16.30	15.90	0.02578	60
65	0.18108	68282	12365	311547	0.03969	869983	16.30	12.74	0.03958	65
70	0.25957	55917	14514	243932	0.05950	558436	16.30	9.99	0.05934	70
75	0.37203	41403	15403	168306	0.09152	314504	16.30	7.60	0.09126	75
80	0.52137	26000	13555	94560	0.14335	146198	16.30	5.62	0.14296	80
85 +	1.00000	12444	12444	51638	0.24099	51638	16.30	4.15	0.23967	85 +

TABLE 3 LIFE TABLE FOR FEMALES

Age, x	$_nq_x$	l_x	$_nd_x$	$_nL_x$	$_nm_x$	T_x	$1000r_x$	$\overset{\circ}{e}_x$	$_nM_x$	Age, x
0	0.02194	100000	2194	98341	0.02231	7405463	3.20	74.05	0.02237	0
1	0.00393	97806	385	390108	0.00099	7307122	3.20	74.71	0.00099	1
5	0.00192	97421	187	486641	0.00038	6917014	13.18	71.00	0.00039	5
10	0.00154	97235	149	485808	0.00031	6430373	0.00	66.13	0.00031	10
15	0.00229	97085	222	484901	0.00046	5944565	10.44	61.23	0.00046	15
20	0.00304	96863	294	483605	0.00061	5459664	5.95	56.36	0.00061	20
25	0.00359	96569	347	482014	0.00072	4976059	0.00	51.53	0.00072	25
30	0.00493	96222	474	479997	0.00099	4494045	1.64	46.70	0.00099	30
35	0.00725	95748	695	477116	0.00146	4014049	0.00	41.92	0.00146	35
40	0.01075	95053	1022	472888	0.00216	3536933	31.58	37.21	0.00215	40
45	0.01638	94031	1540	466573	0.00330	3064045	6.19	32.59	0.00330	45
50	0.02487	92491	2301	457079	0.00503	2597472	0.00	28.08	0.00503	50
55	0.03706	90190	3342	443224	0.00754	2140394	4.80	23.73	0.00753	55
60	0.06115	86848	5311	421980	0.01259	1697170	23.60	19.54	0.01252	60
65	0.10084	81537	8222	388649	0.02116	1275190	23.60	15.64	0.02104	65
70	0.17182	73315	12597	336955	0.03738	886541	23.60	12.09	0.03718	70
75	0.28336	60718	17205	261992	0.06567	549586	23.60	9.05	0.06534	75
80	0.44552	43513	19386	170542	0.11367	287594	23.60	6.61	0.11300	80
85 +	*1.00000	24127	24127	117052	0.20612	117052	23.60	4.85	0.20411	85 +

TABLE 4 POPULATION PROJECTION, USING FIXED AGE-SPECIFIC BIRTH AND DEATH RATES, IN THOUSANDS

Age at last birthday	1970			1975			1980			Age at last birthday
	Total	Males	Females	Total	Males	Females	Total	Males	Females	
0–4	16230	8309	7921	16599	8498	8101	17043	8725	8318	0–4
5–9	15855	8107	7748	16162	8270	7892	16528	8457	8071	5–9
10–14	14144	7230	6914	15822	8088	7734	16129	8250	7879	10–14
15–19	13811	7044	6767	14105	7204	6901	15778	8058	7720	15–19
20–24	14074	7184	6890	13750	7001	6749	14042	7159	6883	20–24
25–29	12458	6399	6059	14002	7135	6867	13679	6953	6726	25–29
30–34	13323	6880	6443	12385	6351	6034	13919	7081	6838	30–34
35–39	12406	6341	6065	13214	6810	6404	12284	6286	5998	35–39
40–44	12467	6222	6245	12257	6245	6012	13056	6708	6348	40–44
45–49	12224	5746	6478	12242	6081	6161	12035	6104	5931	45–49
50–54	8204	3803	4401	11884	5538	6346	11896	5860	6036	50–54
55–59	10666	4881	5785	7842	3574	4268	11358	5204	6154	55–59
60–64	10206	4609	5597	9911	4404	5507	7288	3225	4063	60–64
65–69	8642	3807	4835	9075	3920	5155	8818	3746	5072	65–69
70–74	6497	2608	3889	7172	2980	4192	7539	3069	4470	70–74
75–79	4242	1533	2709	4824	1800	3024	5315	2056	3259	75–79
80–84	2435	850	1585	2625	861	1764	2980	1011	1969	80–84
85+	1399	451	948	1552	464	1088	1680	470	1210	85+
All ages	189283	92004	97279	195423	95224	100199	201367	98422	102945	All ages

TABLE 5 OBSERVED AND PROJECTED VITAL RATES

Rates per thousand	Observed			Projected						Stable	
				1970		1975		1980			
	Total	Males	Females	Males	Females	Males	Females	Males	Females	Males	Females
Birth	18.08	19.12	17.09	18.77	16.82	18.63	16.77	18.50	16.76	18.99	17.74
Death	10.69	11.51	9.92	11.74	10.70	11.88	11.24	11.98	11.61	11.67	10.41
Increase	7.39	7.62	7.17	7.03	6.12	6.74	5.53	6.52	5.15		7.3278

TABLE 6 RATES STANDARDIZED ON THREE STANDARD COUNTRIES

Standardized rates per thousand	England and Wales, 1961			United States, 1960			Mexico, 1960		
	Total	Males	Females	Total	Males	Females	Total	Males	Females
Birth	16.67	17.39*	15.72	16.97	16.37*	16.27	19.28	15.77*	18.71
Death	11.21	11.76*	10.70	9.17	10.52*	7.88	4.84	8.86*	3.88
Increase	5.46	5.64*	5.02	7.80	5.85*	8.39	14.44	6.91*	14.83

TABLE 7 VITAL STATISTICS AND RATES INFERRED FROM AGE DISTRIBUTIONS (FEMALES)

Vital statistics		Thompson				Bourgeois-Pichat					Coale	
		Age range	NRR	1000r	Interval	Age range	NRR	1000b	1000d	1000r		
TFR	2.63	0–4	1.19	6.50	27.43	5–29	1.13	15.71	11.28	4.43	1000b	17.08
GRR	1.28	5–9	1.13	4.52	27.40	30–54	1.15	16.49	11.23	5.27	1000d	9.27
NRR	1.23	10–14	1.10	3.55	27.35	55–79	1.56	36.67	20.24	16.44	1000r	7.81
Generation	28.18	15–19	1.13	4.37	27.28	*20–44	0.91	12.42	16.07	-3.65	1000k_1	20.45
Sex ratio	105.5										1000k_2	0.27

TABLE 8 LESLIE MATRIX AND ITS ANALYSIS (FEMALES)

Start of age interval	Sub-diagonal	First row	Percent in stable population	Fisher values	Total reproductive values	Net maternity function	Matrix equation coefficient
0	0.99630	0.00000	8.508	1.043	8107228	0.00000	0.00000
5	0.99829	0.00009	8.171	1.085	7518326	0.00000	0.00009
10	0.99813	0.03491	7.864	1.128	7646158	0.00018	0.03472
15	0.99733	0.19710	7.566	1.136	7845754	0.06926	0.19567
20	0.99671	0.36465	7.274	0.975	5929029	0.32208	0.36103
25	0.99581	0.33640	6.989	0.634	4099665	0.39999	0.33197
30	0.99400	0.20015	6.710	0.308	1878588	0.26396	0.19668
35	0.99114	0.08670	6.429	0.111	701718	0.12941	0.08469
40	0.98665	0.02296	6.143	0.025	166534	0.03998	0.02222
45	0.97965	0.00237	5.843	0.002	10834	0.00447	0.00227
50	0.96969	0.00003	5.518	0.000	192	0.00006	0.00003
55	0.80457		22.985				

Parameters

	Integral	Matrix
λ_1	1.0373	1.0373
λ_2	0.3914	0.3955
	+0.7813	+0.7568i
r_1	0.0073	0.0073
r_2	-0.0270	-0.0316
	+0.2213	+0.2178i
c_1		883780
c_2		197219
		-460053i
$2\pi/y$	28.396	28.844
Δ	4.643	

European Free Trade Association, 1955

TABLE 1 DATA INPUT TO COMPUTATIONS

Age at last birthday	Population Total	Males	%	Females	%	Births, by age of mother	Deaths Total	Males	Females	Age at last birthday
0	1356307	694925	1.7	661382	1.5	0	50479	28571	21908	0
1–4	5367344	2749636	6.6	2617708	5.9	0	13021	6894	6127	1–4
5–9	7256236	3709126	9.0	3547110	8.0	0	4283	2474	1809	5–9
10–14	6377662	3253196	7.9	3124466	7.1	75	2884	1721	1163	10–14
15–19	5763608	2910220	7.0	2853388	6.5	72205	4314	2846	1468	15–19
20–24	5687189	2849767	6.9	2837422	6.4	387678	5958	3917	2041	20–24
25–29	5931054	2949811	7.1	2981243	6.7	435143	6965	4225	2740	25–29
30–34	6362875	3121420	7.5	3241455	7.3	305653	8912	5128	3784	30–34
35–39	5563536	2725009	6.6	2838527	6.4	151632	10458	5902	4556	35–39
40–44	6181706	3017792	7.3	3163914	7.2	54537	17541	9958	7583	40–44
45–49	6091868	2970128	7.2	3121740	7.1	4768	27978	16386	11592	45–49
50–54	5621696	2699174	6.5	2922522	6.6	57	43276	26357	16919	50–54
55–59	4824318	2210333	5.3	2613985	5.9	0	58340	35635	22705	55–59
60–64	4062525	1792304	4.3	2270221	5.1	0	78737	46306	32431	60–64
65–69	3387744	1449904	3.5	1937840	4.4	0	106019	58594	47425	65–69
70–74	2631879	1092910	2.6	1538969	3.5		133895	68683	65212	70–74
75–79	1771553	710595	1.7	1060958	2.4		151469	72575	78894	75–79
80–84	905688	348752	0.8	556936	1.3	726377 M	125431	55416	71015	80–84
85+	429053	147100	0.4	281953	0.6	685371 F	100904	37086	63818	85+
All ages	85573841	41402102		44171739		1411748	951864	488674	463190	All ages

TABLE 2 LIFE TABLE FOR MALES

Age, x	$_nq_x$	l_x	$_nd_x$	$_nL_x$	$_nm_x$	T_x	$1000r_x$	$\overset{\circ}{e}_x$	$_nM_x$	Age, x
0	0.03993	100000	3993	97117	0.04111	6652544	0.00	66.53	0.04111	0
1	0.00996	96007	956	381282	0.00251	6555427	0.00	68.28	0.00251	1
5	0.00332	95051	316	474467	0.00067	6174145	4.60	64.96	0.00067	5
10	0.00265	94735	251	473080	0.00053	5699679	23.60	60.16	0.00053	10
15	0.00489	94484	462	471349	0.00098	5226599	12.28	55.32	0.00098	15
20	0.00685	94022	644	468545	0.00137	4755249	0.00	50.58	0.00137	20
25	0.00714	93378	666	465250	0.00143	4286704	0.00	45.91	0.00143	25
30	0.00819	92712	759	461731	0.00164	3821454	5.23	41.22	0.00164	30
35	0.01078	91953	991	457440	0.00217	3359724	1.11	36.54	0.00217	35
40	0.01637	90962	1489	451389	0.00330	2902283	0.00	31.91	0.00330	40
45	0.02728	89473	2441	441821	0.00552	2450894	5.27	27.39	0.00552	45
50	0.04795	87032	4174	425565	0.00981	2009073	19.40	23.08	0.00975	50
55	0.07805	82859	6467	399197	0.01620	1583508	24.18	19.11	0.01612	55
60	0.12198	76391	9319	359892	0.02589	1184311	11.74	15.50	0.02584	60
65	0.18451	67073	12376	305593	0.04050	824419	11.74	12.29	0.04041	65
70	0.27285	54697	14924	236968	0.06298	518826	11.74	9.49	0.06284	70
75	0.40676	39773	16178	158065	0.10235	281858	11.74	7.09	0.10213	75
80	0.56017	23595	13217	83015	0.15922	123792	11.74	5.25	0.15890	80
85+	1.00000	10378	10378	40777	0.25450	40777	11.74	3.93	0.25211	85+

TABLE 3 LIFE TABLE FOR FEMALES

Age, x	$_nq_x$	l_x	$_nd_x$	$_nL_x$	$_nm_x$	T_x	$1000r_x$	$\overset{\circ}{e}_x$	$_nM_x$	Age, x
0	0.03237	100000	3237	97717	0.03312	7152428	0.00	71.52	0.03312	0
1	0.00930	96763	900	384482	0.00234	7054711	0.00	72.91	0.00234	1
5	0.00254	95863	244	478708	0.00051	6670229	3.88	69.58	0.00051	5
10	0.00186	95620	178	477655	0.00037	6191521	21.33	64.75	0.00037	10
15	0.00257	95442	246	476630	0.00052	5713867	9.11	59.87	0.00051	15
20	0.00359	95196	342	475167	0.00072	5237237	0.00	55.20	0.00072	20
25	0.00459	94855	435	473229	0.00092	4762070	0.00	50.20	0.00092	25
30	0.00582	94420	550	470790	0.00117	4288841	3.71	45.42	0.00117	30
35	0.00800	93870	751	467589	0.00161	3818051	0.76	40.67	0.00161	35
40	0.01192	93119	1110	463019	0.00240	3350462	0.00	35.98	0.00240	40
45	0.01842	92010	1695	456117	0.00372	2887443	4.09	31.38	0.00371	45
50	0.02862	90315	2585	445538	0.00580	2431326	11.85	26.92	0.00579	50
55	0.04271	87730	3747	429959	0.00871	1985788	16.07	22.64	0.00869	55
60	0.06944	83983	5832	406448	0.01435	1555829	19.85	18.53	0.01429	60
65	0.11626	78151	9086	369608	0.02458	1149381	19.85	14.71	0.02447	65
70	0.19333	69065	13352	313718	0.04256	779773	19.85	11.29	0.04237	70
75	0.31581	55713	17595	235624	0.07467	466055	19.85	8.37	0.07436	75
80	0.48195	38118	18371	143545	0.12798	230431	19.85	6.05	0.12751	80
85+	1.00000	19747	19747	86886	0.22728	86886	19.85	4.40	0.22634	85+

TABLE 4 POPULATION PROJECTION, USING FIXED AGE-SPECIFIC BIRTH AND DEATH RATES, IN THOUSANDS

Age at last birthday	1960			1965			1970			Age at last birthday
	Total	Males	Females	Total	Males	Females	Total	Males	Females	
0–4	6716	3442	3274	6710	3439	3271	6950	3562	3388	0–4
5–9	6671	3416	3255	6664	3414	3250	6658	3411	3247	5–9
10–14	7237	3698	3539	6554	3406	3248	6647	3404	3243	10–14
15–19	6359	3241	3118	7217	3685	3532	6535	3394	3241	15–19
20–24	5738	2893	2845	6330	3222	3108	7184	3663	3521	20–24
25–29	5656	2830	2826	5706	2873	2833	6295	3199	3096	25–29
30–34	5893	2927	2966	5619	2808	2811	5669	2851	2818	30–34
35–39	6311	3092	3219	5846	2900	2946	5574	2782	2792	35–39
40–44	5500	2689	2811	6240	3052	3188	5779	2862	2917	40–44
45–49	6071	2954	3117	5401	2632	2769	6127	2987	3140	45–49
50–54	5910	2861	3049	5889	2845	3044	5240	2535	2705	50–54
55–59	5352	2532	2820	5627	2684	2943	5607	2669	2938	55–59
60–64	4464	1993	2471	4949	2283	2666	5201	2419	2782	60–64
65–69	3586	1522	2064	3939	1692	2247	4362	1938	2424	65–69
70–74	2769	1124	1645	2932	1180	1752	3219	1312	1907	70–74
75–79	1885	729	1156	1985	750	1235	2103	787	1316	75–79
80–84	1019	373	646	1087	383	704	1147	394	753	80–84
85 +	508	171	337	574	183	391	614	188	426	85 +
All ages	87645	42487	45158	89369	43431	45938	91011	44357	46554	All ages

TABLE 5 OBSERVED AND PROJECTED VITAL RATES

Rates per thousand	Observed			Projected						Stable	
				1960		1965		1970			
	Total	Males	Females	Males	Females	Males	Females	Males	Females	Males	Females
Birth	16.50	17.54	15.52	16.77	14.89	16.70	14.89	17.23	15.45	16.73	15.65
Death	11.12	11.80	10.49	12.17	11.22	12.51	11.84	12.89	12.36	13.74	12.66
Increase	5.37	5.74	5.03	4.61	3.67	4.19	3.05	4.34	3.09		2.9977

TABLE 6 RATES STANDARDIZED ON THREE STANDARD COUNTRIES

Standardized rates per thousand	England and Wales, 1961			United States, 1960			Mexico, 1960		
	Total	Males	Females	Total	Males	Females	Total	Males	Females
Birth	15.08	16.40*	14.19	15.32	15.51*	14.66	17.49	14.38*	16.94
Death	12.46	12.61*	12.35	10.28	11.18*	9.23	5.72	9.52*	4.84
Increase	2.61	3.79*	1.83	5.04	4.33*	5.42	11.78	4.85*	12.11

TABLE 7 VITAL STATISTICS AND RATES INFERRED FROM AGE DISTRIBUTIONS (FEMALES)

Vital statistics		Thompson				Bourgeois-Pichat					Coale	
TFR	2.37	Age range	NRR	1000r	Interval	Age range	NRR	1000b	1000d	1000r	$1000b$	19.26
GRR	1.15	0–4	1.07	2.57	27.42	5–29	1.25	16.81	8.50	8.31	$1000d$	7.80
NRR	1.09	5–9	1.14	4.91	27.38	30–54	0.99	14.72	15.18	-0.46	$1000r$	11.45
Generation	28.16	10–14	0.99	-0.22	27.33	55–79	1.46	30.85	16.71	14.14	$1000k_1$	51.58
• Sex ratio	106.0	15–19	0.91	-3.34	27.25	*50–74	1.48	31.79	17.21	14.58	$1000k_2$	0.72

TABLE 8 LESLIE MATRIX AND ITS ANALYSIS (FEMALES)

Start of age interval	Sub-diagonal	First row	Percent in stable population	Fisher values	Total reproductive values	Net maternity function	Matrix equation coefficient	Parameters		
									Integral	Matrix
0	0.99276	0.00000	7.494	1.045	3425650	0.00000	0.00000	λ_1	1.0151	1.0151
5	0.99780	0.00003	7.329	1.068	3789064	0.00000	0.00003	λ_2	0.3778	0.3848
10	0.99785	0.02958	7.204	1.087	3395390	0.00006	0.02930		+0.7509	+0.7277 i
15	0.99693	0.18905	7.082	1.075	3066044	0.05855	0.18587	r_1	0.0030	0.0030
20	0.99592	0.33007	6.955	0.896	2542350	0.31518	0.32526	r_2	-0.0347	-0.0389
25	0.99484	0.28065	6.823	0.567	1690459	0.33533	0.27542		+0.2209	+0.2169 i
30	0.99320	0.17247	6.687	0.284	920151	0.21552	0.16839	c_1		437104
35	0.99022	0.08250	6.543	0.109	308595	0.12126	0.08001	c_2		355200
40	0.98509	0.02194	6.382	0.024	77228	0.03875	0.02106			249675 i
45	0.97681	0.00181	6.194	0.002	5881	0.00338	0.00171	$2\pi/\gamma$	28.439	28.972
50	0.96503	0.00002	5.960	0.000	72	0.00004	0.00002	Δ	3.914	
55	0.78820		25.348							

European Free Trade Association, 1960

TABLE 1 DATA INPUT TO COMPUTATIONS

Age at last birthday	Population					Births, by age of mother	Deaths			Age at last birthday
	Total	Males	%	Females	%		Total	Males	Females	
0	1489636	765017	1.8	724519	1.6	0	47475	27085	20390	0
1–4	5673970	2908928	6.7	2765042	6.0	0	9887	5443	4444	1–4
5–9	7393254	3778032	8.8	3615222	7.9	0	3537	2144	1393	5–9
10–14	7107680	3618579	8.4	3489101	7.6	195	2699	1659	1040	10–14
15–19	6434969	3252682	7.5	3182287	7.0	104556	4413	3112	1301	15–19
20–24	5754592	2873099	6.7	2881493	6.3	460559	5377	3823	1554	20–24
25–29	5627440	2830285	6.5	2797155	6.1	471872	5608	3586	2022	25–29
30–34	5834063	2902044	6.7	2932019	6.4	304513	7138	4322	2816	30–34
35–39	6122352	2995087	6.9	3127265	6.8	166947	10963	6400	4563	35–39
40–44	5787232	2902114	6.7	2885118	6.3	48250	14375	8327	6048	40–44
45–49	6065072	2985405	6.9	3079667	6.7	3772	25841	15312	10529	45–49
50–54	5893826	2850651	6.6	3043175	6.7	21	41632	25731	15901	50–54
55–59	5344310	2525723	5.9	2818587	6.2	0	62583	40054	22529	55–59
60–64	4485632	2009823	4.7	2475809	5.4	0	84034	51326	32708	60–64
65–69	3612981	1536899	3.6	2076082	4.5	0	107403	60714	46689	65–69
70–74	2782692	1129751	2.6	1652941	3.6		135181	70215	64966	70–74
75–79	2021599	777793	1.8	1243806	2.7		153537	71809	81728	75–79
80–84	981573	360707	0.8	620866	1.4	802671 M	138155	58898	79257	80–84
85+	472187	161492	0.4	310695	0.7	758014 F	116215	42022	74193	85+
All ages	88885060	43164111		45720949		1560685	976053	501982	474071	All ages

TABLE 2 LIFE TABLE FOR MALES

Age, x	$_nq_x$	l_x	$_nd_x$	$_nL_x$	$_nm_x$	T_x	$1000r_x$	$\mathring{e}_x$	$_nM_x$	Age, x
0	0.03441	100000	3441	97463	0.03531	6752442	3.60	67.52	0.03540	0
1	0.00741	96559	716	384159	0.00186	6654980	3.60	68.92	0.00187	1
5	0.00283	95843	271	478537	0.00057	6270811	0.63	65.43	0.00057	5
10	0.00230	95572	219	477348	0.00046	5792274	14.38	60.61	0.00046	10
15	0.00479	95352	457	475704	0.00096	5314926	22.14	55.74	0.00095	15
20	0.00664	94895	630	472930	0.00133	4839222	12.67	51.00	0.00133	20
25	0.00632	94265	595	469853	0.00127	4366292	0.00	46.32	0.00127	25
30	0.00742	93670	695	466695	0.00149	3896439	0.00	41.60	0.00149	30
35	0.01063	92975	988	462533	0.00214	3429744	0.00	36.89	0.00214	35
40	0.01425	91987	1311	456929	0.00287	2967211	0.00	32.26	0.00287	40
45	0.02535	90676	2299	448174	0.00513	2510282	0.00	27.68	0.00513	45
50	0.04430	88377	3915	432970	0.00904	2062108	7.14	23.33	0.00903	50
55	0.07676	84462	6484	407247	0.01592	1529138	18.58	19.29	0.01586	55
60	0.12073	77978	9414	367589	0.02561	1221891	15.60	15.67	0.02554	60
65	0.18086	68564	12400	313020	0.03962	854302	15.60	12.46	0.03950	65
70	0.27017	56164	15174	243510	0.06231	541282	15.60	9.64	0.06215	70
75	0.37578	40990	15403	166355	0.09259	297772	15.60	7.26	0.09232	75
80	0.57687	25587	14760	90079	0.16386	131417	15.60	5.14	0.16328	80
85+	•1.00000	10826	10826	41338	0.26190	41338	15.60	3.82	0.26021	85+

TABLE 3 LIFE TABLE FOR FEMALES

Age, x	$_nq_x$	l_x	$_nd_x$	$_nL_x$	$_nm_x$	T_x	$1000r_x$	$\mathring{e}_x$	$_nM_x$	Age, x
0	0.02750	100000	2750	97996	0.02806	7294138	3.49	72.94	0.02814	0
1	0.00638	97250	620	387214	0.00160	7196141	3.49	74.00	0.00161	1
5	0.00192	96630	186	482685	0.00039	6808927	0.00	70.45	0.00039	5
10	0.00149	96444	144	481863	0.00030	6326243	12.41	65.60	0.00030	10
15	0.00205	96300	197	481033	0.00041	5844380	18.73	60.69	0.00041	15
20	0.00270	96103	259	479899	0.00054	5363347	12.35	55.81	0.00054	20
25	0.00361	95844	345	478397	0.00072	4883449	0.00	50.95	0.00072	25
30	0.00479	95498	458	476419	0.00096	4405052	0.00	46.13	0.00096	30
35	0.00727	95041	691	473585	0.00146	3928634	0.14	41.34	0.00146	35
40	0.01043	94350	984	469473	0.00210	3455049	0.00	36.62	0.00210	40
45	0.01696	93365	1583	463157	0.00342	2985549	0.00	31.98	0.00342	45
50	0.02583	91782	2370	453386	0.00523	2522418	3.48	27.48	0.00523	50
55	0.03934	89411	3517	438923	0.00801	2069032	12.20	23.14	0.00799	55
60	0.06440	85894	5532	416707	0.01328	1630109	21.93	18.98	0.01321	60
65	0.10738	80362	8629	381785	0.02260	1213403	21.93	15.10	0.02249	65
70	0.18054	71733	12951	327980	0.03949	831618	21.93	11.59	0.03930	70
75	0.28491	58782	16748	253587	0.06604	503637	21.93	8.57	0.06571	75
80	0.48442	42035	20363	158756	0.12826	250050	21.93	5.95	0.12766	80
85+	1.00000	21672	21672	91293	0.23739	91293	21.93	4.21	0.23880	85+

TABLE 4 POPULATION PROJECTION, USING FIXED AGE-SPECIFIC BIRTH AND DEATH RATES, IN THOUSANDS

Age at last birthday	1965			1970			1975			Age at last birthday
	Total	Males	Females	Total	Males	Females	Total	Males	Females	
0–4	7655	3923	3732	8004	4102	3902	8474	4343	4131	0–4
5–9	7121	3650	3471	7611	3898	3713	7957	4075	3882	5–9
10–14	7378	3769	3609	7107	3641	3466	7595	3888	3737	10–14
15–19	7089	3606	3483	7359	3756	3603	7089	3629	3460	15–19
20–24	6409	3234	3175	7060	3585	3475	7328	3734	3594	20–24
25–29	5726	2854	2872	6378	3213	3165	7026	3562	3464	25–29
30–34	5597	2811	2786	5596	2835	2861	6343	3191	3152	30–34
35–39	5791	2876	2915	5555	2786	2769	5654	2810	2844	35–39
40–44	6059	2959	3100	5730	2841	2889	5497	2752	2745	40–44
45–49	5693	2847	2846	5960	2902	3058	5537	2787	2850	45–49
50–54	5899	2884	3015	5536	2750	2786	5798	2804	2994	50–54
55–59	5627	2681	2946	5632	2713	2919	5284	2587	2697	55–59
60–64	4956	2280	2676	5217	2420	2797	5220	2449	2771	60–64
65–69	3979	1711	2268	4393	1941	2452	4624	2061	2563	65–69
70–74	2980	1196	1784	3280	1331	1949	3516	1510	2006	70–74
75–79	2050	772	1278	2196	817	1379	2417	910	1507	75–79
80–84	1200	421	779	1218	418	800	1305	442	863	80–84
85 +	523	166	357	641	193	448	652	192	460	85 +
All ages	91732	44640	47092	94573	46142	48431	97516	47726	49790	All ages

TABLE 5 OBSERVED AND PROJECTED VITAL RATES

Rates per thousand	Observed			Projected						Stable	
				1965		1970		1975			
	Total	Males	Females	Males	Females	Males	Females	Males	Females	Males	Females
Birth	17.56	18.60	16.58	18.51	16.57	19.00	17.10	19.41	17.57	19.50	18.35
Death	10.98	11.63	10.37	11.99	11.08	12.33	11.67	12.54	11.93	11.58	10.42
Increase	6.58	6.97	6.21	6.53	5.49	6.67	5.42	6.87	5.64		7.9235

TABLE 6 RATES STANDARDIZED ON THREE STANDARD COUNTRIES

Standardized rates per thousand	England and Wales, 1961			United States, 1960			Mexico, 1960		
	Total	Males	Females	Total	Males	Females	Total	Males	Females
Birth	17.03	18.46*	16.03	17.31	17.38*	16.57	20.03	16.10*	19.41
Death	11.85	12.11*	11.62	9.72	10.75*	8.60	5.23	9.19*	4.31
Increase	5.17	6.36*	4.41	7.59	6.63*	7.97	14.81	6.91*	15.10

TABLE 7 VITAL STATISTICS AND RATES INFERRED FROM AGE DISTRIBUTIONS (FEMALES)

Vital statistics		Thompson				Bourgeois-Pichat					Coale	
		Age range	NRR	$1000r$	Interval	Age range	NRR	$1000b$	$1000d$	$1000r$		
TFR	2.68	0–4	1.15	5.28	27.44	5–29	1.45	18.35	4.70	13.65	$1000b$	
GRR	1.30	5–9	1.20	6.75	27.40	30–54	0.91	12.10	15.71	-3.61	$1000d$	
NRR	1.25	10–14	1.14	4.80	27.35	55–79	1.55	35.90	19.59	16.31	$1000r$	
Generation	27.70	15–19	1.03	0.95	27.27	*50–74	1.49	32.40	17.61	14.79	$1000k_1$	
Sex ratio	105.89										$1000k_2$	

TABLE 8 LESLIE MATRIX AND ITS ANALYSIS (FEMALES)

Start of age interval	Sub-diagonal	First row	Percent in stable population	Fisher values	Total reproductive values	Net maternity function	Matrix equation coefficient	Parameters		
									Integral	Matrix
0	0.99479	0.00000	8.730	1.051	3667780	0.00000	0.00000	λ_1	1.0404	1.0404
5	0.99830	0.00007	8.347	1.099	3974135	0.00000	0.00007	λ_2	0.3662	0.3727
10	0.99828	0.03871	8.009	1.146	3997202	0.00013	0.03845		+0.7822	+0.7559i
15	0.99764	0.22660	7.684	1.153	3670010	0.22465	0.22465	r_1	0.0079	0.0079
20	0.99687	0.38649	7.368	0.964	2777811	0.37255	0.38226	r_2	-0.0293	-0.0342
25	0.99586	0.32065	7.059	0.599	1674572	0.39197	0.31615		+0.2266	+0.2225i
30	0.99405	0.18491	6.757	0.287	841640	0.24032	0.18156	c_1		416020
35	0.99132	0.08244	6.455	0.105	328192	0.12279	0.08046	c_2		-48240
40	0.98655	0.02113	6.151	0.023	65615	0.03813	0.02044			270675i
45	0.97890	0.00145	5.832	0.001	4533	0.00276	0.00139	$2\pi/y$	27.728	28.234
50	0.96810	0.00001	5.487	0.000	20	0.00002	0.00001	Δ	5.297	
55	0.80033		22.122							

European Free Trade Association, 1965

TABLE 1 DATA INPUT TO COMPUTATIONS

Age at last birthday	Total	Males	%	Females	%	Births, by age of mother	Total	Males	Females	Age at last birthday
0	1644381	845144	1.9	799237	1.7	0	42408	24263	18145	0
1–4	6257656	3207638	7.2	3050018	6.5	0	8526	4660	3866	1–4
5–9	7072237	3623732	8.1	3448505	7.3	0	3473	2125	1348	5–9
10–14	6654222	3398470	7.6	3255752	6.9	320	2576	1576	1000	10–14
15–19	7210692	3663826	8.2	3546866	7.5	150716	5212	3672	1540	15–19
20–24	6508624	3260287	7.3	3248337	6.9	534541	5242	3732	1510	20–24
25–29	5883790	2969036	6.7	2914754	6.2	506907	5266	3449	1817	25–29
30–34	5678120	2871252	6.5	2806868	6.0	292682	6494	4084	2410	30–34
35–39	5771806	2884867	6.5	2886939	6.1	153041	10007	6064	3943	35–39
40–44	6123850	3012993	6.8	3110857	6.6	48746	16745	9934	6811	40–44
45–49	5475926	2682684	6.0	2793242	5.9	3346	22933	13792	9141	45–49
50–54	5926441	2859161	6.4	3067280	6.5	23	40888	25593	15295	50–54
55–59	5633905	2682227	6.0	2951678	6.3	0	64149	41076	23073	55–59
60–64	4949092	2289338	5.1	2659754	5.7	0	93766	59868	33898	60–64
65–69	3943059	1686209	3.8	2256850	4.8	0	117691	69129	48562	65–69
70–74	2987887	1192157	2.7	1795730	3.8		141330	74239	67091	70–74
75–79	2159265	800144	1.8	1359121	2.9		156841	73590	83251	75–79
80–84	1063977	373171	0.8	690806	1.5	869166 M	142512	59511	83001	80–84
85+	578087	184283	0.4	393804	0.8	821156 F	132590	46988	85602	85+
All ages	91523017	44486619		47036398		1690322	1018649	527345	491304	All ages

TABLE 2 LIFE TABLE FOR MALES

Age, x	$_nq_x$	l_x	$_nd_x$	$_nL_x$	$_nm_x$	T_x	$1000r_x$	$\overset{\circ}{e}_x$	$_nM_x$	Age, x
0	0.02802	100000	2802	97921	0.02862	6807882	4.09	68.08	0.02871	0
1	0.00576	97198	560	387172	0.00145	6709961	4.09	69.03	0.00145	1
5	0.00291	96638	282	482486	0.00058	6322788	16.82	65.43	0.00059	5
10	0.00232	96356	223	481265	0.00046	5840303	0.00	60.61	0.00046	10
15	0.00500	96133	481	479531	0.00100	5359037	3.24	55.75	0.00100	15
20	0.00571	95652	545	476911	0.00115	4879506	19.90	51.01	0.00114	20
25	0.00580	95106	551	474179	0.00116	4402595	11.50	46.29	0.00116	25
30	0.00709	94555	670	471189	0.00142	3928417	1.38	41.55	0.00142	30
35	0.01046	93885	982	467146	0.00210	3457228	0.00	36.82	0.00210	35
40	0.01637	92903	1521	460990	0.00330	2990082	3.88	32.19	0.00330	40
45	0.02541	91382	2322	451601	0.00514	2529092	0.00	27.68	0.00514	45
50	0.04386	89060	3906	436365	0.00895	2077492	0.00	23.33	0.00895	50
55	0.07406	85154	6306	411220	0.01534	1641127	6.07	19.27	0.01531	55
60	0.12357	78848	9743	371251	0.02624	1229906	17.98	15.60	0.02615	60
65	0.18707	69105	12927	314343	0.04112	858646	17.98	12.43	0.04100	65
70	0.27058	56178	15200	243392	0.06245	544303	17.98	9.69	0.06227	70
75	0.37460	40977	15350	166358	0.09227	300911	17.98	7.34	0.09197	75
80	0.56464	25627	14470	90411	0.16005	134553	17.98	5.25	0.15947	80
85+	1.00000	11157	11157	44142	0.25275	44142	17.98	3.96	0.25498	85+

TABLE 3 LIFE TABLE FOR FEMALES

Age, x	$_nq_x$	l_x	$_nd_x$	$_nL_x$	$_nm_x$	T_x	$1000r_x$	$\overset{\circ}{e}_x$	$_nM_x$	Age, x
0	0.02227	100000	2227	98373	0.02264	7394714	3.73	73.95	0.02270	0
1	0.00503	97773	492	389675	0.00126	7296341	3.73	74.63	0.00127	1
5	0.00194	97281	189	485934	0.00039	6906667	16.14	71.00	0.00039	5
10	0.00153	97092	149	485094	0.00031	6420733	0.00	66.13	0.00031	10
15	0.00217	96944	210	484208	0.00043	5935638	0.00	61.23	0.00043	15
20	0.00233	96733	225	483123	0.00047	5451430	19.14	56.36	0.00046	20
25	0.00312	96508	301	481828	0.00062	4968308	13.98	51.48	0.00062	25
30	0.00428	96207	412	480080	0.00086	4486479	0.05	46.63	0.00086	30
35	0.00681	95795	652	477476	0.00137	4006400	0.00	41.82	0.00137	35
40	0.01089	95143	1036	473307	0.00219	3528924	1.07	37.09	0.00219	40
45	0.01624	94107	1528	466972	0.00327	3055617	0.00	32.47	0.00327	45
50	0.02465	92578	2282	457592	0.00499	2588646	0.00	27.96	0.00499	50
55	0.03844	90297	3471	443456	0.00783	2131053	6.08	23.60	0.00782	55
60	0.06219	86826	5400	421654	0.01281	1687598	21.86	19.44	0.01274	60
65	0.10295	81426	8383	387672	0.02162	1265944	21.86	15.55	0.02152	65
70	0.17233	73043	12587	335331	0.03753	878272	21.86	12.02	0.03736	70
75	0.26823	60456	16215	263388	0.06157	542891	21.86	8.98	0.06125	75
80	0.46323	44240	20494	169756	0.12072	279503	21.86	6.32	0.12015	80
85+	1.00000	23747	23747	109748	0.21638	109748	21.86	4.62	0.21737	85+

TABLE 4 POPULATION PROJECTION, USING FIXED AGE-SPECIFIC BIRTH AND DEATH RATES, IN THOUSANDS

Age at last birthday	1970 Total	1970 Males	1970 Females	1975 Total	1975 Males	1975 Females	1980 Total	1980 Males	1980 Females	Age at last birthday
0–4	8451	4333	4118	8791	4507	4284	9012	4520	4392	0–4
5–9	7864	4031	3833	8409	4309	4100	8748	4483	4265	5–9
10–14	7058	3615	3443	7847	4021	3826	8391	4298	4093	10–14
15–19	6636	3386	3250	7038	3602	3436	7825	4006	3819	15–19
20–24	7183	3644	3539	6611	3368	3243	7011	3582	3429	20–24
25–29	6482	3242	3240	7152	3623	3529	6582	3348	3234	25–29
30–34	5854	2950	2904	6449	3221	3228	7117	3600	3517	30–34
35–39	5639	2847	2792	5813	2925	2888	6404	3194	3210	35–39
40–44	5709	2847	2862	5576	2809	2767	5749	2886	2863	40–44
45–49	6021	2952	3069	5612	2789	2823	5482	2752	2730	45–49
50–54	5329	2592	2737	5860	2852	3008	5462	2695	2767	50–54
55–59	5667	2694	2973	5096	2443	2653	5603	2688	2915	55–59
60–64	5229	2422	2807	5259	2433	2826	4727	2205	2522	60–64
65–69	4383	1938	2445	4630	2050	2580	4659	2060	2599	65–69
70–74	3258	1306	1952	3617	1501	2116	3820	1588	2232	70–74
75–79	2225	815	1410	2425	892	1533	2687	1026	1661	75–79
80–84	1311	435	876	1352	443	909	1473	485	988	80–84
85 +	629	182	447	778	212	566	804	216	588	85 +
All ages	94928	46231	48697	98315	48000	50315	101556	49732	51824	All ages

TABLE 5 OBSERVED AND PROJECTED VITAL RATES

Rates per thousand	Observed Total	Observed Males	Observed Females	Projected 1970 Males	Projected 1970 Females	Projected 1975 Males	Projected 1975 Females	Projected 1980 Males	Projected 1980 Females	Stable Males	Stable Females
Birth	18.47	19.54	17.46	19.84	17.79	19.61	17.67	19.38	17.57	20.38	19.15
Death	11.13	11.85	10.45	12.12	11.10	12.36	11.67	12.43	11.81	10.85	9.64
Increase	7.34	7.68	7.01	7.72	6.69	7.24	6.00	6.95	5.76		9.5267

TABLE 6 RATES STANDARDIZED ON THREE STANDARD COUNTRIES

Standardized rates per thousand	England and Wales, 1961 Total	Males	Females	United States, 1960 Total	Males	Females	Mexico, 1960 Total	Males	Females
Birth	17.62	19.31*	16.59	17.94	17.98*	17.17	20.92	17.12*	20.27
Death	11.39	11.95*	10.87	9.32	10.65*	8.00	4.89	9.07*	3.93
Increase	6.23	7.36*	5.72	8.61	7.33*	9.17	16.03	8.05*	16.35

TABLE 7 VITAL STATISTICS AND RATES INFERRED FROM AGE DISTRIBUTIONS (FEMALES)

Vital statistics		Thompson Age range	NRR	1000r	Interval	Bourgeois-Pichat Age range	NRR	1000b	1000d	1000r	Coale 1000b
TFR	2.78	0–4	1.23	7.52	27.44	5–29	1.19	16.08	9.73	6.35	1000d
GRR	1.35	5–9	1.14	4.92	27.40	30–54	0.87	10.58	15.83	−5.25	1000r
NRR	1.30	10–14	1.08	2.91	27.35	55–79	1.49	33.17	18.50	14.65	$1000k_1$
Generation	27.41	15–19	1.16	5.46	27.28	*50–74	1.37	27.09	15.43	11.67	$1000k_2$
Sex ratio	105.85										

TABLE 8 LESLIE MATRIX AND ITS ANALYSIS (FEMALES)

Start of age interval	Sub-diagonal	First row	Percent in stable population	Fisher values	Total reproductive values	Net maternity function	Matrix equation coefficient	Parameters	Integral	Matrix
0	0.99567	0.00000	9.135	1.049	4038344	0.00000	0.00000	λ_1	1.0488	1.0488
5	0.99827	0.00012	8.672	1.105	3811120	0.00000	0.00012	λ_2	0.3590	0.3660
10	0.99817	0.05040	8.254	1.161	3779966	0.00023	0.05009		+0.7874	+0.7505i
15	0.99776	0.24501	7.855	1.167	4139110	0.09995	0.24309	r_1	0.0095	0.0095
20	0.99732	0.40069	7.473	0.969	3147942	0.38622	0.39565	r_2	−0.0289	−0.0339
25	0.99637	0.32933	7.105	0.598	1742008	0.40708	0.32513		+0.2286	+0.2245i
30	0.99458	0.18611	6.750	0.282	792550	0.24319	0.18308	c_1		418703
35	0.99127	0.08126	6.401	0.101	292860	0.12296	0.07950	c_2		−145600
40	0.98662	0.01998	6.050	0.021	66372	0.03603	0.01937			−352283i
45	0.97991	0.00143	5.691	0.001	4021	0.00272	0.00137	$2\pi/y$	27.486	27.993
50	0.96911	0.00001	5.317	0.000	20	0.00002	0.00001	Δ	6.542	
55	0.80689		21.296							

European Members of Comecon, 1955

TABLE 1 DATA INPUT TO COMPUTATIONS

Age at last birthday	Population Total	Males	%	Females	%	Births, by age of mother	Deaths Total	Males	Females	Age at last birthday
0	1977723	1013487	2.3	964236	2.0	0	146517	83052	63465	0
1–4	7736383	3959534	8.9	3776849	7.8	0	25980	13551	12419	1–4
5–9	8448638	4306343	9.7	4142295	8.5	0	7292	4152	3140	5–9
10–14	7060021	3576145	8.0	3483876	7.2	509	4787	2894	1893	10–14
15–19	7620367	3829814	8.6	3790553	7.8	177537	8119	5109	3010	15–19
20–24	7508293	3761923	8.4	3746370	7.7	718877	11359	7132	4237	20–24
25–29	7430553	3625133	8.1	3805420	7.8	633893	12680	7393	5287	25–29
30–34	6940576	3234159	7.3	3706417	7.6	396403	13593	7382	6211	30–34
35–39	4537865	2063487	4.6	2474378	5.1	148392	10817	5531	5285	35–39
40–44	6051958	2751880	6.2	3300078	6.8	70530	21140	11180	9960	40–44
45–49	6499783	3036681	6.8	3463102	7.1	6629	32525	18376	14149	45–49
50–54	5713491	2692247	6.0	3021244	6.2	407	45838	26730	19108	50–54
55–59	4820922	2160716	4.8	2660206	5.5	1	60568	34839	25729	55–59
60–64	3763902	1571139	3.5	2192763	4.5	0	73032	38999	34033	60–64
65–69	2862702	1225478	2.7	1637224	3.4	0	96531	48375	48155	65–69
70–74	2023159	874444	2.0	1148715	2.4		114925	54476	60449	70–74
75–79	1238079	527436	1.2	710643	1.5		111344	49752	61592	75–79
80–84	596023	246733	0.6	349290	0.7	1112090 M	82533	35770	46763	80–84
85 +	438303	109053	0.2	329250	0.7	1041188 F	55630	21926	33704	85 +
All ages	93268741	44565832		48702909		2153278	935220	476629	458591	All ages

TABLE 2 LIFE TABLE FOR MALES

Age, x	$_nq_x$	l_x	$_nd_x$	$_nL_x$	$_nm_x$	T_x	$1000r_x$	$\overset{\circ}{e}_x$	$_nM_x$	Age, x
0	0.07712	100000	7712	94106	0.08195	6321473	0.00	63.21	0.08195	0
1	0.01356	92288	1252	365512	0.00342	6227367	0.00	67.48	0.00342	1
5	0.00474	91036	432	454104	0.00095	5861855	31.33	64.39	0.00096	5
10	0.00404	90605	366	452144	0.00081	5407752	10.77	59.68	0.00081	10
15	0.00665	90239	600	449793	0.00133	4955607	0.00	54.92	0.00133	15
20	0.00944	89639	846	446141	0.00190	4505814	3.69	50.27	0.00190	20
25	0.01015	88793	901	441742	0.00204	4059673	13.05	45.72	0.00204	25
30	0.01138	87891	1001	437008	0.00229	3617932	54.05	41.16	0.00228	30
35	0.01334	86891	1159	431706	0.00269	3180923	13.27	36.61	0.00268	35
40	0.02012	85731	1725	424625	0.00406	2749218	0.00	32.07	0.00406	40
45	0.02984	84006	2507	414233	0.00605	2324593	0.00	27.67	0.00605	45
50	0.04876	81500	3974	398303	0.00998	1910360	23.65	23.44	0.00993	50
55	0.07820	77525	6063	373397	0.01624	1512056	37.26	19.50	0.01612	55
60	0.11785	71463	8422	337376	0.02496	1138659	30.48	15.93	0.02482	60
65	0.18123	63041	11425	287805	0.03970	801284	30.48	12.71	0.03947	65
70	0.27138	51616	14007	223676	0.06262	513479	30.48	9.95	0.05230	70
75	0.38250	37608	14385	151728	0.09481	289803	30.48	7.71	0.09433	75
80	0.53086	23223	12328	84567	0.14578	138075	30.48	5.95	0.14497	80
85 +	*1.00000	10895	10895	53508	0.20361	53508	30.48	4.91	0.20105	85 +

TABLE 3 LIFE TABLE FOR FEMALES

Age, x	$_nq_x$	l_x	$_nd_x$	$_nL_x$	$_nm_x$	T_x	$1000r_x$	$\overset{\circ}{e}_x$	$_nM_x$	Age, x
0	0.06274	100000	6274	95327	0.06582	7010557	0.00	70.11	0.06582	0
1	0.01303	93726	1221	371369	0.00329	6915229	0.00	73.78	0.00329	1
5	0.00371	92505	344	461664	0.00074	6543860	29.41	70.74	0.00075	5
10	0.00271	92161	250	460184	0.00054	6082197	8.23	66.00	0.00054	10
15	0.00396	91911	364	458699	0.00079	5622013	0.00	61.17	0.00079	15
20	0.00564	91547	516	456498	0.00113	5163314	0.00	56.40	0.00113	20
25	0.00692	91030	630	453626	0.00139	4706816	0.00	51.71	0.00139	25
30	0.00838	90400	757	450175	0.00168	4253190	41.34	47.05	0.00168	30
35	0.01064	89643	954	445948	0.00214	3803016	9.39	42.42	0.00214	35
40	0.01498	88689	1329	440292	0.00302	3357067	0.00	37.85	0.00302	40
45	0.02025	87360	1769	432659	0.00409	2916775	4.52	33.39	0.00409	45
50	0.03127	85591	2677	421715	0.00635	2484116	19.87	29.02	0.00632	50
55	0.04749	82914	3938	405411	0.00971	2062401	21.97	24.87	0.00967	55
60	0.07548	78976	5961	381266	0.01564	1656991	29.41	20.98	0.01552	60
65	0.13861	73015	10120	341609	0.02963	1275725	29.41	17.47	0.02941	65
70	0.23489	62895	14773	279020	0.05295	934115	29.41	14.85	0.05262	70
75	0.35792	48121	17224	197670	0.08713	655096	29.41	13.61	0.08667	75
80	0.49725	30898	15364	114270	0.13445	457425	29.41	14.80	0.13388	80
85 +	1.00000	15534	15534	343155	0.04527	343155	29.41	22.09	0.10236	85 +

TABLE 4 POPULATION PROJECTION, USING FIXED AGE-SPECIFIC BIRTH AND DEATH RATES, IN THOUSANDS

Age at last birthday	1960 Total	Males	Females	1965 Total	Males	Females	1970 Total	Males	Females	Age at last birthday
0–4	10056	5155	4901	10126	5191	4935	10334	5298	5036	0–4
5–9	9603	4913	4690	9941	5093	4848	10010	5129	4881	5–9
10–14	8417	4288	4129	9567	4892	4675	9905	5072	4833	10–14
15–19	7031	3558	3473	8381	4265	4116	9527	4867	4660	15–19
20–24	7571	3799	3772	6985	3529	3456	8327	4231	4096	20–24
25–29	7448	3725	3723	7510	3761	3749	6928	3494	3434	25–29
30–34	7362	3586	3776	7379	3685	3694	7441	3721	3720	30–34
35–39	6867	3195	3672	7284	3543	3741	7300	3540	3650	35–39
40–44	4473	2030	2443	6768	3143	3625	7179	3485	3694	40–44
45–49	5928	2685	3243	4381	1980	2401	6628	3066	3562	45–49
50–54	6296	2920	3376	5742	2581	3161	4244	1904	2340	50–54
55–59	5428	2524	2904	5982	2737	3245	5459	2420	3039	55–59
60–64	4454	1952	2502	5011	2280	2731	5525	2473	3052	60–64
65–69	3305	1340	1965	3907	1665	2242	4392	1945	2447	65–69
70–74	2289	952	1337	2647	1042	1605	3125	1294	1831	70–74
75–79	1407	593	814	1593	646	947	1844	707	1137	75–79
80–84	705	294	411	801	331	470	908	360	548	80–84
85 +	1205	156	1049	1420	186	1234	1622	209	1413	85 +
All ages	99845	47665	52180	105425	50550	54875	110698	53315	57383	All ages

TABLE 5 OBSERVED AND PROJECTED VITAL RATES

Rates per thousand	Observed Total	Males	Females	Projected 1960 Males	Females	1965 Males	Females	1970 Males	Females	Stable Males	Females
Birth	23.09	24.95	21.38	23.73	20.30	22.30	19.24	22.09	19.22	22.05	20.44
Death	10.03	10.69	9.42	11.11	11.13	11.39	11.81	11.67	12.48	12.32	10.71
Increase	13.06	14.26	11.96	12.62	9.17	10.92	7.43	10.42	6.74		9.7332

TABLE 6 RATES STANDARDIZED ON THREE STANDARD COUNTRIES

Standardized rates per thousand	England and Wales, 1961 Total	Males	Females	United States, 1960 Total	Males	Females	Mexico, 1960 Total	Males	Females
Birth	18.95	22.59*	17.77	19.27	20.90*	18.36	22.48	20.92*	21.68
Death	13.26	14.26*	13.38	11.30	12.26*	10.40	7.33	9.34*	6.44
Increase	5.70	8.33*	4.38	7.98	8.64*	7.96	15.15	11.58*	15.25

TABLE 7 VITAL STATISTICS AND RATES INFERRED FROM AGE DISTRIBUTIONS (FEMALES)

Vital statistics		Thompson Age range	NRR	$1000r$	Interval	Bourgeois-Pichat Age range	NRR	$1000b$	$1000d$	$1000r$	Coale	
TFR	2.98	0–4	1.32	10.26	27.39	5–29	1.03	17.30	16.22	1.08	$1000b$	21.11
GRR	1.44	5–9	1.17	5.85	27.35	30–54	0.95	13.76	15.52	-1.76	$1000d$	10.39
NRR	1.31	10–14	1.01	0.46	27.29	55–79	2.35	83.73	52.12	31.62	$1000r$	10.72
Generation	27.36	15–19	1.15	5.11	27.21	*50–74	2.16	67.59	39.15	28.44	$1000k_1$	42.55
Sex ratio	106.8										$1000k_2$	0.68

TABLE 8 LESLIE MATRIX AND ITS ANALYSIS (FEMALES)

Start of age interval	Sub-diagonal	First row	Percent in stable population	Fisher values	Total reproductive values	Net maternity function	Matrix equation coefficient	Parameters	Integral	Matrix
0	0.98922	0.00000	9.314	1.098	5203871	0.00000	0.00000	λ_1	1.0499	1.0499
5	0.99679	0.00020	8.776	1.165	4825672	0.00000	0.00019	λ_2	0.3407	0.3524
10	0.99677	0.05287	8.332	1.227	4274224	0.00039	0.05214		+0.7650	+0.7386i
15	0.99520	0.26832	7.910	1.234	4677757	0.10388	0.26372	r_1	0.0097	0.0097
20	0.99371	0.40328	7.498	1.006	3768810	0.42356	0.39447	r_2	-0.0355	-0.0401
25	0.99239	0.30771	7.096	0.617	2349686	0.36538	0.29909		+0.2304	+0.2251i
30	0.99061	0.18771	6.707	0.313	1159815	0.23281	0.18106	c_1		481223
35	0.98732	0.09148	6.328	0.124	306027	0.12932	0.08741	c_2		319913
40	0.98266	0.02624	5.951	0.030	98432	0.04550	0.02475			-665975i
45	0.97471	0.00231	5.570	0.003	8875	0.00400	0.00214	$2\pi/y$	27.276	27.910
50	0.96134	0.00015	5.171	0.000	494	0.00027	0.00014	Δ	6.622	
55	0.81707		21.347							

[549]

European Members of Comecon, 1960

TABLE 1   DATA INPUT TO COMPUTATIONS

Age at last birthday	Population Total	Males	%	Females	%	Births, by age of mother	Deaths Total	Males	Females	Age at last birthday
0	1732500	891182	1.9	841318	1.7	0	94051	53446	40605	0
1–4	7488239	3847661	8.3	3640578	7.2	0	15775	8471	7304	1–4
5–9	9573508	4909859	10.6	4663649	9.3	0	5665	3374	2291	5–9
10–14	8245189	4209611	9.1	4035578	8.0	722	3951	2494	1457	10–14
15–19	6951261	3521358	7.6	3429903	6.8	183104	6151	4213	1938	15–19
20–24	7123200	3468552	7.5	3654648	7.3	663585	9145	5054	3091	20–24
25–29	7305698	3653025	7.9	3652673	7.3	500542	10422	6572	3850	25–29
30–34	7272367	3546636	7.6	3725931	7.4	283207	12157	7320	4837	30–34
35–39	6744484	3129075	6.7	3615409	7.2	142292	14530	8056	6474	35–39
40–44	4342468	1979369	4.3	2363099	4.7	32541	12611	5862	5749	40–44
45–49	6014672	2756334	5.9	3258338	6.5	3699	27620	15188	12432	45–49
50–54	6105179	2851659	6.1	3253520	6.5	308	44036	25779	18257	50–54
55–59	5383526	2515340	5.4	2868186	5.7	0	63242	38350	24892	55–59
60–64	4374731	1912023	4.1	2462708	4.9	0	82425	47134	35291	60–64
65–69	3195455	1319709	2.8	1875746	3.7	0	97417	50622	46795	65–69
70–74	2371541	949518	2.0	1422023	2.8		120551	57171	63480	70–74
75–79	1610033	641958	1.4	968075	1.9		123340	55035	68905	75–79
80–84	617527	242482	0.5	375045	0.7	934938 M	98450	41684	56766	80–84
85+	278229	103161	0.2	175068	0.3	875062 F	67069	26536	40533	85+
All ages	96729807	46448312		50281495		1810000	909308	464351	444947	All ages

TABLE 2   LIFE TABLE FOR MALES

Age, x	$_nq_x$	l_x	$_nd_x$	$_nL_x$	$_nm_x$	T_x	$1000r_x$	$\overset{\circ}{e}_x$	$_nM_x$	Age, x
0	0.05730	100000	5730	95548	0.05997	6539937	0.00	65.40	0.05997	0
1	0.00875	94270	825	374673	0.00220	6444390	0.00	68.36	0.00220	1
5	0.00342	93445	319	466427	0.00068	6069717	10.72	64.96	0.00069	5
10	0.00298	93126	277	464985	0.00060	5603290	32.49	60.17	0.00059	10
15	0.00599	92849	555	462963	0.00120	5138305	18.18	55.34	0.00120	15
20	0.00869	92293	802	459514	0.00175	4675342	0.00	50.66	0.00175	20
25	0.00896	91491	819	455432	0.00180	4215828	0.00	46.08	0.00180	25
30	0.01028	90671	932	451097	0.00207	3760396	13.37	41.47	0.00205	30
35	0.01287	89739	1155	445932	0.00259	3309299	55.68	36.88	0.00257	35
40	0.01722	88584	1526	439359	0.00347	2863367	9.01	32.32	0.00347	40
45	0.02721	87058	2368	429834	0.00551	2424009	0.00	27.84	0.00551	45
50	0.04428	84690	3750	414829	0.00904	1994174	0.00	23.55	0.00904	50
55	0.07398	80940	5988	390778	0.01532	1579345	24.12	19.51	0.01525	55
60	0.11713	74952	8779	353998	0.02480	1188568	32.23	15.86	0.02465	60
65	0.17656	66173	11683	302815	0.03858	834570	32.23	12.61	0.03835	65
70	0.26335	54489	14350	237110	0.06052	531755	32.23	9.76	0.06021	70
75	0.35535	40140	14263	165288	0.08629	294645	32.23	7.34	0.08573	75
80	0.60059	25876	15541	89710	0.17323	129357	32.23	5.00	0.17191	80
85+	*1.00000	10335	10335	39647	0.26068	39547	32.23	3.84	0.25723	85+

TABLE 3   LIFE TABLE FOR FEMALES

Age, x	$_nq_x$	l_x	$_nd_x$	$_nL_x$	$_nm_x$	T_x	$1000r_x$	$\overset{\circ}{e}_x$	$_nM_x$	Age, x
0	0.04655	100000	4655	96446	0.04826	7019048	0.00	70.19	0.04825	0
1	0.00798	95345	761	379169	0.00201	6922602	0.00	72.61	0.00201	1
5	0.00244	94584	231	472345	0.00049	6543434	9.59	69.18	0.00049	5
10	0.00181	94354	170	471350	0.00036	6071088	30.29	64.34	0.00036	10
15	0.00283	94183	266	470298	0.00057	5599738	9.34	59.46	0.00057	15
20	0.00422	93917	396	468642	0.00085	5129440	0.00	54.62	0.00085	20
25	0.00526	93521	492	466418	0.00105	4660799	0.00	49.84	0.00105	25
30	0.00647	93029	602	463711	0.00130	4194381	0.00	45.09	0.00130	30
35	0.00897	92427	829	460170	0.00180	3730670	43.73	40.36	0.00179	35
40	0.01211	91598	1109	455402	0.00244	3270501	7.82	35.70	0.00243	40
45	0.01891	90489	1711	448449	0.00382	2815098	0.00	31.11	0.00382	45
50	0.02773	88778	2462	438147	0.00562	2366649	6.93	26.66	0.00561	50
55	0.04270	86316	3686	423058	0.00871	1928503	18.70	22.34	0.00868	55
60	0.06993	82630	5778	399843	0.01445	1505445	36.61	18.22	0.01433	60
65	0.11889	76852	9137	363081	0.02516	1105602	36.61	14.39	0.02495	65
70	0.20306	67716	13750	305740	0.04497	742521	36.61	10.97	0.04464	70
75	0.30605	53965	16516	229985	0.07181	436781	36.61	8.09	0.07118	75
80	0.55277	37449	20701	135543	0.15272	206796	36.61	5.52	0.15135	80
85+	*1.00000	16749	16749	71253	0.23506	71253	36.61	4.25	0.23153	85+

TABLE 4 POPULATION PROJECTION, USING FIXED AGE-SPECIFIC BIRTH AND DEATH RATES, IN THOUSANDS

Age at last birthday	1965 Total	Males	Females	1970 Total	Males	Females	1975 Total	Males	Females	Age at last birthday
0–4	8555	4395	4160	8803	4522	4281	9436	4847	4589	0–4
5–9	9152	4701	4451	8491	4359	4132	8736	4485	4251	5–9
10–14	9549	4895	4654	9128	4686	4442	8469	4346	4123	10–14
15–19	8218	4191	4027	9516	4873	4643	9098	4665	4432	15–19
20–24	6913	3495	3418	8172	4160	4012	9464	4837	4627	20–24
25–29	7075	3438	3637	6866	3464	3402	8116	4123	3993	25–29
30–34	7249	3618	3631	7021	3405	3516	6813	3431	3382	30–34
35–39	7203	3506	3697	7181	3577	3604	6955	3366	3589	35–39
40–44	6661	3083	3578	7113	3454	3659	7090	3524	3566	40–44
45–49	4263	1936	2327	6539	3016	3523	6982	3379	3603	45–49
50–54	5843	2660	3183	4143	1869	2274	6353	2911	3442	50–54
55–59	5827	2686	3141	5580	2506	3074	3956	1761	2195	55–59
60–64	4990	2279	2711	5402	2433	2969	5175	2270	2905	60–64
65–69	3872	1636	2236	4411	1949	2462	4778	2082	2596	65–69
70–74	2613	1033	1580	3164	1281	1883	3599	1526	2073	70–74
75–79	1732	662	1070	1908	720	1188	2310	893	1417	75–79
80–84	919	348	571	989	359	630	1091	391	700	80–84
85 +	304	107	197	454	154	300	490	159	331	85 +
All ages	100938	48669	52269	104881	50787	54094	108911	52997	55914	All ages

TABLE 5 OBSERVED AND PROJECTED VITAL RATES

Rates per thousand	Observed Total	Males	Females	Projected 1965 Males	Females	1970 Males	Females	1975 Males	Females	Stable Males	Females
Birth	18.71	20.13	17.40	19.20	16.73	19.47	17.11	20.24	17.95	18.08	16.97
Death	9.40	10.00	8.85	10.46	9.66	11.01	10.53	11.37	11.09	13.36	12.25
Increase	9.31	10.13	8.55	8.74	7.07	8.46	6.59	8.87	6.87		4.7172

TABLE 6 RATES STANDARDIZED ON THREE STANDARD COUNTRIES

Standardized rates per thousand	England and Wales, 1961 Total	Males	Females	United States, 1960 Total	Males	Females	Mexico, 1960 Total	Males	Females
Birth	15.96	18.35*	14.96	16.24	17.24*	15.47	19.59	16.95*	18.90
Death	12.84	12.92*	13.08	10.69	11.20*	9.87	6.29	8.90*	5.43
Increase	3.13	5.43*	1.88	5.55	6.04*	5.60	13.30	8.06*	13.47

TABLE 7 VITAL STATISTICS AND RATES INFERRED FROM AGE DISTRIBUTIONS (FEMALES)

Vital statistics		Thompson Age range	NRR	$1000r$	Interval	Bourgeois-Pichat Age range	NRR	$1000b$	$1000d$	$1000r$	Coale
TFR	2.51	0–4	1.28	9.22	27.41	5–29	1.35	19.88	8.74	11.14	$1000b$
GRR	1.21	5–9	1.35	10.93	27.38	30–54	1.14	17.19	12.47	4.72	$1000d$
NRR	1.13	10–14	1.18	5.95	27.32	55–79	2.02	61.16	35.03	26.13	$1000r$
Generation	26.49	15–19	1.03	0.99	27.24	*15–39	0.91	13.99	17.56	-3.58	$1000k_1$
Sex ratio	106.84										$1000k_2$

TABLE 8 LESLIE MATRIX AND ITS ANALYSIS (FEMALES)

Start of age interval	Sub-diagonal	First row	Percent in stable population	Fisher values	Total reproductive values	Net maternity function	Matrix equation coefficient	Parameters Integral	Matrix
0	0.99313	0.00000	7.980	1.064	4767409	0.00000	0.00000	λ_1 1.0239	1.0239
5	0.99789	0.00020	7.740	1.097	5114323	0.00000	0.00020	λ_2 0.2870	0.3033
10	0.99777	0.05144	7.543	1.125	4539941	0.00041	0.06089	+0.7570	+0.7261i
15	0.99648	0.26940	7.351	1.089	3734871	0.12138	0.26638	r_1 0.0047	0.0047
20	0.99525	0.36556	7.154	0.831	3038063	0.41139	0.36020	r_2 -0.0422	-0.0479
25	0.99420	0.24443	6.954	0.465	1696676	0.30900	0.23970	+0.2417	+0.2350i
30	0.99236	0.13229	6.753	0.217	807985	0.17040	0.12898	c_1	537032
35	0.98964	0.06092	6.545	0.082	296226	0.08755	0.05894	c_2	683737
40	0.98473	0.01712	6.326	0.019	45606	0.03032	0.01639		561936i
45	0.97703	0.00141	6.084	0.002	5133	0.00246	0.00133	$2\pi/y$ 25.999	25.733
50	0.96556	0.00011	5.806	0.000	370	0.00020	0.00010	Δ 5.971	
55	0.78800		23.765						

European Members of Comecon, 1965

TABLE 1 DATA INPUT TO COMPUTATIONS

Age at last birthday	Population Total	Males	%	Females	%	Births, by age of mother	Deaths Total	Males	Females	Age at last birthday
0	1594574	819304	1.7	775270	1.5	0	56987	32729	24258	0
1–4	6529519	3347614	7.0	3181905	6.2	0	9311	5161	4150	1–4
5–9	9198150	4704127	9.8	4494023	8.7	0	4755	2793	1962	5–9
10–14	9450221	4824431	10.0	4625790	9.0	702	3959	2451	1508	10–14
15–19	7975527	4055817	8.4	3919710	7.6	177655	6181	4217	1964	15–19
20–24	6830482	3447999	7.2	3382483	6.6	578890	7484	5368	2116	20–24
25–29	7216819	3599514	7.5	3617305	7.0	447394	8797	5895	2902	25–29
30–34	7227639	3610181	7.5	3617458	7.0	241300	10910	7027	3883	30–34
35–39	7152151	3475562	7.2	3676589	7.1	114419	14614	8956	5658	35–39
40–44	6576986	3044369	6.3	3532617	6.8	33718	18963	10923	8040	40–44
45–49	4111891	1867812	3.9	2244079	4.3	2024	17597	9871	7825	45–49
50–54	5911988	2690280	5.6	3221708	6.2	175	39774	22952	16822	50–54
55–59	5799063	2677448	5.6	3121615	6.0	0	64017	38404	25613	55–59
60–64	4958163	2271017	4.7	2687146	5.2	0	91655	55142	36513	60–64
65–69	3792533	1605901	3.3	2186632	4.2	0	116975	63779	53196	65–69
70–74	2559976	1007883	2.1	1552093	3.0		129262	62164	67098	70–74
75–79	1825516	691972	1.4	1133544	2.2		140928	61272	79655	75–79
80–84	705360	262711	0.5	442649	0.9	819498 M	115317	47699	67618	80–84
85 +	323046	112932	0.2	210114	0.4	776779 F	84485	32303	52182	85 +
All ages	99739604	48116874		51622730		1596277	942071	479106	462965	All ages

TABLE 2 LIFE TABLE FOR MALES

Age, x	$_nq_x$	l_x	$_nd_x$	$_nL_x$	$_nm_x$	T_x	$1000r_x$	$\overset{\circ}{e}_x$	$_nM_x$	Age, x
0	0.03875	100000	3875	97012	0.03995	6699963	0.00	67.00	0.03995	0
1	0.00614	96125	590	382779	0.00154	6502951	0.00	68.69	0.00154	1
5	0.00296	95535	283	476965	0.00059	6220172	0.00	65.11	0.00059	5
10	0.00254	95251	242	475695	0.00051	5743207	14.19	60.30	0.00051	10
15	0.00522	95009	495	473907	0.00105	5267512	32.55	55.44	0.00104	15
20	0.00776	94513	734	470787	0.00156	4793605	10.47	50.72	0.00155	20
25	0.00816	93779	765	467020	0.00164	4322819	0.00	46.10	0.00164	25
30	0.00969	93015	901	462906	0.00195	3855799	1.50	41.45	0.00195	30
35	0.01283	92113	1182	457764	0.00258	3392893	14.40	36.83	0.00258	35
40	0.01795	90931	1632	450817	0.00362	2935128	58.39	32.28	0.00359	40
45	0.02614	89299	2334	441079	0.00529	2484312	6.81	27.82	0.00528	45
50	0.04184	86965	3638	426450	0.00853	2043332	0.00	23.49	0.00853	50
55	0.06945	83327	5787	403276	0.01435	1616783	1.85	19.40	0.01434	55
60	0.11552	77540	8957	366705	0.02443	1213507	28.83	15.65	0.02428	60
65	0.18219	68583	12495	312090	0.03993	846802	28.83	12.35	0.03972	65
70	0.26874	56087	15073	243258	0.06196	533853	28.83	9.52	0.06168	70
75	0.36470	41014	14958	167916	0.08908	290585	28.83	7.08	0.08855	75
80	0.62235	26056	16215	88676	0.18287	122669	28.83	4.71	0.18155	80
85 +	*1.00000	9840	9840	33993	0.28948	33993	28.83	3.45	0.28604	85 +

TABLE 3 LIFE TABLE FOR FEMALES

Age, x	$_nq_x$	l_x	$_nd_x$	$_nL_x$	$_nm_x$	T_x	$1000r_x$	$\overset{\circ}{e}_x$	$_nM_x$	Age, x
0	0.03056	100000	3056	97669	0.03129	7204346	0.00	72.04	0.03129	0
1	0.00520	96944	504	386311	0.00130	7106676	0.00	73.31	0.00130	1
5	0.00218	96440	210	481675	0.00044	6720355	0.00	69.68	0.00044	5
10	0.00163	96230	157	480753	0.00033	6238691	13.28	64.83	0.00033	10
15	0.00251	96073	241	479791	0.00050	5757927	30.82	59.93	0.00050	15
20	0.00313	95832	300	478439	0.00063	5278136	7.39	55.08	0.00063	20
25	0.00400	95532	382	476748	0.00080	4799697	0.00	50.24	0.00080	25
30	0.00535	95150	509	474546	0.00107	4322949	0.00	45.43	0.00107	30
35	0.00767	94640	725	471504	0.00154	3848402	0.79	40.65	0.00154	35
40	0.01141	93915	1072	467077	0.00229	3376898	47.00	35.96	0.00228	40
45	0.01731	92843	1607	460452	0.00349	2909821	5.64	31.34	0.00349	45
50	0.02579	91235	2353	450705	0.00522	2449359	0.00	26.85	0.00522	50
55	0.04034	88882	3586	436135	0.00822	1998654	9.53	22.49	0.00821	55
60	0.06638	85296	5662	413503	0.01369	1562519	32.24	18.32	0.01359	60
65	0.11600	79634	9237	376790	0.02452	1149016	32.24	14.43	0.02433	65
70	0.19716	70397	13880	318925	0.04352	772226	32.24	10.97	0.04323	70
75	0.30270	56517	17108	241491	0.07084	453301	32.24	8.02	0.07027	75
80	0.55623	39409	21920	142324	0.15402	211810	32.24	5.37	0.15276	80
85 +	*1.00000	17489	17489	69486	0.25169	69486	32.24	3.97	0.24835	85 +

TABLE 4 POPULATION PROJECTION, USING FIXED AGE-SPECIFIC BIRTH AND DEATH RATES, IN THOUSANDS

Age at last birthday	1970			1975			1980			Age at last birthday
	Total	Males	Females	Total	Males	Females	Total	Males	Females	
0–4	7907	4042	3865	8507	4349	4158	9046	4524	4422	0–4
5–9	8080	4142	3938	7864	4018	3846	8463	4324	4139	5–9
10–14	9178	4692	4486	8062	4131	3931	7847	4008	3839	10–14
15–19	9422	4806	4616	9150	4674	4476	8039	4116	3923	15–19
20–24	7938	4029	3909	9378	4775	4603	9107	4643	4464	20–24
25–29	6791	3420	3371	7892	3997	3895	9323	4736	4587	25–29
30–34	7169	3568	3601	6745	3390	3355	7839	3962	3877	30–34
35–39	7164	3570	3594	7106	3528	3578	6686	3353	3333	35–39
40–44	7065	3423	3642	7077	3516	3561	7019	3475	3544	40–44
45–49	6462	2979	3483	6939	3349	3590	6950	3440	3510	45–49
50–54	4003	1806	2197	6289	2880	3409	6752	3238	3514	50–54
55–59	5662	2544	3118	3834	1708	2126	6022	2723	3299	55–59
60–64	5395	2435	2960	5269	2313	2956	3568	1553	2015	60–64
65–69	4387	1938	2449	4775	2078	2697	4667	1974	2593	65–69
70–74	3099	1248	1851	3580	1507	2073	3898	1615	2283	70–74
75–79	1871	696	1175	2263	862	1401	2609	1040	1569	75–79
80–84	1033	365	668	1060	367	593	1281	455	826	80–84
85 +	317	101	216	466	140	326	479	141	338	85 +
All ages	102943	49804	53139	106256	51582	54674	109595	53420	56175	All ages

TABLE 5 OBSERVED AND PROJECTED VITAL RATES

Rates per thousand	Observed			Projected						Stable	
				1970		1975		1980			
	Total	Males	Females	Males	Females	Males	Females	Males	Females	Males	Females
Birth	16.00	17.03	15.05	17.38	15.44	18.37	16.43	18.35	15.54	15.77	14.71
Death	9.45	9.96	8.97	10.53	9.85	11.10	10.73	11.43	11.22	14.25	13.19
Increase	6.56	7.07	6.08	6.85	5.59	7.27	5.70	6.92	5.32		1.5208

TABLE 6 RATES STANDARDIZED ON THREE STANDARD COUNTRIES

Standardized rates per thousand	England and Wales, 1961			United States, 1960			Mexico, 1960		
	Total	Males	Females	Total	Males	Females	Total	Males	Females
Birth	14.22	15.65*	13.41	14.45	14.75*	13.86	17.62	14.22*	17.10
Death	12.48	12.33*	12.62	10.22	10.78*	9.30	5.52	8.90*	4.65
Increase	1.73	3.32*	0.79	4.24	3.97*	4.56	12.10	5.32*	12.45

TABLE 7 VITAL STATISTICS AND RATES INFERRED FROM AGE DISTRIBUTIONS (FEMALES)

Vital statistics		Thompson				Bourgeois-Pichat					Coale
		Age range	NRR	$1000r$	Interval	Age range	NRR	$1000b$	$1000d$	$1000r$	
TFR	2.24	0–4	1.07	2.50	27.43	5–29	1.48	20.69	6.26	14.43	$1000b$
GRR	1.09	5–9	1.31	10.07	27.39	30–34	1.38	22.24	10.27	11.97	$1000d$
NRR	1.04	10–14	1.35	10.98	27.34	55–79	1.99	60.82	35.41	25.41	$1000r$
Generation	26.32	15–19	1.16	5.40	27.26	*20–44	0.92	13.12	16.36	-3.24	$1000k_1$
Sex ratio	105.50										$1000k_2$

TABLE 8 LESLIE MATRIX AND ITS ANALYSIS (FEMALES)

Start of age interval	Sub-diagonal	First row	Percent in stable population	Fisher values	Total reproductive values	Net maternity function	Matrix equation coefficient	Parameters		
									Integral	Matrix
0	0.99524	0.00000	7.092	1.037	4103699	0.00000	0.00000	λ_1	1.0076	1.0075
5	0.99811	0.00018	7.005	1.059	4718490	0.00000	0.00018	λ_2	0.2831	0.2973
10	0.99798	0.05344	6.939	1.060	4902336	0.00036	0.05309		+0.7630	+0.7314 i
15	0.99718	0.25434	6.872	1.015	3976569	0.10582	0.25214	r_1	0.0015	0.0015
20	0.99647	0.34666	6.801	0.761	2572854	0.39845	0.34269	r_2	-0.0412	-0.0473
25	0.99538	0.22383	6.725	0.408	1477275	0.28693	0.22049		+0.2431	+0.2369 i
30	0.99359	0.11496	6.644	0.180	651942	0.15404	0.11272	c_1		586811
35	0.99061	0.04778	6.551	0.063	230818	0.07140	0.04655	c_2		-84274
40	0.98584	0.01229	6.440	0.014	48900	0.02169	0.01186			981926 i
45	0.97881	0.00112	6.301	0.001	2746	0.00202	0.00107	$2\pi/y$	25.847	25.518
50	0.96767	0.00006	6.121	0.000	216	0.00012	0.00006	Δ	6.927	
55	0.78421		26.510							

CHAPTER 19

Male-Dominant Computations

The preceding tables have all been based on numbers of births by age of mother, and have assumed nothing about ages of fathers. The female-dominant model, to which analysis is inevitably limited by such data, takes it that with persistence of the observed rates the number of births will be proportional to the number of women in each age category.

For the nine populations on the following pages we were able to obtain births by age of father. The life tables are not affected, of course, but most of Tables 4–8 involve fertility and are somewhat different from those based on births by age of mother. The Tables 4–8 that follow are based on the same data as shown in Table 1 of the corresponding printout with female dominance, except that the column of Table 1 for births by age of mother is replaced by births by age of father. Births by age of father are given in Table M.

TABLE M
Births by age of father for seven countries.

Age group	Canada, 1966 (excluding Newfoundland)	United States, 1966			Peru, 1963
		Total	Nonwhite	White	
<15	0	94	65	29	0
15–19	8,948	188,435	45,780	142,655	9,131
20–24	80,683	1,053,241	188,537	864,704	78,104
25–29	110,098	1,030,046	155,347	874,699	114,094
30–34	82,360	648,766	98,104	550,662	100,001
35–39	52,791	394,618	63,554	331,064	71,070
40–44	25,484	186,199	34,589	151,610	43,316
45–49	9,363	69,623	16,229	53,394	4,290
50–54	2,779	22,630	6,240	16,390	1,207
55–59	800	12,622	4,599	8,023	0
60–64	212	0	0	0	0
65–69	108	0	0	0	0
Total	373,626	3,606,274	613,044	2,993,230	421,213

Age group	Belgium, 1966	Hungary, 1967	England and Wales, 1964	New Zealand, 1966
15–19	2,458	2,512	17,572	1,796
20–24	31,648	37,166	168,856	14,092
25–29	48,599	52,869	284,175	19,714
20–34	35,875	31,516	208,112	12,140
35–39	20,343	15,687	116,398	7,569
40–44	8,921	6,490	55,151	3,168
45–49	2,290	1,579	16,890	1,142
50–54	700	696	6,292	390
55–59	182	250	2,526	120
60–64	55	121	0	36
65–69	25	0	0	21
Total	151,096	148,886	875,972	60,188

Canada, 1966

TABLE 4 POPULATION PROJECTION, USING FIXED AGE-SPECIFIC BIRTH AND DEATH RATES, IN THOUSANDS

Age at last birthday	1971 Total	1971 Males	1971 Females	1976 Total	1976 Males	1976 Females	1981 Total	1981 Males	1981 Females	Age at last birthday
0–4	1917	981	936	2159	1105	1054	2466	1262	1204	0–4
5–9	2121	1089	1032	1910	977	933	2150	1100	1050	5–9
10–14	2229	1136	1093	2116	1086	1030	1905	974	931	10–14
15–19	2023	1034	989	2221	1130	1091	2109	1081	1028	15–19
20–24	1773	894	879	2012	1026	986	2209	1121	1088	20–24
25–29	1417	703	714	1764	887	877	2000	1017	983	25–29
30–34	1206	600	606	1409	698	711	1753	880	873	30–34
35–39	1207	611	596	1198	595	603	1398	691	707	35–39
40–44	1247	628	619	1194	603	591	1185	587	598	40–44
45–49	1212	599	613	1225	614	611	1173	590	583	45–49
50–54	1036	511	525	1176	576	600	1190	591	599	50–54
55–59	923	458	465	989	480	509	1123	541	582	55–59
60–64	743	367	376	858	415	443	920	435	485	60–64
65–69	582	279	303	664	316	348	768	358	410	65–69
70–74	440	200	240	491	223	268	561	253	308	70–74
75–79	322	140	182	339	144	195	378	161	217	75–79
80–84	193	83	110	213	86	127	224	88	136	80–84
85 +	128	51	77	142	53	89	157	55	102	85 +
All ages	20719	10364	10355	22080	11014	11066	23669	11785	11884	All ages

TABLE 5 OBSERVED AND PROJECTED VITAL RATES

Rates per thousand	Observed Total	Observed Males	Observed Females	Projected 1971 Males	Projected 1971 Females	Projected 1976 Males	Projected 1976 Females	Projected 1981 Males	Projected 1981 Females	Stable Males	Stable Females
Birth	19.14	19.56	18.72	20.38	19.35	22.00	20.78	23.41	22.03	21.56	20.23
Death	7.52	8.78	6.25	8.93	6.68	9.06	7.01	9.16	7.28	10.06	8.74
Increase	11.62	10.77	12.47	11.45	12.67	12.94	13.77	14.25	14.75	11.4991	

TABLE 6 RATES STANDARDIZED ON THREE STANDARD COUNTRIES

Standardized rates per thousand	England and Wales, 1961 Total	Males	Females	United States, 1960 Total	Males	Females	Mexico, 1960 Total	Males	Females
Birth	19.01	20.16	16.90*	18.26	19.02	17.09*	18.73	19.27	19.74*
Death	10.15	10.88	9.62*	8.33	9.69	7.02*	4.46	5.43	4.77*
Increase	8.87	9.28	7.28*	9.93	9.33	10.07*	14.27	13.83	14.98*

TABLE 7 VITAL STATISTICS AND RATES INFERRED FROM AGE DISTRIBUTIONS (MALES)

Vital statistics		Thompson Age range	NRR	$1000r$	Interval	Bourgeois-Pichat Age range	NRR	$1000b$	$1000d$	$1000r$	Coale	
TFR	2.95	0–4	1.55	16.44	27.37	5–29	2.35	31.65	−0.05	31.70	$1000b$	24.57
GRR	1.51	5–9	1.77	21.14	27.33	30–54	1.28	18.88	9.87	9.01	$1000d$	8.69
NRR	1.42	10–14	1.69	19.00	27.25	55–79	1.62	27.86	9.96	17.90	$1000r$	15.88
Generation	30.62	15–19	1.53	14.83	27.10	40–69	1.75	33.17	12.36	20.81	$1000k_1$	0.
Sex ratio	105.4										$1000k_2$	0.

TABLE 8 LESLIE MATRIX AND ITS ANALYSIS (MALES)

Start of age interval	Sub-diagonal	First row	Percent in stable population	Fisher values	Total reproductive values	Net paternity function	Matrix equation coefficient	Parameters	Integral	Matrix
0	0.99562	0.00000	10.267	1.056	1093798	0.00000	0.00000	λ_1	1.0592	1.0597
5	0.99727	0.00000	9.641	1.125	1232008	0.00000	0.00000	λ_2	0.4318	0.4310
10	0.99535	0.01234	9.069	1.196	1185177	0.00000	0.01226		+0.7680	+0.7427i
15	0.99199	0.15340	8.514	1.261	1111739	0.02451	0.15160	r_1	0.0115	0.0116
20	0.99143	0.36755	7.966	1.184	847785	0.27869	0.36033	r_2	−0.0253	−0.0305
25	0.99209	0.39279	7.449	0.875	532448	0.44197	0.38178		+0.2117	+0.2090i
30	0.99051	0.26942	6.970	0.517	309478	0.32159	0.25979	c_1		103304
35	0.98623	0.15496	6.512	0.266	165842	0.19799	0.14801	c_2		130122
40	0.97789	0.07359	6.057	0.120	74276	0.09802	0.06933			372803i
45	0.96256	0.03168	5.587	0.050	26894	0.04063	0.02664	$2\pi/y$	29.677	30.063
50	0.93962	0.01232	5.072	0.020	9833	0.01264	0.00838	Δ	5.515	
55	0.77816		16.896							

[556]

TABLE 4 POPULATION PROJECTION, USING FIXED AGE-SPECIFIC BIRTH AND DEATH RATES, IN THOUSANDS

Age at last birthday	1971 Total	1971 Males	1971 Females	1976 Total	1976 Males	1976 Females	1981 Total	1981 Males	1981 Females	Age at last birthday
0–4	18905	9648	9257	21844	11148	10696	24905	12710	12195	0–4
5–9	19776	10093	9683	18835	9608	9227	21762	11101	10661	5–9
10–14	20765	10556	10209	19736	10069	9667	18797	9585	9212	10–14
15–19	19334	9813	9521	20692	10505	10187	19666	10020	9646	15–19
20–24	17648	8871	8777	19217	9727	9490	20565	10412	10153	20–24
25–29	13515	6561	6954	17528	8785	8743	19084	9632	9452	25–29
30–34	11385	5576	5809	13413	6496	6917	17394	8698	8696	30–34
35–39	10743	5258	5485	11270	5505	5765	13277	6413	6864	35–39
40–44	11528	5609	5919	10581	5158	5423	11101	5401	5700	40–44
45–49	12103	5842	6261	11259	5442	5817	10334	5005	5329	45–49
50–54	11190	5365	5825	11665	5564	6101	10851	5183	5668	50–54
55–59	10092	4800	5292	10570	4963	5607	11019	5147	5872	55–59
60–64	8568	3992	4576	9271	4267	5004	9714	4412	5302	60–64
65–69	6969	3149	3820	7534	3346	4188	8157	3577	4580	65–69
70–74	5253	2236	3017	5744	2428	3316	6215	2580	3635	70–74
75–79	3915	1571	2344	3968	1553	2415	4340	1686	2654	75–79
80–84	2414	943	1471	2570	947	1623	2609	937	1672	80–84
85 +	1507	556	951	1756	619	1137	1877	622	1255	85 +
All ages	205610	100439	105171	217453	106130	111323	231667	113121	118546	All ages

TABLE 5 OBSERVED AND PROJECTED VITAL RATES

Rates per thousand	Observed Total	Observed Males	Observed Females	Projected 1971 Males	Projected 1971 Females	Projected 1976 Males	Projected 1976 Females	Projected 1981 Males	Projected 1981 Females	Stable Males	Stable Females
Birth	18.41	19.24	17.62	21.11	19.22	23.20	21.09	24.42	22.22	22.92	21.40
Death	9.51	10.98	8.11	11.14	8.73	11.10	9.06	10.85	9.14	10.10	8.58
Increase	8.90	8.27	9.51	9.96	10.50	12.10	12.04	13.56	13.08	12.8195	

TABLE 6 RATES STANDARDIZED ON THREE STANDARD COUNTRIES

Standardized rates per thousand	England and Wales, 1961 Total	Males	Females	United States, 1960 Total	Males	Females	Mexico, 1960 Total	Males	Females
Birth	19.42	20.53	16.96*	18.66	19.39	17.09*	20.11	20.63	19.79*
Death	11.36	12.41	10.47*	9.33	10.99	7.72*	4.99	6.14	5.60*
Increase	8.06	8.13	6.49*	9.33	8.40	9.37*	15.11	14.49	14.19*

TABLE 7 VITAL STATISTICS AND RATES INFERRED FROM AGE DISTRIBUTIONS (MALES)

Vital statistics		Thompson Age range	NRR	1000r	Interval	Bourgeois-Pichat Age range	NRR	1000b	1000d	1000r	Coale
TFR	3.02	0–4	1.53	15.88	27.33	5–29	2.36	30.75	−1.12	31.87	1000b
GRR	1.55	5–9	1.73	20.39	27.27	30–54	0.90	10.91	14.99	−4.08	1000d
NRR	1.45	10–14	1.65	18.17	27.17	55–79	1.29	20.69	11.14	9.55	1000r
Generation	29.03	15–19	1.51	14.51	26.98	*40–64	1.31	21.34	11.45	9.89	$1000k_1$
Sex ratio	104.85										$1000k_2$

TABLE 8 LESLIE MATRIX AND ITS ANALYSIS (MALES)

Start of age interval	Sub-diagonal	First row	Percent in stable population	Fisher values	Total reproductive values	Net paternity function	Matrix equation coefficient	Parameters Integral	Parameters Matrix
0	0.99583	0.00000	10.866	1.061	10309896	0.00000	0.00000	λ_1 1.0662	1.0668
5	0.99763	0.00001	10.138	1.137	11632022	0.00000	0.00001	λ_2 0.3797	0.3792
10	0.99515	0.02610	9.475	1.217	11612845	0.00002	0.02593	+0.7920	$+0.7648\,i$
15	0.99118	0.22244	8.834	1.278	11249857	0.05184	0.21991	r_1 0.0128	0.0129
20	0.99030	0.42350	8.203	1.138	7941574	0.38799	0.41500	r_2 −0.0260	−0.0316
25	0.99007	0.37792	7.611	0.772	4510303	0.44202	0.36674	+0.2247	$+0.2221\,i$
30	0.98724	0.23654	7.059	0.428	2362097	0.29147	0.22726	c_1	941677
35	0.98107	0.12373	6.529	0.208	1245179	0.16306	0.11736	c_2	180641
40	0.97029	0.05344	6.001	0.092	588914	0.07167	0.04973		$3108625\,i$
45	0.95247	0.02345	5.455	0.043	258451	0.02779	0.01857	$2\pi/y$ 27.957	28.289
50	0.92503	0.01170	4.868	0.022	122733	0.00934	0.00746	Δ 5.394	
55	0.76637		14.960						

[557]

United States, 1966 (Nonwhite)

TABLE 4 POPULATION PROJECTION, USING FIXED AGE-SPECIFIC
BIRTH AND DEATH RATES, IN THOUSANDS

Age at last birthday	1971 Total	1971 Males	1971 Females	1976 Total	1976 Males	1976 Females	1981 Total	1981 Males	1981 Females	Age at last birthday
0–4	3236	1632	1604	3902	1968	1934	4652	2346	2306	0–4
5–9	3204	1614	1590	3217	1622	1595	3878	1955	1923	5–9
10–14	3060	1527	1533	3194	1608	1586	3208	1616	1592	10–14
15–19	2701	1347	1354	3046	1518	1528	3180	1599	1581	15–19
20–24	2277	1129	1148	2677	1330	1347	3019	1499	1520	20–24
25–29	1635	782	853	2248	1109	1139	2642	1306	1336	25–29
30–34	1353	632	721	1607	764	843	2208	1083	1125	30–34
35–39	1268	584	684	1322	614	708	1568	741	827	35–39
40–44	1291	585	706	1226	560	666	1277	588	689	40–44
45–49	1259	580	679	1232	552	680	1169	528	641	45–49
50–54	1085	501	584	1178	534	644	1153	508	645	50–54
55–59	948	440	508	989	446	543	1075	476	599	55–59
60–64	749	350	399	833	376	457	868	381	487	60–64
65–69	582	272	310	609	274	335	678	295	383	65–69
70–74	374	165	209	439	193	246	460	194	266	70–74
75–79	292	121	171	275	113	162	321	131	190	75–79
80–84	190	81	109	204	80	124	191	74	117	80–84
85 +	189	79	110	222	87	135	240	87	153	85 +
All ages	25693	12421	13272	28420	13748	14672	31787	15407	16380	All ages

TABLE 5 OBSERVED AND PROJECTED VITAL RATES

Rates per thousand	Observed Total	Observed Males	Observed Females	1971 Males	1971 Females	1976 Males	1976 Females	1981 Males	1981 Females	Stable Males	Stable Females
Birth	26.09	27.29	24.97	29.94	27.32	32.79	29.96	34.40	31.56	33.38	31.67
Death	9.73	11.30	8.27	11.13	8.57	10.78	8.63	10.31	8.53	9.05	7.34
Increase	16.36	15.99	16.70	18.81	18.75	22.00	21.33	24.10	23.03	24.3269	

TABLE 6 RATES STANDARDIZED ON THREE STANDARD COUNTRIES

Standardized rates per thousand	England and Wales, 1961 Total	Males	Females	United States, 1960 Total	Males	Females	Mexico, 1960 Total	Males	Females
Birth	28.83	30.15	23.44*	27.60	28.37	23.53*	29.35	29.80	27.49*
Death	14.84	15.98	15.08*	12.41	14.18	10.81*	7.29	8.60	6.69*
Increase	13.99	14.17	8.37*	15.19	14.19	12.71*	22.06	21.19	20.80*

TABLE 7 VITAL STATISTICS AND RATES INFERRED FROM AGE DISTRIBUTIONS
(MALES)

Vital statistics		Thompson Age range	NRR	$1000r$	Interval	Bourgeois-Pichat Age range	NRR	$1000b$	$1000d$	$1000r$	Coale
TFR	4.47	0–4	2.07	27.67	27.15	5–29	3.21	41.58	−1.57	43.15	$1000b$
GRR	2.26	5–9	2.20	29.85	27.02	30–54	0.99	12.10	12.49	−0.39	$1000d$
NRR	2.02	10–14	2.04	25.98	26.84	55–79	1.25	18.07	9.75	8.32	$1000r$
Generation	28.99	15–19	1.75	16.40	26.59	*40–64	1.24	18.07	10.13	7.94	$1000k_1$
Sex ratio	102.55										$1000k_2$

TABLE 8 LESLIE MATRIX AND ITS ANALYSIS (MALES)

Start of age interval	Sub-diagonal	First row	Percent in stable population	Fisher values	Total reproductive values	Net paternity function	Matrix equation coefficient	Parameters	Integral	Matrix
0	0.99358	0.00000	15.155	1.111	1774849	0.00000	0.00000	λ_1	1.1293	1.1307
5	0.99677	0.00007	13.308	1.265	1942780	0.00000	0.00007	λ_2	0.3538	0.3478
10	0.99394	0.04827	11.723	1.436	1949692	0.00014	0.04781		+0.8327	+0.8082i
15	0.98748	0.33179	10.298	1.580	1823855	0.09547	0.32660	r_1	0.0243	0.0246
20	0.98212	0.57250	8.987	1.438	1236488	0.55773	0.55650	r_2	−0.0200	−0.0256
25	0.97736	0.48373	7.801	1.009	736584	0.55527	0.46181		+0.2338	+0.2329i
30	0.97033	0.31983	6.738	0.618	431046	0.36834	0.29842	c_1		105792
35	0.95903	0.19152	5.779	0.355	257419	0.22850	0.17340	c_2		60113
40	0.94274	0.10219	4.898	0.197	138963	0.11830	0.08873			372086i
45	0.92178	0.06058	4.081	0.116	71455	0.05916	0.04110	$2\pi/y$	26.873	26.980
50	0.88978	0.03861	3.324	0.070	38084	0.02304	0.02064	Δ	6.986	
55	0.75741		7.907							

United States, 1966 (White)

TABLE 4 POPULATION PROJECTION, USING FIXED AGE-SPECIFIC
BIRTH AND DEATH RATES, IN THOUSANDS

Age at last birthday	1971 Total	1971 Males	1971 Females	1976 Total	1976 Males	1976 Females	1981 Total	1981 Males	1981 Females	Age at last birthday
0–4	15694	8028	7666	18032	9224	8808	20431	10451	9980	0–4
5–9	16573	8480	8093	15642	7998	7644	17971	9189	8782	5–9
10–14	17705	9027	8678	16542	8461	8081	15612	7980	7632	10–14
15–19	16632	8465	8167	17645	8985	8660	16486	8422	8064	15–19
20–24	15371	7742	7629	16537	8395	8142	17544	8910	8634	20–24
25–29	11881	5780	6101	15279	7675	7604	16438	8323	8115	25–29
30–34	10032	4944	5088	11806	5732	6074	15183	7612	7571	30–34
35–39	9473	4673	4800	9948	4891	5057	11709	5671	6038	35–39
40–44	10237	5024	5213	9351	4596	4755	9821	4811	5010	40–44
45–49	10844	5262	5582	10025	4890	5135	9158	4474	4684	45–49
50–54	10105	4864	5241	10484	5029	5455	9692	4674	5018	50–54
55–59	9141	4359	4782	9580	4517	5063	9941	4671	5270	55–59
60–64	7820	3643	4177	8437	3892	4545	8845	4033	4812	60–64
65–69	6386	2877	3509	6926	3073	3853	7475	3283	4192	65–69
70–74	4882	2072	2810	5301	2233	3068	5754	2386	3368	70–74
75–79	3622	1449	2173	3697	1442	2255	4016	1554	2462	75–79
80–84	2224	862	1362	2365	866	1499	2416	861	1555	80–84
85+	1336	482	854	1556	536	1020	1661	539	1122	85+
All ages	179958	88033	91925	189153	92435	96718	200153	97844	102309	All ages

TABLE 5 OBSERVED AND PROJECTED VITAL RATES

Rates per thousand	Observed Total	Observed Males	Observed Females	Projected 1971 Males	Projected 1971 Females	Projected 1976 Males	Projected 1976 Females	Projected 1981 Males	Projected 1981 Females	Stable Males	Stable Females
Birth	17.37	18.16	16.60	19.92	18.11	21.91	19.88	23.06	20.94	21.43	19.94
Death	9.48	10.93	8.09	11.14	8.76	11.14	9.15	10.95	9.28	10.45	8.96
Increase	7.88	7.23	8.51	8.78	9.35	10.77	10.73	12.11	11.66	10.9757	

TABLE 6 RATES STANDARDIZED ON THREE STANDARD COUNTRIES

Standardized rates per thousand	England and Wales, 1961 Total	Males	Females	United States, 1960 Total	Males	Females	Mexico, 1960 Total	Males	Females
Birth	18.23	19.32	16.04*	17.52	18.25	16.17*	18.90	19.44	18.70*
Death	10.96	12.00	10.04*	8.97	10.61	7.42*	4.68	5.81	5.47*
Increase	7.26	7.32	6.00*	8.56	7.64	8.75*	14.22	13.63	13.23*

TABLE 7 VITAL STATISTICS AND RATES INFERRED FROM AGE DISTRIBUTIONS
(MALES)

Vital statistics		Thompson Age range	NRR	1000r	Interval	Bourgeois-Pichat Age range	NRR	1000b	1000d	1000r	Coale
TFR	2.84	0–4	1.46	14.04	27.36	5–29	2.26	29.37	−0.81	30.18	1000b
GRR	1.46	5–9	1.67	19.02	27.30	30–54	0.88	10.76	15.29	−4.53	1000d
NRR	1.38	10–14	1.60	17.08	27.20	55–79	1.30	20.94	11.29	9.65	1000r
Generation	29.04	15–19	1.48	13.82	27.03	*45–69	1.40	24.62	12.25	12.37	1000k_1
Sex ratio	105.33										1000k_2

TABLE 8 LESLIE MATRIX AND ITS ANALYSIS (MALES)

Start of age interval	Sub-diagonal	First row	Percent in stable population	Fisher values	Total reproductive values	Net paternity function	Matrix equation coefficient	Parameters	Integral	Matrix
0	0.99625	0.00000	10.232	1.053	8545665	0.00000	0.00000	λ_1	1.0564	1.0569
5	0.99777	0.00000	9.641	1.117	9711213	0.00000	0.00000	λ_2	0.3843	0.3849
10	0.99534	0.02278	9.097	1.184	9690853	0.00001	0.02264		+0.7867	+0.7598 i
15	0.99169	0.20706	8.564	1.234	9441155	0.04528	0.20486	r_1	0.0110	0.0111
20	0.99139	0.40354	8.032	1.096	6706750	0.36445	0.39595	r_2	−0.0266	−0.0321
25	0.99172	0.36450	7.531	0.740	3781739	0.42744	0.35455		+0.2233	+0.2204 i
30	0.98934	0.22630	7.063	0.402	1941775	0.28167	0.21830	c_1		843569
35	0.98366	0.11572	6.609	0.189	994179	0.15494	0.11044	c_2		108757
40	0.97337	0.04790	6.148	0.079	448964	0.06593	0.04497			2762889 i
45	0.95578	0.01936	5.660	0.034	183738	0.02401	0.01582	$2\pi/y$	28.140	28.512
50	0.92873	0.00880	5.116	0.017	82053	0.00764	0.00582	Δ	5.087	
55	0.76599		16.307							

TABLE 4 POPULATION PROJECTION, USING FIXED AGE-SPECIFIC BIRTH AND DEATH RATES, IN THOUSANDS

Age at last birthday	1968			1973			1978			Age at last birthday
	Total	Males	Females	Total	Males	Females	Total	Males	Females	
0–4	2053	1054	999	2397	1231	1166	2816	1446	1370	0–4
5–9	1842	931	911	1974	1014	960	2305	1184	1121	5–9
10–14	1613	810	803	1825	922	903	1957	1005	952	10–14
15–19	1294	661	633	1599	803	796	1811	915	896	15–19
20–24	1093	554	539	1278	653	625	1579	793	786	20–24
25–29	920	461	459	1075	545	530	1258	643	615	25–29
30–34	789	391	398	904	453	451	1056	535	521	30–34
35–39	658	331	327	771	382	389	882	442	440	35–39
40–44	565	279	286	641	323	318	751	372	379	40–44
45–49	454	226	228	547	269	278	622	312	310	45–49
50–54	382	187	195	436	216	220	526	257	269	50–54
55–59	304	148	156	363	176	187	415	204	211	55–59
60–64	232	112	120	281	135	146	335	160	175	60–64
65–69	197	97	100	206	98	108	249	118	131	65–69
70–74	124	57	67	170	82	88	178	83	95	70–74
75–79	86	37	49	101	45	56	139	65	74	75–79
80–84	48	21	27	64	27	37	75	33	42	80–84
85 +	34	17	17	46	22	24	60	28	32	85 +
All ages	12688	6374	6314	14678	7396	7282	17014	8595	8419	All ages

TABLE 5 OBSERVED AND PROJECTED VITAL RATES

Rates per thousand	Observed			Projected						Stable	
				1968		1973		1978			
	Total	Males	Females	Males	Females	Males	Females	Males	Females	Males	Females
Birth	38.36	39.51	37.21	39.71	37.66	40.02	38.17	40.61	38.94	40.20	39.53
Death	10.03	10.28	9.77	10.09	9.61	10.27	9.96	10.45	10.25	10.73	10.06
Increase	28.34	29.23	27.44	29.62	28.04	29.75	28.21	30.16	28.69	29.4656	

TABLE 6 RATES STANDARDIZED ON THREE STANDARD COUNTRIES

Standardized rates per thousand	England and Wales, 1961			United States, 1960			Mexico, 1960		
	Total	Males	Females	Total	Males	Females	Total	Males	Females
Birth	39.94	42.55	30.79*	38.61	40.42	30.98*	36.87	38.12	37.73*
Death	13.00	12.19	26.46*	11.92	11.93	18.05*	9.42	9.81	8.93*
Increase	26.94	30.36	4.33*	26.69	28.50	12.93*	27.45	28.31	28.80*

TABLE 7 VITAL STATISTICS AND RATES INFERRED FROM AGE DISTRIBUTIONS (MALES)

Vital statistics		Thompson				Bourgeois-Pichat					Coale	
		Age range	NRR	$1000r$	Interval	Age range	NRR	$1000b$	$1000d$	$1000r$	$1000b$	43.52
TFR	6.14	0–4	2.30	30.61	27.25	5–29	2.48	43.71	10.09	33.61	$1000d$	10.99
GRR	3.16	5–9	2.36	32.23	27.16	30–54	2.36	43.12	11.26	31.86	$1000r$	32.53
NRR	2.55	10–14	2.25	29.28	27.08	55–79	3.15	82.60	40.12	42.47	$1000k_1$	0.
Generation	31.77	15–19	2.23	29.70	26.96	*30–54	2.36	43.12	11.26	31.86	$1000k_2$	0.
Sex ratio	106.5											

TABLE 8 LESLIE MATRIX AND ITS ANALYSIS (MALES)

Start of age interval	Sub-diagonal	First row	Percent in stable population	Fisher values	Total reproductive values	Net paternity function	Matrix equation coefficient	Parameters		
									Integral	Matrix
0	0.96201	0.00000	16.776	1.199	1136484	0.00000	0.00000	λ_1	1.1587	1.1592
5	0.99107	0.00000	13.922	1.445	1170744	0.00000	0.00000	λ_2	0.5515	0.5491
10	0.99160	0.01866	11.902	1.690	1078525	0.00000	0.01779		+0.8121	+0.7947i
15	0.98758	0.20923	10.181	1.953	1066380	0.03558	0.19781	r_1	0.0295	0.0296
20	0.98473	0.51898	8.673	2.039	951027	0.36003	0.48455	r_2	-0.0037	-0.0069
25	0.98149	0.66589	7.368	1.768	716492	0.60907	0.61223		+0.1949	+0.1932i
30	0.97782	0.62166	6.238	1.275	425905	0.61539	0.56098	c_1		55883
35	0.97391	0.49521	5.262	0.749	219857	0.50507	0.43696	c_2		79702
40	0.96604	0.23823	4.421	0.282	66026	0.36735	0.20472			76243i
45	0.95528	0.03380	3.684	0.043	8569	0.04209	0.02807	$2\pi/y$	32.246	32.515
50	0.94184	0.00885	3.036	0.009	1488	0.01404	0.00702	Δ	2.140	
55	0.82435		8.537							

Belgium, 1966

TABLE 4 POPULATION PROJECTION, USING FIXED AGE-SPECIFIC
BIRTH AND DEATH RATES, IN THOUSANDS

Age at last birthday	1971			1976			1981			Age at last birthday
	Total	Males	Females	Total	Males	Females	Total	Males	Females	
0–4	747	382	365	780	399	381	823	421	402	0–4
5–9	772	396	376	745	381	364	777	397	380	5–9
10–14	774	396	378	771	395	376	743	380	363	10–14
15–19	731	373	358	772	395	377	768	393	375	15–19
20–24	710	361	349	729	371	358	769	392	377	20–24
25–29	624	319	305	706	359	347	724	368	356	25–29
30–34	574	293	281	621	317	304	702	356	346	30–34
35–39	616	312	304	569	290	279	616	314	302	35–39
40–44	653	328	325	609	308	301	563	286	277	40–44
45–49	653	324	329	642	321	321	598	301	297	45–49
50–54	502	246	256	634	312	322	623	309	314	50–54
55–59	512	247	265	478	230	248	603	292	311	55–59
60–64	532	247	285	473	221	252	441	206	235	60–64
65–69	481	213	268	468	207	261	416	185	231	65–69
70–74	382	158	224	396	165	231	385	160	225	70–74
75–79	252	96	156	281	108	173	290	112	178	75–79
80–84	137	50	87	152	53	99	169	59	110	80–84
85 +	80	27	53	85	27	58	95	29	66	85 +
All ages	9732	4768	4964	9911	4859	5052	10105	4960	5145	All ages

TABLE 5 OBSERVED AND PROJECTED VITAL RATES

Rates per thousand	Observed			Projected						Stable	
				1971		1976		1981			
	Total	Males	Females	Males	Females	Males	Females	Males	Females	Males	Females
Birth	15.81	16.53	15.11	16.76	15.28	17.36	15.85	17.91	16.40	17.79	16.53
Death	12.10	13.13	11.11	13.29	11.84	13.34	12.34	13.31	12.64	12.48	11.23
Increase	3.71	3.41	4.01	3.46	3.45	4.01	3.51	4.59	3.76	5.3078	

TABLE 6 RATES STANDARDIZED ON THREE STANDARD COUNTRIES

Standardized rates per thousand	England and Wales, 1961			United States, 1960			Mexico, 1960		
	Total	Males	Females	Total	Males	Females	Total	Males	Females
Birth	15.56	16.49	14.88*	14.97	15.59	15.32*	15.69	16.14	16.99*
Death	11.60	12.17	11.05*	9.44	10.82	8.25*	4.92	5.91	6.46*
Increase	3.97	4.33	3.83*	5.53	4.77	7.07*	10.77	10.23	10.54*

TABLE 7 VITAL STATISTICS AND RATES INFERRED FROM AGE DISTRIBUTIONS
(MALES)

Vital statistics		Thompson				Bourgeois-Pichat					Coale	
		Age range	NRR	$1000r$	Interval	Age range	NRR	$1000b$	$1000d$	$1000r$		
TFR	2.42	0–4	1.18	6.20	27.38	5–29	1.46	19.77	5.81	13.96	$1000b$	18.39
GRR	1.24	5–9	1.24	8.01	27.34	30–54	1.25	19.86	11.47	8.39	$1000d$	10.23
NRR	1.17	10–14	1.19	6.48	27.25	55–79	1.26	24.58	16.03	8.55	$1000r$	8.15
Generation	30.07	15–19	1.15	4.94	27.10	*5–29	1.46	19.77	5.81	13.96	$1000k_1$	5.20
Sex ratio	105.3										$1000k_2$	0.

TABLE 8 LESLIE MATRIX AND ITS ANALYSIS (MALES)

Start of age interval	Sub-diagonal	First row	Percent in stable population	Fisher values	Total reproductive values	Net paternity function	Matrix equation coefficient	Parameters		
									Integral	Matrix
0	0.99550	0.00000	8.560	1.043	393901	0.00000	0.00000	λ_1	1.0269	1.0272
5	0.99741	0.00000	8.294	1.076	407644	0.00000	0.00000	λ_2	0.4227	0.4230
10	0.99638	0.00840	8.051	1.109	398129	0.00000	0.00835		+0.7685	+0.7447i
15	0.99419	0.13032	7.808	1.135	396376	0.01669	0.12893	r_1	0.0053	0.0054
20	0.99313	0.32637	7.555	1.036	316597	0.24116	0.32101	r_2	-0.0262	-0.0310
25	0.99272	0.34619	7.303	0.729	205446	0.40086	0.33817		+0.2136	+0.2108i
30	0.99089	0.21764	7.056	0.391	119396	0.27549	0.21105	c_1		45516
35	0.98665	0.10938	6.805	0.176	57735	0.14661	0.10511	c_2		21932
40	0.97856	0.04448	6.535	0.068	22512	0.06360	0.04217			47034i
45	0.96251	0.01556	6.224	0.024	6150	0.02075	0.01333	$2\pi/y$	29.418	29.801
50	0.93602	0.00532	5.831	0.008	2263	0.00591	0.00364	Δ	3.239	
55	0.75423		19.978							

TABLE 4 POPULATION PROJECTION, USING FIXED AGE-SPECIFIC BIRTH AND DEATH RATES, IN THOUSANDS

Age at last birthday	1972			1977			1982			Age at last birthday
	Total	Males	Females	Total	Males	Females	Total	Males	Females	
0–4	737	379	358	797	410	387	838	431	407	0–4
5–9	634	326	308	734	377	357	793	408	385	5–9
10–14	720	369	351	634	326	308	733	377	356	10–14
15–19	936	478	458	718	368	350	632	324	308	15–19
20–24	843	428	415	932	475	457	714	365	349	20–24
25–29	738	371	367	839	425	414	926	471	455	25–29
30–34	690	338	352	734	368	366	833	421	412	30–34
35–39	684	332	352	684	334	350	728	364	364	35–39
40–44	724	353	371	676	327	349	676	329	347	40–44
45–49	734	350	384	710	345	365	663	319	344	45–49
50–54	551	256	295	714	338	376	691	333	358	50–54
55–59	563	259	304	527	242	285	684	320	364	55–59
60–64	603	276	327	523	235	288	491	220	271	60–64
65–69	480	215	265	532	235	297	462	200	262	65–69
70–74	368	157	211	389	166	223	433	182	251	70–74
75–79	223	85	138	261	105	156	276	111	165	75–79
80–84	107	40	67	126	45	81	148	56	92	80–84
85 +	52	19	33	55	19	36	65	22	43	85 +
All ages	10387	5031	5356	10585	5140	5445	10786	5253	5533	All ages

TABLE 5 OBSERVED AND PROJECTED VITAL RATES

Rates per thousand	Observed			Projected						Stable	
				1972		1977		1982			
	Total	Males	Females	Males	Females	Males	Females	Males	Females	Males	Females
Birth	14.60	15.60	13.66	16.29	14.31	17.44	15.41	17.29	15.36	15.34	14.26
Death	10.74	11.46	10.07	12.27	11.13	12.81	11.89	13.19	12.56	14.72	13.64
Increase	3.86	4.14	3.59	4.02	3.18	4.64	3.51	4.10	2.81	0.6172	

TABLE 6 RATES STANDARDIZED ON THREE STANDARD COUNTRIES

Standardized rates per thousand	England and Wales, 1961			United States, 1960			Mexico, 1960		
	Total	Males	Females	Total	Males	Females	Total	Males	Females
Birth	13.62	14.54	12.09*	13.08	13.72	12.45*	14.07	14.58	13.94*
Death	12.52	12.39	12.60*	10.28	11.22	9.20*	5.63	6.52	7.29*
Increase	1.10	2.15	−0.51*	2.80	2.50	3.26*	8.44	8.05	6.65*

TABLE 7 VITAL STATISTICS AND RATES INFERRED FROM AGE DISTRIBUTIONS (MALES)

Vital statistics		Thompson				Bourgeois-Pichat					Coale
		Age range	NRR	$1000r$	Interval	Age range	NRR	$1000b$	$1000d$	$1000r$	$1000b$
TFR	2.13	0–4	0.87	−5.18	27.36	5–29	1.22	19.36	12.09	7.27	$1000d$
GRR	1.10	5–9	1.05	1.81	27.31	30–54	1.31	22.07	11.94	10.14	$1000r$
NRR	1.02	10–14	1.41	12.55	27.24	55–79	1.84	57.40	34.83	22.57	$1000k_1$
Generation	30.79	15–19	1.27	8.50	27.11	*10–34	1.61	25.00	7.38	17.62	$1000k_2$
Sex ratio	106.86										

TABLE 8 LESLIE MATRIX AND ITS ANALYSIS (MALES)

Start of age interval	Sub-diagonal	First row	Percent in stable population	Fisher values	Total reproductive values	Net paternity function	Matrix equation coefficient	Parameters		
									Integral	Matrix
0	0.99497	0.00000	7.357	1.049	324863	0.00000	0.00000	λ_1	1.0031	1.0036
5	0.99780	0.00000	7.291	1.058	371714	0.00000	0.00000	λ_2	0.3936	0.3932
10	0.99638	0.00716	7.246	1.065	488332	0.00000	0.00711		+0.7709	+0.7462^i
15	0.99354	0.12906	7.191	1.066	443896	0.01422	0.12767	r_1	0.0006	0.0007
20	0.99237	0.31247	7.116	0.941	346557	0.24112	0.30710	r_2	−0.0289	−0.0341
25	0.99136	0.30602	7.034	0.621	219825	0.37307	0.29846		+0.2197	+0.2172^i
30	0.98891	0.16911	6.945	0.305	108248	0.22386	0.16351	c_1		53817
35	0.98470	0.07593	6.841	0.131	48896	0.10316	0.07260	c_2		−134835
40	0.97665	0.02951	6.710	0.052	20436	0.04204	0.02778			67041^i
45	0.96660	0.01201	6.527	0.022	6671	0.01352	0.00955	$2\pi/y$	28.594	28.933
50	0.94636	0.00577	6.284	0.010	3130	0.00558	0.00364	Δ	6.051	
55	0.75049		23.458							

TABLE 4   POPULATION PROJECTION, USING FIXED AGE-SPECIFIC
BIRTH AND DEATH RATES, IN THOUSANDS

Age at last birthday	1969			1974			1979			Age at last birthday
	Total	Males	Females	Total	Males	Females	Total	Males	Females	
0–4	4363	2241	2122	4542	2333	2209	4690	2409	2281	0–4
5–9	3997	2050	1947	4349	2233	2116	4528	2325	2203	5–9
10–14	3434	1760	1674	3990	2046	1944	4342	2229	2113	10–14
15–19	3303	1689	1614	3425	1754	1671	3980	2039	1941	15–19
20–24	3695	1885	1810	3291	1680	1611	3413	1745	1668	20–24
25–29	3068	1535	1533	3680	1875	1805	3279	1672	1607	25–29
30–34	2964	1507	1457	3055	1527	1528	3664	1865	1799	30–34
35–39	2927	1501	1426	2946	1496	1450	3035	1515	1520	35–39
40–44	3018	1524	1494	2897	1483	1414	2917	1479	1438	40–44
45–49	3355	1673	1682	2966	1493	1473	2847	1453	1394	45–49
50–54	2795	1367	1428	3262	1615	1647	2884	1442	1442	50–54
55–59	3049	1459	1590	2667	1284	1383	3112	1517	1595	55–59
60–64	2803	1307	1496	2821	1310	1511	2467	1153	1314	60–64
65–69	2340	1035	1305	2474	1099	1375	2490	1101	1389	65–69
70–74	1699	653	1046	1925	793	1132	2034	842	1192	70–74
75–79	1176	410	766	1258	436	822	1418	529	889	75–79
80–84	683	212	471	727	222	505	779	237	542	80–84
85 +	424	112	312	465	116	349	497	122	375	85 +
All ages	49093	23920	25173	50740	24795	25945	52376	25674	26702	All ages

TABLE 5   OBSERVED AND PROJECTED VITAL RATES

Rates per thousand	Observed			Projected						Stable	
				1969		1974		1979			
	Total	Males	Females	Males	Females	Males	Females	Males	Females	Males	Females
Birth	18.48	19.57	17.44	19.54	17.49	19.71	17.75	19.42	17.58	21.24	20.01
Death	11.28	11.92	10.67	12.29	11.44	12.52	11.80	12.66	12.00	10.17	8.94
Increase	7.20	7.65	6.77	7.25	6.05	7.20	5.94	6.75	5.59	11.0727	

TABLE 6   RATES STANDARDIZED ON THREE STANDARD COUNTRIES

Standardized rates per thousand	England and Wales, 1961			United States, 1960			Mexico, 1960		
	Total	Males	Females	Total	Males	Females	Total	Males	Females
Birth	18.32	19.49	17.22*	17.63	18.43	17.67*	18.31	18.91	19.84*
Death	11.12	11.95	10.31*	9.05	10.60	7.70*	4.61	5.61	5.99*
Increase	7.20	7.54	6.91*	8.57	7.83	9.97*	13.71	13.30	13.85*

TABLE 7   VITAL STATISTICS AND RATES INFERRED FROM AGE DISTRIBUTIONS
(MALES)

Vital statistics		Thompson				Bourgeois-Pichat					Coale
		Age range	NRR	1000r	Interval	Age range	NRR	1000b	1000d	1000r	1000b
TFR	2.85	0–4	1.24	7.94	27.41	5–29	1.21	17.07	9.94	7.13	1000d
GRR	1.47	5–9	1.11	3.90	27.36	30–54	0.92	12.74	15.74	−3.00	1000r
NRR	1.40	10–14	1.06	1.98	27.28	55–79	1.85	57.45	34.60	22.86	1000k_1
Generation	30.13	15–19	1.16	5.50	27.13	*20–44	0.85	11.81	17.65	−5.84	1000k_2
Sex ratio	106.16										

TABLE 8   LESLIE MATRIX AND ITS ANALYSIS (MALES)

Start of age interval	Sub-diagonal	First row	Percent in stable population	Fisher values	Total reproductive values	Net paternity function	Matrix equation coefficient	Parameters		
									Integral	Matrix
0	0.99637	0.00000	10.133	1.053	2056558	0.00000	0.00000	λ_1	1.0569	1.0574
5	0.99796	0.00000	9.545	1.118	1874440	0.00000	0.00000	λ_2	0.4363	0.4344
10	0.99657	0.01161	9.005	1.185	1916642	0.00000	0.01155		+0.7910	+0.7663i
15	0.99468	0.14845	8.484	1.246	2259348	0.02310	0.14710	r_1	0.0111	0.0112
20	0.99480	0.37191	7.978	1.168	1795199	0.27110	0.36657	r_2	−0.0203	−0.0254
25	0.99471	0.40766	7.503	0.848	1239936	0.46205	0.39972		+0.2133	+0.2110i
30	0.99262	0.26710	7.055	0.470	673559	0.33739	0.26051	c_1		201509
35	0.98818	0.13496	6.621	0.217	327559	0.18364	0.13066	c_2		−108560
40	0.98002	0.05528	6.185	0.089	151445	0.07768	0.05289			−285148i
45	0.96536	0.02188	5.730	0.036	53106	0.02810	0.01866	$2\pi/y$	29.450	29.776
50	0.93959	0.00918	5.229	0.016	26295	0.00922	0.00646	Δ	7.562	
55	0.76059		16.533							

TABLE 4 POPULATION PROJECTION, USING FIXED AGE-SPECIFIC
BIRTH AND DEATH RATES, IN THOUSANDS

Age at last birthday	1971			1976			1981			Age at last birthday
	Total	Males	Females	Total	Males	Females	Total	Males	Females	
0–4	313	160	153	356	182	174	406	208	198	0–4
5–9	305	156	149	313	160	153	354	181	173	5–9
10–14	300	153	147	305	156	149	311	159	152	10–14
15–19	266	136	130	300	153	147	303	155	148	15–19
20–24	243	124	119	265	135	130	298	151	147	20–24
25–29	192	98	94	243	124	119	264	134	130	25–29
30–34	169	86	83	191	97	94	242	123	119	30–34
35–39	148	76	72	168	85	83	189	96	93	35–39
40–44	161	83	78	147	75	72	166	84	82	40–44
45–49	157	80	77	157	81	76	144	73	71	45–49
50–54	142	70	72	153	77	76	153	78	75	50–54
55–59	131	64	67	134	65	69	145	72	73	55–59
60–64	112	55	57	122	58	64	125	59	66	60–64
65–69	88	42	46	99	47	52	107	49	58	65–69
70–74	65	28	37	72	32	40	81	36	45	70–74
75–79	43	16	27	48	19	29	52	21	31	75–79
80–84	27	10	17	27	9	18	30	10	20	80–84
85 +	15	5	10	16	5	11	17	5	12	85 +
All ages	2877	1442	1435	3116	1560	1556	3387	1694	1693	All ages

TABLE 5 OBSERVED AND PROJECTED VITAL RATES

Rates per thousand	Observed			Projected						Stable	
				1971		1976		1981			
	Total	Males	Females	Males	Females	Males	Females	Males	Females	Males	Females
Birth	22.43	22.94	21.93	24.04	22.90	25.58	24.33	26.60	25.28	26.02	24.76
Death	8.86	9.82	7.90	9.51	7.95	9.35	7.95	9.23	7.88	8.32	7.06
Increase	13.57	13.12	14.02	14.52	14.94	16.24	16.37	17.37	17.40	17.7027	

TABLE 6 RATES STANDARDIZED ON THREE STANDARD COUNTRIES

Standardized rates per thousand	England and Wales, 1961			United States, 1960			Mexico, 1960		
	Total	Males	Females	Total	Males	Females	Total	Males	Females
Birth	22.47	23.81	20.70*	21.60	22.50	20.87*	22.59	23.24	24.41*
Death	11.46	12.20	10.77*	9.33	10.83	7.92*	4.74	5.78	5.48*
Increase	11.01	11.62	9.93*	12.27	11.67	12.95*	17.85	17.47	18.93*

TABLE 7 VITAL STATISTICS AND RATES INFERRED FROM AGE DISTRIBUTIONS
(MALES)

Vital statistics		Thompson				Bourgeois-Pichat				Coale	
		Age range	NRR	$1000r$	Interval	Age range	NRR	$1000b$	$1000d$	$1000r$	$1000b$	25.60
TFR	3.49	0–4	1.65	18.68	27.38	5–29	2.17	29.86	1.24	28.63	$1000b$	25.60
GRR	1.79	5–9	1.78	21.37	27.33	30–54	1.09	14.22	10.99	3.23	$1000d$	7.00
NRR	1.70	10–14	1.66	18.40	27.25	55–79	2.00	49.20	23.57	25.63	$1000r$	18.60
Generation	29.85	15–19	1.57	15.85	27.10	*35–59	1.29	19.04	9.71	9.33	$1000k_1$	4.18
Sex ratio	105.4										$1000k_2$	0.

TABLE 8 LESLIE MATRIX AND ITS ANALYSIS (MALES)

Start of age interval	Sub-diagonal	First row	Percent in stable population	Fisher values	Total reproductive values	Net paternity function	Matrix equation coefficient	Parameters		
									Integral	Matrix
0	0.99560	0.00000	12.230	1.069	159593	0.00000	0.00000	λ_1	1.0925	1.0932
5	0.99754	0.00000	11.135	1.174	173146	0.00000	0.00000	λ_2	0.4289	0.4259
10	0.99528	0.01789	10.158	1.286	168133	0.00000	0.01777		+0.8209	+0.7946i
15	0.99211	0.19610	9.246	1.394	166957	0.03554	0.19384	r_1	0.0177	0.0178
20	0.99294	0.46451	8.389	1.325	125387	0.35215	0.45554	r_2	-0.0153	-0.0207
25	0.99277	0.48511	7.618	0.960	80098	0.55892	0.47238		+0.2179	+0.2158i
30	0.99005	0.31140	6.916	0.535	38987	0.38584	0.30104	c_1		12871
35	0.98680	0.16099	6.262	0.255	19930	0.21624	0.15409	c_2		2683
40	0.97802	0.06806	5.651	0.108	8477	0.09194	0.06428			29413i
45	0.96329	0.02980	5.055	0.046	3389	0.03662	0.02465	$2\pi/y$	28.839	29.121
50	0.93787	0.01266	4.453	0.019	1342	0.01268	0.00839	Δ	4.105	
55	0.76935		12.886							

[564]

PART V

QUALIFICATIONS AND SOURCE NOTES

CHAPTER 20

On the Quality of Demographic Data

The total effort represented by the numbers in this book is large, and only a minute fraction of it was contributed by the authors whose names are on the cover. Countries spend large sums on censuses in which tens of thousands of enumerators request information from householders; in some countries the entire body of postal employees, school teachers, and other public servants take part. Nationwide registration systems record births and deaths, requiring active participation of householders, as well as of doctors, hospitals, undertakers, and others. Large staffs and costly equipment code and tabulate the individual returns that come out of census and registration. The work is guided by skilled statisticians.

Yet when statisticians survey their own demographic data they realize that every number is subject to error. As national statisticians deserve the main credit for the data in this book, they have the main responsibility for the errors in them. Guided by their statements and other evidence, we list and discuss here some of the sources of error. The discussion, like the whole of the book, is confined to data on population, births and deaths, classified by age and sex. The many other variables taken up in demography—from marriage to income to cause of death—are not discussed here.

The numbers of births and deaths are interpreted by calculating rates per unit or per thousand population. Typically a census or an estimate of population size based on a census provides the denominator for a fraction of which births or deaths is the numerator. To use vital statistics for demographic purposes we need to know something about the accuracy attained in censuses (Deming, 1944).

Definitions: What Is To Be Counted?

Accuracy and error can only be thought about relative to a definition of what is to be counted. In the United States, Canada, and a number of other countries, the objective of a census is to count the resident population, sometimes called the *de jure* population. This means that all persons who are usually or legally resident in the country are counted, including those who have homes in the country but are away, say as tourists abroad, at the time of the census. Similarly, foreign residents who happen to be travelling in the country are disregarded. The question of residence arises similarly in determining who should be enumerated in each state, city, or other local area.

Elaborate rules are needed to cover the many special cases. Are college students to be counted at the college they are attending or at the home of their parents who are supporting them? What about a person who maintains two homes in different towns? The United States rules omit from the count citizens absent from the country for extended periods of time. Reading the formal rules makes a person wonder to what extent they are effectively followed, and in a good census this question is answered by resurvey of a sample.

An alternative widely used in European and other countries is to count the *de facto* population, the people who happen to be physically present in the country at the moment of the count. Conceptually, the *de facto* method is easier; determining the number of living persons at the instant when the census is taken (midnight of April 23, 1961, in the last census of England and Wales) requires the resolution of no delicate conceptual issues.

If the *de facto* method is easier to think about abstractly, and requires a shorter book of rules, it is more difficult to execute in a large country in which the actual enumeration goes on over a period of weeks. It requires reconstructing the situation at the point of time when the census occurred, and for this the enumerator often lacks data—the tourist has left by the time the enumerator gets to the place where he was, and no adequate record of him exists. The *de facto* census is ideally taken in a single day, and this ideal can be approached with a cooperative and compactly distributed population. In some countries the ordinary life of the country is halted while the count takes place, and people are not allowed to leave their homes until they have been counted.

Aside from the difficulty of stopping everything while the census is taken, the *de facto* count is conceptually not as satisfactory for many purposes as a count of the resident population, and this is the main reason for putting up with the rules that are part of the *de jure* method.

Of especial importance for us is the requirement that whatever definition is applied for the count of population be applied also to the counts of births and deaths. On any estimate of exposure, the construction of the denominator of a death rate for

EXHIBIT 3

Outline of United States 1970 Census activities by date.

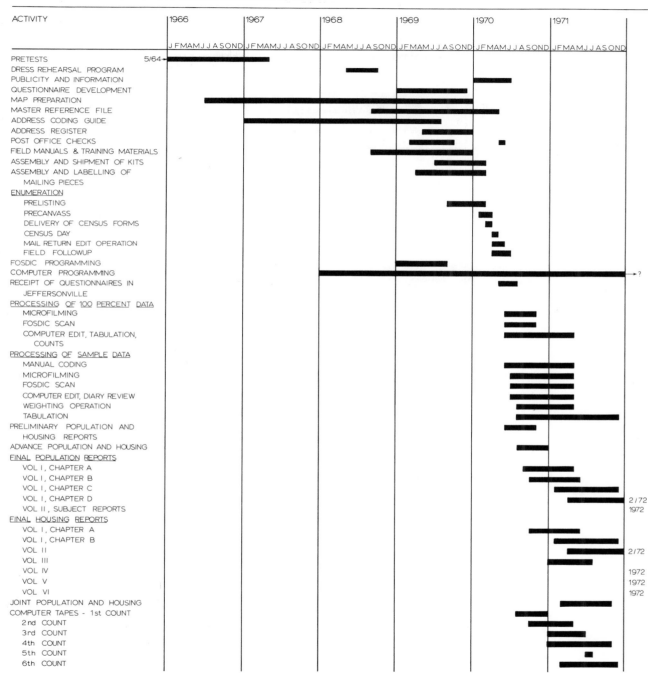

EXHIBIT 4

United States 1970 Census questionnaire.

ANSWER THESE QUESTIONS FOR

DO NOT MARK THIS COL-UMN

Line No.

1. WHAT IS THE NAME OF EACH PERSON
who was living here on Wednesday, April 1, 1970 or
who was staying or visiting here and had no other home?

Print names in this order

Head of the household
Wife of head
Unmarried children, oldest first
Married childen and their families
Other relatives of the head
Persons not related to the head

2. HOW IS EACH PERSON RELATED TO THE HEAD OF THIS HOUSEHOLD?

Fill one circle.

If "Other relative of head," <u>also</u> give exact relationship, for example, mother-in-law, brother, niece, grandson, etc.

If "Other not related to head," <u>also</u> give exact relationship, for example, partner, maid, etc.

---

(1) Last name _____

First name _____ Middle initial

○ Head of household   ○ Roomer, boarder, lodger
○ Wife of head   ○ Patient or inmate
○ Son or daughter of head   ○ Other not related to head— *Print exac relations*
○ Other relative
   of head— *Print exact*
    relationship →

---

(2) Last name _____

First name _____ Middle initial

○ Head of household   ○ Roomer, boarder, lodger
○ Wife of head   ○ Patient or inmate
○ Son or daughter of head   ○ Other not related to head— *Print exac relations*
○ Other relative
   of head— *Print exact*
    relationship →

---

(3) Last name _____

First name _____ Middle initial

○ Head of household   ○ Roomer, boarder, lodger
○ Wife of head   ○ Patient or inmate
○ Son or daughter of head   ○ Other not related to head— *Print exac relations*
○ Other relative
   of head— *Print exact*
    relationship →

---

example, the question in regard to the inclusion of data on an individual must always be: If this person were to die in this place, would he be included in the death statistics?

Steps in the Taking of a Census

The census operation requires the collaboration of respondents, enumerators, and census officials. We include Exhibit 3 to show the reader the sequence of steps in the taking of a census; it has been especially provided by the United States Bureau of the Census as a summary of its 1970 census operation.

No part of government expenditure in the United States is more carefully watched than the census budget. The cost of the 1960 Census of Population and Housing was $91,000,000 (plus some costs shared with the Census of Agriculture). Planning and geographic work accounted for $11,000,000 of this; field enumeration for $64,000,000; data processing for $13,000,000; and publication and evaluation for just less than $2,000,000 each (U.S. Bureau of the Census, 1966). The volume of detailed work accomplished for a total·cost of about 50 cents per inhabitant is impressive.

ACH PERSON IN YOUR HOUSEHOLD

3. SEX	4. COLOR OR RACE		DATE OF BIRTH				8. WHAT IS EACH PERSON'S MARITAL STATUS?
			5. Month and year of birth and age last birthday	6. Month of birth	7. Year of birth		
Fill one circle	Fill one circle. If "Indian (American)," also give tribe. If "Other," also give race.		Print	Fill one circle	Fill one circle for first three numbers	Fill one circle for last number	Fill one circle
Male ○ Female ○	○ White ○ Negro or Black ○ Indian (Amer.) Print tribe ➤	○ Japanese ○ Hawaiian ○ Chinese ○ Korean ○ Filipino ○ Other– Print race	Month _____ Year _____ Age _____	○ Jan.-Mar. ○ Apr.-June ○ July-Sept. ○ Oct.-Dec.	○ 186- ○ 192- ○ 187- ○ 193- ○ 188- ○ 194- ○ 189- ○ 195- ○ 190- ○ 196- ○ 191- ○ 197-	○ 0 ○ 5 ○ 1 ○ 6 ○ 2 ○ 7 ○ 3 ○ 8 ○ 4 ○ 9	○ Now married ○ Widowed ○ Divorced ○ Separated ○ Never married
Male ○ Female ○	○ White ○ Negro or Black ○ Indian (Amer.) Print tribe ➤	○ Japanese ○ Hawaiian ○ Chinese ○ Korean ○ Filipino ○ Other– Print race	Month _____ Year _____ Age _____	○ Jan.-Mar. ○ Apr.-June ○ July-Sept. ○ Oct.-Dec.	○ 186- ○ 192- ○ 187- ○ 193- ○ 188- ○ 194- ○ 189- ○ 195- ○ 190- ○ 196- ○ 191- ○ 197-	○ 0 ○ 5 ○ 1 ○ 6 ○ 2 ○ 7 ○ 3 ○ 8 ○ 4 ○ 9	○ Now married ○ Widowed ○ Divorced ○ Separated ○ Never married
Male ○ Female ○	○ White ○ Negro or Black ○ Indian (Amer.) Print tribe ➤	○ Japanese ○ Hawaiian ○ Chinese ○ Korean ○ Filipino ○ Other– Print race	Month _____ Year _____ Age _____	○ Jan.-Mar. ○ Apr.-June ○ July-Sept. ○ Oct.-Dec.	○ 186- ○ 192- ○ 187- ○ 193- ○ 188- ○ 194- ○ 189- ○ 195- ○ 190- ○ 196- ○ 191- ○ 197-	○ 0 ○ 5 ○ 1 ○ 6 ○ 2 ○ 7 ○ 3 ○ 8 ○ 4 ○ 9	○ Now married ○ Widowed ○ Divorced ○ Separated ○ Never married

Crucial to the completeness of a census is organization of the thousands of enumerators. The central element of organization is assigning to each an area for whose coverage he is responsible. The areas must be nonoverlapping and exhaustive, and they must be designated unambiguously, so as to have effectively the same boundaries on the ground that they have in the office. The office base maps for the 1960 Census of the United States totalled 250,000 square feet, and a copy of the appropriate area had to be made for each of the 159,000 enumerators. Designing the division into areas required skilled and painstaking geographic work.

An early phase in any census is devising the questionnaires. Questions are proposed by users of the census, definitions of the needed terms are worked out, field tests are conducted, the questions are modified and retested, in a sequence extending through five or more years prior to the census date. (Exhibit 4 gives part of the final questionnaire for the United States 1970 Census, so drawn up as to be transferable to magnetic tape by optical sensing. The procedures to be used are described by Kaplan, 1970.)

When all this has been done the questions and definitions must be communicated to the enumerators through a kind of training ladder. For the census taken in the United States in 1960, the training started February 3–11 with a session in Washington for 39 chief instructors. These chief instructors went into the field and between February 22 and March 4 trained 405 technical officers in 15 places. The technical officers in their turn trained 10,348 crew leaders at 399 training sites throughout the

United States. Finally the crew leaders trained 159,321 enumerators and 9,948 field reviewers in 5,604 training sites (U.S. Bureau of the Census, 1966).

The possibilities for distortion as concepts were passed down this training ladder were minimized by the written and pictorial materials used at all stages to accompany the oral instruction. But no training effort could eliminate the idiosyncrasies of the 159,000 enumerators at the bottom of the ladder as they interacted with 60,000,000 respondents. Their recruitment was crucial, for everything depended on their grasp of the instructions and their patience in applying them. The supply of competent people available for only a few weeks of work is limited. Hired enumerators are usually paid so much per schedule turned in—to pay them by time would be impossibly expensive, though it is practicable for crew leaders and reviewers. This affects the amount of effort an enumerator will make to get the facts straight on a given respondent.

Most enumeration is not accomplished by direct questioning of the enumeratee, but by reports concerning him given by a third person who is the respondent—wife, mother, child, or landlady. If the landlady does not know her lodger's age she ought to say so, and the enumerator ought to come back when the lodger is likely to be home and ask him; or at least he ought to leave a card that could be mailed with the needed information. Understandably, in a high proportion of such cases the respondent will instead be asked to make a guess, or the enumerator will provide a suggestion: "Is he about 40?" Experiments conducted by the U.S. Bureau of the Census show that respondents will agree with a wide range of such suggestions and hence that it is important that discretion and restraint be used by the enumerator in making them.

The method of enumeration used and the form of payment have much to do with the completeness of the census. The enumerator, carrying a map of the area for which he is responsible, starts his rounds, and collects data at the houses where someone answers the doorbell. He may only receive eight cents per name, but this represents a satisfactory rate per hour when there are plenty of households where someone is present to answer the questions immediately. On the first round through his area he skims the cream, and then he has to face less rewarding work. Following instructions he will try to keep up with callbacks from the beginning. As he continues his work he encounters a continually rising proportion of not-at-homes—until, finally he is left with the task of returning again and again to the households where everyone is absent most of the time. His return per hour goes steadily downward. The most persistent enumerator has a quitting point, and the point is generally short of complete coverage. He is required at the end to turn back a list of the addresses he has not been able to cover, and these are the target of subsequent effort by hourly paid employees.

The great difficulties of such enumeration, and especially the errors contributed by interposing an enumerator (and perhaps an additional person, such as a landlady) between the respondent and the census form, have led the Bureau of the Census towards using self-enumeration for the 1970 census. Self-enumeration has been practiced in the highly literate countries of western Europe for many decades, and tests conducted by the Bureau of the Census showed that a high quality of response could on the whole be attained by this method in the United States.

The method adopted for 1970 is to establish a list of dwellings in an area in cooperation with the post office, then to mail a short questionnaire, to be filled out by the occupants at their convenience. The facts concerning lodgers are more likely to be reported by themselves, rather than by the landlady. The questionnaires are then mailed back to the local census office in prepaid envelopes, and checked off on a list. Those dwellings listed for which no response is recorded are then visited by an enumerator. The scheme seems well designed to enlist the help of the literate and cooperative majority of the population. The traditional method of enumeration is reserved for those who are illiterate or unwilling to complete and return the questionnaire. If half or more of the households fill out and return questionnaires, the census cost is lower on the 1970 procedure. But the principal aim is accuracy rather than reduction of cost.

In many countries the task of hiring enumerators is avoided, and an apparent economy is achieved by requiring school teachers and other public servants to do the enumeration as part of their regular duties. Sometimes these employees recognize that they are performing an important national duty in enumerating their area, and are fully as persistent as specially hired enumerators; sometimes they are considerably less effective.

Sampling is a feature of modern censuses. Using a sample permits more care to be taken in interviewing the subjects selected, and the reduction of response error can more than offset the sampling error incurred. Hence we have the seeming paradox of a sample that is not only less expensive but also more accurate than a complete enumeration.

In the censuses of the twentieth century an increasing degree of mechanization has been applied, and official statistical agencies in the United States and elsewhere have led in developing and introducing modern equipment. In the first mechanized procedure, the primary census information as provided by the enumerator was edited by clerks, punched on cards, the cards were sorted and counted to provide the desired statistical distributions, and these in turn were made into printer's copy, and set in type as the census tables. The procedure was better than the hand counts it displaced, but inaccuracy and delay were compounded at each step. Tabulation work sometimes took up most of the ten-year interval between censuses, so that the results were largely of only historical interest by the time they became available to the public.

Speedier compilation is made possible today by machine-readable enumeration forms from which tapes are made directly; these tapes are immediately read into computers. The computers in their turn produce tables, and the tables are printed by photo-offset without typesetting or the need for proofreading. The interval between enumeration and the release of results is greatly shortened, an achievement made possible by extended advance preparation in computer programming and other tasks.

The modern input arrangements are less subject to error than the handwork that they replaced. They permit more elaborate and effective analysis of the questionnaires for inconsistencies, more realistic filling of gaps in the returns, and more efficient estimates of totals from samples.

Some years back it seemed that wages were the most important factor in determining which census procedures would be the cheapest. With clerical wages less than $50 per month hand compilation would be cheapest; with wages between $50 and $200, the use of punch cards and unit record equipment would be indicated; with wages higher than $200 computers would be economical. Subsequent decrease in costs of computer operations has changed this, and handwork has become relatively less advantageous in both accuracy and cost.

Much ingenuity has gone into the improvement of censuses around the world in recent years, with the United States Bureau of the Census especially active in devising and testing new procedures. It has led in the introduction of sampling; machine-readable questionnaires; computer editing, tabulation and printing; self-enumeration; and other ways of increasing accuracy and lowering cost. These are being adopted in many other countries.

At the same time census-taking has become more difficult because of modern changes in patterns of work and residence. When most people lived on farms and rarely spent a night away from home, the process of census-taking was simpler than it is today; extensive travel, highly specialized occupations, and frequent change of jobs and residence make the task much more difficult.

Analysis of Age Misstatement

Table N shows parts of the age distribution for males in three countries, with an apparent diminution of accuracy (at least on this evidence) as we go from the United States to Thailand and from Thailand to Turkey. If we want to make more delicate comparisons among countries or ages we can form an index, relating age 30, for example, to the mean of ages 29, 30 and 31. Such an index of error of statement appears in Table O, a more compact version of Table N in its bearing on the points here raised.

Combining indexes for all ages together (U.S. Bureau of the Census, 1966)

TABLE N

Numbers of males reported at certain ages in the census of three countries.

Age, in years	United States, April 1, 1960	Thailand, April 25, 1960	Turkey, October 23, 1955
49	1,041,333	92,157	54,812
50	1,004,142	90,505	188,536
51	972,235	82,112	80,175
. . .	. . .	. . .	. . .
69	506,168	20,759	12,120
70	494,297	27,154	58,943
71	477,620	15,737	13,958

Source: *United Nations Demographic Yearbook*, 1962.

TABLE O

Index of age misstatement for three countries: ratio of given age to mean of three ages around it.

Age, in years	United States, April 1, 1960	Thailand, April 25, 1960	Turkey, October 23, 1955
50	0.998	1.025	1.748
70	1.003	1.280	2.080

Source: Table N.

provides a comparison of proportionate misstatement in the successive United States censuses:

1930	4.3	1950	2.2
1940	3.0	1960	0.8

The strikingly better performance of the United States 1960 census on this test is partly due to the question asked. In 1960, rather than asking the respondent his age at last birthday, the questionnaire requested that he provide the month and year of his birth. (In the 1970 census both questions were asked.) Which form of question is preferable depends on whether more people know their year of birth (and calculate their age from that) or know their age (and calculate their year of birth from their age).

The smaller index of error in the United States in 1960 than in previous censuses does not by itself prove greater accuracy. Tests such as concentration on even ages are no substitute for re-enumeration of a sample by more skilled enumerators (post-enumeration survey), as discussed later in this chapter.

Given that census responses to the question of the person's age tend to be concentrated at the even ages and subject to other errors, little seems to be lost by grouping ages in tabulation. Most censuses publish data in the age intervals 0, 1–4, 5–9, . . . , at last birthday, and we have followed them in the tables in this book. But given also that some smoothing is required, and that grouping ages is a first step toward such smoothing, the question may still be asked whether this particular grouping is optimum in the face of the errors that typically occur.

From some viewpoints it is not. Consider the tendency of people to give an even rather than an odd number of years in stating their age at last birthday, and suppose that this results in the number of persons included in all even ages being high by a fixed amount ϵ and those in odd ages low by ϵ. If ages are otherwise correctly reported, five-year age intervals starting with 0 will be too high, and those starting with 5 will be low. For example, since the age interval 50–54 contains three even ages—50, 52, and 54—and the age interval 55–59 contains only two even ages—56 and 58—the number of persons of age 50–54 would be overstated by about ϵ, and the number 55–59 understated by the same amount.

The concentration on ages that are multiples of 5 is usually greater than that on multiples of 2. Here any fixed amount by which the multiple of 5 draws from the two neighboring ages will not alter the size of the five-year group. If, for example, age 50 has drawn from ages 49 and 51, and age 55 has drawn from ages 54 and 56 in the same degree, then the total number of persons stated as in the 50–54 age group will be correct. But concentration on multiples of 10 tends to increase the same groups that are already too large by virtue of the concentration on even numbers.

Missing Infants

A second nearly universal tendency that makes censuses inaccurate is under-reporting of very young children. They may be omitted altogether, or reported to be of an older age.

Some of the shortfall in the reporting of infants is due to stating that children are one year old when they are approaching their first birthday. If all children older than 51 weeks (and less than one year) are said to be one year old, then the number younger than one year will be short by about 2 percent. Presumably this tendency exists at all ages: persons who are 29 years and 51 weeks old tend to report their age as 30 years, but this tendency is offset by persons who are 30 years and 51 weeks old reporting their age as 31. Only at the youngest age is there nothing to offset this tendency. Theory for making the comparison is shown on page 583.

The under-reporting of infants is seen in the ratio of the less than one year age group to the 1–4 age group; this ought to be more than 0.25 insofar as the population is increasing and is subject to positive mortality. Yet for few populations does the ratio rise as high as 0.25, even among European countries with a long census tradition. The ratio of the less than 1, P_0, to the 1–4, $_4P_1$, is found from 1968 records to be

$$\frac{P_0}{_4P_1} = 0.244 \text{ for Austria,}$$
$$= 0.241 \text{ for England and Wales}$$
$$= 0.244 \text{ for Ireland}$$
$$= 0.259 \text{ for New Zealand,}$$

On the closed-population stable model of Chapter 2, the ratio ought to be about 0.26. In general the ratio is too low for the discrepancy with that from the model to be accounted for by declining births over the five years prior to the census.

Problems of Age-reporting in Africa and Asia

A thorough study of age-reporting in African censuses and surveys is provided by Van de Walle (Van de Walle, 1968). He collects African data in physiological age intervals: up to puberty, puberty to menopause, after menopause—categories once extensively used in certain colonial areas. (The Indonesian Census of 1930 classified children as "not yet able to walk," "able to walk but below puberty," etc.)

Van de Walle finds such counts to be unusable. One test he applies is whether the proportion below puberty, 40.4 percent in Zambia, 45.7 percent in Rwanda, varies with the birth rate; it turns out to vary in directions that do not correlate with what is known of the birth rates. This, and the difficulty of dealing statistically with age boundaries so vaguely defined, have discouraged our use of such categories.

Overstatement at Oldest Ages

The fact that social security benefits begin at age 65 leads some persons in the United States who are just a little younger than that to overstate their age to the census enumerator in the hope of qualifying sooner. In fact, a census is not an admissible proof of age (at least not until 30 or more years have gone by). Comparisons of successive censuses have shown that the numbers of persons counted in the 55–64 age group are too small, and those in the 65–69 group too large (Spiegelman, 1968).

At ages older than these the exaggeration continues, especially among less educated populations. It can be studied (Myers, 1966) by the use of two successive censuses; projecting forward from the early census tells how many centenarians, say, are expected at the later one. Myers found that not much more than one-third of those persons who claimed to be older than 100 years actually were that old. Because of such inaccuracy, we have terminated all tables in this volume with the group 85+.

Our calculations do not show the effects of age exaggeration of older persons to be serious, at least up to age 80. Table P compares the observed United States, 1967, male population at ages greater than 50 with the projection from 1962. The differences are small and partly accounted for by immigration.

TABLE P
Observed United States, 1967, age distribution of males older than 50 years, compared with projection from 1962, using 1962 age-specific birth and death rates.

Age, in years	Observed, in thousands	Projected, in thousands	Observed less projected, in thousands
50–54	10,773	10,723	50
55–59	9,523	9,492	31
60–64	8,048	8,024	24
65–69	6,501	6,481	20
70–74	5,177	5,175	2
75–79	3,785	3,764	21
80–84	2,160	2,125	35
85+	1,173	1,225	−52

Source: Observed data from page 360 of this book; projected data from Keyfitz and Flieger (1968), page 159.

Post-censal Estimates

Since censuses are too expensive to be taken frequently, we have actual population counts, to use as denominators in ratios, for only about one out of ten years. And as we have just seen, even the actual counts have errors. For other years, denominators must be estimated. (A strong case can be made for taking censuses every five years, as Canada and a few other countries now do.) Thus in most of the tables of this book, as in demographic calculations generally, the denominators must be sought in estimates.

Since population estimates used here and elsewhere are based on censuses they contain all the errors of censuses and others besides. To see what these other errors are, note that in principle a post-censal estimate is made by starting with the numbers published in the preceding census, adding births and immigration, and subtracting deaths and emigration, all age by age and for each sex.

As an example of the calculation, consider the components of the change in population size of Canada in the period 1961–66, summarizing all ages together (Table Q). As presented the calculation does not allow for emigration, on which

TABLE Q

Components of change of size of population, Canada, 1961–66 (Newfoundland included).

Census population as of June 1, 1961	18,238,000
Births, June 1, 1961 to June 1, 1966	2,249,000
Deaths, June 1, 1961 to June 1, 1966	731,000
Natural increase = Births − Deaths	1,518,000
Immigration, June 1, 1961 to June 1, 1966	539,000
Census + Natural Increase + Immigration	20,295,000

Source: *Canada Year Book*, 1968.

Canada does not gather statistics. For most years we would simply have to guess the emigration. The 1966 census reported a total population of 20,015,000 persons. This permits an inference on emigration as the difference between the last number in Table Q and the 1966 census count: 20,295,000 − 20,015,000 = 280,000 persons.

The accuracy of this emigration estimate cannot be very high. If the 1966 census was better enumerated than the 1961 census the improvement would have caused an understatement in emigration in the bookkeeping. Suppose the 1966 census was one percent more complete than that of 1961; then the true emigration would have been 480,000. A one percent improvement in the census would have made the inferred emigration 40 percent short; fortunately, our work did not need separate estimates of emigration.

Though the post-censal estimates must depend on a guess at emigration in Canada and some other countries, these estimates can be improved after the next census by taking account of the adjustment for closure. At the very least the adjustment can be allocated back among the several years. This means that many of the population numbers contained in this book will be improved by national agencies after they have tabulated their 1970 census.

If a census age distribution is projected forward by births and deaths the census pattern of misstatement will not be preserved. In particular the understatement at ages less than five years will move up to ages 5–9 after five years. This qualifies some of the remarks made earlier about understatement of age of infants; the error pattern of censuses is not necessarily the same as that of intercensal estimates.

Population Shifted to Mid-period

The population counts of this volume are presented less for their own interest than as denominators of birth and death rates. They provide measures of exposure to the risk of birth and death. Ideally we need the number of people (age by age and for each sex) who, *if* they had died in the time in question, *would have been counted* in the death statistics. Where death statistics are compiled for residents of each country—not including, for example, tourists from other countries—this means that we need the number of person-years of residence in a country during 1968— not counting tourists—for interpreting its deaths of 1968.

The ideal datum of person-years of residence is not directly provided for any country. The closest generally feasible approximation is the mid-period population, and this will be equivalent to person-years of residence if the population increases or decreases by uniform *amounts* during the whole period. Insofar as the population is changing in a constant *ratio* the mid-period population will tend to be low. If the rate of increase is 3 percent, for example, and the period is 5 years, the mid-period population underestimates average exposure by about one part in 1000.

If n is the width of the time interval, and r the (supposed uniform) rate of increase of the population, then the mid-period number times n understates exposure by a fraction $r^2n^3/24$.

Some countries publish mid-year estimates, and for those that do not we interpolated. For some populations, we had official estimates for two successive years, say as of May 1, and we then took the weighted arithmetic mean as the mid-year number; for 1967 we would take 10 times the population at May 1, 1967, add twice the population as of May 1, 1968, then divide by 12. If we had to extrapolate as much as a year beyond the latest official estimates, we used birth and death data in a population-accounting similar to that of Table Q, but broken down by age and sex.

Conclusion: Accuracy of Censuses

We have mentioned that sources of error may lie in the several steps of taking a census, the further manipulation of the census results, the production of the official post-censal estimates, or in the production—by the authors of this book—of the mid-year figures of each period used.

Notwithstanding the doubts expressed in the preceding sections, most of the population figures of this book appear relatively trustworthy. Data on births and deaths are more difficult to collect, and data on births suffer from especially large errors.

Increasing the census figures to compensate for incompleteness of enumeration could increase the inaccuracy of birth and death rates if births and deaths are incompletely recorded and left unadjusted. Lacking separate information on completeness of data on births, we did not undertake to correct censuses on the basis of re-enumeration results.

Birth and Death Registrations

In the federal arrangements of the United States and Canada, censuses are the task of the national government, while the states and provinces are responsible for the primary recording of what are called vital statistics, including births and deaths. (This division of responsibility for demographic statistics is not universal: in England and Wales the national government, through the office of the Registrar-General, takes the census and also records births and deaths; in India the several states are responsible for census-taking as well as for the vital statistics.)

Although each state of the United States and each province of Canada legislates for birth and death registration, a considerable degree of coordination has been attained. Standard birth and death certificates have been devised, and a copy of every birth and death certificate is sent to the national statistical agency for tabulation.

Definitions and Accuracy of Birth Statistics

The definition of a statistical entity must be sharp and detailed, particularly at certain boundaries. For instance, we saw that, where a census is taken on the basis of legal residence, "residents" had to be distinguished from nonresidents who are in the country as tourists. For the current census of the United States, persons included are those born before April 15, 1970, who are still alive on that date. If the enumerator fails to observe such definitions the resulting numbers will not be what they purport to be: a count of the resident population as of April 15, 1970. And what is serious about this for our purpose is that the census will not provide the right number to compare with the number of births.

For counting births a main definition is that distinguishing between a child born alive that subsequently dies and a child born dead. The latter, called a stillbirth, does not qualify as a birth at all. In the attempt to make this definition sharp the World Health Organization recommended to countries that a live birth be specified as "the complete expulsion or extraction from its mother of a product of conception, irrespective of the duration of pregnancy, which after such separation, breathes or shows any other evidence of life such as beating of the heart, pulsation of the umbilical cord, or definite movement of voluntary muscles, whether or not the umbilical cord has been cut or the placenta is attached; each product of such a birth is considered live born" (quoted in Spiegelman, 1968). This painfully detailed attempt at specification has been adopted by most national statistical agencies. Nonetheless we can only conclude in examining infant mortality ratios that countries must vary considerably in interpreting this definition. The apparently low infant mortality of some countries is evidently due to the omission from both birth and death records of children born alive who die in the first hours or minutes after birth. The infant mortality rates shown in column 18 of the Summary Table (Part II) and the probabilities of dying in the first year of life are to be regarded with suspicion for many countries.

Such omission from birth and death records affects infant mortality greatly, but has little effect on the computed rate of increase of a population. In fact, the choice of the moment of birth for the demographic accounting is arbitrary; we can at least imagine registration systems and analysis based on counting from the moment of conception, or at another extreme counting from the first birthday. But the moment of birth, arbitrary or not, is now universally adopted as the zero point, and no one seriously suggests changing it.

A grosser problem in the study of birth rates is that in most of the world a registration system is either altogether lacking, or is formally present but in practice disregarded by an unspecified proportion of parents. The selective bias of class and region weighs heavily on the published results. Children born to illiterate parents in rural areas without medical facilities are often unregistered, notwithstanding laws making registration unconditionally compulsory. The districts of Indonesia show birth rates ranging from 10 per thousand to 45 per thousand, a variation in completeness of registration rather than in fertility.

Literate populations, especially those in cities, attain high standards of birth registration. That the law imposes the obligation of registering births on parents is probably less important than the parents' concern that their child's future rights of citizenship, as well as his age, be attested by the birth certificate. In Canada and some other countries the existence of government allowances for children draws attention to registration, even where the registration is not formally a condition for receiving the allowance. Moreover, most children in cities in rich countries are born in hospitals, and hospital personnel routinely register the births.

Moriyama (1946; also Jaffe, 1951) discusses the shift from births at home to births in hospitals during the ten years 1935–44; at the beginning of this period 36.9 percent of births in the United States took place in hospitals and other institutions, at the end, 75.6 percent. For the four months preceding the 1940 census it was found that births in hospitals were 98.5 percent registered, those at home only 86.1 percent registered. By 1966 only about 2 percent of the total occurred outside of hospitals in the United States (U.S. Department of Commerce, 1968).

Less than 30 percent of the world's population lives in areas in which birth registration can seriously be claimed to be complete (Keyfitz and Flieger, 1968). If this could be taken as a proper 30 percent sample all would be well; unfortunately it is far from representative. The areas in which registration is complete are those that are the richest, most literate, most urban. The demographer is under obligation to seek data for the other 70 percent of the world's population, not only because it is the majority, but because it is known to be growing faster, and hence facing more immediate and more serious demographic problems.

Comparison of Births with Census

As an example of the way in which demographic data are redundant that shows how this redundancy can be of service, consider the number of individuals younger than five years old from the census or estimated population, and the number of births. Assume that migration is negligible.

If the number of births in the year with which we are concerned, say year zero, is B_0, then the population younger than one year old expected at the end of the year is $B_0 L_0 / l_0$, where l_0 is the radix or starting number of the life table, and L_0 is the number younger than one year old in the stationary life table population. The mid-year population will be somewhat less than this; if growth is uniform at rate r the factor $e^{-r/2}$ is required. Hence we ought to be able to compare the observed mid-year population P_0 with $B_0 e^{-r/2} L_0 / l_0$, once B_0, r, and L_0/l_0 are available to us. The question of how to take advantage of the relation is practically important but theoretically indeterminate unless we know more than has just been said. But since omissions are more common in demographic data than are duplications, which applies both to the census and to birth registrations, we might consider whichever is higher to be correct and adjust the other one upwards to this.

In fact we can do much better by bringing in more comparisons. If stability cannot be assumed, but we have registered births in years $-1, -2, \ldots, -9$, then we can write as approximations,

$$_5P_0 \cong \left(\frac{B_{-1} + B_0}{2} \right) \frac{L_0}{l_0} + \ldots + \left(\frac{B_{-5} + B_{-4}}{2} \right) \frac{L_4}{l_0}, \tag{38}$$

$$_5P_5 \cong \left(\frac{B_{-6} + B_{-5}}{2} \right) \frac{L_5}{l_0} + \ldots + \left(\frac{B_{-10} + B_{-9}}{2} \right) \frac{L_9}{l_0},$$

as long as the death rates implicit in the life table L's are applicable. If these are under suspicion we can revert to recorded deaths over the period, as the last stage in this progressive weakening of assumptions.

In some countries censuses are more or less completely enumerated, while birth registrations are grossly deficient. India is an example: her 1961 census showed 13,562,045 children younger than one year old, and the births reported for 1960 were 8,070,000 and for 1961 were 8,360,000 (Data from United Nations Demographic Yearbook, 1964). True the births were for a registration area in which only 90 percent of the population lived, but the gap is far from closed if we multiply the registered births by 100/90. Moreover, the births should be higher by the number of deaths of infants younger than one year up to the time of the census.

Other countries, including Canada up to recent times, have the opposite sort of result: their births are reported as higher than the enumerated population younger than one year old.

In preparing the tables of this book, when the age distribution gave a very different birth rate from that observed, and the several methods, each making somewhat different assumptions, agreed with one another, we took the liberty of adjusting the births. In all instances a note warns the reader that an adjustment has been made and tells him how much it was.

Inferring the Life Table and Births

In some instances we were faced with the problem of what to do when we had an age distribution and no life table, that is, neither number of births nor number of deaths was reliably given. We wanted to avoid the arbitrary selection of a life table, or if arbitrary selection was inevitable, we wanted to mitigate its worst effects. Our technique was to use in reverse a technique for making model tables due to Brass and Coale (1968). By this technique the age distribution can tell us *both* what birth rate *and* what life table are applicable.

Brass and Coale show how to produce sets of model life tables by linear transformation. They start by changing $p(a) = l(a)/l_0$, the probability of living from birth to age a, into a function called the *logit*. The logit function of x is defined as

$$\text{logit } [x] = \frac{1}{2} \ln \frac{1 - x}{x};$$

since a probability ranges over the interval zero to unity, the logit of a probability ranges over infinity to minus infinity. The main point to note here is that for every $p(a)$ we can find a logit $[p(a)]$, and for every logit we can find a $p(a)$, and in each direction the answer is unique.

Brass and Coale then make up a two-parameter set of model tables working from one standard $p_s(a)$:

$$\text{logit}[p(a)] = \alpha + \beta \text{ logit}[p_s(a)] \tag{39}$$

In this linear relation any α and β provide a model table. By rearranging we obtain

$$p(a) = 1 / \left[1 + e^{2\alpha} \left(\frac{1}{p_s(a)} - 1 \right)^{\beta} \right]$$

as the explicit form for the set of model tables generated by varying the values of α and β, given a standard table $p_s(a)$.

Now if stability may be assumed we can again apply the relation that connects the life table with the age distribution,

$$c(a) = be^{-ra}p(a),$$

where $c(a)da$ is the proportion of the population between ages a and $a + da$, b is the intrinsic birth rate, and r is the intrinsic rate of natural increase. Our final result then is obtained by entering the Brass and Coale model value for $p(a)$ into the relation just given:

$$c(a) = be^{-ra}p(a)$$
$$= \frac{be^{-ra}}{1 + e^{2\alpha}\left(\dfrac{1}{p_s(a)} - 1\right)^{\beta}} \tag{40}$$

Aside from the standard life table $p_s(a)$ this has four constants, b, r, α and β. If it can be identified with an observed age distribution we ought to be able to solve for the constants. We may take an arbitrary standard life table as $p_s(a)$ to begin with, but then let the age distribution adjust it for us by providing α and β. This is as close to raising oneself by one's bootstraps as demography permits; having nothing but a census age distribution, a mere cross section, it provides the life table, births, and deaths.

In practice the procedure is conditioned by the selection of $p_s(a)$; it would be too much to expect the result to be invariant with respect to the standard. But if the b and r vary less with $p_s(a)$ on this process than they do on the Bourgeois-Pichat method described in the program INFER, that is to say, if the introduction of α and β makes the result less sensitive to the arbitrary choice of standard, then we have a clear gain through the use of the Brass and Coale system.

It turns out that this is true for the demographic data on some populations, and for those we used the method described. An example of this was Indonesia. We tried as the input standard $p_s(a)$ the Coale and Demeny (1966) Model West male tables. Let us write $\mathring{e}_{s0} = \int_0^\omega p_s(a)da$ to identify the input table. Then

with input $\mathring{e}_{s0} = 40$, output $\mathring{e}_0$ was 44.9;
with input $\mathring{e}_{s0} = 45$, output $\mathring{e}_0$ was 44.1;
with input $\mathring{e}_{s0} = 50$, output $\mathring{e}_0$ was 42.4.

Over a range of 10 years in the input $\mathring{e}_{s0}$ the output $\mathring{e}_0$ ranged over only 2.5 years. For input values outside of 40–50 years (for example, $\mathring{e}_{s0} = 35$ or $\mathring{e}_{s0} = 55$), the least-squares fitting process that we used did not converge. With some other age distributions, including that of India, 1961, the output varied as much as the input, so that we could not compel the ages in these instances to help us in selecting the life table. (The least-squares fitting of (40) to given age distributions was programmed by Prithwis Das Gupta and Geoffrey McNicoll.)

Age of Mother Partially Given

Some filling-out of the data was required where the age of mother was available only in ten-year age groups, or otherwise incomplete from the viewpoint of the programs we had developed. For example, we sometimes had to find a ratio into which the ten-year interval 25–34 could be split. From the distribution in ten-year or other intervals we ascertained μ and σ^2 and used the well-known function (41) to obtain the ratio of the two halves of the group to be split. In each age interval the number of births taking place at age of mother a to $a + da$ was assumed to be

$$B(a)da = B_0 \frac{c^k a^{k-1} e^{-ca}}{\Gamma(k)} da, \tag{41}$$

where $\Gamma(k)$ is the gamma function, sufficiently well approximated for our purposes by $\Gamma(k) = (2\pi/k)^{1/2} k^k exp(-k + 1/12k)$. The constants c and k may be defined in terms of μ and σ^2, the mean and variance, respectively, of the distribution of births by age of mother, by (Keyfitz, 1968):

$$c = \mu/\sigma^2$$
$$k = \mu^2/\sigma^2.$$

In short, knowing the mean and variance of the distribution, we could find c and k, and knowing these and the total births B_0, we can integrate (41) to provide the births by age of mother in five-year age groups.

Illegitimate Births

Most countries include illegitimate births in tabulations by age of mother, but if age of mother is omitted for the illegitimate births we are obliged to assume some distribution. Since most illegitimate births occur to young mothers it would be entirely inappropriate to distribute them according to the ages of legitimate births, as we might first think of doing. We looked up distributions of illegitimate births for those countries that showed them, and then for those countries that did not we distributed according to a nearby or similar country that did.

Illegitimate births by age of father present a more difficult problem. A few countries do publish tables of these, however, for those instances in which the father is known, and we supposed the distribution of illegitimate births by age of father to be the same in other countries.

Since the single and married populations are not separately shown, we require no distinction between legitimate and illegitimate births in the analyses of this book. But all births are needed in all tables. The registration of an illegitimate birth as legitimate does us no harm, but omissions, which are undoubtedly high for illegitimate births, do damage the results. The problem of counting illegitimate births merges with the problem of completeness of birth registration in general, and can only be handled by the overall tests of completeness already described.

Completeness of Death Statistics

Those populations that in other regards qualified for inclusion in this book generally have more or less complete records of deaths, at least of adults. Life tables for ages beyond 5 or 10 years are less suspect than most statistics. Death certificates are filled out under medical or other professional auspices and in circumstances considerably more solemn then the filling out of the census questionnaire. If our life tables are in error for ages older than 5 years it is more likely through the inadequacy of the estimate of the population exposure than of the deaths.

Similar confidence in regard to records on younger children's deaths is more difficult to sustain. Through uncertainty on the application of the definition, a number, highly variable from one country to another, of children who are born alive and then die are not mentioned either in birth or death statistics. This makes international comparisons of infant mortality very difficult, and such comparisons are probably the weakest in this book. Good though Taiwan's health services may have become, and excellent as its statistics appear to be in other regards, we cannot believe that its 1966 infant mortality is 20.19 per thousand births while that of the United States, 1966, is 23.72.

External evidence has been available to us. The life table made for Mexican deaths, and shown in this volume, may be checked against a series prepared by E. Arriaga that uses no data in common with ours. Arriaga found the population increase between successive censuses and used this along with the census age distributions; his series shows as expectation of life for males in 1960, 56.4, and for females, 59.6 years. Our figures for 1966, based on official registrations, are 59.5 and 62.8 for males and females, respectively. The increase of 3 years in the expectation of life during the six years from 1960 to 1966 is typical of progress in Latin America. The latest $\overset{\circ}{e}_0$ for Mexico shown by the United Nations, for 1956, is 55.14 for males and 57.93 for females (United Nations Demographic Yearbook, 1967). This was calculated locally and appears to be consistent both with Arriaga's figures and with ours.

However, even at the point where demographic measurement is at its best, in respect of adult mortality for industrial countries, some of our results are on the edge of credibility. Consider male mortality in the United States and Spain as an instance. Our figures for 1967 show an expectation of life at age zero for the United States of 66.98 and for Spain of 69.24. The difference in favor of Spain does not disappear with age, for the expectation at age 10 is 59.08 for the United States and 61.69 for Spain. The result is not an accident of the particular year; our calculation for 1966 shows 66.75 for the United States and 69.25 for Spain. It is not due to any subtle effect of the stationary age distribution since when both countries are standardized on the United States rates of 1960 the United States for 1967 shows 10.80 deaths per thousand and Spain 9.43. The difference has persisted over time and in other calculations than ours. The official United States life tables of 1960 show $\mathring{e}_0 = 66.6$ years, and those of Spain for that year show 67.32 (United Nations Demographic Yearbook, 1967). For females the differences are less, or else in the other direction.

Of course, all these comparisons are not independent, even though they cover different ages, years, and methods of calculation. They all depend in common on the Spanish registration system. The question is whether Spanish male mortality is lower than that of the United States, or whether in Spain some deaths are omitted from registration or ages are overstated. Evidence to answer this will have to be sought elsewhere. We did include Spain in the detailed printout with some hesitation.

An example of lower credibility is the male mortality of Romania, 1966. When we made a life table out of the data on male deaths and population provided officially we obtained an $\mathring{e}_0$ of 71.26 years, compared with the expectation of white males in the United States, 1966, of 67.61, and that of the aggregate 1965 European Common Market of 67.99. Standardizing on the rates of the United States, 1960, by the indirect method gives 10.66 deaths per thousand of United States whites and only 9.71 for Romania. While it is not impossible that Romanian mortality is about 10 percent lower than that of the United States, it is much more probable that a fraction of Romanian deaths were unregistered. The registration omissions are apparently greater for males, since the $\mathring{e}_{70}$ for males is 17.76 years, compared with 14.99 for females, reversing the sex differential shown by nearly all populations (including Romania in six earlier periods). Moreover, the male $\mathring{e}_0$ for Romania had been slowly rising since 1957, and by 1964 had reached 66.69, and then suffered a slight drop to 66.57 in 1965. We could not see any reason why it should rise by $4\frac{1}{2}$ years in 1965–66. Romania seemed below the line of acceptability, and we omitted its detailed analysis among the Main Tables of Part IV but left it in the Summary Table of Part II.

Numbers of deaths that on the surface look perfectly satisfactory appear defective when computations of the kind undertaken here are made.

Overall Consistency—Mexico and Other Examples

Let us study the birth data for Mexico, 1966, and obtain some feeling of how much we ought to trust them. The total given is 1,940,565. The sex ratio is 107.2 males per hundred females, somewhat high in relation to other countries; is there some under-reporting of female births? If this is the error, then to bring the sex ratio to the more usual 105 males per hundred females we would need about 20,000 more female births, about one percent of the total.

When the number of births is applied in the usual way (see discussion in Chapter 10) to estimate the net reproduction rate R_0—the ratio of one female generation to the preceding female generation if the given age-specific rates of birth and death continue—we find that Mexico, 1966, stands at $R_0 = 2.71$. The children younger than 5 years in the population estimate provide—through the calculation of Thompson's index (discussed in Chapter 15)—a net reproduction rate of 2.47. The fact that the R_0 obtained from births is higher than that from the children younger than 5 years in the population count increases confidence in the births; censuses are often short at the youngest ages, and being short at these ages even by 9 percent need not discredit the census altogether, and certainly does not challenge the birth registrations.

Going on, accordingly, to a further use of the life table and age distributions, let us compare the slope of the Mexican female age curve for ages 5–29 with the slope of the same ages in the life table. The mechanics of this process were worked out by J. Bourgeois-Pichat and programmed by us in INFER. It gives a birth rate of 43.34 per thousand, compared with the official 43.96 (or 42.5 for females). Before congratulating ourselves on the closeness of the result we ought to see whether the age distribution is approximately stable; unless it is, the closeness of the numbers could be merely a coincidence.

One way of ascertaining stablity is to compare the observed age distribution with that which would be given if the population were actually stable, by the life table and the rate of increase, the difference between the two distributions being the index of dissimilarity, designated Δ. The definition of the index Δ is that it is the sum of the positive differences between the two percentage distributions (see page 30). For Mexico, 1966, we find it to be 1.5, meaning that only 1.5 percent of the one distribution would have to be shifted to other classes in order to make it identical with the other. This is among the lowest in the 752 calculations shown in the index of this volume.

But the part of the age distribution we made use of is only that from 5–29. Here the agreement between the observed and the stable is especially close:

Age	Observed population	Stable population	Departure of observed from stable
5–9	32,710	32,415	295
10–14	27,120	27,026	94
15–19	22,350	22,571	−221
20–24	18,380	18,788	−408
25–29	15,380	15,582	−202

This gives us confidence in the application of the Bourgeois-Pichat device to ages 5–29. We could not have as much confidence in it for older ages, since the observed Mexican age distribution departs more from the stable as we get to older ages, and hence we will not lean on the 38.61 per thousand for ages 30–54.

We can obtain a better fit to the observed ages by allowing for changes in birth rates. The theory used does not assume stability, but does suppose that the change in the birth rate has been systematic with simple linear and quadratic components. The program checks to see if these conditions have been approximately observed, and, if they have not, it deletes the computation. We are perfectly within our rights in using a method that is not always correct, provided that we obtain an objective indication of when it is applicable.

In this instance it is applicable, and it gives a birth rate of 45.71 per thousand, somewhat above that of the birth registrations. This, along with what we have previously found by working on the age distribution, suggests that the registered births are only slightly low.

Aside from the internal evidence of any one date, we can compare two censuses to see if the net rate of increase from one to the next is consistent with the net rate of increase implied by births and deaths of 1966. Of the two last censuses of Mexico, that of June 8, 1960, showed 34,923,000 persons, that of June 6, 1950, 25,791,000 persons. We are told (United Nations Demographic Yearbook, 1967) that the 1960 census was short by 3 percent; having no information on the completeness of the 1950 census we are inclined to assume it the same. The increase between 1950 and 1960 is at about

$$\sqrt[10]{\frac{34,923,000}{25,791,000}} - 1$$

or 3.1 percent per year. This is lower than the 34.35 per thousand of the birth and death data, but since mortality has been steadily dropping, the two cannot be regarded as inconsistent.

The sound operation of Mexico's statistical system is confirmed by the internal checks that we have performed. Let us take a case that is more difficult. We do not have information for the whole of Cameroon, but we do have data on west Cameroon, which has a population of 1,031,000 according to a sample survey taken during 1964. The death rate is high, 25.7 per thousand, with expectation of life at birth for males of 34.3 years, and for females of 38.1 years. We have nothing with which to compare this death rate, and can only say that it is among the highest in our list of 752 populations. The main challenge possible would be over-registration of deaths, which we have no reason to suspect.

The births reported are 51,201, or 49.7 per thousand. The value of Thompson's index for the ages 0–4 is somewhat higher than the net reproduction rate calculated from births and deaths. The Bourgeois-Pichat estimates of births from ages 5–29 and from 30–54 are both more than 50, and the estimate under "Coale" is more than 60. This last is plainly high, and the previous figures are under suspicion since the age distribution is not stable. Nonetheless we can say from this evidence that the birth rate of 49.67 is of the right order of magnitude. Other parts of French-speaking tropical Africa are estimated by Brass and Coale (1968) to be at about this level, including 49.1 as the birth rate in Upper Volta, and 54.6 for Dahomey. On the other hand, they estimate only 36 as the birth rate of northern Cameroon. This is a different part of the country, and we have no opinion on how homogeneous Cameroon is.

For the Philippines we think the reader will go less astray with births inferred from the age distribution than with those officially published. Official births for 1960, as reported through the United Nations Demographic Yearbook (1965) are 810,904. This gives a rate of 30 per thousand population. We estimated 1,291,000, a rate of 47 per thousand (page 410). The Coale measure gives 44, the Thompson measure gives about 41, the Bourgeois-Pichat, based on ages 5–29, gives 47. (See Chapter 11 for details of the use of these methods.)

Confirmation comes from an outside source. Frank Lorimer (1966) uses survey enquiries to calculate the total fertility rate, the number of children ever born per woman of completed fertility, and finds 6.80, compared with our 6.71.

Summary for Births and Deaths

In the United States and Canada the physician or hospital authorities fill out birth and death certificates, in consultation with parents or relatives of the deceased. The local registrar or the city or county health department verifies that a certificate has been properly prepared, makes a copy for local use, and passes the certificate up the line to the state or provincial registrar. This registrar in his turn makes a copy for the National Center for Health Statistics in the United States and the Dominion Bureau of Statistics in Canada, which prepare and publish the official vital statistics. Similar procedures are used in European countries, and birth and death statistics for most countries of Europe and North America are very nearly complete. Qualifications on this principally apply to infants who die shortly after birth.

For other continents serious problems of incomplete registration, especially of births, are present.

Our precautions against error started with the punching of totals as well as numbers at each age. This permitted the computer to check the punching before proceeding to calculate life tables and other quantities. Such precautions of a mechanical nature are necessary, but hardly sufficient, conditions that the data here contained be accurate. We were nonetheless surprised at how often the computer told us that official figures did not add to their purported totals.

Our contribution to knowledge of accuracy of data is through computing in sets of related demographic statistics. An investigator can verify copying; he can obtain officially collected materials from the most impeccable sources; he can study footnote qualifications on the material with assiduity, and still not know how close the statistics come to the facts. Such is the difficulty of dealing with isolated figures.

But with births, deaths, and population for a given area, all by age and sex, we can do more. Though the death data may withstand the most intensive examination when looked at by themselves, their use with the population numbers to construct a life table that has an expectation at age 0 of 90 years shows them to be wrong. This happened to us more than once, and we eliminated all data giving such gross errors from our collection. In other instances an error is less gross, and we include the material even though we do not believe it, so that the reader may judge its accuracy for himself. A main resource for this is Table 7 of the printouts, in which rates obtained from the observed number of births are compared with rates based on the age distribution and deaths. The use of Table 7 requires judgment, since when the age distribution is far from stable, the indirect methods of inference can produce impossible results. When the several estimates of Table 7 agree with one another, they may permit the reader to improve on the officially counted births.

Documentation

The following notes to the printout tables show the sources of the data, such qualifications on their accuracy and meaning as we could ascertain, and the adjustments we had to make. Distributing data for which some information, such as age, was not stated was frequently necessary and is not separately mentioned each time. Most of the notes refer to the Main Tables, but a few apply to populations given in the Summary Table only; however, we have not attempted to include the notes for all of the 752 populations of the Summary Table.

Ideally, notes are shown at the foot of the same page as the numbers that they qualify, but the method of production of this book required that they be printed in a separate section.

Some of the points in the notes below are trivial, but we include them nonetheless, even down to the statement that three births were of unstated sex, if this was what the official source said. We tried not to be discouraged by a frequent suspicion that the topics chosen for annotating are an arbitrary selection from among the much larger number of qualifications that actually apply to the data.

ALGERIA 1965

POPULATION:
ESTIMATED DE JURE POPULATION OF
APRIL 1966 BASED ON A 10 PER CENT
SAMPLE OF CENSUS RETURNS; DYB 1967,
TAB.5, PP.132-3. ADJUSTED TO MID-
YEAR 1965.

BIRTHS BY AGE OF MOTHER:
PROVISIONAL FIGURES FOR ALGERIAN
POPULATION ONLY; DYB 1967, TAB.9,
P.245. INFLATED BY 4.5 PER CENT
TO INCLUDE BIRTHS TO NON-ALGERIAN
POPULATION AND TO ADJUST FOR PROBABLE
UNDERENUMERATION.

BIRTHS BY SEX:
ESTIMATE BASED ON 1965 SEX RATIO;
DYB 1965, TAB.22, P.534.

DEATHS:
FIGURES FOR ALGERIAN POPULATION ONLY;
DYB 1967, TAB.20, PP.380-1. INFLATED
BY 4 PER CENT TO INCLUDE DEATHS TO
NON-ALGERIAN POPULATION. AGE GROUPS
65 AND OLDER EXTRAPOLATED.

BIRTHS AND DEATHS EXCLUDE LIVE BORN
INFANTS WHO DIED BEFORE REGISTRATION
OF BIRTH.

CAMEROON (WEST) 1964

POPULATION:
PROVISIONAL ESTIMATE OF DE JURE
POPULATION OBTAINED THROUGH SAMPLE
SURVEY IN 1964; DYB 1967, TAB.5,
PP.132-3.

BIRTHS BY AGE OF MOTHER:
ESTIMATES BASED ON BIRTHS REPORTED
BY WOMEN AGED 10-49 FOR TWELVE-MONTH
PERIOD PRECEDING 1964 SAMPLE SURVEY
OF POPULATION; DYB 1967, TAB.9, P.245.

BIRTHS BY SEX:
ESTIMATE BASED ON 1957 SEX RATIO;
DYB 1965, TAB.22, P.534.

DEATHS:
ESTIMATED ANNUAL AVERAGES BASED ON
DEATHS REPORTED FOR TWELVE-MONTH
PERIOD PRIOR TO 1964 SAMPLE SURVEY OF
POPULATION; DYB 1967, TAB.20,
PP.380-1.

POPULATION AND DEATHS 70 AND OLDER
EXTRAPOLATED.

MADAGASCAR 1966

POPULATION:
ESTIMATE OBTAINED THROUGH SAMPLE
SURVEY CONDUCTED BETWEEN MAY AND
SEPTEMBER, 1966; DYB 1967, TAB.5,
PP.140-1. ADJUSTED TO MID-YEAR.
AGE GROUPS 70 AND OLDER EXTRAPOLATED.

BIRTHS BY AGE OF MOTHER:
DYB 1967, TAB.9, P.246.

BIRTHS BY SEX:
ESTIMATE BASED ON 1961 SEX RATIO;
DYB 1965, TAB.22, P.535.

DEATHS:
DYB 1967, TAB.20, PP.382-3. AGE
GROUPS 70 AND OLDER EXTRAPOLATED.

BIRTHS AND DEATHS ARE ESTIMATES BASED
ON REPORTS FOR TWELVE-MONTH PERIOD
PRECEDING SAMPLE SURVEY OF POPULATION.

MAURITIUS 1966
(EXCLUDING DEPENDENCIES)

POPULATION:
MID-YEAR ESTIMATE; DYB 1967, TAB.5,
PP.140-1.

BIRTHS BY AGE OF MOTHER:
DYB 1967, TAB.9, P.246.

BIRTHS BY SEX:
ESTIMATE BASED ON 1964 SEX RATIO;
DYB 1965, TAB.22, P.535.

DEATHS:
DYB 1967, TAB.20, PP.384-5. BY YEAR
OF REGISTRATION.

REUNION 1963

POPULATION:
PROVISIONAL MID-YEAR ESTIMATE
EXCLUDING MIGRATORY BALANCE; DYB 1965,
TAB.6, PP.168-9. AGE GROUPS 70 AND
OLDER EXTRAPOLATED.

BIRTHS BY AGE OF MOTHER:
DYB 1965, TAB.13, P.302. AGE
CLASSIFICATION BASED ON DIFFERENCE
BETWEEN BIRTH YEARS OF CHILD AND
MOTHER.

BIRTHS BY SEX:
DYB 1965, TAB.22, P.536.

DEATHS:
DYB 1965, TAB.43, PP.744-5.

BIRTHS AND DEATHS EXCLUDE LIVE BORN
INFANTS WHO DIED BEFORE REGISTRATION
OF BIRTHS.

SEYCHELLES 1960

POPULATION:
CENSUS OF APRIL 7, 1960; DYB 1967,
TAB.5, PP.144-5. ADJUSTED TO MID-
YEAR.

BIRTHS BY AGE OF MOTHER:
OBTAINED FROM BIRTH RATES; CF. DEMO-
GRAPHIC HANDBOOK FOR AFRICA, MARCH
1968, TAB.15, P.75.

BIRTHS BY SEX:
DYB 1965, TAB.22, P.536.

DEATHS:
  OBTAINED FROM DEATH RATES; CF. DEMO-
  GRAPHIC HANDBOOK FOR AFRICA, MARCH
  1968, TAB.21, P.95. AGE GROUPS 80
  AND OLDER EXTRAPOLATED.

SOUTH AFRICA 1961
  (COLORED AND WHITE POPULATIONS)

  POPULATION:
    MID-YEAR ESTIMATES; DYB 1965,
    TAB.6, PP.170-1.

  BIRTHS BY AGE OF MOTHER:
    DYB 1965, TAB.13, P.302.

  BIRTHS BY SEX:
    DYB 1965, TAB.22, P.536.

  DEATHS:
    DYB 1966, TAB.18, PP.362-3.

TUNISIA 1960

  POPULATION:
    MID-YEAR ESTIMATE OBTAINED FROM
    TOTAL POPULATION OF JULY, 1961 AND
    AGE STRUCTURE OF 1956 CENSUS; CF.
    DEMOGRAPHIC HANDBOOK FOR AFRICA.
    MARCH, 1968, TAB.3, P.13, AND DYB 1967,
    TAB.5, PP.148-9. AGE GROUPS 60 AND
    OLDER EXTRAPOLATED. POPULATION 0-4
    DIVIDED INTO "UNDER 1" AND "1-4"
    ACCORDING TO AGE PATTERN OF LYBIA 1964;
    CF. DYB 1967, TAB.5, P.140.

  BIRTHS BY AGE OF MOTHER:
    DYB 1967, TAB.9, P.248. ADJUSTED TO
    CONFORM TO BIRTH RATE ESTIMATED FROM
    AGE STRUCTURE.

  BIRTHS BY SEX:
    DYB 1965, TAB.22, P.537.

  DEATHS:
    DYB 1967, TAB.20, PP.386-7.

  BIRTHS AND DEATHS BY YEAR OF
  REGISTRATION, OBTAINED FROM CIVIL
  REGISTERS OF QUESTIONABLE RELIABILITY.
  DATA EXCLUDE REFUGEES TEMPORARILY IN
  COUNTRY.

CANADA 1966
  (EXCLUDING NEWFOUNDLAND)

  POPULATION:
    CENSUS OF JUNE 1, 1966; DOMINION
    BUREAU OF STATISTICS, CAT. NO.92-610,
    VOL.I (1-10), "POPULATION AGE GROUPS,"
    TAB.19, PP.19-1 FF. ADJUSTED TO MID-
    YEAR.

  BIRTHS BY AGE OF MOTHER:
    DOMINION BUREAU OF STATISTICS,
    VITAL STATISTICS 1966. TAB.B9,
    P.78.

  BIRTHS BY AGE OF FATHER:
    OP. CIT., TAB.B10, P.79. ILLEGITIMATE

AND AGE NOT-STATED BIRTHS DISTRIBUTED
ACCORDING TO AGE PATTERN OF ILLEGITI-
MATE BIRTHS IN NORWAY 1963; CF. DYB 1965,
TAB.26, P.584.

BIRTHS BY SEX:
  OP. CIT., TAB.B1, P.60.

DEATHS:
  OP. CIT., TAB.D7, PP.108-11.

CANADA 1967
  (EXCLUDING NEWFOUNDLAND)

  POPULATION:
    ESTIMATE FOR JUNE 1, 1967; DOMINION
    BUREAU OF STATISTICS. AGE GROUPS
    "UNDER 1" AND "1-4"; SPECIAL TABULATIONS
    COURTESY OF DOMINION BUREAU OF
    STATISTICS, OTTAWA, JULY 1969.
    ADJUSTED TO MID-YEAR.

  BIRTHS AND DEATHS:
    SPECIAL TABULATIONS; COURTESY OF DOMINION
    BUREAU OF STATISTICS, OTTAWA,
    JULY 1969.

CANADA 1968
  (EXCLUDING NEWFOUNDLAND)

  BIRTHS AND DEATHS:
    SPECIAL TABULATIONS; COURTESY OF DOMINION
    BUREAU OF STATISTICS, OTTAWA,
    JULY 1969.

COSTA RICA 1966

  POPULATION:
    MID-YEAR ESTIMATE; COURTESY OF
    UNITED NATIONS, DEMOGRAPHIC AND
    SOCIAL STATISTICS BRANCH, STATISTICAL
    OFFICE, NEW YORK, AUGUST 1969.
    AGES UNDER 5 DIVIDED INTO "UNDER 1"
    AND "1-4" ACCORDING TO AGE PATTERN
    OF 1963; CF. DYB 1967, TAB.5, P.154.

  BIRTHS BY AGE OF MOTHER:
    DYB 1967, TAB.9, P.248. INFLATED
    BY 2.7 PER CENT TO CONFORM TO BIRTH
    RATE ESTIMATED FROM AGE STRUCTURE.

  BIRTHS BY SEX:
    ESTIMATE BASED ON 1964 SEX RATIO;
    DYB 1965, TAB.22, P.538.

  DEATHS:
    DYB 1967, TAB.20, PP.388-9.

DOMINICAN REPUBLIC 1966

  POPULATION:
    MID-YEAR ESTIMATE OBTAINED
    THROUGH PROJECTION OF 1960 MID-YEAR
    POPULATION WITH FIXED AGE-SPECIFIC
    BIRTH AND DEATH RATES; CF. KEYFITZ
    AND FLIEGER, WORLD POPULATION: AN
    ANALYSIS OF VITAL DATA. CHICAGO:
    UNIVERSITY OF CHICAGO PRESS, 1968,
    P.99.

BIRTHS BY AGE OF MOTHER:
DYB 1967, TAB.9, P.248.

BIRTHS BY SEX:
ESTIMATE BASED ON 1962 SEX RATIO;
DYB 1965, TAB.22, P.538.

DEATHS:
DYB 1967, TAB.20, PP.388-9.

BIRTHS AND DEATHS BY YEAR OF
REGISTRATION.

EL SALVADOR 1961

POPULATION:
CENSUS OF MAY 2, 1961; DYB 1967,
TAB.5, PP.154-5. ADJUSTED TO MID-
YEAR.

BIRTHS BY AGE OF MOTHER:
DYB 1965, TAB.13, P.305.

BIRTHS BY SEX:
DYB 1965, TAB.22, P.538.

DEATHS:
DYB 1962, TAB.19, PP.538-9. FIGURES
INCLUDE 20 RESIDENTS WHO DIED
OUTSIDE OF COUNTRY.

GREENLAND 1960

POPULATION:
CENSUS OF DECEMBER 31, 1960:
DYB 1967, TAB.5, PP.156-7. ADJUSTED
TO MID-YEAR.

BIRTHS BY AGE OF MOTHER:
DYB 1965, TAB.13, P.305.

BIRTHS BY SEX:
DYB 1965, TAB.22, P.538.

DEATHS:
DYB 1963, TAB.24, PP.564-5.

BIRTH AND DEATH DATA ARE OF UNKNOWN
RELIABILITY.

GRENADA 1961

POPULATION:
MID-YEAR ESTIMATE OBTAINED THROUGH
PROJECTION OF 1960 CENSUS POPULATION,
ADJUSTED TO MID-YEAR AND CORRECTED
FOR UNDERENUMERATION; CF. DYB 1967,
TAB.5, PP.156-7.

BIRTHS BY AGE OF MOTHER:
DYB 1965, TAB.13, P.305. INFLATED
BY 11 PER CENT TO CONFORM TO BIRTH
RATE ESTIMATED FROM AGE STRUCTURE.

BIRTHS BY SEX:
ESTIMATE BASED ON MALE AND FEMALE
BIRTHS REGISTERED FOR 1961; CF. DYB
1965, TAB.22, P.350.

DEATHS:
DYB 1966, TAB.18, PP.370-1.

BIRTHS AND DEATHS BY YEAR OF
REGISTRATION.

GUATEMALA 1964

POPULATION:
PROVISIONAL ESTIMATE FOR APRIL 18,
1964, BASED ON A 5 PER CENT SAMPLE
OF CENSUS RETURNS; DYB 1967, TAB.5,
PP.156-7. ADJUSTED FOR 5 PER CENT
UNDERENUMERATION AND PROJECTED TO
MID-YEAR.

BIRTHS BY AGE OF MOTHER:
DYB 1966, TAB.8, P.223.

BIRTHS BY SEX:
ESTIMATE BASED ON 1963 SEX RATIO;
DYB 1965, TAB.22, P.538.

DEATHS:
DYB 1966, TAB.18, PP.372-3.

HONDURAS 1966

POPULATION:
MID-YEAR ESTIMATE; ANUARIO ESTADISTICO
1966. TEGUCIGALPA, 1968, TAB.B7, P.44.

BIRTHS BY AGE OF MOTHER:
OP. CIT., TAB.C6, P.70. INFLATED BY
4 PER CENT TO CONFORM TO BIRTH RATE
ESTIMATED FROM AGE STRUCTURE.

BIRTHS BY SEX:
OP. CIT., TAB.C4, P.63.

DEATHS:
OP. CIT., TAB.C10, P.73.

POPULATION AND DEATHS 75 AND OLDER
EXTRAPOLATED.

JAMAICA 1963

POPULATION:
END-YEAR ESTIMATE; ANNUAL ABSTRACT
OF STATISTICS 1967. NO.26, TAB.12,
P.12. ADJUSTED TO MID-YEAR. AGE
GROUPS 80 AND OLDER EXTRAPOLATED.

BIRTHS BY AGE OF MOTHER:
OP. CIT., TAB.22, P.25. INFLATED
BY 2 PER CENT TO CONFORM TO BIRTH
RATE ESTIMATED FROM AGE STRUCTURE.

BIRTHS BY SEX:
OP. CIT., TAB.21, P.24.

DEATHS:
OP. CIT., TAB.26, P.28. AGE GROUP
"UNDER 1"; CF. TAB.25, P.27.

MEXICO 1966

POPULATION:
PROVISIONAL MID-YEAR ESTIMATE;
DYB 1967, TAB.5, PP.158-9. AGE
GROUPS 80 AND OLDER EXTRAPOLATED.

BIRTHS BY AGE OF MOTHER:
ESTIMATES BASED ON CONFINEMENTS
RESULTING IN LIVE BIRTHS, RECORDED
BY YEAR OF REGISTRATION; CF. DYB 1967,
TAB.9, P.249. CONFINEMENTS OF MOTHERS
AGED 40 AND OVER DIVIDED INTO CONFINE-
MENTS OF MOTHERS AGED 40-44 AND 45 AND
OLDER ACCORDING TO PATTERN OF PANAMA;
CF. DYB 1967, TAB.9, P.249.

BIRTHS BY SEX:
ESTIMATE BASED ON 1963 SEX RATIO;
DYB 1965, TAB.22, P.539.

DEATHS:
DYB 1967, TAB.20, PP.309-10.

NICARAGUA 1965

POPULATION:
PROVISIONAL MID-YEAR ESTIMATE;
DYB 1967, TAB.5, PP.160-1. AGE
GROUPS 75 AND OLDER EXTRAPOLATED.

BIRTHS BY AGE OF MOTHER:
DYB 1967, TAB.9, P.249.

BIRTHS BY SEX:
ESTIMATE BASED ON 1964 SEX RATIO;
DYB 1965, TAB.22, P.539.

DEATHS:
DYB 1967, TAB.20, PP.130-1.

BIRTHS AND DEATHS BY YEAR OF
REGISTRATION.

PANAMA 1966
(EXCLUDING CANAL ZONE)

POPULATION:
MID-YEAR ESTIMATE; DYB 1966, TAB.5,
PP.148-9.

BIRTHS BY AGE OF MOTHER:
DYB 1967, TAB.9, P.249.

BIRTHS BY SEX:
IBID.

DEATHS:
DYB 1967, TAB.20, PP.390-1

DATA EXCLUDE INDIAN JUNGLE POPULATION
NUMBERING 62,187 IN 1960.

ST. KITTS-NEVILLE-ANGUILLA 1961

POPULATION:
MID-YEAR ESTIMATE OBTAINED THROUGH
PROJECTION OF 1960 CENSUS POPULATION
ADJUSTED TO MID-YEAR; CF. DYB 1967.
TAB.5, PP.162-3.

BIRTHS BY AGE OF MOTHER:
DYB 1965, TAB.13, P.308. INFLATED
BY 21 PER CENT TO CONFORM TO BIRTH
RATE ESTIMATED FROM AGE STRUCTURE.

BIRTHS BY SEX:
ESTIMATE BASED ON MALE AND FEMALE

BIRTHS REGISTERED FOR 1961;
CF. DYB 1965, TAB.22, P.539.

DEATHS:
DYB 1966, TAB.18, PP.376-7.

BIRTHS AND DEATHS BY YEAR OF
REGISTRATION.

TRINIDAD AND TOBAGO 1967

POPULATION, BIRTHS, AND DEATHS:
SPECIAL TABULATIONS; COURTESY OF
CENTRAL STATISTICAL OFFICE,
PORT-OF-SPAIN, JULY 1969.

UNITED STATES 1966
(TOTAL, NON-WHITE, AND WHITE POPULATIONS)

POPULATION:
ESTIMATED RESIDENT POPULATIONS OF
JULY 1, 1966; VITAL STATISTICS OF
THE UNITED STATES 1966. VOL.II:
"MORTALITY," PART A, SECTION 6,
TAB.6-2, P.6-15.

BIRTHS BY AGE OF MOTHER:
OP. CIT., VOL.I: "NATALITY,"
SECTION 1, TAB.1-52, P.1-83.

BIRTHS BY AGE OF FATHER:
OP. CIT., TAB.1-56, P.1-119. AGE
NOT-STATED BIRTHS DISTRIBUTED
ACCORDING TO AGE PATTERN OF ILLE-
GITIMATE BIRTHS IN NORWAY 1963;
CF. DYB 1965, TAB.26, P.584.

BIRTHS BY SEX:
OP. CIT., TAB.1-49, PP.1-55 F.

DEATHS:
OP. CIT., VOL.II: "MORTALITY,"
PART A, SECTION 1, TAB.1-25,
PP.1-100 F.

UNITED STATES 1967
(TOTAL POPULATION)

POPULATION:
ESTIMATED TOTAL RESIDENT POPULATION
OF JULY 1, 1967. SPECIAL TABULATION;
COURTESY OF U.S. BUREAU OF THE CENSUS,
NATIONAL POPULATION ESTIMATES AND
PROJECTIONS BRANCH, WASHINGTON, D.C.,
JULY 1969.

BIRTHS AND DEATHS:
SPECIAL TABULATIONS; COURTESY OF
NATIONAL CENTER FOR HEALTH STATISTICS,
DEPARTMENT OF HEALTH, EDUCATION, AND
WELFARE, WASHINGTON, D.C., JULY 1969.

ARGENTINA 1964

POPULATION:
MID-YEAR ESTIMATE OBTAINED THROUGH
INTERPOLATION BETWEEN 1961 AND 1965
DATA; CF. DYB 1963, TAB.5, PP.190-1.
AND DYB 1966, TAB.5, PP.152-3. AGE
GROUPS 70 AND OLDER EXTRAPOLATED.

BIRTHS BY AGE OF MOTHER:
PROVISIONAL ESTIMATES; DYB 1966,
TAB.8, P.224.

BIRTHS BY SEX:
DYB 1965, TAB.22, P.540. ADJUSTED
TO TOTAL SHOWN FOR BIRTHS BY AGE
OF MOTHER.

DEATHS:
DYB 1967, TAB.20, PP.392-3.

CHILE 1967

POPULATION, BIRTHS, AND DEATHS:
SPECIAL TABULATIONS; COURTESY OF
DIRECCION DE ESTADISTICO Y CENSOS,
SANTIAGO, AUGUST 1960.

COLOMBIA 1965

POPULATION:
MID-YEAR ESTIMATE OBTAINED THROUGH
PROJECTION OF 1964 CENSUS POPULATION;
CF. DYB 1967, TAB.5, PP.166-7.

BIRTHS BY AGE OF MOTHER:
DYB 1966, TAB.8, P.224. BASED ON
BAPTISMAL RECORDS. INFLATED BY
4 PER CENT TO CONFORM TO BIRTH RATE
ESTIMATED FROM AGE STRUCTURE.

BIRTHS BY SEX:
ESTIMATE BASED ON 1964 SEX RATIO;
DYB 1965, TAB.22, P.540.

DEATHS:
DYB 1966, TAB.18, PP.350-1. BASED ON
BURIAL PERMITS.

ECUADOR 1965

POPULATION:
MID-YEAR ESTIMATE OBTAINED THROUGH
INTERPOLATION BETWEEN AGE DISTRIBUTION
DERIVED FROM 3 PER CENT SAMPLE OF 1962
CENSUS AND PROVISIONAL MID-YEAR ESTIMATE
FOR 1966. CF. DYB 1967, TAB.5, PP.166-7.

BIRTHS BY AGE OF MOTHER:
DYB 1967, TAB.9, P.250. DATA OBTAINED
FROM CIVIL REGISTERS OF QUESTIONABLE
RELIABILITY.

BIRTHS BY SEX:
ESTIMATE BASED ON 1964 SEX RATIO;
DYB 1965, TAB.22, P.540.

DEATHS:
DYB 1967, TAB.20, PP.392-3. TEN-YEAR
AGE GROUPS SPLIT INTO FIVE-YEAR GROUPS
ACCORDING TO AGE PATTERN OF URUGUAY 1965;
CF. DYB 1967, TAB.20, PP.394-5.

POPULATION 70 AND OLDER AND DEATHS 65 AND
OLDER EXTRAPOLATED. DATA EXCLUDE NOMADIC
INDIAN TRIBES.

FRENCH GUIANA 1964

POPULATION:
PROVISIONAL MID-YEAR ESTIMATE;
DYB 1967, TAB.5, PP.166-7. AGE
GROUPS 75 AND OLDER EXTRAPOLATED.

BIRTHS BY AGE OF MOTHER:
DYB 1966, TAB.8, P.224.

BIRTHS BY SEX:
ESTIMATE BASED ON 1963 SEX RATIO;
DYB 1965, TAB.22, P.540.

DEATHS:
DYB 1966, TAB.18, PP.380-1.

BIRTHS AND DEATHS EXCLUDE LIVE-BORN
INFANTS WHO DIED BEFORE REGISTRATION
OF BIRTH.

GUYANA 1961
(FORMERLY BRITISH GUIANA)

POPULATION:
MID-YEAR ESTIMATE OBTAINED THROUGH
EXTRAPOLATION BASED ON POPULATION
OF 1958 AND CENSUS POPULATION OF
APRIL 7, 1960; CF. DYB 1960, TAB.5,
PP.202-3, AND DYB 1967, TAB.5, PP.168-9.

BIRTHS BY AGE OF MOTHER:
DYB 1967, TAB.9, P.250. ADJUSTED TO
TOTAL SHOWN FOR BIRTHS BY SEX.

BIRTHS BY SEX:
DYB 1965, TAB.22, PP.392-3.

BIRTHS AND DEATHS BY YEAR OF REGISTRATION.
DATA EXCLUDE AMERINDIAN POPULATION.

PERU 1963

POPULATION:
MID-YEAR ESTIMATE OBTAINED THROUGH
INTERPOLATION BETWEEN CENSUS OF
JULY 2, 1961, AND 1965 MID-YEAR
ESTIMATE; CF. DYB 1967, TAB.5, PP.168-9.

BIRTHS BY AGE OF MOTHER:
DYB 1967, TAB.9, P.250. INFLATED BY
10 PER CENT TO CONFORM TO BIRTH RATE
ESTIMATED FROM AGE STRUCTURE.

BIRTHS BY AGE OF FATHER:
UNION PANAMERICANA, AMERICA EN
CIFRAS 1967. WASHINGTON, D.C., 1968,
TAB.202-16, PP.90-1. AGE NOT-STATED
BIRTHS DISTRIBUTED ACCORDING TO AGE
PATTERN OF ILLEGITIMATE BIRTHS OF 1960;
CF. DYB 1965, TAB.26, P.579. INFLATED
BY 10 PER CENT TO CONFORM TO BIRTH RATE
ESTIMATED FROM AGE STRUCTURE.

BIRTHS BY SEX:
ESTIMATE BASED ON MALE AND FEMALE BIRTHS
REGISTERED FOR 1963; CF. DYB 1965,
TAB.22, P.540.

DEATHS:
DYB 1967, TAB.20, PP.392-3.

BIRTHS AND DEATHS BY YEAR OF
REGISTRATION. POPULATION AND DEATHS
75 AND OLDER EXTRAPOLATED. ALL DATA
EXCLUDE INDIAN JUNGLE POPULATION
ESTIMATED AT 100,830 IN 1961.

URUGUAY 1963

POPULATION:
ESTIMATE BASED ON 5 PER CENT SAMPLE
OF 1963 CENSUS. ADJUSTED FOR 2.05
PER CENT UNDERENUMERATION AND SHIFTED
TO MID-YEAR; CF. DYB 1967, TAB.5,
PP.168-9.

BIRTHS BY AGE OF MOTHER AND DEATHS:
SPECIAL TABULATIONS; DEMOGRAPHIC AND
SOCIAL STATISTICS BRANCH, NEW YORK,
AUGUST 1969. BIRTHS INFLATED BY
27 PER CENT TO CONFORM TO BIRTH RATE
ESTIMATED FROM AGE STRUCTURE.

BIRTHS BY SEX:
ESTIMATE BASED ON 1963 PERU SEX RATIO;
CF. DYB 1965, TAB.22, P.540.

VENEZUELA 1965

POPULATION:
MID-YEAR ESTIMATES; UNION PANAMERICANA,
AMERICA EN CIFRAS 1967. WASHINGTON, D.C.,
1968, TAB.201-04, P.20. AGE GROUP 0-4
DIVIDED INTO "UNDER 1" AND "1-4" ACCORDING
TO PATTERN OF 1961 CENSUS; CF. DYB 1967,
TAB.5, P.170. AGE GROUPS 70 AND OLDER
EXTRAPOLATED.

BIRTHS BY AGE OF MOTHER:
UNION PANAMERICANA, AMERICA EN CIFRAS
1967. TAB.202-15, PP.88-9.

BIRTHS BY SEX:
OP. CIT., TAB.202-14, P.87.

DEATHS:
OP. CIT., TAB.202-24, P.111.

DATA EXLUDE INDIGENOUS JUNGLE POPULATION
ESTIMATED AT 31,800 IN 1961.

CEYLON 1967

POPULATION, BIRTHS, AND DEATHS:
SPECIAL TABULATIONS; COURTESY OF
DEPARTMENT OF CENSUS AND STATISTICS,
COLOMBO, AUGUST 1969.

CHINA (TAIWAN) 1966
(TOTAL POPULATION)

POPULATION:
MID-YEAR ESTIMATE; TAIWAN DEMOGRAPHIC
FACTBOOK 1966, (OCTOBER, 1967), TAB.1,
PP.2-3.

BIRTHS BY AGE OF MOTHER:
OP. CIT., TAB.7, PP.178-9.

BIRTHS BY SEX:
IBID.

DEATHS:
OP. CIT., TAB.21, PP.382-5.

BIRTHS AND DEATHS BY YEAR OF
REGISTRATION. POPULATION AND DEATHS
80 AND OLDER EXTRAPOLATED.

CHINA (TAIWAN) 1966
(URBAN, SEMI-URBAN, RURAL)

POPULATION:
MID-YEAR ESTIMATES; TAIWAN DEMOGRAPHIC
FACTBOOK 1966, (OCTOBER, 1967), TAB.2,
PP.54-5.

BIRTHS BY AGE OF MOTHER:
OP. CIT., TAB.7, PP.178-81.

BIRTHS BY SEX:
OP. CIT., TAB.7, PP.178-201.

DEATHS:
OP. CIT., TAB.22, PP.437, 439, 441.
FOR DEFINITION OF "URBAN PLACES"
"SEMI-URBANIZED COMMUNITIES", AND
"RURAL COMMUNITIES"; CF. OP. CIT.,
P.16.

BIRTHS AND DEATHS BY YEAR OF
REGISTRATION. POPULATION AND DEATHS
80 AND OLDER EXTRAPOLATED.

HONG KONG 1966

POPULATION:
MID-YEAR ESTIMATE; DYB 1967, TAB.5,
PP.172-3. AGE GROUPS 80 AND OLDER
EXTRAPOLATED.

BIRTHS BY AGE OF MOTHER:
ESTIMATES BASED ON HOSPITAL AND
NURSING HOME RECORDS; CF. R. FREEDMAN
AND A.L. ADLAKHA, "RECENT FERTILITY
DECLINES IN HONG KONG: THE ROLE OF THE
CHANGING AGE STRUCTURE." POPULATION
STUDIES, VOL.22, 1968, TAB.11, P.196.

BIRTHS BY SEX:
ESTIMATE BASED ON 1964 SEX RATIO;
DYB 1965, TAB.22, P.541.

DEATHS:
DYB 1967, TAB.20, PP.394-5.

INDONESIA 1961
(INCLUDING WEST IRIAN)

POPULATION:
FIGURES ARE BASED ON ONE PER CENT SAMPLE
OF CENSUS OF OCTOBER 31, 1961; CF.
DYB 1967, TAB.5, PP.174-5. ADJUSTED TO
MID-YEAR AND INCREASED BY 700,000,
ESTIMATED POPULATION OF WEST IRIAN.

BIRTHS AND DEATHS:
ESTIMATES INFERRED FROM CENSUS AGE
DISTRIBUTION AND LIFE TABLE. SEE
SECTION 4.1 FOR DETAILS.

ISRAEL 1967
(JEWISH POPULATION)

POPULATION AND BIRTHS BY AGE OF MOTHER:
SPECIAL TABULATIONS; COURTESY OF
CENTRAL BUREAU OF STATISTICS,
JERUSALEM, JULY 1969.

BIRTHS BY SEX:
STATISTICAL ABSTRACT OF ISRAEL, 1968,
NO. 19, TAB.C/20, P.70.

DEATHS:
OP. CIT., TAB.C/29, P.79.

JAPAN 1966

POPULATION:
ESTIMATE OF OCTOBER 1, 1966;
DYB 1967, TAB.5, PP.174-5. ADJUSTED
TO MID-YEAR.

BIRTHS BY AGE OF MOTHER:
JAPAN STATISTICAL YEARBOOK 1968,
TAB.16, P.39.

BIRTHS BY SEX:
SPECIAL TABULATION; COURTESY OF
BUREAU OF STATISTICS, OFFICE OF
THE PRIME MINISTER, TOKYO, JULY 1969.

DEATHS:
DYB 1967, TAB.20, PP.396-7.

DATA REFER TO JAPANESE NATIONALS
IN JAPAN.

KUWAIT 1966

POPULATION:
MID-YEAR ESTIMATE OBTAINED FROM
PROVISIONAL TOTAL POPULATION FIGURE
FOR MID-1966 AND AGE STRUCTURE OF
1965; CF. DYB 1966, TAB.2, P.106, AND
DYB 1967, TAB.5, PP.176-7.

BIRTHS BY AGE OF MOTHER:
ESTIMATED FIGURES; DYB 1967, TAB.9,
P.251. 1622 LATE REGISTRATIONS ADDED.

BIRTHS BY SEX:
ESTIMATE BASED ON 1964 SEX RATIO;
DYB 1965, TAB.22, P.542.

DEATHS:
DYB 1967, TAB.20, PP.396-7. OBTAINED
FROM CIVIL REGISTERS OF QUESTIONABLE
RELIABILITY. AGE GROUPS 75 AND OLDER
EXTRAPOLATED.

MALAYSIA (WEST) 1966
(ALL RACES AND RACIAL SUBGROUPS)

POPULATION:
MID-YEAR ESTIMATE FOR 1967;
DEPARTMENT OF STATISTICS, "ESTI-
MATES OF POPULATION FOR WEST MALAYSIA,"
KUALA LUMPUR, TAB.1, PP.37-9.
ADJUSTED TO MID-1966.

BIRTHS AND DEATHS:
SPECIAL TABULATIONS; COURTESY OF
DEPARTMENT OF STATISTICS, KUALA
LUMPUR, APRIL 1969.

POPULATION AND DEATHS FOR AGE GROUPS 70
AND OLDER EXTRAPOLATED.

RYUKYU ISLANDS 1965

POPULATION:
CENSUS OF OCTOBER 1, 1965;
DYB 1967, TAB.5, PP.180-1.
ADJUSTED TO MID-YEAR.

BIRTHS BY AGE OF MOTHER:
DYB 1966, TAB.8, P.226. INFLATED
BY 9.3 PER CENT TO CONFORM TO
BIRTH RATE ESTIMATED FROM AGE
STRUCTURE.

BIRTHS BY SEX:
ESTIMATE BASED ON 1964 SEX RATIO;
DYB 1965, TAB.22, P.542.

DEATHS:
DYB 1966, TAB.18, PP.390-1. INFLATED
BY 51 PER CENT TO CONFORM TO DEATH
RATE CONSONANT WITH AGE STRUCTURE.

DATA EXCLUDE U.S. CITIZENS STATIONED
IN THE AREA. BIRTHS AND DEATHS BY YEAR
OF REGISTRATION. BIRTH AND DEATH FIGURES
EXCLUDE LATE REGISTRATIONS AND INFANTS
WHO DIED BEFORE REGISTRATION OF BIRTH.

SARAWAK 1961

POPULATION:
CENSUS OF JUNE 14, 1960; DYB 1967,
TAB.5, PP.178-9. FIGURES EXCLUDE
TRANSIENTS AFLOAT. AGE GROUPS 75
AND OLDER EXTRAPOLATED. ADJUSTED TO
MID-1961.

BIRTHS BY AGE OF MOTHER:
DYB 1965, TAB.13, P.313. INFLATED
BY 40 PER CENT TO CONFORM TO BIRTH
RATE ESTIMATED FROM AGE STRUCTURE.

BIRTHS BY SEX:
ESTIMATE BASED ON MALE AND FEMALE
BIRTHS REGISTERED FOR 1961; CF.
DYB 1965, TAB.22, P.542.

DEATHS:
DYB 1966, TAB.18, PP.388-9.
INFLATED BY 50 PER CENT TO CONFORM
TO DEATH RATE CONSONANT WITH AGE
STRUCTURE.

RECORDED BIRTHS AND DEATHS ARE ESTIMATES
BASED ON CIVIL REGISTERS OF UNKNOWN
RELIABILITY.

SINGAPORE 1966, 1967, 1968

POPULATION, BIRTHS, AND DEATHS:
SPECIAL TABULATIONS; COURTESY OF

DEPARTMENT OF STATISTICS, REPUBLIC
OF SINGAPORE, JULY 1969.

AUSTRIA 1966, 1967, 1968

POPULATION, BIRTHS, AND DEATHS:
SPECIAL TABULATIONS; COURTESY OF
OESTERREICHISCHES STATISTISCHES
ZENTRALAMT, VIENNA, JULY 1969.

BELGIUM 1966

POPULATION:
ESTIMATE OF DECEMBER 31, 1966:
SPECIAL TABULATION, COURTESY OF
INSTITUT NATIONAL DE STATISTIQUE,
BRUSSELS, JULY 1969. ADJUSTED TO
MID-YEAR.

BIRTHS BY AGE OF MOTHER:
ANNUAIRE STATISTIQUE DE LA BELGIQUE,
TOME 88, P.57.

BIRTHS BY AGE OF FATHER:
LEGITIMATE BIRTHS ONLY: OP. CIT.,
P.78. ILLEGITIMATE AND AGE NOT-
STATED BIRTHS DISTRIBUTED ACCORDING TO
PATTERN OF NORWAY 1963; CF. DYB 1965,
TAB.26, P.584.

BIRTHS BY SEX:
ANNUAIRE STATISTIQUE DE LA BELGIQUE,
TOME 88, P.78.

DEATHS:
SPECIAL TABULATION; COURTESY OF
INSTITUT NATIONAL DE STATISTIQUE,
BRUSSELS, JULY 1969.

BULGARIA 1966

POPULATION:
ESTIMATE OF DE JURE POPULATION AT
MID-YEAR; DYB 1967, TAB.5, PP.184-5.

BIRTHS BY AGE OF MOTHER:
DYB 1967, TAB.9, P.252.

BIRTHS BY SEX:
IBID.

DEATHS:
DYB 1967, TAB.20, PP.398-9.

BULGARIA 1967, 1968

POPULATION, BIRTHS, AND DEATHS:
SPECIAL TABULATIONS; COURTESY OF
CENTRAL STATISTICAL OFFICE, SOFIA,
SEPTEMBER 1969.

CZECHOSLOVAKIA 1967

POPULATION, BIRTHS, AND DEATHS:
SPECIAL TABULATIONS, COURTESY OF
FEDERAL STATISTICAL OFFICE, PRAGUE,
JULY 1969.

DENMARK 1967

POPULATION, BIRTHS, AND DEATHS:
SPECIAL TABULATIONS; COURTESY OF
DEPARTMENT OF STATISTICS,
COPENHAGEN, SEPTEMBER 1969.

FINLAND 1966
(TOTAL, URBAN, AND RURAL)

POPULATION, BIRTHS, AND DEATHS:
SPECIAL TABULATIONS; COURTESY OF
CENTRAL STATISTICAL OFFICE OF
FINLAND, HELSINKI, JULY 1969.

FRANCE 1967

POPULATION, BIRTHS, AND DEATHS:
SPECIAL TABULATIONS; COURTESY OF
INSTITUT NATIONAL DE LA STATISTIQUE
ET DES ETUDES ECONOMIQUES, PARIS,
JULY 1969.

GERMANY (EAST) 1967
(INCLUDING EAST BERLIN)

POPULATION, BIRTHS, AND DEATHS:
SPECIAL TABULATIONS; COURTESY OF
STAATLICHE ZENTRALVERWALTUNG FUER
STATISTIK, BERLIN, SEPTEMBER 1969.

GERMANY (WEST) 1967
(INCLUDING WEST BERLIN)

POPULATION, BIRTHS, AND DEATHS:
SPECIAL TABULATIONS; COURTESY OF
STATISTISCHES BUNDESAMT, WIESBADEN,
JULY 1969.

GREECE 1966

POPULATION:
DYB 1967, TAB.5, PP.188-9.
AGE CLASSIFICATION BASED ON YEAR OF
BIRTH RATHER THAN ON COMPLETED YEARS
OF AGE. INCLUDING ALIEN ARMED FORCES IN
COUNTRY BUT EXCLUDING GREEK FORCES
STATIONED OUTSIDE COUNTRY.

BIRTHS BY AGE OF MOTHER:
DYB 1967, TAB.9, P.253.

BIRTHS BY SEX:
IBID.

DEATHS:
DYB 1967, TAB.20, PP.400-1.

GREECE 1967

POPULATION:
MID-YEAR ESTIMATE; STATISTICAL YEARBOOK OF
GREECE 1968, TAB. II-6, P.20. AGE GROUP
"UNDER 5" DIVIDED INTO "UNDER 1" AND "1-4"
ACCORDING TO AGE PATTERN OF 1966; CF.
DYB 1967, TAB.5, P.188.

BIRTHS BY AGE OF MOTHER:
   OP. CIT., TAB.II-15, P.31.

BIRTHS BY SEX:
   ESTIMATE BASED ON 1966 SEX RATIO;
   DYB 1967, TAB.9, P.253.

DEATHS:
   STATISTICAL YEARBOOK OF GREECE 1968,
   TAB.II-18, P.33.

GREECE 1968

POPULATION, BIRTHS, AND DEATHS:
   SPECIAL TABULATIONS; COURTESY OF
   NATIONAL STATISTICAL SERVICE OF GREECE,
   ATHENS, JULY 1969.

HUNGARY 1967

POPULATION:
   ESTIMATE OF JANUARY 1, 1967;
   DEMOGRAFIAI EVKOENVY 1967,
   TAB.1.7, P.15. ADJUSTED TO MID-YEAR.

BIRTHS BY AGE OF MOTHER:
   OP. CIT., TAB.4.4, P.78.

BIRTHS BY AGE OF FATHER:
   STATISTICAL YEARBOOK OF HUNGARY
   1967, TAB.20, P.19. ADJUSTED TO
   EXCLUDE STILLBIRTHS. TEN-YEAR AGE
   GROUPS BROKEN DOWN INTO FIVE-YEAR
   GROUPS ACCORDING TO PATTERN OF
   1964; CF. DYB 1965, TAB.48, P.509.

BIRTHS BY SEX:
   DEMOGRAFIAI EVKOENVY 1967, TAB.4.10,
   P.81.

DEATHS:
   OP. CIT., TABS.5.3 THROUGH 5.5,
   PP.115-17.

ICELAND 1965

POPULATION:
   MID-YEAR ESTIMATE OF DE JURE
   POPULATION; DYB 1967, TAB.5,
   PP.188-9.

BIRTHS BY AGE OF MOTHER:
   DYB 1967, TAB.9, P.253.

BIRTHS BY SEX:
   ESTIMATE BASED ON 1964 SEX RATIO;
   DYB 1965, TAB.22, P.545.

DEATHS:
   DYB 1966, TAB.18, PP.398-9.

IRELAND 1968

POPULATION, BIRTHS, AND DEATHS:
   SPECIAL TABULATIONS; COURTESY OF
   CENTRAL STATISTICS OFFICE, DUBLIN,
   JULY 1969.

ITALY 1966

POPULATION, BIRTHS, AND DEATHS:
   SPECIAL TABULATIONS; COURTESY OF
   ISTITUTO CENTRALE DI STATISTICA,
   ROME, SEPTEMBER 1969.

LUXEMBOURG 1966

POPULATION:
   RECENSEMENT DE LA POPULATION
   AU 31 DECEMBRE 1966, SERVICE
   CENTRAL DE LA STATISTIQUE ET
   DES ETUDES ECONOMIQUES, LUXEMBOURG,
   DECEMBER 1968, TAB.203, P.85. ADJUSTED
   TO MID-YEAR.

BIRTHS BY AGE OF MOTHER:
   DYB 1967, TAB.9, P.254.

BIRTHS BY SEX:
   IBID.

DEATHS:
   PROVISIONAL FIGURES; DYB 1967,
   TAB.20, PP.402-3.

MALTA 1966

POPULATION:
   MID-YEAR ESTIMATE; DYB 1967, TAB.5,
   PP.190-1.

BIRTHS BY AGE OF MOTHER:
   DYB 1967, TAB.9, P.254.

BIRTHS BY SEX:
   IBID.

DEATHS:
   DYB 1967, TAB.20, PP.402-3.

DATA INCLUDE CIVILIAN NATIONALS TEMPORARILY
OUTSIDE COUNTRY AND EXCLUDE NON-MALTESE
FORCES IN COUNTRY.

NETHERLANDS 1967

POPULATION, BIRTHS, AND DEATHS:
   SPECIAL TABULATIONS; COURTESY OF
   NETHERLAND CENTRAL BUREAU OF
   STATISTICS, THE HAGUE, JULY 1969.

NORWAY 1967

POPULATION, BIRTHS, AND DEATHS:
   SPECIAL TABULATIONS; COURTESY OF
   STATISTISK SENTRALBYRA, OSLO.
   JULY 1969.

POLAND 1965

POPULATION:
   ESTIMATE OF DECEMBER 31, 1964;
   DYB 1967, TAB.5, PP.194-5. AGE
   GROUPS 0-5 AND 75 AND OLDER DIVIDED

ACCORDING TO AGE STRUCTURE ESTIMATED
FOR MID-1966; CF. IBID. ADJUSTED TO
MID-YEAR.

BIRTHS BY AGE OF MOTHER:
DYB 1967, TAB.9, P.254. FIGURES FOR
MOTHERS UNDER 16 AND 16-19 ADJUSTED
TO UNDER 15 AND 15-19.

BIRTHS BY SEX:
ESTIMATE BASED ON 1964 SEX RATIO;
DYB 1965, TAB.22, P.545.

DEATHS:
DYB 1967, TAB.20, PP.402-3.

PORTUGAL 1966

POPULATION:
DYB 1967, TAB.5, PP.194-5.

BIRTHS:
DYB 1967, TAB.9, PP.254-5. TOTAL
INCLUDES 1,106 LIVE BIRTHS OF UNKNOWN
LEGITIMACY NOT DISTRIBUTED BY
AGE OF MOTHER.

DEATHS:
DYB 1967, TAB.20, PP.404-5.

PORTUGAL 1967, 1968

POPULATION, BIRTHS, AND DEATHS:
SPECIAL TABULATIONS; COURTESY OF
NATIONAL STATISTICAL INSTITUTE,
LISBON, JULY 1969.

DATA REFER TO EUROPEAN PORTUGAL AND
ADJACENT ISLANDS.

SPAIN 1967

POPULATION, BIRTHS, AND DEATHS:
SPECIAL TABULATIONS; COURTESY OF
INSTITUTO NACIONAL DE ESTADISTICA,
MADRID, JULY 1969.

POPULATION 0-4 DIVIDED INTO "UNDER 1"
AND "1-4" IN PROPORTION 1:3.762.

SWEDEN 1967

POPULATION, BIRTHS, AND DEATHS:
SPECIAL TABULATIONS; COURTESY OF
STATISTISKA CENTRALBYRAN, STOCKHOLM,
SEPTEMBER 1969.

SWITZERLAND 1967

POPULATION:
"WOHNBEVOELKERUNG DER SCHWEIZ
NACH ALTERSKLASSEN UND GESCHLECHT,
FORTSCHREIBUNG AUF DEN 1. JANUAR
1967: SCHWEIZER UND AUSLAENDER."
EIDGENOESSISCHES STATISTISCHES AMT,
BERN, JULY 1967. ADJUSTED TO MID-YEAR.

BIRTHS AND DEATHS:
SPECIAL TABULATIONS; COURTESY OF
EIDGENOESSISCHES STATISTISCHES AMT,
BERN, JULY 1969.

UNITED KINGDOM 1964
(ENGLAND AND WALES)

POPULATION:
MID-YEAR ESTIMATE; CENTRAL STATISTICAL
OFFICE, MONTHLY DIGEST OF STATISTICS
NO.235, JULY 1965, TAB.12, P.12. AGES
UNDER 5 DIVIDED INTO "UNDER 1" AND "1-4"
ACCORDING TO AGE PATTERN OF 1965; CF.
ANNUAL ABSTRACT OF STATISTICS, NO.105,
1968, TAB.8, P.8.

BIRTHS BY AGE OF MOTHER:
PROVISIONAL FIGURES; DYB 1965, TAB.13,
P.321.

BIRTHS BY AGE OF FATHER:
DYB 1965, TAB.18, P.509. AGE NOT-STATED
BIRTHS DISTRIBUTED ACCORDING TO PATTERN
OF ILLEGITIMATE BIRTHS; CF. OP. CIT.,
TAB.26, P.548.

BIRTHS BY SEX:
DYB 1965, TAB.18, P.509.

DEATHS:
PROVISIONAL FIGURES; DYB 1965, TAB.43,
PP.760-1.

UNITED KINGDOM 1966
(ENGLAND AND WALES)

POPULATION:
CENTR. STAT. OFFICE, ANNUAL ABSTRACT
OF STATISTICS, NO.105, 1968,
TAB.8, P.8.

BIRTHS BY AGE:
OP. CIT. TAB.20, P.22.

BIRTHS BY SEX:
OP. CIT. TAB.24, P.24.

DEATHS:
DYB 1967, TAB.20, PP.404-5.

UNITED KINGDOM 1967, 1968
(ENGLAND AND WALES)

POPULATION, BIRTHS, AND DEATHS:
SPECIAL TABULATIONS; COURTESY OF
GENERAL REGISTER OFFICE, LONDON,
JULY 1969.

DEATH FIGURES ARE PROVISIONAL ESTIMATES.

UNITED KINGDOM 1967
(ENGLAND AND WALES, URBAN AND RURAL
DISTRICTS)

POPULATION, BIRTHS, AND DEATHS:
SPECIAL TABULATIONS; COURTESY OF

GENERAL REGISTER OFFICE, LONDON,
JULY 1969.

DEATH FIGURES FOR TEN-YEAR AGE GROUPS
SPLIT INTO FIVE-YEAR GROUPS USING
NEWTON'S DIFFERENCE FORMULA. POPULATION
AND DEATHS FOR AGE GROUPS 75 AND OLDER
EXTRAPOLATED.

UNITED KINGDOM 1966
(NORTHERN IRELAND)

POPULATION:
MID-YEAR ESTIMATE; DYB 1967,
TAB.5, PP.196-7.

BIRTHS BY AGE OF MOTHER:
ESTIMATES BASED ON TOTAL BIRTHS
AND ASSUMED MEAN AND VARIANCE OF
NET MATERNITY FUNCTION CORRESPONDING
TO IRELAND (REPUBLIC) 1960; CF. KEYFITZ
AND FLIEGER, WORLD POPULATION: AN ANALYSIS
OF VITAL DATA. CHICAGO: UNIVERSITY OF
CHICAGO PRESS, 1968, TAB.7, P.387, AND
CENTRAL STATISTICAL OFFICE, ANNUAL
ABSTRACT OF STATISTICS, NO.105, 1968,
P.25.

BIRTHS BY SEX:
ANNUAL ABSTRACT OF STATISTICS, NO.105,
1968, P.25.

DEATHS:
DYB 1967, TAB.20, PP.404-5. BY YEAR OF
REGISTRATION.

UNITED KINGDOM 1966
(SCOTLAND)

POPULATION:
MID-YEAR ESTIMATE; CENTRAL STATISTICAL
OFFICE, ANNUAL ABSTRACT OF STATISTICS,
NO.105, TAB.8, P.9.

BIRTHS BY AGE OF MOTHER:
DYB 1967, TAB.9, P.255.

BIRTHS BY SEX:
IBID.

DEATHS:
DYB 1967, TAB.20, PP.404-5.

BIRTHS AND DEATHS BY YEAR OF
REGISTRATION.

YUGOSLAVIA 1966

POPULATION, BIRTHS, AND DEATHS:
SPECIAL TABULATIONS; COURTESY OF
UNITED NATIONS, DEMOGRAPHIC AND
SOCIAL STATISTICS BRANCH, STATISTICAL
OFFICE, NEW YORK, AUGUST 1969.

AUSTRALIA 1967

POPULATION, BIRTHS, AND DEATHS:
SPECIAL TABULATIONS; COURTESY OF
COMMONWEALTH BUREAU OF CENSUS
AND STATISTICS, CANBERRA, AUGUST 1969.

FIJI ISLANDS 1966

POPULATION:
MEAN OF END-YEAR ESTIMATES; DYB 1967,
TAB.5, PP.200-1.

BIRTHS BY AGE OF MOTHER:
DYB 1967, TAB.9, P.255.

BIRTHS BY SEX:
ESTIMATE BASED ON 1964 SEX RATIO;
DYB 1965, TAB.22, P.546.

DEATHS:
DYB 1967, TAB.20, PP.406-7.

BIRTHS AND DEATHS BY YEAR OF REGISTRATION.
FIGURES ARE OF UNKNOWN RELIABILITY.

NEW ZEALAND 1966

POPULATION, BIRTHS BY AGE OF MOTHER, DEATHS:
SPECIAL TABULATIONS; COURTESY OF
DEPARTMENT OF STATISTICS, WELLINGTON,
JUNE 1969.

BIRTHS BY AGE OF FATHER:
NEW ZEALAND YEARBOOK 1968, P.92.
LEGITIMATE BIRTHS ONLY. ILLEGITIMATE
BIRTHS DISTRIBUTED ACCORDING TO AGE
PATTERN OF ILLEGITIMATE BIRTHS IN
NORWAY 1963; CF. DYB 1965, TAB.26,
P.584.

DATA COVER MAORI AND NON-MAORI POPULATIONS.

NEW ZEALAND 1967, 1968

POPULATION, BIRTHS, AND DEATHS:
SPECIAL TABULATIONS; COURTESY OF DEPART-
MENT OF STATISTICS, WELLINGTON, JUNE,
1969.

DATA COVER MAORI AND NON-MAORI POPULATIONS.

MONTREAL (CANADA) 1966

POPULATION:
CENSUS OF JUNE 1, 1966; DOMINION
BUREAU OF STATISTICS, CAT. NO.92-610,
VOL.I (1-10), "POPULATION AGE GROUPS,"
TAB.22. ADJUSTED TO MID-YEAR.

BIRTHS BY AGE OF MOTHER:
ESTIMATES OBTAINED FROM TOTAL BIRTHS
AND ASSUMED MEAN AND VARIANCE OF NET
MATERNITY FUNCTION CORRESPONDING TO
CHICAGO 1959-61 (WHITE POPULATION);
CF. KEYFITZ AND FLIEGER, WORLD POPULATION:
AN ANALYSIS OF VITAL DATA. CHICAGO: UNI-
VERSITY OF CHICAGO PRESS, 1968, P.28.

BIRTHS BY SEX AND DEATHS:
SPECIAL TABULATIONS; COURTESY OF
DOMINION BUREAU OF STATISTICS, OTTAWA,
JULY 1969.

TORONTO (CANADA) 1966
POPULATION, BIRTHS, AND DEATHS:
CF. MONTREAL 1966.

VANCOUVER (CANADA) 1966

  POPULATION, BIRTHS, AND DEATHS:
    CF. MONTREAL 1966.

CHICAGO 1959
  TOTAL, NON-WHITE AND WHITE POPULATIONS

  BIRTHS AND DEATHS:
    SPECIAL TABULATIONS; COURTESY OF
    BUREAU OF STATISTICS, ILLINOIS
    DEPARTMENT OF HEALTH, 1967.

CHICAGO 1960
  TOTAL, NON-WHITE AND WHITE POPULATIONS

  POPULATION:
    CENSUS POPULATION OF APRIL 1; UNITED
    STATES CENSUS OF POPULATION AND HOUSING
    1960, PART 15 (ILLINOIS), TAB.20,
    P.15-79. ADJUSTED TO MID-YEAR.

  BIRTHS BY AGE AND SEX:
    VITAL STATISTICS, ILLINOIS 1960, TAB.A,
    P.6.

  DEATHS:
    SPECIAL TABULATION; COURTESY OF
    BUREAU OF STATISTICS, ILLINOIS
    DEPARTMENT OF HEALTH, 1967.

CHICAGO 1961
  TOTAL, NON-WHITE AND WHITE POPULATIONS

  BIRTHS BY AGE AND SEX:
    VITAL STATISTICS, ILLINOIS 1961, TAB.A,
    P.1.

  DEATHS:
    SPECIAL TABULATION; COURTESY OF
    BUREAU OF STATISTICS, ILLINOIS
    DEPARTMENT OF HEALTH, 1967.

DISTRICT OF COLUMBIA 1959

  BIRTHS BY AGE OF MOTHER:
    U.S. VITAL STATISTICS 1959, VOL.I,
    TAB.39B, P.258.

  BIRTHS BY SEX:
    OP. CIT., VOL.I, TAB.30, P.229.

  DEATHS:
    OP. CIT., VOL.II, TAB.77B, P.236.

DISTRICT OF COLUMBIA 1960

  POPULATION:
    CENSUS POPULATION OF APRIL; UNITED
    STATES CENSUS OF POPULATION AND
    HOUSING 1960, PART 10 (DISTRICT OF
    COLUMBIA), TAB.16, P.10-12. ADJUSTED
    TO MID-YEAR.

  BIRTHS BY AGE OF MOTHER:
    U.S. VITAL STATISTICS 1960, VOL.I,
    TAB.2-14, P.2-29.

  BIRTHS BY SEX:
    OP. CIT., TAB.2-4, P.2-7.

  DEATHS:
    OP. CIT., VOL.II, PART B, TAB.9-5.
    P.9-165.

DISTRICT OF COLUMBIA 1961

  BIRTHS BY AGE OF MOTHER:
    U.S. VITAL STATISTICS 1961, VOL.I,
    TAB.2-11, P.2-25.

  BIRTHS BY SEX:
    OP. CIT., TAB.2-4, P.2-9.

  DEATHS:
    OP. CIT., VOL.II, PART B, TAB.9-5,
    P.9-156.

KAOHSIUNG (TAIWAN) 1966

  POPULATION:
    MID-YEAR ESTIMATE; TAIWAN DEMOGRAPHIC
    FACTBOOK 1966, (OCTOBER, 1967), TAB.1,
    PP.2-3.

  BIRTHS BY AGE OF MOTHER:
    OP. CIT., TAB.7, PP.178-9.

  BIRTHS BY SEX:
    IBID.

  DEATHS:
    OP. CIT., TAB.21, PP.386-9.

  BIRTHS AND DEATHS BY YEAR OF REGISTRATION.
  POPULATION AND DEATHS 80 AND OLDER EXTRA-
  POLATED.

TAIPEI (TAIWAN) 1966

  POPULATION:
    MID-YEAR ESTIMATE; TAIWAN DEMOGRAPHIC
    FACTBOOK 1966, (OCTOBER, 1967, TAB.1,
    PP.2-3.

  BIRTHS BY AGE OF MOTHER:
    OP. CIT., TAB.7, PP.178-9.

  BIRTHS BY SEX:
    IBID.

  DEATHS:
    OP. CIT., TAB.21, PP.382-5.

  BIRTHS AND DEATHS BY YEAR OF REGISTRATION.
  POPULATION AND DEATHS 80 AND OLDER EXTRA-
  POLATED.

DJAKARTA (INDONESIA) 1964

  POPULATION, BIRTHS AND DEATHS:
    PARTLY HYPOTHETICAL DATA, BASED ON
    1961 CENSUS AND OFFICIAL BIRTHS AND
    DEATH REGISTRATIONS ADJUSTED FOR
    INCOMPLETENESS.

COPENHAGEN (DENMARK) 1966

POPULATION:
ESTIMATE OF OCTOBER 15, 1966;
STATISTISK ARSBOG FOR KOBENHAVN,
FREDERIKSBERG OG GENTOFTE SAMT
OMEGNSKOMMUNERNE 1967, TAB.13, P.18.
ADJUSTED TO MID-YEAR.

BIRTHS BY AGE OF MOTHER:
STATISTISK ARSBOG FOR KOBENHAVN,
FREDERIKSBERG OG GENTOFTE SAMT
OMEGNSKOMMUNERNE 1968, TAB.31, P.36.
ADJUSTED TO EXCLUDE 98 STILLBIRTHS.

BIRTHS BY SEX:
OP. CIT., TAB.28, P.31.

DEATHS:
OP. CIT., TAB.34, P.39.

DATA ARE FOR KOBENHAVN STAD ONLY.

HELSINKI (FINLAND) 1966

POPULATION, BIRTHS, AND DEATHS:
SPECIAL TABULATIONS; COURTESY OF
CENTRAL STATISTICAL OFFICE OF FINLAND,
HELSINKI, JULY 1969.

BERLIN-EAST (GERMANY) 1961

POPULATION:
ESTIMATE OF DECEMBER 31, 1960;
STATISTISCHES JAHRBUCH DER HAUPTSTADT
DER DEUTSCHEN DEMOKRATISCHEN REPUBLIK,
BERLIN, 1962 (2.JAHRGANG), PP.17-8.
ADJUSTED TO MID-1961.

BIRTHS BY AGE OF MOTHER:
OP. CIT., 1963 (3.JAHRGANG), TAB.16,
P.314. AGE CLASSIFICATION BY AGE OF
MOTHER ON JANUARY 1, 1961. BIRTHS BY
SINGLE YEARS OF MOTHERS' AGE ADJUSTED
BY HALF A YEAR.

BIRTHS BY SEX:
OP. CIT., 1963 (3.JAHRGANG), TAB.13,
P.312.

DEATHS:
OP. CIT., 1965 (5.JAHRGANG), TAB.26,
P.325.

BERLIN-WEST (GERMANY) 1961

POPULATION:
ESTIMATED DE JURE POPULATION OF JUNE 6,
1961; DYB 1963, TAB.5, PP.210-11.
ADJUSTED TO MID-YEAR.

BIRTHS BY AGE OF MOTHER:
DYB 1965, TAB.13, P.317. AGE
CLASSIFICATION BASED ON DIFFERENCE
BETWEEN BIRTH YEARS OF CHILD AND
MOTHER.

BIRTHS BY SEX:
DYB 1965, TAB.22, P.544.

DEATHS:
DYB 1962, TAB.19, PP.548-9.

BIRTHS AND DEATHS INCLUDE RESIDENTS OF
WEST BERLIN TEMPORARILY IN THE FEDERAL
REPUBLIC OF GERMANY AND EXCLUDE ALIEN
ARMED FORCES AND NON-RESIDENT CIVILIANS
TEMPORARILY IN BERLIN.

BERLIN-WEST (GERMANY) 1967

POPULATION, BIRTHS, AND DEATHS:
SPECIAL TABULATIONS; COURTESY OF
STATISTISCHES BUNDESAMT, WIESBADEN,
JULY 1969.

DUESSELDORF (GERMANY) 1966

POPULATION:
ESTIMATED RESIDENTIAL POPULATION
OF DECEMBER 1; STATISTISCHES JAHRBUCH
DER LANDESHAUPTSTADT DUESSELDORF,
62.JAHRGANG, BERICHTSJAHR 1966,
TABS.13-15, PP.11-12. ADJUSTED TO
MID-YEAR.

BIRTHS BY AGE OF MOTHER:
LEGITIMATE LIVE BIRTHS OF RESIDENT
MOTHERS; OP. CIT., TAB.37, P.23.
ADJUSTED TO INCLUDE 766 ILLEGITIMATE
BIRTHS.

BIRTHS BY SEX:
OP. CIT., TAB.32, P.21.

DEATHS:
OP. CIT., TAB.43, P.26. TEN-YEAR AGE
GROUPS DIVIDED INTO FIVE-YEAR GROUPS
BY FITTING FREE-HAND CURVE TO AGE
SPECIFIC DEATH RATES. AGE GROUPS 70
AND OLDER EXTRAPOLATED.

HAMBURG (GERMANY) 1966

POPULATION:
RESIDENTIAL POPULATION OF JANUARY 1,
1967; FREIE HANSESTADT HAMBURG,
STATISTISCHES JAHRBUCH 1966/67, TAB.13,
P.11. ADJUSTED TO MID-YEAR.

BIRTHS BY AGE OF MOTHER:
LIVE BIRTHS TO MOTHERS AGED 15-45;
OP. CIT., TAB.22, P.25. AGE
CLASSIFICATION BASED ON DIFFERENCE
BETWEEN BIRTH YEARS OF CHILD AND MOTHER.

BIRTHS BY SEX:
OP. CIT., TAB 24, P.25.

DEATHS:
OP. CIT., TAB.44, P.36.

STOCKHOLM (SWEDEN) 1960

POPULATION:
ESTIMATE OF NOVEMBER 1, 1960;
STATISTISK ARSBOK FOR STOCKHOLMS

STAD 1961, TAB.17, P.15. ADJUSTED TO
MID-YEAR.

BIRTHS BY AGE OF MOTHER:
OP. CIT., TAB.50, P.59.

BIRTHS BY SEX:
OP. CIT., TAB.48, P.57.

DEATHS:
OBTAINED FROM DEATH RATES; OP. CIT.,
TAB.57, P.62. DEATHS TO CHILDREN UNDER 1
AND TOTAL DEATHS; CF. OP. CIT., TAB.55,
P.63.

LONDON (UNITED KINGDOM) 1967

POPULATION:
ESTIMATED HOME POPULATION OF JUNE 30,
1967. SPECIAL TABULATION; COURTESY OF
GENERAL REGISTER OFFICE, LONDON, JULY
1969.

BIRTHS BY AGE OF MOTHER AND SEX:
SPECIAL TABULATIONS; CF. POPULATION.

DEATHS:
SPECIAL TABULATION; CF. POPULATION.
FIGURES ARE PROVISIONAL ESTIMATES.
TEN-YEAR AGE GROUPS SPLIT INTO FIVE-YEAR
GROUPS THROUGH USE OF NEWTON'S DIFFERENCE
FORMULA.

POPULATION AND DEATHS 75 AND OLDER EXTRA-
POLATED. ALL DATA REFER TO "GREATER LONDON."

SYDNEY (AUSTRALIA) 1966

POPULATION, BIRTHS AND DEATHS:
SPECIAL TABULATIONS; COURTESY OF
COMMONWEALTH BUREAU OF CENSUS
AND STATISTICS; CANBERRA, AUGUST 1969.

DATA REFER TO SYDNEY METROPOLITAN AREA.

CENTRAL AMERICA 1964-66

COSTA RICA 1966
GUATEMALA 1964
HONDURAS 1966
NICARAGUA 1965
PANAMA 1966

WEST INDIES 1963-64

BARBADOS 1963
GUADALOUPE 1964
JAMAICA 1963
MARTINIQUE 1963
PUERTO RICO 1964
SANTA LUCIA 1963
TRINIDAD AND TOBAGO 1964

EUROPEAN COMMON MARKET 1955, 1960, 1965

BELGIUM
FRANCE
GERMANY (WEST)
ITALY
LUXEMBOURG
NETHERLANDS

EUROPEAN FREE TRADE ASSOCIATION 1955,
1960, 1965

AUSTRIA
DENMARK
ENGLAND AND WALES
NORWAY
PORTUGAL
SCOTLAND
SWEDEN
SWITZERLAND

EUROPEAN MEMBERS OF COMECON, 1955, 1960,
1965

BULGARIA
CZECHOSLOVAKIA
GERMANY (EAST)
HUNGARY
POLAND
ROMANIA

EUROPE 1955, 1960, 1965
EXCLUDING ALBANIA, U.S.S.R.,
AND NORTHERN IRELAND

AUSTRIA
BELGIUM
BULGARIA
CZECHOSLOVAKIA
DENMARK
ENGLAND AND WALES
FINLAND
FRANCE
GERMANY-EAST   (INCLUDING EAST BERLIN)
GERMANY-WEST   (INCLUDING WEST BERLIN)
GREECE
HUNGARY
ICELAND
IRELAND (REPUBLIC)
ITALY
LUXEMBOURG
MALTA AND GOZO
NETHERLANDS
NORWAY
POLAND
PORTUGAL
ROMANIA
SCOTLAND
SPAIN
SWEDEN
SWITZERLAND
YUGOSLAVIA

References

Arriaga, E. E., 1968. *New Life Tables for Latin American Populations in the Nineteenth and Twentieth Centuries.* Population Monograph Series, No. 3. Berkeley: Institute of International Studies, University of California.

Bourgeois-Pichat, J., 1957. "Utilisation de la notion de population stable pour mesurer la mortalité et la fécondité des populations des pays sous-développés," *Bulletin de l'Institut International de Statistique* (Actes de la 30ᵉ Session).

———, 1968. *The Concept of a Stable Population: Application to the study of Populations of Countries with Incomplete Demographic Statistics.* Population Studies, No. 39. New York: United Nations.

Brass, W., and A. J. Coale, 1968. "Methods of analysis and estimation," in W. Brass et al., *The Demography of Tropical Africa.* Princeton: Princeton University Press.

Canada Year Book, 1968. Ottawa: The Queen's Printer.

Coale, A. J., 1955. "The population of the United States in 1960 classified by age, sex, and color—a revision of census figures," *Journal of the American Statistical Association, 50:* 16–54.

———, 1963. "Estimates of various demographic measures through the quasi-stable age distribution," *Emerging Techniques in Population Research: Proceedings of the 1962 Annual Conference of the Milbank Memorial Fund,* 175–193.

———, and P. Demeny, 1966. *Regional Model Life Tables and Stable Populations.* Princeton: Princeton University Press.

Coale, A. J., and P. Demeny, 1967. *Methods of Estimating Basic Demographic Measures from Incomplete Data.* Manual IV. New York: United Nations.

Coale, A. J., and E. M. Hoover, 1958. *Population Growth and Economic Development in Low-Income Countries.* Princeton: Princeton University Press.

Coale, A. J., and M. Zelnik, 1963. *New Estimates of Fertility and Population in the United States.* Princeton: Princeton University Press.

Davis, K., 1967. "Population policy: Will current programs succeed?" *Science, 158:* 730–739.

Deming, W. E., 1944. "On errors in surveys," *American Sociological Review, 9:* 359–369.

Duncan, O. D., R. P. Cuzzort, and Beverley Duncan, 1961. *Statistical Geography.* Glencoe, Illinois: The Free Press.

Euler, L., 1760. "Recherches générales sur la mortalité et la multiplication du genre humain," *Mémoires de l'Académie Royale des Sciences et Belles Lettres (Belgium), 16:* 144–164.

Fisher, R. A., 1929, 1958. *The Genetical Theory of Natural Selection.* 2nd Rev. Ed. New York: Dover Publications, 1958. (First published in 1929.)

Frejka, T., 1968. "Reflections on the demographic conditions needed to establish a U.S. stationary population growth," *Population Studies, 22:* 379–397.

Greville, T. N. E., 1943. "Short methods of constructing abridged life tables," *Record of the American Institute of Actuaries, 32:* 29–43.

———, 1949. "On the derivation of discrete interpolation formulas," *Transactions of the Society of Actuaries, 1:* 343–357.

Hauser, P. M. (ed.), 1969. *The Population Dilemma.* The American Assembly, Columbia University. 2nd Ed. Englewood Cliffs, New Jersey: Prentice-Hall.

Hawley, A. H., 1950. *Human Ecology.* New York: Ronald Press.

Jaffe, A. J., 1951. *Handbook of Statistical Methods for Demographers.* U. S. Bureau of the Census. Washington, D. C.: U. S. Government Printing Office.

Kaplan, D. L., 1970. "Plans for the 1970 Census of Population and Housing," *Demography, 7:* 1–18.

Keyfitz, N., 1965. "Age distribution as a challenge to development," *American Journal of Sociology, 70:* 659–668.

———, 1968. *Introduction to the Mathematics of Population.* Reading, Massachusetts: Addison-Wesley.

———, 1970. "Finding probabilities from observed rates, or how to make a life table," *The American Statistician, 24:* 28–33.

———, and W. Flieger, 1968. *World Population: An Analysis of Vital Data.* Chicago: University of Chicago Press.

Keyfitz, N., D. Nagnur, and D. Sharma, 1967. "On the interpretation of age distributions," *Journal of the American Statistical Association, 62:* 862–874.

Kitagawa, E. M., 1964. "Standardization comparisons in population research," *Demography, 1:* 296–315.

Leslie, P. H., 1945. "On the use of matrices in certain population mathematics," *Biometrika, 33:* 183–212.

———, 1948. "Some further notes on the use of matrices in population mathematics," *Biometrika, 35:* 213–245.

Lorimer, F., 1966. "Analysis and projections of the population of the Philippines," *First Conference on Population, 1965.* Quezon City: Population Institute, University of the Philippines.

Lotka, A. J., 1907 "Relation between birth and death rates," *Science,* N. S. *26:* 21–22.

———, 1922. "The stability of the normal age distribution," *Proceedings of the National Academy of Sciences, 8:* 339–345.

———, 1939. *Théorie analytique des associations biologiques.* Part II. *Analyse démographique avec application particulière à l'espèce humaine.* Actualités Scientifiques et Industrielles, No. 780. Paris: Hermann et Cie.

———, 1948. "Application of recurrent series in renewal theory," *Annals of Mathematical Statistics, 19:* 190–206.

Moriyama, I. M., 1946. "Estimated completeness of birth registration: United States, 1935 to 1944." United States Public Health Service, National Office of Vital Statistics, *Vital Statistics—Special Reports, 23:* 223–227.

Myers, R. J., 1940. "Errors and bias in the reporting of ages in census data, "*Transactions of the Actuarial Society of America, 41 (2):* 395–415.

——, 1966. "Validity of centenarian data in the 1960 census," *Demography, 3:* 470–476.

Notestein, F. W., et al., 1944. *The Future Population of Europe and the Soviet Union.* Geneva: League of Nations.

Petersen, W., 1969. *Population.* 2nd Ed. New York: The Macmillan Company.

Potter, R. G., 1970. "Births averted by contraception: An approach through renewal theory," *Theoretical Population Biology, 1:* 251–272.

Rogers, A., 1968. *Matrix Analysis of Interregional Population Growth and Distribution.* Berkeley: University of California Press.

Scarborough, J. B., 1958. *Numerical Mathematical Analysis.* 4th Ed. Baltimore: Johns Hopkins Press.

Spiegelman, M. 1968. *Introduction to Demography.* 2nd Ed. Cambridge: Harvard University Press.

Tabah, L., 1968. "Représentations matricielles de perspectives de population active," *Population, 23:* 437–476.

United Nations, 1961–1968. *Demographic Yearbook.* 13th to 18th issues. New York: United Nations.

United States Bureau of the Census, 1963. *The Current Population Reinterview Program: Some Notes and Discussion.* Technical Paper No. 6. Washington, D. C.: U. S. Government Printing Office.

——, 1966. *1960 Censuses of Population and Housing: Procedural History.* Washington, D. C.: U. S. Government Printing Office.

——, 1968. *Statistical Abstract of the United States: 1968.* 89th Ed. Washington, D. C.: U. S. Government Printing Office.

Van de Walle, E., 1965. Comment on the article by N. Keyfitz entitled "Age distribution as a challenge to development," *American Journal of Sociology, 70:* 549–557.

——, 1968. In W. Brass, et al., *The Demography of Tropical Africa.* Princeton: Princeton University Press.

Wicksell, W. D., 1931. "Nuptiality, fertility, and reproductivity," *Scandinavisk Aktuarietidskrift,* 125–157.

Index